A BIBLIOGRAPHY OF THE WORKS OF
SAMUEL JOHNSON

A

BIBLIOGRAPHY

OF

THE WORKS OF

SAMUEL JOHNSON

Treating his published works from
the beginnings to 1984

COMPILED BY

J. D. FLEEMAN

Prepared for publication by James McLaverty

VOLUME 2
1760–1816

CLARENDON PRESS · OXFORD

OXFORD

UNIVERSITY PRESS

Great Clarendon Street, Oxford OX2 6DP

Oxford University Press is a department of the University of Oxford.
It furthers the University's objective of excellence in research, scholarship,
and education by publishing worldwide in

Oxford New York

Athens Auckland Bangkok Bogotá Buenos Aires Calcutta
Cape Town Chennai Dar es Salaam Delhi Florence Hong Kong Istanbul
Karachi Kuala Lumpur Madrid Melbourne Mexico City Mumbai
Nairobi Paris São Paulo Singapore Taipei Tokyo Toronto Warsaw

and associated companies in Berlin Ibadan

Oxford is a registered trade mark of Oxford University Press
in the UK and in certain other countries

Published in the United States
by Oxford University Press Inc., New York

British Library Cataloguing in Publication Data

Data available

Library of Congress Cataloging in Publication Data
Fleeman, J. D. (John David)
A bibliography of the works of Samuel Johnson, 1709–1784/
compiled by J.D. Fleeman.
Includes bibliographical references (p.   )
1. Johnson, Samuel, 1709–1874—Bibliography.
I. Johnson, Samuel, 1709–1784. II. Title.
Z8455.8.F54 2000 [PR3533] 016.828′609—dc21   98–51336
ISBN 0–19–812269–1 (v. 1)
ISBN 0–19–812270–5 (v. 2)

1 3 5 7 9 10 8 6 4 2

Typeset by Hope Services (Abingdon) Ltd.
Printed in Great Britain
on acid-free paper by
Biddles Ltd., Guildford and King's Lynn

Contents

For an alphabetical list of works included in the bibliography,
see the Index of Items

VOLUME 2 (1760–1816)

January–December 1760

The following items have been attributed to SJ:

January 12. *Preliminary Address*, 'To the PUBLIC.'

References: E.L. McAdam, *RES* xviii (1942), 197–207. The *Public Ledger* was noticed by Payne's *Universal Chronicle* (58.4Id/1, above), no. 96, and repeated in 97, 98, for Jan. 26–Feb. 2, 1760, p. 40, from which it appears that the proprietor was William Faden. This opening address 'To the Public' is reprinted there.

January 14. Advertisement for Newbery's *World Displayed* (59.10WDA, above)

References: *Life* i. 546. This advt. was reprinted on the final leaf of *The Idler* (1761; 58.4Id/2, above).

December 2, 9 and 16. Three Essays by the 'Weekly Correspondent', viz.

(i) On Authors

(ii) On the Coronation This essay was reprinted in *Gents. Mag.* xxx (Dec. 1760), 554–5

(iii) Tom Stucco

References: E.L. McAdam, *RES* xviii (1942), 197–207. The attribution is corroborated by Thomas Percy in a note that SJ was 'Weekly Correspondent in the first Year of the Public Ledger' (Bodl: MS Percy 87).

Notes: The *Public Ledger* was a daily newspaper, published at 2½d.

According to Hawkins (*Life87*, 518) the 'conductor' of the paper (? = editor), was Hugh Kelly (cited in *Life* iii. 113 n. 3). Newbery's involvement is surveyed in Welsh 40–4, 336, and Roscoe, *Newbery* (1973), A430.

[Engr. t.] THE | Britiſh Magazine | OR | Monthly Repository | FOR | Gentlemen & Ladies. | VOL. I [– &c.]. | [Engr. vignette of Sheldonian Theatre, Oxford] | LONDON. | Printed for James Rivington & James Fletcher, at the | Oxford Theatre; & H. Payne, at Dryden's Head, in | PATER NOSTER ROW.

January 37–9   'The Bravery of the English Common Soldier'.

References: Unattributed in *British Magazine*, but acknowledged by SJ by inclusion in 3rd edn. of *The Idler* (1767; 58.4Id/4, above). *BUCOP* (1955), i. 419b; Roscoe, *Newbery* (1973), A54.

Notes: The essay was reprinted in *London Chronicle* (1 June 1767), *Lloyd's Evening Post* and the *Caledonian Mercury* (4 June 1767), and in the *Court*

Miscellany (May 1767), 253–4; a later reprint is in the *Town & Country Magazine; or Universal Repository* (Apr. 1778), 205–6, all probably from *The Idler*, 3rd. edn. (1767; 58.4Id/4, above).

The *British Magazine* was edited by Tobias Smollett (*Lit. Anec.* viii. 497), with assistance from others including Goldsmith (*Lit. Anec.* iii. 465). It ran to the 8th vol. in 1767. Smollett had helped to secure the discharge of Frank Barber from the Navy in July 1759 (*Life* i. 348–9), and this doubtless strengthened SJ's acquaintance.[1]

Welsh 177, noted that 'Newbery's seventh share in the British Magazine was valued at £10. 10s. in the schedule of assets when he made an arrangement with his creditors' (see further *idem*, 39–40 and 309).

Various Johnsonian pieces were reprinted here from time to time:

I. (1760), January 25–6: *Idler* 88 (orig. 89), 'What have ye done?' (with a brief but favourable editorial comment on SJ)

March 148–50: *Idler* 96 (orig. 97), 'Hacho King of Lapland' (by T. Warton), No. V, 264: *Idler* 103 (orig. 104), 'The last Idler'

November 646–48: Introduction to the *Proceedings of the Committee . . . for cloathing French Prisoners of War* (60.8FP/1, below), as: 'Essay on Charity'.

This publication is sometimes confused with another of the same name, edited by 'Sir' John Hill, and published by C. Corbett, which ran in the late 1740s and early 1750s (see further *BUCOP* & *Supp.* (1962), s.nn.). The 1750 numbers were printed by David Henry, successor to Edward Cave, and some numbers of SJ's *Rambler*, entitled 'The Moralist' appeared therein.

Copies: O (Hope adds 1158–65, vols. 1–8);

USA: CtY[2] (**1**. imperfect: vols. 1–2; **2**. vols. 1 & 3), DFo (vol. 1), ICU (vols. 3, 6, 8), IU, MB (vols. 1–2), TxU (vols. 1–2); *Can*: CaOHM (vol. 1 'Rippey'); *UK*: BMp (vols. 1–2), L (vol. 1), LCu (vol. 1).

---

[1] See *Daily Advertiser* (14 Feb. 1757; 57.2DA, above). Smollett's involvement did not become general knowledge until 1769, when these letters were published in *Letters between the Duke of Grafton and John Wilkes, Esq;* (1769), i. 59–60, and reprinted in *St James's Chronicle* (25 July 1769) and the *Court Miscellany*, v (July 1769), 352 (*Letters of Smollett*, ed. Knapp (Oxford, 1970), 75–77). Smollett's letter of 16 March 1759, to Wilkes, was reprinted in *European Mag.* vii (March 1785), 190. In his MS list of SJ's writings, Isaac Reed noted s.d. 1759, 'See Wilks's Letters.' D.J. Greene is more sceptical of SJ's writing for Smollett (*Works* (Yale), x. 279).

60.2LSA   Letters for Society of Artists   1760

Between 19 Jan. and 26 Feb. 1760, SJ drafted a letter for the signature of Francis Hayman, President of the Society of Artists of Great Britain, asking for the use of the rooms of the Society for the Encouragement of Arts and Sciences for their annual Exhibition on 7–19 April 1760.

References: *Walpole Society*, vi (1917–18), 113–23, 'The Papers of the Society of Artists of Great Britain' (minutes of meetings of 19 Jan. and 26 Feb. 1760); Clifford, in *Augustan Milieu* (1970), 333–48; Brownell, *Johnson's Attitude to the Arts* (1989), 47–50.

Notes: Text of SJ's letter and a 'Plan' advertising the proposed exhibition, in *Walpole Society*, 118. The opening paragraph of the 'Plan' at least, is also SJ's; Brownell reasonably attributes the whole. SJ was thanked 'for his great assistance to the Committee of Artists' in the minutes of 12 May 1760. See 60.12LSA and 62.5SA/1, below.

60.2LB   Brumoy's Greek Theatre   1759

THE | GREEK THEATRE | OF | FATHER BRUMOY. | TRANSLATED | By Mrs. CHARLOTTE LENNOX. | [rule] | IN THREE VOLUMES. | [rule] | VOL. I [– III]. | [double rule] | LONDON: | Printed for Meſſ. MILLAR, VAILLANT, BALDWIN, CROWDER, | JOHNSTON, DODSLEY, and WILSON and DURHAM. | MDCCLIX.

3 vols., 4°

I. π⁴ ᵖa–c⁴ d², ²a–d⁴ e–p⁴ B–3H⁴ (3H4 blk), ($2 signed; 'VOL. I.' on $1), 290 leaves.

Pp. π1 t., π1ᵛ blk, π2–3 Dedication dh: TO HIS | ROYAL HIGHNESS| GEORGE, | PRINCE OF WALES. (signed 'JUNE 4. | 1759 CHARLOTTE LENNOX.'), π3ᵛ blk, π4 Advertisement, π4ᵛ blk, on ᵖa1 *i* ii–xxviii Preface, on ²a1 ²i ii–cxx A Discourse upon the Theatre of the Greeks., &c., on B1 *1–5* 6–96 *97* Oedipus, *98* blk, *99–103* 104–196 Electra, *197–201* 202–54 Philoctetes, *255–8* 259–336 Hyppolytus, *337–41* 342–422 Iphigenia, *423–24* (3H4) blk.

Pagination: unnumbered π⁴, ᵖa1 i, ²a1 i, xxii, lxxv, 1–5, 68, 79, 88, 97–103, 159, 163, 175, 197–201, 251, 255–8, 317, 325, 337–41, 409, 423–4; on ᵖc3: xxi as xx.

Press-figures: ᵖd2(xxvii)–7, ²a3ᵛ(vi)–2, ²a4ᵛ(viii)–4, ²b3(xiii)–5, ²c4ᵛ(xxiv)–1, ²d1ᵛ(xxvi)–6, ²d4ᵛ(xxxii)–5, e2ᵛ(xxxvi)–4, f2ᵛ(xliv)–4, g3(liii)–1, h4ᵛ(lxiv)–2, i3ᵛ(lxx)–6, k2ᵛ(lxxvi)–7, k3ᵛ(lxxviii)–6, l2(lxxxiii)–5, l4ᵛ(lxxxviii)–5, m2ᵛ(xcii)–7, n3ᵛ(cii)–3, o2ᵛ(cviii)–5, o4(cxi)–1, p2ᵛ(cxvi)–5, B4(7)–6, C1ᵛ(10)–4, D4(23)–4, E4(31)–6, F4(39)–5, G3(45)–5, G4(47)–7, H3ᵛ(54)–6, I4(63)–7, K3(69)–6, L3(77)–2, M2ᵛ(84)–5, N4(95)–6, O4(103)–2, P2ᵛ(108)–7, Q4(119)–6, R2ᵛ(124)–2, S2ᵛ(132)–1, T3(141)–4, U3ᵛ(150)–4, X2ᵛ(156)–4, Y2ᵛ(164)–6, Z1ᵛ(170)–5, 2A1ᵛ(178)–6, 2B4ᵛ(192)–5, 2D3ᵛ(206)–4, 2D4ᵛ(208)–4, 2E2ᵛ(212)–4, 2F3ᵛ(222)–1, 2F4ᵛ(224)–2, 2G4ᵛ(232)–5, 2H1ᵛ(234)–5, 2I2ᵛ(244)–1, 2K1ᵛ(250)–4, 2K3(253)–5, 2L4(263)–2, 2M1ᵛ(266)–2, 2O1ᵛ(282)–5, 2P2ᵛ(292)–5, 2Q3(301)–6, 2S1ᵛ(314)–5, 2T3ᵛ(326)–5, 2Y3ᵛ(350)–2, 2Z2ᵛ(356)–1, 3A2ᵛ(364)–7, 3B2ᵛ(372)–4, 3B4(375)–1,

3C3(381)–1,   3D3ᵛ(390)–5,   3E1ᵛ(394)–7,   3F4ᵛ(408)–6,   3G3ᵛ(414)–6, 3H1ᵛ(418)–1, 3H2ᵛ(420)–5; unfigured: ᵖa–c, 2C, 2N, 2R, 2U, 2X.

Catchwords: ᵖa2 eloquence. (elegance.), ᵇxiii n. ₐPIECES, ("~,), ᶠxli knot₍, (~*,), 7 I (if I), 19 OEDIPUS. (TIRESIAS.), 80 ₐwherein ("~), 88 contagion₍ (~,), 104 part₍ (~.), 105 ELECTRA. (GOVERNOR.), 129 ELECTRA. (CHORUS.), 133 CLY- (CRYSOTHEMIS.), 140 *om.* (ELECTRA.), 231 PHILOC- (NEOPTOLEMUS.), 260 ₐHe ([*He*]), 261 *om.* (HIPPOLYTUS.), 296 [tempe-] rance₍ (~,), 296 n. [that] this (that this), 299 [pre-] fence₍ (~,), 314 thee₍ (~,), 319 Now₍ (~,), 322 Phedra₍ (~,), 323 [mo-] derns, (~₍), 325 [con-] fidant₍ (~,), 332 ₐPour ("~), 336 *om.*, 341 thou₍ (~,), 368 IPHI- (CLYTEMNESTRA.), 393 ₐSCENE (*~), 406 him₍ (~,), 406 n. Surely₍ (~,).

Explicit: 422 END of the FIRST VOLUME.

II. *A*1 B–3Y⁴ 3Z², ($2 signed; 'VOL. II.' on $1), 271 leaves.

Pp. A1 *i* t., *ii* blk, on B1 *1–5* 6–66 Iphigenia, *67–71* 72–125 Alcestis, *126* blk, *127* ½t Part the Second, Eschylus., *128–29* 130–37 Prometheus, *138* 139–44 The Seven Chiefs, *145* 146–56 The Persians, *157* 158–76 Agamemnon, &c., *177* 178–84 The Eumenides, *185* 186–94 The Suppliants, *195* ½t Sophocles, *196–7* 198–211 Ajax, *212* 213–29 Antigone, *230* 231–50 Oedipus at Colona, *251* 252–73 The Trachiniennes, *274* 275–96 Hercules on Mt. Oeta, *297* 298–403 Hercules dying, *305* ½t Euripides, *306* blk, *307–9* 310–26 Hecuba, *327* 328–46 Orestes, *347* 348–75 Phoenicians, *376* 377–88 Thebaid, *389* 390–3 Antigone, *394* 395–402 Thebaid [by Racine], *403* Jocasta . . . of Dolce, *404* 405–50 Medea, &c., *451* 452–69 Andromache, *470* 471–88 The Suppliants, *489* 490–503 Rhesus, *504* 505–18 Trojan Captives, *519–520* The Troades.

Pagination: unnumbered A1, 1–5, 61, 67–71, 118, 126–9, 138, 145, 157, 172, 177, 185, 195–7, 212, 230, 251, 274, 297, 305–9, 327, 347, 376, 389, 394, 403–4, 428, 442, 449, 451, 470, 489, 504, 519; 300 as 301 at inner margin, 301 as 300, 302 as 301, 323 as 223; first '2' of 222 *sometimes inverted*.

Press-figures: B3(5)–2,   B3ᵛ(6)–7,   C1ᵛ(10)–1,   D3(21)–6,   E1ᵛ(26)–3, F2ᵛ(36)–4, G2ᵛ(44)–3, H2ᵛ(52)–5, I4(63)–1, K3(69)–5, L2ᵛ(76)–4, M4ᵛ(88)–6, N4(95)–5, O2ᵛ(100)–4, P4ᵛ(112)–4, Q4ᵛ(120)–6, R2ᵛ(124)–2, S1ᵛ(130)–7, T1ᵛ(138)–5, U3ᵛ(150)–1, X3ᵛ(158)–4, Y1ᵛ(162)–4, Z3(173)–1, 2A2ᵛ(180)–1, 2B1ᵛ(186)–1,   2B4ᵛ(192)–3,   2C4ᵛ(200)–4,   2D2ᵛ(204)–5,   2E1ᵛ(210)–2, 2F1ᵛ(218)–5,   2G3ᵛ(230)–5,   2H3ᵛ(238)–2,   2I1ᵛ(242)–6,   2K4ᵛ(256)–5, 2L4ᵛ(264)–2, 2M2ᵛ(268)–1, 2N4ᵛ(280)–5, 2O4ᵛ(288)–5, 2Q1ᵛ(298)–7, 2R3(309)–7, 2S3ᵛ(318)–6, 2T2ᵛ(324)–2, 2U3(333)–7, 2X3ᵛ(342)–3, 2Y4ᵛ(352)–6,   2Z4(359)–2,   2Z4ᵛ(360)–4,   3A4(367)–5,   3B1ᵛ(370)–7, 3C3(381)–2,   3D3ᵛ(390)–2,   3E2ᵛ(396)–1,   3F4ᵛ(408)–1,   3G3(413)–2, 3H4ᵛ(424)–1,   3I4(431)–6,   3K3ᵛ(438)–3,   3L3ᵛ(446)–1,   3M2ᵛ(452)–1, 3N1ᵛ(458)–3,   3O3ᵛ(470)–7,   3P2ᵛ(476)–5,   3Q3ᵛ(486)–1,   3R2ᵛ(492)–6,

3S2ᵛ(500)–3,   3T3ᵛ(510)–3,   3U3(517)–5,   3X3ᵛ(526)–2,   3Y2ᵛ(532)–4,
3Y4(535)–6, 3Z1ᵛ(538)–1; 2P unfigured.

Catchwords: 13 *om* (to), 33 n. ₐ*fud-* ("*a fudden*), 43 ORESTES. (IPHIGE-
NIA.), 51 THOAS. (IPHIGENIA.), 53 n. Jupiter₍ (~,), 72 DEATH₍ (~.), 84
ALCESTIS. (~,), 87 Shades; (~,), 91 HERCULES. (ADMETUS.), 120
now₍ (~:), 122 them₍ (~,), 123 (a ((as), 150 ₍fad ("~), 157 [expect-] ed (ted),
173 He₍ (~,), 175 no (not), 186 imitate₍ (~.), 197 **Mota (*"~), 203 ₍ing ("~),
307 ₍your ("~), 212 ₍of ("which), 216 ₍It ("~), 219 ₍his ("~), 233 deftiny₍ (~.),
245 [Fu-] ries₍ (~,), 250 TRACHI- (THE | TRACHIENNES), 262 ₍peo-
("people), 264 ₍"Incu- (*"Incubuitque), 267 [fuf-] fer (fuffer), 277 Rotrou₍ (~,),
278 ₍Vin- ("Vincere), 279 ₍Elle ("~), 280 ₍which ("Felix), 286 ₍Qu' une ("Qu'
une), 313 "buried ("under), 320 [per-] plexity₍ (~;), 324 ₍from ("~), 327 fad
("~), 328 hair (to), 364 ₍be- ("befieged), 360 ₍buck- ("bucklers,), 391 [odi-] ous₍
(~,), 400 ₍ CRE- ("CREON), 408 felf₍ (~:), 420 [lon-] ger ("~), 458 ₍Qu' il
("Qu' il), 463 [de-] clares₍ (~,), 467 "Tour ('~), 472 all (the), 473 ₍is ("~), 480
adds₍ (~,), 516 ₍oh, ("~₍), 525 ₍mur- ("murmuring), 528 ₍favour ("~), 536
[compaf-]fion₍ (~.).
Explicit: 540 END of VOL. II.

III. *A*² B–2X⁴ *2X⁴ 2Y–3P⁴, ($2 signed, 3P2 as 2P2; 'VOL. III.' on $1), 246
leaves.

Pp. A1 *i* Advertisement, *ii* blk, *iii* t., *iv* blk, on B1 *1* 2–21 The
Bacchanalians, *22* 23–36 The Heraclidae, *37* 38–60 Helena, *61* 62–85 Ion, *86*
87–120 Hercules Mad, &c., *121* ½t Part the Third., *122–3* 124–61 Dissertation
dh: A | DISSERTATION | UPON THE GREEK COMEDY., ht: A
DISSERTATION | UPON THE GREEK COMEDY., *162* 163–66 dh:
PRELIMINARY | OBSERVATIONS., *167* 168–74 Annals of the
Peloponesian War, *175* ½t: Comedies of Aristophanes, *176* blk, *177* 178–96
Acharnenses, *197* 198–217 The Knights, *218* 219–59 The Clouds, *260* 261–80
Wasps, *281* 282–302 Peace, *303* 304–*344 Birds, on 2Y1 *345* 346–56 Feasts of
Ceres, *357* 358–64 Lysistrata, *365* 366–84 Frogs, *385* 386–401 Female Orators,
402 403–5 Life of Conon, *406* 407–27 Plautus, *428* 429–40 Conclusion dh:
THE | GENERAL CONCLUSION., ht: GENERAL CONCLUSION.,
441 442–78 Cyclops of Euripides, *479* Advertisement of errata, *480* blk.

Pagination: unnumbered A², 1, 22, 37, 61, 86, 106, 121–3, 162, 167, 175–7,
197, 218, 260, 281, 303, 345, 357, 365, 385, 402, 406, 428, 441, 452, 479–80;
*2X⁴ is numbered as *337–*344 (*341 as *401) in duplication of 2X, thereafter
numeration is regular; 447 as 44.

Press-figures: B4(7)–2,   C1ᵛ(10)–3,   D4(23)–5,   E4(31)–4,   F1ᵛ(34)–1,
G1ᵛ(42)–2,   G4ᵛ(48)–2,   H2ᵛ(52)–1,   I2ᵛ(60)–1,   K3ᵛ(70)–1,   L2ᵛ(76)–1,
M2ᵛ(84)–3,   M3ᵛ(86)–2,   N4ᵛ(96)–1,   O4ᵛ(104)–1,   P2ᵛ(108)–2,   P4(111)–3,
Q3(117)–1,   R4(127)–3,   S3(133)–3,   T3ᵛ(142)–1,   2I3ᵛ(246)–3,   2K4ᵛ(256)–3,
2L4(263)–3,   2M3ᵛ(270)–3,   2O3ᵛ(286)–5,   2P4(295)–5,   2Q4(303)–3,

2Q4ᵛ(304)–7,   2R4(311)–5,   2T4(327)–1,   2U4ᵛ(336)–7,   2X3(341)–5,
2X4(343)–6,   *2X1ᵛ(*338)–5,   2Y2ᵛ(348)–2,   2Y4(351)–7,   2Z3ᵛ(358)–3,
3A4(367)–2,   3B3ᵛ(374)–7,   3C1ᵛ(378)–4,   3C2ᵛ(380)–2,   3D1ᵛ(386)–4,
3D3(389)–5,   3G1ᵛ(410)–5,   3I3ᵛ(430)–1,   3K3ᵛ(438)–1,   3L3ᵛ(446)–4,
3M4ᵛ(456)–4,   3N2ᵛ(460)–1,   3N4(463)–4,   3O4ᵛ(472)–5,   3P1ᵛ(474)–4,
3P3(477)–4; unfigured: A, U–2H, 2N, 2S, 3E–F, 3H.

Catchwords: 17 ₍ₐ₎himſelf ("~"), 20 races₍ₐ₎, (~*,), 25 ₍ₐ₎ever ("~"), 28 n. ₍ₐ₎is ("~"), 29 [volun-] tary, (tarily,), 33 ₍ₐ₎mounted ("~"), 89 "With (₍ₐ₎~"), 162 ₍ₐ₎ It (III. It), 184 *Athenians*₍ₐ₎. (~*.), 213 papers₍ₐ₎ (~.), 224 [firſt dignity in the] ſtate, (dignity in the ſtate,), 284 ₍ₐ₎peace, ("~,), 295 ₍ₐ₎fight- ("fighting), 300 he (the), 306 [con-] ₍ₐ₎ceived ("~"), 307 [imme-] ₍ₐ₎diately ("~"), 308 ₍ₐ₎Greece; ("~;), 317 [com-] panion₍ₐ₎: (~*;), 357 prize₍ₐ₎ (~,), 374 ₍ₐ₎Euri- ("Euripides."), 389 ₍ₐ₎When ("~"), 393 ſhaped₍ₐ₎ (~,), 399 "he (₍ₐ₎~"), 403 ₍ₐ₎fidelity ("~"), 407 GHRE- (CHREMYLUS), 436 activity₍ₐ₎ (~,), 437 Odeſſy₍ₐ₎ (~,), 474 CHORUS.(~,).

Explicit: 478 *FINIS*.

Paper: White, laid; demy (uncut: 11 × 8¾ in.); wmk.: Fleur-de-lys + VI.

Type: Pica (4.4 mm). Flowers used *passim* in rows as underlines, sub-divisions, &c., and arranged to form tpp.

References: *Life* i. 345 (Courtney 97); CH 143; Hazen 91–4; Small, *Lennox* (1935), 216–20, 257–8; Isles, *HLB* xix (1971), 52, no. 20 & n.; J. Gray, 'Dr Johnson, Charlotte Lennox, and the Englishing of Father Brumoy', *MP* lxxxiii (1985), 142–50; ESTC: t127806.

Notes: (i) *Catchwords*. Many (e.g. I. 19, 105, 129, 231, 296; II. 43, 51, 91, 157, 267, 280, 313; III. 224) are vestiges of proof revision in the type, for though they do not catch with the correct word, there is often a catch with the first word in an adjacent line, either on the same page or on the next, showing that the shift of a whole line in corrected proof has not led to a corresponding adjustment of the catchword itself.[1]

(ii) *Publication*: Announced on 21 February 1760 at £2. 2s. (*London Chronicle*, and *Gents. Mag.* xxx (Feb. 1760), 96/71). A preliminary notice that 'Next Month will be published . . . ' had appeared in *London Chronicle* 24 Jan. 1760. The date on the tt. is unusual for a book published early in the following year, but it is probable (in view also of the date of the Dedication), that some last-minute adjustments held it back after the tt. had been printed, e.g. the extra section in vol. 3; other difficulties are perhaps adumbrated by the closing 'Advertisement' in III. 479, which invites the reader to correct the 'several errors of the press.'

(iii) *Contributions* (cf. 'Advertisement' at I. π4): Hamilton Boyle, 6th E. of Cork & Orrery contributed the 'Preface' and was otherwise involved, as his MS commonplace books and correspondence with CL show.[2]

James Grainger translated the 'Cyclops', and John Bourryeau contributed the prefatory notice thereto (*Life* ii. 534); Gregory Sharpe translated and wrote notes on the 'Frogs', and an unnamed 'young gentleman' wrote on the 'Birds' and 'Peace' (*London Chronicle*, 21 Feb. 1760). Johnson contributed the 'Dedication' (attributed by CH 143); the translations of the 'Dissertation upon Greek Comedy' (III. 123–61), and the 'General Conclusion' (III. 428–40) are attributed to 'the celebrated author of the Rambler' in the '*Advertisement*' (III. A1ᵛ).[3]

SJ's own copy was lot 64 at the sale of his books (Christie, 16 Feb. 1785) to 'Wr[?igh]t' for 8s., but is yet untraced.

Copies: O (2 δ 759–61, uncut);

USA: [CLU], CSmH (223889), CtY (Gd 5.7 Beinecke), DFo (PA 3461. B7 Cage), DLC (pres. by Charlotte Lennox to 'Andrew Stone, Secretary to the Duke of Newcastle'),[4] Hyde[2] (**1**. 'Henry Erskine, 1st E of Rosslyn';[5] **2**. 'Coote'), ICN (Pres. CL to 'Earl of Corke, Febʳʸ. 14ᵗʰ. 1760'),[6] ICU, [IEN], IU (Nickell: 'R.W. Chapman'), [KyU], [Liebert = CtY], MB, [MdBP], MH (*EC75.B8348. Eg759), [MiD, NjNbS], NjP, NN[2], [ODW], PPL ('Mackenzie'), [PPM], PPU, ViU; *Can*: CaOHM; *UK*: AWn, BRc, BMp (560444), C, E (DNS 787–9), [Es], Eu, L (75. f. 8–10), MRc.

¹ Fleeman, in *Studies in the Eighteenth Century* (1979), 207–21.
² MS. DFo: (N. b. 42-3), dated '1758' and 'Finished in George Street Westminster after various interruptions, particularly the death of my wife. May 27ᵗʰ. 1759'; Christie (Orrery), 21 Nov. 1905, 668– Sparks, £1. 10s.
³ The attribution of the 'Dissertation on the Greek Comedy' and the 'General Conclusion' was repeated by *European Mag.* vii (March 1785), 190; the former only, is also given to him in Reed's MS list (Ljh).
⁴ Thomas Pelham-Holles (1693–1768*), 1st D of Newcastle. The Duchess was CL's patron.
⁵ 1st E of Rosslyn (cr. 1801), was Alexander Wedderburn (1733–1805*), on whose death the title devolved to his nephew, 2nd E, Sir James St. Clair Erskine (1762–1837*). The 'Henry' is a problem.
⁶ John Boyle (1707–62*), 5th E of Cork & Orrery, dedicatee of CL's *Shakspeare Illustrated* (53.5LSI, above).

60.3H   Something for Lord Charles Hay   ?1760

SJ told JB, 'I wrote something for Lord Charles; and I thought he had nothing to fear from a court-martial. I suffered a great loss when he died; he was a mighty pleasing man in conversation, and a reading man. The character of a soldier is high' (*Life* iii. 9). Langton also reported that 'When Lord Charles Hay, after his return from America, was preparing his defence to be offered to the Court-Martial which he had demanded, having heard Mr. Langton as high in expressions of admiration of Johnson, as he usually was, he requested that Dr. Johnson might be introduced to him; and Mr. Langton having mentioned it to Johnson, he very kindly and readily agreed; and being presented by Mr. Langton to his Lordship, while under arrest, he saw him several times; upon one of which occasions Lord Charles read to him what he had prepared, which Johnson signified his approbation of, saying, "It is a very good soldierly defence." Johnson said, that he had advised his Lordship, that as it was in vain to contend with those who were in possession of power, if they would offer him the rank of Lieutenant-General, and a government, it would be better judged to desist from urging his complaints. It is well known that his Lordship died before the sentence was made known.' (*Life* iv. 23).[1]

Hay had criticised his Commander-in-Chief, John Campbell, 4th Earl of Loudoun (1705–82*), who was superseded in 1758, for dilatory tactics at Halifax, NS, and was sent home on 31 July 1757, to be tried, though the court did not convene until February 1760. Hay died on 1 May 1760 (*Gents. Mag.* xxx (May 1760), 249), before the King, to whom the case was referred, had reached a decision. Hay was the second son of the 3rd Marquess of Tweeddale, a Major-general, veteran of Fontenoy, Colonel of the 33rd Foot, and third in command in the American campaign.[2]

Croker (*Life* (1848), 497), added details, including a contemporary declaration by a Mr Calcraft, 'a personal friend of Lord Charles', that Hay had gone mad and was therefore sent home. Whatever the causes, there was a court martial, and Croker reported: 'I have looked over the original minutes of this court-martial, and can find nothing that can be supposed to have been written by Johnson.' adding 'He meant, perhaps, some defence in the press.' (*l.c.s.*).

Since no such publication has yet been identified, this entry is placed shortly before Hay's death, though it is clear that SJ might have written and perhaps published 'something' at almost any time between July 1757 and April 1760.

[1] See further Langton to JB, 17 Dec. 1790 (Waingrow, *Corr.* 372–3), and *c*.30 July 1793 (Waingrow, *Corr.* 554, and *Corr. of JB with Club*, ed. Fifer, 391).
[2] Sir J.B. Paul, ed., *Scots Peerage* (Edinburgh: Douglas, 1904–14), iii. 461, and *Journey* (1985), 206, and further 288, where SJ dined on 17 Aug. 1773, with Archibald Murray, Lord Henderland, whose wife, Jean Hay, was a first cousin of Lord Charles, though neither SJ nor JB made any mention of this. Whether his 'madness' was real or not, the topic would have been delicate. Hay's contretemps with his C-in-C is briefly noticed by Col. David Stewart, *Sketches of the Character . . . of the Highlanders of Scotland*, 2 vols. (Edinburgh, 1822), i. 280.

60.4MM The Monthly Melody 1760

[Engr. t.] The Monthly Melody: or polite Amusement for Gentlemen and Ladies; being a Collection of Vocal and Instrumental Music composed by Dr. Arne. London. Printed for G. Kearsly. MDCCLX. 'J. Ellis fculp.'

2°, *a*² b² B² D–H² ²H² K² M–N², 24 leaves.

Pp. Engr. t. + a1 *i*–ii Dedication (signed 'THE PROPRIETORS. March 30, 1730') dh: [hp of flowers] | TO | HIS ROYAL HIGHNESS, | PRINCE EDWARD., ht: DEDICATION., *iii* iv–vi Introduction dh: [hp of flowers] | THE | COMPLEAT MUSICIAN. | [orn. strip] | CHAP. I. | [orn. strip] | INTRODUCTION., ht: INTRODUCTION., 7–48 text and engr. music (*infra*).

Pagination: [↑] except i–vi, but (↑) 41.

Press-figures: none.

Catchwords: ii *om*. (THE), 37 well (when), 44 fenator, (Senator,).

Explicit: 48 FINIS.

Paper: White, laid; Pot (uncut: 12½ × 7½ in.); wmk: PRO PATRIA VREYHEYT LVG (bB ²H KMN), Britannia + crowned GR (DEFGH). Both papers are found in the plates.

Type: Dedication: Great primer (5.6 mm), Introd. and text: English (4.5 mm).

Plates: There are 2 series of engr. music plates, the first of 37 plates, the second of 35. Several extant copies are imperfect in that various plates have been removed. In the second series there is no leaf 19, but two are numbered '23'.

Series 1: 1. 'Ketty the nonpareil'; 2. A Ballad in the Modern Taste ('One Morning young Roger . . . '); 3–4. Bacchanalian Song ('Bacchus God of Mirth . . . '); 5–6. Aria, the words by Metastasio, set by Sigʳ. Cocchi; 7. Kitty for the Guittar; 8. Spring an Ode; 9. The Lucky Fall; 10. Nancy Crow; 11. The Way to Keep Him; 12–13. Sung by Miss Brent in the Character of the fine Lady in Lethe (*To be continued in our next*); 14. Nancy Crow for the Guitar; 15. Peggy Wynne; 16. Duetto 1. for two German Flutes by Dr. Arne; 17. The Shepherd; 18. The Shepherdess; 19. Damon & Cinthia. A Dialogue; 20. The Honest Fellow; 21. The Comparison; 22–23. Celia's Complaint; 24. A celebrated Italian Song; 25. Sung by Mr Lowe at Vaux-Hall ('Resolv'd on her Poet . . . '); 26–27. Mrs. Scott's Song in the Desart Island (*R. Alderman Sculpt*.); 28. Affectation. A Cure for Love (*Alderman*); 29. The Fruitless Endeavour; 30. The Prudent Nymph & Treacherous Swain; 31. Strephon of the Hill (*Alderman*); 32–33. The Lover's Petition; 34. The Caution; 35. The Phoenix; 36–37. Peggy or the fickle Fair.

Series 2: 1. Loves True Object; 2. The Honest Lover; 3. An antient Ballad, new set to Musick ('Despairing beside a clear Stream'); 4. The Virgin Unmask'd; 5. The Tender Lover; 6. A favourite Air by Sigʳ. D. Giardini ('Voi Amante . . . '); 7–8. The Joys of Harvest; 9. Inconstancy Requited; 10. A Love Rhapsody; 11–12. The Inamorata; 13. Retirement; 14. The Wish; 15. Love's Elegy; 16. The Prudent Lover; 17. A Pastoral Song; 18. A favourite Air by Sigʳ. Giardini ('A se de mali mici . . . '); [No number 19]; 20–21. The Amorous Beggar; 22. Female Advice; 23. The Lost Shepherd; ²23. The Remonstrance; 24. An Italian Song ('Fancilina sinnamora . . . '); 25. The Charms of Silvia; 26. Clarinda; 27. Advice from Experience; 28. A Dialogue; 29. An Italian Song ('E mentre il siordottore . . . '); 30. Love Ill Requited; 31. Grief for the past, ineffectual; 32–33. Love, our Greatest Blessing; 34. The Kind Request; 35. Air in Demetrio. For the Guitar.

References: Courtney 98 (citing *Life* ii. 2); Hazen 243–6; ESTC: t167511.

Notes: Published 1 April 1760 (*London Chronicle*), and as monthly numbers (on the first of each month) at 1s. each, comprising one signature of the text (containing a 'chapter' on some musical topic), and two or three songs. Some of the songs were republished as *Songs from the Monthly Melody*, arranged by Adam Carse [1939].

The Dedication is hesitantly attributed to SJ on the strength of *Life* ii. 2, and the reference to 'Edward, Duke of York', but the style is unimpressive; nevertheless no other musical work so dedicated has been found. Percy also thought SJ had contributed to a work of this kind: 'Preface or Dedication to some Music for the German Flute' (O: Percy 87).

Copies: BMp (55908);

USA: CtY (Music School), DLC, DFo (imperfect), ICN (imperfect), NN, NIC, MB, [ViW]; *UK*: L (MusG.34), Lrcm (imperfect), O (Mus. 2 c.48).

60.4BD/1   Baretti's Italian Dictionary, first edition   1760

(a) [First state] A | DICTIONARY | OF THE | ENGLISH and ITALIAN | LANGUAGES. | By *JOSEPH BARETTI.* | Improved and augmented with above TEN THOUSAND WORDS, | omitted in the laſt EDITION of *Altieri.* | To which is added, | An ITALIAN and ENGLISH GRAMMAR. | VOLUME I [– II]. | [double rule] | LONDON: | Printed for C. HITCH and L. HAWES, R. BALDWIN, W. JOHNSTON, W. OWEN, | J. RICHARDSON, G. KEITH, T. LONGMAN, S. CROWDER and Co. | P. DAVEY and B. LAW, and H. WOODGATE and S. BROOKES. | MDCCLX.

(b) [Second state] A | DICTIONARY . . . &c., as above, . . . LONDON: | Printed for J. RICHARDSON, in Pater-noſter-row. | MDCCLX.

2 vols., 4°

I. π1 A⁴ a–d⁴ e1, B–4T⁴ 4U1, ($2 (–A2) signed; 'VOL. I.' on $1 (–C, D, F–S)), 371 leaves.

Pp. π1 t., π1ᵛ blk, on A1–2 Dedication dh: TO HIS | EXCELLENCY | DON FELIX, | Marquis of ABREU and BERTODANO, | Ambaſſador Extraordinary and Plenipotentiary | from his Catholick Majeſty to the King of | Great Britain. | MY LORD, &c. ('London, January the | 12th, 1760. J. BARETTI.'), A2ᵛ blk, A3–4 Preface dh: THE | PREFACE., A4ᵛ blk, on a1 *i* ii–xxxiv Grammar dh: GRAMMATICA | DELLA | LINGUA INGLESE. | [row of 45 flowers], on B1 (–4U1ᵛ, unpaged) Text of Dictionary (Italian-English) dh: [double rule] | DIZIONARIO | ITALIANO ed INGLESE, |PARTE PRIMA | NELLA QUALE | *L' ITALIANO precede L' INGLESE.* | [rule] |THE | *ITALIAN* and *ENGLISH* | DICTIONARY | PART the FIRST. | CONTAINING | The Italian before the Engliſh.

Pagination: a–e only, roman.

Press-figures: A3–3, A3ᵛ–4, a3(ᵛ)–7, b3ᵛ(xiᵛ)–1, c4ᵛ(xxiᵛ)–4, d1ᵛ(xxᵛi)–5, d3(xxix)–4, B3ᵛ–8, B4ᵛ–1, C2ᵛ–1, C3ᵛ–5, D3ᵛ–1, E3–8, F3–8, K3–8, L2ᵛ–6, N2ᵛ–6, O1ᵛ–3, P3ᵛ–2, P4ᵛ–3, Q1–2, R1ᵛ–1, S4ᵛ–2, T2ᵛ–8, T4–3, U4–4,

U4^v–3, X3^v–8, Y4^v–4, Z1^v–2, Z3–1, 2A1^v–4, 2A2^v–3, 2B3–8, 2B3^v–4, 2D1^v–8, 2D2^v–7, 2E2^v–4, 2E3^v–7, 2F3^v–3, 2G4–4, 2H1^v–4, 2I3^v–4, 2K1^v–5, 2K3–7, 2L1^v–6, 2M3–5, 2N1^v–3, 2O2^v–5, 2O3^v–8, 2P2–2, 2P3–3, 2Q2^v–3, 2R3–3, 2S2^v–8, 2S4–7, 2T2^v–6, 2T3^v–2, 2U3–1, 2U3^v–4, 2X4–5, 2X4^v–6, 2Y1^v–3, 2Z3^v–5, 2Z4^v–3, 3A1^v–3, 3A4^v–7, 3B3^v–4, 3B4^v–3, 3C1^v–3, 3C2^v–4, 3D2^v–3, 3D3^v–7, 3E1^v–4, 3E3–2, 3F1^v–2, 3G2^v–5, 3H3–6, 3I1^v–2, 3K4^v–7, 3L4–3, 3M1^v–1, 3M4^v–2, 3N3–4, 3N4–8, 3O1^v–3, 3P4–4, 3Q1^v–3, 3R4–1, 3S1^v–3, 3S2^v–1, 3T1^v–2, 3T4^v–1, 3U2^v–5, 3U4–6, 3X1^v–1, 3Y3^v–1, 3Y4^v–7, 3Z1^v–3, 3Z2^v–2, 4A3^v–4, 4B2–8, 4B2^v–3, 4C1^v–8, 4C3–4, 4D4–4, 4D4^v–1, 4E4–1, 4F3–4, 4G4^v–3, 4H4^v–7, 4I3^v–3, 4K1^v–1, 4L1^v–1, 4L2^v–7, 4M1^v–4, 4M4^v–8, 4N2^v–1, 4O3^v–1, 4P1^v–3, 4Q2^v–1, 4R3^v–1, 4S2–6, 4S2^v–7, 4T2–6, 4T2^v–2; Unfigured: e, G–I, M, 2C, 4U, and sometimes d3 (xxix).

Catchwords: C2 Addo- (Addomesticame'nto,), d3 Albe- (Alberino,), H4^v Gia (Già), L3^v Bighero, (Bi' ghero,), O1^v Can- (Ca' ntero,), Q1^v Cre- (Cerfo' glio,), S4^v Con$_\wedge$ (con,), T2 Condure (Condurre), U2 Contra- (~,), X2 Corsía [*stet* 's'] (Corsia), 2C2^v (di- (Disumaa'rsi), 2C4^v Domo, (Do' mo,), 2F1 Fa- (Fa' cola,), 2H1 Fo- [*hyphen dropt*] (Focacciuo' la), 2H4 R$_\wedge$nder (Render), 2M1 Salaro (salario), 2R1 Intes- (Inte' ssere), 2R4^v K. (L.), 3A3 Nichi-(Ni' chilo,), 3N3 Ricalta (Ricolta), 4A4^v with (*cloath*,), 4D4^v Spi- [*hyphen dropt*] (Spigo' so,), 4H4 ohimè (Ohimè), 4S2^v Un- (Vnghiu' to,), 4U1 U$_\wedge$o (Uno).

Explicit: 4U1v *FINE* del Primo Tomo.

II. π1 2π^2 a–e^4 A–4P^4 4Q^2, ($2 signed; 'Vol. II.' on $1 (–B,D; as 'Vol. I.' on F,G)), 361 leaves.

Pp. π1 *i* Italian t.: DIZIONARIO | DELLE | LINGUE | ITALIANA ed INGLESE | *Di GIUSEPPE BARETTI*. | Più di dieci mila Vocaboli ſi ſono aggiunti che l'*Altieri* avera | laſciati fuora. | Queſta Edizione contiene una Grammatica della due Lingue. | VOLUME II. | [double rule] | LONDON: | Printed for J. Richardson, in Pater-noſter-row. | MDCCDLX., π1^v *ii* blk, 2π1 *iii* iv–v Prefazione dh: [double rule] | PREFAZIONE., *vi* blk, on a1 ^2i ii–xxxix Grammar dh: [double rule] | A | GRAMMAR | OF THE | ITALIAN TONGUE. | [row of flowers], *xl* blk, on A1 Dictionary (English-Italian) dh: [double rule] | THE | *ENGLISH* and *ITALIAN* | DICTIONARY: | Part the Second | CONTAINING | The Engliſh before the Italian. | [rule] | DIZIONARIO | INGLESE ed ITALIANO: | Parte Seconda, | NELLA QUALE | *L' INGLESE precede L' ITALIANO*., 4Q2^v blk.

Pagination: 2π and a–e only, roman.

Press-figures: 2π1(iii)–1, 2π1^v(iv)–5, a1^v(^{2}ii)–8, a2^v(^{2}iv)–6, b3^v(xiv)–2, c1^v(xviii)–1, d4(xxxi)–4, e3(xxxvii)–4, e4(xxxix)–3, A4^v–5, B2^v–3, B3^v–6, C1^v–6, C2^v–3, D1–2, D3^v–8, E3^v–5, E4^v–4, F1^v–8, G1^v–6, H4^v–6, I2–3, I4^v–8, K2^v–4, L3^v–1, L4^v–2, M2^v–2, M3^v–5, N1^v–2, N2^v–4, O3^v–6, O4–2, P1–4, Q1^v–6, Q2^v–5, R3^v–8, S4^v–7, T3–3, U3^v–4, X2^v–4, Y1^v–2, Z1^v–2,

Z4ᵛ–8, 2A3–8, 2B4–3, 2C1ᵛ–2, 2C4ᵛ–4, 2D1–3, 2D1ᵛ–1, 2E2ᵛ–2, 2F2ᵛ–7, 2F4–5, 2G1ᵛ–3, 2G4ᵛ–2, 2H1ᵛ–5, 2H3–2, 2I2ᵛ–2, 2I3ᵛ–4, 2K3ᵛ–4, 2K4ᵛ–2, 2L3–7, 2M3–2, 2N2ᵛ–4, 2O1–7, 2O4–8, 2P1ᵛ–4, 2Q2ᵛ–3, 2R1ᵛ–1, 2S3–7, 2T3–3, 2U1ᵛ–8, 2U4ᵛ–1, 2X2–2, 2Y3ᵛ–4, 2Y4ᵛ–3, 2Z2ᵛ–8, 2Z3ᵛ–1, 3A2–4, 3B4ᵛ–4, 3C4–3, 3D3–4, 3E3–1, 3E3ᵛ–2, 3F2–8, 3F2ᵛ–1, 3G2ᵛ–2, 3H1ᵛ–8, 3I2ᵛ–2, 3K2–2, 3L1ᵛ–3 [*inverted*], 3L3–4, 3M1ᵛ–1, 3N1ᵛ–1, 3N3–2, 3O3–3, 3P2ᵛ–1, 3P4–2, 3Q1ᵛ–2, 3R2ᵛ–1, 3R4–4, 3S4ᵛ–2, 3T3ᵛ–3, 3U4–4, 3X2ᵛ–1, 3X3ᵛ–2, 3Y2ᵛ–7, 3Y4–3, 3Z3–8, 4A1ᵛ–3, 4B2ᵛ–8, 4C2ᵛ–2, 4C4–8, 4D3–7, 4E2ᵛ–2, 4E4–4, 4F1ᵛ–1, 4F2ᵛ–8, 4G3–6, 4G4–3, 4H1ᵛ–1, 4H2ᵛ–4, 4I3–7, 4K1ᵛ–1, 4L2ᵛ–3, 4L4–4, 4M2–5, 4N4–3, 4O2ᵛ–1, 4P1ᵛ–3; unfigured: 4Q.

Catchwords: xx Com- (*Simple*), xxvi Effere (E'ffere), xxxii even (fyllable), xxxiii *om*. (By), xxxix *om*. (THE), B3ᵛ T (To), C3 An- (A'ngelot,), D3 A littl‸ (~ little), F4 *fi* (A), K1 Bran- [*broken sort*] (Brant), N4 Chew- (Che' wing,), P2 Cock- (Co' ckered,), S1 T (To), T2 *monto*, (*monte*,), T3 [*slipt*], U2ᵛ To (The), X4 T (To), Z1 Debout, (Devóut,), 2B1 To [*inverted*], 2B3 Draft, (~‸), 2I2 [*len-*] *ti*, (*li*,), 2K3 Gaudy, (Ga'udy,), 2L3 Vain‸ (Vainglorious,), 2M3ᵛ [*met-*] *te*‸ (*tere*), 2M4ᵛ Gur- (Gu'rnard), 2O2ᵛ Here‸ (He'refrom,), 2Q2 Imbol- (Imbo'ldened,), 2Q4 Im-(To), 2R1 Incon- (Inco'ngruous,), 3A3ᵛ pro- (Proverbial), 3A4ᵛ Mi'ngle- (Mingle-), 3C1ᵛ Murk' (Murk,), 3G1 Pan- (Pa'nnier,), 3I4 Play- (Pla'ying,), 3L3 Prey (Preying), 3M1 Pro- (Profligateness,), 3M2 Pro- (Prôphecy), 3M3ᵛ Pu'b- (A Pu'blican), 3Q1 To (*rare*), 3T2 *ufa*‸*o* (*ufato*), 3X1 *om*. (Sharper), 3Z4 So'v- (Sovereignty), 4C3ᵛ Stum- (Stu'mble,), 4D4 Swal- (Swa'llow,), 4E4 T (To), 4I3ᵛVague, (~‸), 4M3ᵛ Usa- (U'sager,).

Explicit: 4Q2 *FINIS*.

Paper: White, laid; La. post (uncut: 10¾ × 8½ in.); no vis wmk.

Type: Preface: gt. primer, Grammar &c.: pica (rom. and ital., text: bourgeois (2 cols./p.).

References: *Life* i. 353 (Courtney 98–99); CH 144; Hazen 6–7; Collison-Morley, *Giuseppe Baretti* (1909), 101, 107; Piccioni, 13, no. 18; ESTC: n003080 and n008657 (discriminating the variant tt.).

Notes: The printer has not been identified. The work was published at £2. bound on 24 April 1760 (*London Chronicle*). There is no evidence to determine the precedence of the states of the title. The fuller version (**a**) is, as Hazen pointed out, the same as that of the advt. in the *London Chronicle*, but discrepancies between advts and published imprints are common enough.

The English Grammar in vol. 1, though in Italian, is based on Johnson's Grammar (1755; 55.4D/1, above), as Baretti acknowledges in his own Preface:

The Learners therefore may be assured that the two Grammars I here offer them are not raked together from those three works, as that of one Palermo lately published. Mine, such as they are, are intirely new. That of Mr. Samuel Johnson prefixed to his English Dictionary, and that of

Buonmattei were my guides.

JB's attribution of the Dedication to SJ (*Life* i. 353) in 1791 (i. 192), was anticipated by Isaac Reed in *Works* (1788), xiv. 482, who noted it in his MS attributions (MS: Ljh), though not in the notes in *European Mag.* vii (March 1785), 190–1. Attention was again drawn to it by W. Davis in *NQ*, 2nd ser. xi (1861), 207–8.

Copies:[1] O (303 u. 103–4, (**b**));

(**a**) *USA*: CSmH (83117), CtY (Hb.48.177), Hyde[2] (**1**. 'James Boswell 1769' – 'R.W. Rogers'; **2**. R.B. Adam, lacks 'Prefazione' in vol. 2), [Liebert = CtY], MH (*EC75 B2377.760d), NIC, PPL; *Can*: CaOHM; *UK*: ABu, BRu (vol. 2 only), L (1332. g.2–3), SAN (ˢAG35.B3);

(**b**) *USA*: DFo (187705), [Liebert = CtY], MB (*B.4111.9); *UK*: DUu, Eu, Gu, Op, JDF ('James Walwyn' – 'Richard Samuel White', vol. 1 only); *Aust*: CNL (DNS 1902).

---

[1] SJ's own copy, Christie (Johnson), 16 Feb. 1785, 439, went to Hoole for £1. 1s., but is untraced.

60.4BD/2   Baretti's Italian Dictionary, second edition   1771

A | DICTIONARY | OF THE | ENGLISH and ITALIAN | LANGUAGES. | By *JOSEPH BARETTI*. | Improved and augmented with above TEN THOUSAND WORDS, | omitted in the laſt EDITION of *Altieri*. | To which is added, | An ITALIAN and ENGLISH GRAMMAR. | A NEW EDITION. | VOLUME I [–II]. | [parallel rule] | LONDON: | Printed for W. Strahan; J. and F. Rivington; W. Johnston; Hawes, Clarke, and | Collins; W. Owen; G. Keith; S. Crowder; T. Longman; B. Law; | T. Davies; T. Becket and Co.; Wilson and Nicol; J. Aalmon; | Robinson and Roberts; T. Cadell; and P. Elmsley. | MDCCLXXI.

2 vols., 4°

I. π1 A⁴ a–d⁴ e1, B–4T⁴ 4U1, ($2 (3R2 as 2R2) signed; 'Vol. I.' on $1 (–BCDE,2K,3M)), 371 leaves.

Pp. π1 t., π1ᵛ blk, A1–2 Dedication (as 60.4BD/1, 1760, above), A2ᵛ blk, A3–4 Preface (as 60.4BD/1, above), on B1 text A–IZZ, on 2S1 text L–ZUR (Dhh &c. as first edition).

Press-figures: A3ᵛ–3, a1ᵛ(ii)–3, a4ᵛ(viii)–5, b3ᵛ(xiv)–7, b4ᵛ(xvi)–5, c4ᵛ(xxiv)–3, d3ᵛ(xxx)–6, B2ᵛ–8, C4–1, C4ᵛ–4, D1ᵛ–3, E3ᵛ–2, F2ᵛ–6, F3ᵛ–7, G2ᵛ–6, H3ᵛ–1, I1ᵛ–1, I4ᵛ–3, K3ᵛ–8, L2ᵛ–1, L3ᵛ–3, M2–1, N3–1, N4–3, O3–3, P1ᵛ–5, P2ᵛ–8, Q3ᵛ–8, Q4ᵛ–3, R1ᵛ–1, S2ᵛ–8, S4–2, T3ᵛ–3, U3ᵛ–7, U4ᵛ–3, X3–8, Y3–3, Y3ᵛ–7, Z1ᵛ–8, Z3–3, 2A3ᵛ–3, 2B2ᵛ–5, 2B4–8, 2C3ᵛ–1, 2C4ᵛ–8, 2D3ᵛ–1, 2E3–7, 2E3ᵛ–8, 2F1ᵛ–6, 2F4ᵛ–5, 2G1ᵛ–8, 2G3–7, 2H1ᵛ–8, 2H3–7, 2I4–7, 2K2ᵛ–3, 2K3ᵛ–8, 2L3–6, 2M4–7, 2N2ᵛ–5, 2N4–8, 2O1ᵛ–1, 2O4ᵛ–3, 2P1ᵛ–2, 2P2ᵛ–1, 2P3ᵛ–3, 2Q3–6, 2Q3ᵛ–1, 2R3–3, 2R3ᵛ–5, 2S3ᵛ–5, 2S4ᵛ–3, 2T4–5, 2U4–8,

2X3^{v}–3, 2Y4^{v}–3, 2Z1^{v}–7, 3A2^{v}–5, 3B3^{v}–3, 3C1^{v}–3, 3D3^{v}–7, 3D4^{v}–5, 3E2^{v}–3, 3E4–6, 3F4–3, 3G2^{v}–5, 3G3^{v}–6, 3H1^{v}–1, 3I1^{v}–3, 3I2^{v}–1, 3K1^{v}–7, 3L3–7, 3L3^{v}–3, 3M1^{v}–8, 3M4^{v}–[?], 3N1^{v}–7, 3N3–5, 3O4–1, 3O4^{v}–8, 3P4–2, 3P4^{v}–3, 3Q1^{v}–7, 3Q4^{v}–2, 3R3^{v}–7, 3S1^{v}–6, 3S3–[?], 3T1^{v}–1, 3T3–6, 3U1^{v}–7, 3X2^{v}–7, 3X3^{v}–1, 3Y3–7, 3Z1^{v}–3, 4A3^{v}–3, 4B1^{v}–3, 4C4^{v}–6, 4D3^{v}–6, 4D4^{v}–1, 4E1^{v}–7, 4E4^{v}–1, 4F3–3, 4F4–2, 4G1^{v}–1, 4G3–7, 4H3^{v}–7, 4H4^{v}–1, 4I3–2, 4I4–1, 4K1^{v}–5, 4K4^{v}–1, 4L1^{v}–3, 4L2^{v}–5, 4M1^{v}–7, 4N3–1, 4O3^{v}–7, 4O4^{v}–1, 4P4–6, 4Q1^{v}–2, 4Q2^{v}–7, 4R2^{v}–3, 4R3^{v}–5, 4S3–6, 4S4–7, 4T3^{v}–3; *note 3 figures in 2P.*

Catchwords: D2 Ch'avén (Che avéndo), D3^{v} Aallé- (Allegro), M1^{v} Bota're, (~$_{\wedge}$), N1 *om.* (C.), S4^{v} [ammaeſtra-] re, (~$_{\wedge}$), Z3 M'è (M'e), 2B4^{v} Diſpórre (Diſporre), 2C2 Dilvário (Diſvário), 2I2^{v} Furbac- (Furba'ccio,), 2L4^{v} Grondea (Grondéa), 2Q1 Inna'n- (Innazitra'tto,), 3A3^{v} Nichi- (Ni'chilo,), 3L3 ra- (gione,), 3N3 Ricalta (Ricolta), 3R3^{v} *om.* (SACCU'CCIO,), 3S2^{v} Sha- (Sbalordire), 4A4^{v} *with* (*cloath*,), 4F1^{v} *pity*$_{\wedge}$ (~,), 4H4 ohimè (Ohimè), 4I4^{v} noſce (noſche), 4N3^{v} Tras- (Transmuta'to,).

Explicit: 4U1^{v} *FINE* del PRIMO TOMO.

II. π^{2} a–e^{4} A–4P^{4} 4Q^{2}, ($2 (d1 as b) signed; 'Vol. II.' on $1 (–L,U)), 360 leaves.

Pp. π *i* t., *ii* blk, *iii*–iv Prefazione, on a1 *i* ii–xxxix A Grammar of the Italian Tongue, *xl* blk, on B1 text A–GYV, on 2N1 text H–QUO, on 3O1 text R–Z, 4Q2^{v} blk.

Press-figures: π2–7, π2^{v}–4, a3^{v}(vi)–4, b1^{v}(x)–6, c3(xxi)–6, c3^{v}(xxii)–4, d2^{v}(xxviii)–7, d4(xxxi)–8, e3(xxxvii)–1, B4^{v}–6, C2^{v}–1, D3^{v}–6, E4–6, F3^{v}–1, F4^{v}–2, G1^{v}–1, H3^{v}–1, H4^{v}–2, I4–1, K1^{v}–6, K3–7, L3–2, L3^{v}–1, M4–2, M4^{v}–1, N3^{v}–7, O4–2, P1^{v}–7, Q1^{v}–4, Q3–1, R4^{v}–6, S3–7, S3^{v}–7, T1^{v}–2, T3–6, U2–7, X1^{v}–1, Y2V–2, Z3^{v}–4, 2A4–1, 2A4^{v}–6, 2B1^{v}–7, 2B2^{v}–2, 2C2^{v}–3, 2C3^{v}–6, 2D2^{v}–6, 2D4–2, 2E3–1, 2F4–1, 2F4^{v}–6, 2G4–8, 2H2^{v}–6, 2H3^{v}–8, 2I4^{v}–2, 2K3^{v}–1, 2L4^{v}–1, 2M2^{v}–2, 2M4–4, 2N2^{v}–1, 2N4–4, 2O1^{v}–6, 2O4^{v}–2, 2P2^{v}–7, 2P3^{v}–6, 2Q2^{v}–1, 2Q4–6, 2R1^{v}–4, 2R4^{v}–6, 2S2^{v}–7, 2S3^{v}–6, 2T3–7, 2T3^{v}–7, 2U2^{v}–7, 2U4–1, 2X3–6, 2X3^{v}–7, 2Y4–4, 2Y4^{v}–6, 2Z1^{v}–4, 2Z3–6, 2Z4^{v}–6, 3A2^{v}–7, 3B3^{v}–4, 3C3–2, 3C3^{v}–4, 3D2^{v}–6, 3E3–6, 3E3^{v}–7, 3F3^{v}–7, 3G3–4, 3H3^{v}–4, 3I3^{v}–7, 3I4^{v}–6, 3K4^{v}–4, 3L3–4, 3M2^{v}–1, 3N3–7, 3N3^{v}–6, 3O3–6, 3O3^{v}–4, 3P3^{v}–4, 3Q1^{v}–4, 3Q4^{v}–6, 3R4–1, 3S3–2, 3S3^{v}–4, 3T4–6, 3U1^{v}–6, 3U4^{v}–1, 3X1^{v}–6, 3X2^{v}–2, 3Y3^{v}–1, 3Z4–4, 3Z4^{v}–6, 4A3^{v}–1, 4A4^{v}–4, 4B3^{v}–1, 4C3–2, 4C3^{v}–1, 4D2^{v}–6, 4D3^{v}–4, 4E3^{v}–4, 4F2^{v}–1, 4F4–1, 4G1^{v}–1, 4H4^{v}–1, 4I1^{v}–1, 4I4^{v}–4, 4K3^{v}–4, 4K4^{v}–6, 4L4–1, 4L4^{v}–4, 4M2^{v}–4, 4M4–2, 4N2^{v}–1, 4O3^{v}–1, 4P1^{v}–7; *note 3 figures in* 2Z.

Catchwords: d1^{v} (xxvi) Eſſere (E'ſſere), d4^{v} (xxxii) even (ſyllable), e2^{v} (xxxvi) Italians, (lians,), e4 (xxxix) *om.* (THE), D2 *om.* (To), F1 *om.* (Foot-), F2 A b$_{\wedge}$ (A barber's), F2^{v} B'AR- (BA'RRACAN,), Q4 CONDUC- (CONDU'CTRESS,), R2 *one*$_{\wedge}$ (~,), T3^{v} [glimmer-] ing$_{\wedge}$ (~;), 2A1 H (He), 2C4^{v} Elder$_{\wedge}$ (~,), 2G1 Fell$_{\wedge}$ (~,), 2M3 *om.* (*brontolare*,), 2M3^{v} [*mol*-] *om.* (*to*),

2N2 *vezzofamente*ᴧ (~,), 2O3ᵛ ᴧo (To), 2Q2 Imbol- (Imbo'lden,), 2Q4 Im- (To Impu'rple,), 2R1 Incon- (Irco'ngruous,), 2S4 *om.* (or), 2T3 *om.* (To), 2U3ᵛ ᴧ*ia*ᴧ (*fcialacquare*,), 2X1 Length- (Le'ngthening,), 2X2ᵛ Lightᴧ (Light-), 3A4ᵛ Mi'ngle- (Mingle-), 3B2 Tᴧ (To), 3D1 Thᴧ (The), 3E4 *om.* (To), 3E4ᵛ Oli- (O'rigine,), 3F2ᵛ *querica* (*quercia*), 3N2 Puᴧ (Putredinous,), 3N3 Quarᴧ (Quarter), 3N4ᵛ *om.* (R.), 3S3 Sakeᴧ (Saker), 3T2ᵛ SCRA'LLᴧ (SCRA'LLED,), 3X1 Sharpeᴧ (Sharper), 4A3 *infetti*ᴧ (~,), 4D4 Swal- (Swa'llow,), 4G2 To'll- (Tollbooth,), 4I3ᵛ Vague, (~ᴧ), 4K3 Viᴧ (Vi'olin,), 4K3ᵛ [Ita-] lian (ian), 4M2ᵛ Usa- (U'sager,), 4N1 Deadᴧ (Dead-), 4N2 War- (Wa'rworn,), 4N3 Thᴧ (The), 4N3ᵛ weakᴧ (~]), 4P2 Tᴧ (To).

Explicit: 4Q2 *FINIS.*

Paper: White, laid; Printing demy (uncut: 11 × 8¾ in.); wmk.: Fleur-de-lys.

Type: Preface: gt. primer, Grammar: pica, text: bourgeois, 3 cols./p.

References: Courtney 99; Piccioni 13, no. 18; ESTC: t081920.

Notes: 1,000 copies of vol. 1 were printed by William Strahan in May 1771 (L: Add. MS 48803, fo. 36), though he had earlier recorded that 70 sheets had been worked off by 1 Jan. 1771 (Add. MS 48808, fo. 1).

According to the *Petition of the Booksellers for Relief from the Expenses of Correction and Improvement* (2 leaves, 4°, ?1778),[1] which lists the costs of correcting various books, is the note:

Baretti's Italian Dictionary, 2d. Edition	£236 – 0 – 0	
– – – – – – – – – 3d Edition, to Mr Baretti	*105 – 0 – 0*	
	341 – 0 – 0	

The revisions were apparently extensive, but the work was successful. In Mary Richardson's Trade Sale of 18 Sept. 1766 (Longman's), lots 24 and 25 each of 6th shares, were sold to Davies for £8. 13s., and to Beckett for £8 respectively; lot 26 was an 8th share which went to Rivington for £6.

The dedicatee, Joseph Antonio de Abreu et Bertodano, was an international lawyer and Spanish envoy to the Court of St James from 1754 until 1760; he died in 1775, and consequently this is the last edition to include SJ's Dedication.[2]

Subsequent editions of Baretti's *Dictionary* in his lifetime (d. 1789), were: London: Nourse, 'New Edition' 1778 (Piccioni, *Bibliografia Analitica* (1942), 13, no. 18; ESTC: t083922); Venezia, 1778; London 'corrected by Peter Ricco Rota' 1790. Thereafter the *Dictionary* was modified by other compilers though Baretti's name was usually linked with the work, as: Venezia, 1796; Londra, 1798; Firenze, 1816 (ed. J. Roster); London, 1820; Londra 'Settima Edizione', 1824; Livorno, 1828–9; Londra 'Ottava Edizione', 1831; Firenze (with Walker's 'Pronunciation') 1832; Londra 'Nona Edizione', 1839; London (ed. John Davenport), 1854; London 1868, and doubtless others.

Copies: O (Vet. A5 d. 1038–9, 'Jo: Oates' — 'Edward Oates' — 'William Edward Oates 1897');

USA: MB, [MeB, NPV], PPL; *UK*: BMp, BRu, Cf, Csj, E (K. 101.d; ^{II}4Z *misb.* before 4U), Gu, L (1480. bb. 15, vol. 1 only), MRc, Om.

¹ O: (4° x. 136 Jur. (13)), formerly 'Isaac Reed'.
² Friedrich Hausmann, *Repertorium der diplomatischen Vertreter aller Länder* (Zürich, 1950), ii (1716–63), 388.

60.5FBB   Flloyd's Bibliotheca Biographica   1760

Flloyd's *Bibliotheca Biographica: a Synopsis of Universal Biography, Ancient and Modern. Containing a circumstantial and curious Detail of the Lives, Actions, Opinions, Writings, and Characters of the most celebrated Persons, of both Sexes, of all Ranks, in all Countries, and in all Ages: Alphabetically disposed* . . . London: Printed for J. Hinton; L. Davis and C. Reymers; R. Baldwin, and J. Wallter [!]. MDCCLX.

3 vols., 8°

Notes: The Dedication to John Boyle, 5th E. of Cork and Orrery has sometimes been attributed to SJ, but without internal or external supporting evidence. Publication was in May 1760, at 18s. (*Gents. Mag.* xxx (May 1760), 251/36). See also 62.11FC/1 (1762), below.

References: ESTC: t145165.

Copies: O (Vet. A5 e. 281–83); *USA*: DLC, ICU, MB, NIC; *UK*: C.

60.8FP/1   Hollis's Committee for French Prisoners   1760

PROCEEDINGS OF THE COMMITTEE | APPOINTED TO MANAGE THE CONTRIBUTIONS | BEGUN AT LONDON DEC. XVIII MDCCLVIIII | FOR CLOATHING FRENCH PRISONERS OF WAR. | [rule] | HOMO SVM: HVMANI NIHIL À ME ALIENVM PVTO. TER. | [rule] | LONDON | PRINTED BY ORDER OF THE COMMITTEE | MDCCLX.

2°, *A*² B–C² D1, ²A–O², ($1 signed), 35 leaves.

Pp. A1 t., A1ᵛ blk, on A2 *i–ii* Introduction dh : INTRODUCTION., on B1 *iii* iv–xiii Proceedings dh: PROCEEDINGS., *xiv* blk, on ²A1 Subscribers (unpaged) dh: APPENDIX. No. I. | A | LIST | OF THE | SUBSCRIBERS | FOR CLOATHING | FRENCH PRISONERS OF WAR., ht: APPENDIX No. I. (APPENDIX. only on ²A1ᵛ and ²D2), on ²E2 dh: APPENDIX No. II. | THE | THANKS | OF THE | FRENCH PRISONERS., ht: APPENDIX No. II (APPENDIX. only on ²F2ᵛ), on ²H1ᵛ dh: APPENDIX No. III. | GENERAL ACCOUNT. ht: APPENDIX No. III., on ²K1 dh: APPENDIX. No. IV. | ACCOUNT | OF SEVERAL | PUBLIC and PRIVATE COLLECTIONS | Made in different Parts of the KINGDOM, | FOR

CLOATHING | FRENCH PRISONERS OF WAR., ht: APPENDIX No. IV.

Pagination: [↑], none in ²A–O; *Press-figures*: none.

Catchwords: ii *om.* (PROCEEDINGS), xiii *om.* (APPENDIX), *no cwds in* ²E–F1; ²G1ᵛ *om.* (Boroughbridge,), ²H2ᵛ *om.* (Cloaths), ²I2 *om.* (Brought).

Explicit: ²O2ᵛ FINIS.

Paper: White, laid; Foolscap (uncut: 13¼ × 8¼ in.); wmk.: PRO PATRIA VRYHEYT + LVG; Britannia and crowned GR.

Type: Introduction: great primer (5.6 mm), text: english (4.25 mm).

References: *Life* i. 353 (Courtney 99); CH 144; Hazen 189; *Tinker* 1341; *Rothschild* 1247; ESTC: t147649; Blackburne, *Memoirs of Thomas Hollis* (1780), i. 88 (MS of Hollis's diary at MH); Clifford, in *Johnson, Boswell and their Circle* (1965), 99–110; W.H. Bond, in *Johnson and his Age*, ed. J. Engell (1984), 83–105.

Notes: The scheme was promoted and managed largely by Thomas Hollis from January 1760 onwards (frequent notices of the Committee and its activities are found in the *London Chron.*).[1] Johnson composed the 'Introduction'. John Payne (d. 1787, above 58.2PT) of the Bank of England, was also involved and was presumably the treasurer for the committee as well as the publisher. The subscribers include 'Mr Hanway £1. 1s.' and 'Samuel Whitbread, Esq; £25'. The progress of the enterprise is traceable in Hollis's diary, and some effect was noticed in *Gents. Mag.* xxx (Feb. 1760), 101 'Monday 18 — A distribution was made of 100 suits of new cloaths, among the *French* prisoners in the city of *York*, from the charitable collection of the city of *London*, for that purpose.' Hollis received 'a M.S. of Mr. Johnson's, composed at my request & for which I have presented him with five Guineas, which MS. I hope will be allowed to serve as an Introduction to the before mentioned publication, notwith-standing that another Introduction has been already agreed upon by the Committee.' (MS *Diary*, fo. 75–75ᵛ, s.d. 19 June 1760). Throughout July Hollis negotiated with Payne about the publication, enlisted SJ as a member of the Society for promoting Arts and Commerce (25 July), and saw the publication of this piece at the beginning of August.

SJ's 'Introduction' was reprinted in the *British Mag.* i (Nov. 1760), 646–8 (above, 60.2BM), as an 'Essay on Charity'.

Hollis sponsored the publication which was 'committed to the care of Mr. Payne', and the Committee resolved that 'printed copies of the proceedings of this charity should be deposited in the British Museum, and in the several Universities of the British Empire' (*Proceedings*, xiii). These library copies are usually bound in full red morocco, gilt extra, together with Belle-Isle's *Letters*, 1759.[2] Many are inscribed by Hollis himself, who sometimes added to the letter at K2: 'A letter which does honor to Britain & to human nature.' (e.g. in copies at CSmH 'Robinson', and Hyde 'Sterne').[3] His diary records his employment in 'preparing various copies of the Proceedings . . . to give away' on 6–18 August.

On 11 August Baretti took 'a dozen copies . . . which he has promised to dis-perse, obligingly, in Spain & Portugal' (*Diary*, fo. 90). On 9 Sept. Hollis pre-pared a copy for William Pitt, with the inscription, 'To the Right honourable William Pitt, Minister of Britain, able, active, faithful, magnanimous, fortunate, this book is presented by an Englishman, a Lover of freedom & beneficence.' (*Diary*, fo. 95).[4] Another copy, formerly the property of George Milne, Esq; of New York, was sold at Christie's (June 1992).

Copies: O (AA 44 Art. Seld. Subt. 'For the Bodleian Library from the Committee', and docketed: 'Rec^d. Novr 28° 1760 Entered', + *BelleIsle*);

USA: CSmH (54796, 'To Sir Thomas Robinson Bar.',[5] marbled wraps, uncut), CtY[2] (**1**. 'For the Library of Yale College' + *BelleIsle*; **2**. marbled wraps, uncut), Hyde ('To Laurence Sterne A.M. &c.' marbled wraps, uncut; R.B. Adam), IU (Nickell), MH[2] (**1**. *fEC75 J6371 A760c. 'For the public library of Harvard College in New England. From the Committee for cloathing French prisoners of war.' + *Belle-Isle*;[6] **2**. 'To Sir James Grey Bar.'[7] with quotation from Akenside), [G. Milne, Esq;], NIC ('Leeds Public Library' — 'R.W. Chapman' — 'H. W. Liebert'), [NjP, NNU], L.R. Rothschild, Esq; ('To Jonathan Mayhew, D.D. of Boston in N. England learned, ingenious, active'), [PU]; *Can*: CaOHM (D 1805; 'Middle Temple' — 'Arthur G. Rippey');

UK: Eu (*U.17.29), Gu (in Bh9——d.10: 'For the Public Library of the University of Glasgow' + *Belle-Isle*), L[2] (**1**. C. 59.i.6(2); **2**. 102. k.9), [Llp, Lrcp], [L.F. Powell], SAN (In. ^sDC 133. 6F7), [WNs]; *Eir*: Dt (P.b.43 no. 2; + *BelleIsle*).

---

[1] In the *Catalogue Général des Manuscrits des Bibliothèques de France*, xlv (1915), 506, 'Bibliothèque d' Aix', is '1565 (1430). f. 25 Lettres d' un Anglois à l' auteur du projet d' une souscription pour les prisonniers français'. This entry remains to be pursued.

[2] Charles Louis Fouquet, Duc de Belleisle (1684–1761), was the conqueror of Prague in the War of the Austrian Succession. An account of this work is given in *London Chron.*, 6–8 Nov. 1759, 446.

[3] Both these copies were sold at Hodgson's, 25 Nov. 1920, lot 11 ('Robinson') for £30, and lot 12 ('Sterne') for £51, the latter acquired by R.B. Adam.

[4] This copy is unlocated, as is another in wrappers which once belonged to L.F. Powell, and which he had purchased in Italy in the 1920s, presumably one of those distributed by Baretti.

[5] Robinson was 1st Bt of Rokeby, see Shakespeare, below 65.10SP/1, *Copy*: NPM.

[6] This copy has smoke-prints on inserted leaves, of Hollis's Liberty emblems. W.H. Bond, *Thomas Hollis of Lincoln's Inn* (Cambridge: Cambridge University Press, 1990), 40, and illus. 66–7.

[7] Sir James Gray (d. 1773*), envoy to the K of Naples, 1753–61.

60.8FP/2   Hollis's Committee for French Prisoners,   1951
                 French translation

Johnson's 'Introduction' is translated into French, and published by 'J. G. L.' as 'Un Siècle avant Solférino', in *Revue Internationale de la Croix Rouge* [Geneva], lxxxii (December 1951), 'Chronique' 969–71.

In J.G.L.'s Introductory note the translation is attributed to 'le regretté J. C. de Watteville', and is described:

Nos lecteurs constateront combien ces lignes, admirable dans leur sobriété, demeurent actuelles. Ils verront également que, cent ans exactement avant Solférino, Samuel Johnson professait, à propos des prisonniers de guerre et de l' aide qu' on doit leur apporter, des opinions qui vont loin; elles annoncent, en effet, la grande idée qui, trouvant un terrain favorable, va bientôt donner naissance au mouvement universel de la Croix Rouge.

References: Greene, *Samuel Johnson* (1970), 85, 229, was the first to notice this translation.

Copies: O (*Revue* &c.).

60.10JCM   Robert James on Canine Madness   1760

A | TREATISE | ON | CANINE MADNESS. | By R. JAMES, M.D. | [row of 22 orn. flowers of 4 circles each, a 23rd of 3 circles only] | Solet autem ex eo vulnere, ubi parum occurſum eſt | aquæ timor naſci, ὑδροφοβιαν Græci appellant: Miſerri- | mum genus morbi: in quo ſimul æger et ſiti et aquæ | metu cruciatur; quo oppreſſis in anguſto ſpes eſt. | CELSUS. L. 5 C. 27. | [row of 24 orn. flowers of 4 circles each] | [small orn. device of flowers] | LONDON: | Printed for J. NEWBERY, at the Bible and Sun in St. | Paul's Church-yard. | M DCC LX.

8°, *A*⁴ B–O⁸ P⁸ (± P3) Q–R⁸ S⁴, ($4 (−S3,4) signed), 136 leaves.

Pp. A1 t., A1ᵛ blk, A2 *i* ii–vi Dedication dh: TO | HIS GRACE THE | DUKE OF KINGSTON, | MARQUIS OF DORCHESTER, | EARL OF KINGSTON, | VISCOUNT NEWARK, | BARON PIERREPONT, of HOLME PIERREPONT, | Lieutenant General of His Majeſty's Forces, | AND | Knight of the Moſt Noble Order of the Garter. | MY LORD, ht: DEDICATION., (vi. ROBERT JAMES.), on A1 *1* 2–257 text dh: [Hp of flowers] | A | TREATISE | ON | CANINE MADNESS., rt: A TREATISE ON | CANINE MADNESS., 258–64 Postscript.

Pagination: no errors; *Press-figures*: none.

Catchwords: 28 ˏtongue, ("∼,), 36 andˏ (∼,), 48 tho' (though), 49 yearˏ(∼,), 56 Thus (THUS), 74 ˏTHE ('∼), 122 *om.* (SIR,) 129 ˏ *A ſure* ('∼ ∼), 135 ˏI think ('∼ ∼), 156 THOˏ ('THOUGH), 158 'ſighedˏ ('∼,), 216 [de-] teſtablyˏ (teſtable,), 227 BUTˏ (∼,), 232 wouldˏ (∼,), 238 *Lumine* (*Summe*), 243 'headˏ ('∼,), 246 IN- (Innumerable), 253 *The* (THE).

Explicit: 264 *FINIS*.

Paper: White, laid; La. post (uncut: 8¼ × 5¼ in.); wmk.: fleur-de-lys.

Type: English (4.5 mm).

References: Welsh 241; Roscoe, *Newbery* (1973), A258; ESTC: t057163.

Notes: The work is an expansion of James's earlier study, *A New Method of preventing and curing the Madness caused by the Bite of a Mad Dog. Laid before the Royal Society in February 1741*, London: T. Osborne, 4°, 1741 (*Gents. Mag.* xi (May 1741), 280/23 at 1s.) of which there are copies in *UK*: Cq, Eu, Gu, L (7660. d.27), MC), and of which a second edition was published in 1743 (*UK*: [Es], Gu, O (1572 e.1)).

The attribution of the 'Dedication' to SJ is doubtful, though it was supported by Hazen, and a connection with James is very plausible.[1] The association of anti-vivisectionist opinions as there displayed, with those of *Rambler* 6, and more especially with *Idler* 17, are in its favour, but the clumsinesses of the style and the awkward conduct of the tenor of the piece give pause.[2] Yet it may be conceded that SJ could have modified a draft by James. Sentences and phrases which might be his are, however, entangled with the rest, and SJ could not easily have restrained himself from mending the whole; nevertheless James (as a slightly older schoolfellow) was probably wilfully independent enough to have invited SJ's aid to accept it only in part. I am reluctant, however, to adopt it as a canonical piece.

The book was announced in *Gents. Mag.* xxx (Oct. 1760), 491, no. 15, and reviewed in the same periodical (Dec. 1760), 547–9, where the price was noticed as 4s. 6d.

Copies: O (1572 e.14);

USA: CtY, DLC ('F. C. Cherry, '37'), G. Goldberg, Esq; ICU, [Liebert = CtY], MH, NN, [ICJ, NAM, NNC, PPCP, PPM, PUV]; *Can*: CaOHM; *UK*: C ('S. W. Warneford E Coll: Univ: Oxon.'[3]), Cf, Eu (G.4.25), Gu, L, [Lrcs, Lrcp], MRu, NCu, REu.

---

[1] Hazen proposed the attribution in an address (1971), but never published his arguments; it is repeated, obliquely, by P. Rogers, *The Augustan Vision* (London: Weidenfeld, 1974), 236, but no evidence is adduced. The dedicatee was Sir Evelyn Pierrepont (1711–73*), 2nd D. of Kingston.
[2] Supposed by Brain, *London Hospital Gazette* (Feb. 1947), 14–20, to be an attack on the experiments of William Hunter on the lacteal glands (described in 1746–7), and corroborated by his brother John in 1758, but cf. Wiltshire, *Samuel Johnson in the Medical World* (1991), 128–38.
[3] Philanthropist, 1763–1855*.

60.12LSA   Letter for the Society of Artists   1760

On 25 Nov. 1760 the Society, by the agency of Reynolds, asked SJ to draft a letter to the Society for the Encouragements of Arts and Sciences, asking for the further use of their rooms for the annual exhibition in June 1761.

References: *Walpole Society*, vi (1917–18), 113–23, 'The Papers of the Society of Artists of Great Britain' (minutes of meetings of 25 Nov., 8 Dec. 1760, and 16 Jan. 1761); Clifford, in *Augustan Milieu* (1970), 333–48; Brownell, *Johnson's Attitude to the Arts* (1989), 49–50.

Notes: The text of the letter is given in *Walpole Society*, vi. 122, and is partly quoted by [Charles Taylor], *Literary Panorama*, iii (1808), cols. 1014–15. Neither of these letters is noticed by Chapman in *Letters*, or in Hyde i.

For SJ's further involvement with the Society, see below 62.5SA/1.

60GM30   Gentleman's Magazine, Vol. XXX   1760

October 453–6   Account of a Book, entitled, 'An historical and critical Enquiry into the Evidence produced by the Earls of Moray and Morton against Mary Queen of Scots. With an Examination of the Rev. Dr. Robertson's Dissertation, and Mr. Hume's History, with respect to that Evidence.'

References: *Life* i. 21, 354 (Courtney 99).

Notes: Attributed to SJ by Percy as '[Review] of Titler's Book on the evidence concern^g. Qu. Mary's Letters in the Gent. Mag^e.' (O: Percy 87), and by Isaac Reed in his MS (Ljh), '[1761 *sic*] Review of Tytler's Queen Mary' and in his note sent to JB (Waingrow, *Corr.* 317). William Tytler's *Enquiry*, was published in Edinburgh in 1760.

61.1LG   The London Gazette   1761

January 6–10, p. 1   An Address of the Painters, Sculptors, and Architects to George III. on His Accession to the Throne of these Kingdoms.

References: *Life* i. 352 (Courtney 99); Clifford, in *The Augustan Milieu* (1970), 333–48; Liebert, *YULG* lviii (1984), 140–2; Brownell, *Johnson's Attitude to the Arts* (1989), 50–1. This piece is also included in Percy's list of attributions: 'The Address of the Painters to the King at the beginning of this reign' (O: Percy 87).

Notes: The address was quickly reprinted by other newspapers. The following list makes no claims to completeness: *London Chron.*, 10–13 January; *Lloyd's Evening Post*, 9–12 January, and *London Evening Post*, 10–13 January, both record the presentation of the Address, but do not print the text. The latter and the *Public Advertiser*, 14 January, printed verses on SJ's Address (Clifford, 343).

Copies: L; *USA*: CtY, MH; *UK*: E.

61.3LH/1   Lennox's Henrietta, second edition   1761

HENRIETTA. | BY | Mrs. CHARLOTTE LENNOX. | [rule] | IN TWO VOLUMES. | VOL. I [–II]. | [rule] | The SECOND EDITION, Corrected. | [rule] | [Lozenge of flowers] | [double rule] | LONDON: | Printed for A. MILLAR, in the Strand. | MDCCLXI.

2 vols., 12°

I. A⁴ B–L¹² M⁸, ($6 (−A1,3,4, M5,6) signed; 'VOL. I.' on $1 (−AG)), 132 leaves.

Pp. A1 *i* t., *ii* blk, *iii–vi* Dedication dh: TO HER GRACE | The Ducheſſ of Newcaſtle., ht: DEDICATION. ('LONDON, | Nov. 20, 1760. Charlotte Lennox.'), *vii–viii* Contents dh: [double rule] | CONTENTS., ht. (viii) CONTENTS., on B1 *1* 2–255 text dh: [double rule] | HENRIETTA. | BOOK THE FIRST. | [rule], ht. HENRIETTA., *256* blk.

Pagination: 48 as 84, 226 as 126, 228 as 128.

Press-figures: B12(23)–1, B12ᵛ(24)–5, C11(45)–4, C12(47)–5, D8(63)–2, D11(69)–5, E7(85)–1, E11ᵛ(94)–5, F11ᵛ(118)–5, G8(135)–4, H5ᵛ(154)–1, H7(157)–2, I7(181)–1, K2ᵛ(196)–5, K11ᵛ(214)–4, L8ᵛ(232)–2, L11ᵛ(238)–5, M1ᵛ(242)–2, M2ᵛ(244)–1.

Catchwords: i, ii, vi *om.*, 2 *om.* ("Who), 9 ˏap- ("appearance), 11 ˏCourtney ("∼), 14 ˏfriends; ("∼;), 51 ˏcare. ("∼.), 60 ˏher ("∼), 140 "No, ("∼ˏ), 150 [impa-] "tiently. (ˏ∼.), 151 "ˏ ("I), 155 ˏOh, ("∼,), 185 ˏhad ("∼), 190 "ſelf (ˏ∼), 234 "Miſſ(ˏ∼), 235 ˏhave ("∼), 239 ˏtake. ("∼.), 245 *om.* ("I).

Explicit: 255 END of VOL. I. | [inverted triangle of flowers].

II. A⁴ B–O¹² P², ($6 signed; 'VOL. II.' on $1), 162 leaves.

Pp. A1 *i* t., *ii* blk, *iii–viii* Contents dh: [double rule] | THE | CONTENTS | OF THE | SECOND VOLUME. | [rule], ht: CONTENTS., on B1 *1* 2–315 text dh: [parallel rule] | HENRIETTA. | BOOK THE THIRD. | [rule], ht: HENRIETTA., *316* blk.

Pagination: 5 unnumbered.

Press-figures: B12ᵛ(24)–4, C6ᵛ(36)–2, C11ᵛ(46)–1, D12(71)–1, D12ᵛ(72)–1, E6ᵛ(84)–3, E11ᵛ(94)–4, F1ᵛ(98)–3, F6ᵛ(108)–5, G12(143)–5, H1ᵛ(146)–5, I5ᵛ(178)–4, K1ᵛ(194)–4, K11(213)–2, L6ᵛ(228)–5, L11ᵛ(238)–2, M12ᵛ(264)–4, N8(279)–2, O1ᵛ(290)–1, P1ᵛ(314)–4.

Catchwords: i–ii *om.*, 20 "yet ('∼), 30 "Abont ("About), 71 "hˏ ("her), 139 ˏYou ("∼), 144 'No ("∼), 165 ˏas ("∼), 174 "Hen- (ˏHenrietta), 313 *om.* (of).

Explicit: 315 THE END.

Paper: White, laid; La. post (uncut: 7 × 4¼ in.); no vis. wmk.

Type: Dedication: gt. primer (5.7 mm), leaded; text: sm. pica (3.6 mm), leaded; Contents: (italic) bourgeois (3.0 mm).

References: CH 145; Hazen 98–102; Small, *Lennox* (1935), 23–9, 127–8; *Tinker* 1345; Isles, *HLB* xix (1971), 58–60; ESTC: t139652.

Notes: SJ wrote the 'Dedication' (which was not in the first edn. 1758 (ESTC: t072179); see CL's letter to Dss. of Newcastle, 6 Oct. 1760, L: Add. MS 33067, fo. 23; cited by Hazen). The dedicatee was Henrietta (d. 1776), duchess of Sir Thomas Pelham-Holles (1693–1768*), 1st D. of Newcastle. Isles, *HLB* xix (1971), 58–60, shows CL's involvement with the Newcastle family: she christened her daughter (1765–?1782) Henrietta Holles. This novel was drama-tized by CL as *The Sister* in 1769. It was published 19 March 1761 (*Lond. Chron.*), at 6s. bound or 5s. in boards.

Copies: O (256 f. 2731–2, 'To Her Grace the Dutchess of Leeds From the Author'[1]);

USA: CSmH, Hyde, ICU, [Liebert = CtY], MH, NjP; *UK*: C, L (12611. aaa. 21), Lv (Dyce 5747, pres.), MRu.

[1] Mary Godolphin, granddaughter of John Churchill, 1st D. of Marlborough, and d. of Francis, 2nd E of Godolphin (1678–1766*), m. 1740, Thomas Osborne (b. 1713), 4th D of Leeds.

61.3LH/2   Lennox's Henrietta, Harrison's Novelist's Magazine, Vol. XXIII   1788

[Engr. t.] THE | [BL] **Novelist's Magazine.** | VOL. XXIII. | *CONTAINING* | Raſſelas, Prince of Abiſſinia. | Henrietta. | Nourjahad. | Felicia to Charlotte. | The Creole. | The Inviſible Spy. | [vign.] | LONDON: | Printed for Harriſon and Co. N°. 18, Paternoſter Row. 1788.

[Title] HENRIETTA. | BY MRS. LENNOX. | IN TWO VOLUMES. | [device of flowers] | LONDON: | Printed for HARRISON and C°. N° 18, Paternoſter Row. | M DCC LXXXVIII.

8°, *A*1–3 B–U⁴ X1, ($1 signed), 80 leaves.

Pp. A1 *1* t., *2* blk, *3* Dedication, *4* blk, *5* 6–160 text.

Pagination: 28, 75, 103, 125 unnumbered.

Press-figures: none; *Catchwords*: unrecorded.

Explicit: 74 END OF THE FIRST VOLUME. 160 FINIS.

Paper: White with bluish tinge, laid; Demy (uncut: 8¾ × 5⅝ in.); no vis. wmk.

Type: Bourgeois (2.9 mm).

Plates: 4 plates.

'Plate I. . . . E. F. Burney del. Anker Smith sculp. Published as the Act directs by Harrison & Co. Augᵗ 1. 1787' (facing p. 84).

'Plate II. . . . E. F. Burney . . . I. Milson sc. . . . Sepᵗ 1. 1787' (p. 126).

'Plate III. . . . E. F. Burney . . . Milson sculp. . . . Octʳ. 1. 1787' (p. 59).

'E. F. Burney . . . Anker Smith sculp. . . . Novʳ. 1. 1787' (p. 50).

References: ESTC: t088672 ('1787').

Notes: The three preliminary leaves form H2–4 of the last ½-sheet of SJ's *Rasselas* (59.4R/14, above), and the final leaf is the first of the ½-sheet which forms the prelims. of *Nourjahad*.

The dates of the plates give some guidance to the issuance of the four sections of alternately 2 (with a plate) and 3 signatures to purchasers.

Copies: BMp;

USA: MB, NN, PBm, [RPB], TxU; *UK*: C, Eu, L (1207. e. 4/3), NCu ('1787').

61.3LH/3   Lennox's Henrietta, Dublin   1786

Not seen, but a Dublin edn. in 2 vols. 12°, Printed by M. Mills, is reported in ESTC: n032858, with copies at *USA*: IaU, IEN.

61.3LH/4   Lennox's Henrietta, Cooke's edition   [?1805]

[Hollow] HENRIETTA, | By Mrs LENNOX, | AUTHOR OF | *THE FEMALE QUIXOTE.* | TWO VOLUMES IN ONE. | [short parallel rule] | [BL] **Cooke's Edition.** | [short total rule] | [device: book with lyre and trumpet] | [parallel rule] | EMBELLISHED WITH SUPERB ENGRAVINGS. | [total rule] | [BL] **London:** | Printed for C. COOKE, No. 17, Paternoster-Row, | And fold by all the Bookfellers in | Great Britain.

18°, A–2D⁶ ($3 signed), 162 leaves.

Pp. A1 t., A1ᵛ blk, A2 *3* 4–144 text, 144 END OF THE FIRST VOLUME., *145* 146–323 text vol. 2, 323 FINIS. | [metal tp.], *324* blk.

Notes: (ESTC: n032859). SJ's 'Dedication' is not reprinted in this edn.
Copies: L (012635. d.2); *USA*: [CLU], IU, MH, [NNU, NRY].

61.2LH/TF/1   Lennox's Henrietta,   1760
                       French translation

Henriette. Traduit de l' Anglois. Lausanne: chez Antoine Chapuis; aux dépens de Marc-Michel Rey. Amsterdam, 1760

2 vols., 12°. Not seen.

I. Pp. ii + 298; II. Pp. ii + 355.

References: Streeter, *Eighteenth-Century English Novel in French Translation* (1970), 199.

Notes: The translator was Gaspard Joël Monod whose first edn. appeared in 1758. The date implies that this is a version of the first edn. (1758) of *Henrietta*, which makes it unlikely that SJ's 'Dedication' appears in it.

Another issue has a cancelled t. with the imprint: 'Londres, et se trouve à Paris, Chez Duchesne. 1760' (ESTC: t120567); *UK*: L (1607/5666).

Copies: Not examined (J. Burmester, *Cat.* 16 (1991), 179, £200).

61.3CR11   Critical Review, Vol. XI   1761

April 304–14

Review of Capt. Joseph Otway's Translation of Comte Lancelot Turpin de Cressé's *Essai sur l' Art de la Guerre* (1754), as article X. '*An Essay on the Art of War. Translated from the* French *of Count* Turpin, *by Captain* Joseph Otway. In Two volumes. 4to. Pr. 1*l.* 16*s. Johnston.*'

References: A memorandum in JB's papers (CtY: M 155:1) records, 'He reviewed (authority of Mr Reed from Wright Printer in Critical Review Hawkesworth's Oronooko — Otway's Art of War.'[1] When JB came to assemble material for the published *Life*, he appears to have overlooked or disregarded this note. Otway's translation was published in April (*Gents. Mag.* xxxi (Apr. 1761), 190b). There is nothing in this review to associate it with SJ, though he quoted from the book in his 'Essay on the Bravery of the English Common Soldier' (60.2BM/1, Jan. 37–9, above).[2] Many military treatises were published about this time as a consequence of the Seven-years War, but there are no pertinent reviews which might be given to SJ. His resolutions on 18 Sept. 1760, include 'Send for books on Hist. of war' but that does not afford much assistance with a problem of this sort (*Diaries* 71).

[1] I am indebted to Prof. M. Waingrow for this information. See also above 59.12CR8, for the review of Hawkesworth. The printer was presumably Thomas Wright who had worked until 1766, with Archibald Hamilton (fl. 1736–93), founder and printer of the *Critical Review* (Plomer, s.nn.), and became printer of the *Westminster Mag.* (*Lit. Anec.* ii. 666–7, iii. 399). Isaac Reed did not record this attribution himself in his MS List (Ljh), nor is it in the list he sent to JB (Waingrow, *Corr.* 317); he may have acquired it at a late date.

[2] The 'Mrs Otway' mentioned in SJ's *Diaries*, 126 and refs. (2 Jan. 1770), and 136 (30 March 1771), and her son (*Letters*, 25 March 1773, Hyde, ii. 25), may have been some connections of the Captain, but even such an acquaintance cannot prove SJ's authorship of a review. See *Works* (Yale), x. 279 n.

61.4SL/1 Sophronia 1761

SOPHRONIA: | OR, | LETTERS | TO THE | LADIES. | [device of flowers] | LONDON: | Printed for WILLIAM JOHNSTON, in | *Ludgate-ſtreet*. 1761.

12°, A⁶ B–L¹² M⁴ (M4 blk), ($5 (–A1,4,5, M3) signed), 130 leaves.

Pp. A1 t., A1ᵛ blk, A2 iii–xii Preface, on B1 *1* 2–245 text, *246* blk, *247–8* (M4) blk.

Pagination: no errors; *Press-figures*: none; *Catchwords*: unrecorded.

Explicit: 245 FINIS.

Notes: Publication is noticed in *Gents. Mag.* xxxi (Apr. 1761), 190, at 3s. ESTC: t117042. For attribution, see 61.4SL/4.

Copies: L (1155. c.35);

USA: CLU-C, ICN, InU, MiU, NjP, PU; *UK*: O (Vet. A5 f.3055, 'Madam, Your acceptance of these Letters is desired by yʳ most hum. Servᵗ, J: N:' — 'Elizabeth Roberts' — 'Union 1786' — 'Mr. N. Georges Coffee House Strand London. 1810', &c.)

61.4SL/2   Sophronia, Dublin   1763

Sophronia: or, Letters to the Ladies. Dublin: Printed for D. Chamberlaine in Smock-Alley, James Hunter and J. Mitchell, in Sycamore-Alley. M.DCC͵LXIII.

12°, A–K¹², ($5 signed), 120 leaves; Pp. A1 *i* t., *ii* blk, iii–viii Preface, on A5 *9* 10–237 text, *8–40* Catalogue of Books sold by David Chamberlaine.

Notes: There is nothing in this work to associate it with SJ. ESTC: t107101.

Copies: L (12654. k.46);

USA: CSmH, CtY; *Can*: CaOHM; *UK*: C.

61.4SL/3   Sophronia, second edition   1775

Sophronia: or, Letters to the Ladies. The Second Edition. London: Printed for J. Bew, No. 28, Pater-noſter-Row. 1775

12°, A⁶ B–L¹² M⁴ (M4 blk), ($5 (–A1,4,5, M3) signed), 130 leaves.

Notes: This edn. collates as 1761, (61.4SL/1 above), but the t. is integral without any suggestion of a cancellation for a reissue. ESTC: t107096.

Copies: L (12654. l.12, + MS notes); *USA*: MH, PU.

61.4SL/4   Sophronia, 'second' edition   1780

Sophronia: or, Letters to the Ladies . . . With a Preface by Dr Johnson. . . . London: J. Bew . . . MDCCLXXX.

Notes: In *JNL* ix (1 Feb. 1949), 10, this titular attribution in the second edn. was pointed out, but no corroborating evidence is known, and neither the style nor the subject matter offers anything to suggest that the attribution has any force. The copy to which the 1949 note refers is not traced.

Copies: Unlocated.

61.8GC   Gwynne on the Coronation   1761

THOUGHTS | ON THE | CORONATION | Of his preſent MAJESTY | KING GEORGE THE THIRD. | OR, | Reaſons offered againſt confining the Proceſſion to | the uſual Track, and pointing out others more | commodious and proper. | To which are prefixed, | A Plan of the different Paths recommended, with the Parts | adjacent, and a Sketch of the Proceſſion. | Moſt humbly ſubmitted to Conſideration. | *LONDON:* | Printed for the PROPRIETOR, and ſold by F. NOBLE, oppoſite *Gray's Inn* | Gate, *Holbourn*; J. NOBLE, in St. *Martin*'s Court, near *Leiceſter*-Square; | W. BATHOE, near *Exeter-Change*, in the *Strand*; and H. YATES, | at the *Royal-Exchange*. | [short rule] | M DCC LXI. | [Price One Shilling and Six-pence.]

Note: An early state of the title reads: perfixed,

2°, *A*² B², ($1 signed), 4 leaves.

Pp. *1* t., *2* ADVERTISEMENT., *3* 4–8 text dh: THOUGHTS | ON THE | CORONATION, *&c*., ht: THOUGHTS *on the* CORONATION., + 1 engr. fold. plate.

Pagination: no errors; *Press-figures*: none.

Catchwords: 3 [be-] fore, 5 Streets, 7 A, 7 n. At$_\wedge$.

Explicit: 8 *FINIS*.

Paper: White, laid; Crown (uncut: 15¼ × 10 in.); wmk.: Strasburg lily + LVG, countermark: IV.

Type: Advertisement: english (4.5 mm), text: gt. primer (5.6 mm), notes: sm. pica (3.6 mm).

Plate: Plate area 14 × 16½ in. (356 × 419 mm), paper as for text; 'Sketch of the Proceſſion Usually Observed in the Coronation of our KINGS & QUEENS to Gether with a PLAN Pointing out Several new Paths and their Parts adjacent.' Coloured with hand-painted pink and yellow lines.

References: *Life* i. 316 (Courtney 100); CH 144; Hazen 41; Hobbs, *NQ* ccvii (1962), 22–4; Harris 214–17, esp. 227; Brownell *Johnson's Attitude to the Arts* (1989), ch. x; ESTC: t085342.

Notes: A 'Second Edition' was advertised in *Lond. Chron.*, 8 Aug. 1761. No copy is recorded bearing those words, and yet it seems implausible that the mere correction of the misprint in the title should have led to the use of that expression. The Coronation took place on 22 September, and this pamphlet was again advertised in *Gents. Mag.* xxxi (Oct. 1761), 479.[1]

F. & J. Noble were the proprietors of a circulating library which specialized in books for children, but of H. Yates nothing seems to be known. William Bathoe (d. Oct. 1768; *Plomer* 19) was succeeded by his [?]son Samuel, who perhaps figures as 'Mr. Bathoe' in the publication of Gwynne's later *London & Westminster Improved*, 1766 (66.7GLW/1, below).

SJ's contribution of corrections and improvements was reported by JB and in both Reed's MS list (Ljh), and in that sent to him in 1790 by JB (Waingrow, *Corr.* 317). Hazen believed SJ responsible for the first four paragraphs (41).

Copies: O² (**1**. D 8.23 Art, 'perfixed'; uncut, orig. blue wraps, inscr: 'Mithas 1761'; **2**. Gough Westm. 20 (14) 'prefixed');

USA: [IEN]; *UK*: L² (**1**. 604. i. 30; **2**. 604. m. 45; both states of t.).

---

[1] L: Add. MS 6307, fo. 35, is a collection of newspaper cuttings and notes relative to the coronation of George III. Hazen also confessed his puzzlement over the 'Second Edition' (41 n.).

61.8BA/1a   Life of Ascham, Bennet's Ascham,   1761
                         first edition, first issue

THE | ENGLISH WORKS | OF | *ROGER ASCHAM,* | Preceptor to Queen ELIZABETH: | CONTAINING, | I. A Report of the Affairs of Germany, and the Em- | peror Charles's Court. | II. Toxophilus, or the School of Shooting. | III. The Schoolmaster, or perfect Way of bringing up Youth, | illuſtrated by the late learned Mr. Upton. | IV. Letters to Queen Elizabeth and others, now firſt | publiſhed from the Manuſcripts. | With Notes and Observations, and the Author's Life. | [rule] | By JAMES BENNET, | Maſter of the Boarding-School at Hoddesdon in Hertfordshire. | [double rule] | LONDON: | Printed for R. and J. Dodsley, in Pall-Mall, and J. Newbery, in St. Paul's Church-Yard. | [short rule] | M,DCC,LXI.

4°, A⁴ χ1 b–c⁴ B–3D⁴ 3E², ($2 (−2B2, 2Y2) signed), 211 leaves.

Pp. A1 *1* t., *2* blk, *3–4* Dedication dh: [Engr. hp Arms of Ashley Cooper, 'F. Garden Sculp'] | TO | The RIGHT HONOURABLE | ANTHONY ASHLEY COOPER, | Earl of Shaftesbury, Baron Ashley, Lord | Lieutenant and Custos Rotulorum | of Dorsetshire, F. R. S. | My LORD, on A3 *5–8* Subscribers dh: [double rule] | A LIST of SUBSCRIBERS., ht: A LIST of SUBSCRIBERS., on χ1 *9* dh: ADDITIONAL SUBSCRIBERS., *10* blk., on b1 *i* ii–xvi Life of Ascham dh: [double rule] | THE | LIFE | OF | *ROGER ASCHAM.*, rt: THE LIFE OF | ROGER ASCHAM. (on xvi THE LIFE OF, &c.), on B1 *1* 2–395 text (various dhh. and htt. *passim*), rt: THE WORKS OF | ROGER ASCHAM., *396* blk.

Pagination: b–c roman; (↑) 53, 55; [↑] 177–9, 189, 191, 199, 349–60, 363–7, 369–95; blanks pp. 2, 10, 50, 52, 60, 188, 262, 348, 362, 368, 396.

Press-figures: A3ᵛ–3, b3ᵛ(vi)–1, b4(vii)–2, c1ᵛ(x)–4, B4ᵛ(8)–1, C4(15)–2, D4(23)–8, E1ᵛ(26)–8, F4(39)–2, G4(47)–4, H4(55)–4, I1ᵛ(58)–1, K1ᵛ(66)–8, L3(77)–4, M1ᵛ(82)–6, M4(88)–3, N3ᵛ(94)–2, N4ᵛ(96)–7, O1ᵛ(98)–7, P4(111)–6, Q3(117)–1, R3ᵛ(126)–7, S4(135)–6, T1ᵛ(138)–3, U1ᵛ(146)–1, X3(157)–3, Y2(163)–4, Z3(173)–3, Z4(175)–4, 2A2ᵛ(180)–3, 2A4(183)–5, 2B3(189)–2, 2B4(191)–8, 2C1ᵛ(194)–3, 2D1ᵛ(202)–7, 2D3(205)–4, 2E3ᵛ(214)–4, 2E4ᵛ(216)–4, 2F3(221)–4, 2G3ᵛ(230)–4, 2H1ᵛ(234)–3, 2I1ᵛ(242)–1, 2K4(255)–2, 2K4ᵛ(256)–4, 2L4(263)–6, 2M1ᵛ(266)–3, 2M2ᵛ(268)–4, 2N1ᵛ(274)–2, 2N3(277)–3, 2O2ᵛ(284)–4, 2P4(295)–4, 2P4ᵛ(296)–2, 2Q1ᵛ(298)–1, 2Q3ᵛ(302)–1, 2Q4ᵛ(304)–4, 2R1ᵛ(306)–4, 2S1ᵛ(314)–1, 2T1(321)–2, 2T4(327)–1, 2U2ᵛ(332)–1, 2U4(335)–4, 2X1ᵛ(338)–5, 2X4ᵛ(344)–4, 2Y4ᵛ(352)–4, 2Z4(359)–3, 2Z4ᵛ(360)–4, 3A2ᵛ(364)–3, 3A3ᵛ(366)–6, 3B4ᵛ(376)–2, 3C3(381)–1, 3D4ᵛ(392)–6, 3E1ᵛ(394)–1; *NB* three figures in 2Q.

Catchwords: A4v THE (χ1 ADDITIONAL), 48 *om.* (For), 62 day‸ (∼,), 71

Both (—*Both*), 130 thermes, (*~,), 175 THE (The), 178 DIVÆ (*~), 272 n. fciebam, ("~,), 358 C. GUAL- (D. GUALTIERI).

Explicit: 395 FINIS.

Paper: White, laid; La. post (uncut: 10½ × 8½ in.); no vis. wmk.

Type: Dedication: great primer (5.6 mm), Life and text: english (4.7 mm), notes: sm. pica (3.5 mm).

References: Courtney 100; CH 144; Hazen 19–23; Welsh 199, 244; *Life* i. 464, 550–2; Roscoe, *Newbery* (1973), A17; Katterfeld, *Roger Ascham* (1879), App. II, 358 no. 9; Tannenbaum *Roger Ascham* (1937); ESTC: t140586.

Notes: See 'Proposals' (57.12PBA/1, above), for notes on the slow progress of this work. William Strahan printed 750 copies in July 1761, but a further 1,000 receipts for subscribers in August, suggesting that sales and subscriptions (at £1. 1s.), were sluggish. 307 subscribers (among whom were Thomas Bowdler, Mrs Gardiner, Mr John Hawkins, Mr John Hoole, Rev. Mr. Merrick, Mr Samuel Richardson ('2 *books*'), Thomas Sheridan, Edward Southwell, and Hon. Robt. Walpole, but not SJ) took 383 copies, but the work was readvertised in 1762 (*Lond. Chron.*, 7 Jan.) and in 1763 at 10s. 6d., again with little success, since the second issue (61.8BA/1b, below) was prepared in 1767.

Of James Bennet little is known. His connection with Hoddesdon implies an acquaintance with John Hoole, and suggests that he may have been a Quaker.[1] Verses addressed to the memory of 'Mr. Bennet' by John Scott of Amwell, in 1769, perhaps refer to him (*Lit. Illus.* v (1828), 795). Both Hoole and Scott were among the subscribers. Joseph Cockfield, himself a Quaker, in a letter to Weeden Butler on 8 Aug. 1768, after a visit to Hertfordshire, mentions 'An unhappy poor person, who was formerly my schoolmaster, partly through the hardship of the times, and in a good degree through his own misconduct, was lately under confinement' (*Lit. Illus.* v. 784–5). Cockfield adds that he relieved his former tutor's distress (*tempora mutantur*). If Bennet was the man, then he apparently died in 1768 or 1769.

Johnson's contribution was the 'Life' of Ascham, which, as Hazen observed, derives from Edward Grant's *Oratio* (1576).[2] It is incorporated in the 2nd edn. by Kippis, of *Biographia Britannica* (1779–91), s.n. Tom Davies, who became involved with the publication in the second issue (below 61.8BA/1b), asserted that SJ was editor as well as biographer, and Percy corroborated this in his MS notes on Boswell's *Life* (1791) (O: MS Percy d. 11, fo. 8),[3] as did Isaac Reed in his MS list in Ljh, where he noted the second issue, giving merely '1767 Ascham's Works'.[4] Powell marshalled the evidence for SJ's editorial responsibility in *Life* i. 464, 550–2.

A reduced facsimile of the section containing the 'Life' only was incorporated in *Early Biographical Writings of Dr. Johnson*, Gregg International Publishers Ltd. 1973 (61.8BA/5, below).

Copies: O (Douce A. 566);

USA: CSmH (1. 21145; and 2. 139806 consisting of the 'Life' only), CtY,

DFo ('George Rose'), [DLC (? lost)], Hyde (R.B. Adam), ICN, ICU, [Liebert[2] (**1**. 'James Bennet to the Reverend Dr. Birch'[5]; **2**. BM dupl.) + CtY ?], MBAt, MH, MiU, NcD, NIC, NjP, NNC, PPL, L.R. Rothschild, Esq; TxU, [MHi, MeB, NB, OU, OkU]; *Can*: CaOHM (D 1652), [CaBVaU];

UK: BMp, BRu, Cf, Ck, Csj, DUu, E, En, Eu, GRA (Newcome), Gu, L (632. 1. 12, 'Thomas Birch' + MS notes), [Lg], LVp, MRc, MRu, NCu, SAN, Y[2]; *Aust*: CNL; *Eir*: Dt.

[1] 'James Bennet, Master of the Grammar School, Hoddesdon' is among the subscribers to Christopher Smart's *Poems*, 4°, 1752.
[2] Grant's *Oratio* (1576) is described by W.A. Jackson in the *Pforzheimer Library* (1940), item 13. SJ also refers (para. 46), to Grant's edn. of Ascham's letters, *Ioannis Sturmii, Hieronymi Ossorii, aliorumque epistolae, ad Rogerum Ascham aliosque nobiles Anglos missae, ab E.G. collectae & nunc primum editae* (London, 1589). It was this book, or perhaps William Elstob's *Rogeri Aschami Epistolarum libri quatuor. Accessit Ioannis Sturmii, aliorumque ad Aschamum, Anglosque alios eruditis Epistolarum liber unus* (Oxford, 1703), which was lot 58 in Johnson's sale, Christie (Johnson), 16 Feb. 1785, sold to 'King' for 3s.
[3] Referring to *Life* (1791), i. 253: 'B. does not know that J. corrected the press & was the real Editor of Ascham's Works, w[ch]. go under the name of *Bennet* who kept an academy. NB. This employ'd him in [1762 and *deleted*] 1763 & perhaps part of 1762.'
[4] *European Mag.* vii (March 1785), 191–2, also noted 'In the next year [*sc.* 1767], he furnished Mr. Bennet with all the new materials introduced into his edition of Roger Ascham's Works.'
[5] Ifan Kyrle Fletcher, *Catalogue* 161 (Sept. 1953), item 6, @ £5. 5s.

61.8BA/1b   Life of Ascham, Bennet's Ascham,   [1767]
first edition, second issue

[½t] THE | WORKS | OF | ROGER ASCHAM.
[Title *as first issue*, 61.8BA/1a, 1761, prec.] . . . the Em- | peror CHARLES the FIFTH's COURT . . . LONDON: | Printed for T. DAVIES, in RUSSELL-STREET, COVENT-GARDEN, | And J. DODSLEY, in PALL-MALL.
4°, A[4] (−A1 + χ²) b–c⁴ B–3D⁴ 3E² (&c., as prec.), 213 leaves.
Pp. [A]χ1 ½t, χ1[v] blk, χ2 t., χ2[v] blk, on A2 Dedication, &c., on A3–4[v] Subscribers, on b1 Life, &c., as prec. 61.8BA/1a, above.
References: Courtney 100; CH 144; Hazen 19–23; Katterfeld, *Roger Ascham* (1879), no. 10; ESTC: t140587.
Notes: This issue is distinguished by the new ½t and undated t., and by the absence of the single leaf of 'Additional Susbcribers'; in all other respects it comprises sheets from the first issue of 1761, 61.8BA/1a, above. The date of publication was established by Chapman, *RES* v (1929), 69–70 from one of Davies's catalogues of 1767. It was sold at 12s. This second issue was noticed in the *Monthly Review*, xxxviii (1768), 147.
Copies: O (Vet. A5 d.1141, 'F. Moysey');
USA: CtY², DFo, Hyde², IU, [Liebert = ? CtY], MH ('Thomas Hollis' inscr: 'Written by Mr. Johnson (Dictionary Johnson)'), [NB], NIC, NPM, [OCl],

PPAmP ('John Darby'), [PPULC]; *Can*: CaOHM (D.349); *UK*: Abb ('1767'), ABu, BMp, C, Cp, Cq, Ct, [Es], L (90. e.11), Oef.

61.8BA/2   Life of Ascham, Ascham's Works   1815

THE | ENGLISH WORKS | OF | ROGER ASCHAM, | PRECEPTOR TO QUEEN ELIZABETH. | A NEW EDITION. | [medium rule] | "He that will write well in any tongue, must follow this coun- | sel of Aristotle, To speak as the common people do, to think as wise men do." Toxophilus. | [medium rule] | LONDON: PRINTED FOR WHITE, COCHRANE, AND CO. | HORACE's HEAD, FLEET-STREET. | [short rule] | MDCCCXV.

8°, π² a⁸ b⁶ B–2A⁸ 2B⁴ 2C⁸, ($2 signed), 212 leaves.

Pp. *i* t., *ii* coloph: 'Printed by S. Hamilton, Weybridge, Surrey.', *iii–iv* Advertisement ('London Jan. 1815.'), on a1 ²*i* Contents, *ii* blk, *iii* iv–xxviii Life of Ascham, on B1 *1* ½t, *2* blk, *3* 4–391 text, 391 coloph. and 'FINIS.', *392* blk.

References: Courtney 100; Katterfeld, *Roger Ascham* (1879), no. 11.

Notes: According to Giles, *The Whole Works of Roger Ascham* (1865), I. vii, the editor of 1815 was J.G. Cochrane (1781–1852*), cataloguer of the Abbotsford library.[1] Giles added that although only 250 copies of this edn. were printed ('Advertisement'), some were reissued with a new ½t and undated t. Katterfeld noted this alleged reissue (no. 12 'Zweite Ausgabe Cochranes'), adding that he had never seen a copy: nor have I. It may be a ghost arising from a confused rec- ollection of the undated second issue of 61.8BA/1b [1767], above. Giles himself quoted liberally from SJ's Life of Ascham, though not *in extenso*.

Copies: O (8° Q. 32.BS);

USA: DFo, MB, [MdBJ, MdBP], MH, [MHi], NIC, NN, PPU, [ScU]; *UK*: BAT, BMp, BRu, BRp, C, Csj, Ct, E, En, [Es], Eu, Gp, Gu, L (94. e.23), LEu, NOW, ONu, SAN; *Eir*: Dt.

SJ's Life of Ascham was reprinted in 61.8BA/3–5.[2]

[1] The *Abbotsford Catalogue* notably gives the correct date '1767' for the copy of the second issue of Bennet's edn. (61.8BA/1b, above), though Cochrane gives no indication of his source.
[2] It is **not** included in *The Cambridge English Classics. English Works of Roger Ascham. Roger Ascham English Works Toxophilus Report of the Affaires and State of Germany The Scholemaster*. Edited by William Aldis Wright, M.A., Cambridge at the University Press. 1904. *Copies*: L (12270. dd.1); O (2698 e. 29).

61.8BA/3   Life of Ascham, Memoir of Roger Ascham   1886

A Memoir of Roger Ascham. Edited with an Introduction by James H. Carlisle. Boston: Chautauqua Press. 1886

References: Clifford & Greene 13:2. (Not seen).
Copies: *USA*: CtY, DLC.

61.8BA/4   Life of Ascham, Two Great Teachers   1890

Two Great Teachers. Johnson's Memoir of Roger Ascham; and Selections from Stanley's Life and Correspondence of Thomas Arnold of Rugby. Syracuse, [New York] C. W. Bardeen. 1890.

   References: Clifford & Greene 13:2.

   Notes: The Introduction here is by James H. Carlisle (61.8BA/3, 1886, above), but SJ's Life of Ascham (pp. 11–33), and the Dedication (pp. 33–4) are printed from Bennet's edn.

   Copies: *USA*: MH (Educ. 101. 3.8).

61.8BA/5   Life of Ascham, facsimile   1977

A facsimile of the 'Life' from the first edn. was included in *Samuel Johnson: Early Biographical Writings*, Gregg International: Farnborough, Hants. 1977, pp. 497–512. ISBN: 0-576-02301-9.

61.8BA/TJ/1   Life of Ascham, Japanese translation   1975

A Japanese translation by Hitoshi Suwabe was published in Tokyo in 1975.

62.3KC   Kennedy's Chronology   1762

A | COMPLETE SYSTEM | OF | Astronomical Chronology, | Unfolding the Scriptures. | IN WHICH | [2 cols., col. a:] I. The Chronology of the Maforetic Hebrew Text | is proved, by Aftronomical Arguments, to be | genuine and authentic, without Error, and with- | out Corruption. | II. The Date of the Creation is fixed. | III. The Year, Month, Day of the Month, and | Day of the Week, in which the Ifraelites went | out of Egypt, are afcertained. | IV. It is clearly proved, that at the going out of | Egypt the original Sabbath was changed by Di- | vine Legiflative Authority. | V. It is proved, that our Saviour rofe from the | Dead on the Seventh Day of the Week, in the | [vertical double rule; col. b:] uninterrupted Series of Weeks from the Creation, | and that the original Seventh Day, or Patriarchal | Sabbath, revived with him. | VI. It is proved, that our Saviour gave up the | Ghoft upon the Crofs, on the very Month, Day, | Hour, and Minute, on which the Pafchal Lamb | was ordered, by the Law, to be flain. | VII. The Chronology of the Five Books of Mofes | is compleated in all its Particulars. | VIII. The Aftronomical Epocha of the Gofpel, | and the Year, Months, and Day of Christ's | Death, are determined. | [full rule] | [across the full measure] *Si origo mundi in notitiam hominum veniffet exordium inde fumeremus.* Censorinus. | *Ethnicis nullum tempus propriè hiftoricum audiat, nifi quod primam Olympiadem fequitur. Nos autem, qui | Mofaicis gaudemus ratiociniis ab ipſo primo homine mundoque condito hiſtorias noſtras exordiamur. Et | idcirco totum temporis, quod ab ipſis motuum cœleſtium carceribus ad hanc uſque metam ſive tempus preſens | effluxerit, hiſtoricum jure nominamus.* Bev. Chronolog. Inſtitut. | [rule] | By JOHN KENNEDY, | Rector of Bradley in *Derbyſhire.* | [parallel rule] | *LONDON:* | Printed by E. ALLEN, in Bolt-Court, Fleet-Street; | For Meſſrs. Davis and Reymers, in *Holborn;* W. Owen, in *Fleet-Street;* | and T. Hope, behind the *Royal Exchange.* | [short rule] | M. DCC. LXII.

4°, π² (*)–(***)⁴ a–b⁴ d⁴ B–4Y⁴ 4Z⁴ (±4Z4), †–††² χ1, ($2 signed), 395 leaves.

Pp. π1 t., π1ᵛ blk, π2–2ᵛ Dedication dh: TO THE | KING | SIR, ht: DEDICATION., on (*)1–(***)4 Analysis dh: [hp] | AN | ANALYSIS | OF THE | ENTIRE WORK. | [rule], ht: *An* ANALYSIS *of the Entire* WORK., (***)4ᵛ blk, on a1 *i* ii–xxiii Introduction dh: [Hp] | INTRODUCTORY | DISCOURSE., ht: INTRODUCTORY DISCOURSE., *xxiv* blk, on B1 *1* 2–69 text dh: [hp] | THE | CHRONOLOGY | OF THE | WORLD, | From the Creation to the Year of our Lord 1761., ht: *The Chronology of the World.,* 70 blk, *71* 72–113 text dh: A | COLLECTION | OF ALL THE | TEXTS of SCRIPTURE, | BOTH FROM | The OLD and NEW TESTA MENT, | Relative to its Chronology. | [rule], *114* blk, 115–21 text dh: [double rule] | DISSERTATION I., 122–35 Dissertation II (dh as prec.), 136–310 Dissertation III (dh. as prec.), 311–598 Dissertation IV. (ht as prec.), 599–728 Dissertation V (ht. as prec.), on †1 i–viii Tables dh: A | Solar and Lunar KALENDAR | OF THE | CHAOTIC YEAR; | . . . &c., + 5 folding ½ sheet tables, on χ1 errata., χ1ᵛ blk.

Pagination: (↑) i–viii; 345 as 354 [*inverted*].

Press-figures: none.

Catchwords: None in Tables pp. 1–68, or in final tables; (***)1 ˄Of (—Of), (***)1ᵛ ˄Of (—Of), (***)2 ˄Of (—Of), (***)3 ˄Sun (—Sun), xx (2.) The ((3.) ~), 89 The (Now), 134 I (It), 281 terminate˄ (~,), 305 *To* (*In*), 427 *om.* (TABLE), 728 *om.* (A).

Explicit: 728 ΔΟΧΑ ΜΟΝΩ ΤΩ ΘΕΩ. | SOLI DEO GLORIA. (*See below*).

Paper: White, laid; La. post (uncut: 10½ × 8¼ in.); Var. wmks.: (**a**) fleur-de-lys, (**b**) Arabesque; so at least two distinct stocks.

Type: Dedication: double pica (7.1 mm), text: english (4.5 mm), notes: sm. pica (3.3 mm). Orn. hpp. on A1, B1; headstrip on (*)1, tp. on (**)4ᵛ, factotum on a1. Complex typography employing astronomical symbols, calculations, tabulations and lists with many rules, and Greek letters.

Plates: (5) Five folding tables (= ½ sheet each), 17⅝ × 11½in. No vis. wmk. Tables 1–4 are entitled SCRIPTURAL KALENDAR. I [–IV]., and 5. as KALENDAR of the EXODUS.

References: Life i. 366, 547 (Courtney 101); CH 145; Hazen 74–7; *Boswell in Extremes,* 240; ESTC: t111126.

Notes: There are two states of the cancelled leaf (4Z4) distinguished by the penultimate line of Greek in the *Explicit* which is either (a) 75 mm or (b) 62 mm long. In the longer version *iotas* stand at the ends of the last three words, and since these are erroneous it may be assumed that (a) is the earlier state. Alternatively, though less probably, Allen may have printed the *cancellanda* as a pair in two settings, but the differences would surely have involved more than the Greek, and discrepancies should have been more evident.

The two stocks of paper are perhaps not significant since the book is large, the printing complex (with many tables and symbols), and consequently slow, and the printer's premises were relatively small.

Johnson contributed the 'Dedication' to George III, and the closing paragraph, both of which JB identified as his. The cancellation was doubtless made to include this exordium. Edmund Allen, the printer, was SJ's landlord and neighbour in Bolt Court (*Life*);[1] last-minute work involving a cancel would have been easy to effect. The 'Dedication' was reprinted by George Gleig in *Works*, xv (1789), 486–7, but Reed printed the uncanonical Preface to Kennedy's *A New Method . . .* (1751), in his *Works*, xiv (1788), 156–63, with the evasive note, 'Ascribed to Dr Johnson on the authority of Hawkins's Life of Johnson. E[ditor]',[2] though Reed's MS list of SJ's works (Ljh) unequivocally states '1762 . . . Dedication to Kennedy's Scripture Chronology . . .' and the Dedication is accepted in the list sent to him in 1790 by JB (Waingrow, *Corr.* 317). It is not however mentioned in the articles in *European Mag.* vii (1785). The 'Dedication' apparently secured a gift of £50 from the King to Kennedy.[3] The book was published 29 March 1762 at £1. 3s. sewed, or £1. 5s. bound (*St James's Chron.*).

SJ's own copy was lot 66 in his Sale (Christie, 16 Febr. 1785), and sold to 'Price' for 3s. It was the copy which JB read on 22 March 1772, and in which he identified SJ's contributions. Kennedy (1698–1782*), with his wife, had spent 40 years of research on his book which involved him in considerable controversy with, among others, James Ferguson (1710–76*), the astronomer, and John Jackson (1686–1763*), the polemic theologian.

Copies: O ((a), 107 d.5, 'Liber Coll. Univ. in Academiâ Oxōn.');

(a) *USA*: [Liebert = CtY]; *UK*: Cf, Ck, E, Eu, MRc;

(b) *USA*: CtY ('Sam. Kettilby DD.'), IU, [Liebert = CtY], NIC ('J. D. Hastings'), [PPAt], PPL; *UK*: C, DUu, Ep (uncut, 'Cha: Gray'), Yc.

[Undifferentiated: *USA*: Hyde, MH (KG. 13353), NN (*YIV), NNC, NjP, RPB; *UK*: L (6. d.6)].

---

[1] His death, on 28 July 1784, is noticed in *Gents. Mag.* liv (July 1784), 558.

[2] Hawkins's comments were vague: 'a life of the author, a dedication, preface, or an introduction tending to recommend it' (*Life87* 517). If Reed relied only on this, and on Hawkins's version of the title, 'Kennedy's "Scripture Chronology"', it is unsurprising that he lighted on *A New Method of Stating and Explaining the Scripture Chronology* of 1751. His MS list retained the title 'Scripture Chronology' (Ljh), when 'Astronomical Chronology' would have been clearer.

[3] Birch to Hardwicke, 24 July 1762 (L: Add. MS 35399).

62.5SA/1   Society of Artists' Catalogue   1762

[Engr. t. plate area: 8½ × 6¹⁄₁₆ in. 'Champion sc.'] A | CATALOGUE | of the | [BL] **Pictures, Sculptures, Models, Drawings, Prints, &c.** | Exhibited by the | SOCIETY of ARTISTS | *OF* | [BL] **Great-Britain,** | AT THE | Great Room, in Spring Gardens, Charing Cross. | [BL] **May the 17th, Anno 1762.** | Being the Third year of their Exhibition. | [Vignette: Angel presenting gifts to Britannia, triple tree of Arts behind; motto: 'AUREA SI TULERIS DONA | MINORA FERES. MART.' and 'S. Wale inv. et del. C. Grignion Sculp.']

4°, *A*² B–E², ($1 (–A) signed), 10 leaves.

Pp. Engr. t. + A1 pp. 3 iv–vi Preface dh: [hp of flowers] | *PREFACE.*, ht: *PREFACE.*, on B1 *1* 2–16 catalogue dh: [hp of flowers] | A | CATALOGUE, *&c.* | [row of flowers]

Pagination: [↑] 3, (↑) 2–16; *Press-figures*: none.
Catchwords: 1 Mr. (Mrs.), 6 Mr. (88ₐ Mr.).
Explicit: vi tp. [flowers]; 16 *FINIS*.
Paper: White, laid; La. post (10½ × 8¼ in.); fleur-de-lys in t., no vis. wmk. in A–E.
Type: Preface: gt. primer (5.5 mm), leaded, text: pica (4.1 mm).
Plate: Title as above.
References: *Life* i. 363 (Courtney 101); CH 145; Hazen 200–5; Hilles, *Literary Career of Reynolds* (1936), 24–5; Clifford, in *Augustan Milieu* (1970), 333–48; Charles Taylor,[1] *The Literary Panorama* (1808), iii. 1016–18; 'The Papers of the Society of Artists of Great Britain' *The Walpole Society*, vi (1917–18), 113–23 is drawn from the minute books of the Society (now Lra); Brownell, *Johnson's Attitude to the Arts* (1989), 46–55, 129; ESTC: t028778, t072122.

Notes: In the course of the Exhibition the sale of articles, and changes in the contents, led to revision of the Catalogue itself. Some changes are listed in Hazen, but all are confined to the lists themselves in sigg. B–E, and do not affect sig. A which carries SJ's Preface. The variant states of B–E therefore are not of importance to the Johnsonian, though the art historian may find them of interest. This suggests that a large number of copies of sig. A were printed off, but that the reprinting of B–E involved a smaller number, and was *ad hoc*. Taylor (col. 1018) reported that 10,488 copies of the catalogue were sold at 1s. each: at least 10,500 copies of sig. A must therefore have been printed.

The Preface and the motto on the engr. t. are Johnson's (Hazen, 202).[2] The Preface was first included by Thomas Davies in *Miscellaneous and Fugitive Pieces* (1773), ii. 151–2 (73.12DM/1, below), and as Bookseller to the Royal Academy he may have had special information. The notice of this collection in *Gents. Mag.* xliv (Nov. 1774), 525, explicitly gave the Preface to SJ. It is in Isaac Reed's MS list of SJ's works (Ljh), and was printed by him in *Works*, xiv (1788), 355–6

(87.3W/1.3/1, below), though it is not mentioned in his notes in the *European Mag*. vii (1785).[3]

SJ was elected to the Society 1 December 1756, and became involved with this exhibition in January 1760 when the Committee invited him to revise their letter requesting the use of the rooms of the Society for the Encouragement of Arts, &c. (*Walpole Society*, vi. 113 ff., Clifford, and Brownell, ch. iv, *passim*., above 60.2LSA and 60.12LSA), and Taylor, evidently unaware of Davies's or Reed's attribution in 1773 and 1788, prefixed his reprinting of the Preface with the note:

> March 16. 1762 . . . The preface to the catalogue this year was "presented" by Mr Reynolds. — Was it his own composition, or that of Dr Johnson? If by the latter, it has escaped Boswell and the collectors of the Dr.'s work; we shall therefore insert it entire . . .

The date is taken from the minute books (MSS: Lra; cf. Clifford, 344 ff.).

Copies: O[3](1–2. Johnson d.610[2]; 3. G.Pamph. 1804 (5));

USA: CtY[2] (1. Lewis: 'Horace Walpole'), [Liebert = ? CtY], NN; *UK*: L[3], [Lra], Lv[3], Oam.

SJ's Preface was later reprinted in 62.5SA/2–62.5SA/7.

---

[1] Charles Taylor (1756–1823*) was the son of Isaac (1730–1807*) who was the last secretary of the Society.
[2] SJ may have suppplied other mottos for other catalogues. This, from Martial, *Epigr*. xiv and xc (with modifications), is surely SJ's. Cf. Brownell, *Johnson's Attitude to the Arts* (1989), 54, n. 22.
[3] It was added by Reed to the list of SJ's Works which JB sent to him for corroboration (Waingrow, *Corr*. 317).

62.5SA/2   Society of Artists' Catalogue,   1808
                              The Literary Panorama

Charles Taylor, *The Literary Panorama*, iii (1808), cols. 1016–17.

62.5SA/3   Society of Artists' Catalogue, Memoirs of   1813
                            Sir Joshua Reynolds

James Northcote, *Memoirs of Sir Joshua Reynolds* (1813).

62.5SA/4   Society of Artists' Catalogue,   1818
                            Life of Sir Joshua Reynolds

James Northcote, *The Life of Sir Joshua Reynolds*, 2nd edn., 2 vols. (1818), i. 100–2.

| 62.5SA/5 | Society of Artists' Catalogue, Patronage of British Art | 1845 |

John Pye, *Patronage of British Art, an Historical Sketch* (1845), 106–9.

| 62.5SA/6 | Society of Artists' Catalogue, History of the Royal Academy | 1862 |

William Sandby, *History of the Royal Academy* (1862), i. 37–8.

| 62.5SA/7 | Society of Artists' Catalogue, Society of Artists | 1907 |

Algernon Graves, *The Society of Artists of Great Britain* (1907), 303–6.

62.7WP   Proposals for Anna Williams's Miscellanies   [1762]

PROPOSALS | For PRINTING by SUBSCRIPTION, | ESSAYS, | IN | VERSE and PROSE. | By ANNA WILLIAMS. | [rule] | CONDITIONS. | I. THE Essays will make One Volume in Quarto. | II. THE Price will be Five Shillings, to be paid for at the | Time of Subſcribing. | [rule] | I *Received* | *being the whole Payment for* | *Book.*

4°, $2 (unsigned), 2 leaves.

Pp. *1* t., *2* ADVERTISEMENT., *3–4* sample text dh: [double rule] | THE | PETITION.

Pagination: none. *Press-figures*: none; *Catchwords*: *3* Content
Paper: White, laid; Crown (uncut: 10¼ × 7½ in.); wmk.: fleur-de-lys.
Type: Great primer (5.5 mm).
References: Courtney 112; Prospectuses no. 25.
Notes: The project was first moved in 1750 when 'Proposals' were published in *Gents. Mag.* xx (1750), '423' (50GM/20, above), but the proposed work was changed from 8° to 4°, and support dwindled (*Johns. Misc.* ii. 172–3). In summer 1762 a new subscription was mounted,[1] and this date agrees with '1762' pencilled on one of the extant copies.

Strahan's account for the book (66.4WM/1, below) records 'Proposals for D° at different times £1. 1s.' suggesting different impressions, though the scarcity of copies affords little evidence. The distribution seems not to have been sufficiently wide, as Cockfield reported (*Lit. Illus.* v (1828), 761–2), though Grainger in 1766 recalled having 'subscribed a great many years ago' (*Lit. Illus.* vii (1848), 294). The 'Advertisement' to the eventual book apologized for the delayed publication.

Copies: O² (Johnson, 'Thomas Percy': **1**. Complete with names of subscribers in Percy's hand; **2**. Receipt form cut away).

¹ *Letters of Mrs Carter*, ed. Pennington (1817), i. 164–5 ('July, 8, 1762'), and J. Grainger to Percy, 4 Dec. 1766 (*Lit. Illus.* vii (1848), 294).

62.11FC   DuFresnoy's Tables   *1762*

(a) CHRONOLOGICAL TABLES | OF | UNIVERSAL HISTORY, | Sacred and Profane, Ecclefiaftic and Civil; | FROM THE | CREATION OF THE WORLD, | TO THE | Year One thoufand Seven hundred and Forty-three. | WITH A | PRELIMINARY DISCOURSE | ON | The fhort Method of Studying History; | AND | A Catalogue of Books neceffary for that Purpose; | With fome REMARKS on them. | By Abbé LENGLET DUFRESNOY. | In TWO PARTS. | Tranflated from the laft French Edition; and continued down to the | Death of King George II. | PART THE FIRST [– SECOND]. | [bevelled parallel rule] | LONDON: | Printed for A. Millar, J. Newbery, R. Baldwin. W. Johnston, | D. Wilson, S. Crowder and Co. T. Jefferys, A. Hamilton, | J. Coote, H. Payne and Co. T. Becket and Co. and J. Walter. | MDCCLXII.
Var: (b) Ecclefiaftical . . . Baldwin, . . . (as in vol. 2)
  2 vols., 8°.

I. π⁴ (π2 + ☜2) a–g⁸ h⁴ i² B–X⁸ Y⁴ Y*², ($4 (a4ᵛ as a4, –d4, K2 as L2, P3 as P, –S4, T2,3,4) signed), 234 leaves.
  Pp. π1 ½t, π1ᵛ blk, π2 t., π2ᵛ blk, on ☜1 paged *–**** Table of Chapters, on π3 v–vi Dedication dh: To the RIGHT HONOURABLE the EARL | OF POMFRET. ('THOMAS FLLOYD. Sept. 8, 1762.'), vii–viii Preface dh: THE PREFACE., on b1 pp. i–cxxiii Preliminary Discourse, *cxxiv* blk, on B1 *1* 2–320 text Chronological Tables, on Y1 pp. 321–32 Indexes.
  Pagination: iii as ii, xciv as cxiv, 146–7 as 136–7, 150–1 as 140–1, 154–5 as 144–5, 158 as 148, 159 as 449, 169 unnumbered, 284 as 184, 322 as 22 (mis-numbered 146–59 confined to L(i)).
  Press-figures: d5(xli)–2, d5ᵛ(xlii)–1, g3ᵛ(lxxxvi)–1, U6(299)–3, U6ᵛ(300)–3, X3ᵛ(310)–3, X6ᵛ(316)–3.
  Catchwords: not recorded; *Explicit*: not recorded.

II. π² a⁴ A–2H⁸, ($4 signed; 'Part. II.' on $1 (–M, 2B–2H)), 254 leaves.
  Pp. π1 ½t, π1ᵛ blk, π2 t., π2ᵛ blk, on a1 iii–iv Advertisement, on a2 viii–x Table of Articles, on B1 *1* 2–496 text Chronological Tables.
  Pagination: 193 unnumbered.
  Press-figures: B6(11)–1, G5ᵛ(90)–3, G6ᵛ(92)–3, H4ᵛ(104)–3, H6(107)–3, I5(121)–1, I5ᵛ(122)–3, K4(135)–2, K4ᵛ(136)–2, L3ᵛ(150)–1, L4ᵛ(152)–1.
  Catchwords: not recorded; *Explicit*: not recorded.

Paper: White, laid; La. Post (8¼ × 5¼ in.) [or demy (8¾ × 5⅝ in.)].

Type: not recorded.

References: Hazen, *TLS*, 28 June 1934, 460; CH 146; Hazen 84–9; *Tinker* 1346; Welsh 185–6; Roscoe, *Newbery* (1973), A291; D'Israeli, *Curiosities* (1823), ii. 328–45; Sherbo, in *English Writers of the 18th Century* (1971), 122–42; ESTC: t139561.

Notes: The section signed ☜ in vol. 1 is variously placed, but should precede the Dedication. *Tinker* noted the variant (b) in the t., and some resetting of the Preface, i.e. I. π⁴.

The translation was made by Thomas Flloyd (*Life* i. 457),[1] and the book was published 19 November 1762, at 12s. (*Lloyd's Evening Post*), where as Hazen observed, it was 'Recommended by Samuel Johnson.' The same expression accompanied the notice in *Gents. Mag.* xxxii (Dec. 1762), 602. Millar was the paymaster. Despite the recommendation it appears not to have sold well, for Roscoe notes an advertisement in 1764 at 10s. Hazen noted (87) that the newspaper advertisement named 'H. Payne and W. Cropley' instead of the 'H. Payne and Co.' of the imprint.

The 'Preface' was first attributed to SJ by Hazen in *TLS*, 28 June 1934, 460, and repeated with the hesitant addition of the 'Dedication' in *SJ's Prefaces and Dedications* (1937). Chapman, in CH, accepted the 'Preface' but rejected the 'Dedication'. Sherbo (1971), 132–3, rejected both. It is difficult to dissociate SJ from the 'Preface' though it is probably not entirely his, and it must be conceded that the evidence for SJ's connection is far from overwhelming. SJ's own copy was, with Thomas Warton on Spenser, lot 29 in his sale, Christie 18 Feb. 1785, and went to Backhouse for 15s. 6d. It is untraced. For an associated, and rejected, attribution, see Flloyd's *Bibliotheca Biographica*, 60.5FBB, above

Copies: [(a) L.F. Powell = ? Hyde].

USA: (a) Hyde ('Holdsworth'); (b) CtY (Tinker), DLC, [Liebert = ? CtY], NjP ('Witherspoon'), PPL;

[Undifferentiated: IU, MH, NN (vol. 1, only), NNC];

UK: (a) ABu, Csj, Ct, E, LVu;

(b) En, Eu, Gu, NCu, SAN;

[Undifferentiated: BAT, L, MRc].

---

[1] Waingrow, *MS of Life* i. 319, reports that JB's journal, 9 May 1776, recorded, 'One of his friends Floyd [SJ was afraid had been] whipt as a thief in Moorfields.' There was evidently an old acquaintance between them.

62GDP   Proposals for Anchitell Grey's Debates   [1762]

In the Beginning of May *next, will be ready to deliver,* | In TEN VOLUMES, Octavo, | Price TWO POUNDS TEN SHILLINGS, in Sheets, | THE | DEBATES | OF THE | HOUSE OF COMMONS, | From the Year 1667, to the Year 1694. | (To which the Right Hon. the late and prefent Speakers, | with many worthy Members, have been pleafed to fubfcribe) | COLLECTED | By the Hon. *Anchitell Grey*, Efq; | Who was Thirty Years Member for the Town of *Derby*, | Chairman of feveral Committees, and decyphered | *Coleman*'s Letters for the Ufe of the Houfe. | Printed for Meff. Henry and Cave, at *St John's Gate.* | [rule] | To the PUBLIC. [&c.]

8°, $1, 1 leaf.

Pp. *1–2* t. and SJ's Address.

Pagination: (↑) 2.

Paper: White, laid; demy (uncut: 8¾ × 5⅝ in.); no vis. wmk.

Type: Text: bourgeois (3.0 mm).

References: Courtney 19; Prospectuses 24; Brack, *Shorter Prose* (s.d. 1745); ESTC: t077856.

Notes: The unique copy of this notice bears the pencilled date '1762'. In the edn. of Grey's *Debates* dated 1763, the names of Henry and Cave stand in the imprints, but when that work was reissued in 1769 with cancelled tt. the imprints bore the names of Thomas Becket and P. A. DeHondt. This notice therefore refers to the 1763 edn., and suggests that the '1762' is probably correct.

This separate publication is slightly revised from the text of *Gents. Mag.* xv (March 1745), 135–42 (45GM15, above), and the revisions are discussed by Brack.

Copies: O (Johnson; b. 162).

62GM32   Gentleman's Magazine, Vol. XXXII   1762

February 81–82

An Account of the Detection of the Imposture in Cock-Lane

References: D. Grant, *Cock Lane Ghost* (1965), 71–2; O M Brack, *Shorter Prose.*

Notes: Sent also to the newspapers. Reprinted in *Works*, xv (1789), 487 (87.3W/1.4, below) having been attributed to SJ by Hawkins, *Life87*, 483. It is unlikely that SJ was responsible for the whole account, but he may have contributed to it.

June 295

Brief notice of Charlotte Lennox's *Sophia*

This short and sympathetic notice of CL's novel, is plausibly Johnson's, but there is nothing to support the attribution save circumstances.

63.1PC/1a   Poetical Calendar   1763

[½t] THE | POETICAL CALENDAR. | VOL. I. [–XII]. | FOR JANUARY [– DECEMBER].

[Title] THE | POETICAL CALENDAR. | CONTAINING | A COLLECTION | of fcarce and valuable | PIECES OF POETRY: | With Variety of | ORIGINALS AND TRANSLATIONS, | BY THE MOST EMINENT HANDS. | Intended as a Supplement to | MR. DODSLEY's COLLECTION. | Written and Selected | By FRANCIS FAWKES, M.A. | And WILLIAM WOTY. | IN TWELVE VOLUMES. | LONDON: | Printed by DRYDEN LEACH; | For J. Coote, at the King's Arms, in Pater-nofter-Row. | MDCCLXIII.

Note: The two lines (Intended . . . COLLECTION.) referring to Dodsley's *Collection* are omitted from the tt. of vols. 3–12.

12 vols., 8°

I. (January): A⁴ B–H⁸ I⁴, ($4 (–B2, E2, G4, I3,4) signed), 64 leaves.

Pp. A1 *i* ½t, *ii* blk, *iii* t., *iv* blk, *v*–vi dh: ADVERTISEMENT. (dated 'Dec. 24. 1762'), *vii*–viii Contents, on B1 *1* 2–120 text dh: THE | POETICAL CALENDAR. (no htt. or rtt.).

Pagination: [↑], i–v, vii, 1 unnumbered; *Press-figures*: none.

Catchwords: 8 Or₍ (~,), 51 *om.* (PART), 52 Youths₍ (~,), 65 ₍EUPOLIS' ("~'), 75 *om.* (HYMN.), 86 *om.* (Let), 87 *om.* (ON).

Explicit: 120 END OF VOL. I.

II. (February): *A*² B–H⁸ I⁴ K², ($4 (–E2,3, H3, I3,4, K2) signed; 'Vol. II.' on $1 (as 'II,' on D, as 'II₍' on FI)), 64 leaves.

Pp. A1 *i* ½t, *ii* blk, *iii* t., *iv* blk, on B1 *1* 2–122 text dh: THE | POETICAL CALENDAR., on K2 *v*–vi CONTENTS.

Pagination: [↑]; *Press-figures*: none.

Catchwords: 8 *om.* (DEITY.), 21 Then₍ (~,), 25 *om.* (With), 53 *om.* (Thy), 55 *om.* (what), 73 *om.* (whimfically), 95 *om.* (Thither), 101 *om.* (PEACE.), 110 *om.* (A), 112 TRUTH₍ (LOVE₍), 114 *om.* (Curs'd), 116 *om.* (In), 117 *om.* (Tho',), 122 CON- (CONTENTS.).

Explicit: 122 END OF VOL. II.

III. (March): *A*² B–H⁸ I⁴ K², ($4 (–B2,4 C2, G4, I3,4, K2) signed; 'Vol. III.' on $1), 64 leaves.

Pp. A1 *i* ½t, *ii* blk, *iii* t., *iv* blk, on B1 *1* 2–123 text dh: THE | POETICAL CALENDAR., *124* CONTENTS.

Pagination: [↑]; *Press-figures*: none.

Catchwords: *om.* pp. 3, 6, 7, 10, 11, 14, 15, 19, 82, 87, 88, 89, 90, 91, 92, 93, 94, 108, 112, 114, 116, 120, 122.

Explicit: 124 END OF VOL. III.

IV. (April): *A²* B–H⁸ I⁴ K², ($4 (–G2,3,4, I3,4, K2) signed; 'Vᴏʟ. IV.' on $1), 64 leaves.

Pp. A1 *i* ½t, *ii* blk, *iii* t., *iv* blk, on B1 *1* 2–123 text dh: THE | POETICAL CALENDAR., *124* CONTENTS.

Pagination: [↑]; *Press-figures*: none.

Catchwords: *om.* pp. 18, 41, 80, 83, 85, 89, 91, 114; 96 THE (EPISTLE), 97 And (But).

Explicit: 124 END OF VOL. IV.

V. (May): *A²* B–H⁸ I⁴ K², ($4 (–D3, F2,3,4, G2, I3,4, K2) signed; 'Vᴏʟ. V.' on $1 (K as 'VI.')), 64 leaves.

Pp. A1 *i* ½t, *ii* blk, *iii* t., *iv* blk, on B1 *1* 2–123 text dh: THE | POETICAL CALENDAR., *124* CONTENTS.

Pagination: [↑]; *Press-figures*: none.

Catchwords: *om.* pp. 2, 15, 24, 27, 37, 41, 43, 44, 48, 50, 57, 61, 67, 68, 69, 70, 71, 77, 78, 79, 82, 83, 84, 93, 117, 118, 119, 120, 123; 32 Still˄ (~,), 116 SWEET˄ (SWEET-WILLIAM,). *Note*: GEMINI on 123 is not a cwd.

Explicit: 124 END OF VOL. V.

VI. (June): *A²* B–H⁸ I⁴ K², ($4 (–B3, E2, F3, H2, I2,3,4, K2) signed; 'Vᴏʟ. VI.' on $1), 64 leaves.

Pp. A1 *i* ½t, *ii* blk, *iii* t., *iv* blk, on B1 *1* 2–122 text dh: THE | POETICAL CALENDAR., *123*–124 CONTENTS.

Pagination: [↑]; *Press-figures*: none.

Catchwords: *om.* pp. 5, 9, 21, 31, 32, 46, 51, 52, 54, 69, 70, 74, 76, 77, 80, 84, 89, 91, 92, 93, 96, 99, 100, 107, 110, 115, 116; 17 And˄ (~,), 111 ˄ODE (AN ODE), 112 That (AIR. | Hence !).

Explicit: 124 END OF VOL. VI.

VII. (July): *A²* B–H⁸ I⁴ K², ($4 (–B4, D2,3,4, F4, I3,4, K2; B5 as B4) signed; Vᴏʟ. VII.' on $1), 64 leaves.

Pp. A1 *i* ½t, *ii* blk, *iii* t., *iv* blk, on B1 *1* 2–123 text dh: THE | POETICAL CALENDAR., *124* CONTENTS.

Pagination: [↑]; *Press-figures*: none.

Catchwords: *om.* pp. 5, 11, 12, 13, 14, 15, 22, 25, 35, 36, 37, 38, 41, 60, 62, 63, 71, 72, 73, 74, 76, 77, 109; 17 Thou˄ (~,), 48 AND (AN), 69 But˄ (~,), 111 The (Th' affrighted).

Explicit: 124 END OF VOL. VII.

VIII. (August): *A²* B–H⁸ I⁴ K², ($4 (–B3, C2,3,4, E2, G2, I3,4, K2) signed; 'Vᴏʟ. VIII.' on $1), 64 leaves.

Pp. A1 *i* ½t, blk, *iii* t., *iv* blk, on B1 *1* 2–122 text dh: THE | POETICAL CALENDAR., *123*–124 CONTENTS.

Pagination: [↑]; *Press-figures*: none.

Catchwords: *om.* pp. 5, 6, 19, 20, 21, 22, 23, 24, 25, 26, 28, 29, 31, 32, 38, 40,

41, 42, 43, 51, 58, 63, 64, 68, 73, 83, 89, 90, 119; 54 ˌBold (*~), 60 Bedold (Behold), 112 AN- (XIV. ANOTHER,), 115 ˌSeven (*~).

Explicit: 124 END OF VOL. VIII.

IX. (September): *A*² B–H⁸ I⁴ K², (\$4 (–B3,4, F2, I3,4, K2) signed; 'VOL. IX.' on \$1), 64 leaves.

Pp. A1 *i* ½t, *ii* blk, *iii* t., *iv* blk, on B1 *1* 2–123 text dh: THE | POETICAL CALENDAR., *124* CONTENTS.

Pagination: [↑]; *Press-figures*: none.

Catchwords: *om.* pp. 6, 7, 8, 9, 67, 86, 88, 89, 90, 91, 105, 106, 112, 119; 33 Butˌ (~,), 34 Nervousˌ (~,), 51 Thusˌ (~,), 54 Butˌ (~,), 85 "Andˌ ("~,).

Explicit: 124 END OF VOL. IX.

X. (October): *A*² B–H⁸ I⁴ K², (\$4 (–B2,4, F2, G3, H3,4, I3,4, K2) signed; 'VOL. X.' on \$1), 64 leaves.

Pp. A1 *i* ½t, *ii* blk, *iii* t., *iv* blk, on B1 *1* 2–122 text dh: THE | POETICAL CALENDAR., *123*–124 CONTENTS.

Pagination: [↑]; *Press-figures*: none.

Catchwords: *om.* pp. 3, 7, 8, 9, 10, 11, 30, 36, 41, 46, 47, 66, 67, 85, 100, 101, 102, 103, 104, 105, 112, 118, 119; 87 HORACE, (HOR.), 93 Epiftlesˌ (~,).

Explicit: 124 END OF VOL. X.

XI. (November): *A*² B–H⁸ I⁴ K², (\$4 (–G3, H4, I3,4, K2) signed; 'VOL. XI.' on \$1), 64 leaves.

Pp. A1 *i* ½t, *ii* blk, *iii* t., *iv* blk, on B1 *1* 2–122 text dh: THE | POETICAL CALENDAR., *123*–124 CONTENTS.

Pagination: [↑]; *Press-figures*: none.

Catchwords: *om.* pp. 16, 31, 46, 50, 54, 57, 58, 74, 85, 88, 89, 95, 103, 112; 24 ˌGay- (*Gay-), 69 ˌWith (*With), 79, TO (THE), 82 Inˌ (Inconftant), 94 ˌODE (*~), 102 ˌSALT (*~).

Explicit: 124 END OF VOL. XI.

XII. (December): A⁴ B–H⁸ I⁴, (\$4 (–B3, D2, F2,3, I3,4) signed; 'VOL. XII.' on \$1), 64 leaves.

Pp. A1–2 advert for 'The Poetical Magazine, or, Muses Monthly Companion.' on A3 *i* ½t, *ii* blk, *iii* t., *iv* blk, on B1 *1* 2–112 text dh: THE | POETICAL CALENDAR., on I1 *113*–120 Index.

Pagination: [↑]; *Press-figures*: none.

Catchwords: *om.* pp. 5, 6, 24, 25, 26, 29, 34, 35, 36, 47, 48, 66, 67, 70, 71, 73, 102, 105; 22 A (AD), 57 "ˌAnd ("(~), 76 Sˌ (S.), 80 ˌPRO- (*PROLOGUE.).

Explicit: 120 END OF VOL. XII.

Paper: White, laid; Pot (uncut: 6¼ × 3¾in.); wmk.: VREYHEYT | PRO PATRIA.

Type: Text: sm. pica (3.3 mm), leaded; Contents and footnotes: brevier (2.4 mm).

References: *Life* i. 382–3 (Courtney 101); CH 146; H. B. Forster, *Supplements to Dodsley* (1980), 1–2; Wendorf, *PBSA* lxxiv (1980), 95–115; ESTC: t146608.

Notes: As usual with part issues there was some reprinting and reissuance of individual volumes.

The undertaking was largely promoted by Fawkes.[1] H.W. Garrod first pointed out that vol. 11 represents the first collection of the poems of William Collins, an account of whom (save for the opening para. by James Hampton; cf. Wendorf (1980)), was contributed by SJ to vol. 12 (December), 107–12. This was reprinted in *Gents. Mag.* xxxiv (Jan. 1764), 234, and later incorporated into the *Lives of the Poets*. It was given to SJ in *European Mag.* vii (Mar. 1785), 191.

Other Johnsonian pieces are in verse: I. (Jan.), 17 'A Winter's Walk' (*Poems*[2] 101–3); IV. (Apr.), 3–4 'An Ode' ('Stern Winter now by Spring repress'd', *Poems*[2] 101–3). Hawkesworth's verses 'Winter. An Ode' in I (Jan.), 3–4, and 'Autumn' in IX (Sept.), 5–6, have sometimes been attributed to SJ (*Poems*[2] 462–3), and the 'Evening Ode to Delia' in IX (Sept.), 11, is doubtfully his (*Poems*[2] 452–3).

SJ's further involvement in this publication is perhaps slight: the account of Collins is the only certainty; the Eulogy on Garrick, VII (July), 47–8 was by John Duncombe, and Sir Thomas Browne's 'Evening Hymn' from *Religio Medici* ('Sleep is a death . . . &c.') in XI (Nov.), 121–2, was no expression of SJ's sentiments on that topic.[2]

Copies: O (8° K. 275–80 BS, 'George Chalmers', imperfect, vols. 3, 7, 8 are '2nd.');

USA: CSmH, CtY, DFo, DLC (> 4 vols.), ICN, ICU (imperfect, vols. 3–9 '2nd'), IU, [Liebert (> 6 vols. 'R. W. Chapman') = ? CtY], MB (imperfect, vols. 3–6 '2nd.'), MH[2] (1. 17466.4, > 6 vols.; 2. *46.2318 'Robert Southey, Keswick 6 Jan[y]. 1836'), NIC, NN[2], PPM, TxU (> 4 vols.), [WaSU]; *Can*: CaOHM (> 6 vols. 'Colquhoun of Luss'); *UK*: BMp (283887, > 4 vols. 'Olivia Adee' — 'Charles Awdry'), C[2] (1. XIV.20.44–7, > 4 vols.; 2. Z.721 d.76.1–7, imperfect, lacks vols. 4–8), L[2] (1. G.18357–62, > 6 vols.; 2. 238. e.3, imperfect, vols. 3–5, 8–9 '2nd.'), LEu (DML S.218, imperfect, lacks vols. 3–4; 5–6, 8–9 '2nd.').

[1] R.V. Taylor, *Biographia Leodiensis* (1865), 174–7.
[2] Cf. his note on *Measure for Measure*, III. i. 17, in *Works* (Yale), vii. 193, though he was less disturbed by it at the close of *Adventurer* 39 (20 Mar. 1753).

63.1PC/1b   Poetical Calendar, second 'edition'   1763

This series carries the words 'Second Edition' on the tt., but most volumes are reissues. Sets are often mixed. This 'Second Edition' in any case, is confined to vols. 3–9 in which only vol. 3 is dated 'MDCCLXIV.' H.B. Forster, *Supplements to Dodsley* (1980), 2; ESTC: t146609.

63.1PC/2   Poetical Calendar, Flowers of Parnassus   1769

In 1769 sheets of vols. 2–3 were reissued with cancel titles as 'The Flowers of Parnassus . . . In Two Volumes. London, Printed for the Editor and Sold by all the Booksellers.'

Copy: CtY (Ib.55 Td.769. F1–2).

63.2HT/1   Hoole's Tasso, first edition   1763

Jerusalem Delivered; | An Heroick Poem: | Tranflated from the ITALIAN | OF | TORQUATO TASSO, | By JOHN HOOLE. | VOL. I [– II]. | [Engr. vignettes I: 'Vol. 1. Book 2ᵈ. A Walker del. et Sculpᵗ.—', II: 'Vol. II. B. 18. A Walker del. et Sculpᵗ.—'] | LONDON, | Printed for the Author: | And fold by R. and J. Dodsley, in *Pall-mall*; P. Vaillant, | in the *Strand*; T. Davies, in *Ruffell Street, Covent Garden*; | J. Newbery, in *St. Paul's Church Yard*; Z. Stuart, in | *Pater-nofter-Row*; J. Brotherton, at the *Royal Exchange*; | D. Prince, at *Oxford*; and W. Thurlbourn and J. | Woodyer, at *Cambridge*. MDCCLXIII.

2 vols., 8°

I. a⁴ (–a4 + 'e1') ²a⁸ (–²a8 = e1) ³a⁸ b–c⁸, B–Y⁸, ($4 (a2 as a, —²a2, ²a in brackets, b2,4 as B2,4), signed; 'Vol. I.' on $1), 203 leaves.

Pp. a1 *i* t., *ii* blk, *iii* iv–v Dedication dh: TO THE | QUEEEN. | MADAM, ('John Hoole'), ht: DEDICATION., *vi* blk, on e1 ½t: JERUSALEM DELIVERED; | AN | HEROICK POEM., e1ᵛ Errata, on ²a1–7ᵛ (7 leaves unpaged) Subscribers dh: [double rule] | SUBSCRIBERS., on ³a1 ²i–xv Preface dh: [double rule] | PREFACE., ht: PREFACE., *xvi* blk, on b1 xvii–xlviii Life dh: [double rule] | THE | LIFE | OF | *TASSO*., ht: *The Life of* TASSO., on B1 *1* 2–336 text of bks. I–X dh: JERUSALEM DELIVERED. | [rule] | BOOK I. | [rule], ht: Jerusalem Delivered. Book. I. [&c.].

Pagination: ²a⁸ (Subscribers) unpaged, and pp. xvi, 1 &c. (first of each new book): 33, 68, 96, 129, 167, 200, 242, 273, 310; [↑] 31 and ᵇ1 (= xvii).

Press-figures: ³a7(xiii)–1, b3ᵛ(xxii)–4, c2ᵛ(xxxvi)–5, B5(9)–4, C7(29)–4, D8ᵛ(48)–1, E8(63)–4, F8ᵛ(80)–1, G7(93)–1, H8ᵛ(112)–4, I7ᵛ(126)–4, L4ᵛ(152)–3, N7ᵛ(190)–3, N8ᵛ(192)–4, O8ᵛ(208)–3, P1ᵛ(210)–4, Q3ᵛ(230)–4, R7(253)–3, S1ᵛ(258)–1, T7ᵛ(286)–4, U7ᵛ(302)–3, U8ᵛ(304)–1, X6(315)–5, Y8(335)–4.

Catchwords: xliv Cardina, (Cardinal͜), 21 Th (This), 23 To (Whate'er), 47 And͜ (~,), 96 And͜ (~,), 97 Some͜ (~,), 101 Whe͜ (~,), 119 As (At), 121 O͜ (O!), 124 While͜ (~,), 136 When͜ (~,), 153 The (Thefe), 186 In (Thou), 223 O͜ could (O! ~), 275 *om*. (Elected), 289 "Till (͜~), 315 Who͜ (~,).

Explicit: 336 *The* End *of* VOL. I.

II. *A*1 (?= I. a4) B–2A⁸, ($4 signed; 'VOL. II.' on $1 (–R, Z)), 185 leaves.

Pp. A1 *i* t., *ii* blk, on B1 *1* 2–326 text of bks XI–XX, dhh and htt as vol. 1., 327–67 Index dh: [double rule] | INDEX., ht: INDEX., *368* blk.

Pagination: [↑] 327; unnumbered 1, 29, 66, 93, 121, 145, 171, 202, 236, 279; 216 *misinked*; 339 *sometimes* 33.

Press-figures: B3ᵛ(6)–3, C4ᵛ(24)–3, C8(31)–8, D5ᵛ(42)–4, E6ᵛ(60)–2, F1ᵛ(66)–2, G5ᵛ(90)–2, H1ᵛ(98)–5, I3ᵛ(118)–5, I6ᵛ(124)–4, K6(139)–5, K7(141)–2, L8(159)–5, M3ᵛ(166)–4, N5ᵛ(186)–5, P1ᵛ(210)–5, Q4ᵛ(232)–5, R8ᵛ(256)–5, S8ᵛ(272)–5, T5ᵛ(282)–4, U5(297)–5, X1ᵛ(306)–5, Y2ᵛ(324)–4, Y8(335)–5, Z6(347)–5, 2A7ᵛ(366)–5.

Catchwords: 1 While (You), 17 Nor (Now), 49 When (Then), 83 A dreadful (A direful), 102 *Ubald*ₐ (~,), 135 Andₐ (~,), 161 Ah [*broken* 'h'], 249 Nowₐ (~,), 292 Difguis'dₐ (~,), 309 I (It), 338 DESCRPTIONSₐ (~,).

Explicit: 367 *FINIS*.

Paper: White, laid; Demy (uncut: 8¾ × 5½ in.); no vis. wmk.

Type: Dedication: great primer (5.6 mm), leaded, Preface: english (4.45 mm), Life and text: pica (3.9 mm), Index: long primer (3.2 mm), 2 cols./p. Tpp I. xv, 336; II. 367.

References: *Life* i. 383 (Courtney 101); CH 146; Hazen 62–6; Welsh 237, 313; Roscoe, *Newbery* (1973), A581; Hoole, *Anecdotes respecting the Life of John Hoole* (1803); *Booklist* 88; Subscriptions no. 61; ESTC: t133777.

Notes: Early specimens prepared by Hoole were noticed as 'now in the Press; the first Book of which has been printed, and presented by the Author, Mr. *Hoole*, to his Friends', in *Gents. Mag.* xxxi (Sept. 1761), 422–3. No such specimens have been found. They presumably solicited subscriptions too.

SJ furnished the 'Dedication' of which the holograph MS remained in the Hoole family until 1930 (*MS Handlist* 87; *MS Index* JoS 181). In his 'Preface', Hoole acknowledged the encouragement of SJ and the assistance of Hawkesworth. SJ was a subscriber, but his copy (Hyde), also has a presentation inscription. In this copy the *Errata* are printed on ³a7ᵛ with the dh. as 'ERRAT', and there is neither list of Subscribers nor ½t signed 'e'. This ½t signed 'e' is variously placed, and was evidently an afterthought since it was not printed until the List of Subscribers was completed.

500 copies of the edn. were printed between June 1761 and March 1762 by William Bowyer (O: MS. Don b. 4, fo. 175).[1] The first copy was delivered to Hoole on 4 Jan. 1763, and others to the trade throughout the spring, presumably for subscribers of whom there were 332 who took 352 copies. Hoole gave a copy to the Queen (Charlotte, of Mecklenburg-Strelitz), his dedicatee, on 28 May 1763 (*Gents. Mag.* xxxiii (May 1763), 256 s.d.). The work was not advertised until 1 June 1763 (*Lond. Chron.*), priced at 10s. 6d. sewed, and 12s. bound, and was reviewed by John Langhorne in the *Monthly Review*, xxix (1763), 106,

182, 251, and 321, and anonymously in *Gents. Mag.* xxxiii (June 1763), 266–8, with further 'Observations' in xxxiv (Feb. 1764), 85–6.

Copies: O (Vet. A5 e. 1295–6, 'Marg^t Howes' — Oxford City Library);

USA: CSmH (359931), CtY (*no Subscribers*), G. Goldberg, Esq; Hyde³ (1. Inscr: 'To Mr Samuel Johnson from the Author John Hoole'; *Booklist* 88), ICN, [Liebert ('William Baker') = ? CtY], MH, [MoU], NIC, NjP, [OCl], PPL, TxU (*no Subscribers*); *Can*: CaOHM (B 14561–2, 'Sam¹. Thoyts' — 'John Samworth'); *UK*: BRc, L (11429. d.16), SAN.

---

¹ This account shows that 500 was the nominal size of the edn., but the record of copies distributed reveals an edn. of at least 590.

63.2HT/2   Hoole's Tasso, second edition   1764

[½tt, in both vols.] JERUSALEM DELIVERED; | AN | HEROIC POEM:
   Stet: POEM:
[Title] JERUSALEM DELIVERED; | AN | HEROIC POEM: | Tranſlated from the Italian of | TORQUATO TASSO, | By JOHN HOOLE. | VOL. I [–II]. | THE SECOND EDITION. | [Engr. vignette as 1st edn. 63.2HT/1, above] | LONDON: | Printed for R. and J. DODSLEY, P. VAILLANT, | T. DAVIES, J. NEWBERY and Z. STUART. | MDCCLXIV.
   2 vols., 12°

I. π² A¹² a¹² b⁴ B–L¹² M⁶ (M6 blk), ($6 (–A2, b3,4, M4,5,6) signed; 'VOL. I.' on $1), 156 leaves.
   Pp. π1 ½t, π1ᵛ blk, π2 *i* t., *ii* blk, on A1 *iii–v* Dedication dh: TO THE | QUEEN. | MADAM, ht: DEDICATION., *vi* blk, on A3 *vii* viii–xxi Preface dh: [double rule] | PREFACE., ht: PREFACE., *xxii* blk, xxiii–lxiii Life dh: [double rule] | THE | LIFE | OF | TASSO*., ht: THE LIFE OF TASSO., on B1 *1* 2–250 text of bks I–X dh: JERUSALEM DELIVERED. | [rule] | BOOK. I. [&c.], *251–2* (M6) blk.
   Pagination: [↑] xiii; unnumbered: π², A1–2, vii, xxii, and first p. of each book: 1, 25, 51, 72, 96, 120, 149, 181, 204, 231.
   Press-figures: A8ᵛ(xviii)–9, a1ᵛ(xxviii)–5, b4(lvii)–9, b4ᵛ(lviii)–1, B11ᵛ(22)–4, C11ᵛ(46)–8, C12ᵛ(48)–*, D2ᵛ(52)–4, E6ᵛ(84)–1, E11ᵛ(94)–*, F5ᵛ(106)–6, F8ᵛ(112)–1, G7ᵛ(134)–9, G12ᵛ(144)–4, H8(159)–1, H8ᵛ(160)–*, I5ᵛ(178)–9, K7ᵛ(206)–9, K11(213)–1, L8(231)–*.
   Catchwords: 3 Tancrea (Tancred), 34 Yon͔ (~'), 43 T (To), 95 JERUSA (JERUSALEM), 133 And͔ (~,), 211 Theſe͔ (~,), 242 But͔ (~,).
   Explicit: 250 The END of VOL. I.

II. *A*² B–L¹² M–P⁶, ($6/3 (–DEGI 6) signed; 'VOL. II.' on $1 (B1 as 'VOL.')), 146 leaves.

Pp. A1 *i* ½t, *ii* blk, *iii* t., *iv* blk, on B1 *1* 2–244 text of bks XI–XX (dh and ht as vol. 1), 245–87 Index dh: [double rule] | INDEX., *288* blk.

Pagination: [↑] 245; new books unpaged at 1, 22, 50, 70, 91, 109, 129, 152, 178, 210.

Press-figures: H7(157)–4, K5ᵛ(202)–4, L7(229)–4, L11ᵛ(238)–3, O4(271)–2.

Catchwords: 2 Then₍ (~,), 48 ₍Till ('Till), 160 Thus₍ (~,), 187 Come₍ (~,), 250 *Armida*₍ (~,), 266 HERMIT₍ (—gives), 281 Sᴘᴇᴇᴄʜᴇs₍ (~,), 282 Sᴘᴇᴇᴄʜᴇs₍ (~,).

Explicit: 287 FINIS.

Paper: White, laid; La. post (uncut: 7 × 4½ in.); wmk: fleur-de-lys.

Type: Dedication: english (4.7 mm), leaded, Preface: sm. pica (3.7 mm), leaded, Life and text: long primer (3.2 mm), leaded. Index 2 cols./p.

References: Hazen 65; Roscoe, *Newbery* (1973), A 581; ESTC: t129222.

Notes: The infrequent press-figures in vol. 2 imply shared printing. The small size of the first edn. and the publication by subscription probably led to an early reprint for the wider market. It was noticed in *Gents. Mag.* xxxiv (Feb. 1764), 85 n., 'A new edition of this work is now in the press', and published at 5s. sewed. SJ's 'Dedication' is unchanged.

Copies: O (Vet. A5 f.2867–8, 'E Libris Caroli Walters');

USA: MH², PPL (lacks tt.), PPU; *Can*: CaOHM (B 5195–6); *UK*: Gu (BC4——k 29–30), Om.

63.2HT/3   Hoole's Tasso, third edition   1767

[½t] JERUSALEM DELIVERED; | AN HEROIC POEM.
    Stet: POEM.
[Title] JERUSALEM DELIVERED; | AN | HEROIC POEM: | Tranflated from the Italian of | TORQUATO TASSO, | BY JOHN HOOLE. | VOL. I [– II]. | THE THIRD EDITION. | [engr. vignette as 63.2HT/1 above] | LONDON: | Printed for T. DAVIES, in Ruffel-Street, Covent-Garden; | and J. DODSLEY, in Pall-Mall. | MDCCLXVII.

    2 vols., 12°

I. A¹² (–A1,2 + *A*1.2) B–N¹² (N12 blk), ($5 signed; 'Vᴏʟ. I.' on $1), 156 leaves.

Pp. A1 *i* ½t, *ii* blk, *iii* t., *iv* blk, on A3 *v–vii* Dedication, *viii* blk, *ix* x–xxi Preface, *xxii* blk, *xxiii* xxiv–lix Life of Tasso, *lx* blk, on C7 *1* 2–250 text of bks. I–X, *1–2* (N12) blk.

Pagination: 1st p. of each book unpaged 1, 25, 51, 72, 96, 120, 149, 181, 204, 231.

Press-figures: A7ᵛ(xiv)–1, A12ᵛ(xxiv)–2, B7(xxxvii)–3 [*inverted*], B8(xxxix)–1, C12(11)–2, D12(35)–2, E1ᵛ(38)–5, E2ᵛ(40)–2, F7(73)–2, G1ᵛ(86)–2,

G11(105)–4,   H2^v(112)–2,   I12^v(156)–2,   K2^v(160)–4,   L5^v(190)–3, M11^v(226)–4, N7^v(242)–3, N11(249)–4.

Catchwords: xxxiii *om.* (There), 133 nd$_\wedge$ (~,), 175 Orman (Ormano), 178 Thefe$_\wedge$ (~,), 191 Here$_\wedge$ (~,), 211 Thefe$_\wedge$ (~,), 242 But$_\wedge$ (~,), 247 A (At).

Explicit: 250 The END of the FIRST VOLUME.

II. A^{12} (–A1,2 + *A*1.2) B–M^{12}, ($5 signed; 'VOL. II.' on $1), 144 leaves.

Pp. A1 ½t, A1^v blk, A2 t., A2^v blk, on A3 *1* 2–244 text bks XI–XX, 245–84 Index.

Pagination: [↑] 245; Unpaged A1–2, and 1st page of each new book 1, 22, 50, 70, 91, 109, 129, 152, 178, 210; 138 as 831, 227 as 22, 240 as 40.

Press-figures: A12(19)–5, B11^v(42)–5, C11^v(66)–4, D1^v(70)–4, E2^v(96)–3, E8(107)–5, F11^v(138)–[?], G8(155)–5, G8^v(156)–3, H11^v(186)–3, I1^v(190)–3, K6(223)–2, K6^v(224)–3, L8(251)–5, L12^v(260)–3, M11(281)–3, M12(283)–2.

Catchwords: 2 Then$_\wedge$ (~,), 48 $_\wedge$Till ('Till), 84 But$_\wedge$ (~,), 92 while$_\wedge$ (~,), 107 So$_\wedge$ (~,), 120 Hafte$_\wedge$ (~!), 135 On (One), 160 Thus$_\wedge$ (~,), 187 Come$_\wedge$ (~,), 256 *Guafco*, (*Guelpho*,), 271 *Rinaldo*$_\wedge$ (~,), 277 [*God-*]*frey*$_\wedge$ (~,).

Explicit: 284 FINIS.

Paper: White, laid; Demy (uncut: 7½ × 4⅞ in.); no vis. wmk.

Type: Dedication: pica (4.0 mm), leaded, Preface: Long primer (3.3 mm), leaded, Life and text: bourgeois (3.2 mm), leaded; Index 2 cols./p.

References: ESTC: t133778.

Notes: There is no obvious reason for the cancellation of the ½tt and tt.

Dodsley acquired a ½-share of the copyright of this work from Thomas Davies in January 1766 for £31. 10s.,[1] and retained an interest in subsequent edns. (Tierney, 70).

Copies: O (Antiq. f.E 1767/4–5, 'E. S. Dodgson, 1912');
USA: CtY, PPL, TxU; *Can*: CaOHM (B 14263–4); *UK*: C, L (239. h.40).

[1] Untraced document in Sotheby (Pocock), 10 May 1875, 48, @ 4s. 6d.

63.2HT/4   Hoole's Tasso, fourth edition   1772

[½t] JERUSALEM DELIVERED; | AN | HEROIC POEM.

   [Title] JERUSALEM DELIVERED; | AN | HEROIC POEM: | Tranflated from the Italian of | TORQUATO TASSO, | BY JOHN HOOLE. | VOL. I [– II]. | THE FOURTH EDITION. | [Engr. vignette as 63.2HT/1, above] | LONDON: | Printed for J. DODSLEY, in Pall-Mall; and T. DAVIES, | in Ruffell-Street, Covent-Garden. | M.DCC.LXXII.
   2 vols., 12°

I. A–N^{12} (N12 blk), ($5 (–A1,2,4) signed; 'VOL. I.' on $1 (–A)), 156 leaves.

Pp. A1 *i* ½t, *ii* blk, *iii* t., *iv* blk, *v–vii* Dedication dh: [2 double rules] | TO THE | QUEEN. | MADAM, *viii* blk, on A4 *ix* x–xxi Preface, *xxii* blk, *xxiii* xxiv–lix Life of Tasso, *lx* blk, on C7 *1* 2–250 text of bks I–X, *251–2* (N12) blk.

Pagination: unpaged i–ix, xxxiii, lx; new bk. 1, 25, 51, 72, 96, 120, 149, 181, 204, 231, 252–2; 165 as 169.

Press-figures: none.

Catchwords: xxxiii *om*. (There), 186 Who͵ (~,), 191 Here͵ (~,), 211 Thefe͵ (~,), 244 Alone͵ (~,), 247 A (At).

Explicit: 250 The END of the FIRST VOLUME.

II. A–M¹², ($6 (–A1,2) signed; 'VOL. II.' on $1 (–AEI)), 144 leaves.

Pp. A1 *i* ½t, *ii* blk, *iii* t., *iv* blk, on A3 *1* 2–244 text bks XI–XX, on L5 245–84 Index.

Pagination: [↑] 245; unpaged i–iv, 1, 22, 50, 70, 91, 109, 129, 152, 178, 210; 175 as 157, 221 as 223, 230 as 123, 260 [*2 dropt*], 271 as 272.

Press-figures: A7(9)–3, A8(11)–4, B1ᵛ(22)–3, C7(57)–5, D12(91)–6, E12ᵛ(116)–3, F1ᵛ(118)–7, G11(161)–6, G12(163)–6, H11ᵛ(186)–6, I12(211)–5, I12ᵛ(212)–7, K1ᵛ(214)–3, K2ᵛ(216)–5, L12(259)–5, M11ᵛ(282)–7.

Catchwords: 2 Then͵ (~,), 15 Now (Not), 17 Dare (Dear), 19 No (Not), 30 ͵Till ('Till), 63 At (All), 92 While͵ (~,), 102 *om*. (But), 126 Alcide (Alcides'), 168 Where'e (Where'er), 180 Tancred͵ (~,), 187 Come͵ (~,), 227 Or, (~͵), 231 A hun (A hundred), 243 Th (Thy), 255 *Chriſtians*, (~͵), 264 *Godfrey*, (~͵), 272 *Rinaldo*, (~͵), 280 SPEECH (——*Argantes'*).

Explicit: 284 FINIS.

Paper: White, laid; Demy (uncut: 7 × 4½ in.); no vis. wmk.

Type: Dedication: pica (4.0 mm), leaded, Preface, Life and text: long primer (3.2 mm), leaded, Index and notes: brevier (2.5 mm). Vignette as 63.2HT/1 ('A. Walker del. et fculp.').

Notes: Bowyer printed 1,000 copies of vol. 2 for Dodsley in Oct. 1771 (O: MS Don. b.4, fo. 175),[1] so that the date on the tt. may be anticipatory, or it was published early in 1772. ESTC: t084059.

Copies: JDF ('J.F. Katenkamp');

USA: NN, TxU ('Richard Heber'); *UK*: HLu.

---

[1] The total of copies recorded as distributed by Bowyer was 997.

63.2HT/5 Hoole's Tasso, fifth edition 1783

[½t] JERUSALEM DELIVERED; | AN | HEROIC POEM. | [short swelled rule] | VOL. I [– II].

[Title] JERUSALEM DELIVERED; | AN | HEROIC POEM: | Tranſlated from the ITALIAN of | *TORQUATO TASSO*, | BY JOHN HOOLE. | IN TWO VOLUMES. | VOL. I [– II]. | [short swelled rule] | THE FIFTH EDITION, | WITH NOTES. | [short swelled rule] | LONDON: | PRINTED FOR J. DODSLEY, IN PALL-MALL. | M.DCC.LXXXIII.

2 vols., 8°

I. a–c⁸ B–Y⁸ Z², ($4 (–Z2) signed; 'Vᴏʟ. I.' on $1 (–a)), 194 leaves.

Pp. a1 *i* ½t, *ii* blk, *iii* t., *iv* blk, *v–vi* Dedication to the Queen, *vii–*viii ADVERTISEMENT | BY THE TRANSLATOR, | TO THE PRESENT EDITION. ('May 23, 1783'), ht: ADVERTISEMENT., *ix* x–xviii Preface, *xix* xx–xlvii Life of Tasso, *xlviii* blk, on B1 *1* ½t: THE | FIRST BOOK | OF | JERUSALEM DELIVERED., *2* blk, *3* 4–339 text bks I–X dh: THE | FIRST BOOK | OF | JERUSALEM DELIVERED., ht: JERUSALEM DELIVERED. B. I. [&c.], *340* blk.

Pagination: unpaged i–vii, ix, xix, xlviii, 1–3, 36–9, 73–5, 102–5, 135–7, 166–9, 204–7, 246–9, 277–9, 313–15, 340; blank ii, iv, xlviii, 36, 102, 166, 204, 246, 340; 302–3 as 202–3.

Press-figures: a5ᵛ(x)–5, b4ᵛ(xxiv)–6, b6(xxvii)–3, c7ᵛ(xlvi)–6, B8(15)–7, B8ᵛ(16)–9, C7(29)–6, C7ᵛ(30)–1, D1ᵛ(34)–5, D8ᵛ(48)–1, E5ᵛ(58)–7, F1ᵛ(66)–10, G3ᵛ(86)–2, G8ᵛ(96)–9, H2ᵛ(100)–2, H6(107)–3, I5ᵛ(122)–6, I6ᵛ(124)–5, K6(139)–3, L7(157)–1, M6ᵛ(172)–5, M8(175)–3, N7ᵛ(190)–3, N8ᵛ(192)–5, O2ᵛ(196)–5, O8(207)–1, P2ᵛ(212)–10, P7ᵛ(222)–3, Q2ᵛ(228)–1, Q3ᵛ(230)–10, R5ᵛ(250)–9, R7(253)–3, S5ᵛ(266)–5, S8ᵛ(272)–2, T5(281)–6, T8(287)–3, U1ᵛ(290)–6, X1ᵛ(306)–9, Y6(331)–9, Y7(333)–3, Z1ᵛ(338)–5.

Catchwords: xxv Alphonſo˄ (~,), 4 Thou˄ (~,).

Explicit: 339 END OF THE TENTH BOOK.

II. *A*² B–2A⁸ 2B⁶, ($4 (–2B4) signed; 'Vᴏʟ. II.' on $1 (–Z)), 192 leaves.

Pp. A1 *i* ½t, *ii* blk, *iii* t., *iv* blk, on B1 *1* ½t: THE | ELEVENTH BOOK | OF | JERUSALEM DELIVERED., *2* THE ARGUMENT., *3* 4–335 text of bks XI–XX dh: THE | ELEVENTH BOOK | OF | JERUSALEM DELIVERED., ht: JERUSALEM DELIVERED. B. XI. [&c.], *336* blk, on Z1–2B6 Index (unpaged) dh: [double rule] | INDEX., ht: INDEX., 2B6ᵛ blk.

Pagination: unpaged: A², 1–3, 29–31, 65–7, 92–5, 122–5, 148–51, 176–9, 213–15, 248–51, 290–3, Z1–2B6; blanks 92, 122, 148, 176, 248, 290, 336, 2B6ᵛ.

Press-figures: B5ᵛ(10)–10, C5ᵛ(26)–6, D2ᵛ(36)–2, D5ᵛ(42)–5, E7ᵛ(62)–3, F7ᵛ(78)–5, G5ᵛ(90)–6, G8ᵛ(96)–10, H4ᵛ(104)–1, H6(107)–10, I3ᵛ(118)–1, K8(143)–9, L5ᵛ(154)–7, L8ᵛ(160)–9, M1ᵛ(162)–3, M7(173)–1, N2ᵛ(180)–3, N8(191)–6, O7ᵛ(206)–3, P5ᵛ(218)–5, P7(221)–10, Q1ᵛ(226)–3, R1ᵛ(242)–6, S5ᵛ(266)–3, S6(268)–7, T6(283)–2, T6ᵛ(284)–7, U6ᵛ(300)–7, X5ᵛ(314)–3, X6ᵛ(316)–6, Y7(333)–7, Z2ᵛ–1, 2A6ᵛ–10, 2B1ᵛ–3, 2B5ᵛ–7.

Catchwords: 23 Al (All), 80 O king ! (O King !), Z6 Cʏᴘʀᴇss˄ (~,).

Explicit: 2B6 FINIS.

Paper: White, laid; La. post (uncut: 8¼ × 5¼ in.); no vis. wmk.

Type: Dedication: english (4.6 mm), leaded, Advertisement and text: pica (4.2 mm), notes: sm. pica (3.6 mm), index: long primer (3.2 mm).

Plates: 2, at I. 9 by Anker Smith, after Stothard, and II. 225, by [William] Sharp, after Stothard.

References: ESTC: t145056.
Copies: O (Vet. A5 e.5171, 'Sir Robert Laurie');
USA: ICN, MH, TxU; *Can*: CaOHM (B 3661–2); *UK*: C (Nn. 26. 23–4), Gu, L (84. e.11–12).

63.2HT/6   Hoole's Tasso, sixth edition   1787

Jerusalem Delivered: An Heroic Poem. Translated from the Italian of Torquato Tasso, By John Hoole. The Sixth Edition. London: For J. Dodsley
2 vols.
References: ESTC: n006701.
Not examined.
Copies: *UK*: DUc, LEu.

63.2HT/7   Hoole's Tasso, seventh edition   1788

Jerusalem Delivered: An Heroic Poem. Translated from the Italian of Torquato Tasso, By John Hoole. The Seventh Edition, with Notes. Dublin: Printed by James Moore, No. 45, College-Green.
2 vols., 12°
References: ESTC: n028973.
Not examined.
Copies: *USA*: [PPAmP], PPL; *Can*: CaOHM (B 405; vol. 2 only).

63.2HT/8   Hoole's Tasso, 'seventh' edition   1792

[½t] JERUSALEM DELIVERED; | AN | HEROIC POEM: | [short swelled rule] | VOL. I [– II].
   [Title] JERUSALEM DELIVERED; | AN | HEROIC POEM: | Tranſlated from the Italian of | *TORQUATO TASSO,* | By JOHN HOOLE. | IN TWO VOLUMES. | VOL. I [– II]. | THE SEVENTH EDITION, | WITH NOTES. | [medium swelled rule] | LONDON: | Printed for J. DODSLEY, in Pall-Mall. | [short double rule] | M.DCC.XCII.
   2 vols., 8°

   I. a–c⁸ B–Y⁸ Z², ($4 (–a1,2) signed; 'Vol. I.' on $1), 194 leaves.
   Pp. a1 ½t, a1ᵛ blk, + Engr. front. + a2 t., a2ᵛ blk, on a3 *v–vi* Dedication: TO THE | QUEEN., *vii–*viii Advertisement ('May 23, 1783.'), a4 *ix* x–xviii Preface, *xix* xx–xlvii Life of Tasso, *xlviii* blk, on B1 *1* ½t Book I, *2* Argument, *3* 4–339 text, *340* blk.
   Pagination: Fly tt. and first pp. of each book are unnumbered, viz. i–vii, ix,

xix, xlviii, 1–3, 36–9, 73–5, 102–5, 135–7, 166–9, 204–7, 246–9, 277–9, 313–15, 340; blk pp: ii, iv, xlviii, 36, 102, 166, 204, 246, 340; no errors.

Press-figures: a5(ix)–3, a8(xv)–*, b2ᵛ(xx)–x, b7ᵛ(xxx)–3, c5ᵛ(xlii)–x, B6(11)–x, C4ᵛ(24)–§, D7(45)–x, D7ᵛ(46)–4, E1ᵛ(50)–2, E4ᵛ(56)–x, F7ᵛ(78)–1, G8ᵛ(96)–1, H5ᵛ(106)–*, H8ᵛ(112)–2, I1ᵛ(114)–x, K7ᵛ(142)–2, L7(157)–8, M1ᵛ(162)–9, N7ᵛ(190)–*, O1ᵛ(194)–2, P5ᵛ(218)–*, Q7(237)–2, Q7ᵛ(238)–3, R6ᵛ(252)–1, R7ᵛ(254)–x, S2ᵛ(260)–3, S3ᵛ(262)–1, T6(283)–2, U6ᵛ(300)–1, X6(315)–8, Y5ᵛ(330)–4, Z1ᵛ(338)–3.

Catchwords: no errors.

Explicit: 339 THE END OF THE TENTH BOOK.

II. *A*² B–2A⁸ 2B⁶, ($4 (–2B4) signed; 'Vol. II.' on $1), 192 leaves.

Pp. A1 ½t, A1ᵛ blk, + Engr. front. + A2 t., A2ᵛ blk, on B1 *1* ½t Book XI, *2* Argument, *3* 4–335 text, *336* blk, on Z1–2B6ᵛ (unpaged) Index.

Pagination: unnumbered: i–iv, 1–3, 29–31, 65–7, 92–5, 122–5, 148–51, 176–9, 213–15, 248–51, 290–3, 336 and Index; blk pp. 92, 148, 122, 177, 248, 290, 336; no errors.

Press-figures: B7ᵛ(14)–2, B8ᵛ(16)–*, C5(25)–*, C6(27)–3, D6(43)–2, E3ᵛ(54)–3, F7ᵛ(78)–*, G1ᵛ(82)–2, H7ᵛ(110)–1, I1ᵛ(114)–2, K6(139)–x, L7ᵛ(158)–1, M1ᵛ(162)–*, N6ᵛ(188)–5, N7ᵛ(190)–9, O6(203)–5, P6(219)–5, P7(221)–4, Q8(239)–1, R3ᵛ(246)–2, S6(267)–3, S7(269)–1, T6(283)–1, U5ᵛ(298)–8, X8(319)–1, Y7ᵛ(334)–8, Z7–2, 2A8–9, 2B2ᵛ–x.

Catchwords: no errors.

Explicit: 335 THE END OF THE TWENTIETH AND LAST BOOK. 2B6ᵛ FINIS.

Paper: White, wove (foxed); medium (uncut: 9 × 5¾ in.); no vis. wmk.

Type: Preface: english (4.6 mm), Advertisement and text: pica (4.0 mm, leaded 3.5 mm), Preface, notes and Argument: sm. pica (3.5 mm).

Plates: Front. to each vol. 1. (Gabrield directing Godfrey) 'Vol. 1. Page 9.' 'Stothard. delin. Anker Smith sculpt.'; 2. (Rinaldo slaying Armida) 'Vol. 2 Page. 225' 'Stothard delin Sharp sculp.'

References: ESTC: t126454.

Copies: Op;

USA: [ChSU], CSmH (433105), NN, PPL, TxU; *Can*: CaOHM (B 4279–80); *UK*: E (Dry. 581), L, LCu, [PER], WIS.

63.2HT/9   Hoole's Tasso, J. Johnson, octavo   1797

JERUSALEM DELIVERED: | An Heroic Poem. | TRANSLATED FROM THE ITALIAN OF | *TORQUATO TASSO,* | By John Hoole. | [short swelled rule] | WITH FOUR ELEGANT ENGRAVINGS, | [double rule] | IN TWO VOLUMES. — VOL. I [– II]. | *LONDON:* | Printed for J. Johnson; T.

N. Longman; Cadell & | Davies; J. Walker; W. Otridge & Son; R. Lea; | J. Nunn; J. Cuthell; Ogilvy & Son; Lack- | ington, Allen, & Co. and Vernor & Hood. | [short rule] | 1797.

2 vols., 8°

I. π^2 a–c^8 d^4, 1–17^8, (unsigned), 166 leaves.

Pp. π1 blk + Engr. front. + π2 t., π2^v blk, on a1 *iii–iv* Dedication to the Queen, *v* vi–xviii Preface, *xix* xx–lviii Life of Tasso, on 1_1 *17* ½t, *18* Argument, *19* 20–286 text bks I–X.

Pagination: unpaged between books, 43–5, 71–3, 94–7, 121–3, 146–9, 210–13, 235–7, 264–7; blk: 94, 146, 210, 264; 154 as 54.

Press-figures: none; *Catchwords*: none.

Explicit: 42, 93, 120, 145 END OF THE FIRST [–SECOND –THIRD –FOURTH –FIFTH] BOOK., 176 [double rule] | END OF THE FIFTH [*sic* = 6th] BOOK. | [double rule], 209 [double rule] | END OF THE SEVENTH [–EIGHTH –NINTH –TENTH] BOOK‸ | [double rule].

II. π1 *1–19*^{8} *20*^{4} (*20*$_4$?=π1), 157 leaves.

Pp. Engr. front. + π1 t., π1^v blk, on 1_1 *1* ½t, *2* Argument, *3* 4–264 text bks XI–XX, *265–312* Index (48 pages unnumbered).

Pagination: unpaged 24–7, 54–7, 77–9, 99–101, 118–21, 140–3, 166–9, 194–7, 228–31; blk: 24, 54, 118, 140, 166, 194, 228.

Press-figures: none; *Catchwords*: none.

Explicit: 23 [double rule] | END OF THE ELEVENTH [–TWELFTH – THIRTEENTH –FOURTEENTH –FIFTEENTH –SIXTEENTH –SEVENTEENTH –EIGHTEENTH –NINETEENTH –TWENTIETH AND LAST] BOOK. | [double rule] *312* THE END.

Paper: White, wove; demy (8¾ × 5½ in.); wmk.: (prelims) R D, (vol. 1) R D, var: 7 LEPARD 9.

Type: Dedication: long primer (3.3 mm) Hoole's 'signature' in civilité, Preface, Life, text &c: bourgeois (2.8 mm) leaded. Index (2 cols./p.): minion (2.4 mm).

Plates: (4): I. Front ('Vol. I. page 5. Kirk E.W. Thomson. Published by John Walker Sepr 1797'), 23 (Stothard delin. Anker Smith sculp.); II. Engr. front. ('Frontispiece to Vol. II. See Page 260 Published as the Act directs by Vernor and Hood. Novr 1. 1797. Kirk delin. Ridley sculp.'), 176 (Stothard delin. Sharp sculp.)

References: ESTC: t133776.

Notes: SJ's *Dedication*, I. *iii–iv*. This is the first edn. in which the firm of Vernor & Hood is involved. An undated note from Hoole (d. 1803), to [? Thomas] 'Hood' asking him to send a copy to 'Mr Corbett' probably refers to this, or the 1802 edn. (Eu: MS La. II. 422/ 118).

Copies: O (Vet. A5 f.3063, 'Hobart');

USA: CSmH (324858), CtY, MH, PPU²; *UK*: L² (**1**. 11427. c.26, **2**. (Large Paper) 11422. ff. 24), LCu, [PER], WIS; *Eir*: Dt.

63.2HT/10   Hoole's Tasso, J. Johnson, duodecimo   1797

JERUSALEM DELIVERED: | An Heroic Poem. | TRANSLATED FROM THE ITALIAN OF | *TORQUATO TASSO*, | By John Hoole. | [short swelled rule] | WITH FOUR ELEGANT ENGRAVINGS, | [double rule] | IN TWO VOLUMES. — VOL. I [– II]. | *LONDON:* | Printed for J. Johnson; T. N. Longman; Cadell & | Davies; J. Walker; W. Otridge & Son; R. Lea; | J. Nunn; J. Cuthell; Ogilvy & Son; Lack- | ington, Allen, & Co. and Vernor & Hood. | [short rule] | 1797.

2 vols., 12°
References: ESTC: n001308.
Notes: Not seen, but reported by ESTC with copies at *USA*: MBSuf, IU.

63.2HT/11   Hoole's Tasso, Associated Booksellers   1797

Jerusalem Delivered: An Heroic Poem. Translated from the Italian of Torquato Tasso, By John Hoole. London: Printed for the Associated Booksellers, J. Walker, J. Cuthell, Vernor and Hood, Ogilvy and Son, Lackington, Allen and Co., and J. Nunn. 1797.

2 vols., 8°
References: ESTC: n000220.
Notes: Not seen, but reported in ESTC.
Copies: *USA*: PU; *UK*: LU; *Eir*: Dt.

63.2HT/12   Hoole's Tasso, J. Johnson   1799

Jerusalem Delivered: An Heroic Poem. Translated from the Italian of Torquato Tasso, By John Hoole. London: J. Johnson.

Not Examined.
Copies: *USA*: MH.

63.2HT/13   Hoole's Tasso, 'eighth' edition   1802

Jerusalem Delivered; An Heroic Poem. Translated from the Italian of Torquato Tasso, By John Hoole. In Two Volumes. Vol. I [– II]. The Eighth Edition, with Notes. London: Printed by T. Bensley, Bolt Court, Fleet Street, for J. Johnson; Cuthell and Martin; Otridge and Son; J. Walker; R. Lea; J. Nunn;

Lackington, Allen, and Co.; Longman and Rees; Cadell and Davies; Vernor and Hood; J. Mawman; and W.J. and J. Richardson. 1802.
[vol. 2: . . . Hood; and J. Mawman . . .]
2 vols., 8°

I. *a*⁸ b–c⁸ B–Y⁸ Z², ($2 signed), 194 leaves.
Pp. *i* ½t + engr. front + *iii* t., *v–vi* SJ's Dedication to the Queen, *vii*–viii Advertisement ('May 23. 1783'), *ix* x–xviii Preface, *xix* xx–xlvii Life of Tasso, on B1 *1–3* 4–339 text bks I–X, *340* coloph: 'T. Bensley, Printer, Bolt Court, Fleet Street, London.'

II. *A*² B–2A⁸ 2B⁶, ($2 signed), 192 leaves.
Pp. A1 ½t + engr. front. + A2 t., on B1 *1–3* 4–335 (222 as 22) text bks XI–XX, *336* blk, on Z1–2B6ᵛ Index, 2B6ᵛ THE END. and coloph. as vol. 1.

Plates: as in 1797 (63.2HT/9, above); SJ's 'Dedication' at I. *v–vi*.
Copies: O (8° I. 161–2 BS);
USA: CSmH (436695), MH (vol. 2 only), NN, TxU.

63.2HT/14   Hoole's Tasso, 'eighth' edition,   1803
royal paper

Jerusalem Delivered; An Heroic Poem. Translated from the Italian of Torquato Tasso, By John Hoole. In Two Volumes. Vol. I [– II]. The Eighth Edition, with Notes. London: Printed by T. Bensley, Bolt Court, Fleet Street, for J. Johnson; Cuthell and Martin; Otridge and Son; J. Walker; R. Lea; J. Nunn; Lackington, Allen, and Co.; Longman and Rees; Cadell and Davies; Vernor and Hood; J. Mawman; and W.J. and J. Richardson. 1803.
Notes: Royal paper (10 × 6¼ in.) issue of prec. 1802 (63.2HT/13, above).
Copies: O (Broxb. 36. 12–13, 'John Hely-Hutchinson'; goffered, gilt, in red, blue and brown morocco, gilt extra, silk end pp.);
USA: CSmH (69992), CtY, MH, NN, NPM, TxU; *UK*: L (1163. i.17), LEu.

63.2HT/15   Hoole's Tasso, J. Johnson   1807

Jerusalem Delivered; An Heroic Poem. Translated from the Italian of Torquato Tasso. By John Hoole. In Two Volumes. Vol. I [–II]. A New Edition, with Notes. London: Printed for J. Johnson; Vernor, Hood, and Sharpe; W. J. and J. Richardson; W. Otridge and Son; J. Walker; Cuthell and Martin; R. Lea; J. Nunn; Lackington, Allen, and Co.; Longman, Hurst, Rees, and Orme; Cadell and Davies; J. Mawman; and J. Murray; At the Union Printing-Office, St John's Square, by W. Wilson. 1807.
2 vols., 12°

I. *A*² B–N¹² O⁶ P⁴, ($6 (–O4,5,6, P3,4) signed; 'VOL. I.' on $1), 156 leaves.

Pp. *i* ½t + Engr. front. ('Shelley pinxᵗ. Thompson sculp.') + *iii* t., on B1 *1–2* Dedication, *3–4* Advertisement ('*May* 23, 1783'), 5 6–16 Preface, *17* 18–50 Life of Tasso, *51* ½t, *52* Argument, *53* 54–305 text bks I–X, 305 coloph: 'W. Wilson, Printer, St. John's-Square.', *306* blk, *307–8* advts.

Pagination: ½tt and 1st pp. each book, 112 unnumbered; 122, 200, 232, 256, 284, 306 blk.

Press-figures: B5ᵛ(10)–2, C1ᵛ(26)–6, C2ᵛ(28)–1, D11ᵛ(70)–1, E5ᵛ(82)–2, F7ᵛ(110)–2, G8(135)–1, I12(191)–1, K8(207)–3, L5ᵛ(226)–2, M1ᵛ(242)–2, N12(287)–1, P1ᵛ(302)–2.

Catchwords: none.

II. *A*² B–O¹² P⁴ ($6 (–P4) signed; 'VOL. II.' on $1), 162 leaves.

Pp. *i* ½t + Engr. front ('Kirk delin. Ridley sculp') + *iii* t., on B1 *1* ½t, *2* Argument, *3* 4–263 text bks XI–XX, *264* blk, on N1–P4 Index, on P4 coloph. as vol. 1, P4ᵛ blk.

Pagination: as vol. 1; 52, 74, 98, 140, 168, 196, 264, and P4ᵛ blk; 256 as 56 (2 *broken* and *inverted*).

Press-figures: B5ᵛ(10)–2, C1ᵛ(26)–2, D5ᵛ(58)–1, F3ᵛ(102)–3, I11ᵛ(190)–3, L12(239)–2, O11ᵛ–2, O12ᵛ–1, P2ᵛ–2.

Catchwords: none.

Explicit: P4 [medium double rule] | THE END. | [medium double rule].

Paper: White, wove; wmk.: H S | 1807.

Plates: as fronts. (Shelley & Thompson, and Kirk & Ridley).

Notes: Printed by William Wilson (Todd 215, 232). SJ's 'Dedication' at I. 1–2.

Copies: O (28523 f. 39; 'Maria Eleanora Giffard Nerquis 1808');

USA: MB; *UK*: L (11427. c.27, annotated).

63.2HT/16   Hoole's Tasso,   1809
Suttaby's Miniature Library

[Engr. t.] Jerusalem Delivered An Heroic Poem, Translated from the Italian of Torquato Tasso By John Hoole. Complete in One Volume. [Vignette 'Drawn by R. Cook. 'Engraved by J. Fittler, A.R.A.'] London: Published by Wm. Suttaby; Crosby & Cᵒ. and Scatcherd and Letterman, Stationers Court. 1809. C & R. Baldwin, Printer.

12°, *A*² B–X¹² Y⁸, ($1,2,5 (–Y5) signed), 250 leaves.

Pp. A1 blk + engr. front and t. ('London Publish'd by W. Suttaby May 31, 1809'), A2 t., on B1 *1–2* Dedication, *3* 4–12 Preface, *13* 14–41 Life of Tasso, *42* blk, *43–5* 46–465 text bks I–XX, *466* blk, *467* 468–501 Index, *502* blk.

Press-figures: B8(15)–3, C3ᵛ(30)–4, D12ᵛ(72)–3, E8ᵛ(88)–3, F11(117)–4,

G11(141)–2, H4ᵛ(152)–3, I8ᵛ(184)–4, K2ᵛ(196)–2, L11(237)–4, M8(255)–3, P9ᵛ(330)–3, Q12ᵛ(360)–3, R11(381)–3, S8ᵛ(400)–3, T12(431)–3, U12ᵛ(456)–3, X12(479)–3, Y2ᵛ(484)–3.

Notes: Uncut: 5¾ × 3¼in., wmk.: CT | 1808; Ptd. bds: [Within orn. rules] Jerusalem Delivered. | AN | HEROIC POEM. | Translated from | TORQUATO TASSO, | BY | JOHN HOOLE. | COMPLETE IN ONE VOLUME. | [double rule] | LONDON: | Published by W. SUTTABY, B. CROSBY | and Co., and SCATCHERD and LET- | TERMAN, *Stationers'-Court*. | 1809. | Price 4s.

Copies: O (28523 f.5, boards, uncut); *USA*: MH; *UK*: BMp.

63.2HT/17   Hoole's Tasso, English Poets,   1810
ed. Chalmers

The Works of the English Poets, From Chaucer to Cowper; including the Series Edited with Prefaces, Biographical and Critical, By Dr. Samuel Johnson: and the most approved translations. The Additional Lives by Alexander Chalmers, F.S.A. In Twenty-one volumes. Vol. XXI. Hoole's Ariosto and Tasso. Mickle's Lusiad. London: Printed for J. Johnson; J. Nichols and Son; R. Baldwin, F. and C. Rivington; W. Otridge and Son; Leigh and Sotheby; R. Faulder and Son; G. Nicol and Son; T. Payne; G. Robinson; Wilkie and Robinson; C. Davies; T. Egerton; Scatcherd and Letterman; J. Walker; Vernor, Hood, and Sharpe; R. Lea; J. Nunn; Lackington, Allen, and Co.; J. Stockdale; Cuthell and Martin; Clarke and Sons; J. White and Co.; Longman, Hurst, Rees, and Orme; Cadell and Davies; J. Baker; John Richardson; J. M. Richardson; J. Carpenter, B. Crosby; E. Jeffery; J. Murray; W. Miller; J. and A. Arch; Black, Parry, and Kingsbury; J. Booker; S. Bagster; J. Harding; J. Mackinlay; J. Hatchard; R. H. Evans; Matthews and Leigh; J. Mawman; J. Booth; J. Asperne; P. and W. Wynne; and W. Grace. Deighton and Son at Cambridge, and Wilson and Son at York. 1810.

8°, *A*⁴ (–A4 = 3O1) B–3L⁸ 3M⁴ 3N⁴ 3O1, ($1 signed), 460 leaves.

Pp. A1 Gen. t., A2 t. Orlando Furioso, A3 *vii*–viii Contents, viii coloph: 'C. Whittingham, Printer, Goswell Street, London' (as 3O1ᵛ below), on B1 *1* ½t Orl. Fur., *2* blk, *3* Dedication, *4* blk, *5* 6–18 Preface, *19* 20–36 Life of Ariosto, *37* 38–40 General View, *41* 42–382 text of *Orlando Furioso* (2 cols./p.), *383*–4 Postscript ('15 May 1783'), on 2C1 *385* ½t Jer. Del., *386* blk, *387* SJ's Dedication to the Queen, *388* Advertisement to 5th edn. ('May 23, 1783', 63.2HT/5, above), *389* 390–404 Preface, *405* 406–516 text of Jer. Del. (2 cols./p.), *517* ½t Mickle's *Lusiad*, *518* blk, *519* 520–8 Introduction, *529* 530–97 History of Discovery of India &c., *598* 599–605 Life of Camoens, *606* 607–24 Dissertation &c., *625* 626–30 Appendix, *631* 632–783 Mickle's *Lusiad* (2

cols./p.), *784* coloph: 'Printed by Richard Taylor and Co. Shoe Lane, Fleet Street', on 3E1 Gen. Index (2 cols./p.), on 3O1ᵛ coloph: (as A3ᵛ, viii, above).
    Copies: O (280 i. 405);
    USA: CtY (Ib55. t810.21), MH; *UK*: L (11613. c.1).

63.2HT/18   Hoole's Tasso, first American edition   1810

Jerusalem Delivered: an Heroic Poem, Translated from the Italian of Torquato Tasso, by John Hoole. First American, from the Eighth London Edition. With Notes. Newburyport, [Mass.] Published and sold by Edward Little and Co.; Exeter [NH], Printed by C. Norris and Co. and E. C. Beals. 1810.
    Copies: MH² (1. Ital. 7472. 2. 8);
    USA: CtY (Hd 117. 334), MB, NN.

63.2HT/19   Hoole's Tasso, 'tenth' edition   1811

Jerusalem Delivered. An Heroic Poem. Translated from the Italian of Torquato Tasso. By John Hoole. The Tenth Edition. London. 1811.
    Not examined.
    Copies: *USA*: ICN, NN, TxU, ViU; *UK*: LEu, NOu.

63.2HT/20   Hoole's Tasso   1816

Jerusalem Delivered. An Heroic Poem. Translated from the Italian of Torquato Tasso. By John Hoole. London. 1816
    Not seen.
    Copies: Unlocated.

63.2HT/21   Hoole's Tasso   1818

Jerusalem Delivered. An Heroic Poem. Translated from the Italian of Torquato Tasso. By John Hoole. London. 1818
    Not seen.
    Copies: Unlocated.

63.2HT/22   Hoole's Tasso, Suttaby, Evance & Fox   1819

[Engr. t.] Jerusalem Delivered An Heroic Poem, Translated from Torquato Tasso. By John Hoole. Complete in One Volume. [vign.] London: Published by Suttaby, Evance & Fox, Stationers Court, and Baldwin, Cradock & Joy, Paternoster Row: 1819.

12°, B–T¹² U⁶, ($1,5; $5 as $2), 222 leaves.

Pp. Engr. port. ('London, Published by Suttaby, Evance & Fox, Stationers Court, May 31, 1819') and engr. t. (vign. 'Drawn by R. Cook. Engraved by Wm Finden . . . Book XVI pa. 321') + on B1 *1*–2 SJ's 'Dedication' to the Queen, *3* 4–12 Preface, *13* 14–34 Life of Tasso, *35* ½t Bk. 1, *36* Argument, *37* 38–418 text of Jer. Del., *419* 420–43 Index, 443 coloph: 'Corrall, Printer, Charing Cross', *444* blk.

Paper: white, wove; Pot (uncut: 5 × 3⅛ in.).
Copies: CtY (Hd 17. 335), NN.

63.2HT/23 Hoole's Tasso 1821

Jerusalem Delivered. An Heroic Poem. Translated from the Italian of Torquato Tasso, By John Hoole. London. 1821
Not examined.
Copies: *USA*: DFo.

63.2HT/24 Hoole's Tasso, Rivington 1822

Jerusalem Delivered. An Heroic Poem. Translated from the Italian of Torquato Tasso, By John Hoole. London. F.C. and J. Rivington. 1822
Not examined.
Copies: [L (11472. aa.33) ? **lost**]; *USA*: CtY, DFo.

63.4CR Critical Review, Vol. XV 1763

April 314–18 Review of 'Telemachus, A Mask. By the Rev. George Graham, M.A., Fellow of King's-College, Cambridge.'
References: *Life* i. 411 (Courtney 102–3).
Notes: Attributed also by Percy in his short list: 'Review of Graham's Telemachus' (O: Percy 87).

63.7KS Dr King's Speech at the Oxford Encænia 1763

References: Philip, *BLR* viii (1969), 122–3, and Greenwood, *BLR* viii (1971), 285–8.
Notes: In his letter of 15 March 1763 to Revd Dr John Douglas, Dr Richard Powney alludes to SJ's writing or supplying an 'English oration' for Dr William King, Principal of St Mary Hall, Oxford (L: Egerton MS, 2813, fo. 60ᵛ and 63ᵛ).

SJ had not heard King's notorious jacobite ('Redeat') speech in 1749 (*Life* i.

279–80, n. 5) delivered at the opening of the Radcliffe Camera, but he clapped his hands till they were sore at King's equally jacobitical address to the Oxford Convocation for the installation of John Fane (?1682–1762*), 7th Earl of Westmorland, as Chancellor on 7 July 1759 (*Life* i. 281, 348, and *Letters* i. 123 n. 2).[1]

King made a speech at the Oxford Encænia on 8 July 1763, but no text is recorded.[2] If Powney was right, this is the likeliest 'English oration' from SJ, for, though most formal Oxford addresses were in Latin, the Encænia was a wider public occasion, and English may have been used. Greenwood argues that King's jacobitism was much abated by 1763 and that the speech was likely to attract notice for its Hanoverian sympathies, but his further contention that this precludes SJ's involvement is weak. SJ would not have allowed his own opinions to inhibit him from praise of George III when he was writing for a commission.[3] Without a text however, the matter must be left in doubt.

[1] *Gents. Mag.* lv (Apr. 1785), 288, and Ditchfield, *NQ* ccxxxiv (1989), 66–8. King's jacobitism was undisguised, cf. *A New Speech from the Old Trumpeter of Liberty Hall*, 1756 (O: Gough Adds. Oxon. 8° 60).
[2] An account of it is given in *Jackson's Oxford Journal*, 9 July 1763, and a further observation is in the letter of 1 August 1763 from Charles Godwyn to John Hutchins in Nichols, *Lit. Anec.* viii (1815), 236 (cited by Greenwood, *BLR* viii (1971), 285–8).
[3] The decline of SJ's jacobitism may be charted in Greene's *The Politics of SJ* (1960), and in his edition of *Works* (Yale), x. 142 and 193, both referring to 1756.

64.7LC   London Chronicle   1764

July 3–5, pp. 12 [20 and 28]   Review of James Grainger's *The Sugar Cane. A Poem.*

References: *Life* i. 553 (Courtney 103); Hazen 168–71 gave the first three paragraphs to SJ and the remainder to Percy. Since SJ was not impressed by the poem,[1] it is likely that he was persuaded to this review by Percy. SJ's autograph of this piece, annotated by Percy, is MS Hyde (*MS Handlist* 88; *MS Index* JoS 299 and PeT 399).[2]

Copies: O (N 22863 d.1), &c. [see *BUCOP*].

[1] *Life* i 453, and *passim*, and Anderson, *Life of Samuel Johnson* (1815), 297–8. Cole (ed.), *General Correspondence of JB*, iii. (1993), 328. Fifer (ed.), *Corr. . . . Club* (1976), pp. 328–9, and 331 n., canvasses the story of the poems and the development of the text.
[2] Waingrow, *Corr.* 318. The wording of this entry in JB's list (1790), is exactly the same as in Reed's MS list (MS: Ljh).

64.10CR   Critical Review, Vol. XVIII   1764

October 270–77   Review of Grainger's *The Sugar Cane. A Poem.*

References: Courtney 103, citing *Gents. Mag.* n.s. xxviii (1847), 251–2; Hazen 168–71; see also *London Chronicle*, 5 July 1764, above.

December 458–62   Notice of 'The Traveller, or a Prospect of Society.'
  References: Life i. 481–2 nn. (Courtney 103).
  Copies: O (Hope adds. 522–618 +)

64.12GT/1a   Goldsmith's Traveller, first state   1764

(a) [First state] THE | TRAVELLER, | OR A | PROSPECT of SOCIETY. | A POEM. | [double rule] | LONDON: | Printed for J. NEWBERY, in St. Paul's Church-yard. | M DCC LXIV.

  4°, *A*² B–F² G1, ($1 signed), 13 leaves.

  Pp. A1 t., A1ᵛ blk, A2 Dedication dh: THIS | POEM | IS INSCRIBED TO THE | REV. HENRY GOLDSMITH, M.A. | BY | HIS MOST AFFECTIONATE BROTHER, | OLIVER GOLDSMITH. (single sentence), A2ᵛ blk, on B1 *1* 2–22 text.

  Pagination: no errors; *Press-figures*: none.
  Catchwords: 2 That‸ (~.).
  Explicit: 22 THE END.
  Paper: White, laid; La. post (10½ × 8¼ in.); no vis. wmk.
  Type: Great primer, leaded (5.6 mm).
  References: Courtney 113; Goldsmith, *A Prospect of Society*, ed. Todd (1954); Welsh 227; Roscoe, *Newbery* (1973), A199; *Tinker* 1101; *Rothschild* 1024; *Sterling* 399; Todd, *SB* vii (1955), 103–11; Arthur Friedman (ed.), *Works of Goldsmith* (1966), iv. 238–41; ESTC: t146158.
  Notes: The four states of 64.12GT/1 differ in the prelims (A²) only. This, the first state, was published on 19 December 1764 (Welsh), and is dated 1764. Todd, *SB* vii (1955), 103–11, identified four states of the first edn., and his distinctions have been adopted here. The cogency of his argument enforces the sequence as chronological. Friedman differed as to the order of the 3rd and 4th. Boswell's copy of the 'Fifth' edn., 12° (Hyde; 64.12GT/7, below), is inscribed:

> In Spring 1783 Dr. Johnson at my desire marked with a pencil the lines in this admirable Poem which he furnished viz. l. 18 on p. 23 and from the 3 line on the last page to the end except the last couplet but one. "These (he said) are all of which I can be sure." (*Poems*² 438, *Life* ii. 478).

SJ's contribution is established as l. 420, and the last ten lines (429–38) except for 435–6, but his own account varies. On 23 Oct. 1773 he told JB 'he had not written more than twenty lines' of it (*JB Journal of a Tour* (1961), 347). Reynolds, however, was told by SJ 'the utmost that I have wrote in that poem, to the best of my recollection, is not more than eighteen lines' (Leslie and Taylor, *Reynolds* (1865), ii. 458). Akenside attributed ll. 3–4 to SJ (Prior, *Life of Malone* (1860), 413–14), but no reasons are given.

  SJ's lines are not in the earlier version found as disordered proof-sheets by Bertram Dobell and published by him as: *A Prospect of Society by Oliver*

Goldsmith, being the earliest form of his Poem. Now first reprinted from the Unique Original, with a reprint of the first edition of The Traveller. Edited by Bertram Dobell. London, Published by the Editor, 77 Charing Cross Road, W.C., 1902. These sheets are now L (C.58. g.7).

Goldsmith received £21 for the work. The dedication is of one sentence only. Johnson himself reviewed the poem in *Critical Review*, xviii (Dec. 1764), 458–62 (above; *Courtney* 103).

Copies: CSmH (Todd, *SB* vii (1955), 111).

64.12GT/1b   Goldsmith's Traveller, second state   1764

(b) [Second state] THE | TRAVELLER, | OR A | PROSPECT of SOCIETY. | A POEM. | INSCRIBED TO THE | REV. HENRY GOLDSMITH. | BY | OLIVER GOLDSMITH, M.B. | [double rule] | LONDON: | Printed for J. NEWBERY, in St. Paul's Church-yard. | M DCC LXIV.

4° π1 a² B–F² G² (–G1 ?= π1), 14 leaves.

Pp. π1 t., π1ᵛ blk, on a1 *i* ii–iv Dedication dh: TO THE | REV. HENRY GOLDSMITH., (6 paragraphs), on B1 *1* 2–22 text, (as 64.12GT/1a, above).

Paper, Type, &c., all as 64.12GT/1a, above.

Notes: Still dated 1764, but 4 lines added to t., and text of dedication enlarged to six paragraphs. The CSmH copy has a ½t (as 64.12GT/1c–d, below, with '[Price Two Shillings.]' at the foot. It may be a sophistication.

Copies: CSmH ('From the Author', var.), NN-B (Todd, *SB* vii (1955), 111).

64.12GT/1c   Goldsmith's Traveller, third state   1765

(c) [Third state] [½t] THE | TRAVELLER; | OR, A | PROSPECT of SOCIETY. | [Price One Shilling and Six Pence.]

[Title] THE | TRAVELLER, | OR A | PROSPECT of SOCIETY. | A | POEM. | INSCRIBED TO THE | REV. MR. HENRY GOLDSMITH. | BY | OLIVER GOLDSMITH, M.B. | [double rule] | LONDON: | Printed for J. NEWBERY, in St. Paul's Church-yard. | M DCC LXV.

4°, π² a² B–G², ($1 signed), 16 leaves.

Pp. π1 ½t, π1ᵛ blk, π2 t., π2ᵛ blk, on a1 *i* ii–iv Dedication dh: TO THE | REV. HENRY GOLDSMITH., ht: DEDICATION., on B1 *1* 2–22 text dh: [two double rules] | THE | TRAVELLER, | OR A | PROSPECT of SOCIETY., ht: THE TRAVELLER., *23–4* 2 pp. Newbery's advts.

Pagination: unpaged π1–2, i, 1, 23–4; *Press-figures*: none.

Catchwords: *om.* iv, 2 That˄ (~,).

Explicit: 22 THE END.

Paper, Type, &c., as 64.12GT/1a, above.

Notes: Differing from 64.12GT/1b, above only in the ½t (punctuation). Friedman considered this the fourth rather than the third state (*Works of Goldsmith*, iv. 239 n. 3).
Copies: NjP, NN-B (Todd, *SB* vii (1955), 111).

64.12GT/1d   Goldsmith's Traveller, fourth state   1765

(**d**) [Fourth state] [½t] THE | TRAVELLER, | OR A | PROSPECT of SOCIETY. | [Price One Shilling and Six Pence.]
[Title] THE | TRAVELLER, | OR A | PROSPECT of SOCIETY. | A | POEM. | INSCRIBED TO THE | REV. MR. HENRY GOLDSMITH. | BY | OLIVER GOLDSMITH, M.B. | [double rule] | LONDON: | Printed for J. NEWBERY, in St. Paul's Church-yard. | M DCC LXV
4°, π² a² B–G², ($1 signed), 16 leaves.
Pp. π1 ½t, π1ᵛ blk, π2 t., π2ᵛ blk, on a1 *i* ii–iv Dedication (as 64.12GT/1c, above), on B1 *1* 2–22 text, *23–24* Newbery's advts. (all as 64.12GT/1c, above).
Notes: Friedman considered this to be the third rather than the fourth state (*Works of Goldsmith*, iv. 239 n. 3).
Copies: MH, NN-B³, L.R. Rothschild, Esq; ViU (Todd, *SB* vii (1955), 111).

64.12GT/1e   Goldsmith's Traveller, facsimile   1970

A facsimile of the first edn. was published from L copy by the Scolar Press, Menston, Yorks., 1970, together with the Dobell proofs of 'A Prospect of Society'. The subsequent fortunes of *The Traveller* cannot be the business of a bibliography of Johnson, but there are several early edns., of which four are quartos, matching the first in typography and style, varying in minor details and with different edition statements on the tt., but all dated '1765'
Copies: O (2799 d.295);
USA: CtY; *UK*: Ct, Eu, Gu, L (T. 12*(1)), LVu, Lu, MRu.

64.12GT/2   Goldsmith's Traveller, second edition   1765

... THE SECOND EDITION ... J. NEWBURY, ...
Collation and contents follow 64.12GT/1c, except text runs to 23, *24* blk.
References: Roscoe, *Newbery* (1974), A199 (2); Friedman, *Works of Goldsmith* (1966), iv. 239, noted as revised text; ESTC: t146159. Note 'NEWBURY' on t.
Copies: O (13 θ. 9 (1), 'R.W.C[hapman]').

64.12GT/3   Goldsmith's Traveller, third edition   1765

... THE THIRD EDITION ... J. NEWBURY, ...

References: Roscoe, *Newbery* (1973), A199 (3); Friedman, *Works of Goldsmith* (1966), iv. 240; ESTC: t146160. A reimpression of 64.12GT/2, above with F2 a cancel.

Copies: O² (**1**. G.P. 1731 (5); **2**. G.P. 1740 (20)).

64.12GT/4   Goldsmith's Traveller, fourth edition   1765

... Rev. Mr. HENRY GOLDSMITH ... [parallel rule] | THE FOURTH EDITION. | [total rule] | LONDON: | Printed for J. NEWBERY, in St. Paul's Church-Yard. | M DCC LXV.

Notes: Welsh 227 noted publication as 6 August 1765; Roscoe, *Newbery* (1973), A199 (4); ESTC: t146161; Friedman, *Works of Goldsmith* (1966), iv. 240 noted as a new edn. from a new setting of type, based on 64.12GT/3, above, unrevised but with some degeneration of the text. Collation and contents as 64.12GT/2.

Copies: O (13 θ. 9 (2), 'R.W.C[hapman]'), LVu.

64.12GT/5   Goldsmith's Traveller, fifth edition   1768

THE | TRAVELLER; | OR, A | ... [as 64.12GT/4, above] THE FIFTH EDITION. ... Printed for F. NEWBERY, jun. and Co. at the Bible and Sun, No. 65, the | North Side of St. Paul's Church-Yard. | M DCC LXVIII.

Notes: Welsh 227; Roscoe, *Newbery* (1973), A199 (5); ESTC: t146162; Friedman, *Works of Goldsmith* (1966), iv. 240, printed from 64.12GT/4, above and unrevised.

Copies: O (G.P. 1487 (27)), MRu.

64.12GT/6   Goldsmith's Traveller, sixth edition   1770

THE | TRAVELLER; | OR, A | PROSPECT OF SOCIETY. | A | POEM. | BY | OLIVER GOLDSMITH, M.B. | [rule] | THE SIXTH EDITION CORRECTED. | [double rule] | *LONDON*: | Printed for T. CARNAN and F. NEWBERY, jun. at No. 65, | in St. Paul's Church-Yard. | M DCC LXX.

Collation and contents as 64.12GT/2.

Press-figures: a1ᵛ(ii)–2, B2ᵛ(4)–2, C2(7)–3, D2(11)–2, E2(15)–3, F2(19)–2, G1ᵛ(22)–1.

Notes: Welsh 227; Roscoe, *Newbery* (1973), A199 (6); ESTC: n014032; Friedman, *Works of Goldsmith* (1966), iv. 240 noted this as the last revised by OG, though he lists two further editions dated 1770. See further Friedman, *SB* xiii (1960), 234–5.

Copies: O (Firth d. 4(6)); LEu², MRp², MRu; *Eir*. Dt (48 c.134 no. 8).

64.12GT/7 Goldsmith's Traveller, 'fifth' edition 1770

THE | TRAVELLER: | OR, A | PROSPECT of SOCIETY. | A | POEM, | INSCRIBED TO THE | REV. MR. HENRY GOLDSMITH. | BY | OLIVER GOLDSMITH, M.B. | [bevelled parallel rule] | THE FIFTH EDITION. | [bevelled total rule] | LONDON: | Printed for W. GRIFFIN, at Garrick's Head, in | Catharine-ſtreet. Strand. | [short rule] | M DCC LXX.

12°, A–B⁶, ($3 (−A1) signed), 12 leaves.

Pp. A1 *i* t., *ii* blk, *iii* iv–vi Dedication, on A4 7 8–24 text.

References: ESTC: t177311; Friedman, *Works of Goldsmith* (1966), iv. 236. Probably a piracy.

Notes: This is Boswell's copy, referred to in the Notes to 64.12GT/1a, above.

Copies: O (G.P. 2928 (3); *USA*: Hyde ('James Boswell').[1]

---

[1] Sotheby (Auchinleck), 23 June 1893, 293 (with Goldsmith's *Deserted Village*), Sotheran, £36; — R. B. Adam.

64.12GT/8 Goldsmith's Traveller, Dublin 1767

. . . Dublin: Printed by George Faulkner. M DCC LXVII.

8°, *A*⁴ B⁴ C², 10 leaves (A1 blk). ESTC: n014036.

Copies: CtY; *Eir*: Dt (23 p.67, no. 1).

64.12GT/9 Goldsmith's Traveller, Dublin 1770

12°, π1 *A*² B⁴ C², ($1 signed), 9 leaves. Pp. π1 *i* t., *ii* blk, on A1 iii–iv Dedication, A2 *1* 2–13 text, *14* blk. *Tinker* 1102; ESTC: n014035 (and six further editions).

Copies: O (Vet A5 e.3714); *USA*: CtY.

64GH Preface to Guthrie's History 1764–7

A GENERAL | HISTORY of the WORLD, | FROM THE | CREATION to the preſent Time. | CONTAINING | All the EMPIRES, KINGDOMS, and STATES; their REVO- | LUTIONS, FORMS of GOVERNMENT, LAWS, RELIGIONS, | CUSTOMS and MANNERS; the PROGRESS of their LEARN- | ING, ARTS, SCIENCES, COMMERCE and TRADE; | Together with | Their CHRONOLOGY, ANTIQUITIES, PUBLIC BUILDINGS, and | CURIOSITIES of NATURE and ART. | [rule] | By WILLIAM GUTHRIE, Eſq; | JOHN GRAY, Eſq; | And others eminent in this Branch of Literature. | [rule] | —*cui lecta potenta erit res* | *Nec faciunda deſeret tunc, nec lucidus orde.* HOR. | [rule] | VOLUME I [– XII]. | [double rule] | LONDON: | Printed for J. NEWBERY, R. BALDWIN, S.

CROWDER, J. COOTE, | R. WITHY, J. WILKIE, J. WILSON and J. FELL, W. NICOLL, | B. COLLINS, and R. RAIKES. | [short rule] | MDCCLXIV.

12 vols., 8°.

I. A–2M⁸ 2N⁴, ($4 (–2N3,4) signed), 284 leaves.

Pp. A1 *i* t., *ii* blk, on A2 iii–xvi Preface, on B1 1–551 text: A General History of the World, *552* blk.

Notes: The 'Preface' is attributed to SJ by Richard Harrison in *Book Lore*, i (1884), 21, and repeated in *Bookworm*, i (1888), 381, without any supporting evidence.[1] The attribution is wholly unconvincing: the Preface is apologetic in tone and devoid of SJ's forceful manner.

The work was translated into German in 1762, and published in Leipzig by Weidemann, and again in 1785 as: **Allgemeine Weltgefchichte. Im Englifchen herausgegeben von Wilh. Guthrie und Joh. Gray** . . . **übersetzt und verbeßert von Christian Gottlob Heyne** . . . Troppau, 1785–1808, 94 Bde. 8°, (E); but this has no Johnsonian significance.

References: ESTC: t138428.

Copies: E (E.98.1); *UK*: L (9007. dd.12).

---

[1] Mentioned without support by Sherbo, *SB* xl (1987), 207–19, esp. 209.

65.2PR/1   Percy's Reliques, first edition   1765

RELIQUES | OF | ANCIENT ENGLISH POETRY: | CONSISTING OF | Old Heroic BALLADS, SONGS, and other | PIECES of our earlier POETS, | (Chiefly of the LYRIC kind.) | Together with fome few of later Date. | VOLUME THE FIRST [–SECOND – THIRD]. | [Engr. vignette DURAT OPUS VATUM] | LONDON: | Printed for J. DODSLEY in Pall-Mall. | M DCC LXV.

3 vols., 8°

I. *A*⁸ b⁸ (–b7,8) B⁸ (± B1) C⁸ (± C2,7) D–F⁸ G⁸ (± G4,5) H–Y⁸ Z⁴, ($4 (+C7, G5) signed; 'VOL. III.' on $1 (+C2,7, G4,5)), 186 leaves.

Pp. A1 *i–ii* blk + Engr. front. + A2 *iii* t., *iv* blk, *v* vi–viii Dedication dh: [Engr. hp: arms of Northumberland] | TO | THE RIGHT HONOURABLE | ELIZABETH | COUNTESS OF NORTHUMBERLAND: | IN HER OWN RIGHT | BARONESS PERCY, LUCY, POYNINGS, FITZ-PAYNE, | BRYAN, AND LATIMER. | MADAM, ('THOMAS PERCY.'), ix–xiv Preface dh: The PREFACE., ht: PREFACE., xv–xxiii dh: AN ESSAY | ON THE ANCIENT ENGLISH MINSTRELS., rt: AN ESSAY ON THE | ANCIENT ENGLISH MINSTRELS., *xxiv* blk, *xxv–xxvii* Contents dh: CONTENTS OF VOLUME THE FIRST., ht: CONTENTS, *xxviii* Epigraph (from Sidney's *Defence of Poetry*), on B1 *1* 2–329 text dh: [Engr. hp.] |

[BL] ANCIENT | SONGS and BALLADS, | *&c.* | SERIES THE FIRST. | BOOK. I., rt: ANCIENT SONGS | AND BALLADS., *330* 331–44 Glossary dh: A GLOSSARY | OF THE OBSOLETE AND SCOTTISH WORDS IN | VOLUME THE FIRST., ht: A GLOSSARY.

Pagination: (↑) vi–ix, xv; unnumbered i–v, xi, xxiv–xxviii, 1, 117, 231, 330; empty parens. xxv; 337 sometimes as 33.

Press-figures: A6ᵛ(xii)–2, b3ᵛ(xxii)–2, B2(3)–4, C6(27)–4, C8ᵛ(32)–1, D2ᵛ(36)–4, E8(63)–2, F5ᵛ(74)–2, G8(95)–3, H3ᵛ(102)–4, H8ᵛ(112)–1, I1ᵛ(114)–3, K8(143)–4, L5ᵛ(154)–3, L8ᵛ(160)–4, M5ᵛ(170)–4, N1ᵛ(178)–1, N4ᵛ(184)–3, P5(217)–4, P8(223)–3, Q8(239)–3, R6(251)–4, S2ᵛ(260)–3, T1ᵛ(274)–4, U3ᵛ(294)–3, X1ᵛ(306)–3, Y6(331)–2, Z1ᵛ(338)–2.

Catchwords: *om.* pp. i–iv, viii, and at end of each bk. 116, 230, 329. 17 ∧ THE (II. | THE), 31 *om.* (III. | THE), 98 *om.* (XI. | EDOM), 148 "New ("Now), 160 ∧ THE (II. | ∼), 171 ∧ TAKE (V. | ∼), 182 whereas (wheras), 198 *om.* (X. | THE), 217 Even [? *om.*], 231 *om.* (an), 247 III∧ THE (III. | ∼), 254 Earle (Earl), 255 *om.* (She), 273 Whom (Whome), 298 *om.* (XIV. | GILDEROY), 316 XIX. RIO (XIX. GENTLE), 317–21 [*on alternate pp.*], 322 *om.* (Like), 327 To- (And), 336 Laitl (Langſome).

Explicit: 344 THE END OF VOLUME THE FIRST. | [Engr. tp.]

II. *A*⁴ B–M⁸ N⁸(± N7) O–T⁸ U⁸ (± U2.3.4.5.6.7) X⁸ (± X4) Y–2A⁸, ($4 (+N7) signed; 'Vᴏʟ. II.' on $1 (+N7, U2,3,4, X4)), 188 leaves.

Pp. A1 ½t: RELIQUES | OF | ANCIENT ENGLISH POETRY. | VOL. II., A1ᵛ blk, A2 t., A2ᵛ blk, on A3 pp. i–iii Contents dh: CONTENTS OF VOLUME THE SECOND., ht: CONTENTS., *iv* Epigraph (from Selden's *Table Talk*), on B1 *1* 2–371 text dh: [Engr. hp.] | [BL] Ancient | SONGS and BALLADS, | *&c.* | SERIES ᴛʜᴇ SECOND. | BOOK. I., rt: ANCIENT SONGS | AND BALLADS. (as ANTIENT pp. 6, 100; as SNGOS p. 296), *372* 373–84 Glossary dh: A GLOSSARY | OF THE OBSOLETE AND SCOTTISH WORDS IN | VOLUME THE SECOND., ht: A GLOS-SARY., + Engr. leaf of music.

Pagination: (↑) i; unpaged A1–2, iv, 1, 103, 259. Pp. nos 113–128 *om.* at end of sig. H (p. 112), and beginning of sig. I (129 and seqq.).¹ 145 may be 451, 153 as 351, 299 as 296.

Press-figures: B2ᵛ(4)–2, B5(9)–2, B6(11)–3, C7(29)–3, D7(45)–3, E8(63)–2, F1ᵛ(66)–3, F6ᵛ(76)–2, G2ᵛ(84)–2, H1ᵛ(98)–2, K8ᵛ(160)–2, L3ᵛ(166)–2, M4ᵛ(184)–2, N5ᵛ(202)–3, N6ᵛ(204)–1, O7ᵛ(222)–1, P7(237)–1, Q7(253)–2, Q8(255)–3, R5ᵛ(266)–3, R8ᵛ(272)–2, S3ᵛ(278)–3, S5(281)–2, T3ᵛ(294)–3, T5(297)–2, U3ᵛ(310)–3, X2ᵛ(324)–2, X5ᵛ(330)–4, Y2ᵛ(340)–3, Y8(351)–2, Z7(365)–2, Z8(367)–3, 2A5(377)–4. *Note*: 3 figg. in B, none in I; U3 a cancel.

Catchwords: *om.* A1–2, 102, 258, 371; 25 *om.* (VI. | THE), 47 IX. Sir (∼ | SIR), 56 Then (King), 60 *om.* (XI. | HARPALUS), 77 Awaye (waye), 79 ∧Why

("~), 85 Suc (Such), 131 IV. Q₂ (~. ~.), 133 ₍In ("~), 160 So (Soe), 161 FITS₍ (~,), 169 *om.* (IX. | THE), 174 XII. FANCY (XI. ~), 197 Wo (WOE), 200 XV. A. (~.~₍), 208 'Another' ('~₍), 209 THE (XVII. | ~), 227 Bu (But), 231 "*and* ("*in*), 300 *om.* (I'll), 318 *om.* (AN), 324 XVI. TO (XIV. ~), 354 XXII. TH (~. THE), 373 Couthen, (~.), 380 Sitteth₍ (~.).

Explicit: 384 THE END OF VOLUME THE SECOND. | [Engr. tp.]

III. A⁴ (±A1) b⁸ c⁴ B⁸ (± B1,3) C–F⁸ G⁸ (± G3.4.5.6) H⁸ (± H4), I–O⁸ P⁸ (± P3) ²P⁸ Q–S⁸ T⁸ (± T6,7) U–X⁸ Y⁸ (± Y2; −Y6,7,8) Z⁸ ∗∗², ($4 (b–c as i–iv/i–ii, A3 as A2, P2 as Q2, ²P1 as '[2d P]', ²P2–4 as '[P]'2–4) signed; 'VOL. III.' on $1 (+A3, B3, G3,4, H4, P3, T6,7, Y2)), 199 leaves.

Pp. A1 ½t [*as vol. 2, except:* . . . VOL. III.], A1ᵛ blk, A2 t., A2ᵛ blk, A3 (as 'A2') pp. *i* ii–iii Contents dh: CONTENTS OF VOLUME THE THIRD., ht: CONTENTS., *iv* Epigraph (Addison, *Spectator* 70), on b1 ²*i* ii–xxiv, *1* 2–323 text dh: [Engr. headp.] | [**BL**] **Ancient** | SONGS AND BALLADS, | &c. | SERIES ᴛʜᴇ THIRD. | BOOK I., rt: ANCIENT SONGS | AND BALLADS., *324* 325–31 Glossary dh: A GLOSSARY | OF THE OBSOLETE AND SCOTTISH WORDS IN | VOLUME THE THIRD., ht: A GLOSSARY., 332 ADDITIONS AND CORRECTIONS., 333–46 ADDITIONS AND CORRECTIONS | IN VOLUME I., rt: ADDITIONS, &c. | ᴛᴏ VOLUME I. AND II. (337–41 ᴛᴏ VOLUME II., 343–5 ᴛᴏ VOLUME III.), ∗∗1–1ᵛ Errata (unpaged), ∗∗2 ADVERTISEMENT,² ∗∗2ᵛ TO THE BINDER.³

Pagination: (↑) i, 332, 333; unpaged A1–2, iv, ᵇi, 1, 103, 213, 324, ∗∗²; in ²P pp. 225–40 are in brackets and the same pp. nos. are repeated in sig. Q; 153 as 119, 173 as 137, 206 as 260, 341 as 241.

Press-figures: A3ᵛ(ii)–4, b3ᵛ(vi)–1, c3(xxii)–3, B3ᵛ(6)–2, C1ᵛ(18)–3, D5(41)–∗, D5ᵛ(42)–2, E8(63)–2, F5ᵛ(74)–5, H7ᵛ(110)–2, I5ᵛ(122)–5, I6ᵛ(124)–3, K3ᵛ(134)–3, K7(141)–2, L7(157)–3, L8(159)–2, M6(171)–4, N3ᵛ(182)–2, N5(185)–4, O1ᵛ(194)–3, O2ᵛ(196)–4, P1ᵛ(210)–2, ²P8(239)–4, Q6ᵛ(236)–3, Q8(239)–1, R3ᵛ(246)–2, S8(271)–3, T1ᵛ(274)–1, T6ᵛ(284)–3, T8ᵛ(288)–2, U4ᵛ(296)–3, U7ᵛ(302)–2, X5ᵛ(314)–2, Y5ᵛ(330)–2, Z5ᵛ(346)–4; G unfigured, D5 and T8ᵛ sometimes unfigured, B3, T6 are cancels.

Catchwords: *om.* A1–2, 102, 212, 323; iii [*na-*] *tions*₍. (~∗.), xiv V. (PART V.), xix *in* (*In*), xxiv THE BOY (I. ~ ~), 41 *om.* (VI. | a), 46 O (Or [*in some copies*]), 48 *om.* (They), 61 The (Seeſt), 92 XIX. GIL (XX. | ~), 112 Sirrah, (Sirra,), 113 At (Att), 142 *om.* (The), 144 O where- (O wherfore), 145 Oh, (~₍), 167 The (Not), 168 Well (And), 174 Rejoicing (Rejoycing), 177 A (XIX. | ~), 185 Therefore (Therfore), 197 XXIII. The (~. THE), 224 II. LOVE ([II.] GEORGE), [240] III. ST. GEO. (II. | ST. GEORGE), 229 And (The), 236 Where (You), 241 Now₍ (~,), 304 *om.* (Who), 332 *om.* (ADDITIONS), 346 *om.* (ERRATA), 348 *om.* (ADVERTISEMENT), 349 *om.* (TO).

Explicit: 346 THE END OF VOLUME THE THIRD. | [Engr. tp].

Paper: White, laid; Sm. post (uncut: 7½ × 4¾ in.); no vis. wmk.

Type: Dedication: pica (4.0 mm), leaded; Preface and introd. essays: long primer (3.4 mm), text and footnotes: bourgeois (3.1 mm), Glossary: nonpareil (2.2 mm), 2 cols./p.

Plates: All engr. 'S. Wale del. C. Grignion Sculp.' and placed as follows:

I. Front. Minstrel scene, 'Non Omnis Moriar'; plate size: 150 × 92 mm
    Title: vignette 'DURAT OPUS VATUM' 71 × 82 mm
    A3 (v) Hp: Northumberland arms 'Esperance en Dieu' 55 × 82 mm
    B1 (1) Hp: Chevy Chase — hunting scene[4] 61 × 86 mm
    I3 (117) Hp: Shakespeare with harper and singer[5] 61 × 98 mm
    Q4 (231) Hp: Friar of Orders Grey 55 × 92 mm
    Z4ᵛ (344) Tp. 'See Page 230' 82 × 73 mm
II. Title: vignette (as vol. 1) 71 × 82 mm
    B1 (1): Destruction of 'Magna Charta' 51 × 92 mm
    H3ᵛ (102): Luther, Pope and Cardinal 51 × 92 mm
    R1ᵛ (258): Time rescuing Truth 'Occulta Veritas Tempore Patet' 53 × 83 mm
    2A8ᵛ (384) Tp. 'See Pag. 66. &c' 63 × 88 mm
    Final leaf of music: 'The Notes referred to Vol. 2ᵈ. pag. 24' and 'To come in at the End of Vol. 2ᵈ.'[6] 134 × 83 mm
III. Title: vign. (as vol. 1) 71 × 82 mm
    b1 (i): King Arthur's Court 56 × 85 mm
    H4 (103): Guy of Warwick and the giant 52 × 80 mm
    P3 (213): St George and the dragon (Alnwick Castle in background) 54 × 85 mm
    Z5ᵛ (346) Tp. Robin Goodfellow 66 × 84 mm

References: *Life* i. 554–5, iv. 555–6 (Courtney 111); CH 148; Hazen 158–68; *Rothschild* 1521; *Tinker* 1662; H. B. Wheatley's n. in Sotheran's *Catalogue* (1917), 227; Powell, *Library*, 4th ser. ix (1928), 113–37; Munby, *New Colophon*, 1 (1948), 404–7; Baine, *HLB* v (1951), 246–51; H. Hecht, *Percy und Shenstone: Ein Briefwechsel* (1909), and *Correspondence of Thomas Percy and Richard Farmer*, ed. Brooks (1946); *Correspondence of Thomas Percy and Thomas Warton*, ed. Robinson (1951); J.D. Carver, 'Thomas Percy and the Making of the *Reliques* . . . 1756–65', B.Litt. thesis (Oxford, 1973); B. H. Davis, *Thomas Percy* (1989); Smith, *MS Index* 'Percy', ESTC: t084936.

Notes: The contract for the work is printed by Hecht (p. 54).[7] Production and publication were long delayed.[8] It was almost certainly printed by John Hughs in an edn. of 1,500 (*Correspondence of Thomas Percy and Thomas Warton*, ed. Robinson, 119). The type ornament found on the *cancellandum*[9] of III.Y6 is found in Hughs's edn. of Edward Moore's *Poems, Fables & Plays*, 1756 (p. 61), in Dyer's *Poems*, 1761 (p. 83), and in the 6th edn. of Dodsley's *Collection*, 1763 (i. 2).[10] Printing began in 1762. TP sent Warton part of the first sheet on 28 Feb. 1762, and a second sheet on 25 April. This was part of the original first vol. which TP later changed to become Vol. III. Conversely his original third vol. became vol. I.[11] There is no ½t to vol. 1, and that for vol. 3 is a *cancellans*. TP presented a copy to the Countess of Northumberland on 22 November 1764, but the finished work was not published until 12 February 1765, at 10s. 6d., bound (*St James's Chronicle*). It was reviewed in *Gents. Mag.* xxxv (Apr. 1765), 179–83.

SJ furnished the Dedication.[12] He had visited TP at Easton Mauduit in summer 1764 when TP's diary for 13 Aug. 1764 records, 'Preparing dedication of old ballads' (B.H. Davis, *Thomas Percy* (1989), ch. vi, esp. 125). Other assistance was less overt, though there can be little doubt that he advised with the Glossary and that the work was discussed generally.[13] In his Preface TP made acknowledgement: 'To the friendship of Mr. JOHNSON he owes many valuable hints for the conduct of the work' (p. xxiii).[14]

Copies: O[5] (1. Douce P. 276–77, Proof-sheets of vols. 2–3 'Richard Farmer'; 2. Don. f. 120–22, 'Ham Court'[15] with *cancellanda* in vol. 1; 3. Vet. A5 e.1457–9 'To the Earl of Hardwicke these Volumes are with great respect presented by The Editor'; 4. Godwyn 8° 515–17; 5. Douce P. 264–66, 'George Keate'[16]);

USA: CLU-C, CSmH ('Beverley Chew'), [CSt], CtY[6] (inc. copy marked by TP for 2nd edn. 1767 'Liebert'[17]), [DCU], DFo, DLC (imperfect), Eddy, [FTaSU], Hyde[3] (1. 'Hungerford'; 2. 'R. B. Adam'; 3. 'L.F. Powell' with *cancellantia* I. G4,5, II. X4), IaU ('Lilly'), ICN ('Bonaparte'), ICU (vols. 1, 3 misbound), [InU], IU, [KU], MH[2] (inc. TP's marked copy at MS Eng. 893, fold. 275[18]), [MiU, MWiW-C, NBuU, NcD], NIC, NjP, [NLD], NN-B, NPM ('William Constable'), [OC, OrP], PPL, [TxHU], TxU[2], ViU (imperfect), [WU]; *Can*: CaOHM; *UK*: AWn, C ('Eliza Heathcote, 1765'), Csj, Ct (Rothschild, 'Edward Gibbon'), DUu ('Routh'), E[2], Gu, JDF ('Benir. Sparrow', lacks final leaves *₊*[2] of vol. 3), L[2] (1. 11621. bb.8–10 + MS notes; 2. 11626. bbb.36, vol. 3 imperfect), LEu[2], LVu, MRu, NCu; *Aust*: CNL (DNS 6051).

---

[1] The missing page numbers would have occupied a complete 8° gathering, which suggests either a miscalculation in casting off, or (less probably, I think) that some matter was at some stage suppressed. See Percy's 'Advertisement' at the end of vol. 3, below, n. 5

[2] This reads: 'The Editor's distance from the press has occasioned some mistakes and confusion in the Numbers of several Poems, and in the Reference from one Volume to another: the latter will be set right by the Table of Errata, and the former by the Tables of Contents. In the Second Volume, page 129 follows page 112; this was merely an oversight in the Printer; nothing is there omitted.'

[3] This reads: 'The Binder is desired to take Notice that the marginal Numbers of the 1st and 3d Volumes are wrong: that the Sheets marked VOL. I. are to be bound up as VOLUME THE THIRD: and that those noted VOL. III. as VOLUME THE FIRST.'

[4] This engraving is mentioned in James Grainger's letter to Percy, 22 Jan. 1764 (*Lit. Illus.* vii (1848), 285).

[5] See Percy to Farmer, 31 Dec. 1763 (*Correspondence of TP & Richard Farmer*, ed. Brooks (1946), 62).

[6] Percy to Farmer, 28 Feb. 1764 (*Correspondence of TP & Richard Farmer*, ed. Brooks (1946), 68, 70).

[7] Tierney (ed.), *Correspondence of Robert Dodsley* (1988), 522, adumbrates this document, dated 22 May 1761.

⁸ See Tierney (ed.), *Correspondence of Robert Dodsley* (1988), 292–3 n. 8, 324 n. 1, 466–7 n. 6, and n. 12 below.

⁹ This uncancelled leaf is preserved in Farmer's copy, now O (Douce P. 276).

¹⁰ Sale, *Samuel Richardson* (1950), 296–7.

¹¹ Cf. n. 3, above; a thorough account of the composition of this edition is given in J.D. Carver, 'Thomas Percy and the Making of the *Reliques* . . . 1756–65', B. Litt. thesis (Oxford, 1973).

¹² Percy's original version was rewritten by SJ as is revealed in the proof-sheets at MH (see Baine, *HLB* v (1951), 246–51). TP considered SJ's contribution as revision, and was therefore unwilling to disclaim it as his own (Carver (1973), 29–30, and TP to Anderson, 18 June 1800, *Correspondence*, ed. W.E.K. Anderson (1988), 26). He obliged Boswell to cancel a leaf in the *Life* (1791) in which JB gave the Dedication to SJ (*Life* iv. 555–6), but both overlooked a mention in JB's Index which made the attribution plain. TP's vexation is recorded in his MS notes on *Life* 1791: 'See Index *Percy*. The Illiberal Manner of pointing to yᵉ Dedicatⁿ. of the Reliques, & the false Motive he assigns in p. 273' (O: MS Percy d. 11, fo. 9). SJ had already dedicated Charlotte Lennox's *Memoirs of Madame de Maintenon* (1757), to the Countess (57.3LMM/1, above).

¹³ The conjunction of SJ's work on Shakespeare with TP's collection, is implied in a note on 'Shakespearean illustration from Percy's Ballads', in *Gents. Mag.* xxxv (Apr. 1765), 179–83. See n. 14, next below.

¹⁴ TP later minimized SJ's involvement, e.g. to Robert Anderson, 18 June 1800, *Correspondence*, ed. Anderson (1988), 26, 'I declare that I do not recollect that a single expression, sentiment, or observation of any kind besides [the Dedication], was suggested by him in the whole 3 Volumes.'

¹⁵ 1m S of Upton on Severn; Pull Court, seat of Berens–Dowdeswell is another mile further S.

¹⁶ Friend of Voltaire, (1729–97*).

¹⁷ 'Recent Acquisitions', *YULG* lii (1978), 92.

¹⁸ Baine, *HLB* v (1951), 246–51, describes these papers.

65.2PR/2   Percy's Reliques, second edition, Dublin   1766

[Engr. t.] RELIQUES | OF | ANCIENT ENGLISH POETRY | CONSISTING OF | Old Heroic Ballads Songs, and other | Pieces of our earlier Poets, | Chiefly of the Lyric kind | Together with fome few of later Date | VOLUME THE I [–III]. | [Vignette as 65.2PR/1, above, DURAT OPUS VATUM 'Geo. Byrne Sculpt.'] | DUBLIN | Printed for P. Wilson in Dame Street, | and | E. Watts in Skinner Row, MDCCLXVI.

Stet: Ballads˄ Songs, . . .

3 vols., 12°

I. π² A–N¹² O⁴ (–O4 ? blk), ($5 (H3,4,5 as G3,4,5) signed; 'Vol. I.' on $1), 162 leaves.

Pp. π1 Engr. front. ('Non Omnis Moriar') and π2 engr. t. + A1 i–iv Dedication dh: [double rule] | TO | THE RIGHT HONOURABLE | ELIZABETH | COUNTESS OF NORTHUMBERLAND: | IN HER OWN RIGHT | BARONESS PERCY, LUCY, POYNINGS, FITZ- | PAYNE, BRYAN, AND LATIMER. | Madam,, v–x Preface dh: THE | PREFACE., ht: PREFACE., xi–xx essay dh: AN ESSAY | ON THE ANCIENT ENGLISH MINSTRELS., rt: AN ESSAY ON THE | ANCIENT ENGLISH MINSTRELS., *xxi–xxiii* Contents dh: CONTENTS | OF | VOLUME THE FIRST., ht: CONTENTS., *xxiv* Epigraph (Sidney), on B1 1–277 text dh: [double rule] | ANTIENT | SONGS and BALLADS, |

&c. | SERIES the FIRST. | BOOK I., rt: ANCIENT SONGS | AND BALLADS. (as 'ANTIENT' pp. 2, 4, 26, 28, 50, 52, 94, 108, 110, 134, 154, 160, 180, 194, 204, 226, 252, 254, 274; 'ACNIENT' 10; and 'ANCIENT SONGS, &c.' 197; 'BALADLS.' 253), *278* 279–94 Glossary dh: A | GLOSSARY | OF THE OBSOLETE AND SCOTTISH WORDS | IN VOLUME THE FIRST., ht: GLOSSARY.

Pagination: (↑) i–v, xi; [↑] 1, 196; unpaged 101, 278.

Press-figures: none.

Catchwords: *om.* pp. iv, 100, 195, 277; xvii [COUN-] "TRIE͵ ("~*:"), xxi 2. *Th* (2. *The*), xxiv ANCIENT (ANTIENT), 54 Tha (That), 137 Come (And), 138 THE (II. | ~), 179 *obſerved͵* (~†), 231 impatience (Impatience), 241 Thus͵ (~,), 285 Laith. (L. | ~.).

Explicit: 294 THE END OF VOLUME THE FIRST.

II. *A*1 B–O¹² (O12 ? blk), ($5 (L2 as 2L) signed; 'VOL. II.' on $1 (−C, N)), 157 leaves.

Pp. Engr. t. + A1 *i*–ii Contents dh: CONTENTS OF VOLUME THE SECOND., ht: CONTENTS., on B1 1–295 text dh: [double rule] | ANCIENT | SONGS and BALLADS, | *&c.* | SERIES the SECOND | BOOK I., rt: ANCIENT SONGS | AND BALLADS. ('ANCIENT SONGS, &c.' 88, 205), *296* blk, 297–310 Glossary dh: A GLOSSARY | OF THE OBSOLETE AND SCOTTISH WORDS IN | VOLUME THE SECOND., ht: A GLOSSARY.

Pagination: [↑] 1, 89, 204; unnumbered i, 296; 283 *inverted*, 293 as 239.

Press-figures: none.

Catchwords: *om.* pp. ii, 203, 295; 9 YOURE (I. I. | ~), 10 He (2. | ~), 21 FOR (V. ~), 42 SIR (IX. | SIR), 58 Robin (Robin), 80 An (And), 96 *homilies͵* (~,), 120 The (Then), 130 "Amonge ("Among), 186 'I wis ("~ ~), 224 *faith.*" ("~,'), 243 Yea͵ (~,), 287 BUSK (*A.* ~), 297 Blent͵ (~.), 298 Coſt͵ (~.), 302 I-lore͵ (~-~,), 304 N͵ Nathles͵ (~. ~.), 305 Q͵ Quat͵ (~. ~.), Wer͵ (~.).

Explicit: none.

III. *A*1 a¹² B–N¹² O², ($5 signed; VOL. III.' on $1), 159 leaves.

Pp. Engr. t. + A1 Contents dh: CONTENTS OF VOLUME THE THIRD., ht: CONTENTS., on a1 i–xxiv Essay, on B1 1–284 text dh: [double rule] | ANCIENT | SONGS and BALLADS, | *&c.* | SERIES the THIRD. | BOOK I., rt: ANCIENT SONGS | AND BALLADS. ('ANTIENT' xxiv, 2, 24, 38, 42, 60, 62, 88, 96, 110, 118, 144, 150, 160, 178, 202, 238, 252, 262, 268; 'ANCIENT SONGS, &c.' 87, 181), *285* 286–92 Glossary dh: A | GLOSSARY | OF THE OBSOLETE AND SCOTTISH WORDS IN | VOLUME THE THIRD., ht: A GLOSSARY.

Pagination: [↑] i, 86; unpaged A1, 180, 285; *Press-figures*: none.

Catchwords: *om.* pp. 85, 179, 284; iii Dwarfs͵ (~*,), 55 XI. PHIL- (~ | *PHILLIDA), 126 Uproſe (Up roſe).

Explicit: 292 THE END OF VOLUME THE THIRD.

Paper: White, laid; ? Carré (uncut: 7 × 4½ in.); wmk.: J CAILLARD | MOYEN DANGOUMOIS + Grapes.
Type: Dedication: pica (4.1 mm), leaded, Preface, text &c.: long primer (3.1 mm).
Plates: I. front and title, II. and III. titles.
References: Hazen 166; ESTC: t083734.
Copies: O (Vet. A5 f. 1320–22);
USA: CtY, ICN, MH, NIC, PPL; *UK*: BAT, L (11623. bb. 26–8); *Eir*: Dt (149 d. 188–90).

65.2PR/ 3a   Percy's Reliques, 'second' edition   1767

[½t] RELIQUES | OF | ANCIENT ENGLISH POETRY. | VOL. I [– III].
[Title] RELIQUES | OF | ANCIENT ENGLISH POETRY: | CONSISTING OF | Old Heroic Ballads, Songs, and other | Pieces of our earlier Poets, | (chiefly of the Lyric kind.) | together with fome few of later Date. | THE SECOND EDITION. | VOLUME THE FIRST [–SECOND –THIRD]. | [Vignette as 65.2PR/1, 1765, above] | LONDON: | Printed for J. Dodsley in Pall-Mall. | M DCC LXVII.
3 vols., 8°

I. A⁸ a–d⁸ B–2A⁸ 2B², ($4 (–A1,2, b3, 2B2; A5 as A4) signed; 'Vol. i.' on $1 (as 'VOL. 1.' on B1)), 226 leaves.
Pp. A1 *i* ½t, *ii* blk, *iii* blk, *iv* Engr. front. ('Non Omnis Moriar' as 1st edn. 65.2PR/1, 1765. above: 'S. Wale del. C. Grignion Sculp.'), *v* t., *vi* blk, *vii* viii–x Dedication dh: [Engr. hp.] | TO | THE RIGHT HONOURABLE | ELIZ-ABETH | COUNTESS OF NORTHUMBERLAND: | IN HER OWN RIGHT | BARONESS PERCY, LUCY, POYNINGS, FITZ-PAYNE, | BRYAN, AND LATIMER. | Madam,, (p. x 'MDCCLXV'), ht: DEDICA-TION., xi–xvi Preface dh: The PREFACE., ht: PREFACE. (p. xvi 'MDC-CLXV'), xvii Advertisement dh: ADVERTISEMENT. | TO | THE SECOND EDITION. (dated 'MDCCLXVI'), *xviii* Note, *xix* xx–xxxviii Essay dh: AN | ESSAY | ON THE | ANCIENT ENGLISH MINSTRELS., rt: AN ESSAY ON THE | ANCIENT ENGLISH MINSTRELS., xxxix–lxxvi Notes dh: NOTES AND ILLUSTRATIONS | REFERRED TO IN THE | FOREGOING ESSAY., rt: NOTES ON THE | FOREGOING ESSAY., *lxxvii–lxxix* Contents dh: CONTENTS OF VOLUME THE FIRST., ht: CONTENTS., *lxxx* Epigraph (Sidney), on B1 *1* 2–347 text dh: [Engr. hp.] | [BL] ANCIENT | SONGS AND BALLADS, | &c. | SERIES THE FIRST. | BOOK I., rt: ANCIENT SONGS | AND BALLADS. ('AND BALLADS.' 80; 'ANCIENT SONGS, &c.' 124, 248), *348* 349–65 Glossary

dh: A GLOSSARY | OF THE OBSOLETE AND SCOTTISH WORDS IN | VOLUME THE FIRST., ht: A GLOSSARY., *366* 367–70 Addenda dh: ADDITIONS | TO | The Essay on the Origin of the | English Stage., *371–2* ERRATA.

Pagination: (↑) viii–xi, xxxix, 367–70; [↑] xvii; unnumbered i–vii, xviii–xix, lxxii, lxxvii–lxxx, 1, 125, 249, 348, 366; xxvii as xxvli, 143 as 141.

Press-figures: A3ᵛ(vi)–3, A8(xv)–1, a7ᵛ(xxx)–1, a8ᵛ(xxxii)–2, b7(xlv)–3, b8(xlvii)–2, c5(lvii)–2, c8(lxiii)–3, d3ᵛ(lxx)–4, B5ᵛ(10)–4, C7ᵛ(30)–1, D3ᵛ(38)–4, D6ᵛ(44)–1, E8(63)–3, F5(73)–3, F5ᵛ(74)–4, G8(95)–3, H6(107)–2, H8ᵛ(112)–1, I8(127)–4, I8ᵛ(128)–1, K4ᵛ(136)–2, K8(143)–3, L7ᵛ(158)–3, L8ᵛ(160)–1, M7ᵛ(174)–1, N7ᵛ(190)–1, O3ᵛ(198)–2, P8(223)–2, Q5(233)–2, Q8(239)–3, R6ᵛ(252)–1, S5ᵛ(266)–2, T6(283)–1, T7(285)–3, U1ᵛ(290)–3, U7(301)1, X7ᵛ(318)–3, Y1ᵛ(322)–3, Z5ᵛ(346)–4, 2A1ᵛ(354)–1, 2A8ᵛ(368)–2.

Catchwords: *om.* A1–3, x, xvii, xviii, 124, 140, 248, 261, 347, 362, 365, 370–1; 336–40 as for parallel texts; xix anceſtorsₐ (~†), xxvi centuryₐ (~*), lxv [an-] ₐteriorite ("tériorité), 17 II. THE (~. | The), 83 Ahₐ (~!), 172 ₐTHE (II. | ~), 189 My (HE. | ~), 190 King (SHE. | ~), 199 Whereas (Wheras), 261 *om.* (O), 284 When (Much), 353 Gairₐ (G. | ~.), 362 *om.* (Thair), 364 Y-cloped. (Y-cleped.).

Explicit: 370 THE END OF VOLUME THE FIRST. | [Engr. tp.]

II. *A*⁴ B–S⁸ T⁸ (± T3) U–Z⁸ 2A–2C⁸, ($4 signed; 'Vol. II.'on $1), 204 leaves.

Pp. A1 ½t, A1ᵛ blk, A2 t., A2ᵛ blk, A3 i–iii Contents dh: CONTENTS OF VOLUME THE SECOND., ht: CONTENTS., *iv* Epigraph (Selden), on B1 *1* 2–382 text dh: [Engr. hp.] | [BL] ANCIENT | SONGS AND BALLADS, | *&c.* | SERIES THE SECOND. | BOOK I., rt: ANCIENT SONGS | AND BALLADS., *383* 384–98 Glossary dh: A GLOSSARY | OF THE OBSOLETE AND SCOTTISH WORDS IN | VOLUME THE SECOND., ht: A GLOSSARY., 398–400 Addenda ht: POST-SCRIPT., + 1 leaf engr. music.

Pagination: (↑) i, 399, '340' [=400]; unnumbered A1–2, iv, 1, 43, 267, 383; 19 as 25, 400 as 340.

Press-figures: A3(i)–3, A3ᵛ(ii)–2, B7ᵛ(14)–1, C8(31)–3, E6(59)–1, F5(73)–1, F8(79)–3, G6ᵛ(92)–1, H2ᵛ(100)–3, H8(111)–2, H8ᵛ(112)–3, I2ᵛ(116)–3, I8(127)–4, K7(141)–2, K8(143)–4, L1ᵛ(146)–1, L4ᵛ(152)–4, M6(171)–2, N1ᵛ(178)–1, O6ᵛ(204)–2, O8(207)–3, P6(219)–3, Q5ᵛ(234)–2, Q7(237)–3, R3ᵛ(246)–2, S1ᵛ(258)–1, T1ᵛ(274)–3, T3ᵛ(278)–3, T7(285)–1, U6(299)–2, X8(319)–2, Y5ᵛ(330)–1, Z3ᵛ(342)–2, 2A6(363)–1, 2B1ᵛ(370)–3, 2C2ᵛ(388)–4, 2C5ᵛ(394)–2. *Note*: unfigured: D; 3 figg. in T; T3 a cancel.

Catchwords: *om.* A1–2, 25, 110, 266, 373; iv [BL] RELIQUES (ANCIENT), 23 A (At), 37, 39 He· (~.), 90 AS (XVI. | ~), 179 THE (The), 309 ₐNow ("~), 317 IX. Sir (~. | SIR), 390 Maden. (M. | ~.).

Explicit: 400 THE END OF VOLUME THE SECOND. | [Engr. tp].

III. *A*⁴ b–c⁸ B–Z⁸ 2A⁴ *2B*1, ($4 (−M3, 2A3,4) signed; 'Vᴏʟ. III.' on $1), 201 leaves.

Pp. A1 ½t, A1ᵛ blk, A2 t., A2ᵛ blk, A3 i–iii Contents dh: CONTENTS OF VOLUME THE THIRD., ht: CONTENTS., *iv* Epigraph (Addison), on b1 ²*i* ii–xxxii, *1* 2–346 text dh: [Engr. hp.] | [BL] ANCIENT | SONGS AND BALLADS, | *&c.* | SERIES THE THIRD. | BOOK I., rt: ANCIENT SONGS | AND BALLADS. ('ANCIENT SONGS, &c.' 98, 346; smaller font xxvi–xxvii), *347* 348–56 Glossary dh: A GLOSSARY | OF THE OBSOLETE AND SCOTTISH WORDS IN | VOLUME THE THIRD., ht: A GLOSSARY., 357–8 dh: ADDITIONAL NOTES., *359–60* Dodsley's advts. dh: BOOKS | Printed and Sold by J. Dᴏᴅsʟᴇʏ, in | Pall-Mall, London.

Pagination: (↑) ᴬi, 357; [↑] 358; unnumbered A1–2, ᴬiv, ᵇi, 1, 99, 215, 347.

Press-figures: b6ᵛ(xii)–1, b8(xv)–4, c5(xxv)–4, c8(xxxi)–3, B6(11)–3, C8(31)–2, D1ᵛ(34)–3, E3ᵛ(54)–3, E8ᵛ(64)–2, F2ᵛ(68)–2, F8(79)–3, G2ᵛ(84)–2, G8(95)–3, H4ᵛ(104)–3, H5ᵛ(106)–2, I4ᵛ(120)–3, I6(123)–2, K2ᵛ(132)–3, K8(143)–2, L8(159)–3, M4ᵛ(168)–2, M5ᵛ(170)–1, N6(187)–2, O6(203)–2, O6ᵛ(204)–1, P7ᵛ(222)–1, Q1ᵛ(226)–1, R5ᵛ(250)–2, T1ᵛ(274)–3, U1ᵛ(290)–3, X1ᵛ(306)–3, Y8(335)–3, Z2ᵛ(340)–2, Z8(351)–3, 2A3(357)–1. Unfigured: S.

Catchwords: *om.* A1–2, ᴬiii, 48, 98, 130, 162, 164, 165, 169, 171, 172, 173, 212, 214, 239, 265, 337, 356; ᴬiv [BL] RELIQUES (ANCIENT), ᵇxiii Lʏᴏɴ∧, (∼ (*o*),), xxvii 17. The (∼. *The*), 125 She∧ (∼,), 129 O hooly∧ (∼ ∼,), 144 Oh, (∼∧), 151 Bu (But), 185 Therfore∧ (∼,), 193 And∧ (∼,), 262 VII. HENCE (∼. | THE), 277 IX. TO (XI. | ∼), 278 X. VA- (XII. | VALENTINE), 344 XIX. ∧L' AMOUR (∼. | 'L' AMOUR).

Explicit: 358 THE END OF VOLUME THE THIRD. | [Engr. tp].

Paper: White, laid; Sm. post (uncut: 7½ × 4¾ in.); no vis. wmk.

Type: Dedication: pica (4.1 mm), leaded; Prefatory essays and text: bourgeois (3.1 mm), footnotes and glossary: brevier (2.6 mm).

Plates: As first edn. 65.2PR/1, 1765, above.

References: Hazen 166; ESTC: t083735.

Notes: Published December 1767 (*Lond. Chron.*, 3 Dec. 1767).

Copies: O (Douce P. 261–3);

USA: CtY, IU, NN-B, TxU; *UK*: BRu, L³ (1. 1162. d.4–6; 2. 11605. aaa.28; 3. G. 18374–6), Om.

65.2PR/3b   Percy's Reliques, 'second' edition,   1767
Four Essays

FOUR ESSAYS, | AS IMPROVED AND ENLARGED | IN THE | SECOND EDITION | OF THE | Rᴇʟɪ Qᴜᴇs of Aɴᴄɪᴇɴᴛ | ENGLISH

POETRY. | *VIZ.* | I. On the Ancient English Minstrels. | II. On the Ancient Metrical Romances. | III. On the Origins of the English Stage. | IV. On the Metre of Pierce Plowman's Vifions. | [short rule] | MDCCLXVII.

8°, a–c⁸ d⁶, ²b–c⁸, A⁸, ²A⁸, ³A⁸, ($4 signed), 70 leaves.

Pp. *1–3* 4–60 Minstrels, *1–2* 3–32 Romances, *1–2* 3–16 Stage, *1* 2–4, *1–3* 4–15 *16* Piers Plowman.

Notes: A few copies of the *Essay on the Ancient English Minstrels* (I), *On the Ancient Metrical Romances* (II), and on the *Origin of the English Stage* (III) which had been criticized by Samuel Pegge for their historical weakness (B.H. Davis, *Thomas Percy* (1989), 153–6), and which were extensively revised by TP for the 'second' edn., were separately printed. ESTC: t083746.

Copy: CaOHM (B 15653, TP: 'From the Author'; AD: 'Revᵈ. Dr. Percy' and 'And: Ducarel June 4 1767').[1]

---

[1] Andrew Coltee Ducarel (1713–85*), antiquarian and Keeper of the Lambeth library; another presentation copy was lot 2718 at Sotheby's (William Pickering), 7 August 1854.

65.2PR/4   Percy's Reliques, 'third' edition   1775

[½t] RELIQUES | OF | ANCIENT ENGLISH POETRY. | VOL. I [–III].

[Title] RELIQUES | OF | ANCIENT ENGLISH POETRY: | CONSISTING OF | Old Heroic Ballads, Songs, and other | Pieces of our earlier Poets, | Together with fome few of later Date. | THE THIRD EDITION. | VOLUME THE FIRST [–SECOND –THIRD]. | [Engr. vignette as 65.2PR/1, 1765, above] | LONDON: | Printed for J. Dodsley, in Pall Mall. | M DCC LXXV.

Var: (vols. 2–3) . . . Pall-Mall.

3 vols., 8°

I. A⁸ b–e⁸ f1, B⁸ C⁸ (± C6) D–H⁸ I⁸ (± I7) K–2A⁸ 2B⁴, ($4 (−A1,2,3) signed; 'Vol. I.' on $1 (−A)), 229 leaves.

Pp. A1 *i* ½t, *ii* blk, *iii* blk, *iv* Engr. front. ('Non Omnis Moriar'), *v* t., *vi* blk, *vii* viii–x Dedication dh: [Engr. hp. arms] | TO | THE RIGHT HONOURABLE | ELIZABETH, | COUNTESS OF NORTHUMBERLAND: | IN HER OWN RIGHT | BARONESS PERCY, LUCY, POYNINGS, FITZ-PAYNE, | BRYAN, AND LATIMER. | MADAM, ('MDCCLXV'), xi–xvi Preface dh: The PREFACE. ('MDCCLXV'), xvii–xviii dh: ADVERTISEMENT | TO | THE THIRD EDITION. ('MDCCLXXV'), *xix* xx–xxxix Essay dh: AN | ESSAY | ON THE | ANCIENT ENGLISH MINSTRELS., rt: AN ESSAY ON THE | ANCIENT ENGLISH MINSTRELS., xl–lxxviii Notes dh: NOTES and ILLUSTRATIONS | REFERRED TO IN THE | FOREGOING ESSAY.,

rt: NOTES ON THE | FOREGOING ESSAY. ('NOTES, &c.' xli, 'NOTES
ON THE &c.' lxxviii), *lxxix–lxxxi* Contents dh: CONTENTS OF VOLUME
THE FIRST., ht: CONTENTS., *lxxxii* Epigraph (Sidney), on B1 *1* 2–349
text dh: [Engr. hp.] | [BL] **RELIQUES** | OF ANCIENT POETRY, | *&c.* |
SERIES THE FIRST. | BOOK I., ht: ANCIENT POEMS (*om.* 127, 251),
350–68 Glossary dh: A GLOSSARY | OF THE OBSOLETE AND
SCOTTISH WORDS IN | VOLUME THE FIRST., ht: A GLOSSARY.,
on 2B1 *371* 372–5 Addenda dh: ADDITIONS | TO | THE ESSAY ON THE
ORIGIN OF THE ENGLISH STAGE., rt: ADDITIONS TO ESSAY | ON THE
ENGLISH STAGE., 376 dh: ADDITIONAL NOTES., *377* dh: BOOKS |
PUBLISHED BY J. DODSLEY, | IN PALL-MALL., *378* Errata.

Pagination: (↑) viii–xi, xl; [↑] xvii; unpaged i–vii, xix, lxxix–lxxxii, 1, 127, 251;
369–70 om. from numeration; 208 as 08.

Press-figures: A7(xiii)–7, A7ᵛ(xiv)–6, b5(xxv)–9, b5ᵛ(xxvi)–7, c7(xlv)–6,
c7ᵛ(xlvi)–9, d2ᵛ(lii)–9, d8(lxiii)–6, e6(lxxv)–9, e6ᵛ(lxxvi)–10, B7ᵛ(14)–3,
B8ᵛ(16)–5, C6ᵛ(28)–9, D6ᵛ(44)–3, D8(47)–2, E6(59)–1, E7(61)–3, F5ᵛ(74)–5,
F7(77)–6, G8(95)–2, H1ᵛ(98)–1, H6ᵛ(108)–4, I6(123)–4, K8(143)–7,
L4ᵛ(152)–1, L8(159)–4, M1ᵛ(162)–2, N8ᵛ(192)–3, O4ᵛ(200)–1, O8(207)–5,
P5(217)–7, P8(223)–6, Q6(235)–7, R5ᵛ(250)–[?], R6ᵛ(252)–4, S2ᵛ(260)–3,
S7ᵛ(270)–5, T2ᵛ(276)–2, T8(287)–6, U2ᵛ(292)–4, U7ᵛ(302)–3, X2ᵛ(308)–1,
X8(319)–4, Y5ᵛ(330)–5, Z1ᵛ(338)–6, 2A6(363)–10, 2B2ᵛ(374)–6.

Catchwords: *om.* i–vi, x, xviii, 126, 142, 250, 368, 375–77; xix [an-] ceſtors₍₎,
(~†,), xxvi century₍₎, (~*,), xxxv ₍₎feet, ("~,), 17 II. THE (II. | THE), 26 A
FYTTE. (THE), 149 Se (Set), 191 ₍₎My (HE. | ~), 192 King (SHE. | ~), 338
"En ('En), 351 Blude₍₎ (~.), 352 Byſte. (C.), 367 Worthe. (Worthè.).

Explicit: 376 THE END OF THE FIRST VOLUME. | [Engr. tp].

II. *A*⁴ B–2C⁸ 2D², ($4 (−2D2) signed; 'VOL. II.' on $1), 206 leaves.

Pp. A1 ½t, A1ᵛ blk, A2 t., A2ᵛ blk, on A3 i–iii Contents dh: CONTENTS
OF VOLUME THE SECOND., ht: CONTENTS., *iv* Epigraph (Selden), on
B1 *1* 2–384 text dh: [Engr. hp.] | [BL] **RELIQUES** | OF ANCIENT
POETRY, | *&c.* | SERIES THE SECOND. | BOOK I., ht: ANCIENT
POEMS. (*om.* 113, 269), 385–99 Glossary dh: A GLOSSARY | OF THE
OBSOLETE AND SCOTTISH WORDS IN | VOLUME THE
SECOND., ht: A GLOSSARY., 400–3 dh: ADDITIONS | TO | THE ESSAY
ON PIERCE PLOWMAN'S VISIONS., rt: ADDITIONS TO ESSAY | ON
ALLITERATIVE METRE., 404 dh: POST-SCRIPT., + 1 engr. leaf music.

Pagination: (↑) i; unpaged A1–2, 1, 113, 269; 389 as 386.

Press-figures: B7ᵛ(14)–4, B8ᵛ(16)–3, C5(25)–1, C7ᵛ(30)–6, D7ᵛ(46)–4,
E1ᵛ(50)–4, F1ᵛ(66)–3, F8ᵛ(80)–6, G1ᵛ(82)–6, G5(89)–3, H6ᵛ(108)–7,
H8(111)–4, I5ᵛ(122)–5, I8ᵛ(128)–4, K6ᵛ(140)–1, K7ᵛ(142)–3, L3ᵛ(150)–6,
L5(153)–4, M6ᵛ(172)–4, M8(175)–5, N8(191)–4, N8ᵛ(192)–6, O7ᵛ(206)–1,
O8ᵛ(208)–7, P1ᵛ(210)–1, P4ᵛ(216)–3, Q5(233)–3, Q8(239)–6, R4ᵛ(248)–2,

R6(251)–1, S1ᵛ(258)–5, S2ᵛ(260)–4, T8(287)–4, U8(303)–6, X6(315)–8, X8ᵛ(320)–6, Y7(333)–1, Y7ᵛ(334)–4, Z1ᵛ(338)–7, Z8ᵛ(352)–8, 2A6(363)–1, 2B8(383)–8, 2C5ᵛ(394)–7, 2C8ᵛ(400)–9, 2D1ᵛ(402)–9.

Catchwords: *om.* A1–2, 112, 268, 399; 132 *om.* (No), 181 THE (The), 196 When (Whan), 247 "His ("Her), 292 TRUTH· (~.), 387 ˏDaleˏ (D. | ~.), 399 *i.e.* (Felay.).

Explicit: 404 THE END OF VOLUME THE SECOND. | [Engr. tp].

III. A⁸ b⁸ c⁴ d² B–Z⁸ 2A⁴, ($4 (–A1,2, c3,4, d2, H2, 2A3,4) signed; 'Vol. III.' on $1 (–A)), 202 leaves.

Pp. A1 ½t, A1ᵛ blk, A2 t., A2ᵛ blk, on A3 i–iii Contents dh: CONTENTS OF VOLUME THE THIRD., ht: CONTENTS., *iv* Epigraph (Addison), *v* vi–xxxix Essay on Ancient Metrical Romances dh: [Engr. hp.] | [BL] RELIQUES | OF | ANCIENT ENGLISH POETRY, | *&c.* | SERIES the THIRD. | BOOK I., ht: ANCIENT POEMS., *xl* blk, on B1 1–349 text ht: ANCIENT POEMS. (*om.* 100, 216), 350–59 Glossary dh: GLOSSARY | OF THE OBSOLETE AND SCOTTISH WORDS IN | VOLUME THE THIRD., ht: A GLOSSARY., *360* dh: ADDITIONAL NOTES.

Pagination: (↑) i; unpaged A1–2, iv–v, xl, 56, 100, 216, 360; 276 as 27.

Press-figures: A5ᵛ(vi)–7, b7(xxv)–7, b8(xxvii)–6, c3(xxxiii)–10, c4(xxxv)–7, d2ᵛ(xxxviii)–7, B7(13)–6, B7ᵛ(14)–5, C3ᵛ(22)–3, C8ᵛ(32)–1, D5(41)–3, D7ᵛ(46)–9, E2ᵛ(52)–9, E8(63)–1, F6ᵛ(76)–10, F7ᵛ(78)–4, G5ᵛ(90)–5, G8ᵛ(96)–1, H1ᵛ(98)–10, I7(125)–9, K6(139)–10, K6ᵛ(140)–8, L7(157)–8, L8(159)–7, M7(173)–3, M8(175)–7, N6ᵛ(188)–7, N7(190)–1, O5ᵛ(202)–7, O8ᵛ(208)–10, P5(217)–8, P5ᵛ(218)–1, Q5ᵛ(234)–10, Q7(237)–9, R8(255)–10, R8ᵛ(256)–3, S1ᵛ(258)–7, S7(269)–10, T2ᵛ(276)–2, T7ᵛ(286)–9, U2ᵛ(292)–7, U7ᵛ(302)–6, X6(315)–9, X7(317)–2, Y7(333)–7, Y7ᵛ(334)–6, Z7ᵛ(350)–6.

Catchwords: *om.* A1–2, xxxix, 48, 99, 215, 359; xix Lyonˏ, (~ (q),), 20 Peaceˏ (~,), 49 All (And), 126 Sheˏ (~,), 130 O hoolyˏ (~ ~,), 155 This (Go), 178 Pair (Paire), 185 Therforeˏ (~,), 218 *Th* (*The*), 278 IX. TO (XI. | ~), 279 X. VA- (XII. | VALENTINE), 347 XIX. ˏL' AMOUR (XIX. | 'L' AMOUR), 356 Rade. (R. | ~.).

Explicit: *360* THE END OF VOLUME THE THIRD. | [Engr. tp].

Paper: White, laid; crown (uncut: 7½ × 5 in.); no vis. wmk.

Type: Dedication: pica (4.0 mm), leaded; Preface, essays, Text &c.: bourgeois (3.1 mm), Footnotes, Glossary &c.,: brevier (2.6 mm).

Plates: As in first edn. 65.2PR/1, above.

References: Hazen 166; B.H. Davis, *Thomas Percy* (1989), 213; ESTC: t082693.

Notes: TP was paid £21 for this enlarged edn. on 21 June, 1774 (Powell, *Library* 4th ser. ix (1928), 136). It ran to 1,000 copies, and was published in December 1775 (Davis, 234 n. 52). The dedicatee, Elizabeth, Countess of Northumberland, died in 1776, so that this is the last of the edns. of *Reliques* to print SJ's Dedication in her lifetime; thereafter TP changed it to address her memory from the '4th' edn. 1794–5 onwards.[1] It was omitted from the important German translation (probably by J.G. Herder, 1744–1803), published in Frankfurt, 1767.

The bibliographical history of later edns. of the *Reliques* is beyond the scope of these notes, but many, if not most, of subsequent edns. include SJ's 'Dedication' in one or other version.

Copies: O^2 (1. Percy 58, incl. proofs of vol. 2; **2**. Douce P. 273–5);
USA: CtY, PPL ('Benjamin Franklin'); *UK*: L (239. 1.23), SAN.

---

[1] Robert Anderson, apparently unconscious of the history of the Dedication, regretted the change (Letter to TP 28 Sept. 1799, *Lit. Illus.* vii (1848), 81; *Percy Letters* (1988), 20–1, see also pp. 1071–2, above).

65.9TE   Henry Thrale's Election Addresses   1765

23 September
'To the worthy Electors of the Borough of SOUTHWARK'
Election address for Henry Thrale in Southwark by-election.
Published in *Public Advertiser*, 24, 25, 26, 27, 28, and 30 Sept., also in *St James's Chron.*, 25–6, 26–8 Sept.
References: [*Life* iii. 440, Courtney 152–3]; Fleeman, in *Johnson, Boswell and their Circle* (1965), 171–2.[1]

1 October
'To the worthy Electors of the Borough of SOUTHWARK'
Published in *Public Advertiser*, 1, 2, 3 Oct. (dated '1 Oct.') and 4, 5, 7, 8, 9, 10, 11, 12, 14, 15, 16, 17, 18, 19, 22, 24, 26, 28, and 30; 1, 11, and 19 Nov. (dated '4 Oct.'); and in *St James's Chron.*, 3–5, 5–8, 8–10 Oct.
References: Fleeman, in *Johnson, Boswell and their Circle* (1965), 172.

20 November
'To the worthy Electors of the Borough of Southwark'
Printed handbill corrected in SJ's autograph in AWn (MS 11103D; *MS Handlist* 95; *MS Index* JoS 191).
References: Fleeman, in *Johnson, Boswell and their Circle* (1965), 173.

19 December
'To the Worthy ELECTORS of the BOROUGH of SOUTHWARK'
Printed handbill, in Hyde Collection.
References: Fleeman, in *Johnson, Boswell and their Circle* (1965), 174.

24 December
Thrale's Notice of thanks

Published in *Public Advertiser*, 24, 25, 26 Dec. MS draft in SJ's autograph in AWn (MS 11103D; *MS Handlist* 96, *MS Index* JoS 192).

References: Fleeman, in *Johnson, Boswell and their Circle* (1965), 174–5.

Notes: The evidence for SJ's composition of all these pieces is not unchallengeable, but he was evidently closely involved with HT's electioneering.

[1] For details of election results, see *Members of Parliament. A Return dated 1 March 1878 for return of names from 1696 to the present time*. Gerald Nowell. Printer to the House of Commons. 1878.

65.10SP/1   Shakespeare, first edition   1765

THE | PLAYS | OF | WILLIAM SHAKESPEARE, | IN EIGHT VOLUMES, | WITH THE | CORRECTIONS and ILLUSTRATIONS | OF | Various COMMENTATORS; | To which are added | NOTES by SAM. JOHNSON. | [double rule] | LONDON: | Printed for J. and R. TONSON, C. CORBET, H. WOODFALL, | J. RIVINGTON, R. BALDWIN, L. HAWES, CLARK and | COLLINS, W. JOHNSTON, T. CASLON, T. LOWNDS, | and the Executors of B. DODD. | M,DCC,LXV.

Stet: LOWNDS,

8 vols., 8°

I. π^2 (= E1.8) A–D^8 E^8 (–E1.8,7) a–f^8 g^4 B–U^8 X^8 ($\pm$ X4,6) Y–2H^8 2I^4, [B5, O8 and P8 *occasionally* cancels], (\$4 signed (A–E in brackets); 'VOL.I.' on \$1), 335 leaves.

Pp. Engr. front. + π1 t., π1^v blk, π2 vol. t: THE | PLAYS | OF | WILLIAM SHAKESPEARE. | VOLUME the FIRST, | CONTAINING, | The TEMPEST. | A MIDSUMMER-NIGHT's DREAM. | The TWO GENTLEMEN of VERONA. | MEASURE for MEASURE. | The MERCHANT of VENICE. | [double rule] | LONDON: [*imprint* as gen. t., above], π2^v blk, on A1–E5 (37 leaves unpaged) Preface dh: [double rule] | PREFACE., ht: PREFACE., E5^v blk, on a1 *i*–ii Dedication of First Folio dh: TO THE MOST NOBLE | AND | INCOMPARABLE PAIRE | OF BRETHREN, | WILLIAM | Earle of PEMBROKE, *&c*, . . . [&c.], ht: (ii) THE PLAYERS DEDICATION., on a2 *iii*–iv Preface to First Folio dh: THE | PREFACE | OF THE PLAYERS. | To the great variety of Readers., ht: (iv) PREFACE BY THE PLAYERS., on a3 *v* vi–xxi Pope's Preface dh: MR. POPE's | PREFACE., ht: Mr. POPE's PREFACE., on b3^v *xxii* xxiii–li dh: Mr. THEOBALD's | PREFACE., ht: Mr. THEOBALD's PREFACE., on d2^v *lii* liii–lv dh: Sir T. HANMER's PREFACE., ht: Sir T. HANMER's PREFACE., on d4^v *lvi* lvii–lxxii dh: Dr. WARBURTON's | PREFACE., ht: Dr. WARBURTON's PREFACE., on e5 *lxxiii* lxxiv–xcii Life by Rowe dh: SOME | ACCOUNT of the LIFE, &c. | OF | Mr. WILLIAM SHAKESPEAR. | Written by Mr. ROWE. rt: Some ACCOUNT of the LIFE, &c. | of Mr.

WILLIAM SHAKESPEAR. (xcii 'Some *ACCOUNT of the Life, &c.*'), on f7 *xciii*–xciv Grant of Arms, on f8 *xcv* xcvi–xcix Will dh: SHAKESPEARE's WILL, | Extracted from the Regiſtry of the Arch- | biſhop of *Canterbury.*, ht: SHAKESPEARE's WILL., on g2ᵛ c Horse-holding anecdote, on g3 *ci* cii–ciii Ben Jonson's verses, *civ* blk, on B1 *1* ½t: THE | TEMPEST., *2* Dramatis Perſonæ., *3* 4–85 text dh: THE | TEMPEST*. | [rule], ht: THE TEMPEST., *86* Epilogue, *87* ½t: A | MIDSUMMER-NIGHT's | DREAM., *88* Dramatis Perſonæ., *89* 90–176 text dh: A Mɪᴅsᴜᴍᴍᴇʀ-Nɪɢʜᴛ's | DREAM. | [rule], ht: A MIDSUMMER-NIGHT's DREAM., *177* ½t: THE TWO | GENTLEMEN | OF | *VERONA.*, *178* Dramatis Perſonæ., *179* 180–259 text dh: THE | TWO GENTLEMEN | OF | VERONA. | [rule], rt: THE TWO GENTLEMEN | OF VERONA., *260* blk, *261* ½t: MEASURE | FOR MEASURE., *262* Dramatis Perſonæ., *263* 264–382 text dh: MEASURE ғᴏʀ MEASURE*. | [rule], ht: MEASURE FOR MEASURE., *383* ½t: THE | MERCHANT | OF | *VENICE.*, *384* Dramatis Perſonæ., *385* 386–488 text dh: THE | MERCHANT of VENICE. | [rule], rt: THE MERCHANT | OF VENICE. (488 'THE MERCHANT, &c.').

Pagination: A–E (SJ's Preface) unpaged; [↑] xciv, c, cii–ciii.

Press-figures: A1ᵛ–4, A2ᵛ–2, B1ᵛ–4, C1ᵛ–9, C6ᵛ–8, D2ᵛ–2, D7ᵛ–1, E4–3, E4ᵛ–8, a8(xv)1, a8ᵛ(xvi)–8, b2ᵛ(xx)–2, b7ᵛ(xxx)–8, c1ᵛ(xxxiv)–8, c2ᵛ(xxxvi)–6, d7(lxi)–5, d7ᵛ(lxii)–2, e7ᵛ(lxxviii)–2, f5(lxxxix)–4, f8(xcv)–2, B3ᵛ(6)–5, B4ᵛ(8)–1, C6(27)–3, C7(29)–6, D8(47)–3, E7(61)–5, E8(63)–1, F1ᵛ(66)–3, F7(77)–8, G7ᵛ(94)–3, H8(111)–1, I2ᵛ(116)–2, I8(127)–8, K5ᵛ(138)–2, K8ᵛ(144)–4, L4ᵛ(152)–3, L8(159)–1, M8(175)–5, N3ᵛ(182)–3, O7ᵛ(206)–2, P3ᵛ(214)–6, P7(221)–1, Q2ᵛ(228)–3, Q8(239)–4, R1ᵛ(242)–3, R4ᵛ(248)–6, S8ᵛ(272)–3, T2ᵛ(276)–2, U8(303)–3, X7(317)–1, X7ᵛ(318)–5, Y7(333)–4, Y8(335)–3, Z1ᵛ(338)–4, Z8ᵛ(352)–1, 2A8ᵛ(368)–4, 2B2ᵛ(372)–2, 2B6(379)–5, 2C7ᵛ(398)–4, 2D8ᵛ(416)–6, 2E8(431)–2, 2F8(447)–1, 2G7(461)–4, 3G7ᵛ(462)–1, 2H1ᵛ(466)–5, 2H6ᵛ(476)–8, 2I3(485)–8; unfigured g.

Catchwords: E5 *om.* (TO), a1v *om.* (THE), g2 *om.* (*To*), g2v *om.* (TO), 1 *om.* (Dramatis), 63 ⌄No (⁹No), 86 *om.* (Dramatis), 88 *om.* (A), 107 ⌄And (⁵~), 177 *om.* (Dramatis), 195 [pul-] ling⌄ (~,), 197 *Speed*⌄ (~.), 261 *om.* (Dramatis), 262 *om.* (MEASURE), 276 nA (And), 286 Sir⌄ (~,), 334 ſure (*Duke.*), 383 *om.* (Dramatis), 413 Gra. (~⌄), 442 ⌄The (⁴~), 465 ⌄Anthonio, (—Anthonio,). 334 *catches* with l. 2 of 335.

Explicit: 488 The Eɴᴅ of the Fɪʀsᴛ Vᴏʟᴜᴍᴇ.

II. *A*1 (= I. E7) B–2N⁸ (2N8 blk), ($4 signed; 'Vᴏʟ. II.' on $1), 281 leaves.

Pp. A1 t: THE | PLAYS | OF | WILLIAM SHAKESPEARE. | VOLUME the SECOND, | CONTAINING, | AS YOU LIKE IT. | LOVE's LABOUR's LOST. | The WINTER's TALE. | TWELFTH-NIGHT: or, WHAT YOU WILL. | The MERRY WIVES of WINDSOR. | LONDON: | Printed for J. and R. Tᴏɴsᴏɴ, . . . &c. [as gen. t.], A1ᵛ blk, on

B1 *1* ½t: AS YOU LIKE IT. | A | COMEDY., *2* Dramatis Perſonæ.*, *3* 4–108 text dh: AS YOU LIKE IT. | [rule], ht: AS YOU LIKE IT., *109* ½t: LOVE's LABOUR's LOST. | A | COMEDY., *110* Dramatis Perſonæ., *111* 112–229 text dh: LOVE's LABOUR's LOST. | [rule], ht: LOVE's LABOUR's LOST., *230* blk, *231* ½t: THE | WINTER's | TALE., *232* Dramatis Perſonæ., *233* 234–349 text dh: THE | WINTER's TALE.¹ | [rule], ht: THE WINTER's TALE., *350* blk, *351* ½t: TWELFTH-NIGHT: | OR, | WHAT YOU WILL., *352* Dramatis Perſonæ., *353* 354–448 text dh: TWELFTH-NIGHT: | OR, | WHAT YOU WILL. | [rule], rt: TWELFTH-NIGHT: OR, | WHAT YOU WILL. (448 'TWELFTH-NIGHT.'), *449* ½t: THE | MERRY WIVES | OF | WINDSOR., *450* Dramatis Perſonæ., *451* 452–557 text dh: THE | ¹MERRY WIVES | OF | WINDSOR. | [rule], rt: THE MERRY WIVES | OF WINDSOR., *558* blk, + (2N8) blk.

Pagination: 252 unnumbered, 394 as 594.

Press-figures: B7ᵛ(14)–1, C8(31)–8, D8(47)–2, D8ᵛ(48)–8, E3ᵛ(54)–1, E4ᵛ(56)–4, F1ᵛ(66)–1, F8ᵛ(80)–2, G1ᵛ(82)–1, G4ᵛ(88)–5, H3ᵛ(102)–8, I8ᵛ(128)–2, K5(137)–5, L4ᵛ(152)–4, M2ᵛ(164)–8, M7ᵛ(174)–1, N3ᵛ(182)–1, O5ᵛ(202)–8, P8(223)–2, Q8ᵛ(240)–2, R7ᵛ(254)–8, S1ᵛ(258)–5, T7(285)–8, U8ᵛ(304)–8, X7ᵛ(318)–4, Y7(333)–8, Y7ᵛ(334)–5, Z5ᵛ(346)–1, 2B6(379)–4, 2C8ᵛ(400)–2, 2E1ᵛ(418)–3, 2E8ᵛ(432)–8, 2F1ᵛ(434)–4, 2F6ᵛ(444)–3, 2G8ᵛ(464)–3, 2H6(475)–3, 2H8ᵛ(480)–4, 2I5ᵛ(490)–3, 2K3ᵛ(502)–3, 2K7(509)–2, 2L1ᵛ(514)–1, 2N5ᵛ(554)–8, 2N6ᵛ(556)–5; unfigured 2A, 2D, 2M.

Catchwords: *om.* A1, 1–2, 109, 230–2, 350–1, 449–50; 24 *Clo.* But ['l' *inverted*] (*Clo.* ~), 83 ₐSCENE (⁴SCENE), 113 Soₐ (~,), 149 *Enter* (*Prin.*), 176 n. read, (~ₐ), 199 He (*Biron.*), 303 *Dor.* (*Clo.*), 353 ₐThat (²~), 367 n. Howeverₐ (~,), 371 ₐ*Oli.* (⁵~), 372 ₐLook (⁶~), 413 ₐput (—put).

Explicit: 557 The END of the SECOND VOLUME.

III. *A*² B–2B⁸ 2C⁸ (± 2C2) 2D–2I⁸ 2K⁴ [C5 and Y3 *occasionally* cancels], ($4 signed; 'VOL. III.' on $1 (+A1)), 254 leaves.

Pp. A1 Gen. ½t: THE | PLAYS | OF | WILLIAM SHAKESPEARE., A1ᵛ blk, on A2 t: THE | PLAYS | OF | WILLIAM SHAKESPEARE. | VOLUME the THIRD, | CONTAINING, | The TAMING of the SHREW. | The COMEDY of ERRORS. | MUCH ADO ABOUT NOTHING. | ALL's WELL, THAT ENDS WELL. | The LIFE and DEATH of KING JOHN. | [double rule] | LONDON: | Printed for J. and R. TONSON, . . . [&c. as vol. 1, above], A2ᵛ blk, on B1 *1* ½t: THE | TAMING | OF THE | SHREW., *2* Characters *in the* Induction. [&] Dramatis Perſonæ, *3* 4–14 *15* 16–99 text dh: THE | TAMING of the SHREW. | [rule], rt: THE TAMING | OF THE SHREW., *100* blk, *101* ½t: THE | COMEDY | OF | ERRORS., *102* Dramatis Perſonæ, *103* 104–70 text dh: THE | COMEDY of ERRORS. | [rule], rt: THE COMEDY | OF ERRORS., *171* ½t: MUCH ADO | ABOUT | NOTHING., *172* Dramatis Perſonæ, *173* 174–273 text dh:

MUCH ADO ABOUT NOTHING.[1] | [rule], rt: MUCH ADO | ABOUT NOTHING., *274* blk, *275* ½t: ALL's WELL, | THAT | ENDS WELL., *276* Dramatis Perſonæ., *277* 278–398 text dh: ALL's WELL, that ENDS WELL. | [rule], rt: ALL's WELL | THAT ENDS WELL., *399* dh: EPILOGUE., *400* blk, *401* ½t: THE | LIFE and DEATH | OF | KING *JOHN.*, *402* Dramatis Perſonæ., *403* 404–504 text dh: The LIFE and DEATH of | KING *JOHN.* | [rule], ht: KING JOHN.

Pagination: 137 as 13, 269 as 66, 347 unnumbered, 445 as 454, 475 as 47, 476 as 479.

Press-figures: B7(13)–4, B7ᵛ(14)–8, C5ᵛ(26)–9, C7ᵛ(30)–4, D3ᵛ(38)–4, E6(59)–4, F5v(74)–3, F7(77)–8, G5ᵛ(90)–1, G7(93)–2, H5ᵛ(106)–4, H8ᵛ(112)–2, I4ᵛ(120)–6, I7ᵛ(126)–4, K7ᵛ(142)–2, L7ᵛ(158)–2, M7ᵛ(174)–8, N7(189)–6, N7ᵛ(190)–5, O7ᵛ(206)–4, O8ᵛ(208)–3, P5(217)–7, P8(223)–8, Q6(235)–6, Q8ᵛ(240)–2, R1ᵛ(242)–3, R2ᵛ(244)–1, S3ᵛ(262)–3, T5ᵛ(282)–1, T6ᵛ(284)–3, U5(297)–5, X6ᵛ(316)–2, X8(319)–5, [*Cancellans* Y3ᵛ(326)–2], Y7(333)–6, Y7ᵛ(334)–4, Z6(347)–2, Z6ᵛ(348)–6, 2A8(367)–8, 2A8ᵛ(368)–5, 2B7(381)–8, 2B7ᵛ(382)–2, 2D1ᵛ(402)–2, 2D8ᵛ(416)–4, 2E7ᵛ(430)–4, 2F7ᵛ(446)–4, 2G3ᵛ(454)–3, 2G8ᵛ(464)–4, 2H1ᵛ(466)–6, 2H8ᵛ(480)–5, 2I1ᵛ(482)–3; unfigured 2C, 2K.

Catchwords: *om.* A1, 1, 100–1, 171, 274–5, 400–1; 79 To (For), 172 MUCH (MUCH), 203 n. [Cir-] cumſtances, (~‸), 253 *Ciaud.* (*Claud.*), 276 ALL's (ALL's), 289 ‸He (⁵~), 297 ‸For (¹Fortune), 307 *Par.* (*Ber.*), 349 your (Lordſhip), 375 n. This (The), 382 n. ‸*ſtink*, (⁷*Indeed*,), 402 ‸THE (¹The), 408 ‸And (⁴~), 415 And (Againſt), 464 ‸Turn- (⁵Turning).

Explicit: 557 The END of the THIRD VOLUME.

IV. *A*² B–E⁸ F⁸ (± F3) G–Z⁸ 2A⁸ (± 2A7), 2B⁸ (± 2B4) 2C–2P⁸ (2P8 blk), ($4 (–Q4) signed; 'VOL. IV.' on $1 (+A1)), 298 leaves.

Pp. A1 Gen. ½t: THE | PLAYS | OF | WILLIAM SHAKESPEARE., A1ᵛ blk, A2 t: THE | PLAYS | OF | WILLIAM SHAKESPEARE. | VOLUME FOURTH, | CONTAINING, | The LIFE and DEATH of RICHARD the SECOND. | The FIRST PART of KING HENRY the FOURTH. | The SECOND PART of KING HENRY the FOURTH. | The LIFE of KING HENRY the FIFTH. | The FIRST PART of KING HENRY the SIXTH. | [double rule] | LONDON: | Printed for J. and R. TONSON, . . . [&c. as vol. 1], A2ᵛ blk, on B1 *1* ½t: THE | LIFE and DEATH | OF | *RICHARD* | THE | SECOND., *2* Dramatis Perſonæ., *3* 4–105 text dh: The LIFE and DEATH of | KING *RICHARD* II. | [rule], ht: KING RICHARD II., *106* blk, *107* ½t: The FIRST PART of | *HENRY* IV. | WITH THE | LIFE and DEATH | OF | HENRY, *Sirnam'd* HOT-SPUR., *1108* Dramatis Perſonæ., *109* 110–230 text dh: The FIRST PART of | *HENRY* IV. | [rule], ht: THE FIRST PART OF | KING HENRY IV., *231* ½t: The SECOND PART of | *HENRY* IV. | Containing his DEATH: | AND THE | CORONATION |

OF | King *HENRY* V., *232* Dramatis Perſonæ., *233–4* dh. and ht: INDUCTION., *235* 236–356 text dh: The Sᴇᴄᴏɴᴅ Pᴀʀᴛ of *HENRY* IV⁶. | [rule], rt: THE SECOND PART OF | KING HENRY IV., *357–8* dh. and ht: EPILOGUE., *359* ½t: THE | LIFE | OF | *HENRY* V., *360* Dramatis Perſonæ., *361–2* dh. and ht: PROLOGUE., *363* 364–487 text dh: The LIFE of | King *HENRY* V. | [rule], ht: KING HENRY V., *488* blk, *489* ½t: THE | FIRST PART | OF | *HENRY* VI., *490* Dramatis Perſonæ., *491* 492–589 text dh: The Fɪʀsᴛ Pᴀʀᴛ of | King *HENRY* VI. | [rule], rt: THE FIRST PART OF | KING HENRY VI., *590* blk, + 1 blk leaf (2P8).

Pagination: no errors.

Press-figures: B7ᵛ(14)–4, C7ᵛ(30)–4, D2ᵛ(36)–6, D7ᵛ(46)–5, E7ᵛ(62)–6, F8ᵛ(80)–1, G8(95)–5, G8ᵛ(96)–7, H8ᵛ(112)–4, I8(127)–4, K7ᵛ(142)–4, L7ᵛ(158)–8, L8ᵛ(160)–3, M4ᵛ(168)–1, M7ᵛ(174)–4, N8(191)–2, O2ᵛ(196)–3, O8(207)–4, P7ᵛ(222)–8, Q2ᵛ(228)–6, R8(255)–2, R8ᵛ(256)–4, S2ᵛ(260)–8, T7ᵛ(286)–4, U7ᵛ(302)–4, X3ᵛ(310)–8, Y5ᵛ(330)–7, Z5(345)–6, Z6(347)–7, 2A5(361)–2, '2A7ᵛ(366)–2, 2A8(367)–6, 2B6(379)–8, 2B8ᵛ(384)–4, 2C6(395)–4, 2D5(409)–3, 2D7ᵛ(414)–4, 2E7(429)–2, 2F8(447)–4, 2G7ᵛ(462)–4, 2H7ᵛ(478)–3, 2I8(495)–4, 2K7ᵛ(510)–3, 2L1v(514)–8, 2L8ᵛ(528)–3, 2M6ᵛ(540)–8, 2N1ᵛ(546)–2, 2O8(575)–3, 2P6ᵛ(588)–2.

Catchwords: *om.* A1–2, 1–2, 106–8, 231–2, 234, 359–60, 488–90; 15 n. ſub-ſtitutes‸ (~,), 48 ‸SCENE (2~), 51 ‸To ([~), 64 Then (Than), 76 ‸And (⁵~), 83 ‸To (*~), 84 Thou‸ (~‸), 125 ‸A ('~), 152 valiant‸ (~,), 179 ‸And (⁶~), 217 ‸He (¹~), 307 ‸Con~ (*Conſtrue), 374 n. ſhew‸ (~,), 381 ‸And (⁴~), 382 ‸We'll (⁶~), 388 ‸For (⁹~), 391 ‸Trea- (⁷Treaſon), 396 I hop'd‸ (~ ~,), 403 ‸Shall (²~), 414 ‸SCENE (*~), 491 ‸Brandiſh (²~).

Explicit: 589 The Eɴᴅ of the Fᴏᴜʀᴛʜ Vᴏʟᴜᴍᴇ.

V. *A²* B–2G⁸ 2H⁸ (± 2H8) 2I⁸ (2I8 blk), ($4 signed; 'Vᴏʟ. V.' on $1), 250 leaves.

Pp. A1 Gen. ½t: THE | PLAYS | OF | WILLIAM SHAKESPEARE., A1ᵛ blk, A2 t: THE | PLAYS | OF | WILLIAM SHAKESPEARE. | VOLUME the FIFTH, | CONTAINING | The Sᴇᴄᴏɴᴅ Pᴀʀᴛ of KING HENRY the SIXTH. | The Tʜɪʀᴅ Pᴀʀᴛ of KING HENRY the SIXTH. | The LIFE and DEATH of RICHARD the THIRD. | The LIFE of KING HENRY the EIGHTH. | LONDON: | Printed for J. and R. Tᴏɴsᴏɴ, . . . [&c. as vol. 1], A2ᵛ blk, on B1 *1* ½t: THE | SECOND PART | OF | HENRY VI., *2* Dramatis Perſonæ., *3* 4–115 text dh: ¹The Sᴇᴄᴏɴᴅ Pᴀʀᴛ of | King *HENRY* VI. | [rule], rt: THE SECOND PART OF | KING HENRY VI., *116* blk, *117* ½t: THE | THIRD PART | OF | *HENRY* VI. | With the DEATH of the | Dᴜᴋᴇ of *YORK*., *118* Dramatis Perſonæ., *119* 120–225 text dh: ¹The Tʜɪʀᴅ Pᴀʀᴛ of | King *HENRY* VI.² | [rule], rt: THE THIRD PART OF | KING HENRY VI., *226* blk, *227* ½t: THE | LIFE and DEATH | OF | *RICHARD* III., *228* Dramatis Perſonæ., *229* 230–368 text dh: THE |

¹LIFE and DEATH of | King *RICHARD* III. | [rule], ht: KING RICHARD III., *369* ½t: THE | LIFE | OF | *HENRY* VIII., *370* blk, *371–2* Dramatis Perſonæ., *373–4* dh and ht: PROLOGUE., *375* 376–491 text dh: The LIFE of | King *HENRY* VIII. | [rule], ht: KING HENRY VIII., *492*–493 dh and ht: EPILOGUE., *494* blk.

Pagination: no errors.

Press-figures: B7ᵛ(14)–4, C1ᵛ(18)–4, D8ᵛ(48)–2, E7ᵛ(62)–8, F3ᵛ(70)–7, G2ᵛ(84)–4, G5ᵛ(90)–2, H5ᵛ(106)–8, I1ᵛ(114)–7, K5ᵛ(138)–3, L3ᵛ(150)–7, M7ᵛ(174)–7, N8(191)–7, O1ᵛ(194)–1, O8ᵛ(208)–7, P2ᵛ(212)–3, Q5(233)–3, Q7ᵛ(238)–4, R2ᵛ(244)–4, R7ᵛ(254)–7, S7ᵛ(270)–3, T8(287)–1, U7(301)–1, X1ᵛ(306)–5, Y8(335)–4, Z1ᵛ(338)–8, 2A8(367)–1, 2B4ᵛ(376)–4, 2B5ᵛ(378)–1, 2C3ᵛ(390)–5, 2D5(409)–2, 2D7ᵛ(414)–8, 2E8(431)–5, 2E8ᵛ(432)–6, 2F6(443)–3, 2F8ᵛ(448)–2, 2G6(459)–6, 2I3ᵛ(486)–5, 2I4ᵛ(488)–4; unfigured 2H.

Catchwords: *om.* A1–2, 1–2, 116–18, 226–8, 369–70; 35 *Both*: (∼.), 68 ∧ Would (¹∼), 102 Should (Shouldſt), 105 *York*∧ (∼.), 140 ∧And (⁶∼), 181 ∧Did (¹∼), 211 ∧which (⁵∼), 229 ∧He (²∼), 246 ∧Of (⁵∼), 249 ∧Hear (¹∼), 253 They∧ (∼,), 283 ∧Thus (¹∼), 315 ∧Rude (*∼), 347 ∧Look (¹∼), 381 ∧He (⁴∼), 385 ∧I (³∼), 387 ∧ (⁶∼), 390 ∧From (⁵∼), 432 ∧Do (³∼), 463 ∧SCENE (⁴∼).

Explicit: 493 The END of the FIFTH VOLUME.

VI. *A²* B–Q⁸ R⁸ (± R4) S⁸ (± S1,8) T–2R⁸ 2S², ($4 (+R4, S8, −2S2) signed; 'VOL. VI.' on $1 (+R4, S8)), 316 leaves.

Pp. A1 Gen. ½t: THE | PLAYS | OF | WILLIAM SHAKESPEARE., A1ᵛ blk, A2 t: THE | PLAYS | OF | WILLIAM SHAKESPEARE. | VOLUME SIXTH, | CONTAINING, | The LIFE and DEATH of KING LEAR. | TIMON of ATHENS. | TITUS ANDRONICUS. | The TRAGEDY of MACBETH. | CAIUS MARCIUS CORIOLANUS. | [double rule] | LONDON: | Printed for J. and R. TONSON, . . . [&c. as vol. 1], A2ᵛ blk, on B1 *1* ½t: THE | LIFE *and* DEATH | OF | KING *LEAR*., *2* Dramatis Perſonæ., *3* 4–163 text dh: KING *LEAR*. | [rule], ht: KING LEAR., *164* blk, *165* ½t: TIMON | OF | *ATHENS*., *166* Dramatis Perſonæ., *167* 168–276 text dh: TIMON *of* ATHENS. | [rule], ht: TIMON OF ATHENS., *277* ½t: TITUS ANDRONICUS., *278* Dramatis Perſonæ., *279* 280–365 text dh: TITUS ANDRONICUS. | [rule], ht: TITUS ANDRONICUS., *366* blk, *367* ½t: THE | TRAGEDY | OF | *MACBETH*., *368* Dramatis Perſonæ., *369* 370–484 text dh: *MACBETH*. | [rule], ht: MACBETH., *485* ½t: C. MARCIUS | CORIOLANUS., *486* Dramatis Perſonæ., *487* 488–627 text dh: CORIOLANUS. | [rule], ht: CORIOLANUS., *628* blk.

Pagination: 446 as 46, 581 as 58.

Press-figures: B7(13)–2, B7ᵛ(14)–3, C1ᵛ(18)–1, D1ᵛ(34)–2, E1ᵛ(50)–1, F6ᵛ(76)–6, F8(79)–5, G3ᵛ(86)–1, G8ᵛ(96)–8, H1ᵛ(98)–1, H2ᵛ(100)–5, I8(127)–8, K8(143)–4, L1ᵛ(146)–6, M7ᵛ(174)–2, N3ᵛ(182)–8, N8(192)–4, O1ᵛ(194)–1, P2ᵛ(212)–8, P8(223)–2, Q6ᵛ(236)–2, Q8(239)–2, R2ᵛ(244)–3,

R8(255)–6, S2ᵛ(260)–1, S5ᵛ(266)–7, T7(285)–8, U1ᵛ(290)–1, X8(319)–5, Y5ᵛ(330)–6, Z2ᵛ(340)–3, 2A5(361)–6, 2B6ᵛ(380)–8, 2C5ᵛ(394)–4, 2C8ᵛ(400)–7, 2D6(411)–1, 2D6ᵛ(412)–3, 2E5ᵛ(426)–8, 2F5ᵛ(442)–7, 2F8ᵛ(448)–1, 2G4ᵛ(456)–1, 2H5(473)–3, 2I8(495)–3, 2K1ᵛ(498)–1, 2K2ᵛ(500)–3, 2L7ᵛ(526)–2, 2M7(541)–2, 2N1ᵛ(546)–3, 2O1ᵛ(562)–2, 2P7ᵛ(590)–8, 2P8ᵛ(592)–2, 2Q8(607)–4, 2R4ᵛ(616)–4, 2R8(623)–9.

Catchwords: *om.* A1–2, 1, 164–6, 277–8, 366–8, 485; superior figg. *om.* 18, 48, 54, 60, 96, 112, 113, 146, 170, 180, 217, 319, 324, 343, 356, 374, 378, 385, 394, 405, 408, 415, 522, 579, 581, 583; 168 Shew (Shews), 235 Baſe₍ₐ₎ (~,), 238 thou (*~), 276 TITU₍ₐ₎ (TITUS), 439 *Lady*₍ₐ₎ (~.), 449 *Ap.* (*Apparition*), 473 Come (—Come), 519 ₍ₐ₎At (*~).

Explicit: 627 The END of the SIXTH VOLUME.

VII. *A*² B–2M⁸ 2N², ($4 (–2N2) signed; 'VOL. VII.' on $1), 276 leaves.

Pp. A1 Gen. ½t: THE | PLAYS | OF | WILLIAM SHAKESPEARE., A1ᵛ blk, A2 t: THE | PLAYS | OF | WILLIAM SHAKESPEARE. | VOLUME the SEVENTH, | CONTAINING, | JULIUS CÆSAR. | ANTONY and CLEOPATRA. | CYMBELINE. | TROILUS and CRESSIDA. | [double rule] | LONDON: | Printed for J. and R. TONSON, . . . [&c. as vol. 1], A2ᵛ blk, on B1 *1* ½t: JULIUS CÆSAR., *2* Dramatis Perſonæ., *3* 4–102 text dh: *JULIUS CÆSAR.* | [rule], ht: JULIUS CÆSAR., *103* ½t: ANTONY | AND | CLEOPATRA., *104* Dramatis Perſonæ., *105* 106–254 text dh: *ANTONY* | AND | *CLEOPATRA.* | [rule], ht: ANTONY AND CLEOPATRA., *255* ½t: CYMBELINE | A | TRAGEDY., *256* Dramatis Perſonæ., *257* 258–404 text dh: CYMBELINE. | [rule], ht: CYMBELINE., *405* ½t: TROILUS | AND | CRESSIDA., *406–7* dh and ht: PROLOGUE., *408* Dramatis Perſonæ., *409* 410–547 text dh: TROILUS *and* CRESSIDA. | [rule], ht: TROILUS AND CRESSIDA., *548* blk.

Pagination: 501 unnumbered.

Press-figures: B5ᵛ(10)–3, C2ᵛ(20)–8, D5(41)–3, D5ᵛ(42)–6, E1ᵛ(50)–1, E7(61)–6, F6(75)–9, G1ᵛ(82)–2, G2ᵛ(84)–1, H2ᵛ(100)–2, H7ᵛ(110)–6, I7ᵛ(126)–1, K5(137)–6, K5ᵛ(138)–1, L1ᵛ(146)–6, L6ᵛ(156)–5, M8(175)–7, M8ᵛ(176)–9, N1ᵛ(178)–7, O7(205)–1, O7ᵛ(206)–9, P5ᵛ(218)–6, Q2ᵛ(228)–1, Q7ᵛ(238)–4, R7ᵛ(254)–2, S6ᵛ(268)–6, T8ᵛ(288)–2, U6(299)–3, X7(317)–3, X7ᵛ(318)–7, Y3ᵛ(326)–3, Z6(347)–4, Z6ᵛ(348)–1, 2A2ᵛ(356)–7, 2B7ᵛ(382)–1, 2B8ᵛ(384)–6, 2C1ᵛ(386)–2, 2D1ᵛ(402)–1, 2D6ᵛ(412)–9, 2E2ᵛ(420)–8, 2E3ᵛ(422)–7, 2F5ᵛ(442)–7, 2F8ᵛ(448)–4, 2G4ᵛ(456)–9, 2G5ᵛ(458)–2, 2H1ᵛ(466)–2, 2I6ᵛ(492)–8, 2I8(495)–3, 2K5ᵛ(506)–4, 2K8ᵛ(512)–8, 2L1ᵛ(514)–4, 2M1ᵛ(530)–3; unfigured 2N.

Catchwords: *om.* A1–2, 1–2, 104, 254–5, 405, 408; superior figg. *om.* 47, 105, 109, 111, 136, 154, 196, 219, 227, 242, 300, 303, 352, 453, 468, 485, 490, 503; 369 Bu (But), 411 As, (Hard), 452 Th (There's), 504 Let (⁴*Æne.*), 509 Ma (Manly), 532 *om.* (I am), 544 *Hio.* (*Dio.*).

Explicit: 547 The End of the Seventh Volume.

VIII. *A*² B–I⁸ K⁸ (± K7) L⁸ M⁸ (± M1) N⁸ (± N7) O–P⁸ Q⁸ (± Q6) R–X⁸ Y⁸ (± Y5) Z–2L⁸, ($4 signed; 'Vol. VIII.' on $1 (+K7, N7, Q6, Y5)), 266 leaves.

Pp. A1 Gen. ½t: THE | PLAYS | OF | WILLIAM SHAKESPEARE., A1ᵛ blk, A2 t: THE | PLAYS | OF | WILLIAM SHAKESPEARE. | VOLUME EIGHTH, | CONTAINING, | ROMEO and JULIET. | HAMLET, PRINCE of DENMARK. | OTHELLO, the MOOR of VENICE. | LONDON: | Printed for J. and R. Tonson, . . . [&c., as vol. 1], A2ᵛ blk, on B1 *1* ½t: ROMEO | AND | JULIET., *2* blk, *3* PROLOGUE., *4* Dramatis Perfonæ., *5* 6–125 text dh: Romeo *and* Juliet. | [rule], ht: ROMEO *and* JULIET., *126* blk, *127* ½t: HAMLET | Prince *of* Denmark., *128* Dramatis Perfonæ., *129* 130–316 text dh: HAMLET | Prince *of* Denmark. | [rule], rt: HAMLET, | PRINCE OF DENMARK., *317* ½t: OTHELLO, | THE | MOOR of *VENICE.*, *318* Dramatis Perfonæ., *319* 320–473 text dh: ¹OTHELLO, | The Moor of Venice. | [rule], rt: OTHELLO, | THE MOOR OF VENICE., *474* blk, on 2H6–2L8 (27 leaves, 53 unnumbered pp.) Appendix dh: [double rule] | APPENDIX., ht: APPENDIX to VOL. I. [&c. –VIII.], 2L8ᵛ blk.

Pagination: 189 as 18.

Press-figures: B4ᵛ(8)–9, B6(11)–2, C1ᵛ(18)–*, D2ᵛ(36)–2, D7ᵛ(46)–4, E6(59)–8, F8(79)–3, G3ᵛ(86)–8, G8ᵛ(96)–3, H2ᵛ(100)–8, H5ᵛ(106)–9, I1ᵛ(114)–6, I5(121)–7, L3ᵛ(150)–6, L5(153)–3, M1(161)–3, M8ᵛ(176)–9, N1ᵛ(178)–1, N8ᵛ(192)–6, O1ᵛ(194)–9, O2ᵛ(196)–1, P3ᵛ(214)–9, P6ᵛ(220)–4, Q5(233)–2, Q7ᵛ(238)–8, R1ᵛ(242)–1, R5(249)–9, S7ᵛ(270)–8, S8ᵛ(272)–7, T1ᵛ(274)–9, T2ᵛ(276)–8, U6(299)–7, U8ᵛ(304)–2, X3ᵛ(310)–3, X8ᵛ(320)–2, Y1ᵛ(322)–4, Y7(333)–2, Z5(345)–2, Z5ᵛ(346)–4, 2A5ᵛ(362)–2, 2B6(379)–4, 2B7(381)–1, 2C7ᵛ(398)–3, 2C8ᵛ(400)–4, 2D6(411)–1, 2D8ᵛ(416)–4, 2E7(429)–6, 2E7ᵛ(430)–3, 2F2(435)–2, 2G5(457)–3, 2H2ᵛ(468)–4, 2H3ᵛ(470)–6, 2I5ᵛ–2, 2I8ᵛ–8, 2K2ᵛ–7, 2L8–4; unfigured K.

Catchwords: *om.* A1–2, 1–2, 4, 126–8, 317, 474, 2L2ᵛ, 2L4ᵛ; superior figg. *om.* 53, 71, 94, 107, 108, 116, 135, 136, 155, 177, 207, 230, 231, 233, 259, 264, 267, 294, 318, 341, 345, 387, 392; 286 Ham, (~.), 466 *And* [*d* slipt].

Explicit: none.

Paper: White, laid; Demy (uncut: 8½ × 5½ in.), wmk.: fleur-de-lys.

Type: Prefatory matter and text: pica (4.0 mm), (SJ's Preface is leaded 1.1 mm); footnotes, appendix &c.: long primer (3.0 mm).

Plate: Engr. port. of Shakespeare (after Droeshout in F1), within oval: ribbon at top 'WILLIAM SHAKESPEARE', 'G Virtue Sculpsit' and 'Obᵗ. Anº. Dom. 1616 Æta. 53.'

References: Courtney 103–4, 107–8; Jaggard 501; CH 146–7; Hazen, *TLS*, 24 Dec. 1938, 820; Eddy, *PBSA* lvi (1962), 428–44; ESTC: t138601. SJ's labours are outlined by Eastman, *MLN* lxiii (1948), 512–15, and expanded by Sherbo, *SJ: Editor of Shakespeare* (1956), esp. 8–14; more detailed observations by Johnston in *Yearbook of English Studies*, vi (1976), 80–91, and in *Greene Centennial Essays* (1984), and by Seary in *Johnson after 200 Years* (1986).

Notes: The cancels are discussed by Hazen and Eddy. There are 15 regular cancels, viz. I. X4 (311–12), X6 (315–16), III. 2C2 (387–8), IV. F3 (69–70), 2A7 (365–6), 2B4 (375–6), V. 2H8 (479–80), VI. R4 (247–8), S1 (257–8), S8 (271–2), VIII. K7 (141–2), M1 (145–6), N7 (173–4), Q6 (235–6), Y5 (329–30); and five occasional ones: I. B5 (9–10), O8 (207–8), P8 (223–4), III. C5 (25–6), Y3 (325–6). These five are irregularly represented, and no set is recorded which contains them all. The cancels were effected primarily to soften some criticisms of Warburton. Percy preserved some of the *cancellanda* in his copy (viz. I. X4, X6, VI. R4, S1, S8); H.W. Liebert's second copy had *cancellanda* of I. B5, and III. C5. JDF copy shows I. P8 *cancellans*. A copy 'lacking the cancels' was Sotheby (27 Feb. 1978), 128, Quaritch, £130, but is untraced: it was probably a 2nd edn. (65.10SP/2a, below).

Some account of proof revision in SJ's Preface is offered by Sherbo, *BJRL*, xxxv (1952–3), 206–10, and by Fleeman, in *Studies in the Eighteenth Century* (1979), 207–21, esp. 215–17.

There are no General ½tt in vols. 1–2, but each vol. has a particular t. listing the contents. The main t. is found in vol. 1 only.

The work was offered by subscription (see *Proposals*, 56.6SP/1, above), but the number of subscribers is unknown (*Life* iv. 111).[1] Four receipts only are known to survive:

(a) No. 8, 'Thos. Hay Esqr' (PPRF)
(b) No. 27, 'The Revd. Mr Seward' (O: GA Staffs 4° 8, p. 487)
(c) No. 660, 'Earl of Loudoun' (CSmH: LO 9626)[2]
(d) No. 831 'Ld. B. Bertie . . . March 16, 1759' (Rippey – CaOHM ?)

The MS agreement, dated 2 June 1756, between Jacob Tonson and SJ is LICj.

This edn. was printed by William Strahan: 150 sheets were in print by 1 Jan. 1759, and 156 sheets were worked off by 1 Jan. 1761.[3] Strahan's complete account shows the first 6 vols. printed by Dec. 1761, and the work finished in Sept. 1765, in an edn. of 1,000 copies (L: Add. MS 48802A, fo. 20v). The account is complex because printing occupied several years. The work was published, and presumably distributed to subscribers, on 10 October 1765, at 2 gns a copy, but Tonson had already set a second edn. (65.10SP/2a) in hand about mid-September.

The reception was almost uniformly favourable. Kenrick was the main antagonist (*Life* i. 498, 556), and cf. McGuffie *SJ in the British Press 1749–1784* (1976), 37 ff.

Copies: O² (**1**. Malone Adds. 50 e. 19–26; **2**. Percy 7–14 'Thomas Percy');

USA: CSmH, CtY, DFo ('The present of the Bishop of Lichfield & Coventry to N. Kilvert 1777',[4] 'This copy was a present from Bp. Warburton to

Mr Hurd (afterwards Bishop of Lichfield & Worcester) upon its' publication 1765. See the Warburton Letters Page 366. 8vo.', 'E. Jordan Worcester'), DLC ('Thomas Cowper Esq. Overleigh'), Hyde[2] (**1**. 'David Garrick'; **2**. 'R. B. Adam'), ICN, IU, [Liebert[2] (**1**. uncut, 'Tho. Bowles Feb[y] 11. 1767')], MH, NIC, NjP, NN ('John St. Aubyn, Bt.'), NPM ('To Sir Thomas Robinson Bart. the kindest Promoter of this Edition, these Volumes were presented by the Editor.'[5]), NRo; *Can*: CaOHM (B 2500–7, 'Andrew Anderson a present from Mr Jas. Cullen October 1766'); *Japan*: [Kyoto]; *UK*: ABu, BMp (666865, vol. 1. imperfect, lacking I–K[8], 'Charles James Fox'), C, Cp (lacks vol. 2), Ct, DUu, E, [Es], Eu ('Halliwell-Phillipps'), JDF ('Wm. Mitford'), L (11761. c.15), Om ('F.P. Wilson'); *Aust*: CNL (DNS 6912).

[1] Fleeman, in *Writers, Books, and Trade* (1994), 355–65.
[2] On the verso of this document, in the same hand as entered Loudoun's name is the docket: 'Mr Johnsons Receipt for a new edition of Shakespeares works Payed to Sir Thomas Rob[?in]son London Janua[r]y 30[th] 1759. £1 — 1 — ::'.
[3] William Strahan's Journals 1751–77, in PPAmP (1958.140 MS).
[4] PR.2752.1765a. c1. There are contemporary annotations in vol. 1, perhaps by Warburton; Richard Hurd was Bp. of Coventry and Lichfield, 1775–81 when he was translated to Worcester. The last inscription is in a 19th-century hand.
[5] *Booklist* 139. This inscription is not in SJ's hand. Tonson may have considered himself to be the 'Editor'.

65.10SP/2a   Shakespeare, second edition   1765

THE | PLAYS | OF | WILLIAM SHAKESPEARE, | IN EIGHT VOLUMES, | WITH THE | CORRECTIONS and ILLUSTRATIONS | OF | Various COMMENTATORS; | To which are added | NOTES by SAM. JOHNSON. | [double rule] | LONDON: | Printed for J. and R. TONSON, H. WOODFALL, J. RIVINGTON, | R. BALDWIN, L. HAWES, CLARK and COLLINS, T. LONGMAN, | W. JOHNSTON, T. CASLON, C. CORBET, T. LOWNDS, | and the Executors of B. DODD. | M,DCC,LXV.

Variants: II. . . . COLLINS, C. CORBET, | W. JOHNSTON, T. CASLON, T. LONGMAN, T. LOWNDS | and the Executors of B. DODD. . . .

III–VIII. . . . J. and R. TONSON, C. CORBET, H. WOODFALL, | J. RIVINGTON, R. BALDWIN, L. HAWES, CLARK and | COLLINS, W. JOHNSTON, T. CASLON, T. LOWNDS, | and the Executors of B. DODD. . . .

Stet: LOWNDS,

8 vols., 8°

I. A[8] a–k[8] B–2H[8] 2I[4], ($4 (–A1,2, G4, S3, 2I3,4) signed; 'VOL. I.' on $1), 332 leaves.

Pp. Engr. front. (Port. of Shakespeare 'G. Virtue Sculpsit') + A1 t., A1[v] blk, A2 t. vol. 1 (as 1st edn. 65.10SP/1, above), A2[v] blk, on A3 pp. v–lxxii SJ's Preface dh: [double rule] | PREFACE., ht: PREFACE., *lxxiii*–lxxiv

Dedication to First Folio, *lxxv*–lxxvi Preface of the Players (from First Folio), *lxxvii* lxxviii–xciii Pope's Preface, xciv–cxxiii Theobald's Preface, cxxiv–cxxvii Hanmer's Preface, cxxviii–cxliv Warburton's Preface, cxlv–clxiv Rowe's Life of Shakespeare, *clxv*–clxvi Grant of Arms, *clxvii* clxviii–clxxi Shakespeare's Will, clxxii Horse-holding anecdote, *clxxiii* clxxiv–clxxv Ben Jonson's verses, *clxxvi* blk, on B1 *1* ½t Tempest, *2* Dram. Pers., *3* 4–85 text: The Tempest, *86*, Epilogue, *87* ½t Midsummer Night's Dream, *88* Dram. Pers., *89* 90–176 text Midsummer Night's Dream, *177* ½t Two Gentlemen, *178* Dram. Pers., *179* 180–259 text Two Gentlemen of Verona, *260* blk, *261* ½t Measure for Measure, *262* Dram. Pers., *263* 264–382 text Measure for Measure, *383* ½t Merchant of Venice, *384* Dram. Pers., *385* 386–488 text Merchant of Venice.

Pagination: [↑] v, xciv, cxxiv, cxxviii, cxlv, cxlvi, 'clii', 'cliv', 'clv'; clxx–clxxv as cl–clv; clxxvi, 260 blk.

Press-figures:[1] A6ᵛ(xii)–2, a4ᵛ(xxiv)–3, b8ᵛ(xlviii)–4, c7(lxi)–2, d6(lxxv)–3, e4ᵛ(lxxxviii)–2, f3ᵛ(cii)–4, g6ᵛ(cxxiv)–2, h5ᵛ(cxxxviii)–2, i8(clix)–3, k7(cliii)–2, B8ᵛ(16)–2, C6ᵛ(28)–2, D8ᵛ(48)–4, E2ᵛ(52)–2, F7ᵛ(78)–2, G6(91)–4, H1ᵛ(98)–2, H7ᵛ(110)–[*sometimes*]2, I7ᵛ(126)–2, K5ᵛ(138)–4, L2ᵛ(148)–4, M6ᵛ(172)–4, N7(189)–4, O5ᵛ(202)–4, P8ᵛ(224)–2, Q7ᵛ(238)–2, R3ᵛ(246)–2, S8ᵛ(272)–3, T6ᵛ(284)–2, U5ᵛ(298)–2, X5ᵛ(314)–2, Y1ᵛ(322)–4, Z6(347)–3, 2A8ᵛ(368)–2, 2B3ᵛ(374)–3, 2C8ᵛ(400)–2, 2D7ᵛ(414)–2, 2E4ᵛ(424)–4, 2F1ᵛ(434)–4, 2G4ᵛ(456)–3, 2H1ᵛ(466)–4, 2I3(485)–2.

Catchwords: *om.* on ½t and Dram. Pers. p. of each play; superior figg. *om.* pp. 63, 107, 442; xxxii Nations [*in last line of text*, not *in direction line*], lxxii *om.* (TO), lxxiv *om.* (THE), xciv Thought; (~:), ciii becauf (becaufe), 'cli' *om.* (*To*), 'clii' *om.* (TO), 15 n. fays, (fay,), 85 PI- (EPILOGUE.), 86 *om.* (A), 88 *om.* (A), 100 a merry, (~ ~.), 155 But, (~,), 195 [pul-] ing, (~,), 276 An (And), 284 *sometimes om.* (*Ang.*), 286 Sir, (~,), 323 marriage, (marriage-dowry;), 362 Harp. (~,), 415 *Laur.* (*Laun.*), 465 ,Anthonio, (—*Anthonio*,).

Explicit: 488 The END of the FIRST VOLUME.

II. *A²* B–2N⁸ (2N8 blk), ($4 (–Q4) signed; 'VOL. II.' on $1), 282 leaves.
Pp. A1 ½t: THE | PLAYS | OF | WILLIAM SHAKESPEARE., A1ᵛ blk, A2 t. to vol. 2, A2ᵛ blk, on B1 *1* ½t As You Like It, *2* Dram. Pers., *3* 4–108 text As You Like It, *109* ½t Love's Labour's Lost, *110* Dram. Pers., *111* 112–229 text Love's Labour's Lost, *230* blk, *231* ½t Winter's Tale, *232* Dram. Pers., *233* 234–349 text Winter's Tale, *350* blk, *351* ½t Twelfth Night, *352* Dram. Pers., *353* 354–448 text Twelfth Night, *449* ½t Merry Wives of Windsor, *450* Dram. Pers., *451* 452–557 text Merry Wives of Windsor, *558* blk, *559–60* (2N8) blk.

Pagination: 230, 350, 558–60 blk.

Press-figures: [*Two variant series of figg. in* Sigg. B–H; *see* Note *below*], Series 1: B6ᵛ(12)–2, C2ᵛ(20)–2, D2ᵛ(36)–1, E5(57)–2, F1ᵛ(66)–2, G8(95)–1, H2ᵛ(100)–2; Series 2: B8(15)–1, C7ᵛ(30)–4, C8ᵛ(32)–4, D5ᵛ(42)–1, E3ᵛ(54)–4, F8ᵛ(80)–4, G3ᵛ(86)–1, H2ᵛ(100)–1; I5(121)–4, K6(139)–1, L5(153)–4,

M5(169)–4, M6(171)–2, N5(185)–3, O1ᵛ(194)–4, P6(219)–4, Q8(239)–4, R8ᵛ(256)–4, T8(287)–4, U8(303)–1, X7ᵛ(318)–1, Y8ᵛ(336)–1, Z2ᵛ(340)–4, 2A5(361)–1, 2B5(377)–4, 2C6ᵛ(396)–1, 2D2ᵛ(404)–4, 2E6ᵛ(428)–4, 2F2ᵛ(436)–1, 2F3ᵛ(438)–4, 2G3ᵛ(454)–4, 3G5(457)–1, 2H2ᵛ(468)–1, 2H3ᵛ(470)–4, 2I6(491)–4, 2I7(493)–1, 2K5(505)–4, 2L4ᵛ(520)–4, 2M7(541)–1, 2N3ᵛ(550)–4; unfigured S.

Catchwords: *om.* at ½tt and Dram. Pers. pp, 113 So‸ (∼,), 199 He (*Biron.*), 288 n. manner‸ (∼,), 367 n. however‸ (∼,), 372 Look (⁶∼), 413 ‸pot (—put), 549 n. [PUR-] PLE‸ (∼,).

Explicit: 557 The END of the SECOND VOLUME.

III. *A²* B–2I⁸ 2K⁴, ($4 (–H3, 2K3,4) signed; 'VOL. III.' on $1), 254 leaves.

Pp. A1 ½t (as vol. 2), A1ᵛ blk, A2 t. (vol. 3), A2ᵛ blk, on B1 *1* ½t Taming of the Shrew, *2* Dram. Pers., *3* 4–14 *15* 16–99 text Taming of the Shrew, *100* blk, *101* ½t Comedy of Errors, *102* Dram. Pers., *103* 104–70 text Comedy of Errors, *171* ½t Much Ado about Nothing, *172* Dram. Pers., *173* 174–273 text Much Ado, *274* blk, *275* ½t All's Well that Ends Well, *276* Dram. Pers., *277* 278–398 text All's Well, *399* Epilogue, *400* blk, *401* ½t King John, *402* Dram. Pers., *403* 404–504 text King John.

Pagination: blk. 100, 274, 400; unpaged 15, 399; 208 as 176, 465 as 495.

Press-figures: [*Two variant series* in B–F] B6ᵛ(12)–4, C *unfigured*, D1ᵛ(34)–1, E3ᵛ(54)–1, E5(57)–4, F6(75)–4, *Series* 2: B6ᵛ(12)–2, C8(31)–4, D5(41)–4, E3ᵛ(54)–2, F *unfigured*; G5ᵛ(90)–1, H5(105)–4, I4ᵛ(120)–4, I7ᵛ(126)–2, K2ᵛ(132)–4, L4ᵛ(152)–1, M2ᵛ(164)–1, N1ᵛ(178)–4, N8(192)–1, O5ᵛ(202)–1, P5ᵛ(218)–1, P6ᵛ(220)–1, Q8(239)–4, R7(253)–4, S8(271)–4, T7(285)–2, U1ᵛ(290)–1, X1ᵛ(306)–4, Y2ᵛ(324)–1, Y6ᵛ(332)–1, Z7ᵛ(250)–1, 2A5(361)–1, 2B3ᵛ(374)–1, 2B7(381)–4, 2C6(395)–1, 2D7(413)–1, 2D8(415)–4, 2E4ᵛ(424)–1, 2G2ᵛ(452)–1, 2H1ᵛ(466)–4, 2I5(489)–1, 2K2ᵛ(500)–2; unfigured 2F.

Catchwords: *om.* A1–2, 1 and ½tt and Dram. Pers., superior figg. *om.* pp. 289, 297, 402, 408, 464; 1 *om.* (Characters), 131 n. *(not‸)* ((∼,)), 135 n. to (be), 169 Come‸ (∼,), 173 conflict‸ (∼,), 231 For‸ (∼,), 280 n. makes (make), 325 n. This‸ (∼,), 349 your (Lordſhip), 353 which (Which), 363 he‸ (∼,), 415 And (Againſt), 417 K. *Philip.* (K. *Philp.*), 475 confound- (founded).

Explicit: The END of the THIRD VOLUME.

IV. *A²* B–2P⁸ (2P8 blk), ($4 (–Q4) signed; 'VOL. IV.' on $1), 298 leaves.

Pp. A1 ½t (as. vol. 2), A1ᵛ blk, A2 t. (vol. 4), A2ᵛ blk, on B1 *1* ½t Richard II, *2* Dram. Pers., *3* 4–105 text Richard II, *106* blk, *107* ½t 1 Henry IV., *108* Dram. Pers. *109* 110–230 text 1 Henry IV., *231* ½t 2 Henry IV., *232* Dram. Pers., *233* 234 *235* 236–356 text 2 Henry IV., *357–8* Epilogue, *359* ½t Henry V., *360* Dram. Pers., *361–2* Prologue, *363* 364–487 text Henry V., *488* blk, *489* ½t 1 Henry VI., *490* Dram. Pers., *491* 492–589 text 1 Henry VI., *590* blk, + *591–2* 1 blk leaf;

Pagination: blk. 106, 488, 590–2; 457 as 574, 586 as 686.

Press-figures: B2ᵛ(4)–4, C1ᵛ(18)–4, D7(45)–1, D8(47)–4, E5ᵛ(58)–4, E6ᵛ(60)–2, F2ᵛ(68)–4, G5(89)–1, H8ᵛ(112)–2, I8ᵛ(128)–2, K4ᵛ(136)–2, K8(143)–1, L4ᵛ(152)–1, L6(155)–2, M7(173)–4, N8ᵛ(192)–1, O2ᵛ(196)–4, O8(207)–1, P5ᵛ(218)–4, Q1ᵛ(226)–1, Q7(237)–4, R8(255)–4, S3ᵛ(262)–4, T1ᵛ(274)–1, T4ᵛ(280)–4, U1ᵛ(290)–2, U5(297)–1, X4ᵛ(312)–1, Y5ᵛ(330)–2, Z5(345)–4, 2A1ᵛ(354)–3, 2B3ᵛ(374)–2, 2C2ᵛ(388)–1, 2C3ᵛ(390)–4, 2D6ᵛ(412)–1, 2E1ᵛ(418)–1, 2F2ᵛ(436)–2, 2G4ᵛ(456)–2, 2G7ᵛ(462)–1, 2H7ᵛ(478)–2, 2H8ᵛ(480)–1, 2I6ᵛ(492)–4, 2K8ᵛ(512)–1, 2L3ᵛ(518)–1, 2M3ᵛ(534)–1, 2M8ᵛ(544)–4, 2N5ᵛ(554)–4, 2O2ᵛ(564)–1, 2O3ᵛ(566)–4, 2O7ᵛ(574)–4, 2P2ᵛ(580)–4, 2P3ᵛ(582)–1; *Note*: three figures in 2O.

Catchwords: *om.* A1–2, ½tt and Dram. Pers., 234, 488; superior figg. *om.* pp. 48, 76, 125, 179, 209, 217, 362, 381, 382, 391, 403, 491; 15 n. fubftitutes‸ (∼,), 64 Then (Than), 83 ‸To (*∼), 105 THE (The), 111 which (what), 117 *P. Henry.* (*P. Harry.*), 127 Rut (But), 152 valiant‸ (∼,), 156 *om.* (yet), 174 To‸ (To-morrow), 277 *Pift*, (∼.), 279 For (Fear), 307 ‸Con- (*Conftrue), 320 courage‸ (∼;), 374 n. fhew‸ (∼,), 413 ‸SCENE (*∼), 451 Leave (Leaving), 453 except‸ (Except,), 514 *om.* (For), 531 —Well‸ (∼;), 582 In‸ (Inviron).

Explicit: 589 The END of the FOURTH VOLUME.

V. *A*² B–2I⁸ (2I8 blk), ($4 signed; 'VOL. V.' on $1), 250 leaves.

Pp. A1 ½t (as vol. 2), A1ᵛ blk, A2 t. (vol. 5), A2ᵛ blk, on B1 *1* ½t 2 Henry VI., *2* Dram. Pers., *3* 4–115 text 2 Henry VI., *116* blk, *117* ½t 3 Henry VI., *118* Dram. Pers., *119* 120–225 text 3 Henry VI., *226* blk, *227* ½t Richard III., *228* Dram. Pers., *229* 230–368 text Richard III., *369* ½t Henry VIII., *370* blk, *371–2* Dram. Pers., *373–4* Prologue *375* 376–493 text Henry VIII., *494* blk, *495–6* (2I8) 1 blk leaf.

Pagination: blk. 116, 226, 370, 494–6; 492 unnumbered, 256 as 236, 490 as 9.

Press-figures: B7ᵛ(14)–4, C5ᵛ(26)–4, D6(43)–4, E6ᵛ(60)–4, F5(73)–2, G7(93)–4, G7ᵛ(94)–2, H5ᵛ(106)–4, H8ᵛ(112)–2, I4ᵛ(120)–1, I6(123)–4, K7(141)–4, L6(155)–4, L6ᵛ(156)–2, M2ᵛ(164)–4, M6(171)–1, N3ᵛ(182)–4, O5ᵛ(202)–4, P1ᵛ(210)–4, Q6(235)–1, R6(251)–1, S2ᵛ(260)–1, T2ᵛ(276)–1, T8(287)–4, U1ᵛ(290)–1, X2ᵛ(308)–1, Y1ᵛ(322)–1, Y6ᵛ(332)–4, Z3ᵛ(342)–1, Z6ᵛ(348)–4, 2A3ᵛ(358)–1, 2A4ᵛ(360)–3, 2B7ᵛ(382)–1, 2C7ᵛ(398)–1, 2D5(409)–3, 2D7ᵛ(414)–1, 2E6(427)–3, 2F1ᵛ(434)–3, 2F5(441)–1, 2G6ᵛ(460)–3, 2G7ᵛ(462)–1, 2H5ᵛ(474)–1, 2H6ᵛ(476)–3, 2I5ᵛ(490)–3, 2I6ᵛ(492)–1.

Catchwords: *om.* A1–2, ½tt and Dram. Pers., 226; superior figg. *om.* pp. 68, 140, 181, 211, 229, 246, 249, 283, 347, 381, 385, 387, 390, 432, 461; 91 Kent. (∼‸), 98 *But* (But), 102 Should (Shouldft), 170 *No*; (∼,), 209 And‸ (∼,), 230 And‸ (∼,), 315 ‸Rude (*∼), 365 *om.* (In), 366 Thus‸ (∼,), 375 what (which), 385 2 *Gent.* (2 *Gen.*), 484 *om.* (*King.*).

Explicit: 493 The END of the FIFTH VOLUME.

VI. *A*² B–2R⁸ 2S², ($4 (–2S2) signed; 'VOL. VI.' on $1), 316 leaves.

Pp. A1 ½t (as vol. 2), A1ᵛ blk, A2 t. (vol. 6), A2ᵛ blk, on B1 *1* ½t The Life and Death of King Lear, *2* Dram. Pers., *3* 4–163 text King Lear, *164* blk, *165* ½t Timon of Athens, *166* Dram. Pers., *167* 168–276 text Timon, *277* ½t Titus Andronicus, *278* Dram. Pers., *279* 280–365 text Titus, *366* blk, *367* ½t The Tragedy of Macbeth, *368* Dram. Pers., *369* 370–484 text Macbeth, *485* ½t C. Marcius Coriolanus, *486* Dram. Pers., *487* 488–627 text Coriolanus, *628* blk.

Pagination: blk: pp. 164, 366, 628.

Press-figures: B8(15)–6, C5(25)–7, E4ᵛ(56)–*, F5ᵛ(74)–3, G2ᵛ(84)–1, G6(91)–2, H7ᵛ(110)–8, I8ᵛ(128)–8, K1ᵛ(130)–8, K7(141)–3, L3ᵛ(150)–6, M1ᵛ(162)–6, M7(173)–2, N5(185)–3, N5ᵛ(186)–8, O7(205)–3, O7ᵛ(206)–7, P5ᵛ(218)–7, P8ᵛ(224)–3, Q2ᵛ(228)–3, R3ᵛ(246)–6, S8(271)–4, T7ᵛ(286)–4, U8(303)–6, U8ᵛ(304)–8, X5(313)–6, X5ᵛ(314)–8, Y1ᵛ(322)–8, Y8ᵛ(336)–7, Z4ᵛ(344)–8, Z5ᵛ(346)–1, 2A6(363)–8, 2A8ᵛ(368)–2, 2B2ᵛ(372)–7, 2C2ᵛ(388)–3, 2C5ᵛ(394)–8, 2D6(411)–8, 2E2ᵛ(420)–8, 2E8(431)–7, 2F6(443)–7, 2G1ᵛ(450)–8, 2H6(475)–8, 2H7(477)–7, 2I5(489)–3, 2I6(491)–1, 2K1ᵛ(498)–1, 2K7(509)–3, 2L8(527)–8, 2M2ᵛ(532)–6, 2M8(543)–7, 2N8ᵛ(560)–2, 2O1ᵛ(562)–6, 2O4ᵛ(568)–1, 2P5ᵛ(586)–7, 2P6ᵛ(588)–6, 2Q2ᵛ(596)–4, 2Q8(607)–2, 2R6(619)–4, 2R8ᵛ(624)–8.

Catchwords: *om.* A1–2, blks, ½tt and Dram. Pers. (exc. 486), superior figg. *om.* pp. 18, 47, 54, 60, 96, 112, 113, 146, 170, 180, 217, 237, 300, 319, 343, 356, 374, 378, 385, 394, 405, 408, 415, 579, 581, 583; 63 And (and), 235 Baſe↓ (~,), 270 Be (Beſides), 289 which, (~;), 310 *Ente↓* (*Enter*), 329 Pat. (Patten'd), 374 n. *om.* (the), 399 *Lady↓* (~.), 450 *Ap↓* (*Apparition*), 473 ↓Come (—Come), 488 *om.* (it), 504 *Lart↓* (~.), 613 *Si* (*Sic.*).

Explicit: 627 The END of the SIXTH VOLUME.

VII. *A2* B–2M⁸ 2N², ($4 (–2N2) signed; 'VOL. VII.' on $1), 276 leaves.

Pp. A1 ½t (as vol. 2), A1ᵛ blk, A2 t (vol. 7), A2ᵛ blk, on B1 *1* ½t Julius Cæsar, *2* Dram. Pers., *3* 4–102 text Julius Cæsar, *103* ½t Antony and Cleopatra, *104* Dram. Pers., *105* 106–254 text Antony and Cleopatra, *255* ½t Cymbeline. A Tragedy., *256* Dram. Pers., *257* 258–404 text Cymbeline, *405* ½t Troilus and Cressida, *406–7* Prologue, *408* Dram. Pers., *409* 410–547 text Troilus and Cressida, *548* blk.

Pagination: 548 blk; 125 as 128, 128 as 125.

Press-figures: [*Variant sequence in* B–C] B6ᵛ(12)–4, C8(31)–7, [*alternative sequence*] B7ᵛ(14)–2, C2ᵛ(20)–2; D8(47)–6, E7(61)–4, E8(63)–1, F7(77)–2, F8(79)–S *or* 8, G6(91)–2, G7(93)–4, H6ᵛ(108)–5, I2ᵛ(116)–2, I7ᵛ(126)–3, K8(143)–1, K8ᵛ(144)–6, L3ᵛ(150)–5, L7(157)–7, M1ᵛ(162)–5, N2ᵛ(180)–3, O8(207)–4, P4(216)–3, P5ᵛ(218)–6, Q8(239)–2, R3ᵛ(246)–5, R6ᵛ(252)–4, S1ᵛ(258)–4, S2ᵛ(260)–1, T1ᵛ(274)–4, U2ᵛ(292)–5, U8(303)–4, X4ᵛ(312)–4, Y7(333)–7, Y8(335)–4, Z8(351)–4, Z8ᵛ(352)–7, 2A7(365)–5, 2A8(367)–4, 2B7ᵛ(382)–6, 2C6ᵛ(396)–6, 2G7ᵛ(462)–7, 2H5(473)–4, 2H6(475)–6, 2I3ᵛ(486)–7, 2I8ᵛ(496)–4, 2K5(505)–1, 2K8(511)–3, 2L5(521)–3,

2L7ᵛ(526)–7, 2M6(539)–5, 2M8ᵛ(544)–6; unfigured 2C, 2D–F, 2N. The fig. in F8(79) was first 'S' but later changed to '8'.

Catchwords: *om.* A1–2, ½tt and Dram. Pers.; superior figg. *om.* 47, 105, 109, 111, 136, 154, 196, 219, 227, 242, 300, 303, 352, 453, 467, 485, 490, 503; 33 n. *Calphurnia* (*Caliphurnia*), 384 by (By), 429 And‸ (~,), 504 Let (⁴*Æne.*).

Explicit: 547 The END of the SEVENTH VOLUME.

VIII. A^2 B–2L⁸, ($4 signed; 'VOL. VIII.' on $1), 266 leaves.

Pp. A1 ½t (as vol. 2), A1ᵛ blk, A2 t. (vol. 8), A2ᵛ blk, on B1 *1* ½t Romeo and Juliet, *2* blk, *3* Prologue, *4* Dram. Pers., *5* 6–125 text Romeo and Juliet, *126* blk, *127* ½t Hamlet, Prince of Denmark, *128* Dram. Pers., *129* 130–316 text Hamlet, *317* ½t Othello, the Moor of Venice, *318* Dram. Pers., *319* 320–473 text Othello, *474* blk, on H6–2L8 (53 pp. unpaged) Appendix, 2L8ᵛ blk.

Pagination: 126, 474 and 2L8ᵛ blk; 215 as 214.

Press-figures: B5ᵛ(10)–2, B6ᵛ(12)–1, C7(29)–1, C7ᵛ(30)–6, D7(45)–6, D7ᵛ(46)–8, E5(57)–8, E8(63)–4, F1ᵛ(66)–6, H4ᵛ(104)–3, H7ᵛ(110)–7, I5(121)–1, I6(123)–2, K6(139)–1 [*or* K7(141)–1, K7ᵛ(142)–2], L1ᵛ(146)–2, L7(157)–3, M1ᵛ(162)–4, M2ᵛ(164)–5, N8(191)–4, N8ᵛ(192)–5, O7ᵛ(206)–7, P2ᵛ(212)–2, P7ᵛ(222)–4, Q1ᵛ(226)–6, Q4ᵛ(232)–2, R2ᵛ(244)–4, R7ᵛ(254)–6, S5ᵛ(266)–6, S6ᵛ(268)–7, T7ᵛ(286)–4, T8ᵛ(288)–7, U1ᵛ(290)–4, U5(297)–6, X8(319)–7, Y1ᵛ(322)–2, Y6ᵛ(332)–2, Z2ᵛ(340)–6, Z8(351)–7, 2A6ᵛ(364)–6, 2A8(367)–1, 2B7(381)–4, 2B8(383)–6, 2C6(395)–6, 2C7(397)–7, 2D4ᵛ(408)–2, 2D7ᵛ(414)–6, 2E5ᵛ(426)–7, 2E8(431)–7, 2F6(443)–3, 2G7ᵛ(462)–2, 2G8ᵛ(464)–4, 2H1ᵛ(466)–1, 2H8ᵛ–6 [*or* 2H3ᵛ(470)–4], 2I4ᵛ–7, 2L8–4; unfigured G, 2K; variant figg. in K and 2H, as noted.

Catchwords: *om.* A1–2, ½tt and Dram. Pers. (exc. 318), superior figg. *om.* pp. 53, 71, 94, 107, 108, 116, 135, 136, 155, 177, 207, 230, 232, 234, 259, 264, 268, 318, 341, 387, 392; 240 n. *om.* (is), 391 *Iag* (Iago.), 470 *om.* (I), 2I4 *om.* (P. 312), 2K7ᵛ *om.* (P. 172), 2L2ᵛ *om.* (P. 198), 2L4ᵛ *om.* (P. 374).

Explicit: none.

Paper: White, laid; Demy (uncut: 8½ × 5½ in.); wmk.: fleur-de-lys.

Type: Pref. and text: pica (4.0 mm) (Preface is leaded), footnotes and appendix: long primer (3.0 mm).

Plate: Engr. port. Shakespeare (after Droeshout) in vol. 1, as first edn. 65.10SP/1, above.

References: Courtney 107–8; CH 146–7; ESTC: n012071. This reprint was first noticed by Brett-Smith, *TLS*, 15 May 1919, 265, and elaborated by Eddy, *PBSA* lvi (1962), 428–44.

Notes: This edn. differentiated from edn. 1 (65.10SP/1, above), by the variant imprint, pagination of SJ's Preface, ½tt. in each volume, and absence of cancels. Eddy adds important details of the variation of press-figures, and reveals some reprinting in vols. II. B–G, III. B–F, VII. B–C, and VIII. K and 2H, involving resetting of the text.[2]

750 copies of vols. 2–4 were printed by William Bowyer in Sept–Oct. 1765, the first 68 reams of paper for the work delivered on 19 September (O: MS Don. b. 4, fo. 191ᵛ). This is the earliest date to indicate that Tonson had decided to publish a reprint. Strahan printed 750 copies of vols. 7–8 in Oct. 1765 (L: Add. MS 48802A, fo. 20ᵛ). The work was evidently shared to expedite production: Bowyer's account names 'Mr Reeves' as the printer of 4 sheets in vol. 4. The printer of vols. 1 and 5 is unidentified. The first copies were delivered to Tonson on Monday 4 Nov., and newspaper advts. of 2 and 10 Oct. and 12 Nov. (*Lond. Chron.*), and 12 Nov. (*St. James's Chron.*), suggest that Tuesday 12 Nov. was probably the official date of publication. It was sold at the same price as the first edn., £2. 2s. a set.

Offprints of SJ's Preface were taken from this edn., see below 65.10SP/2b.

Copies: O (Mal. Adds. 50 e. 1–8; lacking some ½tt);

USA: CtY, DFo ('Edward Dowden'), Hyde ('Warde'), ICU, IU, LICj (lacks vol. 1), [Liebert ('Daniel Rolf Munn')], MB, MH (*EC75 J6371. 765sb), NjP, PPL (imperfect), PPRF, PPU, L.R. Rothschild, Esq; TxU²; *UK*: ABu, BMp (2672), JDF ('Mary Lascelles'), Gu, LVu, MRu, Op ('G. B. Hill'); *Aust*: CNL (DNS 6913, lacks vols. 1–2).

---

¹ With the exception of the occasional figure at H7ᵛ, each sheet is figured only once.

² Though Eddy describes these reprinted signatures as a 'Third edition', I consider them to be too few to warrant the expression 'edition', and regard them as variant states of the affected sheets. Our difference is merely terminological.

65.10SP/2b Preface to Shakespeare 1765

[½t] Mr. JOHNSON's | PREFACE | To his EDITION of | SHAKESPEAR's PLAYS. | [Price One Shilling.]

[Title] Mr. JOHNSON's | PREFACE | To his EDITION of | Shakespear's Plays. | [Orn: flower vase] | [double rule] | LONDON: | Printed for J. and R. TONSON, H. WOODFALL, J. RIVINGTON, | R. BALDWIN, L. HAWES, CLARK and COLLINS, T. LONGMAN, | W. JOHNSTON, T. CASLON, C. CORBET, T. LOWNDS, | and the Executors of B. DODD. | M,DCC,LXV.

Stet: LOWNDS

8°, A⁸ a–c⁸ d⁴, ($4 (–A1,2, d3,4) signed), 36 leaves.

Pp. A1 *i* ½t, A1ᵛ *ii* blk, A2 *iii* t., *iv* blk, on A3 v–lxxii text dh: [two rules] | PREFACE., ht: PREFACE.

Pagination: roman; [↑] v.

Press-figures: A6ᵛ(xii)–2, a4ᵛ(xxiv)–3, b8ᵛ(xlviii)–4, c7(lxi)–2, d4(lxxi)–3.

Catchwords: xxxii Nations [*is in last line of text* not *in direction-line*].

Explicit: lxxii FINIS.

Paper: White, laid; Demy (uncut: 8½ × 5½ in.); wmk.: fleur-de-lys.

Type: Pica (4.0 mm), leaded.

References: Courtney 107; CH 148; *Tinker* 1347; *Rothschild* 1249; Eddy, *PBSA* lvi (1962), 432; ESTC: t006431;

Notes: Same setting of type as in 65.10SP/2a, above, of which this is an off-print, except:

1. ½t and t. are reset and differently worded, though imprint remains the same;
2. Sig. d is a whole sheet in vol. 1 (65.10SP/2a, above), but only a ½-sheet here;
3. Press-fig. 3 on d6(lxxiii) of vol. 1, above, is here moved to d4(lxxi), the last leaf of this issue, though it remains in the inner forme of sig. d.
4. The word 'FINIS.' is added here at d4^v (lxxii).

It has sometimes been suggested that this was a small edn., as the sale might have detracted from the sale of the whole edn., and it is often supposed scarce, but the following list of 43 copies hardly supports such an assumption.

The printer is unidentified, though Richard Hett, successor to John Watts, Tonson's regular Shakespearian printer, seems the likeliest candidate. The 'flower vase' ornament in the t. has not yet been identified with a particular printer's stock though it is fairly common in books and pamphlets of the period.

An early note on 'Mr Johnson's Preface to Shakespeare containing 73 pages, but not numbered' is in the Birch papers (L: Add. MS 4254, fos. 99–112).[1]

Copies: O² (**1**. Malone B.50; **2**. G.P. 132(1));

USA: CSmH ('W. H. Hagen'), CtY ('Tinker'), DFo, DLC, G. Goldberg, Esq; Hyde³, [A.A. Houghton (uncut)], IU, [Liebert (wrappers)], MB, MBAt, MH (MS notes), NIC, NjP², NN (no ½t), NN-B ('MacGregor', 'Jerome Kern', 'Owen D. Young'), NNC, NPM², PPRF (wraps, 'J.C. Goodden 1778'), TxU, ViU ('McGeorge'); *Can*: CaOHM (B 15691, 'Rippey', lacks ½t); *Japan*: [Kyoto²]; *UK*: AWn, BMp (2542), Ct (Rothschild), Cq, Gp, Gu, L (11766. bbb.35, no ½t), Lv (Dyce 5289), LICj ('Percy Fitzgerald'), Owo, STA² (2nd. no ½t), Yc; *Aust*: CNL (DNS 4805).

---

[1] I am indebted to Mrs G.I. Hampshire, who drew this item to my attention.

65.10SP/2c   Preface to Shakespeare, facsimile   1969

A facsimile from the L copy (without the ½t), was published by the Scolar Press, Menston, Yorks, 1969.

65.10SP/3   Shakespeare, Dublin   1766

(a) THE | PLAYS | OF | WILLIAM SHAKESPEARE, | IN TEN VOLUMES. | WITH THE | CORRECTIONS and ILLUSTRATIONS |

OF | VARIOUS COMMENTATORS. | To which are added, | NOTES BY SAMUEL JOHNSON, LL.D. | DUBLIN: | PRINTED FOR | A. LEATHLEY, C. WYNNE, P. WILSON, J. EXSHAW, | H. SAUNDERS, J. POTTS, S. WATSON, | J. MITCHELL, and J. WILLIAMS. | [short rule] | M,DCC,LXVI.

(b) [*Volume t.*] THE | PLAYS | OF | WILLIAM SHAKESPEARE. | VOLUME the FIRST, | CONTAINING, | The TEMPEST. | A MIDSUMMER-NIGHT's DREAM. | The TWO GENTLEMEN OF VERONA. | [double rule] | DUBLIN: | Printed for A. LEATHLEY, C. WYNNE, P. WILSON, | J. EXSHAW, H. SAUNDERS, J. POTTS, S. WATSON, | J. MITCHELL, and J. WILLIAMS. | short rule] | MDCCLXVI.

10 vols., 12°

I. π1–3 A^{12} b–f^{12} g1–5, B^8 C–M^{12}, (\$5 (g4^v as g4) signed; 'VOL. I.' on \$1 (–M)), 208 leaves.

Pp. Engr. front. + π1 t., π1^v blk, π2 t. (vol. 1), π2^v blk, π3 blk, π3^v ADVERTISEMENT., on A1 i–liii Preface dh: [orn. hp.] | PREFACE., ht: PREFACE., *liv* blk, *lv*–lvi Dedication of Players to F1, lvii–lviii Preface of Players to F1 dh: [headstrip] | THE | PREFACE | OF THE | PLAYERS. | To the great variety of Readers., ht: PREFACE BY THE PLAYERS., lix–lxxiv dh: [headstrip] | Mr. POPE's PREFACE., ht: Mr. POPE's PREFACE., lxxv–cii dh: [headstrip] | Mr. THEOBALD's | PREFACE., ht: Mr. THEOBALD's PREFACE., ciii–cvi dh: [headstrip] | Sir T. HANMER's | PREFACE., ht: Sir T. HANMER's PREFACE., cvii–cxxii [headstrip] | Dr. WARBURTON's | PREFACE., ht: Dr. WARBURTON's PREFACE., cxxiii–cxli [headstrip] | SOME | ACCOUNT of the LIFE, &c. | OF | Mr. WILLIAM SHAKESPEARE. | Written by Mr. ROWE., rt: Some ACCOUNT of the LIFE, &c. | of Mr. WILLIAM SHAKESPEARE., *cxlii* blk, cxliii–cxliv Grant of Arms, cxlv–cxlix Shakespeare's Will, dh: SHAKESPEARE's WILL., ht: SHAKESPEARE's WILL., cl Horse-holding anecdote, *cli* clii–cliii Jonson's verses, *cliv* blk; on B1 *1* ½t Tempest, *2* Dram. Pers., *3* 4–83 text The Tempest, *84* Epilogue, *85* ½t Midsummer Night's Dream, *86* Dram. Pers., *87* 88–172 text Midsummer Night's Dream, *173* ½t Two Gentlemen of Verona, *174* Dram. Pers., *175* 176–251 text Two Gentlemen, *252–54* ht: ADDITIONAL NOTES.

Pagination: [↑] ^{A}i, lix, ciii, cvii, cxxiii, cxliii–cxlv, cl, clii–cliii; (↑) lvii, lxxv; cliii as clii.

Press-figures: none.

Catchwords: cxxiv upon (Upon), remainder *not checked*.

Explicit: 254 The End of the Firſt VOLUME.

II. π1 A–R^{12} S^{10} T^2, (\$5 (–K4, S4, T2) signed; 'VOL. II.' on \$1 (+A2 *not a cancel*)), 217 leaves.

Pp. π1 t. (as b, above: . . . the SECOND, | CONTAINING, | MEASURE FOR MEASURE. | The MERCHANT OF VENICE. | AS YOU LIKE IT.

| LOVE'S LABOUR'S LOST. | [double rule] . . . &c.), π1ᵛ blk, A1 *1* ½t Measure for Measure, *2* Dram. Pers., *3* 4–116 text Measure for Measure, *117* ½t Merchant of Venice, *118* Dram. Pers., *119* 120–222 text Merchant, *223* ½t As You Like It, *224* Dram. Pers., *225* 226–322 text AYLI, *323* ½t Love's Labour's Lost, *324* Dram. Pers., *325* 326–436 text LLL.

Pagination: no errors; *Press-figures*: none.

Catchwords: not checked; *Explicit*: none.

III. π² A–Q¹² R⁸ S², ($5 (–A3, R4, S2) signed; 'Vᴏʟ. III.' on $1 (+π1)), 204 leaves.

Pp. π1 ½t: THE | PLAYS | OF | WILLIAM SHAKESPEARE., π1ᵛ blk, π2 t. (vol. 3 as **b**, above . . . the THIRD, | CONTAINING, | The WINTER's TALE. | TWELFTH-NIGHT: or, WHAT YOU WILL. | The MERRY WIVES of WINDSOR. | The TAMING of the SHREW. | [double rule] | . . . C. Wʏɴɴᴇ, P. | Wɪʟsᴏɴ, . . . H. Sᴀᴜɴᴅᴇʀs, | Jᴀᴍᴇs Pᴏᴛᴛs, . . . J. | Mɪᴛᴄʜᴇʟʟ, J. Wɪʟʟɪᴀᴍs. | [short rule] | MDCCLXVI., on A1 *1* ½t Winter's Tale, *2* Dram. Pers., *3* 4–112 text Winter's Tale, *113* ½t Twelfth Night, *114* Dram. Pers., *115* 116–204 text Twelfth Night, *205* ½t Merry Wives of Windsor, *206* Dram. Pers., *207* 208–307 text Merry Wives, *308* blk, *309* ½t Taming of the Shrew, *310* Dram. Pers., *311* 312–403 text Shrew, *404* blk.

Pagination: 323 unpaged.

Press-figures: F8ᵛ(136)–2, H7(181)–2, I7(205)–2, N8(303)–2, O7(325)–2, Q7(373)–2.

Catchwords: not checked.

Explicit: 403 Eɴᴅ ᴏꜰ ᴛʜᴇ Tʜɪʀᴅ Vᴏʟᴜᴍᴇ.

IV. π² A–P¹² Q⁴, ($5 (–Q3,4) signed; 'Vᴏʟ. IV.' on $1 (+π1)), 186 leaves.

Pp. π1 ½t (as vol. 3), π1ᵛ blk, π2 t. (as **b** . . . the FOURTH. | CONTAIN-ING, | The COMEDY of ERRORS. | MUCH ADO about NOTHING. | ALL's WELL, that ENDS WELL. | The LIFE and DEATH of KING JOHN. | [double rule] | . . . [as vol. 3] . . . Mɪᴛᴄʜᴇʟʟ, and J. Wɪʟʟɪᴀᴍs. . . . &c., π2ᵛ blk, on A1 *1* ½t Comedy of Errors, *2* Dram. Pers., *3* 4–64 text Errors, *65* ½t Much Ado, *66* Dram. Pers., *67* 68–158 text Much Ado, *159* ½t All's Well, *160* Dram. Pers., *161* 162–273 text All's Well, *274* Epilogue, *275* ½t King John, *276* Dram. Pers., *277* 278–368 text King John.

Pagination: no errors; *Press-figures*: none; *Catchwords*: not checked.

Explicit: 368 The Eɴᴅ of the Fᴏᴜʀᴛʜ Vᴏʟᴜᴍᴇ.

V. *A*² B–O¹² P⁸, ($5 (–P5) signed; 'Vᴏʟ. V.' on $1 (+A1; I1 as 'Vᴏʟ III.')), 166 leaves.

Pp. A1 ½t (as vol. 3), A1ᵛ blk, A2 t. (as **b** . . . the FIFTH. | CONTAINING, | KING RICHARD II. | THE FIRST PART OF KING HENRY IV. | THE SECOND PART OF KING HENRY IV. | [double rule] | . . . Printed for . . . Mɪᴛᴄʜᴇʟʟ, J. Wɪʟʟɪᴀᴍs. . . . &c.), A2ᵛ blk, on B1 *1* ½t Richard II., *2*

Dram. Pers., *3* 4–95 text Richard II., *96* blk, *97* ½t 1 Henry IV., *98* Dram. Pers., *99* 100–210 text 1 Henry IV., *211* ½t 2 Henry IV., *212* Dram. Pers., *213* 214–327 text 2 Henry IV., *328* Epilogue.

Pagination: no errors; *Press-figures*: none; *Catchwords*: not checked.
Explicit: 328 End of the FIFTH VOLUME.

VI. π² A–S¹² T², ($5 (–Q5, T2) signed; 'Vᴏʟ. VI.'on $1 (+π1)), 220 leaves.
Pp. π1 ½t (as vol. 3), π1ᵛ blk, π2 t. (vol. 6 as **b** . . . the SIXTH, | CONTAINING, | KING HENRY V. | THE FIRST PART OF KING HENRY VI. | THE SECOND PART OF KING HENRY VI. | THE THIRD PART OF KING HENRY VI. | [double rule] . . . &c.), π2ᵛ blk, on A1 *1* ½t Henry V., *2* Dram. Pers., *3–4* Prologue, *5* 6–125 text Henry V., *126* blk, *127* ½t 1 Henry VI., *128* Dram. Pers., *129* 130–220 text 1 Henry VI., *221* ½t 2 Henry VI., *222* Dram. Pers., *223* 224–327 text 2 Henry VI., *328* blk, *329* ½t 3 Henry VI., *330* Dram. Pers., *331* 332–435 text 3 Henry VI., *436* blk.

Pagination: no errors; *Press-figures*: none; *Catchwords*: not checked.
Explicit: none.

VII. π1 A–R¹² S⁸, ($5 signed; 'Vᴏʟ. VII.' on $1), 213 leaves.
Pp. π1 t. (as **b** . . . the SEVENTH, | CONTAINING, | The LIFE and DEATH of RICHARD the THIRD. | The LIFE of KING HENRY the EIGHTH. | The LIFE and DEATH of KING LEAR. | [double rule] . . . &c.), π1ᵛ blk, on A1 *1* ½t Richard III., *2* Dram. Pers., *3* 4–137 text Richard III (with notes), *138* blk, *139* ½t Henry VIII., *140* blk, *141–2* Dram. Pers., *143–4* Prologue, *145* 146–256 text Henry VIII., *257–258* Epilogue, *259* ½t King Lear, *260* blk, *261–262* Dram. Pers., *263* 264–416 text Lear, 417–23 Observations, *424* blk.

Pagination: no errors; *Press-figures*: none; *Catchwords*: not checked.
Explicit: 423 END ᴏғ ᴛʜᴇ SEVENTH VOLUME.

VIII. π1 A–R¹² S¹⁰ (S10 blk), ($5 (+S5) signed; 'Vᴏʟ. VIII.' on $1), 215 leaves.
Pp. π1 t. (vol. 8 . . . the EIGHTH, | CONTAINING, | TIMON OF ATHENS. | TITUS ANDRONICUS. | MACBETH. | C. MARCIUS CORIOLANUS. | [double rule] . . .), π1ᵛ blk, on A1 *1* ½t Timon of Athens, *2* Dram. Pers., *3* 4–104 text Timon, *105* ½t Titus Andronicus, *106* Dram. Pers., *107* 108–83 text Titus, *184* blk, *185* ½t Macbeth, *186* Dram. Pers., *187* 188–293 text Macbeth, *294* blk, *295* ½t C. Marcius Coriolanus, *296* Dram. Pers., *297* 298–426 text Coriolanus, *427–28* (S10) blk leaf.

Pagination: 159 as 195.
Press-figures: none; *Catchwords*: not checked.
Explicit: 426 The Eɴᴅ of the Eɪɢʜᴛʜ Vᴏʟᴜᴍᴇ.

IX. π² A–X¹² Y⁶ (Y6 blk), ($5 (–Y4,5) signed; 'Vᴏʟ. IX.' on $1 (+ π1)), 260 leaves.

Pp. π1 ½t: THE | PLAYS | OF | WILLIAM SHAKESPEARE., π1ᵛ blk, π2 t. (as **b**. . . . the NINTH. | CONTAINING, | JULIUS CÆSAR. | ANTONY AND CLEOPATRA. | CYMBELINE. | TROILUS AND CRESSIDA. | [double rule] . . . &c.), π2ᵛ blk, on A1 *1* ½t Julius Cæsar, *2* Dram. Pers., *3* 4–93 text Cæsar, *94* blk, *95* ½t Antony and Cleopatra, *96* Dram. Pers., *97* 98–236 text Antony and Cleopatra, *237* ½t Cymbeline, *238* Dram. Pers., *239* 240–376 text Cymbeline, *377* Collins's verses, *378* blk, *379* ½t Troilus and Cressida, *380–81* Prologue, *382* Dram. Pers., *383* 384–514 text Troilus and Cressida, *515–16* (Y6) blk leaf.

Pagination: 496 as 494.

Press-figures: none; *Catchwords*: not checked.

Explicit: 514 The END of the NINTH VOLUME.

X. π1 A–S¹² T⁴ (T4 blk), ($5 (–T3,4) signed; 'VOL. X.' on $1), 221 leaves.

Pp. π1 t. (as **b** . . . the TENTH. | CONTAINING, | ROMEO and JULIET. | HAMLET, PRINCE of DENMARK. | OTHELLO, the MOOR of VENICE. | [double rule] . . . &c.), π1ᵛ blk, on A1 *1* ½t Romeo and Juliet, *2* blk, *3* Prologue, *4* Dram. Pers., *5* 6–111 text Romeo and Juliet, *112* blk, *113* ½t Hamlet, Prince of Denmark, *114* Dram. Pers., *115* 116–287 text Hamlet, *288* blk, *289* ½t Othello, *290* Dram. Pers., *291* 292–433 text Othello, *434* blk, *435–38* APPENDIX TO VOL. X., *439–40* (T4) blk leaf.

Pagination: no errors; *Press-figures*: none; *Catchwords*: not checked.

Explicit: none.

Paper: White, laid; Grand cornet (uncut: 6⅔ × 3¾ in.); wmk.: R R | E F BABOUIN.

Type: Text: long primer (3.2 mm), footnotes: brevier (2.6 mm).

References: Courtney 108; Jaggard 501; Cole *Irish Booksellers* (1986) 93–4, 243; ESTC: t042453.

Notes: Published November 1766, at £1. 12s. 6d., and announced in Sleater's *Dublin Gazetteer*, 13 Dec. 1766, claiming improvements over the London edns.

Copies: NIC ('Kane O'Hara');

USA: MB (imperfect), [Liebert], NjP; *UK*: L (011768. ff.3).

65.10SP/4   Shakespeare, Woodfall   1768

[½t] THE | PLAYS | OF | WILLIAM SHAKESPEARE.

[Gen. t.] THE | PLAYS | OF | WILLIAM SHAKESPEARE, | IN EIGHT VOLUMES, | WITH THE | CORRECTIONS and ILLUSTRATIONS | OF | various COMMENTATORS; | to which are added | NOTES by SAM. JOHNSON. | [double rule] | LONDON: | Printed for H. Woodfall, C. Bathurſt, J. Beecroft, W. Strahan, | J. and F. Rivington, J. Hinton, Davis and Reymers, R. Bald- | win, Hawes, Clarke and Collins, R.

Horffield, W. Johnfton, | W. Owen, T. Caflon, T. Longman, E. and C. Dilly, C. Cor- | bett, T. Cadell, E. Johnfon, B. White, G. Keith, J. Hardy, | T. Lowndes, T. Davies, J. Robfon, T. Becket, F. Newbery, | and Robinfon and Roberts. M,DCC,LXVIII.

Var: II. Printed *for* H. Woodfall, C. Bathurft, J. Beecroft, W. Strahan, | J. *and* F. Rivington, J. Hinton, Davis *and* Reymers, . . . Clarke *and* Collins, . . . E. *and* C. Dilly, . . . T. Beckett, . . . | *and* Robinfon *and* Roberts. | M DCC LXVIII.

8 vols., 8°

I. A⁸ a–k⁸ B–2H⁸ 2I⁴, ($4 (–A1,2, 2I3,4) signed; 'Vol. I.' on $1), 332 leaves.

Pp. Engr. front. + A1 *i* t., A1ᵛ blk, A2 *iii* t. (vol. 1), *iv* blk, on B1 pp. v–clxxv Prefaces, *clxxvi* blk, *1* ½t Tempest, *2* Dram. Pers., *3* 4–85 text The Tempest, *86* blk, *87* ½t Midsummer Night's Dream, *88* Dram. Pers., *89* 90–176 text Midsummer Night's Dream, *177* ½t Two Gentlemen of Verona, *178* Dram. Pers., *179* 180–259 text Two Gent., *260* blk, *261* ½t Measure for Measure, *262* Dram. Pers., *263* 264–382 text Measure for Measure, *383* ½t Merchant of Venice, *384* Dram. Pers., *385* 386–488 text Merchant.

Pagination: [↑] v, xciv, cxxiv, cxxviii, cxlv, clxvi, clxxii, clxxiv, clxxv; unpaged lxxiii, lxxv, lxxvii, clxv, clxvii, clxxiii; blks. clxxvi, 260; xxxvii as xxxv, 368 [*sometimes*] as 3ₐ8.

Press-figures: A5ᵛ(x)–4, A8ᵛ(xvi)–9, a8(xxxi)–1, a8ᵛ(xxxii)–2, b7(xlv)–8, b7ᵛ(xlvi)–1, c6(lix)–7, d7ᵛ(lxxviii)–3, e8(xcv)–5, f1ᵛ(xcviii), g1ᵛ(cxiv)–4, h2ᵛ(cxxxii)–5, h8(cxliii)–3, i3ᵛ(cl)–4, k4ᵛ(clxviii)–9, k5ᵛ(clxx)–2, B7ᵛ(14)–1, B8ᵛ(16)–2, C2ᵛ(20)–6, C7ᵛ(30)–4, D7ᵛ(46)–2, E7ᵛ(62)–1, E8ᵛ(64)–2, F1ᵛ(66)–1, G8(95)–3, H1ᵛ(98)–9, I7ᵛ(126)–8, K3ᵛ(134)–5, L1ᵛ(146)–6, M3ᵛ(166)–7, M4ᵛ(168)–4, N5ᵛ(186)–8, O7ᵛ(206)–5, P7(221)–2, Q1ᵛ(226)–4, Q2ᵛ(228)–1, R7(253)–2, S5ᵛ(266)–2, S6ᵛ(268)–7, T1ᵛ(274)–9, U7(301)–5, X5ᵛ(314)–8, Y8(335)–2, Z5ᵛ(346)–4, 2A7ᵛ(366)–4, 2B5ᵛ(378)–6, 2B6ᵛ(380)–3, 2C8(399)–6, 2D5(409)–3, 2D5ᵛ(410)–5, 2E8(431)–5, 2F8ᵛ(448)–1, 2G7ᵛ(462)–4, 2G8ᵛ(464)–3, 2H1ᵛ(466)–5, 2H4ᵛ(472)–3; unfigured 2I.

Catchwords: om. A1–2, clxxvi, 1–2, 86–8, 177–8, 260–2, 383; superior figg. *om*. pp. 63, 107, 442; vii *om*. (is), lviii enduredₐ (∼.), lxxii *om*. (TO), lxxiv *om*. (THE), lxxvi *om*. (Mʀ.), xciii *om*. (Mr.), cxxvii *om*. (Dr.), cxlii [*pro*-] "*prietaₐ* ("*prietas*), clxxi *om*. (*Tò*), clxxii *om*. (TO), 100 a merryₐ (∼ ∼,), 108 n. *Didʃt* (*Did'ʃt*), 155 Butₐ (∼,), 155 n. *Fancy*. (∼ₐ), 276 An (And), 286 Sirₐ (∼,), 372 n. it, (∼ₐ), 388 Whichₐ (∼,), 465 ₐ*Anthonio*, (—*Anthonio*,).

Explicit: 488 The End of the First Volume.

II. A² B–2N⁸ (2N8 blk), ($4 signed; 'Vol. II.' on $1), 282 leaves.

Pp. A1 *i* ½t: THE | PLAYS | OF | WILLIAM SHAKESPEARE., *ii* blk, *iii* t. vol. 2 (var. imprint, as above), *iv* blk, on B1 *1* ½t As You Like It, *2* Dram. Pers., *3* 4–108 text AYLI, *109* ½t Love's Labour's Lost, *110* Dram. Pers., *111* 112–229 text LLL, *230* blk, *231* ½t Winter's Tale, *232* Dram. Pers., *233*

234–349 text WT, *350* blk, *351* ½t Twelfth Night, *352* Dram. Pers., *353* 354–448 text TN, *449* ½t Merry Wives of Windsor, *450* Dram. Pers., *451* 452–557 text MWW, *558* blk, *559–60* (2N8) blk leaf.

Pagination: blk. ii, iv, 230, 350, 558–60; 199 as 1, 339 as 3ʌ9, 377 as 37, 478 as 78;

Press-figures: D8(47)–7, E4ᵛ(56)–7, E8(63)–4, Y1ᵛ(322)–1, Y4ᵛ(328)–7, 2A2ᵛ(356)–7, 2A7ᵛ(366)–2, 2B4ᵛ(376)–8, 2E2ᵛ(420)–1, 2G3ᵛ(454)–1, 2N1ᵛ(546)–1, 2N2ᵛ(548)–7.

Catchwords: *om.* i–iv, 1–2, 110, 230–2, 350–1, 449–50; superior figg. *om.* 83, 354, 371, 372; 117 n. *om.* (his), 170 a candleʌ (~ ~,), 176 n. read, (~ʌ), 199 He (*Biron.*), 288 n. mannerʌ (~,), 367 n. howeverʌ (~,), 413 ʌput (—put), 552 Fordʌ (~.).

Explicit: 557 The END of the SECOND VOLUME.

III. *A²* B–2I⁸ 2K⁴, ($4 (–2K3,4) signed; 'VOL. III.' on $1), 254 leaves.

Pp. A1 *i* ½t, *ii* blk, *iii* t. (vol. 3), *iv* blk, on B1 *1* ½t Taming of the Shrew, *2* Dram. Pers., *3* 4–99 text ToS, *100* blk, *101* ½t Comedy of Errors, *102* Dram. Pers., *103* 104–70 text CoE, *171* ½t Much Ado, *172* Dram. Pers., *173* 174–273 text M Ado, *274* blk, *275* ½t All's Well, *276* Dram. Pers., *277* 278–398 text All's Well, *399* Epilogue, *400* blk, *401* ½t K. John, *402* Dram. Pers., *403* 404–504 text K. John.

Pagination: blk: 100, 274, 400; unpaged 15, 399; 54 as 64, 60 as 90, 151 as 15, 453 as 45.

Press-figures: H8(111)–3, P3ᵛ(214)–3, 2D8(415)–4, 2F7(445)–4, 2I1ᵛ(482)–1, 2K2ᵛ(500)–3, 2K4(503)–4.

Catchwords: *om.* i–iv, 1, 100–1, 171, 274–5, 400–1; superior figg. *om.* pp. 287, 297, 408; 38 *om.* (Signior), 74 O mercyʌ (~ ~,), 81 a rabbetʌ (~ ~;), 84 An (And), 130 n. *A* (*An*), 131 n. (*not*ʌ) ((~,)), 172 MUCH (MUCH), 222 n. *om.* (is), 229 *Beat*ʌ (~.), 262 punifhʌ (punifhment;), 276 ALL's (ALL's), 353 which (Which), 386 Th (The), 402 ʌTHE ('The), 437 AC (ACT).

Explicit: 504 The END of the THIRD VOLUME.

IV. *A²* B–2P⁸ (2P8 blk), ($4 signed; 'VOL. IV.' on $1), 298 leaves.

Pp. A1 *i* ½t, *ii* blk, *iii* t., *iv* blk, on B1 *1* ½t Richard II, *2* Dram. Pers., *3* 4–105 text Richard II, *106* blk, *107* ½t 1 Henry IV, *108* Dram. Pers., *109* 110–230 text 1 Henry IV, *231* ½t 2 Henry IV, *232* Dram. Pers., *233–4* Induction, *235* 236–356 text 2 Henry IV, *357–8* Epilogue, *359* ½t Henry V, *360* Dram. Pers., *361–2* Prologue, *363* 364–487 text Henry V, *488* blk, *489* ½t 1 Henry VI, *490* Dram. Pers., *491* 492–589 text 1 Henry VI, *590* blk, *591–2* (2P8) blk leaf.

Pagination: no errors.

Press-figures: D8ᵛ(48)–6, E8(63)–4, F4ᵛ(72)–2, G5(89)–4, H8ᵛ(112)–6, I1ᵛ(114)–6, L6ᵛ(156)–6, M8(175)–6, O7ᵛ(206)–3, P5ᵛ(218)–3, P8ᵛ(224)–1, R8(255)–3, U1ᵛ(290)–4, X5ᵛ(314)–6, 2A6(363)–2, 2B1ᵛ(370)–2, 2C1ᵛ(386)–2,

2E8^v(432)–6, 2F1^v(434)–3, 2G4^v(456)–3, 2G7^v(462)–3, 2H1^v(466)–3, 2I1^v(482)–2, 2M3^v(534)–3, 2O1^v(562)–1.

Catchwords: *om.* i–iv, 1–2, 106–8, 231–2, 359–60, 488–9; superior figg. *om.* 48–83, 125, 179, 209, 219, 234, 307, 362, 381, 382, 388, 391, 403, 413, 491; 8 The (I am), 20 ſhorten (Shorten), 64 Then (Than), 84 Thou# (~₌), 119 n. an (obſervation), 150 Bu₌ (But), 160 *Fal*₌ (~.), 320 courage₌ (~;), 375 Others₌ (~,), 453 Except₌ (~,), 531 —Well₌ (—Well;).

Explicit: 589 The END of the FOURTH VOLUME.

V. *A*² B–2I⁸ (2I8 blk), ($4 signed; 'Vᴏʟ. V.' on $1), 250 leaves.

Pp. A1 *i* ½t, *ii* blk, *iii* t., *iv* blk, on B1 *1* ½t 2 Henry VI, *2* Dram. Pers. *3* 4–115 text 2 Henry VI, *116* blk, *117* ½t 3 Henry VI, *118* Dram. Pers., *119* 120–225 text 3 Henry VI, *226* blk, *227* ½t Richard III, *228* Dram. Pers., *229* 230–368 text Richard III, *369* ½t Henry VIII, *370* blk, *371–2* Dram. Pers., *373–4* Prologue, *375* 376–491 text Henry VIII, *492* 493 Epilogue, *494* blk, *495–6* (2I8) blk leaf.

Pagination: blk: 116, 226, 370, 494–6; 85 as 58, 189 as 18, 298 as 299, 299 as 298 (298–9 ↖), 380 as 0;

Press-figures: B8(15)–3, D8^v(48)–3, E5^v(58)–2, F7^v(78)–2, G6(91)–2, G7(93)–3, H1^v(98)–5 [*inverted*], H6^v(108)–2, I7(125)–2, I8(127)–3, K5^v(138)–2, K8^v(144)–3, L3^v(150)–3, L7(157)–2, M8(175)–2, N8(191)–2, O8(207)–2, P1^v(210)–3, Q2^v(228)–2, Q8(239)–3, R1^v(242)–2, R2^v(244)–3, S8(271)–2, T2^v(276)–4, T6(283)–3, U6(299)–2, X8(319)–4, Y1^v(322)–2, Z3^v(342)–4, 2A8(367)–1, 2B5^v(378)–4, 2C1^v(386)–3, 2D1^v(402)–3, 2E1^v(418)–3, 2E5(425)–4, 2F8(447)–4, 2G3^v(454)–3, 2H3^v(470)–4, 2I3^v(486)–4; unfigured C.

Catchwords: *om.* i–iv, 1–2, 116–18, 226, 228, 369–70; superior figg. *om.* 68, 140, 181, 211, 229, 246, 249, 283, 315, 347, 381, 385, 387, 390, 461; 90 More- (Morever [!]), 119 whereat (Whereat), 135 A (And), 144 oft (Oft), 170 *No*; (~,), 191 ₌*Watch*. (3 ~.), 209 And₌ (~,), 239 *Nor* (~₌), 266 *Thus*₌ (~,), 426 *King*₌ (~.), 433 offers, (Offers,), 471 *King*₌ (~.), 486 I muſt (I miſt).

Explicit: 493 The END of the FIFTH VOLUME.

VI. *A*² B–2R⁸ 2S², ($4 (–2S2) signed; 'Vᴏʟ. VI.' on $1), 316 leaves.

Pp. A1 *i* ½t, *ii* blk, *iii* t., *iv* blk, on B1 *1* ½t King Lear, *2* Dram. Pers., *3* 4–163 text Lear, *164* blk, *165* ½t Timon of Athens, *166* Dram. Pers., *167* 168–276 text Timon, *277* ½t Titus Andronicus, *278* Dram. Pers., *279* 280–365 text Titus, *366* blk, *367* ½t Macbeth, *368* Dram. Pers., *369* 370–484 text Macbeth, *485* ½t C. Marcius Coriolanus, *486* Dram. Pers., *487* 488–627 text Coriolanus, *628* blk.

Pagination: no errors; blk: 164, 367, 628.

Press-figures: B6(11)–1, B8^v(16)–4, C2(19)–3, C7(29)–3, D5(41)–5, D6(43)–2, E3^v(54)–4, E6^v(60)–4, F7^v(78)–2, F8^v(80)–2, G6^v(92)–3, G7^v(94)–3, H4^v(104)–4, H8(111)–4, I7(125)–1, I7^v(136)–4, K6(139)2,

K7(141)–4, L6(155)–5, L8ᵛ(160)–1, M7ᵛ(174)–5, M8ᵛ(176)–5, N1ᵛ(178)–3, N6ᵛ(188)–3, O7(205)–4, O8(207)–2, P1ᵛ(210)–3, P7(221)–3, Q5ᵛ(234)–3, Q7(237)–4, R1ᵛ(242)–3, R8ᵛ(256)–4, S1ᵛ(258)–5, S8ᵛ(272)–2, T4ᵛ(280)–4, T6(283)–4, U4ᵛ(296)–3, U7ᵛ(302)–4, X8(319)–4, X8ᵛ(320)–4, Y7(333)–4, Y7ᵛ(334)–4, Z2ᵛ(340)–4, Z6(347)–2, 2A5ᵛ(362)–1, 2B5(377)–2, 2B6(379)–5, 2C3(389)–4, 2C5ᵛ(394)–5, 2D3ᵛ(406)–4, 2D7(413)–4, 2E2ᵛ(420)–5, 2E5ᵛ(426)–5, 2F6(443)–1, 2F7(445)–2, 2G4ᵛ(456)–5, 2G7ᵛ(462)–5, 2H7(477)–4, 2H7ᵛ(478)–4, 2I5(489)–2, 2I8(495)–5, 2K5(505)–2, 2K5ᵛ(506)–4, 2L6ᵛ(524)–4, 2L8(527)–4, 2M5(537)–4, 2M5ᵛ(538)–4, 2N7ᵛ(558)–4, 2N8ᵛ(560)–5, 2O5ᵛ(570)–4, 2O6ᵛ(572)–2, 2P6ᵛ(588)–2, 2P8(591)–2, 2Q5ᵛ(602)–2, 2Q8ᵛ(608)–4, 2R6ᵛ(620)–5, 2R8(623)–5.

Catchwords: *om.* i–iv, 1, 164–66, 277–78, 366–68, 485; superior figg. *om.* 18, 54, 60, 96, 112, 113, 146, 170, 180, 217, 237, 300, 320, 324, 343, 356, 374, 378, 385, 394, 405, 408, 415, 519, 522, 581, 583; 29 n. reſtored (ſtored), 63 And (and), 235 Baſeₐ (~,), 270 Be (Beſides), 424 n. [de-] vil, (~ₐ), 452 *Macb.* (~,), 473 ₐ Come, (—Come,), 497 *Bru* (~.), 579 ₐ *Sic.* (4. ~.).

Explicit: 627 The END of the SIXTH VOLUME.

VII. *A*² B–2M⁸ 2N², ($4 (–2N2) signed; 'VOL. VII.' on $1), 276 leaves.

Pp. A1 *i* ½t, *ii* blk, *iii* t., *iv* blk, on B1 *1* ½t Julius Cæsar, *2* Dram. Pers., *3* 4–102 text J Cæsar, *103* ½t Antony and Cleopatra, *104* Dram. Pers., *105* 106–254 text Antony and Cleopatra, *255* ½t Cymbeline, *256* Dram. Pers. *257* 258–404 text Cymbeline, *405* ½t Troilus and Cressida, *406–7* Prologue, *408* Dram. Pers., *409* 410–547 text Troilus and Cressida, *548* blk.

Pagination: blk: 548.

Press-figures: B7(14)–1, C4ᵛ(24)–4, C6(27)–1, D7ᵛ(46)–2, E5ᵛ(58)–4, F8(79)–4, G1ᵛ(82)–4, H7ᵛ(110)–1, I2ᵛ(116)–3, K7(141)–4, K8(143)–4, L1ᵛ(146)–4, M2ᵛ(164)–4, N1ᵛ(178)–3, O6(203)–4, P6(219)–4, Q5ᵛ(234)–5, Q8ᵛ(240)–3, R6(251)–2, R6ᵛ(252)–3, S6ᵛ(268)–5, T1ᵛ(274)–4, T6ᵛ(284)–1, U4ᵛ(296)–5, U6(299)–4, X1ᵛ(306)–4, Y3ᵛ(326)–5, Z2ᵛ(340)–1, 2A7ᵛ(366)–1, 2B7ᵛ(382)–4, 2B8ᵛ(384)–5, 2C4ᵛ(392)–1, 2C8(399)–4, 2D7ᵛ(414)–5, 2D8ᵛ(416)–1, 2E2ᵛ(420)–3, 2F2ᵛ(436)–3, 2G1ᵛ(450)–5, 2G7(461)–1, 2H1ᵛ(466)–4, 2H5(473)–3, 2K7(509)–3, 2K8(511)–1, 2L3ᵛ(518)–5, 2L7(525)–1, 2M4ᵛ(536)–3, 2M5ᵛ(538)–1; unfigured 2I.

Catchwords: *om.* i–iv, 103–4, 255–6, 405, 408; superior figg. *om.* 47, 105, 109, 111, 136, 154, 196, 219, 227, 242, 300, 352, 453, 467, 485, 490, 503, 504; 32 n. *Calphurnia* (*Caliphurnia*), 428 And, (~ₐ), 452 *om.* (There's), 480 *om.* (*Neſt.*), 493n herₐ (~.).

Explicit: 547 The END of the SEVENTH VOLUME.

VIII. *A*² B–2L⁸, ($4 signed; 'VOL. VIII.' on $1), 266 leaves.

Pp. A1 *i* ½t, *ii* blk, *iii* t., *iv* blk, on B1 *1* ½t Romeo and Juliet, *2* blk, *3* Prologue, *4* Dram. Pers., *5* 6–126 text Romeo and Juliet, *127* ½t Hamlet, Prince of Denmark, *128* Dram. Pers., *129* 130–316 text Hamlet, *317* ½t

Othello, the Moor of Venice, *318* Dram. Pers., *319* 320–473 text Othello, *474* blk, on 2H6–2L8 (27 leaves unpaged) Appendix, 2L8ᵛ blk.

Pagination: blk: 2, 126, 474; unpaged Appendix; 49 as 64.

Press-figures: B4ᵛ(8)–2, C1ᵛ(18)–2, D6(43)–4, E8ᵛ(64)–1, F1ᵛ(66)–4, G7(93)–4, H3ᵛ(102)–2, I7(125)–2, K7ᵛ(142)–3, L5ᵛ(154)–4, M7ᵛ(174)–2, N8(191)–3, O5ᵛ(202)–2, P8(223)–2, Q3ᵛ(230)–3, R1ᵛ(242)–2, S8(271)–2, T8(287)–3, U8ᵛ(304)–2, X8ᵛ(320)–4, Y8ᵛ(336)–3, Z7ᵛ(350)–3, 2A6(363)–3, 2B4ᵛ(376)–2, 2D4ᵛ(408)–2, 2E5ᵛ(426)–2, 2F2ᵛ(436)–3, 2G7(461)–2, 2H2ᵛ(468)–2, 2I2ᵛ–4, 2K5ᵛ–1, 2L6–4; unfigured 2C.

Catchwords: *om*. i–iv, 1–2, 4, 126–8, 317, 474; superior figg. *om*. 53, 71, 94, 104, 108, 116, 135, 136, 155, 177, 207, 230, 231, 233, 260, 264, 267, 294, 318, 341, 345, 387, 392; 68 Leap, (~ₐ), 115 *Rom*. (~ₐ), 131 *Hor*ₐ (~.), 268 *Horatio*, (~ₐ), 428 *Caf*ₐ (~.), 460 *Æmil* (~.), 2I4 *om*. (P. 312), 2I8ᵛ *domus*, (~ₐ).

Explicit: none.

Paper: White, laid; Demy (uncut: 8½ × 5½ in.); wmk.: fleur-de-lys.

Type: Pref. matter and text: pica (4.0 mm) (SJ's 'Preface' is leaded), nn. and appendix: long primer (3.0 mm).

Plate: Some copies have engr. port. Shakespeare as front. from 1765 edns. (65.10SP/1 or SP/2, above), but the plate seems only an accidental part of this edn.

References: Courtney 108; Jaggard 502; ESTC: t138862.

Notes: Vol. 1 was printed by William Strahan in 750 copies in August 1768 (L: Add. MS 48802B, fo. 25ᵛ). The identity of the other printers is not yet discovered. The enlarged partnership is partly the result of the death of Tonson in 1767, and the consequent sale of his shares, 18 August 1767.

Copies: O (Mal. adds. 50 e. 27–34);

USA: CtY, IU, [Liebert], MB, NjP; *Japan*: [Kyoto]; *UK*: AWn, BAT, Ct, LCu, L (81. c. 20–7), LEu, SHp, SPAg; *Aust*: CNL (DNS 6915).

65.10SP/5   Shakespeare, Dublin   1771

[Engr. t.] [Within a scrolled border] *The* PLAYS *of* | SHAKESPEARE, | *From the* TEXT *OF* | *Dr. S. JOHNSON.* | *With the* Prefaces, Notes *&c: of* | ROWE, POPE, THEOBALD, HANMER, | WARBURTON. JOHNSON. | *And select* Notes *from many other* | CRITICS. | *Alſo the* Introduction *of the laſt Editor* | MR. CAPELL; | *And a* Table *ſhewing his* Various Readings. | VOL. I PART. I [– VI PART II]. | [cartouche and scrolls] | THOMAS EWING. | DUBLIN. 1771.

6 vols. in 12 parts, 8°

I.i. π² a–n⁸ o⁸ (–o6,7,8), B⁸ (± B2), C–H⁸ I⁸ (± I8) K⁸ L⁸ (–L7 = ³D1), ²A–D⁸, ³B⁸ ³C⁴ ³D1 (=L7), ³A⁴, ($4/2 (²D4 as A, ³A *may be unsigned*) signed; 'VOL. I.' on $1), 239 leaves.

Pp. Engr. front. port. of Shakespeare, & t. + π1–1ᵛ Advertisement, π2 Contents, π2ᵛ blk, on a1 *i* ii–lvi SJ's Preface dh: DR. SAMUEL JOHNSON's | PREFACE., ht: PREFACE., *lvii*–lviii Players' Dedication to F1, *lix*–lx Players' Preface to F1, *lxi* lxii–lxxviii Pope's Preface, *lxxix* lxxx–cix Theobald's Preface, *cx* cxi–cxiii Hanmer's Preface, *cxiv* cxv–cxxx Warburton's Preface, *cxxxi* cxxxii–clxxvi Capell's Introduction, *clxxvii* clxxviii–clxxx Table of Quartos, *clxxxi* clxxxii–cci Rowe's Life of Shakespeare, *ccii*–cciii Grant of Arms, *cciv* ccv–ccviii Shakespeare's Will, ccix Horse-holding anecdote, *ccx* ccxi–ccxviii Dedicatory verses, on B1 *1* ½t Tempest, *2* Dram. Pers., *3* 4–81 text Tempest, *82* blk, *83* ½t Midsummer Night's Dream, *84* Dram. Pers., *85* 86–158 text MND, on ²A1 *1* 2–54 Notes on the Tempest, on ²D4 (miss. 'A') *1* 2–35 Notes on MND, *36* blk, on ³A1 *1–8* Textual variants between Johnson and Capell, and errata.

Pagination: blk. 82 (G1ᵛ), 36 (³D1ᵛ);

Press-figures: none;   *Catchwords*: none; *Explicit*: none.

I.ii. π⁴ (± π1, –π2,3,4), M⁸ (± M1) N–P⁸ Q⁸ (± Q8) R⁸ S⁸(± S1) T⁸ (± T5), U⁸ X⁸ (± X6,7), Y⁸ Z⁸ (± Z6,7), 2A⁸ (–2A8 + *1), 2B⁸ (± 2B3), 2C⁸ (± 2C8), 2D⁸ (± 2D7), 2E–2F⁸ 2G⁸ (± 2G6) 2H⁸ (± 2H6,7) 2I⁸ (± 2I1) 2K⁸ 2L⁸ (± 2L2), B⁸ A⁸, ²B–C⁸ ²A⁸ ³C⁸ ³B⁸ ⁴C² ³A⁴, ($4 (²A1 as D, ²A2 as A, ³C4 as A) signed; 'Vol.I.' on $1 (M–2L), 'Vol. I. Part. II.' on $1 (B–³A)), 247 leaves.

Pp. blk and engr. t. + π1 *159* ½t Two Gentlemen of Verona, *160* Dram. Pers., on M1 *161* 162–236 text Two Gent., *237* ½t Measure for Measure, *238* Dram. Pers., *239* 240–333 text Measure for Measure, *334* blk, *335* ½t Merchant of Venice, *336* Dram. Pers., *337* 338–423 text Merchant, *424* blk, *425* ½t As You Like It, *426* Dram. Pers., *427* 428–516 text AYLI, on B1 *1* 2–16 Notes on Two Gent., on A1 *1* 2–50 Notes on Measure for Measure, on ²A2 *1* 2–36 Notes on Merchant, on ³C4 *1* 2–30 Notes on AYLI, on ³A1 (4 leaves unpaged) Textual var. and errata.

Pagination: blk. 334, 424; unpaged ³A⁴; 226 (1st fig. *inverted*), 245 as 145.

Press-figures: 2A8(367)–*.

Catchwords: none; *Explicit*: none.

II.i. B⁸ (± B3) C⁸ (± C6) D⁸ (± D3,5) E⁸ (± E1,3.6) F⁸ (± F5) G⁸ (± G7) H⁸ (± H8) I–K⁸ L⁸ (± L5) M⁸ (± M2) N–Q⁸ R⁸ (± R4) S⁸ T⁸ (± T4) U², ²A–F⁸ ²G⁴ ²H² ²I⁴, ($4 (B–T), $2 (²A–I) signed; 'Vol. II.' on $1), 204 leaves.

Pp. blk and engr. t. + on B1 *1* ½t Love's Labour's Lost, *2* Dram. Pers., *3* 4–96 text LLL, *97* ½t Winter's Tale, *98* Dram. Pers., *99* 100–206 text WT, *207* ½t Twelfth Night, *208* Dram. Pers., *209* 210–91 text TN, *292* blk, on ²A1 *1* 2–49 Notes on LLL, 50 blk, on ²D2 *1* 2–31 Notes on WT, *32* blk, on ²F2 *1* 2–25 Notes on TN, *26* blk, on ²I1 (8 pp.) Textual var. and errata.

Pagination: blk. 292, ²D1ᵛ (50), ²F1ᵛ (32); unpaged ²I⁴; unnumbered ²A3 (5), ²E5ᵛ (22), ²E7ᵛ (2*).

Press-figures: none; *Catchwords*: none; *Explicit*: none.

II.ii. π1 U² (U2 + χ1,²χ²), X⁸ (± X2), Y⁸ (± Y5) Z–2B⁸ 2C⁸ (± 2C5,8) 2D–2M⁸, ²A² ²B–E⁸ ²F⁴ ²G⁴, ($4 (X–2M), $2 (²A–E) signed; 'Vol. II.' on $1 (U–2M), 'Vol. II. Part III.' on $1 (²A–F)), 167 leaves.

Pp. blk and engr. t. + π1 ½t Merry Wives of Windsor, π1ᵛ Dram. Pers., on U1 *295* 296–384 text MWW, *385* ½t Taming of the Shrew, *386* Dram. Pers., *387* 388–477 text ToS, *478* blk, *479* ½t Comedy of Errors, *480* Dram. Pers., *481* 482–541 text Errors, *542–44* blk, on ²A1 *1* 2–34 Notes on MWW, on ²C8 *1* 2–22 Notes on ToS, on ²E3 *1* 2–18 Notes on Errors, *19–20* blk, on ²G1 (8 pp.) Textual var. and errata.

Pagination: blk. 478, 542; 543–4 (2M8), 19–20 (²F4); 305 as 395, 333 as 335, 398 unnumbered, 496 as 596, 514 as 14.

Press-figures: none; *Catchwords*: none; *Explicit*: none.

III.i. B–G⁸ H⁸ (± H4,8) I–K⁸ L⁸ (± L2) M–P⁸ Q⁸ (± Q4) R–S⁸ T⁸ (–T6,7,8), ²A–B⁸, ³B–C⁸ ³D⁴, ⁴A⁴ ⁴B⁸ ⁴C⁴, ($4 (B–T), $2 (²A–⁴C) signed; 'Vol. III.' on $1 (B–T), 'Vol. III. Part. I.' on $1 (²A–⁴C)), 193 leaves.

Pp. blk and engr. t. + on B1 *1* ½t Much Ado, *2* Dram. Pers., *3* 4–89 text M Ado, *90* blk, *91* ½t All's Well, *92* Dram. Pers., *93* 94–188 text All's Well, *189* ½t King John, *190* Dram. Pers., *191* 192–276 275–280 [= 282; 275–6 dupl.] text K. John, on ²A1 *1* 2–24 Notes on M Ado, on ²B5 *1* 2–48 Notes on All's Well, on ⁴A1 *1* 2–28 Notes on K. John, on ²C3 (4 pp) Textual var. and errata.

Pagination: blk. 90, at N1 pp. 175–6 are duplicated; on ⁴B1ᵛ p. 10 unnumbered.

Press-figures: none; *Catchwords*: none; *Explicit*: none.

III.ii. T⁴ U⁸ (–U1,2) X–2B⁸ 2C⁸ (± 2C7) 2D⁸ 2E⁸ (± 2E6) 2F⁸ 2G⁸ (± 2G5) 2H–2M⁸ 2N⁸ (± 2N6), A⁸ B⁴, ²A⁴ B–C⁸, ³A–C⁸, ($4 (U–2N), $2 (A–³C), (T3,4 as U1,2) signed; 'Vol. III.' on $1), 194 leaves.

Pp. blk and engr. t. + on T1 *281* ½t Richard II, *282* Dram. Pers., *283* 284–350, 357–82 text R3, *383* ½t 1 Henry IV, *384* Dram. Pers., *385* 386–486 text 1 Henry IV, *487* ½t 2 Henry IV, *488* Dram. Pers., *489* 490–595 text 2 Henry IV, *596* Epilogue, on A1 *1* 2–24 Notes on Richard II, on ²A1 *1* 2–40 Notes on 1 Henry IV, on ³A1 *1* 2–36 Notes on 2 Henry IV, on ³C3 (12 pp) Textual var. and errata.

Pagination: pagination begins with 357 at 2A1, instead of 351; 491 unnumbered.

Press-figures: none; *Catchwords*: none; *Explicit*: none.

IV.i. B⁸ (± B4) C⁸ (± C3) D–E⁸ F⁸ (± F8) G⁸ (± G1) H–I⁸ K⁸ (± K5) L⁸ (± L7) M⁸ N⁸ (± N4,7) O⁸ (± O2) P⁸ Q⁸ (± Q6) R–S⁸ T⁸ (± T8) U⁸ (± U4,7) X⁸ (–X8), ²A–B⁸ ²C⁴ ²D². ³A⁸ ³B², ⁴A⁸ ⁴B² ⁴C⁴, ($4 (b–X), $2 (²A–⁴B) signed; 'Vol. IV.' on $1), 205 leaves.

Pp. blk and engr. t., + on B1 *1* ½t Henry V., *2* Dram. Pers., *3–5* 6–112 text Henry V, *113* ½t 1 Henry VI, *114* Dram. Pers., *115* 116–208 text 1 Henry VI, *209* ½t 2 Henry VI, *210* Dram. Pers., *211* 212–318 text 2 Henry VI, on ²A1 *1* 2–44 Notes on Henry V, on ³A1 *1* 2–20 Notes on 1 Henry VI, on ⁴A1 *1* 2–19 Notes on 2 Henry VI, *20* blk, on ⁴C1 (8 pp.) Textual var. and errata.

Pagination: blk. ⁴B2ᵛ, 293 as 2ᴧ3.

Press-figures: B4(7)–*, L7(77)–*, N4(103)–8.

Catchwords: none; *Explicit*: none.

IV.ii. π⁴ (–π⁴ + 2π1) Y–Z⁸ 2A⁸ (±2A3) 2B–2C⁸ 2D⁸ (± 2D2) 2E⁸ 2F⁸ (± 2F1) 2G⁸ (± 2G5) 2H–2I⁸ 2K⁸ (± 2K3) 2L⁸ 2M⁸ (± 2M1) 2N⁴ (± 2N1; 2N4 blk), A–B⁸, ²B⁸ ²C⁴ (²C4 blk), *a*⁴ b², ($4 (Y–2N), $2 (A–b; B2 as A) signed; 'Vᴏʟ. IV.' on $1), 151 leaves.

Pp. blk and engr. t., + on 2π1 *319* ½t 3 Henry VI, *320* Dram. Pers., *321* 322–422 text 3 Henry VI, *423* ½t Richard III, *424* Dram. Pers., *425* 426–549 text Richard III, *550* blk, *551–2* (2N4) blk, on A1 *1* 2–17 Notes on 3 Henry VI, *18* blk, on B2 *1* 2–36 Notes on Richard III, *37–8* (²C4) blk, on a1 (12 pp.) textual var. and errata.

Pagination: blk. 550, 551–2 (2N4), 18 (B1ᵛ), 37–8 (²C4); 333 as 334, 336 as 337.

Press-figures: none; *Catchwords*: none; *Explicit*: none.

V.i. B⁸ C⁸ (± C2,6) D⁸ (± D1) E–N⁸ O⁸ (± O6) P⁸ (± P2) Q⁸ R⁸ (± R7,8) S⁸ (± S7) T⁸ (± T5,6) U⁸ (± U6) X–Y⁸ Z⁸ (–Z1,2,3 + Z1,2,3) 2A–C⁸ 2D⁴, ²A–B⁸, ³A–G⁸, ⁴A⁴ ⁴B–D⁸ ⁴E⁴ ⁴F², *a*⁴ b⁴, ($4 (b–2C, C2, Z3 unsigned; 2D3 as 2A3), $2 (²A–b) signed; 'Vᴏʟ. V.' on $1), 315 leaves.

Pp. blk and engr. t., + on B1 *1* ½t Henry VIII, *2* Dram. Pers., *3–5* 6–113 *114* text Henry VIII, *115* ½t King Lear, *116* Dram. Pers., *117* 118–232 text K. Lear, *233* ½t Timon of Athens, *234* Dram. Pers., *235* 236–318 text Timon, on X2 *i* ½t Titus Andronicus, *ii* Dram. Pers., *iii* iv–xxiv, 319–83 text Titus, *384* blk, on ²A1 *1* 2–31 Notes on Henry VIII, *32* blk, on ³A1 *1* 2–111 Notes on Lear, *112* blk, on ⁴A1 1–49 Notes on Timon, *50* blk, on ⁴D7 1–15 Notes on Titus, *16* blk, on a1 (16 pp.) Textual var. and errata.

Pagination: blk. 384, 112 (³G8ᵛ), 50 (⁴D6ᵛ), 16 (⁴F2ᵛ); unpaged a–b⁴; unnumbered 328, 65 (³F1) as 5, 11 (⁴E4) as 1.

Press-figures: none; *Catchwords*: none; *Explicit*: none.

V.ii. π1 2π1 2D² 2E⁸ (± 2E6) 2F–2L⁸ 2M⁸ (± 2M1) 2N⁸ (± 2N3) 2O⁸ (± 2O8) 2P⁸ (± 2P4) 2Q⁸ 2R⁸ (± 2R2) 2S⁸ (± 2S6,7) 2T⁸ (± 2T4), 3A1, A–D⁸ E², ²A⁶ ²B–C⁸, ³B⁸ ³C⁶, ˣD⁴, ($4 (2D–2T, 2π1 as 2D, 2D1 as 2D2, 2C7 as A), $2 (A–D), signed; 'Vᴏʟ. V.' on $1), 197 leaves.

Pp. blk and engr. t., + on 2D1 *385* ½t Macbeth, *386* Dram. Pers., *387* 388–470 text Macbeth, *471* ½t C. Marcius Coriolanus, *472* Dram. Pers., *473* 474–599 text Coriolanus, *600* blk, *601* ½t Julius Cæsar, *602* Dram. Pers., *603*

604–90 text J. Cæsar, on C5 *1* 2–68 Notes on Macbeth, on ²C7 *1* 2–32 Notes on Coriolanus, on ˣD1 (8 pp.) Textual var. and errata.

Pagination: blk 600.

Press-figures: 2E6(401)–†, 2N3(521)–1, 2T2(615)–‡.

Catchwords: none; *Explicit*: none.

VI.i. B–F⁸ G⁸ (± G3) H–I⁸ K⁸ (± K7) L⁸ (± L8) M⁸ (± M8) N⁸ (± N2) O⁸ (± O5) P⁸ (± P2) Q–R⁸ S⁸ (± S3) T⁸ (± T6,8) U⁸ X⁸ (± X4,7) Y⁸ (± Y6) Z⁸ (± Z5,6,7) 2A⁸ (± 2A2,4) 2B², ²A–I⁸ ²K⁶ (2K6 blk), ˣL⁴, ($4 (–²G4) signed; 'VOL. VI.' on $1), 268 leaves.

Pp. blk and engr. t., + on B1 *1* ½t Antony and Cleopatra, *2* Dram. Pers., *3* 4–123 text Antony and Cleopatra, *124* blk, *125* ½t Cymbeline, *126* Dram. Pers., *127* 128–250 text Cymbeline, *251* ½t Troilus and Cressida, *252* blk, *253* Prologue, *254* Dram. Pers., *255* 256–372 text T & Cressida, on ²A1 *1* 2–58 Notes on A & C, on ²D6 1–54 Notes on Cymb., on ²H1 1–41 Notes on T & C, *42* blk, *43–4* (²K6) blk, on ˣL1 (8 pp.) Textual var. and errata.

Pagination: blk. 252, 42 (²K5ᵛ), ²K6; 238 as 239, 239 as 238.

Press-figures: K7(141)–‖, L8(159)–1, T8(287)–§, X4ᵛ(312)–1.

Catchwords: none; *Explicit*: none.

VI.ii. 2B² ²2B⁴ (± ²2B4) 2C⁸ 2D⁸ (± 2D2) 2E⁸ 2F⁸ (± 2F4) 2G–2L⁸ 2M⁸ (± 2M1,3,4) 2N⁸ 2O⁸ (± 2O7), 2P⁸ (± 2P2,4) 2Q–2S⁸ 2T⁸ (± 2T3) 2U⁸ (± 2U3) 2X⁸ (± 1X3,7) 2Y⁸ (± 2Y6) 2Z⁸ 3A⁸ 3B⁴ (3B4 blk), ²A² ²B–D⁸, ³B–G⁸, ⁴B–E⁸, a–b⁴, ²a–n⁸ o², ($4 (2B1 as Bb3, 2B2 as Bb4, ²2B1 as Bb, ²2B2 as Bb2, ²D2 as A, ³G4 as A) signed; 'VOL. VI.' on $1), 406 leaves.

Pp. blk and engr. t., + on 2B1 *373* ½t Romeo and Juliet, *374* blk, *375* Prologue, *376* Dram. Pers., *377* 378–471 text R & J, *472* blk, *473* ½t Hamlet, *474* Dram. Pers., *475* 476–610 text Hamlet, *611* ½t Othello, *612* Dram. Pers., *613* 614–732 text Othello, *733–34* (3B4) blk., on ²A1 *1* 2–37 Notes on R & J, *38* blk, on ²D2 *1* 2–99 Notes on Hamlet, *100* blk, on ³G4 *1* 2–73 Notes on Othello, *74* blk, on a1 (16 pp.) Textual var. and errata; on ²a1 *1* ½t: SHAKESPEARE's | POEMS: | CONTAINING, | 1. VENUS AND ADO-NIS. | II. THE RAPE OF LUCRECE. | III. THE PASSIONATE PIL-GRIM. | IV. SONNETS. | DUBLIN: | PRINTED BY S. POWELL FOR | THOMAS EWING. | M.DCC.LXXI., *2* blk, *3* Dedication of the *Sonnets*, *4* blk, *5* 6–313 text of Poems.

Pagination: 500 as 00, 538 as 358, 614 as 14; in 'Poems' 39–41 and 95 unnumbered, 11 as 12, 68 as 86.

Press-figures: 2O7(577)–¶, ⁴C6ᵛ(38)–2, ⁴C7ᵛ(40)–2, ⁴D3(47)–1.

Catchwords: none; *Explicit*: none.

Paper: White, laid; Pot (uncut: 6¼ × 3¾ in.); wmk.: 1764. *Cancellantia* commonly of a brownish shade and easily distinguished.

Type: Nonpareil (2.1 mm), leaded.

Plates: Same engraved design for all tt., with var. Vol. and Part numbers. Port. of Shakespeare in vol. 1.

References: Jaggard 503; Courtney 108, 110; CH 147; Cole, *Irish Booksellers* (1986), 94, 143; ESTC: t138859.

Notes: The paper, being dated, is probably French, perhaps Tellière (sheet: 15 × 12½ in.), though the dimensions are closer to the English pot.

Cole noted that the work was issued in six or twelve vols., and the signatures at least made a straightforward combination into six. Courtney reported seven vols, presumably the Poems (VI. ii) could form a separate collection.

SJ is not uniformly used. The abundant cancels reflect much *ad hoc* editorial work, as do the selections of notes and commentary. Some editor expended much labour over this edn.: it is a pity he is unidentified. It may be presumed that Samuel Powell was primarily responsible for the printing, though the irregularity of press-figures may indicate some sharing: against that is the uniform type size.[1]

Copies: O (Mal. Adds. 50, fos. 24–35, 12 vols 'Mrs Vesey', full cont. calf); *USA*: Hyde ('Jonathan Boucher' — Adam, full cont. maroon morocco), [Liebert], NjP, NN (vol. 1 only); *Can*: CaOHM (B 11785–97, in 13 vols); *UK*: C, Ct, E, L (11764. aaa.).

---

[1] M. Pollard, *Dublin's Trade in Books* (1989), 181, notes Powell as exclusively a printer.

65.10SP/6   Shakespeare, Bathurst   1773

THE | PLAYS | OF | WILLIAM SHAKESPEARE. | In TEN VOLUMES. | WITH THE | CORRECTIONS and ILLUSTRATIONS | OF | Various Commentators; | To which are added | NOTES by SAMUEL JOHNSON | AND | GEORGE STEEVENS. | With an APPENDIX. | LONDON: | Printed for C. Bathurst, J. Beecroft, W. Strahan, J. | and F. Rivington, J. Hinton, L. Davis, Hawes, Clarke | and Collins, R. Horsfield, W. Johnston, W. Owen, | T. Caslon, E. Johnson, S. Crowder, B. White, T. | Longman, B. Law, E. and C. Dilly, C. Corbett, W. | Griffin, T. Cadell, W. Woodfall, G. Keith, T. | Lowndes, T. Davies, J. Robson, T. Becket, F. New- | bery, G. Robinson, T. Payne, J. Williams, M. | Hingeston, and J. Ridley. | M DCC LXXIII.

10 vols., 8°

I. π^2 A–C^8 D^8 (± D1) E^8 *F^8 F^8 (± F1) G–N^8 ^{2}A–H^8 I^8 (± I5) K–T^8 U^4, ($4 (A–N in brackets (–G4)) signed; 'Vol. I.' on $1), 268 leaves.

Pp. Engr. front. port. + π1 t., π1^v blk, π2 ½t: THE | PLAYS | OF | WILLIAM SHAKESPEARE. | VOLUME the FIRST. | CONTAINING, | PREFACES. | The TEMPEST. | The TWO GENTLEMEN of VERONA. | The MERRY WIVES of WINDSOR. | LONDON: . . . (&c. as above), π2^v blk, on A1 dh: PREFACE., ht: PREFACE., on E2^v dh:

ADVERTISEMENT | TO | THE | READER., ht: ADVERTISEMENT to the READER., on E8 dh: ANCIENT TRANSLATIONS | FROM | CLASSIC AUTHORS., rt: ANCIENT TRANSLATIONS | FROM CLASSIC AUTHORS. (on *F6ᵛ: 'ANCIENT TRANSLATIONS, &c.'), on F1 dh: TO THE | MOST NOBLE ᴀɴᴅ INCOMPARABLE | PAIRE ᴏꜰ BRETHREN, | WILLIAM | Earle of Pᴇᴍʙʀᴏᴋᴇ, &c. Lord Chamberlaine to | the Kings moſt Excellent Majeſtie; | AND | PHILIP | Earle of Mᴏɴᴛɢᴏᴍᴇʀʏ, &c. Gentlemen of his | Majeſties Bed-Chamber. | Both Knights of the Moſt Noble Order of the | Garter, and our ſingular good LORDS., ht: THE PLAYERS DEDICATION, on F2 dh: THE | PREFACE | OF THE | PLAYERS., ht: PREFACE BY THE PLAYERS., on F3 dh: Mr. POPE's | PREFACE., ht: Mr. POPE's PREFACE., on G3ᵛ dh: Mr. THEOBALD's | PREFACE., ht: Mr. THEOBALD's PREFACE., on I2ᵛ dh: Sir T. HANMER's | PREFACE., ht: Sir T. HANMER's PREFACE, on I4ᵛ dh: Dr. WARBURTON's | PREFACE., ht: Dr. WARBURTON's PREFACE., on K5 dh: ADVERTISEMENT | TO THE | READER., ht: ADVERTISEMENT to the READER., on L3ᵛ dh: SOME | Aᴄᴄᴏᴜɴᴛ of the Lɪꜰᴇ, &c. | OF | Mr. WILLIAM SHAKESPEARE. | Written by Mr. ROWE., rt: Some ACCOUNT of the LIFE, &c. | of Mr. WILLIAM SHAKESPEARE. (on L4: 'Some ACCOUNT of the LIFE, &c.'), on M5ᵛ Grant of Arms, on M6ᵛ dh: SHAKESPEARE's WILL., ht: SHAKESPEARE's WILL., on N1 Horse-holding anecdote (signed: 'JOHNSON.'), on N1ᵛ List of Baptisms, Marriages, & Burials, &c., on N2ᵛ Commendatory Verses, on N6ᵛ dh: A LIST OF THE | OLD EDITIONS | OF | SHAKESPEARE's PLAYS., On ²A1 *1* ½t The Tempest, *2* Dram. Pers., *3* 4–99 text The Tempest, *100–1* Epilogue, *102* blk, *103* ½t Two Gentlemen, *104* Dram. Pers., *105* 106–89 text Two Gentlemen, *190* blk, *191* ½t Merry Wives, *192* Dram. Pers., *193* 194–312 text Merry Wives.

Pagination: A–N unpaged, blk 102, 190; 299 as 297, 302 as 303, 303 as 302.

Press-figures: I5(137)–3.

Catchwords: D1ᵛ [acute-] *om.* (neſſ), E4 [throw] light (throw light), *F5 ‿The (*∼), F1ᵛ *om.* (THE), N1 *om.* (†Baptiſms), N6 *om.* (A LIST), N8ᵛ *om.* (THE TEMPEST); *om.* 1–2, 3 *om.* (*Enter*), 27 *om.* (*Hark,*), 28 *om.* (*Fer.*), 29 *om.* (*Pro.*), 45 *om.* (No), 46 *om.* (*While*), 82 *om.* (*Ste.*), 102–4 *om.*, 110 n. So (again), 139 *om.* (*Speed.*), 175 I know‿ (∼,), 189–92 *om.*, 232 *om.* (*Piſt.*), 268 *om.* (*Shal.*), 285 *om.* (SCENE), 288 *om.* (And), 303 *om.* (Like).

Explicit: 312 END ᴏꜰ Vᴏʟᴜᴍᴇ ᴛʜᴇ Fɪʀsᴛ.

II. *A*² B⁸ (± B4) C–2A⁸ 2B⁸ (± 2B5) 2C⁸ (± 2C7) 2D⁸ 2E⁸ (± 2E2) 2F–2H⁸ (2H8 blk), ($4 signed; 'Vᴏʟ. II.' on $1), 242 leaves.

Pp. A1 t., A1ᵛ blk, A2 t. (vol. 2), A2ᵛ blk, on B1 *1* ½t Measure for Measure, *2* Dram. Pers., *3* 4–144 text MfM, *145* ½t Comedy of Errors, *146* Dram. Pers., *147* 148–221 text Errors, *222* blk, *223* ½t Much Ado, *224* Dram. Pers., *225*

226–337 text M Ado, *338* blk, *339* ½t Love's Labour's Lost, *340* Dram. Pers., *341* 342–477 text LLL, *478* blk, *479–80* (2H8) blk.

Pagination: no errors.

Press-figures: B8(15)–1, C6(27)–6, C6ᵛ(28)–4, D5ᵛ(42)–2, D6ᵛ(44)–4, E5(57)–2, F8(79)–2, G3ᵛ(86)–2, G4ᵛ(88)–1, H5ᵛ(106)–1, H7(109)–2, I1ᵛ(114)–1, I6ᵛ(124)–2, K7(141)–1, K8(143)–2, L7(157)–6, L8(159)–7, M5(169)–7, M7ᵛ(174)–2, N5ᵛ(186)–1, N8ᵛ(192)–2, O3ᵛ(198)–8, O4ᵛ(200)–7, P3ᵛ(214)–1, P5(217)–2, Q6(235)–1, R8(255)–6, S7(269)–1, S8(271)–2, T2ᵛ(276)–6, U5ᵛ(298)–7, U8ᵛ(304)–2, X6(315)–2, X7(317)–1, Y6(331)–6, Z3ᵛ(342)–1, Z5(345)–2, 2A6ᵛ(364)–6, 2B1ᵛ(370)–8, 2C1ᵛ(386)–1, 2C4ᵛ(392)–2, 2D7(413)–1, 2D8(415)–2, 2E6(427)–7, 2F3ᵛ(438)–1, 2G3ᵛ(454)–1, 2G8ᵛ(464)–2, 2H1ᵛ(466)–6, 2H2ᵛ(468)–2.

Catchwords: *om.* pp. A1–2, 222–3, 338; 11 I will͵ (~ ~,), 224 ᴍᴜᴄʜ (Mᴜᴄʜ), 248 *Ant͵* (~.), 258 *Pedro.* (*Podro.*), 308 *Dogb.* (*Dogh.*), 355 *Moth͵* (~.), 402 *Hol.* (very), 409 Ay, (~͵), 419 n. *he* (*the*), 434 *Boyet͵* (~.), 465 n. Mr. (Dr.).

Explicit: 488 END OF THE SECOND VOLUME.

III. *A²* B–E⁸ F⁸ (± F7,8) G–S⁸ T⁸ (± T2) U–Z⁸ 2A⁸ (± 2A2) 2B⁸ 2C⁸ (± 2C8) 2D–2F⁸ 2G⁴ (± 2G2), ($4 (−Q2, Z4, 2G3,4) signed; 'Vᴏʟ. III.' on $1), 230 leaves.

Pp. A1 t., A1ᵛ blk, A2 t. (vol. 3), A2ᵛ blk, on B1 *1* ½t Midsummer Night's Dream, *2* Dram. Pers., *3* 4–107 text MND, *108* blk, *109* ½t Merchant of Venice, *110* Dram. Pers., *111* 112–226 text MoV, *227* ½t As You Like It, *228* Dram. Pers., *229* 230–341 text AYLI, *342* blk, *343* ½t Taming of the Shrew, *344* Dram. Pers., *345* 346–456 text ToS.

Pagination: 108, 342 blk.

Press-figures: B5ᵛ(10)–1, C8(31)–2, D6ᵛ(44)–2, D7ᵛ(46)–1, E3ᵛ(54)–2, F5ᵛ(74)–1, F8(79)–2, G1ᵛ(82)–1, G7(93)–2, H8(111)–2, H8ᵛ(112)–1, I7(125)–2, K4ᵛ(136)–2, K6(139)–1, L3ᵛ(150)–1, L5(153)–2, M3ᵛ(166)–2, N6ᵛ(188)–7, N7ᵛ(190)–2, O7ᵛ(206)–2, P3ᵛ(214)–1, P5(217)–2, Q3ᵛ(230)–1, Q5(233)–2, R5(249)–2, S3ᵛ(262)–1, T4ᵛ(280)–1, U1ᵛ(290)–2, X8(319)–1, Y5ᵛ(330)–2, Z2ᵛ(340)–2, Z7ᵛ(350)–1, 2A1ᵛ(354)–4, 2A2ᵛ(356)–6, 2A7(365)–6, 2B4ᵛ(376)–2, 2C6(395)–6, 2D5ᵛ(410)–7, 2D7(413)–6, 2E1ᵛ(418)–2, 2F7(445)–1, 2F8(447)–2, 2F8ᵛ(448)–1, 2G3(453)–8. *Note*: 2A figg. three times.

Catchwords: *om.* A1–2, 2, 108–10, 227, 342–3; superior figg. om. 173, 367, 433, 438; 5 One͵ (~,), 13 O then͵ (~ ~,), 31 n. Again͵ (~,), 34 n. [feve-] ral (of), 50 *Pyr͵* (~.), 98 ͵For ('~), 151 n. propofed, (~.), 165 *A ſong͵* (~,), 217 *om.* (for), 239 *Cel.* (*Col.*), 288 *Jaq.* (*Ja.*), 336 *Roſ.* (*Phe.*), 337 ⁷*Tis* ('*Tis*), 346 n. wit, (~͵), 348 Here͵ (~,), 396 be (Be).

Explicit: 456 END OF THE THIRD VOLUME.

IV. *A²* B–X⁸ Y⁸ (± Y8) Z–2E⁸ 2F⁸ (± 2F6) 2G⁸ 2H⁸ (−2H4.5,6 + 2H4.6 (2H4 + 2H5) ± 2H7) 2I⁸ 2K⁸ (± 2K5) 2L⁸ 2M⁴ (2M4 blk), ($4 (−2C4) signed; 'Vᴏʟ. IV.' on $1), 270 leaves.

Pp. A1 t., A1ᵛ blk, A2 t. (vol. 4), A2ᵛ blk, on B1 *1* ½t All's Well, *2* Dram. Pers., *3* 4–138 text A Well, *139* Epilogue, *140* blk, *141* ½t Twelfth Night, *142* Dram. Pers., *143* 144–253 text T Night, *254* blk, *255* ½t Winter's Tale, *256* Dram. Pers., *257* 258–390 text W Tale, *391* ½t Macbeth, *392* Dram. Pers., *393* 394–533 text Macbeth, *534* blk.

Pagination: blk. 140, 254, 534.

Press-figures: B7ᵛ(14)–1, C7ᵛ(30)–1, D7ᵛ(46)–1, F2ᵛ(68)–2, G4ᵛ(88)–2, H8ᵛ(112)–2, I3ᵛ(118)–2, K5(137)–2, L5(153)–2, M4ᵛ(168)–2, N5(185)–2, O4ᵛ(200)–2, P7(221)–2, Q8(239)–2, R5(249)–2, S6(267)–6, T6(283)–2, U5(297)–2, X4ᵛ(312)–1, X8(319)–2, Y7(333)–2, Z5ᵛ(346)–1, Z7(349)–2, 2A5ᵛ(362)–1, 2B8(383)–2, 2C7ᵛ(398)–1, 2D5(409)–2, 2D7ᵛ(414)–1, 2E1ᵛ(418)–1, 2E5(425)–2, 2F4ᵛ(440)–6, 2G7ᵛ(462)–1, 2H8(479)–1, 2I1ᵛ(482)–4, 2K5ᵛ(506)–2, 2L1ᵛ(514)–6, 2L6ᵛ(524)–7; unfigured E.

Catchwords: om. A1–2, 1–2, 139–42, 253–6, 390–2; 17 To, (To-day), 367 Or, (~,), 393 om. (1 *Witch*.), 532 om. (THIS) 618 n. So (again).

Explicit: 533 END OF THE FOURTH VOLUME.

V. π² A⁸ (± A4,6) B⁸ C⁸ (± C4) D–H⁸ I⁸ (± I1) K⁸ (± K1) L–Q⁸ R⁸ (± R4) S⁸ T⁸ (± T7) U–Z⁸ 2A⁸ (± 2A2) 2B⁸ (± 2B6) 2C⁸ 2D⁸ (± 2D2) 2E⁸ (± 2E1) 2F–2G⁸ 2H⁸ (± 2H8) 2I⁸ (± 2I4), ($4 (−O4) signed; 'VOL. V.' on $1), 258 leaves.

Pp. π1 ½t, π1ᵛ blk, π2 t. (vol. 5), π2ᵛ blk, on A1 *1* ½t King John, *2* Dram. Pers., *3* 4–111 text K. John, *112* blk, *113* ½t Richard II, *114* Dram. Pers., *115* 116–219 text Richard II, *220* blk, *221* ½t 1 Henry IV, *222* Dram. Pers., *223* 224–361 text 1 Henry IV, *362* blk, *363* ½t 2 Henry IV, *364* blk, *365–67* Induction *368* Dram. Pers., *369* 370–509 text 2 Henry IV, *510* blk, *511–12* Epilogue.

Pagination: blk 112, 220, 362, 364, 510.

Press-figures: B4ᵛ(24)–2, C7ᵛ(46)–2, D2ᵛ(52)–2, E4ᵛ(72)–2, F7ᵛ(94)–2, G5ᵛ(106)–2, H5(121)–2, I8ᵛ(144)–2, K4ᵛ(152)–2, L8ᵛ(176)–2, M8(191)–2, N5ᵛ(202)–2, O5ᵛ(218)–2, P4ᵛ(232)–2, Q2ᵛ(244)–2, R8ᵛ(272)–2, S1ᵛ(274)–2, T6ᵛ(300)–2, U8(319)–2, X7(333)–2, Y7ᵛ(350)–2, Z7(365)–2, 2A8ᵛ(384)–2, 2B1ᵛ(386)–2, 2C5ᵛ(410)–2, 2D1ᵛ(418)–2, 2E6ᵛ(444)–2, 2F4ᵛ(456)–2, 2G7ᵛ(478)–2, 2H7(493)–2; unfigured A, 2I. Press-figure 2 only in this vol.

Catchwords: om. π1–2, 1, 111–13, 219–22, 361–4, 510; 3 *Faul*. (*Faulc*.), 48 om. (*Auſt*.), 54 *K. Philip*. (*K. Phil*.), 89 Or (*Faulc*.), 144 n. Shakeſpeare, (~,), 183 om. (*Gard*.), 187 om. (Oh), 199 om. (Thou), 368 om. (ˢTHE), 454 om. (*Weſt*.), 499 om. (*Shal*.);

Explicit: 512 END OF VOLUME THE FIFTH.

VI. π² A⁸ (± A8) B⁸ (± B8) C–G⁸ H⁸ (± H1,3) I⁸ (± I4) K–2H⁸ 2I⁴, ($4 signed; 'VOL. VI.' on $1), 254 leaves.

Pp. π1 ½t (vol. 6), π1ᵛ blk, π2 t., π2ᵛ blk, on A1 1 ½t Henry V., *2* blk, *3–5* Prologue, *6* Dram. Pers., *7* 8–147 text Henry V, *148* blk, *149* ½t 1 Henry VI, *150* Dram. Pers., *151* 152–254 text 1 Henry VI, *255* ½t 2 Henry VI, *256*

Dram. Pers., *257* 258–377 text 2 Henry VI, *378* blk, *379* ½t 3 Henry VI, *380* Dram. Pers., *381* 382–503 text 3 Henry VI, *504* blk.

Pagination: no errors.

Press-figures: A7ᵛ(14)–2, B7ᵛ(30)–2, C6(43)–2, D4ᵛ(56)–2, E3ᵛ(70)–2, F6ᵛ(92)–2, G8(111)–2, H5ᵛ(122)–2, I7ᵛ(142)–2, K8(159)–2, L5ᵛ(170)–2, M7ᵛ(190)–2, N6ᵛ(204)–2, O5(217)–2, O7ᵛ(222)–2, P6(235)–2, Q6(251)–2, R8ᵛ(272)–2, S6ᵛ(284)–2, T8(303)–2, U1ᵛ(306)–2, Y8(351)–2, Z7ᵛ(366)–2, 2A1ᵛ(370)–2, 2B7ᵛ(398)–2, 2C4ᵛ(408)–2, 2D1ᵛ(418)–2, 2E7ᵛ(446)–2, 2F5(457)–2, 2G5ᵛ(474)–2, 2H6(491)–2; unfigured X, 2I. Press-figure 2 only in this vol.

Catchwords: *om.* π1–2, 1–2, 148–50, 254–6, 377–80; 6 *om.* (¹THE), 17 *om.* (Is), 82 *Orl.* (*Or.*), 179 *Alarum.* (*Alarm.*), 411 *Enter* (SCENE), 482 *Glo*₍ₐ₎ (~.), 500 *K. Edw.* (*K. Ed.*).

Explicit: 503 END OF VOLUME THE SIXTH.

VII. A^2 B–O⁸ P⁸ (± P3) Q⁸ R⁸ (± R3) S⁸ (± S6) T–2B⁸ 2C⁸ (± 2C7) 2D⁸ 2E⁸ (± 2E2) 2F⁸, ($4 signed; 'VOL. VII.' on $1), 226 leaves.

Pp. A1 ½t, A1ᵛ blk, A2 t. (vol. 7), A2ᵛ blk, on B1 *1* ½t Richard III, *2* Dram. Pers., *3* 4–154 text Richard III, *155* ½t Henry VIII, *156* Dram. Pers., *157* 158–288 text Henry VIII, *289* ½t Coriolanus, *290* Dram. Pers., *291* 292–447 text Coriolanus, *448* blk.

Pagination: blk 448.

Press-figures: B5(9)–2, C1ᵛ(18)–2, C4ᵛ(24)–1, D7(45)–2, E5(57)–2, F4ᵛ(72)–2, G7ᵛ(94)–2, H6(107)–2, K7ᵛ(142)–2, K8ᵛ(144)–6, L1ᵛ(146)–2, L8ᵛ(160)–6, M6ᵛ(172)–2, N7(189)–2, N8(191)–6, O3ᵛ(198)–1, O4ᵛ(200)–2, P1ᵛ(210)–1, P5(217)–2, Q4ᵛ(232)–2, Q7ᵛ(238)–1, R3ᵛ(246)–2, R5(249)–2, R5ᵛ(250)–1, S6ᵛ(268)–1, T1ᵛ(274)–1, U2ᵛ(292)–1, U6(299)–2, X3ᵛ(310)–1, Y3ᵛ(326)–2, Z8(351)–1, 2A5(361)–6, 2A8(367)–1, 2B8ᵛ(384)–2, 2C3ᵛ(390)–1, 2D2ᵛ(404)–1, 2D5ᵛ(410)–3, 2E5(425)–6, 2E8(431)–4, 2F3ᵛ(438)–6, 2F6ᵛ(444)–4. Unfigured I; *Note*: 3 figg. in R.

Catchwords: *om.* A1–2, 2, 155–6, 288; ₍ₐₐ₎ Dive₍ₐ₎ (—Dive,), 90 ₍ₐ₎Call (—Call), 150 n. *om.* (the), 159 Which (Wh*i*ch), 238 I mean₍ₐ₎ (~ ~,), 296 *om.* (Not), 304 What- (what ever), 424 ₍ₐ₎of ((of).

Explicit: 447 END OF THE SEVENTH VOLUME.

VIII. A^2 B–H⁸ I⁸ (± I3) K⁸ (± K5,8) L–M⁸ N⁸ (± N3) O–P⁸ Q⁸ (± Q2) R–2I⁸ (2I8 blk), ($4 signed; 'VOL. VIII.' on $1), 250 leaves.

Pp. A1 ½t, A1ᵛ blk, A2 t. (vol. 8), A2ᵛ blk, on B1 *1* ½t Julius Cæsar, *2* Dram. Pers., *3* 4–106 text J. Cæsar, *107* ½t Antony and Cleopatra, *108* Dram. Pers., *109* 110–268 text Ant. & Cleopatra, *269* ½t Timon of Athens, *270* Dram. Pers., *271* 272–399 text Timon, *400* blk, *401* ½t Titus Andronicus, *402* Dram. Pers., *403* 404–93 text Titus, *494* blk, *495–6* (2I8) blk leaf.

Press-figures: P2ᵛ(212)–1, Q3ᵛ(230)–?1, Q5(233)–2, R7ᵛ(254)–1, S3ᵛ(262)–1, T8(287)–1, U8(303)–1, X2ᵛ(308)–1, X7ᵛ(318)–2, Y6(331)–1, Z1ᵛ(338)–2,

2A6(363)–2,   2A7(365)–1,   2B5ᵛ(378)–1,   2C4ᵛ(392)–2,   2C7ᵛ(398)–1,
2D8(415)–1,   2E5(425)–2,   2F6ᵛ(444)–2,   2G5(457)–2,   2H5(473)–2,
2H8(479)–1, 2I5ᵛ(490)–2; unfigured B–O.

Catchwords: *om.* A1–2, 1–3, 106–8, 269–70, 399–402; 137n Ye (Yet), 166
Eno. (~,), 167 *Trumpets*ₐ (~.), 200n ₐGo, (—Go,), 237 Dearₐ (~,), 259
Yourſelf (For), 341 Stayₐ (~,), 351 Sheₐ (~,), 366 The (Who), 445n *celada*
(*celeda*).

Explicit: 493 END OF VOLUME THE EIGHTH.

IX. π² A⁸ (± A4) B⁸ (± B5) C⁸ (± C8) D⁸ (± D4) E–2A⁸ 2B⁸ (± 2B2)
2C⁸ (± 2C5) 2D–2F⁸ 2G⁸ (± 2G3) 2H⁸ (± 2H1), ($4 (–D4, K4) signed;
'Vᴏʟ. IX.' on $1), 250 leaves.

Pp. π1 ½t, π1ᵛ blk, π2 t. (vol. 9), π2ᵛ blk, on A1 *1* ½t Troilus and Cressida,
2 blk, *3–5* Prologue, *6* Dram. Pers., *7* 8–150 text T & Cressida, *151* ½t
Cymbeline, *152* Dram. Pers., *153* 154–308 text Cymbeline, *309* ½t King Lear,
310 Dram. Pers., *311* 312–495 text Lear, *496* blk.

Pagination: blk 2, 496; 283 as 2.

Press-figures: C3ᵛ(38)–2, D5ᵛ(58)–2, E4ᵛ(72)–2, F2ᵛ(84)–2, G1ᵛ(98)–2,
H2ᵛ(116)–2, I1ᵛ(130)–2, K7ᵛ(158)–2, L2ᵛ(164)–2, M4ᵛ(184)–2, N3ᵛ(198)–2,
O1ᵛ(210)–2, P6ᵛ(236)–2, Q1ᵛ(242)–2, R1ᵛ(258)–2, S8ᵛ(288)–2, T7ᵛ(302)–2,
U1ᵛ(306)–2, X1ᵛ(322)–2, Y1ᵛ(338)–2, Z8ᵛ(368)–2, 2B7(397)–2; unfigured
A–B, 2A, 2C–2H; press-figure 2 only in this vol.

Catchwords: *om.* π1–2, 1–2, 6, 150–2, 308–10; superior figg. om. 38, 74, 143,
145, 198, 203, 227, 242, 328, 347, 369, 379, 398, 400, 416; 75 *om.* (As), 260
Imogen. (~,), 290 Of (²So), 298 *Imo.* (*Poſt.*), 366 *Stew.* (*Kent.*), 416 Come
(⁴*Come*), 433 Into (If), 438 ₐₐSCENE (['~).

Explicit: 495 END ᴏғ Vᴏʟᴜᴍᴇ ᴛʜᴇ Nɪɴᴛʜ.

X. π² A–K⁸ L⁸ (± L6) M–Z⁸ 2A⁸ (± 2A3) 2B–2D⁸ 2E⁸ (± 2E6) 2F–2I⁸
2K⁴ 2L–2P⁸ 2Q⁶ 2R², ($4 (–2K3,4, 2Q3, 2R2) signed; 'Vᴏʟ. X.' on $1), 310
leaves.

Pp. π1 ½t, π1ᵛ blk, π2 t. (vol. 10), π2ᵛ blk, on A1 *1* ½t Romeo and Juliet, *2*
blk, *3* Prologue, *4* Dram. Pers., *5* 6–141 text R & J, *142* blk, *143* ½t Hamlet,
144 Dram. Pers., *145* 146–353 text Hamlet, *354* blk, *355* ½t Othello, *356*
Dram. Pers., *357* 358–521 text Othello, *522* blk, on 2L2 (46 pp.) Appendix I,
on 2O1 (28 pp.) Appendix II, on 2R1 (4 pp.) Appendix III.

Pagination: blk 2, 142, 354, 522, 2L2–2R2ᵛ unpaged, 376 as m76.

Press-figures: A8(15)–2, B4ᵛ(24)–2, D8ᵛ(64)–2, E8ᵛ(80)–2, F8ᵛ(96)–2,
G7(109)–2, H2ᵛ(116)–2, I2ᵛ(132)–2, K8(159)–2, L2ᵛ(164)–2, M5ᵛ(186)–2,
N6ᵛ(204)–2, O6ᵛ(220)–2, P8(239)–2, Q8ᵛ(256)–2, R2ᵛ(260)–2, S4ᵛ(280)–2,
U1ᵛ(306)–2, X2ᵛ(324)–2, Z3ᵛ(358)–2, 2A4ᵛ(376)–2, 2B1ᵛ(386)–2, 2C8(415)–2,
2E1ᵛ(434)–2, 2E8ᵛ(448)–2, 2L6–4, 2N4ᵛ–3, 2O7ᵛ–4; unfigured C, T, Y, 2D,
2F–2K, 2M, 2P–2R; press-figure 2 only throughout text.

Catchwords: *om.* π1–2, 1–2, 5, 141–4, 353–6, 522; superior figg. om. 17, 24,

27, 29, 34, 44, 46, 84; 18 Though (Through), 19 *om.* (Be), 140 *om.*(THIS), 281 *Haw.* (*Ham.*), 312 *om.* (*Ham.*), 372 n. Virgil (On), 378 *om.* (For), 385 n. *There* (*That*), 437 *om.* (The), 499 Yet (It), 506 *om.* (As), 509 *om.* (*Æmil.*), 510 *om.* (*Gra.*), 515 *om.* (Albeit), 519 *om.* (Remains); 2M1^{v} *Paſſey* (*Paſſy*), 2N2 ASHARD, (~‸), 2N2^{v} the (The), 2N3 ‸periſhed (“~), 2N6 [There ((P. 188)), 2N8^{v} *om.* (The), 2O8^{v} *partition* (*partitions*), 2Q5 (P. 226) ((P. 226. n. 9.)), 2Q6^{v} *om.* (The);

Explicit: 2Q6^{v} THE END.

Paper: White, laid; Royal (uncut: 9¼ × 6 in.); wmk.: fleur-de-lys + LVG.

Type: Text: pica (4.0 mm), SJ's Preface: pica, leaded (1.1 mm); notes: long primer (3.1 mm).

References: Jaggard 503–4; Courtney 104, 108; CH 147; Sherbo, *SJ, Editor of Shakespeare* (1956), ch. 7; T. J. Monaghan, *RES* n.s. iv (1953), 234–48; Sherbo, *PQ* xxxiii (1954), 283–4, in *ECS* vii (1973), 18–39, and *Birth of Shakespeare Studies* (1986), ch. 4; ESTC: t138855.

Notes: Steevens issued Proposals for this edn. dated 1 February 1766 in both folio and quarto O: (JJ: 7-EO2, 24-B12). The numerous cancels (58 in all, 56 affecting the edited text), argue for considerable editorial attention, and it is likely that it was Steevens rather than SJ who gave it, though there are many revisions in SJ's notes. According to the *Petition of the Booksellers for Relief from the Expenses of Correction and Improvement*, 2 leaves 4°, n.d., the following payments were made to editors of Shakespeare:[1]

Mr Rowe	36-10-0
Mr Hughes	28- 7-0
Mr Pope	217-12-0
Mr Fenton	30-12-0
Mr Gay	35-19-6
Mr Whatley	12- 0-0
Mr Theobald	625-10-0
Mr Warburton	500- 0-0
Mr Capel	300- 0-0
Mr Johnson, Copies to the Amount of	375- 0-0
Ditto, a new Edition in 1774	100- 0-0
	2288-10-0

The copy of this edn. at IU contains an inserted printed leaf listing all the cancels.

Copies: O (Malone C. 105–14);

USA: Hyde^{2} (**1**. uncut; **2**. 'R. B. Adam'), IU, [Liebert], NjP, NN, TxU; *Can*: CaOHM; *Japan*: [Kyoto]; *UK*: ABu, C, Ct, [E], Eu, L^{2} (**1**. 642. e. 1, lacks vol. 5; **2**. C.45.a.21, 'S.T. Coleridge'), NOW (8 vols. only), MRu (22347; 'George Steevens' + notes), Oef; *Aust.* CNL (DNS 6917).

¹ The only copy I have seen is O: (4° x. 136 Jur, 'Isaac Reed'). The printed list of charges derives from an undated MS note by Tonson's partner, Somerset Draper, now in DFo (S. a. 163), of which a photograph is reproduced in Foxon and McLaverty, *Pope & the early 18th-Century Book Trade* (1991), 90, fig. 50. A slightly variant version is given in *Lit. Anec.* v (1812), 597, in which the addition is no more accurate than the above, the total of which should read: £2261. 10s. 6d

65.10SP/7   Shakespeare, Bathurst   1778

[Vol. t.] THE | PLAYS | OF | WILLIAM SHAKESPEARE. | VOLUME the FIRST. | CONTAINING | PREFACES, &c. | The TEMPEST. | The TWO GENTLEMEN of VERONA. | The MERRY WIVES of WINDSOR.

[Gen. t.] THE | PLAYS | OF | WILLIAM SHAKESPEARE. | IN TEN VOLUMES. | WITH THE | CORRECTIONS and ILLUSTRATIONS | OF | VARIOUS COMMENTATORS; | TO WHICH IS ADDED | NOTES by SAMUEL JOHNSON | AND | GEORGE STEEVENS. | The SECOND EDITION, | Revised and Augmented. | ΤΗΣ ΦΥΣΕΩΣ ΓΡΑΜΜΑΤΕΥΣ ΗΝ, ΤΟΝ ΚΑΛΛΑΜΟΝ ΑΠΟΒΡΕΧΩΝ ΕΙΣ ΝΟΥΝ. | *Vet. Auct. apud Suidam.* | MULTA DIES, VARIUSQUE LABOR MUTABILIS ÆVI | RETULIT IN MELIUS, MULTOS ALTERNA REVISENS | LUSIT, ET IN SOLIDO RURSUS FORTUNA LOCAVIT. | *Virgil.* | LONDON, | Printed for C. Bathurſt, W. Strahan, J.F. and C. Rivington, | J. Hinton, L. Davis, W. Owen, T. Caſlon, E. Johnſon, S. Crowder, | B. White, T. Longman, B. Law, E. and C. Dilly, C. Corbett, | T. Cadell, H.L. Gardener, J. Nichols, J. Bew, J. Beecroft, | W. Stuart, T. Lowndes, J. Robſon, T. Payne, T. Becket, | F. Newbery, G. Robinſon, R. Baldwin, J. Williams, J. Ridley, | T. Evans, W. Davies, W. Fox, and J. Murray. | MDCCLXXVIII.

10 vols. 8°

I. π² A–H⁸ I⁸ (±I1), K–O⁸ P⁸ (±P8) Q–S⁸ T⁸ (±T6) U⁸ (±U5) X⁸ (±X4) Y⁸, ²B–2A⁸ 2B², ($4 (–2B2, A–Y in brackets) signed; 'VOL. I.' on $1 (+ I2, P8, T6, U5, X4, ²I4)), 372 leaves.

Pp. π1 ½t, π1ᵛ blk, π2 t., π2ᵛ blk, on A1 *1* 2–67 SJ's Preface (signed 67: 'JOHNSON.'), *68* 69–85 Advertisement to the Reader (signed 85: 'STEEVENS.'), *86* 87–101 Ancient translations from classic authors, *102* 103–5 Appendix, *106*–107 Dedication of the Players (from F1), *108*–109 Preface of the Players (from F1), *110* 111–123 Pope's Preface, *124* 125–47 Theobald's Preface, *148* 149–50 Hanmer's Preface, *151* 152–63 Warburton's Preface, *164* 165–74 Steevens's Advertisement to the Reader, *175* 176–90 Rowe's Life of Shakespeare, *191*–192 Grant of Arms, *193* 194–5 Licence for acting (19 May 1603) to Laurence Fletcher and W. Sh., *196* 197–200 Sh's Will, *201* 202–10 Horse-holding anecdote &c., *211*–212 Parish register entries, *213* 214–15 Grainger on portraits of Sh., *216* 217–32 Commendatory poems on Sh., *233* names of actors, *234* 235–47 Ancient edns. of Sh's plays, *248* 249–52 Criticisms of Sh., *253* 254–68 Stationers' Register, *269* 270–346 Attempt to ascertain the order of Plays (signed 346: 'MALONE.'), *347–49* Plays contained in each volume, *350–52* Errata, on B1 *1* ½t Tempest, *2* Dram. Pers., *3* 4–115 text of Tempest, *116–17* Epilogue, *118* blk, *119* ½t Two Gentlemen, *120* Dram. Pers., *121* 122–216 text of Two Gentlemen, *217* ½t Merry Wives, *218* Dram. Pers., *219* 220–372 text of Merry Wives.

Pagination: [↑] 235–47, 249–52, 254–68, 270–346.

Press-figures: R2v(260)–1, S7(285)–7, T1v(290)–6, T4v(296)–2, X2v(324)–8, X4v(328)–4, X5v(330)–1, Y4v(344)–6.

Catchwords: not recorded.

Explicit: 372 END OF VOLUME THE FIRST.

Plates: 1. Front. port. of Shakespeare after Droeshout; 2. facing p. 196 Port of Shakespeare, 3. facing p. 200, Facsimile of Shakespeare's signatures from the Will.

II. *A*2 B–C8 D8 (±D3) E8 (±E4) F–2L8, ($4 signed; 'VOL. II.' on $1 (+ A)), 266 leaves.

Pp. A1 ½t (THE | PLAYS | OF | WILLIAM SHAKESPEARE.), A1v blk, A2 t. (as vol. 1 . . . VOLUME the SECOND. | CONTAINING | MEASURE FOR MEASURE. | COMEDY OF ERRORS. | MUCH ADO ABOUT NOTHING. | LOVE'S LABOUR [*sic*] LOST. | LONDON, &c.), A2v blk, on B1 *1* ½t Measure for Measure, *2* Dram. Pers., *3* 4–162 text of Measure, *163* ½t Comedy of Errors, *164* Dram. Pers., *165* 166–248 text of Comedy, *249* ½t Much Ado, *250* Dram. Pers., *251* 252–74 text of Much Ado, *375* ½t LLL (as 'LOVE's LABOUR's LOST'), *376* Dram. Pers., *377* 378–527 text of LLL, *528* blk;

Press-figures: none; *Catchwords*: not recorded.

Explicit: 527 END OF VOLUME THE SECOND.

III. *A*2 B–H8 I8 (±I8) K–O8 P8 (±P4) Q–2L8 2M4, ($4 (–2M3,4), signed; 'VOL. III.' on $1 (+A1, I8, P4)), 270 leaves.

Pp. A1 ½t (as vol. 2), A1v blk, A2 t. (as vol. 1 . . . VOLUME the THIRD. | CONTAINING | MIDSUMMER-NIGHT'S DREAM. | MERCHANT OF VENICE. | AS YOU LIKE IT. | TAMING THE [*sic*] SHREW. | LONDON, &c.), A2v blk, on B1 *1* ½t MND, *2* Dram. Pers., *3* 4–128 text of MND, *129* ½t Merchant, *130* Dram. Pers., *131* 132–260 text of Merchant, *261* ½t AYLI, *262* Dram. Pers., *263* 264–388 text of AYLI, *389* ½t TAMING OF THE SHREW., *390–91* Characters in the Induction (incl. 4° 1607), *392* blk, *393* 394–536 text of Shrew.

Press-figures: none; *Catchwords*: not recorded.

Explicit: 536 END OF VOLUME THE THIRD.

IV. *A*2 B–S8 T8 (±T8) U–2P8 2Q8 (±2Q2) 2R2, ($4 (–2R2) signed; VOL IV.' on $1 (+T8, 2Q2)), 308 leaves.

Pp. A1 ½t (as vol. 2), A1ᵛ blk, A2 t. (as vol. 1 . . . VOLUME the FOURTH. | CONTAINING | ALL'S WELL THAT ENDS WELL. | TWELFTH NIGHT. | WINTER'S TALE. | MACBETH. | LONDON, &c.), A2ᵛ blk, on B1 *1* ½t All's Well, *2* Dram. Pers., *3* 4–150 text All's Well, *151* ½t TN, *152* Dram. Pers., *153* 154–284 text TN, *285* ½t Winter's Tale, *286* Dram. Pers., *287* 288–437 text WT., *438* blk, *439* ½t Macbeth, *440* Dram. Pers., *441* 442–611 text Macbeth, *612* blk.

Press-figures: T8ᵛ(288)–8; *Catchwords*: not recorded;

Explicit: 611 END OF VOLUME THE FOURTH.

V. *A²* B–O⁸ P⁸ (±P5) Q–2Q⁸ 2R⁴, ($4 (–2R3,4) signed); 'VOL. V.' on $1 (+ P5)), 310 leaves.

Pp. A1 ½t (as vol. 2), A1ᵛ blk, A2 t. (as vol. 1 . . . VOLUME the FIFTH. | CONTAINING | KING JOHN. | KING RICHARD II. | KING HENRY IV. Part I. | KING HENRY IV. Part II. | LONDON, &c.), on B1 *1* ½t K John, *2* Dram. Pers., *3* 4–128 text K. John, *129* ½t Richard II, *130* Dram. Pers., *131* 132–248 text R. II, *249* ½t 1 Hen. IV, *250* Dram. Pers., *251* 252–434 text 1Hen. IV, *435* ½t 2 Hen. IV, *436* Dram. Pers., *437*–39 Induction, *440* Dram. Pers., *441* 442–612 text 2 Hen. IV, *613*–15 Epilogue, *616* blk.

Press-figures: P5ᵛ(218)–4; *Catchwords*: not recorded.

Explicit: 615 END OF VOLUME THE FIFTH.

Plate: folding, f.p. 434: 'Morris Dancing'.

VI. *A²* B–E⁸ F⁸ (±F8) G–2N⁸ 2O⁴ (2O4 blk), ($4 (–2O3,4) signed; 'VOL. VI.' on $1 (+ A1, F8)), 286 leaves.

Pp. A1 ½t (as vol. 2), A1ᵛ blk, A2 t. (as vol. 1 . . . the SIXTH. | CONTAINING | KING HENRY V. | KING HENRY VI. Part I. | KING HENRY VI. Part II. | KING HENRY VI. Part III. | LONDON, &c.), A2ᵛ blk, on B1 *i* ½t Hen. V, *ii* Dram. Pers., *iii* iv–v Chorus, *vi* blk, 7 8–171 text Hen. V, *172* blk, *173* ½t 1 Hen. VI, *174* Dram. Pers., *175* 176–290 text 1 Hen. VI, *291* ½t 2 Hen. VI, *292* Dram. Pers., *293* 294–428 text 2 Hen. VI, *429* ½t 3 Hen. VI, *430* Dram. Pers., *431* 432–566 text 3 Hen. VI, *567*–8 (2O4) blk.

Press-figures: none; *Catchwords*: not recorded.

Explicit: 566 END OF VOLUME THE SIXTH.

VII. *A²* B–R⁸ S⁸ (±S5) T–2I⁸ 2K², ($4 (–2K2) signed; 'VOL. VII.' on $1 (+ A, S5)), 252 leaves.

Pp. A1 ½t (as vol. 2), A1ᵛ blk, A2 t. (as vol. 1 . . . the SEVENTH. | CONTAINING | KING RICHARD III. | KING HENRY VIII. | CORIOLANUS. | LONDON, &c.), A2ᵛ blk, on B1 *1* ½t Richard III, *2* Dram. Pers., *3* 4–174 text of Rich. III, *175* ½t Hen. VIII, *176* Dram. Pers., *177* 178–9 Prologue, *180* blk, *181* 182–323 text Hen. VIII, *324*–325 Epilogue, *326* blk, *327* ½t Coriolanus, *328* Dram. Pers., *329* 330–500 text of Cor.

Press-figures: none; *Catchwords*: not recorded.

Explicit: 500 END OF VOLUME THE SEVENTH.

VIII. *A²* B⁸ (±B2) C–2N⁸ 2O² (2O2 blk), ($4 (–A2, 2O2) signed; 'VOL. VIII.' on $1 (+ a1, B2)), 284 leaves.
Pp. A1 ½t (as vol. 2), A1ᵛ blk, A2 t. (as vol. 1 . . . the EIGHTH. | CONTAINING | JULIUS CÆSAR. | ANTONY AND CLEOPATRA. | TIMON OF ATHENS. | TITUS ANDRONICUS. | LONDON, &c.), on B1 *1* ½t J. Cæsar, *2* Dram. Pers., *3* 4–119 text J. Cæsar, *120* blk. *121* ½t Ant. & Cleo., *122* Dram. Pers., *123* 124–313 text A & C., *314* blk, *315* ½t Timon, *316* Dram. Pers., *317* 318–458 text Timon, *459* ½t Titus, *460* Dram. Pers., *461* 462–562 text of Titus, *563–64* (2O2) blk.
Press-figures: N2ᵛ(180)–2, O8(207)–2, P1ᵛ(210)–7, P7(221)–7, Q2ᵛ(228)–8, R2ᵛ(244)–8, R7ᵛ(254)–1, S2ᵛ(260)–6, S3ᵛ(262)–8, T6(283)–8, T6ᵛ(284)–6, U8ᵛ(304)–8, X1ᵛ(306)–1, X2ᵛ(308)–8, Y3ᵛ(326)–6, Y5(329)–4, Z7ᵛ(350)–7, 2A2ᵛ(356)–2, 2A8(367)–7, 2B1ᵛ(370)–6, 2B2ᵛ(372)–8, 2C5(393)–6, 2C7ᵛ(398)–7, 2D6ᵛ(412)–1, 2D7ᵛ(414)–8, 2E2ᵛ(420)–4, 2F3ᵛ(438)–8, 2F6ᵛ(444)–1, 2G4ᵛ(456)–1, 2H7(477)–7, 2H7ᵛ(478)–7, 2I3ᵛ(486)–8, 2K7(509)–8, 2L5(521)–6, 2L8(527)–8, 2M5ᵛ(538)–8, 2M8ᵛ(544)–6, 2N1ᵛ(546)–7, 2N6ᵛ(556)–6.
Catchwords: not recorded.
Explicit: 562 END OF VOLUME THE EIGHTH.

IX. *A²* B–N⁸ O⁸ (±O2) P–2O⁸ (208 blk), ($4 signed; 'VOL. IX.' on $1 (+ A1, O2)), 290 leaves.
Pp. A1 ½t (as. vol. 2), A1ᵛ blk, A2 t. (as vol. 1 . . . the NINTH. | CON TAINING | TROILUS AND CRESSIDA. | CYMBELINE. | KING LEAR. | LONDON, &c.), A2ᵛ blk, on B1 *1* ½t Troilus, *2* Preface from Q2 1609, *3–5* Prologue, *6* Dram. Pers., *7* 8–170 text Troilus, *171* ½t Cymbeline, *172* Dram. Pers., *173* 174–346 text Cymbeline, *347* ½t Lear, 348 Dram. Pers., *349* 350–573 text Lear, *574–6* blk.
Press-figures: 2O6(571)–8; *Catchwords*: not recorded.
Explicit: 573 END OF VOLUME THE NINTH.

X. *A²* B–E⁸ F⁸ (±F3) G–I⁸ K⁸ (±K7) L–2D⁸ 2E⁸ (2E4 + χ1) 2F–2R⁸ 2S⁴, ($4 (–2S3,4, K7 as K5) signed; 'VOL. X.' on $1 (+ A1, F3, K7)), 319 leaves.
Pp. A1 ½t (as vol. 2), A1ᵛ blk, A2 t. (as vol. 1 . . . the TENTH. | CONTAINING | ROMEO AND JULIET. | HAMLET. | OTHELLO. | LONDON, &c.), A2ᵛ blk, on B1 *1* ½t Romeo & Juliet, *2* blk, *3* Prologue, *4* Dram. Pers., *5* 6–166 text R & J., *167* ½t Hamlet, *168* Dram. Pers., *169* 170–423 text Hamlet, *424* blk, ²Eχ1 *inserted* 'Supplemental Note on *Hamlet*, p. 263 and 420. *The rugged Pyrrhus*, &c.' (signed: STEEVENS.'), on 2E5 *425* ½t Othello, *426* Dram. Pers., *427* 428–629 text Othello, *620* blk, *631–32* 'Vol. X. last Leaf.' (Accidental Omissions, &c. in Vol. I.).
Press-figures: B5ᵛ(10)–1, B8ᵛ(16)–5, C3ᵛ(22)–1, C7(29)–5, D1ᵛ(34)–1,

D6ᵛ(44)–6, E7ᵛ(62)–7, F1ᵛ(66)–7, F2ᵛ(68)–1, G7(93)–2, G7ᵛ(94)–7, H7ᵛ(110)–1, H8ᵛ(112)–5, I8(127)–7, K5ᵛ(138)–2, L4ᵛ(152)–1, L5ᵛ(154)–2, M2ᵛ(164)–5, M7ᵛ(174)–7, N7(189)–5, O4ᵛ(200)–7, O5ᵛ(202)–2, P1ᵛ(210)–5, P8ᵛ(224)–1, Q7(237)–2, Q7ᵛ(238)–5, R5ᵛ(250)–1, R7(253)–7, S1ᵛ(258)–1, S8ᵛ(272)–2, T5ᵛ(282)–1, T6ᵛ(284)–7, U5ᵛ(298)–5, X7(317)–2, X7ᵛ(318)–5, Y1ᵛ(322)–1, Z6(347)–1, Z7(349)–2, 2A6(363)–5, 2A6ᵛ(364)–2, 2B4ᵛ(376)–1, 2B5ᵛ(378)–2, 2C3ᵛ(390)–5, 2D6(411)–5, 2E1ᵛ(418)–2, 2E2ᵛ(420)–5, ²ᴱχ1–3, 2F5ᵛ(442)–5, 2F7(445)–1, 2H7ᵛ(478)–6, 2H8ᵛ(480)–5, 2I5(489)–4, 2I7ᵛ(494)–2, 2K6(507)–1, 2L1ᵛ(514)–3, 2M5(537)–2, 2M7ᵛ(542)–3, 2N6(555)–2, 2N7(557)–3, 2O5(569)–3, 2O6(571)–2, 2P5(585)–6, 2P6(587)–7, 2Q5(601)–6, 2Q7ᵛ(606)–2, 2R8(623)–2, 2R8ᵛ(624)–5, 2S2ᵛ(628)–5; 2G unfigured.

Catchwords: not recorded.

Paper: White, laid; Demy (uncut: 8¾ × 5⅝ in.); wmk.: HV or HA, or AH or VH.

Type: SJ's Preface & text: pica (4.0 mm), leaded (0.8 mm), text (0.5 mm); Prefaces: sm. pica (3.5 mm), leaded (0.2 mm); footnotes: bourgeois (3.0 mm).

Plates: see individual volumes I (3), and V (1).

References: Jaggard 504 (ed. 'Isaac Reed'); Courtney 104, 109; ESTC: t149955.

Notes: The distribution of the press-figures shows some shared printing. Strahan had acquired a sixtieth share in 'Shakespeare's Works' at Hawes & Co.'s sale, 4 April 1776, for £22. 5s. (L: Add. MS 48805, s.d.), to add to his 30th share, acquired at Tonson's sale 18 Aug. 1767, for £60. 17s. 2d. (*ibid.*), making his total holding a 20th. This might well warrant his printing a part of the edn. To this reprint of 65.10SP/6, above, new material was added in the form of a short bibliography of Shakespearian criticism (i. 248–52), Malone's extracts from the Stationers' Company records (i. 253–68), and his chronology of the plays (i. 269–346), but there is no evidence that SJ made any new contribution.

Copies: O (8° P. 145–54 Linc);
UK: En ('Adam Smith'), L² (**1**. C.117.e.3 'Isaac Reed'; **2**. 642. f. 1–10), LCu (+ Malone's Supp. 2 vols), LICj², WIS; *Aust*: CNL (DNS 6918, imperfect).

65.10SP/7/S1   Shakespeare, Malone's Supplement   1780

[½t] SUPPLEMENT | TO THE EDITION OF | SHAKESPEARE's PLAYS | PUBLISHED IN 1778.

[Title] SUPPLEMENT | TO THE EDITION OF | SHAKSPEARE's PLAYS | PUBLISHED IN 1778 | By SAMUEL JOHNSON AND GEORGE STEEVENS. | IN TWO VOLUMES. | CONTAINING | ADDITIONAL OBSERVATIONS | BY SEVERAL OF | THE FORMER

COMMENTATORS: | TO WHICH ARE SUBJOINED | THE GENUINE POEMS | OF THE SAME AUTHOR, | AND | SEVEN PLAYS | THAT HAVE BEEN ASCRIBED TO HIM; | WITH NOTES | By the EDITOR and OTHERS. | *Natura infirmitatis humanæ tardiora funt remedia quam mala*; | *et ut corpora lente augefcunt, cito extinguuntur, fic ingenia ftudia-* | *que oppreſſeris facilius quam revocaveris.* Tacitus. | LONDON, | Printed for C. Bathurſt, W. Strahan, J. F. and C. Rivington, J. | Hinton, L. Davis, R. Horsfield, W. Owen, E. Johnſon, S. Crowder, | B. White, T. Longman, C. Dilly, T. Cadell, J. and T. Bowles, T. | Lowndes, J. Robſon, T. Payne, H. L. Gardner, J. Nichols, J. | Bew, W. Cater, W. Stuart, F. Newbery, G. Robinſon, R. Baldwin, | T. Beecroft, J. Ridley, T. Evans, S. Hayes, and E. Johnſon. | MDCCLXXX.

Note: There are two 'E. Johnson's in the imprint: one is Edward Johnson, successor to Benjamin Dodd (see 1765 imprint, 65.10SP/1, above), the other is Edward Johnston, son of and successor in 1773, to William Johnston.

2 vols. 8°

I. A–D⁸ E⁸ (± E2) F–M⁸ N⁸ (± N2) O–P⁸ Q⁸ (± Q4) R–2C⁸ 2D⁸ (± 2D1) 2E–3B⁸ 3C⁴, ($4 (–A1,2,3, 3C3,4) signed; 'Vol. I.' on $1 (+ A)), 388 leaves.

Pp. A1 ½t, A1ᵛ blk, A2 t., A2ᵛ blk, A3 Contents, A3ᵛ blk, on A4 pp. *i* ii–viii Advertisement ('E. Malone.'), on A8 Errata & Binder's directions, A8ᵛ blk, on B1 *1* 2–371 text dh: SUPPLEMENT., rt: SUPPLEMENTAL | OBSERVATIONS., *372* blk, *373* 374–96 Appendix, *397* ½t Poems, *398* blk, *399* ½t, *400* blk, 401–760 text of Poems of Shakespeare.

Pagination: blk A1ᵛ, A2ᵛ, A3ᵛ, A8ᵛ, 372, 398, 400.

Press-figures: G5ᵛ(90)–4.

Catchwords: *om.* A1–3ᵛ, viii, 372, 397–400, 463–6, 468, 575–80, 707–8, 737–8; superior figg. *om.* 31, 46; 30 day∧ (~,), 64 It (I think), 96 58. *Heaven* (58. *Whilſt*), 146 feven (angels), 192 515. Why (525.—*Maſter*), 202 96. *Like* (96. —*like*), 215 *Deteſter* (*Deteſtor*), 271 ∧En- ("Endure), 365 467. *My* (467. — *My*), 390 means∧ ['s' *inverted*] (means,), 402 *om.* (VENUS), 412 Ah! (~∧), 417 n. ∧It ("~), 424 Or∧ (~,), 477 Where∧ (~,), 483 And (The), 534 Well∧ (~,), 589 She (Look), 743 Cry'd∧ (~,), 746 n. "A ("As).

Explicit: 760 END OF THE FIRST VOLUME.

II. A² B–C⁸ D⁸ (± D8) F⁸ (± F8) G⁸ (± G8) H–S⁸ T⁸ (± T8) U⁸ (± U8) X–2Z⁸ 3A⁶, ($4 (–2S3, + 3A4; F4ᵛ as F4) signed; 'Vol. II.' on $1 (+ D8, F8, T8, U8)), 368 leaves.

Pp. A1 ½t (as vol. 1), A1ᵛ blk, A2 t (as vol. 1 *except*: . . . STEEVENS. | VOLUME THE SECOND. | CONTAINING | PERICLES. | LOCRINE. | SIR JOHN OLDCASTLE. | LORD CROMWELL. | THE LONDON PRODIGAL. | THE PURITAN. | A YORKSHIRE TRAGEDY. | APPENDIX. | LONDON, . . . &c.), A2ᵛ blk, on B1 pp. *1* ½t Pericles, *2*

Persons represented, *3* 4–186 text Pericles, *187* ½t Locrine, *188* Dram. Pers., *189* 190–264 text Locrine, *265* ½t Sir John Oldcastle, *266* blk, *267* Prologue, *268* Dram. Pers., *269* 270–370 text Oldcastle, *371* ½t Lord Cromwell, *372* Dram. Pers., *373* 374–446 text Cromwell, *447* ½t London Prodigal, *448* Dram. Pers., *449* 450–529 text London Prodigal, *530* blk, *531* ½t Puritan, *532* Dram. Pers., *533* 534–627 text Puritan, *628* blk, *629* ½t Yorkshire Tragedy, *630* Dram. Pers., *631* 632–79 text Yorkshire Tragedy, *680* blk, *681* 682–720 Appendix to vol. I., *721* 722–32 Appendix to vol. II.

Pagination: blk A1ᵛ, A2ᵛ, 266, 530, 628, 680; 535 as 435.

Press-figures: none.

Catchwords: *om.* A1–2, 1–2; 10 Sorrow, (~ₐ), 68 ACT. (~ₐ), 72 n. —buₐ (—but), 75 whoₐ (~,), 80 2 *Sai.* (2 *Sail.*), 112 *Cleo·* (*Cle.*), 115 n. "Out ("Our), 155 Hailₐ (~,), 174 bor- (rowed).

Explicit: none.

Paper: White, laid; Royal (uncut: 9½ × 6 in.); no vis. wmk.

Type: Text: pica (4.0 mm), Advertisement: sm. pica (3.8 mm) leaded, Observations: long primer (3.4 mm), footnotes: bourgeois (3.1 mm).

Plates: (3): 1. vol. i., Engr. front. 'The House in Stratford upon Avon in which Shakspeare was born', 'R: Greene del:'; 2. i. 60, Platt of the *Seven Deadly Sins* (fold.); 3. i. 401, Engr. port. 'Henry Wriothesly, Earl of Southampton'.

References: Jaggard 504; Courtney 104, 109; Sherbo, *SJ, Editor of Shakespeare* (1956), 115–16, and *Birth of Shakespeare Studies* (1986), ch. 6; ESTC: t098170.

Notes: These vols. were the work of Edmond Malone and represent his first steps towards becoming the supreme editor of Shakespeare. SJ contributed some notes and corrected others (cf. i. 87, 232 (on *cancellans* Q4ᵛ), 240, 373 and 381). II. G8 is not cancelled in all copies. The *cancellanda* in vol. 2 are not signed, but all bear Binder's Directions. Evidently they were placed not by signatures but by page numbers.

At i. A8, the Binder's Direction reflects problems with the weather: 'When these Books are sewed and put in boards, it is desired that they may not be beaten; and it is recommended not to bind them till next winter.'

Copies: O³ (**1**. Mal. G. I. 22–23, + MS notes; **2**. 8° P. 155–6 Linc.; 3. Douce SS. 81–2; proofs of vol. 1 are Mal. 1058);

USA: Hyde² (**1**. uncut; **2**. 'R. M. Beverly' — 'T. O. Loughlan'), NIC; *Can*: CaOHM (C 755, vol. 2: G8 uncancelled); *Japan*: [Kyoto]; *UK*: ABu, BRu, Ct, DUc, En ('Adam Smith'), [Es], L (686. f. 17–18), LVu, NCu, SAN, WIS; *Aust*: CNL (DNS 6931).

65.10SP/7/S2   Shakespeare, Second Appendix to   1783
                             Malone's Supplement

A | SECOND APPENDIX | TO | Mr. MALONE's SUPPLEMENT | TO THE LAST EDITION | OF | THE PLAYS OF | SHAKSPEARE: | CONTAINING | ADDITIONAL OBSERVATIONS | BY THE EDITOR OF THE SUPPLEMENT. | *—fummi plenâ jam margine libri,* | *Scriptus et in tergo, nec dum finitus, Oreftes.* | JUVEN. | [medium swelled rule] | LONDON: | Printed in the Year MDCCLXXXIII.

8°, *A*² B–I⁴ K², ($2 (-K2) signed), 36 leaves. Pp. i t., *ii* blk, iii 'Advertisement' (signed 'Edm. Malone. Queen Anne Street, East. April 19, 1783.'), iv Quotation from Roscommon, on B1 pp. 1–67 text dh: A SECOND APPENDIX, &c., ht: SECOND APPENDIX., *68* blk.

Pagination: [↑], but (↑) iii.
Press-figures: E2ᵛ(28)–3, F4ᵛ(40)–4, I2ᵛ(60)–4.
Catchwords: *om.* i–iv, 33 VO˰ (VOLUME), 35 "—O˰ ("—O,).
Explicit: 67 THE END.
References: *Lit. Anec.* viii (1814), 133; ESTC: t100656.
Notes: Supporting evidence is adduced for former notes, including some by SJ, but no new Johnsoniana are introduced.
Copies: O² (1. Mal. E. 30 (3); 2. Malone 146).

65.10SP/8a   Shakespeare, Bathurst   1785

THE | PLAYS | OF | WILLIAM SHAKSPEARE. | IN TEN VOLUMES. | WITH THE | CORRECTIONS AND ILLUSTRATIONS | OF | VARIOUS COMMENTATORS; | TO WHICH ARE ADDED | NOTES by SAMUEL JOHNSON| AND | GEORGE STEEVENS. | THE THIRD EDITION, | REVISED AND AUGMENTED BY THE EDITOR OF | DODSLEY's COLLECTION OF OLD PLAYS. | ΤΗΣ ΦΥΣΕΩΣ ΓΡΑΜΜΑΤΕΥΣ ΗΝ, ΤΟΝ ΚΑΛΑΜΟΝ ΑΠΟΒΡΕΧΩΝ ΕΙΣ ΝΟΥΝ. | *Vet. Auct. apud Suidam.* | MULTA DIES, VARIUSQUE LABOR MUTABILIS ÆVI | RETULIT IN MELIUS, MULTOS ALTERNA REVISENS | LUZIT, ET IN SOLIDO RURSUS FORTUNA LOCAVIT. | *Virgil.* | LONDON, | Printed for C. BATHURST, J. RIVINGTON and SONS, | T. PAYNE and SON, L. DAVIS, W. OWEN, B. WHITE and | SON, T. LONGMAN, B. LAW, T. BOWLES, J. JOHNSON, | C. DILLY, J. ROBSON, G. G. J. and J. ROBINSON, | T. CADELL, H. L. GARDNER, J. NICHOLS, J. BEW, | W. STUART, R. BALDWIN, J. MURRAY, A. STRAHAN, | T. VERNOR, J. BARKER, W. LOWNDES, S. HAYES, | G. and T. WILKIE, SCATCHERD and WHITAKER, | T. and J. EGERTON, W. FOX, and E. NEWBERY. | M DCC LXXXV.

Stet: LUZIT [= LUSIT]; Z is wrong fount.
10 vols. 8°.

I. π^2 a^2 A–Y^8 Z^6 (–Z6 ? blk), ^{2}B–E^8 F^8 ($\pm$ F3) G–L^8 M^8 ($\pm$ M6) N–S^8 T^8 ($\pm$ T5) U–2D^8 (2N8 blk), ($^\pi$a A–Z in brackets; \$4 (–K3) signed); 'Vol. I.' on \$1), 394 leaves.

Pp. Engr. front. + π1 t., π1^v blk, π2 ½t: THE | PLAYS | OF | WILLIAM SHAKSPEARE. | VOLUME the FIRST. | CONTAINING | PREFACES, &c. | The TEMPEST. | The TWO GENTLEMEN of VERONA. | The MERRY WIVES of WINDSOR., π2^v blk, on a1 i–iv Advertisement dh: [double rule] | ADVERTISEMENT. ('Nov. 10, 1785.'), on A1 1–67 dh: PREFACE., ht: PREFACE., (signed 67: 'Johnson.'), *68* 69–87 dh: ADVERTISEMENT | TO THE | READER. | (Prefixed to the fecond Edition.), ht: ADVERTISEMENT to the READER., *88* 89–103 ANCIENT TRANSLATIONS | FROM | CLASSIC AUTHORS., ht: ANCIENT TRANSLATIONS., *104* 105–7 dh: APPENDIX., rt: APPENDIX To Mr. COLMAN's | TRANSLATION of TERENCE., *108*–109 Dedication from F1 dh: THE | DEDICATION of the PLAYERS., ht: THE PLAYERS' DEDICATION., *110*–111 Preface to F1, *112* 113–25 dh: Mr. POPE's PREFACE., ht: Mr. POPE's PREFACE., 126–49 dh: Mr THEOBALD's | *PREFACE., ht: Mr. THEOBALD's PREFACE., 150–52 dh: Sir T. HANMER's | PREFACE., ht: Sir T. HANMER's PREFACE., 153–65 dh: Dr. WARBURTON's | PREFACE., ht: Dr. WARBURTON's PREFACE., *166* 167–76 dh: ADVERTISEMENT | TO THE | READER., ht: ADVERTISEMENT to the READER., *177* 178–94 dh: SOME | Account of the Life, &c. | OF | WILLIAM SHAKSPEARE. | Written by Mr. ROWE., rt: Some ACCOUNT of the LIFE, &c. | of Mr. WILLIAM SHAKSPEARE., *195*–196 Grant of Arms, *197* 198–99 Licence for the Globe Theatre, *200* 201–4 dh and ht: SHAKSPEARE's WILL., 205–16 Supplementary biographical anecdotes, *217* 218–19 Extracts from Stratford Registers, ht: Baptisms, Marriages, Burials, &c., *220* 221–22 Extracts from Granger's *Biographical History*, *223* 224–44 dh: Ancient and Modern Commendatory Verses on | SHAKSPEARE., ht: POEMS on the AUTHOR., *245* Names of the original Actors in the Plays of Shakspeare: From the Folio, 1623., *246* 247–60 dh: A LIST OF SUCH | ANCIENT EDITIONS | OF | SHAKSPEARE's PLAYS, | as have hitherto been met with by his different | Editors., *261* 262–66 dh: LIST of Detached PIECES of CRITICISM on | SHAKSPEARE, his Editors, &c., 267–282 dh: EXTRACTS of ENTRIES | ON THE | Books of the Stationers' Company., *283* 284–357 dh: AN | ATTEMPT | TO ASCERTAIN THE | ORDER | IN WHICH THE | PLAYS attributed to SHAKSPEARE | were Written., *358* blk, 359–62 PLAYS, &c. contained in each Volume.

On ^{2}B1 *1* ½t, *2* Dram. Pers., *3* 4–127 text The Tempest, 130–31 Epilogue, *132* blk, *133* ½t Two Gentlemen, *134* Dram. Pers., *135* 136–236 text Two Gentlemen, *237* ½t Merry Wives, *238* Dram. Pers., *239* 240–414 text Merry Wives.

Pagination: (two series): (i) [↑] i–iv, 1, 126, 150, 153, 196, 198–99, 205–16, 221–2, 247–60, 262–66, 268–82, 284–357, 359; 38 unnumbered; (ii) [↑] 130; 76 as 78, 274 as 276 (334 *sometimes* as 4).

Press-figures: a2(iii)–3, A7(13)–1, A8(15)–3, B1ᵛ(18)–7, B4ᵛ(24)–5, C5ᵛ(42)–5, D6(59)–7, D8ᵛ(64)–1, E1ᵛ(66)–6, E4ᵛ(72)–4, F2ᵛ(84)–6, F8(95)–5, G2ᵛ(100)–1, G3ᵛ(102)–5, H3ᵛ(118)–7, H5(121)–6, I2ᵛ(132)–4, I3ᵛ(134)–6, K3ᵛ(150)–4, L3ᵛ(166)–1, L7(173)–3, M2ᵛ(180)–3, M6(187)–6, N4ᵛ(200)–5, O2ᵛ(212)–5, O7ᵛ(222)–3, P8(239)–5, Q5(249)–1, Q7ᵛ(254)–3, R7(269)–3, S2ᵛ(276)–5, T2ᵛ(292)–1, T6(299)–7, U3ᵛ(310)–5, X6(331)–7, X7(333)–3, Y8(351)–7, Z5(361)–3; [2nd. series]: B7ᵛ(14)–2, B8ᵛ(16)–1, C4ᵛ(24)–3, C6(27)–7, D3ᵛ(38)–1, D6ᵛ(44)–3, E6(59)–1, E6ᵛ(60)–2, F1ᵛ(66)–7, F2ᵛ(68)–3, G1ᵛ(82)–2, G2ᵛ(84)–1, H6ᵛ(108)–7, H7ᵛ(110)–2, I2ᵛ(116)–4, I5ᵛ(122)–1, K7ᵛ(142)–4, L8(159)–1, M6ᵛ(172)–1, M8(175)–4, N5ᵛ(186)–4, N8ᵛ(192)–5, O4ᵛ(200)–5, O6(203)–6, P7ᵛ(222)–6, P8ᵛ(224)–4, Q1ᵛ(226)–5, R7(253)–6, S1ᵛ(258)–6, S2ᵛ(260)–1, T2ᵛ(276)–5, T8(287)–6, U6ᵛ(300)–4, U8(303)–1, X7(317)–5, X8(319)–4, Y3ᵛ(326)–1, Y7(333)–7, Z6ᵛ(348)–3, Z7ᵛ(350)–4, 2A7(365)–5, 2A7ᵛ(366)–4, 2B5(377)–1, 2B5ᵛ(378)–7, 2C2ᵛ(388)–3, 2C8(399)–4, 2D4ᵛ(408)–1, 2D6(411)–3.

Catchwords: *om.* π1–2, a1–2, 1–2, 132–4, 237–8; superior figg. *om.* 71, 128, 218; 24, 42, 49, 51, 86, 95, 101, 104, 194, 233, 271, 355, 366, 393, 396, 397; 106n *was* ['s' *slipt*], 119 *om.* (It), 128 her₍ (~*,), 224 And₍ (~,), 288 *Titus* ['t' *inverted*], 298 Hippolita₍ (~,), 309 [of] ſimilar (a ſimilar); ²5 *om.* (Gon.), 30 Side (Side-ſtitches), 58 *Ant*₍ (~.), 66 *Ste.* (But), 79 I do (*Trin.*), 162 *Speed*₍ (~.), 186 And₍ (~,), 247 *Sha*₍ *l.* (Shal.), 254 n. ſtrain₍ (~.), 297 *om.* (SCENE), 300 n. "H₍ ("He), 384 huſband₍ (~,), 385, The (There), 381 n. "Whe ("When), 410 tardy₍ (~:).

Explicit: 414 THE END OF VOL. I.

II. *A*² B–E⁸ F⁸ (± F2) G–2N⁸, ($4 signed; 'Voʟ. II.' on $1), 282 leaves.

Pp. A1 ½t: THE | PLAYS | OF | WILLIAM SHAKSPEARE., A1ᵛ blk, A2 t., A2ᵛ blk, on B1 *1* ½t Measure for Measure, *2* Dram. Pers., *3* 4–170 text Measure, *171* ½t Comedy of Errors, *172* Dram. Pers., *173* 174–257 text Comedy, *258* blk, *259* ½t Much Ado, *260* Dram. Pers., *261* 262–392 text Much Ado, *393* ½t Love's Labour's Lost, *394* Dram. Pers., *395* 396–560 text LLL.

Pagination: blk 258; 64 as 94;

Press-figures: B8ᵛ(16)–1, C7ᵛ(30)–1, D1ᵛ(34)–1, E1ᵛ(50)–0, F5ᵛ(74)–1, G8ᵛ(96)–0, H3ᵛ(102)–1, I3ᵛ(118)–0, I6ᵛ(124)–1, K1ᵛ(130)–0, L3ᵛ(150)–5, M7(173)–5, M7ᵛ(174)–3, N2ᵛ(180)–1, O5(201)–1, O8(207)–0, P4ᵛ(216)–1, Q1ᵛ(226)–7, Q2ᵛ(228)–1, R6ᵛ(252)–7, S3ᵛ(262)–1, S4ᵛ(264)–8, T6(283)–7, T8ᵛ(288)–1, U6(299)–7, U8ᵛ(304)–3, X1ᵛ(306)–7, X2ᵛ(308)–2, Y5ᵛ(330)–3, Y6ᵛ(332)–1, Z6(347)–4, Z7(349)–2, 2A7ᵛ(366)–5, 2A8ᵛ(368)–0, 2B3ᵛ(374)–5, 2B7(381)–6, 2C6(395)–4, 2D2ᵛ(404)–2, 2D8(415)–5, 2E8(431)–9,

2F7ᵛ(446)–4, 2K4ᵛ(504)–6, 2K8(511)–9, 2L7(525)–1, 2L7ᵛ(526)–5, 2M3ᵛ(534)–3 [*inverted*], 2M7(541)–9, 2N6(555)–4, 2N7(557)–8. Unfigg. 2G–I.

Catchwords: *om.* A1–2, 171, 257–9; superior figg. *om.* 71, 193, 224, 241, 263n, 268, 418, 467; 7 That‸ (~,), 18 ‸—like ("—like), 31 Already‸ (~;), 41 officer:— (~;—), 74 Than‸ (~,), 173 *om.* (In), 185 n. So‸ (~,), 234 *E. Ent.* (*E. Ant.*), 237 Come‸ (~,), 260 MUCH (MUCH), 266 n. And‸ (~,), 277 [paint-] ed‸ (~;), 297 Lady‸ (~,), 329 *Verg.* (*Ferg.*), 330 n. 23‸ (~.), 332 knoweſt‸ (~,), 374 *Pedr* (*Pedro*), 385 n. Again, (Agian,), 397 Light‸ (~,), 425 n. *'Feed* ("~), 442 What‸ (~?), 456 n. ‸Prooving ("~), 459 ‸Which ((~), 475 n. One‸ (~,), 482 Biron‸ (~.), 490 *King.* (For), 501 n. Roſaline‸ (~,), 504 For‸ (~,), 531 n. All [2nd 'l' *dropt*], 554 "Franciæ‸ ("~,).

Explicit: 560 END OF VOLUME THE SECOND.

III. *A²* B–Y⁸ Z⁸ (± Z3) 2A–2N⁸, ($4 (–L4) signed; 'VOL. III.' on $1), 282 leaves.

Pp. A1 ½t (as vol. 2), A1ᵛ blk, A2 t., A2ᵛ blk, on B1 *1* ½t Midsummer Night's Dream, *2* Dram. Pers., *3* 4–137 text MND, *138* blk, *139* ½t Merchant of Venice, *140* Dram. Pers., *141* 142–276 text Merchant, *277* ½t As You Like It, *278* Dram. Pers., *279* 280–409 text AYLI, *410* blk, *411* ½t Taming of the Shrew, *412–13* Characters in the Induction, *414* blk, *415* 416–560 text ToS.

Pagination: blk 138, 410; 219 as 216, 497 as 499.

Press-figures: B3ᵛ(6)–4, B4ᵛ(8)–7, C1ᵛ(18)–4, D3ᵛ(38)–2, D8ᵛ(48)–0, E8ᵛ(64)–3, F6(75)–2, F7(77)–1, G1ᵛ(82)–2, G6ᵛ(92)–8, H8ᵛ(112)–3, I8(127)–7, K7ᵛ(142)–8, K8ᵛ(144)–1, L1ᵛ(146)–3, L4ᵛ(152)–4, M2ᵛ(164)–1, M8(175)–2, N3ᵛ(182)–4, O2ᵛ(196)–6, O5ᵛ(202)–3, P5ᵛ(218)–3, Q2ᵛ(228)–4, R6(251)–4, S1ᵛ(258)–1, S2ᵛ(260)–8, T7ᵛ(286)–7, U7ᵛ(302)–3, X4ᵛ(312)–4, Y3ᵛ(326)–4, Z1ᵛ(338)–7, 2A6ᵛ(364)–7, 2B3ᵛ(374)–3, 2B6(379)–2, 2B8ᵛ(384)–1, 2C4ᵛ(392)–4, 2D1ᵛ(402)–3, 2D2ᵛ(404)–7, 2E6(427)–4, 2E6ᵛ(428)–3, 2F1ᵛ(434)–4, 2G4ᵛ(456)–4, 2H5ᵛ(474)–4, 2I8(495)–4, 2K2ᵛ(500)–7, 2L1ᵛ(514)–3, 2L5(521)–4, 2M2ᵛ(532)–9, 2N3ᵛ(550)–3; *Note*: 3 figures in 2B.

Catchwords: *om.* A1–2, 138, 140, 410–11; superior figg. *om.* 95, 226, 380, 384, 413, 454, 526, 532; 2 *om.* (MIDSUMMER-), 11 And (By), 11 n. and (*In*), 19 ‸The ("~), 29 n. *om.* (ſignified), 52 Some‸ (~,), 52 n. A *roundle* (A *roundel*), 55 I mean‸ (~ ~,), 61 n. Parlous‸ (~,), 80 n. And‸ (~,), 86 *Hel.* (*He.*), 90 *Dem.* (And), 102 n. Holinſhed‸ (~,), 115 Go‸ (~,), 127 ‸Tongue, ("~,), 154 *om.* (*Enter*), 202 *A ſong*‸ (~ ~,), 208 For‸ (~,), 265 leaſt‸ (~,), 279 [bro-] *om.* (ther,), 280 birth‸ (~,), 281 *Orla.* (*Oral.*), 305 Should‸ (~,), 334 *Cro.* (*Cor.*), 361 I was‸ (~ ~;), 376 *Orla*‸ (~.), 383 Where‸ (~,), 423 *Lord*‸ (~.), 427 *om.* (*Lord.*), 428 n. "And (³*Who*), 438 Piſa‸ (~,), 450 n. S‸ (She), 472 *Pet*‸ (~.), 516 n. "*Enter.* ("~‸), 522 why‸ (~,), 547 n. "I ("If), 551 *om.* (To), 555 Theſ‸ (Theſe).

Explicit: 560 END OF VOLUME THE THIRD.

IV. A^2 B–2S^8 2T^2, (\$4 (–2T2) signed; 'VOL. IV.' on \$1), 324 leaves.

Pp. A1 ½t (as vol. 2), A1ᵛ blk, A2 t., A2ᵛ blk, on B1 *1* ½t All's Well that End Well, *2* Dram. Pers., *3* 4–155 text All's Well, *156* blk, *157* ½t Twelfth Night, *158* Dram. Pers., *159* 160–293 text 12 Night, *294* blk, *295* ½t Winter's Tale, *296* Dram. Pers., *297* 298–449 text W Tale, *450* blk, *451* ½t Macbeth, *452* Dram. Pers., *453* 454–644 text Macbeth.

Pagination: blk 156, 294, 450; 47 as 74, 260 as 60, 523 *dropt* 3, 622 as 22.

Press-figures: B2ᵛ(4)–5, B8(15)–2, C5(25)–5, C6(27)–1, D3ᵛ(38)–1, D8ᵛ(48)–3, E1ᵛ(50)–2, E5(57)–4, F4ᵛ(72)–5, F7ᵛ(78)–6, G7(93)–6, G7ᵛ(94)–4, H8(111)–4, H8ᵛ(112)–2, I4ᵛ(120)–5, I8(127)–4, K6(139)–1, K6ᵛ(140)–4, L7ᵛ(158)–1, L8ᵛ(160)–4, M7ᵛ(174)–5, N7ᵛ(190)–1, N8ᵛ(192)–1, O2ᵛ(196)–2, O7ᵛ(206)–3, P3ᵛ(214)–5, Q2ᵛ(228)–6, Q7ᵛ(238)–7, R8(255)–2 [*italic fig.*], R8ᵛ(256)–3, S7ᵛ(270)–6, T3ᵛ(278)–2, T6ᵛ(284)–7, U7(301)–7, X5ᵛ(314)–3, X6ᵛ(316)–1, Y6ᵛ(332)–7, Z2ᵛ(340)–3, Z3ᵛ(342)–1, 2A5(361)–7, 2A8(367)–4, 2B8(383)–4, 2C7(397)–2, 2C7ᵛ(398)–5, 2D1ᵛ(402)–2, 2E3ᵛ(422)–7, 2E7(429)–2, 2F5ᵛ(442)–2, 2F8ᵛ(448)–6, 2G4ᵛ(456)–3, 2G8(463)–5, 2H7(477)–5, 2H8(479)–6, 2I2ᵛ(484)–3, 2I8(495)–5, 2K5(505)–2, 2K6(507)–5, 2L3ᵛ(518)–2, 2L5(521)–5, 2M8(543)–2, 2M8ᵛ(544)–3, 2N3ᵛ(550)–2, 2N5(553)–3, 2O5ᵛ(570)–5, 2O7(573)–6, 2P3ᵛ(582)–5, 2P5(585)–2, 2Q3ᵛ(598)–7, 2R2ᵛ(612)–7, 2S3ᵛ(630)–7, 2S5(633)–6.

Catchwords: om. A1–2, 155–7, 294, 296, 450, 452; superior figg. om. 8 n., 14, 124, 125, 129, 162, 409, 463, 465, 503, 510, 526, 538, 578, 587, 602; 2 om. (ALL's), 16 *Pnr.* (*Par.*), 34 in∧ (~:), 39 *Count*∧ (~.), 42 n. [par-] tition∧ (~;), 99 *Wid*∧ (~.), 142 *Ber*∧ (~.), 270 lady∧ (~;), 335 n. Land- (Land∧), 341 *Pau*∧. (*Paul.*), 343 *Leo*∧ (~.), 366 fide∧ (~,), 378 *Ant.* (*Aut.*), 415 But, (~∧), 417 [in-] ftantly, (~∧), 462 n. Mr∧ (~.), 500 *than* (*thank*), 528 The (Will), 568 *Macb.* (*Mac.*), 576 And∧ (~,), 582 1 *Witch*∧ (~ ~.), 585 n. *Chaudron*∧ (~,), 589 1 *Witch*∧ (~ ~.), 591 om. (1 *Witch*.), 605 *Macb.* (*Mal.*), 640 Yet (And).

Explicit: 644 END OF VOLUME THE FOURTH.

V. A^2 B–2S^8 2T^6, (\$4 (B3 as B2, –2T4) signed; 'VOL. V.' on \$1), 328 leaves.

Pp. A1 ½t (as vol. 2), A1ᵛ blk, A2 t., A2ᵛ blk, on B1 *1* ½t King John, *2* Dram. Pers., *3* 4–136 text K. John, *137* ½t Richard II, *138* Dram. Pers., *139* 140–264 text Richard II, *265* ½t 1 Henry IV, *266* Dram. Pers., *267* 268–459 text 1 Hen. IV, *460* blk, *461* ½t 2 Henry IV, *462* blk 463–5 Induction, *466* Dram. Pers., *467* 468–648 text 2 Hen. IV, *649* 650–1 Epilogue.

Pagination: blk 460, 462; [↑] 463; 228 as 223, 327 as 32, 463–4 as 563–4, 520 as 420. Fold. plate inserted facing p. 648.

Press-figures: B7ᵛ(14)–5, C6ᵛ(28)–1, C8(31)–2, D7(45)–1, D8(47)–2, E2ᵛ(52)–2, E7ᵛ(62)–5, F1ᵛ(66)–5, F7(77)–6, G6(91)–7, H8(111)–3, I5ᵛ(122)–5, I7(125)–0, K1ᵛ(130)–3, L2ᵛ(148)–8, L7ᵛ(158)–0, M2ᵛ(164)–3, N3ᵛ(182)–6, O4ᵛ(200)–6, O5ᵛ(202)–3, P6ᵛ(220)–4, Q3ᵛ(230)–4, R6(251)–4,

S1ᵛ(258)–4,   T7ᵛ(286)–3,   2A1ᵛ(354)–1,   2A8ᵛ(368)–2,   2B1ᵛ(370)–5,
2B6ᵛ(380)–0,   2C1ᵛ(386)–9,   2C6ᵛ(396)–0,   2D1ᵛ(402)–9,   2D2ᵛ(404)–2,
2E6ᵛ(428)–4,   2F1ᵛ(434)–0,   2F4ᵛ(440)–4,   2G2ᵛ(452)–7,   2G5ᵛ(458)–0,
2H5ᵛ(474)–6,   2I5(489)–4,   2I6(491)–6,   2K8ᵛ(512)–0,   2L8ᵛ(528)–0,
2M4ᵛ(536)–4,   2M5ᵛ(538)–3,   2N8(559)–5,   2N8ᵛ(560)–6,   2O8ᵛ(576)–1,
2P6(587)–8,   2Q1ᵛ(594)–2,   2R1ᵛ(610)–2,   2S4ᵛ(632)–7,   2S5ᵛ(634)–4,
2T4(647)–6, 2T5(649)–0.

Catchwords: *om.* A1–2, 2, 137–8, 264, 266, 459–60, 462, 466; superior figg.
om. 12, 13 n., 14, 27, 89, 163, 183, 186, 187, 191, 195, 199, 204, 232, 233, 238,
239, 258, 267 n., 272, 357, 369, 409, 410, 413, 420, 430, 432, 446, 554, 581,
613; 7 n. Holinſhe (Holinſhed), 8 *K. John*ᴧ (~. ~.), 23 And, (~,), 55 n. day,
9~.), 72 n. time, (~.), 78 *Hub*, (I would), 108 [Or] Or (Or), 108 n. Or (the),
118 *om.* (let), 120 *om.* (Have), 130 Away, (~,), 157 n. Thu (Thus), 253 That,
(~,), 268 n. e. (i.e.), 308 *Hot*ᴧ (~.), 319 n. *fale* (*falſe*), 324 *Inter* (*Enter*), 327
*Lady*ᴧ (~.), 336 n. *om.* (In), 380 Come, (~,), 389 which, (~,), 399 *om.* (*Hoſt.*),
416 together, (~,), 433 But, (~,), 438 *Fal.* (*P. Henry.*), 457 [man-] er; (ner;),
461 N (INDUCTION), 469 n. So, (~,), 478 n. Ground, (ground.), 499 bear;
(~:), 502 n. Stationer's (Stationers), 510 come; (~?), 519 n. *Heywood*ᴧ (~,), 529
n. [an-] fuſtiad (fuſtian), 530 Again, (~,), 537 *Enter*, (~,), 540 man, (~,), 544
and (And), 548 n. diſeaſe, (*diſeaſe*,), 608 n. hand, (~,), 615 n. *om.* (In), 616 *Sha*
(*Shal.*), 627 graffing, (~,), 634 n. But (but), 639 bottle, (bottle-rogue).

Explicit: 652 END OF VOLUME THE FIFTH.

VI. *A*² B–2O⁸ 2P⁴, ($4 (–2P3,4) signed; 'VOL. VI.' on $1), 294 leaves.

Pp. A1 ½t (as vol. 2), A1ᵛ blk, A2 t., A2ᵛ blk, on B1 *i* ½t Henry V, *ii* Dram.
Pers., *iii* iv–v Chorus (Prologue), *vi* blk, 7 8–180 text Hen. V, *181* ½t 1 Henry
VI, *182* Dram. Pers., *183* 184–301 text 1 Hen. VI, *302* blk, *303* ½t 2 Henry VI,
304 Dram. Pers., *305* 306–442 text 2 Hen. VI, *443* ½t 3 Henry VI, *444* Dram.
Pers., *445* 446–584 text 3 Hen. VI.

Pagination: blk 302; B2ᵛ–B3 roman numerals not affecting sequence.

Press-figures: B5ᵛ(10)–6,   B7(13)–1,   C5(25)–7,   C6(27)–2,   D7(45)–2,
E6ᵛ(60)–7,   F5ᵛ(74)–5,   G2ᵛ(84)–4,   H1ᵛ(98)–5,   H2ᵛ(100)–2,   I3ᵛ(118)–7,
K5ᵛ(138)–1, K6ᵛ(140)–2, L5ᵛ(154)–7, L8ᵛ(160)–4, M5ᵛ(170)–1, M8ᵛ(176)–4,
N7ᵛ(190)–1, N8ᵛ(192)–2, O3ᵛ(198)–3, O4ᵛ(200)–4, P6ᵛ(220)–1, P7ᵛ(222)–2,
Q3ᵛ(230)–2, Q6ᵛ(236)–4, R5ᵛ(250)–4, R7(253)–5, S4ᵛ(264)–5, S6(267)–1,
T3ᵛ(278)–6, T8ᵛ(288)–1, U5(297)–2, U6(299)–5, X4ᵛ(312)–1, X7ᵛ(318)–4,
Y4ᵛ(328)–3, Y7ᵛ(334)–3, Z5(345)–3, Z6(347)–5, 2A3ᵛ(358)–6, 2A8ᵛ(368)–3,
2B5ᵛ(378)–5,   2B8ᵛ(384)–3,   2C2ᵛ(388)–4,   2C7ᵛ(398)–2,   2D8ᵛ(416)–4,
2E3ᵛ(422)–3,   2E4ᵛ(424)–7,   2F5(441)–2,   2F7ᵛ(446)–4,   2G5ᵛ(458)–4,
2G7(461)–3,   2H4ᵛ(472)–4,   2H7ᵛ(478)–6,   2I2ᵛ(484)–5,   2I8(495)–6,
2K6ᵛ(508)–5,   2K7ᵛ(510)–3,   2L7ᵛ(526)–1,   2L8ᵛ(528)–4,   2M3ᵛ(534)–4,
2M6ᵛ(540)–1,   2N1ᵛ(546)–7,   2N7(557)–5,   2O7ᵛ(574)–7,   2O8ᵛ(576)–2,
2P3(581)–7.

Catchwords: *om*. A1–2, i–ii, vi, 181–2, 302–4, 443–4; superior figg. *om*. 26, 33, 51, 56 n., 65, 113, 142, 201, 226, 271, 306, 380, 413, 424, 481, 482, 486, 497, 508, 516, 518; 7 which‸ (~,), 30 n. So, (~‸), 31 n. In (IN), 50 n. *Temper'd*‸ (~,), 64 n. ‸wherein ("~), 162 degree‸ (~.), 300 n. apparent‸ (~,), 336 *Car*. (Cardinal,), 432 That‸ (~,), 452 *York*‸ (~.), 472 I think‸ (~ ~,).

Explicit: 548 END OF VOLUME THE SIXTH.

VII. *A*² B–2D⁸ 2E⁸ (–2E7 + '2G7') 2F–2K⁸, ($4 (–$4 FNOST) signed; 'VOL. VII.' on $1 (+ 2G7)), 258 leaves.

Pp. A1 ½t (as vol. 2), A1ᵛ blk, A2 t., A2ᵛ blk, on B1 *1* ½t Richard III, *2* Dram. Pers., *3* 4–179 text Richard III, *180* blk, *181* ½t Henry VIII, *182* Dram. Pers., *183* 184–5 Prologue, *186* blk, *187* 188–333 text Henry VIII, *334*–335 Epilogue, *336* blk, *337* ½t Coriolanus, *338* Dram. Pers., *339* 340–512 text Cor.

Pagination: blk 180, 185, 336; 334 unnumbered.

Press-figures: B8(15)–1, C7(29)–2, D1ᵛ(34)–2, E2ᵛ(52)–1, G6(91)–4, H1ᵛ(98)–6, I8(127)–6, K3ᵛ(134)–3, K5(137)–2, L5ᵛ(154)–3, M1ᵛ(162)–3, P3ᵛ(214)–2, Q2ᵛ(228)–3, R7ᵛ(254)–4, U1ᵛ(290)–5, U5(197)–4, X2ᵛ(308)–2, Y5ᵛ(330)–2, Z2ᵛ(340)–3, 2A3ᵛ(358)–4, 2B5ᵛ(378)–3, 2B8ᵛ(384)–1, 2C2ᵛ(388)–4, 2C8(399)–1, 2D2ᵛ(404)–6, 2D8(415)–5, 2F8ᵛ(448)–5, 2G6(459)–2, 2G8ᵛ(464)–5, 2H8ᵛ(480)–1, 2I7(493)–1, 2K5ᵛ(506)–4; unfigured F, N, O, S, T, 2E.

Catchwords: *om*. A1–2, 1–2, 180–2, 186, 336–7, superior figg. *om*. 5, 90, 119, 195, 302, 331, 346, 377, 400, 453; 136 *K. Rich*. (*king rich*.), 152 Tel (Tell), 219 *Enter* (*Re-enter*), 240 Follow (*Cham*.), 259 Would (They), 345 *2 Cit*. (*Men*.), 457 *Vol*‸ (~.).

Explicit: 512 END OF VOLUME THE SEVENTH.

VIII. *A*² B–2O⁸ 2P⁴ 2Q², ($4 (–2P3, 2Q2) signed; 'VOL. VIII.' on $1), 296 leaves.

Pp. A1 ½t (as vol. 2), A1ᵛ blk, A2 t., A2ᵛ blk, on B1 *1* ½t Julius Cæsar, *2* Dram. Pers., *3* 4–127 text J. Cæsar, *128* blk, *129* ½t Antony and Cleopatra, *130* Dram. Pers., *131* 132–330 text A & C, *331* ½t Timon of Athens, *332* Dram. Pers., *333* 334–483 text Timon, *484* blk, *485* ½t Titus Andronicus, *486* Dram. Pers., *487* 488–588 text Titus.

Pagination: blk 128, 484.

Press-figures: B6(11)–2, C5ᵛ(26)–3, D8(47)–4, E8(63)–1, F8(79)–1, G5ᵛ(90)–1, G8ᵛ(96)–5, H5ᵛ(106)–2, I1ᵛ(114)–5, K6(139)–2, K7(141)–5, L5(153)–6, M3ᵛ(166)–2, M7(173)–5, N2ᵛ(180)–1, N3ᵛ(182)–5, O7ᵛ(206)–3, P5ᵛ(218)–4, Q5(233)–2, R5(249)–2, S7ᵛ(270)–2, T7(285)–2, U1ᵛ(290)–1, X1ᵛ(306)–2, Y1ᵛ(322)–1, Z6(347)–6, 2A7ᵛ(366)–3, 2B1ᵛ(370)–4, 2C5ᵛ(394)–3, 2D7ᵛ(414)–4, 2D8ᵛ(416)–2, 2E3ᵛ(422)–2, 2F8(447)–1, 2G5ᵛ(458)–2, 2H1ᵛ(466)–5, 2I5ᵛ(490)–5, 2K6(507)–3, 2K7(509)–6, 2L6ᵛ(524)–2, 2L7ᵛ(526)–4, 2M8(543)–6, 2N2ᵛ(548)–6, 2N3ᵛ(550)–3, 2O1ᵛ(562)–1, 2O6ᵛ(572)–2, 2P4(583)–2, 2P5ᵛ(586)–2; unfigured 2Q.

Catchwords: *om.* A1–2ᵛ, 1–2, 128–30, 331–2, 483–6; superior figures *om.* 12, 38, 74, 79, 131, 174, 268, 367, 388, 410, 422, 458, 477, 513; 113 *Pin* (*Pind.*), 126 ∧The ([~), 160 ∧It ((~), 198 He (Her), 203 *Men*∧ (~.), 218 *Eno.* (So), 249 And (Ourſelves), 254 a *feeder*∧ (~ ~,), 336 n. may (be), 366 Honour∧ (~,), 468 n. an (and), 475 2 *Sen.* (3 ~.), 487 And∧ (~,), 492 Reli- (*Tit.*), 493 *Tit.* (Religiouſly), 529 *om.* (That), 541 *Boy*∧ (~.).

Explicit: 588 END OF VOLUME THE EIGHTH.

IX. *A*² B–2Q⁸ 2R⁴ 2S² (2S2 blk), (\$4 (–2R3,4, 2S2) signed; 'VOL. IX.' on \$1), 312 leaves.

Pp. A1 ½t (as vol. 2), A1ᵛ blk, A2 t., A2ᵛ blk, on B1 *1* ½t Troilus and Cressida, *2* Preface, *3–5* Prologue, *6* Dram. Pers., *7* 8–181 text T & C, *182* blk, *183* ½t Cymbeline, *184* Dram. Pers., *185* 186–374 text Cymb., *375* ½t King Lear, *376* Dram. Pers., *377* 378–618 text K. Lear.

Pagination: blk 182; 31 *sometimes* as 3, 266 as 269.

Press-figures: B6(11)–5, B6ᵛ(12)–4, C2ᵛ(20)–5, D8(47)–3, E2ᵛ(52)–1, E6(59)–2, F3ᵛ(70)–4, F4ᵛ(72)–3, G2ᵛ(84)–4, H5ᵛ(106)–1, I1ᵛ(114)–5, K1ᵛ(130)–1, L6(155)–2, L6ᵛ(156)–6, M8(175)–1, O8(207)–1, P2ᵛ(212)–2, Q7(237)–6, Q7ᵛ(238)–1, R6(251)–2, S8ᵛ(272)–7, T2ᵛ(276)–1, T7ᵛ(286)–7, U5(297)–6, U7ᵛ(302)–3, X3ᵛ(310)–1, X8ᵛ(320)–4, Y5(329)–2, Y7ᵛ(334)–8, Z8(351)–3, 2A5ᵛ(362)–6, 2B7ᵛ(382)–3, 2C6(395)–6, 2C7(397)–3, 2D3ᵛ(406)–6, 2D7(413)–3, 2E5ᵛ(426)–4, 2F8(447)–1, 2G7ᵛ(462)–2, 2H5ᵛ(474)–6, 2I7(493)–4, 2K6ᵛ(508)–4, 2L7ᵛ(526)–5, 2M8(543)–4, 2N5(553)–3, 2O2ᵛ(564)–7, 2O5ᵛ(570)–8, 2P8ᵛ(592)–7, 2Q3ᵛ(598)–7, 2Q5(601)–8, 2R4(615)–8; unfigured N, 2S.

Catchwords: *om.* A1–2, 6, 181–4, 375–6; superior figg. *om.* 29, 48, 62, 94, 97, 135, 142, 150, 171, 172, 210, 232, 260, 268, 344, 357, 398, 435, 438, 442, 456, 470, 487, 542, 546, 555, 562, 572, 586, 588, 595, 607; 228 *Clo.* (*Clot.*), 247 n. I (It), 311 Both∧ (~.), 338 more (More), 400 Now∧ (~,), 433 who∧ (~,), 518 n. [de-] vil.∧ (~."), 561 n. ∧.e. (i.e.).

Explicit: 619 END OF VOLUME THE NINTH.

X. *A*² B–3B⁸ 3C² (3C2 blk), (\$4 (–2M4, 3C2) signed; 'VOL. X.' on \$1), 380 leaves.

Pp. A1 ½t (as vol. 2), A1ᵛ blk, A2 t., A2ᵛ blk, on B1 *1* ½t Romeo and Juliet, *2* blk, *3* Prologue, *4* Dram. Pers., *5* 6–180 text R & J, *181* 182–254 The Tragicall Hyſtory of Romeus and Juliet, *255* ½t Hamlet, *256* Dram. Pers., *257* 258–533 text Hamlet, *534* blk, *535* ½t Othello, *536* Dram. Pers., *537* 538–754 text Othello, *755–6* (2S2) blk leaf.

Pagination: blk 2, 534, 755–6; 181, 183 unnumbered, 229 as 239, 297 as 29, 541–559 as 541–555, 714 as 174, 748 as 874.

Press-figures: B5ᵛ(10)–2, C7ᵛ(30)–0, D5ᵛ(42)–2, E7(61)–8, F8ᵛ(80)–5, G1ᵛ(82)–9, G7(93)–4, H8(111)–6, H8ᵛ(112)–9, I5ᵛ(122)–4, K5(137)–5, K5ᵛ(138)–0, L7(157)–2, M7(173)–2, M8(175)–1, N5(185)–0, N5ᵛ(186)–3,

O8(207)–2, O8ᵛ(208)–9, P5(217)–7, P8(223)–1, Q3ᵛ(230)–1, Q6ᵛ(236)–0, R3ᵛ(246)–4, R7(253)–0, S6(267)–7, S7(269)–4, T8(287)–2, U7(301)–8, U8(303)–6, X2ᵛ(308)–6, Y6(331)–1, Y6ᵛ(332)–1, Z6ᵛ(348)–8, Z7ᵛ(350)–4, 2A4ᵛ(360)–9, 2A7ᵛ(366)–6, 2B2ᵛ(372)–8, 2B3ᵛ(374)–5, 2C4ᵛ(392)–5, 2D6(411)–5, 2D8ᵛ(416)–4, 2E1ᵛ(418)–8, 2E8ᵛ(432)–0, 2F4ᵛ(440)–6, 2F5ᵛ(442)–9, 2G7(461)–8, 2H1ᵛ(466)–1, 2H6ᵛ(476)–4, 2I2ᵛ(484)–5, 2K2ᵛ(500)–6, 2L5(521)–4, 2L6(523)–1, 2M5(537)–5, 2M7ᵛ(542)–0, 2N7ᵛ(558)–8, 2O7(573)–8, 2O7ᵛ(574)–7, 2P1ᵛ(578)–0, 2P8ᵛ(592)–4, 2Q4ᵛ(600)–3, 2Q6(603)–8, 2R7ᵛ(622)–6, 2R8ᵛ(624)–7, 2S1ᵛ(626)–6, 2S4ᵛ(632)–4, 2T8ᵛ(656)–5, 2U6ᵛ(668)–3, 2X8(687)–0, 2Y7(701)–6, 2Z5ᵛ(714)–3, 2Z8ᵛ(720)–4, 3A3ᵛ(726)–1, 3B1ᵛ(738)–2, 3B7(749)–7; unfigured 3C.

Catchwords: *om.* A1–2, 1–2, 4, 255–6, 534–6; superior figg. *om.* 18, 30, 36, 44, 55, 57, 63, 64, 132, 137, 138, 152, 156, 260, 266, 269, 277, 280, 312, 327, 329, 332, 365, 423, 432, 455, 462, 482, 540, 550, 567, 575, 579, 594, 611, 641, 649, 750; 8 n. [Gaſ-] coign‸ (~,), 9 n. The (This), 11 *La.* (*L. Cap.*), 32 n. well (wel), 36 n. again‸ (~,), 56 *om.* (Ariſe), 92 n. [epi-] taph‸ (~,), 99 n. printed‸ (~)), 102 *om.* (*Jul.*), 119 What‸ (~,), 124 n. *Anſwer* (*To anſwer*), 128 Look‸ (~,), 130 Thy (*Jul.*), 162 And‸ (~,), 239 For‸ (~,), 248 Feare (Fear), 273 n. heart‸ (~.), 282 n. [im-] portance‸ (~,), 304 *Hor*‸ (~.), 323 *Po*‸ (*Pol.*), 324 *Po.* (*Pol.*), 330 *om.* (what), 333 This‸ (~,), 340 n. I for (I forgot), 356 play‸ (~;), 358 *Wth* (*With*), 366 Fie, (~‸), 371 And‸ (~,), 371 n. ‸You ("~), 372 *om.* (The), 373 n. ‸By ("~), 374 ‸Is ("~), 374 n. *Heat*‸ (~,), 441 and‸ (~,), 474 n. ‸This ("~), 481 n. This (The), 484 Clown. (~‸), 540 n. —I (—*I*), 542 He‸ (~,), 551 *Iago.* (*Enter*), 555 n. *Motio* (*Motion*), 578 A na‸ (A natural), 585 [tor-] ment, (~;), 616 n. ‸*Piſo.* ("~.), 647 n. her‸ (~,).

Explicit: 754 THE END.

Paper: White, laid; Medium (uncut: 9 × 5¾ in.); no vis. wmk.

Type: Advertisement: english (4.4 mm), SJ's Preface: pica (4.0 mm), leaded; prefatory matter: sm. pica (3.5 mm), leaded, text: pica (4.0 mm), footnotes: long primer (3.15 mm).

Plates: (2),[1] 1. I. Front. Port. Shakespeare 'Engraved by JOHN HALL from an ORIGINAL PICTURE in the Poſſeſſion of his Grace the Duke of Chandos. London. Publiſhed as the Act directs March 25ᵗʰ. 1785, by Rivington & Partners.'

2. V. facing 648: folding pl. 'Morris Dancers. From an Ancient Window in the House of George Tollet Esqʳ. at Betley in Staffordshire. J. Keyse Sherwin sculpsit. To be placed at the end of the 2ᵈ. part of K. Henry IV.'

References: Jaggard 504–5; Courtney 104, 109; Sherbo, *Birth of Shakespeare Studies* (1956), ch. 7, and *Isaac Reed* (1989), ch. 6. For the status of this edn. see Woodson, *SB* xxviii (1975), 318–20, and xxxi (1978), 208–10; Sherbo, *SB* xxxii (1979), 241–6, and Woodson, *SB* xxxix (1986), 220–29; ESTC: t138853.

Notes: The corrections made by SJ and published in Malone's *Supplement*, 1780 (65.10SP/7/S, above), are incorporated into this edn., but no new Johnsonian material is here added. This edn., often described as the 'First Variorum', was largely superintended by Isaac Reed whose receipt for £100 for the work from the proprietors, Bathurst, Rivington, &c., is dated 10 Nov. 1785 (MS: DFo (W. b. 475).

Copies: O² (1. Mal. 1059–60 inc. MS notes by 'Edmond Malone'; 2. Mal. adds. 50 e. 9–18, 'M. Bell' — 'R.W. Chapman');

USA: Hyde (3rd. E of 'Egremont'), NjP; *Japan*: [Kyoto]; *UK*: C, DUNu, L (642. f. 11–20), NOu, Oef.

---

[1] In Dobell's *Catalogue* 66 (1941), 19 (at £3. 10s.), was a note from Malone to Rivington, 18 Oct. 1785, relative to Hall's engravings for 'Reed's Shakespeare'.

65.10SP/8b   Shakespeare, Prefatory matter   1788

The prefatory matter in vol. 1, including SJ's Preface, was separately issued in 1788 with a special title, as:

PREFACES, | BY | DIFFERENT EDITORS; | WITH AN ACCOUNT OF | THE LIFE AND WRITINGS OF SHAKESPEAR, | AS PREFIXED BY | JOHNSON AND STEEVENS, | TO THEIR EDITION OF HIS WORKS. | 1785. | [short swelled rule] | LONDON, | PRINTED IN THE YEAR MDCCLXXXVIII.

8°, π1 a2 A–Y⁸ Z⁶ (−Z6 = ? π1), 184 leaves.
Copy: DFo (PR 2894. P7).

EDITIONS OF SHAKESPEARE
AFTER JOHNSON'S DEATH

Few editions of Shakespeare published after Johnson's death are without some of his notes, and many regularly include his Preface, General Observations, and Critical notes. It is beyond the scope of this bibliography to offer descriptions of them. The following list of edns. which contain Johnsonian material does not extend beyond 1800, and is still probably incomplete.

1785–87   Bell's edn. 10 vols. No Johnson. [O]
(Jaggard 505 says '16 vols. 12°' and 20 vols. 12° on fine & regular paper).

1786–90   J. Nichols's edn. 7 vols. No Preface, but a few explanatory notes. [L, O]

1786–94   ed. J. Rann. 6 vols. No Johnson. [O]

65.10SP/9   Shakespeare, Bell's Edition   1788

Bell's edition. 20 vols. SJ's Preface, General Obs., and notes.
  References: Courtney 109. [L², O]

1790   Stockdale's edn. 3 vols. No Johnson. [O]

65.10SP/10   Shakespeare, Malone's edition   1790

Malone's edition. 10 vols. Preface (I. *1* 2–49), and notes in full.
  [Hyde ('Malone' — 'Bindley'), L², O³]

1790   'From Mr Malone's edition.', Rivington, &c., 7 vols.
No Preface, but General Observations and a few notes. [O]

65.10SP/11   Shakespeare, Ayscough's edition   1791

Ed. S. Ayscough, Dublin: William Jones, 2 vols.
  Preface (I. *v* vi–xxxiv), but no notes. [L, O]

65.10SP/12a   Shakespeare, Boydell's edition   [1791]–1800

Boydell's edn. 9 vols. Preface. [L²]
  (There was also a separate issue of SJ's Preface from vol. 1 of this edn.):

65.10SP/12b   Shakespeare, Preface (with Pope's)   ?1793–4

THE | PREFACES | OF | POPE AND JOHNSON | TO THE |
DRAMATIC WORKS | OF | SHAKESPEARE.
  2°, *1–11²*, (unsigned), 22 leaves.
  Pp. *i* t., *ii* blk, *iii* iv–xii Pope's Preface, *xiii* xiv–xliii Johnson's Preface, dh
(and ht): DR. JOHNSON'S PREFACE., *xliv* blk.
  Pagination: roman.
  Press-figures, Catchwords, & Explicit: none.
  Paper: White, wove; Medium ? (18 × 12 in.); wmk.: 1794 | J WHATMAN
  Notes: An offprint from the LP issue of Boydell's edn., c. 1794–5. Boydell's
edn. was printed by William Bulmer.
  Copies: NIC (uncut, blue-grey boards).

1791   London 8 vols. No Johnson.

1792   Edinburgh: W. Gordon. 8 vols. No Johnson (despite t.). Jaggard 506.
[E, O]

65.10SP/13 Shakespeare, second variorum, 1793
fourth edition

London. 'Second Variorum', 4th edn., ed. Isaac Reed.[1]
References: Jaggard 506; Courtney 104
15 vols. Preface and notes in full.
[Hyde ('George Steevens'); *Can*: CaOHM (LP, pres. Steevens to Charles
Burney); *UK*: C, L[3], MRu ('Geo. Steevens'), O[3], Oef].

[1] In vol. 1, p. ix is the note: 'The present editors must also acknowledge, that unless in particular instances, where the voice of the publick had decided against the remarks of Dr. Johnson, they have hesitated to displace them; and had rather be charged with superstititous reverence for his name, than censured for a presumptuous disregard of his opinions.'

65.10SP/14 Shakespeare, Dublin 1794

Dublin: J. Exshaw (reprint of 1793 'Variorum').
16 vols. Preface and notes in full. [CaOHM; L, O]

1795   Glasgow: Blair's edn. 8 vols. No Johnson. [O]

65.10SP/15 Shakespeare, Bioren & Madan, 1795–6
Philadelphia

Philadelphia: Bioren & Madan.[1] 8 vols. Preface and Observations in full.
Jaggard 507. [Hyde]

[1] Evans 29496; 31180. A list of American editions of Shakespeare (December 1889) is in O: (JJ: 'Shakespeare', Box 1). The editor of this edn. is unknown, but after complaining about excessive annotation declared that 'the present edition contains no notes of any kind, except by Dr. Johnson, at the end of each play' (Preface).

1796   London. 8 vols. No Johnson.

1797   London: J. Nichols 8 vols. No Johnson. [O]

1797–1801   Brunswick: C. Wagner. [L: 11766 c. 16]

1798   London: D. Ogilvie & Son. 10 vols. No Preface, but Gen. Observations prefixed to each play. [O]

65.10SP/16 Shakespeare, Tourneisen, Basil 1799-1800

Basil: J. J. Tourneisen. 12 vols. (After Reed, 1793); Preface and notes.
References: Jaggard 508; Courtney 100.
[L[2] (C. 134: dd.1, 'Ludwig Tieck'), O].

65.10SP/17   Shakespeare, Harding's edition   1800

London: T. Bensley. 'Harding's edn.' [A collection of Harding's edd. of individual plays, published 1798–99.]
   12 vols. Preface and selected notes. [L, O]

1800   Berwick 9 vols. No Johnson [O]

65.10SP/TF/1   Shakespeare, French translation   1786

Variétés littéraires, ed. Jean-Baptiste Antoine Suard, 1786, includes a translation of SJ's 'Preface'.

65.10SP/TG/1   Shakespeare, German translation   1816

G.G. Bredows nachgelassene Schriften, ed. J. Kunisch. Breslau, 1816. Not seen. Courtney 107 reports the inclusion of part of SJ's Preface.

65.10SP/TI/1   Shakespeare, Italian translation   1819

Tragedie di Shakespeare tradotte da Michele Leoni. Verona. 1819.
   Courtney 107, notes that the 'first forty-two' pp. of SJ's Preface are here translated in i. 31–74. Not seen.

65.10SP/TI/2   Shakespeare, Italian translation   1960

Samuel Johnson: I. Preface to Shakespeare e altri scritti shakespeariani. Scelta, introduzzi, e note a cura di Agostino Lombardo. Bari, Adriatica. 1960.
   Pp. 329, in *Biblioteca Italiana di testi Inglesi*, 4
   Copy: CtY (Ig. 7K. 765JK).

65.10SP/TJ/1   Shakespeare (Proposals etc.),   1948–9
                        Japanese translation

Translated into Japanese by Ken-ichi Yoshida, published in Tokyo: Shisaku-sha, 1948-9.
   Includes the Proposals (56.6SP/1, above), and the Preface and Notes deriving from 65.10SP/1 (taken from Walter Raleigh's *Johnson on Shakespeare* (Oxford, 1908).
   This was reissued in 1975.

65.10SP/TJ/2   Shakespeare (Proposals etc.),   1978
            Japanese translation

Translated by Makoto Nakagawa, Tokyo: Aratake-shuppan, 1978.[1]
Includes the same material as 65.10SP/TJ/1.

---

[1] I am indebted to Prof. Daisuke Nagashima for information on these versions.

66.4BD/1   Blackrie's Disquisition   1766

In SJ's Diary for 1765 (MS: Hyde; *Diaries*, 90), s.d. 19 March, is the entry, 'corrected Blackrie's sheet'. The editors of *Diaries* conjectured that Blackrie was a compositor working on SJ's *Shakespeare*, but since that work was printed by William Strahan the identification cannot stand, for none of Strahan's men was so named.[1] The name is surely that of an author, and the only possibility seems to be Alexander Blackrie (d. 1772*), an apothecary, who published in 1766, a work exposing the secret of Dr Chittick's cure for gravel:

A | DISQUISITION | ON MEDICINES | THAT DISSOLVE THE STONE | IN WHICH | Dr. Chittick's SECRET | Is CONSIDERED and DISCOVERED. | [rule] | Nullius addictus jurare in verba magiſtri. | Hor. | [rule] | BY | ALEXANDER BLACKRIE. | [bevelled parallel rule] | LONDON: | Printed for D. Wilson, in the Strand. | [medium rule] | M.DCC.LXVI.

12°, *A*² B–F¹² G², ($6 (–C2, D6, E6) signed); 64 leaves.
Pp. *i* t., *ii* blk, *iii* Dedication to 'John Hyde, Esq; of Charterhouse Square', *iv* blk, on B1 *1* 2–123 text, *124* blk.
References: ESTC: n002438.
Notes: The first sheet (sig. B, pp. 1–24) gives a general survey of the topic and includes some mild animadversions on Chittick's secrecy in managing his remedy. It is just, and only just possible that SJ may have 'corrected' it, though it has no marks of his style. SJ's correction, whatever it was, took place scarcely a month before publication which might be thought to argue against the revision of the first sheet of the text, but the piece is a slim pamphlet and would have taken only a short time to work off. Blackrie's second edn. of 1771 (ESTC: t034594) included a long list of subscribers, but there is nothing in it to suggest Johnsonian revision (*Copies*: Eu², L, Ecp, O (Radcl.)). There was a French translation in 1775 (ESTC: n021808). It was reviewed in *Gents. Mag.* xxxvi (Apr. 1766), 191, price 2s., as 'the best practical treatise on the subject that has ever appeared'.
Copies: Eu (*I.32/18)

USA: [DNLM, IEN], NIC, [PPC, PPULC, NNNAM]; *UK*: L (1651/846), MRu, SAN.

¹ The name is not to be found in Strahan's contemporary papers (L: Add. MS 48801 includes a list of his apprentices together with family and personal details); nor does it or any analogy appear among his or anyone else's apprentices in McKenzie *Apprentices* (1978), 339–41.

66.4WM/1   Anna Williams's Miscellanies   1766

MISCELLANIES | IN | PROSE and VERSE. | By ANNA WILLIAMS. | [Ornamental floral spray] | [double rule] | LONDON: | Printed for T. Davies, in Great Ruffel-Street, Covent-Garden. | M,DCC,LXVI.

4°, *A*² B–2A⁴, ($2 signed), 94 leaves.

Pp. A1 *i* t., *ii* blk, *iii–iv* SJ's Advert. dh: [hp.] | ADVERTISEMENT., *iv* Erratum (re. p. 98, l. 12: *not* Johnsonian), on B1 *1* 2–184 text dh: [Headp.] | ESSAYS | IN | VERSE and PROSE. | [rule], ht: *ESSAYS.*, *142* blk, *143* ½t: THE | UNINHABITED ISLAND | FROM THE ITALIAN OF | METASTASIO., *144* blk, *145* 146–7 dh: The ARGUMENT., *148* DRAMATIS PERSONÆ., *149* 150–84 text dh: The UNINHABITED ISLAND.

Pagination: blk 142, 144.

Press-figures: A2(iii)–3, B4(7)–3, B4ᵛ(8)–2, C3(13)–3, C4(15)–2, D1ᵛ(18)–2, E1ᵛ(26)–2, E3(29)–1, F3ᵛ(38)–3, G4(47)–5, H1ᵛ(50)–3, H2ᵛ(52)–9, I2ᵛ(60)–9, I4(63)–7, K1ᵛ(66)–6, K3(69)–3, L1ᵛ(74)–1, M1ᵛ(82)–3, M3(85)–4, N3ᵛ(94)–4, O1ᵛ(98)–9, O4ᵛ(104)–3, P3(109)–9, P4(111)–1, Q1ᵛ(114)–4, R3(125)–6, R4(127)–2, S1ᵛ(130)–1, T2ᵛ(140)–3, U3ᵛ(150)–*F* [swash *inverted*], X3ᵛ(158)–7, X4ᵛ(160)–6, Y2ᵛ(164)–7, Y3ᵛ(166)–4, Z2ᵛ(172)–7, Z3ᵛ(174)–5, 2A1ᵛ(178)–2, 2A2ᵛ(180)–1.

Catchwords: 8 *om.* (A lift), 13 Swift, (~,), 22 The (AN), 27 To (TO), 48 *om.* (The), 56 QUICK (Quick), 65 The (THE), 80 *om.* (BOILEAU), 96 The (RASSELAS), 103 *om.* (To), 141 The (THE), 142–44 *om.*, 148 *om.* (The).

Explicit: 184 FINIS.

Paper: White, laid; Demy (uncut: 11¼ × 8¾ in.); wmk.: arabesque.

Type: Text: great primer (5.5 mm), leaded; footnotes: pica (4.0 mm); ornaments: title, 2, 5, 9, 12, 16, 19, 22, 23, 27, 30, 36, 39, 41, 43, 45, 54, 62, 67, 80, 89, 93, 101, 103, 106, 141, 147.

References: *Life*, ii. 25, 479 (Courtney 111–12); CH 148; Hazen 213–16; *Rothschild* 2571; *Tinker* 1348–9; *Poems²*; *Works* (Yale), xvi. 212 ff; ESTC: t077856.

Notes: 750 copies printed for Anna Williams in March 1766 by William Strahan (L: Add. MS 48802A, fo. 67), the account for which was not settled until 4 December 1769. The finished work was published at 5s. on 1 April 1766 (*Lond. Chron.*). The distribution of press-figg. suggests that the work was printed in sections, as:

I.   B–C, pp. 1–16, figg. 2, 3
II. D–G, pp. 17–48, figg. 1, 2, 3, 5 'Epitaph on Pollio' begins D1 (p. 17)
III. H–L, pp. 49–80, figg. 1, 3, 6, 7, 9 'Excursion' begins H1, no cwd. L4ᵛ (80)
IV. M–N, pp. 81–96, figg. 3, 4 'Boileau to his Gardener' begins M1 (81)
V.   O–T, pp. 97–144, figg. 1, 2, 3, 4, 6, 9 'Rasselas to Imlac' begins O1 (97), wrong cwd. N4ᵛ (96)
VI. U–2A, pp. 145–84, figg. 1, 2, 4, 5, 6, 7 'The Argument' of 'The Uninhabited Island' begins on U1 (145)
VII. A, pp. i–iv, figg. 3 Title & prelims.

For the subscription see 'Proposals', 1750 (50GM/20) and ?1762 (62.7WP) above. According to Lady Knight ('Memoir' in *Johns. Misc.*, ii. 170–6), AW got £150 by this publication, but the figure can hardly be exact since 750 copies at 5s. could produce only £187. 10s. of which £48. 0s. 6d. was due to Strahan for the printing. Nichols reported that '£100 (which was laid out in Bridge-bonds) was added to her little store by the liberality of her subscribers.'[1]

According to Frances Reynolds SJ superintended and corrected the whole edn., and Percy gave him the whole responsibility.[2] The volume represents an important partial collection of SJ's early verse, and is the vehicle for his tale 'The Fountains'. Attribution is complicated, but the following table draws upon contemporary sources, which are discussed and explained in introd. to *Poems²*.[3]

Advertisement	SJ	Tyers (*GM* 84)[4]; *Life*, ii. 25; JBj
1–2 The Ant	SJ	HLT; TP¹; *Works* 87; *Poems²* 153
3 Sonnet. To a Lady of indiscreet Virtue	Percy	TP¹
4–5 To Clara		
6 The Rose		
7–9 The Valley of the Moon		
10 To Miss— . . . Net-work Purse	SJ	EM; Pearch 70; *Life*, *Poems²* 96; JBj
11–12 The Caution		
13–16 To Myrtillis	?SJ	Bell '89; *Poems²* 465 'deny'
17 [Untitled] Epitaph on Pollio, with translation 'Here Pollio lies . . .'		
18–19 The Happy Life	SJ	EM; *Life*; *Poems²* 455, 'doubt'
20–22 On a Young Lady		

23 Epitaph on Claudy Phillips	SJ	TP[1]; *Works* 87; *Life*; *Poems*[2] 89; JBj
24–7 The Wish[5]	HLT	EM
28 To Cleora on her absence[6]	SJ	*Poems*[2] 52
29–30 The True Hero		
31–4 Verses to Mr Richardson	AW & SJ	EM; *Life*; *Poems*[2] 435
35 To Miss S. Grey		
36 Epitaph on Mr Worral	?SJ	TP[1][7]
37 To Marcus		
38–9 Occasioned by the marriage of Miss—		
40–1 An Italian Song		
42–3 On the death of Stephen Grey	AW & SJ	EM; *Life*; *Poems*[2] 431
44–5 On the death of Sir Erasmus Philipps		
46–8 Blondiaux [*prose*]	'Hon Mr Southwell'	TP[2]
49–58 The Excursion	AW & SJ	*Life*; *Poems*[2] 433
59–62 An Ode		
63–5 On the Death of the Patriot Marcus		
66–7 The Petition		
68–70 Reflections on a grave digging	AW & SJ	EM; HLT; *Life*; *Poems*[2] 433
71–3 The Happy Solitude		
74–80 The Three Warnings[8]	HLT	HLT; TP[1]; HMT; EM (doubted); *Thraliana* 225; *Poems*[2] 468
81–9 Boileau to his Gardener	HLT	HLT[9]
90–1 Ode on Friendship	SJ	*GM* 85; JBj (var., from *GM* 43); *Life*; *Poems*[2] 36
92–3 To Laura		
94–6 Epitaph on Sir Thomas Hanmer	SJ	*Hawkins*; *Life*; *Poems*[2] 94
97–101 Rasselas to Imlac	Frances Greville	EM; (? Frances Reynolds, Hazen)
102–3 An Ode	Frances Reynolds	Hazen
104–6 To Miss*** . . . Harpsichord	SJ	Pearch 70; *Poems*[2] 97
107–10 The Nunnery		
111–41 The Fountains [*prose*]	SJ	HLT; RWG; *Thraliana* 205
145–84 The Uninhabited Island	John Hoole	Hoole, *Dramas of Metastasio* (1800), i. xxvi.

Copies: O (13 θ. 189, 'R.W. Greatheed Esq,; 'The gift of Mrs Piozzi.');

USA: CSmH, CtY[2] (1. Tinker 1348 'H.M. Thrale'; 2. Tinker 1349 'James Boswell' jun.), Hyde[3] (1. 'Thomas Percy'; 2. 'Elizabeth Carter'; 3. 'R. B. Adam'), ICN, IU (Nickell), [Liebert (wraps, uncut) = ? CtY], MH, NN, NN-B, TxU; *Can*: CaOHM (C. 3018, 'Sarah Adams' — Rippey); *UK*: [W.R. Batty, no ½t], BFq ('Thomas Percy' — Caledon), BMp (63422 + extraneous engr. port of AW), Ct, Ct-R, [Es], Gu ('Hunter', wraps, uncut), L (78. g.19, 'with advertisement by Johnson'), LICj[2] (1. 'H. L. Piozzi'[10]; 2. 'Percy Fitzgerald'), Ljh ('David Garrick'), Lv[3] (1. Dyce 10617: (a) 'Edmond Malone'; (b) 'Isaac Reed'), [L.F. Powell, blue wraps].

[1] *Lit. Anec.* ii. 179–81. There is an account of AW in *London Mag.* i (Dec. 1783), 517–21.

[2] Frances Reynolds's 'Miscellanies' (MS Hyde: fo. 40; *Johns. Misc.* ii. 279 n.); Percy's annotated copy of AW's *Miscellanies* (Hyde) includes several important notes, see below n. 4.

[3] Printed sources are abbreviated; the following annotated copies are cited: EM (Lv: Malone), HLP (LICj: Mrs Piozzi), HMT (CtY: Tinker 1348, 'Hester M. Thrale'), JBj (CtY: Tinker 1349, 'James Boswell, jun.'), RWG (O: Greatheed), TP[1] (Hyde: 'Thomas Percy'), TP[2] (BFq: 'Thomas Percy').

[4] Adopted in *European Mag.* vii (March 1785), 191, without mention of any other contribution. Reed's MS list (MS: Ljh) also mentions only 'Preface to Mrs. Williams', though JB's list (1790), added 'and several pieces in that Volume' (Waingrow, *Corr.* 318).

[5] A version of Horace's 'Beatus ille' (*Epodes*, ii).

[6] This is a slightly revised version of the text, which I overlooked in editing *Poems*[2], 52–3.

[7] Percy's note reads: 'I also believe that Johnson wrote the Epitaph on Mr. Worrall in p. 36', but no corroboration is offered and TP did not mention it in his other copy, or in the various attributions offered to JB (Waingrow, *Corr. passim*), or to Robert Anderson (*Life of SJ*). The epitaph itself does not compel acceptance, and no one of the name is known to have been associated with SJ, unless perhaps Swift's friend (*Lives*, ed. Hill, iii. 29, n. 4), or perhaps though less likely, John Warrall who entered Pemrboke College, Oxford, in 1720, aged 18 (*Al. Ox.* iv. 1503/12).

[8] *Thraliana* 225. This was dramatized as 'Mrs Thrale's Three Warnings; or, the Moral Tale of Death and the Farmer', and performed in Liverpool with other pieces on 31 December 1793 by Mr — [? Samuel Thomas Russell, according to a playbill (1 sheet, 2°, verso blk), published in Liverpool by Smith, of which the only recorded copy is noticed in J. Burmester, *Catalogue* 15 (1991), 298.

[9] Mrs Thrale's autograph draft of this piece is MRu (MS Eng. 646).

[10] This may be the copy sold at Puttick & Simpson (G. J. Squibb), 9 July 1859, 240, 'with a MS note (respecting Dr Johnson's authorship of one of the Essays) by Mrs Piozzi. Signed H.L.P.', or perhaps, the same with that at Sotheby's (Pocock), 10 May 1875, part 584, with 'MS notes by Mrs Piozzi', which fetched £1.

66.4WM/A/1   Advertisement for Williams's   1766
Miscellanies

Newspaper advertisement for Anna Williams's *Miscellanies*, 1 April

References: O M Brack, *Shorter Prose*.

Note: The newspaper itself in which the notice appeared, is unidentified.

66.4WM/F/1   The Fountains, HLT transcript   [?1766]

Johnson's prose tale was frequently reprinted or taken from the Anna Williams version. See G.J. Kolb (ed.), *Works* (Yale), xvi (1990), 214–49, and R.D. Mayo, *English Novel in the Magazines* (1962), 497, no. 451.

Transcript by HLT in 4° notebook (with lost trans. into Italian?)
UK: MRu (MS Eng. 654).

66.4WM/F/2   The Fountains, HLP transcript   [? 1766]

Transcript by HLP in her 'Piozziana'. *USA*: MH (MS Eng. 1280)[1]

[1] HLT also drafted a 'verse masque' of 'The Fountains' called 'The Two Fountains — a Fairy Tale', of which the scene was set in Dovedale, Derbys. (MRu: MS Eng. 649). Kolb is cool about the identification of HLP with the character of 'Floretta', but there can be no doubt that later in life she used the name of herself. Cf. Clifford, *Hester Lynch Piozzi* (1968), 63 n., and Hayward, *Autobiography*, &c., (1861), ii. 444 ff. The identification was fortified by Sir James Fellowes from conversations with HLP, and in her letter to him of 28 June 1819, she ends her personal comments with 'Ah poor Floretta' (MS Hyde). This may however, be no more than acceptance of a long-standing assumption.

66.4WM/F/3   The Fountains, British Magazine   1766

The British Magazine (May 1766), 227–31, (June 1766), 289–93, [Mayo]. The pagination in 'May' is faulty in sig. L. This version is an abridgement.

66.4WM/F/4   The Fountains, Univeral Museum   1766

The Universal Museum, ii, n.s. (Apr.–May, 1766), [Mayo].

66.4WM/F/5   The Fountains, London Chronicle,   [? 1766]
No. 1476

66.4WM/F/6   The Fountains, Caledonian Mercury   1766

(A part only) *Caledonian Mercury*, 11 June 1766.

66.4WM/F/7   The Fountains, European Magazine   1787

European Magazine, xii (July 1787), 42–7, with editorial note by Isaac Reed that the piece is omitted from *Works*, 1787; Reed included it in his supplementary vol. xiv (1788) published in Nov. 1787 (87.3W/1.3, below).[1]

[1] Reed's note, addressed to the 'Philological Society' is signed [Isaa]C [Ree]D. and it was reprinted in the *Northern Gazette*, the *Hibernian Magazine*, and the *English Lyceum*. 'The Fountains' did not reappear in SJ's Collected *Works* until 1816, 8°, iii. 445–63 (87.3W/13, below), and in the Alnwick ed. 1816, x. 31–44 (87.3W/15, below); Chalmers then included it in 1823, xi. 350–68

(87.3W/18), after which the 12° of 1824, xi. 324–41 (87.3W/20), gave it to Pickering's 'Oxford' ed. 1825, ix. 176–90 (87.3W/22).

66.4WM/F/8   The Fountains, Edinburgh Magazine,   1787
VI (Sept. 1787) [Mayo]

66.4WM/F/9   The Fountains, Northern Gazette, I   1787
(30 Aug. – 13 Sept. 1787) [Mayo]

66.4WM/F/10   The Fountains, Hibernian Magazine,   1787
(Oct. 1787) [Mayo]

66.4WM/F/11   The Fountains, Works, XIV   1788
(1788), 359–76

Cf. 87.3W/1.3/1a.

66.4WM/F/12 The Fountains, English Lyceum (1788),   1788
III, 7 (Jan. 1788) [Mayo]

66.4WM/F/13   The Fountains, Weekly Miscellany   1791
(Glasgow, 1791), V (26 Oct. – 23 Nov.) [Mayo]

66.4WM/F/14   The Fountains (with Rasselas),   1850
Philadelphia, 1850

Cf. 59.4R/207, above, pp. 209–30.

66.4WM/F/15   The Fountains, Baskerville Series   1927

'The Baskerville Series': *The Fountains A Fairy Tale by Dr. Samuel Johnson London Elkin Mathews & Marrot Ltd.* MDCCCCXXVII.
    8°, *A*⁴ B–F⁴, pp. *i–iv* v–vii *viii*, 9–47 *48*. Introduction signed 'H. V. M[arrott].' A limited edition of 510 copies. Published at 6s., April 1927.

66.4WM/F/16   The Fountains, Harmsworth   1978

The Fountains: A Fairy Tale by Samuel Johnson 1709–1784 Illustrated by James Hunt. Felix qui potuit boni Fontem visere lucidum. *Boethius.*
© Thomas Harmsworth Publishing 1978 Printed in Great Britain by the Lincolnshire Publishing Company Limited, St. Benedict Square, Lincoln.
  16 leaves, pp. *1* t., *2* illus., 3–31 text, *32* blk; Coloured illus. pp. (unnumbered): 2, 8, 12, 15, 18, 21, 24, 28, 30. Coloured paper wraps., stapled.
  Type: Title: Dolphin, Foreword: Times italic, text: plantin.
  ISBN. 0-9506012-0-9. Published 28 February 1978, at £1. 90.
  Notes: The epigraph (which stands in *Miscellanies*, 1766), is from Boethius, III. Metre 12, translated by SJ with HLT 'about the year 1765', *Poems*[2] 174.

66.4WM/F/17   The Fountains, Hillside Press,   1982
                    New York

The Fountains | By | Dr. Samuel Johnson | [flowers] | THE HILLSIDE PRESS| BUFFALO, NEW YORK | 1982
  Pp. *i* ½t THE FOUNTAINS, *ii* Port of SJ, *²i* t., *ii* blk, *iii* Limitation notice (250 copies), *iv* blk, *v* vi–xi Preface ('H.V.M[arrott].'), *1* illus. (bird), *2* 3–71 text, *72* Note ('The text for this book was set by hand in 6 pt. Bulmer Roman type and printed on a Rives imported paper at The Hillside Press in the month of September, 1982', *73* blk.
  Notes: Text from 66.4WM/F/15 (1927), above. Bound in full blue morocco, gilt device on front, and spine t. 'THE FOUNTAINS'; 2⅜ × 2 in.
  Copies: *USA*: NIC; *UK*: BMp (965796, 'No. 109').

66.4WM/F/18   The Fountains, St. Lucia,   1984
                    Queensland

The Fountains: A Fairy Tale. St. Lucia, Queensland: Locks' Press. 1984
  ½t: The Fountains A Fairy Tale by Samuel Johnson [illus.] Lock's Press Brisbane 1984
  Pp. *vi* + 35; 15 illus. in text. 50 copies (price: $150A) £95.00. + 8 unbound sheets (nos. 51–58) (@ $100A).
  Type: 18pt. Bembo, handset by Margaret Lock; woodcuts by Margaret Lock.
  Paper: Barcham Green Canterbury toned, laid (120 gsm); 250 × 160 mm.
  Cover: Grey cotton cloth, ptd. paper labels on cover and spine.
  Published by Fred and Margaret Lock, 60 Carmody Rd., St. Lucia, Queensland, Australia 4067, as 50 copies bound, and 8 copies in sheets.

  Copies: *USA*: NIC (No. 20); *UK*: BMp (976645).

66.6AG/1   Adams on the Globes, first edition   1766

A | TREATISE | Defcribing and Explaining the | Construction and Use | OF | New Celestial and Terrestrial | GLOBES. | Defigned to illuftrate, | In the moft Eafy and Natural Manner, | The Phoenomena of the | EARTH and HEAVENS, | And to fhew the | Correspondence of the Two Spheres. | With a great Variety of | Astronomical and Geographical PROBLEMS | occafionally interfperfed. | [rule] | By GEORGE ADAMS, | Mathematical Inftrument-Maker to His Majesty. | [bevelled parallel rule] | LONDON: | Printed for and Sold by the Author, at Tycho Brahe's Head, in Fleet-Street. | [short rule] | M.DCC.LXVI.

8°, *a*⁸ b⁴ (–b4 = R1) *⁴, B–Q⁸ R1, ($1 (ab,*), $4 (–B4, N3) signed; '*' variously placed), 136 leaves.

Pp. A1 *i* t., *ii* blk, *iii–vi* SJ's Dedication dh: TO THE | KING. | SIR,, ht: DEDICATION. (signed: 'GEORGE ADAMS.'), *vii* viii–xiv Preface dh: [double rule] | PREFACE., ht: PREFACE., *xv* xvi–xxii Contents dh: [double rule] | THE | CONTENTS., ht: The CONTENTS., on [*]1 pp. *1* 2–8 Adams's Trade Catalogue dh: A | CATALOGUE | OF | Mathematical, Philofophical, | AND | Optical INSTRUMENTS. | MADE and SOLD by | GEORGE ADAMS, | Mathematical Inftrument-Maker to the KING, | At his Shop the Sign of Tycho Brahe's | Head, in Fleet-ftreet, London. | Where Gentlemen and Ladies may be fupplied with | fuch Inftruments as are either Invented or Impro- | ved by himfelf; and Conftructed according to the | moft perfect Theory., rt: *A* Catalogue *of* | *Mathematical* INSTRUMENTS. (2–3), . . . | *Optical* INSTRUMENTS. (4–5), . . . | *Philofophical* INSTRUMENTS. (6–7), *A* Cat alogue *&c.* (8), on B1 *1* 2–242 text dh: [hp.] | THE | DESCRIPTION and USE | OF THE NEW | CELESTIAL and TERRESTRIAL | GLOBES., rt: Description and Use *of the* | *Celeftial and Terreftrial* Globes. (242: Description *and* Use, *&c.*).

Pagination: no errors; *Press-figures*: none.

Catchwords: om. i–ii, vi *om.* (PREFACE), xix Poeb, (Prob.), xxii THE (A), [*]8 *om.* (THE), 3 twilight. (~,), 126 ecliptic‸ (~,), 236 *om.* (A), 237 *om.* (A), 238 *om.* (A), 239 *om.* (II.), 240 *om.* (III.), 241 *om.* (IV‸).

Explicit: 242 FINIS.

Paper: White, laid; La. post (uncut: 8¼ × 5¼ in.); wmk.: fleur-de-lys + LVG.

Type: Dedication: great primer (5.6 mm), leaded, Preface: english (4.50 mm), leaded, text &c.: small pica (3.4 mm). Orn. hp (725 × 340 mm) and factotum (16 × 16 mm) on p. 1.

Plates: (3) usually folding, but occas. trimmed to size:

1. (facing t.) '*Plate I. To Front the Title.* The New TERRESTRIAL GLOBE, *As improved and Constructed by* GEO: ADAMS. *In* Fleet Street LONDON.'

2. (facing p. 1) '*Plate II. To Front P.1.* The New CELESTIAL GLOBE, *As Improved and Constructed by GEO: ADAMS.* In Fleet Street LONDON.'

3. (facing p. 86) 'Pl. 3 To front p. 86.'

References: Courtney 112; CH 149; Hazen 1–4; *Rothschild* 1; *Tinker* 1350; E.L. Stevenson, *Terrestrial and Celestial Globes* (New Haven, 1921), ii. 184–7, 220, 249; A. Heal, *NQ* clxx (1936), 423; O. Muris & G. Saarmann, *Der Globus im Wandel der Zeiten* (1961), 214–15; ESTC: t070774.

Notes: EU copy establishes the conjugacy of b4 as R1.

The book was published 10 June 1766, at 5s. bound (*Public Advertiser*). 'Tycho Brahe's Head' appears to be no more than an advertising address.[1]

Tyers attributed the Dedication to SJ in *Gents. Mag.* liv (Supp. 1784), 982 and this was repeated in *Gents. Mag.* lv (Jan. 1785), 87, by 'M. G[reen].' [= Nichols] in *Gents. Mag.* lv (Mar. 1785) 188, on the authority of Edmund Allen, the printer, and SJ's neighbour,[2] and independently by Isaac Reed in *European Mag.* vii (Mar. 1785), 191. Reed's MS list of attributions (Ljh) includes the entry, '1767 [Preface *deleted*] Dedication to Adams on Globes', and he repeated it to Boswell (Waingrow, *Corresp.* (1969), 318). Reed's own copy of this book (not traced), was lot 1008 at Sotheby's (Holland) 23 July 1860, and bore his MS note on SJ's authorship of the 'Dedication'.

The earliest globes (18 in. diam.), appear to be of 1769 (Terrestrial) and 1772 (Celestial), and the commonest pairs are by George Adams, jun., 1782. The latter take account of Cooke's discoveries in the early 1770s.

Copies: O (8° Q. 1 Linc.);

USA: CtY, Hyde[2], [Liebert], MiU, NN, NcD, PPL, RPB; *Can*: CaOHM; *UK*: AWu (F 3066), E (Cb. 2.51), Eu (O. 20.89), L (717. f.19), WNs (75c).

---

[1] Adams's MS description of a sundial dated 'Fleet Street N°. 20, June ᵈ. 1768' is C.

[2] Nichols's mention of Allen makes it probable that he was the printer of this book. He had printed Kennedy's *System of Astronomical Chronology* in 1762 (62.3KC/1, above), and was evidently capable of technical and mathematical printing, cf. *Lit. Anec.* viii (1814), 417.

66.6AG/2   Adams on the Globes, second edition   1769

[½t] A | TREATISE | ON THE | New Celeſtial and Terreſtrial | GLOBES.

[Title] A | TREATISE | Dᴇꜱᴄʀɪʙɪɴɢ the CONSTRUCTION, | AND | Exᴘʟᴀɪɴɪɴɢ the USE, | OF | New Cᴇʟᴇꜱᴛɪᴀʟ and Tᴇʀʀᴇꜱᴛʀɪᴀʟ | GLOBES. | Deſigned to illuſtrate | In the moſt Eaſy and Natural Manner, | The Pʜᴏᴇɴᴏᴍᴇɴᴀ of the | EARTH and HEAVENS, | And to ſhew the | Cᴏʀʀᴇꜱᴘᴏɴᴅᴇɴᴄᴇ of the Two Sᴘʜᴇʀᴇꜱ. | With a great Vᴀʀɪᴇᴛʏ of | Aꜱᴛʀᴏɴᴏᴍɪᴄᴀʟ and Gᴇᴏɢʀᴀᴘʜɪᴄᴀʟ PROBLEMS. | [rule] | By GEORGE ADAMS, | Mathematical Inſtrument-Maker to His Mᴀᴊᴇꜱᴛʏ. | [rule] | The SECOND EDITION, | In which a Cᴏᴍᴘʀᴇʜᴇɴꜱɪᴠᴇ Vɪᴇᴡ of the Sᴏʟᴀʀ Sʏꜱᴛᴇᴍ | is given; and the Uꜱᴇ of the GLOBES is farther ſhewn | in the

Explanation of SPHERICAL TRIANGLES. | [bevelled parallel rule] | LONDON: | Printed for and Sold by the AUTHOR, at TYCHO | BRAHE's Head, (N° 60.) in Fleet-Street. | [short rule] | M.DCC.LXIX.

8°, *a*⁸ b⁶ B–M⁸ N⁸ (± N7) O–Z⁸, ($4 (b in brackets) signed), 190 leaves.

Pp. a1 *i* ½t, *ii* blk, *iii* t., *iv* blk, *v–viii* Dedication, *ix* Advertisement, *x* blk, *xi* xii–xvi Preface, on b1 *xvii* xviii–xxviii Contents, xxviii Errata, on B1 *1* 2–345 text, on Z5ᵛ *346–52* Adams's *Catalogue*.

Pagination: 47 and 289 unnumbered, 124 as 224.

Press-figures: none; *Catchwords*: not recorded. *Explicit*: 345 FINIS.

Paper: White, laid; La. post (uncut: 8¼ × 5¼ in.); wmk.: fleur-de-lys + LVG.

Type: Dedication: great primer (5.6 mm), leaded; Preface: pica (3.9 mm), leaded; Contents: Long primer (3.4 mm); text: english (4.5 mm), leaded; footnotes: long primer (3.2 mm).

Plates: (14) 12 on folding leaves (wmk.: posthorn) as:

1. '*Plate I. To front the Title.* The New TERRESTRIAL GLOBE *As improved and Constructed by* GEO: ADAMS *In* Fleet Street LONDON.'
2. '*Plate 2ₐ fronting page 1. The Copernican or* SOLAR SYSTEM.' (fold.)
3. '*Plate 3. Fronting p. 14ₐ* [Ecliptics] '*Goodnight sculp*' (fold.)
4. '*Plate 4. fronting p. 18.*' [Zodiacal seasons] '*Goodnight sculp*' (fold.)
5. '*Plate 5. fronting p. 26.*' [Seasons] '*Goodnight ſculp*' (fold.)
6. '*Plate 6. Fronting p. 31*' [Saturn & Jupiter] '*Goodnight sculp*' (fold.)
7. '*Plate 7. Fronting p. 34ₐ*' [Satellite eclipses] '*Goodnight sculp*' (fold.)
8. '*Plate 8ₐ Fronting p. 40.*' [Atmospheric refraction] '*Goodnight sculp*' (fold.)
9. '*Plate 9. Fronting p. 46.*' [Solar eclipse] '*Goodnight sculp*' (fold.)
10. '*Plate 10ₐ To Front P. 47ₐ* The New CELESTIAL GLOBE, *As Improved and Constructed by* GEO: ADAMS *In* Fleet Street LONDON.'
11. 'Pl. 11ₐ To front p. 138ₐ' [Solar activity] (fold.)
12. '*Plate 12. fronting p. 289ₐ*' [Spherical triangles] '*Goodnight ſculp*' (fold.)
13. '*Plate 13. fronting p. 326ₐ*' [Meridians] '*Goodnight ſculp*' (fold.)
14. '*Plate 14. fronting p. 334ₐ*' [Ecliptics] '*Goodnight ſculp*' (fold.)

References: Courtney 112, Hazen 3; ESTC: t053466.

Notes: Despite the cancellation of N7 the calculation (no. 269, p. 189) is still incorrect (cf. no. 364, p. 138 of first edn., 66.6AG/1, above), in giving the first product as 11 hours instead of zero. A note on this calculation in the first edn. is here omitted.

Copies: L (52. e.17);

USA: DLC, Hyde, [PP]; *UK*: BRu (HKc 131774), MRc (N 8.21), On.

66.6AG/3   Adams on the Globes, third edition   1772

[½t] A | TREATISE | ON THE | New Celeſtial and Terreſtrial | GLOBES.

[Title] A | TREATISE | Describing the CONSTRUCTION | AND | Explaining the USE, | OF | New Celestial and Terrestrial | GLOBES. | Deſigned to illuſtrate, | In the moſt Eaſy and Natural Manner, | The Phoenomena of the | EARTH and HEAVENS, | And to ſhew the | Correspondence of the Two Spheres. | With a great Variety of | Astronomical and Geographical PROBLEMS. | [rule] | By GEORGE ADAMS, | Mathematical Inſtrument-Maker to His Majesty. | [rule] | The THIRD EDITION, | In which a Comprehensive View of the Solar System | is given; and the Uſe of the GLOBES is farther ſhewn | in the Explanation of Spherical Triangles. | [bevelled parallel rule] | LONDON: | Printed for and Sold by the Author, at Tycho | Brahe's Head, Nᵒ. 60, in Fleet-Street. | [short rule] | M.DCC.LXXII.

8°, *a*⁸ b⁴ c² B–Z⁸ 2A⁴ 2B², ($4 (–b3,4, c2, 2A3,4, 2B2; bc in brackets) signed), 196 leaves.

Pp. a1 *i* ½t, *ii* blk, *iii* t., *iv* blk, *v–viii* Dedication, *ix* Advertisement, *x* blk, *xi* xii–xvi Preface, on b1 *xvii* xviii–xxviii Contents, on B1 *1* 2–46 text dh: [hp] | A | COMPREHENSIVE VIEW | OF THE | SOLAR SYSTEM., rt: *A Comprehenſive View | of the Solar Syſtem.*, *47* 48–288 text dh: [hp flowers] | THE | DESCRIPTION and USE | OF THE NEW | Celestial and Terrestrial | GLOBES., rt: *Deſcription and Uſe of the | Celeſtial and Terreſtrial Globes.*, *289* 290–345 text dh: [hp] | THE | USE | OF THE | GLOBES | In the Solution of | Right Angled Spherical *Triangles.*, rt: [*as* pp. 48–288], *346* blk, on Z5 *347–63* Catalogue of Instruments, *364* Advt. for 4th edn. of GA's *Micrographia Illustrata.*

Pagination: 69 as 67; *Press-figures*: none;

Catchwords: *om.* i–iv, viii–x, 339–45, 363; xvi A (THE), 77 PROBLBM (PROBLEM), 190 272ᴧ Having (∼,∼), 216 pointᴧ (–,), 338 A Table (A TABLE).

Explicit: 345 FINIS.

Paper: White, laid; La. post (8¼ × 5¼ in.); wmk.: fleur-de-lys + IV.

Type: Dedication: great primer (5.6 mm), leaded; Preface: pica (3.9 mm), leaded; Contents: long primer (3.4 mm); text: english (4.5 mm), leaded; footnotes: long primer (3.2 mm). Flowers as hpp 1, 47, 289, 347; as factotums 1, 47; and tp. 363.

Plates: As in second edn. 1769, above (66.6AG/2, q.v.).

References: See first edn. 66.6AG/1, above. ESTC: t053464.

Notes: SJ's Dedication to the King is retained. The enlargement of this edn. is owing to the increased length of the final catalogue.

Copies: O (18421 e. 22);

USA: CSmH, [DAU]; *UK*: ABu (MH 52278), [W.R. Batty], DUu, L (08560. de. 64), Oam.

66.6AG/4   Adams on the Globes, fourth edition   1777

[½t] A | TREATISE | ON THE | New Celeſtial and Terreſtrial | GLOBES.

[Title] A | TREATISE | Describing the CONSTRUCTION, | AND | Explaining the USE | OF | New Celestial and Terrestrial | GLOBES. | Deſigned to illuſtrate, | In the moſt Eaſy and Natural Manner, | The Phoenomena of the | EARTH and HEAVENS, | And to ſhew the | Correspondence of the Two Spheres. | With a great Variety of | Astronomical and Geographical PROBLEMS. | [rule] | By GEORGE ADAMS, | Mathematical Inſtrument-Maker to His Majesty. | [rule] | The FOURTH EDITION, | In which a Comprehensive View of the Solar System | is given; and the Uſe of the GLOBES is farther ſhewn | in the Explanation of Spherical Triangles. | [double rule] | LONDON: | Printed for and Sold by the Author, at Tycho | Brahe's Head, N°. 60, in Fleet-Street. | [short rule] | M.DCC.LXXVII.

8°, a^8 b^4 c^2 B–Z^8 2A^4, ($4 (–b3,4, c2, Z3,4, 2A3,4; bc in brackets) signed), 194 leaves.

Pp. a1 *i* ½t, *ii* blk, *iii* t., *iv* blk, *v–viii* Dedication, *ix* Advertisement, *x* blk, *xi* xii–xvi Preface, *xvii* xviii–xxviii Contents, on B1 *1* 2–46 text (Solar System), *47* 48–288 text (Description and Use of the Globes), *289* 290–345 text (Solution of . . . Spherical Triangles), *346* blk, on Z6 *1* 2–14 Adams's Catalogue.

Pagination: 268 as 862; *Press-figures*: none.

Catchwords: *om.* i–iv, 339–45; 216 point‸ (–,), 338 A Table (A TABLE).

Explicit: 345 FINIS.

Paper: White, laid; La. post (8¼ × 5¼ in.); wmk.: fleur-de-lys.

Type: As third edn. 1772 (66.6AG/3, above).

Plates: as 2nd and 3rd edd. 1769, 1772 (66.6AG/2, 66.6AG/3, above), but usually trimmed to avoid folding.

References: Hazen 3; ESTC: n013723.

Notes: This is a lineal and paginatory reprint of third edn. 1772 (66.6AG/3, above), retaining SJ's 'Dedication'.

Copies: O (18421 e. 18);

USA: Hyde ('John R. Digby Beste'), NN, PPAmP, PHi; *UK*: AWn, Csj (A/g. 18.1), Oam.

66.6AG/5   Adams on the Globes, fifth edition   1782

[½t] A | TREATISE | ON THE | New Celeſtial and Terreſtrial | GLOBES.

[Title] A | TREATISE | Describing the CONSTRUCTION, | AND | Explaining the USE | OF | New Celestial and Terrestrial | GLOBES. | Deſigned to illuſtrate, | In the moſt Eaſy and Natural Manner, | The Phoenomena of the | EARTH and HEAVENS, | And to ſhew the | Correspondence of the Two Spheres. | With a great Variety of |

Astronomical and Geographical PROBLEMS. | [rule] | By GEORGE ADAMS, | Mathematical Inſtrument-Maker to His Majesty. |[rule] | The FIFTH EDITION, | In which a Comprehensive View of the Solar System | is given; and the Uſe of the GLOBES is farther ſhewn | in the Explanation of Spherical Triangles. | [double rule] | LONDON: | Printed for and Sold by the Author, at Tycho | Brahe's Head, No. 60, in Fleet-Street. | [short rule] | M.DCC.LXXXII.

8°, *a*⁸ b⁴ B–Z⁸ 2A⁴, ($4 (–b3,4, Z3,4, 2A3,4; b in brackets) signed), 192 leaves.

Pp. a1 *i* ½t, *ii* blk, *iii* t., *iv* t., *v–viii* Dedication, *ix* Advertisement, *x* blk, *xi* xii–xxii Preface, on b1 *i* ii–viii Contents, on B1 *1* 2–345 text (as 4th edn., 66.6 AG/4, above), on Z6 *3* 4–16 Adams's Catalogue.

Pagination: The reptd. Catalogue at the end anticipated two preceding pp.
Press-figures: none.
Catchwords: *om.* i–iv, viii–x, 339–46; 165 *om.* (If), 224 cut (cuts), 338 A TABLE (A TABLE), ²ᴬ9 IN (INSTRUMENTS).
Explicit: 345 FINIS. 2A4ᵛ(14) FINIS.
Paper: White, laid; La. post (as. 4th edn. 1777, prec. 66.6AG/4, above).
Type: As 4th edn. 1777 (66.6AG/4, above), but wholly reset.
Plates: As 4th edn. 1777 (66.6AG/4, above).
References: Hazen 3; ESTC: t127735.
Notes: A close reprint of 4th edn. 66.6AG/4, above, but a new edn.
Copies: O (Vet. A5 e. 4426); *USA*: NjP, PPL.

66.6AG/6   Adams on the Globes   1786

London.[1]   *USA*: NWM, PPU.

[1] An edition was advertised in the *St James's Chronicle*, 15 Jan. 1789.

66.6AG/7   Adams on the Globes, Astronomical and   [? 1789]
                 Geographical Essays

Later editions are recorded, but in 1790 the *Treatise* of the Globes was incorporated with the *Astronomical and Geographical Essays*, of George Adams, the younger (1750–95*), first published in 1789 (*Copies*: O² (1. Rigaud e.2; **2.** Hanson 24), and reprinted 1790 (probably twice), as a 'third' edn., 1795 (O: 1842 e.3), and a 'fifth', revised and enlarged by W. Jones in 1803:

Astronomical and Geographical Essays: containing a full and comprehensive View on a new Plan, of the General Principles of Astronomy; the Use of the Celestial and Terrestrial Globes, exemplified in a greater variety of problems, than are to be found in any other Work; the Description and Use of the most

improved Planetarium, Tellurian, and Lunarium; and also An Introduction to practical Astronomy. By the late George Adams, Mathematical Instrument Maker to his Majesty, &c. The fifth edition, corrected and enlarged By William Jones, F.Am.P.S. London: Printed for, and sold by, W. and S. Jones, Opticians, Holborn. 1803. Price 10s. 6d. in Boards. Printed by W. Glendinning, No. 25, Hatton Garden.
  References: ESTC: t064608.
  Copies: (Hyde; O: Hope 8°.7).

Of the *Treatise* proper, the following editions post-date Johnson's death, but retain his dedication, since George III lived and reigned until 1820.

66.6AG/8   Adams on the Globes   1791

London.   Hazen 3.

66.6AG/9   Adams on the Globes   1795

London.   Hazen 3.

66.6AG/10   Adams on the Globes, London,   1799
                              'fourth edition'

London.   *USA*: MWA.

66.6AG/11   Adams on the Globes, Philadelphia,   1800
                              'fourth edition'

Philadelphia. ESTC: w032024
  USA: CtY, MB, MdBP, MH, MWA, NBuG, NN, PHi, PPULC, PSt, RPJCB, ViLyW, ViU.

66.6AG/12   Adams on the Globes, Whitehall,   1800
                              Pennsylvania

In George Adams, jun., *An Essay on the Use of the Celestial and Terrestrial Globes: Exemplified in a greater variety of Problems, than are to be found in any other Works; exhibiting the general Principles of Dialling and Navigation.* 4th edn. Whitehall (Penn.): William Young.
  8°, pp. viii + 238. [ESTC: w000829; perhaps a reissue of part II. of Adams's *Treatise*.][1]

66.6AG/13   Adams on the Globes,   1810
                              thirteenth edition

A | TREATISE, | DESCRIBING THE CONSTRUCTION AND EXPLAINING THE
USE OF | *NEW CELESTIAL AND TERRESTRIAL* | GLOBES; | Designed
to illustrate, | IN THE MOST EASY AND NATURAL MANNER, | THE
PHENOMENA OF THE EARTH AND HEAVENS, | AND TO SHEW THE
| *CORRESPONDENCE OF THE TWO SPHERES*; | WITH A GREAT VARIETY
OF | ASTRONOMICAL AND GEOGRAPHICAL | [hollow] PROBLEMS.
| [short parallel rule] | *By GEORGE ADAMS, Sen.* | LONG DECEASED. FATHER
TO THE LATE GEORGE ADAMS. | [short total rule] | THE THIRTIETH
EDITION. | In which a Comprehensive View of the Solar System is given; and
the | Use of the GLOBES is farther shewn, in the Explanation | of Spherical
Triangles. | [short swelled rule] | *Now published by* | *DUDLEY ADAMS,* |
GLOBE, AND MATHEMATICAL INSTRUMENT MAKER TO HIS MAJESTY; OPTICIAN |
TO HIS R. H. THE PRINCE OF WALES, &C.; AND BROTHER | TO THE LATE GEORGE
ADAMS. | [short parallel rule] | LONDON: | Printed for, and sold by the
Publisher, No. 60, Fleet-street. | [short rule] | 1810.

8°, a⁸ b⁴ B–Q⁸ R1, ($2 signed), 133 leaves.

Pp. a1 *i* t., *ii* coloph: [short rule] | C. Baldwin, Printer, | New Bridge-street,
London. | [short rule], *iii* iv–v SJ's Dedication dh: TO | THE KING. | [short
parallel rule], *vi* blk, *vii* viii–ix dh: TO | THE PUBLIC. | [short parallel rule]
('Dudley Adams. Fleet Street, Oct. 29, 1810.'), *x* blk, *xi* xii–xvi Preface, on b1
xvii xviii–xxiv Contents, on B1 *1* 2–242 text, 242 explicit: FINIS., and coloph.

Press-figures: a7(xiii)–6, B7(13)–5, B8(15)–1, D1ᵛ(34)–4, E3(53)–5,
E4(55)–1, F1ᵛ(66)–5, F4ᵛ(72)–1, G4ᵛ(88)–3, H4ᵛ(104)–3, I8ᵛ(128)–5,
K1ᵛ(130)–3, K2ᵛ(132)–5, L2ᵛ(148)–5, M7ᵛ(174)–5, N1ᵛ(178)–6, O3(197)–3,
P8ᵛ(224)–3, Q3(229)–4, Q4(231)–2.

References: Hazen 3.
Notes: Numerous engr. folding plates inserted. The quality of printing is poor.
Copies: BMp (53658, uncut); *USA*: [DAU]; *UK*: En, Eu, L (8562. d.4), LVu.

66.6FS   Fordyce's Sermons   1766

SERMONS | TO | YOUNG WOMEN: | IN TWO VOLUMES. |
VOLUME I [– II]. | LONDON: | PRINTED FOR A. MILLAR AND T.
CADELL | IN THE STRAND, J. DODSLEY IN | PALL-MALL, AND J.
PAYNE IN | PATER-NOSTER ROW.| M DCC LXVI.
    2 vols., 8°

I. A⁴ B–R⁸ S⁴ (S4 blk), ($4 (–D4, G2) signed), 136 leaves.

Pp. A1 *i* t., *ii* blk, *iii* iv–vi Preface dh and ht: PREFACE., *vii*–viii CONTENTS., on B1 1–262 text.

II. Not examined.

References: ESTC: t143359.

Notes: Fordyce's *Sermons to Young Women* was a popular title, and was reprinted in London, '3rd. edn. corrected' 1766 (ESTC: t087405), '5th. edn.' 1766 (ESTC: n024231), '6th edn.' 1766 (ESTC: n024238), Dublin, '3rd. edn.' 1766 (ESTC: t178038), Dublin '4th. edn. Sheppard' 1766 (ESTC: t178037), Dublin '4th. edn. Leathley' (ESTC: t123794), London '4th. edn.' 1767 (ESTC: t087402), [Boston] 1767 (ESTC: w024605) reissued: Boston 1767 (ESTC: w026543), Dublin 1767 (ESTC: t133492), Dublin '7th. edn.' (ESTC: n024239), London '5th. edn.' 1768 (ESTC: n024237), '6th. edn.' 1769 (ESTC: n024232), '7th. edn.' 1771 (ESTC: t087406), '10th. edn.' 1786 (ESTC: n039171), Philadelphia 1787 (ESTC: w002988), 1792, 1793, 1794, 1796, and 1800, in Edinburgh 1793–4 ('New edn.'); and perhaps elsewhere. The first edn. was noticed in *Gents. Mag.* xxxvi (June 1766), 288/35, @ 6s. as 'a series of free but affectionate addresses.'

The Preface has sometimes been suggested as by SJ but, despite James Fordyce's acquaintance with and admiration of him, the proposal cannot be accepted in view of the sloppiness of the writing and the extravagant praise of retreat and rural life.[1]

Copies: *USA*: CtY (1977.2918, 'H.W. Liebert'), [ICN], NIC; *UK*: Cq (vol. I only), Eu, [Lu].

[1] Fordyce published a tedious prose epitaph on SJ in *Gents. Mag.* lv (Apr. 1785), 411–12, and an equally tiresome Address 'On the Death of Dr. Samuel Johnson' in his *Addresses to the Deity* (1785), 209–32 (*Life* iv. 411 n.). Fordyce (1720–96*) was one of the numerous family of George Fordyce (1663–1733), provost of Aberdeen, of which David (1711–51*) was a contributor to the *Preceptor*, and Elizabeth (1731–77) was visited by SJ at Durham in August 1773 (Fleeman, *NQ* ccxxi (1986), 59–60). These *Sermons* are perhaps the most unrewarding works it has fallen to my lot to read: that Jane Austen was in any way indebted to them passes belief.

66.7GLW/1   Gwynne's London and Westminster   1766
Improved

LONDON AND WESTMINSTER | IMPROVED, | ILLUSTRATED by PLANS. | To which is prefixed, | A Difcourfe on Publick Magnificence; | WITH | Obfervations on the State of Arts and Artifts in this | Kingdom, wherein the Study of the Polite Arts | is recommended as neceffary to a liberal Education: | Concluded by | Some Propofals relative to Places not laid down in the Plans. | By *JOHN GWYNN*. | —like an entrance into a large city, after a diftant profpect. Remotely, we fee | nothing but fpires of temples, and turrets of palaces, and imagine it the refi- | dence of fplendor, grandeur, and magnificence; but, when we have paffed the | gates, we find it perplexed with narrow paffages, difgraced with defpicable | cottages, embaraffed with obftructions, and clouded with fmoke. Rambler. | LONDON: | Printed for the Author. | Sold by Mr. Dodfley, and at Mr. Dalton's Print-Warehoufe in Pall- | Mall, Mr. Bathoe in the Strand, Mr. Davies in Ruffel-Street, Covent- | Garden, and by Mr. Longman in Pater-nofter-Row. | MDCCLXVI.

4°, a⁴ ²a⁴ B⁴ (± B4) C–G⁴ H⁴ (± H4) I–R⁴ S², ($2 (–S2) signed), 74 leaves.

Pp. a1 *i* t., *ii* blk, *iii–iv* Dedication dh: TO THE | KING. | SIR,, ht: DEDICATION., v–xi Preface dh: [hp of flowers] | PREFACE., ht: PREFACE., xii Contents dh: [row of flowers] | CONTENTS., on ²a3 xiii–xv Introduction dh: [row of flowers] | INTRODUCTION., ht: INTRODUCTION., *xvi* Errata dh: ERRATA., on B1 1–132 text dh: LONDON AND WESTMINSTER | IMPROVED. | [row of flowers] | *A Difcourfe on Publick Magnificence.*, rt: LONDON AND | WESTMINSTER IMPROVED.

Pagination: (↑) v, xii, xiii; [↑] 1.

Press-figures: ²a3(xiii)–2, C3ᵛ(14)–4, D4(23)–4, E4ᵛ(32)–2, F3ᵛ(38)–4, G3ᵛ(46)–3, H3ᵛ(54)–3, I3ᵛ(62)–2, K4(71)–3, L4ᵛ(80)–2, M3(85)–2, N4ᵛ(96)–3, O3(101)–4, P3(109)–3, Q4ᵛ(120)–3, R2ᵛ(124)–4, S2(131)–3.

Catchwords: *om.* iv; 32 The (From), 71 [pic-] true (ture).

Explicit: 132 FINIS.

Paper: White, laid; Demy (uncut: 11¼ × 8¾ in.); wmk.: fleur-de-lys + IV. Plates on heavier paper (below).

Type: Dedication: double pica (6.8 mm); Preface: great primer (5.5 mm), text: english (4.6 mm). Flowers used as hpp. v, xii, xiii, 1, 22, 76, 111, and as tp. 21.

Plates: (4) folding, usually hand coloured in green, ochre, red, and blue; occasionally plain. That they were intended to be coloured is shown by the 'N.B.' on p. xvi. On paper (probably Royal), wmk.: fleur-de-lys + LVG + JW (? J Whatman), trimmed.

I. A PLAN of HYDE PARK with the CITY and LIBERTIES of WEST-MINSTER &c shewing the several IMPROVEMENTS propos'd. (13 × 20⅛ in., fold.)

II. Part of Westminster at large showing the Improvements propos'd about Leicester-Fields, Covent-Garden, the Meuse &c. (13 × 19¼ in., fold.)

III. Part of London shewing the Improvements propos'd about the Mansion-House, Royal Exchange, Moor-Fields, &c. (8¼ × 19¾ in., fold.)

IV. Part of London shewing the Improvements propos'd about London-Bridge, the Custom-House, Tower, &c. (13½ × 20½ in., fold.)

References: *Life*, ii. 25 (Courtney 111); CH 148; Hazen 38–40; *Tinker* 1351; Brownell, *Johnson's Attitude to the Arts* (1989), 127–36; Harris 214–17, **276**; ESTC: t138431.

Notes: The cancellations of B4 and H4 are certain but unexplained since no uncancelled copies are known. The book was published 14 June 1766, at 10s. 6d. bound, or 9s. in boards (*Lond. Chron.*), and *Gents. Mag.* xxxvi (June 1766), 288/26. Hazen noted advts. as late as *Lond. Chron.*, 1 June, 1771 (p. 40). The epigraph is from *Rambler* 14.

For Gwynne, see J. L. Hobbs, *NQ* ccvii (1962), 22–4, and Harris, s.n. SJ provided the 'Dedication' which was, by a slip in proof-correcting, described as 'noble' by JB (*Life*, ii. 25, 479). The attribution was probably first made by Isaac Reed (Waingrow, *Corres.*, 318) who noted it in his MS list at Ljh, and who published the text in his supplementary vol. xiv, *Works*, 1788 (87.3W/1.14). Reed's own copy with a note on SJ's contribution, is untraced.[1] Upcott mistakenly attributed the 'Preface' to SJ, and added that he 'Corrected the proof sheets', but the statement is late and insecure (MH: MS 'Upcottiana' (MS Eng. 1178, vol. ii, fo. 56)).

Francis Douce noted on a fly-leaf: 'The dedication was written by Dr Johnson. Mr Gwynne resided at the end of the garden belonging to the house built and inhabited by Payne the architect, at the N. West end of Saint Martin's lane' (O: Douce).[2] SJ's own copy was lot 647 in his sale, Christie, 16 Feb. 1785, and went to 'Money' for 17s. It is still untraced.

Copies: O² (1. Gough Lond. 265; 2. Douce G. 265);

USA: [CLU-C], CSmH, CtY² (1. Beinecke: uncut), DLC, Hyde³ (1. uncut; 2. 'Mrs Vesey'; 3. 'Grantham De Grey'³), [IaU], IEN, InU, IU (Nickell), [KU], [Liebert² (1. blue boards, uncut 'John Loveday')], MH, NcD, NIC, NjP, NNE, NNU, OO, PPL, TxU; *Can*: CaOHM; *UK*: ABu (uncut, cold.), C, Csj (cold.), E, Eu, Gu, L (191. s.18, cold.), Lg, LVp, LVu, MRp, MRu, Op (boards uncut, 'R. B. Adam'), SAN; *Aust*: CNL (DNS 4194).

---

[1] It was lot 4196 in his sale, King, *Bibliotheca Reediana*, 2 Nov. 1807, with 'MS Note relative to Dr. Johnson's Assistance in this Work', and again lot 1008 in Sotheby (Holland) 23 July 1860.

[2] Other contemporary attributions are noted by Brownell, *Johnson's Attitude to the Arts* (1989), 129 n. 12, who discusses the question pp. 129–35 and is rightly sceptical of SJ's responsibility for much beyond the 'Dedication'.

[3] Thomas Philip Robinson (1781–1859), Baron Grantham, 1st E. De Grey (1833).

66.7GLW/2   Gwynne's London and Westminster   1969
                   Improved, facsimile

A facsimile edition was published by Gregg International, Farnborough, Hants, in 1969.

66.8CL/1   Law Lectures for Robert Chambers   1766

Composed at Oxford during the autumn of 1766 (*Diaries*, 111; 8 Nov. 1766) and winter of 1767 (*Diaries*, 113; 9 Apr. 1767).

References: McAdam, 'Dr Johnson's Law Lectures for Chambers', *RES* xv (1939), 385–91, xvi (1940), 159–68, and his *Dr Johnson and the English Law* (1951); Chambers, *A Course of Lectures on the English Law*, ed. T.M. Curley (1986), i. 4–29.

Notes: McAdam was willing to assign many passages to SJ in his 1951 account, but in his edn. Curley is more conservative in his presentation of the collaboration.

MS: L (Kings MS 80–97).

66.8CL/2   Law Lectures for Robert Chambers,   1824
**   Treatise on Estates and Tenures**

Some parts of the above lectures (Part III), were printed in:

A | TREATISE | ON | ESTATES AND TENURES. | [short swelled rule] | BY THE LATE | SIR ROBERT CHAMBERS, KNT. | CHIEF JUSTICE OF BENGAL. | [short swelled rule] | *EDITED BY* | SIR CHARLES HARCOURT CHAMBERS, Knt. | ONE OF THE JUDGES OF THE SUPREME COURT OF JUDICATURE AT BOMBAY. | [short parallel rule] | LONDON: | PRINTED FOR JOSEPH BUTTERWORTH AND SON, | LAW-BOOKSELLERS, 43, FLEET-STREET; | AND J. COOKE, ORMONDE QUAY, DUBLIN. | [dash] | 1824.

8°, a⁶ B–U⁸ X⁴, ($1 (–a1 + a2, a as *a*) signed), 162 leaves.

Pp. a1 *i* t., *ii* coloph: [rule] | *J. & T. Clarke, Printers, St. John Square, London.*, *iii* iv–ix Preface, *x* blk, *xi*–xii Contents, on B1 pp. *1* 2–18 Introduction, *19* 20–301 text Chapters I–X, *302* blk, *303* 304–11 Index, *312* Errata and coloph. (as p. ii).

Press-figures: U3(293)–1, U6(299)–2, X1ᵛ(306)–1;

Explicit: 301 THE END.

Paper: White, wove; Demy (8⅞ × 5½ in.), no vis. wmk.

Type: Pica (4.0 mm).

References: Chambers, *A Course of Lectures*, ed. T.M. Curley (1986), i. 5, 67–8 (above).

Notes: The 'Preface' refers to this work as 'a portion of the lectures . . . delivered . . . in the University of Oxford'. Curley shows that this volume, published posthumously, represents a small part of the lecture series, confined to the question of private property.

Copies: O (24.120);

USA: DLC, MH(L), PU(L); *UK*: ABu, C (PB8.231), Eu (*E.27.30), Gu (F6—f.3), L (514. e.26), SAN.

66.11CC Considerations on Corn, [1766]
Parliamentary Logick

PARLIAMENTARY LOGICK: | TO WHICH ARE SUBJOINED | TWO SPEECHES, | Delivered in the House of Commons of Ireland, | *AND OTHER PIECES;* | BY THE RIGHT HONOURABLE | WILLIAM GERARD HAMILTON. | WITH AN APPENDIX, CONTAINING | CONSIDERATIONS ON THE CORN LAWS, | BY SAMUEL JOHNSON, LL.D. | NEVER BEFORE PRINTED. | [short parallel rule] | LONDON: | PRINTED BY C. AND R. BALDWIN, | *New Bridge-street,* | FOR THOMAS PAYNE, PALL-MALL. | M.DCCC.VIII.

8° *a*⁸ b⁸ c⁸ (−c8) B–C⁸ D⁸ (± D5) E–R⁸ (R8 blk), ($2 (ˣD5 as D4, M1ᵛ as M2, −M2) signed), 151 leaves.

Pp. Engr. port. front. + a1 *i* t. *ii* blk *iii* dh: CONTENTS., *iv* ERRATA., *v* vi–xlvi dh: PREFACE., ht: PREFACE., on B1 *1* 2–100 text dh: PARLIAMENTARY LOGICK. | [short parallel rule], ht: PARLIAMENTARY LOGICK., *101* ½t: THE | REPRESENTATION | OF THE |LORDS JUSTICES OF IRELAND., *102* Editorial Note, *103* t. THE | REPRESENTATION | OF THE | LORDS JUSTICES OF IRELAND, | Touching the transmission of a Privy-Council Money- | bill, previous to the calling of a new Parliament; | IN TWO LETTERS, | ADDRESSED TO | HIS GRACE, JOHN DUKE OF BEDFORD. | [medium parallel rule] | [motto] | [medium total rule], *104* blk, 105–36 text dh: LETTER I., ht: THE REPRESENTATION, ETC., *137* ½t: A | SPEECH | DELIVERED IN THE | HOUSE OF COMMONS OF IRELAND, | IN NOVEMBER 1761. | [short parallel rule], rt: A SPEECH ON THE | PRIVY-COUNCIL MONEY-BILL. (160: 'A SPEECH, ETC.'), 161–4 text dh: *Journals of the House of Commons of* | Ireland, *vol.* vii. *p.* 108; 23*d January,* | 1762. | [medium parallel rule], rt: MESSAGE TO THE | HOUSE OF COMMONS OF IRELAND. (164: 'MESSAGE, ETC.'), 165–94 text dh: A | SPEECH | DELIVERED IN THE | HOUSE OF COMMONS OF IRELAND, | ON THE SUBJECT OF | A MESSAGE | FROM THE | LORD LIEUTENANT OF IRELAND, | IN FEBRUARY, 1762. | [medium parallel rule], rt: A SPEECH ON RAISING | ADDITIONAL FORCES. (194: 'SPEECH, ETC.', 195–6 text dh: RESOLUTION | OF THE | HOUSE OF COMMONS OF IRELAND, | RESPECTING | THE APPOINTMENT OF THE LORD LIEU- | TENANT, | FEBRUARY 26, 1762. | [medium parallel rule], ht: (196) RESOLUTION, ETC., 197–200 text dh: THE | ANSWER | OF THE | LORD LIEUTENANT | TO THE | ADDRESS OF THE HOUSE OF COMMONS, | FEBRUARY 27, 1762. | [medium parallel rule], rt: ANSWER OF | THE EARL OF HALIFAX. (200: 'ANSWER, ETC.'), *201* ½t: [short parallel rule] | FOUR ODES, | FIRST PRINTED (BUT NOT THEN PUBLISHED) | ABOUT THE YEAR

66.11CC   *Considerations on Corn, Parlimentary Logick*

1752. | [short total rule], *202* blk, *237* ½t: APPENDIX., *238* blk, 239–53 text dh: APPENDIX. | [medium parallel rule] | CONSIDERATIONS ON CORN, | By SAMUEL JOHNSON, LL.D. | [short parallel rule], ht: APPENDIX., *254* coloph: [short parallel rule] | C. and R. Baldwin, Printers, | New Bridge-Street, London. | [short total rule].

Pagination: (↑) 105, 139, 161, 165, 195, 197, 203, 211, 217, 229, 239.

Press-figures: L3ᵛ(150)–3; *Catchwords*: none.

Explicit: 253 THE END.

Paper: Cream, wove (often browned and foxed); ? crown (uncut: 7½ × 5 in.); wmk.: 1804.

Type: Pica (4.0 mm), leaded (1.2 mm).

Plate: Port. of Hamilton, 'I.R. Smith delᵗ. W. Evans sculpᵗ.' entitled: 'The Right Honourable | WILLIAM GERARD HAMILTON, | One of his Majesty's Most Honourable | Privy Council, | And Chancellor of the Exchequer in Ireland.', with imprint: 'Published by T. Payne. Pall Mall, March 1. 1808.'

References: *Life*, i. 519 (Courtney 111); CH 148; *Works* (Yale), x (1977), 301–12; *MS Handlist*, 100; *MS Index* JoS 175.

Notes: Edited by Edmond Malone from Hamilton's papers (d. 1796), the bulk of which passed to the Earl of Donoughmore (Hely-Hutchinson) 1760–95 (*Hist. MSS. Comm.*, 1891).[1] The MS (Hyde, facs. in *Adam Catalogue*, iii (1929), 118 ff.), of SJ's 'Considerations on Corn' bears compositors' marks showing it was used as printer's copy, and is also marked by EM. SJ's piece is discussed by EM (pp. viii–xi) and is dated to 'November 1766'. D.J. Greene (*Works* (Yale) x. 301–4) gives alternative arguments for the same date. The ½t (p. 201) is corrected in the *Errata* (p. iv), to read: 'First printed in quarto, in 1750.'

The book is not scarce. Hamilton's work, *Parliamentary Logick* proved popular, but SJ's 'Considerations' were not included in later versions, e.g. ed. Courtney S. Kenney, Cambridge: W. Heffer & Sons, 1927. It was also translated (without 'Considerations'): **German**: *Parliamentarische Logik*, Tübingen, 1828; Zürich, 1946; Köln, 1949; **French**: *Logique Parliamentaire*, Paris, 1886; **Spanish**: *Logica Parliamentaria*, Buenos Aires, 1943; Madrid, [n.d.]. SJ's 'Considerations' were reprinted together with his *Diary of a Tour in North Wales*, Philadelphia, 1817, q.v. (816DW/2, 1817, below).

For a possible earlier political involvement with Hamilton, see the alleged maiden speech of November 1755 (55.11HS, above).

Copies: O (3809 e. 24);

USA: CSmH, CtY² (1. uncut), DLC, Hyde⁴ (1. uncut), ICU, IEN, IU, [Liebert], MB, MH², [MdBP, NcD], NjP, NPM, OCl, PPL, [PPM], TxU, ViU; *UK*: Abb, BMp, C², [B.S. Barlow ('R.W. Chapman')], E, Eu, Gu², JDF, L (94. e. 3), LEu, MRp, MRu, NCl *Eir*: Dp (Gilbert, p. 434).

---

[1] EM told Burney of the discovery of SJ's MS in Hamilton's papers, in a letter of 8 June 1808 (MS Folger, 14), and made biographical inquiries of Anthony Hamilton, who replied 24 June 1808 (O: MS Malone 38, fos. 263-4), and of Lord Egremont (MS Malone [?], fos. 220-28), to whom he

also declared his intention of publishing a 'curious little volume' as *Parliamentary Logic* (14 Nov. 1806, MS Petworth).

67.1FT/1   Fawkes's Theocritus, first edition   1767

THE | IDYLLIUMS | OF | THEOCRITUS. | TRANSLATED FROM THE GREEK, | WITH | NOTES CRITICAL AND EXPLANATORY | BY FRANCIS FAWKES, M.A. | Τοις Βουκολικοις, πληων ολιγων των εξωθεν, ο θεοκριτος επιτυχες ατος. | LONGINUS. | LONDON: | PRINTED FOR THE AUTHOR, | BY DRYDEN LEACH: | And fold by J. and R. TONSON, J. DODSLEY, R. BALDWIN, L. HAWES | and Co. T. LONGMAN, R. HORSFIELD, S. CROWDER, J. FLETCHER, | T. DAVIES, G. KEARSLEY, JOHNSON and DAVENPORT, ROBINSON | and ROBERTS, W. JOHNSTON, J. RIDLEY, T. and J. MERRIL, and | C. ETHERINGTON. | M DCC LXVII.

8°, A⁸ a⁸ c⁸ ²c⁸ d² B–K⁸ L⁸ (± L2,3 [?6]) M–T⁸, ($4 signed), 178 leaves.

Pp. Engr. front. + A1 *i* t., *ii* blk, *iii–vi* Dedication dh: TO THE | HONOURABLE | CHARLES YORKE. ('Orpington, | January 10, 1767.'), vii–xxi Preface dh: [two double rules] | PREFACE., ht: PREFACE, *xxii* blk. *xxiii* xxiv–xlii Life dh: SOME | ACCOUNT | OF THE | LIFE AND WRITINGS | OF | THEOCRITUS., rt: THE LIFE OF | THEOCRITUS., *xliii* xliv–lvi Essay dh: AN | ESSAY | OF | PASTORAL POETRY. | BY EDWARD BURNABY GREENE, ESQ., rt: AN ESSAY ON | PASTORAL POETRY., on ²c5 List of Subscribers (5 leaves unpaged) dh. and ht: SUBSCRIBERS, on d2 Errata, d2ᵛ Advt. for Fawkes's *Anacreon*; on B1 *1* ½t: THE | IDYLLIUMS | OF | THEOCRITUS, | TRANSLATED FROM THE GREEK., *2* ARGUMENT., *3* 4–267 text dh: [two double rules] | THE | IDYLLIUMS | OF | THEOCRITUS. | [rule], ht: THEOCRITUS., *268* blk, 269–81 Epigrams dh: THE | EPIGRAMS | OF | THEOCRITUS., ht: THEOCRITUS., *282* blk, 283–88 The Combat dh: THE | COMBAT | BETWEEN | POLLUX AND AMYCUS*. | FROM APOLLONIUS, BOOK II., rt: THE COMBAT BETWEEN | POLLUX AND AMYCUS. (288: 'THE COMBAT BETWEEN, &c.').

Pagination: [↑] vii, 269, 283.

Press-figures: A8(xv)–4, a6ᵛ(xxviii)–2, c7(lxi)–1, ²c2ᵛ(lxviii)–3, d1(lxxix)–2, B3ᵛ(6)–3, C5ᵛ(26)–4, D8ᵛ(48)–4, E4ᵛ(56)–3, G5(89)–4, G8(95)–2, H5(105)–2, I5(121)–1, K3ᵛ(134)–2, K8ᵛ(144)–4, L1ᵛ(146)–5, L3(149)–2, L6ᵛ(156)–3, M5ᵛ(170)–3, N1ᵛ(178)–4, O8(207)–4, P5ᵛ(218)–4, Q7ᵛ(238)–3, R7ᵛ(254)–2, R8ᵛ(256)–4, S2ᵛ(260)–4. Unfigured F; *sometimes* R7ᵛ; L figured three times.

Catchwords: only in notes: 24 n. And (Mr.), 197 n. and (—Tantorum), 237 n. Hither‸ (~,).

Explicit: 267 The END of the IDYLLIUMS., 281 The END of the EPIGRAMS., 288 FINIS.

Paper: White, laid; La. post (uncut: 8¼ × 5¼ in.); wmk.: fleur-de-lys.

Type: Dedication: gt. primer (5.6 mm) leaded; text: pica (4.0 mm), footnotes & subscribers: bourgeois (3.3 mm).

Plate: Front. Head of Theocritus on shaded circle, inscr: 'Apud Fulvium Ursinum in Marmore', and 'Grignion sculp.' (area: 90 × 90 mm).

References: CH 149; Hazen and Mabbott, *RES* xxi (1945), 142–6; ESTC: t138182. For Fawkes (1720–77*), see R.V. Taylor, *Biographia Leodiensis* (1865), 174–7.[1] Subscriptions, no. 62.

Notes: The reason for the cancels in sig. L is unclear. In CtY: L2,3 are on evident stubs: other copies are better disguised. L6 is more problematic: it may only have been loosened by the cancellation of L3, but has evidently been detached in many copies. It bears no signature, however.

581 subscribers (including SJ), and 3 institutions took 426 ordinary and 185 large-paper copies: a total of 611 books. Sixteen booksellers named in the imprint took 25 each, accounting for 400 copies. The edn. probably ran to 1,000 copies. There were many Yorkshire subscribers and there are probably more copies to be found in Yorkshire libraries than are recorded below.

The date of publication is unknown, but the date of the 'Dedication' implies it was early in 1767. SJ not only assisted Fawkes (acknowledged in Preface, p. xx: 'The celebrated Mr Samuel Johnson has corrected part of this work and furnished me with some judicious remarks', and cf. nn. pp. 35, 72, 149, and 231; that on 149 is on the cancel L3), but subscribed for a large paper copy which was sold to E. Walker, for 16s. 6d. with lot 563 at Christie's 16 Feb. 1785.[2]

Copies: O (8° Godwyn 493);

USA: CSmH, CtY[2], DLC[2], [G. Goldberg, Esq;], Hyde, ICN, IU, [Liebert (uncut)], MH, NIC, NjP, NN, PPL, PPU (imperfect), TxU; *UK*: C, Cp, Ct, E, [Es], Eu, JDF, L (76 d.4), LEu, MRu, NCu[2], SHp, SHu, Yc.

[1] Among Dawson Turner's papers, Puttick & Simpson, 6 June 1859, lot 592 was 'Fawkes (Francis) translator of Theocritus — Collection of Original Papers, consisting of Translations from Bion, and Anacreon, Odes, Hymns, Epitaph intended for Col. Henry Townshend, 1762, and other papers. — *a parcel*', bought by Lilly for 3s.
[2] The book is not named in the printed catalogue, but the title is inserted in MS in both the Yale and Harvard copies.

67.1FT/2   Fawkes's Theocritus, Poets of Great Britain   1795

The Complete Edition of the Poets of Great Britain, xiii (1795).

67.1FT/3   Fawkes's Theocritus,   1810
                    Chalmers's English Poets

Alexander Chalmers's *English Poets*, (1810), xx.

67.4PG/1 **Payne's Geometry, first edition** 1767

AN | INTRODUCTION | TO | GEOMETRY. | CONTAINING | The moſt uſeful Propoſitions in Euclid, | and other Authors. | Demonſtrated in a clear and eaſy Method, for the Uſe | of Learners. | [rule] | By WILLIAM PAYNE. | [rule] | [device of flowers] | [double rule] | LONDON: | Sold by T. Payne, at the Mews Gate; J. Marks, in | St. Martin's Lane; and M. Hingeston, at Temple | Bar. M DCC LXVII.

4°, π1 A² B⁴ (± B1) C–I⁴ K⁴ (± K2) L–U⁴ X⁴ (± X2) Y–2G⁴, ($2 (A1 as A2) signed), 119 leaves.

Pp. π1 *i* t., *ii* blk, *iii–iv* Dedication dh: TO HIS | ROYAL HIGHNESS | THE | Duke of *YORK.*, ht (iv): DEDICATION., *v* Preface dh: [double rule] | PREFACE., *vi* Errata: 'The Reader is deſired to correct the following Preſs Errors | with his Pen.', on B1 *1* 2–232 text dh: [two double rules] | INTRO-DUCTION | TO | GEOMETRY.

Pagination: (↑); 154 as 254; *Press-figures*: 2A2ᵛ(180)–1.

Catchwords: 6 53.Tri– (62. Triangles), 25 81. A (∼. Corollary. | A), 36 72ₐ Equal (95. ∼), 49 109. Other– (109*. Otherwiſe), 52 111. Other– (111*. Otherwiſe,), 55 113. Other– (113.* Otherwiſe,), 90 Part (PART), 178 275. Si– (275. If), 179 175*. Similar (275*. ∼), 193 *om.* (9. Otherwiſeₐ), 209 Problem (23. Otherwiſe.), 221 *om.* (Problem 34.), 222 Problem (34. Otherwiſe.).

Explicit: 232 FINIS.

Paper: White, laid; Foolscap (uncut: 8½ × 6¼ in.); wmk.: Pro Patria.

Type: Pica (4.0 mm), leaded. Several line diagrams in the text.

References: CH 149; Hazen 151–2; *Life* ii. 482; *Adam Library*, ii. 18 ff.; ESTC: t106919.

Notes: Title (π1) probably printed with cancels (B1, K2, X2) as a sheet, though no copy yet corroborates this. The printer was probably the same as for second edn. (67.4PG/2, below), *viz.* Harris Hart, son of John (Plomer 117–18; Maxted 104), though the absence of press-figures here argues against him. It was published in April 1767, at 7s. 6d. (*London Mag.*). The 'Dedication' was rightly attributed to SJ by R. B. Adam, though Hazen cites some earlier notices (148 n.). The 'Preface' may also have been touched by SJ.[1] SJ's copy was lot 551 in the sale of his books by Christie, 16 Feb. 1785, where it was bought by Charles Marsh, though it cannot be identified in Marsh's sale at Christie's, 1 Feb. 1816. Copies are scarce.

Copies: O (Vet. A5 e. 586, 'R. W. Chapman');

USA: [DAU], Hyde ('R.B. Adam'), MBAt; *UK*: C ('John Sneyd, Bishton, Staffordshire'), Eu, L (1349 f.1), NOu.

---

[1] Para. 2 includes the sentence: 'No man ought to increase the croud of books, without some prospect of increasing or facilitating knowledge'. The verbal repetition ('increase') is un-Johnsonian, and Payne might occasionally aspire to SJ's manner. A single sentence is not adequate for an attribution.

67.4PG/2   Payne's Geometry, second edition   1768

AN | INTRODUCTION | TO | GEOMETRY; | CONTAINING | The
Moſt uſeful Propoſitions in Euclid, | and other Authors. | Demonſtrated in a
clear and eaſy Method, for the Uſe | of Learners. | By WILLIAM PAYNE. |
The Second Edition. | LONDON: | Printed by H. Hart, Popping's Court,
Fleetſtreet. | Sold by T. Payne, at the Mews Gate; and | M. Hingeston, at
Temple Bar. | MDCCLXVIII.

8°, A^2 B–2H⁴ 2I² χ1(? = 2Q4) 2K–2P⁴ 2Q⁴ (–2Q4), ($2 signed), 152 leaves.

Pp. A1 *i* t., *ii* Extract from the *Critical Review, iii* Dedication, iv Preface, on
B1 *1* 2–244 Introduction to Geometry dh: INTRODUCTION | TO |
GEOMETRY., χ1 unpaged leaf = ½t: INTRODUCTION | TO |
MENSURATION., on 2K1 245–98 text *Measuring, &c.*

Pagination: [↑]; (↑) iv.

Press-figures: H2ᵛ(52)–2, K4ᵛ(72)–1, L4ᵛ(80)–1, M1ᵛ(82)–2, N4ᵛ(96)–2,
U4(151)–2, X4ᵛ(160)–2, 2B4ᵛ(192)–2, 2C3ᵛ(198)–1, 2D1ᵛ(202)–2,
2E4ᵛ(216)–2, 2G4ᵛ(232)–1, 2H3ᵛ(238)–2, 2L1ᵛ(254)–2, 2M3ᵛ(266)–1,
2N2ᵛ(272)–1, 2O3ᵛ(282)–1, 2P2ᵛ(288)–1, 2Q1ᵛ(294)–2.

Catchwords: not recorded.

Explicit: Not recorded.

Paper: White, laid; foolscap (uncut: 6¾ × 4¼ in.); wmk.: PRO PATRIA +
GR.

Type: Not recorded.

References: Hazen 152; ESTC: t166902.

Notes: SJ's Dedication to the Duke of York is reprinted, unrevised. The
Introduction to Mensuration was issued separately with its own t., dated 1768
(L: 8503. b.54 (3)). The SAN copy lacks the *Introduction to Mensuration*.

Copies: CU (P 21.7);
USA: CtY, MiU, PPL; *UK*: [AWn], BRu (Maths 66868), [Lsm], LVu (Y76
2.150), SAN (ˢQA451. P2).

67.6HM   Hoole's Metastasio   1767

[Engr. t.] The | Works | OF | Metastasio; | *Translated from the* | Italian, |
By | John Hoole. | Vol. I [– II]. | *London:* | *Printed for T. Davies,* | *in Ruſſel
Street Covent Garden.* | MDCCLXVII.

2 vols., 8°

I. a⁶ B–X⁸ Y⁴ Z², ($4 (–B1, C3, D2,3, E2, F2,3,4, G3, H3,4, I4, M3, N4,
O3,4, S2) signed; 'Vol. I.' on $1), 172 leaves.

Pp. Engr. t. + a1 *i* ii–iv Dedication dh: [Engr. Headp. Vignette of Alnwick
Castle, Northumberland, with motto: 'Esperance en Dieu', 'J. Hall Sculp.'] |
TO THE | DUKE | OF | NORTHUMBERLAND, *&c.* | MY LORD,, ht:
DEDICATION., (signed iv: 'John Hoole.'), *v* vi–xi Preface dh. and ht:

PREFACE., *xii* blk, on B1 *1* ½t: ARTAXERXES., *2* Dram. Pers., *3* 4–118 text dh: [Engr. hp. ARTAXERXES. 'Isaac Taylor del. et ſculp.'], ht: ARTAX-ERXES., *119* ½t THE OLYMPIAD., *120* Dram. Pers., *121* 122–234 text dh: [Engr. hp. THE OLYMPIAD. 'Isaac Taylor del. et ſculp.'], ht: THE OLYMPIAD., *235* ½t HYPSIPILE., *236* Dram. Pers., *237* 238–332 text dh: [Engr. hp. HYPSIPILE. 'Isaac Taylor del. et ſculp.'], ht: HYPSIPILE.

Pagination: 32 as 23;

Press-figures: X8(319)–3, X8ᵛ(320)–3, Y3ᵛ(326)–3, Z2(339)–3;

Catchwords: *om.* iv, xi–xii, 1–2, 118–20; speech-prefixes *om.* 6, 15, 30, 35–6, 39–41, 45, 51, 62–3, 67–8, 72–5, 80, 85, 88, 93–4, 105, 108, 114, 122–3, 126, 138–9, 150, 152, 157, 170, 173–4, 178, 184, 189, 197, 204, 207, 232, 237, 240, 242, 248, 259, 270, 284, 290, 299, 302, 304, 326–7; 13 AR (ARTABAN.), 14 *om.* (Hear), 16 *om.* (ſhall), 21 *om.* (Yet), 25 *om.* (The), 28 *om.* (The), 29 ARTAXERXESₐ (~.), 37 *om.* (SCENE), 50 *om.* (Of), 56 *om.* (I'll), 57 *om.* (Is), 61 *om.* (That), 69 *om.* (Haſt), 71 *om.* (The), 79 *om.* (A), 96 *om.* (If), 101 *om.* (Now), 103 *om.* (Behold), 116 *om.* (The), 132 *om.* (But), 136 *om.* (In), 140 *om.* (SCENE), 165 *om.* (SCENE), 171 *om.* (Of), 183 *om.* (Aſſiſt), 192 *om.* (Who), 194 *om.* (He), 199 *om.* (Methinks), 216 *om.* (They), 218 I ſeekₐ (~ ~,), 258 *om.* (Thou), 260 *om.* (SCENE), 322 *om.* (Forget).

Explicit: 322 END OF THE FIRST VOLUME.

II. B–Z⁸ (Z8 blk), ($4 (–D2,3, F2,3, H4, I2, L2,3, M2, N2,3, R4, T3, Y2) signed; 'VOL. II.' on $1), 176 leaves.

Pp. Engr. t. + on B1 *1* ½t TITUS., *2* Dram. Pers., *3* 4–115 text dh: [Engr. hp. TITUS. 'Isaac Taylor del. et ſculp.'], ht: TITUS., *116* blk, *117* ½t: DEMETRIUS., *118* Dram. Pers., *119* 120–236 text dh: [Engr. headp. DEMETRIUS. 'Isaac Taylor del. et ſculp.'], ht: DEMETRIUS., *237* ½t: DEMOPHOON., *238* Dram. Pers., *239* 240–350 text dh: [Engr. headp. DEMOPHOON. 'Isaac Taylor del. et ſculp.'], ht: DEMOPHOON., *351–2* (Z8) blk.

Pagination: no errors;

Press-figures: C5ᵛ(26)–1, D6(43)–3, D6ᵛ(44)–3, E5ᵛ(58)–1, F3(69)–2, F6(75)–3, G4ᵛ(88)–1, G8(95)–2, H5(105)–1, I5ᵛ(122)–2, I6ᵛ(124)–1, K6(139)–1, L7ᵛ(158)–3, M7(173)–3, M7ᵛ(174)–2, N8(191)–1, O1ᵛ(194)–2, O4ᵛ(200)–3, P5ᵛ(218)–1, Q1ᵛ(226)–3, Q5(233)–1, R5(249)–1, S3ᵛ(262)–1, T3ᵛ(278)–3, T5(281)–1, U5ᵛ(298)–2, X8(319)–1, Y5(329)–3, Y7ᵛ(334)–2, Z2ᵛ(340)–3;

Catchwords: *om.* 1–2, 115–18, 236–8; speech-pfxs. *om.* 4, 27–9, 39–40, 46–7, 54, 64, 66–7, 74, 89, 103, 127–8, 138, 147–8, 179, 181, 192, 203, 205–6, 220–1, 230, 235, 240, 247, 251, 253, 265, 270, 274, 277, 282, 290, 294, 323, 329; 31 *om.* (who), 34 *om.* (SCENE), 35 *om.* (Wait), 43 *om.* (No), 45 *om.* (How), 56 *om.* (I fly), 69 *om.* (Think'ſt), 73 *om.* (Without), 76 *om.* (SCENE), 84 *om.* (The), 91 *om.* (No), 149 *om.* (This), 160 *om.* (SCENE), 163 *om.* (All),

171 *om.* (And), 187 *om.* (At), 223 *om.* (Immortal), 239 *om.* (Apollo), 250 *om.* (I own), 267 *om.* (Exert), 280 *om.* (the), 283 *om.* (SCENE), 287 *om.* (I fee), 292 *om.* (SCENE), 295 But͵ (~,), 300 *om.* (I feek), 306 *om.* (And), 331 *om.* (The), 332 *om.* (O !).

Explicit: 350 END OF THE SECOND VOLUME.

Paper: White, laid; Foolscap (uncut: 7 × 4¼ in.); wmk.: C. Engr. tt. on heavier paper, wmk.: Strasburg bend + LVG (horiz. ch. ll). There may have been a large paper issue.[1]

Type: Dedication: english (4.6 mm), leaded; Preface: pica (4.0 mm), leaded; text: small pica (3.6 mm). Engr. headpp. I. i, 3, 121, 237; II. 3, 119, 239.

References: Hazen 66–8; CH 149; *Tinker* 1352; ESTC: t075038; *MS Handlist* 101; *MS Index* JoS 180.

Notes: Published at 6s. on 20 June 1767 (*Lond. Chron.*).[2] SJ's 'Dedication' was identified when the holograph draft was sold from the estate of Revd A. S. Hoole, of Wroxton, Banbury, at Sotheby 17 Feb. 1930, 184 (now MS Hyde). SJ's own copy of the work was lot 189 in his sale, Christie, 16 Feb. 1785, sold to 'Scot' for 2s. 6d., and is untraced. In the Hoole sale (1930, above), lot 180 was a letter from Metastasio to JH, 13 Oct. 1768 referring to this translation (now MH: TS. 953. * (III. 170)).

An enlarged edn. was published in 3 vols. in 1800, but SJ's Dedication was omitted, the first Duke of Northumberland having died in 1786.[3] In the 1800 'Preface' Hoole acknowledged his translation of 'The Uninhabited Island' in Anna Williams's *Miscellanies*, 1766 (66.4WM/1, above).

Copies: O (3862 f. 1–2, 'K. Yorke');

USA: CSmH (K-D 324, 'J.P. Kemble'), Hyde ('Chr. Rolleston' — 'Lancelot Rolleston'), ICU, [Liebert], MB, MH, NIC, TxU; *UK*: BMp, C, E, LCu (vol. 1 only), L (241. l.1), LEu.

[1] Saunders (Garrick), 23 April 1823, 1483: 'Hoole's *Metastasio*, 2 vols. 1767, Large Paper presentation copy.'

[2] In *A Catalogue of Books . . . to be sold . . . 26 January 1769* by Thomas Davies (O: Vet A5 e.2911(a)), p. 217, Hoole's *Metastasio* is advertised at 7s. Davies told JB in a letter of 28 Apr. 1767, 'I shall publish very soon the 2 first vols. of Hooles Translation of Metastasio' (*General Corr. of JB, 1766–69*, ed. Cole (1993), 151–2.

[3] Hugh (Smithson) Percy, 1st D. of 3rd cr., 1715–86*.

68.1GGM/1   Goldsmith's Good Natur'd Man   1768

THE | GOOD NATUR'D MAN: | A | COMEDY. | As Performed at the | THEATRE-ROYAL | IN | COVENT-GARDEN. | [row of 34 flowers: 58 mm] | BY MR. GOLDSMITH. | [34 flowers: 58 mm] | [floral device: 25 mm] | LONDON: | Printed for W. GRIFFIN, in Catharine-Street, Strand. | MDCCLXVIII.

8°, *A*^{4} b–K^4 L^2, ($2 (–A1, L2) signed), 42 leaves.

Pp. A1 *i* ½t: THE | Good Natur'd Man. | [Price 1s. 6d.], *ii* blk, *iii* t., *iv* blk, *v*–vi Preface dh. & ht: PREFACE., *vii* Prologue dh: PROLOGUE. | WRITTEN BY | Dr. JOHNSON: | SPOKEN BY | Mr. BENSLEY., *viii* Dramatis Personæ., on B1 *1* 2–74 text dh: [2 rows of flowers] | THE | GOOD NATUR'D MAN. | [beaded rule], rt: THE GOOD NATUR'D MAN. | A COMEDY., *75* Epilogue dh: EPILOGUE, | SPOKEN BY | Mrs. BULKLEY., *76* blk.

Pagination: no errors.

Press-figures: A3(v)–3, B4(7)–3*, D1^v(18)–2, E4^v(32)–1*, F3^v(38)–3, I3(61)–3, K4^v(72)–1*.

Catchwords: *om.* i–viii; 23 *om.* (prodigious,), 31 ſcruple. (~‸), 44 ACT, 48 *om.* (*Garnet.*), 54 paſſion‸ (~.).

Explicit: 74 FINIS.

Paper: White, laid; La. post (uncut: 8¼ × 5¼ in.); no vis. wmk.

Type: Preface: english (4.6 mm), Prologue and text: pica (4.0 mm), footnotes: long primer (3.1 mm).

References: Courtney 113; CH 150; Todd, 'The First Editions of *The Good Natur'd Man* and *She Stoops to Conquer*', *SB* xi (1958), 133–42.

Notes: Todd discriminated the several early impressions and the 8 variant states of L^2. The bibliography of Goldsmith is outside the scope of this study, but the following tabulation follows Todd's outline of the distinctions.

Impression No.	Press-figures (by sigg.) A	B	C	D	E	F	G	H	I	K
1. '1768'	3–3	4–3*	–	1^v–2	4^v–1*	3^v–3	–	–	3–3	4^v–1*
2. '1768'	3–3	4–3*	–	4^v–3	4^v–1	3^v–1	–	–	3–3	4^v–1*
3. 'New'	–	–	–	–	–	3^v–1	–	–	3–3	–
4. 'New'	3–1	3–1	1^v–1	2^v–2	–	3^v–2	–	1^v–2	3–2	3–2
5. 'Fifth'	3–3	4–1	1^v–3	2^v–1	3–3	–	–	1^v–3	–	–

Todd adds nicer details from the text, but the above suffice to distinguish most copies. L^2 is more complex since it was apparently printed as a duplicate ½-sheet, each impression involving two settings of type. The last leaf (L2) bears the *Epilogue*, and is something of an afterthought, since p. 74 carries the word 'FINIS.' The 'Epilogue' exhibits the most striking textual differences, sometimes occupying p. 75 only, and sometimes pp. 75–6. Adjustments were evidently made at press, and the sequence and frequency of each is uncertain. Todd presents another table for sheet L, which it is unnecessary to duplicate here. From these tables Todd distinguished copies by the figg. 1–5 from table I for the impression, and by the letters a–h for the states of L^2.

The play was first produced at Covent Garden on 29 Jan. 1768 when Bensley delivered SJ's 'Prologue' (*Life* ii. 45). It was soon printed in the newspapers, apparently first in the *St. James's Chronicle*, 2 Feb. 1768; where the printed text was slightly modified from the hasty transcripts followed by the newspapers (*Poems*[2] 177–9). SJ's authorship of the Prologue was known early, and established by Davies's *Miscellaneous & Fugitive Pieces*, (1773), ii. 298, and confirmed by Steevens in Reed's *Biographia Dramatica* (1782), ii. 268.

Copies: O (Vet A5 e. 2206, *cropt*);
USA: CSmH[4], CtY, DFo, Hyde[3] ICU, IU, [Liebert], MH, PPL, NjP[2], NPM[2], NN, TxU, ViU; *UK*: C[2], E, Gp, L[3], LEu, MRp, MRu.

68.2TE   Henry Thrale's Election Addresses   1768

29 February   Election Address for Henry Thrale
Published in *Public Advertiser* 3 March 1768, and in *Gazetteer & New Daily Advertiser*, 4, 5, 7, and 8 March 1768.
References: Fleeman, in *Johnson, Boswell and their Circle* (1965), 176–7. SJ's draft is MS Hyde (*Letters* 194.1, '29 Feb. 1768', *MS Index* JoS 173) which mentions 'another advertisement', as yet unidentified, but presumably written about this time.

8 March   Election Address for Henry Thrale
'To the worthy Electors of the Borough of SOUTHWARK'
Published in *Public Advertiser*, 9, 10, 11, and 12 March 1768.
References: Fleeman, in *Johnson, Boswell and their Circle* (1965), 177.

14 March   'To the worthy Electors of the Borough of SOUTHWARK'
Published in *Public Advertiser*, 15, 16, 17, 18, 19 and 21 March 1768
References: Fleeman, in *Johnson, Boswell and their Circle* (1965), 178.

23 March   'To the worthy Electors of the Borough of SOUTHWARK'
Published in *Public Advertiser*, 23 March 1768
References: Fleeman, in *Johnson, Boswell and their Circle* (1965), 178.

68.5LB/1   Letter to F.A. Barnard   1823

SJ's Letter to the King's Librarian, Frederick Augusta Barnard, 28 May 1768, advising him on the development of the Royal Library, was denied to JB (*Life* ii. 33n)[1], and was not published until 1823 in the House of Commons papers:

REPORTS | FROM | COMMITTEES: | *IN THREE VOLUMES.* | VOLUME THE FIRST. | [short rule] | EXPIRED LAWS; ROYAL LIBRARY; FOREIGN TRADE; | GAME LAWS; MILITIA ESTIMATES; | MERCHANTS, AGENTS, OR FACTORS; SMALL DEBTS; | &c. | [medium double rule] | Session | 4 *February* — — to — — 19 *July*, | 1823. | [medium double rule] | VOL. IV.

[Sub-t.] REPORT | FROM THE | COMMITTEE | ON | PAPERS RELATING TO | THE | ROYAL LIBRARY, | WHICH | HIS MAJESTY | HAS BEEN GRACIOUSLY PLEASED TO PRESENT | TO THE BRITISH NATION. | [medium parallel rule] | *Ordered, by* The House of Commons, *to be Printed,* | 18 *April* 1823. | [medium total rule].

2°, A–D², ($1 signed), 8 leaves.

Pp. A1 t., A1ᵛ Contents, A2 *3* 4–10 Report ('18 *April* 1823.'), 11–13 Appendix (A): SJ's Letter to Barnard 'May 28, 1768.', 14 Appendix (B) Directions for the reading Room, *15* blk, *16* outer cover (for folding) with t.

Notes: SJ's Letter of 28 May 1768, to F.A. Barnard, adumbrating the desirable features of a great library (*Letters* 206, Hyde, i. 307–14), is printed in the above *Parliamentary Report* for 1823, Session 271, vol. iv. 41.

Copies: O; *UK*: [W.R. Batty], E; *USA*: [Liebert].

¹ JB's request on 10 June 1790, was denied the following day (Waingrow, *Corr.* 322–4). For the history, see J. Brooke, 'The Library of George III', *YULG* lii (1977), 33–45.

68.5LB/2   Letter to F. A. Barnard, facsimile   1955

A Facsimile of the MS (Hyde) of SJ's Letter to Barnard, 28 May 1768, was produced with notes by E.L. McAdam, for the New York 'Johnsonians' in 1955, as *Dr Johnson and the King's Library.*

68.5LB/3   Letter to F. A. Barnard, Toucan Press   1976

Advice on the Formation of a Library. By Dr Johnson. St Peter Port Toucan Press. 1976.

4 leaves, 8pp. (unnumbered), untitled in wraps. Pp. *1–7* text of Letter to Barnard, *8* Typewritten coloph: '100 copies reprinted by The Toucan Press, Mount Durand, St Peter Port, Guernsey, C.I. 1976.' ISBN: 0-85695-077-1.

Copies: O; *UK*: E (HP1. 77. 4264), L (2719. aa.39).

68.12HC/1a   Hoole's Cyrus, first issue   1768

[½t] CYRUS: | A | TRAGEDY. | [Price One Shilling and Sixpence.]

[Title] CYRUS: | A | TRAGEDY. | As it is performed at the | THEATRE ROYAL | IN | COVENT-GARDEN. | BY | JOHN HOOLE. | LONDON: | Printed for T. DAVIES, in Ruffel-Street, Covent-Garden. | M.DCC.LXVIII.

8°, *A*⁴ B–L⁴, ($2 signed), 44 leaves.

Pp. A1 ½t, A1ᵛ blk, A2 t., A2ᵛ blk, A3 *v–vi* Dedication dh: TO THE | DUCHESS | OF | NORTHUMBERLAND, &c. | MADAM, (signed: 'Clement's Inn, | 14 Dec. 1768. | JOHN HOOLE.'), ht: DEDICATION., A4 PROLOGUE., A4ᵛ *Dramatis Perfonæ.*, on B1 *1* 2–79 text dh: [two double rules] | CYRUS: | A | TRAGEDY. | [rule], rt: CYRUS: | A TRAGEDY., *80* EPILOGUE.

Pagination: no errors.

Press-figures: B4ᵛ(8)–1, D4ᵛ(24)–1, F4ᵛ(40)–1.

Catchwords: *om.* between Acts pp. 16, 34, 48, 66, and throughout sig. A, except Dedication, A3(v) 'or'; 3 MANDANE‸ (~.), 12 'Till (‸~), 25 MIRZA‸ (~.), 30 Enter. (~‸), 44 CYRUS‸ (~.).

Explicit: 80 FINIS.

Paper: White, laid; La. post (uncut: 8¼ × 5¼ in.); no vis. wmk.

Type: Dedication: pica (4.1 mm), leaded, text: sm. pica (3.5 mm), leaded, but set close pp. 78–9.

References: CH 150; Hazen 60–2; Nicoll (1952–9), iii. 272; ESTC: t034551.

Notes: Published 20 Dec. 1768, at 1s. 6d. (*Lond. Chron.*). The Dedication was first attributed to SJ by Hazen, and is unchallenged. Some details of the rehearsal and preparation of this work are implied in a letter from Charles Macklin to Garrick, 24 Dec. 1768 (*Corr. of Garrick*, ed. Boaden, i (1831), 327). Hoole's account for his benefit night was part of lot 379 (untraced), at R. H. Evans's sale (Hoole family papers on the d. of Revd Samuel Hoole), 9 December 1839.

Copies: O³ (**1**. Mal B.6(9); **2**. M. adds 108 e.83(3); **3**. M. adds 108 e. 138(4));

USA: CSmH, CtY², DFo², ICN, ICU², InU, [Liebert], MB, MH ('from the Author'), MiU, [MoU], NIC, NjP, NN², NNC, [OrU], PPL, PPU, TxU, ViU, [WU]; *UK*: BAT, BMp, C, Gp, L² (**1**. 643. g.11(9); **2**. 83. a.26(1)), MRp.

68.12HC/1b   Hoole's Cyrus, second issue   1768

CYRUS: | A | TRAGEDY. | As it is performed at the | THEATRE ROYAL | IN | COVENT-GARDEN. | BY | JOHN HOOLE. | SECOND EDITION. | LONDON: | Printed for T. DAVIES, in Ruffel-Street, Covent-Garden. | M.DCC.LXVIII.

8°, *A*⁴ B–L⁴, ($2 signed), 44 leaves.

References: ESTC: n003174.

Notes: Identical in every way with the first issue (68.12HC/1a, above), save for the words 'SECOND EDITION.' on the t. The t. is not a cancel and the change was evidently made at press, perhaps late in the run, perhaps to mislead the Dublin trade (see 68.12HC/2, below), and few copies are recorded. Hazen did not find one (61–2).

Copies: E (Bute 641 (6));

USA: IEN, MH, [NcD, OrU], TxU²; *UK*: BMp, BRu (B128h (69262)), [L]; *Eir*: Dt.

68.12HC/2   Hoole's Cyrus, Dublin   1769

CYRUS: | A | TRAGEDY. | As it is performed at the | THEATRE ROYAL, | IN | COVENT-GARDEN. | BY JOHN HOOLE. | [double rule] | DUBLIN: | Printed for W. and W. Sмith, G. Faulkner, | S. Powell, P. and W. Wilson, J. Exshaw, | H. Saunders, W. Sleater, B. Grierson, | D. Chamberlaine, J. Hoey, jun. J. Potts, | J. Williams, and J. Porter, 1769.

12°, A–B¹² C⁶ D1, ($5 (–C4,5) signed), 31 leaves.

Pp. A1 *1* t., *2* blk. *3–4* Dedication, *5* Prologue dh: PROLOGUE., *6* Dramatis Perſonæ, on A4 *7* 8–61 text, *62* Epilogue dh: EPILOGUE.

Pagination: 8–9 (on A4) as '7–8'; *Press-figures*: none.

Catchwords: 10 Har. (Harpagus), 26 Aud (And).

Explicit: 62 FINIS.

Paper: White, laid; Carré (uncut: 6¾ × 4¼ in.); wmk.: (a) 'MOYEN DANGOUMOIS + grapes'; (b) 'MOYEN DU MARCHAIX + grapes 1767'.

Type: Dedication: small pica (3.6 mm), leaded; text: bourgeois (3.0 mm).

References: Stratman 2393; ESTC: t028339.

Notes: Mixed paper stock, and variant speech-prefix (sigg. A: '*Cyr*.'; BCD: '*Cyrus*.') suggest shared printing in haste from first London issue, so a date early in 1769 is presumed for this publication. SJ's Dedication is reprinted, signed and dated as in 68.12HC/1a, above.

Copies: O³ (**1.** Vet. A5 e.1495(5); **2.** Vet. A5 f.655(5); **3.** Vet. A5 f.1127(2)); *USA*: DFo, [DNLM, InU], NN; *Can*: [CaBVaU]; *UK*: C (Hib. 7.746. 30²).

68.12HC/3   Hoole's Cyrus, third edition   1769

CYRUS: | A | TRAGEDY. | As it is performed at the | THEATRE ROYAL | IN | COVENT-GARDEN. | BY | JOHN HOOLE. | THIRD EDITION. | LONDON: | Printed by T. Davies, in Ruſſel-Street, Covent-Garden. | M.DCC.LXIX.

8°, π² *A*1 B–L⁴, ($2 signed), 43 leaves.

Pp. π1 t., π1ᵛ blk, π2–2ᵛ Dedication, on A1 Prologue, A1ᵛ Dramatis Perſonæ., on B1 *1* 2–79 text dh: [two double rules] | CYRUS: | A | TRAGEDY. | [bevelled rule], rt: CYRUS: | A TRAGEDY., *80* EPILOGUE.

Pagination: no errors; *Press-figures*: none.

Catchwords: *om.* between Acts pp. 16, 34, 48, 66; 12 'Til ('Till).

Explicit: 80 FINIS.

Paper: White, laid; La. post (uncut: 8¼ × 5¼ in.); no vis. wmk.

Type: Dedication: pica (4.1 mm), leaded; text: small pica (3.5 mm), leaded, but set close pp. 76–80.
References: Hazen 62; ESTC: n003175.
Notes: A close reprint of 1st edn. (68.12HC/1a, above).
Copies: O (Vet. A5 e.1853(1), 'James Steuart');
USA: DLC, [InU], NNC, TxU; *UK*: C, LEu.

68.12HC/4   Hoole's Cyrus, 'third' edition   1772

CYRUS: | A | TRAGEDY. | As it is performed at the | THEATRE ROYAL | IN | COVENT-GARDEN. | BY | JOHN HOOLE. | THIRD EDITION. | LONDON: | Printed for T. Davies, in Ruffel-Street, Covent-Garden. | M.DCC.LXXII.
8°, π² *A*1 B–L⁴, ($2 signed), 43 leaves.
Pp. π1 t., π1ᵛ blk, π2–2ᵛ Dedication, on A1 Prologue, A1ᵛ Dramatis Perfonæ., on B1 *1* 2–79 text dh: [two double rules] | CYRUS: | A | TRAGEDY. | [bevelled rule], rt: CYRUS: | A TRAGEDY., *80* EPILOGUE.
References: Hazen 62; ESTC: t034552.
Notes: As for prec. edn. of 1769 (68.12HC/3, above), but a new edn. with reset type and two noticeable variants:
  1. p. 1, dh: . . . TRAGEDY. | [rule]
  2. Catchword: 12 ‚Till
Copies: O (Vet. A5 e.358); *USA*: CtY, DLC, MB; *UK*: BMp, C, L, MRu.

68.12HC/5   Hoole's Cyrus, Bell's British Theatre,   1795
                 Vol. XXIV

Bell's British Theatre, Vol. XXIV. (a) Pp. 72. ESTC: t034553.
  (b) Separately issued, pp. 80. ESTC: t028340.

69.3GNDA   Letter to the Gazetteer   1769

13 March   Letter to the Printer of *The Gazetteer & New Daily Advertiser*
  References: Fleeman, in *Johnson, Boswell and their Circle* (1965), 179–80; MS Hyde (*Handlist* 110). See also *Gents. Mag.* xxxix (March 1769), 161–2.

69.5LC   London Chronicle 29 Apr.–2 May   1769

Apr. 29–May 2, p. 410ᶜ Character of the Revd. Zachariah Mudge, prebendary of Exeter and Vicar of St. Andrew's, Plymouth.
  References: *Life*, iv. 76–7 (Courtney 113).

Notes: Attributed by Thomas Percy (O: Percy 87), who annotated SJ's MS of this 'Character' (*Handlist* 111, from J. Waller, *Catalogue* 82 (1870), 174, £2. 12s. 6d.), which is still untraced.

70.1FA/1a   False Alarm, first edition, first impression   1770

[½t] [row of 36 asterisks, 80 mm] | THE | FALSE ALARM. | [Price One Shilling.] | [row of 36 asterisks, 80 mm]

[Title] THE | FALSE ALARM. | [rule] | [device] | [parallel rule] | LONDON: | Printed for T. CADELL in the Strand. | M D C C L X X.

8°, π² A–F⁴ G², ($4 (–G2) signed), 28 leaves.

Pp. π1 ½t, π1ᵛ blk, π2 *1* t., π2ᵛ *2* blk, on A1 *3* 4–53 text dh: [double rule] | THE | FALSE ALARM., *54* blk.

Pagination: [↑] 4–10, 36–42; (↑) 11–35, 43–53.

Press-figures: A1ᵛ(4)–6, B1ᵛ(12)–4, C4ᵛ(26)–7, D3ᵛ(32)–1, E3ᵛ(40)–7, F4ᵛ(50)–1, G1ᵛ(52)–9.

Catchwords: no errors.

Explicit: 53 FINIS.

Paper: White, laid; Royal (uncut: 9¼ × 6 in.); no vis. wmk.

Type: Pica (4.3 mm), leaded; initial caps begin each para.

References: *Life* ii. 111 (Courtney 113–15); CH 150; *Rothschild* 1250; *Tinker* 1353; Todd, *BC* ii (1953), 59–65; Greene, *SB* xiii (1960), 223–31; *Works* (Yale), x. 313 ff. ESTC: t089378.

Notes: SJ composed the pamphlet 10–11 January 1770. Strahan printed 500 copies within a week (L: Add. MS 48803, fo. 35), and it was published on 16 January at 1s. (*Lond. Chron.*). As is common with such small pamphlets the ½t is often missing.

Copies: O (22774 e.28);

USA: CLU-C (uncut; sophist.), CSmH (uncut), CtY, DLC², G. Goldberg, Esq; Hyde², ICN, ICU, IU, [Liebert = CtY], MB, MH ('Thomas Hollis'), NjP, NN², NIC, NPM, PPAmP, PHi (Af. 364.1, 'Benjamin Franklin'), PPL, PPU, TxU, WiM; *Japan*: [Kyoto]; *UK*: C, Gu, MRu; *Eir*: Dt.

70.1FA/1b   False Alarm, first edition,   1770
second impression

THE | FALSE ALARM. | [rule] | THE SECOND EDITION. | [parallel rule] | LONDON: | Printed for T. CADELL in the Strand. | M D C C L X X.

8°, π² A–F⁴ G², ($2 (–G2) signed), 28 leaves.

Another impression of 70.1FA/1a, above, except for the following details:

Pp. π1 ½t: [row of 36 asterisks, 79 mm] | THE | FALSE ALARM. | [Price

One Shilling.] | [row of 36 asterisks, 79 mm], π1ᵛ blk, . . . &c., as first impression (70.1FA/1a, above).

Press-figures: A3ᵛ(8)–8, B4ᵛ(18)–8, D4ᵛ(34)–9, E3ᵛ(40)–9, F1ᵛ(44)–9 (*sometimes om.*).

Catchwords: 11 felony (probably).

Notes: The first line of type at the head of p. 12, reading: 'felony, is not eligible in Parliament. They', is accidentally omitted producing the disjoined catchword on p. 11. Though Todd reported a single incidence of press-figure 9 on C1ᵛ(20), it is usually missing, leaving sig. C unfigured.

500 copies printed by Strahan soon after the first, and published at 1s. on 6 February 1770 (*Lond. Chron*).

Copies: O (Vet. A5 e.1944);

USA: CLU-C, DLC, Hyde, [Liebert (uncut) = CtY], MH, [MNBedF], NIC, NN, ViU ('Jefferson'; *Sowerby* 2758); *Japan*: [Kyoto]; *UK*: AWn, Ct², E, LEu (½t. inscr: 'Dictʸ Johnson'), STA (uncut); *Aust*: CNL ('Nichol Smith'); *Eir*: Dt.

70.1FA/1c   False Alarm, first edition, third impression   1770

THE | FALSE ALARM. | [rule] | THE SECOND EDITION. | [parallel rule] | LONDON: | Printed for T. CADELL in the Strand. | M D C C L X X.

8°, π² A–F⁴ G², ($2 (–G2) signed), 28 leaves.

A reimpression from the 2nd (70.1FA/1b, above), varying only as follows:

Press-figures: A3ᵛ(8)–2, B4ᵛ(18)–2, C2ᵛ(22)–7, D4(33)–8, E2ᵛ(38)–7, F1ᵛ(44)–7, G1ᵛ(52)–7.

Notes: The ½t agrees with the measurements of the 2nd impression, 70.1FA/1b, above, but the first line of type on p. 12 is here restored. Strahan printed 500 copies which were published at 1s. on 24 February 1770 (*Lond. Chron*.).

Copies: O (Godwyn Pamph. 278 (8));

USA: CSmH (123972, 'From the Author' (*not* SJ)), CtY, DLC, Hyde, IU, [Liebert ('Clement Shorter')], NIC ('Sir Edward Blackett, Bart.'); *Can*: CaOHM; *UK*: Gp, Gu, LVu.

70.1FA/1d   False Alarm, first edition, fourth impression   1770

THE | FALSE ALARM. | [rule| THE SECOND EDITION. | [parallel rule] | LONDON: | Printed for T. CADELL in the Strand. | M D C C L X X.

8°, π² A–F⁴ G², ($4 (–G2) signed), 28 leaves.

A reimpression from the second, above (70.1FA/1b), with the following differences:

Pagination: 51 as '(51ᴧ';

Press-figures: A4(9)–7, B4ᵛ(18)–3, C2ᵛ(22)–5, D4(33)–7, E2ᵛ(38)–7, F1ᵛ(44)–6, G1ᵛ(52)–3.

Notes: ½t as in second impression, 70.1FA/1b, above. Strahan printed 500 copies which were published at 1s. on 13 March 1770 (*London Chron.*).

Copies: O (Vet. A5 e.2458);

USA: CtY (Franklin 770.J62), [Liebert], MB, NIC, PHi, PPL; *UK*: BMp, DUu ('M. J. Routh'), MRp, STA.

70.1FA/2 False Alarm, Dublin 1770

THE | FALSE ALARM. | [medium rule] | [device: ship in sail] | [double rule] | DUBLIN: | Printed for E. LYNCH, Bookſeller, in Skinner-row. | M DCC LXX.

8°, A–C⁸, ($4 (–A1, B3,4) signed), 24 leaves.

Pp. A1 *1* t., *2* blk, *3* 4–48 text dh: [double rule] | THE | FALSE ALARM.

Pagination: (↑) 4–32, [↑] 33–48; *Press-figures*: none.

Catchwords: 39 thoſeᴧ (~,).

Explicit: 48 FINIS.

Paper: White, laid; Carré (uncut: 8¼ × 5½ in.); wmk.: BARAULT | MOYEN | DANGOUMOIS | [grapes].

Type: English (4.5 mm), leaded, but set close in C in slightly larger type (4.6 mm).

References: ESTC: t122458.

Notes: The text follows the second London impression, 70.1FA/1b, above.

Copies: O (Vet. A5 e. 1613);

USA: CtY (uncut), ICU, [Liebert (uncut; now CaOHM?)], NN; *Eir*: Dt.

70.6GD/1a Goldsmith's The Deserted Village 1770

[½t] THE | DESERTED VILLAGE. | [Price 2s.]

[Title] THE | DESERTED VILLAGE, | A | POEM. | By Dr. GOLDSMITH | [Oval engr. vignette of traveller addressing old man, 'The sad historian of the pensive plain.' 'James Taylor del. & sculp.' (85 × 130 mm)] | LONDON: | Printed for W. Griffin, at Garrick's Head, in Catharine-ſtreet, Strand. | MDCCLXX.

4°, π² *A*² B–G², ($1 signed), 16 leaves.

Pp. π1 *i* ½t, *ii* blk, *iii* t., *iv* blk, *v* vi–vii Dedication dh: [two double rules] | TO | SIR JOSHUA REYNOLDS., ht: DEDICATION. ('OLIVER GOLDSMITH'), *viii* blk, on B1 *1* 2–23 text dh: [two double rules] | THE | DESERTED VILLAGE., ht: THE DESERTED VILLAGE., *24* blk.

Pagination: no errors; *Press-figures*: C2(7)–3, F2(19)–2.
Catchwords: *om.* i–viii, 5–9, 11–20; 9 Carelefs (Thus).
Explicit: 23 FINIS.
Paper: White, laid; La. post (uncut: 10½ × 8¼ in.); no vis. wmk.
Type: Great primer (6.0 mm), leaded.
References: *Life* ii. 5–7 (Courtney 113); *Rothschild* 1032; *Sterling* 405; *Tinker* 1122; Friedman, *Works of Goldsmith* (1966), iv. 273–81; ESTC: t088127.

Notes: At least six 4° edd. bear the date '1770' with distinct edition statements on the titles. In the following notes, these designations have been accepted without detailed analysis, but with some clarification from Friedman, 281.

The faulty cwd. 'Carelefs' on p. 9 catches with the same word 2 lines from the foot on the same p. showing that some text (presumably a couplet), was introduced during proofing. It is corrected in later impressions.

According to JB SJ's contribution was the last four lines of the poem.[1]

Copies: O (Don. d. 35);
USA: CLU-C, CSmH³, CtY, ICN, [Liebert], MH, NN-B, NPM⁴, NjP², PPL, TxU; *UK*: BAT, L³, LEu², LVu, MRc (no t.), SHu.

[1] A copy, said to be 'marked by Johnson' was, with a copy of OG's *Traveller*, lot 293 at the Auchinleck sale of Mrs Mounsey's effects, Sotheby &c., 23 June 1893, which went to Sotheran for £36. It presumably was once bound with JB's marked copy of the *Traveller* (64.12GT/7, above), but was subsequently separated.

70.6GD/1b Goldsmith's The Deserted Village, facsimile 1970

A facsimile of the first edition was published by the Scolar Press, Menston, Yorks., 1970. A facsimile with the t. of 70.6GD/1a and the press-Figg. of 70.6GD/2 was published by Noel Douglas Replicas, London, 1927.

70.6GD/2 Goldsmith's The Deserted Village 1770

THE | DESERTED VILLAGE, | A | POEM. | By Dr. *GOLDSMITH* | [Oval engr. vignette of traveller addressing old man, 'The sad historian of the pensive plain.' 'James Taylor del. & sculp.' (85 × 130 mm)] | SECOND EDITION. | LONDON: | Printed for W. Griffin, at Garrick's Head, in Catharine-ftreet, Strand. | MDCCLXX.

Contents: as 70.6GD/1a, above, of which this is partly a reimpression from standing type, but some of the text was revised by OG (Friedman (1966), iv. 281 n. 2, asserting a cancel of E1 or E2, though this is difficult to ascertain).
References: ESTC: t146045.
Press-figures: C2(7)–3, D1^{v}(10)–3 (*inverted*), E2^{v}(16)–3, F2(19)–2.

Copies: O (GP 1728(7), 'Mumford's Coffee House June 8th. 1770');
USA: CLU-C, CSmH, ICN, IU, PPL; *UK*: BAT, C, Csj, Ct, L.

70.6GD/3   Goldsmith's The Deserted Village   1770

THE | DESERTED VILLAGE, | A | POEM. | By Dr. *GOLDSMITH* |
[Oval engr. vign. of traveller addressing old man, 'The sad historian of the pen-
sive plain.' 'James Taylor del. & sculp.' (85 × 130 mm)] | THIRD EDITION.
| LONDON: | Printed for W. Grifin, at Garrick's Head, in Catharine-ftreet,
Strand. | MDCCLXX.
   Contents: as 70.6GD/2, above, of which this is partly (*A–G*), a reimpression
from standing type (Friedman (1966), iv. 281 n. 2).
   Pagination: 8 unnumbered; *Press-figures*: E2(15)–3, G1ᵛ(22)–3.
   Catchword: 5 In.
   References: ESTC: t146044.
   Copies: O (13 θ. 9(3));
   USA: CLU-C, CSmH², PPL; *UK*: C, MRp², MRu.

70.6GD/4   Goldsmith's The Deserted Village   1770

THE | DESERTED VILLAGE, | A | POEM. | By Dr. *GOLDSMITH* |
[Oval engr. vignette of traveller addressing old man, 'The sad historian of the
pensive plain.' 'James Taylor del. & sculp.' (85 × 130 mm)] | FOURTH
EDITION. | LONDON: | Printed for W. Griffin, at Garrick's Head, in
Catharine-ftreet, Strand. | MDCCLXX.
   Contents: as 70.6GD/3, above, of which C–D and some of F are reimpressed
from standing type from 70.6GD/2–3, but the text again revised by OG
(Friedman (1966), iv. 281 n. 2, and *SB* xiii (1960), 146–7).
   Press-figures: D2ᵛ(12)–2.
   References: ESTC: t146046.
   Copies: O² (**1**. 13 θ. 42; **2**. Vet A5 d.509(2)).
   USA: CSmH², DFo, ICN, IU, NN-B, PPL; *UK*: Ct.

70.6GD/5   Goldsmith's The Deserted Village   1770

THE | DESERTED VILLAGE, | A | POEM. | By Dr. *GOLDSMITH* |
[Oval engr. vignette of traveller addressing old man, 'The sad historian of the
pensive plain.' 'James Taylor del. & sculp.' (85 × 130 mm)] | FIFTH
EDITION. | LONDON: | Printed for W. Griffin, at Garrick's Head, in
Catharine-ftreet, Strand. | MDCCLXX.
   Contents: as 70.6GD/4, above, of which this is partly (A–B and some of E) a
reimpression from standing type (Friedman (1966), iv. 281 n. 2).

Press-figures: D2(11)–2, E2ᵛ(16)–2, F2(19)–2.
References: ESTC: t146047.
Copies: O² (**1**. 13 θ. 10 'J. Hunter 2s.'; **2**. Firth d.4(10));
USA: CSmH, IU, PPL; *UK*: C, MRp.

70.6GD/6   Goldsmith's The Deserted Village   1770

THE | DESERTED VILLAGE, | A | POEM. | By Dr. *GOLDSMITH* |
[Oval engr. vignette of traveller addressing old man, 'The sad historian of the
pensive plain.' 'James Taylor del. & sculp.' (85 × 130 mm)] | SIXTH
EDITION. | LONDON: | Printed for W. Griffin, at Garrick's Head, in
Catharine-ſtreet, Strand. | MDCCLXX.
Contents: as 70.6GD/5, above, of which this is partly (D and F) a reimpres-
sion from standing type (Friedman (1966), iv. 281 n. 2).
Press-figures: C2(7)–2, D2(11)–2, E2(15)–2, F2(19)–2.
References: ESTC: t146766.
Copies: O² (**1**. 13 θ. 55; **2**. GP 769(12));
USA: CLU-C, CSmH, DFo, DLC, ICN, MH, NN-B, PPL; *UK*: C, LCu,
MRu.

70.6GD/7   Goldsmith's The Deserted Village   1772

THE | DESERTED VILLAGE, | A | POEM. | By Dr. *GOLDSMITH* |
[Oval engr. vignette of traveller addressing old man, 'The sad historian of the
pensive plain.' 'James Taylor del. & sculp.' (85 × 130 mm)] | SEVENTH
EDITION. | LONDON: | Printed for W. Griffin, at Garrick's Head, in
Catharine-ſtreet, Strand. | MDCCLXXII.
Contents: as 70.6GD/6, above; *Press-figures*: none.
References: ESTC: t146048.
Copies: O² (**1**. 2804 d.22(2); **2**. Vet. A5 d.569(3));
USA: ICN; *UK*: BMp, Gu, LVp, SAN.

70.6GD/8   Goldsmith's The Deserted Village   1775

THE | DESERTED VILLAGE, | A | POEM. | By Dr. *GOLDSMITH* |
[Oval engr. vignette of traveller addressing old man, 'The sad historian of the
pensive plain.' 'James Taylor del. & sculp.' (85 × 130 mm)] | EIGHTH
EDITION. | LONDON: | Printed for W. Griffin, at Garrick's Head, in
Catharine-ſtreet, Strand. | MDCCLXXV.
Contents: as 70.6GD/7, above; *Press-figures*: none.
References: ESTC: t146051.
Copies: O² (**1**. 280 l. 127(2); **2**. Johnson d. 975(3)).

70.11PA   Fictitious Newsletters and Reports,   1770
                        The Public Advertiser

(1) Saturday, 13 October.
'We are at Liberty to assure the Public, that the following Narrative was received on Thursday Night by a Person of Distinction from his Friend at Paris.'
Reprinted: *Middlesex Journal*, Sat. 13 Oct.

(2) Thursday, 18 October.
'A Letter from Scanderoon brings the following Account. . .'
Reprinted: *Middlesex Journal*, Sat. 20 Oct.; *Scots Mag.* xxxii (Oct. 1770), 567; *Universal Mag*, xxiv (1770), 216.

(3) Thursday, 25 October.
'Extract of a private letter from Constantinople.'
Reprinted: *Middlesex Journal*, 25 Oct.; *London Chron.*, 25 Oct.

(4) Thursday, 1 November.
'Extract of a letter from Salonichi.'
Reprinted: no reprint discovered; retracted in *Middlesex Journal*, 17 Nov., and *London Chron.*, 17 Nov.

(5) Thursday, 8 November.
'Extract of a letter from Petersburg.'
Reprinted: *Middlesex Journal*, 8 Nov.; *London Chron.*, 8 Nov.

(6) Tuesday, 13 November.
'Extract of a letter from a Gentleman in the Russian Camp, dated Sept. 4.'
Reprinted: no reprint discovered.

(7) Saturday, 17 November.
'Extract of a letter from Archangel, dated Sept. 5.'
Reprinted: *London Chron.*, 22 Nov.

References: Rizzo, *Library*, 6th ser. viii (1986), 249–64.
Notes: Miss Rizzo supplies a convincing conclusion to the story first noticed in *Gents. Mag.* liii (July 1783), 580–2 and (Aug. 1783), 679–81, that SJ composed such pieces to counter the unqualified faith of Hester Salusbury, HLT's mother, in newspaper reports. The story was repeated in HLP's *Anecdotes* (1786), 83–4 (*Johns. Misc.* i. 235), and in Anderson's *Life of Johnson* (1815), 322–23 n. (*Johns. Misc.* ii. 391–2)[1].
Copies: see *BUCOP*.

---

[1] Anderson gave Sir Brooke Boothby as his authority.

70–71LP   Proposals for William Langley   [? 1771]

In a letter of 17 November 1770 to SJ, William Langley, headmaster of Ashbourne Grammar School, wrote:

Sir,

Mr. Paul Taylor has promised to deliver the papers which accompany this letter safe into your hands. I would have sent them sooner if I had received the translation of the two first Cantos of Lord Lyttelton's Progress of Love. I have been hitherto disappointed and now apprehend I shall not be able to obtain it till I go to Warwickshire which will be about two months hence. I am however unwilling to miss the present opportunity of sending a Copy of what papers are in my Hands, which I have transcribed almost verbatim. There are so many alterations needful, as you will easily observe, but I choose to leave them to your Correction, if you shall think them worthy of that trouble. The Translations of Persius were attempted when my late Friend was very [*hiatus in text*]

You know Sir, the motives from which they were proposed to be offered to the public, and if you shall think them worthy of Publication I must beg the Favour of you to return them to Mr. Paul Taylor or Dr. Taylor, when he shall be in London, who will bring them again to me. If they shall meet with your Approbation you will please to mention in the proposal which you kindly promised to draw up "that no money will be required till the Books are delivered ["]. If it will not be too much Trouble to favour me with a line of your opinion of what I now send you, you will very much oblige Sir

Your most obedient Servant

W L.[1]

The letter evidently refers to some intended publication, probably a translation from some classical author suitable to a schoolmaster, for which Langley had enlisted SJ's assistance, including the drafting of Proposals. No likely Proposals, have been found nor any plausible publication: presumably the enterprise collapsed leaving this ghostly fancy.

---

[1] The MS of this letter is in the Public Library, Derby. I am much indebted to Mr R.C. Smith, of Ashbourne, who brought it and associated material to my attention through the good offices of the late Michael Sadler, also of Ashbourne. Other correspondence between Langley and SJ is in O (MS Don d. 76), and some of it was published by Llewellyn Jewett, in *Gents. Mag.* n.s. xxi (Dec. 1878), 692–712, including this letter (p. 694).

71.3FI/1a   Falkland's Islands, first edition, first state   1771

[½t] [row of 23 flowers, 76 mm] | FALKLAND'S ISLANDS. | [row of 23 flowers, 76 mm] | [Price 1*s*. 6*d*.]

[Title] THOUGHTS | ON THE | LATE TRANSACTIONS |

RESPECTING | Falkland's Iflands. | [ornament] | [double rule] | LONDON: | Printed for T. CADELL, in the Strand. | M DCC LXXI.

8°, *A*² B–K⁴ L², ($2 signed), 40 leaves.

Pp. A1 ½t, A1ᵛ blk, A2 t., A2ᵛ blk, on B1 *1* 2–75 text dh: [parallel rule] | FALKLAND ISLANDS. (*Stet* FALKLAND‸), 76 blk.

Pagination: (↑);

Press-figures: B4ᵛ(8)–2, C3ᵛ(14)–5, D4(23)–5, E4ᵛ(32)–7, F4(39)–2, G4ᵛ(48)–3, H2ᵛ(52)–3, I4ᵛ(64)–7, L1ᵛ(74)–7; K unfigured;

Catchwords: 70 [vio-] lence‸ (~,); *Explicit*: 75 FINIS

Paper: White, laid; Medium (uncut: 9¼ × 5¾ in.); no vis. wmk.

Type: English (4.7 mm), leaded; initial word of each para. in caps, except 'The' (p. 36), and 'Junius' (57).

References: *Life* ii. 135 (Courtney 115–6); CH 150; *Works* (Yale), x. 346–86; *Tinker* 1354–5; McGuffie, *SJ in the British Press* (1976); ESTC: t050220.

Notes: This attack on the whigs, Chatham, Grenville and 'Junius', as warmongers, was composed in late February or early March, presumably at Strahan's instigation, with 'Junius's' letter 42 (30 Jan. 1771), as the provocation. Strahan printed 1,000 copies early in March, though his record is undated (L: Add. MS 48803, fo. 35), and it was published 16 March 1771 (*Lond. Chron.*), but the ministry of Lord North halted the sale and required the removal of an allusion to Grenville on p. 68. The cancellation of the leaf K2, produced the second state (71.3FI/1b, below). Several copies escaped castration, and one such appears to have been the provocation of an attack on SJ by 'A Foe to prostituted Abilities' in *London Evening Post*, 19 Feb. 1771 (McGuffie, *British Press*, 81).[1]

Copies: Hyde ('R.B. Adam', inscr. *not* SJ: 'From the Author');

USA: CtY (Tinker), DLC[2], [Liebert ('R.W. Rogers' — 'A.E. Newton'[2])], NIC ('Herbert H. Smith'), NjP ('R.H. Taylor', inscr. by SJ with the new reading at p. 168[3]); *Can*: CaOHM (C. 2999, Rippey: 'Hon Archᵈ. Grant, 16ᵗʰ March 1771'[4]); *UK*: STA (B/3 Johnson).

---

[1] Other contemporary press notices of this fact appeared in the *Whitehall Evening Post*, 21 March 1771, *Public Advertiser*, 1 April 1771 (repeated in *Lloyd's Evening Post*, 4 April), and apparently independently in *London Evening Post*, 2 April (McGuffie, *SJ in the British Press* (1976), 82–3, s.dd.).

[2] Christie, New York, 12 Feb. 1982, 99 ('Rogers — Newton — Liebert — Gerald E. Slater'), $2,200. Untraced.

[3] *Princeton University Library Chronicle*, xxxviii (1977), 168, illustrated.

[4] Perhaps Archibald Grant (d. 1820), heir and successor to Sir Archibald Grant, 3rd Bt. of Monymusk (d. 1796). The 7th Bt. was also Archibald (b. 1823).

71.3FI/1b   Falkland's Islands, first edition, second state   1771

[½t] [row of 23 flowers, 76 mm] | FALKLAND'S ISLANDS. | [row of 23 flowers, 76 mm] | [Price 1*s*. 6*d*.]

[Title] THOUGHTS | ON THE | LATE TRANSACTIONS | RESPECTING | Falkland's Iſlands. | [ornament] | [double rule] | LONDON: | Printed for T. CADELL, in the Strand. | M DCC LXXI.

8°, *A*² B–I⁴ K⁴ (± K2) L², ($2 signed), 40 leaves.

Pp. A1 ½t, A1ᵛ blk, A2 t., A2ᵛ blk, on B1 *1* 2–75 text dh: [parallel rule] | FALKLAND ISLANDS. ([*Stet*]: FALKLAND‸), 76 blk.

Pagination: (↑);

Press-figures: B4ᵛ(8)–2,   C3ᵛ(14)–5,   D4(23)–5,   E4ᵛ(32)–7,   F4(39)–2, G4ᵛ(48)–3, H2ᵛ(52)–3, I4ᵛ(64)–7, L1ᵛ(74)–7; K unfigured.

Catchwords: 70 [vio-] lence‸ (~,); *Explicit*: 75 FINIS.

Paper: White, laid; Medium (uncut: 9¼ × 5¾ in.); no vis. wmk.

Type: English (4.7 mm), leaded; initial word of each para. in caps, except 'The' (p. 36), and 'Junius' (57).

References: *Life* ii. 135 (Courtney 115–6); CH 150; *Works* (Yale), x. 346–86; *Tinker* 1354–5; ESTC: t050220.

Notes: The cancellation of K2 was effected on or about 16 March 1771, to change the following reference to Grenville on p. 68:

> Let him not however, be depreciated in his grave; he had powers not univer-
> sally possessed; if he could have got the money, he could have counted it.

to read:

> Let him not, however, be depreciated in his grave; he had powers not univer-
> sally possessed; and if he sometimes erred, he was likewise sometimes right.

The studied banality of the change argues for SJ's responsibility, though in his letter to Langton of 20 March 1771 (*Letters* 246, Hyde, i. 356), he affected more nonchalance:

> not many had been dispersed before Lord North ordered the sale to stop. His reasons I do not distinctly know, you may try to find them in the perusal. Before his order a sufficient number were dispersed to do all the mischief, though perhaps not to make all the sport that might be expected from it.

Strahan charged 17s. 6d. for the cancellation 'with Paper', which, in view of his charge of £1 for composing and printing a whole sheet, and 15s. for a Ream of paper, seems rather high for producing no more than 1,000 copies of a single leaf requiring but 125 sheets or a quarter of a ream.

The cancel is the only distinguishing mark between the two issues. It was noticed in the *Whitehall Evening Post* on 21 March 1771, and by other papers soon afterwards (McGuffie, *British Press*, 82–3).

Copies: O (GP. 1185 (12));

USA: CSmH, CtY², G. Goldberg, Esq; Hyde⁴ (x3 uncut), [Liebert (uncut)], IU, NN, NPM, NRU, PHi² (1. Af. 360.2, 'Benjamin Franklin'), PPAmP, TxU, WiM; *Can*: CaOHM (B. 14047, 'Robert Hesketh'); *UK*: [B.S. Barlow ('John Cator')], C, Ct ('Francis Wrangham'), L (C. 38.f.44 (2)), MRu², Oa ('F. H. Egerton').

71.3FI/2   Falkland's Islands, Dublin   1771

[½t] [row of 19 flowers, 80 mm] | THOUGHTS | ON THE | LATE TRANSACTIONS | RESPECTING | Falkland's Iſlands. | [row of 19 flowers, 80 mm]

[Title] THOUGHTS | ON THE | LATE TRANSACTIONS | RESPECTING | Falkland's Iſlands. | [ornament] | [double rule] | DUBLIN: | Printed for J. WILLIAMS, at N° 5, in Skinner- | Row. MDCCLXXI.

8°, π1 A–B⁸ C⁴ D1, ($4 (–A1, C3,4) signed), 22 leaves.

Pp. π1 ½t, π1ᵛ blk, on A1 *1* t., *2* blk, *3* 4–42 text dh: [double rule] | FALKLAND's ISLANDS.

Pagination: [↑]; *Press-figures*: none; *Catchwords*: no errors.

Explicit: 42 FINIS.

Paper: White, laid; Lombard (uncut: 8¾ × 5½ in.); wmk.: DANGOUMOIS | B BRUN MOYEN

Type: Pica (3.8 mm), set close; initial word of each para. in caps.

References: Courtney 116; ESTC: t071571.

Notes: Liebert copy establishes the conjugacy of π1 ≡ D1 as a wrap-round.

Copies: O (Vet. A5 e. 3201(1));

USA: DLC, Hyde, [Liebert (uncut)], NIC; *UK*: MRp (P. 233/1).

71.3FI/3   Falkland's Islands, first edition,   1771
                             second impression

[½t] [row of 23 flowers, 76 mm] | FALKLAND'S ISLANDS. | [row of 23 flowers, 76 mm] | [Price 1*s*. 6*d*.]

[Title] THOUGHTS | ON THE | LATE TRANSACTIONS | RESPECTING | Falkland's Iſlands. | [rule] | THE SECOND EDITION. | [rule] | [ornament] | [double rule] | LONDON: | Printed for T. CADELL, in the Strand. | M DCC LXXI.

8°, *A*² B–K⁴ L², ($2 signed), 40 leaves.

Pp. A1 ½t, A1ᵛ blk, A2 t., A2ᵛ blk, on B1 *1* 2–75 text dh: [parallel rule] | FALKLAND ISLANDS. ([*Stet*:] FALKLAND∧), *76* blk.

Pagination: (↑).

Press-figures: B4ᵛ(8)–7, C3ᵛ(14)–7, D4(23)–5, E4ᵛ(32)–2, F4(39)–2, G4ᵛ(48)–1, H2ᵛ(52)–3, I4ᵛ(64)–5, K4ᵛ(72)–2, L1ᵛ(74)–2.

Catchwords: 70 [vio-] lence∧ (∼,); *Explicit*: 75 FINIS.

Paper: White, laid; Medium (uncut: 9¼ × 5¾ in.); no vis. wmk.

Type: English (4.7 mm), leaded; initial word of each para. in caps, except 'The' (p. 36), and 'Junius' (57).

References: Courtney 115; CH 150; *Tinker* 1356; ESTC: n014397.

Notes: The major part of the type of this edn. is reimpressed from the second issue of the first edn. (71.3FI/1b, above), in which the setting of the *cancellans* of K2 is incorporated. Only at p. 36 is the initial 'THE' correctly in caps.

Strahan printed 1,000 copies of this impression, charging almost twice as much as for the first (L: Add. MS 48803, fo. 35). Some reimpression or over-rrunning (e.g. identical press-figures in sigg. DFH), and featherbedding may be suspected. This edn. was announced in *Daily Advertiser*, 11 Apr. 1771.

Copies: O³ (1. GP. 446; 2. GP. 1085(13); 3. 8° E.88 Art);

USA: CSmH² (1. 123973 'From the Author'; 2. 303302 'R.W. Chapman'), CtY³ (1. 'Benjamin Franklin'), Hyde² (1. uncut ? 'John Loveday'; 2. 'R.B. Adam'), [Liebert], NIC, NN², PPL; *Can*: CaOHM (C. 2147); *Japan*: [Kyoto]; *UK*: BMp, E; *Eir*: Dt.

71.3FI/4   Falkland's Islands, New York   1771

THOUGHTS | ON THE | LATE TRANSACTIONS | RESPECTING | Falkland's Iſlands. | [double rule] | [device of flowers] | [double rule] | LONDON: Printed, | *NEW-YORK*: Re-printed, by H. GAINE, | at his Book-Store and Printing-Office, at the | *Bible* and *Crown*, in *Hanover-Square*. | M,DCC,LXXI.

8°, A–F⁴, ($2 signed), 24 leaves.

Pp. A1 *1* t., *2* blk, *3* 4–48 text.

Paper: ? large post (8¼ × 5¼ in.)

Type: not recorded.

References: Evans 12088; *The Journals of Hugh Gaine*, ed. P. L. Ford (1902); ESTC: w028089.

Notes: On p. 44 the text carries the amended reading of the passage on p. 68 of the first edn. Not examined.

Copies: DLC (F3031. J7. Office, 'By Dr Samuel Johnson Author of the English Dictionary.'); *USA*: [DB], MH, MWA.

71.3FI/5   Falkland's Islands, Thames Bank   1948

DR. JOHNSON | [red] **Thoughts** | on the | [red] **Late Transactions** | respecting | [red] **Falkland's Islands** | [1771] | REPRINTED IN 1948 | by | THE THAMES BANK PUBLISHING COMPANY LIMITED | 1773 LONDON ROAD: LEIGH-ON-SEA: ESSEX | 42 Pages : Annotated | [within a small box of single **red** rules:] TWO | SHILLINGS | NET

$²⁴ (unsigned), 24 leaves.

Pp. *1* ½t, *2* blk, *3* t., *4* blk, 5–6 Preface (signed 'F. N. B.'), 7–41 text, *42* blk, 43–4 Notes, *45*–6 Advts., *47* blk, *48* Note on Falkland's Islands.

Pagination: no errors; *Explicit*: none.

Paper: White, wove, war economy standard; cut: 8½ × 5⅜ in.

Type: Long primer (3.0 mm), leaded: 1.8 mm; notes: minion (2.5 mm).
References: Clifford & Greene 20:74.
Notes: Wire stapled pamphlet, published as a post-war (1939–45) response to
Argentine restlessness over the Falklands.
Copies: L (08157. eee. 55); *USA*: Hyde, MH; *UK*: JDF, LICj.

71.3FI/TF/1   Falkland's Islands, French translation   1771

A French translation is reported by Sabin 36311. Not seen.
*Penseés sur les transactions touchant les isles de Falkland. Traduit de l' anglais
d' après la seconde édition.* Amsterdam. 1771. 8°

71.3FI/TS/1   Falkland's Islands, Spanish translation   1936

A Spanish version is reported by José Torre Revello, *Bibliografía de las Islas
Malvinas*, Buenos Aires, 1953, item 122:
Versión castellana en L N [= *La Nación*, Buenos Aires] 16–21 de marzo de
1936, ano LXVIII, nn. 23.211 – 23.216 con el segiuente título:
SAMUEL JOHNSON, *Una Vieja obra siempre actual*, «Pensiamoentos sobre
las receintes negociaciones acerca de las islas Falkland».

72.2PT   Payne's Trigonometry   1772

ELEMENTS | OF | TRIGONOMETRY, | Plain and Spherical; | Applied
to the moſt uſeful Problems in | Heights and Distances, Astronomy, | and
Navigation: | For the USE OF LEARNERS. | [rule] | By WILLIAM
PAYNE. | [rule] | LONDON: | Printed by H. Hart, in Popping's Court,
Fleet-Street: | And ſold by T. Payne, at the Mews Gate; | and M. Hingeston,
at Temple Bar. | [short rule] | MDCCLXXII.
8°, *A*⁴ B⁸ (B6 + χ1) C–O⁸ P⁴ ²A–I⁸ ²K⁴ ²L², ($4 (–E4, ²A1, ²E1; O4 as N4)
signed), 191 leaves.
Pp. A1 t., A1ᵛ blk, A2–2ᵛ Dedication dh: [double rule] | TO THE |
RIGHT HONOURABLE | *William Henry Naſſau de Zuleiſtein,* | Earl of
Rochford, Viſcount *Tun-* | *bridge,* and one of His Majeſty's | Principal
Secretaries of State. | *My Lord,* [&c.], on A3 pp. i–ii Preface dh: [double rule] |
PREFACE., ht: PREFACE., on A4 ²i–ii Contents dh: [double rule] |
CONTENTS. | BOOK I. | Plain Trigonometry., ht: CONTENTS., on B1
pp. 1–12 13*–14* (= χ1) 13–215 text dh: [two double rules] | PLAIN |
TRIGONOMETRY. | [rule], *216* blk, on ²A1 ²*1* ½t: [rule] | A | TABLE |
OF | LOGARITHMS, | From One to Ten Thousand. | [rule], ²2 blk, 3–65

Logarithms, *66* blk, on ²E1 ½t: A | TABLE | OF | ARTIFICIAL SINES. | AND | TANGENTS | TO EVERY | DEGREE and MINUTE | OF THE | QUADRANT | *The Radius being* 10, 000 000. | [double rule] | LONDON; | Printed in the Year M.DCC.LXXII., 67–155 text, 156 Problems.

Pagination: χ1 (following B6) is 13*–14*. [↑] but ii and ²ii as ↗; (↑) i, ²i;
Press-figures: none;
Catchwords: 3 17 *A* (17. If), 12 53. *In* (*13 Theorem 3. | 56 *In*), *14 Otherwife (53 Corrollary. | *In*), 17 58 Theorem (Theorem 4. | 58.), 19 [e-] qual (equal), 21 there (therefore), 112 DAC (~,), 128 Secondly (*Secondly*), 131 *om.* (The), 132 *om.* (Theorem), &c. Cwds are frequently erroneous.
Explicit: 156 FINIS.
Paper: White, laid; Demy (uncut: 8½ × 5 in.); no vis. wmk.
Type: Dedication & Preface: (*italic*) great primer (5.8 mm), leaded (1.0 mm), text: pica (4.0 mm), leaded (1.6 mm).
Plates: Line blocks inserted at I. facing p. 148; II. facing p. 182; III. facing p. 204.
References: Hazen 152–4; ESTC: t098345.
Notes: The mathematical material appears to have required frequent adjustment in proof so that catchwords are often mislinked. The book was published at 5s. in February 1772 (*Gents. Mag.* xlii (Feb. 1772), 96/60).

Hazen suggested SJ's responsibility for the 'Dedication' but without enthusiasm (148), noting that SJ was associated with Payne's other publications: *Game of Draughts* (56.1PD/1, above), and *Geometry* (67.4PG/1, above), and that there were two copies of this book in SJ's library (Christie, 16 Feb. 1785, 24 and 362). The attribution does not commend itself beyond mere possibility: the piece lacks SJ's usual weight — a quality which he could communicate to light matters (e.g. Payne's *Draughts*, above); Chapman doubted it in *RES* xiv (1938), 359.

Copies: O (Rigaud e. 336);
USA: [Liebert = CtY], MH (Educ.), [NCU]; *UK*: ABu, Eu, L (52 e.5), SAN (no t.); *Eir*: [Dt].

72.2MBG   Latin Motto for Sir Joseph Banks's Goat   1772

Latin motto for Sir Joseph Banks's Goat: 'Versus Collari Capr Domini Banks inscribendi.'
References: Courtney 116; *Poems²* 183–4; *Letters* 272 (Hyde, i. 386).
Notes: Incorporated with SJ's letter to Banks, 27 Feb. 1772, and first published in *European Mag.* xi (July, 1789), 5, and reprinted by Boswell, *Life* (1791), i. 351. An undated facsimile of the holograph letter and the 'distich' was published in Norwich by J.M. Johnson, of which a copy is in the Wellcome Historical Medical Library, but the original remains untraced. Various transcriptions are noticed in *Poems²*, some dated 'March'.

72.4BPH   Boswell's Petition for John Hastie   1772

Patrick Campbell of Knap, Efquire, and others, Appellants.

Mr. John Haftie, *Rector or Head-Mafter of the*⎫ *Refpondent.*
Grammar School *at* Campbelltown.   ⎭

The Refpondent's CASE.

2°, *A²–E²*, (unsigned), 10 leaves.

Pp. A1 *1* 2–6 *7* text Appellants' case, *8–9* blk, *10* folding t., on C2 *1* 2–8 text Respondent's case, *9* blk, *10* docket: bearing t. (as above, and) . . . CASE. To be heard at the Bar of the Houfe of Lords, on *Tuefday*, the 14*th* of *April*, 1772.

Pagination: [↑] Appellants 2–6, (↑) Respondents 2–8.

Press-figures: none; *Catchwords*: none; *Explicit*: none.

Paper: White, laid; foolscap (13½ × 8½ in.); wmk.: crowned fleur-de-lys; LVG + IV.

Type: Appellants: small pica (3.5 mm); respondents: pica (4.1 mm).

References: *Life* ii. 144–5, 183–5, 186; *Boswell Papers* ix. 20 ff.; *Boswell for the Defence* (1960), *passim*, esp. 112, s.d. 11 Apr. 1772; W.H. Bond and D.E. Whitten, in *Eighteenth-Century Studies* (1970), 231–55, esp. no. 720414; ESTC: t112077.

Notes: SJ contributed to the arguments in defence of the pedagogical severity of the Respondent, Hastie. Printed by William Strahan the younger: 'Sat. 11 April, 1772 . . . I went with Mr Spottiswoode to young Strahan's printing-house upon Snow Hill, where Hastie's cause was printing. I made several additions, having carried up Mr. Johnson's *Corpus Juris* with me' (*JB: Defence*, 112). The work is not noticed in Strahan's 'Law Press' Accounts (L: Add. MS. 48807). The text was republished in *Life* (1791), i. 375–77.

Copies: CtY (IIm. B654. Zz772c, 'James Boswell').

72.7BPW/1a   Boswell's Petition for James Wilson   1772

[Drop-head] *July* 1. 1772. | UNTO THE RIGHT HONOURABLE, | The Lords of Council and Seffion, | THE | PETITION | OF | JAMES WILSON late in Haghoufe, | Now Heritor in Kilmaurs, | *Humbly fheweth*,

4°, A–E² F1, ($1 signed), 11 leaves.

Pp. A1 *1* 2–22 text.

Pagination: (↑); *Press-figures*: none;

Catchwords: 1 [Ar-] ‸mour, ("~,), 5 ‸confirmed, ("~,);

Explicit: none.

Paper: White, laid; Demy (uncut: 11¼ × 8¾ in.); wmk.: fleur-de-lys.

Type: Text: pica (4.2 mm), leaded; shoulder notes: long primer (3.2 mm).

References: *Life* ii. 196–200, 496; *Boswell Papers* ix. 203; W.H. Bond and D.E. Whitten, in *Eighteenth-Century Studies* (1970), 231–55, esp. p. 243, no.

720701; Ballantyne, 'Session Papers' M:30 (720701); ESTC: n014544, cf. n014545.

Notes: SJ's contribution was dictated to JB, apparently, though not necessarily, *extempore*, early in May 1772 before JB left London to return to Edinburgh. It was republished in *Life* (1791), i. 382–87. Other papers including Wilson's Petition of 14 January 1772, with an associated Proof, and a Petition of 16 June 1772, relative to the case are in the Kennet collection in Es (M3: 30). Boswell's cause was unsuccessful.

An account of the composition and production of this piece in the case of Wilson v. Smith and Armour, raising the question of 'Vicious Intromission' (*Life*), is given by W.H. Bond in the Introduction to his facsimile edn. of the E copy, below.

Copies: E (Arniston 104 (4)); *USA*: MH (*EC75. B6578C.1772).

72.7BPW/1b   Boswell's Petition for James Wilson,   1971
facsimile

Boswell, Johnson, and the Petition of James Wilson, Cambridge, introduction by W.H. Bond (Printed for the Houghton Library) privately printed for 'The Johnsonians', New York, 1971.

72.12HEIC   Present State of East India   [1772]
Company's Affairs

THE | PRESENT STATE | OF THE | Englifh Eaft-India Company's Affairs, | COMPREHENDING | THE ACCOUNTS | Delivered in by the | COURT OF DIRECTORS TO THE TREASURY, | Which were laid before the | COMMITTEE OF SECRECY, | APPOINTED BY THE | HOUSE OF COMMONS, | Affembled at Weftminfter, in the Sixth Seffion of the | Thirteenth Parliament of | GREAT BRITAIN, | TO ENQUIRE INTO | EAST-INDIA AFFAIRS; | Together with the PLANS propofed by the | DIFFERENT DIRECTORS | FOR THE | Re-eftablifhment of the Company's Affairs, and feveral | other Accounts equally curious and interefting; | DRAWN UP FOR THE | USE OF THE DIRECTORS, *&c.* | [rule] | Under the Infpection of | MR. HOOLE, | AUDITOR OF INDIAN ACCOUNTS. | [rule] | To thefe ACCOUNTS is prefixt, an ADDRESS to the PUBLIC, | difplaying the DESIGNS OF GOVERNMENT on the EAST | INDIA COMPANY'S TERRITORIES in the EAST INDIES. | [total rule] | LONDON: | PRINTED FOR T. EVANS, AT No. 54, PATERNOSTER-Row. | PRICE FIVE SHILLINGS.

8°, *A*⁴ B–C⁸ D⁴ E², ($1 signed), 26 leaves.

Pp. A1 t., A2 *i* ii–vi To the PUBLIC. + 2 inserted fold. sheets + on B1 *1* 2–45 text & accounts, *46* blk.

Paper: White, laid; crown (7½ × 5 in.); wmk.: fleur-de-lys + Strasburg bend.
Type: Address: pica (4.1 mm) *italic*, text: pica roman.
References: Hazen 60 n. 'I think that Johnson may have helped in the composition of the Preface'. ESTC: t203250.
Notes: The Address 'To the PUBLIC' pp. *ii* iii–vi (dated 'London, 21*ft* Dec. 1772.') is surely not by SJ, and Hazen gave no reasons for his suggestion, nor did he promote it to his text. It owes nothing to SJ. Robert Orme (1728–1801*) is a more likely collaborator.
Copies: L (100. m.23/ 1–2); *USA*: CSmH, MH, [NjR]; *UK*: MRu; *Eir*: Dt.

73.4GEP   Verses from Dr. Johnson to Dr. Goldsmith,   1773
General Evening Post

April 1.   'Verses from Dr. Johnson to Dr. Goldsmith'
On *She Stoops to Conquer*, addressed to Goldsmith and signed 'S. J.'
Note: These verses are not by SJ, and the date of publication sufficiently explains their appearance. JB apparently had his clerk, John Lawrie, take a copy from the *London Chron*.
Copies: (CtY: MS Boswell, C 3036).

73.5BLP   Legal argument for Boswell   1773

May 1.   Argument in favour of 'Lay Patronage' in the Church of Scotland.
References: *Life* ii. 149, 242–6.
The argument was dictated to JB who recorded it, despite his reservations. SJ's views were too late for use by JB in his essay in *London Mag.*, 17 April 1773, 181 ff. (*Boswell for the Defence* (1960), 131–2, and Pottle 223), nor were they published until the *Life* (1791), i. 410–13.

73.?6SOE   Lines for William Scott for   ?1773/1774
Oxford Encænia

An untraced letter from William Scott to Robert Chambers, is reported as 'asking for a few lines from Johnson for the Oxford Encænia'.[1] Chambers accompanied SJ to Newcastle in August 1773, and Scott was his companion from Newcastle to Edinburgh (*Journey* (1985), 284–7). Chambers left England for Bengal in 1774 where he remained until 1799, so that this request cannot have been made to him any later than 1773. Scott was a tutor at University College, Oxford, from 1765 to 1775, latterly Senior Tutor of the college, and he became Camden Professor of Ancient History in December 1773 (*Jackson's Oxford Journal*, 4 Dec. 1773). His biographer records that he had no skill in public speaking.[2] Only necessity would lead him to speak at the Encænia, which was held in June, and a likely occasion may have some association with his accession to the chair, perhaps as a public demonstration of his capacity to become a public lecturer, so that the Encænia of the summer of 1773 is possible.[3] Nevertheless such an association cannot be argued as inescapable, and Scott may alternatively have been obliged to speak at the Encænia as a representative of his College in the presentation of graduands.[4]

So far no published record of an Encænia speech by Scott at any date has been found.

[1] The letter was purchased by Messrs. Maggs at Sothebys, 11 Apr. 1938, 414 (with 391) for £400, and appeared thereafter in their *Catalogues* 671 (1939), 466, and 737 (1944), 947, at £600. Its present whereabouts are unknown, and none of the cataloguers gave any detailed description or a complete text.

[2] W.E. Surtees, *The Lives of Lords Stowell and Eldon* (1846), 65. Scott nevertheless delivered at least one public speech at Oxford, *c.*1780, which was published as *Speech on the proposed Fees for Graduation*, Oxford, [n.d.], fol. A copy is O (Bliss B. 417).

[3] It has been suggested, though with little evidence beyond association, that Scott's History lectures showed 'a good deal of the Doctor's [SJ] manner' but this assertion is not borne out by the example quoted in the *Letters of R. Radcliffe and J. James*, ed. M. Evans (1888), 92, cited in *Life* iv. 490.

[4] I am deeply indebted to Mr J.S.G. Simmons, sometime librarian of All Souls College, for his observations on this question. He points out that gentlemen-commoners graduated at Encænia (L.H.D. Buxton and S. Gibson, *Oxford University Ceremonies* (1935), 87–88), and that two such were presented from University College at the Encænia, 1774 (*Jackson's Oxford Journal*, 9 July 1774). He suggests that the tone of the brief extract from the letter might be taken to mean that Scott was not then well-acquainted with SJ, since he used Chambers as an intermediary, so that a date earlier than 1773 is possible. He further reminds me that an election to a chair would not of itself require an address to the Encænia, though Scott's election came after the 1773 Encænia.

73.6MD   Macbean's Dictionary   1773

A | DICTIONARY | OF | ANCIENT GEOGRAPHY, | EXPLAINING | The Local Appellations in Sacred, Grecian, | and Roman History; | EXHIBITING | The Extent of Kingdoms, and Situations of Cities, &c. | And illuftrating | The Allufions and Epithets in the Greek and Roman Poets. | The Whole eftablifhed by proper Authorities, and defigned for | the Use of Schools. | By ALEXANDER MACBEAN, M. A. | [rule] | Πολλῶν δ' ἀνθρώπων ἴδεν ἄϛεα, καὶ νόον ἔγνω. | Homer. | [double rule] | LONDON, | Printed for G. Robinson, in Pater Nofter-Row; and T. Cadell, | in the Strand. 1773.

8°, *A*² B–4K⁴ 4L², ($2 (–4L2) signed), 316 leaves.

Pp. A1 *i* t., *ii* blk, *iii*–iv Preface dh: PREFACE., ht: PREFACE., on B1 text 'Aarassus' to 'Zymna' (314 leaves, unpaged) dh: [two double rules] | A | CLASSICAL GEOGRAPHICAL | DICTIONARY.

Pagination: none.

Press-figures: B2ᵛ–6, F4ᵛ–2, G2ᵛ–2, H1ᵛ–1, I2ᵛ–1, Y1ᵛ–1, Z3ᵛ–1, 2A1ᵛ–7,

2B2^v–7, 2C4^v–2, 2D3^v–7, 2F3–2, 2G2^v–2, 2H1^v–1, 2K1^v–1, 2L2^v–7, 2M1^v–2, 2N2^v–6, 2O3–2, 2Q4^v–4, 2R2^v–4, 2S1^v–4, 2U3–7, 2Y4–7, 2X1^v–6, 2Z3–7, 3A2^v–6, 3B2^v–2, 3C4^v–6, 3D4^v–6, 3E1^v–4, 3F4–8, 3G4–1, 3H1^v–8, 3I4^v–7, 3K1^v–8, 3L4^v–1, 3M2–1, 3N3–6, 3O3^v–8, 3P1^v–6, 3Q3–6, 3R3–6, 3S2^v–8, 3T4–2, 3U2^v–1, 3X3–6, 3Y3^v–8, 3Z4–2, 4A3^v–1, 4B2^v–1, 4C3–2, 4D3–2, 4E4–8, 4F1^v–1, 4G2^v–1, 4H1^v–8, 4I4–1, 4K4–1, 4L1–6.

Catchwords: om. A1–2; C2^v fide (of), O4^v [He-] rodotus; (~,), Q1 Banata, (~.), S2 [Vin-] delicia, (~;), S3 Provincia, (~$_\wedge$), U3 uncertain (whether), Z3 Chaleos, (~.), 2C3 Cothon$_\wedge$ (~,), 2D2 CYANÆAE, (~$_\wedge$), 2D4 Mallea, (Malea,), 2L1^v [Ge-] rion$_\wedge$ (~;), 2P1 Il$_\wedge$ (Illice,), 2T4 om. (M.), 3C2^v fwim-(fwiming [!]), 3H1^v Attali. (~,), 3I2 om. (fit), 3I4^v [He-] catæus, (~;), 3M3^v of (the), 3O4 birth$_\wedge$day (birth-day), 3Z3 om. (T.), 4I2^v [O-] larion, (arion,), 4L3^v Cluverius; (Cluverins;). Unfigured: C–E, K–X, 2E, 2I, 2P, 2T.

Explicit: 4L2^v THE END.

Paper: White, laid; Demy (uncut: 8¾ × 5½ in.); wmk.: fleur-de-lys + IV.

Type: Preface: pica (3.9 mm), leaded, text: brevier (2.7 mm), 2 cols./p. vert. rules.

References: *Life* i. 187, 536, ii. 204 (Courtney 116); CH 150; Hazen 132–6; *Cordell* M-1; ESTC: t031838.

Notes: The book was published 19 June 1773 at 7s. 6d. (*St. James's Chron.*). The 'Preface' is by SJ. His copy was lot 32 at his sale, Christie, 16 Feb. 1785, and went to Bruce for 10s., but is still untraced.[1]

Copies: O (Douce M. 367);

USA: CtY ('Ormathwaite' — 'R.W. Rogers'), DLC, G. Goldberg, Esq; Hyde (Adam), IU, [LNM], MB, MH, NN, NRU, ViU; *Can*: CaOHM, CaOLUI; *UK*: Ct, E, [Es], Eu, L^2 (1. 10001. ee.51; 2. 304. h.5), LEu (Ripon Cathedral), LICj ('John Graham . . . 1805' attributing Preface to SJ), MRu, SAN, STA.

---

[1] This was perhaps William Bruse, bookseller in Clement's Inn Passage, 1785 (*Maxted*, s.n.).

73.8EM   Epitaph on Colin Maclaurin   1773

17 August   Stone on exterior SW wall of Greyfriar's Kirk, Candlemaker's Row, Edinburgh.[1]

The church was badly damaged by fire in 1845 and largely rebuilt, but the stone appears to be original.[2]

References: *Life* v. 49–50, 472.

JB is the only authority for the rejected readings (listed in *Tour*, 1st edn. 1785, 45), and his complete published version in *Tour*, 2nd edn. (1785), 463 n., and 3rd edn. (1786), 38, is accurate except for the reduction of caps to lower case. If the present wall-slab is a replacement, it must of course, derive from JB's printed version.

---

[1] It is next to those of Allan Ramsay (1686–1758*) and Hugh Blair (1718–1800*).

² For the fire see F.H. Groome, *Ordnance Gazetteer of Scotland*, new edn. (1894), ii. 515. Boswell in the *Tour* (3rd edn., 1786), refers to the epitaph as 'engraved on a marble tombstone, in the Grey-Friar's church-yard, in Edinburgh' (p. 38 n.), which does not accord with a stone mounted on a wall. Maclaurin's grave itself is an altar-tomb with but a brief inscription (*Life* v. 472).

73.8LP/1a   Opinion on Literary Property   1773

17 August   SJ offered comments on JB's views which were published by JB in *Scots Mag.* xxxv (Jan.–Feb. 1773), 9, 65,¹ and as a separate pamphlet:

THE | DECISION | OF THE | COURT of SESSION, | UPON THE QUESTION OF | LITERARY PROPERTY; | IN THE CAUSE | JOHN HINTON of LONDON, Bookſeller, Purſuer; | AGAINST | ALEXANDER DONALDSON and JOHN WOOD, | Bookſellers in EDINBURGH, and JAMES MEUROSE, | Bookſeller in KILMARNOCK, Defenders. | PUBLISHED BY | JAMES BOSWELL, Eſq; ADVOCATE, | One of the COUNSEL in the Cauſe. | [parallel rule] | EDINBURGH: | Printed by JAMES DONALDSON, for ALEXANDER DONALDSON, and ſold at | his Shops, N° 48. ST. PAUL's CHURCH-YARD, LONDON, and EDINBURGH; | and by all Bookſellers in SCOTLAND. | M.DCC.LXXIV.

4°, π1 a² A–I², ($1 signed), 21 leaves.

Pp. π1 t., π1ᵛ blk, a1 *i* ii–iv statement of case, on B1 1–37 text, *38* blk.

Pagination: [↑], no errors; *Press-figures*: none.

Catchwords: 24 larceny∧ (~;); *Explicit*: none.

Paper: White, laid; wmk.: fleur-de-lys.

Type: Pica (4.0 mm), leaded (1.6 mm).

References: *Life* v. 50–1, 474–5; ESTC: t088998.

Notes: The extent of SJ's contribution to this publication is not determined, but he and JB certainly exchanged views on the topic. There does not appear to be any direct Johnsonian intervention in this text however.

Copies: E² (1. F.7.c.10; 2. Law).

¹ Pottle 219. An extract is quoted in *Gents. Mag.* lv (May 1785), 344, as by Boswell, without any mention of SJ.

73.8LP/1b   Opinion on Literary Property, facsimile   1925

A facsimile of this pamphlet, together with extracts from the *Life* and a facsimile of SJ's *Letter* 349, to William Strahan, 7 March 1774 (Hyde, ii. 129–31), was published in Buffalo, N.Y., by R.B. Adam, in 1925.

73.10MP   Meditation on a Pudding   1773

24 October

References: *Life* v. 352.

Notes: Recorded by JB on 24 October 1773, and first published in *Tour* (1785), 440–41 as 'I hastily wrote down, in his presence, the following note; which, though imperfect, may serve to give my readers some idea of it.'[1] JB's version was repeated in his 2nd (1785: 440–41) and 3rd edd. of *Tour* (1786: 365–66), and was later printed by Hawkins, *Life87*, 388–89, in a version which diverges from that of JB in so many particulars that it may be from a distinct, though still untraced, source.[2]

[1] JB's MS is mentioned in *JB's Journal of a Tour*, ed. F.A. Pottle and C.H. Bennett (1936 and 1961), 349–50.

[2] A transcript in an unidentified hand, evidently derived from JB's printed text (with some slight deviations), is CtY (MS: Osborn). It does not appear to be the source for Hawkins.

73.10ES   Epitaph on Tobias Smollett   1773

28 October   Revision of draft of a proposed epitaph composed by Commissary James Smollett, which is followed by the text later incised on the base of the obelisk standing at the front of the local school at Renton, Dumbartons.[1]

References: *Life* v. 367, 564; *MS Handlist* 124; *MS Index* JoS 339; *Journey* (1985), 243, 313.

Notes: The draft was prepared by Commissary James Smollett (d. 1775), of Cameron, a cousin of the novelist, and modified by SJ. His adjustments were recorded by JB and first published in *Tour* (1785), 460–61. The document itself is owned by Major Patrick Telfer-Smollett. It is translated in *A Collection of Epitaphs*, 1806 (40GM/10EE/2, above), at i. 66.

[1] It seems probable that the monument has been repaired and the inscription recut since its initial erection, so that the text now visible is perhaps influenced by published versions: JB added the complete text to the 2nd. edn. of his *Tour* (1785), 462-3 n. (*Journey* (1985), 312–13).

73.11EP   Epitaph on Thomas Parnell   1773

22 November   Dictated to JB at Blackshiels.

References: *Life* iv. 54, v. 404, and first published in *Life* (1791), ii. 357.

73.12DM/1   Davies's Miscellaneous and   1773
                      Fugitive Pieces

MISCELLANEOUS | AND | FUGITIVE PIECES. | VOLUME THE
FIRST [– SECOND]. | [rule] | [vol. 1: nearly circular arrangement of flowers,
(28 × 30 mm); vol. 2: inverted trapezium of flowers, (23 × 25 × 13 mm) with
dependent half-curve garland] | [double rule] | LONDON: | Printed for T.
DAVIES, in *Ruſſel-Street, Covent-* | *Garden*, Bookſeller to the Royal Academy.
2 vols., 8°

I. *A*² B–2A⁸ 2B⁴, ($4 (–2B3,4) signed; 'VOL. I.' on $1 (–B1)), 190 leaves.
Pp. A1 t., A1ᵛ blk, A2 Contents dh: CONTENTS | OF THE | FIRST
VOLUME. (last item misnumbered '275' [= 375]), A2ᵛ Advt. (for vol. 3: 'is in
the Press, and will be published very speedily'), on B1 *1* 2–375 text dh: [two
double rules] | A REVIEW OF | A FREE ENQUIRY | INTO THE |
NATURE and ORIGIN of EVIL., *376* blk.
Pagination: 1, 376 unnumbered; [↑] 35, 57, 62, 80, 95, 141, 150, 159, 235,
254, 287, 297, 305, 357;
Press-figures: D6ᵛ(44)–1, G8ᵛ(96)–4, H7ᵛ(110)–2, I2ᵛ(116)–2, K8ᵛ(144)–1,
L2ᵛ(148)–4, M7ᵛ(174)–1, N4ᵛ(184)–4, P3ᵛ(214)–4, Q3ᵛ(230)–2, R1ᵛ(242)–2,
S2ᵛ(260)–1, S5ᵛ(266)–4, T1ᵛ(274)–2, X8ᵛ(319)–4, Y5(329)–2, Z5ᵛ(346)–2,
Z6ᵛ(348)–1, 2A1ᵛ(354)–1, 2A2ᵛ(356)–2, 2B3(373)–1; unfigured B, C, E, F,
O, U.
Catchwords: 56 FOUR (A REVIEW of FOUR LETTERS).
Explicit: 375 END OF THE FIRST VOLUME.

II. *A*² B–Z⁸ 2A⁴, ($4 (–2A3,4) signed; 'VOL. II.' on $1), 182 leaves.
Pp. A1 t., A1ᵛ blk, A2–2ᵛ Contents dh: CONTENTS | OF THE |
SECOND VOLUME., ht: CONTENTS., on A2ᵛ Advt. (as. vol. 1), on B1 *1*
2–360 text dh: [two double rules] | AN | ESSAY | ON THE | ORIGIN and
IMPORTANCE | OF SMALL TRACTS and FUGITIVE PIECES. |
Written for the INTRODUCTION to the | HARLEIAN MISCELLANY.
Pagination: (↑) 21, 55, 87, 151, 153, 192, 240, 262, 291, 350; [↑] 95, 158,
161, 168, 208, 237, 294, 296, 300, 312, 323, 343, 348; (↑] *sic* 10; 35 as 53, 351
at ↖.
Press-figures: B8(15)–4, C3ᵛ(22)–1, D3ᵛ(38)–2, D4ᵛ(40)–1, E4ᵛ(56)–4,
E8(63)–2, F8(79)–4, G1ᵛ(82)–2, G4ᵛ(88)–1, H5(105)–2, H8(111)–2,
I4ᵛ(120)–2, I8ᵛ(128)–1, K8(143)–2, K8ᵛ(144)–1, L5(153)–1, M3ᵛ(166)–2,
M6ᵛ(172)–4, N7ᵛ(190)–2, O6(203)–2, O8ᵛ(208)–2, P1ᵛ(210)–2, Q8ᵛ(240)–1,
R6(251)–2, S2ᵛ(260)–1, T6(283)–4, T7(285)–1, U2ᵛ(292)–2, U5ᵛ(298)–1,
X8ᵛ(320)–1, Y5(329)–1, Y7ᵛ(334)–2, Z7ᵛ(350)–2, Z8ᵛ(352)–1, 2A2ᵛ(356)–1.
Catchwords: 8 AN (AN), 54 *om*. (PREFACE), 287 *om*. (*Sfor*.), 292 When
(Then), 313 Ho (How), 325 *om*. (Mad'ning), 329 ₐIf ('~), 334 *Yet* (Yet).
Explicit: 360: END OF THE SECOND VOLUME.

Paper: White, laid; crown (uncut: 7½ × 5 in.), no vis. wmk.

Type: text: small pica (3.6 mm), footnotes: brevier (2.6 mm). Single quotes as first quotes.

References: Courtney 116–17; CH 150; *Rothschild* 1254; Roscoe, *Newbery* (1973), A271; ESTC: t101912.

Notes: Collected by Davies without permission, whilst SJ was in Scotland (*Life* ii. 270–1; Piozzi, *Anecdotes*, 55), these volumes were first announced as 'In a few Days will be published . . . price 6s. sewed . . . By the Author of the Rambler' in *Lond. Chron.* 23 Nov. 1773, p. 503, but eventually published 23 December 1773 (*Public Advertiser* and *Lond. Chron.*), at 7s., sewed. Vol. III (below) was announced for 'February next'.

The whole of vol. 1 is SJ's, and most of vol. 2, except: *Thoughts on Agriculture*, 161–6; *A Letter to a Bishop, &c.*, 240–61; *Critical Reflections*, 262; *Battle of Wigs*, 323–42; '*Shakespeare*', 343–7; '*Ode to Genius*', 348–9; and '*Translation*', 349–60.

The Table of Contents in vol. 2 does not mention SJ's *Account of the Harleian Library*, 10–20, *Dissertation on Authors*, 21–9, and *Preface to the Artists' Catalogue*, 151–2.

Copies: O (2705 e. 611–12, 'William Leaf 1799' — 'Dauntsey');

USA: CtY, DFo, Hyde² (1. 'R.B. Adam'; 2. 'J. Fazakerley' — 'R.W. Chapman'), ICU, IU, ICN ('R.H. Isham'), [Liebert ('Martin' — 'R.W. Rogers')], MH, NN, NjP; *Japan*: [Kyoto]; *UK*: ABu, AWn, L (12270. aaaa.17, 'Thomas Tyers'), MRu ('Spencer'), NOp, WIS; *Aust*: CNL (DNS).

73.12DM/2a Davies's Miscellaneous and 1774
  Fugitive Pieces, second edition, first issue

[(a) First issue] MISCELLANEOUS | AND | FUGITIVE PIECES. | VOLUME THE FIRST [– SECOND]. | [rule] | THE SECOND EDITION, CORRECTED: | [rule] | [device 12.5 × 2.5 mm] | [double rule] | LONDON, | Printed for T. DAVIES, in Ruffel-Street, Covent- | Garden, Bookfeller to the Royal Academy. | MDCCLXXIV.

Vol. I: . . . CORRECTED:] Vol. II: . . . CORRECTED.

2 vols., 8°

I. *A*² B–2A⁸ 2B⁴, ($4 (–2B3,4) signed; 'VOL. I.' on $1), 190 leaves.

Pp. (as first edn., 73.12DM/1, above, A1 t., A1ᵛ blk, A2 Contents, A2ᵛ advt. (for vol. 3), on B1 *1* 2–375 text, *376* blk.

Pagination: 1, 376 unnumbered; [↑] 57, 62, 95, 150, 159, 235, 254, 287, 297, 357; (↑) 35, 80, 141, 305.

Press-figures: B3ᵛ(6)–6, C2ᵛ(20)–7, C3ᵛ(22)–4, D2ᵛ(36)–7, D3ᵛ(38)–6, E8(63)–6, F1ᵛ(66)–2, G5(89)–2, G8(95)–7, H8(111)–6, I7(125)–1, I7ᵛ(126)–8, K2ᵛ(132)–8, K7ᵛ(142)–2, L6(155)–6, L8ᵛ(160)–2, M5ᵛ(170)–4, M8ᵛ(176)–7,

N6(187)–4, N6ᵛ(188)–7, O2ᵛ(196)–6, O8(207)–2, P8(223)–2, Q2ᵛ(228)–1, R4ᵛ(248)–6, R8(255)–1, S7(269)–4, T1ᵛ(274)–7, T7(285)–2, U7ᵛ(302)–2, X5(313)–6, X6(315)–7, Y1ᵛ(322)–6, Z1ᵛ(338)–2, Z7(349)–1, 2A8ᵛ(368)–7, 2B3(373)–6.

Catchwords: 113 ˏThe ('∼'), 344 Matterˏ (∼,).
Explicit: 375 END of the FIRST VOLUME.

II. *A*² B–Z⁸ 2A⁴, ($4 (–2A3,4) signed; 'Vol.II.' on $1), 182 leaves.
Pp. (as. 73.12DM/1, above) A1 t., A1ᵛ blk, A2–2ᵛ Contents, A2ᵛ advt. for vol. 3, on B1 *1* 2–360 text.
Pagination: A1–2, 1 unnumbered; [↑] 10, 87, 153, 161, 168, 208, 237, 240, 294, 296, 300, 312, 323, 343, 348; (↑) 21, 30, 55, 95, 151, 158, '162', 262, 291, 350; 112 as 96, 192 as 162, 197 as 19.
Press-figures: B7ᵛ(14)–2, C5(25)–6, C8(31)–1, D7ᵛ(46)–6, E2ᵛ(52)–8, F7ᵛ(78)–7, G7(93)–1, H5(105)–1, H6(107)–7, I2ᵛ(116)–6, K5(137)–7, L5(153)–8, L8(159)–1, M7(173)–1, M8(175)–5, N2ᵛ(180)–6, N7(190)–2, O3ᵛ(198)–3, O8ᵛ(208)–5, P1ᵛ(210)–1, P2ᵛ(212)–2, Q6(235)–3, R6(251)–3, R6ᵛ(252)–5, S3ᵛ(262)–2, S4ᵛ(264)–2, T1ᵛ(274)–5, T2ᵛ(276)–1, U2ᵛ(292)–3, U5ᵛ(298)–5, X1ᵛ(306)–5, X2ᵛ(308)–3, Y7(333)–1, Y7ᵛ(334)–3, Z5(345)–1, Z7ᵛ(350)–2, 2A3(357)–2.
Catchwords: 9 AN (Aɴ), 54 *om*. (PREFACE), 62 *om*. (Our), 75 [fa-] tiffied (fied), 88 it (its), 232 *Atroc* (*Atrocis*), 288 *om*. (*Sfor*.), 301 (*d*) Sicne (∼ Since), 252 *om*. (Md'ning), 329 ˏIf ('∼'), 329 n. ˏnious ('∼'), 334 *om*. (Yet).
Explicit: 360 END of the SECOND VOLUME.

73.12DM/2b   Davies's Miscellaneous and   1774
Fugitive Pieces, second edition, second issue

[(b) Second issue: cancel tt.] MISCELLANEOUS | AND FUGITIVE PIECES. | VOLUME THE FIRST [– SECOND]. | [rule] | THE SECOND EDITION, CORRECTED: | [rule] | [device, as 1st issue, above] | [double rule] | LONDON, | Printed for T. Davies, in Ruffel-Street, Covent- | Garden; and Carnan and Newbery, St. Paul's | Church-yard. | MDCCLXXIV.
Vol. I: . . . CORRECTED:] vol. II: CORRECTED.
2 vols., 8°

I. *A*² (± A1) B–2A⁸ 2B⁴, as prec. first issue.
II. *A*² (± A1) B–Z⁸ 2A⁴, as prec. first issue.

Paper: White, laid; (i) double crown (uncut: 7½ × 5 in.); no vis. wmk.; chain-lines horizontal; (ii) crown (uncut: 7½ × 5 in.); wmk.: arabesque. Variously distributed. In O as: (i) I. B–Z, II. B–D, M–Q, (ii) I. A, 2A–2B, II. A, E–L, R–2A. In second issue cancel tt. are on (ii). (i) was presumably left-over stock.

Type: Text: small pica (3.6 mm), footnotes: brevier (2.6 mm).

References: see first edn. (73.12DM/1, above); Roscoe, *Newbery* (1973), A271 (2); ESTC: t101913.

Notes: vols. 1–2 published 28 April 1774 as 'a new and corrected edition' (*Lond. Chron.*), with advts. continuing throughout May–June, and in Aug. 1774. Advts. appeared as late as July 1783. This late date is however an unlikely one for the second issue since the partnership of Carnan & Newbery lasted from only 1769 to 1779 (Roscoe).

Despite the claims of the tt., nothing is revised in this reprint.

Copies: (**a**) First issue: O (2705 e. 404–5, with MS *addenda*);

USA: CtY, ICU, IU, Hyde (Pres. 'T. Davies — Garrick' — Ellsworth — R.B. Adam — R.H. Isham), [Liebert (uncut)], MH, NjP, NN, TxY; *Can*: CaOHM; *Japan*: [Kyoto];

UK: ABu, BMp, C, Cp, Es, L (94. d.22–3), Lu (Sterling), MRp, NCu, NOu; *Aust*: CNL (DNS).

(**b**) Second issue: Oef ('G. A. Thursby'[1]).

[1] G. A. Thursby's copy of the *Lives of the Poets*, 4 vols. 1781 (79.4LP/5, below) was item 175, at £190 in Adam Mills (Cottenham, Cambridge), *Rare Books Catalogue 24* (1993).

73.12DM/3(Vol. 3) Davies's Miscellaneous and Fugitive Pieces, Vol. III 1774

MISCELLANEOUS | AND | FUGITIVE PIECES. | VOLUME THE THIRD. | [rule] | [orn. device of flowers, as vol. 1 (73.12DM/1, above)] | [double rule] | LONDON: | Printed for T. DAVIES, in *Ruſſel-Street, Covent-* | *Garden*, Bookſeller to the Royal Academy; and | CARNAN and NEWBERY, St. Paul's Church Yard. | MDCCLXXIV.

8°, A^4 B–U^8 X^4, ($4 (–A1, B4, X3,4) signed; 'VOL. III.' on $1), 160 leaves.

Pp. A1 *i* t., *ii* blk, iii–viii Contents dh: CONTENTS | OF THE | THIRD VOLUME., on B1 *1* 2–311 text dh: [two double rules] | REVIEW OF MEMOIRS | OF THE | COURT OF AUGUSTUS. | By THOMAS BLACKWELL, J.U.D. Principal of | *Mariſchal-College* in the Univerſity of *Aberdeen*., *312* blk.

Pagination: [↑] 10, 17, 29, 41, 59, 66, 77, 87, 135, 184, 212, 215–16, 218, 220, 234, 245, 249, 278, 280, 282, 290–2, 294, 296, 300–1; (↑) iii, 266, 271, 274, 276; 142 as 42, 235 as 233.

Press-figures: A3(v)–4, B5v(10)–4, C6(27)–2, D5v(42)–1, E6(59)–1, F1v(66)–1, F8v(80)–4, G2v(84)–2, G5v(90)–2, H1v(98)–1, H6v(108)–1, I6(123)–4, I6v(124)–2, K1v(130)–4, K7(141)–2, L4v(152)–1, L8(159)–2, M8(175)–2, M8v(176)–4, N5(185)–4, N6(187)–4, O3v(198)–4, P5v(218)–4, P6v(220)–2, Q1v(226)–2, Q8v(240)–4, R5(249)–4, R7v(254)–2, S5v(266)–4, S7(269)–2, T6(283)–4, T8v(288)–2, U2v(292)–4, U3v(294)–2, X3v(310)–2.

Catchwords: 40 A PHI- (A REVIEW . . .), 76 *om*. (AN), 179 the ('t' *slipt*), 191 ₐIncreafe ('~'), 209 ₐBut ('~'), 218 Andₐ (~,), 241 ₐLet ('~'), 257 ₐWhen ('~'), 309 *om*. (POSTSCRIPT.).

Explicit: 311 FINIS.

Paper: White, laid; double crown stock (i) of prec. (73.12DM/2b, above), (uncut: 7½ × 5 in.); no vis. wmk.

Type: Text: small pica (3.6 mm), footnotes: brevier (2.6 mm).

References: Courtney 116–17; CH 150; Roscoe, *Newbery* (1973), A271 (1); *Rothschild* 1254.

Notes: Despite the notice of 23 Dec. 1773 announcing vols. 1–2, adding 'A Third Volume . . . will be published in February next . . .', and despite similar statements in the advts. in vols. 1–2 themselves, no advt. for vol. 3 (at 3s. 6d. sewed), has been found before the end of May 1774, a whole month after the publication of the second edn. of vols. 1–2 (73.12DM/2, above), when all three vols. are announced at 10s., in *Lond. Chron.*, 31 May 1774, p. 518. The collection in 3 vols. was reviewed in *Gents. Mag.* xliv (Nov. 1774), 524/4, with critical comments on some of the attributions, and the remark of vol. 1, 'Why the Life of Admiral Blake by the same hand, is omitted, we are at a loss to know'.

Only four genuine pieces by SJ are included in this vol: **1**. *Review of* . . . [Blackwell's] *Memoirs of Augustus*, 1–9; **2**. *Observations on the . . . State of Affairs, 1756*, 17–28; **3**. *Life of Sarpi*, 59–65; and **4**. *Preface to Rolt's Dictionary*, 282–9. The *Account of . . . Benvenuto Cellini*, 296–99, and the *Review of Burke's* . . . *Sublime and Beautiful*, 41–58, are no longer thought to be SJ's, despite some contemporary credit in the attribution.

Copies: O² (**1**. 2705 e. 406; **2**. 2705 e. 613);

USA: CtY², DFo, Hyde³, ICN, IU, [Liebert], MH, NN, TxU; *Can*: CaOHM; *Japan*: [Kyoto]; *UK*: ABu, AWn, BMp, C, Cp, [Es], L², Lu, MRc, MRu, NOp, Owo, WIS; *Aust*: CNL (DNS).

73.12DM/4	Davies's Miscellaneous and	1774
	Fugitive Pieces, Dublin	

Miscellaneous and Fugitive Pieces . . .
 Dublin: Sleater, Husband, Walker, Moncrieffe, and Jenkin. 1774
 2 vols., 12°. I. [1] + 320; II. [1] + 302. ESTC: n011614. Not seen.[1]
 Copies: *Fr*: [BN.].

---

[1] J. O'D. Fenning, *Catalogue* 2 (Dublin, 1970), 106, £35.

73.12DM/5   Davies's Miscellaneous and   1804
                        Fugitive Pieces

MISCELLANEOUS | AND | [Hollow] FUGITIVE PIECES: | CONSISTING OF | *Essays, Dissertations, Prefaces, Reviews,* | *Lives, &c. &c.* | [short swelled shaded rule] | By SAMUEL JOHNSON, L.L.D. | [short swelled beaded rule] | To which is prefixed, | *The Life of the Author.* | [dash] | IN TWO VOLUMES. | [dash] | VOL. I [– II]. | [medium swelled rule] | Sheffield: Printed by and for Slater, Bacon and Co. | AND SOLD BY W. BAYNES, G. OFFOR, CROSBY | AND CO. AND LONGMAN AND CO. | LONDON. | 1804.

2 vols., 12°

I. π^4 a–c^6 C–2H^6 2I^4, ($1,3 (–E3) signed; 'VOL.I.' on $1 (–2A)), 200 leaves.

Pp. π1 t., π1^v blk, on π2 *i* Contents, *ii* blk, *iii* iv–vi Advertisement (signed 'J. C.'), *ix* x–xliii Life of Johnson, *xliv* blk, on C1 *1* 2–355 text, *356* blk.

No *press-figures*, or *catchwords*.

II. *A*^{2} B–2K^6 2L^2 (2L2 blk), ($1,3 (–E3, 2G3, 2I3) signed; 'VOL. II.' on $1), 196 leaves.

Pp. A1 t., A1^v blk, A2 Contents, A2^v blk, on B1 *1* 2–386 text, *387–8* (2L2) blk leaf.

No *press-figures*, or *catchwords*.

Paper: white, wove; medium (uncut: 7⅔ × 4½ in.); no vis. wmk.

Type: Pica (3.9 mm), fnn. bourgeois (3.0 mm). Hollow type of tt. recurs in head tt. in text.

References: Courtney 164.

Notes: The identity of 'J. C.' is not known.[1] His 'Advertisement' (I. iv), states: 'In this Edition, the mistakes of Mr. Davies are carefully rectified. Those pieces which evidently were not written by Dr. Johnson are excluded; and several are inserted, which either Mr. Davies overlooked, or they were not then published.'

SJ's contributions to Mrs Lennox's translation of Brumoy (60.2LB/1, above), his 'Preface' to the Artists' Catalogue, 1762 (62.5SA/1, above), his 'Account of Collins' (63.1PC/1, above), his 'Essay on the Epitaphs of Pope' (56.1UV/1, above), and some of SJ's poems (viz. *Drury Lane Prologue*, 1747 (47.10DLP/1), *Prologue to Irene*, 1749, (49.2I/1), *Prologue to 'Comus'*, 1750, (50.4PC/1), *Prologue to 'The Good Natur'd Man'*, 1768, (68.1GM/1), *London*, 1738, (38.5L/1), and *Vanity of Human Wishes*, 1749, (49.1VW/1)), all of which are certainly genuine, are here excluded. Of the pieces here inserted the 'Table of Cebes' (46.3DM/1, above), is not SJ's, but the following are canonical: General Observations on Shakespeare's Plays (i. 130, 65.10SP/1, above), Controversy between Crousaz and Warburton (i. 179, 39.10CP/1, above), Preface to Lobo (i. 240, 35.2LV/1, above), Review of Hanway (i. 295, 56.4LM, above), Review of Warton on Pope (i. 310, 56.4LM, above), Essay on Epitaphs (ii. 38,

40GM/10, above), Reply to Hanway (ii. 47, 56.4LM, above), Bravery of the English Common Soldier (ii. 57, 60.2BM/1, above), Considerations on Blackfriars Bridge (ii. 60, 59.12DG, above), Lives of Morin (ii. 89, 41GM11, above), Cheynel (ii. 96, 50.1St/1, above), and Blake (ii. 196, 40GM10, above). Whoever the editor was he was certainly concerned with an up-to-date determination of the canon, though most of his material is taken from *Works*, 1801 (87.3W/5, below), vols. 2, 8, and 12 (it may even be a made-up collection from the 12° edn., 87.3W/6, below), although the biography of SJ is derived from Murphy's *Essay*, 1792 (87.3W/2, &c., below).

Copies: O (2705 e. 1315–16);

USA: Hyde (uncut), [Liebert (uncut) = CtY]; *UK*: LEu, SHp, STA.

---

[1] If forced to guess, perhaps Joseph Cradock (1742–1826*) might be hazarded.

73EB   Epitaph on Jane Bell   [? 1773]

Memorial slab of white marble, on the south wall of the nave of the parish church of St Peter, Watford, Herts.

According to Sir John Hawkins, who is the only authority for the attribution and for any relevant details, Jane Bell died 'in the month of October, 1771' (*Life87*, 472). The epitaph itself states that she had died in her 53rd year, was the wife of John Bell, Esq., and that he erected the memorial. Hawkins described him as 'a gentleman, with whom he [i.e. SJ] had maintained a long and strict friendship' (*Life87*, 471). Bell's own death is recorded on a smaller slab immediately below that of his wife, as having occurred on 4 August 1796, in his 72nd year.

Neither Jane nor John Bell figures, in any other records of Johnson's life or acquaintance.[1] Hawkins is the only one to associate them, yet he was in a position to know, and it is difficult to disregard so direct an assertion.[2] If John was a brother of Revd. William Bell (1731–1816*), then he at least is mentioned in three of Johnson's letters.[3] If John was over 71 in 1796, then he was born in 1725, and so was an older brother. His death is noticed in *Gents. Mag.* lxvi, 2 (Aug. 1796), 706:

> At his house in Fludyer-street, White-hall, John Bell, esq. many years first commissioner for taking care of sick and wounded seamen, and prisoners of war, and afterwards under-secretary of state to the late Marquis of Downshire.[4]

Such a philanthropic career would have ensured the friendship of SJ, which may have arisen from their involvement with the French Prisoners in 1760 (60.8FP/1, above).

The style of the text is of no great assistance: it is conventional and in English.[5] Hawkins acknowledges that the composition was a combined effort:

> [Bell] wished Johnson, from the outlines of her character, which he should

give him, and his own knowledge of her worth, to compose a monumental inscription for her: he returned the husband thanks for the confidence he placed in him, and acquitted himself of the task in the following fine eulogium, now to be seen in the parish church of Watford in Hertfordshire (*Life87*, 471).

The stone was doubtless erected soon after the death of Jane Bell in 1771, though Boswell appears to place the composition of the epitaph in 1773, so it seems unlikely that Hawkins had access in 1785–7, over twelve years later, to the manuscript which Johnson had then drafted for the widower to use in preparing the memorial. The primary inference is that Hawkins's text derives from the stone, though it remains just possible that he may have used the manuscript from which the text of the stone also descends.

Hawkins's version in *Life87* differs from that of the stone only in some details of capitalization, punctuation, and lineation, notably by creating separate lines for the words 'afflict her,' and 'her friends;' so extending the 22 lines of the stone to 24 lines of print. Hawkins's version, not that of the stone, was followed closely by Isaac Reed in his reprint of it in *Works*, xiv (1788), 541 (87.3W/1.3/1a, below). Reed offered no further comment on the authenticity or the history of the epitaph, though his adoption of it corroborates the attribution. Hawkins's footnote was slightly shortened to read: 'She died in October, 1771.'

¹ The name does not stand in the lost MS list of friends supplied to Croker by Harwood, and published in Croker's *Boswell* (1848), 79.
² Boswell accepted the attribution, and added that John Bell was the brother of Dr William Bell, prebendary of Westminster, who had assured him that the epitaph was indeed the work of SJ. *Life* ii. 204 n.
³ One undated '25 May' [? 1770], to Garrick (169) reserving theatre seats, one of 25 Apr. 1780 to Mrs Thrale, reporting a dinner together (662; Hyde, iii. 244), and one of 3 Jan. 1784 to Taylor, who was also a prebendary of Westminster, and of course, minister of St Margaret's (923).
⁴ Bell's appointment to the commission is noticed in *Gents. Mag.* xliii (Aug. 1773), 416.
⁵ Mrs Piozzi, who also knew of the epitaph, reported that 'They would have it in English, not Latin, which *vex'd* him' (I am ashamed to have lost my note of the source of this remark; it is not in *Thraliana*, and may be a *marginalium*; I have not invented it).

74.7DW Diary of a Journey into North Wales 1776

This excursion began on 5 July and lasted until 30 September 1774. The Holograph MS was not published until 1816, see below 816.DW/1 Diary of a Journey into North Wales, 1816.

74.10P/1 The Patriot, first edition 1774

THE | PATRIOT. | Addreſſed to the | ELECTORS of GREAT BRITAIN. | THEY bawl for Freedom in their ſenſeleſs mood, | Yet ſtill revolt when Truth would fet them free, | Licenfe they mean, when they cry Liberty, | For who loves that muft firft be wife and good. | Milton. | [double rule] | LONDON: | Printed for T. CADELL, in the Strand. | MDCCLXXIV. | [Price 6*d*.]

8°, *A*1 B–E⁴ *F*1, ($2 signed), 18 leaves.

Pp. A1 t., A1ᵛ blk, on B1 *1* 2–33 text dh: [bevelled double rule] | THE | PATRIOT., *34* blk.

Pagination: [↑];

Press-figures: B4(7)–4, C1ᵛ(10)–1, D4ᵛ(24)–2, E1ᵛ(26)–3.

Catchwords: 16 [reprefenta-] tion; (~,).

Explicit: 33 FINIS.

Paper: White, laid; Medium (uncut: 9 × 5¾ in.); no vis. wmk.

Type: English (4.8 mm), leaded.

References: *Life* ii. 285–8 (Courtney 117); CH 151; *Works* (Yale), x. 387 ff.; *Rothschild* 1255; Adams (1980), 74-38a; ESTC: t009708.

Notes: The pamphlet was written in haste in early October perhaps at Strahan's request (*Letters* 363, Hyde, ii. 155).[1] All three editions were printed by him (L: Add. MS 48803, fo. 39), of which the first, of 500 copies, was published 12 Oct. 1774, at 6d. (*Lond. Chron.*). The three editions are discriminated by their press-figures.

Copies: O² (**1**. Gough Cambr. 45 (4) 'Dr S. Johnson' on t. by RG; **2**. Am Lib. 55 b.57);

USA: CSmH² (**1**. 123975 imperfect, 'From the Author' [*not* SJ]), CtY (Franklin 774. J67, uncut), DLC, Hyde³, MH ('Thorndike' — 'd. 19ⁿ octobris. difs Pamphlet ift für den hof, von Dʳ. Johnfon gefchreiben'), [MiU-C], NIC, NN, NPM, PHi (Af. 382.6, 'Benjamin Franklin'), [RPB], TxU; *Can*: CaOHM (C.2542, 'Robert Hesketh'); *UK*: [B.S. Barlow, Esq; ('John Cator')], BMp, C, MRp, Oa, STA.

---

[1] Thomas Campbell, *Diary*, ed. James L. Clifford (Cambridge, 1947), 70; the possible dates are 1 or 8 October.

74.10P/2   The Patriot, second edition   1774

THE | PATRIOT. | Addreffed to the | ELECTORS of GREAT BRITAIN. | They bawl for Freedom in their fenfelefs mood, | Yet ftill revolt when Truth would fet them free, | Licenfe they mean, when they cry Liberty, | For who loves that muft firft be wife and good. | Milton. | THE SECOND EDITION. | [double rule] | LONDON: | Printed for T. CADELL, in the Strand. | MDCCLXXIV. | [Price 6*d*.]

8°, *A*1 B–E⁴ *F*1, ($2 signed), 18 leaves.

Pp. A1 t., A1ᵛ blk, on B1 *1* 2–33 text dh: [bevelled double rule] | THE | PATRIOT., *34* blk.

Pagination: [↑]; *Press-figures*: B4(7)–2, C1ᵛ(10)–4, D4ᵛ(24)–2, E1ᵛ(26)–5.

Catchwords: not recorded;

Explicit: 33 FINIS.

Paper: White, laid; Medium (uncut: 9 × 5¾ in.); no vis. wmk.

Type: English (4.8 mm), leaded.

References: *Life* ii. 285–8 (Courtney 117); CH 151; *Works* (Yale), x. 387 ff.; *Rothschild* 1255; Adams (1980), 74-38b; ESTC: t108415.

Notes: 500 copies were printed by Strahan very soon after the printing of the first edn. (74.10P/1, above), and published 5 Nov. 1774, at 6d. (*Lond. Chron.*). The repeated press-figure in sig. D(o) suggests some overrunning. CSmH (66009) shows that A ≡ F were a conjugate wrap-round.

Copies: BMp ('B. Anderson Mary Hall Ox.'[1]);

USA: CSmH[2] (1. 66009 uncut), CtY (Franklin), DLC, [Liebert], ICU, [MiU-C], NIC, NN[3], ViU; *UK*: [W.R. Batty], C.

[1] No Anderson with the initial 'B' is found in *Al. Ox.*, but William [? Bill] Anderson is reported (ibid, 23/16), as matriculated at Exeter Coll. 1813, aged 16, before migrating to St Mary Hall [Oriel].

74.10P/3   The Patriot, Dublin   1774

THE | PATRIOT. | Addreſſed to the | ELECTORS of GREAT BRITAIN. | Tʜᴇʏ bawl for Freedom in their ſenſeleſs mood, | Yet ſtill revolt when Truth would ſet them free, | Licenſe they mean, when they cry Liberty, | For who loves that muſt firſt be wiſe and good. | Mɪʟᴛᴏɴ. | LONDON, PRINTED; | DUBLIN, REPRINTED. | MDCCLXXIV.

8°, A⁸, ($4 (–A1) signed), 8 leaves.

Pp. A1 *1* t., *2* blk, *3* 4–16 text. Not examined.

References: Courtney 117; Adams (1980), 74-30c; ESTC: n038289.

Notes: ESTC reports copy at InU-Li.

Copies: *USA*: ICN, [MnHi].

74.10P/4   The Patriot, third edition   1775

THE | PATRIOT. | Addreſſed to the | ELECTORS of GREAT BRITAIN. | Tʜᴇʏ bawl for Freedom in their ſenſeleſs mood, | Yet ſtill revolt when Truth would ſet them free, | Licenſe they mean, when they cry Liberty, | For who loves that muſt firſt be wiſe and good. | Mɪʟᴛᴏɴ. | THE THIRD EDITION. | LONDON: | Printed for T. CADELL, in the Strand. | MDCCLXXV. | [Price 6*d*.]

8°, *A*1 B–E⁴ *F*1, ($2 signed), 18 leaves.

Pp. A1 t., A1ᵛ blk, on B1 *1* 2–33 text dh: [bevelled double rule] | THE | PATRIOT., *34* blk.

Pagination: [↑]; 33 unnumbered.

Press-figures: B2(3)–8, C4(15)–6, D1ᵛ(18)–8, E4(31)–1.
Catchwords: not recorded.
Explicit: 33 FINIS.
Paper: White, laid; Medium (uncut: 9 × 5¾ in.); no vis. wmk.
Type: English (4.8 mm), leaded.
References: *Life* ii. 285–8 (Courtney 117); CH 151; *Works* (Yale), x. 387 ff.; *Rothschild* 1255; Adams (1980), 74-38d; ESTC: t012455.
Notes: NIC shows the conjugacy of A ≡ F. 500 copies were printed by Strahan soon after the printing of the first two edd. (74.10P/1–2, above), and published 8 May 1775, at 6d. (*Lond. Chron.*).
Copies: NIC (uncut);
USA: CSmH, CtY (Franklin), DLC², IU, MH (*Ec75. J6371. 774pc), NN (+ Scott's *Remarks*, 1775); *Japan*: [Kyoto]; *UK*: Ct² (1. X. 35.7⁶ 'Francis Wrangham').

74.10P/5 The Patriot, Dublin, second edition   1775

THE | PATRIOT. | Addreſſed to the | ELECTORS of GREAT BRITAIN. | Tʜᴇʏ bawl for Freedom in their ſenſeleſs mood, | Yet ſtill revolt when Truth would ſet them free, | Licenſe they mean, when they cry Liberty, | For who loves that muſt firſt be wiſe and good. | Mɪʟᴛᴏɴ. | DUBLIN: | Printed for E. LYNCH, No. 6, Skinner-Row, | and at the Four-Courts. | MDCCLXXV.

8°, A⁸ B² (–A1 = ? blk), ($4 (–B2) signed), 9 leaves.

Pp. [A1 ? blk], A2 *1* t., *2* blk, on A3 *3* 4–17 text dh: THE | PATRIOT., *18* blk.

Pagination: [↑]; *Press-figures*: none.
Catchwords: 13 [know] that (the).
Explicit: 17 FINIS.
Paper: White, laid; Lombard (uncut: 8¼ × 5¼ in.); no vis. wmk.
Type: English (4.5 mm); 37 line/p. in A (no white lines between paras); 34 line/p. in B, white lines between paras.
References: Adams (1980), 74-30e; ESTC: t177885.
Notes: No copies seen with integral A1.
Copies: O (GP. 327/4, 'Edmond Malone'); *USA*: MB, ICN; *UK*: BMp.

74.10TE Henry Thrale's Election Addresses   1774

1 October   Election Address for Henry Thrale
'To the worthy Electors of the Borough of Sᴏᴜᴛʜᴡᴀʀᴋ'
References: *Life* v. 460 n; *Thraliana*, i. 201, and Piozzi *Anecdotes*, 292–3; Clifford, *Piozzi* (1941), 116 n.; Fleeman, in *Johnson, Boswell and their Circle* (1965), 181–2.

MS draft acquired by the late J.L. Clifford, of New York, from Mrs Herbert Evans, of Brynbella, now NNC (*MS Handlist* 130, *MS Index* JoS 194), published (with minor modifications) in *Public Advertiser*, 1, 3, 4 Oct., and *Daily Advertiser*, 4 Oct. 1774.

4 October   Election Address for Henry Thrale
'To the Worthy Electors of the Borough of Southwark'
References: Clifford, *Piozzi* (1941), 116 n.; Fleeman, in *Johnson, Boswell and their Circle* (1965), 182. Published in *Daily Advertiser*, 6, 7, 8 and 10 October, and *Public Advertiser*, 7 and 10 Oct.

13 October   Address of thanks for Henry Thrale
'To the worthy Electors of the Borough of Southwark'
References: Clifford, *Piozzi* (1941), 116b n; Fleeman, in *Johnson, Boswell and their Circle* (1965), 183. Published in *Public Advertiser* and *Daily Advertiser*, 14 October.

74.10TH/1   Hereford Infirmary Appeal   1774

The Hereford Journal, 20 Oct. 1774. Hereford: Printed and published by C. Pugh.

References: J. Allen, *Bibliotheca Herefordiensis* (1821), 24–5; Hazen and McAdam, *HLQ* iii (1939–40), 359–67; S.H. Martin, 'Ullingswick, the Infirmary and Dr Johnson' *Transactions of the Woolhope Naturalist Field Club* (Hereford), xxxv (1958), 293–8.[1]

Notes: The third address, of 20 Oct. 1774, is SJ's on the evidence of *Thraliana*, 204 n. The text was first published by Hazen and McAdam, 1940. C. Pugh traded from *c*.1762 to 1776, and is recorded in Plomer (s.n.), whose account notices the variety of titles attached to the *Hereford Journal*. Allen also gives a summary history of the newspaper, begun by Pugh in 1770 (24–5). He may be identified with the Charles Pugh, son of Jacob, of Aberedow, Radnorshire, who served apprentice to William Faden, 1751–58 (McKenzie, *Apprentices*, 2801).

Copy: *UK*: HEp.

[1] The front of the present (1965) Hereford City Hospital preserves the facade of Talbot's Infirmary.

74.10TH/2   Hereford Infirmary Appeal   1774

THREE ADDRESSES | TO | THE INHABITANTS OF THE | COUNTY OF HEREFORD, | In FAVOUR of the ESTABLISHMENT of a | PUBLICK INFIRMARY, | IN OR NEAR | THE CITY OF HEREFORD. | [rule] | REPUBLISHED AT THE REQUEST AND EXPENCE OF | THE RIGHT HON. LORD VISCOUNT BATEMAN | LORD LIEUTENANT OF THE SAID COUNTY. | [rule] | BY THOMAS TALBOT, D.D. | RECTOR OF ULLINGSWICK. | [rule] | HEREFORD: | PRINTED BY C. PUGH. MDCCLXXIV.

8°, A^2 B–C^4 D^2 (A1 blk), ($2 (–D2) signed), 12 leaves.

Pp. A1 blk, A2 t., A2^v blk, on B1 1–6 text dh: [bevelled double rule] | A | PROPOSAL | FOR | ERECTING AN INFIRMARY | AT HEREFORD. | [PUBLISHED AT THE MIDSUMMER | SESSIONS, 1763.] (signed 'T.T.'), 7–11 text dh: [bevelled double rule] | AN | ADDRESS | TO THE | INHABITANTS OF HERE- | FORDSHIRE, | TO EXCITE THEM TO BE LIBERAL BE- | NEFACTORS OF THEIR INTENDED | INFIRMARY. | [Publiſhed at the MICHAELMAS SESSIONS, 1764.] (signed 'T.T.'), 12–19 text dh: [bevelled double rule] | An | ADDRESS | TO THE NOBILITY, GENTRY, AND CLERGY | OF THE | COUNTY OF HEREFORD. | [Publiſhed at the MICHAELMAS SESSIONS, 1774.] (signed 'T.T.'), *20* blk.

Pagination: [↑]; *Press-figures*: none; *Catchwords*: no errors.

Explicit: 19 FINIS.

Paper: White, laid; Crown (uncut: 7½ × 5 in.); wmk.: Crowned shield with posthorn + LVG.

Type: Long primer (3.3 mm). Type is as in the initial publications in the *Hereford Journal*, but with lineation adjusted to the new measure.

Notes: This separate pamphlet is not recorded by Allen, though he does mention a booklet of regulations for the infirmary (1778), p. 25. ESTC: t175951.

The progress of the appeal (which was eventually successful), is reported in the *Hereford Journal* for 13, 20 October, 3 and 10 November 1774. There are the following minor variants in SJ's address between the newspaper and this pamphlet:

Heref. Jnl., 20 Oct.	*Three Addresses*
col. 2, §7, 8–9 public | infirmary	P.16, 8 up. Public Infirmary
§8, 7–8 where | by	17, 10 whereby
Final prayer: *My Lords ... Gentlemen,*	MY LORDS ... GENTLEMEN,

Talbot, then an undergraduate at Exeter College, Oxford, was among the subscribers to Husbands's *Miscellany*, 1731 (31.10HM/1, above).

Copies: Heref. County Libr (+ A1 blk);

UK: HEp (lacks A1), O (Gough Heref. 9 (4), lacks A1).

75.1J/1a   Journey, first edition   1775

A | JOURNEY | TO THE | WESTERN ISLANDS | OF | SCOTLAND. | [ornam. floral spray, 20 × 26 mm] | LONDON: | Printed for W. Strahan; and T. Cadell in the Strand. | MDCCLXXV.

8°, A^2 B–C^8 D^8 (± D8) E–T^8 U^8 (± U4) X–$2B^8$, ($4 (+D8, *U4) signed), 194 leaves.

Pp. A1 t., A1^v blk, A2 ERRATA. (11 items, 12 lines), A2^v blk, on B1 *1* 2–384 text dh: [Block of flowers, 13 × 80 mm] | A | JOURNEY | TO THE | WESTERN ISLANDS | OF | SCOTLAND., rt: A JOURNEY TO THE | WESTERN ISLANDS, &c..

Pagination: '48' of *cancellans* D8^v is wrong font (english (4.5 mm) instead of pica (4.4 mm) as in *cancellandum*; 296 as 226 in earlier state of *cancellans* *U4.

Press-figures: B7(13)–6, B8(15)–2, C1^v(18)–6, D6^v(44)–5, *cancellandum* D8(47)–3, *cancellans* D8^v(48)–4, E6(59)–2, E8^v(64)–6, F3^v(70)–4, F7(77)–2, G1^v(82)–6, G7(93)–5, H1^v(98)–6, H8^v(112)–4, I5^v(122)–7, I8^v(128)–1, K3^v(134)–3, K8^v(144)–2, L1^v(146)–7, L5(153)–1, M1^v(162)–7, N4^v(184)–6, N8(191)–7, O5(201)–1, O5^v(202)–6, P5^v(218)–3, Q1^v(226)–7, R7(253)–1, R8(255)–6, S5(265)–4, S5^v(266)–3, T7(285)–6, U2^v(292)–4, U8(303)–6, X1^v(306)–2, X5(313)–3, Y1^v(322)–3, Y8^v(336)–8, Z1^v(338)–4, Z2^v(340)–8, 2A2^v(356)–2, 2A8(367)–6, 2B6(379)–5, 2B6^v(380)–8.

Catchwords: 35 [re-] quired (ruined), 38 [ele-] vat$_\wedge$ on (vation), 195 The (This), 240 I heard (Having heard), 280 I men- (Mention).

Explicit: 384 FINIS.

Paper: White, laid; Medium (uncut: 9¼ × 5¾ in.); no vis. wmk.

Type: Pica (4.4 mm), leaded; white lines between paras., ornament on t., block of flowers as headpiece (p. 1). The orn. on t. is the same as that on *Taxation no Tyranny* (75.3TT/1, below).

References: Courtney 122–3; CH 151–2; *Rothschild* 1257; ESTC: t083702 (undifferentiated); Todd, *SB* vi (1954), 247–54; Fleeman (ed.), *Journey* (1985) Introd & Appx. A.

Notes: Todd's article is the clearest account of production; it is followed and a little expanded in *Journey* (1985). Printing began about 20 June 1774, and SJ read proofs during the summer and autumn. The cancels were made about early December 1774 since frequent offset evidence shows the two *cancellantia* formed a ½-sheet with the t. and errata leaves.[1]

Strahan had printed 2,000 copies (L: Add. MS 48803, fo. 57^v), by about mid-December 1774 when SJ presented copies to the King and to HLT, but at sig. S decided to overrun and reprint a further 2,000 copies which form the 2nd edn. (75.1J/2, below). Nearly 1,200 copies were distributed to the trade on 13 Jan. 1775 (MS Hyde), and publication was announced on 18 Jan. 1775, at 5s. (*Morning Chronicle*). Copies are not scarce.[2]

Copies: O (Gough Scot. 252, with MS note by Richard Gough on p. 48);

USA: CSmH[2] (**1**. 131359 'Robert Hoe'; **2**. 255546 no *errata* leaf), CtY, DLC, Hyde[6] (**1**. 'From the Authour' — H.L. Thrale[3] — Wm Stirling-Maxwell; U4 uncancelled, no *errata* leaf; *Booklist* 145; **2**. pres. by Wm Strahan — 'Sir Archibald Grant of Monymusk'; **3**. uncut, R.B. Adam; **4**. uncut; **5**. Pres. JB to George Dempster; **6**. 'Thomas Hayward Southby' + *cancellandum* D8), ICN ('L. H. Silver'), IU[2], [Liebert[3] (**1**. uncut; **3**. 'Thomas Caldecott'[4] & MS nn.)], MH, NIC, NjP, NN-B[2], NPM[2], NRU, PPRF (uncut, 'W. H. Arnold'), PPU, TxU, ViU, WiM ('Simon Vaughan'); *Can*: CaOHM (B. 14427); *Japan*: [Kyoto]; *UK*: ABu[2], AWn, BMp, C, Cq, Csj, Ct[2] ('To dear Mrs Aston from the Authour' — Rothschild, *Booklist* 146), DUNu (imperfect), E[2] (**1**, HS. 175 'Leeds'; **2**. H35 d.39), En, Es, Eu (EB. 82463, lacks t.), Felbrigg, Gu[3] (**1**. 'Dr William Hunter' *Booklist* 144; **2**. BE.3 ——b.11 lacks *errata* leaf), INV (Fraser Mackintosh), JDF[2], LICj ('To Mr Ryland from the authour' *Booklist* 148), LVu, MRp, MRu, Oef, Op[3] (**1**. SJ: 'To the Master of Pembroke College from the authour' *Booklist* 147;[5] **2**. 'Edward Dowden' — 'George Herbert Vernon'; **3**. imperfect), SHu; *Aust*: CNL (DNS); *Eir*: Dt[2].

---

[1] Hazen, *RES* xvii (1941), 201–3; Fleeman, *PBSA* lviii (1964), 232–8; Kendall; *PBSA* lix (1965); 317–18; and Landon, *PBSA* lxiv (1970), 449–50. The uncancelled version of D8 (pp. 47–8) relative to the roof of Lichfield Cathedral was made public by the *Morning Post*, 20 Feb. 1775, and several owners noted the original reading: Richard Gough (O), Michael Lort (Hyde; also noting the original at U4, p. 296), and John Loveday (p. 48, in Maggs Bros. *Cat.* 1038 (1984), 127).

[2] The copy annotated by James Bindley (biographer of Isaac Reed), was in the J.W. Southgate sale, Southgate, Grimston & Wells, 21 June 1833, lot 503.

[3] Broster , Manchester (Piozzi), 1823, 635; Evans (Craven Ord), 1830, 746.

[4] Sotheby (Caldecott), 26 Aug. 1857, 18.

[5] Wrongly identified as William Adams in my edn. of *Journey* (1985), xxvi. It was in fact given to his predecessor, John Ratcliffe (d. 13 July 1775; *Gleanings* v. 203), bursar in SJ's time at college, who gave it to Edward Bentham, D.D. (1707–76*), of Christ Church, Oxford (cf. *Lit. Anec.* ii. 57).

75.1J/1b   Journey, first edition, facsimile   1968

A facsimile of the above edn. was published by the Scolar Press, Menston, Yorks., with a brief introduction by R.C. Alston. It was issued in both hardback and paperback.

75.1J/2a   Journey, second edition, first issue   1775

A | JOURNEY | TO THE | WESTERN ISLANDS | OF | SCOTLAND. | [ornam. floral spray, 20 × 26 mm] | LONDON: | Printed for W. Strahan; and T. Cadell in the Strand. | MDCCLXXV.

8°, *A*² B–2B⁸, ($4 signed, $1 as '*$'(*–some* B; E, S)), 194 leaves.

Pp. A1 t., A1ᵛ blk, A2 ERRATA. (6 items), A2ᵛ blk, on B1 *1* 2–384 text dh: [Block of flowers, 13 × 80 mm] | A | JOURNEY | TO THE | WESTERN

ISLANDS | OF | SCOTLAND., rt: A JOURNEY TO THE | WESTERN
ISLANDS, &c..

Pagination: '48' on D8ᵛ is still wrong font (english (4.5 mm) instead of pica
(4.4 mm) as in *cancellandum* in 1st edn. (75.1J/1, above).

Press-figures: B8ᵛ(16)–2, C7ᵛ(30)–3, C8ᵛ(32)–4, D1ᵛ(34)–3, D8ᵛ(48)–5,
E8ᵛ(64)–5, F5ᵛ(74)–1, G1ᵛ(82)–6, G2ᵛ(84)–3, H6(107)–5, H7(109)–3,
I2ᵛ(116)–2, I5ᵛ(122)–8, K5(137)–1, K6(139)–3, L6(155)–3, L8ᵛ(160)–8,
M8(175)–6, M8ᵛ(176)–2, N1ᵛ(178)–2, N6ᵛ(188)–1, O6ᵛ(204)–5, O7ᵛ(206)–1,
P7(221)–6, P8(223)–1, Q2ᵛ(228)–6, Q8(239)–1, R6(251)–3, S5(265)–4,
S5ᵛ(266)–3, T5(281)–1, T8ᵛ(288)–8, U2ᵛ(292)–1, U8(303)–2, X3ᵛ(310)–6,
X8ᵛ(320)–5, Y7(333)–3, Y7ᵛ(334)–4, Z1ᵛ(338)–4, Z8ᵛ(352)–2, 2A2ᵛ(356)–5,
2A8(367)–2, 2B6(379)–5, 2B6ᵛ(380)–8.

Catchwords: 191 and (nad), 240 I heard (Having heard), 230 defcription
(defcrition).

Explicit: 384 FINIS.

Paper: White, laid; Medium (uncut: 9¼ × 5¾ in.); no vis. wmk.

Type: Pica (4.4 mm), leaded; white lines between paras., ornament on t.,
block of flowers as headpiece (p. 1) (as 75.1J/1, above).

References: CH 151–2; Todd, *SB* vi (1954), 247–54; *Journey* (1985); *Tinker*
1358; ESTC: t084319 (differentiated only by errata leaf).

Notes: Todd has shown that sigg. S, 2A and 2B are identical with those of
75.1J/1, above, and that p. 336 (Y8ᵛ) and the whole of Z were reimpressed from
standing type with only the addition of an asterisk before the signature in $1,
from the 1st edn. into this 2nd. There are no cancels in this edn. The work of
overrunnning to produce this edn. was begun about 7 Nov. 1774; the other
sheets which had been worked off were reset and reprinted, almost all being distinguished by an asterisk prefixed to $1 (sig. E was overlooked and some copies
of sig. B were missed, but this makes no difference, though it is to be presumed
that the unmarked sigg. represent earlier impressions). Not much attention was
paid to the reprinted text, though some moves were made towards typographical
and orthographical consistency. The errata noticed in the earlier sheets were
corrected in the text, but those ocurring in sig. S or later could not be changed
and so were retained in the errata list on A2. The 2,000 copies were recorded by
Strahan as 'Another Edit.' (L: Add. MS 48803, fo. 57ᵛ). No separate date of
publication is known and in view of its genesis it seems that it was released
without formal notice on the market, probably towards the end of January 1775.

Copies: O² (1. Gough Adds Scot. 8°. 24; 2. Gough Adds Scot. 8°. 895);

USA: CtY² (1. uncut; 2. JB: 'This Book was sent to me by the Author Dr.
Samuel Johnson to be presented to Lord Monboddo' — Tinker; *Booklist* 154),
Hyde³ (1. 'Talbot', uncut; 2. with MS: *MS Index* JoS 57; 3. Adam), IU,
[Liebert⁵ (1. uncut, 'Hopetoun' — 'Terry'; 2. 'David Garrick', 3. 'Richard
Lyster')], MB, MH ('James Boswell'), NIC, NjP³ (1. Taylor, uncut), NN-B
('This book was sent to me by its authour Dr. Samuel Johnson to be presented

to John Maclaurin, esq; advocate. James Boswell.' *Booklist* 153), NRU, PPL ('Lucy Porter'), L.R. Rothschild, Esq; TxU, [MShM]; *Can*: CaOHM² (1. B. 3668, no errata; **2**. B. 14313, 'Harriet Errol' — 'J. Errol'); *Japan*: [Kyoto]; *UK*: ABu (boards, uncut, 'James Macpherson'), BMp, BRp, BRu, C, DUu ('Routh'), DUc, E³, En, Gp², Gu, INV, JDF, LICj², Lsm, Lu (Sterling 'J. Preston'), MRu, Op, Owo, SAN (ʳDA880. H4J7), SHu.

75.1J/2b   Journey, second edition, second issue   '1775'

A | JOURNEY | TO THE | WESTERN ISLANDS | OF | SCOTLAND. | [ornam. small cameo head] | LONDON: | Printed for W. STRAHAN; and T. CADELL in the Strand. | MDCCLXXV.

    8°, *A*² (± A²) B–2B⁸, ($4 signed $1 as '*$'(–*some* B; E, S)), 194 leaves.

    Pp. A1 t., A1ᵛ blk, A2 ERRATA. (6 items), A2ᵛ blk, on B1 *1* 2–384 text dh: [Block of flowers, 13 × 80 mm] | A | JOURNEY | TO THE | WESTERN ISLANDS | OF | SCOTLAND., rt: A JOURNEY TO THE | WESTERN ISLANDS, &c..

    Pagination, Press-figures, Catchwords, and *Explicit* as in first issue (75.1J/2a, above); differing only in the cancellation of the two preliminary leaves which differ in *Paper*: White, wove; no vis. wmk., and *Type*: var. orn. on t.

    References: Courtney 122; *Journey* (1985) Appx. A, 2(b).

    Notes: The unique copy bears a contemporary inscription (not by SJ), 'Pemb: Coll: Library from the Author' (*Booklist* 155), which makes it likely that it was the copy presented to William Adams, then Master of the College, in 1784 (SJ to Cadell, *c.*17 Nov. 1784, *Letters* 1038; Hyde iv. 440–1). Its construction is peculiar, but it may be that when Cadell received the order in 1784 he had only a set of sheets to hand but no suitable copies of *A*², and so arranged to have the special title and errata leaf printed from some convenient copy of the 2nd edn. in order to perfect the gift. The work would have been easy enough: titles and similar leaves with little matter on them were commonly 'prentice work. It is the association with the implied events of 1784 that lead to the description of this version as an issue rather than as a state.

    Copies: Op.

75.1J/3a   Journey, Dublin, Williams, first issue   1775

A | JOURNEY | TO THE | Weſtern Iſlands | OF | SCOTLAND. | By Dr. SAMUEL JOHNSON. | [inverted triangle of flowers, 1.2 × 15 mm] | DUBLIN: | Printed for J. WILLIAMS, No. 21, Skinner-row. | M D C C L X X V.

    12°, A–L¹² M², ($5 signed), 134 leaves.

Pp. A1 *1* t., *2* blk, on A2 *3* 4–268 text dh: [double rule] | A | JOURNEY | TO THE | WESTERN ISLANDS | OF | SCOTLAND. | [rule], rt: A JOURNEY TO THE | WESTERN ISLANDS, &c.

Pagination: 196 as 296; *Press-figures*: none.

Catchwords: 168 [men,] who (men, who), 192 ourfelves. (To be), 193 In (COL.), 250 his (dignity;), 264 [Auchin-] leck (Auchinleck).

Explicit: 268 FINIS.

Paper: White, laid; ? Carré (uncut: 7 × 4½ in.); no vis. wmk.

Type: Sm. pica (3.8 mm), leaded; white lines between paras.

References: [? Courtney 123]; McKinlay, *RGBS* viii (1930), 149; *Adam Library* ii. 22; *Journey* (1985), 3a; Cole, *Irish Booksellers*, 100–1; ESTC: n000735.

Notes: Published 1 Feb. 1775, at 2s. 8½d., or 2s. 2d. in sheets (*Hibernian Journal*), following the text of the first London edn. (75.1J/1, above). The Dublin announcement and the manifest falsity of the London imprint (75.1J/3b, below) argue for the priority of this issue.

Copies: O (Vet. A5 f. 2957);

USA: Hyde ('H. I. R.'), [Liebert[3] (1. 'Samuel Neale')], MH, NIC, NjP, NN; *Japan*: [Kyoto[2]]; *UK*: BMp (818763), E (ABS 1.80.254, 'Elizabeth Ewing — Mrs Potts — D. Lait — Hamilton Macdonald Kings Coll Camb. 85'), En, JDF, L (1507/1483), LICj, [WLApP[2]]; *Aust*: CNL (DNS.4788 = 6864); *Eir*: Dt.

75.1J/3b   Journey, 'Pope'   1775
                  [= Dublin, Williams, second issue]

A | JOURNEY | TO THE | Weftern Iflands | OF | SCOTLAND. | By Dr. SAMUEL JOHNSON. | [inverted triangle of flowers, 11.2 × 15 mm] | LONDON: | Printed for J. POPE. | M.DCC.LXXV.

12°, A–L[12] M[2], ($5 signed), 134 leaves.

References: *Journey* (ed. Chapman, 1924), 480; McKinlay, *RGBS* viii (1930), 149; *Journey* (1985), 3b; Cole, *Irish Booksellers*, 101; ESTC: n000734.

Notes: This issue is identical with Williams's Dublin issue (prec.), save for the last three lines of the title. The leaf is not a cancel, but the imprint has been recomposed. 'J. Pope' is a fiction and is presumably a device to enable Williams the more easily to distribute his copies in Great Britain, at a time when, following Donaldson's case in 1773, the resentment of the London trade was still high against cheap Dublin and Edinburgh reprints.[1]

Copies: O (12 θ. 790);

USA: Hyde ('Henry A. Lloyd' — R.B. Adam), [Liebert = CtY], MH (*EC75 J6371. 775jc), NIC; *Can*: CaOHM (B.12460, 'James Scott 1781'); *UK*: E, LICj ('John Bickersteth'), NOW; *Eir*: Dt (uncut).

---

[1] M. Pollard, *Dublin's Trade in Books* (1989), 82.

75.1J/4   Journey, Dublin, Leathley   1775

A | JOURNEY | TO THE | WESTERN ISLANDS | OF | SCOTLAND. | BY | DOCTOR SAMUEL JOHNSON. | VOL. I [– II]. | DUBLIN: | PRINTED FOR A. LEATHLEY, J. EXSHAW, | H. SAUNDERS, D. CHAMBERLAIN, | W. SLEATER, J. POTTS, T. EWING, | W. WILSON, R. MONCRIEFFE, | AND C. JENKIN. | [short rule] | M,DCC,LXXV.
[Vol. 2] W. SLEATOR,
2 vols., 12°

I. *A*1 B–I¹², ($5 (–C4) signed; 'VOL. I.' on $1 (–BCDE)), 97 leaves.
Pp. A1 t., A1ᵛ blk, on B1 *1* 2–192 text dh: [two rows of flowers] | A | JOURNEY | TO THE | WESTERN ISLANDS | OF | SCOTLAND., rt: A JOURNEY TO THE | WESTERN ISLANDS, &c.
Pagination: no errors; *Press-figures*: none.
Catchwords: 35 [re-] quired (ruined).
Explicit: 192 END of the FIRST VOLUME.

II. *A*1 B¹² (± B1) C–I¹², ($5 (G7 as Y3) signed; 'VOL. II.' on $1), 97 leaves.
Pp. A1 t., A1ᵛ blk, on B1 *25* 26–120, 289–384 text dh: A | JOURNEY, &c., rt: A JOURNEY TO THE | WESTERN ISLANDS, &c.
Pagination: The attempt to keep the pagination and text in step with that of the London 1st edn. 8° (75.1J/1, above) failed in vol. 1 by p. 25, and resumed again in vol. 2 at F1 [= U1 of 75.1J/1] with p. 289, but continues to fail from time to time. 354 as 54.
Press-figures: none.
Catchwords: 72 I heard (Having heard), 112 I men‸ (Mention), 291 th at (that), 313 fome (diftant), 339 we (advanced), 353 aqueduct, (~;).
Explicit: 384 FINIS.

Paper: White, laid; Carré (uncut: 7 × 4½ in.); no vis. wmk.
Type: Pica (3.9 mm), leaded; white lines between paras.
References: [? Courtney 123]; *Journey* (ed. Chapman, 1924), 480–1; *Journey* (1985), 4; ESTC: t147766.
Notes: The printer made an attempt to produce a page-for-page reprint of the 1st London 8° edn. (75.1J/1, above) in a 2 vol. 12° format, but the effort failed after 2 sheets (24 pp.) in vol. 1 (cf. cwdd. in I. 25, 27–30, 76–80, 93, and 178–9), and in vol. 2 where the pagination commenced at 25 the attempt was even less successful, though a new start was again made at F1 (p. 289). This section may have been the work of another printer if the work was shared out to hasten the reprint, though the type is the same.
Published 6 Feb. 1775, at 2s. 8½d, or 2s. 2d. in sheets (*Hibernian Journal*).
Copies: O (Gough Scot. 16°. 16, 'F. Edwards' — 'H. Graham Pollard');
USA: CSmH, CtY, DLC, Hyde, IaU, ICU, [Liebert ('Margᵗ. Evans. 1775')],

MH ('Minerva Rooms, Cork'), NIC, [OrPS]; *Can*: CaOHM (B. 50481); *Japan*: [Kyoto]; *UK*: BMp (460892–3), C (Hib. 7. 775.25), E (PBS 1.76.225, 'Agnes Whitwell 1787'), JDF ('Edm^d. Cullen' — 'Violet, Baroness Leconfield'), L (1507/1488), Lj, MRu ('Edmond Malone. 1776' & nn); *Eir*: Dt; *Fr*: BN.

75.1J/5a   Journey, Dublin, Walker, first issue   1775

A | JOURNEY | TO THE | WESTERN ISLANDS | OF | SCOTLAND. | [rule] | By Dr. SAMUEL JOHNSON. | [rule] | DUBLIN: | Printed by THOMAS WALKER, at Cicero's | Head, in Dame-ftreet, oppofite Caftle- | Market Steps. | [short rule] | M.DCC.LXXV.

12°, A–L¹² M², ($5 signed), 134 leaves.

Pp. A1 *1* t., *2* blk, on A2 *3* 4–268 text dh: [double rule] | A | JOURNEY | TO THE | WESTERN ISLANDS | OF | SCOTLAND. | [rule], rt: A JOURNEY TO THE | WESTERN ISLANDS, &c., (268: 'A JOURNEY, &c.').

Pagination: no errors; *Press-figures*: none.

Catchwords: 72 [preju-] dices. (of), 168 [men,] who (men, who), 192 our-felves, (To), 193 In (COL.), 198 [ter-] tor (ror), 250 his (dignity;), 264 [Auchin-] leck (Auchinleck).

Explicit: 268 FINIS.

Paper: White, laid; Carré (uncut: 7 × 4½ in.); wmk.: Grapes + T BERNARD | FIN | 1770.

Type: Small pica (3.6 mm), leaded; white lines between paras.

References: [? Courtney 123]; *Journey* (Chapman, 1924), 480; McKinlay, *RGBS* viii (1930), 149; *Journey* (1985), 5a; ESTC: t083973.

Notes: The text is directly reprinted from Williams's Dublin edn., 75.1J/3a, above (cf. e.g. catchwords listed above).

Copies: O (Gough Scot. 16°. 22, 'Thomas Mitchell July 15th 1785');
USA: CSmH, CtY, Hyde, [Liebert ('Thomas Hodgson. 1775')], MH (imperfect), [NcCH], NIC, NRU², PPL, TxU²; *Can*: CaOHM (B. 11555, 'J. Smyth'); *UK*: BMp (460894), C, E (Lauriston Cas.), L (579. e.51), LICj; *Aust*: CNL (DNS); *Eir*: Dt (Fag. L.18.16).

75.1J/5b   Journey, Dublin, Walker, second issue   '1775'

A | JOURNEY | TO THE | WESTERN ISLANDS | OF | SCOTLAND. | [medium swelled rule] | [5 rows of flowers] | [short swelled rule] | LONDON: | Printed for W. STRAHAN; and T. CADELL | in the Strand. | MDCCLXXV.

12°, A¹²(±) B–L¹² M², ($5 signed), 134 leaves.

Pp. A1 *1* t., *2* blk, on A2 *3* 4–268 text dh: [3 rows of flowers] | A |

JOURNEY | TO THE | WESTERN ISLANDS | OF | SCOTLAND., rt: A
JOURNEY TO THE | WESTERN ISLANDS, &c.

Pagination: no errors; *Press-figures*: none.

Catchwords: 9 [The] The (The), 11 [roy-] alty‸ (~,), 72 [preju-] dices. (of),
168 [men,] who (men, who), 192 ourfelves, (To), 193 In (COL.), 198 [ter-] tor
(ror), 250 his (dignity;), 264 [Auchin-] leck (Auchinleck).

Explicit: 268 FINIS.

Paper: White, laid; Carré (uncut: 7 × 4½ in.); no vis wmk.

Type: Small pica (3.6 mm), leaded; white lines between paras. Long primer
(3.2 mm) in sig. A only, leaded.

References: [? Courtney 123]; *Journey* (1985), 5b.

Notes: A variant reissue of sheets B–M of Walker's first edn. (75.1J/5a, above)
with a substitute of the first sig. A which follows the text of either Leathley's
Dublin edn. (75.1J/4, above), or of Strahan's first London edn. (75.1J/1, above).
In view of the wording of the t. the latter is more likely. The smaller type of the
substitute sig. A was needed to compress 32 pp. of the London 8° text (sigg.
B–C) into a single 12° sheet. The absence of wmks. is a puzzle but only one
copy is known. The wording of the t. however might easily lead to the conceal-
ment of other copies reported in catalogues, but not examined.

Copies: Andrew Taylor, Esq; ('John Barrow').[1]

[1] I am deeply indebted to Mr Taylor, of Winnipeg, for allowing me to examine this remarkable
copy. John Barrow (1764–1848*, first Bt.), of Ulverston, Lancs., perhaps obtained it locally, which
may account for my failure to discover any notice of such an edn. as this by the metropolitan trade.
Some local trade with Ireland may explain such a provenance. In 1734 James Crockatt testified to
the House of Commons that, on a visit to Preston, Lancs., he had witnessed the arrival in a bookseller's shop of a bale of books from Dublin which were all (pirated) English books (Plomer, s.n.).
Liverpool and other north-western English ports, particularly Whitehaven, were obvious points of
entry for such items, cf. M. Pollard, *Dublin's Trade in Books* (1989), 77–87.

75.1J/6   Journey, new edition   1785

A | JOURNEY | TO THE | WESTERN ISLANDS | OF | SCOTLAND. |
A NEW EDITION. | LONDON: | Printed for A. STRAHAN; and T. CADELL
in the Strand. | MDCCLXXXV.

8°, *A*² B–2B⁸, ($4 signed), 194 leaves.

Pp. A1 t., A1ᵛ blk, A2 Notice correcting allusion to Macleods of Raasay
(dated 'Strand, Oct. 26, 1785.'), A2ᵛ advt. for SJ's *Works* (ed. Hawkins, and
pubd. 1787), on B1 *1* 2–384 text dh: [Block of flowers, 13 × 80 mm] | A |
JOURNEY | TO THE | WESTERN ISLANDS | OF | SCOTLAND., rt: A
JOURNEY TO THE | WESTERN ISLANDS, &c.

Pagination: no errors.

Press-figures: B8(15)–5, C3ᵛ(22)–7, D6(43)–6, E8ᵛ(64)–5, F8(79)–9,
G3ᵛ(86)–3, H8ᵛ(112)–4, I2ᵛ(116)–8, K3ᵛ(134)–8, K7(141)–3, L1ᵛ(146)–5,

M1^v(162)–8, N5(185)–5, O8^v(208)–7, P2^v(212)–7, Q1^v(226)–7, R1^v(242)–8, S7^v(270)–2, T6^v(284)–7, U2^v(292)–7, X8(319)–7, Y8(335)–9, Z6(347)–2, 2A3^v(358)–1, 2B6(379)–3.

Catchwords: 240 I heard (Having heard), 262 piper: (~;).

Explicit: 384 *FINIS*.

Paper: White, laid; Demy (uncut: 8¾ × 5½ in.); no vis. wmk.

Type: Pica (4.4 mm), leaded; white line between paras.

References: Courtney 123; *Journey* (Chapman, 1924), 480–1; *Journey* (1985), 6; ESTC: t083970.

Notes: Andrew Strahan printed 750 copies in October 1785 from the text of the 2nd London edn. (75.1J/2b, above), doubtless to catch the market generated by the popularity of JB's successful *Journal of a Tour to the Hebrides*, published 1 Oct. (Pottle no. 57). It was announced on Saturday, 12 Nov. 1785 (*Public Advertiser*). It probably also helped to recoup the outlay of Strahan and Cadell of £150 which they paid to SJ for the outstanding 2 third shares (at £75 for each third) of the copyright which SJ sold to them on 22 Jan. 1784 (*MS Handlist* 211, *MS Index*, p. 124, col. 1). As the 1st edn. printed after SJ's death it seems to have enjoyed some unwarranted textual authority among early editors.

Boswell's copy 'with MS notes' was recorded in James Bohn's *Catalogue of Ancient & Modern Books* (1840), 4109, at £1. 1s. 'from Heber's collection (i. 3623)'.[1]

Copies: O (Gough adds. Scot. 8° 379);

USA: CtY, Hyde, [Liebert], NIC^2 (2. uncut), NjP^2, NRU; *Can*: CaOHM; *Japan*: [Kyoto]; *UK*: BMp^2, BRu^2, E (NE 4. b.9), [Es], JDF (imperfect lacks Q8), LICj ('Dr. Thos Rowley, J.P.'), Oef, [WLAp], WIS. *Aust*: CNL (DNS. 4790 = 6865); *Fr*: BN.

---

[1] Bohn's same catalogue also reported as item 4110, a copy 'with numerous MS notes for a new edn. by E.H. Barber, Esq. of Thetford', uncut, at £1. 16s.

75.1J/7   Journey, new edition   1791

A | JOURNEY | TO THE | WESTERN ISLANDS | OF | SCOTLAND. | A NEW EDITION. | LONDON: | Printed for A. STRAHAN; and T. CADELL in the Strand. | MDCCXCI.

8°, *A*² B–2B⁸, ($4 signed), 194 leaves.

Pp. A1 t., A1^v blk, A2 Notice correcting allusion to Macleods of Raasay (dated 'Strand, Oct. 26, 1785.'), A2^v advt. for SJ's *Works* (ed. Hawkins, and pubd. 1787), on B1 *1* 2–384 text dh: [Block of flowers, 13 × 80 mm] | A | JOURNEY | TO THE | WESTERN ISLANDS | OF | SCOTLAND., rt: A JOURNEY TO THE | WESTERN ISLANDS, &c..

Pagination: no errors.

Press-figures: B8(15)–5, C4^v(24)–3, D6(43)–4, E7(61)–3, F6(75)–6, G6(91)–1, H6(107)–13, I7^v(126)–4, K5^v(138)–9, L7(157)–9, M5^v(170)–4, N3^v(182)–1, O8(207)–5, P1^v(210)–7, Q1^v(226)–7, R7^v(254)–5, S7^v(270)–9, T8^v(288)–13, U1^v(290)–12, X6(315)–8, Y7^v(334)–11, Z8^v(352)–13, 2A2^v(356)–2, 2B1^v(370)–12.

Catchwords: 240 I heard (Having heard), 262 piper: (~;).

Explicit: 384 THE END.

Paper: Bluish-white, laid; Demy (uncut: 8¾ × 5½ in.); no vis. wmk.

Type: Pica (4.2 mm), leaded; white line between paras.

References: Courtney 123; *Journey* (1985), 7; ESTC: t083971.

Notes: A page-for-page reprint of 1785 (75.1J/6, above). Strahan printed 750 copies for Cadell in August 1791 (L: Add. MS 48811, fo. 2^v). It sold at 6s.

A copy with the title cancelled was reported by Messrs R. & J. Balding (Edinburgh), *Catalogue* 18 (1974), 200, £21, but I have not seen that copy, and am doubtful of the observation.

Copies: O (12 θ. 471);

USA: CLU, CtY, GU, Hyde ('T. Russell Collet 1807' — 'Wm. Fred. D'Arley' — R.B. Adam), [KMK], [Liebert (uncut, 'C.S. Edgeworth')], NH, NIC, NjP, [OrPS], WiM; *Can*: CaOHM (B. 3245); *Japan*: [Kyoto³]; *UK*: BAT, BMp, BRu, C, E (k. 157d), JDF ('J.C. Sharpe' — 'Mrs [Cla]rissa Waterhouse'), Oef, Op (uncut, 'Vernon').

75.1J/8a   Journey, Edinburgh, first issue   1792

[½t] A | JOURNEY | TO THE | WESTERN ISLANDS | OF | *SCOTLAND*.

[Title] A | JOURNEY | TO THE | WESTERN ISLANDS | OF | *SCOTLAND*. | [medium double rule] | A NEW EDITION. | [medium double rule] | EDINBURGH: | PRINTED FOR *LAWRIE & SYMINGTON*, PARLIA- | MENT SQUARE. | [dash] | 1792.

12°, π² A–T⁶ U⁴, ($3 (–U3) signed), 120 leaves.

Pp. π1 ½t, π1^v blk, π2 t., π2^v blk, on A1 *1* 2–235 text dh: A | JOURNEY | TO THE | WESTERN ISLANDS | OF | *SCOTLAND*., rt: A JOURNEY TO THE | WESTERN ISLANDS, &c., *236* blk.

Pagination: no errors; *Press-figures*: none.

Catchwords: 13 country (countrymen.), 36 Auguſt₍ (~,), 72 [thus] piled (G1: thus), 73 A (At), 81 [*pied*] (Raafay), 83 [diminiſh-] ed₍ (~,), 164 know- (knowledge,), 176 te (the), 190 [more] neroſity (generoſity), 218 [Mac-] leod₍ (~,), 230 was₍ (~,), 232 ſchool₍ (~,).

Explicit: 235 FINIS.

Paper: White, wove; La. post (uncut: 7 × 4½ in.); no vis. wmk.

Type: Long primer (3.2 mm), leaded.

References: Courtney 124; McKinlay, *RGBS* viii (1930), 150; *Journey* (1985), 8a; ESTC: t083704.

Notes: The sub-heading p. 36 misprinted as '*LOUGH-NSS.*', and the cwd. 'Raafay' is pied in all copies at p. 81.

Copies: O (Gough adds. Scot. 16° 100);

USA: CtY, G. Goldberg, Esq; Hyde², IU, NIC, [OU]; *Can*: CaOHM (B. 15237); *UK*: BMp (439708, 'J. Stawell'), C, E, Eu, L (10360. e.13).

75.1J/8b   Journey, Edinburgh, second issue   1795

A | JOURNEY | TO THE | WESTERN ISLANDS | OF |*SCOTLAND.* | [medium double rule] | A NEW EDITION. | [medium double rule] | EDINBURGH: | PRINTED FOR R. GORDON N° 30 PARLIAMENT CLOSE. | [short rule] | MDCCXCV.

12°, π1 A–T⁶ U⁴, ($3 (–U3) signed), 119 leaves.

Pp. π1 t., π1ᵛ blk, on A1 *1* 2–235 text dh: A | JOURNEY | TO THE | WESTERN ISLANDS | OF | *SCOTLAND.*, rt: A JOURNEY TO THE | WESTERN ISLANDS, &c., *236* blk.

Pagination: no errors; *Press-figures*: none.

Catchwords: 13 country (countrymen.), 36 Auguſt‸ (~,), 72 [thus] piled (thus), 73 A (At), 81 [*pied*] (Raafay), 83 [diminiſh-] ed‸ (~,), 164 know- (knowledge,), 176 te (the), 190 [more] neroſity (generoſity), 218 [Mac-] leod‸ (~,), 230 was‸ (~,), 232 ſchool‸ (~,).

Explicit: 235 FINIS.

Paper: White, wove; La. post (uncut: 7 × 4½ in.); no vis. wmk.

Type: Long primer (3.2 mm), leaded.

References: McKinlay, *RGBS* viii (1930), 150; *Journey* (1985), 8b; ESTC: t188378.

Notes: The cwd. 'Raafay' is pied at p. 81. The sheets of this 1795 edn. are identical with those of 1792 (75.1J/8a, above), the only differences between the issues being the title, and the absence of any ½t from the 1795 issue.

Copies: BMp (542990, 'Samˡ Luke').

75.1J/9   Journey, second Edinburgh edition   1798

A | JOURNEY | TO THE | WESTERN ISLANDS | OF | *SCOTLAND.* | A NEW EDITION. | [short swelled rule] | EDINBURGH: | PRINTED FOR MUNDELL & SON; AND J. MUNDELL, GLASGOW. | [dash] | 1798.

12°, π² A–M¹², ($6 (K5 as K4) signed), 146 leaves.

Pp. π1 t., π1ᵛ blk, π2 Notice respecting Macleods of Raasay, π2ᵛ blk, on A1 *1* 2–288 text dh: [parallel rule] | A | JOURNEY | TO THE | WESTERN ISLANDS | OF | *SCOTLAND.* | [short swelled rule], rt: A JOURNEY TO

THE | WESTERN ISLANDS, &c. (288: JOURNEY TO THE WESTERN ISLANDS.).

Pagination: no errors.

Press-figures: A12(23)–2, A12ᵛ(24)–2, B7(37)–4, B12(47)–3, C8ᵛ(64)–3, C11ᵛ(70)–4, D12(95)–3, D12ᵛ(96)–2, E11ᵛ(118)–4, E12ᵛ(120)–3, F1ᵛ(122)–2, F12ᵛ(144)–3, G11(165)–3, G12(167)–4, H11(189)–3, I7(205)–2, I12(215)–4, K12(239)–3, K12ᵛ(240)–2, L12(263)–2, L12ᵛ(264)–3, M1ᵛ(266)–3, M2ᵛ(268)–2.

Catchwords: none.

Explicit: 288 THE END.

Paper: Cream, wove; Royal (uncut: 8⅜ × 5⅛ in.); wmk.: '1795'.

Type: Pica (4.0 mm), leaded; white lines between paras.

References: Courtney 124; McKinlay, *RGBS* viii (1930), 150; *Journey* (1985), 9; ESTC: t083705.

Notes: This seems to be a reprint from the London, 1791 ed (75.1J/7, above). In the MS inventory of William Creech's 'Quire Stock & Copyrights, 14 Jan. 1815' (Ep: MS. qYZ. 325. C91), bundle 303 is reported as containing '4 Johnson's Journey, royal 12° Edin. 1798'. ESTC reports an engr. map in some copies but it is an arbitrary insertion.

Copies: O (Gough adds. Scot. 8° 894, 'C. J. H[indle]');

USA: Hyde ('Condover Hall' — 'Reginald Cholmondeley' — R.B. Adam), MH (uncut, 'H. M[urdock]'), NIC, NNC; *Can*: CaOHM; *UK*: BMp, E (Hall 277.d), En (boards, uncut), HLu, L (10369. d.11), LICj.

75.1J/10   Journey, Alnwick   1800

A | JOURNEY | TO THE | WESTERN ISLANDS | OF | [hollow] *SCOTLAND*. | [short parallel rule] | A NEW EDITION. | [short total rule] | [vignette: Traveller with stick and pack passing milestone] | ALNWICK: | *PRINTED BY J. CATNACH*, | FOR J. WALLIS, 46, PATERNOSTER-ROW, LONDON. | 1800. | [short rule] | Price 3s. in boards.

12°, A–2A⁶, ($3 (P3 as P2) signed), 144 leaves.

Pp. A1 *1* t., *2* blk, *3* 4–288 text dh: A | JOURNEY | TO THE | *WEST-ERN ISLANDS* | OF | SCOTLAND., rt: A JOURNEY TO THE | WEST-ERN ISLANDS, &c., (13: WESTERN ISLANDS, &c.; 22: A JOURN‸ TO THE . . .; 46, 50, 70, 72: AJOURNEY TO THE . . .; 124, 142, 154: A JOUNEY TO THE . . .; 288: A JOURNEY TO THE‸).

Pagination: 104 has '1' slipt, 264 as 242.

Press-figures: none; *Catchwords*: none.

Explicit: 288 FINIS | tp. traveller on packhorse.

Paper: White, wove; Demy (uncut: 7½ × 4½ in.); wmk.: WHATMAN | 1799

Type: Sm. pica (3.8 mm); woodcut vign. ornn. on t. and p. 288 are in the style of Bewick.

References: Courtney 124; CC. Burman (1896) 19; *Journey* (1985), 10; ESTC: t083708.

Notes: The vignette woodcuts associate this edn. with the printer of *Rambler*, Montrose, 1800 (50.3R/36, above), and the Alnwick *Idler*, also 1800 (58.4Id/16, above), of which the former states it is printed by David Buchanan, of Montrose, and the latter that it is the work of J. Catnach, of Alnwick. Burman attributes the woodcuts to Bewick.[1]

There is no correction notice referring to the Macleods of Raasay in this edn.

Copies: O (Gough adds. Scot. 16° 99, 'Hen^y Donkin');

USA: G. Goldberg, Esq; Hyde (uncut, 'Edmund Pitts Hopper'), [Liebert], MH, NIC, NRU; *Can*: CaOHM; *UK*: BMp, C (8700 a.177), E² (1. NE 4.a.15; 2. ABS 1.80.4, uncut), L (10370. aa.5), LICj, NCp.

---

[1] *An Account of the Art of Typography, as practised in Alnwick from 1781 to 1815*, by C.C. Burman (1896), 22: 'two woodcuts by Bewick, one of which is given as a head-piece to the preface of Miss Julia Boyd's *Bewick Gleanings*'.

75.1J/11   Journey, Edinburgh   1806

A | JOURNEY | TO THE | WESTERN ISLANDS | OF | *SCOTLAND.* | [short parallel rule] | BY SAMUEL JOHNSON, LL.D. | [short total rule] | A NEW EDITION. | EDINBURGH: | PRINTED FOR BELL & BRADFUTE, JAMES M'CLEISH, AND | WILLIAM BLACKWOOD; GILBERT & HODGES, DUBLIN; AND S. CAMPBELL | NEW YORK. | 1806.

12°, πA² A–R⁶ S², ($3 (πA2 as A3) only, signed; $6 numbered 1–7), 106 leaves. Pp. πA1 t., πA1ᵛ coloph: 'G. CAW, Printer, | Edinburgh.', πA2 Contents dh: CONTENTS. | [short parallel rule], πA2ᵛ blk, on A1 *1* 2–207 text dh: [double rule] | A | JOURNEY | TO | *THE WESTERN ISLANDS* | OF | SCOTLAND. | [short diamond rule], rt: A JOURNEY TO THE | WESTERN ISLANDS, &c., 207 coloph: 'CAW, Printer.', *208* blk.

Pagination: no errors.

Press-figures: $6ᵛ numbered 1–7, but prob. not press-figures.

Catchwords: none.

Explicit: 207 FINIS.

Paper: White, wove; ? foolscap (uncut: 5⅔ × 3¼ in.); wmk.: '1801 | 2' and 'C S | 1804'.

Type: Bourgeois (3.1 mm).

References: *Journey* (1985), 11.

Notes: This is a separate issue of vol. 9 from the Edinburgh edn. of SJ's *Works*, 15 vols. 1806 (87.3W/7, below), in which the text of the *Journey* occupied pp.

133–339; the pages have been re-signed and repaginated for this issue, and the original first leaf (ᵖA1) and final leaf (S3, blk), are removed.

Bell & Bradfute, of Edinburgh, received an order for books from Alexander Angus & Son, of Aberdeen, on 8 November 1808, including, '2 Johnson's Journey thro' Scotland 18ᵐᵒ new ed. qrs. @ 8d.'¹

The reference to the alleged superiority of the Macleods of Dunvegan over the Macleods of Raasay is omitted (p. 72).

Copies: O (Vet. A6 f.133);

UK: JDF ('Caroline Davy' — 'Lucy Catherine Davy Ross May 26ᵗʰ: 79').

¹ E: MS Dep. 317, Box 5. This edn. was still being advertised as 'Lately published' on the final leaf of vol. 2 of SJ's *Lives of the Poets*, 2 vols. 8°, 1821 'Rivington' &c. (79.4LP/33, below), at 4s. 6d.

75.1J/12   Journey, first American edition   1810

A | JOURNEY | TO THE | WESTERN ISLANDS | OF | SCOTLAND. | BY SAMUEL JOHNSON, LL.D. | FIRST AMERICAN EDITION. | Published by Philip H. Nicklin, and Co. Baltimore; Farrand, | Mallory, and Co. Boston; J. Green, Albany; E. Earle, | and B.B. Hopkins and Co. Philadelphia. | Fry and Kammerer, Printers. | 1810.

12°, π² A–Z⁶ 2A⁴, ($1,3 ($3 as $2) signed), 144 leaves.

Pp. π1 t., π1ᵛ blk, π2 Correction notice (Macleods of Raasay), π2ᵛ blk, on A1 *1* 2–284 text dh: A | JOURNEY | TO THE | WESTERN ISLANDS OF SCOTLAND., rt: A JOURNEY TO THE | WESTERN ISLANDS. (284: 'A JOURNEY TO THE, &c.').

Pagination: no errors; *Press-figures*: none; *Catchwords*: none.

Explicit: 284 THE END.

Paper: Rough, cream, wove (uncut: 8¼ × 5⅛ in.), no vis. wmk.

Type: Pica (3.8 mm), leaded.

References: Evans 31692; Courtney 124 ('Philadelphia'), NUC reports MWA copy as 'Philadelphia'; *Tinker* 1359; S&S: 20456 [MMeT, MWA, MWHi].

Notes: The variety of names in the imprint has led to confusion over the origin of this edn., which was certainly printed in Philadelphia, though the first named publishers were in Baltimore, Md. The imprint reflects the varied modes of American distribution at this period, cf *Rasselas* (59.4R/62a, above).

Copies: O (Gough adds. Scot. 8° 1054, uncut);

USA: CSmH, CtY (Tinker), DLC, Hyde² (1. 'R. Fullerton' — R. B. Adam; 2. 'C. I. Danforth'), InU, IU, [Liebert], MH, MWA, NcD, NIC, NjP, NN, NRU (imperfect, lacks A5), PPL, L.R. Rothschild, Esq; WiM [KyLx, MiU-C, OClWHi, PV]; *UK*: BMp, E, L (1508/1551).

75.1J/13 Journey, Edinburgh 1811

A | JOURNEY | TO THE | *WESTERN ISLANDS* | OF | SCOTLAND. | [double rule] | BY SAMUEL JOHNSON, LL.D. | [double rule] | A NEW EDITION. | [medium twisted rule] | [**Black letter**] **Edinburgh:** | PRINTED FOR J. OGLE; M. OGLE, GLASGOW; R. OGLE, AND | T. HAMILTON, LONDON; AND J. JOHNSTON, DUBLIN, | By Thomas Turnbull. | [short rule] | 1811.

12°, A–H¹² (H11,12 blk), ($1 (–A1, +A2) signed), 96 leaves.

Pp. A1 *1* t., *2* blk, on A2 *3* 4–186 text, 186 coloph: '*Thomas Turnbull, Printer, Edinburgh*.' 187–8 2 pp. advts. for books published by J. Ogle, *189–92* (H11–12) blk.

Pagination: no errors.

Press-figures: A12(23)–3, A12ᵛ(24)–1, B2(27)–2, B12(47)–1, B12ᵛ(48)–2, C12(71)–1, C12ᵛ(72)–2, D2(75)–2, D12(95)–2, D12ᵛ(96)–3, E2(99)–2, E12(119)–3, E12ᵛ(120)–1, F2(123)–2, F5(129)–5, F12(143)–2, F12ᵛ(144)–1, G2(147)–2, G11ᵛ(166)–3, G12ᵛ(168)–2, H2(171)–2.

Catchwords: none.

Explicit: 186 orn. tp. 'FINIS'.

Paper: White, wove; demy (uncut: 7½ × 4½ in.); wmk.: 'R T & Co | 1810'.

Type: Sm. pica (3.5 mm); modern face.

References: Courtney 124; McKinlay, *RGBS* viii (1930), 150; *Journey* (1985), 13.

Notes: The distribution of press-figures is unusual in that the third figure does not relate to the inner strip of a 12° by cutting. Ogle's advts. include 'Johnson's Works, 15 vols. royal 18mo.', '——Dictionary, 8vo.', and '—— —— 4 in miniature, 18mo.'

Copies: O (203 g. 210);

USA: Hyde (uncut, 'Launcelot Jefferson' — 'Wm. Dickinson' — R.B. Adam), ICN, [NcU], NIC (boards uncut, 'Charles Lamb'), [OPS]; *Japan*: [Kyoto³]; *UK*: BMp, E², En, Gp, JDF (uncut, blue boards, 'W. M. Calder 1844'), NCp, STA, WIS.

[**75.1J/14** Journal (with McNicol's Remarks) 1812

An edition dated '1812' with McNicol's *Remarks*, reported in W.J. Couper's *Dr Johnson in the Hebrides* (priv. ptd. [offprint from the *Celtic Monthly*], Glasgow, 1916), appears to be an error for the 1817 or 1822 edition, 75.1J/19a or J/19b, below].[1]

---

[1] In *Johnsonian News Letter*, vi. 5 (Dec. 1946), 3, R. A. Hertzberg reported an edition of SJ's 'Western Scotland' published in Kilmarnock as a school text. No such edition has been traced.

75.1J/15   Journey, New York   1812

A TOUR | TO THE | WESTERN ISLANDS, | WITH | ESSAYS | ON | *A VARIETY OF SUBJECTS.* | [short orn. rule] | BY SAMUEL JOHNSON, LL.D. | [short orn. rule]. | *NEW-YORK:* | PUBLISHED BY WILLIAM DURRELL. | [short diamond rule] | 1812.

12° A–P¹² Q⁴ ($1,5 signed; 'VOL. VIII.' on $1), 184 leaves.

Pp. *1* 2–373 text (*190* 191–373 text of *Journey*), 373 coloph: 'JANE AITKEN, PRINTER | No. 71, N. Third-street, Philadelphia.', *374* blk.

Pagination: no errors; *Press-figures*: none; *Catchwords*: none.

Explicit: 373 END OF THE EIGHTH VOLUME.

Paper: White, laid; Demy (uncut: 7½ × 4½ in.); no vis. wmk.

Type: unrecorded, but see *Works*, below.

References: Courtney 124; *Journey* (1985), 14

Notes: A separate issue of vol. 8, from SJ's *Works* (New York, &c.), 1809, (87.3W/10, below). This is the first edn. to give JB's title to SJ's work.

Copies: DLC; *USA*: NN.

[75.1J/16]   Journey, 'sixth' edition, Cadell and Davies   1813

A 'Sixth edition' said to be published by Cadell and Davies, 1813 has not been traced, and is probably a ghost. The first edn. published by that partnership appeared in 1816, 75.1J/17, below. *Journey* (1985), 15.]

75.1J/17   Journey, Cadell and Davies   1816

A | JOURNEY | TO THE | WESTERN ISLANDS | OF | *SCOTLAND.* | A NEW EDITION. | [short swelled rule] | LONDON: | PRINTED FOR T. CADELL AND W. DAVIES, | IN THE STRAND. | 1816.

8°, A⁴ (–A4) B–N⁸ O⁴ P², ($4 (–A1, O3,4, P2) signed), 105 leaves.

Pp. A1 t., A1ᵛ coloph: 'Printed by A. Strahan, | New-Street-Square, London', on A2 *1* 2–208 text dh: A | JOURNEY | TO THE WESTERN ISLANDS | OF | SCOTLAND. | [medium swelled rule], rt: A JOURNEY TO THE | WESTERN ISLANDS, &c., 208 coloph. (as A1ᵛ, above).

Pagination: no errors.

Press-figures: C1ᵛ(22)–4, D7(49)–1, E6ᵛ(64)–12, F2ᵛ(72)–11, G8ᵛ(100)–6, H8ᵛ(116)–10, I5(125)–12, K4ᵛ(140)–1, L8ᵛ(164)–2, M2ᵛ(168)–5, N6(191)–5, O1ᵛ(198)–3, P2(207)–1.

Catchwords: none.

Explicit: 208 THE END.

Paper: White, wove; demy (uncut: 8¼ × 5½ in.); no vis. wmk.

Type: Pica (4.2 mm).

References: *Journey* (1985), 17.

Notes: 500 copies of vol. 8, pp. 205–412, overrun by Strahan from SJ's *Works*, 8° 12 vols. 1816 (87.3W/13, below), printed in August 1816 (L: Add. MS 48816, fo. 147), and published at 6s. in boards 6 Sept. 1816 (*Morning Chronicle*). The statement attributing superiority to the Macleods of Dunvegan over the Macleods of Raasay, is omitted (p. 72).

Copies: E (Hall 193 c);

USA: CtY, Hyde², NIC (uncut, grey boards), NRU, [OClRC]; *Japan*: [Kyoto]; *UK*: Eu (SB. 82463), JDF ('James Dale 1879' — 'Alexander Paterson from James Dale, Abdn, 24th Aug. 1888'), LICj ('Frederick Symonds, Lichfield, 1823').

75.1J/18   Journey, Cadell and Davies   1816

A | JOURNEY | TO THE | Western Islands | OF | SCOTLAND: | BY | Samuel Johnson, LL.D. | [medium parallel rule] | A NEW EDITION. | [medium parallel rule] | LONDON: | PRINTED BY | *Luke Hansard & Sons, near Lincoln's-Inn Fields,* | FOR | T. CADELL AND W. DAVIES, IN THE STRAND. | [short rule] | 1816.

12°, *A*² B–Q⁶ R⁴ (R4 blk), ($3 (–R3) signed), 96 leaves.

Pp. A1 t., A1ᵛ blk, A2 Contents, A2ᵛ blk, on B1 *1* ½t: A | JOURNEY | TO THE | WESTERN ISLANDS | OF | *SCOTLAND:* | 1773., *2* blk, *3* 4–186 text dh: A | JOURNEY | TO THE | WESTERN ISLANDS | OF | SCOTLAND: | [short parallel rule]., ht: A JOURNEY TO THE | WESTERN ISLANDS. (186: A JOURNEY, &c.'), 186 coloph: 'Luke Hansard & Sons, Printers, near Lincoln's-Inn Fields, London.'

Pagination: 141 as 142.

Press-figures: C5ᵛ(22)–*n*, G5ᵛ(70)–*n*, Q6ᵛ(180)–*n*.

Catchwords: none.

Explicit: 186 FINIS.

Paper: White, wove; La. post (uncut: 7 × 4½ in.); no vis. wmk.

Type: Bourgeois (3.2 mm).

References: Courtney 124; *Journey* (1985), 18.

Notes: This is a separate issue of the sheets from *Works*, 12 vol., 1816, 12°, viii, pp. 184–366, and was advertised at 4s. on 6 Sept. 1816 (*Morning Chronicle*). The statement attributing superiority to the Macleods of Dunvegan over the Macleods of Raasay is omitted (p. 66).

Copies: O² (1. Gough adds. Scot. 16° 124, boards, uncut; 2. Gough Adds Scot. 16° 122); *UK*: BMp (383680), Eu (SB. 82463), NCu.

[75.1J/18/Add1   Journey, Philadelphia   1817

No copy of an edition allegedly published in Philadelphia in 1817 has been traced, and it is presumed to be a ghost.]

75.1J/19a   Journey, Glasgow (with McNicol's Remarks),   1817
              first impression

[½t] A | JOURNEY | TO THE | WESTERN ISLANDS | OF | [BL] SCOTLAND. | [rule] | BY SAMUEL JOHNSON, LL.D. | FIRST PUBLISHED IN 1774. [!]

[Title] First issue (a) A | JOURNEY | TO THE | WESTERN ISLANDS | OF | [hollow & shaded] SCOTLAND. | BY SAMUEL JOHNSON, LL.D. | WITH | [Black Letter] Remarks | BY THE REV. DONALD M'NICOL, A.M. | OF LISMORE, ARGYLESHIRE. | [medium double rule] | EMBELLISHED WITH AN ELEGANT PORTRAIT OF JOHNSON. | [medium double rule] | GLASGOW: | [BL] Printed at the Stanhope Press, | BY AND FOR R. CHAPMAN. | Sold by A. & J. M. Duncan, Brash & Reid, J. Smith & Son, W. Turnbull, | D. Niven & Co., M. Ogle, J. Steven, T. Ogilvie, J. Wylie & Co., J. Jones, and J. Sawers. | Also by P. Hill & Co., and A. Constable & Co., Edinburgh. | [medium rule] | 1817.

8°, π⁴ A–3R⁴, ($2 signed), 256 leaves.

Pp. π1 ½t, π1ᵛ blk, π2 *i* t., *ii* blk + Engr. port. of SJ (Engr. by E. Mitchell, after Reynolds, 'Published August 1817, by R. Chapman, Glasgow.') + π3 *iii–iv* Advertisement ('*Glasgow, August,* 1817.'), *v–vi* Contents, on A1 *1* 2–255 text of *Journey* dh: A | JOURNEY | TO THE | [hollow shaded type] WESTERN ISLANDS | OF | SCOTLAND, | [short parallel rule], rt: JOURNEY TO THE | WESTERN ISLANDS., *256* blk, on 2K1 *257* ½t Remarks &c., *258* blk, *259–60* Advertisement, *261* 262–504 text McNicol's *Remarks*, 504 coloph: '[rule] | GLASGOW: [BL] printed by and for R. Chapman. MDCCCXVII.'

Pagination: no errors; *Press-figures*: none; *Catchwords*: none.

Explicit: 504 Orn. tp. with banner: 'FINIS.'

Paper: White, wove; medium (uncut: 9 × 5¼ in.); wmk.: 'C | 1816 | W Balston'. (in π⁴: '1814').

Type: Pica (4.1 mm), leaded; headings in **Black Letter**.

References: Courtney 121; McKinlay, *RGBS* viii (1930), 150; *Journey* (1985), 19a.

Notes: The erroneous reference to the Macleods of Raasay is omitted from this edn. (p. 88). The printed paper spine label reads: JOHNSON'S | *Tour to the Hebrides* | WITH | [BL] **Remarks** | BY | M'NICOL. | [short wavy rule] | PRICE 12s. EXTRA BOARDS.

Copies: O (Gough adds. Scot. 4° 46, uncut);

USA: Hyde² (**2**. uncut), ICN, MH, NIC (uncut), NjP, NN, NRU; *UK*: ABu, BMp, DUu, E, En, Eu ('Mackinnon'), Gp³, Gu², L, LICj (boards, uncut; pres. G.B. Hill, 1901), MRc, MRu, Oef.

75.1J/19b   Journey, Glasgow (with McNicol's   1822
Remarks), second impression

[½t] A | JOURNEY | TO THE | WESTERN ISLANDS | OF | [BL] SCOTLAND. | [rule] | BY SAMUEL JOHNSON, LL.D. | FIRST PUBLISHED IN 1774. [!]

[Title] (i) [First state] A | JOURNEY | TO THE | WESTERN ISLANDS | OF | [hollow & shaded] SCOTLAND. | BY SAMUEL JOHNSON, LL.D. | WITH | [BL] Remarks | BY THE REV. DONALD M'NICOL, A.M. | OF LISMORE, ARGYLLSHIRE. | [medium double rule] | EMBELLISHED WITH AN ELEGANT PORTRAIT OF JOHNSON. | [medium double rule] | LONDON: | PRINTED FOR H. B. FINLAY, | No. 32, Bishopgate-street Within, near the City of London Tavern; | Lackington & Co. Finsbury Square; Ogles & Duncan, Paternoster-row; Cowie & Co. | Poultry; and Simpkin & Marshall, Stationers' Court. | [short wavy rule] | 1822

(ii) [Second state] . . . (as prec.) LONDON: | PRINTED BY H. FINLAY, N°. 52, Bishop-gate-street Within, . . . Stationers' Court. | [short wavy rule] | 1822.

8°, π⁴ (−π1,2 + ²π1.2) A–3R⁴, ($2 signed), 256 leaves.

Pp. (as first state, 75.1J/19a, above): π1 ½t, π1ᵛ blk, π2 *i* t., *ii* blk, Engr. port. of SJ (Engr. by E. Mitchell, after Reynolds, 'Published August 1817, by R. Chapman, Glasgow.') inserted + π3 *iii*–*iv* Advertisement ('*Glasgow, August, 1817.*'), *v*–*vi* Contents, on A1 *1* 2–255 text of *Journey, 256* blk, on R1 *257* ½t, *258* blk, *259–60* Advertisement, *261* 262–504 text McNicol's *Remarks*.

Pagination, and *Explicit* 504, as in prec. 75.1J/19a first state.

Paper: White, wove; medium (uncut: 9 × 5¼ in.); wmk.: 'C | [*variously dated*] 1814 / 1815 / 1816 | W Balston'; cancel t. '1820'.

Type: Pica (4.1 mm), leaded; headings in **Black Letter**.

References: *Journey* (1985), 19b.

Notes: The varying dates in the watermarks show that these 1822 versions are re-impressions rather than reissues.

Copies: Eu (CR. 5. 4. 24);

USA: Hyde (**1**. uncut), [ISU]; *UK*: BMp, Gu, O (Vet. A6 e. 1437), STA.

75.1J/20   Journey, Alnwick   1819

A separate edition of the *Journey*, published by J. Graham, in Alnwick, is noticed by P. Burman in his *An Account of the Art of Typography as Practised in*

Alnwick from 1748 to 1900 (Edinburgh, 1918), 26 and 28. No copy has been seen. If it existed it was probably a separate issue of the sheets of the *Journey* from the Alnwick edn. of SJ's *Works*, 10 vols. 1816 (87.3W/15, below), which was also issued with new tt. in London in 1818. If this is so then it was probably constituted as:

(a) 12°, *A*² B–O⁶ P1–3, ($3 signed), [?] + 81 leaves.

Pp. A1 t., A2 *iii*–iv Contents, on B1 *1* 2–154 text *Journey*.

or as a simple separate issue of vol. ix, as:

(b) 12°, *A*² (± A1) B–2K⁶ 2L⁴ ($3 (–2L3) signed), 198 leaves.

Pp. A1 t., A2 *iii*–iv Contents, on B1 *1* 2–154 text of *Journey, 155* 156–382 text of *Political Essays*, &c., 382 coloph: END OF VOLUME NINTH.

Copy: USA: [? OKentU]. A copy of (b) was K. Spelman (York), *Cat*. 18 (1991), 402, £60, with 'Political Essays, iv + 382 pp.', confirming the identification with *Works* (Alnwick) 1816 and giving the imprint as 'Alnwick. J. Graham. 1819', but mistakenly describing it as '8vo'.[1]

---

[1] I am indebted to Mr David L. Vander Meulen, of the University of Virginia, for drawing this item to my attention. Unhappily I have not traced its present whereabouts.

75.1J/21   Journey, Edinburgh   1819

A | JOURNEY | TO THE | WESTERN ISLANDS | OF | SCOTLAND. | [rule] | BY SAMUEL JOHNSON, LL.D. | [rule] | *A NEW EDITION.* | [short swelled rule] | EDINBURGH: | PRINTED FOR STIRLING & SLADE, | AND | OGLE, ALLARDYCE & THOMSON. | [short rule] | 1819.

12°, π1 A–Q⁶, ($3 (–F2, O2) signed), 97 leaves.

Pp. π1 t., π1ᵛ coloph: 'W. FALCONER, PRINTER, | GLASGOW.', on A1 *i*–ii, *3* 4–192 text

Pagination: no errors; *Press-figures*: none; *Catchwords*: none.

Explicit: 192 FINIS.

Paper: White, wove; La. post (uncut: 7 × 4½ in.); no vis. wmk.

Type: Small pica (3.5 mm), unleaded.

References: Courtney 125; McKinlay, *RGBS* viii (1930), 150; *Journey* (1985), 20.

Copies: E; USA: [? OKentU]; UK: LICj (uncut).

75.1J/22   Journey (and Political Tracts)   1824

(a) A | [BL] JOURNEY | TO THE | WESTERN ISLANDS | OF | [BL] Scotland; | AND | POLITICAL TRACTS. | [short swelled rule] | BY | DR. SAMUEL JOHNSON. | [double rule] | LONDON: | W. BAYNES AND SON, PATERNOSTER-ROW. | [short rule] | 1824.

(b) A Journey . . . With Observations on his Life by Mr. Boswell. London: W. Baynes and Son, . . . J. Bumpus . . . 1824

12°, *A*1 B–2N⁶ 2O², ($3 signed; 'VOL. XII.' on $1), 213 leaves.

Pp. A1 t., A1ᵛ, on B1 *1* 2–216 text of *Political Tracts*, 217–424 text of *Journey*, 424 coloph: 'D. CARTWRIGHT, PRINTER, BARTHOLOMEW CLOSE.'

Pagination: no errors; *Press-figures*: none; *Catchwords*: none.

Explicit: 424 THE END.

Paper: White, laid; Large post (uncut: 6¾ × 4¼ in.); no vis. wmk.

Type: Long primer (3.2 mm), unleaded.

References: Courtney 125; *Journey* (1985), 22.

Notes: A separate issue with cancelled t. of vol. 12 from SJ's *Works*, 12 vols. 12°, 1824 (87.3W/20, below). JDF copy of (a) has ptd. spine label: [parallel rule] | A | JOURNEY | TO THE | WESTERN ISLANDS | OF | SCOTLAND; | AND | POLITICAL TRACTS. | [dash] | BY | DR. JOHNSON. | [total rule]).

Copies: O (Vet. A6 e. 1436);

USA: [NRU]; *UK*: C (Acton d.25.614), E, JDF (a), LICj (a).

75.1J/23   Journey, Glasgow   1825

A | JOURNEY | TO THE | WESTERN ISLANDS | OF | SCOTLAND. | BY SAMUEL JOHNSON, L.L.D. | WITH | [BL] **Remarks** | BY THE REV. DONALD M'NICOL, A.M. | OF LISMORE, ARGYLESHIRE. | GLASGOW:– RICHARD GRIFFIN & CO. | [short rule] | MDCCCXXV.

(b) **var**: . . . ARGYLESHIRE. | LONDON: PRINTED FOR T. TEGG, CHEAPSIDE; AND R. GRIFFIN & CO. GLASGOW. | [short rule] | MDCCCXXV.

12°, A⁴ B–2H⁶, ($3 (–T3) signed), 184 leaves.

Pp. Engr. port. SJ front + on A1 *i* t., *ii* coloph: 'PRINTED BY JAMES STARKE.', *iii* iv–vi OBSERVATIONS | ON THE | LIFE OF DR. JOHNSON. | [dash], rt: OBSERVATIONS ON | THE LIFE OF DR. JOHNSON., *vii* CONTENTS., *viii* blk, on B1 *1* 2–208 text *Journey*, on T3 *209–13* 214–359 text *Remarks*, *359* coloph: [medium rule] | JAMES STARKE, PRINTER, GLASGOW., *360* Advts. as 'Just published for R. GRIFFIN & Co. Chemical Recreations.' &c.

Pagination: vi as vii.

Press-figures: none; *Catchwords*: none.

Explicit: 208 END OF THE JOURNEY., 359 THE END.

Paper: White, wove; Sm. post (uncut: 6⅓ × 3¾ in.); no vis. wmk.

Type: Bourgeois (3.1 mm), leaded (0.2 mm).

Plate: Port. of SJ, 'Kerr Sc. 30 Trongate. JOHNSON | GLASGOW, | Published by Richard Griffin & Co. 1825.'

References: Courtney 121 (erroneously '1852' for 1825); McKinlay, *RGBS* viii (1930), 150; *Journey* (1985), 23.

Notes: DLC report a copy of var. (**b**), which is vindicated by a copy at LICj.

Copies: E; *USA*: CtY, DLC; *UK*: ABu (*82463.Jo.3), LICj², [WLAp].

75.1J/24   Journey, London and Glasgow   1876

[½t] A JOURNEY | TO THE | WESTERN ISLANDS.

[Title] A JOURNEY | TO THE | WESTERN ISLANDS | OF | SCOTLAND | *In 1773.* | BY | SAMUEL JOHNSON, LL.D. | LONDON : HAMILTON, ADAMS, & CO. | GLASGOW: THOMAS D. MORISON. | 1876.

8°, *A*⁴ B–K⁸ (A1 blk), ($1 signed), 76 leaves.

Pp. A1 blk, A2 ½t, A2ᵛ blk, A3 t., A3ᵛ blk, A4 Contents, A4ᵛ blk, on B1 *1* 2–144 text dh: A JOURNEY | TO THE | WESTERN ISLANDS. | [short rule], rt: JOURNEY TO THE | WESTERN ISLANDS., 144 coloph: 'GLASGOW: AIRD AND COGHILL, PRINTERS.'

Explicit: 144 THE END.

Paper: Cream, wove; crown (uncut: 7⅝ × 5 in.); no vis. wmk.

Type: Bourgeois (3.0 mm).

References: Courtney 125; McKinlay, *RGBS* viii (1930), 150.

Notes: The text follows 75.1J/2, above. A paper spine label on the orig. issue in full green fine-ribbed cloth, reads: [within double rules] Journey | to the | Western | Islands. | [short rule] | Johnson.

Copies: O (203 f. 532);

USA: Hyde (uncut, 'James Moir' — 'B.C. F[orbes]'); *UK*: AWn, BMp, C, DUNu ('William John Robertson'), E, En, Eu², JDF, SAN (ˢPR3523. E76).

75.1J/25a   Journey, Cassell's edition   1886

[½t] A JOURNEY TO THE | WESTERN ISLANDS OF SCOTLAND.

[Title] CASSELL's NATIONAL LIBRARY. | [medium rule] | A | JOURNEY | TO THE | Wᴇsᴛᴇʀɴ Isʟᴀɴᴅs | OF | SCOTLAND. | BY | SAMUEL JOHNSON, LL.D. | [device] | CASSELL & COMPANY, LIMITED: | *LONDON, PARIS, NEW YORK & MELBOURNE.* | 1886

16s, *A*¹⁶ B–F¹⁶, ($1 as '$ 51', signed), 96 leaves.

Pp. *1* ½t, *2* List of 51 vols. in 'National Library' weekly series, *3* t., *4* blk, *5* 6–8 Introduction by H[enry]. M[orley]., *9* 10–192 text dh: A JOURNEY TO THE | WESTERN ISLANDS OF SCOTLAND. | [short ornam. rule], 192 coloph: 'Printed by Cassell & Company, Limited, La Belle Sauvage, London, E.C.'

Explicit: none.

Paper: White, wove; ? Demy (uncut: 5½ × 4⅜ in.); no vis. wmk.
Type: Brevier (2.7 mm).
References: Courtney 125.
Notes: Issued as vol. 51 in the 'National Library' series, (**a**) in blue cloth covers ptd. in black with gilt titling, at 6s., and (**b**) ptd. blue paper covers (with advts. on endpp.), at 3d.
  Copies: O (Gough adds. Orkney 16° 2, access. stamp: '14 FEB. 87');
  USA: DLC, MH, [OrSaW]; *UK*: C (access. stamp: '17 Jan. 1887').

75.1J/25b   Journey, Cassell's edition, New York   1887

. . . New York: Cassell and Co. 1887
  Copies: ViU.

75.1J/25c   Journey, Cassell's edition, London   [?1887]

. . . with Carl Moritz's *Travels* (vol. 47 in the 'National Library' series).
  Copies: E (Hall 244.g), JDF.

75.1J/25d   Journey, Cassell's National Library   1889

[as 75.1J/25a, above] . . . SCOTLAND. | . . . LIMITED: | . . . 1889
  P. 2 blk (no advts); coloph: as 75.1J/25a, + '30.889'], and 4pp. advts.
  Copies: ABu, AWn, En (F3/a5, turquoise cloth, blind titling and gilt spine 'A Journey to the Hebrides').

75.1J/25e   Journey, Cassell's edition,   1892
London & New York

Not examined.
  Copies: IU.

75.1J/26 Journey, University Tutorial Series, ed. Thomas [1904]

[BL] **The University Tutorial Series** | Johnson: | A | Journey to the Western | Islands of Scotland. | Edited by E. J. Thomas. M.A. St. Andrews, B.A. Lond., | Editor of Shakespeare, "Much Ado About Nothing." | [device] | London : W. B. Clive, | [BL] **University Tutorial Press Ltd.** | (*University Correspondence College Press*), | 157 Drury Lane, W. C.
  8s, *1*⁸ 2–11⁸ 12⁴, ($1 signed), 92 leaves.

Pp. *1* ½t, *2* advts. 'English Classics', *3* t., *4* blk, *5* Contents, *6* blk, *7* 8–15 Introduction, *16* blk, *17* 18–172 text, *173* 174–83 Notes, *184* blk.

References: Journey (1985), 27.

Notes: Printed pink paper wrappers. The advts. on p. 2 show this edn. sold at 2s. 6d. Thomas's notes are the first to be of any use.

Copies: O (Gough Adds. Scot. 16°. 65; Access. stamp: '16. 1. 1905');
UK: AWu, C, E (R 237.i), LCu, SAN.

75.1J/27   Journey, Paisley, ed. Holmes   [1906]

[½t] A Journey to the | Western Islands of Scotland in 1773

[Title] A Journey to the | Western Islands of Scotland | In 1773 | BY | SAMUEL JOHNSON, LL.D. | [short rule] | With a Preface by D. T. HOLMES, B.A. | [short rule] | PAISLEY: | ALEXANDER GARDNER | [BL] **Publisher by Appointment to the late Queen Victoria.**

8s, *1–3*⁸ 4–7⁸ 8⁸ (± 8⁸) 9–15⁸, ($1 signed), 120 leaves.

Pp. *1* ½t, *2* blk, *3* t., *4* coloph: 'LONDON: SIMPKIN, MARSHALL, HAMILTON, KENT & CO., LTD.' and 'PRINTED IN GREAT BRITAIN BY ALEXANDER GARDNER, LTD., PAISLEY.', *5* 6–13 Preface (signed '*November 1906*. D. T. HOLMES'), *14* blk, *15*–16 Contents, *17* 18–239 text dh: A JOURNEY | TO THE | WESTERN ISLANDS, | 1773. | [medium shaded swelled rule], *240* blk.

References: Courtney 125; McKinlay, *RGBS* viii (1930), 150; *Journey* (1985), 28.

Notes: Sig. 8 is on heavier paper, and ptd. in different type from the rest of the book. There are orn. initials on pp. 5 and 17.

The book was published in green cloth with a ptd. paper spine label in **red** and black, within **red** rules: A | **JOURNEY** | TO THE | **WESTERN** | **ISLANDS** | OF SCOTLAND. | [flower] | **JOHNSON**.

It also had a light green dust-jacket bearing a printed title on the front: [Within double rules]: A Journey to the | Western Islands of | Scotland in 1773 | *By Samuel Johnson, ll.d.* | WITH A PREFACE BY | D. T. HOLMES, B.A. | [ornam: thistle] | PAISLEY: ALEXANDER GARDNER | [BL] **publisher by Appointment to the late Queen Victoria.**

At the head of the spine of the jacket is the title as on the paper label above, and at the tail: ALEX. | GARDNER. The back and flaps are blk.

Daniel Turner Holmes (1863–1955) was Liberal MP for Govan.[1]

Copies: O (Gough Adds. Orkney 8° 39, stamped '1906');
USA: CU, MH; *Can*: [CaBVa]; *UK*: BMp (109997), C, E, JDF², Gp² (1. B591551; but 2. B322147 is dated: '1908').

---

[1] Stenton and Lees, *Who's Who of British Members of Parliament*, ii (1978), 178.

75.1J/28a   Journey, Oxford English Texts,   1924
                            ed. Chapman

Johnson's Journey to the Western Islands of Scotland and Boswell's Journal of a
Tour to the Hebrides with Samuel Johnson, LL.D. Edited by R.W. Chapman.
Oxford University Press. Humphrey Milford. 1924

   Pp. xix + 511; 1–150 text *Journey*, 151–448 text *Tour*, 450–79 Notes, 480–82
Appendix I 'Bibliography', 482–7 Appendixes II–IV, 488–511 Indexes I–III,
512 blk.

   References: Journey (1985), 30.

   Notes: Unluckily printed from uncorrected proofs, but the notes and appendices were the first attempt to settle the bibliographical identity of the early
editions, and to clarify the problems of the text. Published in June 1924, at 12s.,
and on india paper at 17s. 6d.

   Copies: USA: not recorded; *UK*: JDF ('Mary Lascelles').

75.1J/28b   Journey, Oxford Standard Authors,   1931
                            ed. Chapman

Johnson's Journey to the Western Islands of Scotland and Boswell's Journal of a
Tour to the Hebrides with Samuel Johnson, LL.D. Edited by R.W. Chapman.
Geoffrey Cumberlege Oxford University Press London New York Toronto

   Notes: A corrected reimpression from the above (75.1J/28a), without the textual notes, bibliography, or Appendixes. The plates of this impression were
published in January 1931, at 3s. 6d., and frequently reimpressed and reissued
thereafter, e.g. 1948, 1957.

   Copies: CtY (Osborn: annotated by J.M. Osborn after following SJ's route
with L.F. Powell in 1935); F.A. Pottle's copy (pres. by Chapman, 19 Jan. 1931,
and annotated by both, in Wm. Reese, Co., *Cat*. 101 (Sept. 1991), 486, $150).

75.1J/29   Journey, Pilgrim's Books   [1925]

JOHNSON'S | JOURNEY TO THE | HEBRIDES | [Rectangular heraldic
device: 'PHILIP ALLAN'] | LONDON | PHILIP ALLAN & CO., |
QUALITY COURT

   8s, *A*⁸ B–P⁸, ($1 signed), 120 leaves.

   Pp. A1 *i* ½t, *ii* Series Catalogue, *iii* t., *iv* coloph: 'Made and printed in Great
Britain by the Camelot Press Limited, Southampton.', v–vi Foreword, vii
Contents, *viii–ix* Map, *x* type-facs. of 1775 t., on A6 1–228 text ht (rectos):
JOHNSON'S JOURNEY, 229–30 Index.

   Pagination: no errors.

   Explicit: 228 FINIS.

Paper: White, laid; no vis. wmk.
Type: Long primer (3.4 mm), thinly leaded.
References: *Journey* (1985), 31.
Notes: Published both in plain boards at 2s. 6d. in May 1925; and in green morocco with silk place-marker. This is not the first to misrepresent the title of SJ's work (see 75.1J/15, New York, 1812, above). The author of the Foreword ('The text of the present edition is that of the second impression, in which most of the *errata* of the first were corrected' i.e. 75.1J/2), is unidentified; a map is provided and there are a few notes, apparently independent of R.W. Chapman (75.1J/28a, above), but of little use.
Copies: JDF² (both bindings); *USA*: Hyde, NjP; *UK*: AWn, C (1925.6.485), E.

75.1J/30   Journey, Travellers' Library, no. 158   1931

[½t] THE TRAVELLERS' LIBRARY | * | A JOURNEY TO THE | WESTERN ISLANDS OF SCOTLAND
[Title] A JOURNEY TO THE | WESTERN ISLANDS OF SCOTLAND | by | SAMUEL JOHNSON | WITH A FOREWORD BY D. L. MURRAY | [device] | LONDON | JONATHAN CAPE 30 BEDFORD SQUARE

16s, A^{16} B–H¹⁶, ($1 signed), 128 leaves.
Pp. *1* ½t, *2* Publisher's Notice (on the series 'The Travellers' Library'), *3* t., *4* Note on the text, publisher's addresses, and coloph: 'Printed and bound in Great Britain | by the Garden City Press Limited | Letchworth Herts & London | Paper made by John Dickinson & Co. | Limited', 5–6 Contents, 7–10 Foreword (signed: 'D. L. MURRAY.'), 11 ½t, 12–13 Map, 14 Epigraph (*Life* v. 19), 15–256 text.
References: *Journey* (1985), 33.
Notes: The volumes in this series were published at 3s. 6d. each; no. 158 appeared in June 1931. The text follows Chapman's 1931 edn. (75.1J/28b).
Copies: JDF; *USA*: [WaS]; *UK*: AWn, BMp, C (1931.6.230), E, Ep, [STIu].

75.1J/31   Journey, Riverside edition, ed. Wendt, Boston   1965

Johnson's Journey to the Western Islands of Scotland, and Boswell's Journal of a Tour to the Hebrides, edited by Allan Wendt. Riverside Editions. Boston: Houghton Mifflin, 1965.
References: *Journey* (1985), 34; ISBN: 0-395-05181-9.
Notes: Also issued in paperback, as Riverside edition B 86, and issued separately.

75.1J/31   Journey, Yale edition, ed. Lascelles   1971

Samuel Johnson A Journey to the Western Islands of Scotland Edited by Mary Lascelles New Haven and London: Yale University Press 1971
  References: *Journey* (1985), 35; ISBN: 0-300-01251-9.
  Notes: Forming vol. 9 of the Yale edn. of the *Works of Samuel Johnson* with valuable Introduction and notes.

75.1J/32   Journey, Penguin edition   1984

The Penguin English Library. Samuel Johnson A Journey to the Western Islands of Scotland James Boswell The Journal of a Tour to the Hebrides. Edited, with an Introduction and Notes, by Peter Levi Penguin Books 1984
  References: *Journey* (1985), 37; ISBN: 0-14-043.221-3.
  Notes: A slightly adjusted reprint (pp. 35–152) of the text of 75.1J/1, above, with some notes (pp. 413–19).

75.1J/A/1   Abridged Journey, Modern Traveller   1776

The Modern Traveller; being a Collection of Useful and Entertaining Travels, lately made into various Countries: the Whole carefully abridged: Exhibiting a View of the Manners, Religion, Government, Arts, Agriculture, Manufactures and Commerce of the Known World. Illustrated with Maps and ornamental Views. London: T. Lowndes. 1776
  6 vols., 12°
  Journey is abridged in vi. *203* 204–44. On 244 is the note: 'OBSERVATIONS. As Dean Swift wrote well upon a broom-stick, so has Doctor Johnson upon the rocks and naked mountains in Scotland. He writes very laconic, and in two lines says as much as some frothy Frenchmen do in two pages. He has taught the travelled gentlemen what they might have found marvellous in our own country, which they might see with less danger, less expence, and less contamination of mind, than they get in foreign lands.'[1]
  References: Courtney 122; *Journey* (1985), A1; ESTC: n005490.
  Copies: CtY; *USA*: MH, [MnU], NN, [RPB], ViU.

---

[1] The editor was not Josiah Conder (1789–1855*), whose *Modern Traveller* (1825–9) is sometimes confounded with this collection.

75.1J/A/2   Abridged Journey, British Tourists   1798

THE | BRITISH TOURISTS; | OR | TRAVELLER'S | POCKET COMPANION, | THROUGH | ENGLAND, WALES, SCOTLAND, | AND IRELAND. | Comprehending the moſt | *CELEBRATED TOURS* | IN THE | [BL] **British Islands.** | [short parallel rule] | ——My genius ſpreads her wing, | And flies where *Britain* courts the weſtern ſpring; | Where lawns extend, that ſcorn *Arcadian* pride, | And brighter ſtreams than fam'd *Hydaſpes* glide. | *Goldſmith's Traveller.* | [short total rule] | By WILLIAM MAVOR, LL.D. | [medium swelled rule] | VOL. II. | [medium swelled rule] | LONDON: | PRINTED FOR E. NEWBERY, ST. PAUL'S CHURCH- | YARD; AND SOLD BY EVERY BOOKSELLER | IN THE THREE KINGDOMS. | [short rule] | 1798.

6 vols., 18°

II. A^2 B^4 C–2H⁶ 2I1, ($3 (–B3) signed; 'Vol. II.' on $1), 181 leaves.

Pp. Engr. map front. + A1 t., A1ᵛ blk, A2 dh: CONTENTS OF VOL. II. | [short parallel rule], A2ᵛ blk, on B1 *1* 2–179 *Journey* (abridged) dh: JOURNEY | TO THE | *WESTERN ISLANDS* | OF | SCOTLAND, | BY | SAMUEL JOHNSON, LL.D. | PERFORMED IN THE YEAR 1773. | [medium swelled rule], rt: JOHNSON'S JOURNEY | TO THE HEBRIDES. (13: 'JOHNSON'S JOURNEY.'), *180* blk, *181* 182–238 Richard Twiss's Tour in Iceland, *239* 240–302 W. Hutchinson's Excursion to the Lakes, 1773 and 1774, *303* 304–58 William Bray's Tour through some Midland Counties into Derbyshire and Yorkshire in 1777.

Pagination: 68 as 67.

Press-figures: C1ᵛ(10)–3, D6ᵛ(32)–1, F6ᵛ(56)–3, G4ᵛ(64)–1, K6(103)–1, K6ᵛ(104)–2, N1ᵛ(130)–1, N6ᵛ(140)–3, R1ᵛ(178)–2, R4(183)–1.

Catchwords: 14 of (trade), 65 [fa-] mineₐ (~*.), 66 [by] is (the), 171 milesₐ (~,).

Explicit: 358 END OF VOL. II.

Plates: Front.: Engr. (fold. and coloured) map of Ireland 'Published June 23ᵈ. 1798, by E. Newbery, corner of St Pauls Church Yard. Neele sculpᵗ 352 Strand'.

References: Courtney 124; Roscoe, *Newbery* (1973), A334 (2); *Journey* (1985), A2; ESTC: t076192.

Notes: Place headings are omitted, and several passages removed.

Copies: O (GA Gen Top. 16° 289); *USA*: MH, NIC; *UK*: E, Ep.

75.1J/A/3   Abridged Journey, British Tourists   1800

THE | BRITISH TOURISTS; | OR | TRAVELLER'S | POCKET COMPANION, | THROUGH | ENGLAND, WALES, SCOTLAND, |

AND IRELAND. | Comprehending the most | *CELEBRATED TOURS* | IN THE | [BL] **British Islands.** | [short parallel rule] | ——My genius fpreads her wing | . . . [4 lines] | *Goldfmith's Traveller.* | [short total rule] | By WILLIAM MAVOR, LL.D. | [short swelled rule] | VOL. I [– VI]. | SECOND EDITION. | [short swelled rule] | LONDON: | *Printed by J. Swan, and Co. Jerufalem-Court, Gracechurch-Street;* | FOR E. NEWBERY, ST. PAUL'S CHURCH-YARD; | AND SOLD BY EVERY BOOKSELLER | IN THE THREE KINGDOMS. | [short rule] | 1800.

6 vols. 12°

References: Courtney 124; Roscoe, *Newbery* (1973), A 334 (2); *Journey* (1985), A3; ESTC: t166805.

Notes: Vol. vi of this edn. and preceding is dated '1800' and exists in only one edn, though variously attached to this or preceding edn. of vols. 1–5. *Journey* is abridged in ii (1800), *1* 2–164.

Copies: E² (HF 4–9; NE 55 b.8, vol. 2 only);

USA: CtY, DLC, IU, [MeB, NcD], NN, PPL, [PU].

75.1J/A/4 Abridged Journey, British Tourists 1807

BRITISH TOURISTS; | OR, | TRAVELLER's | POCKET COMPANION, | THROUGH | ENGLAND, WALES, SCOTLAND, AND IRELAND. | *Comprehending the most* | CELEBRATED, MODERN, AND RECENT TOURS | IN THE | [BL] **British Islands:** | WITH | SEVERAL ORIGINALS. | [short swelled rule] | IN SIX VOLUMES. | [short swelled rule] | VOL. I [– VI]. | THIRD EDITION, IMPROVED AND MUCH ENLARGED. | [double rule] | By WILLIAM MAVOR, LL.D. &c. &c. | [double rule] | LONDON: | PRINTED FOR RICHARD PHILLIPS, BRIDGE-STREET, BLACK- | FRIARS; AND SOLD BY EVERY BOOK- SELLER IN THE | UNITED KINGDOM. | [short rule] | 1807. | [*Price One Guinea and a Half, in Boards.*]

6 vols., 12°

Notes: *Journey* is abridged in ii. *1* 2–148. Advertisement, II. xvi is dated '1807'; colophon 'Lewis and Hamblin, Printers, Paternoster-row., but in IV: 'J. Adlard, Printer, Duke-street. The paper is watermarked '1805'. For Richard Phillips, see F.S. Herne, 'An old Leicestershire Bookseller' in *Leics. Lit. and Phil. Soc. Journal*, iii (1893), 65–73; F.H.A. Micklewright, *NQ* cxcii (1947), 81–2, and A. Boyle, *NQ* cxcvi (1951), 361–6.

References: *Journey* (1985), A4.

Copies: E.

75.1J/A/5   Abridged Journey, British Tourist's   1809

THE | BRITISH TOURIST'S, | OR, | TRAVELLER'S | POCKET COMPANION, | THROUGH | ENGLAND, WALES, SCOTLAND, AND IRELAND. | *Comprehending the most* | CELEBRATED MODERN TOURS | IN THE | [BL] **British Islands,** | AND | *SEVERAL ORIGINALS.* | [short swelled rule] | IN SIX VOLUMES. | [short swelled rule] | VOL. II. | THE THIRD EDITION, IMPROVED AND MUCH ENLARGED. | [double rule] | By WILLIAM MAVOR, LL.D., &c. &c. | [double rule] | LONDON: | PRINTED FOR RICHARD PHILLIPS, BRIDGE-STREET, BLACK- | FRIARS; AND SOLD BY EVERY BOOKSELLER IN THE | UNITED KINGDOM. | [short rule] | 1809. | [*Price One Pound Sixteen Shillings, in Boards.*]

6 vols., 18°

II. A^2 (± A1) B^2, $^2B^6$ C–$2G^6$ $2H^4$, ($3 (–K2) signed; 'VOL. II.' on $1 (CD, F–K, M–N, P–Q, S–T, X–Y, 2A–2B, 2D–2E); 'VOL. II.' on $1 (ELORUZ, 2C, 2F)), 182 leaves.

Pp. A1 t., A1^v blk, A2 CONTENTS OF VOL. II. | [short parallel rule], A2^v blk, on B1 *1* 2–148 text of *Journey* (abridged), dh: JOURNEY | TO THE | WESTERN ISLANDS | OF | [Hollow type] *SCOTLAND,* | BY | SAMUEL JOHNSON, LL.D. | PERFORMED IN THE YEAR 1773. | [short swelled rule], rt: JOHNSON'S JOURNEY | TO THE HEBRIDES., *149* 150–206 W. Hutchinson, *Excursion to the Lakes*, *207* 208–56 William Bray, *Tour . . . into Derbyshire and Yorkshire*, 1777, *257* 258–310 Arthur Young, *Tour in Ireland*, 1776–1779, *311* 312–60 Thomas Pennant, *Journey from Chester to London . . .* 1780., 360 coloph: '*Printed by Lewis and Hamblin, Paternoster-row.*'

Explicit: 360 END OF VOL. II.

Paper: White, wove; royal (uncut: 6⅞ × 4⅛ in.); wmk.: 'M 1805'.

Type: Bourgeois (3.0 mm), leaded.

References: Courtney 124; *Journey* (1985), A5.

Notes: An introductory note states, 'We have merely shortened some of his digressions . . . or added a few notes', but in fact the text and notes are as in Mavor's first version 1798 (75.1J/A/2, above), of which this is merely a reissue with cancelled tt.

Copies: O (GA Gen. Top. 8° 335, blue boards, uncut); *USA*: MiU, [MnU].

75.1J/A/6   Journey, British Tourist's   1814

The British Tourist's, or, Traveller's Pocket Companion . . . London: Printed by J. Gillet for Sherwood, Neely, & Jones, and B. & R. Crosby, & Co. 1814.

6 vols., 12°

References: *Journey* (1985), A6.

Notes: This is a reissue with new titles, of the 1809 edn. (75.1J/A/5, above). The paper still bears the wmk.: 'M 1805'.
Copies: Unlocated.

75.1J/A/7   Abridged Journey, Abbey Classics,   [1924]
Vol. XXIV

(a) [Within an ornamental block t.] THE | Abbey Classics | [Letterpress] A JOURNEY TO THE | WESTERN ISLANDS | OF SCOTLAND | By SAMUEL JOHNSON | LL.D. | With an Introduction by | JOHN FREEMAN | [Block] Ornamented by Martin Travers. | Published by CHAPMAN & DODD, from their offices | at 66 Gt. Queen Street, In the county of LONDON.
(b) [Within ornamental block, as above, but worn] . . . Martin Travers. Simpkin, Marshall, Hamilton, Kent & Co., Ltd., London, E.C. 4.
(c) [Within ornamental block, as (b) above] . . . Martin Travers. Boston: Small, Maynard & Co. inc. [1925]
8s, A^8 B–Q^8, ($1 signed), 128 leaves.
Pp. *i* ½t, *ii* blk, *iii* t., *iv* coloph: 'PRINTED FOR | CHAPMAN AND | DODD, LTD., BY | CAHILL AND | CO., LTD., IN | DUBLIN. 1924.' (This coloph. absent when t. as (b), above), v Biographical note, vi Bibliography of [dates of major works by] SJ, vii–xvi Introduction (signed 'John Freeman'), on B1 *1* type-facs. of 1775 t. (75.1J/1a, above), *2* blk, 3–240 text (slightly abridged) dh: [orn. hp. dated 'MCMXXII'], 240 orn. tailp.
References: *Journey* (1985), 29.
Notes: The text mainly follows 1785 (75.1J/6, above), but is casually abridged and modified. It was issued in a light-blue cloth, gilt on spine, with 'SIMPKIN' at the tail, in Sept. 1924 at 3s. 6d., and again in March 1925 in 'Lambskin' at 6s.
Copies: JDF² (ab); *USA*: ICU, MH, [OCU, WaU]; DLC (C (Boston), '1925': DA 880 H4J6. 1925); *UK*: AWn, AWu, C, E, Gu, NCp, STIu.

75.1J/A/8   Abridged Journey, Macdonald edition   1983

A Journey to the Western Isles   Johnson's Scottish Journey Retraced by Finlay J. Macdonald   Macdonald & Co London & Sydney 1983
References: *Journey* (1985), 36; ISBN: 0-356-09156-2.
Notes: An abridged text derived from 1785 edn. (75.1J/6, above). The author was a native of the Isle of Harris, which may explain his wording of the title, but he was cavalier with the text and in his annotation. This edn. is to be valued mainly for the photographs (not always correctly located).
Copies: JDF.

75.1J/TF/1   Journey, French translation   1785

In: *Nouveau Recueil de Voyages au Nord de l' Europe et de l' Asie, contenant les Extraits des Relations de Voyages les plus estimés, & qui n' ont jamais été publiés en Français. Ouvrage traduit de différentes langues, par une Société de Gens-de-Lettres, avec des Notes, des éclaircissements, & enrichi de cartes & de beaucoup de vues & dessins gravés par les meilleurs artistes. Tome Second.* A Genève, Chez Paul Barde, Imprimeur-libraire, & se trouve à Paris. Chez Moutard, Imp. Lib. rue des Mathurins. Merigot le jeune, Lib. quai des Augustins. MDCCLXXXV.

This formed vol. ii of a 3 vol. set generally known by this title, but of which vol. i is entitled:

Voyages aux Montagnes d' Ecosse, et aux Isles Hébrides, de Scilly, d' Anglesey, &c. Traduits de l' Anglais par une Société de Gens-de-Lettres, avec les Notes & les éclaircissements nécessairs. Ouvrage enrichi de cartes & de beaucoup de vues & de desseins, gravés par les meilleurs artistes. Tome Premier. A Genève. Chez Paul Barde, Imprimeur-libraire, & se trouve à Paris. Chez Moutard, Imp. Lib. rue des Mathurins. Merigot le jeune, Lib. quai des Augustins. MDCCLXXXV.

3 vols. 8°

II. π^4 A–V^8 X^4 χ1 ($i–iv signed), 169 leaves.

Pp. π1 *i* ½t, *iii* t., *iv* blk, *v*–vj Table des Matières, *vij* Avis au Relieur, on A1 *1*–2 Introductory remarks on SJ's *Journey*, *3* 4–328 text Recueil de Voyages, &c. (p. 152 as 151), *329–30* Errata du second Volume.

Plates: (4): 1. 'Abbaye d' Aberbrothic' (fold. facing p. 16), 2. 'Boulloir de Buchan' (fold. facing p. 32), 3. 'Chute de Foyers' (fold. facing p. 56), and 4. 'Anciens Edifices Danois' (i.e. Broch, or Dùn; fold. facing p. 146).

References: Courtney 123; *Journey* (1985), T2.

Notes: The *Journey* is abridged and translated at ii. 3–328, by the editor and compiler, Pierre-Henri Mallet, who adds an interesting editorial note on SJ (ii. 1–2) praising both his style and 'L' Esprit philosophique'. At ii. 39 the account of the detection of Elgin Cathedral follows the cancelled text of the 1st edn. Iona is printed as '*Jona*' throughout.[1]

Copies: E (Hall 195 f); *USA*: CtY.

---

[1] This feature again points to the translator's use of the first edn. of *Journey* since this form is the first to be met with in it, and subsequent spellings are regularized. Cf. *Journey* (1985), 144 n. 62v.

75.1J/TF/2   Journey, French translation   1804

[½t] VOYAGE | DANS LES HÉBRIDES.

[Title] VOYAGE | DANS LES HÉBRIDES | OU | ILES OCCIDENTALES D' ÉCOSSE, Par le D.ʳ JOHNSON. | TRADUIT DE L' ANGLAIS. | [medium swelled rule] | A PARIS, | CHEZ [5 lines, braced]

COLNET, Libraire, rue du Bac, près celle de Lille. | FAIN Jeune, et Compagnie, Imprimeur, aux ci-devant | Écoles de Droit, place du Panthéon. | MONGIE, Libraire, palais du Tribunat. | DEBRAY, Libraire, place du Muséum. | [short rule] | AN XII.

8°, π⁴ 1–14⁸ 15⁴, ($1 signed), 120 leaves.

Pp. π1 ½t, π1ᵛ coloph: 'DE L'IMPRIMERIE DE FAIN JEUNE ET Cᶜ.', π2 t., π2ᵛ blk, on π3 *i* ii–iij Preface, *iv* blk, on 1₁ *1* 2–228 text dh: [wavy rule] | VOYAGE | DANS LES HÉBRIDES | OU | ILES OCCIDENTALES D' ÉCOSSE. | [short wavy rule], rt: VOYAGE | DANS LES HÉBRIDES., *229–230* Contents, *231–2* (15₄) Colnet's advts.[1]

Pagination: no errors (imperfectly printed figures misread in *Tinker*).

Catchwords: none.

Explicit: 228 FIN.

Paper: White, laid; Moyen (uncut: 8½ × 5½ in.); wmk.: 'DAV'.

Type: St Augustin (4.7 mm), leaded.

References: Courtney 123; Brunet (1860–5), iii. 553; Quérard, *La France Littéraire*, iv (1830), 230 'in-8. 3fr. 50c.'; *Tinker* 1360; *Journey* (1985), T3.

Notes: The translator was Henri-Noël-François Huchet (1782–1861), Comte de Labédoyère. The text is abridged.[2]

Copies: O (G.A. Scot 8° 946);

USA: Hyde[2] (uncut), CtY (Liebert), NIC; *UK*: [W.R. Batty], BMp (848900), E (L.C.256, 'Napoleon'), JDF (boards, uncut; MS spine t.); *Fr*: BN.

[1] Giving Colnet's address as, 'rue du Bac, n° 618, au coin de celle de Lille'.

[2] Nothing more is added to the bibliographical history of French translations by *Johnson & Boswell Voyage dans les Hébrides traduit de l' anglais et annoté par Marcel le Pape . . . Introduction de Maurice Denuzière*, Paris: Collection Outre-Mers, aux Editions de la Différence, 1991 (ISBN: 2-7291-0695-2).

75.1J/TG/1   Journey, German translation   1775

[Fraktur] **Dr. Samuel Johnſon's Reiſen nach den Weſtlichen Inſeln** | **bey** |**Schottland.** | [medium rule, 55 mm] | **Aus dem Engliſchen** | [Engr. vignette reader at table, plate 50 × 80 mm] | [medium rule, 63 mm] | **Mit Churfächſicher Freyheit.** | [rule, 77 mm] | **Leipzig,** | **in der Weygandſchen Buchhandlung.** | **1775.**

8°, A–Q⁸ R⁴, ($5 (–A1, R4) signed), 132 leaves.

Pp. A1 *1* t., *2* blk, *3* 4–264 text.

References: Courtney 123; *Tinker* 1361; *Journey* (1985), T1.

Notes: The work is printed in fraktur throughout, and the text is abridged, but the anonymous translator [? Susanne Thurm, cf. 75.1J/TG.2, below] has supplied some explanatory notes for German readers (pp. 7–8, 11, 26, 32, 38, 44, 58, 77, 80, 90, 99, 119, 132, 171, 196, 230, 253, 256, 259, 264). SJ's copy was included with lot 177 at Christie's, 16 Feb. 1785, which went to 'Money' for

17s. 6d., but remains untraced. It is possible that J.F. Schiller (cousin of the poet) who acted for Weidemann, of Leipzig, and who was often in touch with Thomas Cadell, may have engineered the translation of this work, for which the stimulus was probably the German interest in 'Ossian' reinforced by the publication of Goethe's *Werther* in 1774.[1] The BN Catalogue gives the imprint as 'Leipzig: Gessner und Schramm'.

Copies: O (Don. e. 746);
USA: ICU, [Liebert, wraps. (8½ × 5⅜ in.) = CtY], NNU; [*Fr*: BN].

[1] I derive the idea of Schiller's involvement from Prof. Bernhard Fabian's Lyell Lectures (no. 2, at Oxford, 13 May 1993), of which publication is awaited, though I carry it further than his scrupulosity allowed. Reich, Weidemann's partner, referred to Schiller as his 'agent'. For the interest in 'Ossian' see U. Böker, 'Sprache, literarischer Markt und kulturelle Orientierung', in *Studies in Honour of Otto Heitsch*, ed. T. Kirschner (1991), 305–35, and 'The Marketing of Macpherson' in *Ossian Revisited*, ed. H. Gaskill (1991), 73–93.

75.1J/TG/2   Journey, German translation   1986

Reclams Universal Bibliothek. Band 1132.
    Samuel Johnson Eine Reise zu den Westlichen Inseln von Schottland. 1986 Verlag Philipp Reclam jun. Leipzig.
    'Aus dem Englischen Überarbeitung einer Übersetzung aus dem Jahr 1775 von Susanne Thurm. Mit einen Vorwort und Anmerkungen von Ingrid Kuczynski. Mit einer Karte als Frontispiz und 11 zeitgenössichen Abbildungen.'

75.1MQS   Inscription for Picture of Mary,   1775
**   Queen of Scots**

21 January   Inscription for Picture of Mary, Queen of Scots
    References: *Life* ii. 293 n; *MS Handlist* 133; *MS Index* JoS 210.
    Sent to Boswell with letter of 4 July 1774 (*Letters* 357; Hyde, ii. 146) and revised with that of 21 Jan. 1775 (*Letters* 374; Hyde, ii. 170–1), with SJ's English text accompanying JB's Latin. JB sent a transcription to Reynolds in his letter of 12 Aug. 1775 (Waingrow, *Corr.*, 56–7 and refs). First published by JB in *Life* (1791), i. 445 n.
    No engraving of the picture, commissioned of Gavin Hamilton by JB in 1768, is known bearing SJ's words.[1]
    MS: CtY (Boswell: C 1598).

[1] Hamilton painted the picture in 1768, and was even then waiting for a 'motto' before sending it to be engraved (*Boswell Catalogue* C 1484).

75.2LP   Proposals for Lennox's Works   1775

FEBRUARY 14, 1775. | PROPOSALS | For Printing by Subscription, | Dedicated to THE QUEEN, | A NEW and ELEGANT EDITION, Enlarged and Corrected, | OF | THE ORIGINAL | WORKS | OF | *Mrs CHARLOTTE LENNOX.* | CONSISTING OF | [2 cols., col. a:] The FEMALE QUIXOTE; | SHAKESPEAR Illuftrated; | HENRIETTA; | SOPHIA; | [4-line vertical double rule; col. b:] ELIZA; | The SISTER, a Comedy; | PHILANDER, a Dramatic | Paftoral; | And OTHER PIECES, never before printed. | [medium rule] | CONDITIONS. [&c.]

2°, $1 (unsigned), 1 leaf.

Pp. *1* t. and Conditions and opening of SJ's statement, 2 close of SJ's statement, addresses of booksellers, and receipt form for 1 guinea.

Pagination: [2]; *Press-figures*: none; *Catchwords*: 1 or.

Explicit: none.

Paper: White, laid; Double crown (uncut: 10 × 7½ in.); no vis. wmk.

Type: Title: english and pica (4.7 and 3.9 mm), SJ's statement: english, Conditions &c.: pica.

References: *Life* ii. 289–90, 509 (Courtney 117); *Diaries* 224; Small (1935), 43, 259.

Notes: JB reported that SJ's lost diary had recorded under 2 Jan. 1775, 'Wrote Charlotte's Proposals', and he preserved the only known copy, quoting SJ's statement from it in *Life*. The date on the *Prospectus* is presumably the date of publication. The Conditions were:

I. The work to be in 3 vols. 8°, with engraved frontispiece after Reynolds,

II. Price: 2 gns., one at subscription and one on delivery,

III. Delivery promised in October 1776.

The booksellers involved were: J. Dodsley, in Pall-mall; T. Becket, in the Adelphi; White, in Fleet-street; Wilkie, in St Paul's Church-yard; Mess. Dilly, in the Poultry; Prince, at Oxford; Woodyer, at Cambridge; Frederick, at Bath; Sprange, at Tunbridge; Balfour, in Edinburgh; and Faulkner, in Dublin.

Though Reynolds and SJ were encouraging, the enterprise collapsed and the collection never appeared.[1] It seems to have been set on foot somewhat earlier, for a letter from Hawkesworth to CL of 16 Oct. 1773, shows she had asked his advice about illustrations for a new edn. of the *Female Quixote*, though none appeared until Harrison's edn. of 1783 (52.3LFQ/5, above), and again in Cooke's edn. of [1799] (52.3LFQ/6, above).[2] Neither of these can be considered as authorized edns.

Copies: CtY (MS Boswell, P. 77).

[1] Isles, *HLB* xix (1971), 171–7; SJ *Letters*, Hyde, ii. 201–2. CL's poems were noticed by Elizabeth Carter in a letter of 1752 to Miss Highmore, cited in Thomas Thorpe, *Catalogue of Autographs* (1937), 331, referring to *Poems on several Occasions. Written by a young Lady*. London: S. Paterson, 8°, 1747, dedicated by 'Charlotte Ramsay' to Lady Isabella Finch.
[2] Isles, *HLB* xix (1971), 168–70; MH: (bMS. Eng. 1269 (30–31)).

75.3TT/1   Taxation no Tyranny, first edition   1775

[½t:] [29 flowers, 78 mm] | Taxation no Tyranny. | [29 flowers, 78 mm] | [Price 1s. 6d.]

[Title] Taxation no Tyranny; | AN | ANSWER | TO THE | RESOLUTIONS AND ADDRESS | OF THE | AMERICAN CONGRESS. | [Floral spray orn.] | [double rule] | LONDON, | PRINTED FOR T. CADELL, IN THE STRAND. | MDCCLXXV.

8°, *A*² B–M⁴ N², ($2 (–A1, N2) signed), 48 leaves.

Pp. *i* ½t, *ii* blk, *iii* t., *iv* blk, on B1 *1* 2–91 text dh: [double rule] | TAXA-TION | NO TYRANNY., *92* blk.

Pagination: (↑).

Press-figures: B1ᵛ(2)–1, C2ᵛ(12)–2, D3ᵛ(22)–8, E2ᵛ(28)–1, F2ᵛ(36)–2, G1ᵛ(42)–1, H4ᵛ(56)–2, I4(63)–5, L4ᵛ(80)–5, M2ᵛ(84)–6, N1ᵛ(90)–1; K unfigured.

Catchwords: 28 both, (~;), 86 ruined‸ (~,).

Explicit: 91 FINIS.

Paper: White, laid; Medium (uncut: 9¼ × 5½ in.); no vis. wmk.

Type: English (4.5 mm), leaded; initial word of paras in caps; t. orn. as in *Journey* 1775 (75.1J/1, above).

References: Courtney 125; CH 152; Todd, *BC* ii (1953), 61–5; Greene, *SB* xiii (1960), 223–31, and in *Works* (Yale), x. 401–55; ESTC: t049891.

Notes: 500 copies printed by Strahan in March 1775 (L: Add. MS 48803, fo. 39), and published at 1s. 6d., 8 March 1775 (*Public Advertiser*), corroborated by Garrick in letter to Boswell of that date (*Letters of Garrick*, ed. Little and Kahrl, iii. 993–4, no. 895; CtY: MS Boswell C 1348). The portion given by JB to Lord Hailes is untraced.[1] A fragment of proof was acquired and preserved by JB (MS Hyde; *MS Handlist* 134, *MS Index* JoS 311[2]), and was reproduced in facsimile for 'The Johnsonians' as:

> *Samuel Johnson's Taxation no Tyranny. A Fragment of Proof Copy corrected by the author & preserved by James Boswell*. To Commemorate Dr Johnson's 281ˢᵗ Birthday, at the Grolier Club in New York. MCMXC.

as a keepsake of 250 copies, with notes by Viscount Eccles and Mary Hyde, the Viscountess Eccles, for the meeting on 14 September 1990. No certain identification has yet been made of the 'half dozen copies' in the original unamended state which SJ asked Strahan to lay up for him (*Letters* 381, 1 Mar. 1775, Hyde, ii. 184–5).

Some part of the text is reprinted in the *Universal Mag.* lv (1775), 151–2.

Copies: O (G. Pamph. 327/5 'Edmond Malone');

USA: CSmH² (1. uncut; 2. 'From the Author' [*not* SJ], DLC, Hyde³, IU, [A.A. Houghton, Liebert], MiU(C), NIC, NPM, NN-B² (1. uncut; 2. sophist. (B–L = 2nd. edn.) 'To Mr Parkins | from the author' [*not* SJ]), [NRU, PHi], PPL, ViU, WiM; *Can*: CaOHM (C.2998, 'Rippey'); *Japan*: [Kyoto]; *UK*: AWn, [B.S. Barlow, Esq; ('John Cator')], DUu (Routh), E, L (Ashley 3416).

¹ *Fettercairn* 1127; and *Boswell Catalogue*, L 611, JB to Dalrymple, 21 Nov. 1778.
² D. Buchanan, *The Treasure of Auchinleck* (1975), 309.

75.3TT/2   Taxation no Tyranny, second edition   1775

[½t:] [row of 29 flowers, 78 mm] | Taxation no Tyranny. | [29 flowers, 78 mm] | [Price 1s. 6d.]

[Title] Taxation no Tyranny; | AN | ANSWER | TO THE | RESOLUTIONS AND ADDRESS | OF THE | AMERICAN CONGRESS. | [Floral spray orn. as 75.3TT/1] | [double rule] | LONDON: | PRINTED FOR T. CADELL, IN THE STRAND. | MDCCLXXV.

8°, A² B–M⁴ N², ($2 (–A1, N2) signed), 48 leaves.

Pp. i ½t, ii blk, iii t., iv blk, on B1 *1* 2–91 text dh: [double rule] | TAXATION | NO TYRANNY., *92* blk.

Pagination: (↑).

Press-figures: B4ᵛ(8)–5, C2ᵛ(12)–1, D3ᵛ(22)–5, E2ᵛ(28)–1, F2ᵛ(36)–2, G2ᵛ(44)–1, H4ᵛ(56)–5, I4(63)–2, K4ᵛ(72)–5, M3ᵛ(86)–1; L and N unfigured.

Catchwords: 28 both, (~;), 86 ruined [correct].

Explicit: 91 FINIS.

Paper: White, laid; Medium (uncut: 9¼ × 5½ in.); no vis. wmk.

Type: English (4.5 mm), leaded; as 75.3TT/1, above.

References: Courtney 125; CH 152; *Rothschild* 1258–9; ESTC: t141339.

Notes: Printed in 1,000 copies and published within a few days of the first edn. (75.3TT/1, above) to catch the popular demand. There are minor changes in the text of this edition, though SJ's responsibility for them is uncertain. There was some resetting of type, but sigg. E, F, I, and K (and perhaps G, L) of the first edn. are overrun in this edition. The remainder: B, C, D, H, M, and N were reset, or partly reset. At the top of p. 55 (H4) a line of type was accidentally omitted in this impression, and what stood in 75.3TT/1 as 'authority, and as a seditious conventicle punishable by law, has promulgated' is here printed as: 'authority, has promulgated' (*Works* (Yale), x. 438 n. 2). Such a loss is consonant with the readjustment of type pages.

Copies: O (8° Y. 92 Jur./7);

USA: CtY (Franklin), DLC², Hyde² (1. uncut), ICN, ICU, [Liebert], MH, NIC ('M. Sage', uncut), NPM, PPAmP, TxU; *Can*: CaOHM (B. 12721); *UK*: BMp (574058), MRp, STA.

75.3TT/3   Taxation no Tyranny, third edition   1775

[½t] [row of 29 flowers, 78 mm] | Taxation no Tyranny. | [29 flowers, 78 mm] | [Price 1s. 6d.]

[Title] Taxation no Tyranny; | AN | ANSWER | TO THE |

RESOLUTIONS AND ADDRESS | OF THE | AMERICAN CONGRESS. | THE THIRD EDITION. | [double rule] | LONDON: | PRINTED FOR T. CADELL, IN THE STRAND. | MDCCLXXV.

8°, *A*² B–M⁴ N², ($2 (–A1, N2) signed), 48 leaves.

Pp. *i* ½t, *ii* blk, *iii* t., *iv* blk, on B1 *1* 2–91 text dh: [double rule] | TAXATION | NO TYRANNY., *92* blk.

Pagination: (↑).

Press-figures: B4ᵛ(8)–3, C4(15)–3, D3ᵛ(22)–8, E4(31)–2, F3ᵛ(38)–8, G1ᵛ(42)–8, H4ᵛ(56)–3, I4(63)–8, K2ᵛ(68)–2, L3(77)–8, M4ᵛ(88)–8, N1ᵛ(90)–1.

Catchwords: 28 both; [*correct*], 86 ruined, [*correct*].

Explicit: 91 FINIS.

Paper: White, laid; Medium (uncut: 9¼ × 5½ in.); no vis. wmk.

Type: English (4.5 mm), as in 75.3TT/1, above.

References: Courtney 125; CH 152; Greene, *SB* xiii (1960), 223–31; ESTC: t049888.

Notes: 500 copies printed by Strahan in March 1775 as part of the whole enterprise (see above 75.3TT/1), with overrunning of sigg. D, H, L, M, and N from second edn. (75.3TT/2, above), and resetting of remainder. Greene argues for authorial revision of this edn., with particular reference to readings in sigg. F (*Works*, x. 430t), G (x. 434z), H (x. 438 n. 2), K (x. 442k and n. 7; 443l, m; 445n), L (x. 447s, w–y). That some of these changes are found in the overrun sheets reinforces his argument. It is striking that almost twice as many copies of this edn. survive from a run of 500, than are found of 75.3TT/2 from a run of 1,000. It was announced on 21 March, 1775 (*London Chron.*).

Copies: O (8° Y. 117 Jur./4);

USA: CLU-C, CSmH, CtY³ (1. 'Franklin'), DLC², Hyde (uncut), ICU, IU, [Liebert], MB², MiU(C)² (1. MS note p. 79, l. 14: 'Mrs Macaulay'; 2. uncut, + 4th edn. (75.3TT/4) t.[1]), MH, NIC, NN, OCi, PPAmP, PPL, PPU, TxU² (1. uncut, 'Thomas Percy: A present from the Author', *Booklist* 162), ViU; *UK*: C², Eu², MRu, STA.

---

[1] The press-figures in this copy are eccentric, showing it to be made up of sheets from the different impressions: B4ᵛ(8)–8, C4(15)–8, D3ᵛ(22)–8, E2ᵛ(28)–1, G1ᵛ(42)–1, H2ᵛ(52)–3, K1ᵛ(66)–8, N1ᵛ(90)–2.

75.3TT/4   Taxation no Tyranny, fourth edition   1775

[½t] [row of 23 flowers, 77 mm] | Taxation no Tyranny. | [23 flowers, 77 mm] | [Price 1s. 6d.]

[Title] Taxation no Tyranny; | AN | ANSWER | TO THE | RESOLUTIONS AND ADDRESS | OF THE | AMERICAN CONGRESS. | THE FOURTH EDITION. | [parallel rule] | LONDON: | PRINTED FOR T. CADELL, IN THE STRAND. | MDCCLXXV.

8°, *A*² B–M⁴ N², ($2 (–A1, N2) signed), 48 leaves.

Pp. *i* ½t, *ii* blk, *iii* t., *iv* blk, on B1 *1* 2–91 text dh: [double rule] | TAXATION | NO TYRANNY., *92* blk.

Pagination: (↑).

Press-figures: B1ᵛ(2)–1, C2ᵛ(12)–2, D3ᵛ(22)–8, E2ᵛ(28)–1, F2ᵛ(36)–2, G1ᵛ(42)–1, H4ᵛ(56)–2, I4(63)–5, L4ᵛ(80)–5, M2ᵛ(84)–6, N1ᵛ(90)–1; K unfigured.

Catchwords: 28 both, (∼;), 86 ruined, (∼,).

Explicit: 91 FINIS.

Paper: White, laid; medium (uncut: 9¼ × 5½ in.); no vis. wmk.

Type: English (4.5 mm); as 75.3TT/1, above.

References: Courtney 125; CH 152; R.E. Stiles, *BC* i (1932), 155–6; ESTC: t049889.

Notes: 500 copies printed by Strahan in March 1775 as part of the undertaking of this work (75.3TT/1, above), apparently with some overrunning of sigg. from third edn. (75.3TT/3, above), viz. E, G, I, K, L with the remainder B, C, D, F, H, M and N reset. A few readings in this edn. diverge from its predecessors in B (*Works*, x. 412a), C (x. 413b), D (x. 420j), E (x. 425, l.8 up. 'intitled' 1–3, 'entitled' 4; 427, l.4 'Montesquieu' 1–3, 'Mentesquieu' 4), L (x. 447s). The note by Stiles (1932) above, recorded the variant states of the ½tt which were evidently misplaced in some copies seen by him.

Copies: O (Godwyn Pamph. 278/1, 'Jonathan Boucher');

USA: CLU, CSmH, CtY, DLC ('Jefferson'), [Liebert], MH, NIC, NN, PPAmP; *UK*: Ct² (2. 'Francis Wrangham'), MRu².

75.3TT/5   Taxation no Tyranny, American Archives   1839

American Archives: consisting of A Collection of authentic Records, State Papers, Debates, and Letters and other Notices of Publick Affairs, the whole forming a documentary History of the Origin and Progress of the North American Colonies; of the Causes and Accomplishment of the American Revolution, and of the Constitution of Government for the United States, to the final Ratification thereof. In Six Series. 4th. Series. From the King's Message, of March 7th, 1774, to the Declaration of Independence, by the United States, in 1776. Vol. II. Prepared and Published under Authority of an Act of Congress. Washington. 1839.

2°. Vol. II. cols. 1431–1449 reprint the complete text of *Taxation no Tyranny*, together with various other pamphlets and tracts of 1775, including, at 1449–62 'An Answer to a Pamphlet entitled Taxation no Tyranny', &c.

This 4th series of *American Archives* was published in 5 vols., fol., 1837–53.

References: Sabin, vi. 512–13 (25053).

Notes: The collection was made by Peter Force. *Taxation no Tyranny* does not appear in his earlier *Tracts and other Papers, relating Principally to the Origin, Settlement, and Progress of the Colonies in North America* . . . Washington: Printed by Peter Force, 6 vols. 1836–53. According to Sabin, associated material relative to these collections, is preserved in DLC.

Copies: O (Rhodes House); *USA*: DLC.

75.3TT/6a   Taxation no Tyranny, Wesley's   [1775]
                 Calm Address

A CALM | ADDRESS | TO | *OUR AMERICAN* | COLONIES. | [rule] | By *JOHN WESLEY*, M.A. [rule] | Ne, pueri, ne tanta animis affuefcite bella, | Neu patriæ validas in vifcera vertite vires. | Virgil. | [total rule] | *LONDON*, | Printed by R. Hawes, in *Dorfet-Street*, Spitalfields, | And Sold at the Foundry, Moorfields.

12°, $12 (usigned), 12 leaves; Pp. *1* t., *2* blk, *3* 4–23 text, *24* blk.

References: Courtney 126 (7); ESTC: t143411.

Notes: The bibliographical history of this (as of many of Wesley's publications) is complicated, and this is not the place to clarify it. ESTC: reports many undated [= ? 1775] London edns. before 1800, viz: t016516, t019839, t016518, t016519, n026461, n001727, t016515, Bristol: t187688, t016517, Dublin: t187689, Dundee: n028556, and Salisbury: n046885.

The text is an unacknowledged abridgement of SJ's *Taxation no Tyranny*, as was pointed out by Augustus M. Toplady in his *An Old Fox Tarr'd and Feather'd. Occasioned by Mr. John Wesley's Calm Address* . . . &c. 1775, and repeated by the anonymous author of *Resistance no Rebellion*, 1775. It was not Wesley's first or only plagiary.[1] It was reviewed in the *Critical Review*, xx (Oct. 1775), 305–11, and attacked in the *Public Advertiser*, 23 Oct. 1775. The Virgilian epigraph is from *Aeneid*, vi. 833–4.

Copies: Hyde ('D. Wainter'); *UK*: L, O (GP. 310/5).

[1] He had been successfully sued by Dodsley in 1745 for his usurpation of verses by Edward Young, see H.B. Forster, *BC* xxxii (1983), 425–38, esp. 431–2 item 10, and Tierney, *Dobsley* (1988), 82–3. Wesley also improved the 2nd edn. of his *The Complete English Dictionary*, Bristol: William Pine, 1764, with the aid of SJ's *Dictionary*, but he acknowledged the debt in his 'Preface'.

75.3TT/6b   Taxation no Tyranny, Wesley's   [1775]
                 Calm Address

A CALM | ADDRESS | TO | *OUR AMERICAN* | COLONIES. | By *JOHN WESLEY*, A.M. | A NEW EDITION. | [rule] | Ne, pueri, ne tanta animis affuefcite bella, | Neu patriæ validas in vifcera vertite vires. | Virgil. | [rule] | *LONDON:* | Printed by R. Hawes, in *Dorfet-Street*, Spitalfields, | And Sold at the Foundry, Moorfields.

12°, A–B⁶, ($3 (–A1) signed), 12 leaves.

Pp. A1 *1* t., *2* blk, *3* 4–23 text dh: [hp of flowers] | A CALM | ADDRESS, &c. | [row of flowers], *24* blk.

Pagination: (↑); *Press-figures*: none; *Catchwords*: no errors.

Explicit: 23 THE END.

Paper: White, laid; La. post (uncut: 7 × 4½ in.); no vis. wmk.

Type: Long primer (3.2 mm), leaded (2.0 mm), notes: minion (2.3).

Copies: O (GP. 421/4)

75.3TT/6c   Taxation no Tyranny, Wesley's   [1775]
                              Calm Address

A CALM | ADDRESS | TO | *OUR AMERICAN* | COLONIES. | By *JOHN WESLEY*, A.M. | A NEW EDITION CORRECTED AND ENLARGED. | [rule] | TO WHICH IS ADDED, | A calm Addreſs to AMERICANUS. | By a NATIVE of *AMERICA*. | [rule] | *Ne, pueri, ne tanta animis aſſueſcite bella,* | *Neu patriæ validas in viſcera vertite vires.* | Virgil. | [parallel rule] | *LONDON:* | Printed by R. Hawes, (No. 40) Corner of *Dorſet-Street*, Criſpin-Street, Spitalfields.

12°, $¹² ($6 numbered, –$1), 12 leaves.

Pp. *i* t., *ii* blk, *iii*–iv Preface, *5* 6–16 text dh: [rows of flowers] | A CALM | ADDRESS, &c. | [rule], on $7 ½t: [rule] | A CALM ADDRESS | TO | *AMERICANUS,* | BY | A NATIVE of AMERICA. | [rule], ²*ii* 3–8 text.

Pagination: (↑) 6–16, [↑] ²3–8; *Press-figures*: none; *Catchwords*: 7 voter‸ (~,), 14 on (no).

Explicit: ²8 FINIS.

Paper: White, laid; La. post (7 × 4½ in.); no vis. wmk.

Type: Bourgeois (3.0 mm), roman and italic.

Copies: O (GP. 291/1).

Extracts from *Taxation no Tyranny* were published in various newspapers, including:

Caledonian Mercury, 15, 18, and 20 March 1775

Edinburgh Advertiser, 14, 24 March 1775

Edinburgh Evening Courant, 15 March 1775

London Chronicle, 9, 11 March 1775

Lloyd's Evening Post, 10 March 1775

London Packet, 10, 13, 15, 17, 20, 22, 24, 29, and 31 March 1775

Middlesex Journal, 14, 16, 21, 23, 25, and 28 March 1775

Morning Chronicle, 10, 13 March 1775

Whitehall Evening Post, 14, 16 March 1775

Universal Mag. lvi (March 1775), 151.

75.3TT/TG/1   Taxation no Tyranny,   1777
                     German translation

[Fraktur] Amerikanifches | Archiv, | herausgegeben | von | Julius Auguft
Remer, | Profeffor der Gefchichte. | [medium rule] | Zweyter Band. |
[medium rule] | [scroll device] | [bevelled double rule] | Braunfchweig, | im
Verlage der Fürftl. Waifenhaus=Buchhandlung. | 1777.

8°, a⁴ A–F⁸ G⁴ (G3 + χ1) H–Q⁸ R⁸ (±R8) S⁸ T–U⁴, ($5 (–a1,4,5, G4, T4,
U4) signed; 'Amerik. archiv, 2ter Th.' on $1), 152 leaves.

Pp. a1 *i* t., *ii* blk, *iii–viii* Vorbericht dh: [scroll hp] | Vorbericht | des
Herausgebers., rt: Vorbericht | des Herausgebers. on A1 *1* ½t: I | Schatzung
keine Tiranney. | Eine Antwort | auf | die Entfchlüffe und Adreffen | des |
Amerikanifchen Congreffes. | [medium rule] | Nach der Vierten Ausgabe aus
dem Englifchen | überfetzt., *2* blk, *3* 4–58 text dh: [orn. hp] | Schatzung keine
Tiranney., rt: Antwort auf die Entfchlüffe | des Amerikanifchen Congreffes.,
59 60–294 texts of other translated pieces [vid. inf.], *295–6* errata (incl. 22 in
TnT).

Pagination: ᴳχ1 is a single inserted folded leaf which does not affect the pagination.

Catchwords: 56 [die-] jenigen, (~ₐ).

Paper: Rough, white, laid; Kleine median (uncut: 8½ × 5¼ in.); wmk.:
GEI[?]PEL

Type: Fraktur, brevier (3.6 mm); ornaments on t., ½t and dhh.

References: Metzdorf, *MLN* lxviii (1953), 397–400.

Notes: A companion vol. includes Burke's Speech on the Colonies: 'Herrn
Edmund Burke's Esqu. Rede, womit er seinen Vorschlag einer Aussöhnung mit
den Colonien empfiehlet. Gehalten im Parliament, den 22ten März. 1775.' (pp.
109–219).

The other pieces translated in this volume are:

I. Josiah Tucker, *Demüthige Vorstellen und ernstliche Apellation an
Großbritanien und Ireland*, pp. 59–140 (Adams (1980), 75-144a)

II. *Berufung auf die Gerechtigkeit und den Vortheil der Großbritanischen Nation
und den gegenwärtigen Streitigkeiten mit Amerika, von einem alten Mitgliede des
Parlaments (Nach der vierten Ausgabe . . .)*, pp. 141–208

III. *Zweyte Berufung auf die Gerechtigkeit und den Vortheil des Volks, in Absicht
der Maaßregeln gegen Amerika, von dem Vorfaßer der ersten Berufung. (Nach der
Ausgabe von 1775 . . .)*, pp. 209–94.

The work includes various notes on SJ's style by the translator, e.g. p. 17
'*Ramifications*, ein Wort, das neu gemacht zu seyn scheint',[1] rendered as
'Verbreitungen'.

Copies: NIC (green paper boards, red leather spine label: 'Remers |
Amerikanisches | Archiv. | II. Band.');

USA: CtY (Franklin 777.R28), CU, DLC, MB, MH, [MiU-C], MWA, NN, [OCl, OU, PHi], PPL, [PU, RPJCB].

---

[1] He had evidently not consulted SJ's *Dictionary* where this word is given with citations from Matthew Hale and John Arbuthnot.

75.3BG   W. Bell's Greek Grammar   1775

A NEW | COMPENDIOUS GRAMMAR | OF THE | GREEK TONGUE: | WHEREIN | The ELEMENTS of the LANGUAGE are plainly | and briefly comprized in ENGLISH. | For the Ufe of SCHOOLS and PRIVATE GENTLEMEN, | Whether they have been taught LATIN or not. | BY W. BELL, A.B. | THE THIRD EDITION, WITH ADDITIONS. | [parallel rule] | *LONDON:* | Printed by C. CLARKE, for the | AUTHOR; | And Sold by Meffrs. RICHARDSON and URQUHART, under the Royal | Exchange; J. BUCKLAND, No. 75, Pater-nofter Row; and | G. BURNET, near Arundel-ftreet, in the Strand. | MDCCLXXIX.

12°, π^2 A–C^6 E–N^6 O^4, ($3 (–O3) signed), 78 leaves.

Pp. π1 *i* t., π1^v *ii* blk, *iii*–iv Preface, on A1 *1* 2–150 text, *151* Errors to be corrected, *152* blk.

Pagination: [↑] 5, 97, 112, 135; 27 as 28.

Press-figures: none; *Catchwords*: unrecorded.

Explicit: 150 FINIS.

Paper: White, laid; La. post (7 × 4½ in.); no vis. wmk.

Type: Long primer (3.2 mm); notes and examples: minion (2.5 mm).

Notes: There is no gathering signed D, but the text is continuous, as is shown by the pagination. The first edn. was noticed in *Gents. Mag.* lxxvi (Mar. 1776), 132, as published by Murray @ 2s., but no copy seen. The 'Preface' was attributed to SJ by Richard Harrison in 'Johnsonian Bibliography', *Book Lore*, i (Dec. 1884), 21, and repeated in *Bookworm*, i (1888), 381, without corroborating evidence; cf. Sherbo's discussion, *SB* xl (1987), 207–19 (209); ESTC: t099656. There is nothing to associate it with SJ.

Copies: O (Douce B. 644, = 3rd edn. 12°, 1779).

75.5BL/1   Legal Argument for Boswell   1775

6 May   Legal argument for Boswell on title of 'Doctor of Medicine', a cause between the Aberdeen Infirmary and John Memis, M.D.

References: *Life* ii. 372–3; *JB: Ominous Years*, 62, 100, 148; Brady, *JB: Later Years*, 521 n; Fifer, *Corr. with Club* (1976), 62–4 and refs.

Dictated to JB anent the case of 'Dr [John] Memis', whose draft argument was prepared in Feb.–Apr. 1775, and first published in *Life* (1791), i. 491–2. JB's notes on the case are in his Legal Notebooks (CtY: MS. 27, 29).

No separate publication is known.

75.5BL/2   Legal Argument for Boswell   1775

7 May   Legal argument on the case of Paterson vs. Alexander
'John Paterson and the Town Councillors of Stirling. Case against James Alexander, pretended Provost'.

References: *Scots Mag.* xxxvii (May 1775), 731–2; *Life* ii. 373–4, Brady, *JB: Later Years*, 521 n.

Notes: Dictated to JB 'a few days after' [*sc.* the above], and published in *Life* (1791), i. 492–3. JB's notes are in his Legal Notebooks (CtY: MSS. 27, 29). The case was heard before the Lords in Apr.–May 1775, but was then deferred to the autumn and finally decided in JB's absence in Scotland (*Ominous Years*, 370).

Strahan recorded the printing of the 'Case of John Paterson and Others' on 12 May 1775, comprising 3½ sheets for 'John Spottiswoode Esq.' (L: Add. MS 48803, fo. 63ᵛ). In the customary 4° format this would produce a pamphlet of 14 leaves, 28 pp., but no copy has yet been found.

Copies: Unlocated.

75.5NR   Notice on Macleod of Raasay   1775

On 6 May 1775 SJ wrote to John Macleod of Raasay acknowledging that JB had just showed him Macleod's complaint that his clan had been represented as subordinate to that of Macleod of Macleod (Dunvegan) in the *Journey* (75.1J/1, above, pp. 132–33; *Journey* (1985), 48).[1] He added that 'I have desired Mr. Boswell to anticipate the correction [*sc.* in a future edition] in the Edinburgh papers' (*Letters* 389; Hyde ii. 203). SJ drafted the notice of which the MS is now CtY (MS Boswell 1630; *MS Handlist* 135, *MS Index* JoS 212; facsimiles in *Works* (Yale), ix. 59, and *Journey* (1985), 185). It was published by JB's agency in the *Caledonian Mercury*, 27 May, and the *Edinburgh Advertiser*, 30 May, 1775, and was reprinted by JB in his *Journal of a Tour* (1785), 519–20, and in the 1785 edn. of *Journey* (75.1J/6, above), on A2, where it is dated 'Strand, October 26, 1785.'

---

[1] Macleod's complaint and JB's intermediate correspondence are CtY: MS Boswell, C 1861–2, and L 912. SJ's draft notice is MS Boswell M 133.

75.6ES   Epitaph on Mrs Salusbury   1775

Marble memorial by Joseph Wilton on the S wall of nave of St Leonard's Parish Church, Streatham.[1]

On 20 May 1775 HLT reminded SJ that he owed her 'an Epitaph for that Dear Lady whose Remembrance gives me more delight than many a pretended Lover feels from that of his Mistress' (*Letters* 393a).

The epitaph was composed by SJ at Oxford and sent to HLT on 1 June 1775 (*Letters* 399; Hyde, ii. 215–16). There are ten early versions.

A This MS draft is now MRu². It deliberately left space for the correct dates at the end as: 'Nata . . . 17 Nupta . . . 17 Obijt . . . 17'.

Some delay in the post meant that HLT did not respond immediately, and on 5 June SJ wrote a little petulantly, in French (*Letters* 400; Hyde, ii. 216). To HLT's eventual reply he responded on 7 June:

> You are but a goose at last. Wilton told you that there is room for 350 letters, which are equivalent to twelve lines. If you reckon by lines the inscription has 17. If by letters 579. So that one way you must expel five lines, the other 229 letters. This will perplex us, there is little that by my own choice I should like to spare, but we must comply with the stone.[3]

On 10 June he wrote again, this time from Lichfield: 'I shall adjust the epitaph some way or other. Send me your advice' (*Letters* 405; Hyde, ii. 221), and on the following day:

> Consider the epitaph, which, you know, must be shortened and tell what part you can best spare. Part of it which tells the birth and marriage is formulary, and can be expressed only one way; the character we can make longer or shorter, and since it is too long, may choose what we shall take away. You must get the dates for which you see spaces left (*Letters* 405, 11 June 1775; Hyde, ii. 223).

Henry Thrale apparently objected to any abridgement, and on 16 June HLT wrote:

> Mr Thrale is right in another Affair, he has found out that the Letter of the Epitaph may be made less, and then the Stone will hold more; he will not have your Writing or my Mother's Praises curtailed he says (*Letters* 406a, quoted in Clifford, *Mrs Piozzi*, 126).

To this SJ replied from Lichfield on 19 June:

> Small letters will undoubtedly gain room for more words, but words are useless if they cannot be read. The lines need not all be kept distinct, and some words I shall wish to leave out, though very few. It must be revised before it is engraved (*Letters* 408; Hyde, ii. 229).

B HLT had by now made a copy of SJ's draft (A), but in it she introduced the misreading 'insatiabilis', and added the date of her mother's death '1773'.[4]

C A second draft by HLT generated further misreadings of SJ's hand: 'sentiarum' for *sententiarum*, 'oblectantur' for *oblectaretur*, 'insatiabilis' for *insanabilis*, and 'sperati' for *speram*, and SJ corrected these words, changing the last to *sperans*. This copy however inserted the missing dates to read:

> 'Nata 1706, Nupta 1739, Obiit 1773.–'

It was perhaps prepared with a view to modification of the whole text, for it bears two dockets in HLT's hand:

　　1. 'I have written this over in haste pray correct the mistakes & send it me back by Harry that I may copy it again fair for you to shew Dr. Lawrence', and

　　2. 'Epitaph on Hester Maria Salusbury by Sam: Johnson LLD', this perhaps written much later. (MS Hyde: *MS Handlist* 136c, *MS Index* JoS 203).

D The amended version was then copied by HLT in her *Thraliana*.[5]

E A fair copy of the revised version was presumably made for Wilton the sculptor, but this has not survived.

F The version on the extant stone represents Wilton's rendition of the lost fair copy (E, above). It differs notably from its predecessors by reading 'ut loquenti nunquam' for their *Ut colloquijs nunquam*, 'diri Carcinomatis veneno contabuit' for their *Cancri insanabilis veneno contabuit*, and 'è terris' for simply *Terris*.

G The version given on the stone was first printed by Henry Maty in his *A New Review; with Literary Curiosities* . . . &c., v (May, 1784), 386–7, perhaps directly from the stone, but possibly from (E) if it had survived the activities of the stonecutter.[6]

H When HLT prepared the MS of her *Anecdotes* for publication in 1785 (NPM: MS. MA 322, p. 78), she did not recur to her *Thraliana* because she knew that the text on the stone was a further revised version, and that (F) therefore represented the true final version, but she may also have relied on Maty's version (G) in view of its proximity to the stone and because of the ease of transcription from his printed page into her *Anecdotes* (1785), 131.

I The epitaph was included in Kearsley's *Poetical Works of Johnson* (1785), 195–6 (85.2PW/1, &c., below), with a single unparalleled reading of 'Viribusque vitæ' for *Nexibusque Vitæ*.

J Isaac Reed in *Works*, xiv (1788), 542–3, followed *Anecdotes* (H) above, though it must be conceded that he may have followed Maty (G) since he owned a set of the *New Review*.[7]

　　Later versions are found in Daniel Lysons, *Environs of London*, i, 1792 ('Surrey'), 484–5; Owen Manning and William Bray, *History and Antiquities of the County of Surrey*, 3 vols., iii (1814), 392, and H. W. Bromhead, *The Heritage of St Leonard's Parish Church, Streatham*, 1932, pp. 35–7.

---

[1] Illustrated in Mary Hyde, *The Thrales of Streatham Park* (1977), 119. Hester Maria Salusbury (*née* Cotton, 1707), Mrs Thrale's mother, died 18 June 1773. The original was slightly damaged by a fire in St Leonard's in the 1980s. In 1965 it read: Iuxta sepulta est Hestera Maria | Thomæ Cotton de Combermere Baroneti Cestrienfis Filia, | Ioannis Salusbury, Armigeri Flintienfis, Uxor; | Forma felix, felix Ingenio, | omnibus jucunda, suorum amantifsima; |Linguis Artibusque ita exculta | ut loquenti nunquam deefsent | Sermonis nitor, Sententiarum flosculi, | Sapientiæ gravitas, leporum gratia; | modum servandi adeo perita | ut domestica inter Negotia Literis oblectaretur, | Literarum inter Delicias rem familiarem sedulo curaret. | multis illi multos Annos precantibus, | diri Carcinomatis veneno contabuit, | nexibusque Vitæ paulatim resolutis, | é terris, meliora sperans, emigravit. | Nata 1707, Nupta 1739, Obiit 1773.

² MRu: (MS Eng. 543/20), *BJRL* xix (1935), 235; *MS Handlist* 136, *MS Index* JoS 202.

³ *Letters* 403; Hyde, ii. 220. There is a limit to the diminution of the size of letters to be cut in stone, but marble is more amenable to small sizes than most other kinds. Wilton however would have set his limits.

⁴ MRu: (MS. MR Eng. 543/21); *MS Handlist* 136b, *MS Index* JoS 204, see also *BJRL* xvi (1932) 60–1, and xix (1935), 235.

⁵ MS: CSmH; *Thraliana* i. 7. HLT also recorded an English translation by Murphy, of 14 Jan. 1779, in *Thraliana* 357.

⁶ Robert Ray told HLT that he had seen a version of this epitaph in 1784 on a monument in the Church at Walthamstow (*Thraliana* 829). If so it was copied either from Wilton's monument at Streatham, or perhaps from Maty's published version. I have not verified the story.

⁷ King, *Bibliotheca Reediana*, 2 Nov. 1807, 2558 — Heber, £2. 3s.

75.9–11FJ   Journal of a visit to France   1775

SJ and the Thrales visited France in the autumn of 1775. They set off from Streatham on 15 September and landed at Calais on 17th. Baretti conducted them from Dover to Paris where they arrived on 28 Sept. and stayed until 1 November when they began their return journey which brought them to Calais on 10 November, to Dover on 11th, and thence together back to Streatham on 13th.[1] SJ's record is in a leather bound book bearing 'France 2' on the cover, and with the first entry dated 'Oct. 10. Tu.' This implies a lost volume for the earlier part of the journey from about 15 Sept. to 9 Oct. inclusive, and since 'France 2' ends with the entry for 'Nov. 5. Sunday' there may have been a subsequent notebook covering the last stages of the return.[2]

JB was given the MS by Malone on the instructions of William Scott, SJ's executor, on 21 July 1787, and published the text in *Life* (1791), whence it was repeated in all subsequent edns. of the *Life*. It was sold on the death of JB jun. in 1823 to the E. of Guilford by the agency of Thomas Thorpe, the bookseller, and in the Guilford sale (Evans, 17 Dec. 1835), to Samuel Rogers whose great-nieces presented it to the British Museum (*Athenaeum*, 6, 13, and 27 Aug. 1898) where it remains as L: Add. MS 35299 (*MS Handlist* 138(b), *MS Index* JoS 383). JB commented on the MS, 'I have deposited the original MS. in the British Museum, where the curious may see it' (*Life* i. 509 n.), though its provenance shows that the presentation took much longer.

It was published from the MS by M. Tyson and H. Guppy, *The French Journals of Mrs Thrale and Doctor Johnson* (1932), 168–88 (with a note on the MS, p. 168), and in revising Hill's edn. of Boswell, Powell also consulted the MS and made several corrections to JB's version, *Life* ii. 389–401 (522). The MS was again reprinted by McAdam and Milne in *Works* (Yale), i. 229–56.

¹ Hyde, *The Thrales of Streatham Park* (1977), 143.

² SJ reported to Taylor (*Letters* 440, 16 Nov. 1775; Hyde ii. 276–7) that 'I came back last tuesday from France', indicating that he reached home on Tuesday, 14th November, having spent one day with the Thrales at Streatham. JB commented at the end of the published text, 'Here his journal ends abruptly' (*Life* i. 511).

75.10BP/1a   Baretti's Easy Phraseology   1775

EASY PHRASEOLOGY, | FOR THE USE OF | YOUNG LADIES, | WHO INTEND TO LEARN | THE COLLOQUIAL PART | OF THE | ITALIAN LANGUAGE. | BY | JOSEPH BARETTI, | Secretary for Foreign Correſpondence to the Royal | Academy of Painting, Sculpture, | and Architecture. | LONDON, | Printed for G. Robinson, in Pater-noſter Row; | and T. Cadell, in the Strand. | MDCCLXXV.

8°, π⁴ (π1 + χ1) a⁴ B–3H⁴, ($2 signed), 221 leaves.

Pp. π1 *i* t., *ii* blk, ᵖχ1 *iii*–iv Preface dh: PREFACE., π2 *v* Erratum, π2ᵛ *vi* Dedicatoria dh: [two double rules] | DEDICATORIA | ALLA | Signora ESTERUCCIA., π3 *vii* Dedication dh: [two double rules] | THE | DEDICATORY LETTER | TO | Miſs HETTY., π4–a4ᵛ 'vii–xv' [! = *ix–xvii*] text (English and Italian facing), *xviii* blk, on B1 *1* 2–424 text dh: [two double rules] | DIALOGO PRIMO, | *Tra Eſteruccia e il ſuo Maeſtro.* | DIALOGUE THE FIRST, | Between Hetty and her Maſter.

Pagination: (↑); 306 as ˌ↑), 387 as (↑ˌ.

Press-figures: D1ᵛ(18)–6, E3(29)–6, G1ᵛ(42)–7, L2(75)–7, M3ᵛ(86)–7, P3(109)–6, Q3ᵛ(118)–6, R3ᵛ(126)–1, S4ᵛ(136)–7, T4ᵛ(144)–2, U4ᵛ(152)–2, X4ᵛ(160)–2, Y4(167)–2, Z4ᵛ(176)–7, 2A3ᵛ(182)–7, 2B1ᵛ(186)–6, 2C4ᵛ(200)–1, 2D4ᵛ(208)–7, 2E1ᵛ(210)–8, 2F4ᵛ(224)–8, 2G3ᵛ(230)–1, 2H4(239)–2, 2I2ᵛ(244)–1, 2K3ᵛ(254)–8, 2L3(261)–8, 2M3(269)–6, 2N3ᵛ(278)–8, 2O2ᵛ(284)–6, 2P3(293)–6, 2Q4ᵛ(304)–1, 2R4ᵛ(312)–2, 2S4(319)–1, 2T4(327)–1, 2U4(335)–2, 2X4(343)–8, 2Y2ᵛ(348)–8, 2Z2ᵛ(356)–6, 3A3(365)–1, 3B3(373)–8, 3C1ᵛ(378)–8, 3D3ᵛ(390)–2, 3E3(397)–2, 3F4ᵛ(408)–1, 3G3(413)–1, 3H2ᵛ(420)–6. Unfigured a–C, F, H, K, N, O.

Catchwords: *om.* 5, 13, 34, 39, 42, 71, 77, 82, 100, 101, 126, 314; 16 qualch₍ (qualche), 29 Deh₍ (~,), 41 No, (~:), 90 [mu-] liebre (lièbre), 103 di (sofa di), 128 lark₍ (~,), 142 Ho (Hò), 174 Chᵉ (Che), 181 *M*. Th (*M*. That), 195 [ar-] cipàzza! (arcipàzza!), 259 *other*₍ (~,), 267 Molt (Molto), 272 abou (about), 286 b (I believe), 308 [de-] moliſh (liſh), 329 [beniſ-] ſimo₍ (~,), 341 [qua-] lùnque (lúnque), 348 names? (~ !), 364 *D*. M. Sì (*D. M.* Sì).

Explicit: 424 FINIS.

Paper: White, laid; Demy (uncut: 8¾ × 5½ in.); no vis. wmk.

Type: Sm. pica (3.6 mm), double cols., unleaded.

References: *Life* ii. 290, 509 (Courtney 127); CH 152; Hazen 8–10; Collison-Morley, *Giuseppe Baretti* (1909), 280; ESTC: t083913.

Notes: The book arose from Baretti's teaching Italian to Hester Maria (Queeney) Thrale. Queeney Thrale signed a formal agreement on 8 December 1774, witnessed by SJ and Baretti, to pursue her study of Italian (Lansdowne, *Johnson and Queeney* (1932), 7). Baretti's agreement with George Robinson, dated 4 October 1774, stipulates his preparation of work for a volume of not less than 27 sheets (eventually 27½) for 75 guineas in three instalments, the first paid on delivery of the MS, the second on publication, and the third on any reprinting, with a receipt for the first, dated 6 Oct. 1774 (MS Hyde). The agreement is not reported by Bentley in *SB* xxxv (1982), 67–110, but he points out that the George Robinson archive examined is not complete. Collison-Morley's statement that Baretti got £50 for the work is mistaken. The book was published 5 Oct. 1775 at 6s., bound (*Public Advertiser*), though it is not noticed in *Gents. Mag.* until xlvi (Mar. 1776), 132.

SJ wrote the 'Preface' which stands on the extra inserted leaf $^\pi\chi1$, and later translated Baretti's closing verses into English (*Thraliana*, 210 '1777', *Poems*[2] 201–2; *MS Index* JoS 120–1).

Copies: O (3079 e.9);

USA: CSmH, CtY (imperfect), IU ('H.M. Thrale'), [Liebert], MH, NIC; *UK*: [W.R. Batty, Esq;], C, Csj, L (72. c.12), MRc; *Aust*: CNL.

75.10BP/1b Baretti's Easy Phraseology 1775

An early state, perhaps taken off the press for Baretti's use in his lessons, lacks the inserted leaf $^\pi\chi1$ of SJ's 'Preface', and has a special title:
SMALL TALK | FOR THE USE OF | YOUNG LADIES | THAT WISH TO LEARN | THE COLLOQUIAL PART | OF THE | ITALIAN LANGUAGE. | By JOSEPH BARETTI | SECRETARY for Foreign Correſpondence to the ROYAL | ACADEMY of PAINTING, SCULPTURE, | and ARCHITECTURE. | LONDON, | Printed for G. ROBINSON, in Pater-noſter-Row. | MDCCLXXV.
References: ESTC: t194723.
Notes: The collation here is as for the usual issue, save there is no *erratum* on π2. Only a single copy is recorded: that which belonged to Sophia Streatfeild, now O (Don. e. 120). Queeney Thrale surely had a copy, but if so it is untraced.

75.11MC A Humble Address to the King, 1775
Morning Chronicle

18 November   A Humble Address to the King

From the 'Gentlemen, Merchants, and Traders of . . . Southwark', presented by Henry Thrale, and published in *Morning Chron.*, 20 Nov. 1775, and in the *London Advertiser*, 20 Nov. 1775.

References: Fleeman, in *Johnson, Boswell and their Circle* (1965), 183–4, making an attribution in which I now have less confidence. Accepted by Brack, *Shorter Prose*.

76.1HA/1   Hailes's Annals of Scotland, first edition   1776

[½t] [row of 63 flowers, 127 mm] | ANNALS | OF | SCOTLAND. | [row of 64 flowers, 130 mm]

[Title] ANNALS | OF | SCOTLAND. | FROM | The Accession of MALCOLM III. Surnamed CANMORE, | Tto the Accession of ROBERT I. | By Sir DAVID DALRYMPLE. | EDINBURGH: | Printed by Balfour & Smellie. | FOR | J. MURRAY, No. 32. Fleetſtreet, LONDON. | [short rule] | M.DCC.LXXVI. [M.DCC.LXXIX.]

2 vols., 4°

I (1776): π⁴ A–3D⁴ *3E*1, ($2 (–3A2) signed), 205 leaves.

Pp. π1 ½t, π1ᵛ blk, π2 t., π2ᵛ blk, π3 ADVERTISEMENT., π3ᵛ blk, π4 ERRATA., π4ᵛ blk, on A1 *1* 2–311 text dh: ANNALS | OF | SCOTLAND, | From the ACCESSION of | MALCOLM III. | [beaded rule], htt: var. (Names of Kings &c.), *312* 313–62 Appendixes, *363–9* Tables, *370* 371–401 Chronology, *402* blk.

Pagination: [↑] 46, 101, 162, 185, 222; unnumbered 296, 330, 342, 348, 351, 354, 358, 363–70.

Press-figures: none.

Catchwords: 8 n. "placuit, (ₐ~,), 10 [inha-] bitants. (~*.), 16 After (S. of Durham), 32 [man-] nersₐ (~,), 96 n. *om.* (manifeſt), 131 n. [fa-] ₐciat ('~), 149 Thirlſtaneₐ (~*.), 150 Dervorguil, (~*,), 320 2. *Placitæ* (2. *Placita*), 354 [of] ſucceſſion, (of ſucceſſion,), 360 *om.* (Is), 363–8 *om.*

Explicit: 401 FINIS.

Paper: White, laid; La. post (uncut: 10½ × 8¾ in.); wmk.: fleur-de-lys.

Type: Text: english (4.5 mm), leaded; footnotes: small pica (3.7 mm); shoulder-notes: long primer (3.1 mm).

References: *Life* ii. 178 ff.; ESTC: t082751.

Notes: Dalrymple's MS drafts, and various proofs, the final versions of which are annotated by SJ, are in E: (MS 7228/52–64).[1] JB was the intermediary.[2] These proofs also bear the endorsement, 'Mr James Smellie, Printer, Anchor Close, Edinburgh' (7228/55); John Murray was the publisher, on the recommendation of Gilbert Stewart (E: MS Acc. 7228/23, fos. 90, 94, 96, and 98). The edn. was of 1,000 copies (E: MS Acc. 7228/23, fo. 112; Murray to Dalrymple, 1 Feb. 1776), and vol. 1 was published in London on 15 January 1776 at 15s. in boards (*Scots Mag.* xxxviii (Jan. 1776), 43). Dalrymple became a judge of the criminal court in 1776, and was sufficiently busy with his legal duties for the completion of the second volume to be significantly delayed. It is surprising that there are not more odd volumes extant.

II (1779): π² 2π1 A–3C⁴ 3D² *3E*1, ($2 signed; 'Vol. II.' on $1), 202 leaves.

Pp. π1 ½t: [row of 64 flowers, 129 mm] | ANNALS | OF | SCOTLAND. | [row of 64 flowers, 129 mm], π1ᵛ blk, π2 t., π2ᵛ blk, 2π1 ADVERTISEMENT., 2π1ᵛ blk, on A1 *1* 2–277 text dh: ANNALS | OF | SCOTLAND, | From the

ACCESSION of | ROBERT I. | [beaded rule], *277* 278–329 *330–31* Appendixes, *332* 333–97 text *398* blk.

Pagination: unnumbered 267, 278, 285, 295, 301, 313, 321, 330–2, 349, 358.

Press-figures: none.

Catchwords: 63 The (This), 64 n. Cantire; (~:), 111 'Holy- ('Holy, Land;), 130 mercenaries, (~*.), 143 n. T. (*sometimes* ~,), 212 marches, (~*.), 221 [con-] 'demnation,' ('~*,'), 226 male,, (~*,), 237 n. [re-] 'meavit;' ('remeavit;'), 280 Befides, (~,), 292 flaughtered,; (~*;), 296 I. Alexander (I. If Alexander), 321 No, VI. (~. ~.), 330–2 *om.*, 352 '[one (',~), 368 Bruce, (~,), 391 *om.* (The), 396 abbey (abbay).

Explicit: 397 FINIS.

Paper: White, laid; Demy (uncut: 11¼ × 8¾ in.); wmk.: fleur-de-lys.

Type: Text: english (4.4 mm), footnotes: sm. pica (3.7 mm), shoulder notes: long primer (3.1 mm).

References: ESTC: t141222.

Notes: The conjugacy of II. π^2 with II. $3D^2$ is established by the watermarks and sewing in E (Gray).

It is reasonable to suppose that this vol. was, like vol. 1, printed in an edn. of 1,000 copies by James Smellie, of Edinburgh, though there is no direct evidence on this point. Vol. 2 was published in Feb. 1779 at 12s. 6d. in boards (*Scots Mag.* xli (Mar. 1779), 157–8, review by 'M', and by Gilbert Stuart in the *Monthly Rev.* lx (1780), 183). SJ's name is in Dalrymple's list of presentation copies (E: MS c.5, 499), but no such copy has been recorded. In the 'Inventory of Books in the Parlour at Newhailes' (E: MS Acc. 7228/589, fo. 6), 'opposite the Fire Place East. 1st Row', is noted 'Lord Hailes Miscellaneous Works, Annals of Scotland 5 vols.' which were presumably various duplicates.

Copies: E^2 (**1.** Gray 1374–5; **2.** A 107 b);

USA: CSmH, CtY, DFo, DLC (vol. 1 only), Hyde ('Hew Dalrymple'), ICN, ICU, MBAt, [MeB], MH, MWA, NN, OCl, [OClWHi, PSt], TxU; *UK*: ABu^2, BRp, C^2, Csj, Ct, [Es], Eu^2, Gp^2, Gu, Gt, Innerpeffray, L^2, LEu, MRc, MRu, NCp (vol. 1 only), NCu, O (G. Scot. 141), SAN, WIS; *Eir*: Dt^2.

---

[1] SJ's annotations are in E: (MS 7228/54 and 57), relative to the published texts of *Annals*, I. 234–45, 263–74, and 288–95. He had also read much of the MS (*Corr. of JB with Club*, ed. Fifer (1976), 54). JB's transcriptions of most are now MS Hyde (*Handlist* 132b). JB also read some proofs, and his annotations appear on several (a further fragment annotated by JB is O: MS Don. c.62, fo. 17), though Hailes seems uniformly to have accepted SJ's amendments and to have ignored those by JB. JB retained Hailes's correspondence on the reading of the work, and published some of it in *Life*, cf. *Boswell Catalogue*, s.n. 'Hailes', C 1452 ff., and SJ's *Letters*.

[2] Acknowledged by DD in an undated letter to JB (Eu: MS La. II. 603): 'I am singularly obliged to Dr Johnson for his accurate and useful criticisms. I would that I could profit by his revision of ye whole work, as I have done by his revision of ye Specimen. Had he added some strictures on ye general plan of ye work, it would have added much to his favours . . . As to Fingal, I see a controversy arising & purpose to keep out of its way . . .'. Though undated, the reference to Fingal puts the letter some time after the publication of SJ's *Journey* on 18 Jan. 1775.

76.1HA/2   Hailes's Annals of Scotland, second edition   1797

ANNALS | OF | SCOTLAND. | FROM THE ACCESSION OF MALCOLM III. | TO | THE ACCESSION OF THE HOUSE OF STEWART. | TO WHICH ARE ADDED, | *SEVERAL VALUABLE TRACTS* | RELATIVE TO THE HISTORY AND ANTIQUITIES OF | SCOTLAND. | [double rule] | BY THE LATE SIR DAVID DALRYMPLE, | LORD HAILES. | [double rule] | A NEW EDITION. | IN THREE VOLUMES. | [medium swelled rule] | VOL. I [– III]. | [medium swelled rule] | EDINBURGH: | PRINTED FOR WILLIAM CREECH, | AND T. CADELL AND W. DAVIES, LONDON. | [short parallel rule] | 1797. 3 vols., 8°

I. a⁴ b² A–2X⁴, ($1 (a2 as a) signed; 'VOL. I.' on $1), 182 leaves.

Pp. Engr. front. + a1 *i* t., *ii* blk, *iii* iv–x Preface dh: [double rule] | *PREFACE.* | [double rule], ht: PREFACE., *xi* Contents dh: [double rule] | CONTENTS OF VOL. I. | [double rule], *xii blk*, on A1 *1* 2–343 text dh: [parallel rule] | ANNALS | OF | SCOTLAND, | FROM THE ACCESSION OF | MALCOLM III. | [parallel rule], rt: ANNALS OF SCOTLAND. | MALCOLM III. [&c.], *334* blk, *345* 346–51 *Corrections and Additions by the Author.*, *352* blk.

Pagination: [↑] 51, 55, 75, 113, 124, 178, 203, 325; 84 as 48, 239 as 23, 287 '7' slipt.

Press-figures and *Catchwords*: none.

Explicit: 343 and 351 END OF VOL. I.

II. π² A–3B⁴ (–3B4), ($1 signed; 'VOL. II.' on $1 ('VOL. III.' 2S)), 193 leaves.

Pp. π1 t., π1ᵛ blk, π2 Contents dh: [double rule] | *CONTENTS OF VOL. II.* | [double rule], π2ᵛ blk, on A1 *1* 2–382 text dh: [double rule] | ANNALS | OF | SCOTLAND, | FROM THE ACCESSION OF | ROBERT I. | [double rule], rt: ANNALS OF SCOTLAND. | ROBERT I. [&c.].

Pagination: [↑] 293 as [29ₓ; 45 as 54, 96 as 6, 249 as 492; unnumbered 306.

Press-figures and *Catchwords*: none.

Explicit: 382 END OF VOLUME II.

III π² A–3B⁴ 3C1, ($1 signed; 'VOL. III.' on $1), 195 leaves.

Pp. π1 *i* t., *ii* blk, *iii*–iv Contents dh: [double rule] | CONTENTS OF VOL. III. | [double rule], ht: CONTENTS., on A1 *1* 2–383 text dh: [double rule] | APPENDIX. | No. I. | OF THE LAW OF EVENUS, | AND THE MERCHETA MULIERUM., rt: ANNALS OF SCOTLAND. | APPENDIX. [&c.], *384* blk, *385 Corrections and Obſervations by the Author.*, *386* blk.

Pagination: (↑) 115; unnumbered 22, 30, 35, 42, 45, 48, 53, 59, 66, 77, 84, 96, 104, 106, 114 (blk), 116–25, 145, 198, 246, 253, 258, 263, 272, 275, 278, 324, 337, 340–1, 376, 384 (blk), 386 (blk); 14 as 4, 57 as 59, 85 as 8, 200 as 200, 265–71 as 261–67 (=2L⁴).

Press-figures and *Catchwords*: none.

Explicit: 383 *FINIS*.

Paper: White, wove; wmk.: '1794', '1795', '1796' variously distributed.

Type: Text: pica (3.9 mm), notes: bourgeois (3.1 mm).

Plates: Engr. oval port. of DD 'The Hon^{bl}. Lord Hailes. Painted by Seton Engraved by Bengo'.[1]

References: ESTC: t067790.

Notes: It is likely that II. 3B4 = III. *3C*1, but no copy demonstrates the fact.

DD's annotated copies of the first edn. (76.1HA/1, above; E: MS Acc. 7228/52–3) were not followed in the preparation of this edn. Hailes died in 1792. The identity of the editor of this version is unknown, but he evidently had no access to DD's papers. Exchanges between DD and William Creech relative to his publications are in Er (M/film RH4/26 (P8), and 16078 BK (GD.38)), and in Ep (qYZ.325.C91).

Copies: E (A. 107 d);

USA: [MA], MB, [MdBP], MH, PPL; *UK*: ABu, C, Ck, En, Eu (lacks vol. 3), Gu, L, LVp, O (8° Y.15–17 Art. BS), SAN.

---

[1] Mr Christopher Eimer does not consider this to be a representation of the name of the engraver 'Pingo'.

76.1HA/3   Hailes's Annals of Scotland, third edition   1819

Annals of Scotland, from the Accession of Malcolm III. in the year M.CCC.LXXI. To which are added, Tracts relative to the History and Antiquities of Scotland. By Sir David Dalrymple of Hailes, Bart. Third Edition. Vol. I [– III]. Edinburgh: Printed for Archibald Constable & Co. and Fairbairn & Anderson, Edinburgh; and Hurst, Robinson & Co. London. 1819.

   3 vols., 8°

   I. π^4 A–2F^8 2G^2, Pp. *i–vii* viii, *1* 2–458 *459–68*, text.

   II. π1 2π^2 A–2F^8 2G^2, Pp. *i–vi* 1 2–467 *468*, text.

   III. π^4 A–2H^8, Pp. *i–v* vi–vii *viii*, *1* 2–496, text.

Press-figures are used throughout.

Colophon: on pp. ii, and last p. of text in each vol: 'Printed by Walker and Greig, Edinburgh.'

References: McMullin, *Library*, 6th ser. xii (1990), 236–41, esp. 237.

Notes: McMullin argues that the press-figg. are compounds of two digits each representing a press in the firms of Walker and Greig, and John Ballantyne, and that the sheets were perfected by the combined presses. Such an arrangement is likely to lead to variations in the incidence of the figures.

The text here has been revised in the light of DD's own MS revisions in his copies of 1776–9 (76.1HA/1, above, E: MSS. Acc. 7228/52–3), and secondly by an unidentified editor who has changed the disposition of some notes and appendixes. 'To the present Edition of the *Annals of Scotland* have been added the other Historical Writings of *Sir David Dalrymple, Lord Hailes*, originally published in detached pieces, at various times. *Edinburgh, 1st. May 1819.*' (I. v).

Copies: E (Hist. S.3.H);

USA: CtY, MB, [MdBP], MH, MiU, [NB], PPL, [PPStC], TxU; *UK*: C², DUNu, En, Eu, Gp², [Gt], Gu, L, LVp, MRu, SAN, SHp.

76.1BH/1a   Burney's History of Music, first edition   1776–89

A | GENERAL HISTORY | OF | MUSIC, | FROM THE | EARLIEST AGES to the PRESENT PERIOD. | To which is prefixed, | A DISSERTATION | ON THE | MUSIC of the ANCIENTS. | BY | CHARLES BURNEY, Muſ. D. F.R.S. | VOLUME THE FIRST. | LONDON, | Printed for the Author: And ſold by T. Becket, Strand; J. Robson, | New Bond-Street; and G. Robinson, Paternoſter-Row. | MDCCLXXVI.

4 vols., 4°

I. (1776): π⁴ a–c⁴ B–D⁴ E⁴ (± E4) F⁴ (± F1) G⁴ (± G2) H–K⁴ L⁴ (–L3,4 + L3.4.5.6) *L1 M–2E⁴ *2E–*2F⁴ 2F–3N⁴ 3O⁴ (± 3O3) 3P–3U⁴ 3X⁴ (–3X2.3), (\$2 signed; 'Vol. I.' on \$1), 289 leaves.

Pp. π1 *i* t., *ii* blk, *iii* iv–v Dedication [To the Queen] dh: DEDICATION., ht: DEDICATION., *vi* blk, *vii* viii–xx Preface dh: [two double rules] | PREFACE., *xxi–xxx* List of Subscribers dh: SUBSCRIBERS., *xxxi–xxxii* Contents dh: CONTENTS., on B1 *1* 2–80 *81–*86 81–194 Dissertation dh: DISSERTATION | ON THE | MUSIC | OF THE | ANCIENTS., *195* 196–216 *217–*232 217–495 History dh: A | GENERAL HISTORY | OF | MUSIC., *496* blk, *497* 498–507 Additional notes dh: [two double rules] | ADDITIONAL NOTES., 508–16 dh: [two double rules] | REFLECTIONS | UPON THE | Conſtruction and Uſe of Some particular Musical Instruments of | ANTIQUITY., *517* 518–22 List of Plates dh: A | LIST and DESCRIPTION | OF THE | PLATES to VOL. I., *523–4* Errata & Binder's Directions.

Pagination: no errors. The Binder's Directions state:

There are . . . twenty-six *double pages*, marked with asterisms. Three were occasioned by the late arrival of Mr Bruce's communications, and by other additions to the text, occurring after the text was broken up; and this method of inserting them was preferred to that of giving the reader the trouble of turning to a *Supplement*. As the sheets last printed will not be sufficiently dry to bear beating immediately, the purchasers of this Volume are entreated to let it remain sewed, or in boards, for a few months.

The inserted sections are:

substitutes L3–6	1
*L1	1
Cancels E4, F1, G2, 3O3	4
*2E–*2F⁴	8
	17 leaves

The asterisked page-numbers are *81–*86 (3 leaves L5.6 + *L1 = 6 pp), and *217–*232 (8 leaves *2E–*2F⁴ = 16 pp.), a total of 22 pp. The outstanding 4 pp. of the 26 mentioned in the Directions would occupy 2 leaves, but they are not yet accounted for.

Press-figures: 2Z3(357)–1.

Catchwords: [*Subscribers*]: c1 Miss (Mr. Jackſon), c1ᵛ Robert (Right Hon.), c2 Chriſtopher (Sir James), c2ᵛ John (Hon. Charles), c3 Benjamin (Richard); 16 *Meſon* (M II ~), 17 conſiſting ((*m*) ~), 22 Theſe (—Theſe), 28 *om.* (SECTION), 30 Diatonic. (Diaton.), 32 *om.* (And), 50 *om.* (But), 62 Ariſtoxenus, (~(*b*),), 63 *om.* (D.), 69 *om.* (All), 88 E (ΕΙΣ), 94 *om.* (HYMN), 101 *om.* (M.), 104 do, (~‸), 130 Angellini (Angelini), 133 ‸Ομοφωνοι‸ ("Ομοφωνοι,), 154 *om.* (With), 164 *om.* (As), 170 *om.* (eaſy), 194 *om.* (A), 209 *om.* (in), 212 [ac-] *om.* (count), *226 *om.* (It), *231 [ima-] *om.* (gine), 227 *om.* (This), 242 *om.* (A), 255 *om.* (Sir), 284 *om.* (As), 330 *om.* (trans-dialected), 361 *om.* (There), 363 [inci-] *om.* (dents), 366 *om.* (All), 367 *om.* (had), 379 *om.* (*Of*), 381 *om.* (Pauſanias,), 384 *om.* (Sir), 392 main‸ (~.), 397 *om.* (ſaid), 398 But‸ (~,), 406 *om.* (The), 408 time‸ (~,), 410 *om.* (It), 441 *om.* (The), 442 *om.* (I), 454 *om.* (by), 462 *om.* (Ariſtoxenus), 478 12. (XII.), 481 *om.* (But), 489 *om.* (as), 495 *om.* (ADDITIONAL).

Explicit: 522 END OF THE FIRST VOLUME.

Plates: (9), 1 Front. facing t., and pp. 204 (fold.), *222, 252 (fold.), 275 (fold.), 515 (fold.), 522 (3 = x2 fold. + 1 single leaf). The two folding plates facing p. 522 are each attached to the stubs of 3X2.3.

II. (1777): A | GENERAL HISTORY | OF | MUSIC. | FROM THE | EARLIEST AGES to the PRESENT PERIOD. | BY | CHARLES BURNEY, Muſ.D F.R.S. | VOLUME THE SECOND. | LONDON, | Printed for the Author: And ſold by J. Robson, New Bond-Street; and | G. Robinson, Paternoſter-Row. | MDCCLXXVII.

4°, *A*² B–E⁴ F⁴ (F2 + ˣ'F3') G–3Y⁴ 3Z², ($2 (+ ˣF3) signed; 'Vol. II.' on $1 (+ ˣF3)), 273 leaves.

Pp. A1 t., A1ᵛ blk, A2 Contents, on B1 *1* 2–597 text of History dh: A | GENERAL HISTORY | OF | MUSIC., *598* blk, *599–600* Corrections and Additions.

Pagination: ˣF3 pp. 37–8; 44 (Engr.) ↖; 376 as 476.

Press-figures: B3ᵛ(6)–8, C3(13)–4, D2ᵛ(20)–1, D3ᵛ(22)–2, E2ᵛ(28)–6, F3(37)–7, 3A2ᵛ(366)–7, 3A3ᵛ(368)–8, 3I3ᵛ(432)–4, 3K2ᵛ(438)–5, 3K4(441)–8, 3L4ᵛ(450)–1, 3M3(455)–1.

Catchwords: 1 *om.* (language), 9 *om.* (of), 14 *om.* (The), 16 [by] *om.* (by), 29 *om.* (Boethius,), 32. *om.* (Thefe), 34 *om.* (Tu), 39 *om.* (Of *or.* 41 A few), 41 *om.* (They), 43 *om.* (*SINGING*), 49 *om.* (The), 68 *om.* (I), 164 *om.* (Marchetto), 183 'may ("~), 241 *om.* (*Fo*[*r*]*t*), 243 *om.* (Mi-), 245 No (But | Noftradamus), 252 *om.* (*Comment,*), 253 *om.* (*Out*), 256 *om.* (Be-a-ti), 286 *om.* (fpire!), 287 *om.* (*Ha !*), 290 who (all who), 297 *om.* (*II.*), 300 *om.* (Eager), 306 *om.* (*vous*), 319 [chi-] is (valry), 328 *om.* (But), 331 as ("~), 339 Mufic‸ (~,), 370 ro- (Romances), 378 "There (‸~), 381 [compo-] tions (fitions), 384 *om.* (Owre), 385 *om.* (*Deo*), 389 that‸ (~,), 397 [fa-] milies‸ (~,), 400 *Mufike*‸, (~(*e*),), 405 *om.* (*Pef.*), 406 *om.* (CANON), 407–10 *om.*, 423 *om.* (It), 450 ‸but ("~), 460 *om.* (Indeed), 462 *om.* (Franchinus), 474–6, 478, 491–2, 495–6, 498–500 *om.*, 509 *Da* (Yet), 510 Jofquin, (It will), 512, 520 *om.*, 526 *om.* (PIERRE), 527–32, 534–8, 540–50 *om.*, 551 ‸or ("~), 556–64 *om.*, 568 ‸And ("~), 569 "Lady‸ ("~,), 579–82 *om.*

Explicit: 586 END OF THE SECOND VOLUME.

Plates: (30) Facing t., and pp. 36 (as 'F3' paged '37–38'), 264 ('C. F. Burney fecit'), 480 (2 leaves as '481–4'), 498 (as '499–500'), 502 (2 leaves as '503–6'), 512 (2 leaves as '513–16'), 520 (2 leaves as '521–4'), 530 (as '531–2'), 534 (2 leaves as '535–8'), 540 (5 leaves as '541–50'), 556 (4 leaves as '557–64'), 578 (2 leaves as '579–82'), 586 (6 leaves as '587–97' ['*598*' blk]).

III. (1789): A | GENERAL HISTORY | OF | MUSIC. | FROM THE | EARLIEST AGES to the PRESENT PERIOD. | BY | CHARLES BURNEY, Muf.D. F.R.S. | VOLUME THE THIRD. | LONDON, | Printed for the AUTHOR: And fold by PAYNE and SON, at the Mews-Gate; ROBSON | and CLARK, Bond-Street; and G. G. J. and J. ROBINSON, Paternofter-Row. | MDCCLXXXIX.

4°, *a*² b⁴ B–3Y⁴ 3Z², ($2 (−E2) signed; 'VOL. III.' on $1), 276 leaves.

Pp. a1 *i* t., *ii* blk, *iii–iv* Contents, *v* vi–xi Essay dh: ESSAY | ON | MUSICAL CRITICISM., *xii* blk, on B1 *1* 2–102 *103–*104 103–247 246–7 248–486 477–86 489–576 575–6 577–622 [i.e. 638] text dh: A | GENERAL HISTORY | OF | MUSIC., on 3Y1 *629–50* Index dh: [double rule] | INDEX.

Pagination: 246–7, 477–86, and 575–6 are duplicated; 392 as 382, 398–99 as 388–89, 467 as 367. Inserted leaves of musical examples, though not included in the collation, are included in the sequence of pagination.

Press-figures: a2(iii)–3, b3ᵛ(x)–5, B4(7)–1, C4ᵛ(16)–1, D1ᵛ(18)–1, E3(31)–1, F3ᵛ(40)–1, G4(49)–1, H4ᵛ(60)–1, I2ᵛ(64)–1, K4ᵛ(86)–1, L3(93)–1, M3(107)–1, N1ᵛ(112)–1, O2ᵛ(132)–1, P2ᵛ(144)–1, Q4(155)–1, R1ᵛ(158)–1, S3ᵛ(172)–2, T4(183)–1, U4ᵛ(196)–1, X4(203)–1, X4ᵛ(204)–1, Y3(213)–1, Z3(225)–1, 2A3(243)–2, 2B2ᵛ(250)–2, 2C3ᵛ(260)–1, 2D1ᵛ(264)–1, 2E1ᵛ(278)–2, 2F4(297)–2, 2F4ᵛ(298)–1, 2G1ᵛ(300)–2, 2G4ᵛ(308)–1, 2H3(315)–6, 2I3(327)–6, 2K1ᵛ(332)–1, 2K3(335)–2, 2L3ᵛ(344)–1, 2M1ᵛ(348)–1, 2M3(357)–2, 2N2ᵛ(364)–1, 2O4(375)–2, 2P2ᵛ(380)–1, 2P3ᵛ(382)–2, 2Q3(389)–1, 2Q3ᵛ(390)–3, 2R2ᵛ(396)–8, 2S1ᵛ(402)–3, 2T2ᵛ(418)–3, 2U2ᵛ(426)–1, 2U3ᵛ(428)–2, 2X3(435)–8, 2X3ᵛ(436)–1,

2Y4ᵛ(446)–1,   2Z3(457)–2,   2Z3ᵛ(458)–1,   3A2ᵛ(464)–2,   3A4(367)–6,
3B3(473)–1,   3C3ᵛ(484)–2,   3D3ᵛ(482)–1,   3E2ᵛ(488)–2,   3E3ᵛ(490)–1,
3F4ᵛ(500)–1,   3G3ᵛ(506)–2,   3H4(515)–1,   3I1ᵛ(518)–7,   3I2ᵛ(520)–3,
3K4(531)–3,   3K4ᵛ(532)–2,   3L2ᵛ(536)–6,   3L4(539)–2,   3M3ᵛ(548)–3,
3N4(557)–6,   3N4ᵛ(558)–5,   3O1ᵛ(560)–6,   3P4(575)–6,   3P4ᵛ(576)–3,
3Q2ᵛ(578)–5,   3R2ᵛ(586)–1,   3R4(589)–8,   3S4ᵛ(598)–7,   3T2ᵛ(602)–8,
3U1ᵛ(608)–7,   3U2ᵛ(610)–8,   3X3(619)–2,   3X3ᵛ(620)–8,   3Y1ᵛ(624)–8,
3Y2ᵛ(626)–2.

Catchwords: *om.* before engr. plates and pp. of staff notation, pp. 27–8, 35–6, 47, 55–6, 67–70, 77–82, 90, 95–8, *103–*104, 103–4, 115–18, 125–30, 139–42, 169–70, 177–8, 191–4, 205–8, 215–17, 223–4, 227–32, 237–40, 245–6, 267–72, 279–82, 285–6, 303–4, 309–10, 317–20, 349–54, 378, 383, 405–6, 411–12, 415–16, 449–52, 455–6, 473, 479–80, 543–4, 571–2; 43 "Lyons, (ˌ∼,), 49 ˌfor ('∼), 66 ANTHEM (Anthem), 94 SACRED (Sacred), 102 CANZONET (Canzonet), 114 SPECIMENS (Specimens), 124 MADRIGAL (Madrigal), 190 MOTET (Motetus), 204 MADRIGAL (MADRIGALE), 214 VILLOTAˌ (Villota,), 222 MARDIGAL (Madrigal), 225 always (The), 226 FUGUE (Fuga), 244 MOTET (Motetus.), 264 ſcarceˌ (∼,), 266 MOTET (Motetus.), 276 When (What), 278 EXTRACTS (Extracts), 284 NOËLˌ (NOËL), 293 Page 252. (∼ 262.), 297 Whichˌ (∼,), 308 CHANSON (Chanſon), 316 MADRIGAL (Cantio.), 348 CATCHES (Catch), 369 ˌlearning, ("∼,), 375 "ſceaneˌ ("∼,), 404 PSALM (Pſalm), 410 THE (THE), 414 CANON (Canon), 448 SPECIMENS (Specimens), 454 ANTHEM (Anthem), 478 "them (481 "∼), 478 wasˌ (∼,), 542 FRAGMENTS (Fragments), 556 they (preclude), 570 TINNA NONNAˌ (Tinna Nonna,), 600 churchˌ (∼,), 610 volumeˌ (∼,), 3Y2ᵛ *om.* (G), 3Y3 *om.* (K), 3Y3ᵛ *Menetria*, (*Menetrier*,).

Explicit: 622 END OF THE THIRD VOLUME. 3Z2 END OF THE THIRD VOLUME.

Plates: (59) Facing t. ('R. F. Burney delt. F. Bartolozzi ſculpt. Publishᵈ. as the Act directs April 30ᵗʰ. 1789'), and pp. 26 (as '27–8'), 54 (as '55–6'), 66 (2 leaves as '67–70'), 76 (3 leaves as '77–82'), 88 (as '89–90'), 94 (2 leaves as '95–8'), 102 (2 leaves as '*103–*104, 103–4'), 114 (2 leaves as '115–18'), 124 (3 leaves as '125–30'), 138 (2 leaves as '139–42'), 168 (as '169–70'), 176 (as '177–8'), 190 (2 leaves as '191–4'), 204 (2 leaves as '205–8'), 214 (as '215–16'), 222 (as '223–4'), 226 (3 leaves as '227–32'), 236 (2 leaves as '237–40'), 244 (as '245–6'), 266 (3 leaves as '267–72'), 278 (2 leaves as '279–82' *originally as* '179–82' *but corr. in MS in most copies*), 284 (as '285–6'), 302 (as '303–4'), 308 (as '309–10'), 316 (2 leaves as '317–20'), 348 (3 leaves as '349–54'), 404 (as '405–6'), 410 (as '411–12'), 414 (as '415–16'), 448 (2 leaves as '449–52'), 454 (as '455–6'), 478 (as '479–80'), 542 (as '543–4'), 570 (as '571–2').

IV. (1789): A | GENERAL HISTORY | OF | MUSIC. | FROM THE | EARLIEST AGES to the PRESENT PERIOD. | BY | CHARLES BURNEY, Muſ.D. F.R.S. | VOLUME THE FOURTH | LONDON, |

Printed for the Author: And fold by Payne and Son, at the Mews-Gate; Robson | and Clark, Bond-Street; and G. G. J. and J. Robinson, Paternofter-Row. | MDCCLXXXIX.

4°, a² B–3O⁴ 3P⁴ (± 3P3) 3Q–4N⁴, ($2 signed; 'Vol. IV.' on $1), 326 leaves.

Pp. a1 t., a1ᵛ blk, a2 Contents dh: CONTENTS., on B1 *1* 2–12 text dh: ESSAY | ON THE | EUPHONY | OR SWEETNESS OF LANGUAGES | AND THEIR | FITNESS FOR MUSIC., *13* 14–685 text of History dh: A | GENERAL HISTORY | OF | MUSIC., *686* blk, *687–688* List of Books, *689–700* Index, *701* Errata, *702* blk.

Pagination: 536 as 539, 636 as 656. Inserted leaves of musical examples, though not included in the collation, are included in the sequence of pagination.

Press-figures: B3(5)–1, C4ᵛ(16)–1, D4ᵛ(24)–1, E4(35)–1, F4ᵛ(44)–2, G2ᵛ(48)–1, H3ᵛ(58)–1, H4ᵛ(60)–3, I2ᵛ(64)–1, K2ᵛ(78)–1, K4(81)–2, L3ᵛ(88)–1, M3(99)–3, N2ᵛ(106)–1, N3ᵛ(108)–7, O2ᵛ(114)–2, O3ᵛ(116)–1, P1ᵛ(126)–2, P2ᵛ(130)–3, Q1ᵛ(136)–7, Q4ᵛ(144)–2, R1ᵛ(146)–7, S2ᵛ(164)–8, S4(175)–2, T3(181)–3, U1ᵛ(186)–8, U2ᵛ(188)–6, X2ᵛ(196)–3, X4(199)–2, Y2ᵛ(204)–2, Y3ᵛ(206)–3, Z3(213)–8, Z3ᵛ(214)–6 *or* 7, 2A4(223)–6, 2A4ᵛ(224)–3, 2B3ᵛ(230)–7, 2B4ᵛ(232)–2, 2C1ᵛ(234)–3, 2C3(237)–7, 2D1ᵛ(242)–3, 2D2ᵛ(244)–6, 2E3(253)–2, 2E4(255)–1, 2F4(263)–3, 2F4ᵛ(264)–2, 2G4ᵛ(274)–2, 2H4(281)–7, 2H4ᵛ(282)–8, 2I2ᵛ(286)–5, 2I4(289)–7, 2K4ᵛ(300)–7, 2L2ᵛ(304)–2, 2M1ᵛ(310)–1, 2N3ᵛ(322)–7, 2N4ᵛ(324)–5, 2O2ᵛ(328)–2, 2O3ᵛ(330)–7, 2P2ᵛ(336)–8, 2Q1ᵛ(342)–8, 2R3(353)–8, 2S1ᵛ(358)–3, 2S3(361)–2, 2T2ᵛ(368)–8, 2U3ᵛ(378)–2, 2X4(387)–9, 2X4ᵛ(388)–6, 2Y4(395)–6, 2Z1ᵛ(398)–8, 3A4ᵛ(412)–9, 3B1ᵛ(414)–8, 3B3(417)–9, 3C4(427)–8, 3D1ᵛ(430)–3, 3D2ᵛ(432)–2, 3E1ᵛ(446)–7, 3E3(449)–6, 3F1ᵛ(454)–8, 3F3(457)–9, 3G4(469)–2, 3G4ᵛ(470)–6, 3H1ᵛ(472)–6, 3I4(485)–6, 3I4ᵛ(486)–9, 3K2ᵛ(490)–9, 3L3ᵛ(500)–7, 3M3ᵛ(508)–3, 3N1ᵛ(512)–3, 3N3(515)–8, 3O1ᵛ(520)–3, 3O2ᵛ(522)–2, 3P1ᵛ(528)–5, 3P3ᵛ(532)–7, 3Q2ᵛ(538)–8, 3R1ᵛ(544)–5, 3R2ᵛ(546)–3, 3S3(555)–7, 3T4(565)–8, 3T4ᵛ(566)–3, 3U1ᵛ(568)–6, 3U3(571)–8, 3X1ᵛ(576)–3, 3X4ᵛ(582)–9, 3Y3(587)–9, 3Y3ᵛ(588)–5, 3Z1ᵛ(592)–9, 4A1ᵛ(600)–7, 4B2ᵛ(610)–8, 4B4(613)–9, 4C1ᵛ(616)–3, 4C2ᵛ(618)–8, 4D1ᵛ(624)–5, 4D2ᵛ(626)–8, 4E4ᵛ(638)–8, 4F4ᵛ(646)–7, 4G3(651)–8, 4G3ᵛ(652)–6, 4H3(659)–8, 4H4(661)–3, 4I3ᵛ(668)–5, 4K3ᵛ(676)–5, 4L1ᵛ(680)–7, 4L2ᵛ(682)–9, 4M4ᵛ–6, 4N1ᵛ–8, 4Nᵛ–7.

Catchwords: *om.* at engraved pp. 28, 117–22, 127–8, 137–8, 142–3, 147–50, 153–4, 157–8, 165–8, 171–4, 217, 271–2, 293–4, 437–44, 461–2. Sometimes a cwd. skips the next p. and catches with a later p. designated by '= 00' (giving the p. number where the correct referent is found); 66 but (= 73), 86 J. Peri͵ (~. ~,), 90 fentiments (= 95 ͵entiments), 115 [*Ca-*] *rita*, (*rità*,), 116 Air (Air), 123 TATA, (Il Re), 126 Extract (Extract), 136 Extracts (Extracts), 146 Beauties (Beauties), 152 Fragments (Fragments), 161 *Ma* (*Ricco*), 164 reached, (= 169), 170 Fragments (Fragments), 191 [multi-] ͵tude ("~), 197

"Rich‸ ("~,), 224 author‸ (~,), 226 [fre-] qnently (quently), 246 ‸Mrs. ("~.), 270 Divisions (Divifions), 292 Mrs. (= 295), 348 fhort‸ (~,), 396 *varro*‸ (*varco*,), 407 remains (performance,), 460 Divisions (Vocal Divifions), 465 [irrefifti-] ble‸ (ible,), 466 [Si-] roe‸ (~,), 542 Marcello, (~.), 564 This‸ (~,), 611 fifth‸ (~,), 613 [him-] felf, (~;), 624 The (This), 641 after‸ (~,), 652 Mufic‸ (~,), 662 time‸ (~,), 664 divifions, (~‸), 4M4ᵛ *om.* (L.).

Explicit: 685 FINIS. 4N4ᵛ FINIS.

Plates: (28) Facing t., and pp. 30 (2 leaves as '31–4'), 66 (3 leaves as '67–72'), 90 (2 leaves as '91–4'), 116 (3 leaves as '117–22'), 126 (as '127–8'), 136 (as '137–8'), 146 (2 leaves as '147–50'), 152 (as '153–4'), 156 (as '157–8'), 164 (2 leaves as '165–8'), 170 (2 leaves as '171–4'), 270 (as '271–2'), 292 (as '293–4'), 436 (4 leaves as '437–44'), 460 (as '461–2').

Paper: White, laid; Medium (uncut: 11⅝ × 9 in.); no vis. wmk.

Type: Text: english (4.5 mm), leaded; notes: bourgeois (3.0 mm).

References: *Life* iv. 544 (Courtney 154); CH 153; Hazen 26–30; Lonsdale, *Burney* (1965), 491–4; *Poems²* 220–22; *Letters* 998.1 (to CB, 23 Aug. 84); *Booklist* 32; Subscriptions no. 11; ESTC: t149622.

Notes: Burney issued his Prospectus for this work on 10 Jan. 1774 (*Morning Chronicle*, 5 Apr. 1774),[1] and the progress of the work is documented by Lonsdale, ch. 4.[2] CB's original plan was for two vols. only, but the work expanded and at II. 585–6 he apologized to his subscribers for failing to contain it in 2 vols, and announced a third. The distribution of press-figures in vol. 2, strongly suggests at least two printers. The first volume was announced on 31 January 1776. Lonsdale notes that most of the illlustrations were the work of E. F. Burney, and that many of the drawings are in BL, Prints (Lonsdale, 494).

856 subscribers took 1,047 copies; SJ's copies of vols. 1–2 (all he lived to receive), were lot 322 at his sale (Christie, 16 Feb. 1785) where they were bought by Malone for £1. 19s., who added vols. 3–4 in due course. Vol. 2 is inscribed by SJ: 'Given by the Authour to Sam: Johnson May 16. 1782' (NN-B; *Booklist* 32). The delay between vols. I and II arose from CB's anxiety over Hawkins's rival *History of Music*, published in 5 vols. in November 1776, which led CB to modifications of his own work (Lonsdale, ch. 5).

SJ composed the 'Dedication' to the Queen (I. iii–v), and contributed a verse translation of Euripides' *Medea* 193–203 (II. 340), which CB attributed to 'a learned friend' (*Poems²*).[3] SJ also read proofs, at least of vol. 2 (SJ–HLT, 2 Nov. 1779, *Letters* 641: '[The Doctor] has called twice on me, and I have seen some more sheets — and away we go.' Hyde, iii. 205), and modified CB's Apology (II. 585–6) for the growth of the book (*Letters* 767.4, 18 Mar. 82, to CB: 'A long apology is a tedious thing', Hyde, iv. 21).[4] Some portion of proof was sent to SJ who wrote on it, 'this is an Excellent sheet indeed', leading CB to declare he wished to 'put it up in lavender & shall bequeath it to the Museum or Bodleian library.'[5] CB repaid SJ's assistance with several approving mentions e.g at ii. 41, 219, 343, 354; iii. 49, 339, 341 n., 403, 598 n.; iv. 227, 596.

Copies: O² (**1**. GG. 50–3 Art; **2**. Douce B. subt. 273–6);
USA: CtY², DLC, G. Goldberg, Esq; Hyde, ICN, ICU, [Liebert (uncut, 'David Garrick')], MBAt, MH ('From the Author'), NcU, NjP, NN-B, NN, NPM, PHi, PPL, TxU², ViU; *UK*: E, LICj (lacks vol. 1), Op, WIS (CC.11.3–4, vols. 3–4 only); *Eir*: Dt.

---

¹ Copies in O (Vet. A5 a.15(45)), and CtY. ESTC: t172754 however reports a yet earlier version dated 'London, April 20th. 1773' uniquely represented at Göttingen university library.
² Some preliminary MS notes by CB are in L (Add. MS 48345, fos. 37–40), and a series of notebooks is CtY (MS Osborn); a fragment of corrected proof of 4 pp. is MRu (Eng. MS 655/42).
³ JB recognized this as by SJ but did not mention it in *Life*; *Boswell Catalogue*, MS. M 155:12.
⁴ An erased entry in SJ's MS notebook xiv, fo. 2ᵛ (MS: Op), reads: 'adjusted Burney's apology for his third volume'.
⁵ Lonsdale (1965), 255, quoting CB to Thomas Twining, 11 June 1780. The sheet is not now in the Bodleian and seems not to be in the British Library.

76.1BH/1b   Burney's History of Music,   '1782'
                                    second issue of Vol. II

A | GENERAL HISTORY | OF | MUSIC. | FROM THE | EARLIEST AGES to the PRESENT PERIOD. | BY | CHARLES BURNEY, Muf.D. F.R.S. | VOLUME THE SECOND. | LONDON, | Printed for the AUTHOR: And fold by J. ROBSON, New Bond Street; and G. ROBINSON, Paternofter-Row. | MDCCLXXXII.

4°, *A*² (± A²) B–E⁴ F⁴ (F2 + 'L1') G–3O⁴ 3P⁴ (3P3 + χ²) 3Q⁴ 3R⁴ (3R2 + ²χ1, 3R3 + ³χ²) 3S⁴ (3S2 + ⁴χ², 3S4 + ⁵χ²) 3T⁴ (3T3 + ⁶χ1, 3T4 + ⁷χ²) 3U⁴ (3U1 + ⁸χ1–5, 3U4 + ⁹χ⁴) 3X⁴ 3Y⁴ (3Y3 + ¹⁰χ²) 3Z² (3Z2 + ¹¹χ 1–6), ($2 signed, 'VOL. II.' on $1 (–Z, + 'FL1')), 302 leaves.

Pp. 2 engr. + A1 t., A1ᵛ blk, A2–2ᵛ Contents, on B1 *1* 2–597 text dh: A | GENERAL HISTORY | OF | MUSIC., rt: A GENERAL HISTORY | OF MUSIC., *598* blk, *599* CORRECTIONS and ADDITIONS., *600* blk.

Paper: White, laid (exc. FL1: wove); medium; no vis. wmk.

Type: English, leaded; notes: bourgeois.

Plates: Front. Apollo listening to Pan, 'G. Cipriani inv. F. Bartolozzi fculp.' 2. Port. CB, 'Sir Joshua Reynolds pinxᵗ. F. Bartolozzi Sculpᵗ. Charles Burney Mus: Doc: Oxo. F.R.S. Publifh'd as the Act directs April 1ˢᵗ. 1784.' and as 1st issue 76.1BH/1a vol. 2, above, engr. inserted leaves paginated. On ³ᶻχ1 '587' coloph: 'Engrav'd by T. Straights, Nᵒ. 138 Sᵗ. Martins Lane Charing Crofs London.'

References: Lonsdale, *Burney* (1965), 500; ESTC: n021306.

A reissue with cancelled t. and Contents leaf, of the sheets of the first issue, above. The final leaf 3Z2, bearing the *Corrections and Additions* in the first issue, is missing from many copies of this issue.

The date of the reissue is not established, but the date on the substitute title is false: '1782' is not compatible with the wove paper which is watermarked '1809', or with the use of the short 's' in the *cancellantia* (see Lonsdale 468). 1809 or 1810 are much more likely dates. There is no obvious reason why the date of the reissue should be deliberately misrepresented.

On 30 April 1801 George Robinson paid CB £265. 18s. 10d. on account for the *History of Music*, and again on 10 May 1803, a further £162. 1s. 10d.[1]

Copies: Ep (W.ML.160, 'Joseph Smith "Aequo Animo"');

USA: CLU-C, CSmH, CtY, DFo, DLC, PPL, ViU; *UK*: WIS (CC.11.2).

---

[1] Bentley, *SB* xxxv (1982), 67–110, esp. 86, s.n.

76.1BH/2   Burney's History of Music, second edition   1789

A | GENERAL HISTORY | OF | MUSIC, | FROM THE | EARLIEST AGES to the PRESENT PERIOD. | BY | CHARLES BURNEY, Muf.D. F.R.S. | VOLUME THE FIRST. | THE SECOND EDITION. | LONDON, | Printed for the Author: And fold by Payne and Son, at the Mews-Gate; Robson | and Clark, Bond-Street; and G. G. J. and J. Robinson, Paternofter-Row. | MDCCLXXXIX.

4°, *A*⁴ B–3X⁴ 3*Z*², ($2 signed; 'Vol. I.' on $1), 270 leaves.

Pp. A1 *i* t., *ii* blk, *iii* iv–v Dedication dh: TO THE | QUEEN., ht: DEDICATION., *vi* blk, *vii–viii* Contents dh: CONTENTS., on B1 ²*i* ii–xviii Preface dh: [2 double rules] | PREFACE., on D2 *1* 2–186 Dissertation, *187* 188–485 History, *486* blk, *487* 488–95 Reflections, *496* 497–501 List of Plates, *502* blk, on 3X1 Index, 3Z1ᵛ blk, on 3Z2 Binder's Directions, 3Z2ᵛ blk.

Pagination: 215 as 2ᴧ5.

Press-figures: A4(vii)–2,   3Q3ᵛ(468)–1,   3R2ᵛ(474)–9,   3R4(477)–6, 3S1ᵛ(480)–1, 3S3(483)–3, 3T4(493)–8, 3U3(499)–6, 3X3ᵛ–2.

Catchwords: 10 *Nete* (1.' *Nete*), 15 bottomᴧ (~,), 16 I haveᴧ (~ ~,), 22 *om.* (SECTION), 24 Diatonic. (Diaton.), 32 [deter-] mineᴧ (~.), 69 [inten-] tion-allyᴧ (~,), 75 feet. (~(*i*).), 89 Beholdᴧ (~ !), 92 *om.* (HYMN), 100 the (advantages), 163 *om.* (But), 173 *om.* (There), 201 *om.* (Thefe), 214 *om.* (With), 216 *om.* (It), 260 *om.* (Sir), 291 ᴧThe (—The), 318 *om.* (ORPHEUS), 331 *om.* (Though), 353 *om.* (CHAP.), 356 *om.* (There), 364 *om.* (fays), 388 lefs [*slipt*], 404 us, (~(*d*),), 435 *om.* (After), 452 *om.* (however), 459 *om.* (*Scolia*), 461 HIS- (THE | HISTORY), 463 were (where), 468 Livyᴧ (~(*b*),), 469 robesᴧ (~(*e*),), 473 them ? (~ (*m*)?), 484 and (amufements), 492 The (This), 498 [ap-] pear-anceᴧ (~,).

Explicit: 501 END OF THE FIRST VOLUME. 3Z1 END OF THE FIRST VOLUME.

Paper: White, laid; medium (uncut: 11⅝ × 9 in.); no vis. wmk.

Type: Text: english (4.5 mm), leaded; notes: bourgeois (3.0 mm).

Plates: (11) Facing t. and 196 (fold.), 212, 257 (fold.), 264 ('C. F. Burney fecit'), 276, 325, *502* (2 fold. and 1 other).

References: Hazen 28–9; Lonsdale (1965), 184–7; ESTC: t149621.

Notes: This reprint of vol. 1 was evidently intended to supply customers who may have missed the first edn. of vol. 1 in 1776 yet who acquired vol. 2 in 1777. It has no list of subscribers. There is some revision in CB's 'Preface' which introduces a new allusion to SJ, 'Dr Johnson has well said, that "those who think they have done much, see but little to do" . . .'.

Copies: ABu (SB. *7809 Bur.2; 'Eleanor Henn');

USA: [AlB], CLU-C, CSmH (uncut), [CU], DFo, DLC, ICN, [Liebert, MdBB], MH ('From the author to his beloved and excellent daughter F. B.' — Lowell), [NAurW, NhD, NjN], NNC, [NNU], NRU, [OGH, OClW, PBL, PPP, PP-W, T, TxFTC], ViU, [WaSU]; *UK*: BMp, BRu², Csj (10.3), Ct (L.11.40–3), DUu, Ep (Castle 780.9), Gp, LEu, LICj ('R. Sharpe, organist'), MRu, SAN, SPAg (708 9. fo), WIS (CC.11.1), [Yc]; *Eir*: Dt.

76.1BH/3   Burney's History of Music   1935

A | GENERAL HISTORY | OF | MUSIC | From the earliest Ages to the | Present Period | (1789) | by | CHARLES BURNEY | Mus.D., F.R.S. | VOLUME THE FIRST [– SECOND] | WITH CRITICAL AND HISTORICAL NOTES | by | FRANK MERCER | *London, 1935* | G. T. FOULIS & CO., LTD. | Milford Lane, Strand, W. C. 2.

2 vols., 8°

I. Pp. *1–4* 5–817 *818*.
II. Pp. *1–6* 7–1098.

Colophon: (I. 4, 818; II. 4) 'Made and printed in Great Britain | by the Marshall Press Ltd., | Milford Lane, Strand, London, W.C. 2.'

References: Lonsdale, *Burney* (1965), 500.

Notes: SJ's 'Dedication' is retained at I. 9–10, with '[CHARLOTTE]' inserted after 'QUEEN', and two minor changes (para. 3a. splendor > splendour, and 4c. I can however boast > I can, however, boast). Though this is an avowed abridgement, SJ's translation from Euripides' *Medea* 193–203 (*Poems*² 220–4), is retained at I. 638–9. The phrase in CB's 'Preface' citing SJ's dictum 'Those who think they have done much, see but little to do', is at I. 15, showing that Mercer followed CB's 2nd edn. (76.1BH/2, above); he does not however discuss the bibliographical history of the text of his edn. There is an index.

In Appendix 1 (II. 1027–42) among a selection of letters by CB are printed CB to SJ, 14 Apr. 1755 (1027–8),[1] and CB to Malone, 10 or 18 Oct. 1798 (1032), sending him his 'scribbled [a] sheet of hasty remarks' on vol. 2 of JB's *Life* 1791.

Copies: O (174 e.209–10); *UK*: E (Mus 3).

¹ The text of this letter is not minutely accurate. It was published by Fanny Burney in her *Memoirs of Dr Burney* (1832), i. 122. (Note: two editions of this vol. are pointed out by L.F. Powell, *Life* vi. 478, and Lonsdale (1965) observes: 'Not a page of her *Memoirs* should be trusted implicitly', 455.) The MS draft is Hyde.

76.4PT/1 Political Tracts 1776

POLITICAL | TRACTS. | CONTAINING, | THE FALSE ALARM. | FALKLAND's ISLANDS. | THE PATRIOT; and | TAXATION NO TYRANNY. | Fallitur, egregio quifquis fub principe credit | Servitium, nunquam Libertas gratior extat | Quam fub Rege pio. CLAUDIANUS. | LONDON: | Printed for W. STRAHAN; and T. CADELL in the Strand. | M DCC LXXVI.

8°, *A*² B–R⁸ S⁴, ($4 signed), 134 leaves.

Pp. A1 t., A1ᵛ blk, A2 ½t: THE | FALSE ALARM. | [1770.], A2ᵛ blk, on B1 *1* 2–58 text dh: [double rule] | THE | FALSE ALARM., ht: THE FALSE ALARM., *59* ½t: THOUGHTS | ON THE | LATE TRANSACTIONS | RESPECTING | Falkland's Iflands., *60* blk, *61* 62–142 text dh: [parallel rule] | FALKLAND's ISLANDS., ht: FALKLAND's ISLANDS., *143* ½t: THE | PATRIOT. | Addreffed to the | ELECTORS of GREAT BRITAIN. | They bawl for Freedom in their fenfelefs mood, | Yet ftill revolt when Truth would fet them free, | Licence they mean, when they cry Liberty, | For who loves that muft firft be wife and good. | MILTON. | [1774.], *144* blk, *145* 146–68 text dh: [parallel rule] | THE | PATRIOT., ht: THE PATRIOT., *169* ½t: Taxation no Tyranny; | AN | ANSWER | TO THE | RESOLUTIONS AND ADDRESS | OF THE | AMERICAN CONGRESS. | [1775.], *170* blk, *171* 172–264 text dh: [parallel rule] | TAXATION | NO TYRANNY., ht: TAXATION NO TYRANNY.

Pagination: no errors.

Press-figures: B1ᵛ(2)–6, B6ᵛ(12)–1, C5ᵛ(26)–3, D5(41)–5, D8(47)–6, E1ᵛ(50)–2, F5ᵛ(74)–3, F7(77)–2, G3ᵛ(86)–2, G8ᵛ(96)–7, H5(105)–3, H6(107)–6, I7ᵛ(126)–6, K7(141)–5, L3ᵛ(150)–3, M7ᵛ(174)–1, N6ᵛ(188)–7, O6(203)–7, P1ᵛ(210)–1, Q8(239)–8, Q8ᵛ(240)–3, R8(255)–1, R8ᵛ(256)–2, S1ᵛ(258)–5.

Catchwords: *om.* pp. 58–60, 142–4, 168–70; 71 [pro-] tectₛ ('s' *slipt*), 90 [per-] hasp (haps), 150 to (the), 225 [differ-] ence, (~ₐ).

Explicit: 264 THE END.

Paper: White, laid; medium (uncut: 9 × 5⅝ in.); wmk.: fleur-de-lys.

Type: Text: pica (4.3 mm), leaded; notes: small pica (3.6 mm). White lines between paras., opening with large and small caps.

References: Courtney 127; CH 152; *Tinker* 1362; Adams (1980), 76-71a; ESTC: t130899.

Notes: 750 copies printed for Thomas Cadell by Andrew Strahan in April 1776 (L: Add. MS 48803, fo. 67ᵛ). It was published at 5s.

A few revisions from the earlier versions were effected in the text by SJ, who made several presents of copies: that given to Edmund Hector remains untraced (*Booklist* 165).[1]

Copies: Op² (**1**. SJ: 'To Sir Joshua Reynolds from the Authour' *Booklist* 166; **2**. 'Pemb: Coll: Library 1780');

USA: CLU, CSmH, CtY⁴ (**1**. blue wraps. uncut 'A.E. Newton'), DLC, G. Goldberg, Esq; Hyde⁶ (**1**. SJ: 'To Mr Chamier from the Authour' *Booklist* 164; **2**. uncut; **6**. SJ: 'From the Authour to Mr Boswell', *Booklist* 163²), ICN, ICU, IU (Nickell), [Liebert (uncut)], MH, NIC, NjP, NN-B, NPM, NRU, PPAmP, PPL, TxU; *Can*: CaOHM (B.11246); *Japan*: [Kyoto]; *UK*: [B.S. Barlow, Esq; ('A.S. Cumming, M.D.')], BMp (87287), C, E² (**1**. LC 2156, 'J.R.P. Forrest'), Innerpeffray, INV (Forbes Mackintosh), L (292. k.33), LICj (SJ: 'To the reverend Dr Wetherel Master of University College.' *Booklist* 168), MRp, NCp, O² (**1**. 'T. Warton from the Author' *Booklist* 167), Owo, SAN, WLAp ('James O' Shaughnessy'); *Aust*: CNL; *Eir*: Dt (Lecky A. 7.15).

---

[1] A copy incribed 'From yᵉ Authour', apparently by Hector, and with his further inscription 'Veteris pignus amicitiæ', together with a Hopper bookplate, was, in 1991–92, in the hands of Messrs Ken Spelman, bookseller, York. Walter Carless Hopper (1772–1853), of Lichfield, was Hector's heir. It seems that the book was bought in at the Sotheby sale, 28 Apr. 1887, pt. 750, for it re-emerged in 1991 from a branch of the Meysey-Thompson family.

[2] Sotheby (New York), 14 Feb. 1986, 396.

76.4PT/2   Political Tracts, Dublin   1777

POLITICAL | TRACTS. | CONTAINING, | THE FALSE ALARM. | FALKLAND's ISLANDS. | THE PATRIOT; | AND, | TAXATION NO TYRANNY. | Fallitur, egregio quifquis fub principe credit | Servitium, nunquam Libertas extat | Quam fub Rege pio. Claudianus. | DUBLIN: | Printed for W. Whiteſtone, W. Watſon, E. Lynch, | J. Hoey, J. Williams, W. Colles, W. Wilſon, | T. Walker, C. Jenkin, R. Moncrieffe, P. Wogan, | J. Exſhaw, L. White, J. Beatty, and C. Talbot. | M.DCC.LXXVII.

12°, *A*² B–I¹² K¹² (± K12) L¹² M¹⁰, ($5 (–K4, B5 as B4) signed), 132 leaves.

Pp. A1 t., A1ᵛ blk, A2 ½t: THE | FALSE ALARM. | [1770.], A2ᵛ blk, on B1 *1* 2–58 text dh: [double rule] | THE | FALSE ALARM., ht: THE FALSE ALARM., *59* ½t: THOUGHTS | ON THE | LATE TRANSACTIONS | RESPECTING | Falkland's Iſlands., *61* 62–142 text dh: [double rule] | FALKLAND's ISLANDS., ht: FALKLAND's ISLANDS., *143* ½t: THE | PATRIOT. | Addreſſed to the | ELECTORS of GREAT BRITAIN. | [4 lines . . . Milton.] | [1774.], *144* blk, *145* 146–66 text dh: [parallel rule] | THE | PATRIOT., ht: THE PATRIOT., *167* ½t: Taxation no Tyranny; | AN | ANSWER | TO THE | RESOLUTIONS and ADDRESS | OF THE

| AMERICAN CONGRESS. | [1775.], *168* blk, *169* 170–260 text dh: [double rule] | TAXATION | NO TYRANNY., ht: TAXATION NO TYRANNY.

Pagination: no errors; *Press-figures*: none.

Catchwords: *om.* 58–60, 142–4, 166–8; 53 [bruta-] lity (tality), 64 [that] that (dared), 120 Giant- (~ˌ), 223 [differ-] ence, (~ˌ).

Explicit: 260 THE END.

Paper: White, laid; foolscap [or Tellière] (uncut: 6⅜ × 4¼ in.); no vis. wmk.

Type: Pica (4.0 mm), leaded (1.4 mm).

References: Adams (1980), 76-71b; ESTC: t062630.

Notes: The reason for the cancellation of K12 (pp. 215–16) is unknown. A copy annotated by Charles O'Conor was in Thomas Thorpe's *Catalogue* (1849), ii. 1327, at 10s. 6d.

Copies: O (Don. f. 30);

USA: CSmH, CtY, DLC, [Liebert], Hyde, NIC, NN; *Can*: CaOHM (B. 14396); *Japan*: [Kyoto²]; *UK*: BMp (518401, contemp. mottled sheep), CU (Hib . 7. 777.11), L (1488. bb. 15), NCu; *Eir*: Dt.

76.4PT/3   Political Tracts   1968

The Political Writings of Dr Johnson a selection edited by J.P. Hardy Professor of English, University of New England London: Routledge & Kegan Paul

*A*⁸ B–L⁸ (L8 blk), 88 leaves; Pp. *i* ½t, *ii* blk, *iii* t., *iv* coloph., *v* Dedication., *vi* blk, *vii* Contents, *viii* blk, ix–xxii Introduction, on B4 1–132 text, 133–48 Notes, 149–52 Index, *153–4* (L8) blk.

ISBN: 7100-2936-5 (Hbk), 7100-2937-3 (pbk).

Notes: Reprints the 'Political Tracts' of 1776, and four other essays, with Introduction and explanatory notes.

76.5BL   Legal Argument for Boswell   1776

10 and 13 May   Legal Argument for Boswell on 'Pulpit Censure'.

The Case of the Revd Mr. James Thomson (1699–1790), minister of Dunfermline.

References: *Life* iii. 59–61; JB journal, 4, 10, 13, 15 Feb., and 19 Dec., 1776, *Ominous Years*, esp. 60–1 n., 202.

Notes: JB's MS, taken down from SJ's dictation, is untraced. First published by JB in *Life* (1791), ii. 75–8.

76.6GE/1 Epitaph on Goldsmith 1776

White marble memorial slab by Joseph Nollekens, above the South door ('Poets' Corner') in Westminster Abbey.[1]

Goldsmith died 4 April 1774,[2] but the epitaph was not composed until 1776 (*Poems*[2], 198).[3] Of the Latin epitaph there were three MS versions:

A The rejected version (*Life* iii. 82, 482; *MS Handlist* 144(a); *MS Index* JoS 201; E. of Crawford & Balcarres).[4]

This was composed in early summer 1776, and sent to Reynolds, 16 May 1776 (*Letters* 480, to JR: 'I have sent two copies, but prefer the card', Hyde, ii. 330–1).[5] Reynolds evidently misplaced at least one of the 'copies' for Frances Reynolds asked SJ for a copy,[6] to which he replied on 21 June 1776 (*Letters* 490, Hyde ii. 344–5). The following day he wrote to Reynolds, having failed to recollect the entire text (*Letters* 492, Hyde, ii. 345–6).[7]

B The alternative version as mentioned in SJ to Reynolds, 16 May 1776 (*Letters* 480, Hyde ii. 330–1), in which Percy was to settle the dates (MS untraced, but presumably if it was not entirely lost by JR, it descended to a Reynoldsian source, *Life* iii. 83). If it was lost by JR then it was reconstructed by SJ and sent to Nollekens on 24 Dec. 1776 (*Letters* 505.2, Hyde, ii. 366–7), but there were still blanks 'Where there are dots : : : there must be a space left for the dates which we have <not> yet got at.' This is also mentioned in SJ to Nollekens, 27 Aug. 1777 when the missing details were supplied (**3**. below; *Letters* 539.1, Hyde, iii. 54).[8]

C A copy, presumably from B above, supplied by Frances Reynolds to James Beattie (*Letters* 490–91, Hyde, ii. 344–6), which passed to Sir William Forbes and is now CtY.

The complexity of the textual evolution of this epitaph arises from contemporary uncertainty about the date and place of Goldsmith's birth. In the rejected version A above, the date was left unstated. Percy, as the compiler of a 'Memoir of Goldsmith', and as Johnson's main source of information on Irish matters, pursued inquiries on this point.[9]

---

[1] Photograph in F. E. Halliday, *Doctor Johnson and His World* (1968), 92. According to J.T. Smith, *Nollekens and his Times* (1829), only the bas-relief head of Goldsmith was Nollekens's work; the inscription was cut by a young Irishman, William Arminger. It consists of two panels, set side by side, reading [**Left**]: OLIVARII GOLDSMITH | Poetæ, Phyfici, Historici, | qui nullum fere fcribendi genus | non tetigit, | nullum quod tetigit non ornavit; | five rifus effent movendi, | five lacrimæ, | affectuum potens, at lenis dominator; | ingenio fublimis, vividus, verfatilis; | oratione grandis, nitidus, venuftus; [**Right**]: Hoc monumento memoriam coluit | Sodalium amor, | Amicorum fides, | Lectorum veneratio. | Natus Hiberniæ, Formeiæ Lonfordienfis | in loco cui nomen Pallas, | Nov. xxix, mdccxxxi. | Eblanæ literis inftitutus, | Objit Londini. | Apr. iv. mdcclxxiv.

[2] *Gents. Mag.* xliv (Apr. 1774), 190; Percy noted: 'Goldsmith died 4 April 1774' (O: MS Percy d. 11, fo. 9). The *London Evening Post*, 12 Apr. 1774, reported the opening of a subscription for a memorial to OG, and that SJ was to compose an epitaph. This can have been no more than gossip.

[3] A Greek epitaph was drafted and included in a letter to Langton (5 July 1774, MS Hyde, *Letters* 358, Hyde ii. 147–8, *Poems*[2] 198), and Percy obtained a copy which he supplied to Boswell, 6

March 1787 (*Fettercairn* 696, CtY: MS Boswell, C 2233), having himself obtained it, 'from a Gentleman in this Country to whom Johnson gave it himself, (Mr. Archdall who had been educated under Dr. Sumner at Harrow). I send you Mr. Archdall's own Transcript of it, hoping it will prove a Peace-Offering and restore to me the pleasure of your Correspondence' (Waingrow, *Corr.* 204–5, where this epitaph is confused with the Westminster Abbey Latin epitaph). 'Dr Percy procured J's Greek Epitaph of Goldsmith from Mr Archdale' (O: MS Percy d. 11, fo. 11).

⁴ I am indebted to Lord Crawford for the opportunity to examine this version which is carefully centred and written by SJ across the shorter dimension of of one side of a card (4¾ × 3⅛ in.). It reads:

Olivarij Goldſmith

Poetæ, Phyſici, Hiſtorici,   (tigit,

Qui nullum fere ſcribendi genus non te‸

nullum quod tetigit, non exornavit,

Rerum, ſive naturalium, ſive civilium,

elegans, at gravis ſcriptor,

ſive riſus efsent movendi, ſive lacrimæ,

Affectuum potens, at lenis Dominator;

Ingenia ſublimis, virilum, verſatilis,

Oratione grandis, nitidus, venuſtus,

Hoc monumento memoriam coluit

Sodalium amor, Amicorum fides, Lectorum ve

        (neratio.

Elfiniæ in Hibernia natus 17 . . . Ebla-

næ doctus, obijt Londini 1774

⁵ The Crawford version is on a card so that the other was presumably on some other paper. SJ's 'preference' was evidently not sustained.

⁶ In a letter of 21 June 1776, printed by Croker (*Life* (1831), iii. 446, and (1847), 519), 'Be so good as to favour me with Dr. Goldsmith's Epitaph; and if you have no objection, I should be very glad to send it to Dr. Beattie . . . My brother says he has lost Dr. Goldsmith's Epitaph, otherwise I should not trouble you for it. Indeed I should or I ought to have asked if you had any objection to my sending it, before I did send it.' If the last sentence is disentangled it means she did secure a copy and send it to Beattie, and this is item (C) below, now CtY.

⁷ 'The lines for which I am at a loss are something of *Rerum civilium sivè naturalium.*' These words occur at line 5 on the card in Lord Crawford's possession, above, but are not found on the monument.

⁸ SJ also asked Nollekens for a cast of the head: 'You promised me a cast of the head. If it could be sent to Lichfield directed to Mrs Lucy Porter before I leave the country I should be glad, though the matter is not of such Consequence, as that you should incommode yourself about it.' No such cast is recorded from a Johnsonian source, and Revd J.B. Pearson, Lucy Porter's principal legatee, makes no mention of it.

⁹ Balderston, *The History and Sources of Percy's Memoir of Goldsmith* (1926); Tillotson, *MLR* xxviii (1933), 439–43; Shearer and Tillotson, *Library*, 3rd ser. xv (1934), 224–36, and Weinbrot, *NQ* ccxii (1967), 410–11. Another English translation is in O: (MS Add. Vet. A5 d. 569).

Percy's continued interest is revealed in a letter to Cadell & Davies, 26 Apr. 1797 (CtY: MS Osborn), but Thomas Campbell took up Percy's Memoir (L: Add. MS 42517), which was published in vol.1 of Goldsmith's Collected *Works*, 4 vols. 1801 (Cole (1986), p. 126–7; cf. also Malone to JB, 14 Apr. 1791, Waingrow, *Corr.* 401–2). For subsequent publications, cf. I.L. Churchill, 'Editions of Percy's Memoir of Goldsmith', *MLN* i (1935), 464–5. A modern edn. is by R.L. Harp, in *Salzburg Studies in English Literature: Romantic Reassessments*, lii (Salzburg), 1976.

76.6GE/2a Epitaph on Goldsmith, Poems and Plays, 1777
first issue

POEMS | AND | PLAYS. | BY | OLIVER GOLDSMITH, M.B. | TO
WHICH IS PREFIXED, | THE LIFE OF THE AUTHOR. | DUBLIN: |
Printed for Meſſrs. PRICE, SLEATER, W. WATSON, WHITESTONE, |
CHAMBERLAIN, S. WATSON, BURROWES, POTTS, WILLIAMS, | HOEY,
WILKINSON, SHEPPARD, W. COLLES, W. WILSON, | MONCREIFFE, WALKER,
JENKIN, HALLHEAD, EXSHAW, | SPOTSWOOD, BURNET, P. WILSON, ARMITAGE,
| E. CROSS, HILLARY, WOGAN, MILLS, WHITE, | T. WATSON, TALBOT,
HIGLY, and BEATTY. | M,DCC,LXXVII.

8°, *A*² B–Y⁸ Z², ($2 (–Z2) signed), 172 leaves.

Pp. *i* t., *ii* Notice: 'This Edition contains several Additions and Corrections
never before printed; being the only perfect one ever published of the celebrated
Author's Poems.', *iii* Contents, *iv* blk, on B1 ²*i* ii–x Life dh: [Engr. head of
OG: 'Eſdall ſculp'] | THE | LIFE | OF | OLIVER GOLDSMITH, M.B.*
[footnote: * In these Memoirs, which were published in London, soon after the
death of Dr. Goldsmith, were several mistakes, with respect to our author's age,
the time of his admission into the College of Dublin, &c. which are here corrected from accurate information.'], xi Woty's Epitaph, *xii* blk, on B7 *1* ½t:
POEMS | BY | DR. GOLDSMITH., *2* blk, 3–328 text.

Pagination: unpaged 12–14, 27–8, 32, 48–50, 71–2, 82–4, 94–8, 206–8.

Press-figures: none; *Catchwords*: none.

Explicit: 328 FINIS.

Paper: White, laid; La. post (uncut: 8¼ × 5¼ in.); wmk.: fleur-de-lys + GR
J WHATMAN (Heawood 1846, 1849).

Type: Long primer (3.0 mm), leaded.

References: Cole, *Irish Booksellers* (1986), 125–6; ESTC: t146128.

Notes: The first published version of the epitaph appeared as a footnote, pp.
viii–ix, with the observation that the monument is 'now executed by Mr
Nollikens, an eminent Statuary in London, and is shortly to be placed in
Westminster-abbey, with the following inscription, written by Dr. Samuel
Johnson.' This version, wholly in small capitals, ends with the expanded state-
ment: 'ELFINIÆ IN HIBERNIA NATUS MDCCXXIX. | EBLANÆ
LITERIS INSTITUTUS: | LONDINI OBIIT MDCCLXXIV.' This appears
to be the version known to Percy when he wrote to Malone, 16 June 1785, 'when
he composed Goldsmith's Epitaph, he gave a wrong place for that of his birth
— *Elphin*, which is accordingly so sculptured in Westminster Abbey'.[1] Despite
the Dublin printing, the paper is evidently English. Published 4 Aug. 1777
(*Hibernian Journal*; Cole (1986), 125). The Epitaph is on pp. viii–ix. Malone's
account of OG is indebted (p. viii) to Glover's 'Authentic Anecdotes', published
in the *Universal Mag.* xxvii (May, 1774), and the *Annual Register*, xv (1774).

Copies: O (Vet. A5 e. 470);

USA: CtY, DLC, MH; *UK*: E (HS.188, 'R.H. Isham' — 'Hugh Sharp 1938'[2]), L (12276 c.5).

[1] *Percy Letters*, i ed. A. Tillotson (1944), 25–7, also in Sir James Prior, *Life of Goldsmith* (1837), I. x–xii, and II. 225, and in *Lit. Illus.* viii (1858), 236–7. Percy was wrong as to the wording of the monument, which he had evidently not seen.
[2] Sotheby, 6 June 1938, 54.

76.6GE/2b   Epitaph on Goldsmith, Poems and Plays,   1777
                            second issue

POEMS | AND | PLAYS. | BY | OLIVER GOLDSMITH, M.B. | TO WHICH IS PREFIXED, | THE LIFE OF THE AUTHOR. | PRINTED FOR | [Engr. oval of two allegorical figures on cloud, bearing scrolls, to left 'HISTORY', centre 'PHILOSOPHY', to right 'MISCELLANIES' with cartouche in centre surmounted by bust of Homer, 'W^m. Wilson Bookseller Stationer at Homer's Head N° 6 Dame Street Corner of Palace Street Dublin'] | M, DCC, LXXVII.

This is simply a reissue with cancelled t. of 76.6GE/2a above. Cole (1986), 125 notes that it occurs in both large and ordinary paper issues. ESTC: n011805.

Copies: CtY (La. Paper, 'Thomas James Bulkeley 1785' — 'Portarlington'[1]).

[1] John Dawson, 2nd Visc. Carlow, of Carlow (1744–98), became 1st E of Portarlington, 21 June 1785.

76.6GE/3   Epitaph on Goldsmith, Poems and Plays   1780

[Engr. t., within decorated frame and involved with arabesques] POEMS | AND | PLAYS. | BY | OLIVER GOLDSMITH, M.B. | *to which is Prefixed* | The LIFE of the AUTHOR. | [wavy line] | [BL] **London.** | Printed for B. NEWBERY and | T. JOHNSON St Pauls Church Yard. | MDCCLXXX.

12°, *A*² B–N¹² ($5 (–K5) signed), 146 leaves

Pp. Engr. port. front. and t., on B1 *i* ii–x Life of Goldsmith, on B6 *1* ½t, *2* blk, 3–272 *273–5* text, *276* note.

This is a direct reprint in 12° from Malone's earlier edn. of 1777 (with some minor changes in the 'Life'), and the epitaph is printed as a footnote p. ix.

Copies: O (Don. e. 244);
USA: MH; *Can*: CaOHM²; *UK*: L (11607. b.27), LVp (M 8863).

76.6GE/4   Epitaph on Goldsmith,   '1777'
                  Campbell's Philosophical Survey

A | Philofophical Survey | OF THE | SOUTH | OF | IRELAND, | IN A
SERIES OF LETTERS | TO | JOHN WATKINSON, M.D. | [parallel rule]
| LONDON: | PRINTED FOR W. STRAHAN; AND | T. CADELL IN
THE STRAND. | MDCCLXXVII.

8°, A⁸ B⁸ (±B5, –B7 + 'B7') C–E⁸ F⁸ (–F7 + 'F7') G–M⁸ N⁸ (–N1 + '*N1')
O⁸ (–O5 + 'O5') P–S⁸ T⁸ (–T8 + 'T8') U–2G⁸ 2H⁶, ($4 (+ cancellanda)
signed), 246 leaves.

Pp. A1 *i* t., *ii* blk, *iii–iv* Advertisement ('London May 14, 1777'), *v* vi–xvi
Contents, *xvi* Errata, on B1 *1* 2–466 text of Survey, *467* 468–76 Appendix.

Pagination: 207 *slipt* 7.

Press-figures: A5ᵛ(x)–5,   A6ᵛ(xii)–1,   B6ᵛ(12)–1,   C6(27)–1,   C6ᵛ(28)–*,
D4ᵛ(40)–4,   D8(47)–5,   E1ᵛ(50)–5,   E8ᵛ(64)–1,   F3ᵛ(70)–*,   F7ᵛ(78)–6,
G4ᵛ(88)–‡,   G6(91)–8,   H7(109)–4,   I5(121)–†,   K1ᵛ(130)–7,   K4ᵛ(136)–*,
L5ᵛ(154)–*,   M3ᵛ(166)–1,   N3ᵛ(182)–‡,   N7(189)–‡,   O7ᵛ(206)–4,   P3ᵛ(214)–†,
P7(221)–3,   Q6ᵛ(236)–6,   R7ᵛ(254)–3,   S6(267)–2,   S8ᵛ(272)–5,   U2ᵛ(292)–4,
X7(317)–*,   X8(319)–3,   Y8(335)–†,   Z6(347)–3,   Z7(349)–2,   2A7(365)–6,
2B1ᵛ(370)–†,   2B8ᵛ(384)–8,   2C3ᵛ(390)–8,   2C6ᵛ(396)–1,   2D7ᵛ(414)–†,
2E5ᵛ(426)–4,   2F6(443)–1,   2F8ᵛ(448)–4,   2G2ᵛ(452)–8,   2G7ᵛ(462)–2,
2H6(475)–8.

Catchwords: not recorded.

Explicit: 476 THE END.

Paper: White, laid; La. post (uncut: 8¼ × 5¼ in.); no vis. wmk.

Type: Pica (4.1 mm), leaded (1.2 mm).

Plates: 6: facing t. (fold), pp. 90 (Tower at Kildare), 100 (fold: Abbey at
Kilkenny), 122 (fold: Rock of Cashel), 160 (fold: Crown, sword, and tumulus),
476 (fold: 2 torcs).

Notes: The author was Dr. Thomas Campbell. AWn copy preserves *cancellanda* and shows that B5,7 *cancellanda* were printed as inner fold of 2H.

Despite the date on the t. this book was not published until March 1778,[1]
where the close of the epitaph (pp. 437–8) reads:

    *** in Hibernia natus | Eblanæ literis institutus, | Londini obiit
        MDCCLXXIV.

with a note on p. 437: 'Dr Johnson has honoured the Publisher with a copy,
though the epitaph is not yet finished, the identical spot where Goldsmith was
born being not yet ascertained.'[2] The version of the epitaph published in *Gents.
Mag.* xlix (Jan. 1779), 30 and reprinted in *Scots Mag.* xli (Jan. 1779), 46, agrees
with Campbell's.[3]

References: ESTC: t084447; cf. t085072.

Copies: O³ (1. 8° Q. 59 Linc.; 2. Douce C. 240; 3. Gough Ireland 91);
USA: CSmH, CtY², DLC, ICN, ICU, MB, MH (Br.14117.77; with

cancellans of B7), NjP, TxU; *Can*: CaOHM; *UK*: ABu, AWn (uncancelled), C², DUu, En, Eu, Gu, L³, SAN.

¹ Published 19 March 1778 @ 6s. in boards (*Lond. Chron.*), and noticed in *Gents. Mag.* xlviii (June 1778), 287. William Bewley noticed it in the *Monthly Rev.* lx (Jan. 1779), 8. For some account of this book see Clifford, *Dr Campbell's Diary* (1947), 11–13.

² Clifford (1947), 11, states, without evidence, that William Strahan, the printer of the London edition of Campbell's book, obtained the epitaph for him, apparently on the strength of the word 'Publisher' in Campbell's footnote. It had no such precision of meaning in the 18th century, and is as likely to refer to Campbell himself.

³ The *Gents. Mag.* noted that SJ had given a copy to the publisher, though the epitaph was not yet finished. It was translated in *Gents. Mag.* xlix (Feb. 1779), 85, and again in *Scots Mag.* xlii (Nov. 1780), 607.

76.6GE/5   Epitaph on Goldsmith,   1778
            Campbell's Philosophical Survey
                second edition, Dublin

A | Philofophical Survey | OF THE | SOUTH | OF | IRELAND, | IN A SERIES OF LETTERS | TO | JOHN WATKINSON, M.D. | [parallel rule] | DUBLIN: | Printed for W. Whitestone, W. Sleater, D. Cham- | berlaine, J. Potts, T. Wilkinson, J. Williams, | W. Colles, W. Wilson, C. Jenkin, R. Mon- | creiffe, T. Walker, T. Stewart, W. | Gilbert, R. Jackson, L. White, | J. Beatty, J. Exshaw, | and G. Perrin. | [short rule] | M, DCC, LXXVIII.

8°, A–B⁸ C⁸ (± C4) D–G⁸ H⁸ (± H8) I–S⁸ T⁸ (± T2) U–2D⁸ 2E⁸ (± 2E5) 2F–2H⁸, ($4 (*cancellanda* signed + *) signed), 248 leaves.

Pp. A1 *i* t., *ii* blk, *iii–iv* Advertisement ('May 14, 1777'), *v* vi–xvi Contents, xvii Errata, on B1 *1* 2–467 text, *468* blk, *469* 470–78 Appendix.

Pagination: 278 as 287.

Press-figures: None: asterisks on C4(23), and H8(111) are marks of cancels, and are not press-figg.

Catchwords: not recorded.

Explicit: 478 THE END.

Paper: White laid; Carré or La. post (uncut: 8¼ × 5¼ in.); no vis. wmk.

Type: English (4.5 mm), leaded (1.0 mm).

Plates: Facing pp. 90, 110, 160 (fold), 166, 211, 478 (fold).

Notes: Epitaph at p. 438.

Copies: O (Vet. A5 e. 922);

USA: CSmH, CtY (Franklin; apparently no cancels), DLC, Hyde² (**1.** 'Roper' — 'Dacre'), ICN, IU, MH, NN², [ICJ, NPV, OCl, PPM], TxU; *Can*: CaOHM; *UK*: AWn, C, E (R. 103 f), L (010390. 1.6), MRu.

76.6GE/6   Epitaph on Goldsmith,   1778–9
                      Westminster Abbey

The stone itself was apparently erected in the Abbey in 1778–9,[1] and before the inscription was completed Johnson wrote to Nollekens (*Letters* 539.1, above, 27 Aug. 1777, Hyde, iii. 54), with the final details of Goldsmith's birth:

> I have at last sent you what remains, to put to poor dear Goldsmiths monument, and hope to see it erected at the abbey . . . Natus Hibernia, Forneiæ Lonfordiensis, in loco cui nomen Pallas, Nov. xxix, MDCCXXXI, | Eblanæ literis institutus, | Obiit Londini, Apr. iv. MDCCLXXIV.

The present stone reads at this point:[2]

> Natus Hibernia, Forneiæ Lonfordiensis | in loco cui nomen Pallas, | Nov. XXIX, MDCCXXXI. | Eblanæ literis institutus, | Obijt Londini. | Apr. iv. MDCCLXXIV.

The version on the stone is reprinted in most subsequent editions of Goldsmith, and doubtless elsewhere, including:

> *Poetical and Dramatic Works of Oliver Goldsmith, M.B.* . . . London: H. Goldney, 2 vols. 1780, p. xxxix[3] (O: 2799 e. 426–7).
> *The Bath Chronicle*, 8 July 1784.
> *Poems and Plays of Oliver Goldsmith, M.B.*, Dublin . . . 1785.
> *Essays of Oliver Goldsmith.* Perth: Printed by R. Morison, . . . 7 vols. 1791 (p. 24) (O[2]).
> *Miscellaneous Works of Oliver Goldsmith*, Perth: R. Morison . . . 5 vols. 1792 (O).
> *The Poetical Works of Oliver Goldsmith.* London: Printed for C. Cooke, n.d. [? 1795] (p. xxi) (O[2]).
> *Poems of Goldsmith and Parnell*, [ed. Isaac Reed[4]], London . . . 1795.
> *Essays and Criticisms by Dr Goldsmith* . . . In three volumes. A new edition. [ed. T. Wright, and Isaac Reed].[5] London: Printed for J. Johnson . . . 1798 (II. xxiv).
> *Collected Works of Oliver Goldsmith* . . . ed. Campbell and S. Rose, 4 vols. 1801[6] (O).
> *The Poems and Essays of Oliver Goldsmith, M.B. With sketches of his Life and Writings* . . . Edinburgh: Printed for the Booksellers; by T. MacCleish & Co. 1804. 2 vols. (I. 12, and 'Englished').
> Kearsley's edition of Johnson's *Poetical* Works, 1785, &c., (85.2PW/1, &c., below) pp. 190–91, follows the stone.

Isaac Reed in *Works*, xiv (1788), 543–44, (87.3W/1.3/1a, below), reverts to the version as published by Malone, giving Elphin as Goldsmith's birthplace in 1729: 'Elfiniæ in Hibernia natus MDCCXXIX.' and omitting 'Apr. IV.' from the date of OG's death.

There are other minor textual variants in different versions, most arising in lineation and punctuation.

An English translation is given in *A Collection of Epitaphs*, 1806 (40GM10/EE/2, above), at i. 193.

---

[1] *The Bustle among the Busts; or the Poets-Corner in an Uproar. Occasioned by the Appearance of Dr. Goldsmith's Monument in Westminster-Abbey. A Poem in two Cantos.* By M. MacGregor, Esq. Noticed in the *London Review* (Feb–Mar. 1778), 233–40.

[2] Legible photographs will be found in Roger Ingpen's *Boswell's Life of Johnson*, ii. 657, and in F.E. Halliday, *Doctor Johnson and His World* (1968), 92. An engraving forming the frontispiece to Sir James Prior's *Life of Goldsmith* (1837), differs considerably from the present stone, and erroneously reads in the last line 'MDCCLXXXIV.' It is unreliable: only the present stone ever adorned the walls of the Abbey. Prior's printed version (ii. 527), however, gives the correct text.

[3] Reviewed in *London Review* (Apr. 1780), 268–73, with a hostile notice of the epitaph.

[4] *NCBEL* ii. 1204.

[5] *NCBEL* ii. 1193.

[6] J. Burmester, *Catalogue* 23 (1993), 187, reports an undated letter from Louisa Hamilton, OG's niece, soliciting subscriptions for an edn. of OG's Poems, and Letters addressed to him. The edition seems not to have come to anything, though it is apparent that Louisa Hamilton still had OG's correspondence.

76.8ML/1   Mickle's Lusiad   1776

THE | LUSIAD; | OR, | THE DISCOVERY OF INDIA. | AN | EPIC POEM. | TRANSLATED FROM | The Original Portuguefe of LUIS DE CAMOËNS. | *By WILLIAM JULIUS MICKLE.* | NEC VERBUM VERBO, CURABIS REDDERE, FIDUS | INTERPRES. HOR. ART. POET. | [medium swelled rule] | OXFORD, | PRINTED BY JACKSON AND LISTER; | And Sold by CADELL, in the Strand; DILLY, in the Poultry; BEW, Pater-nofter-Row; | FLEXNEY, Holborn; EVANS, near York-Buildings; RICHARDSON and URQUHART, | under the Royal-Exchange; and GOODSMAN, near Charing-Crofs, LONDON. | [short rule] | M,DCC,LXXVI.

4°, π^2 †a⁴ b–o⁴ p⁴ ($\pm$ p2) q–y⁴ B–U⁴ X⁴ (–X1,2 + X1.2) Y–3E⁴ 3F⁴ ($\pm$ 3F3) 3G–3P⁴ 3Q1, ($2 (–G1) signed), 331 leaves.

Pp. π1 t., π1ᵛ blk, π2 Dedication to the D. of Buccleuch, π2ᵛ blk, on †a1–4 List of Subscribers, †a4ᵛ *Errata*, on b1 *i* ii–clviii Introduction dh: [double rule] | INTRODUCTION | TO THE | LUSIAD. (on p2ᵛ cviii–clviii 'The LIFE of the AUTHOR.'), *clix* clx–clxvii Dissertation, *clxviii* blk, on B1 text *1* 2–484 [= 482] dh: [bevelled parallel rule] | THE | LUSIAD.ᵃ | [medium swelled rule] | BOOK. I., ht: THE LUSIAD. BOOK. I. [&c.].

Pagination: 153–4 *om.* from numeration; blk 42, 84, 144, 232; unnumbered 43, 85, 145, 189, 233, 271, 319, 357, 415; 212–13 and 216–17 as 222–3, 226–7, 246 as 249, 280 as 180, 296 as 266, 330 as 310, 382–3 as 182–3.

Press-figures: none; *Catchwords*: not recorded.

Explicit: 484 THE END.

Paper: White, laid; medium (uncut: 11½ × 9 in.); no vis. wmk.

Type: Text: english (4.5 mm), notes: bourgeois (3.1).

References: *Life* iv. 250–1 (Courtney 127–8); CH 153; Subscriptions no. 13; ESTC: t144002.

Notes: Mickle's papers and correspondence bearing on this work are found mainly at CtY (MSS: Boswell, and Osborn).[1] Proposals for the translation were issued in 8° in March 1771 (*Gents. Mag.* xli (Mar. 1771), 134), with the First Book as a specimen, and promising publication 'in the year 1772'.[2] Another Prospectus ran to only 6pp. with specimens of the type.[3] Mickle's correspondence shows that J. Bew was the printer, and that the edition ran to 1,000 copies, of which 560 subscribers took 612 copies. It was published in August 1776 (*Gents. Mag.* xlvi (Aug. 1776), 367–9, no. 40) and gained £1,000 for the translator.[4] Langhorne noticed it in the *Monthly Review* over a period: liv (1776), 249, 369, and lv (1776), 5.

SJ was a subscriber ('Samuel Johnson, LL.D.') and encourager of the work, and he dictated to WJM the form of acknowledgement printed on p. cliii (x1) of the 'Introduction':

To James Boswell, Esq; he confesses many obligations. To the friendship of Mr Hoole, the elegant translator of Tasso, he is peculiarly indebted. — And while thus he recollects with pleasure the names of many gentlemen from whom he has received assistance or encouragement; he is happy to be enabled to add Dr. Johnson to the number of those, whose kindness for the man, and good wishes for the Translation, call for his sincerest gratitude. Nor must a tribute to the memory of DR. Goldsmith be neglected. He saw a part of this version; but he cannot now receive the thanks of the Translator.

Copies: O (285 d.20, boards, uncut, 'E Libris Richardi Lickorish e Coll: Linc: Oxon:');

USA: CSmH, CtY, DLC, Goldberg, Hyde (uncut), IU, [Liebert ('May 30ᵗʰ 1776 D. Garrick') = CtY], MH², NIC, NN³, PPU, TxU; *Can*: CaOHM (D 1385); *UK*: BRp, C, Ct, E (Hall 199.a), Eu, Gu, L², MRc, MRu, WIS; *Aust*: CNL.

[1] Mostly from the papers of T. Mitchell Ellis (a descendant), at Sotheby &c., 20 May 1968. Other recorded material includes 'Original MS Note Book by Mickle, translator of the Lusiad, relating to that work' at Sotheby (Revd H. White), 5 Feb. 1838, 568 to Wilks, 4s., and (perhaps the same) 'Small MS notebook concerning the Lusiads' at Puttick & Simpson (Law), 19 Mar. 1855, 833. Two letters from Mickle to JB relative to the Lusiads were *Fettercairn* 595–6, and other more extensive exchanges are noticed in *Boswell Catalogue*, L 963.6–967.6 and C 2003–2014.

[2] A copy of the Proposal is MH (Port. 5252.120*), ESTC: n009761. The Specimen translation was noticed in *Gents. Mag.* xli (July 1771), 323–5, by 'X', and by Langhorne in the *Monthly Rev.* xlv (1771), 182; another copy is O: (GP. 1614(13)). An 8° Prospectus of 4 leaves, promising delivery 'some time in May next' is also O: (JJ: 'Prospectuses', Box 2, no. 232a).

[3] Peter Murray Hill, *Catalogue* 44 (1952), 331, £1. 10s. That this was 'Published by John Archer, Bookseller, No. 80 Dame Street . . .' who was the publisher of the so-called 'Third Edition' in Dublin, 1791 (76.8ML/3, below), suggests that this item had little to do with Mickle and was simply a bookselling advertisement. A copy is reported in ESTC: t078028: perhaps the same as that noticed above.

Biographical accounts of Mickle are by Isaac Reed in *European Mag.* i (June 1782), 451–2; John Ireland's 'Introductory Anecdotes' prefixed to his edn. of Mickle's *Poems and a Tragedy* (1794); John Sim's 'Life' in Mickle's *Poetical Works* (1806); R. A. Davenport in *The British Poets* (Chiswick, 1822), vol. lxvi (1822), is apparently less accurate; and S[r] M. Eustace Taylor's *William Julius Mickle (1734–1788): A Critical Study* (Washington 1937). Much new material has since emerged in the Boswell Papers (*Fettercairn* 595–6; CtY: MS Boswell C 2011–2) and in the material secured at Sotheby's (Timothy Mitchell Ellis), 20 May 1968, esp. lots 345–65, by James M. Osborn (now CtY: MS Osborn).

76.8ML/2 Mickle's Lusiad, Oxford 1778

THE | [Hollow type] LUSIAD; | OR, | THE DISCOVERY OF INDIA. | AN | EPIC POEM. | TRANSLATED FROM | The Original Portuguefe of LUIS DE CAMÖENS. | *By WILLIAM JULIUS MICKLE.* | NEC VERBUM VERBO, CURABIS REDDERE, FIDUS | INTERPRES. HOR. ART POET. | THE SECOND EDITION. | [medium swelled rule] | OXFORD, | PRINTED BY JACKSON AND LISTER; | For J. BEW, Pater-nofter-Row; T. PAYNE, Mews-Gate; J. DODSLEY, Pall-Mall; | J. ROBSON, New Bond-Street; J. ALMON, Piccadilly; T. CADELL, Strand; | W. FLEXNEY, Holborn; and J. SEWELL, Cornhill, LONDON. | [short rule] | M.DCC.LXXVIII.

4°, *a*² b–2g⁴ 2h² B–3R⁴, ($2 signed), 368 leaves.

Pp. Engr. allegorical front. ('Design'd & Etch'd by J. Mortimer. Publifhed as the Act directs April 21, 1778') + a1 t., a1[v] blk, a2 Dedication (Duke of Buccleugh, signed 'William Julius Mickle.'), a2[v] blk, on b1 *i* ii–ccxxxvi Introduction &c., on B1 *1* 2–496 text.

Pagination: no errors; *Press-figures*: none; *Catchwords*: not recorded.

Explicit: 496 THE END.

Paper: White, laid; La. post (uncut: 10½ × 8¼ in.); wmk.: fleur-de-lys.

Type: Text & Preface: english (4.7 mm), Dissertation: pica (3.7 mm), notes &c.: bourgeois (3.0 mm).

Plates: Allegorical front., Engr. folding map facing p. lxxi.

References: ESTC: t145625.

Notes: This enlarged second edn. was separately reviewed in *Gents. Mag.* xlviii (Sept. 1778), 427–28.

Copies: O (4° BS. 117);

USA: CSmH², CtY, DFo, IU, MB, MH² (var.), NjP, NN; *Can*: CaOHM; *UK*: AWn, BMp, BRp, C, Cf, Cq, DUu, E (Newb. 3869), [Es], L, LVu, MRp, WIS.

76.8ML/3a   Mickle's Lusiad, Dublin, 'third edition'   1791

THE | LUSIAD: | OR, THE | DISCOVERY OF INDIA. | AN | EPIC POEM. | TRANSLATED FROM THE | ORIGINAL PORTUGUESE OF LUIS DE CAMOËNS. | BY WILLIAM JULIUS MICKLE. | NEC VERBUM VERBO CURABIS REDDERE, FIDUS | INTERPRES. HOR. DE ART. POET. | [medium swelled rule] | VOL. I [–II]. | THE THIRD EDITION. | [medium swelled rule] | DUBLIN: | PRINTED BY GRAISBERRY AND CAMPBELL, | FOR JOHN ARCHER, N°. 80, DAME-STREET. | MDXXCXI.

2 vols. 8°

I. π² a–b⁸ c² B–Y⁸ Z² ²B–F⁸ G², ($2 signed), 232 leaves.

Pp. π1 ½t, + Front. + π2 t., a1 *i* ii–xxxvi Introduction, on B1 ²*xxxiii* xxxiv–xcvii History of the Discovery of India, *xcviii* xcix–cclxxxix (cclxxxix as ccxxxix) History of Portuguese Empire, *ccxc* blk, *ccxci* ccxcii–cccxv (ccxcii as ccxci) Life of Camoens, *cccxvi* blk, *cccxvii* cccxviii–ccclxxv Dissertation, *ccclxxvi* blk, *ccclxxvii* ccclxxviii–cccxci (ccclxxxix–ccxci as ccclxvii, ccclxvii, cccvlxii) Appendix, *cccxcii* blk, on ²B1 pp. *1* 2–83 text *Lusiad* I–II, *Explicit* 83 END OF THE FIRST VOLUME, *84* blk.

II. *A²* B–2I⁸ 2K⁶, ($2 signed), 256 leaves.

Pp. A1 ½t, A2 t., on B1 *1* 2–507 text of *Lusiad* III–X, *Explicit*: 507 THE END., *508* blk.

Paper: White, laid; Lombard (uncut: 8⅜ × 5⅝ in.); wmk.: Grapes + DANGOUMOIS.

Type: Preface: pica (4.0 mm), Introductory matter and text: small pica (3.5 mm), notes: brevier (2.5 mm).

Plate: Front. vol. 1: Oval engr. port. WJM 'Engraved by J. Mannion, from a drawing by Mr. Humphry.'

References: ESTC: 078027.

Notes: The allusion to SJ is at I. ccclxx.

Copies: E (Milc. II.3); *USA*: CtY, MH, NN; *UK*: L (11452. e.36).

76.8ML/3b   Mickle's Lusiad, London, 'third edition'   1793

Not examined.

USA: [DLC]; *Can*: CaOHM (C. 201–2).

**[76.8ML/3/Add1   Mickle's Lusiad, Anderson's   1795
British Poets**

Anderson's British Poets. 1795, vol. xi. does not include the Lusiads with other of Mickle's verses. ESTC: t152376.

Can: CaOHM²; *UK*: O (2804 d.38).]

76.8ML/4   Mickle's Lusiad   1798

The Lusiad: or the Discovery of India. An Epic Poem. Translated from the original Portuguese of Luis de Camoëns. By William Julius Mickle. Nec Verbum, verbo curaris reddere, fidus interpres. Hor. Art. Poet. In two volumes. Vol. I [– II]. The Third Edition. London: Printed for T. Cadell, jun. and W. Davies, in the Strand. 1798.

2 vols., 8°

I. Engr. map and t., + *i* ii–cccli, *ccclii* blk, *1* 2–146, *147* advt. for WJM's Miscellaneous Poems 2nd edn., *148* blk.

II. *i* ½t, *iii* t., *1* 2–444 text.

References: ESTC: t144848.

Note: The allusion to SJ is at I. cccxxxi–cccxxxii.

Copies: O (285 m. 119–20);

USA: DLC, IU, MH, NjP, NN, PHi, ViU; *Can*: CaOHM; *UK*: DUNu, E ([Ag] 3/2.29), En, [Es], L (11452. c.14).

76.8ML/5   Mickle's Lusiad   1809

Published by W. Suttaby; R. Crosby & Co. and Scatcherd & Letterman, Stationers Court. 1809. Coloph: C. Whittingham, Printer, Goswell Street, London.

London. 24°

Note: No allusion to SJ.

Copies: O (28722 g.1);

UK: E (Hall 199.k), L.

76.8ML/6   Mickle's Lusiad, Chalmers's English Poets   1810

See above, Hoole's *Tasso*, 1810 (63.2HT/17), for a description; Mickle's *Lusiads*, with the introductory material, occupies pp. 517–783, of this vol.

Copies: O (280 i.405).

76.8ML/7   Mickle's Lusiad, English Translations   1822

English Translations from ancient and modern Poems by various Authors. London. 1810. vol. 3: The Lusiads. 1822
   Copies: *UK*: L.

76.8ML/8   Mickle's Lusiad, fifth edition   1877

The Lusiads. The Fifth edition, revised, by E. Richmond Hodges, M.C.P.
   London: George Bell and Sons, York Street, Covent Garden. 1877
Coloph: London: Printed by William Clowes and Sons, Stamford Street, and Charing Cross.
   Notes: No allusion to SJ. This is a title uniform with the series of 'Bohn's Standard Library' (Cordasco, *Bohn Libraries* (1951), 100).
   UK: E([Ag] 3/2); L.

76.11SP   Proposals for The Spectator   1776

London, Nov. 30, 1776. | THE SPECTATOR | To be comprized in TWENTY-FOUR Weekly Numbers | AT SIXPENCE EACH. | [medium swelled rule] | *On* Saturday, December 14, *will be publiſhed,* | NUMBER I. | (Containing FIVE SHEETS of LETTER-PRESS) | OF | A NEW AND ELEGANT EDITION | OF | THE SPECTATOR; | CONSISTING OF | ESSAYS ON A VARIETY OF SUBJECTS, | ENTERTAINING, MORAL, AND RELIGIOUS. | [rule] | WRITTEN BY THE LATE Mr. ADDISON | AND OTHERS. | [bevelled parallel rule] | Printed (by *Aſſignment* from JACOB and RICHARD TONSON) | for the *Proprietors,* | And ſold by R. BALDWIN, No. 47, Pater-noſter Row, | And may be had of all the Bookſellers in Town and Country.
   8°, $1 (unsigned), 1 leaf.
   Pp. *1* t., *2* Address 'TO THE PUBLIC.'
   Paper: White, laid; Demy (uncut: 8⅜ × 5 in.); no vis. wmk.
   Type: P. 1 display caps &c. from double pica (7.0 mm) to brevier (2.7 mm); on *2* text: long primer (3.3. mm), leaded.
   References: *Life* i. xiv, ii. 503; Woodruff, *NQ* ccxvi (1971), 61–2.
   Notes: Brought to light by Woodruff. The opening paragraph of the 'Address to the Public' is evidently Johnson's, and on the hitherto unique copy, Isaac Reed has written: 'This Advertizement was drawn up by Dr Johnson'.[1]
   Some part (vols. 5–6) of the edn. was printed by Strahan in 6,000 copies in April 1777 (L: Add. MS 48809, fo. 27ᵛ).
   Copies: L (T 1563/7, 'Isaac Reed' — 'Alexander Chalmers'[2]).

¹ This piece is not noticed by Reed in his presumed articles on SJ's writings published in *European Mag.* vii (1785), nor is it listed in his MS notes in Ljh, or in those supplied to Boswell (Waingrow, s.n.), but the attribution was made, probably by him, in *European Mag.* xvi (July 1789), 5.

² 'These volumes were purchased by me [*sc.* Chalmers] at Isaac Reed's sale £1. 3.' *Brit. Mus. Catal. Accessions* (1835), 183. The item has not been identified in King (*Bibliotheca Reediana*), 2 Nov. 1807, unless it was part of lot 2367 'Johnsoniana, Vol. 1. 1793 etc.' for which Payne (who bought for Chalmers), paid £1. 3s. L: (T1563) now contains 8 items, and a newspaper cutting.

77.1CB   Charade on Thomas Barnard   [1777]

Composed by SJ on Friday, 17 January 1777, when he was unable to attend a meeting of the Club. The card in the possession of the Earl of Crawford is not in SJ's handwriting. The text was first published by JB in *Life*, 2nd. edn. (1793), i. *xviii (Addenda); *Life* iv. 195; *Poems*² 205–6.¹

¹ Letters attacking the craze for charades appeared in the *London Evening Post*, 7 Jan. 1777, and *Morning Post*, 18 Jan. 1777.

77.2PC/1   Zachary Pearce on the Evangelists   1777

[½t] A | COMMENTARY, | WITH | NOTES, | ON THE | FOUR EVANGELISTS | AND THE | ACTS OF THE APOSTLES, &c. | VOL. I –II].

[Title] A | COMMENTARY, | WITH | NOTES, | ON THE | FOUR EVANGELISTS | AND THE | ACTS OF THE APOSTLES; | TOGETHER WITH A NEW TRANSLATION OF | ST. PAUL'S FIRST EPISTLE TO THE CORINTHIANS, | WITH A | PARAPHRASE AND NOTES. | TO WHICH ARE ADDED OTHER | THEOLOGICAL PIECES. | BY ZACHARY PEARCE, D.D. | LATE LORD BISHOP OF ROCHESTER. | TO THE WHOLE IS PREFIXED, | SOME ACCOUNT OF HIS LORDSHIP'S LIFE AND CHARACTER, | WRITTEN BY HIMSELF. | [rule] | PUBLISHED FROM THE ORIGINAL MANUSCRIPTS, | BY JOHN DERBY, A.M. | HIS LORDSHIP'S CHAP-LAIN, AND RECTOR OF SOUTHFLEET AND LONGFIELD. |[rule] | —Πολλῆς πειρας τελευταῖον ἐπιγέννημα | Longinus de Sublim. cap. 6. | Tanta inchoata rea eſt; ut penè vitio mentis tantum opus ingreſſus mihi videar. | Ex Epiſt. Virgilii ad Auguſtum de Æneide ſua. | [rule] | IN TWO VOL-UMES. | [rule] | VOL. I [– II]. | [total rule] | LONDON: PRINTED BY E. COX; | FOR T. CADELL, IN THE STRAND. | M DCC LXXVII.

Vol. II: *omits* 'IN TWO VOLUMES. | [rule]'
2 vols., 4°

I. π⁴ a–h⁴ B–4G⁴, ($2 signed; 'Vᴏʟ. I.' on $1), 336 leaves.
Pp. π1 *i* ½t, *ii* blk, + Engr. port. + *iii* t., *iv* blk, *v–vi* Dedication: 'TO THE

KING.' ('January 6. 1777.'), *vii* Advertisement., *viii* advt. for Pearce's *Discourses*., on a1 ^2i ii–xlv Life of the Author, *xlvi* blk, on f3 *xlv* ½t, *xlviii* blk, *xlix* l–lx *lxi–lxiii* text Dissertation, *lxiv* blk, on B1 *1* 2–599 text Commentaries, *600* blk.

Pagination: unnumbered 208, 294, 458.

Press-figures: g3ᵛ(liv)–2, g4ᵛ(lvi)–1, h1ᵛ(lviii)–1, h2ᵛ(lx)–2, M3ᵛ(86)–2, N3(93)–2, 3K3ᵛ(438)–4, 3K4ᵛ(440)–3, 3L3ᵛ(446)–1, 3L4ᵛ(448)–2, 3M3ᵛ(454)–1, 3N4ᵛ(464)–1, 3O4ᵛ(472)–1, 3P3(477)–2, 3P4(479)–1, 3Q2ᵛ(484)–1, 3R2ᵛ(492)–1, 3S4(503)–2, 3T1ᵛ(506)–2, 3U3(517)–1, 3X4(527)–1, 3Y4(535)–1, 3Z3ᵛ(542)–1, 4A1ᵛ(546)–1, 4B1ᵛ(554)–1, 4C4(567)–1, 4D4(575)–1, 4E4(583)–1, 4E4ᵛ(584)–2, 4F1ᵛ(586)–1, 4G1ᵛ(594)–1.

Catchwords: ii ‸acquainted ('~), xi ‸had ("~), xvi "Deanery, ("~.), *om.* xlv–xlix, lxii Cicilius (Cecilius), *om.* lxiii–lxiv. Cwds throughout this book are inconsistently presented owing to problems arising from a 2-column text and the full-measure footnotes. Only the grosser disparities are here noted: 39 7 But (7 (*b*) ~), 41 For, (14 ~,), 127 *om.* (CHAP.), 158 hatycheata ‸ (~,), 176 36 Naked‸ (~ ~,), 180 17‸ Now (~ ¶ ~), 187 56‸ But (~ (*g*) ~), 189 68 Saying‸ (~ ~,), 194 Chrift‸ (~ ?), 223 [pa-] rable‸ (~,), 236 them‸ (~,), 249 ‸And (16 ~), 256 faith (faid), 343 19 ¶ To (~ ~ And), 360 45‸ See (~ (*b*) ~), 395 right-eoufnefs, (~.), 433 [ekchyno-] menon‸ (~,), 440 66‸ And (~ ¶ ~), 464 29 ¶‸ The (~ ~ (*d*)~), 492 coming‸ (~,), 543 words‸ (~,), 548 24 Verily‸ (~ ~,), 579 35 They (~ Jefus).

Explicit: 599 END OF THE FIRST VOLUME.

II. *A²* B–3I⁴ 3K⁴ (±3K2) 3L–P⁴ 3Q², ($2 (−2S2) signed; 'VOL. II.' on $1), 244 leaves.

Pp. A1 ½t: (as vol. 1 . . . VOL. II.), A1ᵛ blk, A2 t., A2ᵛ blk, on B1 *1* 2–482 text, *482* blk, *483* Errata, *484* blk.

Pagination: [↑] 199, 455, 457, 468; blk 400, 456; unnumbered 197–8, 313–21, 400–3, 416, 453–4, 456; 25 as 27, 272 with first '2' *inverted*.

Press-figures: B3(5)–1, C4ᵛ(16)–1, D1ᵛ(18)–2, D4ᵛ(24)–1, E3ᵛ(30)–1, F3ᵛ(38)–2, F4ᵛ(40)–1, G4(47)–1, H2ᵛ(52)–1, I4(63)–1, K3ᵛ(70)–1, 2D4(207)–2, 2E1ᵛ(210)–2, 2E4ᵛ(216)–1, 2F1ᵛ(218)–1, 2F3(221)–2, 2G2ᵛ(228)–1, 2G3ᵛ(230)–2, 2H1ᵛ(234)–1, 2H3(237)–2, 2I3(245)–1, 2I4(247)–2, 2K4(255)–1, 2K4ᵛ(256)–1, 2L3(261)–2, 2L3ᵛ(262)–1, 2M3(269)–2, 2M4(271)–1, 2N1ᵛ(274)–1, 2N2ᵛ(276)–2, 2O2ᵛ(284)–2, 2O4(287)–1, 2P1ᵛ(290)–1, 2P4ᵛ(296)–2, 2T4(327)–1, 2T4ᵛ(328)–2, 2U1ᵛ(330)–1, 2X4ᵛ(344)–1, 2Y3ᵛ(350)–1, 2Y4ᵛ(352)–2, 2Z3(357)–1, 3A2ᵛ(364)–1, 3A3ᵛ(366)–2, 3B3(373)–2, 3B4(375)–2, 3D3(389)–1.

Catchwords: 4 16 ¶ And (15 ~ ~), 26 6 (*f*) Rather‸ (~ ~ ~,), 33 28 Saying‸ (~ ~,), 69 32 And (~ Send), 99 13 (*x*) Rather‸ (~ ~ ~,), 126 Juftus‸ (~,), 145 foon‸ (~,), 171 king‸ (~,), 182 (I)‸ 17 ‸*The* ((I) V.17. *The*), 183 *minari*‸ (~,),

197–8 *om.*, 245 19 ˌFor (~ (~)), 271 31 ˌ But (~ (G) ~), 296 19 ˌ And (~ (K) ~), 297 27 Forˌ (~ ~,), 298 weˌ (~,), 312–20 *om.*, 399–402 *om.*, 453–4 *om.*, 478 ˌEucharisu ('Eucharisu).

Explicit: 481 FINIS.

Paper: White, laid; wmk.: fleur-de-lys + LVG (Heawood 76).

Type: Dedication: great primer (5.5 mm), leaded; Advertisements and Life: english (4.4) leaded; Commentary: 2 cols./p. pica (4.0 mm), footnotes (full measure): small pica (3.5 mm); Orn. tp. (drummer) I. 134, 172, 247, 306, 414, 449, 474, 507, 526, 545, 571, 592; II. 8, 19, 72, 91, 96, 124, 131, 178, 188.

Plates: Engr. port. of Z. Pearce, front. in I.

References: *Life* iii. 112–3 (Courtney 128); CH 153; Hazen 154–7; *Rothschild* 1516; ESTC: t147627.

Notes: In some copies of vol. II, the inner forme of I⁴ is cancelled by means of pasted-over pages at pp. 58–9 and 62–3. This was apparently to remedy the accidental misprinting of the matter of the outer forme on both sides of the sheeet.

SJ furnished the 'Dedication', and prepared the 'Life of Pearce' from materials left by ZP and gathered together by Derby.[1] It was reprinted in *The Universal Mag.* lx (Feb. 1777), 57–60, though an extract had already appeared in *Lond. Chron.*, 23 Jan. 1777. This book was published at 2 gns. 18 Jan. 1777 (*St James's Chron.*).[2] JB recorded reading 'part of Dr Johnson's life of Pearce' on 31 July and again on 6 October 1777, in booksellers' shops (*JB: Extremes*, 136, 188).[3] Perhaps he thought it too expensive.

Copies: O (FF. 32–3 Jur.);

USA: CtY ('T. Jervis 1804' — R.W. Rogers, I⁴ mispaged), DLC, Hyde ('Rev. John Hopton' II. 3I2 (pp. 427–8) mutil.), ICN, ICU, [Liebert ('D. of Newcastle, Clumber Park' — 'R.W. Chapman')], MB, MH (C 1316.28.5), NjP, NN, PPL², [PPLT, PPM. PPP]; *UK*: ABu, BMp (161441), C, Ccc, Cf, Ck, Cp, Cq, Csj², Ct(R), DUc, E, En, Eu, Gu, L (5. f. 10–11), LEu, LVu², MRp, MRc, MRu; *Eir*: Dt.

---

[1] Boswell's attribution perhaps relied to some degree on Isaac Reed, whose MS list of SJ's works (MS: Ljh) reported '1777 Dedication & Life to Pearce's Commentary'; see also Waingrow, *Corr.* 319. It is not however, mentioned in the appropriate place in *European Mag.* vii (Apr. 1785), 249–50.

[2] A memorandum of an agreement between George Robinson and John Darby, dated 24 July 1777, for the preparation of 4 vols. of Pearce's Sermons in the sum of £200, is MS Hyde: (R.B. Adam, extra-illus. *Letters*, vi. 73), cf. William Upcott, *Original Letters &c.*, [priv. ptd.], 1836, p. 50 (O: Mus Bibl. III. 4° 36), and 'Advertisement' in *Commentary*, I. vii.

[3] JB had identified them as SJ's by 2 Aug. 1777 when he wrote to Lord Hailes asking him if he recognized SJ's hand (CtY: MS Boswell, L 608).

77.2PC/2   Life of Zachary Pearce   1816

[½t] [medium rule] | THE | LIVES, *&c.* | [medium rule]
[Title] THE | [BL] Lives | OF | DR. EDWARD POCOCK, | THE

CELEBRATED ORIENTALIST, | BY DR. TWELLS; | OF | DR. ZACHARY PEARCE, | BISHOP OF ROCHESTER, | AND OF | DR. THOMAS NEWTON, | BISHOP OF BRISTOL, | BY THEMSELVES; | AND OF THE | REV. PHILIP SKELTON, | BY MR. BURDY. | [medium rule] | IN TWO VOLUMES. | VOL. I [– II]. | [medium rule] | **[BL]** **London:** | PRINTED FOR F. C. AND J. RIVINGTON, | NO. 62, ST. PAUL'S CHURCH YARD; | *By R. and R. Gilbert, St. John's Square, Clerkenwell.* | [short rule] | 1816

2 vols., 8°

I. *A*⁴ B–2E⁸ 2F⁴ (2F4 blk), ($2 signed; 'VOL. I.' on $1), 224 leaves.

Pp. A1 *i* ½t, *ii* blk, *iii* t., *iv* blk, *v–vii* Preface dh & ht: PREFACE. (vii: 'A.C. | *Nov. 1816.*'), *viii* blk, on B1 *1* 2–356 text dh: THE | LIFE | OF THE | REV. AND MOST LEARNED | *DR. EDWARD POCOCK.* | [medium wavy rule], rt: THE LIFE OF | DR. EDWARD POCOCK., *357* ½t: THE LIFE | OF | *DR. ZACHARY PEARCE*, | LATE LORD BISHOP OF ROCHESTER., *358* blk, *359* 360–438 text dh: (as ½t), rt: THE LIFE OF | DR. ZACHARY PEARCE., *439–40* (2F4) blk.

Pagination: 69 as 96.

Press-figures: B5ᵛ(10)–9, C7(29)–6, C7ᵛ(30)–2, D4ᵛ(40)–2, E8(63)–9, E8ᵛ(64)–*, F1ᵛ(66)–9, F6ᵛ(76)–6, G7(93)–1, G8(95)–*, H8(111)–1, I6ᵛ(124)–4, I8(127)–5, K5(137)–2, L3ᵛ(150)–3, L7(157)–9, M1ᵛ(162)–6, M6ᵛ(172)–8, N5ᵛ(186)–5, N7(189)–1, O4(199)–4, O4ᵛ(200)–2, P1ᵛ(210)–5, P8ᵛ(224)–1, Q2ᵛ(228)–9, Q6(235)–1, R6(251)–9, R7(253)–1, S7(269)–9, S7ᵛ(270)–2, T7(285)–5, T8(287)–2, U2ᵛ(292)–6, U7ᵛ(302)–5, X4(311)–6, Y5(329)–6, Z3ᵛ(342)–*, Z8ᵛ(352)–1, 2A8(367)–7, 2B8(383)–5, 2C2ᵛ(388)–1, 2C6(395)–7, 2D5ᵛ(410)–5, 2E7ᵛ(430)–8, 2F1ᵛ(434)–2.

Catchwords: vii–viii *om.*, 16 "side‸ ("~,), 42 "half‸ ("~,), 55 *om.* (years), 93 as (he), 109 *om.* ("judge;), 119 visitors‸ (~,), 125 then‸ (~,), 127 [per-] ‸petual ("~), 134 ‸quiet ("~), 158 [profes-] sors‸ (~,), 202 [af-] ‸feacted, ("~,), 203 ‸happen ("~), 232 "Hebrew ("Canonship), 258 ‸an ("~), 264 offices (of), 277 year‸ (~,), 292 Oldenburg; (~:), 214 ‸and ("~), 329 [al-] ways‸ (~,), 348 [mate-] rials, (~‸), 356–8 *om.*, 361 "‸whom ('"~), 380 by ("the), 381 ‸judgment ("~), 390 "give ("him), 401 " 'is, ("‸ ~,).

Explicit: 438 THE END OF VOL. I.

II. *A*² B–2K⁸, ($2 signed; 'VOL. II.' on $1), 258 leaves.

Pp. A1 *i* ½t, *ii* blk, *iii* t., *iv* blk, on B1 *²i* ½t: THE | LIFE | OF | *DR. THOMAS NEWTON,* | LATE LORD BISHOP OF BRISTOL, | WRITTEN BY HIMSELF., *ii* blk, *iii* iv–vii Preface, *viii* blk, on B5 *9* 10–248 text dh: SOME | ACCOUNT | OF THE | *LIFE OF DR. THOMAS NEWTON,* | LATE LORD BISHOP OF BRISTOL; | WITH | ANECDOTES OF SEVERAL OF HIS FRIENDS. | [medium wavy rule] | [motto, from Martial.] | [medium wavy rule], *249* ½t:THE | LIFE | OF THE

LATE | *REV. PHILIP SKELTON;* | WITH SOME CURIOUS ANECDOTES, | BY SAMUEL BURDY, A.B. | [short parallel rule] | *Virtus post funera vivit.*, *250* blk, *251* 252–3 Preface (253: '*Down, January* 10, 1792.'), *254* blk, *255* 256–504 text, *505–12* (2K5–8, 4 leaves unp.) Index, *512* coloph: 'Printed by R. and R. Gilbert, St. John's Square, London.'

Pagination: no errors.

Press-figures: B5ᵛ(10)–2, C7ᵛ(30)–2, D7(45)–9, E1ᵛ(50)–5, F4(71)–5, G3ᵛ(86)–5, H8(111)–1, I7ᵛ(126)–*, K6(139)–*, L6ᵛ(156)–8, M4(167)–5, N8(191)–6, O7ᵛ(206)–2, P7ᵛ(222)–1, Q5ᵛ(234)–8, R8(255)–5, S3ᵛ(262)–4, T7ᵛ(286)–8, U8ᵛ(304)–4, X7ᵛ(318)–1, Y7(333)–8, Z7(349)–3[*or* ? 5], 2A1ᵛ(354)–8, 2B2ᵛ(372)–2, 2B5ᵛ(378)–1, 2C4ᵛ(392)–4, 2D7ᵛ(414)–7, 2E8(431)–1, 2E8ᵛ(432)–7, 2F2ᵛ(436)–8, 2F7ᵛ(446)–*, 2G4(455)–†, 2G6ᵛ(460)–3, 2H7ᵛ(478)–9, 2I3(485)–8, 2I8(495)–*, 2K5–4, 2K6–2.

Catchwords: i–ii *om.*, 52 ‸be ("~), 67 "acted ('~), 68 "posts ("post), 101 Oswald‸ (~:), *269–70 om.* (PREFACE.), 258 *Quem* (Quem), 321 "something‸ ("~;), 352 account‸ (~,), 466 offered‸ (~,), 504 *om.* (INDEX).

Explicit: 2K8ᵛ (*512*) FINIS

Paper: White, wove; wmk.: '1814'.

Type: Pica (4.1 mm), notes: long primer (3.4).

Notes: This collection was the work of Alexander Chalmers, perhaps as an extension from his labours on the *General Biographical Dictionary* (1812–17), and was published in November 1816 (*Gents. Mag.* lxxxvi (Nov. 1816), 209).[1] SJ's Life of Pearce is reprinted at I. 359–438.

Copies: O (8° X. 178–9 BS); *USA*: CtY² (1. Im. J637. +777p.2; 2. pagination disorderly in vol. 2); *UK*: Gu, SAN, SHu.

[1] *Lit. Illus.* viii (1858), 629.

77.2LC/1 Defence of James's Fever Powders, 1777
London Chronicle

20 February A Defence of Dr James's Fever Powders.

References: Hazen 71.

Notes: The Powders had suffered from the general belief that they had brought about Goldsmith's death in 1774,[1] and James and Newbery were anxious to restore the credit of this once-popular and profitable remedy.[2] The final paragraph is by SJ.

Copies: O (N. 22863 d.1); [see further in *BUCOP*].

[1] James and his powders were vigorously attacked by William Hawes, Apothecary, in *An Account of the late Dr Goldsmith's Illness, so far as relates to the Exhibition of Dr James's Powders*, 3 edd. 4° 1774. (cf. *Bibliotheca Osleriana* (1929), 4871); which reached a 4th edn. by 1780. It was addressed to Burke and Reynolds, and cited Dr George Fordyce and Dr John Turton who, with Hawes, attended Goldsmith, as having urged him to take the fatal dose, *Life* iii. 500–1.

² Newbery published a 4° leaflet advertising his patent medicines (including James's Powders at No. 1) on one side, and carrying a testimonial to their efficacy in 'A very extraordinary case of rheumatism', from Robert Arthington, of Leeds, dated July 6, 1774 (O: JJ. Labels 3). Robert Cole had Newbery's account books (Feb. 1768–July 1798) for his sales of the powders (Puttick & Simpson, 29 July 1861, lot 714), which reappeared in the same rooms at J. Carnaby's sale, 25 Nov. 1886, as lot 351. They are still untraced. For the history of this once popular remedy, see R.B. Dickens, 'Dr James's Fever Powders', *Life and Letters*, ii (1929), 36–47, and J.K. Crellin, 'Dr James's Fever Powders', *Transactions of British Soc. for Hist. of Pharmacy*, i (1974), 136–43.

77.2LC/2   Defence of James's Fever Powders,   1777
Dissertation on Fevers

A | DISSERTATION | ON | FEVERS, | AND | Inflammatory Distempers. | THE EIGHTH EDITION. | To which are now firſt added, | From Papers which he was preparing to publiſh before his Death, | A | Vindication | OF THE | Fever Powder, | And a Short | TREATISE | ON THE | Disorders of Children. | [medium swelled rule] | By the late R. JAMES, M.D. | [medium swelled rule] | LONDON: | Printed for Francis Newbery, Junior, | in St. Paul's Church-Yard. | M.DCC.LXXVIII.

8°, *A*⁴ B–L⁸, ($4 (–L3) signed), 84 leaves.

Pp. A1 t., A1ᵛ blk, A2–2ᵛ ADVERTISEMENT., A3–4ᵛ CONTENTS., on B1 *1* 2–60 text dh: [hp flowers] | A | DISSERTATION | ON | FEVERS, | AND | Inflammatory Disorders., rt: A DISSERTATION ON FEVERS | AND INFLAMMATORY DISORDERS., on E7 *61* ½t: A | VINDICATION | OF THE | FEVER POWDER., *62* blk, *63* 64–148 text dh: [hp flowers] | A | VINDICATION, &c., rt (64–133): A VINDICATION OF THE | FEVER POWDER., (134–47): OF ADMINISTERING | THE FEVER POWDER., on L3 *149* ½t: A SHORT | TREATISE | ON THE | DISORDERS | OF | CHILDREN., *149* blk, *150* 151–60 text dh: [hp flowers] | A SHORT | TREATISE | ON THE | DISORDERS | OF | CHILDREN*., rt: ON THE DISORDERS | OF CHILDREN.

Pagination: [–] 148; *Press-figures*: none.
Catchwords: 23 At (Aт), 60 AN (A), 84 th (the), 91 In (Iғ), 117 [dou-] ble, (~;), 120 IF (Iғ).
Explicit: 160 FINIS.
Paper: White, laid.
Type: Text: pica (4.0 mm), leaded (1.0 mm); notes: bourgeois (3.0 mm).
References: *Life* iii. 4 n. 2; Hazen 71; Roscoe, *Newbery* (1973), A256(8); Welsh 241–2; ESTC: t028066.
Notes: James's *Dissertation on Fevers* was first published by Newbery in 8° in 1748, with a second edition in 12° in 1749, a third edition also 12° in 1755, a fourth 8° in 1758, a fifth, 12° in 1761, a sixth, 12° in 1764, and a seventh, 12° in 1770. SJ's 'Defence' of the powders, of which the reputation suffered after the death of Goldsmith, was first published in the *Lond. Chron.* 20 February 1777

(77.2LC/11, above). There are allusions to 'Miss Eccles' (pp. 10 ff),[1] Colley Cibber (22), and Sir Thomas Robinson in 1774 (55).

Roscoe notes what appears to be a reissue, dated '1849', in Lrcs: not seen. One of the Eu copies (H.20/31) has an engr. front. port. of James in an oval frame, facing right over a caduceus and Medicinal Dictionary, 'D͞ʀ. JAMES| From an Original Bust by Scheemaker. W. Walker Del et Sculp. Published Nov. 1ˢᵗ 1778.' It seems to be an intruder.

Copies: O (12 θ. 1973);

USA: DLC, MB, MH (Tr. 2069), PPL; *UK*: C, Eu², Gu, L (7561 bbb.21), [Lrcp, Lrcs, Lrmchs], NCu.

---

¹ Cf. *Booklist* 138, for this unidentified lady.

77.3SP   Shaw's Proposals   1777

MARCH 1777. | PROPOSALS | For Printing by Subscription, | INSCRIBED, BY PERMISSION, | To the Right Honourable the Earl of *Eglinton:* | AN | ANALYSIS | OF THE | Scotch CELTIC Language. | By WILLIAM SHAW, | NATIVE OF ONE OF THE HEBRIDES. | The Book will be elegantly printed in One Volume in Quarto. | Price Half a Guinea, to be paid at the Time of fubfcribing. | The Books will be delivered in November 1777, by J. Murray, Fleet-Street, | J. Donaldson, Arundel Street, Strand, and Richardson and Urquhart, | No. 91, Royal Exchange, London; C. Elliot, Edinburgh, and Dunlop | and Wilson, Glafgow, where Subfcriptions are alfo received.

4°, $1 (unsigned), 1 leaf.

Pp. $1 t. (as above), $1ᵛ statement (as below):

Though the Earfe Dialect of the Celtic Language has, from the | earlieft Times, been fpoken in Britain, and ftill fubfifts in the Northern | Parts and adjacent Iflands, yet by the Negligence of a People rather warlike | than lettered, it has hitherto been left to the Caprice and Judgment of every | Speaker, and has floated in the living Voice, without the Steadinefs of Ana- | logy or Direction of Rules. An Earfe Grammar is an Addition to the Stores | of Literature, and its Author hopes for the Indulgence always fhewn to thofe | that attempt to do what was never done before. If his Work fhall be found | defective, it is at leaft all his own; he is not like other Grammarians a Com- | piler or Tranfcriber; what he delivers, he has learned by attentive Obfervation | among his Countrymen, who perhaps will be themfelves furprized to fee | that Speech reduced to Principles, which they have ufed only by Imitation. |

The Ufe of this Book will however not be confined to the Mountains and | Iflands; it will afford an important and pleafing Subject of

Speculation, to | thofe whofe Studies lead them to trace the Affinity of Languages, and the | Migrations of the ancient Races of Mankind. |

As this Book is intended for the curious and the learned, a few Copies | more than what are fubfcribed for will be printed. |

The Subfcribers Names will be printed.

Paper: White, laid; foolscap (uncut: 8½ × 6¼ in.); no vis. wmk.

Type: Title display from 32 pt. to long primer (10 pt), i.e. 13 mm to 3.4 mm; Statement in pica (3.9 mm), widely leaded (3.5 mm).

References: *Life* iii. 107, 488 (JB's text is not scrupulously accurate; Courtney 129); CH 154 (had not seen a copy); Powell, in *Johnsonian Studies* (1962), 9–13; K.D. Macdonald, *TGSI* 1 (1976–8), 1–19.

Notes: In his letter of 24 April 1777 to JB giving an account of himself and of his undertaking, Shaw wrote:

> I was advis'd after consulting my friends who said it was easier to get 200 half guineas than 400 Crowns, to price it at half a guinea — The price has not here been objected to and as I have got some subscriptions here at y^t price I mean to keep it at the same in Scotland — The book cost labour & time in the Composition, it will probably never have another Impression & in a few years will be met w^t only in the Libraries of the Curious. . . . When I don't get money I gladly take their names — I have got about 60.[1]

The advice was sound. In the event Shaw mustered 182 subscribers who took 296 copies. For the published work see Shaw's *Analysis*, 1778 (78.7SA/1, below).

Copies: O² (**1**. Gough Gen. Top. 366 f. 552; **2**. O-JJ 'Prospectuses');

USA: CtY (P 78; 'James Boswell'), Hyde ('James Boswell' — 'Talbot de Malahide' — Malahide Castle).[2]

---

[1] *Boswell Catalogue* (CtY: MS Boswell C 2482, *Fettercairn* 772), in reply to a letter from JB (CtY: MS Boswell L 1154, *Fettercairn* 1284).

[2] Another copy was sold at Parke-Bernet (New York), 4 October 1961, 356, for $600, but is untraced.

77.5KW/1   **[Prologue to] Kelly's Word to the Wise**   **1770**

A | WORD to the WISE, | A | COMEDY. | AS IT WAS PERFORMED | AT THE | THEATRE ROYAL, in DRURY-LANE. | [rule] | Written by HUGH KELLY, | of the Middle-Temple, | Author of False Delicacy. | [rule] | [Orn. device of flowers] | [parallel rule] | LONDON, | PRINTED FOR THE AUTHOR, | AND SOLD BY | J. DODSLEY, IN PALL-MALL; J. AND E. DILLY, IN | THE POULTRY; G. KEARSLEY, IN LUDGATE-STREET; | AND T. CADELL, IN THE STRAND. | M DCC LXX.

Stet: J. AND E. DILLY,
8°, *a*⁴ b–d⁴ ²d² B–O⁴ (O4 blk), ($2 (–²d2) signed), 70 leaves.

Pp. a1 *i* t., *ii* Paste-on *Errata* slip, *iii* iv–xix Address to the Public, *xx–xxx*
Subscribers, *xxxi* Dedication, *xxxii* blk, *xxxiii–xxxiv* Prologue, *xxxv* Dramatis
Personæ, *xxxvi* blk, on B1 *1* 2–99 text Word to the Wise, *100* blk, *101–2*
Epilogue, *103–4* (O4) blk.

Press-figures: a3(v)–*, b1ᵛ(x)–*, c2(xix)–*, d1ᵛ(xxvi)–3, ²d1ᵛ(xxxiv)–*,
C3ᵛ(14)–2, D3ᵛ(22)–2, H4ᵛ(56)–3, I4(63)–3, K2ᵛ(68)–3, L1ᵛ(74)–3,
M3ᵛ(86)–3, N3ᵛ(94)–3, O1ᵛ(98)–3.

Catchwords: iii ‸*parties*, ("~,), xii ‸feem ("~), 21 *om.* (ACT II.), 35 There‸
(~,), 51 Mifs (Lᴜᴄʏ.), 59 ‸ Wɪʟʟᴏᴜɢʜʙʏ. (Mifs ~.), 61 *om.* (mifs), 64 fafe
(‸afe), 70 For‸ (~,).

Paper: White, laid; La. post (uncut: 8¼ × 5 in.); no vis. wmk.

Type: Prelims: bourgeois (3.1 mm), leaded (0.2), text: pica (4.0 mm), leaded
(0.2).

References: *Poems*² 209–11; Subscriptions no. 33.

Notes: The play *A Word to the Wise* was composed and produced in 1770, and
was published by subscription. Because Kelly was manager of the *Public Ledger*
he had political opponents and the 1770 productions were disrupted. It was
revived after Kelly's death on 3 February 1777 for the benefit of his widow and
five children. Performances, at which SJ's 'Prologue' was delivered, were given
on 13 and 29 May (*Public Advertiser*, 27, 28, and 29 May 1777, the *Gazetteer &
New Daily Advertiser*, 29 May 1777, and *Morning Chron.* 28 May 1777, the latter reporting that SJ had furnished the 'Prologue' for the occasion). His generosity in supplying the 'Prologue' had however been noticed already on 26
May, by both the *London Packet* and *Morning Chron.*

A transcript of the 'Prologue' dated 27 May 1777, made for Thomas Harris,
is in the Larpent Collection (CSmH: LA 434; *MS Index* JoS 68).[1] The published play itself does not include SJ's 'Prologue'.

The 'Address to the Public' was wrongly attributed to SJ in Tregaskis,
Catalogue 780 (19—?). 836 subscribers took 1918 copies; the list includes the
names of James Boswell, Dr and Mrs Dodd, 'Mr Johnson', 'Dr. J.' (4 copies),
and Thomas Percy, with a large number of American Kellys. A blank receipt
form for 5s. for a copy of the play, signed by Kelly, is C (Munby: 'Hutton'
Collection). SJ's 'Prologue' is not printed with this edn., nor is it in the second
edn. published by Edward and Charles Dilly, 1773 (MH; E (Bute)), nor with
the play in Bell's *British Library*, 12°, xxiii (1795) (MH).

Copies: MH (17473.35, 'F. R. C. Grant');
USA: CtY, NIC, TxU²; *UK*: C, E (H. 28 d.7(2)). L², O.

Johnson's 'Prologue' was printed in the following newspapers:

30 May 1777   *London Packet, Morning Chron.* (with review).
31 May 1777   *Gazetteer, London Chron., London Evening Post, Morning Post,*

Public Advertiser, *St James's Chron.*, *Whitehall Evening Post.* Boswell preserved a cutting of SJ's 'Prologue' from the *Morning Post* (CtY: MS Boswell, P 76).

May 1777	*Westminster Mag.* iv. 273.
7 June 1777	*Caledonian Mercury.*
9 June 1777	*Edinburgh Evening Courant.*
12 June 1777	Edinburgh *Weekly Mag.* xxv. 369.
June 1777	*Gentleman's Mag.* xlvii. 286; *Scots Mag.* xxxix. 325.
July 1777	*London Mag.* lvi. 375–6.
1777	*Annual Register* (p. 198).

References: Courtney 128; *Poems*² 209–11; McGuffie, *SH in the British Press* (1976), 209–10.

---

¹ I am indebted to Mr Robert D. Dunn, of the University of Toronto, for drawing this item to my attention in 1986, and to his published account in *ELN* xxv (1987–8), 28–35.

77.5KW/2   Prologue to Kelly's Word to the Wise   1778

THE | WORKS | OF | HUGH KELLY. | [short swelled rule] | TO WHICH IS PREFIXED | THE LIFE OF THE AUTHOR. | [swelled rule] | LONDON: | Printed for the AUTHOR's WIDOW; | And fold by T. CADELL, in the Strand; J. RIDLEY, in St. James's | Street; and N. CONANT, in Fleet Street. | [short rule] | M,DCC,LXXVIII.

4°, Engr. front. + A⁴ a⁴ b² B–3Q⁴ 3R², ($2 signed), 256 leaves.

Pp. *i–xx*, on B1 *1* ½t, *2* blk, *3* Dedication, *4* blk, *5–6* SJ's Prologue, *7* 8–492 text.

Pagination: 483 as 487.

Press-figures: A3(v)–4, A3ᵛ(vi)–1, B4(7)–5, C3ᵛ(14)–1, D4ᵛ(24)–7, E2ᵛ(28)–9, E4(31)–†, F2ᵛ(36)–6, F4(39)–8, G1ᵛ(42)–1, H4(55)–†, I4ᵛ(64)–5, K1ᵛ(66)–4, L3ᵛ(78)–8, M3(85)–5, M4(87)–3, N1ᵛ(90)–4, O4(103)–2, P2ᵛ(108)–†, P3ᵛ(110)–1, Q1ᵛ(114)–8, R3(125)–7, R4(127)–2, S1ᵛ(130)–2, S2ᵛ(132)–*, T4(143)–2, U1ᵛ(146)–*, X4(159)–2, Y3ᵛ(166)–†, Z1ᵛ(170)–7, Z4ᵛ(176)–†; 2A1ᵛ(178)–2, 2A3(181)–†, 2B4ᵛ(192)–4, 2C4ᵛ(200)–9, 2D4(207)–4, 2E4ᵛ(216)–2, 2F2ᵛ(220)–†, 2F4(223)–6, 2G3(229)–†, 2H4(239)–5, 2I1ᵛ(242)–7, 2I3(245)–2, 2K3(253)–5, 2K4(255)–2, 2L2ᵛ(260)–5, 2L4(263)–4, 2M1ᵛ(266)–2, 2N2ᵛ(276)–4, 2N3ᵛ(278)–3, 2O1ᵛ(282)–9, 2P1ᵛ(290)–5, 2P4ᵛ(296)–6, 2Q1ᵛ(298)–7, 2R4ᵛ(312)–1, 2S4(319)–1, 2T2ᵛ(324)–4, 2U1ᵛ(330)–1, 2X3(341)–9, 2Y3ᵛ(350)–2, 2Z2ᵛ(356)–9, 2Z3ᵛ(358)–6; 3A4(367)–3, 3B3(373)–7, 3C3ᵛ(382)–1, 3D3(389)–9, 3E2ᵛ(396)–5, 3F4(407)–5, 3G3ᵛ(414)–7, 3H3(421)–5, 3H4(423)–5, 3I2ᵛ(428)–9, 3I4(431)–6, 3K2ᵛ(436)–4, 3L2ᵛ(444)–6, 3M3ᵛ(454)–9, 3M4ᵛ(456)–8, 3N3ᵛ(462)–9, 3O3ᵛ(470)–4, 3O4ᵛ(472)–8, 3P4(479)–3, 3Q2ᵛ(484)–8, 3R2(491)–1.

Explicit: 492 FINIS.

Paper: White, laid; La. post (uncut: 10½ × 8¼ in.); no vis. wmk.

Type: English (4.4 mm), leaded (1.0 mm).
References: *Life* iii. 113–14 (Courtney 128).
Notes: SJ's 'Prologue', delivered on 13 and 29 May 1777, is at pp. x–xi. The version in J's *Poetical Works*, 1785 (85.2PW/1, below) was followed in *Works*, 1787 (87.3W/1, below), xi. 349, but Hawkins in *Life87* (87.3W/1.1/1, below) followed this version directly (77.5KW/2). 296 subscribers took 338 copies. Though SJ is not among them, it is hard to believe he did not contribute.
Copies: O (Vet. A5 d. 142);
USA: CtY, DFo, DLC, [Liebert], MB, MH, NN, PPU; *UK*: BMp, L (79 k.9), LVu, NOu.

77.5KW/3   Prologue to Kelly's Word to the Wise   1825

Richard Ryan, *Dramatic Table Talk*, 3 vols. 1825 (i. 166–7).
Copies: Hyde.

(1)   DODD'S SPEECH TO THE COURT

SJ's involvement with Dodd's case emerges from newspaper accounts which appear at intervals, so that the observance of strict chronology loses narrative coherence. These minor items are therefore treated together in the following notes, though it should be remembered that SJ was concerned with various other literary matters as the Dodd affair progressed.[1] There are sixteen sections: Speech to the Court; Account of Himself; Declaration to a Friend; Petition of the City; Convict's Address; Letter to North; Letter to Mansfield; Petition of Mrs Dodd; Petition to the King; Johnson's Letter to the King; Johnson's Observations; Last Solemn Declaration; Introduction to Occasional Papers; Conclusion to Occasional Papers; Occasional Papers; Sources and Doddiana.

---

[1] Recurrent references are made to Chapman's edn. of *Papers written by Dr Johnson and Dr Dodd in 1777* (1926), of which the original MSS to which Chapman refers are now in the Hyde Collection, to the *Occasional Papers by the late William Dodd*, published by George Kearsley [1777] (77.7DOP, below), to the *Index of English Literary Manuscripts*, III.ii, ed. Margaret M. Smith (1989), to the note by Metzdorf in *HLB* vi (1952), 393–6, and especially to A.D. Barker, 'Samuel Johnson and the Campaign to Save William Dodd', *HLB* xxxi (1983), 147–80. Other contemporary publications are listed briefly at the end of this entry.

77.5DS/1   Dodd's Speech, Gazeteer   1777

Dodd's *Speech to the Court*, addressed to the Recorder of the City of London. 'I now stand before you . . .' (MS Hyde) [Mon. 16 May 1777][1]

17 May *Gazetteer & New Daily Advertiser*, *Public Advertiser*, *Whitehall Evening Post*.

¹ A MS copy of this speech is DFo (MA 114, fos. 13–16). On this same day Dodd wrote a letter to Manley, Lord Chesterfield's attorney (BL Add MS 24419, fo. 9), and sent a note to Dilly, the bookseller, from 'Newgate' (Brick Row Bookshop, *Catalogue* 29 (Sept. 1927), 94b).

77.5DS/2   Dodd's Speech, folio   1777

dh: Dr. DODD's | SPEECH | WHICH | He delivered to the Judge, before he received | Sentence of DEATH.

2°, $1, (unsigned), 1 leaf. Pp. *1* text in 2 cols., *2* blk.

Paper: White, laid; Pot (12 × 7½ in.); no vis. wmk.

Type: Drop-head display from 2-line great primer (11.5 mm) caps to double pica (7.3 mm); text: bourgeois (3.0 mm).

References: Chapman (1928), no. 1; *Letters* 519 (to Taylor, 19 May 77; Hyde, iii. 25); A.D. Barker, *HLB* xxxi (1983), 160; ESTC: t12822.

Notes: Apparently later than the newspaper reports of the sentencing which took place on 16 May.

Copies: L (C. 127. i.1.1).

Reprints: *Gents. Mag.* xlvii (May 1777), 226–7 (published *c.*14 June)

Scots Mag. xxxix (July 1777), 384–5

Reed, *Account of the Life and Writings of William Dodd*, (25 June) 1777, 67–70

The Convict's Address, 2nd edn. (26 June), 1777, 25–8

Duncombe, *Historical Memoirs of William Dodd*, (3 July) 1777, 55–8

Reed, *An Account of the Life* &c., 2nd edn. (1 Aug.) 1777, 67–70

Thoughts of a Citizen of London, (30 Aug.), 1777, 23–4

Dr Dodd's Address to his Unhappy Brethren, [1777], 18–20

A Narrative of the late William Dodd, Bath [1777], 11–12

[Reed] *Johnson's Works*, xiv (1788), 378–80.

(2)   DODD'S ACCOUNT OF HIMSELF

'The greatest Affliction I have known . . .' [Sat. 21 May 1777]

? [11 July] *Occasional Papers* (77.7DOP, below), 7–11

References: Chapman (1928), no. 4.

Reprints: Cooke, *Life of Johnson*, 1st edn. 1785, 130–3; 2nd edn. 1785, 174–82

[Reed], *SJ's Works*, xiv (1788), 399–402 ('May 21. 1777').

(3)   DODD'S DECLARATION TO A FRIEND

'Though I acknowledge in all its atrocity . . .' [Sat. 21 May 1777]
[11 July] *Occasional Papers* (77.7DOP, below), 12–13
    Reprints: Cooke, *Life of Johnson*, 1st edn. 1785, 133–4; 2nd edn. 1785, 183–6
    [Reed], *SJ's Works*, xiv (1788), 402–3.

(4)   PETITION OF THE CITY
[*OR* THE CITIZENS] OF LONDON

'Most humbly sheweth, that William Dodd, Dr. of Laws, now lying . . .' [5 June 1777]
    (i) SJ's first MS draft 'To the &c.' (MS Hyde; *MS Index* JoS 237)
    (ii) SJ's second MS draft (L: Add. MS 5420; *MS Index* JoS 238)[1]
    (iii) Transcript by JB of (ii), above (CtY: MS Boswell, M 156:5)
Presented 12 June (*Morning Chronicle*, 13 June).
[27 Aug. 1777] *Thoughts of a Citizen of London on the Conduct of William Dodd*, 17–18.
    References: Chapman (1928), no. 10; A.D. Barker (1983), 163–5, 169–70 reports that it was presented by Lord North on 26 June, to the Privy Council (*Public Advertiser*, 27 June)
    Reprints: *Lloyd's Evening Post*, 27 June, 1777.

---

[1] Waingrow, *Corr.* 384–5. SJ's authorship of a Petition for Dodd is reported in the *Morning Post*, 3 July 1777.

(5) THE CONVICT'S ADDRESS, PREACHED AT
NEWGATE. FRI. 6 JUNE 1777[1]

The true chronological sequence of the following items has proved difficult to determine since few were regularly advertised, beyond the first two edns (**1** and **2** below). The remainder have therefore been arranged alphabetically by place of publication.

---

[1] On the next day Dodd composed verses, 'Pearly Fount and pebbly Rill, . . .' entitled 'The Adieu' (MS Hyde), docketed by Weeden Butler: 'Written by him in *Newgate*, was found among his papers and is dated 7th June 1777'.

77.6CA/1a   Dodd, Convict's Address, first edition,   1777
first issue

THE | Convict's ADDRESS | TO | His Unhappy Brethren. | Delivered in the Chapel of NEWGATE, on | FRIDAY, JUNE 6, 1777. | [rule] | *I acknowledge my Faults: and my Sin is ever before me.* | PSALM li. 3. | [total rule] | LONDON: | Printed for G. KEARSLY, at N° 46, in Fleet-Street. | [short rule] | M.DCC.LXXVII. | [Price One Shilling.]

8°, A–C⁴, ($2 (–A1) signed), 12 leaves.

Pp. A1 *1* t., *2* blk, *3* Dedication dh: *To the Reverend Mr.* VILLETTE, | *Ordinary of* NEWGATE. ('*Friday, June 6,* | 1777.'), *4* blk, *5* 6–24 text dh: [total rule] | AN | ADDRESS, &c. | [rule], rt: *The* CONVICT'S ADDRESS | *to his Unhappy Brethren.* (24: *The* CONVICT'S ADDRESS, *&c.*).

Pagination: no errors; *Press-figures*: none.

Catchwords: 11 [Imprifon-] men (ment), 19 th a∧ [*slipt*] (that).

Explicit: 24 [small crown].

Paper: White, laid; La. post (uncut: 8¼ × 5¼ in.); wmk.: fleur-de-lys.

Type: English (4.5 mm), leaded (1.0 mm). Small crown on p. 24.

References: Courtney 128; CH 153–5; *Rothschild* 1260; *Tinker* 1363; ESTC: t060725.

Notes: Printed by Kearsley as recorded in a MS note by Isaac Reed, '16 April 1782 Kearsley told me these anecdotes That Dr Johnson actually wrote the Convicts Address. That it was printed by him (K) & the profit arising from it – amounted to 87*l*' (MH: *EC75.R2518. 777ic; cf. Metzdorf, *HLB* vi (1952), 395). Published Thurs. 19 June 1777 (*Public Advertiser*), and reviewed in Kenrick's *London Review*, iii (Aug. 1777), 152, which praised the style, condemned the contents, and attributed it to SJ. Edmund Allen's transcript of SJ's 'Postscript' is MS Hyde (*MS Index* JoS 178; Chapman, 15).[1]

Copies: L² (1. C.108. bbb.41(1); 2. 4474. c.58);

USA: CSmH (44251(1) 'James Boswell' jun.), CtY² (1. JB's copy, (*Fettercairn* 1597) = P 73; uncut in blue wraps, marked by SJ showing Dodd's additions), Hyde³, MB, MiU, NIC ('Liebert'), NN, NN-B, TxU; *UK*: BMp (225144), C, Ct(R), O.

[1] A MS copy of the whole (though the handwriting is not identified), was lot 276 in Sotheby's (Revd H.S. Cotton, Ordinary of Newgate), 17 June 1839, (with other Doddiana, lots 266–75).

77.6CA/1b   Dodd, Convict's Address, first edition,   1777
second issue

THE | Convict's ADDRESS | TO | His Unhappy Brethren. | Delivered in the Chapel of NEWGATE, on | FRIDAY, JUNE 6, 1777. | By WILLIAM DODD, LL.D. | [rule] | SECOND EDITION. | To which is added, | His GENUINE

SPEECH to the COURT previous | to his receiving Sentence of [**Black Letter**] **Death.** | [rule] | *I acknowledge my Faults: and my Sin is ever before me.* | PSALM li. 3. | [total rule] | LONDON: | Printed for G. KEARSLY, at N° 46, in Fleet-Street. | [short rule] | M.DCC.LXXVII. | [Price One Shilling.]

   8°, A–C⁴ D², ($2 (–A1, D2) signed), 14 leaves.

   Pp. A1 *1* t., *2* blk, *3* Dedication: 'To the Rev. Mr. Villette.', *4* blk, *5* 6–24 text, 25–28 'Speech to the Court' (no. 1, above).

   Pagination: [↑] 25–8.

   Press-figures: none; *Catchwords*: As 77.6CA/1, above; *Explicit*: none.

   Paper: White, laid; La. post (uncut: 8¼ × 5¼ in.); wmk.: fleur-de-lys.

   Type: As 77.6CA/1a above. Orn. tp. 28 usually a small crown (as p. 24), but L (1416. f.30) has a group of flowers.

   References: Courtney 128–9; CH 153–4; ESTC: t139001 (O copy **3**. is recorded separately as t186132).

   Notes: A reissue of the sheets of the first edn. with the addition of Dodd's name on the t., and with the addition of D² (pp. 25–8) carrying Dodd's 'Speech to the Court on receiving Sentence of Death'. The variant tp. and variant footprint on p. 25 (D1), where the 'D' is placed under '*heard*' (crown), or 'heard' (flowers), may arise from the printing of this *addendum* as a duplicate ½-sheet. Published on Thurs. 26 June 1777 (*Public Advertiser*), the day before WD's execution.

   Copies: O³ (**1**. 12 θ. 882; **2**. Vet A5 e.531(2); **3**. Vet A5 e.4521(3));

   USA: CtY² (flowers & crown), [Liebert² (flowers & crown)], IU, MH (*EC75 D6618. B781d, 'Isaac Reed'), NIC (flowers), [OU]; *Can*: CaOHM (B. 1720); *UK*: ABu (flowers), C (flowers), Ct² (flowers & crown), L (1416 f.30, flowers), MRp (crown); *Ger*: GOT (not seen).

77.6CA/2   Dodd, Convict's Address, Bath   [1777]

A Narrative of the late William Dodd, Doctor of Laws, heretofore Prebend of Brecon, and Chaplain in ordinary to His Majesty; containing Genuine Memoirs of his Life — &c. &c. &c. Bath: Printed and Sold by W. Gye, in Westgate Buildings; Sold also by A. Tennant and S. Hazard Bath; T. Mills Bristol; T. Burrough Devizes; J. Matthews London; and all other Booksellers, in *England*. Price Four-Pence.

   8°, A–B⁴, ($4 (–B3,4) signed), 12 leaves.

   Pp. A1 *1* t., *2* 3–4 Sketch of the Life of the Rev. Dr. Dodd, 4–7 Account of his Apprehension, and Examination . . . February 8, 1777, 7–11 Trial of Dr Dodd, 11–12 Dr Dodd's Speech to the Judge, 13 Copy of a Letter from . . . the Countess of Huntingdon (May 1777), 14–21 Dr Dodd's Sermon to his Unhappy Brethren, 22–4 An Account of Dr Dodd's Execution. 24 Epitaph on Dr Dodd.

Notes: No press-figures. Pendred records Gye as a printer in 1785 (p. 23), and 'Miles' as a bookseller in Bristol (p. 24), who may be the same as Plomer's 'T. Mills' of Bath.

Copies: BAT (39:57 + other pieces); *UK*: [? MRp].

77.6CA/3   Dodd, Convict's Address, Dublin   1777

THE | Convict's ADDRESS | TO | His Unhappy Brethren. | Delivered in the Chapel of NEWGATE, on | FRIDAY, JUNE 6, 1777. | [rule] | *I acknowledge my Faults: and my Sin is ever before me.* | PSALM li. 3. | [parallel rule] | DUBLIN: | PRINTED BY W. SPOTSWOOD, | FOR THE COMPANY OF BOOKSELLERS. | [short rule] | M.DCC.LXXVII.

8°, A–C⁴, ($2 (–A1) signed), 12 leaves.

Pp. A1 *1* t., *2* blk, *3* Dedication, *4* blk, *5* 6–24 text.

References: ESTC: n027325.

Notes: This reprints the first London version for it makes no mention of the appended 'Speech to the Court' (no. 1, above), which was added to the second London issue. William Spotswood was a publisher of the *Dublin Chronicle* for 1770 (Plomer). The 'Company of Booksellers' regulated copyright in Dublin from about 1774 until the mid-1790s (M. Pollard, *Dublin's Trade in Books* (1989), 168–9).

Copies: Hyde.

77.6CA/4   Dodd, Convict's Address, Edinburgh   1777

THE LAST AND GREAT | SERMON, | Of the Rev. Dr WILLIAM DODD, | Prea- | ched in the Chapel of *Newgate*-prifon, late | Minifter at *Bloomsberry*-Chapel in *London*, to | his Convict Brethren on Friday the 6th of | *June*, 1777, a fhort time before he fuffered. | From *Pfal.* li. 3, *I acknowledge my faults, and my fin is | ever before me.* | With his Letters of Addrefs to the Rev. Mr. VILETTE, | *Ordinary* in *Newgate*-prifon, in order for publica- | tion. | Likewife his Solemn Declaration wrote | by himfelf for his laft Speech, and | given in a Letter at the place of | Execution, *June* 27 1777. | [woodcut: 3 figures holding books, right-hand figure in clerical dress] | *Printed in Niddery's-wynd.* 1777. | (*Price One-penny.*)

Stent: Bloomsberry . . . VILETTE

8°, A⁸, (A2ᵛ as 'A2'), 8 leaves.

Pp. A1 *1* t., *2* blk, 3 dh: Dr WILLIAM DODD's ADDRESS | *To the Rev. Mr* VILETTE, 4–15 Convict's Address, dh: *Dr DODD's laft* SERMON, *&c.,* 15–16 dh: *Dr.* DODD's *laft folemn* DECLARATION. (i.e. no. 12, below).

Pagination: (↑); *Press-figures*: none; *Catchwords*: none; *Explicit*: 16 FINIS.

Paper: White, laid; Foolscap (uncut: 6¾ × 4¼ in.); no vis. wmk.

Type: Long primer (3.3 mm), leaded.
Notes: Inelegantly written and hastily printed chapbook, e.g. on p. 16 is the following note:

N.B. It is hoped and expected, that all ranks of men, in whose hands this Awful Sermon may come into, will take care, and steer by the fatal Rock, on which this great man has split upon; for through all England, there was not a more popular Clergyman in his day, and one who has left many valuable books of his own writings, for the good of succeeding generations. Witness DODD upon Death.

This does not contain WD's 'Speech to the Court' (no. 1, above), and appears to descend from the first London issue. Item 12 ('Last Solemn Declaration') is taken from Villette's *Genuine Account* of 3 July.

The printer is unidentified despite the given address. Alexander Robertson and James Spottiswoode (Bushnell, *Scottish Engravers* (1949), *s.nn.*) are unlikely to have been responsible for so ill-printed a piece, nor indeed is C. McLean.[1]
Copies: E (RB. s. 832(1)).

[1] Carnie, *SB* xv (1962), 108.

77.6CA/5 Dodd, Convict's Address, Edinburgh 1777

THE | TRIAL | OF | WILLIAM DODD, *L.L.D.* | WITH | An ACCOUNT of his BEHAVIOUR during his | Confinement, and on the Day of his Execution: | ALSO, | The PETITIONS prefented to His MAJESTY | on his Behalf, His ADDRESS to his Fellow Convicts, | and LAST SOLEMN DECLARATION. | To the whole is prefixed, | An ACCOUNT of his LIFE and WRITINGS. | [parallel rule] | EDINBURGH: | Printed in the Year M.DCC.LXXVII.

8°, a⁴ A–F⁴ G1, ($2 signed), 29 leaves.
Pp. a1 *i* t., *ii* blk, *iii* iv–v Account of the Life and Writings of the Reverend Dr. Dodd, vi–vii A List of his Works, *viii* blk, on B1 *1* 2–35 The Trial. . . &c., 35 Dedication (To Villette, of 'Addsess' [!] to the Convicts), 36–46 Convict's Address, 47–9 Account of WD's last hours, 49 Last Solemn Declaration (no. 12, dated 'June 27, 1777'), *50* blk.
Pagination: [↑]; *Press-figures*: none.
Paper: White, laid; La. post (8¼ × 5¼ in.); no vis. wmk.
Notes: The Account of the Trial (pp. 1–25) includes: 32 Petition of the City (no. 4), 32–3 Petition of the Jury, 33–5 Petition of . . . Borough of Southwark.
Copies: Ep (G 9443.K; blue wraps, uncut); *UK*: E (Hall 149. c.1, imperfect), Gt.

[77.6CA/6   Dodd, Convict's Address, Gainsborough   1777

There is a rumour of such an edition, though no copy has been traced. It is not reported in ESTC, and is presumably a ghost.
  Copies: Unlocated.]

77.6CA/7   Dodd, Convict's Address, ? London   [1777]

THE | CONVICT's ADDRESS | TO HIS | UNHAPPY BRETHREN: | BEING A | SERMON | PREACHED BY | The Rev. Dr. DODD, | FRIDAY, June 6, 1777, | In the Chapel of NEWGATE, | While under Sentence of Death, | For FORGING the Name of the EARL of | CHESTERFIELD on a Bond for 4200*l*. | [double rule] | Sold by the Bookfellers and News-Carriers. | [Price Two-Pence.]
  8°, $⁸, (unsigned), 8 leaves; Pp. $1 *1* t., *2* Dedication, 3–16 text.
  References: ESTC: t093967.
  Notes: A chapbook.
  Copies: L (4405. g.14); *USA*: NPM (7005. W/22/A).

77.6CA/8   Dodd, Convict's Address, ? London   [1777]

The Address of the Rev. Dr. Dodd, to his unhappy brethren, delivered in the Chapel of Newgate, on Friday the 6th of June, 1777. To which is added a Letter from the Countess of Huntingdon to the unfortunate Divine. Also an Account of his Execution. [n.p., n.d. = ? London, 1777].
  12°, Pp. 24. Not examined.
  References: ESTC: n042287.
  Copies: [MBAt].

77.6CA/9   Dodd, Convict's Address, ? London   [1777]

The Convict's Address to his unhappy Brethren, delivered in the Chapel of Newgate, on Friday, June 6, 1777. [n.p., n.d. = ? London, 1777].
  8°, Pp. 16. Not examined.
  References: ESTC: n027328.
  Copies: [NN].

77.6CA/10   Dodd, Convict's Address, London   1777

Dr. DODD's ADDRESS | TO | His Unhappy Brethren. | Delivered in the Chapel of NEWGATE, on | FRIDAY, JUNE 6, 1777. | To which are added | His

GENUINE SPEECH to the Court previous | to his receiving Sentence of DEATH. | His SOLEMN DECLARATION, | which he delivered to the Ordinary of Newgate at the | Place of Execution on the 27th of June, 1777. | And a short ACCOUNT of | His LIFE and WRITINGS. | [rule] | *I acknowledge my Faults: and my Sin is ever before* | *me.* PSALM li. 3. | [rule] | LONDON: Printed in the Year 1777. | [Price Threepence]

12°, A–B⁶, ($3 (–A1,2) signed), 12 leaves.

Pp. A1 *1* t., *2* blk, *3* Dedication to Villette ('Friday, June 6, 1777'), *4* blk, *5* 6–17 [Convict's] Address, 18–20 Speech to the Court (no. 1, above), 21–4 Last Solemn Declaration (no. 12, below). *Pagination*: (↑).

References: ESTC: t095460.

Copies: O (24773 e. 206(3)); *UK*: DUc (XXIII.G.1.13), L.

77.6CA/11   Dodd, Convict's Address, [? London]   1777

Dr DODD's | EXHORTATION | TO HIS | FELLOW PRISONERS, | DELIVERED | In the CHAPEL of NEWGATE, | JUNE 6, 1777. | [rule]

8°, $⁸, (unsigned), 8 leaves.

Pp. $1 *1* t., *2* blk, *3* Dedication to Villette ('Friday, June 6, 1777.'), *4* blk, 5–16 The Address. *Pagination*: (↑).

References: ESTC: t165657.

Copies: MRu (R 111727.4).

77.6CA/12   Dodd, Convict's Address, [? London]   1777

A | SERMON | PREACHED | In Newgate to the Convicts, | FROM | Pfal. li. 3 *I acknowledge my faults and my fin is ever before me.* | [rule] | By the late Reverend WILLIAM DODD, *L.L.D.* | [rule] | A | Few Days before his Execution. | Printed, M DCC LXXVII.

12°, A⁶, ($3 (–A1,2) signed), 6 leaves.

Pp. A1 *1* t., *2* 3–12 text: A Sermon. *Pagination*: (↑).

Copies: Gu (Mu.56 ——i.2(10)).

77.6CA/13   Dodd, Convict's Address, [London]   [1777]

The True and Genuine Account of the Trial And all the most material transactions respecting the Rev. Dr. Dodd . . . To which is added The Convict's Address . . . [London 1777]

8°, A–G⁴, ($2 signed), 28 leaves.

Pp. A1 *1* t., *2* Advertisement, 3–32 Trial &c., 33–5 Sentence and WD's Speech to the Court ('I now stand before you . . .'), 35–56 Convict's Address.

Pagination: [↑] 3, 17, 26, 33, 37, 42, 46, 48, 53–4, 56; (↑) 4–16, 18, 20–25, 27–32, 34–6, 38–41, 43–5, 47, 49–52, 55; [↑] 19.

Notes: A chapbook.

Copies: O (Vet. A5 f.1621); *USA*: MH (Law).

77.6CA/14   Dodd, Convict's Adress, Villette's edition   1777

Exhortations and Prayers selected from Rossell's Prisoner's Directory, for the Instruction and Comfort of Malefactors under Imprisonment for Capital Offences, and more especially those who are under Sentence of Death; containing suitable Directions for the Improvement of their Minds in Prison; and as a due Preparation for Death and a future State: to which is prefixed, An Exhortation to Convicted Criminals by William Dodd. The whole published by the Rev. John Villette, Ordinary of Newgate. 1777.

8°. Not seen.

References: Reed, ed., *Dodd's Thoughts* (3rd edn. 1789), xxxiv, no. 55 (77.6WD/S/35).

Copies: Unlocated.

77.6CA/15   Dodd, Convict's Address,   [1777]
                    first Newcastle edition

THE | CONVICT's ADDRESS | TO HIS | UNHAPPY BRETHREN, | Delivered in the CHAPEL of NEWGATE, | JUNE 6, 1777.| By Dr. DODD. | [parallel rule] | NEWCASTLE UPON TYNE: | Sold by T. ROBSON and Co. Lion's-head, Side; the Bookfellers in Town | and Country; and the Diftributors of the Newcaftle Journal. | [Price THREE-PENCE.]

8°, A–B⁴, ($2 (–A1) signed), 8 leaves.

Pp. A1 *1* t., *2* blk, *3* Dedication, *4* blk, on A3 *5* 6–15 Convict's Address, *16* blk.

References: CH 153–4; Welford, *Archaeologia Aeliana*, 3rd ser. iii (1907), 89; *Tinker* 1363; ESTC: n027330.

Notes: The publisher of the *Newcastle Journal* was Isaac Thompson, a printer (fl. 1737–76; Plomer, s.n.), which he had founded in 1739. Pendred recorded the paper as 'Printed by G. Temple' in 1785.

Copies: CaOHM (B.15704, 'Rippey'); *USA*: CtY, L.R. Rothschild, Esq.

77.6CA/16   Dodd, Convict's Address,   1777
                    second Newcastle edition

THE | CONVICT's ADDRESS | TO HIS | UNHAPPY BRETHREN, | Delivered in the CHAPEL of NEWGATE, | JUNE 6, 1777.| By Dr. DODD. |

[parallel rule] | The SECOND EDITION Corrected. | [parallel rule] | *NEWCASTLE UPON TYNE:* | Sold by T. ROBSON and Co. Lion's-head, Side; the Bookſellers in Town | and Country; and the Diſtributors of the Newcaſtle Journal. | [Price THERE-PENCE.]

Stet: THERE-PENCE.

8°, *A*⁴ B⁴, ($1 B only signed), 8 leaves.

Pp. A1 *1* t., *2* blk, *3* Dedication to Villette, *4* blk, *5* 6–15 Convict's Address

dh: [double rule] | *The ADDRESS.* | "I acknowledge my faults; and my ſin is ever before me." | Psalm li. 3., *16* blk.

Pagination: [↑]; *Press-figures*: none; *Catchwords*: no errors; *Explicit*: 15 FINIS.
Paper: White, laid; crown (7½ × 5 in.); no vis. wmk.
Type: Pica (4.1 mm), unleaded.
References: Welford, *Archaeologia Aeliana*, 3rd ser. iii (1907), 89, s.d. '1777' also reports a 'Third Edition' by Robson; ESTC: t204555.
Notes: The t. is evidently not a cancel, so this is presumably a reimpression with a modified t., the changes produced the misprinted price.
Copies: O (GP. 2833 (5)); *UK*: NCp (L252.21476).

77.6CA/17   Dodd, Convict's Address, Salisbury   1777

A | SERMON, | PREACHED BY | The Rev. Dr. DODD, | *(Under Sentence of Death)* | In the CHAPEL of NEWGATE, on | Friday, June 6, 1777. | TO HIS | UNHAPPY BRETHREN. | [rule] | *I acknowledge my Faults: and my Sin is ever before me.* | Psalm li. 3. | [double rule] | SALISBURY: | Printed and Sold by COLLINS and JOHNSON, on the | New-Canal. 1777.

12°, A⁶ B⁴, ($3 (–A1, B3) signed), 10 leaves.

Pp. A1 *1* t., *2* blk, *3* Dedication, *4* blk, *5* 6–20 Convict's Address.

Paper: Small post (6⅓ × 3¾ in.).
References: Courtney 128; ESTC: t073547.
Notes: The combination of [Benjamin] Collins and 'Johnson' is not noticed by historians of the book-trade, but Pendred (1785) records, 'Johnson, *printer and Bookseller*' in Salisbury (p. 34).
Copies: L (4473. aaa.47(12)); *USA*: Hyde (R.B. Adam), IU; *Can*: CaOHM (B. 15703, 'Rippey').

77.6CA/18   Dodd, Convict's Address, Taunton   1777

THE | CONVICT's ADDRESS | TO | His Unhappy Brethren. | Delivered in the Chapel of Newgate, on | Friday, June 6, 1777. | [rule] | *I acknowledge my Faults: and my Sin is ever before me.* | Psalm. LI. 3. | [total rule] | Sold by A. Gray, in *Taunton*, and by other | Bookſellers. | [short rule] | M.DCC.LXXVII. | [Price Three-Pence]

8°, *A*⁴ B–C², ($1 signed), 8 leaves.

Pp. A1 *1* t., *2* blk, *3* Dedication to Villette, *4* blk, *5* 6–16 text dh: [total rule] | AN | ADDRESS, &c. | [orn. rule].

Pagination: no errors; *Press-figures*: none.

Catchwords: 12 n. [I] add (that).

Explicit: 16 none. [Tp. of flowers].

Paper: White, laid; La. post (8¼ × 5¼ in.); wmk.: Garter arms.

Type: Sm. pica (3.8 mm), but in sig. C long primer (3.2 mm).

References: ESTC: t204717.

Copies: O (12 θ. 1351(2), with MS list of Doddiana).

[77.6CA/19   Dodd, Convict's Address, Whitehaven

This, like the 'Gainsborough' edition, is rumoured to exist, though no copy has been found and it is not reported in ESTC.

Copies: Unlocated.]

77.6CA/20   Dodd, Convict's Address   [1810]

The Reverend Dr. Dodd's Earnest Address to his Fellow Convicts, which he delivered in the Chapel of Newgate, a few days before he was executed. Together with his last prayer, left in his own hand-writing the night before he suffered. To which is added an address to young persons. Norwich: Lane and Co. [n.d.]

Notes: Not seen, but cited in Ken Spelman (York), *Catalogue* 25 (1993), 379 (with Dodd's *Reflections on Death*[1] from the same place and publisher), £50.00, described as 12°, pp. 35 + (1), so presumably 3 sigg. in 12s.

Further reprintings of the Convict's Address were often included with Dodd's *Thoughts in Prison*, q.v. (16) Sources, below, 77.6WD/S.

---

[1] First published 1763, but frequently reprinted (Roscoe, *Newbery* (1973), A127).

77.6CA/21/A   Dodd, Convict's Address (Abridged)   1777

Abridged versions and extracts were published in the Magazines:

(a) *Gents. Mag.* xlvii (June 1777), 293–4, s.d. '27 June'.

(b) *Scots Mag.* xxxix (June 1777), 330.

(c) *The Universal Mag.* lx (June 1777), 324–7.

(6)   LETTER I: 'TO LORD NORTH'
[= LORD BATHURST,
THE LORD CHANCELLOR]

'I have committed . . .' [Sun. 8 June 1777]
    (i) SJ's MS draft 'My Lord . . .' (MS Hyde; *MS Index* JoS 236).
    (ii) Dodd's autograph copy (HMC Bathurst (1923), 15; *not seen*).
Presented to the Privy Council, with Letter II (7, below), on Fri. 13 June, but
rejected.
[11 July] *Occasional Papers*, 14–16.
    References: Chapman (1928), no. 8; A.D. Barker (1983), 164.
    Reprints: Cooke, *Life of Johnson*, 1st edn. 1785, 134–5; 2nd edn. 1785,
187–90.
    [Reed], *SJ's Works*, xiv (1788), 403–4 ('June 11, 1777').

(7)   LETTER II: TO LORD MANSFIELD

'Not many days are now to Pass . . .' [Wed. 11 June 1777]
[5 July] *Observations on the Case of Dr Dodd* (Bew), 32 (77.6WD/S/22, below).
[11 July] *Occasional Papers*, 17–18.
    References: Chapman (1928), no. 9, A.D. Barker (1983), 164.
    Reprints: Cooke, *Life of Johnson*, 1st edn. 1785, 135–6; 2nd edn. 1785, 191–4.
    [Reed], *SJ's Works*, xiv (1788), 405–6 ('June 11, 1777').

(8)   PETITION OF MRS MARY DODD
TO THE QUEEN

'Madam, It is most humbly represented . . .'
    (i) SJ MS draft 'To the Queen most excellent Majesty . . .' (MS Hyde; *MS Index* JoS 229).
[11 July] *Occasional Papers*, 21–2.
    References: Chapman (1928), no. 27; A.D. Barker (1983), 165.
    Reprints: Cooke, *Life of Johnson*, 1st edn. 1785, 137–8; 2nd edn. 1785, 199–201.
    Hawkins: *Life87*, 526.
    [Reed], *SJ's Works*, xiv (1788), 407–8.

(9) PETITION OF WILLIAM DODD
TO THE KING

'It is most humbly represented . . .' [Sun. 22 June 1777]

(i) SJ MS draft 'To the Kings &c.' (MS Hyde; *MS Index* JoS 235)[1]

Composed by SJ on Sun. 22 June (*Life* iii. 144–5; *Letters* 521–2; Hyde iii. 30–1).[2]

Pres. by Earl Percy on 25 June (*Whitehall Evening Post*, 26 June), though *Public Advertiser*, 27 June, reported that it was pres. to George III by Lord North 'yesterday'.[3] Attributed to SJ in *Morning Post*, 3 July.[4]

[11 July] *Occasional Papers*, 19–20.

[1 August] Reed: [2nd issue] *Account of the Life and Writings of William Dodd*, 89–90 n.

References: Chapman no. 4.

Reprints: Cooke, *Life of Johnson*, 1st edn. 1785, 135–6; 2nd edn. 1785, 195–8.

Hawkins, *Life87*, 524–5.

[Reed], *SJ's Works*, xiv (1788), 406–7.

[1] In Puttick & Simpson's autograph sale, 10 March 1862, lot 188 was 'W. Dodd, ALS to Mr Manley, Lord Chesterfield's attorney, 16 May 1777, and copy of Johnson's Letter to the King for William Dodd'. For Dodd's letter to Manley, see 77.5DS/1 n.1, above; a copy of SJ's *Letter* 521, by Edmund Allen, is now MS Hyde (Hyde iii. 30).

[2] SJ originally wrote, 'This day will be conveyed to the Secretary of State . . .', so that the pencilled date (perhaps by Edmund Allen), on the MS 'June 25' which Chapman dismissed as 'of no authority' is apparently the date on which the letter written by SJ was intended to be published in the papers. Since it uses the expression 'This day . . .' (originally 'This morning . . .') it must have been composed by SJ on Tuesday 24th, or perhaps in the evening of Monday 23rd. See further n. 3, below.

[3] The *St James's Chronicle*, 26 June stated, 'A Report was circulated through the Town yesterday [= 25th] that Earl Percy had promised to deliver to his Majesty the Petition [for Dodd] . . . His Lordship . . . delivered it in person at the Secretary of State's Office on Tuesday last [= 24th].' This implies that SJ's announcement was intended for publication on Wednesday, 25 June.

[4] This article by 'A Lover of Impartial Justice' may have been by Philip Thicknesse (cf. *Lit. Illus.* iv (1822), 523–4, and his *Memoirs and Anecdotes* (1788)), giving an account of the intended rescue of Dodd. He is also credited with the 'Note on the Death of Dr Dodd' in *Gents. Mag.* lx (1790), ii. 1066 (Kuist 148c). For Thicknesse, see *Lit. Anec.* ix (1815), 256–88.

(10) JOHNSON'S LETTER TO THE KING,
COMPOSED FOR DODD, 22 JUNE 1777

'May it not offend your Majesty . . .'

The original is untraced, but Boswell printed it in *Life* (1791), ii. 137–8 (iii. 144–5).

(11) JOHNSON'S OBSERVATIONS ON THE PROPRIETY OF PARDONING WILLIAM DODD

'Yesterday was presented to the Secretary of State . . .' [Wed. 25 June 1777][1]

(i) MS Hyde 'This day will be conveyed . . .' (*MS Index* JoS 231).

(ii) 8°, $1, 1 leaf unsigned, Pp. *1* text dh: 'Dʀ. DODD., &c.', *2* blk.

Copy: CtY: (Boswell P75; JB: 'This paper copies of which were given about in London and inserted in the Newspapers was written by Dr. Johnson.')

(iii) 24–25 June *London Chronicle*.

(iv) 26 June 1777, *Gazetteer*.

References: Chapman (1928), no. 24; A.D. Barker (1983), 172.

Reprints: Cooke, *Life of Johnson*, 1st edn. 1785, 139–40; 2nd edn. 1785, 205–9.

Hawkins: *Life87*, 527–8.

[Reed], *SJ's Works*, xiv (1788), 409–11.

---

[1] These are not the same as the comments reported in the *Public Advertiser*, 27 May 1777 (McGuffie, *SJ in the British Press* (1976), 209).

(12)   DODD'S LAST SOLEMN DECLARATION

'To the words of dying men . . .' [Wed. 25 June 1777]

Composed by SJ on 25th and delivered by Dodd to Villette just before his execution on Friday 27 June.[1]

(i) [5 July] Villette: *A Genuine Account of the Behaviour and Dying Words of William Dodd, LL.D.*, 22–4; 2nd edn. [10 July], 4th edn. [22 Aug.], (77.6WD/S/12, below).

(ii) *Gents. Mag.* xlvi (July 1777), 341–2.

(iii) *Westminster Mag.* v (July 1777), 359–60.

(iv) *Scots Mag.* xxxix (July 1777), 387.

(v) [1 August] Reed: [2nd issue: 77.6WD/S/1b, below] *An Account of the Life and Writings of William Dodd*, 89–90 (& n.).

(vi) [30 August] *Thoughts of a Citizen of London on the Conduct of Dr. William Dodd*, 42 (77.6WD/S/57, below).

(vii) *The Convict's Address*, Edinburgh, 1777, 49.

(viii) *Dr Dodd's Address*, 1777, 21–4.

(ix) *A Relation of Dr Dodd's Behaviour*, 1777, 12–13 (77.6WD/S/23, below).

(x) *An Authentic Account of the Late unfortunate Dr Dodd*, 26–8 (77.6WD/S/6, below).

References: Chapman (1928), no. 23 ('To the words of a dying man . . .'); A.D. Barker (1983), 171–2.

Reprints: [Reed], *SJ's Works*, xiv (1788), 411–2 ('June 27, 1777').

(13)　　'INTRODUCTION' TO THE OCCASIONAL PAPERS [PUBD. 11 JULY 1777]

'What is to be expected . . .'.
(i) Edmund Allen's transcript is MS Hyde (*MS Index* JoS 232).
[11 July] *Occasional Papers*, 5–6.
References: Chapman (1928), no. 31.
Reprints: Cooke, *Life of Johnson*, 1st edn. 1785, 130; 2nd edn. 1785, 171–3.
[Reed], *SJ's Works*, xiv (1788), 398–9.

(14)　　CONCLUSION TO THE OCCASIONAL PAPERS

'Such were the last thoughts . . .'.
(i) SJ's MS draft (MS Hyde; *MS Index* JoS 233).
(ii) [11 July] *Occasional Papers*, 23–4.
References: Chapman (1928), no. 29.
Reprints: Cooke, *Life of Johnson*, 1st edn. 1785, 138–9; 2nd edn. 1785, 202–4.
[Reed], *SJ's Works*, xiv (1788), 408–9.

(15)　　OCCASIONAL PAPERS

77.7DOP　　Dodd, Occasional Papers　　　　　1777

[½t] [rule] | Occaſional PAPERS. | BY THE LATE | WILLIAM DODD, LLD. | [rule] | [Price One Shilling.]
　[Title] OCCASIONAL | PAPERS, | BY THE LATE | WILLIAM DODD, LLD. | [rule] | [Orn: 2 bees over basket of flowers] | [double rule] | LONDON: | Printed for G. KEARSLY, at Nº. 46, in Fleet-Street. | [short rule] | M.DCC.LXXVI. | Entered in the Hall-Book of the Company of Stationers.]
　Stent: LLD. (*bis*) . . . KEARSLY
　8°, *A*⁴ B–C⁴, ($2 (–B2) signed), 12 leaves.
　Pp. A1 *1* ½t, *2* blk, *3* t., *4* blk, *5* 6–24 text dh: [total rule] | Occaſional PAPERS. | BY THE LATE | WILLIAM DODD, LLD. | [rule].

1309

Pagination: [↑], no errors; *Press-figures*: none.

Catchwords: 18 To ([Dr. Dodd's Petition preſented by his Brother.] | To).

Explicit: 24 Tp. orn.

Paper: White, laid; Demy (uncut: 8¾ × 5½ in.); wmk.: fleur-de-lys (in E).

Type: Small pica (3.5 mm), leaded (1.2).

References: 'Occasional papers by William Dodd', *TLS*, 7 Dec. 1922; 'A Unique Dr. Johnson Item', *BMQ* iv (1929), 78–9; CH 154; A.D. Barker (1983), 175; *Life* iii. 143 shows that JB had seen a copy, but see my note in *Edinburgh Bib. Soc. Transactions*, vi. (1993), 55–6; ESTC: t095446.

Reprints: Cooke, *Life of Johnson*, 1st edn. 1785, 128–9; 2nd edn. 1785, 171–209.

[Reed], *SJ's Works*, xiv (1788), 398–411, from a copy of *Occasional Papers*.

Notes: Announced for publication 'Tomorrow at Noon' in *Public Advertiser*, Fri. 11 July 1777, but withdrawn, see *Life* iii. 496–7. Printed items (no. **13**) 'What is to be expected . . .' (5–6), (**2**) 'The greatest affliction . . .' (7–11), Dodd's Declaration (**3**) 'Though I acknowledge in all its atrocity . . .' (12–13), Letter I (**6**), 'I have committed . . .' (14–16), Letter II (**7**) 'Not many days . . .' (17–18), Dodd's Petition (**9**) 'It is most humbly . . .' (19–20), Mrs Dodd's Petition (**8**) (21–22), (**14**) 'Such were the last thoughts . . .' (23–4).

These were gathered together by Kearsley who claimed to publish them for the benefit of Mrs Dodd. She however refused to allow the publication of material over her husband's name but not written by him, and the edn. was stopped.[1] Chapman asserted that 500 copies were printed.

The copy given to Lord Hailes is annotated by JB, p. 16, Letter I: 'To the Lord Chancellor.', and p. 17, Letter II: 'To Lord Mansfield'; JB also marked SJ's closing Observations with an 'X' at the word *petitions* and wrote below: 'Every one of these Papers was <wr>itten by Dr. Johnson, except Dr. <Do>dd's Account of himself, and <hi>s Declaration.'

Copies: L (C.40. g.24).

UK: E (Nha. 0179 (11), James Boswell + MS notes — David Dalrymple, Lord Hailes).[2]

---

[1] The story of the supression of the publication is told in Cooke's *Life of Johnson* (1784), 128–9, and 2nd edn. 1785, 166–70. In *Papers Written by Dr Johnson and Dr Dodd in 1777* (1926), at §30, Chapman printed a lettter from 'Mr Winterbottom' to Edmund Allen thanking him for halting the publication.

Barker notes that the piece was announced in the *Public Advertiser* (11 July), as 'Original Papers . . .', and suggests that the change to 'Occasional' was probably effected by SJ (*HLB* xxxi (1983), 175).

[2] That JB parted with this copy to Hailes (d. 1792), probably with his letter of 10 March 1778 (CtY: MS Boswell, L 610), strongly suggests that he had another copy with even more authentic notes on SJ's contribution, presumably marked by SJ himself; see Fleeman, *Edinburgh Bib. Soc. Transactions*, vi (1993), 55–6.

(16)   SOURCES AND DODDIANA

77.6WD/S/1a   Isaac Reed's Account of Dodd,   1777
               first issue

[½t] AN | ACCOUNT | OF THE | LIFE AND WRITINGS | OF | Dr.
WILLIAM DODD. | [Price ONE SHILLING.]
[Title]: AN | ACCOUNT | OF THE | LIFE AND WRITINGS | OF |
WILLIAM DODD, LL.D. | [rule] | [8-Line motto from Shakespeare] | [dou-
ble rule] | LONDON: | Printed for M. Hingeston in the Strand, | and J.
Williams in Fleet-ſtreet. | MDCCLXXVII.

8°, π1 a⁴ B–F⁸ (–F8 = π1), ($4 signed), 44 leaves; Pp. π1 ½t, π1ᵛ blk, a1 *i*
t., *ii* blk, iii–v Preface ('May 31, 1777'), vi–viii Postscript ('June 16, 1777'), on
B1 1–77 text, *78* blk, (67–70 **(1)** 'I now stand before you . . .', 83–4 **(9)** Dodd's
Petition to the King, 89–90 n. **(12)**'To the words of dying men . . .'; Reed's
notes on pp. 84 and 88–9 offer covert attributions of these two pieces to SJ).[1]

Notes: Published 27 June 1777 (*Publ. Adv.*, and *Morn. Chron.*, 25 June); A.D.
Barker (1983), 148–9. Noticed in *Gents. Mag.* xlvii (July 1777), 341/57. Reed's
Account begins the attempt at a bibliography of Dodd's writings.[2] ESTC:
t075463.
Copies: L (1132. b.72).

[1] Reed's interest in the Dodd affair was considerable. At the sale of his books by King, *Bibliotheca
Reediana*, 2 Nov. 1807 (and 38 following days), lots. 2034, 5984, 5999, 6001, 6004, 6101, 6795–6
exhibited material relative to Dodd. SJ's involvement seems however to have been known early
enough to the literary world. An untraced letter of George Steevens to Michael Lort, 29 June 1777,
on Chatterton, also gave some account of Johnson's part (recorded in Puttick & Simpson (Robert
Cole), 29 July 1861, 1050, and P & S (Johnston), 12 Aug. 1863, 308).
[2] Addenda were proposed in *Gents. Mag.* xlvii (Sept. 1777), 421–22, by 'Historicus', a signature
used by Richard Gough in 1802 (Kuist 68c) and therefore attributed to him in this note by E.L. de
Montluzin (*SB* xliv (1991), 271–302, esp. 298–99), but the pseudonym is not very distinctive.

77.6WD/S/1b   Isaac Reed's Account of Dodd,   1777
               second issue

[½t & Title] as preceding (77.6WD/S/1a)
8°, π1 a⁴ B–E⁸ F⁸ (–F8 = π1) G–H⁸, ($4 signed), 60 leaves; Pp. a1 *i* t., *ii*
blk, iii–v Preface ('May 31, 1777'), vi–viii Postscript ('June 11, 1777'), on B1
1–77 text, *78* blk, on G1 77–108 Appendix.

Notes: G1 apparently intended to replace F7 (F8 still forms the ½t), since part
of text on F7 is repeated on G1.[1] Published 1 Aug. (*Gazetteer & New Daily
Advertiser*, as 'An Impartial Account . . .' though the word 'Impartial' occurs on
no copies of either ½t. or t.). The supplementary material in the Appendix (no.
9) 'Petition' (83–4n), and **(12)** 'To the words of dying men' (89–90 n.), was
issued separately at 6d. (*Gents. Mag.* xlvii (Aug. 1777), 389/74; A.D. Barker

(1983), 150 n.). Both genuine pieces are ascribed to a 'celebrated writer'.² To the footnote pp. 91–2, Reed noted in the Harvard copy (Metzdorf, *HLB* vi (1952), 395), 'This Note added by Mr Nicholls the Printer'.

Copies: L² (1. G. 14464, 'by Mr Isaac Reed of Staple-Inn'; 2. 1416. f.29 with F7 present); *USA*: MH (*EC75. R2518. 777ic, IR: 'By Isaac Reed of Staple Inn' & other MS notes).

¹ Metzdorf, *HLB* vi (1952), 393–6, esp. 394 n. 3.
² See *Bibliotheca Grenvilliana* (Payne & Foss), ii (1848), 381.

77.6WD/S/2   Citizen of London's Account of Dodd   1777

AN | ACCOUNT | OF THE | LIFE, DEATH, and WRITINGS, | OF THE | Rev. Dr. DODD, | Who was EXECUTED at Tyburn, | On FRIDAY the 27th of June, 1777, | for the forging of a BOND of | Four Thousand Two Hundred Pounds | IN THE NAME OF THE | EARL of CHESTERFIELD. | WITH | OBSERVATIONS on his CASE, | SHEWING THE | CAUSE of his Unhappy END, | AND | REMARKS on the PETITIONS | presented in his Favour. | With suitable and Useful REFELXIONS | On the Whole. | [rule] |By a CITIZEN of LONDON. | [rule] | PRINTED in the YEAR 1777. | Price Six-ence ˄

[*Stent*]: REFELXIONS ... Pence˄ *Note*: Pence. (in O).
12°, π1 A⁸ B⁴ C⁸ D⁴ E⁶ F⁶ (–F6 = ? π1), 36 leaves.
Pp. π1 t., π1ᵛ blk, on A1 *1* 2–70 text.
Pagination: (↑); *Explicit*: 70 *FINIS*.
Notes: (**1**) WD's Defence pp. 31–3, 'I now stand before you' 33–4, (**4**) Petition of Lord Mayor &c., 35–6, Petition of Gentlemen &c., 36–7; (**5**) Convict's Address pp. 40–52. The text offers a full account of WD's trial and career largely derived from contemporary newspapers, and attributes the origins of the Magdalen Hospital to SJ's *Rambler* 107 (p. 11). ESTC: t095440.
Copies: O (Vet. A5 f.366(1)); L (1132. b.72).

77.6WD/S/3   Life and Writings of Dodd   1777

An Account of the Life and Writings of the Rev. William Dodd, L.L.D. In which is included the original and present State of the Magdalen Charity; the Society for the relief of Prisoners confined for small Debts; and of the Society for recovering Persons drowned, apparently dead; the Motives on which they were instituted, with how far Dr Dodd was concerned in their several laudable Institutions, and the benefits that have arose therefrom. Also an impartial Account of the whole Proceedings of his late unfortunate Transaction, &c. The whole intended to shew him as a proper Object of Mercy. London. Printed for J. Wenman, No. 144, Fleet-Street.

References: A.D. Barker (1983), 167 n. 86; ESTC: n003727.
Notes: Published 27 June (*St James's Chronicle*); reviewed with Reed's *Account* in *Gents. Mag.* xlvii (June 1777), 341/56. Wenman had been Kearsley's apprentice.
Copies: Unlocated.

| 77.6WD/S/4 | The Apparition | [1777] |

The Apparition, or Dr. Dodd's Last Legacy — Addressed to Lord ——.
London: J. Bell, in Bell-Yard. 4°. 1s.[1]

---

[1] *Westminster Mag.* v (Oct. 1777), 594, 'an invidious and a stupid performance'.

| 77.6WD/S/5a | [Mary Bosanquet], An Aunt's Advice to a Neice | 1780 |

[Mary Bosanquet:] An Aunt's Advice to a Neice . . . to which is added a Correspondence with the late Rev. Dr. Dodd. . . . 1780.
Notes: I am indebted to Mr Alan Harding, sometime of Pembroke College, Oxford,[1] for the following observations:

'Mary Bosanquet was prominent in the Evangelical Revival, and there are a number of references to her in both the Journals and the Letters of John Wesley. Her main significance however, was her marriage, after a courtship of twenty-five years, to the Rev. John Fletcher, Vicar of Madely in Shropshire. Fletcher, who was Swiss by birth, was a central figure in the Revival: he was the first President of the Countess's [of Huntingdon] training college at Trevecca, until the Calvinistic Controversies of 1770 when he resigned his position and became one of the chief apologists on the Wesleyan side. He was designated by Wesley as his successor, but predeceased him in 1785.' Mr Harding continues, citing 'a letter to the Countess of Huntingdon dated June 10, 1777, and written by John Sparke, an apothecary of Titchfield Street and one of the Countess's principal agents in London. "After applying to others," he says, "Lady Montague came to me to go with your letters to poor Dr Dodd." Sparke describes how he had found Dodd in a better frame of mind than he had expected and that he had asked for the Countess's prayers. Sparke ends by saying that he has heard that some of the Gospel Ministers have refused to visit him, but hopes that "they cannot think his crimes greater in God's sight than their own, or too great for the Lord to pardon".' The original of the Countess's letter is not discovered.

Some exchanges between WD and Mary Bosanquet were included in later edd. of *Thoughts in Prison*, q.v., below. ESTC: t127061
Copies: Hyde.

77.6WD/S/5b   [Mary Bosanquet],   1780
An Aunt's Advice to a Neice, second edition

[Mary Bosanquet:] An Aunt's Advice to a Neice . . . to which is added a Correspondence with the late Rev. Dr. Dodd. Second Edition. Leeds . . . 1780. 12°, pp. ii + 75. Not seen. ESTC: t162724.

77.6WD/S/5c   [Mary Bosanquet],   1784
An Aunt's Advice to a Neice

[Mary Bosanquet:] An Aunt's Advice to a Neice . . . to which is added a Correspondence with the late Rev. Dr. Dodd. . . . 1824
Notes: The letters to Dodd occupy pp. 97–106.
Copies: L (4405. c.34).

77.6WD/S/6   An Authentic Account of Dodd   1777

An Authentic Account of the Late unfortunate Doctor William Dodd. Rochester: T. Fisher. 1777
Notes: WD's Last Solemn Declaration (no. **12**) pp. 26–8. ESTC: t1096459.
Copies: Hyde; *UK*: L (5804. c.12).

77.6WD/S/7   Authentic Memoirs of Dodd   [? 1777]

Authentic Memoirs of the Life of William Dodd, LL.D. Who was executed at Tyburn, on Friday, June 17, 1777. With the Particulars of his Trial and Execution, and a Review of the Arguments, for and against his suffering the Sentence of the Law. To which is added a Letter from Lady Huntingdon, to the unfortunate Convict. The Third Edition. Salisbury: Printed and Sold by Jos. Hodson. Sold also by Mess. Linden and Hodson, Southampton; Mrs. Willis, Ringwood; Mrs. Clarke, Cranborne; Mr. Lacy, Warminster; Mr. Spalding, Trowbridge; Mr. Stuart, Bradford; Miss Noyes, Andover; and the Newsmen. [? 1777]
12°, A^2 B–E^6, ($3 signed), 26 leaves. Pp. *1* blk, *2* woodblock port. of WD., *3* t., *4* blk, on B1 *1* 2–48 text.
Notes: There is nothing Johnsonian in this pamphlet. ESTC: t115014 (cf. t164319).
Copies: L (1452. e.12, 'Jos: Harrington').

77.6WD/S/8   A Dialogue in the Shades   1777

A Dialogue in the Shades, between a Reverend Divine and a Welsh member of
Parliament, both lately deceased. London: J. Bew, 4°, is announced for publication 'next week' in the *Whitehall Evening Post*, 3–5 July 1777.[1] ESTC: t080571.

[1] Not seen, but reviewed in *Westminster Mag.* v (Nov. 1777), 594, giving it 'wit, humour, and
character'. A poem similarly titled was submitted to the *Town & Country Magazine*, but was too late
for insertion (June, 1777, 282).

77.6WD/S/9   Evidences of Christianity Not   1777
Weakened

The Evidences of Christianity not weakened by the Frailty of its Ministers. A
Sermon. . . preached at Bristol . . . June 29, 1777 . . . by . . . John Camplin.
London: Rivington. 1777.
   Notes: Priced at 6d; ESTC: t073222.
   Copies: L; *USA*: MH (*EC75 D6618 B781d, 'Isaac Reed').

77.6WD/S/10   A Full and Circumstantial   1777
Account of Dodd

A Full and Circumstantial Account of the Trial of the Rev. William Dodd . . .
London: Richardson and Urquhart. n.d. [1777]. 8°.
   Notes: Published in March 1777 (A.D. Barker (1983), 156); ESTC: t064231.
   Copies: L (1417. b.12); O² (1. 12 θ. 1351(1); 2. GP 945(2)); *USA*: MH
(*EC75 D6618.B781d, 'Isaac Reed').

77.6WD/S/11   A Full and Particular   [? 1777]
Account of Dodd

A Full and Particular Account of . . . Dodd London: J. Anderson
   Notes: Includes Convict's Address (pp. 45–56). ESTC: t095438.
   Copies: [L (1417. b.12)]

77.6WD/S/12   John Villette's Genuine   1777
Account of Dodd

A GENUINE | ACCOUNT | OF THE | Behaviour and Dying Words | OF |
WILLIAM DODD, LL.D. | Who was Executed at Tyburn for FORGERY, | on
FRIDAY the 27th of JUNE, 1777. |[rule] | By the Reverend JOHN VILLETTE,

| ORDINARY of NEWGATE. | [double rule] | LONDON: | Printed for the AUTHOR, and Sold by J. BEW, | No 28, Pater-nofter Row; and likewife at the | Author's Houfe, No 1, Newgate-Street. | [short rule] | M.DCC.LXXVII. | [Price SIX-PENCE.]

8°, A–C⁴, ($2 (–A1) signed), 12 leaves; Pp. A1 *1* t., *2* blk, *3* 4–24 text.

References: A.D. Barker (1983), 175–6.

Notes: Published 5 July 1777 (*Public Advertiser*) and noticed in *Gents. Mag.* xlvii (July 1777), 341–2/58. All copies carry Villette's authenticating signature.[1] Dodd's Last words (no. **12**) are here printed pp. 22–4. ESTC: t040748 (cf. n018090, t040749, n001789).

There seems, however, to have been at least one piracy of this piece, cf. 77.6WD/S/13, below.

[1] This was customary since the publication of the Dying Words of condemned criminals was a lucrative business for the Ordinary. The advertisements stress this point, 'N.B. To prevent any false Copy being obtruded on the Public, each Pamphlet will be signed by the Ordinary, in his own Hand-writing.' Cf. Alkon, in *The Unknown Samuel Johnson*, edd. J.J. Burke and D. Kay (1983), 113–30.

77.6WD/S/13a	A Relation of Dodd's Behaviour in Newgate	1777

A Relation of Dr Dodd's Behaviour in Newgate . . . Printed in the Year 1777, 12°. This account also printed no. **11** (pp. 12–13) (L: 1132. a.43, attr. to Villette), see below. ESTC: t046693.

Copies: O (8° U. 134 Jur), L (698. d.23(3)); *USA*: MH (*EC75 D6618 B781d, 'Isaac Reed').

77.6WD/S/13b	A Relation of Dodd's Behaviour in Newgate	1777

. . . Second edition, 1777. Not seen. Published: 11 July (*Public Advertiser*).

77.6WD/S/13c	A Relation of Dodd's Behaviour in Newgate	1777

. . . Third edition. 1777. Not examined. *References*: Maggs Bros. *Cat.* 1038, 'Samuel Johnson' (1984), 372.

Copies: L: 1372. d.11 (3).

77.6WD/S/13d   A Relation of Dodd's   1777
                         Behaviour in Newgate

. . . Fourth edition. 1777. Not seen.

77.6WD/S/14   A Genuine and Authentic   1777
                         Account of Dodd

A Genuine and Authentic Account of the Life, Trial . . . of Dr Dodd. London: 1777. 8°. ESTC: t184727.
   Copies: O (270 f.910(8)).

77.6WD/S/15   The Genuine Life and Trial of Dodd   ?1777

The genuine Life and Trial of . . . William Dodd, for forgery, at the Old Bailey . . . 1777. London: T. Trueman. [1777]. 8°. ESTC: n001834.
   Copies: L (6494 b. 58(4)).

77.6WD/S/16   Genuine Memoirs of Dodd   1777

Genuine Memoirs of the Rev. Dr Dodd; containing many curious Anecdotes which were never before published; Together with an Account of the Forgery of a Bond of 4200*l*. on the Earl of Chesterfield. With the exact Particulars of his Trial at the Old Bailey. London. Printed for John Whitaker, No. 3, Mitre-Court Fleet-ftreet, and by all the Booksellers in Town and Country. [1777]
   8°, A–H⁴ (–H4 ? blk), 32 leaves.
   Notes: Published early March 1777 (A.D. Barker (1983), 149), and noticed in *Gents. Mag.* xlvii (March 1777), 136. It contains no Johnsonian texts. ESTC: t195346, t095448.
   Copies: L (113. c.20).

77.6WD/S/17   John Duncombe's
                         Historical Memoirs

Historical Memoirs of the Life and Writings of the late Rev. William Dodd, L.L.D. From his Entrance at Clare-Hall, Cambridge in 1745 to his fatal Exit at Tyburn, June 27, 1777. London: Printed for Fielding and Walker n.d. [1777]
   12°, 58 pp.
   Notes: There is a ½t, and should also be an *errata* slip. Published: 3 July (*Public Advertiser*), and noticed in *Gents. Mag.* xlvii (July 1777), 339–41/55.

Attributed to Duncombe by Isaac Reed (MH copy, below), and in *Lit. Anec.* viii (1814), 277. A.D. Barker (1983), 150 n. and 176. ESTC: t036322.

    Copies: O (Vet. A5 e.4103(3)), L (1372. d.11(1) imperfect); *USA*: Hyde, MH (*EC75 D6618. B781d, 'Isaac Reed', inscr: 'By John Duncombe, A.M.').

77.6WD/S/18　　　A Letter to Messrs. Fletcher　　　1777
and Peach

A Letter to Messrs. Fletcher and Peach of the City of London; on their negoti-ation with Dr Dodd; which has unhappily deprived Society &c. &c. London: Printed for, and Sold by G. Kearsley at No. 46, Fleet-Street; and B. Bristow, at No. 85, in Great Tower-Street. MDCCLXXVII.

    4°, *A*1 B–H², ($1 signed), 15 leaves; Pp. A1 t., A1ᵛ blk, on B1 *1* 2–27 Letter, *28* blk. (Pagination irregular as [↑] 2–3, 7–9, 15, 17–19, 21; (↑) 4–6, 10–14, 16, 20, 22–27.)

    References: ESTC: t118295.

    Notes: Wrongly attributed to SJ, but by Matthew Dawes (A.D. Barker (1983), 173).[1]

    Copies: L (1243. k.7).

---

[1] McAdam, *MP* xli (1944), 183–7. Barker cites *Public Advertiser*, 24 June 1777.

77.6WD/S/19　　　Life and Writings of Dodd　　　1777

The Life and Writings of the Rev. William Dodd, L.L.D. . . . &c. London: Printed for Joseph Wenman, No. 144, Fleet-street, 1777. [Price One-Shilling.]

    8°, π1 A–D⁴ E² F–I⁴ (–I4 ? = π1), ($2 (–E2) signed), 34 leaves.

    Pp. π1 *i* t., *ii* blk, on A1 1–36 Life &c., 37–66 Trial &c., 66 FINIS.

    Notes: Extracts from *Convict's Address* 64–66. ESTC: n003727.

    Copies: O (GP 2124 (6)).

77.6WD/S/20　　Memoirs of the Late William Dodd　　1777

'Memoirs of the late William Dodd' in *Town and Country Mag.* lx (July 1777), 372–77.

77.6WD/S/21　　　A New Song [on Dodd]　　　[?1777]

A New Song. [on Dr Dodd] [n.d.] Brs. 2°.

    Notes: A.D. Barker (1983), 154. ESTC: t039944, t039943.

    Copies: L (1872. a.1(18*)), Rox. III. 425.

77.6WD/S/22   Observations on the Case of Dodd   1777

Observations on the Case [Conduct?] of Dr Dodd London: J. Bew
  Notes: Published: 5 July (*Public Advertiser*); ref. 32 n. to 'a most pathetic petition, written by a very masterly hand' in the Petition to Mansfield (no. 7). A.D. Barker (1983), 174. ESTC: n010125.
  Copies: MH (*EC75 D6618 B781d, 'Isaac Reed').

77.6WD/S/23   Dodd's Behaviour in Newgate   1777

A Relation of Dr Dodd's Behaviour in Newgate. n.p. 1777. 8°.
  Notes: Cp. above, Villette's *Genuine Account*, 77.6WD/S/12. ESTC: t046693.
  Copies: L (1132 a.43), O (Vet. A5 f.366(2)).

77.6WD/S/24   Remarks on Sanguinary Laws   1777

'Remarks on Sanguinary Laws' in the *Gazetteer & New Daily Advertiser*, 7 July 1777, with reference to *Rambler* 114, proposing SJ as reviser of the statutes involving capital punishment.

77.6WD/S/25   Serious Reflections upon   1777
                              Dodd's Trial

Serious Reflections upon Dr Dodd's Trial for Forgery: with some Observations and Remarks upon his Case, in a Letter by a Clergyman . . . London: Printed for J. Wilkie, St. Paul's Church Yard. MDCCLXXVII. 8°.
  Notes: Published: 27 June (*St James's Chronicle*; A.D. Barker (1983), 174, gives 28 June), at 1s. ESTC: n021217.
  Copies: O (GP 2786 (11)); MH (*EC75 D6618 B781d, 'Isaac Reed').

77.6WD/S/26   A Sketch of the Life of Dodd   1777

'A Sketch of the Life of Rev. Dr. Dodd', *Westminster Mag.* v (March 1777), 118–20 (and a *Letter* by 'Cantab' in v (April 1777), 186).

77.6WD/S/27   Particulars of the late Dr Dodd   1777

'Particulars of the late Dr Dodd', *Westminster Mag.* v (July 1777), 359–60.
  Notes: Includes his 'Last Solemn Declaration' (12).

77.6WD/S/28   A Tear of Gratitude   1777

A Tear of Gratitude, to the Memory of the Unfortunate Dr Dodd, A Poem. [orn.] London: Printed for F. Newbery, in the Corner of St Paul's Church-Yard, Ludgate-Street. MDCCLXXVII. [Price Six-Pence.]

4°. *A*² B–D² (–D2 ? blk), ($1 signed), 7 leaves.

Pp. A1 *1* ½t, *2* blk, *3* t., *4* blk, on B1 5–14 text.

Pagination: [↑]; *Press-figures*: none; *Catchwords*: 7 Proclami (Proclaim).

Explicit: 14 FINIS.

Notes: Published: 8 July (*Gazetteer & New Daily Advertiser*). There is nothing of SJ here.

Copies: O (13 θ. 166(4)).

77.6WD/S/29   Dodd's Thoughts in Prison,   1777
  first edition

THOUGHTS IN PRISON: | IN FIVE PARTS. | VIZ. | THE IMPRISONMENT. | THE RETROSPECT. | PUBLICK PUNISHMENT. | THE TRIAL. | FUTURITY. | By the Rev. WILLIAM DODD, LLD. | TO WHICH ARE ADDED, | HIS LAST PRAYER. | Written in the Night before his Death: | AND | OTHER MISCELLANEOUS PIECES. | [medium swelled rule] | —Thefe evils . . . [5 lines] . . . the Suppliant ! MILTON. | [medium swelled rule] | LONDON: | Printed for EDWARD and CHARLES DILLY, in the Poultry; | and G. KEARSLY, at N° 46, in Fleet-Street. | MDCCLXXVII.

8°, *A*⁴ (–A4 = χ1) B–2C⁴ (2C3 + χ1) 2D–2E⁴ 2F⁴ (–2F4), 116 leaves.

Pp. A1 t., A1ᵛ blk, A2 *i*–iii Advertisement, *iv* blk, on B1 *1* 2–206 text of *Thoughts*, + ²ᶜχ1 inserted 'To front Page 206.', *207* 208–32 Pieces &c., 232 Errata. A1, χ1 unnumbered, 78–80 omitted.

Notes: No Johnsonian items included in this edn. which was prepared by Weeden Butler (*Gents. Mag.* xlvii (Sept. 1777), 421–2, and lxiii (March 1793), i. 233–4; A.D. Barker (1983), 177.)[1] It was noticed in the *London Review*, iii (Sept. 1777), 226–9. Later edd. became the pendants for various Johnsonian pieces (see below). ESTC: t050180.

Copies: O (2799 e. 353);

USA: Hyde, MH; *Can*: CaOHM; *UK*: E ([Ai] 2/238), Eu, L (698. d.23(2)).

---

[1] Isaac Reed transcribed a note from Dodd, dated 16 June 1777, asking Kearsley to supply him with a copy of *Thoughts on the Last Day* (MS: MH).

77.6WD/S/30   Dodd's Thoughts in Prison   [? 1777]

THOUGHTS in PRISON: | In FIVE PARTS. | VIZ. The IMPRISONMENT. The Trial. | The RETROSPECT. FUTURITY. | PUBLIC PUNISHMENT. | By the Rev. WILLIAM DODD, L.L.D. | TO WHICH ARE ADDED, | HIS LAST PRAYER, | Written in the Night before his Death; | AND | Other MISCELLANEOUS PIECES. | [rule] | —— These evils . . . [5 lines] . . . Suppliant ! Milton. | [rule] | *BOSTON :* | Printed by Robert Hodges, at his Office, in *Mar- | fhall's Lane*, near the *Bofton Stone*. [n.d.]

4s. *A*⁴ (–A1 ? blk/½t) B–2F⁴, ($1 signed), 115 leaves.

Pp. A2 t., A2ᵛ blk, A3–4 Dedication: 'TO THE REVEREND | JOSEPH WILLARD, | President of Harvard Univerfity:' (signed: 'ROBERT HODGE.'), *vi* blk, *vii*–viii Advert., on B1 *9* 10–206 text, *207* ½t, *208* blk, *209* 210–23 miscellaneous pieces, *224* 225–32 WD's last prayer.

Explicit: 232 THE END.

Notes: Presumably edited by R. Hodge. There is nothing of SJ in this compilation.

Copies: O (Vet. K5 e.8; cont. sheep; 'Richᵈ Wrann' — 'W.M. Legate Feb. 14ᵗʰ 1807' — Alfred Harmsworth), L (11633. b.15); *USA*: MH, NjP; CaOHM.

77.6WD/S/31   Soliloques ou Lamentations   1777
                    du docteur Dodd

Soliloques ou Lamentations du docteur Dodd dans sa prison, suivis du Discours addressé à ses Juges avant de subir son supplice. [Trans: ? de Laujuirais] A Moudon Chez' La Société Typographique. 1777.

8°.

Copies: O (Vet. D5. f.147).

77.6WD/S/32   Dodd's Thoughts in Prison   1778

Thoughts in Prison. To which are added, his last Prayer, written in the Night before his Death; and other Miscellaneous Pieces. Dublin: Printed for Messrs. S. Price, W. Sleater, W. Whitestone, . . . &c. 1778

12°, pp. 251.

Notes: H. Sotheran, *Cat.* 1018 (Spring 1991), 30, £300, inscr: 'Jno. McGarry' on t., and bkpl. of 'Arthur Melville Clark'. It is apparently a reprint of the first edn. and contains nothing by SJ. ESTC: n014345.

77.6WD/S/33   Dodd's Thoughts in Prison,   1780
                              French translation

MÉDITATIONS | DE | DODD | DANS SA PRISON: | *EN CINQ PARTIES*; | I. L' EMPRISONNEMENT. | II. LA REVUE DU PASSÉ. | III. LE CHATIMENT PUBLIC. | IV. L' INTERROGATOIRE. | V. L' AVENIR. | TRADUIT DE L' ANGLOIS | PAR M. L * * *. | — — Thefe evils I deferve, and more | Acknowledge them from God inflicted on me | Juftly; yet despair not of his final pardon, | Whofe ear is ever open, and his eye | Gracious to re-admit the fuppliant ! | MILTON. | [Asterism] | A AMSTERDAM, | *Chez D. J. CHANGUION.* | M D C C L X X X.

Stet: PUBLIC.

8°, *⁸A–L⁸ (–L8 ? blk), ($5 signed), 95 leaves.

Pp. *i* ½t MÉDITATIONS | DE | DODD | DANS SA PRISON., *ii* blk, *iii* t., *iv* blk, *v*–vi Avertissement ('Guillaume Dodd.'), *vii* viii–xvi Avertissement du Traducteur, on A1 *1* 2–174 text.

Paper: White, laid; Moyen (uncut: 9 × 5½ in.); wmk.: MOYEN DAN GOUMOIS

Type: Philosophie (3.5 mm), leaded (2.7).

Notes: Translated by 'M. L***' [D. Levade ?]. There is nothing of SJ in this work.

Copies: O (Vet. B5. d.5; marbled wraps, uncut); *USA*: Hyde.

77.6WD/S/34   Dodd's Thoughts in Prison,   1781
                              second edition

THOUGHTS IN PRISON: | IN FIVE PARTS. | VIZ. | THE IMPRISONMENT. | THE RESTROSPECT. | PUBLICK PUNISHMENT. | THE TRIAL. FUTURITY. | By the Rev. WILLIAM DODD, LL.D. | TO WHICH ARE ADDED, | HIS LAST PRAYER, | Written in the Night before his Death. | THE CONVICT'S ADDRESS TO HIS | UNHAPPY BRETHREN: | AND | OTHER MISCELLANEOUS PIECES. | WITH AN ACCOUNT OF THE AUTHOR, | AND A LIST OF HIS WORKS. | [short swelled rule] | [5-line quotation from Milton] | [rule] | THE SECOND EDITION. | [double rule] | LONDON: | PRINTED FOR CHARLES DILLY, IN THE POULTRY; | AND G. KEARSLEY, AT N° 46, IN FLEET STREET. | MDCCLXXXI.

12°, a¹² b⁶ B–I¹², ($6 (–b4,5,6, H4 as H) signed), 114 leaves.

Pp. Engr. front. port. Dodd + a1 *i* t., *ii* blk, iii–iv Advertisement, v–xxv Account of the Author, *xxvi* blk, xxvii–xxxiii List of the Writings of Dr Dodd, *xxxiv* blk, xxxv–xxxvi Advertisement originally prefixed to Prison Thoughts, on B1 1–141 *142* Thoughts in Prison, *143* 144–55 Miscellaneous Pieces, *156* blk, *157* 158–78 Convict's Address, 179–84 Dodd's Last Prayer, &c., 185–92 Letters.

Notes: Edited by Isaac Reed, with considerable additions to the first edn., above.[1] A.D. Barker (1983), 177. The List of Dodd's writings attempts a bibliography of Dodd, still a desideratum. ESTC: t133880.

Copies: O (12 θ. 515(1)); BMp, L, Lv (Dyce 3114); MH.

[1] *Lit. Anec.* viii (1814), 91–2, and *Lit. Illus.* v (1828), 733–4, though the reference at 734 n. cannot be to this edn. Metzdorf, *HLB* vi (1952), 393–6.

77.6WD/S/35   Dodd's Thoughts in Prison,   1789
                        third edition

THOUGHTS IN PRISON: | IN FIVE PARTS. | VIZ. *The Impriſonment. The Retroſpect. Public Puniſhment. The Trial. Futurity.* | By the Rev. WILLIAM DODD. LL.D | TO WHICH ARE ADDED, | HIS LAST PRAYER, | Written in the Night before his Death; | THE CONVICT'S ADDRESS TO HIS | UNHAPPY BRETHREN; | AND OTHER | *MISCELLANEOUS PIECES.* | WITH | AN ACCOUNT OF THE AUTHOR, AND | A LIST OF HIS WORKS. | "—Theſe evils I deſerve . . ." [5 lines verse] *Milton.* | THE THIRD EDITION, | WITH ADDITIONS. | [medium swelled rule] | LONDON: | PRINTED FOR C. DILLY, IN THE POULTRY. | M DCC LXXXIX.

8°, *a*² b–c⁸ B–O⁸, ($4 signed), 122 leaves.

Pp. a1 t., a2 iii–iv Advertisement, v–xxvii Account of the Author (xxv–xxvii 'To the words of dying men . . .' (June 25, 1777; **12**), *xxviii* blk, xxix–xxxiv List of Writings, xxxv–xxxvi Advertisement to Prison Thoughts, on B1 1–141 text, *142* postscript, *143* ½t Pieces &c., *144* blk, 145–55 text, *156* blk, *157* ½t Convict's Address (**5**), *158* blk, 159 To Villette, *160* blk, *161* 162–79 text, *180* blk, 181–6 Dodd's last prayer, 187–95 Letters, 196–9 Dodd's Account of Himself (**2**), 199–200 Declaration 'Though I acknowledge in all its atrocity . . .' (**3**), 200–2 Letter I (**6**), 202–3 Letter II (**7**), 203–4 Dodd's Petition (**9**), 205–6 Mrs Dodd's Petition (**8**), 206–7 'Such were the last thoughts . . .' (**14**), 207–8 'Yesterday was presented . . .' (**11**); (p. 207 as 107), 208 FINIS.

References: ESTC: t050182.

Copies: O (1419 f. 1945(1)), L (11633. a.14), JDF; *USA*: MH.

77.6WD/S/35/Add1   Dodd's Thoughts in Prison,   1789
                         Russian translation

РАЭМЫЩПЄНЇЯ Додда И СоТоВанїя его въ Темницо St Petersburg 1789.

Reprinted in 1795. Not seen.

Copies: Unlocated.

77.6WD/S/36   Dodd's Thoughts in Prison,   1793
                          fourth edition

Thoughts in Prifon, | IN FIVE PARTS, | VIZ. *The Imprifonment - The Retrofpect - Public Punifhment - The Trial - Futurity*, | By the Rev. WILLIAM DODD, LL.D. | To which are added, | HIS LAST PRAYER, | Written in the Night before his Death; | THE CONVICT'S ADDRESS TO HIS | UNHAPPY BRETHREN; | AND | *OTHER MISCELLANEOUS PIECES*: | WITH | AN ACCOUNT OF THE AUTHOR, | AND A LIST OF HIS WORKS. | "—-Thefe evils . . . [5 lines] . . . the Suppliant." Milton. | THE FOURTH EDITION. | [double rule] | LONDON: | PRINTED FOR C. DILLY, IN THE POULTRY. | [short rule] | 1793.

12°, *A*² B–L¹² M¹⁰, ($6 (–K5,6, M6) signed), 132 leaves.

Pp. Engr. port. WD ('T. Trotter Sculp. Publish'd Dec. 1ˢᵗ 1788. by C. Dilly') + A1 *i* t., *ii* blk, *iii*–iv Advertisement to 4th edn., on B1 *1* 2–31 dh: [parallel rule] | AN | ACCOUNT | OF | *THE AUTHOR*. | [medium swelled rule], rt: *An Account | of the author.*, *32* blk, on C5 *33*–4 Advertisement Originally Prefixed to the Prison Thoughts., on C6 *35* 36–178 text, Thoughts in Prison &c., *179* Postscript, *180* blk, *181* ½t: Pieces found among the Author's Papers in Prison . . . &c., 182–92 text of verses, *193* ½t Convict's Address, *194* blk, 195 Dedication to Villette, *196* blk, *197* 198–217 text (5), *218* blk, *219* 220–25 Dodd's Last Prayer, *226* blk, *227* 228–52 Miscellaneous pieces, 253–9 List of the Writings of Dr Dodd, *260* blk.

Notes: Items **1**: 16–20, **11**: 28–31, **5**: Convict's Address 193–217, **2**: 237–40, **3**: 241–2, Letter I (**6**): 242–4, Letter II (**7**): 244–5, **9**: 246–7, **8**: 248–9, **13**: 249–50, **10**: 250–2. ESTC: t050183.

Copies: E (I.39/2.h), L² (**1**. 475 a.51; **2**. 1477 aa.30); *Can.*: CaOHM.

77.6WD/S/37   Dodd's Thoughts in Prison, Exeter,   1794
                         New Hampshire

Thoughts in Prison . . . Exeter, New Hampshire. Odiorne. 1794. 12°.
    Not examined. ESTC: w028291.
    Copies: MH (*EC75.D6618.777te), NjP.

77.6WD/S/38   Dodd's Thoughts in Prison,   [1796]
                          Cooke's edition

Cooke's Pocket Edition of the Sacred Classics. . . . London: C. Cooke.
    18°, pp. 142 + 2 engr. illus. Convict's Address pp. 96–107. ESTC: t050185.
    Copies: *UK*: AWn, BAT, BRu, L (11631 a.15); *USA*: Hyde; *Can*: CaOHM.

77.6WD/S/39   Dodd's Thoughts in Prison, Bath   1796

Thoughts in Prison . . . Bath: For the Booksellers. 1796.
  16°, Engr. port. front. + iv + 186; Convict's Address pp. 141–57. ESTC:
t050184.
  Copies: *UK*: L, LVu (P749.2.499); *USA*: Hyde, MH.

77.6WD/S/40   Dodd's Thoughts in Prison,   1801
new edition

Thoughts in Prison. A New Edition. London: Published for the Booksellers;
and printed and sold by Henry Mozley, Market Place, Gainsborough. 1801.
  12°, A² B–Q⁶ R⁴ (–R4 ? blk), ($3 signed), 95 leaves.
  Pp. A1 t., A2 *iii*–iv Advert., on B1 *1* 2–19 Account of the author, *20*–21
Advert. to Prison Thoughts, *22* blk, *23* 24–132 text of Prison Thoughts, *133*
134–40 Misc. pieces, *141* ½t Convict's Address, *142* to Villette, *143* 144–57
text Convict's Address, *158* 159–62 Last Prayer, *163* 164–70 correspondence,
171 172–6 WD's Account of Himself, 174–5 WD's Declaration, 176–7 Letter
to North, 178–9 Letter to Mansfield, 180–1 WD's Petition, 182–3 Mrs D's
Petition, 184 SJ: 'Such were the last thoughts', 185–6 SJ's Observations on
Pardoning WD. 186 *Explicit*: THE END. Coloph: 'Printed by Henry Mozley,
Market-Place, Gainsborough.'
  Copies: O (280 f. 2664).

77.6WD/S/41   Dodd's Thoughts in Prison,   1806
London

Thoughts in Prison . . . London J. Brambles, and printed by H. Mozley,
Gainsborough. 1806.
  12°, Engr. port. front. + iv + 202. Convict's Address, pp. 155–72.
  Copies: Hyde.

77.6WD/S/42   Dodd's Thoughts in Prison,   1806
Philadelphia

Thoughts in Prison . . . Philadelphia: Robert Johnson. 1806
  12°. Not examined.
  Notes: Convict's Address, pp. 140–54.
  Copies: Hyde (uncut, 'Robert F. Metzdorf'), MH.

77.6WD/S/43   Dodd's Thoughts in Prison   1808

Thoughts in Prison, In Five Parts, viz. . . . By the Rev. William Dodd, LL.D. To which are added, his last prayer, written in the Night before his Death; the Convict's Address to his unhappy Brethren; and other miscellaneous Pieces; with some Account of the Author. . . . London: Printed for J. Mawman, 23, Poultry. 1808. [J.G. Barnard, Printer, Snow-Hill.]

12°, *A*1 B–O⁸ P²; Pp. A1 t., A1ᵛ blk, on B1 *1* 2–180 Thoughts, *181* ½t Convict's Address, *182* Dedication to Villette, *183* 184–93 text, *194* 195–212 misc. pieces, including: Account of Himself (**2.** 204–6), Declaration (**3.** 206), Letter I (**6.** 207–8), Letter II (**7.** 208–9), Dodd's Petition (**9.** 209–10), Mrs Dodd's Petition (**8.** 210–11), Conclusion (**14.** 211), 'Yesterday was presented' (**11.** 212).

Copies: L (11641. aaa.26).

77.6WD/S/44   Dodd's Thoughts in Prison   1808

Thoughts in Prison. In Five Parts, viz. . . . By the Rev. William Dodd, LL.D. London: Printed for J. Mawman; J. Walker; Scatcherd and Letterman; Longman, Hurst, Rees, and Orme; Vernor, Hood, and Sharpe; B. Crosby and Co. and Sherwood, Neely, and Jones. 1808. J.G. Barnard, Printer, Skinner-Street.

Notes: A reissue of prec. with cancelled t.
Copies: L (11641. bb.25).

77.6WD/S/45   Dodd's Thoughts in Prison,   1808
Philadelphia

Thoughts in Prison . . . Philadelphia: B and T. Kite. 1808.[1]
Not examined.
Copies: MH (*EC75 D6618. 777tj), NjP.

---

[1] As late as 1829 in Moses Thomas's *Philadelphia Trade Sale* (8 Sept. 1829), John Grigg, of Philadelphia, was offering 50 copies of 'Dodd's Prison Thoughts' at 25¢ to the Trade and 75¢ retail (MWA). I have found no copy of any impression or edn. with that date.

77.6WD/S/46   Dodd's Thoughts in Prison   1809

Thoughts in Prison, in Five Parts . . . to which are added his Last Prayer, The Convict's Address to his Unhappy Brethren, and other Miscellaneous Pieces. With some Account of the Author, and a Letter from Dr. Johnson, sent after Dr. Dodd's Death to the Public Papers. London: Printed for J. Mawman; J.

Walker; Scatcherd & Letterman; Longman, Hurst, Rees, and Orme; Vernor, Hood, and Sharpe; B. Crosby and Co. and Sherwood, Neeley, and Jones. 1809. J.G. Barnard, Printer, Skinner Street.

12°, *A*1 B–O⁸ P², ($4 signed), 107 leaves.

Pp. Engr. front. + A1 t., on B1 *1* 2–169 Thoughts, *170–1* 172–80 Miscellaneous pieces, *173* ½t, *174* To Villette, *175* 176–93 Convict's Address, *194* 195–7 Last Prayer, *198* 199–203 Correspondence, *204* 205–6 Account of Himself, 206 WD's Declaration, 207–8 Letter to Lord North, 208–9 Letter to Mansfield, 209–10 WD's Petition, 210–11 Mrs D's Petition, 211 SJ's Conclusion 'Such were the last thoughts', 212 SJ on Propriety of Pardoning WD.

Copies: O (2799 f.399, pres. R.W. Chapman), MRp; *USA*: CtY.

77.6WD/S/47   Dodd's Thoughts in Prison   1812

Thoughts in Prison. In Five Parts. . . . To which are added His Last Prayer, Written in the Night before his Death; the Convict's Address to his unhappy Brethren; and other miscellaneous Pieces; with some Account of the Author. Gainsborough: Printed by and for H. Mozley, 1812.

12°, A–P⁶, ($3 signed), 90 leaves; Pp. Engr. front. 'Publish'd By H. Mozley, Gainsborough, 1 Oct. 1805.' + A1 t., A1ᵛ blk, A2 *iii*–iv Advertisement, *5* 6–24 Account of the Author, *25* 26–140 Thoughts, *141* ½t Convict's Address, *142* Dedication to Villette, *143* 144–56 text Convict's Address, 157–61 Last Prayer, 168–70 Account of Himself (2), 171 Declaration (3), 172–3 Letter I (6), 173–4 Letter II (7), *175*–76 WD's Petition (9), *177*–78 Mrs D's Petition (8), 178 Conclusion (14), 179–80 SJ on Propriety of Pardoning WD (11).

Copies: L (11644 ee.23), LICj ('J.A. Lovat Fraser', uncut).

77.6WD/S/48   Dodd's Thoughts in Prison   1813

Thoughts in Prison . . . London: Printed and sold by Dean & Munday, 35 Threadneedle Street. 1813.

12°. Not examined.

Copies: E (YY.7/3), L (11632. a.11), WIS.

77.6WD/S/49   Dodd's Thoughts in Prison,   1813
Edinburgh

[Engr. t.] Thoughts in Prison &c. By the Revᵈ William Dodd L.L.D. [vignette] –Low on earth And mingled with my native dust, I cry. Pag. 28. Edinburgh, Published by Oliver & Boyd.

[Title] Thoughts in Prison, by the Rev. W. Dodd, LL.D. With the Life of the Author, his last prayer, and other miscellaneous pieces. –Cautious shun The Rocks on which he split. Cleave close to God, Your Father, sure Protector, and Defence: Forsake not his lov'd service; and your cause He never will forsake. Vide Prison Thoughts. Edinburgh: Printed by Oliver & Boyd, Caledonian Press, Netherbow. 1813.

12°, A–M⁶ N² O1, ($3 (–A2,3, B2,3, C2, N2) signed), 75 leaves.

Pp. Engr. t. + A1 *i* t., *ii* blk, *iii*–iv Advertisement, *v* vi–xvi Life of Dodd, on B3 *17* 18–124 Thoughts in Prison, on L3 125–35 Convict's Address (5), 135–8 Dr Dodd's Last Prayer, 139–43 Letters, 144–5 Dodd's Account of Himself (May 21, 1777: 'The greatest affliction. . .' 2), 146 Dodd's Declaration ('Though I acknowledge. . .' 3), 146–7 Letter I (6), June 8, 1777 ('I have committed. . .'), 147–8 Letter II (7), June 11, 1777 ('Not many days are now to Pass . . .'), 148–9 Dr Dodd's Petition ('It is most humbly represented . . .' 9), 149–50 Mrs Dodd's Petition ('Madam, It is most humbly represented. . .' 8), 150 Conclusion ('Such were the last thoughts . . .' 14).

Copies: *UK*: E, L, JDF.

77.6WD/S/50 Dodd's Thoughts in Prison   1814

Thoughts in Prison by the Rev. W. Dodd, LL.D. With the Life of the Author, His last Prayer, and other miscellaneous Pieces. — Cautious shun The Rocks on which he split. Cleave close to God, Your Father, sure Protector, and Defence: Forsake not his lov'd service; and your cause He never will forsake. Vide Prison Thoughts. London: Printed and sold by J. Bailey, 116, Chancery Lane; and may be had of most Booksellers. 1814.

12°, A–M⁶ N1, ($3 signed), 72 leaves.

Pp. Engr. front. WD + A1 t., A2 *iii*–iv Advert., *v* vi–xvi Life of WD, on B3 *17* 18–114 Thoughts, 115–21 Miscellaneous pieces, 122–32 Convict's Address, 132–5 Last prayer, 135–40 correspondence, 140–2 WD Account of Himself, 142 Solemn Declaration, 143 Letter to Lord North, 144 Letter to Lord Mansfield, 144–5 WD's Petition, 145–6 Mrs D's petition, 146 SJ Conclusion: 'Such were the last thoughts'.

Explicit: 146 THE END. Coloph: 'J. Bailey, Printer, 116, Chancery-Lane.'

Copies: O (1419 f. 1962 (1)), L.

77.6WD/S/51 Dodd's Thoughts in Prison   1815

Thoughts in Prison; in five Parts, viz. The Imprisonment, the Retrospect, Public Punishment, The Trial, Futurity. By William Dodd, L.L.D. To which are added his Last Prayer, . . . the Convict's Address . . . and other miscellaneous Pieces: with an Account of the Author. [Epigraph from Milton]. London: Printed for J. Mawman; Longman, Hurst, Rees, Orme, and Brown;

Baldwin, Cradock, and Joy; Sherwood, Neely, and Jones; Gale, Curtis, and Fenner; and J. Walker and Co.; by T. Miller, 5, Noble-street, Cheapside. 1815.

12°, a^{10} B–K^{12}, ($1,2 ($2 as $5) signed), 118 leaves.

Pp. a1 ½t, a2 t., a3 *iii*–iv Advertisement, *v* vi–xviii Account of Author, *xx* Advt. to Prison Thoughts, on B1 *1* 2–169 text Prison Thoughts, 170–80 misc. pieces, *181* ½t Convict's Address, *182* To Villette, *183* 184–93 Convict's Address, *194* 195–7 Last Prayer, *198* 199–203 correspondence, *204* 205–6 Account of Himself, 206 Declaration, 207–8 Letter to Lord North, 208–9 Letter to Mansfield, 209–10 Dodd's petition, 210–11 Mrs Dodd's petition, 211–12 SJ on Propriety of Pardoning WD, *213–15* advts., *216* blk.

Copies: ABu, E², Eu, L, O (8° BS. P.31); *Eir.* Dt.

77.6WD/S/52   Dodd's Thoughts in Prison   1818

Thoughts in Prison; in five parts, viz. The Imprisonment, The Retrospect, Public Punishment, The Trial, Futurity. By William Dodd, LL.D. To which are added, His Last Prayer, the Convict's Address to his Unhappy Brethren; and other Miscellaneous Pieces. With some account of the author. These evils I deserve, and more; . . . [5 lines] . . . Gracious to re-admit the Suppliant. Milton. Printed at the Chiswick Press, by C. Whittingham. Sold by R. Jennings, Poultry; T. Tegg, Cheapside, London; and J. Sutherland, Edinburgh. 1818.

8°, π² a⁸ B–K⁸ L², ($1 signed), 84 leaves.

Pp. Engr. t. + π1 *i* t., *ii* blk, *iii*–iv Advertisement, on a1 *v* vi–xviii Account of the Author, xix Advertisement to Prison Thoughts, *xx* blk, on B1 *1* 2–107 Prison Thoughts, *108* 109–15 Miscellaneous Pieces, *116* blk, *117* ½t Convict's Address (5), *118* To Villette, *119* 120–30 text, 130–4 Last Prayer, 134–9 Letters, 139–41 Account of Himself ('The greatest affliction . . .' 2), 141–2 Declaration ('Though I acknowledge . . .' 3), 142–3 Letter I (6), 143–4 Letter II (7), 144–5 Dodd's Petition (9), 145–6 Mrs Dodd's Petition (8), 146 Conclusions ('Such were the last thoughts . . .' 14), 147–8 SJ's Observations on Pardoning WD ('Yesterday was presented . . .' 11).

Notes: Convict's Address, pp. 117–48.

Copies: AWn, BAT, JDF, L (11659. de.31(1)); *USA*: Hyde.

77.6WD/S/53   Dodd's Thoughts in Prison   1822

Thoughts in Prison . . . London: Chiswick Press. 1822.

12°. [reissue of prec.].

Copies: L (11632. a.48(1)).

77.6WD/S/54   Dodd's Thoughts in Prison   1823–4

Thoughts in Prison . . . London: Chiswick Press. 1823–4
  Engraved t. dated '1824'. 8° [reissue of prec.]
  Copies: L (11658 de.37).

77.6WD/S/55   Dodd's Thoughts in Prison,   1827
                              Dove's English Classics

Dove's English Classics.
  Blair's Grave. Gray's Elegy. Porteus on Death. Dodd's Prison Thoughts.
[vignette 'Perseverantia et amicis'] London: Printed and published by J. F.
Dove, St. John's Square. 1827.
  *A*² B–H¹² I¹⁰, ($1,5 (–I5 + I4) signed), 96 leaves.
  Engr. front. & engr. t. + A1 t., A2 ½t The Grave, on B1 *1* 2–23 Blair, *24*
blk, *25–7* 28–30 Gray's Elegy, *31–3* 34–44 Porteus's Death, *45* ½t: Thoughts in
Prison, *46* blk, *47–48* Advertisement, *49* 50–61 Account of the Author, 62–3
'To the words of dying men . . .' (**12**, above), *64* Advertisement to Prison
Thoughts, *65* 66–148 text, *149* Postscript, *150* blk, *151* 152–6 Miscellaneous
Pieces, *157* ½t Convict's Address (**5**), *158* To Villette, *159* 160–9 text, 170–3
Dodd's last prayer, 173–8 Letters, *179* 180–1 Dodd's Account of himself ('The
greatest affliction and oppression to my mind . . .' **2**), 181 'Though I acknow-
ledge in all its atrocity . . .' (**3**), 182 Letter I (**6**), 183 Letter II (**7**), 184 Dodd's
Petition (**9**), 185 Mrs Dodd's Petition (**8**), 186 'Such were the thoughts . . .'
(**14**), 187–8 'Yesterday was presented . . .' (**11**).
  Notes: The printed boards advertise Dove's English Classics, inc. this vol. at
3s.
  Copies: JDF.

77.6WD/S/56   Dodd's Thoughts in Prison   1842
                              (with The Grave etc.)

[Engr. t.] The Grave by Blair, The Elegy by Gray, The Prison Thoughts by
Dodd, On Death by Porteus, and the Night Thoughts, &c. by Edward Young,
LL.D. [Vignette] London: Published by Scott, Webster & Geary,
Charterhouse Square. 1842.
  Dodd's *Thoughts*, &c., pp. 35–151. The Account of Dodd, pp. *38* ff. includes
'I now stand before you' (45–6; no. **1**, above), and 'To the words of dying men'
(51–2; **12**, above).
  Notes: Scott, Webster & Geary, were Dove's successors.
  Copies: BMp, L.

77.6WD/S/56/ADD1 Dodd's Prison Thoughts   1846

[Engr. t. in dec. frame] PRISON | [Hollow] THOUGHTS. | [wavy rule] | BY THE | REV. W. DODD, D.D. | [wavy rule] | CHELSEA: | PUBLISHED BY W. TOBY. | [short rule] | 1846.

8s. [. . .] *F*⁴ G–R⁸ ($2 signed), 92 leaves.

Pp. Steel engr. front & t. + *89* 90–224 text, 225–34 miscellaneous pieces, 235–55 Convict's Address, 256–62 Last Prayer, 263–72 correspondence, 272 *Explicit*: THE END.

Notes: Miniature book, extracted from some larger collection, and furnished with special t. and front.

Copies: O (Vet A6 g.46; 4⅝ × 2⅞ in. Ribbed mauve cloth, blind dec. covers, gilt device on front cover and gilt titling on spine; all edges gilt; 'Hezia Peache Sepᵗ 10ᵗʰ 1853').

77.6WD/S/57   Thoughts of a Citizen of   1777
                        London on Dodd

Thoughts of a Citizen of London on the Conduct of Dr Dodd in his Life and Death. With Remarks on the several Petitions presented in his Favour; the Arguments of the Court of Common Council of the City of London on the Occasion considered; and some Queries addressed to the Right Hon. the Lord Mayor and the Court on the Subject. With Reflexions on some Passages of the ordinary of Newgate's Account of Dr Dodd's Conversation in Newgate, and going to Execution. Shewing that the dangerous and hurtful Doctrine, of Christians who have past their whole Lives in Wickedness being saved at the last Hour by applying to Christ, has no Foundation either in the Nature of Things or the Scriptures. London: Printed for W. Owen. '1767' [= 1777].

8°, Pp. *1–3* 4–8, 17–48. (Erratum on *2* is itself erroneous).

Includes 23–4 Dodd's Address to the Court, No. **1** ('I now stand before you . . .'), 24–5 Petition of the Lord Mayor &c. (**4**,) 25 Petition of the Jury, 25–6 Petition of the Borough of Southwark, 42 Dodd's Last solemn Declaration ('To the words of dying men . . .' **12**) dated 'June 27, 1777'.

Notes: Misdated '1767' Published: 30 Aug. (*Gazetteer & New Daily Advertiser*; A.D. Barker (1983), 156 n. 30 says '27 August', and suggests Robert Goadby as author, 174).¹ ESTC: n014351.

Copies: MH ('Isaac Reed' with MS note p. 31), Hyde; *UK*: BAT, En, Lv (Forster 2520).

---

¹ Goadby (1723–78), published a pamphlet in defence of the sentence on Dodd, *Lit. Anec.* iii (1812), 724.

77.6WD/S/58   The Trial and the Life of Dodd   1777

The Trial and the Life of the Rev. Dr Dodd. [Part 1] London. 1777
8°, A–F⁴, ($2 (–A1) signed), 24 leaves; Pp. *1* t., *2* blk, *3* 4–48 text, 48 FINIS.
Notes: No Johnsonian texts. ESTC: t097390.
Copies: L² (1. 1131. c.14 (3); 2. Rox. III. 425).

77.6WD/S/59   The Trial of Dodd, Dublin   ?1777

The Trial of the Rev. Doctor Dodd at the Old Bailey, on Saturday the 22d Day of February, 1777, For Forging a Bond in the Name of the Right Hon. Philip, Earl of Chesterfield, for 4200 l. Taken in Short Hand, by a Barrister. Dublin: Printed for John Beatty and Christopher Jackson, No. 32, Skinner-Row. 8°.
8°, A–F⁴, ($2 signed), 24 leaves; Pp. A1 *1* t., *2* blk, *3* 4–48 text.
Pagination: (↑); *Explicit*: 48 FINIS.
References: ESTC: t195641.
Copies: O (Vet. A4 e. 2521).

77.6WD/S/60   The Trial of Dodd, Edinburgh   1777

The Trial of William Dodd, L.L.D. With an Account of his Behaviour during his Confinement and on the Day of Execution; Also, the Petitions, his Address . . . and Last Solemn Declaration, &c. &c. Edinburgh: Printed in the Year M.DCC.LXXVII.
See above 77.6CA/5.

**77.6WD/S/61   The Proceedings in the King's   1777
Commission**

The Whole Proceedings in the King's Commission of the Peace . . . 19 February 1777. Taken in Short hand by Joseph Gurney . . . No. III. Pt. I. . . . London: William Richardson . . . S. Bladon. 4°.
Notes: Dodd's Trial pp. 94–118, with errata slip; advertised as 'Dr Dodd's Trial . . . &c.' ESTC: t199141.
Copies: Hyde; *UK*: Lll.

**77.6WD/S/62   Der unglückliche Prädicant   [? 1777]
zu London**

[Fraktur] **Der unglückliche Prädicant zu London / in grabfchariftlichen Gedanken lebhaft abgefchildert.** [Engr. vignette of sheepstealer and parson on gallows] Welcher Alldorten auf feiner mit eigener Hande ausgefertigten Erzfalfchen, und fehr viel betragenden Wechfelbriefen alfo fchändlich ift aus-bezahlet worden / nemlich am 27ften Junii 1777. London, Aus dem Englischen in das Hochdeutfche übersetzt per A. S. d. M. P.

4°, $2, Pp. *1* t., *2* Vorläufig= von deffen Herkommen und Verbrechten gründlicher Bericht., *3–4* Grabfchriftliche Gedanken (Verse: 2 cols./p.).

Notes: Partly in verse. There are no Johnsonian allusions.

Copies: L (11517. dd.25(9).

77.9BL   Boswell's Petition for Joseph Knight   1777

23 September   Petition for Joseph Knight, a Negro

References: *Life* iii. 200–3, 212–14; *JB: Extremes*, 182–3, 204 and n.

Notes: Knight was freed in Jan. 1778. SJ's argument arose from that deployed in court by John Maclaurin,[1] but was not published until the 2nd. edn. of *Life* (1793), in the supplementary leaves prefixed to vol. I, pp. *xiv–xvi (p. xiv as *ix'), JB having mislaid his notes during the printing of both the first and second editions.

---

[1] Waingrow, *Corr.* 429–30; and *Life* (refs. above), showing that JB was not himself engaged in the hearing.

78.5RD/1a   Reynolds's Seven Discourses   1778

[½t] [row of 21 flowers, 75 mm.] | SEVEN | DISCOURSES | DELIVERED IN THE | ROYAL ACADEMY | BY THE | PRESIDENT. | [row of 21 flowers, 75 mm.]

[Title] SEVEN | DISCOURSES | DELIVERED IN THE | ROYAL ACADEMY | BY THE | PRESIDENT. | [rule] | Omnia fere quæ præceptis continentur, ab ingeniofis | hominibus fiunt: fed cafu quodam magis, quàm Sci- | entiâ. Ideoque doctrina & animadverfio adhibenda | eft, ut ea quæ interdum fine ratione nobis occurrunt, | fempre in noftra poteftate fint; & quoties res poftula- | verit, a nobis ex præparato adhibeantur. | Aquila Roman. *de Fig. Sententiar.* | *apud* Junium. | [double rule] | LONDON: | Printed for T. Cadell, in the Strand, Bookfeller | and Printer to the Royal Academy. | M DCC LXXVIII.

8°, *A*⁴ B–X⁸ Y⁴, ($4 (–Y3,4) signed), 168 leaves.

Pp. A1 ½t, A1ᵛ blk, A2 t., A2ᵛ blk, A3–4ᵛ Dedication dh: TO | THE KING., on B1 *i* ½t A Discourse, &c., *ii* blk, *iii*–iv Address: 'To the Members', 5–326 text, *327–8* (Y4) Cadell's advts.

Pagination: [↑]; 30 *slipt*; ½tt. 27–8, 65–6, 99–100, 149–50, 191–2, 253–4; blks 26, 64, 148, 190, 252; unnumbered 67, 101, 151, 193, 255.

Press-figures: B4ᵛ(8)–2, B7ᵛ(14)–2, C3ᵛ(22)–5, C7(29)–7, D2ᵛ(36)–2, D5ᵛ(42)–2, E5(57)–5, E7ᵛ(62)–2, F7(77)–7, F8(79)–5, G3ᵛ(86)–2, G4ᵛ(88)–5, H6ᵛ(108)–5, H7ᵛ(110)–2, I2ᵛ(116)–7, I5ᵛ(122)–1, K3ᵛ(134)–5, K8ᵛ(144)–7, L4ᵛ(152)–2, L8(159)–2, M5(169)–1, M6(171)–1, N2ᵛ(180)–2, N6(187)–2, O4ᵛ(200)–5, O7ᵛ(206)–5, P1ᵛ(210)–1, P4ᵛ(216)–1, Q3ᵛ(230)–7, Q8ᵛ(240)–7, R5ᵛ(250)–5, R8ᵛ(256)–5, S7(269)–5, S7ᵛ(270)–5, T5ᵛ(282)–5, T7(285)–5, U8(303)–1, U8ᵛ(304)–7, X5ᵛ(314)–1, X7(317)–7, Y2ᵛ(324)–5, Y4(327)–7.

Catchwords: 128 ₐprac- ("practiſed).

Explicit: 326 FINIS.

Paper: White, laid; Demy (uncut: 8¾ × 5⅝ in.), wmk.: fleur-de-lys.

Type: Dedication: 2-line great primer (8.5 mm), Address: great primer (5.7 mm), text: English (4.5 mm), notes: small pica (3.6 mm).

References: *Life* ii. 2 n. (Courtney 129); CH 154; Hazen 195–7; Northcote (1819) 315; *Diaries* 288; *Rothschild* 1740; Hilles, *Literary Career of Reynolds* (1936), and in *Eighteenth Century Studies* (1970), 267–77; Todd, *BC* vii (1958), 417–18; ESTC: 047974.

Notes: SJ composed the Dedication to the King. He also made some stylistic revisions in at least one later *Discourse*, viz. XI (1783) (*MS Index*, JoS 337–8; Hilles, 135, and 82.12RD, below). Occasionally some closing passages are reminiscent of SJ but the community of view and JR's own style preclude detailed attribution to SJ.

The volume was published 19 May 1778, @ 5s. in boards (*Public Advertiser*). The brief notice in *Gents. Mag.* xlviii (Nov. 1778), 592 is confined to the quotation of the entire Dedication 'as a model to dedicators'.[1]

SJ's 'Dedication' was not included in any of the translations of this work. *Life* iii. 485, suggests Baretti may have been the translator of the Italian version of the Discourses (78.5RD/TI/1, below); cf. Hilles, above (1970), 273; or in the French (2 vols. 1787) and Italian (1787) versions sent to Catherine the Great, 4 Aug. 1789 (Hilles, *ibid.* 273), or in the Russian translation by Ivan Tatischer, published at St Petersburg: 'At the Printing Office of the School of Mines, 1790' (8°, pp. 292; Hilles, *ibid.* 274–5). This is not a scarce item.

Copies: O (170 k.159);

USA: CSmH, CtY², DFo (JR: 'To Mr Gawler from the Author'), Hyde⁴ (1. Pres. JR to Robert Jephson; 2. 'H.M. Keith 1816'² — L.F. Powell; 3. 'Maria Clara Lechmere' — R.B. Adam; 4. Cotton — J. Leslie), ICN, ICU, [InU, IU, [Liebert (E. of Portarlington)], MH, NjP (R.W. Rogers), [PBm], PPL, PPU; *Can*: CaOHM²; *UK*: [W.R. Batty²], BRu, C, Ct, E, Eu, JDF, L (126. k.1), LEu, NCu; *Eir*: Dt²; *Aust*: CNL (DNS 6552).

---

[1] This seems to be the first notice of SJ in the *Gents. Mag.* after John Nichols had become the major shareholder with the purchase of a quarter share from David Henry on 1 July 1778, for £330 (C: MS Nichols Sharebook (ex A.N.L. Munby), sub 'G').

[2] Hester Maria ('Queeney') Thrale m. 1808, Admiral Viscount Keith.

78.5RD/1b   Reynold's Seven Discourses, facsimile   1971

Joshua Reynolds Seven Discourses 1778   Scolar Press 1971 Printed and published by the Scolar Press, Menston, Yorks, in 1971, with an Introduction signed Richard Woodfield.

Copies: E, O (1701 e. 453; red cloth, gilt spine titling).

78.5RD/2   Reynolds's Discourses, Works   1797

The Works of Sir Joshua Reynolds, Knt. Late President of the Royal Academy; containing his Discourses, Idlers, A Journey to Flanders and Holland (now first published) and his Commentary on Du Fresnoy's Art of Painting, printed from his revised copies (with his last corrections and additions,) In two volumes. To which is prefixed an Account of the Life and Writings of the Author, by Edmond Malone, Esq. one of his executors . . . Volume the first [– second]. London: Printed for T. Cadell, jun. and W. Davies, in the Strand. M DCC XCVII.

2 vols., 4°.

Notes: Edited by Malone. SJ's Dedication 'To the King', I. *i–ii*. SJ's Dedication is not always included in Reynolds's Works. It is not present in the following: **1**. The Literary Works of Sir Joshua Reynolds, To which is prefixed a Memoir . . . by Henry William Beechey. London: T. Cadell, Strand; W. Blackwood and Son. Edinburgh. 1835. 2 vols. *Copies*: O (35. 146–7); **2**. Discourses on Painting and the fine Arts, delivered at the Royal Academy, by Sir Joshua Reynolds, Kt. London. Printed for Jones and Co. 3, Acton Place, Kingsland Road. 1825. 8°. *Copies*: O (170 n. 164(2)); **3**. [Engr. t.] The Discourses of Sir Joshua Reynolds. Illustrated by Explanatory Notes & Plates by John Burnet, F.R.S. London. James Carpenter, Old Bond Street. 1842. 4°.

Copies: O (2 Δ 326); **4**. Everyman Library No. 118. Fifteen Discourses delivered in the Royal Academy by Sir Joshua Reynolds. London: Published by J.M. Dent & Co and in New York by E.P. Dutton & Co. [1906] *Copies*: O (1701 f.33); **5**. 'John Long's Carlton Classics'. Discourses by Sir Joshua Reynolds with Biographical Introduction by Hannaford Bennett London John Long Norris Street, Haymarket MCMVIII *Copies*: O (1701 f.56).

References: ESTC: t000594.

Copies: O (BB. 42–3, Art. Seld).

78.5RD/3   Reynolds's Discourses, Works   1798

The Works of Sir Joshua Reynolds, Knight; late President of the Royal Academy: containing his Discourses, Idlers, A Journey to Flanders and Holland and his Commentary on Du Fresnoy's Art of Painting; printed from his revised copies, (with his last corrections and additions,). In three volumes. To which is added an Account of Life and Writings of the Author, by Edmond Malone, Esq. . . . Volume the first [–third]. London: Printed for T. Cadell, jun. and W. Davies, in the Strand. 1798

3 vols., 8°.

Notes: Malone's revised and expanded edition; SJ's Dedication at I. *i*–ii. ESTC: t052793.

Copies: O (Vet. A5 e.1945, lacks v.2).

78.5RD/4   Reynolds's Discourses, Works   1801

The Works of Sir Joshua Reynolds, Knight; late President of the Royal Academy: containing his Discourses, Idlers, A Journey to Flanders and Holland, and his Commentary on Du Fresnoy's Art of Painting; printed from his revised copies, (with his last corrections and additions) In three volumes. To which is prefixed an Account of the Life and Writings of the Author, by Edmond Malone, Esq. . . . The third edition corrected . . . London: Printed for T. Cadell, jun. and W. Davies, in the Strand, By H. Baldwin and Son, New Bridge-Street. 1801.

3 vols., 8°.

Notes: SJ's Dedication 'To the King' at I. *i*–ii.

Copies: O (1701 e. 374–6).

78.5RD/5   Reynolds's Discourses, Works   1809

The Works of Sir Joshua Reynolds, Knight; late President of the Royal Academy. Containing his Discourses, Idlers, A Journey to Flanders and Holland, and his Commentary on Du Fresnoy's Art of Painting, printed from his revised copies, (with his last Corrections and Additions) In three volumes. To which is prefixed an Account of the Life and Writings of the Author. By Edmond Malone, Esq. . . . The Fourth Edition Corrected. . . . Volume the First [–Third]. London: Printed for T. Cadell and W. Davies, in the Strand, By C. and R. Baldwin, New Bridge-Street. 1809.

3 vols., 8°. SJ's Dedication, I. *i*–ii.

Copies: O (1701 e.307–9, 'H.D. Acland' — R.W. Chapman).

78.5RD/6   Reynolds's Discourses, Works   1819

The Literary Works of Sir Joshua Reynolds, Kt. Late President of the Royal Academy. Containing his Discourses, Papers in the Idler, the Journal of a Tour through Flanders and Holland, also his Commentary on Du Fresnoy's Art of

Painting, printed from the Author's revised copies, with his last corrections and additions. In three volumes. To which is prefixed some Account of the Life, by Edmond Malone, Esq. London: Printed for T. Cadell and W. Davies in the Strand, Booksellers to the Royal Academy. 1819.

3 vols., 8°. SJ's Dedication is in I. *i–ii*.
Notes: The Memoir of JR is by Joseph Farington.
Copies: O (1701 d. 111–13); Op.

78.5RD/7   Reynolds's Discourses   [1820/25]

Sharpe's British Prose Writers
[Engr. t.] SIR JOSHUA REYNOLDS'S | DISCOURSES. | VOL. I. | [Engr. vign. port. of JR 'Sir J. Reynolds pinx. G. Murray sc.'] | LONDON, PUBLISHED BY JOHN SHARPE, PICCADILLY. | 1820.
[Engr. t. vol. 2] DISCOURSES | AT THE | ROYAL ACADEMY | BY SIR JOSHUA REYNOLDS KN^T. | VOL. II. | [Vignette easel &c.] | LONDON: | PUBLISHED BY JOHN SHARPE, PICCADILLY. | 1820.
[Titles] DISCOURSES | DELIVERED AT THE | ROYAL ACADEMY, | BY SIR JOSHUA REYNOLDS, K_T. | [short rule] | VOL. I [– II] . | [short rule] | M DCCC XXV.
Sir Joshua Reynolds's Discourses. Vol. I [– II]. London: Published by John Sharpe, Piccadilly.
2 vols., 12°

I. B–G^{12}, ($1,5 ($5 as $2) signed; 'VOL.I.' on $1), 72 leaves.
Pp. Engr. t. + B1 *1* t., *2* coloph: '[rule] | C. & C. WHITTINGHAM, Chiswick.', *3* SJ's Dedication ('[1778]'), *4* JR's Dedication to the Academy, *5* 6–142 text, *143*–144 'Index', 144 coloph. as p. 2.

II. B–G^{12} H^{10}, ($1,5 ($5 as $2) signed; 'VOL. II.' on $1), 82 leaves.
Pp. Engr. t. + on B1 *1* t., *2* coloph., *3* 4–161 text, *162* blk, *163*–164 Index, 164 coloph.

Notes: Part of the series of Sharpe's 'British Prose Writers', cf. *Sermons*, 1819 (88.5S/13, below).[1] This collection is of 15 Discourses.
Copies: O (170 n. 164(2)); *UK*: JDF.

[1] At M. & S. Thomas's *Philadelphia Trade Sale* (5 Sept. 1825), Messrs Wells & Lilly, of Boston, offered 25 copies of 'Prose Writers' (9 vols.), including 'Reynolds's Discourses' and 'Johnson's Sermons', folded [= in sheets] at $1.25 retail. I have seen no American edition of this date.

78.5RD/8   Reynolds's Discourses, Boston   1821

The Discourses of Sir Joshua Reynolds . . . Boston, 1821.
   Not examined.
   Copies: Unlocated.

78.5RD/9   Reynolds's Discourses, Works   1824

The Complete Works of Sir Joshua Reynolds, first President of the Royal
Academy. With an original Memoir, and Anecdotes of the Author. [Epigraph:
2 lines, Cicero] In Three Volumes. Volume I [-III]. London: Printed for
Thomas M'Lean, 26 Haymarket. 1824.
   3 vols. 8°; coloph: 'Howlett and Brimmer, Printers, Frith Street, Soho.'
   Note: SJ's Dedication is I. *xcix–xcc*.
   Copies: O (1701 f.69), Op (G.B. Hill).

78.5RD/10   Reynolds's Discourses   1837

The Discourses of Sir Joshua Reynolds . . . London, 1837.
   Not examined.
   Copies: Unlocated.

[78.5RD/11   Reynolds's Discourses   1842

The Discourses of Sir Joshua Reynolds. Illustrated by explanatory Notes &
Plates by John Burnet, F.R.S. London: James Carpenter, Old Bond Street.
1842
   4°. SJ's Dedication is omitted.
   Copies: E, O, Op.]

78.5RD/12a   Reynolds's Discourses, Works   1845

The Literary Works of Sir Joshua Reynolds, containing his Discourses, Idlers,
A Journey to Flanders and Holland (now first published) and his Commentary
on Du Fresnoy's Art of Painting, printed from his revised copies, corrected . . .
with . . . an Account of the Life and Writings of the Author. London: Henry
G. Bohn. 1845.
   2 vols., 8°. Pp. I: viii + 463 *464*; II: *iv* + 495 *496*.
   Notes: Not examined. SJ's 'Dedication, is I. 301–2. Beechey's Memoir was
first published in 1835.[1]
   Copies: Unlocated.

¹ This is the earliest of Bohn's editions of which I have a note. Subsequent reimpressions of the plates are recorded below, but there may well be more.

78.5RD/12b   Reynolds's Discourses, Works   1846

The Literary Works of Sir Joshua Reynolds, First President of the Royal Academy. To which is prefixed a Memoir of the Author, with remarks on his professional Character, illustrative of his Principles and Practice, By Henry William Beechey. In two Volumes. New and improved Edition. London: Henry G. Bohn, York Street, Covent Garden. 1846.

Notes: A reimpression of the above. Not examined.

78.5RD/12c   Reynolds's Discourses, Works   1852

The Literary Works of Sir Joshua Reynolds, First President of the Royal Academy. To which is prefixed a Memoir of the Author, with remarks on his professional Character, illustrative of his Principles and Practice, By Henry William Beechey. In two Volumes. New and improved Edition. London: Henry G. Bohn, York Street, Covent Garden. 1852.

Notes: A reimpression of 78.5RD/12a, above; 2 vols., 8°. SJ's 'Dedication' is at i. 301–2.

Copies: Op.

78.5RD/12d   Reynold's Discourses, Works,   1867
Bohn's Library

Bohn's Library. The Literary Works of Sir Joshua Reynolds, containing his Discourses, Idlers, A Journey to Flanders and Holland (now first published) and his Commentary on Du Fresnoy's Art of Painting, printed from his revised copies, corrected . . . with . . . an Account of the Life and Writings of the Author. London: Henry G. Bohn. 1867.

2 vols., 8°. Not examined, but presumably a reimpression of 78.5RD/12a, above.

[78.5RD/13   Reynolds's Life and Discourses, Ohio   1853

The Life and Discourses of Sir Joshua Reynolds, First President of the Royal Academy. Ohio. 1853

Not seen.]

78.5RD/14   Reynolds's Discourses, Parchment Library   1884

'Parchment Library'

The Discourses of Sir Joshua Reynolds. Edited and annotated by Edmund Gosse. London: Kegan Paul, Trench & Co. MDCCCLXXXIIII.

8°, Pp. [Etched port. of JR] + *i–v*, vi–xi Preface, *xiii* Biographical Note, *xv* xvi–xvii Contents, on *1* SJ's Dedication, *3* JR to Royal Academy, *5* 6–290 15 Discourses, *291–3* 294–99 Notes, *301* coloph: 'Chiswick Press:– C. Whittingham and Co., Tooks Court, Chancery Lane.'

Notes: Published in vellum 7s. 6d., parchment or cloth 6s. Printed green dust jacket. SJ's Dedication p. 1.

Copies: O (170 f.11; white vellum, red and black titling, deckle edges; in light-blue slipcase; *UK*: E; *USA*: Hyde.

78.5RD/15   Reynolds's Discourses, Camelot Series   1887

The Camelot Series. (Monthly Shilling Volumes).

[½t] **[BL] The Camelot Series.** Edited by Ernest Rhys. Reynolds's Discourses.

[Title] Sir Joshua Reynolds's Discourses: Edited with an Introduction, by Helen Zimmern. Walter Scott: London: 24 Warwick Lane, Paternoster Row. 1887

8s, a^8 b^8 379–396^8, ($1 signed), 160 leaves.

Pp. a1 *i* t., *ii* blk, *iii* t., *iv* blk, *v*–vi Contents, *vii* viii–xxvi Introduction, *xxvii* SJ's Dedication, *xxviii* blk, *xxix* JR's Dedication to the Royal Academy, *xxx* blk, *xxxi* ½t Discourses., *xxxii* blk, on 379_1 *1* 2–283 text, 283 coloph: 'Printed by Walter Scott, Felling, Newcastle-upon-Tyne.', *284* blk, *285–8* advts.

References: J.R. Turner, *SB* xliv (1991), 323–31 sheds some preliminary light on the Walter Scott company.

Notes: The signatures show that this collection formed part of a larger collection in the 'Camelot Series'. JR's *Idlers* are included (pp. 269–83), and SJ's 'Dedication' (dated '[1778]'), is printed at p. xxvii. Issued in red cloth and black titling.

Copies: O (1701 f.15); *UK*: E, JDF ('Will Tomlinson').

78.5RD/16a   Reynolds's Discourses,   1888
Cassell's National Library

Cassell's National Library, No. 109

Cassell's National Library. Seven Discourses on Art. By Sir Joshua Reynolds. Cassell & Company, Limited: London, Paris, New York & Melbourne. 1888

16s. A^{16} B–F^{16}, ($1 as '$–109'), 96 leaves.

Pp. A1 *1* ½t Seven Discourses on Art, *2* advts., *3* t., *4* blk, *5* 6–8 Introduction, *9* SJ's Dedication, *10* JR's Dedication to the Academy, *11* 12–192 text of Discourses, 192 coloph: 'Printed by Cassell & Company, Limited, La Belle Sauvage, London, E.C.'

Copies: O (1701 f.12); *USA*: TxU, [MWelC]; *UK*: E, Gp (D.443480), JDF.

78.5RD/16b   Reynolds's Discourses,   1888
                   Cassell's National Library, New York

An undated New York issue of National Library, 109, is tentatively dated to 1888. Not examined.

Copies: CtY, MiU.

78.5RD/16c   Reynolds's Discourses,   1891
                     Cassell's National Library

Cassell's National Library, no. 109
   The Discourses of Sir Joshua Reynolds. London: Cassell & Co.
   16s.
   Notes: SJ's 'Dedication', p. 9. This is a reissue of the above 78.5RD/16a.
   Copies: *USA*: MH, [RPB]; *UK*: AWu, LVu.

78.5RD/17   Reynolds's Discourses, ed. Fry   1905

Discourses delivered to the students of the Royal Academy by Sir Joshua Reynolds, Kt. With Introduction and Notes by Roger Fry. [vignette] London Seely & Co. Limited 38 Great Russell Street 1905.

   8°, pp. xxxii + 445 text, coloph. *446*: The Riverside Press Limited, Edinburgh., + *447–8* advts. With illustrations.

   Notes: SJ's Dedication p. xxix.

   Copies: O (1701 e. 132; green cloth, white titling and decoration + green dust jacket, price: 7s.).

78.5RD/18   Reynolds's Discourses, New   [1906]
                       Universal Library

The New Universal Library
   Discourses on Art delivered to the students of the Royal Academy by Sir Joshua Reynolds. London. George Routledge & Sons, Limited New York: E.P. Dutton & Co. [1906]

Pp. i–viii, 1–240 15 Discourses, 241–8 Index. Coloph: (248) 'Printed by J. W. M'Laren and Co., Edinburgh.'

Notes: SJ's Dedication, p. xxi.

Copies: E, O (1701 f.31; grey cloth, gilt spine titling, grey printed dust jacket, priced 1s.; Accession date: '27.8.1906').

78.5RD/19   Reynolds's Discourses, ed. Dobson   1907

The Discourses of Sir Joshua Reynolds, to which are added his Letter to 'The Idler'. With an Introduction by Austin Dobson, Hon. LL.D. Edinburgh ['Worlds Classics' device] Henry Frowde Oxford University Press London, New York and Toronto. 1907.

Coloph: 'Printed by Ballantyne, Hanson & Co. At the Ballantyne Press, Edinburgh.'

Note: SJ's 'Dedication', p. xxi.

Copies: O (1701 f.55; green cloth, gilt spine titling; red printed dust jacket; price 1s.).

78.5RD/20   Reynolds's Discourses, Glasgow   1924

The Discourses of Sir Joshua Reynolds. P.R.A. Printed for the Royal Academy of Arts by Robert Maclehose and Company Ltd. At the University Press, Glasgow, and published by Macmillan and Company Ltd. London. MCMXXIV.

8°, Pp. *i* ½t + [Front. port. of JR] + *iii* t., *iv* coloph: 'Printed in Great Britain by Robert Maclehose and Co. Ltd. The University Press, Glasgow.' *v* Preface, vii–xxv Introduction, *xxvii* ½t 'Discourses', xxix–xxx SJ's dedication, xxxi–xxxiii Contents, xxxv JR to Royal Academy, *1* 2–280 15 Discourses, 281–2 *283* Index.

Notes: The Introduction is signed by 'W.R.M. L[amb].', and SJ's 'Dedication' is printed pp. xxix–xxx.

Copies: Hyde (Adam); *UK*: E, O (1701 d.106).

78.5RD/21   Reynolds's Discourses, ed. Olsen   [1945]

The Discourses of Sir Joshua Reynolds, edited by E. Olsen. Chicago. n.d. [1945]

Not examined.

Notes: 'Longinus'' Treatise *Of the Sublime* is included in translation.

Copies: Unlocated.

78.5RD/22a   Reynolds's Discourses, ed. Wark   1959

Sir Joshua Reynolds Discourses on Art Edited by Robert R. Wark. Huntington Library San Marino California 1959.
8s.
Notes: SJ's 'Dedication' is printed at p. 3.
Copies: O (1701 d.260); *USA*: Hyde.

78.5RD/22b   Reynolds's Discourses, ed. Wark   1975

Sir Joshua Reynolds Discourses on Art Edited by Robert R. Wark. Huntington Library San Marino California Yale University Press 1975
8s.
Notes: SJ's 'Dedication' is on p. 3, but there are additions to the notes in this edn. ISBN: 0-300-01823-1. This edition was also reissued in paperback in 1981 (ISBN: 0-300-02775-3).
Copies: O (1701 d. 435); Op.

78.5RD/TF/1   Reynolds's Discourses,   1909
French translation

Les Discours de Sir Joshua Reynolds. Traduit par L. Dimier. Paris, 1909. Not seen.
Copies: Unlocated.

78.5RD/TG/1   Reynolds's Discourses,   1893
German translation

Ed. E.Leisching, 1893. Not seen.
Copies: Unlocated.

[78.5RD/TI/1   Reynolds's Discourses,   1778
Italian translation

[Engr. t.] Delle Arti del Disegno Discorsi del Cav. Giosuè Reynolds Presidente della R. Acad. di Londra ec. Trasportati dall' Inglese nel Toscano idioma In Firenze MDCCLXXVIII.
12°, *6 (–*1 + Engr. t.) A–K¹², ($6 signed), 126 leaves.
Pp. Engr. t. + *2 III–XI L' Editore a chi legge, XII blk, on A1 1–2 JR's Dedication to the Academicians, 3–240 text of seven 'Discorsi'.
Notes: In the copy examined, a blank leaf stands between *6 and A1: if it had

a partner then the initial gathering was of 8 leaves, of which the first is lost (? ½t), and the second replaced by the engr. t., but the t. leaf is followed by a leaf signed '*2' and paged 'III' so that a ½t and t. would have disrupted the sequence.

SJ's 'Dedication' is omitted. The translation is attributed to Baretti.

Copies: E (X.46.g).]

78.7SA/1a   Shaw's Analysis of the Galic Language   1778

AN | ANALYSIS | OF THE | GALIC LANGUAGE. | By WILLIAM SHAW, A.M. | —Forfan et hæc olim meminiffe juvabit. | Virg. | [short swelled rule] | LONDON: | Printed for the Author, by W. and A. Strahan; | And fold by J. Donaldson in the Strand; and C. Elliot, Edinburgh. | M DCC LXXVIII.

4°, *a*⁴ b–c⁴ B–U⁴ X², ($2 (S2 as R2, –X2) signed), 90 leaves.

Pp. a1 *i* t., *ii* blk, *iii* Dedication to the Earl of Eglinton (signed 'W. SHAW.'), *iv* blk, *v* vi–viii List of Subscribers dh: [parallel rule] | SUB SCRIBERS NAMES., ht: SUBSCRIBERS NAMES., *ix* x–xxiv Introduction dh: [parallel rule] | INTRODUCTION., ht: INTRODUCTION., on B1 *1* 2–156 text dh: [parallel rule] | AN | ANALYSIS | OF THE | GALIC LANGUAGE. | [rule], rt: AN ANALYSIS OF | THE GALIC LANGUAGE.

Pagination: [↑] 125–56; unnumbered i–v, ix, 11, 102–3, 113; ii, iv, 102 blk.

Press-figures: a3ᵛ(vi)–2, b4(xv)–4, b4ᵛ(xvi)–2, c4(xxiii)–4, B4ᵛ(8)–3, C4(15)–5, D4ᵛ(24)–8, E4(31)–7, E4ᵛ(32)–8, F3ᵛ(38)–‡, G1ᵛ(42)–6, G4ᵛ(48)–9, H4ᵛ(56)–6, I4(63)–8, K2ᵛ(68)–8, L3(77)–3, M3ᵛ(86)–4, N3ᵛ(94)–1, O1ᵛ(98)–3, P3ᵛ(110)–3, Q3ᵛ(118)–‡, Q4ᵛ(120)–4, R3ᵛ(126)–2, S3ᵛ(134)–4, T3(141)–‡, U1ᵛ(146)–7, U2ᵛ(148)–6, X2(155)–4.

Catchwords: viii *om.* (INTRODUCTION.), xxiv *om.* (AN), 9 *Sdiuiz- (Sduir-)*, 25 Singular (*Definitely.*), 47 *Active* (ACTIVE), 48–53 *Bha* (*Ro*), 56–9 *Chru-* (Do), 65 *Dfhend* (*Indicative*), 67 Future (*Indicative.* | Future.), 69 *Bha* (*Indicative.*), 71 Perfect. (*Indicative* | Perfect.), 101 *om.* (AN), 103 Imith (Imich), 112 BOOK (AN), 119 Sio- (Sior-), 125 *om.* (*Specimens*), 152 *om.* (A).

Explicit: 156 FINIS.

Paper: White, laid; medium (uncut: 11½ × 9 in.); no vis. wmk.

Type: English (4.6 mm), leaded; footnotes: long primer (3.2 mm).

References: *Life* iii. 106, 107, 488 (Courtney 129, 153); 'Memoirs of Dr. Samuel Johnson', *NQ*, 2nd ser. v (1858), 377–8; *Life* (ed. Napier, 1884) 'Preface'; K. D. Macdonald, *TGSI* 1 (1979), 1–19; ESTC: t084356.

Notes: William Strahan printed 350 copies in December 1777 (L: Add MS 48809, fo. 7), and it was published in July 1778 (*Edinburgh Weekly Mag.*, 22 July 1778, 92–4). There were 182 subscribers (including JB, Gibbon, Langton, Pennant, Percy, and Adam Smith, but not SJ), who took 296 copies, leaving 54 for public sale. See 'Proposals', 77.3SP, above.

Shaw's 'Preface' includes several verbal borrowings from SJ's 'Proposals', and some echoes of SJ's description of Iona from the *Journey*. 'To the advice and encouragement of Dr. Johnson, the friend of letters and humanity, the Public is indebted for these sheets' (p. xxiii). This was also noticed in the Edinburgh *Weekly Mag.* 22 July 1778, 92–4. On pp. 141–5 is 'Mr. Pope's *Messiah translated into Galic Rhime.*' See also Shaw's *Memoirs of Johnson* (1785), 149–51. The Dedication is Shaw's work.[1]

Copies: E² (1. K 119.b; 2. Oss. 204);

USA: CtY, ICN, InU, [Liebert (boards, uncut)], MH (3275.10), NcU, NIC, NRU, [PPM]; *Can*: [CaBViV]; *UK*: ABu, AWn, C, [Es], Eu⁴, Gu², L⁵, O (4° BS. 157), SAN.

---

[1] To Archibald Montgomerie (1726–96*), 11th E., who is mentioned in the book as one 'who has a taste for the [Gaelic] language, as well as an attachment to the people'.

78.7SA/1b   Shaw's Analysis of the Galic Language,   1972
                                facsimile

A Facsimile in the Series 'English Linguistics 1500–1800', ed. R. C. Alston, No. 356, Scolar Press Limited, Menston, England. 1972. ISBN: 85417-874-0
   This reprint is taken from the C copy, above.

78.7SA/2a   Shaw's Analysis of the Galic Language,   1778
                                second edition

[½t] [rule] | AN | ANALYSIS | OF THE | GALIC LANGUAGE. |[rule] [Title] AN | ANALYSIS | OF THE | GALIC LANGUAGE. | By WILLIAM SHAW, A.M. | [rule] | —Forsan et hæc olim meminisse juvabit. | Virg. | [rule] | THE SECOND EDITION. | EDINBURGH: | Printed by W. and T. Ruddiman; | For R. Jamieson, Parliament-fquare. | [short rule] | M,DCC,LXXVIII.

   8°, *a*⁴ b⁴ C–X⁴ Y², ($1 signed), 86 leaves.

   Pp. a1 *i* ½t, *ii* blk, *iii* t., *iv* 'Entered at STATIONERS' HALL, | According to Act of Parliament.', *v* vi–xviii Introduction dh: [double rule] | INTRODUCTION., ht: INTRODUCTION., on C2 *19* 20–171 text dh: [double rule] | AN | ANALYSIS | OF THE | GALIC LANGUAGE. | [rule], rt: AN ANALYSIS OF | THE GALIC LANGUAGE., *172* blk.

   Pagination: [↑] 165; unnumbered i–iv, 19, 28–9, 116–17, 127, 164, 172; blk: 28, 116, 164, 172.

   Press-figures: none.

   Catchwords: 19 *om.* (CHAP. II.), 56 *So*ₐ (~,), 62, 64, 70 *Bha* (*Subjunctive*), 63, 65, 71, *Ro* (*Indicative*), 66, 73 *Ro* (*Subjunctive*), 77 *Bithibh*, [slipt], 87

Perfect. (Perf.), 105 ‚*Of* (6.*Of*), 118 *Dhoirt* (Dhoirt), 126 BOOK (AN | ANALYSIS . . .), 145 [*ul-*] *trâ* (*trà*), 148 [*var* '&'].

Explicit: 171 FINIS.

Paper: White, laid; La. post (uncut: 8¼ × 5¼ in.); wmk.: fleur-de-lys + IV.

Type: Scotch face: small pica (3.5 mm), leaded (2.0 mm).

References: ESTC: t149618.

Notes: No information on the Ruddimans' printing has emerged, but this was presumably published after the London edition of July, perhaps in the autumn of 1778.

Copies: E (HM.109(2));

USA: CSmH (322051, no ½t), CtY, DLC, Hyde ('James Marie Crolly, Newcastle on Tyne 1844'), ICN, ICU, MH, NN, [PPAmP, PPL-R]; *Can*: CaOHM; *UK*: ABu², AWn, BMp, C, DUu, En³, Eu³, JDF (no ½t, 'Henry Davidson' — 'I Stole this Book from Robert D. Thompson, Dingwall'), L (872. 1.22), LVp, MRc, Mu², O² (1. 8° Y.511.BS; 2. Douce S. 797), SAN²; *Aust*: CNL (DNS 6989); *Eir*: Dp.

78.7SA/2b   Shaw's Analysis of the Galic Language,   1787
'third' edition

[½t] AN | ANALYSIS | OF THE | GALIC LANGUAGE.

[Title] AN | ANALYSIS | OF THE | GALIC LANGUAGE. | BY WILLIAM SHAW, A.M. | [rule] | *Forſan et hæc olim meminiſſe juvabit.* | VIRG. | [rule] | THE THIRD EDITION. | [Parallel rule] | *LONDON:* | PRINTED FOR R. JAMESON, NO. 227, STRAND, | NEAR TEMPLE BAR. | [short double rule] | MDCCLXXXVII.

8°, *a*⁴ (± a2) b⁴ C–X⁴ Y², ($1 signed), 86 leaves.

Pp. a1 *i* ½t, *ii* blk, on a2 (cancel) *iii* t., *iv* blk, on a3 *v* vi–xviii Introduction, *19* 20–171 text of *Analysis* &c., *172* blk.

Pagination &c., see prec. 78.7SA/2a, above.

References: ESTC: t162620.

Notes: This is a reissue with cancel t., of the second edn. (78.7SA/2a, prec.)

Copies: Gu (BG51 ——l.11).

78.10EC   Epitaph on Dr Collier   1778

Dr Arthur Collier (1707–77), who had taught classics to Mrs Thrale, and to her daughters Hester (Queeney) and Sophia, died on 23 May 1777 (*Gents. Mag.* xlvii (May 1777), 248). On 15 October 1778 SJ wrote to HLT: 'As to Dr Collier's Epitaph, Nollikens has had it so long, that I have forgotten how long. You never had it.' Chapman supposed that Mrs Thrale's not having seen it pre-cluded it being an epitaph on Collier himself, and conjectured it was one composed by Collier for his dog Pompey, on whom HLT had sometime composed verses.[1] But this is more reasonably interpreted by Redford as an epitaph on Collier composed by SJ. SJ was acquainted with Collier, and though there was little affinity between them, that need not have precluded an epitaph.[2] The mention of Nollekens however, supposes a lapidary inscription.

References: Letters 583 (Hyde, iii. 126–8); Clifford, *Mrs Piozzi* (1968), 25–7, 36, 168 & refs.

Notes: No inscription or text has yet been traced.

---

[1] Clifford calls her 'Epistle from Pompey', dated 3 Sept. 1762 (MRu: MS Rylands 647.3), an 'elegy' which implied the demise of the dog at a much earlier date, unless, as is common, Collier owned several dogs in succession and gave all the same name. All this, however, gives little support to the proposal that SJ composed an epitaph on any of them, a suggestion which strikes me as wholly unlikely in view of SJ's known seriousness about such memorials.

[2] Collier's friendship with James (Hermes) Harris, the pseudo-phililogist would have counted little in his favour with SJ, but HLT's strong loyalty to Collier probably prevented overt hostilities. The Misses Collier who gained SJ's assistance in securing their inheritance were no relation of Dr Collier who was the son of Dr Arthur, metaphysician and rival of Bp. Berkeley. For the wronged ladies, see H.W. Liebert, *Dr. Johnson and the Misses Collier* (1949), and *Gleanings* ix (1939), 25 ff., 75, 228.

78ME/1   More's Sir Eldred, second edition   1778

[½t] Sɪʀ ELDRED ᴏꜰ ᴛʜᴇ BOWER: | A | LEGENDARY TALE. | IN TWO PARTS.

[Title] Sɪʀ ELDRED ᴏꜰ ᴛʜᴇ BOWER, | AND THE | BLEEDING ROCK: | TWO LEGENDARY TALES. | By Miss HANNAH MORE. | [rule] | The Sᴇᴄᴏɴᴅ Eᴅɪᴛɪᴏɴ, corrected. | [rule] | Of them who, wrapt in Earth ſo cold, | No more the ſmiling day ſhall view, | Shou'd many a tender tale be told, | For many a tender thought is due. | Lᴀɴɢʜᴏʀɴᴇ. | [medium swelled rule] | Pʀɪɴᴛᴇᴅ ꜰᴏʀ T. CADELL, ɪɴ ᴛʜᴇ Sᴛʀᴀɴᴅ. | MDCCLXXVIII.

8°, π1 *A*² B–G⁴ *H*1, ($2 signed), 28 leaves.

Pp. π1 ½t, π1ᵛ blk, A1 t., A1ᵛ blk, A2–2ᵛ Dedication: TO | DAVID GARRICK, Bʀɪsᴛᴏʟ. ('Bʀɪsᴛᴏʟ, Dec. 14, 1775. HANNAH MORE.'), on B1 *1* 2–35 text (Part I. 1–16, Part II. 17–35) dh: [bevelled parallel rule] | Sɪʀ ELDRED ᴏꜰ ᴛʜᴇ BOWER: | A | LEGENDARY TALE. | [medium swelled rule], ht: SIR ELDRED OF THE BOWER., *36* blk, *37* ½t: THE | BLEEDING ROCK, | A | LEGENDARY TALE. | ——The annual wound allur'd | The Syrian damſels to lament his fate, | In amorous ditties all a ſummer's day; | While ſmooth Adonis from his native Rock | Ran purple to the ſea, ſuppos'd with blood | of Thammuz yearly wounded. Mɪʟᴛᴏɴ., *38* blk, *39* 40–49 text dh: [bevelled parallel rule] | THE | BLEEDING ROCK, | A | LEGENDARY TALE. | [medium swelled rule], ht: THE BLEEDING ROCK., *50* advts: 'BOOKS printed for T. CADELL, in the Sᴛʀᴀɴᴅ.'

Pagination: [↑] 17; *Press-figures*: none; *Catchwords*: no errors.

Explicit: 35 THE END., 49 THE END.

Paper: White, laid; Demy (8¾ × 5⅝ in.), or La. post (8¼ × 5¼ in.); no vis. wmk.

Type: Dedication: english (4.7 mm), text: pica (4.0 mm), leaded (3.7 mm), notes: bourgeois (3.0 mm).

References: W. Roberts, *Memoirs of Hannah More* (1834), i. 64; Liebert, in *New Light on Johnson*, ed. Hilles (1959), 233–45; *Poems²* 439–41; ESTC: t048322.

Notes: It is likely that the prelims and final leaf formed a ½-sheet, though the copies examined are bound so as to conceal the distribution of the leaves. It is probable that they were printed as $4 so that $1 could be folded back into last place as *H*1.

Liebert showed that this edn. incorporated textual revisions and a new stanza by SJ from the first edn. 4°, of 1776 [q.v., below]. His findings were vindicated by the emergence of a portion of the printed text (said to be a proof) of the 1776 edn. with SJ's autograph revisions of the stanza 'My scorn has oft the dart repel'd . . .'[1] The revised versions are printed in Liebert's note and in *Poems²*.

Copies: O² (**1.** G.P. 1294 (7); **2.** Vet. A5 e. 1635(2), 'Miss Stewart, Grandtully'); *USA*: CSmH, CtY, [Liebert], NjP, PPL; *UK*: C, L.

First Edition 1776

Sɪʀ ELDRED ᴏꜰ ᴛʜᴇ BOWER, | AND THE | BLEEDING ROCK: | TWO LEGENDARY TALES. | [med. swelled rule] | Bʏ Mɪss HANNAH MORE. | [med. swelled rule] | Of them who, wrapt in Earth ſo cold, | No more the ſmiling day ſhall view, | Shou'd many a tender tale be told, | for many a tender thought is due. Lᴀɴɢʜᴏʀɴᴇ. | [med. swelled rule] | LONDON: | PRINTED FOR T. CADEL, IN THE STRAND. | MDCCLXXVI.

4°, *A*² B–N² O1, ($1 signed), 27 leaves.

Pp. A1 *i* t., *ii* blk, *iii*–iv Dedication ('To David Garrick, Esq. Hannah More, Bristol, Dec. 14th. 1775.'), on B1 *1* 2–35 text Sir Eldred, *36* blk, *37* ½t: The Bleeding Rock: a legendary Tale. [6 lines. Milton], *38* blk, *39* 40–9 text Bleeding Rock, *50* advts.

Pagination: no errors; *Press-figures*: none.

Catchwords: iii I ſhall (I may), 16 Sɪʀ (PART II. | ONCE), 28 Yet͇ (~,).

Explicit: 35, 49 THE END.

Paper: White, laid; La. post (10½ × 8¼ in.), no vis. wmk.

Type: Great primer (5.5 mm), notes: pica (4.0 mm).

References: ESTC: t048321.

Notes: on p. 28, l. 1 the letters 'LDRED' are hand-stamped after 'Sir E'.

There was a Dublin reprint of this first edn., also dated 1776 (ESTC: t062588), of which copies are: *USA*: CSmH, [Liebert = ? CtY], NIC; *UK*: C, L; *Eir*: Dp.

Langhorne reviewed the work in *Monthly Rev.* liv (1776), 89-99.

Copies: O (2805 d. 2(5)); *UK*: C, Lu, MRu, Osj.

¹ This appears to be the stanza (printed as the 49th), mentioned in Hannah More's letter of Jan. 1776, cited by Liebert, from Roberts's *Memoirs* (1834), i. 64; Sotheby &c., 19 July 1993, 173, with other documents descending from Hannah More's sister.

78ME/2   More's Sir Eldred   [1800]

Sir Eldred of the Bower; a legendary tale, in two parts, by Hannah More. And Edwin and Emma, by Mr. Mallet. Manchester: Printed and sold by G. Bancks; sold also by Lee and Hurst. n.d.

12°, Pp. 24. Not examined.
References: ESTC: t143010.
Notes: Though unexamined, this edn. is likely to reprint the text of the second edn. as revised by SJ, rather than that of the first of 1776 (above).
Copies: [L (012611. de. 1(3)].

79.3BC/1   Baretti's Carmen Seculare   [1778]

[medium swelled rule] | THE | INTRODUCTION | TO THE | CARMEN SECULARE. | [medium swelled rule]

8°, A⁸ (A8 blk), ($2,3 signed), 8 leaves.

Pp. A1 *1* t., *2* blk, *3* 4–14 text dh: [double rule] | JOSEPH BARETTI | TO THE | ENGLISH READER., *15–16* (A8) blk leaf.

Pagination: no errors; *Press-figures*: none; *Catchwords*: no errors.
Explicit: 14 [tp.].
Paper: White, laid; La. post (uncut: 8¼ × 5¼ in.); no vis. wmk.
Type: Pica (3.6 mm), leaded (1.2 mm).
References: *Life* iii. 373; Collison-Morley (1909), 321–3; Piccioni, *Bibliografica Analitica* 27 (no. 31); *Poems²* 218–19; Brownell, *Johnson's Attitude to the Arts* (1989), 33; ESTC: t083923.
Notes: G.B. Hill, on SJ's *Letters* 592 (to HLT, 21 Nov. 78; Hyde iii. 144), reported Baretti as writing:

The musical scheme was the *Carmen Seculare*, that brought £150 in three nights, and three times as much to Philidor, whom I got to set it to music. It would have benefited us both, if Philidor had not proved a scoundrel, greatly more than those sums.¹

Revd William Tasker was also involved with this production.² On p. 13 is a note: 'The Translation, together with the original, will be distributed at the place of performance, which will be at Free-Masons-Hall, the last Friday of February next' [= 26 Feb. 1779]. The performance, which SJ attended, was noticed in *Public Advertiser* 3 Mar., *Gen. Advertiser*, and *Morning Chron.* 6 Mar. A parody appeared in *General Evening Post*, 22 Apr. 1779, which was announced, in *London Evening Post*, 27 Apr. 1779, and again in the *Morning*

Post 25 May 1779, as a separate publication (McGuffie, *British Press* (1976), 207, and 232–3). Baretti's version was reprinted in his *Opere* (Laterza, 1933), no. 13, pp. 305–15 (Piccioni). SJ's English version of the 'Epilogue' is pp. 13–14.

Copies: O³ (1. GP 1443(2) + final A8 (blk); **2.** GP 1884(4); **3.** GP 2784(8)); *USA*: CSmH (124558), Hyde (sewn), NjP; *UK*: [E], L (11630. c.12 (8)), [Lu].

---

¹ Hill was quoting from Baretti's annotated copy of H.L. Piozzi's edn. of SJ's *Letters* (1788), now L (see 88.3L/1, below). The first performance was reported in *Public Advertiser*, 3 March 1779. 'Philidor' was the pseudonym of François André Danican (1726–95*), chess-player and composer. The score for this work was published in Paris [1779] in 237 pp. as *Carmen Seculare; poëme seculaire*, and reprinted in the 1790s and again in 1805. See further in Grove's *Dictionary of Music, &c.*, s.n. 'Baretti', where I. Fenlon gives *Katarinæ Aug. Piæ Felici Ottomannicæ Tauricæ Musagetæ Q. Horatii Flacci Carmen sæculare lyricis concentibus restitutum A.D. Philidor D.D.D.*, London, 1778, as the earliest appearance, with several later versions.
² *Life* iii. 373–4, and *Boswell, Laird of Auchinleck*, 56–7 (s.d. '16 March 1779').

79.3BC/2   Baretti's Carmen Seculare   [1779]

THE | CARMEN SECULARE | OF | *HORACE.* | [*Price One Shilling.*]
4°, *A*² B–G², ($1 signed), 14 leaves.
Pp. A1 *1* t., *2* blk, *3* 4–10 text, dh: JOSEPH BARETTI | TO THE | ENGLISH READER., ht: INTRODUCTION., on C2 *1* ½t: CARMEN SECULARE, | SIVE | POLYMETRUM SATURNIUM | IN LUDOS SECULARES., 2/2 – 9/9 text [Latin & English *en face*], ht: CARMEN SECULARE. | THE SECULAR POEM., *10* blk.
Pagination: from C2ᵛ ff [↑]; *Press-figures*: none.
Catchwords: 6 [*Uterque* (ₐ~), 6 [*Both* (ₐ~).
Explicit: C1ᵛ (10) [tp.], 8 FINIS. 9 THE END.
Paper: White, laid; La. post (uncut: 10½ × 8¼ in.); no vis. wmk.
Type: Introd. pica (3.7 mm), leaded (2.0 mm).
References: Collison-Morley (1909), 321–3; Piccioni, *Bibliografica Analitica* (1942), 27 (no. 31); *Poems*² 218–19; Brownell *Johnson's Attitude to the Arts* (1989) 33; ESTC: n026946.
Notes: SJ's translation of the 'Epilogue' on pp. 9–9. Baretti's Address as in 79.3BC/1, omitting the footnote p. 13 (cited above). The text was reprinted in *European Mag.* xi (June 1787), 451, whence it was adopted by Isaac Reed in *Works* (Supp.), xiv, 546.
Copies: O (GP. 1727 (19));
USA: CSmH (84177; 'Ingelby', annot. with names of performers¹), CtY, Hyde,² [Liebert].

---

¹ Opposite SJ's verses on pp. 9–9 is written: 'Manzoletto'.
² With a MS note on the t.: 'With Notes & translation in English by Joseph Baretti — author of the Italian & Spanish Dictionaries, Grammar &c. — Composed with the view of being Sung to Music written by the Celebrated *Phillidor* the Chess Player—'.

79.3BC/3   Baretti's Carmen Seculare   [1788]

THE | CARMEN SECULARE | OF | *HORACE.* | Set to Muſic by Mr.
PHILIDOR.

4°, A–B⁴ C², ($2 (–C2) signed), 10 leaves.

Pp. A1 *i* t., *ii* Persons, iii–v Introduction, *6–7* 8–19 text [Latin & English *en
face*], *20* blk.

Pagination: no errors; *Press-figures*: none; *Catchwords*: not recorded.

Explicit: not recorded.

Paper: White, laid; Small post (uncut: 9½ × 7⅝ in.).

Type: not recorded.

References: *Poems²* 218–19.

Notes: This version was performed at the Installation of the Knights of the
Bath (*Gents. Mag.* lviii (Apr. 1788), 459, s.d. '19 May'), corroborated on p. v of
the 'Introduction'. The text of SJ's 'Epilogue' varies from the 1779 versions,
reading 'England‚' for 'England,' (l. 3). A note at p. 19 offering copies of the
score, suggests the publishers were 'Longman and Broderip, in Cheapside and
the Haymarket.'

Copies: *USA*: Hyde, [Liebert (brown wraps, trimmed) = CtY].

79.4LP/1.1   [Lives of the Poets],   1779
                        Works of the English Poets

THE | WORKS | OF THE | ENGLISH POETS. | WITH | PREFACES, |
BIOGRAPHICAL AND CRITICAL, | BY SAMUEL JOHNSON. |
[medium swelled rule] | VOLUME THE FIRST [– FIFTY-EIGHTH]. |
[medium swelled rule] | LONDON: | PRINTED BY H. HUGHS; | FOR C.
BATHURST, J. BUCKLAND, W. STRAHAN, J. RIVING- | TON AND
SONS, T. DAVIES, T. PAYNE, L. DAVIS, W. OWEN, | B. WHITE, S.
CROWDER, T. CASLON, T. LONGMAN, | B. LAW, E. AND C.
DILLY, J. DODSLEY, H. BALDWIN, | J. WILKIE, J. ROBSON, J.
JOHNSON, T. LOWNDES, | T. BECKET, G. ROBINSON, T.
CADELL, W. DAVIS, | J. NICHOLS, F. NEWBERY, T. EVANS, J. RID-
| LEY, R. BALDWIN, G. NICOL, LEIGH AND | SOTHEBY, J. BEW,
N. CONANT, | J. MURRAY, W. FOX, J. BOWEN. | M DCC LXXIX.

    58 vols, 8°

Contents: I–II Cowley, II–V Milton, VI–VIII Butler, VIII Waller, IX Denham
& Sprat, X Rochester, Roscommon, & Yalden, XI Otway, Duke, & Dorset, XII
Halifax, Stepney, & Walsh, XIII–XVI Dryden, XVII–XIX Dryden's *Virgil*, XX
Garth & King, XXI J. Philips, Smith & Pomfret, XXII Hughes, XXIII
Addison, XXIV Blackmore, XXV Sheffield & Lansdowne [= Granville], XXVI
Rowe & Tickell, XXVII–XXVIII Rowe's *Lucan*, XXIX Congreve & Fenton,
XXX–XXXI Prior, XXXII–XXXIV Pope, XXXV–XXXVI Pope's Homer

(*Iliad*), XXXVII–XXXVIII Pope's Homer (*Odyssey*), XXXIX–XL Swift,
XLI–XLII Gay, XLIII Broome & Pitt, XLIV Parnell & A. Philips, XLV
Savage, XLVI Watts, XLVII Somervile, XLVIII Thomson, Hammond, &
Collins, L–LII Young, LIII Dyer & Mallet, LIV Shenstone, LV Akenside,
LVI Lyttelton, West, & Gray, LVII–LVIII *Index* (dated '1781') see below.

Printing: The printing was shared among ten printers

H. Baldwin	XXIII, XXVI–XXVIII, XXXVII–XXXVIII, L–LII	9
G. Bigg	XLVII–XLIX	3
J.D. Cornish	XVII–XVIII	2
E. Cox	IX–XII, XXV, XXIX	6
H. Goldney	XXII, XLV	2
R. Hett	XIII–XVI, XLIII	5
H. Hughs	I–VIII, XXI, XXXV–XXXVI, XLVI	12
J. Nichols	XX, XXIV, XXX–XXXI, XXXIX–XLII, LVII–LVIII	10
J. Rivington	XIX, XLIV, LIII–LVI	6
W. & A. Strahan	XXXII–XXXIV	3
		58

Paper: White, laid; Foolscap (uncut: 6¾ × 4½ in.); wmk.: Pro Patria 'G R' crowned.

Type: Pica (4.0 mm), leaded; smaller text in long primer (3.4 mm).

Plates: The Binder's Directions in *Prefaces* I, *c1 (79.4LP/1.2, below), show that 28 engraved portraits were prefixed to the volumes of the following:

Cowley (I), Milton (III), Butler (VI), Waller (VIII), Denham (IX), Otway (XI), Dryden (XIII), Garth (XX), J. Philips (XXI), Hughes (XXII), Addison (XXIII), Blackmore (XXIV), Buckingham (XXV), Rowe (XXVI), Congreve (XXIX), Prior (XXX), Pope (XXXII), Swift (XXXIX), Gay (XLI), Broome (XLIII), Parnell (XLIV), Watts (XLVI), Thomson (XLVIII), Young (L), Dyer (LIII), Shenstone (LIV), Akenside (LV), Lyttelton (LVI).

References: Courtney 130–41; CH 156–8; ESTC: t092171.

Notes: Some minor variations in imprints e.g. 'F. NEWBERY,' in XII, and in the omission of 'H. BALDWIN,' from LVI–LVII (*Index*, 1781) after his death.

Composition: John Bell's collection of *The Poets of Great Britain*, 109 vols. Edinburgh: At the Apollo Press, 1776–82, was the provocation for this collection, which was intended to preserve the London trade's notion of copyright, as Dilly's letter to JB of 26 Sept. 1777 shows (*Life* iii. 110–11), but Dilly's letter is partisan in denigrating the quality of the Martins' printing.[1]

John Bell's letter of defence against an attack by 'Benevolus' in the *London Evening Post*, 1 April 1779 (the day after the publication of the London *Works*), stated that the 42 London booksellers had divided their property into shares at £50 each (*London Evening Post*, 7 April 1779). These 42 shareholders (36 named in the imprint + 6 printers whose names are distributed as noticed above), produced a capital of £2,100. The eventual edn. of 1,500 copies, was retailed at £7. 10s. per set. According to SJ's letter of 25 Oct. 1779 to HLT (637; Hyde iii. 198–99), referring to Bowen's four shares, each share was worth 15 copies, so that 42 shares accounted for 630 copies. This is so irregular that there must have been more than 42 shares, more likely 100 variously distributed among the 42 names. 100 shares at £50 implies a capital of £5,000 which is much in excess of reasonable production costs. Strahan printed 1,500 copies of vols. XXXII–XXXIV ('Pope's Poems') in August 1778 for £102. 15s. (L: Add. MS 48809, fo. 25). If this is reckoned at £34. 5s. per volume, then the whole series of 58 should have cost in the region of £2,020. 15s. To this may be added the first four vols. of SJ's 'Prefaces', a further £137, producing some £2,157. 15s. for which a subscribed capital of £5,000 is extravagant. A capital subscription of 42 x £50 = £2100 is more reasonable. There is further evidence for an initial share holding of 100. John Nichols's Sharebook (MS: C), records 'Johnson's Lives of the Poets 5/100ths. produces 75 in 1500', so that a 100th must have produced 15 copies as discount to the shareholder, which agrees with SJ's letter of 25 Oct. 1779 (*Letters* 637, Hyde iii. 198–9). Furthermore George Robinson paid John Murray £31 on 29 October 1778 for a 100th share in the 'First edition of the Lives of the Poets'.[2] All these references to 100ths strongly imply that the original shareholding was indeed 100, and in this case the subscription of £50 by 42 shareholders producing £2100, means that a 100th share was initially valued at £21, and that each 100th share represented 15 copies from the edn. of 1,500.[3]

The Collection was labelled 'Johnson's Poets' on the spines of bound sets, following the printed paper spine labels of the original publications in blue paper wrappers.[4] Though SJ objected,[5] it is clear that his name was an important factor in the establishment of copyright and in the publicity.[6] John Nichols asserted SJ's close involvement with the collection.[7]

Copies: O (2804 f. 96–163).[8]

---

[1] See Bonnell, *MP* lxxxv (1987–8), 128–52. I am greatly indebted to Professor Bonnell for his advice on this aspect of the genesis of SJ's Collection, and for allowing me to read his dissertation (Ph.D. University of Chicago, 1983). Dilly's letter to JB is CtY (MS Boswell, C 1075).

[2] MS: CaOHM ('Rippey'); I am indebted to Mr Rippey, the then owner, for information about this document.

[3] See also p. 1356, below.

[4] H.W. Liebert owned vols. XIII–XVI, 'Dryden', in this condition.

[5] 'It is great impudence to put Johnsons Poets on the back of books which Johnson neither recommended nor revised. He recommended only Blackmore on the Creation and Watts. How then are they Johnson's? This is indecent.' (*Life* iv. 35 n., *MS Handlist* 157, exhibited at Arts Council (Yung, *SJ, 1709–1784*, 1984), item 97, MS: MH; and *Letters* 670; Hyde iii. 226–7).

[6] His 'Prefaces' were inalienable, and so were intended to defend the texts of the Poets. Compare the negotiations involved with Tonson's claim for Shakespearian copyright, 45.4SP/1, above.

[7] Note by JN on p. 22 of article by 'Anti-Stiletto' in *Gents. Mag.* lvi (Jan. 1786), 17–23.

[8] No list has been kept of copies of this collection which is to be found in most libraries. Samuel Rogers's set of '55 volumes —— with all faults' was sold as lot 1868 at his sale by Puttick & Simpson, 10 March 1868.

79.4LP/1.2 [Lives of the Poets], Prefaces, 1779
first instalment (Vols I–IV)

PREFACES, | BIOGRAPHICAL | AND | CRITICAL, | TO THE |
WORKS | OF THE | ENGLISH POETS. | BY SAMUEL JOHNSON. |
[medium swelled rule] | VOLUME THE FIRST [–FOURTH]. | [medium
swelled rule] | LONDON: | PRINTED BY J. NICHOLS; | FOR C.
BATHURST, J. BUCKLAND, W. STRAHAN, J. RIVING- | TON AND
SONS, T. DAVIES, T. PAYNE, L. DAVIS, W. OWEN, | B. WHITE, S.
CROWDER, T. CASLON, T. LONGMAN, | B. LAW, E. AND C.
DILLY, J. DODSLEY, H. BALDWIN, | J. WILKIE, J. ROBSON, J.
JOHNSON, T. LOWNDES, | T. BECKET, G. ROBINSON, T.
CADELL, W. DAVIS, | J. NICHOLS, F. NEWBERY, T. EVANS, J.
RID- | LEY, R. BALDWIN, G. NICOL, LEIGH AND | SOTHEBY, J.
BEW, N. CONANT, | J. MURRAY, W. FOX, J. BOWEN. | M DCC
LXXIX.
  4 vols., 8°

  I. a² *b² *c² B–L⁸ M⁴ b–i⁸, ($4 (–M3,4) signed), 154 leaves.
  Pp. on a1 *i* General t., *ii* blk, *iii* ½t: PREFACES | TO | COWLEY | AND
| WALLER., *iv* blk, on *b1 v–vii ADVERTISEMENT. ('March 15, 1779.'),
viii blk, on *c1 ix–x *Directions to the Binder.*, xi Errata, *xii* blk, on B1 text 1–165
Cowley dh: [double rule] | COWLEY., ht: COWLEY., *166* blk, *167–68* (M4)
blk, on b1 text 1–128 Waller dh: [double rule] | WALLER., ht: WALLER.
  Pagination: [↑] v–vii, ix–x, B1: 1, b1: 1.
  Press-figures: *b1ᵛ(vi)–4, B1ᵛ(2)–3, B6ᵛ(12)–4, C1ᵛ(18)–5, D4ᵛ(40)–4,
D7ᵛ(46)–7, E7ᵛ(62)–1, E8ᵛ(64)–7, F6(75)–5, F6ᵛ(76)–3, G2ᵛ(84)–3,
G7ᵛ(94)–5, H1ᵛ(98)–5, H7(109)–1, I6(123)–1, I7(125)–2, K3ᵛ(134)–1,
K7(141)–2, L3ᵛ(150)–4, L5(153)–2; b2ᵛ(4)–5, b3ᵛ(6)–5, c3ᵛ(22)–5, c7(29)–2,
d3ᵛ(38)–3, d5(41)–1, e3ᵛ(54)–6, e8ᵛ(64)–3, f4ᵛ(72)–3, f7ᵛ(78)–1, g3ᵛ(86)–3,
g4ᵛ(88)–6, h1ᵛ(98)–3, i1ᵛ(114)–7, i4ᵛ(120)–5.
  Catchwords: *Cowley*: 4 It (This); *Waller*: 64 In (To).

  II. a² b–p⁸, ²b–c⁸ ²d⁴, ($4 (–²d3,4) signed; on ²bc1 'VOL. VI.'), 134 leaves.
  Pp. *i* t., *ii* blk, *iii* ½t: PREFACES | TO | MILTON | AND | BUTLER.,
iv blk, on b1 1–223 text Milton dh: [double rule] | MILTON., ht: MILTON.,
224 blk, on ²b1 1–39 text Butler dh: [double rule] | BUTLER., ht: BUTLER.,
40 blk.
  Pagination: [↑] pp. b1: 1, ²b1: 1.
  Press-figures: b5(9)–2, b8ᵛ(16)–7, c3ᵛ(22)–1, d2ᵛ(36)–7, e4ᵛ(56)–3, f1ᵛ(66)–4,
f8ᵛ(80)–1, g3ᵛ(86)–6, g8ᵛ(96)–3, h3ᵛ(102)–6, h5(105)–2, i1ᵛ(114)–5,
i2ᵛ(116)–3, k8(143)–1, l5(153)–1, m2ᵛ(164)–6, m3ᵛ(166)–7, n2ᵛ(180)–7,
o5ᵛ(202)–5, o6ᵛ(204)–5, p7(221)–2, p7ᵛ(222)–7; ²b2ᵛ(4)–3, ²b6(11)–5,
²c6ᵛ(28)–4, ²c7ᵛ(30)–3, ²d1ᵛ(34)–4.

Catchwords: *Butler*. 16 on (of).

III. a² b–e⁸ f⁸ (± f8) g–z⁸ (z8 blk), ($4 (+ 'f8') signed), 178 leaves.

Pp. *i* t., *ii* blk, *iii* ½t: PREFACE | TO | DRYDEN., *iv* blk, on b1 1–349 text Dryden dh: [double rule] | DRYDEN., ht: DRYDEN., *350* blk, *351–2* (z8) blk.

Pagination: [↑] p. 1; 303 dropping final 3.

Press-figures: b2ᵛ(4)–7, b6(11)–1, c1ᵛ(18)–7, c2ᵛ(20)–2, d1ᵛ(34)–4, d6ᵛ(44)–1, e2ᵛ(52)–4, e3ᵛ(54)–2, f5ᵛ(74)–1, g4ᵛ(88)–2, g6(91)–1, h8ᵛ(112)–2, i5(121)–1, k6(139)–4, k6ᵛ(140)–7, l1ᵛ(146)–7, m5(169)–1, m5ᵛ(170)–4, n3ᵛ(182)–6, n6ᵛ(188)–4, o2ᵛ(196)–2, o5ᵛ(202)–5, p7ᵛ(222)–3, q1ᵛ(226)–4, q7(237)–3, r3ᵛ(246)–1, r6ᵛ(252)–4, s7ᵛ(270)–1, s8ᵛ(272)–3, t1ᵛ(274)–4, u4ᵛ(296)–2, u8(303)–5, x4ᵛ(312)–4, x7ᵛ(318)–1, y5ᵛ(330)–1, z6(347)–1, z6ᵛ(348)–5.

Catchwords: 224 'Till (ᴧTill), 336 [ap-] peal; (∼:).

Notes: *Rothschild* 1261 preserves the *cancellandum* of f8, as do the proofs (L).

IV. a² b–c⁸ (Denham), b⁸ (Sprat), b⁸ c⁶ (Roscommon), b–c⁸ (Rochester & Yalden), b⁸ (Otway & Duke), b–c⁸ d² (d2 blk) (Dorset, Halifax, Stepney, & Walsh), b⁸ (b8 blk) (Garth), b⁶ (King), b–c⁸ d⁶ (d6 blk) (J. Philips), b–e⁸ (Smith), b² (Pomfret), b⁸ (b8 blk) (Hughes), ($4 signed), 160 leaves.

Pp. *i* t., *ii* blk, *iii* ½t: PREFACES | TO| DENHAM, SPRAT, ROSCOMMON, | ROCHESTER, YALDEN, OTWAY, | DUKE, DORSET, HALIFAX, | STEPNEY, WALSH, GARTH, | KING, J. PHILIPS, SMITH, | POMFRET, HUGHES., *iv* blk, on b1 texts 1–31 Denham dh: [double rule] | DENHAM., ht: DENHAM., *32* blk, on b1 1–15 Sprat, *16* blk, on b1 1–27 Roscommon, *28* blk, on b1 1–20 Rochester, on c3 1–12 Yalden, on b1 1–12 Otway, on b7 1–4 Duke, on b1 1–9 Dorset, *10* blk, on b6 1–12 Halifax, on c4 1–6 Stepney, on c7 1–5 Walsh, *6* blk, d2 blk leaf, on b1 1–13 Garth, *14* blk, b8 blk leaf, on b1 1–11 King *12* blk, on b1 1–42 J. Philips, on b1 1–64 Smith, on b1 1–4 Pomfret, on b1 1–13 Hughes, *14* blk, b8 blk.

Dropheads: all are standardized as: [double rule] | NAME., and all htt are as NAME.

Pagination: [↑] pp. 1 of Denham, Sprat, Roscommon, Rochester, Yalden, Otway, Duke, Dorset, Garth, King, J. Philips, Smith, Pomfret, & Hughes; (↑) pp 1 of Halifax, Stepney, & Walsh.

Press-figures: (Denham) b6(11)–2, b7(13)–3, c6ᵛ(28)–4, c7ᵛ(30)–2; (Sprat) b3ᵛ(6)–2, b7(13)–7, (Roscommon) b5ᵛ(10)–4, b8ᵛ(16)–5, c1ᵛ(18)–2, c5(25)–7, (Rochester & Yalden) b3ᵛ(6)–4, c3ᵛ(2)–1, c7(9)–4, (Otway & Duke) b7(1)–1, (Dorset, Halifax, Stepney, & Walsh) b2ᵛ(4)–2, b3ᵛ(6)–3, c2ᵛ(10)–3, (Garth) b3ᵛ(6)–7, b5(9)–2, (King) b2ᵛ(4)–2, b4(7)–5, (J. Philips) b6(11)–5, b6ᵛ(12)–3, c5ᵛ(26)–2, d1ᵛ(34)–6 [*see Note below*], (Smith) b3ᵛ(6)–7, b4ᵛ(8)–4, c5ᵛ(26)–3, c8ᵛ(32)–2, d2ᵛ(36)–2, d7ᵛ(46)–7, e2ᵛ(52)–7, e7ᵛ(62)–6, (Pomfret) *no figures*, (Hughes) b5(9)–1.

Catchwords: *Denham*: 15 ‸Thofe ("∼").

Note: The construction of this vol. from several short 'Lives' allowed the printer to combine some in single sheets. Roscommon c^8 lacks the innermost fold which formed d^2 of Walsh (of which the second leaf is a blank), King b^6 was a whole sheet of which the innermost fold formed Pomfret b^2. Similarly the 'Advertisement' in vol. 1 signed *b^2 was the innermost fold of J. Philips d^8, an arrangement made at SJ's own suggestion.[1] The press-figures in sig. d of J. Philips therefore include I. *b1^v(vi)–4 as recording the working of the outer forme (d4^v) with the inner recorded in Philips d1^v(34)–6.

A fragment of MS notes for 'J. Philips' is L (*MS Index* JoS 221).

Paper: White, laid; Foolscap (uncut: 6¾ x 4¼ in.); wmk.: Crown + 'G R'.

Type: Pica (4.0 mm), leaded. Flowers often used a tpp. I. vii, Cowley 165, Waller 120, 128; II. Milton 149, 150, 223, Butler 39; III. Dryden 168, 316, 349; IV. Sprat 15, Roscommon 27, Rochester 20, Yalden 12, Otway 12, Duke 4, Dorset 9, Halifax 12, Stepney 6, Walsh 5, Garth 13, King 11, Philips 18, 42, Smith 62, 64, Pomfret 4. Swelled rule at Denham 11; thick head-rules at Walsh 1, King 1, Smith 1, and Hughes 1.

References: Courtney 140–41; CH 155–58; *Rothschild* 1252.

Notes: For a chronology of composition, see W. McCarthy, *PQ* lx (1981), 53–67.[2] JB acquired the MSS (*JB: Extremes*, 19 May 1778, p. 350). Only those of Rowe (Hyde), and Pope (NPM) are extant. Most of the proofs of the 'Prefaces' are Lv.[3] Thomas Percy noted on Boswell's *Life* (1791), ii. 344 [= 345] (*Life* iv. 35): 'In March 1781 Johnson finished his Lives of y^e Poets for 200 ll. & the Booksell^{rs} after^{wds} gave him 100 ll. more' (O: MS Percy d. 11, fo. 14^v). The printing began with 'Cowley' in Dec. 1777,[4] and the four volumes were presented to George III by 10 March 1779 (*Letters* 606, Hyde, iii. 155–6), though the whole edn. was at that time 'not quite printed'. These four vols. were announced as published in *Lond. Chron.*, 31 March 1779.[5] SJ did not record publication until 2 April (*Diaries* 294). A copy of these four vols. annotated by Isaac Reed, was lot 224 at Evans, 19 Apr. 1819. A brief MS note refers to Nichols's share:

October 17. 1778

Two Months after date I promise to pay Mr Nichols or Bearer Seventy two Pounds value rec^d. in printing Johnson's Poets.

£72 – 0 – 0 Tho: Cadell.[6]

The 'Prefaces' were not sold separately from the *Works of the English Poets* (79.4LP/1.1, above), so that an invoice from Robert Faulder to Bell & Bradfute, of Edinburgh, 29 April 1780, for '6 Johnson's Prefaces' which is marked 'not to be had', need not mean that the instalment was sold out, but merely that these 4 vols. could not be obtained as a separate item (cf. *Lives* (1905), ed. G.B. Hill, I. xxvi, n.).

For further details and copies, see below under the second instalment of 1781 (79.4LP/4).

¹ 1 March 1779, *Letters* 603 (Hyde iii. 152), to Nichols; *Life* iv. 36

² Other details may be found canvassed in Hilles, *PQ* xlviii (1969), 226–33, and Battersby, *SB* xxiii (1970), 179–83.

³ The extant proofs are listed in Fleeman, *Library*, 5th ser. xvii (1962), 213–30, and reviewed by Middendorf, in *Eighteenth Century Studies*, ed. W. H. Bond (1970), 89–106. A microfilm of the Lv proofs is at O: (Films 291). They, like the MSS, were acquired by JB through the agency of Frank Barber, but the proofs escaped in the Boswell sale, 1823. The *Rothschild* 1261, vol. 3 ('Dryden') is not a proof but an early (retaining the *cancellandum* of f8) annotated copy of that vol. (*Booklist* 171).

⁴ Nichols in *Gents. Mag.* lv (Jan. 1785), 9, and advertisements in *Lond. Chron.* 17–20, 20–22 Oct. 1778.

⁵ Other notices were in the *Gazetteer*, 18 Mar.; *Lond. Chron.*, 20 Mar.; *Gazetteer*, 2 Apr.; *Morning Chron.*, 2 Apr.; *Lond. Chron.* 6 Apr.; and *Lond. Evening Post*, 6 Apr.

⁶ This document was owned in 1960 by F.S. Bradburn, Esq; of Blundellsands, Lancs., who kindly communicated its details to me. It appears to refer to the first instalment (4 vols.) of the 'Prefaces' (79.4LP/1.2 (1779)), above, at £18 per volume.

79.4LP/2a(i)   Lives of the Poets, first instalment,   1779
first Dublin edition, first issue, first state

THE | LIVES | OF THE | ENGLISH POETS; | AND A | CRITICISM | ON THEIR | WORKS. | [medium swelled rule] | BY SAMUEL JOHNSON. | [medium swelled rule] | DUBLIN: | Printed for Meſſrs. WHITESTONE, WILLIAMS, COLLES, WILSON, | LYNCH, JENKIN, WALKER, BURNET, HALLHEAD, | FLIN, EXSHAW, BEATTY, and WHITE. | [short swelled rule] | M,DCC,LXXIX.

8°, *A*² B–2L⁸ 2M⁶ (2M6 blk), ($2 signed; 'VOL. I.' on C1 only), 272 leaves.

Pp. *i* t., *ii* blk, *iii* Contents, *iv* blk, on B1 pp. ²i–ii ADVERTISEMENT. ('March 15, 1779.'), on B2 text 3–77 Cowley, *78* blk, 79–136 Waller, 137–230 Milton, 231–47 Butler, *248* blk, 249–394 Dryden, *395* 396–406 Denham, 407–12 Sprat, 413–23 Roscommon, *424* blk, 425–33 Rochester, *434* blk, 435–9 Yalden, *440* blk, 441–46 Otway, 447–8 Duke, 449–52 Dorset, 453–7 Halifax, *458* blk, 459–61 Stepney, *462* blk, 463–6 Walsh, *466* blk, 467–72 Garth, 473–7 King, *478* blk, 479–97 J. Philips, *498* blk, 499–527 Smith, *528* blk, 529–30 Pomfret, 531–6 Hughes.

Dropheads: All are in the form: [parallel rule] | NAME.

Pagination: 143–44 repeated on L1, 395 unnumbered, 245 as 445; [↑] i–ii, 3, 79, 137, 231, 249, 407, 413, 425, 435, 441, 447, 449, 453, 459, 463, 467, 473, 479, 499, 529, 531.

Press-figures: B4ᵛ(8)–3, B5ᵛ(10)–2, C5(25)–2, C8(31)–1, D7(45)–3, D8(47)–1, E4(55)–1, E7(61)–2, F6ᵛ(76)–2, F8(79)–3, G7(93)–2, G7ᵛ(94)–3, H5(105)–2, H7ᵛ(110)–3, I5(121)–3, I7ᵛ(126)–2, K7(141)–2, K8(143)–3, L4ᵛ(150)–2, L5ᵛ(152)–3, M3(163)–3, M6(169)–2, N3ᵛ(180)–2, N7(187)–3, O1ᵛ(192)–1, O5(199)–2, P4(213)–2, P8ᵛ(222)–3, Q3ᵛ(228)–2, Q4ᵛ(230)–3, R1ᵛ(240)–2, R6ᵛ(250)–3, S1ᵛ(256)–2, S4ᵛ(262)–1, T4(277)–2, T6ᵛ(282)–3, U4(293)–3, U6ᵛ(298)–1, X5(311)–1, X8(317)–2, Y7(331)–1, Z8ᵛ(350)–1,

2A1ᵛ(352)–1,   3F3ᵛ(436)–3,   2F6ᵛ(442)–2,   2G2ᵛ(450)–2,   2H5(471)–3,
2H7ᵛ(476)–2,   2I3(483)–3,   2I8(493)–2,   2K5(503)–1,   2K7ᵛ(508)–3,
2L5ᵛ(520)–2, 2L8ᵛ(526)–3; 2B–2E, 2M *unfigured*.

Catchwords: ii *om.* (COWLEY.), 71 words‸ (~,), 277 copies (copiecs), 280
Spartan‸ (~.), 354 [Re-] for mers (formers), 360 *om.* (The), 370 There (Thefe),
373 *om.* (He), 391 *om.* ("perpetually), 392 *om.* ("you), 394 *om.* (DENHAM.),
398 *om.* (His), 402 *om.* (The), 411 *om.* (expreffed), 412 *om.* (ROSCOMMON.),
418 ‸man, ("~,), 423 *om.* (ROCHESTER.), 432 *om.* (Abfque), 439 *om.*
(OTWAY.), 477 J. PHILIPS. (‸ PHILIPS.), 488 *om.* (of).

Explicit: 536 THE END.

Paper: White (some sheets are bluish-grey), laid, of varying texture
(rough/smooth) and thickness; Carré (uncut: 8¼ × 5¼ in. 210 × 132 mm);
wmk.: Grapes + P G | F DANGOUMOIS.

Type: English (4.5 mm), unleaded; 2-line caps. pp. 24, 26, 30–32, 34, 35, 37,
38, 39, 40, 42, 116; flowers 19, 131, 199, 247, 320, 381, 392, 446, 481, 483,
487, 514; rules: parallel 3, 79, 137, 231, 249, 395, 407, 413, 425, 435, 441, 447,
449, 453, 459, 463, 467, 473, 479, 499, 529, 531; swelled 237, 379, 399, 400.

References: Courtney 141 (with facs. t. in 1925 edn.); *Tinker* 1364; Cole,
PBSA lxxv (1981), 235–55 (esp. 245–6), reports publication in October 1779;
ESTC: t116665 (3 vols); t183621.

Notes: A reprint from the first instalment of the *Prefaces* (79.4LP/1.2, above),
without the errata. At B2ᵛ, p. 4, l. 3 erroneously reads: 'partaking his posterity' (=
prosperity), and on Q8ᵛ the ht. erroneously reads: 'MILTON.' for 'BUTLER.'

The ESTC entry does not discriminate the various states of this vol. or of its
associates.

Copies: O (12 θ. 1742);

USA: CtY² (Tinker), Hyde, ICU, [Liebert ('Brackenbury')], NjP ('A.E.
Newton' — 'Robert H. Taylor'), MH (A1258.1.5.5, 'Thomas Caldecott' + MS
notes — 'R.H. Isham'), NIC, TxU; *Can*: CaOHM; *Japan*: [Kyoto]; *UK*: C
(Hib.5.779.15), JDF ('Mathews'), LICj (1887), MRu, Oef; *Eir*: Dt² ('Noel
Jameson' — 'Kells Ingram'). [Not discriminated: *UK*: Ljh].

79.4LP/2a(ii)   Lives of the Poets, first instalment,   1779
first Dublin edition, first issue, second state

Title: as first state (79.4LP/2a(i), above, *except*: short ornamental dotted rule
above the date.

8°, *A*² B⁸ (±B2) C–P⁸ Q⁸ (±Q8) R–2L⁸ 2M⁶, (as first state), 272 leaves.

Contents &c., as in first state, *except* cancellations:

1. B2 (pp. 3–4) changing p. 4, l. 3 to read 'partaking his prosperity'.

2. Q8 (pp. 237–8) to correct the headline on 238 from 'MILTON.' to
'BUTLER.'.

3. The two *cancellanda* are marked with asterisked signatures.
Copies: Eir: Dt² (**1**. T. Press H. 3.25; **2**. T. Press H. /9/2, 'Edw. Stopforth 1791' with B2 uncancelled);
USA: CLU-C (B2 uncancelled, but Q8 cancelled), CtY (Im J637.779g. 'Jn. Smith 1801'), NIC; *Can*: [CaOHM ('Arminella & William Sharman' — 'Rippey')]; *UK*: BMp² (**1**. 460244; **2**. 60638, 'Samuel Parr. The Gift of my inge-nious and excellent Friend Daniel Braithwaite Esqr. January 15 — 1779. With sincere esteem and regard, I give this precious relique, to Ann Parker, who was deservedly considered as a Freind, by my late Wife, Jane Parr, & my beloved children Sarah Ann Wynne, & Catharine Jane Parr — may we all meet again in a better world ! Samuel Parr May 11th 1818 —').

79.4LP/2a(iii)   Lives of the Poets, first instalment,   1779
first Dublin edition, first issue, third state

Title: as second state, 79.4LP/2a(ii) above
8°, *A*² B–2L⁸ 2M⁶ (2M6 blk), ($2 signed; 'VOL. I.' on $1), 272 leaves.
Contents, &c. As in second state above with the corrected readings on B2ᵛ (p. 4), l. 3 'partaking of his prosperity', and Q8 (headline 'BUTLER.') on inte-gral leaves.
Copies: O (12 т. 1760; 'W. Kellett');
USA: CSmH (370494), CtY (Im. J637. 779g), [Liebert], NIC.

79.4LP/2b   Lives of the Poets, first instalment,   1780
first Dublin edition, second issue

THE | LIVES | OF THE | ENGLISH POETS: | AND A | CRITICISM | ON THEIR | WORKS. | BY SAMUEL JOHNSON. | PRINTED FOR | [Engraved oval vignette: two allegorical female figures supporting an oval car-touche surmounted by a bust of Homer, inscribed: 'Wm Wilson, | Bookseller & Stationer | at Homer's head | No 6 Dame Street | the Corner of | Palace Street, | [**BL**] Dublin.'] | MDCCLXXX.
Collation and *Contents* as in first issue, second state (79.4LP/2a(ii), above) i.e. with cancels at B2 and Q8, and the above version of the t. which is also a sin-gleton, presumably a cancel of the earlier A1, though as a singleton it may be prefixed to any state of the contents as noticed above.
Wilson's engraved vignette is found in different states:[1]
(a) as above,
(b) as above with the names of the artists: 'G.B. Cypriani inv. F. Bartolozzi fculp.'
(c) as above with an abbreviated address: 'Wm. Wilson | Bookseller | and | Stationer | Dublin.'

References: ESTC: t116666 (3 vols. without discrimination).
Copies: O² (**1**. Vet. A5 e. 1713; **2**. Vet. A5 e. 2293);
USA: Hyde, [Liebert (a, and no cancels)], NIC; *UK*: LICj (1888), LVu, STA; *Eir*: Dt² (**1**. Jameson; **2**. B2 uncancelled 'Kells Ingram' — 'W.G. Paul').

---

¹ Examples of these engraved vignettes are in a collection of printing miscellanea derived from William Hutton (1723–1815), bookseller, of Birmingham, formerly in the possession of the late A.N.L. Munby, of King's College, Cambridge, and now C.

79.4LP/2c   Lives of the Poets, first instalment,   1781
first Dublin edition, third issue

Title: as first state of first issue (79.4LP/2a(i) above), but reading 'VOL. I.' above the imprint, and dated '1781'.
Copies: CtY (Im J637.779Kc.1, 'G. Maltby, 1790').

79.4LP/2d   Lives of the Poets, first instalment,   1795
first Dublin edition, fourth issue

THE | LIVES | OF THE | ENGLISH POETS: | AND | *A CRITICISM* | ON THEIR | WORKS. | *BY SAMUEL JOHNSON* | LONDON: | [short swelled rule] | PRINTED FOR R. DODSLEY, PALL-MALL. | [short rule] | M DCC XCV.

Collation and *Contents* as in first issue, second state (79.4LP/2a(ii), above), save that this title is a cancel. Robert Dodsley had died in 1764; his brother James died in 1797. The name 'Dodsley' recurs in other unauthorized reprints during the 1790s.¹
References: Rowan, *BC* i (1952), 174.
Notes: It is likely that this title was attached to other collations of the sheets of this Dublin edn., as in MH copy (below).
Copies: CtY (Ib. 55. f779d);
USA: [Liebert (±B2,Q8) = CtY], MH (10453.2* has this t. prefixed to sheets in which B2 is in the erroneous uncancelled first state as 79.4LP/2a(i), above, but Q8 in the integral corrected third state (79.4LP/2c, above), NN.

---

¹ See e.g. *Rambler*, [? 1800] (50.3R/25c), 1794 (50.3R/26), and their associates, and Abridged *Dictionary*, 1798 (56.1DA/19).

79.4LP/3   Lives of the Poets, first instalment,   1781
                  second Dublin edition

THE | LIVES | OF THE MOST EMINENT | ENGLISH POETS; | WITH | CRITICAL OBSERVATIONS | ON THEIR | WORKS, | BY SAMUEL JOHNSON. | [medium swelled rule] | IN THREE VOLUMES. | [medium swelled rule] | THE FIRST VOLUME. | [triple rule] | DUBLIN: | Printed for Meffrs. WHITESTONE, WILLIAMS, COLLES, WILSON, | LYNCH, JENKIN, WALKER, BURNET, HALLHEAD, | FLIN, EXSHAW, BEATTY, and WHITE. | [medium swelled rule] | M,DCC,LXXXI.

8°, *A*² B–2L⁸ 2M⁶ (2M6 blk), ($2 signed), 272 leaves.

Pp. *i* t., *ii* blk, *iii* Contents, *iv* blk, on B1 pp. i–ii ADVERTISEMENT. ('March 15, 1779.'), on B1 text 3–77 Cowley, *78* blk, 79–136 Waller, 137–232 Milton, 233–49 Butler, *250* blk, 251–396 Dryden, *397* ½t: DENHAM., *398* blk, 399–408 Denham, 409–14 Sprat, 415–25 Roscommon, *426* blk, 427–35 Rochester, *436* blk, 437–41 Yalden, *442* blk, 443–48 Otway, 449–50 Duke, 451–4 Dorset, 455–9 Halifax, *460* blk, 461–3 Stepney, *464* blk, 465–7 Walsh, *468* blk, 469–74 Garth, 475–9 King, *480* blk, 481–99 J. Philips, *500* blk, 501–29 Smith, *530* blk, 531–2 Pomfret, 533–8 Hughes, *539–40* (2M6) blk leaf.

Dropheads: All are in the form: [rule] | NAME., with rules as: medium parallel pp. 3, parallel pp. 399, 409, 415, and double: pp. 79, 137, 233, 251, 427, 437, 443, 449, 451, 455, 461, 465, 469, 475, 481, 501, 531, 533.

Pagination: 285 (2 *slipt*), 329 (9 *slipt*), 338–9 as 336–7, 342–3 as 340–1, 346–7 as 344–5, 350–1 as 348–9 [all inner forme of sig. Z], 396–7 repeated at 2C7 [½t 'DENHAM.'], 399 (2nd 9 *slipt*), 441 as 41; (↑) i, ii, 3; [↑] 79, 137, 233, 251, 397, 409, 415, 427, 437, 443, 449, 451, 455, 461, 465, 469, 475, 481, 501, 531, 533.

Press-figures: none.

Catchwords: ii *om.* (COWLEY.), 87 *ˮTher‸ (*ˮThere), 103 imagination‸ (∼,), 183 Th‸ (The), 396 *om.* (DENHAM.), 398 [em-] ployments‸ (∼.), 408 *om.* (SPRAT.), 414 *om.* (ROSCOMMON.), 425 *om.* (ROCHESTER.), 441 *om.* (OTWAY.), 479 J. PHILIPS. (‸ PHILIPS.).

Explicit: 538 THE END.

Paper: White, laid; Demy (? or Lombard; uncut: 8¾ × 5½ in.); wmk.: Grapes + 'GABER'.

Type: text: english (4.5 mm), unleaded; 2-line caps. at new paras. pp. 24, 26, 30–5, 37–40, 42, 166; flowers pp. 19, 131, 201, 249, 322, 383, 394, 448, 483, 485, 489, 516; rules (see *Dropheads* above).

References: Courtney 141; ESTC: t183621 alleges a cancelled t.

Notes: This is a wholly reset reprint from the first Dublin edn. (79.4LP/2) above, but reset and published as a companion to the Dublin edn. of the second instalment of the 'Prefaces' (79.4LP/5, var. 1 of t., 1781), below.

Copies: JDF; *USA*: NIC ('Rippey').

79.4LP/4   [Lives of the Poets], Prefaces,   1781
                  second instalment (Vols. V–X)

PREFACES, | BIOGRAPHICAL | AND | CRITICAL, | TO THE | WORKS | OF THE | ENGLISH POETS. | BY SAMUEL JOHNSON. | [medium swelled rule] | VOLUME THE FIFTH [–TENTH]. | LONDON: | PRINTED BY J. NICHOLS; | FOR C. BATHURST, J. BUCKLAND, W. STRAHAN, J. RIVING- | TON AND SONS, T. DAVIES, T. PAYNE, L. DAVIS, W. OWEN, | B. WHITE, S. CROWDER, T. CASLON, T. LONGMAN, | B. LAW, C. DILLY, J. DODSLEY, J. WILKIE, J. ROB- | SON, J. JOHNSON, T. LOWNDES, G. ROBINSON, | T. CADELL, J. NICHOLS, E. NEWBERY, | T. EVANS, J. RIDLEY, R. BALDWIN, | G. NICOL, LEIGH AND SOTHEBY, | J. BEW, N. CONANT, J. MURRAY, | W. FOX, J. BOWEN. | M DCC LXXXI.

Note: This imprint varies from that of the first instalment (79.4LP/1.2, above), in that Edward Dilly (d. 11 May 1779), H. Baldwin (? retired *c*.1781), T. Becket (bankrupt 5 Jan. 1779) and W. Davis (retired *c*.1780), are omitted, leaving 34 names.

6 vols., 8°

V. a², Addison A–B⁸ C⁸ (±C8) D–K⁸ L1, Blackmore ²A–C⁸ D⁴ (2D4 blk), Sheffield ³A⁸ B², ($4 (+ a2, Addison 'C8', Blackmore ²D3,4, Sheffield ³B2) signed; 'VOL. V.' on a2), 121 leaves.

Pp. *i* t., *ii* blk, *iii* ½t: PREFACES | TO | ADDISON, | BLACKMORE, | AND | SHEFFIELD., *iv* blk, on A1 1–162 Addison, on ²A1 1–53 Blackmore, *54* blk, *55–56* (²D4) blk, on ³A1 1–20 Sheffield.

Dropheads: in the form: [double rule] | NAME., except Sheffield as: '[double rule] | SHEFFIELD, | BUCKINGHAMSHIRE., and htt. as: 'NAME.'

Pagination: [↑] pp. 1 (×3).

Press-figures: (Addison) A5(9)–1, B1ᵛ(18)–5, C6(43)–3, C6ᵛ(44)–5, 'C8'ᵛ(48)–1, D4ᵛ(56)–2, D7ᵛ(62)–4, E2ᵛ(68)–1, E3ᵛ(70)–3, F8(95)–3, F8ᵛ(96)–2, G3ᵛ(102)–7, H1ᵛ(114)–2, H4ᵛ(120)–7, I1ᵛ(130)–4, I2ᵛ(132)–1, K2ᵛ(148)–4, (Blackmore) A1ᵛ(2)–2, B1ᵛ(18)–4, C2ᵛ(36)–2, C8(47)–2, (Sheffield) A3ᵛ(6)–5, A8ᵛ(16)–1.

Catchwords: *Addison*: 12 calld (called), 82 Pope₍ₐ₎ (~*,).

Plate: The engr. port. of SJ is properly prefixed to this vol. since it was not engraved until after the proprietors had agreed to publish an edn. in 4 vols. 8°, on 12 March 1781 (79.4LP/5, below). Copies which have the port. in vol. 1 (79.4LP/1.2, above), have therefore been rebound.

Notes: A *cancellandum* of C8 in 'Addison' is still unlocated.

VI. a², Granville A–C⁸ D⁴, Rowe ²A–B⁸ (B8 blk), Tickell ³A–B⁸ C⁶, Congreve ⁴A–B⁸ C⁴ (C4 blk), Fenton ⁵A⁸ B², Prior ⁶A–D⁸, ($4 (–Granville D2,3, Tickell C4, Congreve C3,4, Fenton B2) signed; 'VOL. VI.' on a2), 130 leaves.

Note: B² of Fenton was printed as the innermost fold of Hammond (A4.5) in vol. 9 (see below); the remaining fractions in this vol. viz. Granville D⁴ and Congreve C⁴ form a whole sheet. The missing bifolium from Tickell C⁶ is not identified, unless it formed a² of this or another vol.

Pp. *i* t., *ii* blk, *iii* ½t: PREFACES | TO | GRANVILLE, | ROWE, TICKELL, | CONGREVE, FENTON, | AND | PRIOR., *iv* blk, on A1 1–56 Granville, on ²A1 1–30 Rowe, *31–2* (2B8) blk, on ³A1 pp. 1–43 Tickell, *44* blk, on ⁴A1 pp. 1–38 Congreve, *39–40* (4C4) blk, on ⁵A1 pp. 1–19 Fenton, *20* blk, on ⁶A1 pp. 1–63 Prior, *64* blk.

Dropheads: in form: [double rule] | NAME., and htt. as 'NAME.'

Pagination: [↑] pp. 1 (×6).

Press-figures: (Granville) A1ᵛ(2)–1, B1ᵛ(18)–4, B5(25)–3, C8(47)–4, (Rowe) A6(11)–4, B1ᵛ(18)–2, (Tickell) A3ᵛ(6)–2, A6ᵛ(12)–1, B6(27)–7, B6ᵛ(28)–1, C2ᵛ(36)–1, C5ᵛ(42)–3, (Congreve) A1ᵛ(2)–2, A2ᵛ(4)–4, B5(25)–4, B5ᵛ(26)–2, C3(37)–1, (Fenton) A4ᵛ(8)–3, A7ᵛ(14)–2, (Prior) A4ᵛ(8)–3, B7ᵛ(30)–5, C3ᵛ(38)–2, C4ᵛ(40)–4, D2ᵛ(52)–4, D7ᵛ(62)–2.

Catchwords: *Granville*: 24 *om.* (PREFACE), 50 *om.* ("The), 51 *om.* (Tho'), 52 ˏThe ((6) The), 54 *om.* (On), (Prior) 1 *om.* (He).

Notes: The MS of Rowe is extant (MS Hyde; *Handlist* 169, *MS Index* JoS 227).

VII. a² A–Z⁸ 2A⁴ (2A4 blk), ($4 (–2A3,4) signed; 'VOL. VII.' on a2), 190 leaves.

Pp. *i* t., *ii* blk, *iii* ½t PREFACE | TO | POPE., *iv* blk, on A1 text 1–373 Pope dh: [double rule] | POPE., ht: POPE., *374* blk, *375–6* (2A4) blk lf.

Pagination: [↑] p. 1.

Press-figures: A2v(4)–6, A8(15)–2, B5ᵛ(26)–2, B8ᵛ(32)–4, C5ᵛ(42)–3, D3ᵛ(54)–7, D7(61)–4, E6ᵛ(76)–3, E8(79)–1, F7(93)–4, F8(95)–2, G4ᵛ(104)–3, H3ᵛ(118)–3, H8ᵛ(128)–4, I7(141)–3, I7ᵛ(142)–4, K8(159)–1, K8ᵛ(160)–7, L7(173)–2, L8(175)–2, M1ᵛ(178)–1, M8ᵛ(192)–2, N8ᵛ(208)–7, O7ᵛ(222)–2, O8ᵛ(224)–6, P4ᵛ(232)–2, P5ᵛ(234)–5, Q7(253)–2, Q7ᵛ(254)–1, R6ᵛ(268)–6, S4(279)–3, T6(299)–6, U5ᵛ(314)–4, U8ᵛ(320)–6, X1ᵛ(322)–4, Y1ᵛ(338)–3, Y2ᵛ(340)–1, Z7(365)–6, Z7ᵛ(366)–7.

Catchwords: 131 "in (*commas damaged*);

Notes: Preliminary MS notes for Pope are L (*Handlist* 170a; *MS Index* JoS 222) and Lv (*Handlist* 170b; *MS Index* JoS 223). The MS of Pope (partly in HLT's hand) is NPM (*Handlist* 171; *MS Index* JoS 224), and the proofs (presented by SJ to Fanny Burney) are Hyde (*Handlist* 174; *MS Index* JoS 225).

VIII. *a*², Swift A–G⁸, Gay ²A–B⁸ (B8 blk), Broome ³A⁶, Pitt ⁴A⁴, Parnell ⁵A⁴ B², A. Philips ⁶A⁸ B⁴, Watts ⁷A⁸ B⁴, ($4 (– Broome ³A4, Pitt ⁴A3,4, Parnell ⁵A3,4, B2, Philips ⁶B3,4, Watts ⁷B3,4) signed; 'VOL. VIII.' on a2), 114 leaves.

Notes: Watermarks suggest the conjugacy of Pitt A⁴ with Parnell A⁴. It is also likely that Broome A⁶ enclosed Parnell B², and that A. Philips B⁴ was conjugate with Watts B⁴, but there is not yet watermark evidence in confirmation.

Pp. *i* t., *ii* blk, *iii* ½t: PREFACES | TO | SWIFT, GAY, | BROOME, PITT, | PARNELL, A. PHILIPS, | AND | WATTS., *iv* blk, on A1 text 1–112 Swift, ^{2}A1 pp. 1–30 Gay, *31–2* (^{2}B8) blk, on ^{3}A1 1–12 Broome, on ^{4}A1 1–7 Pitt, *8* blk, on ^{5}A1 1–11 Parnell, *12* blk, on ^{6}A1 1–23 A. Philips, *24* blk, on ^{7}A1 1–24 Watts.

Dropheads: all as : [double rule] | NAME., and htt: as NAME. On ^{6}A1 A. Philips is printed simply as 'PHILIPS.' and again in htt. without any initial.

Pagination: [↑] pp. 1 (×7).

Press-figures: (Swift) A4^v(8)–3, A8(15)–2, B4^v(24)–7, B5^v(26)–3, C5^v(42)–5, C7(45)–1, D3^v(54)–4, E2^v(68)–1, E8(79)–3, F2^v(84)–1, F8(95)–5, G6(107)–4, G6^v(108)–3, (Gay) A3^v(6)–3, B1^v(18)–1, B2^v(20)–2, (Broome) A3^v(6)–4, A4^v(8)–1, (A. Philips) A5(9)–1, (Watts) A2^v(4)–1, A6(11)–4, B3^v(22)–1.

Catchwords: no errors.

IX. a^2, Savage b–k^8 l^2, Somervile A^4, Thomson ^{2}A–B^8 C^4, Hammond ^{3}A^6, Collins ^{4}A^8 (A8 blk), ($4 (–Savage l2, Somervile A3,4, Thomson ^{2}C3,4, Hammond ^{3}A4) signed; 'VOL. IX.' on a2), 114 leaves.

Note: Hammond A^6 enclosed B^2 of Fenton (vol. 6). Watermarks suggest the conjugacy of Somervile A^4 and Thomson C^4, but the conjugacy of Savage l^2 is not yet identified.

Pp. *i* t., *ii* blk, *iii* ½t: PREFACES | TO | SAVAGE, SOMERVILE, | THOMSON, HAMMOND, | AND | COLLINS., *iv* blk, on b1 text 1–147 Savage, *148* blk, on A1 1–7 Somervile, *8* blk, on ^{2}A1 1–40 Thomson, on ^{3}A1 1–11 Hammond, *12* blk, on ^{4}A1 1–14 Collins, *15–16* (A8) blk leaf.

Dropheads: as [double rule] | NAME., and htt as: NAME.

Pagination: [↑] pp. 1 (×5), and Hammond 9.

Press-figures: (Savage) b6(11)–5, b8^v(16)–7, c5^v(26)–7, d1^v(34)–6, d5(41)–1, e7(61)–1, e7^v(62)–5, f8^v(80)–6, g1^v(82)–2, g6^v(92)–3, h2^v(100)–5, h6(107)–4, i7(125)–2, i8(127)–1, k3^v(134)–1, (Somervile) A2^v(4)–1, (Thomson) A2^v(4)–2, A5^v(10)–1, B5(25)–5, C1^v(34)–3, (Hammond) A2^v(4)–4, A5^v(10)–1, (Collins) A3^v(6)–3, A5(9)–4.

Catchwords: *Savage*: 32 ‿Gentlemen ('∼'), 49n Say‿ (∼,); *Thomson*: 30 *om.* (The).

X. a^2, Young A–D^8 E^8(±E5) F–G^8 H^2 (H2 blk), Dyer ^{2}A^4, Mallet ^{3}A^8, Shenstone ^{4}A^8 B^2, Akenside ^{5}A^8 B^2 (B2 blk), Lyttelton ^{6}A^8 B^4 (B4 blk), West ^{7}A^8, Gray ^{8}A–C^8 D^4 ($4 (– Young H2, Dyer ^{2}A3,4, Shenstone ^{4}B2, Akenside ^{5}B2, Lyttelton ^{6}B3,4, Gray ^{7}D3,4) signed; 'VOL. X.' on a2), 140 leaves.

Notes: The blanks are usually present, so were evidently not used to print the *cancellans* of Young E5. This bears the press-fig. 4 on E5^v (74) which makes it improbable that it was printed in multiple settings, and very likely that it formed part of a whole sheet: the problem is, which one?

Pp. *i* t., *ii* blk, *iii* ½t: PREFACES | TO | YOUNG, DYER, | MALLET, SHENSTONE, | AKENSIDE, LYTTELTON, | WEST, AND GRAY., *iv* blk, on A1 text 1–113 Young, *114* blk, *115–16* (H2) blk leaf, on ²A1 1–8 Dyer, on ³A1 1–16 Mallet, on ⁴A1 1–20 Shenstone, on ⁵A1 1–18 Akenside, *19–20* (B2) blk leaf, on ⁶A1 1–22 Lyttelton, *23–24* (B4) blk leaf, on ⁷A1 1–15 West, *16* blk, on ⁸A1 1–56 Gray.

Dropheads: as [double rule] | NAME., and htt: NAME.

Pagination: [↑] pp. 1 (×8).

Press-figures: (Young) A3ᵛ(6)–5, B2ᵛ(20)–1, B3ᵛ(22)–5, C4ᵛ(40)–3, C6(43)–1, D3ᵛ(54)–7, D6ᵛ(60)–1, 'E5'ᵛ(74)–4, F2ᵛ(84)–4, F6(91)–1, G6ᵛ(108)–2, G7ᵛ(110)–5, (Dyer) A2ᵛ(4)–1, A3ᵛ(6)–2, (Mallet) A5ᵛ(10)–1, (Shenstone) A3ᵛ(6)–2, A4ᵛ(8)–4, (Akenside) A8ᵛ(16)–2, (Lyttelton) A3ᵛ(6)–5, A6ᵛ(12)–3, B1ᵛ(18)–7, (West) A3ᵛ(6)–3, A4ᵛ(8)–5, (Gray) A7(13)–7, A8(15)–1, B5ᵛ(26)–7, B8ᵛ(32)–1, C5ᵛ(42)–1, C7(45)–5, D1ᵛ(50)–3 (*inverted*), D3(53)–1.

Catchwords: Young: 34 *o*ₐ (*of*), 88 *om.* (In), 110 proudₐ (~,); *Gray*: 37 *om.* (To), 39 ₐA brace (*~ ~), 55 ₐ "Througₐ (VIII. "Through).

Notes: The cancel at E5 (Young, pp. 73–4) was made by Herbert Croft; the *cancellandum* is preserved in the proof sheets in Lv. In *Gents. Mag.* li (1781), 318, are listed the passages which SJ is said to have struck out of Croft's 'Life of Young'.

Paper: White, laid; foolscap (as in 79.4LP/1.2, above); (uncut: 6¾ × 4¼ in.); wmk.: Pro Patria + G R.

Type: Pica (4.0 mm), leaded (2.3 mm, as in 79.4LP/1.2, above). In IX Savage is set in smaller type, viz. long primer (3.4 mm), leaded thinly (0.5 mm). Some pica Greek in VIII. Parnell. Flowers in V. Addison, 91, 159, 162, Blackmore 43, 48, 49, 53, Sheffield 20; VI. Granville 24, 36, 44, 56, Rowe 30, Tickell 15, 16, 40, 43, Congreve 38, Fenton 16, 17, 19, Prior 41, 63; VII. Pope 221, 222, 272, 273, 332, 333, 339, 340, 373; VIII. Swift 82, 83, 109, 110, 112, Gay 30, Broome 12, Pitt 7, Parnell 11, A. Philips 23, Watts 24; IX. Savage 147, Somervile 7, Thomson 38, 40, Hammond 8, 9, 11, Collins 14; X. Young 102, 103, 113, Dyer 8, Mallet 16, Shenstone 20, Akenside 11, 18, Lyttelton 22, West 11, 15, and Gray 20, 21, 36, 37, 48, 56.

References: Courtney 141, see 79.4LP/1.2, above.

Notes: Each 'Life' was printed as a unit according to the original intention of prefixing them to the appropriate volumes in the 'Works' (79.4LP/1.1, above), yet some were so short that it was practicable to combine them into single sheets. The original binder distributed the sections according to a leaf of instructions sometimes found in I. pp. ix–x:

> Dr Johnson's Lives of the Poets are to be sewed in Ten separate Volumes; viz. . . . [with a List of vols. I–X with Contents]. The Two Volumes of Index are to be lettered Vol. LVII and Vol. LVIII.

This leaf cannot have been issued until 1781 since the *Index* vols. were not published until that year, and of course the contents of vols V–X were not known until they were completed.

The independent fractions of sheets have been noticed under the collations of individual vols. above, but may be summarized

1. a^2 prelims to each vol.	12 leaves
2. VI. Tickell C^6 [*press figs*: 1 (o), 3 (i)]	6
3. VII. Pope 2A^4	4
4. IX. Savage l^2	2
5. X. Young H^2, Dyer A^4, Shenstone B^2, Akenside B^2	
[*press figs*: Dyer 1 (o), 2 (i)]	10
6. X. *Cancellans* E5 [pr. fig. 4]	1
	Total 37 leaves.

This amounts to 4 whole sheets and 3 leaves. It is possible that some copies may eventually reveal more as to these conjugacies, but this is the present state of knowledge.[1] The press-figures offer little assistance towards the following speculative reconstruction:

1. VI. Tickell C^6 ≡ IX. Savage l^2 [p-f: 1(o), 3(i)] 1 sheet
2. VII. Pope 2A^4 ≡ X. Dyer A^4 [p-f: 1(o), 1(i)] 1 sheet
3. X. Young H^2 ≡ Shenstone B^2 ≡ Akenside B^2 (? + 2 blk) [*No* p-f.] 1 sheet
4. V–X. 6 × a^2 (prelims) ≡ X. Young 'E5' (? + 1 blk) [p-f: 4] 1½ sheets

There is nothing in the copies examined to contradict this proposal, though that does not constitute strong evidence, since small fractions might have reached the binder in a rather haphazard way, yet had that been the case more confusion in examined copies might have been found.

Publication: The composition was completed on 5 March 1781 when SJ wrote to Strahan about payment (*Letters* 713; Hyde, iii. 325). A week later the proprietors met and agreed to produce a separate edn. in 4 vols. 8° (79.4LP/5, below). The six vols. of *Prefaces* together with the two vols. of the *Index* (57–58) were published on 15 May 1781 at £1. (*Public Advertiser*).[2]

Copies: O (2804 f. 154–63);

USA: CSmH, CtY (pres. Joshua Reynolds), DFo, Hyde[5] (1. vols. 1–2 pres Fanny Burney; 2. pres. Dr Lawrence; 3. pres. Thomas Percy; 4. 'Broughton'; 5.; also proofs of 'Pope' (vol. 7) pres. Fanny Burney), ICU, IU (*Prefaces* bound before appropriate vols. of *Works*), [Liebert[2] 1. uncut, marbled wraps.; 2. 'George Gilpin'], MH ('Murdock'), NIC, NjP, TxU; *Can*: CaOHM[2] (1. 'R. Wilson'; 2. 'Mrs Smith' — 'Selborne'); *UK*: ABu, BMp (96741–50, 'Edmund Hector'[3]), C, Csj, Ct (Rothschild: pres. 'Mrs Davenant' *Booklist* 176), E[2] (1.; 2. lacks vol. 2), Eu[2] (1. complete; 2. lacks vols. 4,9), JDF[3] (1. 'Stephen Nash' lacks vol. 6; 2. lacks vol. 2; 3. vols. 3–4 only), Gu[2] (1. uncut), LICj, LVu, MRc, Oef, Op (1–2 only, 'Richard Jebb'); *Aust*: CNL (DNS 6910–19); *Ger*: GöttU.

---

[1] The fractions of sheets were sure to cause trouble in binding: Pickering & Chatto, *General Catalogue* 686 (1991), 257, report a set in which the D^4 of Granville (vol. 6), is misbound with Gray, vol. 10.

² On 13 March 1781 Charles Dilly wrote to James Beattie telling him that the *Prefaces* will be out 'by the end of the month' (ABu: MS Beattie C 354). Beattie's copy is untraced. Beattie negotiated the sale of it with William Creech, in August 1788 (ABu: MSS Beattie B 289, 290, and C 572).

³ Acquired by Lt.-Col. Francis R.C. Grant from the Meysey-Thompson sale at Sotheby's, 1887, and noticed in *The Academy*, 25 June 1887, p. 44. *Booklist* 177. They do not figure in Grant's sale, Sotheby, 7 May 1900.

79.4LP/5   Lives of the Poets, second London edition   1781

THE | LIVES | OF THE MOST EMINENT | ENGLISH POETS; | WITH | CRITICAL OBSERVATIONS | ON THEIR | WORKS. | By SAMUEL JOHNSON. | IN FOUR VOLUMES. | [short swelled rule] | VOLUME I [–IV]. | [short swelled rule] | LONDON: | PRINTED FOR C. BATHURST, J. BUCKLAND, W. STRAHAN, J. RIVING- | TON AND SONS, T. DAVIES, T. PAYNE, L. DAVIS, W. OWEN, B. WHITE, | S. CROWDER, T. CASLON, T. LONGMAN, B. LAW, C. DILLY, | J. DODSLEY, J. WILKIE, J. ROBSON, J. JOHNSON, T. LOWNDES, | G. ROBINSON, T. CADELL, J. NICHOLS, E. NEWBERY, | T. EVANS, P. ELMSLY, J. RIDLEY, R. BALDWIN, G. NICOL, | LEIGH AND SOTHEBY, J. BEW, N. CONANT, W. NICOLL, | J. MURRAY, S. HAYES, W. FOX, AND J. BOWEN. | M DCC LXXXI.

4 vols., 8°

I. a⁴ B–2H⁸, ($4 (–a1,3,4) signed; VOL. I.' on $1 (–L)), 244 leaves.

Pp. Engr. port. front. + *i* t., *ii* blk, iii–v ADVERTISEMENT., *vi* blk, vii Contents, *viii* blk, on B1 text *1* ½t, *2* blk, 3–102 Cowley, *103* ½t, *104* blk, 105–22 Denham, *123* ½t, *124* blk, 125–268 Milton, *269* ½t, *270* blk, 271–95 Butler, *296* blk, *297* ½t, *298* blk, 299–311 Rochester, *312* blk, *313* ½t, *314* blk, 315–32 Roscommon, *333* ½t, *334* blk, 335–42 Otway, *343* ½t, *344* blk, 345–427 Waller, *428* blk, *429* ½t, *430* blk, 431–2 Pomfret, *433* ½t, *434* blk, 435–40 Dorset, *441* ½t, *442* blk, 443–6 Stepney, *447* ½t, *448* blk, 449–74 J. Philips, *475* ½t, *476* blk, 477–80 Walsh.

Half-titles, Dropheads &c: ½tt in the form: [medium (56 mm) swelled rule] | NAME. | [medium swelled rule], but Pomfret (429), Stepney (441), and Walsh (475) have short (31 mm) swelled rules. Dhh. as: [rule *var*.] | NAME., htt: NAME. The rules differ as follows: double rules pp. 3, 125, 299, 335, 345, 431, 443, 477, total rules pp. 105, 271, 315, 435, and parallel rule p. 449. Htt. as: NAME. At intermediate points in the text there are swelled rules pp. 28, 421 and 460.

Pagination: [↑] iii–v, vii, 3, 105, 125, 271, 299, 315, 335, 345, 431, 435, 443, 449, 477.

Press-figures: a2ᵛ(iv)–4, B5(9)–1, B5ᵛ(10)–2, C4ᵛ(24)–4, C8(31)–2, D6(43)–5, D7(45)–4, E2ᵛ(52)–2, F3ᵛ(70)–3, F6ᵛ(76)–4, G8ᵛ(96)–4, H1ᵛ(98)–6, H2ᵛ(100)–2, I2ᵛ(116)–6, I3ᵛ(118)–3, K2ᵛ(132)–2, K6(139)–3,

L5ᵛ(154)–5, L8ᵛ(160)–4, M1ᵛ(162)–3, M4ᵛ(168)–4, N5ᵛ(186)–2, N6ᵛ(188)–5, O6ᵛ(204)–4, O8(207)–6, P8ᵛ(224)–6, Q4ᵛ(232)–4, Q8(239)–5, R7(253)–2, S6(267)–3, S8ᵛ(272)–1, T1ᵛ(274)–4, T2ᵛ(276)–2, U2ᵛ(292)–3, U7ᵛ(302)–5, X3ᵛ(310)–1, X7(317)–4, Y4ᵛ(328)–2, Z5(345)–2, Z5ᵛ(346)–5, 2A5ᵛ(362)–2, 2A7(365)–4, 2B6ᵛ(380)–2, 2C1ᵛ(386)–6, 2C6ᵛ(396)–1, 2D7ᵛ(414)–5, 2D8ᵛ(416)–2, 2E2ᵛ(420)–6, 2E6(427)–4, 2F3ᵛ(438)–3, 2F7(445)–1, 2G4ᵛ(456)–2, 2G8(463)–4, 2H2ᵛ(468)–1, 2H3ᵛ(470)–3.

Catchwords: 117 meaning (g *slipt*), 357 ‸"There (* "∼).
Explicit: 480 END OF THE FIRST VOLUME.

II. *a*² B–2G⁸ 2H⁴, ($4 (–2H3,4) signed; Vᴏʟ. II.' on $1), 238 leaves.
Pp. *i* t., *ii* blk, iii Contents, *iv* blk, on B1 text pp. *1* ½t, *2* blk, 3–218 Dryden, *219* ½t, *220* blk, 221–61 Smith, *262* blk, *263* ½t, *264* blk, 265–7 Duke, *268* blk, *269* ½t, *270* blk, 271–8 King, *279* ½t, *280* blk, 281–90 Sprat, *291* ½t, *292* blk, 293–300 Halifax, *301* ½t, *302* blk, 303–9 Parnell, *310* blk, *311* ½t, *312* blk, 313–20 Garth, *321* ½t, *322* blk, 323–42 Rowe, *343* ½t, *344* blk, 345–444 Addison, *445* ½t, *446* blk, 447–55 Hughes, *456* blk, *457* ½t, *458* blk, 459–71 Sheffield, *472* blk.

Half-tt, dropheads & headtt: As vol. 1, above, with medium swelled rules in all ½tt in the form: [medium swelled rule] | NAME. | [medium swelled rule], dhh. as: [double rule] | NAME., except total rules pp. 221 (Smith) and 271 (King). Htt. as: 'NAME.'

Pagination: [↑] pp. iii, 3, 221, 265, 271, 281, 293, 303, 313, 323, 345, 447, 459.

Press-figures: B5ᵛ(10)–3, B7(13)–2, C5ᵛ(26)–5, C7(29)–9, D6ᵛ(44)–9, D8(47)–3, E6(59)–2, E6ᵛ(60)–5, F1ᵛ(66)–3, F2ᵛ(68)–10, G5ᵛ(90)–5, G7(93)–10, H3ᵛ(102)–5, H8ᵛ(112)–10, I4ᵛ(120)–2, I5ᵛ(122)–3, K6(139)–5, K8ᵛ(144)–2, L1ᵛ(146)–3, L2ᵛ(148)–2, M5(169)–10, M8(175)–5, N1ᵛ(178)–5, N6ᵛ(188)–9, O7(205)–10, O8(207)–3, P1ᵛ(210)–10, P5(217)–2, Q3ᵛ(230)–10, Q6ᵛ(236)–9, R6(251)–5, R8ᵛ(256)–3, S1ᵛ(258)–10, S2ᵛ(260)–5, T5ᵛ(282)–2, T6ᵛ(284)–3, U5ᵛ(298)–2, U8ᵛ(304)–9, X6(315)–5, X7(317)–3, Y4ᵛ(328)–10, Y5ᵛ(330)–9, Z6(347)–2, Z6ᵛ(348)–3, 2A1ᵛ(354)–9, 2A8ᵛ(368)–5, 2B5(377)–2, 2B7ᵛ(382)–10, 2C1ᵛ(386)–5, 2C4ᵛ(392)–3, 2D8(415)–10, 2D8ᵛ(416)–9, 2E3ᵛ(422)–1, 2E6ᵛ(428)–2, 2F5(441)–3, 2F8(447)–5, 2G1ᵛ(450)–9, 2G8ᵛ(464)–10, 2H1ᵛ(466)–2.

Catchwords: 35 ‸Obſerve, ("∼,), 151 Ther‸ (There), 347 Addiſon‸‸ (∼*,), 395 ‸Addiſon's ("∼), 420 ‸Oh! ("∼!).
Explicit: 471 END OF THE SECOND VOLUME.

III. *a*² B–2G⁸ (2G8 blk), ($4 (–a1) signed; 'Vᴏʟ. III.' on $1 (–a)), 234 leaves.
Pp. *i* t., *ii* blk, iii Contents, *iv* blk, on B1 text pp. *1* ½t, *2* blk, 3–42 Prior, *43* ½t, *44* blk, 45–69 Congreve, *70* blk, *71* ½t, *72* blk, 73–106 Blackmore, *107* ½t, *108* blk, 109–18 Fenton, *119* ½t, *120* blk, 121–39 Gay, *140* blk, *141* ½t, *142* blk, 143–57 Granville, *158* blk, *159* ½t, *160* blk, 161–8 Yalden, *169* ½t, *170*

blk, 171–80 Tickell, *181* ½t, *182* blk, 183–7 Hammond, *188* blk, *189* ½t, *190* blk, 191–4 Somervile, *195* ½t, *196* blk, 197–378 Savage, *379* ½t, *380* blk, 381–451 Swift, *452* blk, *453* ½t, *454* blk, 455–62 Broome, *463–4* (2G8) blk leaf.

Half-tt, dropheads & headtt: As vol. 1 with ½t in form: [short swelled rule] | NAME. | [short swelled rule], and dhh. as: [parallel rule] | NAME. Htt. as: NAME.

Pagination: 186 as 168, 378 *sometimes* unnumbered (see *Note* below under *Press-figures*); [↑] pp. iii, 3, 45, 73, 109, 121, 143, 161, 171, 183, 191, 197, 381, 455.

Press-figures: B7(13)–5, B8(15)–8, C8(31)–1, D3^v(38)–1, D4^v(40)–3, E2^v(52)–8 *or* 9, F2^v(68)–7, F7^v(78)–4, G6(91)–5, G7(93)–1, H7(109)–4, H8(111)–1, I1^v(114)–2, I5(121)–3 *or* 1, K5^v(138)–2, K8^v(144)–4, L1^v(146)–4, L6^v(156)–1, M3^v(166)–3, M8^v(176)–1, N4^v(184)–4, N5^v(186)–1, O4^v(200)–6 *or* 1, O7^v(206)–5, P1^v(210)–2, Q6^v(236)–5, Q7^v(238)–6, R1^v(242)–1 *or* 2, R4^v(248)–4 *or unfigured*, S4^v(264)–6, S7^v(270)–4, T4^v(280)–7, T8(287)–5, U6(299)–7, U8^v(304)–8, X1^v(306)–1, X5(313)–4, Y5^v(330)–1, Y8^v(336)–2, Z8(351)–5, Z8^v(352)–4, 2A1^v(354)–5, 2A5(361)–6, 2B5^v(378)–5 *or unfigured*, 2B8^v(384)–4, 2C5^v(394)–2, 2C6^v(396)–6, 2D6(411)–1, 2D7(413)–8, 2E7(429)–5, 2E8(431)–2, 2F6^v(444)–7, 2F8(447)–5, 2G5^v(458)–7, 2G7(461)–8.

Note: p. 378 (2B5^v) figured '5' has no p. number, but unfigured is correctly numbered; none of the variant numbers heralds a cancel.

Catchwords: 19 na (an), 24 whigs$_\wedge$ (~*,), 60 *om.* (CONGREVE.), 106 *om.* (FENTON.), 135 *ana* (*and*), 456 fourth, (~$_\wedge$).

Explicit: 462 END OF THE THIRD VOLUME.

IV. a² B–2I⁸ 2K⁴ *2L²*, ($4 signed; 'VOL. IV.' on $1 (+ a2)), 256 leaves.

Pp. *i* t., *ii* blk, *iii* Contents, *iv* blk, on B1 text pp. *1* ½t, *2* blk, 3–240 Pope, *241* ½t, *242* blk, 243–47 Pitt, *248* blk, *249* ½t, *250* blk, 251–74 Thomson, *275* ½t, *276* blk, 277–92 Watts, *293* ½t, *294* blk, 295–310 A. Philips, *311* ½t, *312* blk, 313–19 West, *320* blk, *321* ½t, *322* blk, 323–31 Collins, *332* blk, *333* ½t, *334* blk, 335–9 Dyer, *340* blk, *341* ½t, *342* blk, 343–56 Shenstone, *357* ½t, *358* blk, 359–431 Young, *432* blk, *433* ½t, *434* blk, 435–45 Mallet, *446* blk, *447* ½t, *448* blk, 449–60 Akenside, *461* ½t, *462* blk, 463–85 Gray, *486* blk, *487* ½t, *488* blk, 489–503 Lyttelton, *504* blk, 505 Advt. for the 'Poets' and SJ's *Prefaces*, *506* blk, *507* Four printed spine labels for these four vols., *508* blk.

Half-tt, dropheads and headtt: ½t in the form: [medium swelled rule] | NAME. | [medium swelled rule], dhh. as: [double rule] | NAME. pp. 3, 243, 251, 277, 323, 449, 461; parallel rule pp. 295, 313, 343, 435; total rule pp. 335, 359, 489.

Pagination: [↑] iii, 3, 243, 251, 277, 295, 313, 323, 335, 343, 359, 435, 449, 463, 489, 505.

Press-figures: B8(15)–5, C2^v(20)–3, C8(31)–2, D8(47)–5, E2^v(52)–5,

E8(63)–1,   F7(77)–3,   F8(79)–2,   G7ᵛ(94)–4,   H2ᵛ(100)–3,   H6(107)–5,
I7ᵛ(126)–4, I8ᵛ(128)–5, K8(143)–1, L1ᵛ(146)–4, L7(157)–3, M3ᵛ(166)–5,
M4ᵛ(168)–4, N1ᵛ(178)–1, N7(189)–4, O2ᵛ(196)–5, P1ᵛ(210)–1, Q1ᵛ(226)–1,
R2ᵛ(244)–2, S7ᵛ(270)–1, T6(283)–5, U1ᵛ(290)–1, X2ᵛ(308)–2, X6(315)–4,
Y4ᵛ(328)–2, Y5ᵛ(330)–5, Z1ᵛ(338)–2, 2A7ᵛ(366)–3, 2B2ᵛ(372)–4, 2B8(383)–1,
2C1ᵛ(386)–5,   2C5(393)–2,   2D8ᵛ(416)–6,   2E1ᵛ(418)–5,   2E2ᵛ(420)–3,
2F3ᵛ(438)–5,   2G6(459)–3,   2G8ᵛ(464)–5,   2H1ᵛ(466)–2,   2I6(491)–2,
2K3(501)–3.

Catchwords: 214 *om.* (THE), 407 Popeₐ (∼,), 495 Abuot (About).

Explicit: 503 FINIS.

Paper: White, laid; Medium (uncut: 9 × 5¾ in.); no vis. wmk.

Type: Text: pica (4.5 mm) throughout, leaded (1.5 mm); quotes in small pica
(4.0 mm), leaded (1.3 mm), and some in long primer (3.3 mm) e.g. Pope, IV. 53.

2-line caps begin subsections and each new 'Life' at I. 34, 37, 42, 43, 44, 46,
48, 50, 51, 52, 53, 55, 401; II. 3, 221, 265, 271, 281, 293, 303, 313, 323, 345,
447, 459; III. 3, 45, 73, 109, 121, 143, 161, 171, 183, 191, 197, 381, 455; IV. 3,
243, 251, 277, 295, 313, 323, 335, 343, 359, 435, 449, 463, 489. Greek II. 304.

Plate: Port. of SJ as front. in I. a slightly larger version of the engr. for *Prefaces*
(79.4LP/4, above), taken from Reynolds's 1778 portrait (*Life* iv. 450 no. IV).[1] It
occurs in two states, with and without the imprint: 'London. Printed as the Act
directs June 8th. 1781'.

References: Courtney 141–2; ESTC: t146734.

Notes: The Dublin reprints of the first instalment of the *Prefaces* offered a
sharp challenge to the London proprietors who would not sell SJ's *Prefaces* without the *Works* to which the Prefaces were their copyright defence.[2] In view of
the Dublin edns. however they determined on their own edn., and chose a general title which inspired that of one of the states of the Dublin edn. of vols.
II–III (below, 79.4LP/6a, with the words 'the most eminent'). This phrase perhaps derives from SJ's own suggestions made in an undated note to Nichols
(*Letters* 729.2; Hyde, iii. 347), though Nichols was presumably the final arbiter.

The agreement to publish this edn. was drawn up on 12 March 1781. It
reads:

> At a Meeting of the Committee on the Poets at the Grecian Coffeehouse,
> March 12 1781 Present, Messrs. Dodsley, Rivington, Dilly, Evans,
> Robinson, Conant, Nicol, T. Davies, Cadell, and J. Nichols
> It is agreed that an Edition of the Lives shall be printed, as soon as pos-
> sible, in Four Volumes 8vo No 3000; to be ready for Delivery at the First
> of May at farthest.
> It is intended that the Volumes shall make 25 or 26 Sheets
> The Volumes shall be printed by Mr Strahan; Mr Hughs, Mr. J.
> Rivington, and J. Nichols.
> The Paper to be bought by Messrs. Longman, Rivington, Conant, and J.
> Nichols

That a Head of Dr Johnson be engraved, under the Direction of Mr
Robinson, for the Four Volumes; and a smaller Head of the Doctor to be
engraved, under the Direction of Mr Dilly, for the small Edition. Both
Plates to be engraved from a new Drawing, [to be taken] and that Sir
Joshua Reynolds be requested to permit a Drawing to be taken.

That Mr. Reed be desired to draw up an Assignment, to Mr Cadell if that
is sufficient; otherwise to the whole Body of Partners.

On the verso, in a single column, are the signatures:

T. Cadell, Jas. Dodsley, Thos Longman, Chs Dilly, T Evans, Geo:
Robinson, N Conant, George Nicol, Thomas Davies, J Nichols.[3]

The naming of four printers implies one for each vol, but of vol. III only is there
any certainty for it is recorded in Strahan's accounts (L: Add. MS 48809, fo. 25,
and 48810, fo. 46[v]) as printed in 3,000 copies in June 1781. It seems likely that
Nichols printed vol. I because the surviving annotated made-up copy (largely) of
that vol. now NN-B (*Booklist* 185, *MS Index* JoS 216) descends from John
Nichols. It is clear that Strahan did not print the prelims to vol. III.

In preparing this edn., the sequence of the 'Lives' was adjusted in conformity
with the then known dates of the deaths of the individual poets. The text is very
slightly revised, perhaps by Nichols, since most of the changes affect minor historical details and the correction of dates.

The four vols. were published in June 1781 ('shortly' in *Public Advertiser*, 5
June 1781), at £1. 1s. in boards, and as Thursday was then (as now) a popular
day for publication, 7th June seems most probable.

A copy of this edn. with the autograph letter of James Thomson (4 Oct.
1747, *Thomson* § 40–2, iv. 266–70) inserted, was lot 322 at Parke-Bernet, N.Y.,
(Carnan), 22 Oct. 1953. Of the copy given to John Wilkes (*Life* iv. 107,
Booklist, 184), only vol. I survives, and is now Hyde.[4]

Copies: O (279 e. 78–81);

USA: CLU-C[2] (1. uncut), CSmH, CtY[2] (both uncut[5]), CtY (Brit. Art.
'Joshua Reynolds'), Hyde[5] (×3 uncut), ICN (Silver: uncut), ICU, IU, [Liebert[4]
(1. 'H. L. Piozzi'; 2. 'Robert Smith')], MH[2] (1. 'R. Sneyd, Keele'; 2. boards,
uncut, 'J.H. Schaffner'), NIC[2], NjP ('Robert H. Taylor'), NN-B, NPM (Pres.
SJ: 'John Wesley' *Booklist* 183), NRU, PPL, PPM, TxY[3], ViU; *Can*: CaOHM[2]
('Rippey'); *Japan*: [Kyoto]; *UK*: BMp (431681), BRu (no vol. 4), Ck (Keynes),
Cq, DUc, E (Hall 193.d), En (vol. 2 only), JDF (vols. 1–3 'J. R. Cuthbert,
1793', vol. 4 'E.S. Sitwell, 1783'), L, LICj, Ljh[2] (1. Brett – Esher; 2. 'Hon.
Theobald Fitzwalter Butler'), Lu (Sterling), MRp, MRu, NCu, Oa, Oef, Op,
STA, WIS; *Eir*: Dt; *Fr*: BN.

---

[1] SJ did not much like it, ''Tis surly Sam', he said to JB when they looked at it on 2 June 1781
(perhaps in consequence of this reproduction, *Boswell, Laird of Auchinleck* (1977), 369).

[2] In their announcement of the edn. in *Public Advertiser* 5 June 1781, the proprietors congratu-
lated themselves on having beaten the Dublin booksellers whose edn. of the second instalment of
the 'Prefaces' (79.4LP/6) was published in July, but it was a close run thing.

³ *MS Handlist*, 176; formerly owned by the late Arthur A. Houghton, Esq; of New York, to whom I am indebted for permission to transcribe and publish it.
  ⁴ Formerly Alan G. Thomas, Sotheby, 21 June 1993, 196.
  ⁵ In CtY: (Beinecke/1980/78), vol. 3 comprises mixed sheets from this and from 79.4LP/7 (below), and vol. 4 has only a² from this ed. with following sheets of 79.4LP/9 (below); 'Geo. Mace' — 'Thomas Battersbee'.

79.4LP/6a   Lives of the Poets, second instalment,   1781
           first Dublin edition, first issue

THE | LIVES | OF THE | ENGLISH POETS; | AND A | CRITICISM | ON THEIR | WORKS. | [medium swelled rule] | BY SAMUEL JOHNSON. | [medium swelled rule] | VOL. II [–III]. | DUBLIN: | Printed for Meſſrs. WHITESTONE, WILLIAMS, COLLES, WILSON, | LYNCH, JENKIN, WALKER, BURNET, HALLHEAD, | FLIN, EXSHAW, BEATTY, and WHITE. | [short swelled rule] | M,DCC,LXXXI.

[*Var.* 1] THE | LIVES | OF THE MOST EMINENT | ENGLISH POETS; | WITH | CRITICAL OBSERVATIONS | ON THEIR | WORKS. | BY SAMUEL JOHNSON. | [medium swelled rule] | IN THREE VOLUMES. | [medium swelled rule] | THE SECOND [–THIRD] VOLUME. | [triple rule] | DUBLIN: | Printed for Meſſrs. WHITESTONE, WILLIAMS, COLLES, WILSON, | LYNCH, JENKIN, WALKER, BURNET, HALLHEAD, | FLIN, EXSHAW, BEATTY, and WHITE. | [short swelled rule] | M,DCC,LXXXI.

Note: As this title is integral, it is presumably a press-variant, and so there is some likelihood that other versions with minor typographical differences may be found.

2 vols., 8°

II. *A*² B–2E⁸ 2F⁸ (2F3 + ˣ2F⁸) 2G–2I⁸, ($4 (ˣ2F1,2 as '2F4,5') signed; 'VOL. II.' on $1 (+ ˣ2F4)), 258 leaves.

Pp. *i* t., *ii* blk, *iii* Contents, *iv* blk, on B1 text 1–86 Addison, 87–114 Blackmore, 115–25 Sheffield, *126* blk, 127–56 Granville, 157–73 Rowe, *174* blk, 175–98 Tickell, 199–219 Congreve, *220* blk, 221–30 Fenton, 231–65 Prior, *266* blk, 267–438 *439–*454 Pope, 439–96 Swift.

Dropheads: in the form: [parallel rule] | NAME., with htt. as: NAME., except Sheffield as : [parallel rule] | SHEFFIELD | BUCKINGHAMSHIRE., and medium parallel rule p. 127.

Pagination: [↑] pp. 1, 87, 115, 127, 157, 175, 199, 221, 231, 267, 439; 496 *sometimes* 196. The insert in 2F of an extra 8 leaves, is paged *439–*454 and carries the Essay on the Epitaphs of Pope, from the *Universal Visiter*, q.v. (56.1UV/1, above).

Press-figures: none. There is some faint sign of a '1' on Rowe p. 167 (M4) in NIC (1779 a. c.1), but a press-figure is doubtful.

Catchwords: 64 long, (~;), 303 em₍ₐ₎ (employment), 307 But₍ₐ₎ (~,), 361 drawn (*drawn*), 438 THE (*THE*), *451 [vul-] gar (vulgar).

Explicit: 496 END OF THE SECOND VOLUME.

Notes: Contents misdirect Blackmore to p. 89 [= 87].

III. π^2 a^8 A–2C^8 ($2 (*occas.* + C3) signed; 'VOL. II.' on $1), 218 leaves.

Pp. *i* t., *ii* blk, *iii* Contents, *iv* blk, on a1 *1 2–16 Gay, on A1 pp. *17 18–22 Broome, 23–26 Pitt, 27–32 Parnell, on B1 pp. 1–13 A. Philips, *14* blk, 15–27 Watts, *28* blk, 29–185 Savage, *186* blk, 187–90 Somervile, 191–212 Thomson, 213–19 Hammond, *220* blk, 221–29 Collins, *230* blk, 231–95 Young, *296* blk, 297–301 Dyer, *302* blk, 303–12 Mallet, 313–25 Shenstone, *326* blk, 327–37 Akenside, *338* blk, 339–51 Lyttelton, *352* blk, 353–63 West, *364* blk, 365–99 Gray (386, 394 blk), *400* blk.

Dropheads: as: [parallel rule] | NAME., and htt. as: NAME., but A. Philips simply as: 'PHILIPS.'

Pagination: Sigs. a and A are *addenda* and the duplicated pagination is the result of placing them in their correct sequence. The affected Lives of Gay, Broome, Pitt, and Parnell are all from *Prefaces* VIII (79.4LP/4, above).[1] The additional pagination is supplied with asterisks and brackets (single for numbers placed ↗), as follows: [*↑] (a) 1, (A) 17, [↑] (A) 23, 27, (B–) 15, 29, 187, 191, 213, 221, 231, 297, 303, 313, 327, 339, 353, 365; [↗₍ₐ₎ (a) 2–16, (A) 18–22, 24–6, 28–32.

Press-figures: none.

Catchwords: none between 'Lives'; no errors.

Explicit: 399 FINIS.

Paper: White, laid; Carré (uncut: 8¼ × 5 ³⁄₁₆ in.); wmk.: Grapes + P G | F DANGOUMOIS. In II. A & ˣ2F, wmk.: Grapes + F [. . . ?] MET.

Type: Text: english (4.7 mm), leaded (II. insert ˣ2F English, unleaded); quots. Long primer (3.3 mm), leaded (II. insert ˣ2F, bourgeois (2.8 mm) in different face). White lines divide paras. exc. in II. ˣ2F where set close. Flowers II. 50, 109, 112, 183, 230, 253, 382, 408, 481, 495, *none* in III.; parallel rules II. 1, 87, 115, 157, 199, 221, 231, 267, 439, III. (a) *1, (A) *17, 23, 27, (B–) 1, 15, 29, 187, 191, 213, 221, 231, 297, 303, 313, 327, 339, 353, 365; medium parallel rules II. 127.

References: Courtney 141; *Tinker* 1364; Rowan, *BC* i (1952), 174.

Notes: There was only one edn. of vols. II–III of the Dublin printing of the second instalment of *Prefaces* (79.4LP/4) and all copies are dated to 1781. They were published in July 1781 (Cole, *PBSA* lxxv (1981), 245–6).

It appears from the version of Pope (II.) that the printer had acquired sheets of SJ's 'Preface' *without* the appended 'Criticism on Pope's Epitaphs' from the *Universal Visiter*, which occupied the last 2½ sheets of *Prefaces* VII. Pope's *Letter to Bridges* (*Prefaces*, vii. 333–39) is omitted from this edn., and it begins on X7 of *Prefaces* VII. The cwd. on p. 332 of *Prefaces* VII, is 'THE' and this is copied by the Dublin printer at II. 438, but when the insert ˣ2F was prepared it was not noticed that it began with '*THE*'. The identity of paper in the prelims and insert in II. (as well as the distinctive typography), shows that they were printed at a late stage in the production, doubtless when both vols. were virtually complete.

The inserted a + A in III. containing Gay, Broome, Pitt, and Parnell, shows that the vol. was planned to begin as usual with sig. B (A. Philips) but that at some point it was discovered that these four had been overlooked. Perhaps it was supposed they would find a place in II. which contains 11 'Lives' . With these four it would have contained 15; III. contains 19 and without them would have contained 15, so matching vol. II. The Dubliners probably reckoned at first on dividing the 30 'Lives' into two vols. of 15 each, but then found the proportions were unequal, especially when they had missed the Essay on the 'Epitaphs of Pope'. If this is plausible, it is likely that A. Philips, beginning with III. sig. B was already set up, so that the extra 'Lives' had to be inserted before it. Such awkwardness would have been more likely if both vols. were being composed and worked off simultaneously.

Copies: O² (1. 12 т. 1743–44; 2. Vet. A5 e. 2294–95);

USA: CLU-C ('Brown of New Hall'), DLC, Hyde², ICU, IU, [Liebert], MH², NIC² (1. 'Rippey'; 2. 'Academiæ Belfastiensis'), NjP, NRU, TxU, ViU; *Can*: CaOHM; *Japan*: [Kyoto]; *UK*: BMp (460245–6), JDF, L (11613. bb.11), [unidentified Ljh]; *Eir*: Dt ('Kells Ingram' — 'W.G. Paul').

---

[1] It may be that the Dubliners were working from a defective copy of vol. 8 of *Prefaces*, either incomplete or in unbound sheets, or (perhaps more likely) that the work was shared between printers to expedite production so that this section was overlooked or its printer misdirected.

79.4LP/6b   Lives of the Poets, second instalment   1781
first Dublin edition, second issue

THE | LIVES | OF THE | ENGLISH POETS: | AND A | CRITICISM | ON THEIR | WORKS. | BY SAMUEL JOHNSON. | VOL. II [–III]. | PRINTED FOR | [Oval engr. vignette of 2 allegorical figures supporting a cartouche: 'Wᵐ. Wilson, | Bookseller & Stationer | at Homer's head | No 6 Dame Street | the Corner of | Palace Street, | [BL] **Dublin**.' (G.B. Cypriani inv. F. Bartolozzi sculp.] | MDCCLXXXI.

This is a cancel t. attached to the sheets of the first issue, described above 79.4LP/6a. There are variant versions of Wilson's engraved vignette plate, see above 70.4LP/2b. The only copies examined so far bear the vignette as above, but there may well be others in different states.

Copy: *Eir*: Dt; *USA*: Hyde.

79.4LP/7a   Lives of the Poets, third edition   1783

THE | LIVES | OF THE MOST EMINENT | ENGLISH POETS; | WITH | CRITICAL OBSERVATIONS | ON THEIR | WORKS. | By SAMUEL JOHNSON. | IN FOUR VOLUMES. | A NEW EDITION, CORRECTED. | [short swelled rule] | THE FIRST [–FOURTH] VOLUME. | [short swelled rule] | LONDON: | PRINTED FOR C. BATHURST, J. BUCKLAND, W. STRAHAN, J. RIVING- | TON AND SONS, T. DAVIES, T. PAYNE, L. DAVIS, W. OWEN, B. WHITE, | S. CROWDER, T. CASLON, T. LONGMAN, B. LAW, C. DILLY, | J. DODSLEY, J. WILKIE, J. ROBSON, J. JOHNSON, T. LOWNDES, | G. ROBINSON, T. CADELL, J. NICHOLS, E. NEWBERY, | T. EVANS, P. ELMSLY, R. BALDWIN, G. NICOL, LEIGH | AND SOTHEBY, J. BEW, N. CONANT, W. NICOLL, | J. MURRAY, S. HAYES, W. FOX, AND J. BOWEN. | MDCCLXXXIII.

4 vols., 8°

I. a⁴ B–T⁸ U⁸ (±U8) X–2F⁸ 2G⁴ (–2G4 = 'U8'), ($4 signed; 'VOL.I.' on $1 (+ 'U8')), 231 leaves.

Pp. Engr. front. 1 leaf + a1 p. *i* title, *ii* blank, iii–v Advertisement dh: [double rule] | ADVERTISEMENT. (no date), ht: ADVERTISEMENT. *vi* blank, vii dh: CONTENTS | OF THE | FIRST VOLUME., *viii* blank, on B1 1–100 text Cowley dh: [treble rule] | COWLEY., ht: COWLEY., 101–18 Denham dh: [double rule] | DENHAM., ht: DENHAM., 119–262 Milton dh: [double rule] | MILTON., ht: MILTON., 263–88 Butler dh: [double rule] | BUTLER., ht: BUTLER., 289–302 Rochester dh: [double rule] | ROCHESTER., ht: ROCHESTER., 303–20 Roscommon dh: [double rule] | ROSCOMMON., ht: ROSCOMMON., 321–8 Otway dh: [double rule] | OTWAY., ht: OTWAY., 329–412 Waller dh: [double rule] | WALLER., ht: WALLER., 413–14 Pomfret dh: [double rule] | POMFRET., ht: POM-FRET., 415–20 Dorset dh: [double rule] | DORSET., ht: DORSET., 421–24 Stepney dh: [parallel rule] | STEPNEY., ht: STEPNEY., 425–50 J. Philips dh: [double rule] | J. PHILIPS., ht: J. PHILIPS., 451–4 Walsh dh: [double rule] | WALSH., ht: WALSH.

Dropheads &c: as: [double rule] | NAME., *except*: [triple rule] on p. 1, and [parallel rule] on p. 421; htt. as: NAME.

Pagination: [↑] pp. iii–v, vii, 1, 101, 119, 263, 289, 303, 321, 329, 413, 415, 421, 425, 451.

Press-figures: a2ᵛ(iv)–4, B1ᵛ(2)–5, C3ᵛ(22)–7, C6ᵛ(28)–5, D5(41)–3, D6(43)–7, E1ᵛ(50)–5, E7(61)–1, F2ᵛ(68)–3, F3ᵛ(70)–7, G7(93)–7, G7ᵛ(94)–7, H7(109)–6, H8(111)–3, I6ᵛ(124)–6, I8(127)–8, K5ᵛ(138)–1, K7(141)–5, L1ᵛ(146)–3, L5(153)–1, M5ᵛ(170)–5, M8ᵛ(176)–6, N1ᵛ(178)–7, N2ᵛ(180)–1, O2ᵛ(196)–6, P5(217)–5, P6(219)–7, Q4ᵛ(232)–7, Q5ᵛ(234)–1, R3ᵛ(246)–5, R5(249)–3, S5ᵛ(266)–7, S6ᵛ(268)–5, T3ᵛ(278)–*sometimes* 5, T5(281)–1,

U4^v(296)–3, X7(317)–7, X8(319)–6, Y4^v(328)–3, Y6(331)–5, Z3^v(342)–5, Z7(349)–6, 2A2^v(356)–1, 2A6(363)–5, 2B6^v(380)–3, 2B7^v(382)–1, 2C8(399)–1, 2C8^v(400)–3, 2D2^v(404)–7, 2D6(411)–5, 2E5(425)–1, 2F8(447)–4, 2F8^v(448)–5.

Catchwords: 209 [wor-] ſhip$_\wedge$ (~.), 240 He (But), 341 $_\wedge$"Mere (*"~).

Explicit: 454 END OF THE FIRST VOLUME.

Type: Rules are doubles at 101, 119, 263, 289, 303, 321, 329, 413, 415, 425, 451; treble at 1; parallel at 421, and swelled at 436. J. Philips ends (450) with 6 asterisks.

II. a² B–2E⁸ 2F⁴, ($4 (–2F3,4) signed; 'VOL. II.' on $1), 222 leaves.

Pp. al *i* title, *ii* blank, iii dh: CONTENTS | OF THE | SECOND VOLUME., *iv* blk, on Bl text pp. 1–214 Dryden dh: [parallel rule] | DRY-DEN., ht: DRYDEN., 215–55 Smith dh: [parallel rule] | SMITH., ht: SMITH., 256–8 Duke dh: [parallel rule] | DUKE., ht: DUKE., 259–66 King dh: [parallel rule] | KING., ht: KING., 267–76 Sprat dh: [parallel rule] | SPRAT., ht: SPRAT., 277–84 Halifax dh: [parallel rule] | HALIFAX., ht: HALIFAX., 285–91 Parnell dh: [double rule] | PARNELL., ht: PARNELL., 292–300 Garth dh: [parallel rule] | GARTH., ht: GARTH., 301–20 Rowe dh: [parallel rule] | ROWE., ht: ROWE., 321–420 Addison dh: [parallel rule] | ADDISON., ht: ADDISON., 421–8 Hughes dh: [parallel rule] | HUGHES., ht: HUGHES., 429–40 Sheffield dh: [parallel rule] | SHEFFIELD, | BUCKINGHAMSHIRE., ht: SHEFFIELD.

Dropheads &c: as: [double rule] | NAME. p. 285, but: [parallel rule] pp. 1, 215, 256, 259, 267, 277, 292, 301, 321, 421, and 429, and: [swelled rule] p. 216.

Pagination: [↑] pp. iii, 1, 215, 256, 259, 267, 277, 285, 292, 301, 321, 421, 429.

Press-figures: B2^v(4)–10, B3^v(6)–3, C7^v(30)–6, C8^v(32)–7, D7^v(46)–5, D8^v(48)–4, E5^v(58)–10, E7(61)–5, F2^v(68)–6, F8(79)–3, G3^v(86)–*sometimes* 7, G7(93)–3, H1^v(98)–5, H8^v(112)–7, I2^v(116)–5, I6(123)–3, K2^v(132)–9, K5^v(138)–3, L7^v(158)–10, L8^v(160)–3, M7(173)–6, M8(175)–9, N5(185)–10, N8(191)–5, O6^v(204)–7, P5^v(218)–10, P6^v(220)–5, Q5^v(234)–7, Q8^v(240)–9, R1^v(242)–10, R2^v(244)–3, S4^v(264)–5, S8(271)–3, T1^v(274)–10, T4^v(280)–5, U5(297)–9, U5^v(298)–7, X5^v(314)–3, X6^v(316)–10, Y6(331)–9, Y7(333)–7, Z3^v(342)–9, Z8^v(352)–7, 2A6(363)–2, 2A7(365)–10, 2B1^v(370)–3, 2B4^v(376)–5, 2C8(399)–10, 2C8^v(400)–7, 2D3^v(406)–2 *or* 10, 2D7(413)–5, 2E7^v(430)–5, 2E8^v(432)–3, 2F4(439)–7. The variant figures in 2D(i) are not associated with variant settings of type in Rowe.

Catchwords: 199 $_\wedge$unhappy ("~), 200 $_\wedge$to ("~), 324 Addiſon$_\wedge$ (~*,).

Explicit: END OF THE SECOND VOLUME.

III. *A*² B–G⁸ H⁸ (H6 + *H7'.8) I–2E⁸, ($4 signed; 'VOL. III.' on $1), 220 leaves.

Pp. on A1 p. *i* title, *ii* blank, iii CONTENTS | OF THE | THIRD VOLUME., *iv* blank, on B1 1–40 Prior dh: [parallel rule] | PRIOR., ht: PRIOR., 41–64 Congreve dh: [parallel rule] | CONGREVE., ht: CONGREVE., 65–98 Blackmore dh: [parallel rule] | BLACKMORE., ht: BLACKMORE., 99–108, 109*–12* 'Fenton' dh: [parallel rule] | FENTON., ht: FENTON., 109–27 Gay dh: [parallel rule] | GAY., ht: GAY., 128–42 Granville dh: [parallel rule] | GRANVILLE., ht: GRANVILLE., 143–50 Yalden dh: [parallel rule] | YALDEN., ht: YALDEN., 151–60 Tickell dh: [parallel rule] | TICKELL., ht: TICKELL., 161–5 Hammond dh: [parallel rule] | HAMMOND., ht: HAMMOND., 166–70 Somervile dh: [parallel rule] | SOMERVILE., ht: SOMERVILE., 171–352 Savage dh: [parallel rule] | SAVAGE., ht: SAVAGE., 353–424 Swift dh: [parallel rule] | SWIFT., ht: SWIFT., 425–32 Broome dh: [total rule] | BROOME., ht: BROOME.

Dropheads &c: as: [parallel rule] | NAME. pp. 1, 41, 65, 99, 109, 128, 143, 151, 161, 166, 171, 353; [total rule] pp. 425.

Pagination: 109*–112* are an *addendum* to Fenton.

Press-figures: B7(13)–7, B7ᵛ(14)–9, C1ᵛ(18)–6, C7(29)–5, D6(43)–4, D8ᵛ(48)–1, E2ᵛ(52)–9, F7(77)–7, F8(79)–1, G3ᵛ(86)–6, H2ᵛ(100)–†, H6(107)–*, 'H7ᵛ(*110)–‡, I3ᵛ(118)–7, I8ᵛ(128)–5, K6(139)–7, K7(141)–5, L6ᵛ(156)–7, L7ᵛ(158)–6, M1ᵛ(162)–9, M7(173)–7, N8(191)–6, N8ᵛ(192)–5, O1ᵛ(194)–5, O7(205)–4, P1ᵛ(210)–9, P2ᵛ(212)–6, Q1ᵛ(226)–7, Q7(237)–4, R1ᵛ(242)–9, R8ᵛ(256)–6, S3ᵛ(262)–7, S7(269)–5, T2ᵛ(276)–*, T6(283)–†, U3ᵛ(294)–7, U5(297)–†, X3ᵛ(310)–4, X6ᵛ(316)–†, Y2ᵛ(324)–*, Y8(335)–†, Z2ᵛ(340)–9, Z7ᵛ(350)–*, 2A7(365)–‡, 2A8(367)–1, 2B6(379)–†, 2B7(381)–8, 2C7(397)–†, 2C8(399)–2, 2D8(415)–†, 2D8ᵛ(416)–2, 2E1ᵛ(418)–8, 2E6ᵛ(428)–7.

Catchwords: 22 Whigs, (~*,), 104 [uſe-] ful (~,), 108 GAY. (109*: WHATEVER), *112 (109: GAY.), 413 "Dr. (*"~.), 420 to ("~).

Explicit: 432 END OF THE THIRD VOLUME.

IV. a² B–2H⁸ 2I⁴, ($4 (–2I3,4) signed; 'VOL. IV' on $1 (–a)), 246 leaves.

Pp. a1 *i* t., *ii* blk, iii dh: CONTENTS | OF THE | FOURTH VOLUME., *iv* blk, on B1 1–238 text Pope dh: [parallel rule] | POPE., ht: POPE., 239–44 Pitt dh: [parallel rule] | PITT., ht: PITT., 245–68 Thomson dh: [parallel rule] | THOMSON., ht: THOMSON., 269–84 Watts dh: [parallel rule] | WATTS., ht: WATTS., 285–300 A. Philips dh: [parallel rule] | A. PHILIPS., ht: A. PHILIPS., 301–8 West dh: [parallel rule] | WEST., ht: WEST., 309–17 Collins dh: [parallel rule] | COLLINS., ht: COLLINS., 318–22 Dyer dh: [parallel rule] | DYER., ht: DYER., 323–36 Shenstone dh: [parallel rule] | SHENSTONE., ht: SHENSTONE., 337–422 Young dh: [parallel rule] | YOUNG., ht: YOUNG., 423–34 Mallet dh: [parallel rule] | MALLET., ht: MALLET., 435–46 Akenside dh: [parallel rule] | AKENSIDE., ht: AKENSIDE., 447–69 Gray dh: [parallel rule] | GRAY., ht:

GRAY., 470–84 Lyttelton dh: [parallel rule] | LYTTELTON., ht: LYTTELTON., 485 Advt. for the 'Poets' and 'Preface' in 69 vols., *486* NEW BOOKS publiſhed by J. NICHOLS., *487* Four spine labels for the 4 vols. of this ed., *488* blk.

Dropheads &c: as: [parallel rule] | NAME. pp. 1, 239, 245, 269, 285, 301, 309, 318, 323, 337, 423, 435, 447, 470; [swelled rule] pp. 441, and [flowers] p. 140.

Pagination: [↑] pp. iii, 1, 239, 245, 269, 285, 301, 309, 318, 323, 337, 423, 435, 447, 470.

Press-figures: B4ᵛ(8)–2, B7ᵛ(14)–6, C7ᵛ(30)–4, C8ᵛ(32)–1, D3ᵛ(38)–2, E6ᵛ(60)–1, E7ᵛ(62)–5, F5(73)–5, F7ᵛ(78)–4, G7(93)–1, H5ᵛ(106)–3, I6ᵛ(124)–2, K7ᵛ(142)–2, K8ᵛ(144)–4, M4ᵛ(168)–3, N1ᵛ(178)–3, N2ᵛ(180)–1, O3ᵛ(198)–2, P3ᵛ(214)–2, P7(221)–4, Q1ᵛ(226)–2, Q2ᵛ(228)–3, R1ᵛ(242)–4, R8ᵛ(256)–1, S4ᵛ(264)–2, S6(267)–4, T1ᵛ(274)–3, T7(285)–1, U8(303)–7, U8ᵛ(304)–6, X8(319)–7, X8ᵛ(320)–4, Y1ᵛ(322)–3, Y5(329)–4, Z1ᵛ(338)–8, Z2ᵛ(340)–2, 2A3ᵛ(358)–3, 2A7(365)–8, 2B5ᵛ(378)–8, 2B6ᵛ(380)–5, 2C8(399)–1, 2D1ᵛ(402)–1, 2D7(413)–4, 2E6ᵛ(428)–5, 2E7ᵛ(430)–6, 2F8(447)–4, 2F8ᵛ(448)–7, 2G5(457)–7, 2G8(463)–3, 2H1ᵛ(466)–1, 2H7(477)–2, 2I1ᵛ(482)–3. Sheet L is *unfigured*.

Catchwords: 208 THE (The), 459 GRAY‿ (GRAY's), 484–[487] *om*.

Explicit: 484 FINIS.

Paper: White, laid; Medium (uncut: 9 × 5¾ in.); wmk. rarely vis., perhaps Pro Patria.

Type: Despite different printers, text throughout is english (4.5 mm), with quotations in small pica (4.0 mm), occasionally in long primer (3.3 mm). Initial 2-line caps begin paragraphs in 'Cowley' (I. 32, 35, 40, 41, 42, 44, 46, 48, 49, 50, 51, and 53, and again 385), but not elsewhere.

References: Courtney 142; CH 159–60; ESTC: t004514.

Notes: The reason for the cancellation of I. U8 (pp. 303–4) is unknown. Offsets in JDF (Ilchester) copy of I: Roscommon, 'U8' (pp. 303–4) on 2G3ᵛ, and of 2G3ᵛ on 'U8', and of a1 (title) on 'U8'ᵛ, show that U8 formed a whole sheet with a and 2G. Offsets in JDF (Mayo) copy show that III. N8ᵛ (p. 192) is set on A1 (title). CH noted (p. 159), that *H7.8 are sometimes misbound between A1.2 and together formed a ½-sheet. The extra leaves of III. *H7.8 carry an addendum to Fenton and were apparently printed as Savage (N8ᵛ) was going through the press.[1] Vol. III was printed in 'November' (Strahan's ledger, L: Add. MSS 48809, fo. 25, and 48810, fo. 46ᵛ), but the four volumes were not announced for publication until February 1783 (*Lond. Chron.* 8 Feb. 1783), at 1 gn. (£1.1s.) the set.

SJ's receipt for £100. for the revision of this edn. is CtY (*MS Handlist* 195). The text of these 'Lives' is revised, as is that of Young, by Herbert Croft (see L copy, below).

Copies: O (279 e. 103–6). Sets of this edn. are common.[2]

USA: CSmH, CtY[2] (**1**. 'J. Reynolds' — 'F.W. Hilles'), Hyde, ICU, [Liebert], MBAt, MH (Pres. SJ: 'Lucas Pepys' *Booklist* 188, Lowell), NIC, TxU, WiM, [CU, NhM, OCU, PPB]; *Can*: CaOHM; *Japan*: [Kyoto]; *UK*: ABu, BMp (434438), BRu (vol. 1: 2F4 misp, –2F5), Eu, En[2] (B16/b1), [Es], JDF[2] (**1**. 'Ilchester'; **2**. 'Mayo'), Gu, [PR], L (C.28. h.1–4, 'Herbert Croft' + MS revisions of Young), LCu, LICj, Ljh ('S.A. Hale, Oct. 1838' — 'Chas. Blailie' — 'R. Fullard'), Oef, WLAp; *Fr*: BN (vol. 3 only).

---

[1] Strahan's charge for this vol. covers 27½ sheets at £2. 2s. per sheet only, so that no extra charge is made for the inserted bifolium.

[2] HLP's annotated copy was lot 735a in Pt. I of the Jerome Kern sale, Anderson Galleries (N.Y.), 7 Jan. 1927. I have not traced it. A copy 'interleaved with numerous notes by Malone, and one of Dr Johnson' was lot 1211 at Evans, *Bibliotheca Heberiana*, pt. VIII (29 Feb. 1836), and went for £2. It is also untraced.

79.4LP/7b   Lives of the Poets, Additions and   1783
Corrections in third London edition

THE PRINCIPAL | ADDITIONS and CORRECTIONS | IN THE THIRD EDITION OF | Dr. JOHNSON's | LIVES OF THE POETS; | COLLECTED TO COMPLETE | THE SECOND EDITION.

8°, 2L–2O⁴, ($2 signed; 'VOL. IV.' on $1 (–2N)), 16 leaves.

Pp. *505* t. (+ sig. and Dir. line), *506* blk, 507–34 text dh: [parallel rule] | ADDITIONS *and* CORRECTIONS., ht: ADDITIONS IN VOL. I. (508–11), . . . VOL. II. (512–15), . . . VOL. III. (516–20), . . . VOL. IV. (521–34), *535–6* blk.

Pagination: [↑] 507.
Press-figures: 2L3ᵛ(510)–4, 2M4(519)–1, 2N4ᵛ(528)–1, 2O1ᵛ(530)–7.
Catchwords: 522 WATT∧ (WATTS.).
Paper: White, laid; medium (as. 79.4LP/7a, above); no vis. wmk.
Type: English and pica.
References: *Life* iv. 63 (Courtney 142); CH 159; *Tinker* 1366.
Notes: These leaves were intended to supplement 79.4LP/5, and to be bound in vol. IV after sig. 2K. The publication of 79.4LP/7a (1783), so soon after 1781 evidently led to complaints. This supplement was apparently compiled by Nichols from SJ's marked copy of 1781 used in preparation of 1783, of which vol. I (imperfect) only, survives (NN-B: *Booklist* 185). Nichols acknowledged his responsibility in *Lit. Anec.* vi (1812), 633 n. 23. It is noticed in *Gents. Mag.* liii (March 1783), 239–41, and largely reprinted in *London Mag.* li (Sept. 1783), 248–53.

Copies are fairly scarce, so the edn. perhaps ran to no more than 500; few exist separately, most being bound in copies of 79.4LP/5, vol. IV.
Copies: O (279 e. 81*); *USA*: Hyde³, NN; *UK*: Op.

79.4LP/8a   The Works of the English Poets,   1790
                              second edition

THE | WORKS | OF THE | ENGLISH POETS. | WITH | PREFACES, |
BIOGRAPHICAL AND CRITICAL, | BY SAMUEL JOHNSON. |
[medium swelled rule] | VOLUME THE FIRST [–SEVENTY-FIFTH]. |
[medium swelled rule] | LONDON: | PRINTED BY JOHN NICHOLS; |
FOR J. BUCKLAND, J. RIVINGTON AND SONS, T. PAYNE AND |
SONS, L. DAVIS, B. WHITE AND SON, T. LONGMAN, B. LAW, | J.
DODSLEY, H. BALDWIN, J. ROBSON, C. DILLY, T. CADELL, | J.
NICHOLS, J. JOHNSON, G. G. J. AND J. ROBINSON, | R. BALDWIN,
H. L. GARDNER, P. ELMSLY, T. EVANS, | G. NICOL, LEIGH AND
SOTHEBY, J. BEW, N. CONANT, | J. MURRAY, J. SEWELL, W.
GOLDSMITH, W. RICHARDSON, | T. VERNOR, W. LOWNDES, W.
BENT, W. OTRIDGE, T. AND | J. EGERTON, S. HAYES, R.
FAULDER, J. EDWARDS, G. AND | T. WILKIE, W. NICOLL,
OGILVY AND SPEARE, SCATCHERD | AND WHITAKER, W. FOX,
C. STALKER, E. NEWBERY. 1790.
  75 vols., 8°

I–VI *Prefaces* (see separate entries, below), VI–IX Cowley, IX Denham,
X–XII Milton, XIII–XIV Butler, XV Rochester, Roscommon, & Otway, XVI
Waller, XVII Pomfret, Dorset, Stepney, J. Philips, & Walsh, XVIII–XXI
Dryden, XXII–XXIV Dryden's *Virgil*, XXV Smith, Duke, & King, XXVI King,
Sprat, & Halifax, XXVII Parnell, XXVIII Garth & Rowe, XXIX Rowe's *Lucan*,
XXX Addison, XXXI Hughes, XXXII Sheffield & Prior, XXXIII–XXXIV
Prior, XXXIV Congreve, XXXV Blackmore & Fenton, XXXVI–XXXVII Gay,
XXXVIII Lansdowne (*alias* Granville), XXXIX Yalden, Tickell, & Hammond,
XL–XLI Somervile, XLI Savage, XLII–XLIV Swift, XLIV Broome,
XLV–XLVII Pope, XLVIII–LI Pope's *Homer*, LII–LIII Pitt, LIV–LV
Thomson, LV–LVI Watts, LVII A. Philips & West, LVIII Collins & Dyer,
LIX Shenstone, LX–LXII Young, LXIII Mallet & Akenside, LXIV Akenside,
Gray, & Lyttelton, LXV Moore & Cawthorne, LXVI–LXVII Churchill,
LXVIII Falconer, LXIX Cunningham & Green, LXX Goldsmith & P.
Whitehead, LXXI Armstrong & Langhorne, LXXII Johnson & W.
Whitehead, LXXIII N. Whitehead & Jenyns, LXXIV–LXXV *Index*.
  The various volumes were printed by different printers as evidenced by the
first lines of the imprints on each title:

H. Baldwin	XIX–XXIV, LXVIII, LXXI	8
R. Blyth	XLVIII–LI, LXIII–LXIV	6
M. Brown	LII–LVI, LXXII	6
J. Davis	XXXI–XXXVI	6
H. Goldney	XXXVII–XLI	5

A. Hamilton	LVII–LXII	6
Henry Hughs	VII–XII	6
John Nichols	I–VI, LXXIV–LXXV	8
Rivington & Marshall	XIII–XVIII, LXIX–LXX	8
T. Spilsbury and Son	XLII–XLVI	5
Andrew Strahan	XXV–XXX, XLVII	7
T. Wright	LXV–LXVII, LXXIII	4
		75

Paper: White, laid; foolscap (uncut: 6¾ × 4¼ in.); no vis. wmk.

Type: Texts: long primer (3.2 mm).

Plates: See below 79.4LP/8b.

References: Courtney 141; ESTC: t152606.

Notes: The various notes in this edn. signed 'E'[ditor] are by Isaac Reed, who was responsible for the additional non-Johnsonian Lives. Also incorporated are the notes of Sir John Hawkins ('H') from his edn. of Johnson's *Works*, 1787 (q.v., 87.3W/1, below), and some supplied by John Nichols ('N').

Printing: Andrew Strahan's account for the printing of vols. XXV–XXX and XLVII (with titles), shows that the first series (XXV–XXX) were printed in 1,500 copies in September 1788, and the remaining vol. (XLVII) in December 1789 (L: Add. MS 48809, fo. 99ᵛ). A letter from Samuel Hayes to James Lackington (who was not a shareholder), of 28 Jan. 1790 (MS Hyde), refers to the distribution of this edn.:

Mr J. Lackington

Sir

The Partners in the New Edition of Dr Johnsons Poets will be summon'd to divide the book the latter End of next Week, it is printed on a fine foolscap made on Purpose for this work by Watman & Co. the number of volumes (including the additional Poets, with their Lives & Portraits) is I think 75 but I am not quite certain, and the Price will be finally fixed by the Partners next week. You shall have some of them at the Price they are put in Lots at the first Capital Sale agreeable to your Proposal, therefore you will be please[d] to find the Articles I mark'd from your Catalogue as soon as Convenient.

I am

your Obedᵗ. Servt.

332 in Oxford Street.   Samuel Hayes.

Thursd. Jan 28/ 90

Some scraps of memoranda in the Hyde Collection show that John Nichols was the paymaster for this edn. His sharebook records his ownership of 5/100 shares which, he noted, 'produces 75 in 1500; & 18 of the Works in 1250' (MS: C (formerly owned by A.N.L. Munby, of King's College)). These notes also show that the production cost per set of 75 vols. was £4. 18s. 4½d.

Copies: O (2804 f. 11–79);

USA: CLU-C, CSmH, DFo, DLC, Hyde, [Liebert], MH (Child), NRU, [OU], PPL; *UK*: ABu, BMp, Eu (9700–774, ex-En), L, LVu, MRu, NCu, Op (lacks vols. 61–2 Young); [JDF: 18 odd. vols. VII, XI, XVI, XIX, XXIII–XXV, XXVII–XXX, L–LI, LVIII, LXV, LXVII, LXXII].

79.4LP/8b Prefaces to the Works of the English Poets,   1790
             companion to second edition of Works

[½t] THE | WORKS | OF THE | ENGLISH POETS. | WITH | PREFACES, | BIOGRAPHICAL AND CRITICAL, | BY SAMUEL JOHNSON. | AND | A POETICAL INDEX. | [medium swelled rule] | IN SEVENTY-FIVE VOLUMES. | [medium swelled rule]

[Title] THE | WORKS | OF THE | ENGLISH POETS. | WITH | PREFACES, | BIOGRAPHICAL AND CRITICAL, | BY SAMUEL JOHNSON. | [medium swelled rule] | VOLUME THE FIRST [–SIXTH]. | [medium swelled rule] | LONDON: | PRINTED BY JOHN NICHOLS; | FOR J. BUCKLAND, J. RIVINGTON AND SONS, T. PAYNE AND | SONS, L. DAVIS, B. WHITE AND SON, T. LONGMAN, B. LAW, | J. DODSLEY, H. BALDWIN, J. ROBSON, C. DILLY, T. CADELL, | J. NICHOLS, J. JOHNSON, G. G. J. AND J. ROBINSON, | R. BALDWIN, H.L. GARDNER, P. ELMSLY, T. EVANS, | G. NICOL, LEIGH AND SOTHEBY, J. BEW, N. CONANT, | J. MURRAY, J. SEWELL, W. GOLDSMITH, W. RICHARDSON, | T. VERNOR, W. LOWNDES, W. BENT, W. OTRIDGE, T. AND | J. EGERTON, S. HAYES, R. FAUL-DER, J. EDWARDS, G. AND | T. WILKIE, W. NICOLL, OGILVY AND SPEARE, SCATCHERD | AND WHITAKER, W. FOX, C. STALKER, E. NEWBERY. 1790.

6 vols., 8°

I. a–b⁴ B–X⁸ (–X8 ? blk), ($4 (–a2 = t., b2,3,4) signed; 'VOL. I.' on $1), 168 leaves.

Pp. *i* ½t, *ii* blk, Front. 1 leaf inserted, *iii* t., *iv* blk, v–vii Advertisement, viii Contents, ix–x Portraits, on b2–4 3 leaves. spine labels, on B1 *1* ½t: THE | LIVES | OF THE MOST EMINENT | ENGLISH POETS; | WITH | CRITICAL OBSERVATIONS | ON THEIR WORKS., *2* blk, 3–4 Advertisement to 1783 edn. (79.4LP/7, above), 5–101 Cowley, 102–17 Denham, 118–255 Milton, 256–81 Butler, 282–93 Rochester, 294–309 Roscommon, 310–17 Otway, *318* blk, *319–20* (X8) ? blk.

Dropheads &c: as: [short swelled rule] | NAME., pp. 5, 102, 118, 256, 282, 294, 310.

Pagination: [↑] v–ix, 1, 3, 5, 102, 118, 256, 282, 294, 310.

Press-figures: a3ᵛ (vi)–5.

Catchwords: 70 [enu-] meration, (~;), 87 tha‸ (that), 140 1642‸ (~.), 208 Thomas‸ (~,), 306 Hi‸ (His).
Explicit: 317 END OF VOL. I.

II. *A*² B–X⁸ Y², ($4 signed; 'VOL. II.' on $1), 164 leaves.
Pp. *i* t., *ii* blk, *iii* Contents, *iv* blk, on B1 1–78 Waller, 79–81 Pomfret, 82–7 Dorset, 88–91 Stepney, 92–116 J. Philips, 117–20 Walsh, 121–324 Dryden.
Dropheads &c: as prec.
Pagination: [↑] iii, 1, 79, 82, 88, 92, 117, 121.
Press-figures: none.
Catchwords: 8 marry; (~,), 38 influence, (fluence,), 87 TEP- (STEPNEY.), 103 focial (focial), 142 This (The), 250 the (the *flipt*), 273 [reputa-] ion (tion).
Explicit: 324 END OF VOL. II.

III. *A*² B–X⁸ Y², ($4 (B8 as C3) signed; 'VOL. III.' on $1), 164 leaves.
Pp. *i* t., *ii* blk, *iii* Contents, *iv* blk, on B1 1–39 Smith, 40–2 Duke, 43–9 King, 50–8 Sprat, 59–66 Halifax, 67–72 Parnell, 73–80 Garth, 81–99 Rowe, 100–197 Addison, 198–205 Hughes, 206–17 Sheffield, 218–55 Prior, 256–78 Congreve, 279–310 Blackmore, 311–23 Fenton, *324* blk.
Dropheads &c: as: [short swelled rule] | NAME. pp. 1, 40, 43, 50, 59, 67, 73, 81, 198, 206, 218, 256, 279, 311; *The rule is omitted on* p. 100.
Pagination: [↑] iii, 1, 40, 43, 50, 59, 67, 73, 81, 100, 198, 206, 218, 256, 279, 311.
Press-figures: none.
Catchwords: 15 took, (~;), 88 [pre-] face‸; (~*;), 234 propofals‸, (~*,), 236 Nec (Necnon), 267 to (‸o), 276 Of [f *flipt*].
Explicit: 323 END OF VOL. III.

IV. *A*² B–U⁸ X², ($4 signed; 'VOL. IV.' on $1), 156 leaves.
Pp. *i* t., *ii* blk, *iii* Contents, *iv* blk, on B1 1–19 Gay, 20–33 Granville, 34–41 Yalden, 42–50 Tickell, 51–5 Hammond, 56–60 Somervile, 61–233 Savage, 234–300 Swift, 301–7 Broome, *308* blk.
Dropheads &c: as: [short swelled rule] | NAME., pp. 1, 20, 34, 42, 51, 56, 61, 234, 301.
Pagination: [↑] iii, 1, 20, 34, 42, 51, 61, 234, 301; 56 as [↑]; 28 '8' *inverted*, 191 as 189.
Press-figures: none.
Catchwords: 294 lawful [*2nd* l *flipt*].
Explicit: 307 END OF THE FOURTH VOLUME.

V. *A*² B–X⁸ Y², ($4 signed; 'VOL. V.' on $1), 164 leaves.
Pp. *i* t., *ii* blk, *iii* Contents, *iv* blk, on B1 1–230 Pope, 231–5 Pitt, 236–58 Thomson, 259–73 Watts, 274–88 A. Philips, 289–95 West, 296–304 Collins, 305–9 Dyer, 310–23 Shenstone, *324* blk.

Dropheads &c: as: [short swelled rule] | NAME. pp. 1, 231, 236, 259, 274, 289, 296, 305, 310.

Pagination: 229 as '22'; [↑] iii, 1, 231, 236, 259, 274, 289, 296, 305, 310.

Press-figures: none.

Catchwords: 48 (We‸ ((~,), 64 [pub-] lifhed‸ (~.), 191 Effay‸ (~,), 249 Prologue, (logue,), 262 life‸ (~.), 270 piety, (~.).

Explicit: 323 END OF THE FIFTH VOLUME.

VI. a² B–S⁸ T⁴ ($4 signed; 'VOL. VI.' on $1), 142 leaves.

Pp. *i* t., *ii* blk, iii Contents, *iv* blk, on B1 1–85 Young, 86–96 Mallet, 97–108 Akenside, 109–30 Gray, 131–44 Lyttelton, 145–8 Moore, 149–51 Cawthorne, 152–7 Churchill, 158–9 Falconer, 160–2 Lloyd, 163–6 Cunningham, 167–8 Green, 169–74 Goldsmith, 175–7 P. Whitehead, 178–9 Armstrong, 180–1 Langhorn, 182–6 Johnson, 187–93 W. Whitehead, 194–8 Jenyns, 199–279 Index, *280* blk.

Dropheads &c: as: [short swelled rule] | NAME., pp. 1, 86, 97, 109, 145, 149, 152, 158, 160, 163, 167, 169, 178, 180, 182, 187, 194, and 199 INDEX &c.; no rule p. 131.

Pagination: 148 as '178'; [↑] iii, 1, 86, 97, 109, 131, 145, 149, 152, 158, 160, 163, 167, 169, 175, 178, 180, 182, 187, 194, 199.

Press-figures: N2ᵛ(180)–5, N7ᵛ(190)–3, O2ᵛ(196)–3, O8(207)–3, P3ᵛ(214)–5, P4ᵛ(216)–3, Q5ᵛ(234)–3, R1ᵛ(242)–5, R5(249)–3, S1ᵛ(258)–5, S7(269)–6, T3ᵛ(278)–5.

Catchwords: 43 ‸whom (—whom), 240 [per-] formance, (mance,), 256 epi-taph (Epitaph).

Explicit: 279 END OF THE SIXTH VOLUME.

Paper: (cf. Hayes's letter to Lackington, quoted 79.4LP/8a, above); White, laid; foolscap (uncut: 6¾ × 4¼ in.), Whatman; no vis. wmk.

Type: Small pica (3.5 mm).

Plates: 32 engr. portraits of poets precede the individual Lives and are directed in I. ix to be placed as facing the pp. noted below:

I. (5 plates): Cowley 'Hall Sculp.' (1), Denham 'Collier fculp.' (102), Milton 'Bartolozzi Sculp:' (118), Butler 'Sherwin Sculp:' (256), Otway 'Hall fculp.' (310).

II. (3 plates): Waller 'Caldwall Sculp.' (1), J. Philips 'Collyer Sculp.' (92), Dryden 'I Sherwin Sculp.' (121).

III. (9 plates): Parnell (67), Garth 'Painted by Sʳ. G. Kneller. Engraved by J. Caldwall. From a Picture in the pofsefsion of W. Bromfield Esqʳ.' (73), Rowe 'From a Buft in Weftminfter Abbey. J.M. Delattre fculpᵗ' (81), Addison 'G. Kneller pinxit F. Bartolozzi fculp.' (100), Hughes 'Caldwall fulp' (198), Sheffield ('Buckingham') 'Hall Sculp.' (206), Prior 'Hall Sculp.' (218), Congreve 'Caldwall Sculp.' (256), Blackmore 'Hall fculp.' (279).

IV. (3 plates): Gay 'Hall Sculp.' (1: wrongly named as 'Gray' in I. ix), Swift 'Walker Sculp:' (234), Broome 'Cook Sculp.' (301).

V. (5 plates): Pope 'Jarvis pinx^t. Caldwall fculp.' (1), Thomson 'Ætatis 25. Aikman Pinxit Delattre fculp^t.' (236), Dr. Watts 'Bartolozzi fculp.' (259), Dyer (305), Shenstone 'Cook Sculp.' (310).

VI. (7 plates): Young 'Cook Sculp.' (1), Akenside 'Cook Sculp.' (97), Lyttelton 'Collyer Sculp.' (131), Churchill 'Cook fculp.' (152), Cunningham 'Cook fculp.' (163), Armstong 'Cook fculp.' (178), Johnson (182).

References: Courtney 141.

Notes: The fluctuating incidence of press-figg. is a problem if the assignment of printers in the imprints is to be relied on.

The last 14 Lives in vol. 6 are not by SJ, though frequently attributed to him in minor edns. of the individual poets, but are the work of Isaac Reed.[1]

Copies: O (2804 f. 5–10);

USA: CLU-C, CSmH, DFo, DLC, Hyde, [Liebert], MH (Child), NRU, [OU], PPL; *Can*: CaOHM; *Japan*: [Kyoto]; *UK*: Eu (SC 9700–6, ex-En), MRu, NCu, Op (lacks vol. 2); [JDF vols. 1 and 6 only].

[1] Sherbo, *Isaac Reed, Editorial Factotum* (1989), 113 and ref.

79.4LP/9 Lives of the Poets, new edition 1790–91

THE | LIVES | OF THE MOST EMINENT | ENGLISH POETS, | WITH | CRITICAL OBSERVATIONS | ON THEIR | WORKS. | By SAMUEL JOHNSON. | [medium swelled rule] | A NEW EDITION, CORRECTED. | [medium swelled rule] | IN FOUR VOLUMES. | VOL. I [–IV]. | [parallel rule] | LONDON: | Printed for J. Rivington & Sons, L. Davis, B. White & Son, T. Longman, | B. Law, J. Dodfley, H. Baldwin, J. Robfon, C. Dilly, T. Cadell, J. Nichols, | J. Johnfon, G. G. J. & J. Robinfon, R. Baldwin, H.L. Gardner, | P. Elmfley, G. Nicol, Leigh & Sotheby, J. Bew, J. Murray, J. Sewell, | W. Goldfmith, T. Payne, W. Richardfon, T. Vernor, W. Lowndes, | W. Bent, W. Otridge, T. & J. Egerton, S. Hayes, R. Faulder, J. Edwards, | G. & T. Wilkie, W. Nicol, Ogilvy & Speare, Scatcherd & Whitaker, | J. Evans, W. Fox, C. Stalker, and E. Newbery. | 1790.

Var: vols. 3–4: . . . 1791.

4 vols., 8°

I. (1790), A^4 (? A1 blk) B–2G^8, ($4 signed; 'VOL. I.' on $1), 236 leaves.

Note: In O: ±X1 is undoubted, affecting Rochester pp. 305–6.

Pp. Engr. front. 1 leaf + *i* t., *ii* blk, iii Contents (misdirecting Rochester to 292 = 299), *iv* blk, 3–4 Advertisement to 1783 edn., on B1 1–464 text Cowley–Walsh.

Dropheads &c: as [short swelled rule] | COWLEY., &c.

Pagination: [↑] 1, 105, 123, 272, 299, 312, 339, 431, 435, 461, ₍↑] 425, (↑) 330; 139 as 136, 348 as '48'.

Press-figures: A3(3)–2, B6(11)–1, B6ᵛ(12)–4, C5(25)–2, D1ᵛ(34)–2, D4ᵛ(40)–7, E5(57)–2, E5ᵛ(58)–4, F5ᵛ(74)–4, F7(77)–2, G4ᵛ(88)–2, G7ᵛ(94)–3, H6ᵛ(108)–4, I6ᵛ(124)–3, I7ᵛ(126)–4, K5(137)–1, K6(139)–3, L1ᵛ(146)–2, L2ᵛ(148)–7, M1ᵛ(162)–4, M7(173)–2, N7(189)–7, N7ᵛ(190)–3, O5(201)–2, O5ᵛ(202)–6, P6(219)–6, P8ᵛ(224)–3, Q6ᵛ(236)–6, R8(255)–1, S2ᵛ(260)–1, S6(267)–5, T2ᵛ(276)–5, T3ᵛ(278)–7, U1ᵛ(290)–1, U2ᵛ(292)–6, X3ᵛ(310)–3, X8ᵛ(320)–1, Y5ᵛ(330)–3, Z2ᵛ(340)–5, Z8(351)–1, 2A6ᵛ(364)–7, 2A7(365)–5, 2B1ᵛ(370)–5, 2B7(381)–3, 2C5ᵛ(394)–6, 2D1ᵛ(402)–3, 2D8ᵛ(416)–7, 2E6(427)–7, 2E7(429)–3, 2F5(441)–6, 2F7ᵛ(446)–7, 2G7(461)–5, 2G8(463)–3.

Catchwords: 60 written‸ (~,), 101 [ma-] jeſtick‸ (~,), 112 ‸But ("~), 174 [Cho-] rus‸ (~,), 178 importance‸ (~,), 351 ‸"There (*"~), 390 "that‸ ("~,).

Explicit: 464 END OF VOL. I.

II. *A*² B–2F⁸ 2G⁴, ($4 signed; 'VOL. II.' on $1), 230 leaves.
Pp. *i* t., *ii* blk, iii Contents, *iv* blk, on B1 1–452 Dryden–Sheffield.
Pagination: [↑] iii, 1, 283, 431; (↑) 222, 263, 266, 273, 291, 298, 307, 372, 440; 293 as '29', 406 as '06'.
Press-figures: B8ᵛ(16)–4, C1ᵛ(18)–4, C7(29)–3, D7ᵛ(46)–7, E4ᵛ(56)–4, E8(63)–3, F3ᵛ(70)–2, F5(73)–4, G5ᵛ(90)–1, G8ᵛ(96)–3, H2ᵛ(100)–7, H8(111)–6, I6(123)–6, I7(125)–1, K3ᵛ(134)–1, K5(137)–3 (*inverted*), L1ᵛ(146)–3, L7(157)–1, M3ᵛ(166)–1, M7(173)–3, N8(191)–5, O2ᵛ(196)–7, O7ᵛ(206)–3, P8(223)–3, P8ᵛ(224)–6, Q2ᵛ(228)–6, Q5(234)–7, R8(255)–1, S1ᵛ(258)–6, T2ᵛ(276)–7, T7ᵛ(286)–1, U2ᵛ(292)–7, U5ᵛ(298)–5, X8(319)–6, X8ᵛ(320)–1, Y1ᵛ(322)–7, Z6(347)–5, 2A1ᵛ(354)–7, 2A7(365)–6, 2B8(383)–6, 2B8ᵛ(384)–5, 2C2ᵛ(388)–1, 2C8(399)–3, 2D1ᵛ(402)–3, 2D7(413)–7, 2E2ᵛ(420)–7, 2F7(445)–2, 2F8(447)–1, 2G1ᵛ(450)–1.

Catchwords: 16 ‸light- ("lightning), 221 *om.* (SMITH.), 370 O‸ (Of), 408 "there (" *slipt*).

Explicit: 452 END OF THE SECOND VOLUME.

III. *A*² B–2E⁸ 2F², ($4 signed; 'VOL. III.' on $1), 220 leaves.
Pp. *i* t., *ii* blk, iii Contents, *iv* blk, on B1 1–436 Prior–Broome.
Dropheads &c.: as [parallel rule] |PRIOR., &c.
Pagination: [↑] 1, 41, 65, 99, 113, 132, 147, 155, 165, 170, 175, 358, 429; 223 as '232'.
Press-figures: B7(13)–2, C1ᵛ(18)–2, D7(45)–2, E7ᵛ(62)–2, F1ᵛ(66)–2, G1ᵛ(82)–2, H1ᵛ(98)–2, I1ᵛ(114)–2, K7ᵛ(142)–2, L1ᵛ(146)–2, M1ᵛ(162)–6, M6ᵛ(172)–5, N7ᵛ(190)–5, O7ᵛ(206)–6, P8('232' = 223)–6, Q3ᵛ(230)–13, R1ᵛ(242)–5, S8(271)–5, T7ᵛ(286)–5, U6ᵛ(300)–2, X6(315)–3, Y6(331)–2, Z8(351)–2, 2A7(365)–5, 2A8(367)–2, 2B1ᵛ(370)–2, 2C5ᵛ(394)–2, 2D1ᵛ(402)–2, 2E7(429)–2, 2F1ᵛ(434)–2.

Catchwords: *om.*; 26 (PRIOR), 40 (CONGREVE.), 56 (CONGREVE‸), 64 (BLACKMORE.), 91 (BLACKMORE,), 108 (WHATEVER), 112 (GAY.),

123 "acted ("in), *om.*: 131 (GRANVILLE.), 146 (YALDEN.), 154 (TICK-ELL.), 164 (HAMMOND.), 169 (SOMERVILE.), 174 (SAVAGE.), 278 "Mifcellany" ("~*"), *om.*: 357 (SWIFT.), 410 (WHEN), 428 (BROOME.).
Explicit: 436 END OF THE THIRD VOLUME.

IV. *A²* B–2H⁸ 2I⁶, ($4 signed; 'Vol. IV.' on $1), 248 leaves.
Pp. *i* t., *ii* blk, iii Contents (misdirecting 'Akenside' to 445 = 441), *iv* blk, on B1 1–491 Pope–Lyttelton, *492* blk.
Pagination: 44 unnumbered; [↑] 1, 241, 247, 287, 303, 311, 320, 326, 341, 430, 441, (↑) 271, 454, 477.
Press-figures: B7ᵛ(14)–2, C3ᵛ(22)–2, D3ᵛ(38)–2, E8(63)–2, F6(75)–2, G6(91)–2, H1ᵛ(98)–2, I1ᵛ(114)–2, K1ᵛ(130)–2, L3ᵛ(150)–2, M1ᵛ(162)–2, N1ᵛ(178)–2, O8(207)–2, P1ᵛ(210)–2, Q5ᵛ(234)–2, R1ᵛ(242)–2, S8(271)–2, T5ᵛ(282)–2, U3ᵛ(294)–2, X7ᵛ(318)–2, Y3ᵛ(326)–2, Z3ᵛ(342)–2, 2A3ᵛ(358)–5, 2B3ᵛ(374)–2, 2C2ᵛ(388)–2, 2D1ᵛ(402)–2, 2E1ᵛ(418)–2, 2F5(441)–2, 2G8(463)–2, 2H1ᵛ(466)–13, 2H7(477)–4, 2I1ᵛ(482)–11.
Catchwords: *om.*: 140 (THE), 240 (PITT.), 243 (AT), 246 (THOMSON.), 271 (WATTS.), 286 (A. PHILIPS.), 302 (WEST.), 310 (COLLINS.), 319 (DYER.), 325 (SHENSTONE.), 340 (YOUNG.), 386 [hu-] ₐan (man), *om.*: 422 (OF), 429 (MALLET.), 440 (AKENSIDE.), 453 (GRAY.), 476 (LYTTELTON.).
Explicit: 491 THE END.

Paper: White, laid; Medium (uncut: 9 × 5¾ in.); no vis. wmk.
Type: Pica (4.3 mm), leaded.
Plate: Engr. port. of SJ. front. in ornam. oval: 'SAMUEL JOHNSON, LL.D. Publifhed as the Act directs. Augᵗ. 24ᵗʰ. 1791 by T. Cadell, Strand.'
References: Courtney 142; ESTC: t116667.
Notes: Vols 3–4 (dated 1791) were printed by Andrew Strahan in Jan. 1791 in 1,000 copies; the paymaster was Thomas Cadell (L: Add. MS 48811, fo. 26). Annotations are signed 'H'[awkins], and 'R'[eed].
Copies: O (279 e. 135–38, 'William Forsteen');
USA: Hyde (lacks I. A⁴; 'Sir John Shaw' — 'Sir Edward Dering' — 'R.B. Adam'), IU, [Liebert], MH (10453.5.15), WiM; *Can*: CaOHM (B. 6865–68); *Japan*: [Kyoto]; *UK*: BMp (431798–80), C (Yorke e. 97–100), LICj, SAN, WLAp.

79.4LP/10   Lives of the Poets, ? Piracy   1793

THE | LIVES | OF THE MOST EMINENT | ENGLISH POETS; | WITH | CRITICAL OBSERVATIONS | ON THEIR | WORKS. | [rule] | By SAMUEL JOHNSON. | [rule] | IN FOUR VOLUMES. | [rule] | A NEW EDITION, CORRECTED. | [rule] | [short (22 mm) rule] | VOL. I [–IV]. | [short (22 mm) rule] | LONDON: | Printed for J. Buckland, C. Bathurst, and | T. Davies. | [short (23 mm) rule] | mdccxciii.

4 vols., 12°

I. π⁴ A–Y⁶ Z², ($3 signed; 'VOL. I.' on $1), 138 leaves.

Pp. *i* blk, *ii* woodcut port. SJ., ²*i* t. *ii* blk, *iii–iv* Advertisement, *v* Contents, *vi* blk, on A1 1–61 Cowley, 62–72 Denham, 73–153 Milton, 154–68 Butler, 169–76 Rochester, 177–86 Roscommon, 187–91 Otway, 192–240 Waller, 241–2 Pomfret, 243–6 Dorset, 247–9 Stepney, 250–65 J. Philips, 266–8 Walsh.

Dropheads: as: [rule] | NAME., but rules vary as: triple rules pp. 1, 62, 73, 154; double rules 169, 187, 192, 241, 243, 250, 266; total rules 177; parallel rule 247.

Pagination: (↑) iv; [↑] 1, 62, 73, 154, 169, 177, 187, 192, '141' [=241], 243, 247, 250, 266; 53 as 52, 143 as 431, 241 as 141 (correct in *Contents*).

Press-figures: none.

Catchwords: 23 *om.* (An), 145 in ('i' *slipt*), 167 Nor (would), 237 10ₐ O pouer-tie, (10. O ~,).

Explicit: 268 END OF THE FIRST VOLUME.

II. π² A–S⁶ T⁶ (±T3) U–X⁶ Y⁴, ($3 (F3 as F5) signed; 'VOL. II.' on $1), 132 leaves.

Pp. *i* t., *ii* blk, *iii* Contents, *iv* blk, on A1 1–128 Dryden, 129–52 Smith, 153–4 Duke, 155–8 King, 159–64 Sprat, 165–9 Halifax, 170–3 Parnell, 174–8 Garth, 179–89 Rowe, 190–248 Addison, '294' [249]–53 Hughes, 254–60 Sheffield.

Dropheads: rules as: triple pp. 1; double pp. 129, 155, 159, 165, 170, 174, 179, 254; parallel pp. 153, 190, '294' [= 249].

Pagination: [↑] 1, 129, 153, 155, 159, 165, 170, 174, 179, 190, '294' [=249], 254; 187 *sometimes* as 107 (both states in ENLS), 249 as 294 (corr. in *Contents*).

Press-figures: none.

Catchwords: 12 "walk ('walk = 2 *single quotes*), 15 ₐmorality ("~), 122 "Ifₐ ("~,), 245 eₐ | mulation ('e' *sometimes slipt*) (emulation).

Explicit: 260 END OF THE SECOND VOLUME.

III. π² A–X⁶ Y², ($3 (C3 as C5) signed; 'VOL. III.' on $1), 130 leaves.

Pp. *i* t., *ii* blk, *iii* Contents, *iv* blk, on A1 1–24 Prior, 25–39 Congreve, 40–59 Blackmore, 60–7 Fenton, 68–79 Gay, 80–88 Granville, 89–93 Yalden, 94–9 Tickell, 100–3 Hammond, 104–6 Somervile, 107–211 Savage, 212–51 Swift, 252–6 Broome.

Dropheads: rules as triple pp. 1; double pp. 25, 40, 68, 80, 89, 94, 100, 104, 107; total pp. 60, 252; parallel p. 212.

Pagination: [↑] 1, 25, 40, 60, 68, 80, 89, 94, 100, 104, 107, 212, 252; 85–86 (sig. H1) as '87–88', 101 unnumbered (*corr.* in E: BCL), 103 as '203'.

Press-figures: none.

Catchwords: 81 "you (1st ' *slipt*), 138 *let*ₐ, (~*,).

Explicit: 256 END OF THE THIRD VOLUME.

IV. π^2 A–Z^6 2A^4, ($3 signed; 'VOL. IV.' on $1), 144 leaves.

Pp. *i* t., *ii* blk, *iii* Contents, *iv* blk, on A1 1–139 Pope, 140–3 Pitt, 143–56 Thomson, 157–65 Watts, 166–74 A. Philips, 175–9 West, 180–5 Collins, 186–88 Dyer, 189–96 Shenstone, 197–247 Young, 248–54 Mallet, 255–61 Akenside, 262–74 Gray, 275–83 Lyttelton, *284* blk.

Dropheads: rules as triple p. 1; double pp. 140, 157, 166, 175, 186, 197, 248, 255, 275; parallel pp. 143, 180; total pp. 189, 262.

Pagination: [↑] 1, 140, 143, 157, 166, 175, 180, 186, 189, 197, 248, 255, 262, 275; 44 unnumbered (*corr.* E: NG), 198 as 168, 242 as 224.

Press-figures : none.

Catchwords: 34 [plea-] ˌſure ("~), 127 ˌ*On* (IV. ~), 159 [ſacred] "labours ("~ ~), 162 [cen-] ſure. (ˌure.), '224' [=242] *om.* (Is), 249 [Pro-] logue (logue 'l' *ſlipt*).

Explicit: 283 FINIS.

Paper: White, laid; ? Demy or medium (uncut: 7⅝ × 4¾ in.); wmk.: fleur-de-lys + GR (see *Note* below).

Type: Long primer (3.2 mm), thinly leaded (0.3 mm). Despite the appearance of this work it does not seem to have been shared among different printers.

References: Courtney 142; ESTC: t116684.

Notes: The cancel of II. T3 ('Addison' pp. 221–2) is not apparent in all copies, though observable in Hyde. The execrable portrait of SJ, the shabby appearance of the printing, and that all the respectable booksellers named in the imprint were already dead invite the description of a piracy.[1] All had figured as senior proprietors in the earlier edns. (79.4LP/1–8, above). The origin of this edn. is unknown but from the uncertain size of the paper: sheet = 22⅞ × 19 in. it may be suspected that it is Dutch (Groot mediaan) and if so perhaps of Scotch provenance.

Copies: O (Vet. A5 f. 1870–73);

USA: CSmH (vol. 2 only), DFo, DLC, [GEU '1791', no port. *DUC*], Hyde, IU, [Liebert], MH (10453.6), NIC (uncut), [? PPL]; *Japan*: [Kyoto]; *UK*: AWn, BMp (472458–61), C, E^2 (1. BCL B.5492–5; 2. NG. 1570 a.3), JDF; *Ger*: [Gött.U].

---

[1] Buckland ('of irreproachable integrity', *Lit. Anec.* iii (1812), 719) died in 1790, Bathurst in 1786, and Davies in 1785. Buckland's son, James (McKenzie, *Apprentices* 1314) appears not to have traded independently.

79.4LP/11   Lives of the Poets   1794

[½t] THE | LIVES | OF THE MOST EMINENT | ENGLISH POETS. | WITH | CRITICAL OBSERVATIONS | ON THEIR | WORKS.

[Title] THE | LIVES | OF THE MOST EMINENT | ENGLISH POETS. | WITH | CRITICAL OBSERVATIONS | ON THEIR |

WORKS. | [medium swelled rule] | By SAMUEL JOHNSON. | [medium swelled rule] | A NEW EDITION, CORRECTED. | IN FOUR VOLUMES. | VOL. I [–IV]. | [double rule] | LONDON: | Printed for T. Longman, B. Law, J. Dodſley, H. Baldwin, | J. Robſon, J. Johnſon, C. Dilly, G. G. & J. Robinſon, T. Cadell, | P. Elmſly, J. Nichols, R. Baldwin, H.L. Gardner, T. Payne, | F. & C. Rivington, W. Otridge, J. Sewell, W. Goldſmith, | W. Richardſon, R. Faulder, Leigh and Sotheby, G. Nicol, | W. Lowndes, W. Bent, S. Hayes, G. & T. Wilkie, C. Davis, | W. Nicoll, J. Matthews, J. Egerton, W. Fox, J. Edwards, | Ogilvy & Speare, Scatcherd & Whitaker, J. Evans, Vernor & Hood, | Clarke and Son, E. Newbery, and H. Murray. | 1794. | *(Drawback.)*

Var: . . . Clark, & Son, in vols. 3–4.

4 vols., 8°

I. A⁴ B–2E⁸ 2F², ($4 signed; 'VOL. I.' on $1 (+ A, –G)), 222 leaves.

Pp. *i* ½t, *ii* blk, Engr. port. SJ. front. inserted + A2 *iii* t., *iv* blk, ²iii Contents ²*iv* blk, 3–4 Advertisement to 1783 edn. (79.4LP/7), on B1 text 1–96 Cowley, 97–112 Denham, 113–254 Milton, 255–79 Butler, 280–91 Rochester, 292–307 Roscommon, 308–15 Otway, 316–95 Waller, 396–7 Pomfret, 398–403 Dorset, 404–7 Stepney, 408–32 J. Philips, 433–6 Walsh.

Pagination: 310 as '3‚0', 338 as '3g8'; [↑] iii, ᴬ3, ᴮ1, 97, 113, 255, 280, 292, 308, 316, 396, 408; (↑) 398, 404, 433.

Press-figures: A4('3')–1, B1ᵛ(2)–5, B2ᵛ(4)–3, C5(25)–2, C7ᵛ(30)–7, D1ᵛ(34)–7, E4ᵛ(56)–1, F5ᵛ(74)–1, F7(77)–5, G4ᵛ(88)–3, G5ᵛ(90)–1, H2ᵛ(100)–5, H6(107)–6, I6ᵛ(124)–3, K2ᵛ(132)–6, K5ᵛ(138)–7, L4ᵛ(152)–1, M8ᵛ(176)–7, N3ᵛ(182)–4, N6ᵛ(188)–2, O5(201)–5, O6(203)–4, P1ᵛ(210)–3, P8ᵛ(224)–5, Q8(239)–6, R7(253)–2, S5ᵛ(266)–2, T7(285)–6, T8(287)–7, U5ᵛ(298)–5, X5ᵛ(314)–2, X8ᵛ(320)–7, Y1ᵛ(322)–5, Y6ᵛ(332)–2, Z3ᵛ(342)–5, 2A5ᵛ(362)–2, 2A7(365)–6, 2B1ᵛ(370)–3, 2B8ᵛ(384)–6, 2C7ᵛ(398)–2, 2D3ᵛ(406)–5, 2D7(413)–1, 2E7ᵛ(430)–2, 2F1ᵛ(434)–2.

Catchwords: 36 N, (No), 64 When (He), 71 n. ‚magnifici ("~), 292 [cer-] tain, (~.), 323 [poe-] try, (~;), 335 [de-] clared, (~*,).

Explicit: 436 END OF VOL. I.

II. A⁴ (A1 blk) B–2E⁸, ($4 signed; 'VOL. II.' on $1), 220 leaves.

Pp. A1 blk, on A2 *i* ½t (as. vol. 1), *ii* blk, ²*i* t., *ii* blk, iii Contents, *iv* blk, on B1 1–209 Dryden, 210–49 Smith, 250–2 Duke, 253–9 King, 260–8 Sprat, 269–76 Halifax, 277–83 Parnell, 284–91 Garth, 292–310 Rowe, 311–410 Addison, 411–18 Hughes, 419–31 Sheffield, *432* blk.

Pagination: 412 as 142; [↑] iii, 1; (↑) 210, 250, 253, 260, 269, 277, 284, 292, 311, 411, 420.

Press-figures: B2ᵛ(4)–3, C1ᵛ(18)–4, D8ᵛ(48)–2, E6ᵛ(60)–2, F1ᵛ(66)–4, G8ᵛ(96)–1, H5ᵛ(106)–2, I1ᵛ(114)–4, I2ᵛ(116)–5, K7ᵛ(142)–3, L5ᵛ(154)–7, M5ᵛ(170)–2, N7ᵛ(190)–3, O6(203)–6, P7(221)–1, P7ᵛ(222)–6, Q2ᵛ(228)–3,

R1ᵛ(242)–1, R4ᵛ(248)–6, S1ᵛ(258)–7, T8(287)–1, U1ᵛ(290)–5, U4ᵛ(296)–2, X8ᵛ(320)–3, Y3ᵛ(326)–6, Z8ᵛ(352)–6, 2A1ᵛ(354)–5, 2A2ᵛ(356)–7, 2B2ᵛ(372)–7, 2B3ᵛ(374)–3, 2C1ᵛ(386)–7, 2D1ᵛ(402)–5, 2D4ᵛ(408)–1, 2E1ᵛ(418)–7, 2E5(425)–2.

Catchwords: 320 verſe‸ (~,) 390 [ima-] ‸gine ? ("~?).

Explicit: 431 END OF THE SECOND VOLUME.

III. *A*² B–2C⁸ 2D⁶, ($4 signed; 'VOL. III.' on $1), 208 leaves.

Pp. *i* t., *ii* blk, *iii* Contents, *iv* blk, on B1 1–38 Prior, 39–61 Congreve, 62–92 Blackmore, 93–105 Fenton, 106–23 Gay, 124–37 Granville, 138–45 Yalden 146–54 Tickell, 155–9 Hammond, 160–3 Somervile, 164–335 Savage, 336–402 Swift, 403–409 Broome, *410* blk, *411* advts., *412* blk.

Pagination: [↑] 1, 39, 62, 93, 106, 124, 138, 146, 155, 160, 164, 336, 403.

Press-figures: B7ᵛ(14)–11, C6ᵛ(28)–14, D8(47)–14, E1ᵛ(50)–5, F8(79)–5, G7(93)–6, H2ᵛ(100)–6, I6ᵛ(124)–10, K7ᵛ(142)–13, L5(153)–6, M2ᵛ(164)–10, N6(187)–8, O5(201)–4, P1ᵛ(210)–13, Q2ᵛ(228)–13, R7(253)–13, S1ᵛ(258)–13, T3ᵛ(278)–10, U2ᵛ(292)–13, X2ᵛ(308)–13, Y3ᵛ(326)–6, Y8ᵛ(336)–1, Z2ᵛ(340)–13, 2A8(367)–13, 2B2ᵛ(372)–13, 2C7ᵛ(398)–13, 2D4(407)–10.

Catchwords: *om.* with each new 'Life' pp. 38, 61, 92, 105, 123, 137, 145, 154, 159, 163, 335, 402; 400 *om.* (IN).

Explicit: 409 END OF THE THIRD VOLUME.

IV. *A*² B–2F⁸ 2G², ($4 signed; 'VOL. IV.' on $1), 228 leaves.

Pp. *i* t., *ii* blk, *iii* Contents, *iv* blk, on B1 1–225 Pope, 226–30 Pitt, 231–53 Thomson, 254–67 Watts, 268–81 A. Philips, 282–8 West, 289–96 Collins, 297–301 Dyer, 302–14 Shenstone, 315–96 Young, 397–406 Mallet, 407–18 Akenside, 419–39 Gray, 440–52 Lyttelton.

Pagination: [↑] 1, 226, 231, 254, 268, 282, 289, 297, 302, 315, 397, 407, 419, 440.

Press-figures: B1ᵛ(2)–5, C2ᵛ(20)–10, D5ᵛ(42)–5, E5(57)–2, F3ᵛ(70)–2, G8(95)–6, H1ᵛ(98)–13, I5ᵛ(122)–13, K3ᵛ(134)–13, L8(159)–10, M3ᵛ(166)–13, N6ᵛ(188)–13, O8(207)–13, P1ᵛ(210)–13, Q1ᵛ(226)–13, R8(255)–6, S3ᵛ(262)–13, T1ᵛ(274)–5, U1ᵛ(290)–3, X3ᵛ(310)–13, Y3ᵛ(326)–3, Z6ᵛ(348)–13, 2A8(367)–3, 2B6ᵛ(380)–10, 2C4ᵛ(392)–3, 2D8ᵛ(416)–7, 2E7ᵛ(430)–2, 2F5ᵛ(442)–1, 2G1ᵛ(450)–4.

Catchwords: *om.* before new 'Lives' pp. 225, 230, 253, 267, 281, 288, 296, 301, 314, 396, 406, 418, 439; 264 wishing‸ (~,), 276 ſhower‸ (~,), 437 "enough‸." ("~*.").

Explicit: 452 THE END.

Paper: White, laid; Demy (uncut: 8¾ × 5½ in.); wmk.: '1794'.

Type: I–II text: english (4.6 mm), leaded; notes: long primer (3.4 mm); III–IV text: pica (4.2 mm); notes: long primer (3.3 mm).

Plate: I. Engr. port. SJ after Reynolds, 'SAMUEL JOHNSON, LL.D. Published as the Act directs Augᵗ. 24ᵗʰ. 1791 by T. Cadell Strand.'

References: Courtney 142–43; ESTC: t122612.

Notes: 1,000 copies of vols. 3–4 were printed in November 1794 by Andrew Strahan for Cadell & Davies who were the paymasters (L: Add. MS 48811, fo. 39). There are no ½tt. in these vols.

There is no confirmatory evidence for a cancellation of I1, or of R⁸ in vol. I.

In this edn. the notes of 1790 are repeated but those formerly signed 'E'[ditor] are now signed 'R'[eed]; this identification makes Reed's responsibility unlikely, and the text contains a number of misprints which suggest that little editorial attention was paid to the proofreading.

The advt. leaf at the end of vol. 3 includes notices for:

1. *The Rambler*, 12th edn. 1793 (50.3R/24) @ 12s, 13th edn. 3 vols. 8°, 1794 (50.3R/28) @ £1. 1s.

2. *The Idler*, 5th edn. 2 vols. 12°, 1790 (58.4Id/7) @ 6s.

3. *Journey*, 8°, 1791 (75.1J/7), 6s.

4. *Political Tracts*, 1776, (76.4PT/1) 5s.

5. *Rasselas*, 9th edn. 12°, 1793 (59.4R/21) @ 2s. 6d.

6. *Dictionary*, 2 vols. fol. (5th edn. 1784) (55.4D/6) @ £4. 10s., and 2 vols. 4°, 6th edn. 1785 (55.4D/8) @ £3. 3s.

7. Abridgement of *Dictionary*, one large volume 8°, 10th edn. 1794 (56.1DA/16) @ 9s.

8. Works, ed. Murphy, 12 vols. 1792 (87.3W/2) @ £4. 4s., with

9. *English Poets & Prefaces*, 75 vols. 1790 (79.4LP/8a–b), @ £11. 5s. in boards;

10. Hawkins's Life of SJ, 1787 (87.3W/1.1/1), @ 8s.

11. Murphy's *Essay*, 1791–2 (87.3W/2.1/1), @ 5s.

12. HLP's *Letters*, 2 vols. 1788, @ 14s. (88.3L/1), and

13. HLP's *Anecdotes*, 1785 @ 5s.

Copies: O (Don. e. 604–7);

USA: Hyde, ICU, IU, [Liebert ('R.B. Sheridan'[1]), MH[2] (1. 10453.6.1), NIC, NjP, PPA, WiM; *Can*: CaOHM (B.7686–9;? *var* imprint); *UK*: BMp (504769–72, 'The gift of Ann Johnson of Arley, to her Son Thomas Johnson of Brazen Nose College Oxford'[2]), E (Saltoun 136–9), En (B16/b1, 'Students Library Selkirk No. 149'), Felbrigg, MRc (928.21.J4), Op ('Willm. Wilson').

---

[1] The bookplate and signature in this copy are suspect.
[2] Matriculated at BNC 1814, aged 18, d. 1834, *Al. Ox.* 758/24.

79.4LP/12a   Lives of the Poets, Dublin,   1795–1800
                        Moore's edition, first issue

THE | WORKS | OF THE | [hollow] POETS | OF | *GREAT BRITAIN AND IRELAND.* | WITH | PREFACES, | BIOGRAPHICAL AND CRITICAL. | [short swelled rule] | BY SAMUEL JOHNSON. | [short swelled rule] | VOLUME THE FIRST [–EIGHTH], | CONTAINING |

THE LIVES OF THE POETS, | WITH | *CRITICISMS ON THEIR WORKS.* | [parallel rule] | DUBLIN: | [short total rule] | PRINTED FOR J. MOORE, NO. 45, COLLEGE-GREEN. | [short rule] | 1795.

Note: DUBLIN: | PRINTED . . . &c. in vols. 2–8.

[*Var.* t. vol. 1]: THE | LIVES | OF THE | [hollow]: POETS| OF | *GREAT BRITAIN AND IRELAND*; | AND A | CRITICISM | ON THEIR | WORKS. | [short swelled rule] | BY SAMUEL JOHNSON. | [parallel rule] | DUBLIN: | [short total rule] | PRINTED FOR J. MOORE, NO. 45, COL-LEGE-GREEN. | [short rule] | 1795.

8 vols., 8°

I. *A*² B–O⁴ *O⁴ P1, P–4T⁴ 4U² ($2 (–$2 S–2A, 2C–2G, 3R–4M, 4Q, 4S–T) signed; 'VOL. I.' on $1), 357 leaves.

Pp. *i* t., *ii* blk, *iii* Contents, *iv* blk, on B1 text *1* 2–40 dh: [parallel rule] | ENGLISH POETS. | [total rule] | COWLEY. | [medium parallel rule], 40–46 Denham, *47* 48–93 Milton, 94–102 Butler, 102–6 Rochester, 106–12 Roscommon, 112 113*–114* Otway, *113* 114–44 Waller, *145* Pomfret, *146* 147–8 Dorset, *149*–150 Stepney, *151* 152–60 J. Philips, *161*–162 Walsh, *163* 164–243 Dryden, *244* 245–59 Smith, *260* Duke, *261* 262–3 King, *264* 265–7 Sprat, *268* 269–70 Halifax, *271* 272–3 Parnell, *274* 275–7 Garth, *278* 279–84 Rowe, *285* 286–324 Addison, *325* 326–8 Hughes, *329* 330–3 Sheffield, *334* 335–49 Prior, *350* 351–8 Congreve, *359* 360–71 Blackmore, *372* 373–7 Fenton, *378* 379–84 Gay, *385* 386–90 Granville, *391* 392–3 Yalden, *394* 395–7 Tickell, *398* 399 Hammond, *400*–401 Somervile, *402* 403–67 Savage, *468* 469–93 Swift, *494* 495–6 Broome, *497* 498–586 Pope, *587*–588 Pitt, *589* 590–7 Thomson, *598* 599–603 Watts, *604* 605–9 A. Philips, *610* 611–12 West, *613* 614–16 Collins, *617*–618 Dyer, *619* 620–4 Shenstone, *625* 626–59 Young, *660* 661–3 Mallet, *664* 665–8 Akenside, *669* 670–77 Gray, *678* 679–82 Lyttelton, *683*–684 Moore, *685* Cawthorne, *686* 687–8 Churchill, *689* Falconer, *690*–691 Lloyd, *692*–693 Cunningham, *694* Green, *695*–696 Goldsmith, *697*–698 P. Whitehead, *699* Armstrong, *700* Langhorn, *701*–702 Johnson, *703* 704–5 W. Whitehead, *706*–707 Jenyns, *708* blk.

Pagination: 113–14 *repeated*; dhh. unnumbered at 47, 113, 145, 146, 149, 151, 161, 163, 244, 260, 261, 264, 268, 271, 274, 278, 285, 325, 329, 334, 350, 359, 372, 378, 385, 391, 394, 398, 400, 402, 468, 494, 497, 587, 589, 598, 604, 610, 613, 617, 619, 625, 660, 664, 669, 678, 683, 685, 686, 689, 690, 692, 694, 695, 697, 699, 700, 701, 703, & 706.

Press-figures: Z3ᵛ(182)–2, 2A1ᵛ(186)–2, 2B4ᵛ3(200)–2, 2E4(223)–2.

Catchwords: 50 *om.* (— a quo), 53 that (wanting [cf. 1.4]), 114* *om.* (WALLER.), 270 PARNELL. (~:), 317 "Now ('~), 376 *om.* (I condole), 437 charity‸ (~.), 472 ‸what ("~), 548 *om.* (of), 588 *om.* (THOMSON.), 626 ‸one ("~), 651 Yet‸ (~,), 656 of (OF).

Explicit: none.

Note: The remaining vols. II–VIII contain the *Works* of the Poets reprinted from the London edn. of *Works* & *Prefaces* in 75 vols. edited by Isaac Reed (79.4LP/8a, above). The additional 'Lives' and the annotations of 'N', 'H', and 'E' [=Reed] are adopted from the same source. The different dates on the volumes suggest a slow publication: II 1793; III 1797; IV 1800; V 1801; VI 1801; VII 1801; VIII 1802

Paper: White, wove; ? Carré [? Medium] (uncut: 9 × 5¾ in.); wmk.: uncertain: ? M / W / N / Z. Probably of French origin.

Type: Small pica (3.6 mm), leaded, quotations in bourgeois (3.1 mm). Intermediate sections of text separated by medium swelled rules; dhh on new pp. preceded by parallel rules.

References: Courtney 143 (dated '1795'); ESTC: t187039.

Notes: *O⁴ P1, bearing part of *Rochester* and all of *Roscommon* and *Otway*, is an insert, perhaps simply because *Otway* was overlooked in the initial printing.

Copies: O (8 vols: Vet. A5 e. 534–41);
USA: Hyde, NIC; *UK*: BMp (822769–76), JDF (vol. 1 only), Ljh (6 vols.); *Eir*: Dp (Gilbert), Dt (186 q.21–8).

97.4LP/12b   Lives of the Poets, Dublin,   1795
                            Moore's edition, second issue

There was an issue 'Printed for R. Dodsley . . . 1795', but I have not made an examination of the recorded copy. ESTC: n020396.

Copies: CaOHM (C.1486); [? MH].

79.4LP/12c   Lives of the Poets, Dublin,   1800
                            Moore's edition, third issue

THE LIVES | OF THE | MOST EMINENT | ENGLISH POETS, | WITH CRITICAL OBSERVATIONS ON THEIR WORKS: | [medium parallel rule] | [BL]: **By Samuel Johnson, L.L.D.** | [medium total rule] | *COMPLETE IN ONE VOLUME.* | [medium parallel rule] | LONDON: | PRINTED FOR ANDREW MILLER, IN THE STRAND. | [short diamond rule] | 1800.

This t. leaf on a white wove paper, is a cancel prefixed to the sheets of Moore's 1795 edn., 79.4LP/12a, above. An unlocated copy was: Faulkner-Grierson (Dublin), *Cat.* 22 (1972), 305, £25.

In BMp however the volume appears to be a new setting, as:

8°, *A*1 B–4U⁴, ($2 signed), 353 leaves; Pp. A1 t., A1ᵛ blk, on B1 *1* 2–682 Lives (Cowley–Lyttelton), *683* 684–704 Additional Lives (Moore–Jenyns). The associated 5 vols. of Works, include the Poets in SJ's collection, but not the works of the 'Additional' poets.

Copies: O (Harding C. 3411–8);

USA: NN; *Can*: CaOHM² (**1**. C. 2092–8; **2**. C. 2150–6); *UK*: BMp (468223–30, 8 vols. inc. *Works of Poets*), L, Ljh (4 vols. 'Cecil Harmsworth').

79.4LP/13   Lives of the Poets, Montrose   1800

THE | LIVES | OF THE | *MOST EMINENT* | ENGLISH POETS; | WITH | CRITICAL OBSERVATIONS | ON THEIR WORKS; | [short parallel rule] | By SAMUEL JOHNSON. | *IN FOUR VOLUMES.* | [double rule] | EMBELLISHED WITH ELEGANT ENGRAVINGS. | [double rule] | VOL. I [–IV]. | [woodblock vignette: bush, pick, and spade, cottages behind] | MONTROSE: | Printed by D. Buchanan, Sold by him, *&* by W. Creech, | P. Hill, W. Mudie, *&* A. Constable, Edinburgh. | [short rule] | M,DCCC.

[*Var.*] . . . VOL. I. | [woodblock vignette: shaded weir] | MONTROSE: | Printed . . . *&* by W. Mudie, | *&* G. Gray, Bookfellers, Edinburgh. . . .

. . . II. | [woodblock vignette: snow scene with cottage]

or: [woodblock vignette: traveller and wayside cross]

. . . III. | [woodblock vignette: traveller and wayside cross]

or: [woodblock vignette: shaded weir]

. . . IV. | [woodblock vignette: snow scene with cottage] | MONTROSE: | Printed . . . Buchanan, . . . Creech, | P. Hill, W. Mudie, *&* A. Constable, Edinburgh. . . .

4 vols., 18°

I. π^4 (–π4 = 2D1) A–2C⁶ 2D1, (\$3 (–E2,3, F2,3, K2,3; 2B2 as 2B3) signed; 'Vol. I.' on \$1), 160 leaves.

Pp. *i* t., *ii* blk, *iii–iv* Advertisement (n.d.), v Contents, *vi* blk, on A1 pp. *1* 2–70 Cowley, 71–82 Denham, 83–179 Milton, 180–97 Butler, 198–207 Rochester, 208–19 Roscommon, 220–5 Otway, 226–83 Waller, 284–5 Pomfret, 286–9 Dorset, 290–2 Stepney, 293–310 J. Philips, 311–13 Walsh.

Dropheads: as: COWLEY. | [medium parallel rule] &c., with medium parallel rules pp. 1, 71, 83, 180, 198, 208, 220, 226, 284, 286, 293, 311; double rule p. 290. ht: 189 and 243; Htt. 189 ('Butler') and 243 ('Waller') read 'MILTON.'

Pagination: 256 as 156; [↑] iv, v, 208, 226, 286, 290, 311; (↑) 71, 83, 180, 198, 220, 284, 293.

Catchwords: 33 Awake, (~,), 98 *om.* ("ftrong), 121 [ver-] bal, (~.), 157 religion, (~,), 190 [amu-] fed, (~,), 226 [Winchef-] "ter, ("~,), 233 ,not ("~), 242 [inter-] ,courfe ("~), 244 [re-] ,vealed ("~), 258 ,he ("~), 299 *om.* (that), 311 Dryden, (~,).

Explicit: 313 END OF THE FIRST VOLUME. | [woodblock vignette: lounger by waterfall and and tower].

II. π² A–2B⁶ 2C⁴, ($3 (H2 as G2, –H3, 2C2 as 2C3) signed; 'VOL. II.' on $1), 156 leaves.

Pp. *i* t., *ii* blk, iii Contents, *iv* blk, on A1 *1* 2–149 Dryden 150–78 Smith, 179–80 Duke, 181–5 King, 186–92 Sprat, 193–8 Halifax, 199–203 Parnell, 204–9 Garth, 210–23 Rowe, 224–93 Addison, 294–9 Hughes, 300–8 Sheffield.

Dropheads: medium parallel rules pp. 1, 179, 204, 210, 224, 300; full parallel rule p. 193; medium total rules pp. 150, 181, 186, 294; full double rule p. 199.

Pagination: [↑] iii, 150, 179, 181, 186, 193, 199, 204, 210, 224, 294, 300.

Catchwords: 10 "King‸ ("~,), 13 [pretend-] ‸ed ("~), 15 ‸With ("~), 18 reverenced‸ (~,), 27 *om.* ("whoever,"), 37 cenfure‸ (~;), 64 *om.* ("will), 79 who‸ (~,), 80 manner‸ (~,), 90 Ye‸ (yet), 100 [tedi-] ous‸ (~;), 116 ‸for ("~), 117 others, (other,), 218 [com-] ‸pany‸ ("~.) 219 "teftimony (‸~), 247 part‸ (~,), 255 *under* (*d ascender broken*), 270 within (neither), 282 *om.* ("feems,), 283 "laft; ("~?), 285 "O Marcia‸ ("~ ~,), 286 [eve-drop-] "ping‸ ("~,), 289 *om.* (It), 306 topicks‸ (~;).

Explicit: 308 END OF THE SECOND VOLUME. [*no* woodblock].

III. π² A–2B⁶ 2C⁴ (–2C4 ? blk), ($3 (–M2) signed; 'VOL. III.' on $1), 156 leaves.

Pp. *i* t., *ii* blk, iii Contents, *iv* blk, on A1 1–28 Prior, 29–45 Congreve, 46–69 Blackmore, 70–9 Fenton, 80–93 Gay, 94–104 Granville, 105–10 Yalden, 111–17 Tickell, 118–21 Hammond, 122–5 Somervile, 126–252 Savage, 253–300 Swift, 301–6 Broome, *307–8* (2C4) blk.

Dropheads: medium parallel rules at pp. 1, 29, 46, 70, 80, 94, 111, 118; short parallel rules at pp. 105, 122, 126, 253.

Pagination: 270 unnumbered; [↑] iii, 29, 70, 105, 111, 118, 301; (↑) 1, 46, 80, 94, 253.

Catchwords: 13 ‸A ("~), 39 *om.* (CONGREVE), 54 ‸or, ("~,), 55 ‸in- ("interefts,), 56 [fpi-] ‸rits, ("~,), 58 ‸concern ("~), 59 [uncharita-] ble, ("~,), 62 "certain‸ ("~,), 77 appear- (ed), 86 [Doc-] ‸tor ("~), 90 inventor‸ (~;), 99 (1710,) ((1710),), 131 affords‸ (~,), 145 laudable‸ (~,), 177 increafe‸ (~,), 181 [thought-] leffnefs‸ (~,), 224 [in-] dignation‸ (~,), 225 ‸fmall ("~), 268 ranks, (~‸), 298 "which ("he).

Explicit: 306 END OF THE THIRD VOLUME. | [woodblock: churchyard and inscribed stone: 'LUCE'].

IV. π² A–2E⁶ 2F², ($3 (–2A2) signed; 'VOL. IV.' on $1), 172 leaves.

Pp. *i* t., *ii* blk, iii Contents, *iv* blk, on A1 *1* 2–164 Pope, 165–8 Pitt, 169–86 Thomson, 187–97 Watts, 198–208 A. Philips, 209–14 West, 215–21 Collins, 222–5 Dyer, 226–35 Shenstone, 236–97 Young, 298–305 Mallet, 306–14 Akenside, 315–30 Gray, 331–40 Lyttelton.

Dropheads: medium total rules pp. 1, 165; short parallel rules pp. 169, 215, 331 (also in text p. 95); medium parallel rules pp. 187, 198, 209, 222, 226, 236, 298, 306, 315.

Pagination: 214 as 241; [↑] 165, 169, 215, 226, 236, 306, 315, 331; (↑) 187, 198, 209, 222, 298.

Catchwords: 12 ˏthe ("~), 41 "of (ˏ~), 56 ˏdetect- ("detecting), 84 "If ("March), 115 fcholastickˏ (~,), 135 *place* ˏ (~,), 140 [verfifica-] tionˏ (~,), 247 [re-] ˏceived ("~), 259 *om.* (of), 264 piety, (~;), 282 whomˏ (~,), 294 madeˏ (~,), 336 lifeˏ (~,).

Explicit: 340 FINIS.

Colophon: 340 [2-line brace] D. Buchanan | Montrose.

Paper: White, wove; Demy 18° gives uncut leaf: 5⁵⁄₁₆ × 3¾ in. which agrees with extant copies (5⁷⁄₁₆ × 3⁹⁄₁₆ in.); no vis. wmk. means that the format is problematic, but the dimensions of extant copies accord better with Demy 18° than with the nearest 12° in Small Post which gives uncut: 6⅓ × 3¾ in.).

Type: Bourgeois (3.2 mm), thinly leaded (0.3 mm). Swelled rule at I. 301; short parallel rule IV. 95.

Plates: I. front. Port of SJ in oval: 'JOHNSON Engraved for Johnfon's Lives of the Poets: Publifhed by D. Buchanan Montrofe.'

Milton, Butler, Rochester, Otway, Waller: 'Engᵈ by Kirkwood & Sons Engraved for Johnfon's Lives of the Poets; Published by D. Buchanan Montrofe.'

II. Dryden, Parnell, Rowe, Addison (as above: Kirkwood &c.), except 'Parnell': 'Engraved for Johnson's Lives of the Poets, By D. Buchanan Montrose'

III. Congreve, Gay, Swift (as. 'Parnell' above, vol. 2)

IV. Pope, Thomson, Akenside, Gray (as: Kirkwood, &c. above), Watts, Young, & Lyttelton (as 'Parnell', vol. 2 above).

Woodblocks: Cp. *Rambler*, Montrose 1800 (50.3R/36, above), for several of these blocks and other ornaments from Buchanan's stock. Of those listed under 50.3R/36, nos. 9 (snow scene and cottage), 10 (traveller and wayside cross), and ? 2, recur here.

References: Courtney 143; ESTC: t116681 and n020399 (discriminating only imprints of vol. 1).

Notes: The faulty catchword at II. 270 suggests an intriguing possibility that the error derives from MSS, as may perhaps II. 283 also.

The printed Catalogue of William Creech's Stock-in-Trade (7 July 1815), p. 24 includes '34 Lives. 4 Vols. 18mo. fine Montrose. 1800', and '3 Ditto. 4 Vols. 18mo.' reflecting Creech's involvement in the publication, and presumably a significant Scottish distribution (E: MS Acc. 5000, no. 1413).

Copies: E (S. 127 i);

USA: [Liebert], MH (vol. 1 only, 10453.6.5), NIC, PBa, PU; *Japan*: [Kyoto]; *UK*: JDF (*var* tt.), Gu.

79.4LP/14 Lives of the Poets 1801–1800

THE | LIVES | OF THE MOST EMINENT | ENGLISH POETS. | WITH | CRITICAL OBSERVATIONS | ON THEIR | WORKS. | [short parallel rule] | By *SAMUEL JOHNSON.* | [short total rule] | A NEW EDITION, CORRECTED. | IN FOUR VOLUMES. | VOL. I [–IV]. | [parallel rule] | *LONDON:* | *Printed by Nichols and Son, Red-Lion-Paſſage, Fleet-Street,* | For H. Baldwin, J. Johnſon, G. G. and J. Robinſon, P. Elmſly, | J. Nichols, R. Baldwin, H.L. Gardner, J. Sewell, F. and C. | Rivington, W. Otridge and Son, W. J. and J. Richardſon, | Leigh and Sotheby, R. Faulder, G. and W. Nicol, T. Payne, | W. Lowndes, G. Wilkie, C. Davis, J. Matthews, T. Egerton, | Ogilvie and Son, J. Scatcherd, J. Walker, E. Newbery, Vernor | and Hood, J. Deighton, J. Nunn, Lackington Allen and Co. | J. Stockdale, J. Cuthell, D. Walker, Clarke and Son, R. Lea, | Longman and Rees, Cadell jun. and Davies, J. Barker, T. Hurſt, | S. Bagſter, J. Harding, J. Hatchard, and R.H. Evans. | 1801. [–1800.]

Var: vols. 3–4 . . . Printed by A. Strahan, Printers-Street, London. . . . 1801. 4 vols., 12°

I (1801). A⁴ B–N¹² O⁴ P1, ($6 signed; 'VoL. I.' on $1), 153 leaves.

Pp. *i* ½t: THE | LIVES | OF THE MOST EMINENT | ENGLISH POETS. | WITH | CRITICAL OBSERVATIONS | ON THEIR | WORKS., *ii* blk, Engr. port. front. 1 leaf inserted, *iii* t., *iv* blk, v–vi Advertisement to 1783 edn., vii Contents, *viii* blk, on B1 pp. 1–298 texts Cowley–Walsh.

Pagination: (↑) v, vii, 1, 68, 79, 174, 200, 211, 270, 272, 276, 279.

Press-figures: none.

Catchwords: 64 "And‸ ("~,), 160 Diſcontent, (The Perſons), 154 Clarke, (~*,), 246 ‸reſerved ("~).

Colophon: 298 *Printed by* NICHOLS *and* SON, | *Red Lion Paſſage, Fleet Street, London.*

Explicit: 298 END OF THE FIRST VOLUME.

II (1801). A² (A2 + χ1) B–N¹², ($6 signed; 'VoL. II.' on $1 (+ A1)), 147 leaves.

Pp. *i* ½t, *ii* blk, *iii* t., *iv* blk, v Contents, *vi* blk, on B1 pp. 1–287 text Dryden–Sheffield, *288* blk.

Pagination: 179 unnumbered; (↑) v, 1, 169, 189, 207, 274.

Press-figures: B7(13)–4, C2ᵛ(28)–5 C11ᵛ(46)–4, D6ᵛ(60)–4, E7ᵛ(86)–5, F8ᵛ(112)–1, G5ᵛ(130)– *sometimes* 3, H12ᵛ(168)–5, I8(183)–4, K11ᵛ(214)–5, L5ᵛ(226)–4, L6ᵛ(228)–5, M12(263)–4. N *unfigured*.

Catchwords: no errors.

Colophon: 287 as vol. 1.

Explicit: 287 END OF THE SECOND VOLUME.

III (1800). A^2 B–M^{12} N^{10}, ($6 (–N6) signed; 'VOL. III.' on $1), 144 leaves.

Pp. *i* t., *ii* blk, *iii* Contents, *iv* blk, on B1 pp. 1–284 texts Prior–Broome.

Pagination: ($\uparrow$) 1, 87, 97, 234, 280.

Press-figures: $B6^v$(12)–15, $C6^v$(36)–4, $C11^v$(46)– *sometimes* 12, $E2^v$(76)–15, E12(95)–10, $F1^v$(98)–13, $F12^v$(120)–9, $G9^v$(138)–11, $G12^v$(144)–9, H7(157)–10, $H11^v$(166)–8, $I1^v$(170)–10, $K11^v$(214)–11, $K12^v$(216)–13, L7(229)–6, $M12^v$(264)–13, $N2^v$(268)–15. D *unfigured*.

Catchwords: 12 [propo-] fals, (~*,), 17 ₍and ("~), 52 ₍he ("~), 86 *om.* (GRANVILLE.), 87 which₍ (~,), 96 *om.* (YALDEN.), 193 (O! le₍ ((O! let), 233 *om.* (SWIFT.), 279 *om.* (BROOME.).

Colophon: 284 *Printed by A. Strahan, Printers-Street, London.*

Explicit: 284 END OF THE THIRD VOLUME.

IV (1800). A^2 B–O^{12} P^6, ($6 (–P5,6) signed; 'VOL. IV.' on $1), 164 leaves.

Pp. *i* t., *ii* blk, *iii* Contents, *iv* blk, on B1 pp. 1–322 texts Pope–Lyttelton, *323–4* Advts. for various of SJ's Works (as in 79.4LP/11, above).

Pagination: 143 unnumbered; ($\uparrow$) 1, 160, 189, 213, 290, 298, 313.

Press-figures: B12(23)–15, C8(39)–10, $C8^v$(40)–13, D12(71)–5, $D12^v$(72)–11, $E11^v$(94)–15, $F6^v$(108)–6, $G12^v$(144)–13, $H6^v$(156)–8, $I7^v$(182)–14, K12(215)–5, $L11^v$(238)–5, $L12^v$(240)–2, M12(263)–15, $N8^v$(280)–10, O7(301)–4, $P4^v$(320)–4.

Catchwords: 44 ₍and ("~), 159 *om.* (PITT.), 188 *om.* (A. PHILIPS.), 212 *om.* (SHENSTONE.), 289 *om.* (AKENSIDE.), 297 *om.* (GRAY.), 312 *om.* (LYTTELTON.).

Colophon: 324 as vol. 3.

Explicit: 322 THE END.

Paper: White, wove; La. post (uncut: 7 × 4½ in.); wmk.: '1799', '1800'.

Type: Small pica (3.6 mm), set close. Some 'Lives' separated by full parallel rules.

Plates: 31 engr. portraits:

I. Front. port. of SJ: 'SAM^L. JOHNSON L.L.D. Sir Josh. Reynolds Pinx^t. T. Trotter Sculp.', 2. 'COWLEY. Hall Sculp.', 3. 'DENHAM. Collier fculp.', 4. 'MILTON. Bartolozzi Sculp.', 5. 'BUTLER. Sherwin Sculp:', 6. 'OTWAY. Hall fculp.', 7. 'WALLER. Caldwall Sculp.', 8. 'J. PHILIPS. Collyer Sculp.'.

II. Front. 'CUNNINGHAM. Cook fculp.', 10. 'DRYDEN. I. Sherwin Sculp.', 11. 'PARNELL. Hall Sculp^t.', 12. 'GARTH. Painted by S^r. G. Kneller. Engraved by J. Caldwall. From a Picture in the Pofsefsion of W. Bromfield Esqr.', 13. 'ROWE. From a Buft in Weftminfter Abbey. J.M. Delattre fculp^t.', 14. 'ADDISON. G. Kneller pinxit. F. Bartolozzi fculp.', 15. 'HUGHS. Caldwall fculp.', 16. 'BUCKINGHAM. Hall Sculp.'

III. Front. 'CHURCHILL. Cook fculp.', 18. 'PRIOR. Hall Sculp.', 19. 'CONGREVE. Caldwall Sculp.', 20. 'BLACKMORE. Hall fculp.', 21. 'GAY. Hall Sculp.', 22. 'SWIFT. Walker Sculp:', 23. 'BROOME. Cook Sculp.'

IV. Front. 'POPE. Jarvis Pinxᵗ. Caldwall ſculp.', 25. 'THOMSON. Ætatis 25. Aikman pinxit. Delattre ſculpᵗ.', 26. 'Dʳ. WATTS. Bartolozzi ſculp.', 27. 'DYER. Hall Sculp.', 28. 'SHENSTONE. Cook Sculp.', 29. 'YOUNG. Cook Sculp.', 30. 'AKENSIDE. Cook Sculp.', 31. 'LYTTELTON. Collyer Sculp.'

References: Courtney 143.

Notes: 1,500 copies of vols. 3–4 were printed for Cadell & Davies by Andrew Strahan in Dec. 1800 (L: Add. MS 48811, fo. 39). That the work was carried out at the turn of the year explains the discrepant dates in the titles. The Book-Trade year corresponded to that of the Law courts (and the present academic year), so that books printed in Michaelmas Term were usually dated in anticipation of the coming calendar year. Nichols as befitted a senior member of the Trade, followed this custom, Strahan as a younger man, perhaps did not.[1]

Annotations are signed 'H'[awkins], 'N'[ichols], and 'R'[eed].

Copies: O (Vet. A6 e. 1141);[2]

USA: DLC, Hyde ('Henry Tomkinson', uncut), IU; *UK*: JDF ('E libris H. Barnard Reg: Coll: Alumni — 1805 The Gift of W. Heath'), Ljh ('Harriet E. Pollard, August 1825' — Pres. to House by Dora H. Moffett, 9 Apr. 1919), Op (Vernon, lacks vol. 4); *Fr*: BN.

---

[1] Cf. *Lit. Anec.* iii (1812), 249 n., and Hearne's *Remarks and Collections*, iv. 251, 'so 'tis dated, according to the usual Way of the Booksellers'.

[2] R.W. Chapman told D. Nichol Smith (27 Jan. 1920), that S.C. Roberts had a copy of this edn. (letter in Courtney, *Aust*: CNL), but it is not traced.

79.4LP/15   Lives of the Poets   1801

THE | LIVES | OF THE MOST EMINENT | ENGLISH POETS. | WITH | CRITICAL OBSERVATIONS | ON THEIR | WORKS. | [short parallel rule] | By *SAMUEL JOHNSON*, LL.D. | [short total rule] | A NEW EDITION, CORRECTED. | IN THREE VOLUMES. | VOL. I [–III]. | [parallel rule] | *LONDON:* | *Printed by Nichols and Son, Red-Lion-Paſſage, Fleet-Street,* | For H. Baldwin, J. Johnſon, G. G. and J. Robinſon, P. Elmſly, | J. Nichols, R. Baldwin, H.L. Gardner, J. Sewell, F. and C. | Rivington, W. Otridge and Son, W. J. and J. Richardſon, Leigh and | Sothebys, R. Faulder, G. and W. Nicol, T. Payne, W. Lowndes, G. Wilkie, C. Davis, J. Matthews, T. Egerton, Ogilvie and Son, | J. Scatcherd, J. Walker, E. Newbery, Vernor and Hood, J. Deigh- | ton, J. Nunn, Lackington Allen and Co. J. Stockdale, J. Cuthell, | D. Walker, Clarke and Son, R. Lea, Longman and Rees, Cadell jun. | and Davies, Murray and Highley, J. Barker, T. Hurſt, S. Bagſter, | J. Harding, J. Hatchard, and R.H. Evans. | 1801.

Stet: Sothebys,

3 vols., 8°

I. a⁴ B–2F⁸ 2G⁴ 2H², ($4 (–a1,2, 2G3,4, 2H2) signed; 'VOL. I.' on $1), 234 leaves.

Pp. *i* ½t: THE | LIVES | OF THE MOST EMINENT | ENGLISH POETS. | WITH | CRITICAL OBSERVATIONS | ON THEIR | WORKS., *ii* blk, *iii* t., *iv* blk, v–vi Advertisement to 1783 edn., vii Contents, *viii* blk., on B1 pp 1–71 Cowley, 72–83 Denham, 84–182 Milton, 183–200 Butler, 201–10 Rochester, 211–22 Roscommon, 223–8 Otway, 229–84 Waller, 285–6 Pomfret, 287–90 Dorset, 291–3 Stepney, 294–311 J. Philips, 312–14 Walsh, 315–460 Dryden.

Pagination: no errors; (↑) v, vii, 1, 72, 84, 183, 201, 211, 223, 229, 285, 287, 291, 294, 312, 315.

Press-figures: G7ᵛ(94)–2, N2ᵛ(180)–3, N5ᵛ(186)–1, O2ᵛ(196)–1, O6(203)–5, P3ᵛ(214)–1, P7(221)–2, Q7(237)–3, Q8(239)–5, R7(253)–2, S2ᵛ(260)–1, S8(271)–5, T2ᵛ(276)–1, T3ᵛ(278)–5, U7ᵛ(302)–1, U8ᵛ(304)–3, X3ᵛ(310)–1, X8ᵛ(320)–3, Y2ᵛ(324)–5, Y7ᵛ(334)–3, Z8(351)–5, Z8ᵛ(352)–1, 2A7(365)–4, 2B3ᵛ(374)–2, 2C1ᵛ(386)–5, 2D6ᵛ(412)–1, 2D7ᵛ(414)–2, 2E5(425)–1, 2E8(431)–4, 2F5(441)–1, 2F7ᵛ(446)–2, 2G3(453)–3; *unfigured*: B–F, H–M, 2H.

Catchwords: 128 *that*ᴧ (~,), 256 made; (~:), 320 ᴧMonk] ("~]), 368 "Jefferies, ("~;).

Explicit: 460 END OF THE FIRST VOLUME.

Colophon: 460 [medium parallel rule] | *Printed by* NICHOLS *and* SON, | *Red-Lion-Paſſage, Fleet Street, London.*

II. a² B–2C⁸ 2D² (±2D2), ($4 signed; 'VOL. II.' on $1), 204 leaves.

Pp. *i* t., *ii* blk, iii Contents, *iv* blk, on B1 pp. 1–28 Smith, 29–30 Duke, 31–5 King, 36–42 Sprat, 43–8 Halifax, 49–53 Parnell, 54–9 Garth, 60–72 Rowe, 73–141 Addison, 142–7 Hughes, 148–56 Sheffield, 157–84 Prior, 185–201 Congreve, 202–25 Blackmore, 226–35 Fenton, 236–49 Gay, 250–60 Granville, 261–6 Yalden, 267–73 Tickell, 274–7 Hammond, 278–80 Somervile, 281–404 Savage.

Pagination: (↑) iii, 1, 29, 31, 36, 43, 49, 54, 60, 73, 142, 148, 157, 185, 202, 226, 236, 250, 261, 267, 274, 278, 281.

Press-figures: B7ᵛ(14)–2, D7ᵛ(46)–2, G3ᵛ(86)–2, H3ᵛ(102)–5, I2ᵛ(116)–5, I8(127)–2, K1ᵛ(130)–5, K5(137)–2, L7(157)–2, M8ᵛ(176)–3, N1ᵛ(178)–5, O1ᵛ(194)–2, P1ᵛ(210)–5, P2ᵛ(212)–3, Q8(239)–3, R4ᵛ(248)–5, R7ᵛ(254)–3, S7ᵛ(270)–4, S8ᵛ(272)–3, T7(285)–4, T7ᵛ(286)–2, U8(303)–3, U8ᵛ(304)–4, X5ᵛ(314)–3, X7(317)–5, Y8(335)–2, Z7(349)–2, Z7ᵛ(350)–5, 2A2ᵛ(356)–5, 2A8(367)–2, 2B5ᵛ(378)–5, 2C2ᵛ(388)–5; *unfigured*: C, E–F, 2D.

Catchwords: 107 "Pope, (ᴧ~,), 149 "whichᴧ ("~,), 231 Popeᴧ (~*;), 235 *om.* (GAY.), 302 *Dealer*, (~*,).

Explicit: 404 END OF THE SECOND VOLUME.

Colophon: 404 (as vol. 1, above).

III. a² B–2B⁸ 2C⁴ (2C4 ? blk), ($4 signed; 'VOL. III.' on $1), 198 leaves.

Pp. *i* t., *ii* blk, iii Contents, *iv* blk, on B1 pp. 1–48 Swift, 49–53 Broome, 54–217 Pope, 218–20 Pitt, 221–37 Thomson, 238–48 Watts, 249–58 A. Philips, 259–64 West, 265–71 Collins, 272–5 Dyer, 276–85 Shenstone, 286–346 Young, 347–54 Mallet, 355–63 Akenside, 364–79 Gray, 380–9 Lyttelton, *390* blk.

Pagination: (↑) iii, 1, 49, 54, 218, 238, 249, 259, 265, 272, 276, 286, 347, 355, 364, 380; [↑] 221; 269 as 296, 287 as 278.

Press-figures: B1ᵛ(2)–5, B8ᵛ(16)–3, C6(27)–1, C7(29)–5, D1ᵛ(34)–5, D5(41)–3, E1ᵛ(50)–5, E2ᵛ(52)–4, F6ᵛ(76)–2, G1ᵛ(82)–5, G7(93)–2, H2ᵛ(100)–5, H7(110)–1, I2ᵛ(116)–4, I7ᵛ(126)–3, K1ᵛ(130)–4, L8ᵛ(160)–4, M6(171)–1, M8ᵛ(176)–5, P8(223)–2, Q8(239)–3, Q8ᵛ(240)–4, R6ᵛ(252)–2, S6(267)–2, T8(287)–2, U3ᵛ(294)–5, U5(297)–1, Y8(335)–2, 2B3ᵛ(374)–4; *unfigured*: NOXZ 2A 2C.

Catchwords: 138 "If ("March . . . | "If), 199 *On* (I. | ~), 220 *Om.* (THOM-SON.), 289 "that⌄ ("~,), 320 Who⌄ (~,), 369 ⌄voyages ("~).

Explicit: 389 THE END.

Colophon: 389 (as vol. 1, above).

Paper: White, wove; Demy (uncut: 8¾ × 5⅞ in.); wmk.: '1800', '1801' + WS.

Type: Text: pica (4.0 mm), quotes: sm. pica (3.5 mm), footnotes: long priner (3.2 mm).

References: Courtney 143.

Notes: These volumes are a separate issue of the sheets of vols. IX–XI of SJ's *Works*, 8°, 1801 in 12 vols. ed. Murphy (87.3W/5, below), with new prelims, Binders Directions on $1 adjusted from 'IX–XI' to 'I–III', and some type adjustments and alterations in the last pp. of each vol. viz. I. 2H2ᵛ, II. 2D2 (a cancel), and III. 2C⁴ here loses the press-figure 6 from 2C1ᵛ (inner forme) in *Works*.

Copies: OPc ('Vernon');

USA: Hyde ('Henry Mills Thornton'), [Liebert = CtY], NIC, NjP; *Japan*: [Kyoto]; *UK*: ABu, Gp (B.153829), SAN, [SPu, STIu, WLAp].

79.4LP/16   Lives of the Poets, Philadelphia   1803

The Lives of the Poets. A New Edition, corrected. 'Philadelphia. Published for Benjamin Johnson and Samuel F. Bradford . . . Coale and Oliver, printers.'

2 vols. Not examined.

I. (pp. 225–6 as 125–6).

II. (309 as 368).

References: S&S: 4455 [MSher]

Copies: MH (10453.6.7*); *USA*: CtY, ICU, [Liebert], MWA, NjP, [NRU, PHi, PP], PPL, [PSC], PU, ViU.

79.4LP/17   Lives of the Poets,   1804
                      Moore's second Dublin edition

THE | LIVES | OF THE | [hollow] POETS | OF | *GREAT BRITAIN AND IRELAND;* | AND A | CRITICISM | ON THEIR | WORKS. | [medium parallel rule] | *BY DR. SAMUEL JOHNSON.* | [medium parallel rule] | [BL] **Dublin:** | PRINTED BY PAT. WOGAN, OLD-BRIDGE | [short diamond rule] | 1804.

8°, *A*1 B–4U⁴, 353 leaves.

Pp. A1 t., A1ᵛ blk, on B1 *1* 2–704 text. No press-figures. The t. on a bluish laid paper, is a singleton, but is not a cancel prefixed to the reissued sheets of Moore's 1795 edn. (79.4LP/12a, above), for these sheets are a distinct setting from the former.

Plate: Engr. front. port. of SJ 'Painted by Sir Joshua Reynolds. G. Shea Scᵗ. Published by P. Wogan, Old Bridge, Dublin.'

References: Courtney 143.

Copies: O (2804 d. 52–59); *USA*: NIC, NjP; *UK*: L (10804. p. 27); *Eir*: Dt.

79.4LP/18   Lives of the Poets,   1805–6
                      Works of the British Poets, ed. Park

THE | LIVES | OF THE MOST EMINENT | ENGLISH POETS, | WITH | *CRITICAL OBSERVATIONS* | ON THEIR | WORKS. | [short double rule] | BY SAMUEL JOHNSON, LL.D. | [short total rule] | VOL. I [–VII]. | [parallel rule] | *LONDON:* | [BL] **Printed at the Stanhope Press,** | BY CHARLES WHITTINGHAM, | *Union buildings, Leather Lane*; | FOR JOHN SHARPE, OPPOSITE YORK-HOUSE, | PICCADILLY. | [short swelled rule] | 1805.

Var. dates: II. . . . 1805. III., IV., V., VI., VII. . . . 1806.

7 vols., 16°

I. *A*² B–K⁸ L⁶, ($1 signed; 'VOL. I.' on $1), 80 leaves.

Pp. Engr. front. + *1* t., *2* blk, *3* Advertisement ('Piccadilly, November 1, 1805.'), *4* Contents, on B1 *5* 6–63 text dh: THE | LIVES OF THE POETS. | [short parallel rule] | *COWLEY.* | [short swelled rule], ht: COWLEY., *64* 65–73 Denham [dh. and ht. as prec.], *74* 75–160 Milton [dh. and ht. as prec.].

Dropheads: as [short parallel rule] | *NAME.* | [short swelled rule].

Pagination: no errors.

Colophon: 160 [double rule] | C. WHITTINGHAM, *Printer*, Union Buildings, Leather Lane. | [double rule].

Explicit: 160 END OF VOL. I.

II. *A*² B–H⁸ I1, ($1 signed; 'VOL. II.' on $1), 59 leaves.

Pp. Engr. front. + *1* t., *2* blk, *3* Contents, *4* blk, on B1 *5* 6–20 Butler, *21* 22–6 Rochester, *27* 28–36 Roscommon, *37* 38–41 Otway, *42* 43–90 Waller, *91*–92 Pomfret, *93* 94–6 Dorset, *97* 98–9 Stepney, *100* 101–15 J. Philips, *116* 117–18 Walsh, [dhh. and htt. as vol. 1].

Pagination: no errors; *Colophon*: 118 as vol. 1.
Explicit: 118 END OF VOL. II.

III. *A*² B⁴ C–N⁸ O⁶ (O6 blk), ($1 signed; 'VOL. III.' on $1), 100 leaves.

Pp. Engr. front. + *1* t., *2* blk, *3* Contents, *4* blk, on B1 *5* 6–134 Dryden *135* 136–59 Smith, *160*–161 Duke, *162* 163–5 King, *166* 167–71 Sprat, *172* 173–6 Halifax, *177* 178–80 Parnell, *181* 182–6 Garth, *187* 188–98 Rowe, [dhh. and htt. as vol. 1], *199–200* blank leaf.

Pagination: no errors; *Colophon*: 198 as vol. 1.
Explicit: 198 END OF VOL. III.

IV. *A*² B–L⁸ M⁶, ($1 signed; 'VOL. IV.' on $1), 88 leaves.

Pp. Engr. front. + *1* t., *2* blk, *3* Contents, *4* blk, on B1 *5* 6–66 Addison, *67* 68–72 Hughes, *73* 74–80 Sheffield, *81* 82–105 Prior, *106* 107–20 Congreve, *121* 122–40 Blackmore, *141* 142–9 Fenton, *150* 151–61 Gay, *162* 163–71 Granville, *172* 173–6 Yalden, [dhh. and htt. as vol. 1].

Pagination: no errors; *Colophon*: 176 as vol. 1.
Explicit: 176 END OF VOL. IV.

V. *A*² B–L⁸ M⁶, ($1 signed; 'VOL. V.' on $1), 88 leaves.

Pp. Engr. front. + *1* t., *2* blk, *3* Contents, *4* blk, on B1 *5* 6–10 Tickell, *11* 12–13 Hammond, *14* 15–16 Somervile, *17* 18–128 Savage, *129* 130–71 Swift, *172* 173–6 Broome, [dhh. and htt. as vol. 1].

Pagination: no errors; *Colophon*: 176 as. vol. 1.
Explicit: 176 END OF VOL. V.

VI. *A*² B–K⁸ L⁴, ($1 signed; 'VOL. VI.' on $1), 78 leaves.

Pp. *1* t., *2* blk, *3* Contents, *4* blk, on B1 *5* 6–152 Pope, *153* 154–5 Pitt, *156* blk. [dhh. and htt. as vol. 1].

Pagination: no errors; *Colophon*: 178 as vol. 1;
Explicit: 155 END OF VOL. VI.

VII. *A*² B² C–L⁸, ($1 signed; 'VOL. VII.' on $1), 76 leaves.

Pp. Engr. front. + *1* t., *2* blk, *3* Contents, *4* blk, on B1 *5* 6–19 Thomson, *20* 21–9 Watts, *30* 31–8 A. Philips, *39* 40–3 West, *44* 45–49 Collins, *50* 51–2 Dyer, *53* 54–61 Shenstone, *62* 63–115 Young, *116* 117–22 Mallet, *123* 124–30 Akenside, *131* 132–44 Gray, *145* 146–52 Lyttelton, [dhh. and htt. as vol. 1].

Pagination: no errors; *Colophon*: 152 as. vol. 1;
Explicit: 152 FINIS.

Paper: White, wove; Probably crown (uncut: 5 × 3¾ in.); no vis. wmk.

Type: Brevier (2.5 mm).

Plates: 17 engr. plates, all portrait busts of the following poets (the first mentioned is the front. to each vol.):

I. Cowley, Denham, Milton: *all* 'Engraved by Anth^y. Cardon from a Drawing by Thomas Uwins, after the Originals of Sir Peter Lely and R. White, and Published 2nd. Novr. 1805, by John Sharpe; Piccadilly.'

II. J. Philips, Butler, Waller *all* as I. above: '. . . after the Authentic Originals of G. Soest & S^r. Godfrey Kneller . . . 1st. Decr. 1805, . . .'.

III. Garth, Dryden, Parnell *all* as I above: '. . . after the Originals of Sir Godfrey Kneller &c. . . . 1st. Jany. 1806 . . .'.

IV. Prior, Addison, Gay *all* as I above: '. . . after the Originals of Richardson, Zinck and Kneller . . . 1st. Feby. 1806 . . .'.

V. Swift: 'Engraved by Anthony Cardon, from the Mezzotinto of Andrew Miller; after the Original Painted at Dublin, 1739, by Francis Bindon. Published 1st. March 1806, . . .'.

VI. Pope: 'Painted by Sir Godfrey Kneller. Engraved by Anthony Cardon. Published 1st. April 1806, . . .'.

VII. Young, Gray, Thomson *all* as I above: '. . . after the most authentic Originals and Published 1st. Jany. 1806, . . .'.

References: Courtney 143.

Notes: The Advertisement in vol. 1 states that this edn. is intended as a companion to 'the series of British Poets', edited by Thomas Park, 1805–6.

These 7 vols. are variously bound, usually in three, sometimes in four.

Copies: O² (1. Douce I. 30–32, 3 vols.; 2. Byw. Adds. 53);

USA: DLC (4 vols.), ICU (7 vols.), MH (10453.7; 3 vols.), NjP (4 vols.), NN; *Can*: CaOHM; *Japan*: [Kyoto]; *UK*: ABu (3 vols.), BMp (7 vols. 382033–9), Ct (4 vols.), En (3 vols. 'David Welsh'), JDF (3 vols.).

79.4LP/19   Lives of the Poets (from Works)   1806

THE | LIVES | OF THE MOST EMINENT | ENGLISH POETS. | WITH | CRITICAL OBSERVATIONS | ON THEIR | WORKS. | [medium parallel rule] | BY *SAMUEL JOHNSON*, LL. D. | [medium total rule] | A NEW EDITION, CORRECTED. | IN THREE VOLUMES. | VOL. I [–III]. | [parallel rule] | *LONDON:* | *Printed by J. Nichols and Son, Red-Lion-Paſſage, Fleet-Street*; | For J. Johnſon, J. Nichols and Son, R. Baldwin, F. and C. Rivington, | Otridge and Son, W. J. and J. Richardſon, Leigh and Sotheby, R. Faulder, | G. Nicol, and Son, T. Payne, W. Lowndes, Wilkie and Robinſon, C. Davis, | T. Egerton, Scatcherd and Letterman, J. Walker, Vernor and Hood, | R. Lea, J. Deighton, J. Nunn, Lackington Allen and Co. J. Stockdale, | Cuthell and Martin, Clarke and Son, Wynne and Son, Longman

Hurſt | Rees and Orme, Cadell and Davies, J. Barker, T. Booker, Carpenter and Co. | E. Jeffery, W. Miller, J. and A. Arch, Blacks and Parry, S. Bagſter, J. Harding, | Payne and Mackinlay, J. Hatchard, R. Phillips, R.H. Evans, and Matthews | and Leigh. | 1806.

Var. imprint: '*Printed by Luke Hansard, near Lincoln's-Inn Fields;* | For J. Johnson . . . &c.' presumably derives by some mistake, from *Works* 1806 (87.3W/8, below), for these vols. of *Lives* should all be Nichols's work, and in the Control copy (O), the colophons all read: 'Printed by NICHOLS and SON, | Red Lion-Paſſage, Fleet-Street, London.'

3 vols., 8°

I. a⁴ B–2F⁸ 2G⁶, ($4 signed; 'VOL. I.' on $1), 234 leaves.

Pp. Engr. front. + *i* t., *ii* blk, iii–v Advertisement to 1783 edn., *vi* blk, vii Contents, *viii* blk, on B1 pp. 1–71 Cowley, 72–83 Denham, 84–182 Milton, 183–200 Butler, 201–10 Rochester, 211–22 Roscommon, 223–8 Otway, 229–84 Waller, 285–6 Pomfret, 287–90 Dorset, 291–3 Stepney, 294–311 J. Philips, 312–14 Walsh, 315–460 Dryden.

Pagination: no errors.

Press-figures: B5(9)–2, C2ᵛ(20)–3, D4ᵛ(40)–2, D7ᵛ(46)–5, H6ᵛ(108)–2, K6ᵛ (140)–5, T8(287)–5, U8(303)–3.

Catchwords: not recorded.

Explicit: 460 END OF THE FIRST VOLUME.

II. a² B–2C⁸ 2D², ($4 signed; 'VOL. II.' on $1), 204 leaves.

Pp. *i* t., *ii* blk, iii Contents, *iv* blk, on B1 pp. 1–28 Smith, 29–30 Duke, 31–5 King, 36–42 Sprat, 43–8 Halifax, 49–53 Parnell, 54–9 Garth, 60–72 Rowe, 73–141 Addison, 142–7 Hughes, 148–56 Sheffield, 157–84 Prior, 185–201 Congreve, 202–25 Blackmore, 226–35 Fenton, 236–49 Gay, 250–60 Granville, 261–6 Yalden, 267–73 Tickell, 274–7 Hammond, 278–80 Somervile, 281–404 Savage.

Pagination: no errors.

Press-figures: Q3ᵛ(230)–2, X8(319)–2.

Catchwords: not recorded.

Explicit: 404 END OF THE SECOND VOLUME.

III. a² B–2B⁸ 2C⁴ (2C4 blk), ($4 signed; 'VOL. III.' on $1), 198 leaves.

Pp. *i* t., *ii* blk, iii Contents, *iv* blk, on B1 pp. 1–48 Swift, 49–53 Broome, 54–217 Pope, 218–20 Pitt, 221–37 Thomson, 238–48 Watts, 249–58 A. Philips, 259–64 West, 265–71 Collins, 272–5 Dyer, 276–85 Shenstone, 286–346 Young, 347–54 Mallet, 355–63 Akenside, 364–79 Gray, 380–9 Lyttelton, *390* blk, *391–92* blk leaf.

Pagination: no errors; *Press-figures*: none; *Catchwords*: not recorded.

Explicit: 389 THE END.

Paper: Demy (uncut: 8¾ × 5½ in.)

Type: Pica (4.0 mm).
Plate: Engr. port. SJ. front. vol. 1.
References: Courtney 143.
This is a separate issue of the sheets of vols. IX–XI of SJ's *Works* ed. A. Chalmers, 12 vols. 8°, London, 1806 (87.4W/8, below), as the press-figures, colophons, &c., demonstrate. The tt. are reset, Binder's Direction lines and vol. refs. are adjusted from 'IX–XI' to 'I–III'. Annotation includes some signed 'C'[halmers].
Copies: O (279 d. 104);   *USA*: CSmH, Hyde ('Henry Stephen Fox, 1806'), MH, NIC, [PP]; *Japan*: [Kyoto]; *UK*: BMp (496039–41), Cp.

79.4LP/20   Lives of the Poets,   1806
                   Edinburgh (from Works)

THE | LIVES | OF THE MOST EMINENT | ENGLISH POETS. | WITH | *CRITICAL OBSERVATIONS* | OF THEIR | WORKS. | [short parallel rule] | BY SAMUEL JOHNSON, LL. D. | [short total rule] | VOL. I [–IV]. | [parallel rule] | EDINBURGH: | PRINTED FOR BELL & BRADFUTE, JAMES M'CLEISH, AND | WILLIAM BLACKWOOD; | GILBERT & HODGES, DUBLIN; AND S. CAMPBELL, NEW YORK. | 1806.
    4 vols. 18°

    I. *A²* B–2D⁶, ($3 signed; 'Vᴏʟ. I.' on $1), 158 leaves.
    Pp. *i* t., *ii* coloph: 'G. Cᴀᴡ, Printer, | Edinburgh.', *iii* Contents, *iv* blk, on B1 pp. *1–2* Advertisement, *3* 4–70 Cowley dh: | LIVES | OF THE | *ENGLISH POETS.* | [short swelled rule] | COWLEY. | [short parallel rule], ht: COWLEY., *71* 72–82 Denham dh: [double rule] | DENHAM. | [short diamond rule], ht: DENHAM., *83* 84–178 Milton, *179* 180–95 Butler, *196* 197–205 Rochester, *206* 207–17 Roscommon, *218* 219–23 Otway, *224* 225–80 Waller, *281–282* Pomfret, *283* 284–6 Dorset, *287* 288–9 Stepney, *290* 291–307 J. Philips, *308* 309–10 Walsh.
    Dropheads: The conjunction of a double rule and diamond rule occurs throughout, save on p. 308 where there is no diamond rule.
    Pagination: 198 *sometimes* as 98.
    Press-figures: none, but there are sheet numbers at every third signature (reflecting the 18° imposition) as: B6ᵛ(12)–1, E6ᵛ(48)–2, H6ᵛ(84)–3, L6ᵛ(120)–4, O6ᵛ(156)–5, R6ᵛ(190)–6, U6ᵛ3(226)–7, Z6ᵛ(262)–8, 2C6ᵛ(298)–9.
    Catchwords: None throughout.
    Colophons: ii: G. Cᴀᴡ, Printer, | Edinburgh. 310 [short rule] | G. Cᴀᴡ, Printer.
    Explicit: 310 END OF THE FIRST VOLUME.

II. *A*² B–2C⁶, ($3 signed; 'VOL. II.' on $1), 152 leaves.

Pp. *i* t., *ii* coloph., *iii* Contents, *iv* blk, on B1 pp. *1* 2–145 Dryden, *146* 147–73 Smith, *174*–175 Duke, *176* 177–80 King, *181* 182–7 Sprat, *188* 189–92 Halifax, *193* 194–7 Parnell, *198* 199–203 Garth, *204* 205–16 Rowe, *217* 218–85 Addison, *286* 287–91 Hughes, *292* 293–300 Sheffield.

Dropheads: as vol. 1.

Pagination: as. vol. 1., 192 as 19.

Sheet-numbers: B6ᵛ(12)–1, C6ᵛ(48)–2, F6ᵛ(60)–3, I6ᵛ(96)–4, M6ᵛ(132)–5, P6ᵛ(168)–6, S6ᵛ(204)–7, X6ᵛ(240)–8, 2A6ᵛ(276)–9.

Colophon: as vol. 1: ii, 300.

Explicit: 300 END OF THE SECOND VOLUME.

III. *A*² B–X⁶ Y² Z⁴ 2A–2B⁶ 2D⁴ ($3 (–Z3) signed; 'VOL. III.' on $1), 142 leaves.

Pp. *i* t., *ii* coloph., *iii* Contents, *iv* blk, on B1 pp. *1* 2–28 Prior, *29* 30–45 Congreve, *46* 47–68 Blackmore, *69* 70–8 Fenton, *79* 80–91 Gay, *92* 93–102 Granville, *103* 104–8 Yalden, *109* 110–15 Tickell, *116* 117–19 Hammond, *120* 121–2 Somervile [ht (121): 'SOMERVILLE.'], *123* 124–244 Savage, *245* 246–91 Swift, *292* 293–6 Broome.

Dropheads: as vol. 1.

Pagination: 182 as 812, 294 as 264.

Sheet-numbers: B6ᵛ(12)–1, E6ᵛ(48)–2, H6ᵛ(84)–3, L6ᵛ(120)–4, O6ᵛ(156)–5, R6ᵛ(192)–6, U6ᵛ(228)–7, 2A6ᵛ('264' = 294)–8, 2D4ᵛ(296)–9.

Colophons: as vol. 1: ii, 296.

Explicit: 296 END OF THE THIRD VOLUME.

IV. *A*² B² C–2F⁶ 2G⁴ (? 2G4 blk), ($3 (–2G3) signed; 'VOL. IV.' on $1), 168 leaves.

Pp. *i* t., *ii* coloph., *iii* Contents, *iv* blk, on B1 pp. *1* 2–162 Pope, *163* 164–6 Pitt, *167* 168–83 Thomson, *184* 185–94 Watts, *195* 196–204 A. Philips, *205* 206–10 West, *211* 212–17 Collins, *218* 219–21 Dyer, *222* 223–30 Shenstone, *231* 232–92 Young, *293* 294–300 Mallet, *301* 302–9 Akenside, *310* 311–24 Gray, *325* 326–34 Lyttelton.

Dropheads: as. vol. 1; *Pagination*: no errors.

Sheet-numbers: E6ᵛ(40)–1, H6ᵛ(76)–2, L6ᵛ(112)–3, O6ᵛ(148)–4, R6ᵛ(184)–5, U6ᵛ(220)–6, Z6ᵛ(256)–7, 2C6ᵛ(292)–8, 2F6ᵛ(328)–9.

Colophons: as vol. 1: ii, 334.

Explicit: 334 END OF THE FOURTH VOLUME.

Paper: White, wove; Demy (uncut: 5⅞ × 3¾ in.); wmk.: '1804' 'C S'. There was an issue on Royal paper (see note below), which should produce an uncut leaf of 6⅔ × 4⅙ in.

Type: Long primer (3.2 mm), leaded (0.3 mm); quotations in brevier (2.6 mm), leaded (0.2 mm).

Notes: The unexpected structure of III. Y² Z⁴ &c. is clear: Y1.2 are conjugate, and there is sewing between Z2.3. *Swift* begins on Z1, and it may be that the printer at first supposed the vol. would end with *Savage* on Y2ᵛ (244), or perhaps the printing was shared and the sigg. were stretched to make up a shortfall, though there is no other evidence for it.

This is a separate issue of vols. X–XIV of SJ's *Works*, 15 vols. 18°, Edinburgh, &c., 1806, (q.v. 87.3W/7, below), with adjusted Direction lines and new prelims.

Disappointingly there is no account in the papers of Bell & Bradfute (E: MS Dep. 317), which could establish the size of the edn. either of the *Works* or of this issue, though calculations of share entitlements are made on the basis of proportions from a total of 1,500 which may represent the total production. Nevertheless if the publishers were to avoid broken sets, the *Lives* must have been overprinted in some round number. The present scarcity of copies is an uncertain basis for guesswork.

An order from Alexander Angus, bookseller in Aberdeen, to Bell & Bradfute, 8 Nov. 1808 (E: MS Dep. 317, Box 5), includes '2 Johnson's Lives of the Poets 4 Vol. 18mo. *new and neat edn.* qrs. @ 7/-.' J.M. Robertson of Glasgow also offered this edn. for sale in their Trade catalogue of 1807, p. 7. Ogle & Aikman's *Catalogue of Books in Quires, offered to the Trade* (*c*.1807), p. 16, show a Trade price of 10s. 6d. for the Royal paper issue, and 7s. 8d. for the demy. Both these catalogues are E: MS Acc. 5000, no. 1388.

The printed paper spine labels read: [parallel rule] | JOHNSON'S | LIVES | OF THE | ENGLISH POETS. | NEW EDITION, | In Four Volumes. | 1806. | *Price* 12*s*. | [short rule] | VOL. I [–IV]. | [total rule].

Copies: E² (**1**. BCL. B5685–88 boards, uncut, ptd. spine labels; **2**. NG. 1567 d.3).

79.4LP/21   Lives of the Poets (from Works)   1810

THE | LIVES | OF THE MOST EMINENT | ENGLISH POETS. | WITH | CRITICAL OBSERVATIONS | ON THEIR | WORKS. | [medium parallel rule] | By *SAMUEL JOHNSON*, LL.D. | [medium total rule] | A NEW EDITION, CORRECTED. | IN THREE VOLUMES. | VOL. I [–III]. | [parallel rule] | *LONDON:* | *Printed by J. Nichols and Son, Red Lion Passage, Fleet Street;* | For J. Nichols & Son; F. & C. Rivington; W. Otridge & Son; Leigh & | Sotheby; G. Nicol & Son; T. Payne; G. Robinson; Wilkie & Robinson; | C. Davis; T. Egerton; Scatcherd & Letterman; J. Walker; Vernor, | Hood, & Sharpe; R. Lea; J. Nunn; Lackington, Allen, & Co.; J. | Stockdale; J. Cuthell; Clarke & Sons; J. White & Co.; Longman, | Hurst, Rees, & Orme; Cadell & Davies; J. Barker; John Richardson; | J. M. Richardson; J. Carpenter; B. Crosby; E. Jeffery; J. Murray; W. | Miller; J. & A. Arch; Black, Parry, & Kingsbury; J. Booker; S. Bag- | ster; J. Harding; J. Mackinlay; J. Hatchard; R.

H. Evans; Matthews | & Leigh; J. Mawman; J. Booth; J. Asperne; R. Scholey; R. Baldwin; | Sherwood, Neely, & Jones; J. Johnson & Co.; and T. Underwood— | Deighton & Son, at Cambridge; and Wilson & Son, at York. | [short rule] | 1810.

3 vols., 8°

I. a⁴ B–2F⁸ 2G⁴ 2H², ($2 signed; 'Vᴏʟ. I.' on $1), 234 leaves.

Pp. Engr. port. SJ. front. inserted + *i* t., *ii* blk, iii–v Advertisement to 1779–80 edn. [i.e. 'Prefaces' 79.4LP/1.2], *vi* blk, vii Contents, *viii* blk, on B1 pp. 1–460 text Cowley–Dryden.

II. a² B–2C⁸ 2D², ($2 signed; 'Vᴏʟ. II.' on $1), 204 leaves.

Pp. *i* t., *ii* blk, iii Contents, *iv* blk, on B1 pp. 1–404 text Smith–Savage.

III. a² B–2B⁸ 2C⁴ (2C4 ? blk), ($2 signed; 'Vᴏʟ. III.' on $1), 198 leaves.

Pp. *i* t., *ii* blk, iii Contents, *iv* blk, on B1 pp. 1–389 text Swift–Lyttelton, *390* blk, *391–2* (2C4) ? blk.

Paper: White, wove; Demy (uncut: 8¾ × 5⅝ in.); no vis. wmk.

Type: Pica (4.1 mm).

References: Courtney 143.

Notes: This is a separate issue, with adjusted headings to Contents, binder's directions, and reset titles, of the sheets of vols. 9–11 of SJ's *Works*, ed. Chalmers, 12 vols. 8°, 1810 (87.3W/12, below).

In J. Mawman's trade catalogue of July 1809, this edn. was offered as 'Johnson's Lives, 3 vols. 8vo. [Trade] 0. 13. 6. [retail] 1. 1. 0.' Vernor, Hood, & Sharpe also offered it in their *Catalogue* (Jan.–July, 1810), at '14s. 6d. [Trade and] 1. 1s. 0. sells in boards' (E: MS Acc. 5000, no. 1389).

Copies: Hyde ('E. Litchford' — 'Swan');

USA: CSmH, NIC;   *UK*: BMp (467490–3, 'Charles Walter Lyon'), Ep (PR.503.J69), NCp; *Aust*: CNL.

79.4LP/22   Lives of the Poets   1810
           Works of the English Poets, ed. Chalmers

The Works of the English Poets, From Chaucer to Cowper; including the Series Edited with Prefaces, Biographical and Critical, By Dr. Samuel Johnson: and the most approved translations. The Additional Lives by Alexander Chalmers, F.S.A. In Twenty-one volumes. Vol. I [– XXI]. [Summary Contents] London: Printed for J. Johnson; J. Nichols and Son; R. Baldwin, F. and C. Rivington; W. Otridge and Son; Leigh and Sotheby; R. Faulder and Son; G. Nicol and Son; T. Payne; G. Robinson; Wilkie and Robinson; C. Davies; T. Egerton; Scatcherd and Letterman; J. Walker; Vernor, Hood, and Sharpe; R. Lea; J. Nunn; Lackington, Allen, and Co.; J. Stockdale; Cuthell and

Martin; Clarke and Sons; J. White and Co.; Longman, Hurst, Rees, and Orme; Cadell and Davies; J. Baker; John Richardson; J.M. Richardson; J. Carpenter, B. Crosby; E. Jeffery; J. Murray; W. Miller; J. and A. Arch; Black, Parry, and Kingsbury; J. Booker; S. Bagster; J. Harding; J. Mackinlay; J. Hatchard; R.H. Evans; Matthews and Leigh; J. Mawman; J. Booth; J. Asperne; P. and W. Wynne; and W. Grace. Deighton and Son at Cambridge, and Wilson and Son at York. 1810.

21 vols., 8°

The Lives are reprinted as: Addison ix. 485–520, Akenside xiv. 53–6, Blackmore x. 313–23, Broome xii. 3–5, Butler viii. 87–94, Collins xiii. 191–3, Congreve x. 257–65, Cowley vii. 3–40, Denham vii. 223–9, Dorset viii. 339–40, Dryden viii. 423–91, Duke ix. 211–12, Dyer xiii. 221–2, Fenton x. 385–9, Garth ix. 419–21, Gay x. 427–33, Granville (Lansdowne) xi. 3–7, Gray xiv. 137–43, Halifax ix. 331–3, Hammond xi. 137–8, Hughes x. 3–5, King ix. 237–9, Lyttelton xiv. 161–5, Mallet xiv. 3–6, Milton vii. 271–342, Otway viii. 279–81, Parnell ix. 345–7, A. Philips xiii. 99–103, J. Philips viii. 367–75, Pitt xii. 365–6, Pomfret viii. 303, Pope xii. 51–128, Prior x. 105–18, Rochester viii. 231–4, Roscommon viii. 255–60, Rowe ix. 457–62, Savage xi. 243–98, Sheffield x. 73–6, Shenstone xiii. 257–61, Smith ix. 165–76, Somervile xi. 149–50, Sprat ix. 309–11, Stepney viii. 349–50, Swift xi. 345–66, Thomson xii. 405–12, Tickell xi. 97–99, Waller viii. 3–27, Walsh viii. 401–2, Watts xiii. 3–7, West xiii. 135–7, Yalden xi. 59–61, Young xiii. 339–66.

References: Courtney 147; *CBEL* ii. 260

Notes: In Chalmers's diary, s.dd.[1]

'1805. *August* 8. — My Biog. labours interrupted by my engaging to prepare a new edition of Johnson's Poets, with additional Poets and Lives, translations, &c. This was a work of great labour, and not completed before 1809–10.

1809. *November* 3. — Finished my labours on the Poets. The proprietors very liberally voted me 600 guineas — just double of what I originally asked.

1814. *November* 8. — A most scurrilous and malignant attack on my edition of the Poets now appeared in the *Quarterly Review*, but neither the scurrility nor malignity surprised me, when I found who had written it.'

Chalmers incorporated his own Life of Johnson in xvi. 549–70, followed by SJ's Poems pp. 571–624.[2]

Copies: O (Camera); *USA*: CSmH, DLC; *Japan*: [Kyoto]; *UK*: Eu (.82108 Cha, uncut: 10 × 6 in.), Gp, L, LCu, MRu, [NOu], Oef.

[1] [James Chalmers (1814–96) ed.] *In Memoriam Alexander Chalmers, F.S.A. Editor of the Biographical Dictionary. Born 1759. Died 1834.* [priv. ptd., Aberdeen, 1884: copy in ENLS at NC 277 e. 17]. The 'Memoir' is taken from *Gents. Mag.* NS. iii (Feb. 1835), 207–10, supplemented by extracts from Chalmers's own diaries, of which the originals are as yet untraced, entitled 'Memoranda', p. 27 ff.
[2] Chalmers first evidenced his admiration of SJ in his Account of Dr Johnson's Character, compiled from SJ's own writings and signed 'Amerus', in *Gents. Mag.* lviii (1788), 300–3.

79.4LP/23   Lives of the Poets, Charlestown,   1810
Massachusetts

THE | LIVES | OF | THE MOST EMINENT | ENGLISH POETS; | WITH | CRITICAL OBSERVATIONS | ON THEIR | WORKS. | [medium parallel rule] | BY SAMUEL JOHNSON, L. L. D. | [medium total rule] | IN TWO VOLUMES. | VOL. I [–II]. | [short parallel rule] | CHARLESTOWN. | PRINTED AND SOLD BY SAMUEL ETHERIDGE, Jun'r. | [short dotted (16) rule] | 1810.

Var. PUBLISHED By S. ETHERIDGE, Jun. AND J. R. WELD. | [short dotted (16) rule] | 1810.

2 vols., 8°

I. *1*⁴ 2–55⁴, ($1 numbered; 'VOL. I.' on $1), 220 leaves.

Pp. *i* t., *ii* blk, *iii*–iv Original Advertisement to the First Edition, 1779, 1780., *v* Contents, *vi* blk, on 1₄ *1* 2–432 text Cowley–Sheffield, *433–4* Etheridge's advts., 'Boston, June 1, 1810.'

Pagination: blanks pp. 50, 126, 196, 200, 216, 320, 340, 352, 358, 374, 422; unnumbered: 1, 51, 59, 127, 139, 145, 153, 157, 195, 197, 201, 203, 217, 219, 321, 341, 343, 347, 353, 357, 359, 365, 375, 423, 427.

Explicit: 432 END OF THE FIRST VOLUME.

II. *1*² 2–57⁴, ($1 numbered; 'VOL. II.' on $1), 226 leaves.

Pp. *i* t., *ii* blk, *iii* Contents, *iv* blk, on 2₁ *1* 2–448 text Prior–Lyttelton.

Pagination: 321 as 221; blanks 56, 66, 74, 86, 174, 324, 328, 340, 348, 356, 366, 370, 378; unnumbered 1, 21, 33, 49, 57, 67, 75, 79, 83, 87, 89, 175, 211, 325, 329, 341, 349, 357, 361, 367, 371, 379, 421, 426, 432, 442.

Explicit: 448 THE END.

References: [Courtney 143–44];[1] S&S: 20458 ('Etheridge' only in imprint to vol. 1): CSt, DLC, MB, MWA, MdU, NN, NPla, OCL, ViU), 20457 ('Etheridge & Weld' in imprint): MEahnW, MWA, ViU).

Notes: The variant imprints occur in combination in the two vols. S&S (working from library catalogues), apparently record the version of vol. 1 only. This feature was noticed too late to be checked in all copies noted below. For earlier American editions and distribution, see 79.4LP/16 and 20, above.

Copies: CtY (Im. J637. 779R: 'Etheridge' only in 1–2);

USA: CSmH (E only), DLC, Hyde (E), [InU, KyU, Liebert = CtY], MB, MH (10453.8; E & W, E in vol. 2), [MiU], MWA² (1. E; 2. E & W), NjP, NN, [NRU, OCl, PU, RPB, ScU], ViU (E).

---

[1]   Courtney's reference to 'Alston' as the place of publication is a puzzle, unless it is some kind of aural error for 'Charlestown'. No edition is known with 'Alston' in the imprint.

79.4LP/24   Lives of the Poets, New York (from Works)   1811

(A): THE | LIVES | OF | THE MOST EMINENT | ENGLISH POETS; | WITH | CRITICAL OBSERVATIONS | ON THEIR | WORKS. | [short parallel rule] | BY SAMUEL JOHNSON, L. L. D. | [short total rule] | IN THREE VOLUMES. | VOL. I [–III]. | [medium ornamental rule] | *NEW YORK*: | PUBLISHED BY WILLIAM DURRELL. | [short ornamental rule] | 1811.

(B): *Var.* PHILADELPHIA: | PUBLISHED BY JOHNSON AND WARREN, 147 Market Street. 1811.

(C): *Var.* THE | LIVES | OF | THE MOST | [hollow, shaded] EMI-NENT ENGLISH POETS; | WITH | CRITICAL OBSERVATIONS | ON | *THEIR WORKS.* | [medium rule] | BY SAMUEL JOHNSON, L.L.D. | [medium rule] | IN THREE VOLUMES. | VOL. I [–III]. | [medium total rule] | *PHILADELPHIA:* | PUBLISHED BY BENJAMIN C. BUZBY, No. 28, NORTH | THIRD STREET; AND BENJAMIN WARNER, No. 171, | MARKET STREET. | [short total rule] | 1819 (see 79.4LP/30, below).

3 vols., 12°

I. A^2 B–R^{12} S^{10} (S10 blk), ($6 (–S6) signed; 'VOL. I.' on $1), 204 leaves.
Pp. *1* t., *2* blk, *3* Original Advertisement to 1779–80, *4* Contents ('of the NINTH Volume'), on B1 *7* 8–408 text Cowley–Dryden, *409–10* (S10) blank.
Colophon: 408 [rule] | A. FAGAN, PRINTER.
Explicit: none.

II. π^2 A–P^{12}, ($6 (H4 as K4) signed ; 'VOL. II.' on $1), 182 leaves.
Pp. *1* t., *2* blk, *3* Contents ('of the SECOND Volume'), *4* blk, on A1 *5* 6–363 text Smith–Savage, *364* blk.
Colophon: 363 JANE AITKEN, PRINTER. | No. 7, N. Third-street, Philadelphia.
Explicit: 363 END OF THE SECOND VOLUME.

III. π^2 A–O^{12} P^6, ($6 (–P2,4,6, P3 as P2) signed; 'VOL. III.' on $1), 176 leaves.
Pp. *1* t., *2* blk, *3* Contents ('THIRD Volume'), *4* blk, on A1 *5* 6–351 text Swift–Lyttelton, *352* blk.
Colophon: 351 as vol. 2.
Explicit: 351 END OF THE THIRD VOLUME.

References: S&S: 23120 (New York: LNH, MHi, MWA, MWal, N, PU); 23121 (Philadelphia: MWA, NjNbS, PU, ViLxW).
Notes: This is a separate issue of vols. IX–XI of Durrell's edn. of J's *Works*, 12 vols. New York, 1809–11 (87.3W/10, below), as the colophons and faulty dh. to the Contents leaf of vol. 1 show. The variant tt. reflect distribution issues.
Copies: CtY (Im J637. 779S);

USA: MWA² (**1**. NY; **2**. Philad.), NjP (Philad.), ViU; *UK*: O (279 e. 298: vol. 1 as **A**, 2–3 as **C** *without* colophons, see 79.4LP/30, below).

79.4LP/25　　　Lives of the Poets, Edinburgh　　　1815

THE | LIVES | OF THE MOST EMINENT | ENGLISH POETS: | WITH | CRITICAL OBSERVATIONS | ON THEIR | [BL] **Works.** | [short parallel rule] | BY SAMUEL JOHNSON, LL. D. | [short total rule] | TO WHICH ARE ADDED | A LIFE OF THE AUTHOR, | AND HIS | POETICAL WORKS. | [short parallel rule] | IN FOUR VOLUMES. | VOL. I [–IV]. | [short total rule] | EDINBURGH: | PRINTED FOR PETER HILL, PRINTER TO THE CHURCH | OF SCOTLAND. | 1815. 4 vols., 12°

I. π1 2π1 A–2A⁶ 2B², ($3 (–2B2) signed; 'VOL. I.' on $1), 148 leaves.
Pp. *ᵀi* t., *ii* blk, *iii* Contents, *iv* blk, on A1 *ᴬi* ii–xxx Life of Johnson, *xxxi*–xxxiii Original Advertisement to 1779–80 edn., on C5 *33* 34–292 text Cowley–Walsh.
Colophon: 292 [medium parallel rule] | GLASGOW: | Printed by and for R. Chapman. |1814.
Explicit: 292 END OF VOLUME FIRST.

II. π1 2π1 A–2A⁶ 2B², ($3 (–2B2) signed; 'VOL. II.' on $1), 148 leaves.
Pp. *i* t., *ii* blk, *iii* Contents, *iv* blk, on A1 *1* 2–291 text Dryden–Congreve, *292* blk. Coloph. 291 as vol. 1, above.
Explicit: 291 END OF VOLUME SECOND.

III. π1 2π1 A–Y⁶ Z⁴, ($3 (–Z3) signed; 'VOL. III.' on $1), 138 leaves.
Pp. *i* t., *ii* blk, *iii* Contents, *iv* blk, on A1 *1* 2–272 text Blackmore–Collins. Coloph: 272 as vol. 1.
Explicit: 272 END OF VOLUME THIRD.

IV. π1 2π1 A–2B⁶ 2C⁴, ($3 signed; 'VOL. IV.' on $1), 156 leaves.
Pp. *i* t., *ii* blk, *iii* Contents, *iv* blk, on A1 *1* 2–226 text Pope–Lyttelton, *227* ½t: [medium parallel rule] | THE | [BL] **Poetical Works** | OF | SAMUEL JOHNSON. | *Collated with the best Editions.* | [medium total rule]., *228* blk, *229* 230–307 text of SJ's Poems, *308* blk, (p. 307 *sometimes* as 30). Coloph: 307 as vol. 1.
Explicit: 307 [ornamental scroll: FINIS].

Paper: White, wove (some foxing); Demy (uncut: 7⅝ × 4¾ in.); wmk.: '1813'.
Type: Small pica (3.8 mm), thinly leaded (c. 1.0 mm).
References: Courtney 144.
Notes: The watermark and the colophon, together with the disjunct leaves

forming the prelims, strongly suggest a reissue of an edn. of 1813 or 1814 (paper), but no such edn. has yet been traced.

Copies: JDF (orig. blue boards, uncut; paper spine labels: [wavy rule]. | JOHNSON's | *LIVES* | of the | POETS, | including his | *Poetical Works*. | [short rule] | IN FOUR VOLS. | Price 18s. *boards*. | [short rule] | VOL. I [–IV]. | [wavy rule]); *USA*: CtY, Hyde ('Frank Lyon'; orig. boards. uncut + labels), [Liebert]; *UK*: E (R. 160 h), SAN.

79.4LP/26   Lives of the Poets (from Works)   1816

THE | LIVES | OF THE MOST EMINENT | ENGLISH POETS. | WITH | CRITICIAL OBSERVATIONS | ON THEIR | WORKS. | [medium parallel rule] | By SAMUEL JOHNSON, LL. D. | [medium total rule] | *A NEW EDITION, CORRECTED*. | IN THREE VOLUMES. | VOL. I [–III]. | [medium swelled rule] | LONDON: | PRINTED FOR NICHOLS AND SON; F. C. AND J. RIVINGTON; A. STRAHAN; NICOL | AND SON; G. WILKIE; C. DAVIS; T. EGERTON; J. DEIGHTON; J. NUNN; LACK- | INGTON AND CO.; J. CUTHELL; CLARKE AND SONS; SCATCHERD AND LETTERMAN; | LEIGH AND SOTHEBY; LAW AND WHITTAKER; LONGMAN, HURST, REES, ORME, | AND BROWN; CADELL AND DAVIES; J. OTRIDGE; J. BOOKER; CARPENTER AND | SON; E. JEFFERY; J. AND A. ARCH; BLACK AND CO.; J. BLACK AND SON; J. BOOTH; | JOHN RICHARDSON; S. BAGSTER; J.M. RICHARDSON; J. MURRAY; J. HARDING; | J. HATCHARD; R.H. EVANS; J. MAWMAN; R. SCHOLEY; BALDWIN, CRADOCK, | AND JOY; J. ASPERNE; SHERWOOD, NEELEY AND JONES; GALE AND FENNER; | RODWELL AND MARTIN; R. SAUNDERS; WALKER AND EDWARDS; AND SIMPKIN | AND MARSHALL. | 1816.

3 vols. 8°

I. a⁴ B–2F⁸ 2G⁴ 2H², ($4 signed; 'VOL. I.' on $1), 234 leaves.

Pp. Engr. port. of SJ front. + *i* t., *ii* blk, *iii* iv–v Orig. advert. to 1779–80 edn., *vi* blk, *vii* Contents, *viii* coloph: 'Printed by A. Strahan, | New-Street-Square, London.' on B1 *1* 2–460 text Cowley–Dryden, 460 coloph. as p. viii.

Pagination: 243 *wrong font* 2.

Press-figures: B2ᵛ(4)–9, B6(11)–7, C3ᵛ(22)–7, C4ᵛ(24)–6, D2ᵛ(36)–4, D3ᵛ(38)–6, E4ᵛ(56)–4, E8(63)–9, F2ᵛ(68)–10, F8(79)–12, G4ᵛ(88)–1, G7ᵛ(94)–5, H6ᵛ(108)–9, H7ᵛ(110)–6, I1ᵛ(114)–5, I4ᵛ(120)–6, K4ᵛ(136)–1, K8(143)–6, L6(155)–7, M7(173)–9, M7ᵛ(174)–11, N5ᵛ(186)–1, N6ᵛ(188)–4, O5(201)–11, O5ᵛ(202)–7, P8(223)–12, P8ᵛ(224)–10, Q6(235)–2, Q6ᵛ(236)–7, R5(249)–1, R6(251)–6, S1ᵛ(258)–4, S5(265)–1, T7(285)–7, T8(287)–12, U8(303)–1, U8ᵛ(304)–4, X3ᵛ(310)–4, X4ᵛ(312)–9, Y5ᵛ(330)–9, Y7(333)–10,

Z1^v(338)–12, Z5(345)–8, 2A5^v(362)–12, 2A6^v(364)–11, 2B7^v(382)–12, 2B8^v(384)–4, 2C4^v(392)–4, 2D2^v(404)–4, 2D7^v(414)–12, 2E4^v(424)–4, 2E8^v(432)–9, 2F3^v(438)–4, 2F6^v(444)–12, 2G4(455)–8, 2H1^v(466)–2.

Catchwords: None throughout.

Explicit: 460 END OF THE FIRST VOLUME.

II. *A*² B–2C⁸ 2D⁴, ($4 signed; 'Vol. II.' on $1), 206 leaves.

Pp. *i* t., *ii* blk, *iii* Contents, *iv* coloph. as vol. 1, on B1 *1* 2–408 text Smith–Savage, 408 coloph. as vol. 1.

Pagination: 204 as 420, 247 *wrong font* 7.

Press-figures: B2^v(4)–9, B6(11)–5, C1^v(18)–5, C4^v(24)–1, D2^v(36)–6, D6(43)–1, E2^v(52)–9, E7^v(62)–11, F6(75)–5, F6^v(76)–12, G5(89)–10, G8(95)–12, H1^v(98)–10, H8^v(112)–7, I1^v(114)–5, I2^v(116)–10, K6^v(140)–11, K8(143)–10, L3^v(150)–2, L7(157)–10, M5^v(170)–4, M7(173)–12, N3^v(182)–8, N4^v(184)–4, O3^v(198)–1, O5(201)–1, P4^v(216)–12, P6(219)–8, Q5(233)–4, Q7^v(238)–12, R1^v(242)–2, R8^v(256)–10, S8(271)–7, S8^v(272)–4, T1^v(274)–9, T2^v(276)–2, U8(303)–9, U8^v(304)–5, X7^v(318)–7, X8^v(320)–11, Y2^v(324)–12, Y7^v(334)–9, Z4^v(344)–1, Z7^v(350)–11, 2A6^v(364)–7, 2A8(367)–5, 2B5^v(378)–5, 2B7(381)–7, 2C5^v(394)–9, 2C8^v(400)–5, 2D3(405)–10, 2D4(407)–2.

Explicit: 408 END OF THE SECOND VOLUME.

III. *A*² B–2B⁸ 2C⁴, ($4 signed; 'Vol. III.' on $1), 198 leaves.

Pp. *i* t., *ii* blk, *iii* Contents, *iv* coloph. as vol. 1, on B1 *1* 2–391 text Swift–Lyttelton, 391 coloph. as vol. 1, *392* blk.

Press-figures: B6(11)–1, B7(13)–9, C5(25)–1, C8(31)–7, D1^v(34)–12, D6^v(44)–11, E1^v(50)–11, E7(61)–10, F6^v(76)–7, F8^v(80)–5, G7^v(94)–10, G8^v(96)–7, H7(109)–7, H8(111)–10, I8^v(128)–5, K6(139)–1, K6^v(140)–11, L8(159)–9, L8^v(160)–10, M6^v(172)–11, M8(175)–7, N2^v(180)–5, N8(191)–7, O3^v(198)–11, P1^v(210)–5, P5(217)–9, Q2^v(228)–6, R5(249)–9, R7^v(254)–5, S3^v(262)–1, S7(269)–7, T3^v(278)–9, T4^v(280)–2, U3^v(294)–4, U6^v(300)–12, X3^v(310)–1, X8^v(320)–3, Y5^v(330)–5, Y8^v(336)–9, Z6(347)–1, Z7(349)–2, 2A6(363)–12, 2A8^v(368)–3, 2B5^v(378)–9, 2B8^v(384)–3.

Explicit: 391 THE END.

Paper: White, wove; Demy (uncut: 8¾ × 5⅝ in.); no vis. wmk.

Type: Pica (4.2 mm).

Plate: Engr. port. of SJ ('Blinking Sam') in oval; 'W. Evans sculpsit'.

References: Courtney 144.

Notes: This is a separate issue of 500 copies of the overrun sheets of vols. ix–xi of J's *Works*, 12 vols. 8°, London, 1816 (87.3W/13, below), with new tt. and adjusted Contents and Binder's direction lines, worked off in August 1816 (Strahan: L: Add. MS 48816, fo. 147). Chalmers added notes by Malone to this edn. It was published 6 September 1816, at £1. 4s. (*Morning Chronicle*).

Copies: Hyde ('George Porcher' — 'R.B. Adam'; Fore-edge paintings on each

vol. 1: Lichfield, 2. St Andrews, 3. Iona. Boxed: with arms on covers and box);
USA: [Liebert = CtY]; *Can*: CaOHM; *Japan*: [Kyoto]; *UK*: AWu, BMp
(482664–6, 'John Graham Janr^y 1818'), O (Vet. A6 e.530), SAN (^sPR.553.
J6E16).

79.4LP/27   Lives of the Poets (from Works)   1816

The Lives of the most eminent English Poets. With critical observations on
their Works . . . 1816

3 vols., 12°. Not examined.

Notes: An offprint of vols. ix–xi, from ? *Works*, 1816, 12 vols. 18° (87.3W/14,
below), announced in 'Large Paper' at 12s. in boards.

Copies: Unlocated.

79.4LP/28a   Lives of the Poets, Edinburgh   1818

THE | LIVES | OF THE MOST EMINENT | [hollow] ENGLISH
POETS: | WITH | [BL] **Critical Observations** | ON THEIR | WORKS. |
BY SAMUEL JOHNSON, LL.D. | [medium wavy rule] | *IN FOUR
VOLUMES.* | [medium wavy rule] | VOL. I [–IV]. | EDINBURGH: |
PRINTED FOR | JAMES SAWERS, CALTON-STREET. |
M.DCCC.XVIII.

4 vols., 12°

I. π² a¹² A–N¹², ($5 signed; 'VOL. I.' on $1), 170 leaves.
Pp. Engr. front. + *i* t., *ii* coloph: [medium rule] | Printed by R. Chapman,
Glasgow., *iii* Contents, *iv* blk, on a1 ^a*i* ii–xxi Life of J., *xxii* blk, *xxiii*–xxiv
Orignal advert. to 1790–80 edn., on A1 *1* 2–311 text Cowley–Walsh, 311
Explicit: END OF VOLUME FIRST., coloph: [rule] | R. Chapman, Printer,
Glasgow., *312* blk.

II. π² A–N¹² (N12 blk), ($5 (–A3) signed; 'VOL. II.' on $1), 158 leaves.
Pp. *i* t., *ii* coloph. as I. ii, *iii* Contents, *iv* blk, on A1 *1* 2–310 text
Dryden–Granville, 310 *Explicit*: END OF VOLUME SECOND., coloph. as
I. 311, *311*–*12* (N12) blk.

III. π² A–N¹², ($5 signed; 'VOL. III.' on $1), 158 leaves.
Pp. *i* t., *ii* coloph. as I. ii, *iii* Contents, *iv* blk, on A1 *1* 2–316 text
Congreve–Thomson, 316 *Explicit*: END OF THE THIRD VOLUME.,
coloph. as I. 311.

IV. π² A–N¹² O⁴, (O2 blk), ($5 signed; 'VOL. IV.' on $1), 162 leaves.
Pp. *i* t., *ii* coloph. as I. ii, *iii* Contents, *iv* blk, on A1 *1* 2–314 text
Collins–Lyttelton, 314 *Explicit*: [orn. scroll tp. FINIS.], coloph. as I. 311,
315–*16* (O2) blk, on O3 pp. *1* 2–4 advts.

Press-figures: none throughout; *Catchwords*: none throughout.

Paper: White, wove; ? Crown (uncut: 6¾ × 4 in.); no vis. wmk.
Type: Long primer (3.2 mm), thinly leaded (0.8 mm).
Plate: Port. SJ: 'Painted by Sir Joshua Reynolds. E. Mitchell sculpt. Edinburgh Published by James Sawers. 1818.'
Notes: Though this edn. emanates from the same shop as 79.4LP/25 (1815, above), it is not a reissue or reimpression of that edn.

The advts. include 'Johnson's Lives of the most Eminent English Poets, corrected Edition, 4 vols. foolscap, [£]1. 0. 0.' and 'Johnson's Journey to the Western Islands of Scotland, with Remarks by M'Nicol, demy 8vo, Elegant Edition, with fine portrait. [£] 0. 12. 0.' and Proposals for Sawers's edn. of a *Scottish Dictionary*.

Copies: E² (**1**. Jac.V. 5/1; **2**. BCL 5512 vol. 1 only, uncut, + ptd. spine label (1½ × 1 in.): [double rule] | JOHNSON'S | [**BL**] **Lives** | of the | POETS | [wavy rule] | VOL. I. [?–IV.] | [wavy rule] | *Price 20s.* | [double rule]);

USA: Hyde, ICN, ICU, MH (10453.15 vol. 4 only), ViU (imperfect); *Japan*: [Kyoto]; *UK*: BMp (473355–8), Ct, JDF, NORp (John Clare, pres. Lord Radstock), O (Vet. A6 f.787 (1–4)), Op ('Stoke Newington PL').

79.4LP/28b   Lives of the Poets   1819

THE | LIVES | OF THE MOST EMINENT | [Hollow] ENGLISH POETS: | WITH | CRITICAL OBSERVATIONS | ON THEIR | WORKS. | [short swelled rule] | BY SAMUEL JOHNSON, L.L.D. | [short swelled rule] | IN FOUR VOLUMES. | VOL. I [–IV]. | [medium parallel rule] | *LONDON:* | PRINTED BY J. CHAPMAN, FOR SHARPE AND SON; J. BUMPUS; | BALDWYN AND CO.; AND J. SAWERS, EDINBURGH. | [short rule] | 1819.

4 vols., 12°

This is a reissue of the sheets of 79.4LP/28a above, with cancel tt. printed on wove paper, wmk.: 'H SMITH & SON 1818'. Colophons and advts. remain unchanged.

Copies: Hyde ('S. Green Smith' — 'R.B. Adam'; boards, uncut, lacking O2.3 in vol. 4, retaining port. front. as 79.4LP/28a, above); *USA*: [Liebert = CtY], MH (vol. 4 only).

79.4LP/29   Lives of the Poets,   1819
Encyclopædia of British Literature

[General title] THE | ENCYCLOPÆDIA | OF | BRITISH LITERATURE; | OR, | A METHODICAL EDITION | OF THE MOST ESTEEMED | WORKS IN THE ENGLISH LANGUAGE: | CLASSED

UNDER THE DEPARTMENTS OF | HISTORY; NATURAL HISTORY; BIOGRAPHY; POETRY; | PLAYS; NOVELS; VOYAGES; TRAVELS; SERMONS; | PERIODICAL PAPERS; MORAL, RELIGIOUS, POETICAL, | AND METAPHYSICAL TREATISES; | AND | MISCELLANEOUS WRITINGS. | EACH DEPARTMENT FORMING A SERIES OF VOLUMES. | [double rule] | [BL] **Biography,** | VOL. I [–II]. | JOHNSON's LIVES OF THE POETS. | [double rule] | *LONDON:* | STEREOTYPED AND PRINTED BY AND FOR J. FERGUSSON, | 42, Newman Street, Oxford Street; | AND SOLD BY ALL BOOKSELLERS. | [short rule] | 1819.

[Title] THE LIVES | OF THE | MOST EMINENT | ENGLISH POETS. | WITH | CRITICAL OBSERVATIONS | ON | THEIR WORKS. | [short rule] | BY SAMUEL JOHNSON, LL.D. | [short rule] | IN TWO VOLUMES. | VOL. I [–II]. | [double rule] | [BL] **Encyclopaedia of British Literature.** — *Biography, vol. I [–II]*. | [double rule] | *LONDON:* | STEREOTYPED AND PRINTED BY AND FOR J. FERGUSSON, | 42, Newman Street, Oxford Street; | AND SOLD BY ALL BOOKSELLERS. | [short rule] | 1819.

2 vols., 6s

I. A^6 (–A1,2 + π^4) B–2Q^6, ($3 signed; 'VOL. I.' on $1), 236 leaves.

Pp. Engr. front. inserted + on $^A\pi 1$ *i* Gen. t., *ii* blk, *iii* t., *iv* blk, *v* Advertisement to Encyclopædia 'London, November, 1819.', *vi* blk, *vii* Contents vol. 1, *viii* blk, on A3 *5* Advertisement, *6* blk, *7* 8–468 text Cowley–Prior, 468 coloph: [wavy rule] | Stereotyped and Printed by James Fergusson, Newman Street, Oxford Street.', *Explicit*: END OF THE FIRST VOLUME.

II. π^4 A–2N^6 2O^4 (2O4 blk), ($3 signed; 'VOL. II.' on $1), 224 leaves.

Pp. *i* Gen. t., *ii* blk, *iii* t., *iv* blk, *v* Advertisement ('Nov. 1819.'), *vi* blk, *vii* Contents, *viii* blk, on A1 pp. *1* 2–437 text Congreve–Lyttelton, 437 coloph. as vol. 1, *Explicit*: END OF JOHNSON'S LIVES OF THE POETS., *438* blk, *439–40* (2O4) blk.

Paper: White, wove; Demy (uncut: 7½ × 4⅞ in.); wmk.: '1818'.

Type: Bourgeois (2.9 mm), thinly leaded (0.6 mm).

Plate: Port. of SJ: 'Samuel Johnson, L.L.D. Engraved by J. Hawksworth, from the original picture by Sir Joshua Reynolds, for the Encyclopædia of British Literature. Published Decr. 1. 1819. by J. Fergusson Newman Street.'

References: Courtney 144.

Notes: The plates were reimpressed and published in London in 1822 (79.4LP/36), in Halifax in 1835 (79.4LP/52) and 1836 (79.4LP/53), and in Glasgow in 1839 (79.4LP/55).

Copies: E (Dav. I. 4. 15);

UK: Eu (R.7.1–2, lacks gen. t. in vol. 1), O (10 θ. 88–89), SAN.

79.4LP/30   Lives of the Poets, Philadelphia   1819

THE | LIVES | OF | THE MOST | [hollow] EMINENT ENGLISH POETS; | WITH | CRITICAL OBSERVATIONS | ON | *THEIR WORKS.* | [medium rule] | BY SAMUEL JOHNSON, L.L.D. | [medium rule] | IN THREE VOLUMES. | VOL. I [–III]. | [medium total rule] | *PHILADELPHIA:* | PUBLISHED BY BENJAMIN WARNER, No. 171, MARKET | STREET; AND BENJAMIN C. BUZBY, No. 28, NORTH | THIRD STREET. | [short total rule] | 1819.

Var. PUBLISHED BY BENJAMIN C. BUZBY, No. 28, NORTH | THIRD STREET; AND BENJAMIN WARNER, No. 171, | MARKET-STREET. | [short total rule] | 1819.

3 vols., 12°

I. A^2 B–R^{12} S^{10} (S10 blk), ($6 (–B5, C6, D5,6, H3,5; M6 as M5, S4 as 4S) signed; 'VOL. IX.' on $1), 204 leaves.

Pp. *i* t., *ii* blk, *iii* Advertisement to 1779–80 edn., *iv* Contents, on B1 7 8–408 text Cowley–Dryden, 408 coloph: 'A. FAGAN, PRINTER.' No *explicit.*

Pagination: pp. 5–6 om. from sequence; misnumbering in some copies (e.g Hyde), of sig. R (o): 367 as 365, 370–1 as 368–9, 372 as 373, 374–5 as 372–3, 378–9 as 376–7, 382–3 as 380–1, 386–7 as 384–5, and 390 as 388.

II. π^2 A–2G^6 ($1,3, $3 as $2 (L3 as 2L, M3 as 2M) signed; 'VOL. II.' on $1), 182 leaves.

Pp. *i* t., *ii* blk, *iii* Contents, *iv* blk, on A1 7 8–363 text Smith–Savage, 363 *Explicit*: END OF THE SECOND VOLUME., *364* blk.

III. A–2F^6 2G^2, ($1,3, $3 as $2; 'VOL. III.' on $1), 176 leaves.

Pp. *i* t., *ii* blk, *iii* Contents, *iv* blk, on A3 *5* 6–351 (57 unnumbered, 271 as 171, 304 as 204) text Swift–Lyttelton, 351 *Explicit*: END OF THE THIRD VOLUME., *352* blk.

References: S&S: 48383 ('Buzby & Warner': CBPSR, CoCorS, MuHi, ScY); 48384 ('Warner & Buzby': CrW, ViRu, ViSwc).

Notes: The presence of Abraham Fagan's name, and the eccentric direction line (Vol. IX) in vol. 1, suggest a reissue of sheets from a Collected edn. of *Works*, by Durrell, New York, 1809–11 (q.v. above 79.4LP/24, and *Works*, 87.3W/10, below). Such stigmata have been eliminated from vols. 2–3. There is a good deal of mispagination in different copies and some missignings, probably more than are reported above.[1]

Copies: Hyde^2 (**1. B-W** 'Laura M. Riley'; **2. W-B** 'Sylvanus Plympton');

USA: (**B-W**): MWA, NN, NRU, PPL, ViU; (**W-B**): CSmH, [Liebert = CtY], MH (10453.12), MWA, NIC (uncut), NjP, NRU, PLC, [CtHT-W, MeAU, MiD, NBU, NcD, NIC, NNC, OCIWHi, OO, PPA, PU, ScU]; *UK*: O (279 e. 298; vol. 1 as 79.4LP/24, above; vols. 2–3 as here, without 1811 colophons).

79.4LP/31   Lives of the Poets (from Works)   1820

THE | LIVES | OF THE MOST EMINENT | ENGLISH POETS, | WITH | CRITICAL OBSERVATIONS | ON THEIR WORKS. | BY | SAMUEL JOHNSON, LL.D. | [short swelled rule] | *A New Edition, Corrected and Revised.* | IN THREE VOLUMES. | VOL. I [–III]. | [medium total rule] | LONDON: | PRINTED FOR G. WALKER, J. AKERMAN, E. EDWARDS; W. ROBINSON AND SONS, | LIVERPOOL; E. THOMSON, MANCHESTER; J. NOBLE, HULL; J. WILSON, | BERWICK; W. WHYTE AND CO. EDINBURGH; AND R. GRIFFIN | AND CO. GLASGOW. | [short rule] | 1820.

3 vols., 8°

I. π⁴ (−π⁴ + π1,2,3) B⁸ (±B1) C–2F⁸ *2G*1 (±*2G*1), ($1 signed; 'LIVES OF THE POETS, VOL. I.' on B1, 'VOL. IX.' on $1 (−N, P)), 228 leaves.

Pp. *i* t., *ii* blk, *iii*–iv Advertisement, *v* Contents, *vi* blk, on B1 *1* 2–447 (110 as 10, 383–4 dupl., 413 as 41, 425 unnumbered, 440–1 as 450–1) text Cowley–Dryden, 447 END OF THE LIVES OF THE POETS, VOL. I., *448* blk.

Catchwords: none throughout.

II. π² (±π²) B⁸ (±B1) C–2C⁸ 2D1(±2D1), ($1 signed; 'LIVES OF THE POETS, VOL. II.' on B1, 'VOL. X.' on $1 (−2D)), 203 leaves.

Pp. *i* t., *ii* blk, *iii* Contents, *iv* blk, on B1 *1* 2–402 (321 as 320) text Smith–Savage, 402 END OF THE LIVES OF THE POETS, VOL. II.

III. π² (−π² + π1,2) B⁸ (±B1) C–2B⁸ 2C² *2D*1, ($3 (−B3, I3, K3, N3, O3, S3, Z3; P3 as P4) signed; 'VOL. XI.' on $1, 'LIVES OF THE POETS, VOL. III.' on B1 ('. . . IV.' on C1), 197 leaves.

Pp. *i* t., *ii* blk, *iii* Contents, *iv* blk, on B1 *1* 2–389 (89 as 9, 319–20 as 219–20) text Swift–Lyttelton, 389 END OF THE LIVES OF THE POETS, VOL. III. and coloph: 'Printed by J. Haddon, Tabernacle Walk.'

Paper: White, wove; demy (uncut: 8¾ × 5⅝ in.); wmk.: '1819' but in cancellantia: '1820'.

Type: pica (4.1 mm), leaded (1.0 mm).

Notes: A separate issue of the sheets of vols. ix–xi of SJ's *Works*, 8°, 12 vols. 1820 (87.3W/17, below), with cancels to adjust titles, and *explicit* refs. to vol. nos; the Binder's direction lines were largely overlooked. The type of the cancels is very slightly different from that of the rest of the text.

Copies: O (279 e. 132–4);

USA: Hyde ('Marianne Colston' — 'Edward Francis Colston'), [Liebert = CtY], MH (10453.16), NN (dated to '1821').

79.4LP/32 Lives of the Poets, British Classics 1820

THE | LIVES | OF | THE ENGLISH POETS; | BY | SAMUEL JOHNSON, LL. D. | IN TWO VOLS. | [short swelled rule] | VOL. I [–II]. | [medium rule] | LONDON: | Printed for F. C. and J. Rivington; J. Nunn; Cadell | and Davies; Longman, Hurst, Rees, Orme, and | Brown; G. & W.B. Whittaker; J. Richardson; | J. Walker; Newman and Co.; Lackington and | Co.; Black, Kingsbury, Parbury, and Allen; | J. Black and Son; Sherwood, Neely, and Jones; | Baldwin, Cradock, and Joy; J. Robinson; E. | Edwards; Simpkin and Marshall; R. Scholey; | and G. Cowie. | 1820.

2 vols., 24°

I. *A*² B–Z¹², ($1,5, $5 as $2; 'VOL. I.' on $1 (–CD)), 266 leaves.

Pp. Engr. front. & engr. t. ([BL] THE | **Lives of the Poets** | by | SAMUEL JOHNSON, L.L.D. | *in Two Volumes.* | VOL. I. | [vignette: 'T. Uwins del. W. Finden sculp. (Quot. from 'Cowley')] | LONDON. | Printed for F. C. & I. Rivington, and | the other Proprietors. | 1820.) 2 leaves + *i* t., *ii* blk, *iii* Contents, *iv* blk, on B1 *1* 2–528 text Cowley–Sheffield, 528 coloph: '[short rule] | Printed by J.F. Dove, St. John's Square.', *Explicit*: END OF VOL. I.

II. *A*² B–Z¹² 2A², ($1,5 &c. as vol. 1, signed; 'VOL. II.' on $1), 268 leaves.

Pp. Engr. front. & engr. t. (as vol. 1 but vignette: Savage and his mother) 2 leaves + *i* t., *ii* blk, *iii* Contents, *iv* blk, on B1 *1* 2–531 [in some copies: 2–543 (482–93 *om.* from pagination)], 531 coloph. (as vol. 1), *Explicit*: THE END., *532* blk.

Paper; White, wove; ? double crown (cut leaf: 5 × 2⅞ in.); no vis. wmk.

Type: Ruby (2.0 mm), thinly leaded.

Plates: I. front. of blind Milton: 'T. Uwins del. W. Finden sculp. Printed for F. C. & I. Rivington & the other Proprietors.'; II. front. of Swift directing the Studies of Miss VanHomright, as. vol. 1.

References: Courtney 144.

Notes: The annotations are signed by 'C'[halmers], 'H'[awkins], 'N'[ichols], and 'R'[eed].

Copies: O (Vet. A6 f.284, 'British Classics');

USA: Hyde ('R.F. Metzdorf', with faulty pagination in vol. 1), [Liebert = CtY], [GEU]; *UK*: BMp (366394–5), C (8450 e. 6–7), E (Gray 1429–30), JDF², NCu, Op (Vernon, vol. 1 only, ptd. boards: [within beaded rules]: LIVES | OF | THE ENGLISH POETS; | BY | SAMUEL JOHNSON,

LL.D. | IN TWO VOLS. | [medium rule] | VOL. I. | [medium rule] |
LONDON: | [*imprints as above*] | 1820. | (*Price 9s.*).

79.4LP/33   Lives of the Poets, Rivington   1821

THE | LIVES | OF THE MOST EMINENT | ENGLISH POETS: |
WITH | CRITICAL OBSERVATIONS | ON THEIR | WORKS. | [short
double rule] | By SAMUEL JOHNSON, LL.D. | [short double rule] | *A NEW
EDITION, CORRECTED.* | IN TWO VOLUMES. | VOL. I [–II]. | [short
parallel rule] | *LONDON:* | PRINTED FOR F. C. AND J. RIVINGTON;
W. NICOL AND SON; J. NUNN; C. DAVIS; | T. EGERTON; J.
CUTHELL; SCATCHERD AND LETTERMAN; LONGMAN, HURST,
| REES, ORME, AND BROWN; CADELL AND DAVIES; W. AND T.
CLARKE; LACK- | INGTON AND CO.; J. BOOKER; W. CARPENTER;
E. JEFFERY; J. AND A. ARCH; | BLACK AND CO.; J. BOOTH; J.
RICHARDSON; J.M. RICHARDSON; J. MURRAY; | J. HARDING;
HATCHARD AND SON; R.H. EVANS; J. MAWMAN; R. SCHOLEY; |
BALDWIN, CRADOCK, AND JOY; J. ASPERNE; SHERWOOD,
NEELY, AND JONES; | RODWELL AND MARTIN; R. SAUNDERS; E.
EDWARDS; SIMPKIN AND MARSHALL; | W. MASON; W. MACKIE;
J. DEIGHTON AND SONS, CAMBRIDGE; WILSON AND | SON,
YORK; AND FAIRBAIRN AND ANDERSON, AND STIRLING AND
SLADE, | EDINBURGH. | [short rule] | 1821.

2 vols., 8°

I. A⁴ B–2F⁸ (2F8 ? blk), ($2 signed; 'VOL. I.' on $1), 228 leaves.

Pp. *i* t., *ii* coloph: 'C. Baldwin, Printer, | New Bridge-street, London.', *iii*
iv–v Original Advertisement to 1779–80 edn., *vi* blk, *vii* Contents (*Smith* misdirected to p. 232 [= 332]), on B1 1 2–446 text Cowley–Sheffield, 446 coloph.
as p. ii above, *Explicit*: END OF VOL. I., *447–8* (2F8) ? blk.

Press-figures: B3(5)–5, B5ᵛ(10)–7, C4(23)–2, C6ᵛ(28)–7, D8(47)–2,
E4(55)–5, E7(61)–7, F8(79)–7.

II. *A*² B–2F⁸ 2G⁴, ($2 signed; 'VOL. II.' on $1), 230 leaves.

Pp. *i* t., *ii* coloph. as vol. 1, *iii* Contents, *iv* blk, on B1 *1* 2–454 text
Prior–Lyttelton, 454 coloph. as vol. 1, *Explicit*: *455–6* advts. for various of SJ's
Works.

Pagination: each new Life begins with an unnumbered p.; *Press-figures*: none.

Paper: White, wove; Demy (uncut: 8¾ × 5½ in.); wmk.: '1819'.

Type: Orig. Advertisement: english (4.6 mm), text: small pica (3.6 mm),
leaded (1.0 mm).

Notes: The brief run of press-figures in vol. 1 in a book published at this date,
is puzzling. Some of the annotation is signed 'M' [= Malone].

Copies: En (B16/b1; half red morocco and marbled boards, t.e.g., device 'J H');

USA: Hyde ('Luxmoore' — 'Dolphin'; tan morocco, gilt), MH (10453.16), NIC, NjP, [LU]; *Can*: CaOHM (?'Rippey'); *UK*: BMp (473979–80, 'Margaret Scott From Wm. Scott 12 June 1826'), Eu, O (Vet A6 e.531).

79.4LP/34   Lives of the Poets, Walker   1821

THE | LIVES | OF THE MOST EMINENT | ENGLISH POETS: | WITH | CRITICAL OBSERVATIONS | ON THEIR | WORKS. | [medium rule] | BY SAMUEL JOHNSON, LL.D. | [medium rule] | A NEW EDITION, CORRECTED AND REVISED. | IN THREE VOLUMES. | VOL. I [–III]. | [medium parallel rule] | LONDON: | PRINTED FOR G. WALKER, J. AKERMAN, E. EDWARDS; G. AND J. | ROBINSON, LIVERPOOL; E. THOMSON, MANCHESTER; J. NOBLE, | HULL; J. WILSON, BERWICK; W. WHYTE AND CO. EDINBURGH; | AND GRIFFIN AND CO. GLASGOW. | [short rule] | 1821.
    3 vols., 8°

    I. π1 a² B–2F⁸ 2G⁶, ($2 signed; 'VOL. I.' on $1), 233 leaves.
    Pp. *i* t., *ii* coloph: 'London: printed by Thomas Davison, Lombard-street, Whitefriars.', *iii* Contents, *iv* blk, *v*–*vi* Advertisement, on B1 pp. *1* 2–459 (433 as 483) text Cowley–Dryden, 459 *Explicit*: END OF VOL. I., *460* coloph. as p. ii.

    II. *A*² B–2C⁸ 2D⁶ (2D6 blk), ($2 signed; 'VOL. II.' on $1), 208 leaves.
    Pp. *i* t., *ii* coloph. [as vol. 1 *except* 'Printed'], *iii* Contents, *iv* blk, on B1 pp. *1* 2–410 text Smith–Savage, 410 *Explicit*: END OF VOL. II., *411–12* (2D6) blk.

    III. *A*² B–2B⁸ 2C⁴ (2C4 blk), ($2 signed; 'VOL. III.' on $1), 198 leaves.
    Pp. *i* t., *ii* coloph. [as vol. 1], *iii* Contents, *iv* blk, on B1 pp. *1* 2–389 text Swift–Lyttelton, 389 *Explicit*: THE END., *390* coloph. [as vol. 1], *391–92* (2C4) blk.

    Paper: White, wove; Demy (uncut: 8¾ × 5½ in.); wmk.: '1820'.
    Type: Pica (4.1 mm), leaded (0.7 mm).
    References: Courtney 144.
    Copies: JDF; *USA*: [Liebert = CtY], [MH, NN]; *UK*: NOu.

79.4LP/35   Lives of the Poets, British Poets,   1822
                        Chiswick edition

The British Poets. Including Translations. In one hundred volumes. [I. Chaucer, Vol. 1. &c.] Chiswick: Printed by C. Whittingham, College House;

for J. Carpenter, J. Booker, Rodwell and Martin, G. and W.B. Whittaker, R. Triphook, J. Ebers, Taylor and Hessey, R. Jennings, G. Cowie and Co, N. Hailes, J. Porter, B.E. Lloyd and Son, C. Smith, and C. Whittingham. 1822.

References: Courtney 147; *CBEL* ii. 26.

Notes: SJ's 'Lives' are supplemented by S. W. Singer, R. A. Davenport, &c. They are distributed as follows: XIII–XV Cowley, 'Life' xiii. *1* 2–61; XVI–XVIII Milton, 'Life' xvi. *1* 2–90, XIX–XX Waller, 'Life' xix. *9* 10–55, XX Denham, 'Life' xx. *95* 96–104, Roscommon, 'Life' xx. *243* 244–52, XXI–XXII Butler, 'Life' xxi. *5* 6–20, XXIII–XXV Dryden, 'Life' xxiii. *5* 6–126, XXVI Addison, 'Life' xxvi. *7* 8–64, J. Phillips, 'Life' xxvi. *171* 172–86, XXVII Garth, 'Life' xxvii. *7* 8–12, Tickell, 'Life' xxvii. *123* 124–8, XXVIII Smith, 'Life' *7* 8–30, Blackmore, 'Life' xxviii. *53* 54–72, XXIX Pomfret, 'Life' *7*–8, Fenton, 'Life' xxix. *137* 138–45, XXX–XXXI Prior, 'Life' xxx. *5* 6–28, XXXII–XXXIII Gay, 'Life' xxxii. *5* 6–16, XXXIV A. Philips, 'Life' *7* 8–15, Parnell, 'Life' xxxiv. *119* 120–22, West, 'Life' xxxiv. *215* 216–18, XXXV Savage, 'Life' *5* 6–110, XXXVI Somerville, 'Life' *5* 6–7, XXXVII–XXXIX Swift, 'Life' xxxvii. *5* 6–45, Broome, 'Life' xxxix. *209* 210–13, XL–XLII Pope, 'Life' xl. *5* 6–144, XLIII–XLIV Thomson, 'Life' xliii. *5* 6–18, XLIV Collins, 'Life' xliv. *183* 184–8, XLVII–XLVIII Shenstone, 'Life' xlvii. *5* 6–14, Mallet, xlviii. 'Life' *93* 94–8 (misattributed to SJ and Herbert Croft), XLIX–LII Young, 'Life' xlix. *5* 6–56, LIII–LIV Akenside, 'Life' liii. 6–12, Dyer, 'Life' liv. *107* 108–10, LV Gray, 'Life' lv. *7* 8–20, LVI Lyttelton, 'Life' lvi. *7* 8–14, LXIII Hammond, 'Life' *11* 12–14, [LXVII Johnson, by S.W. Singer].

Copies: O (2804 f. 180–279).

79.4LP/36   Lives of the Poets, Christie   1822

The Lives of the most eminent English Poets. With critical Observations on their Works. By Samuel Johnson, LL.D. In Two Volumes. Vol. I [–II]. **London**: Published by James Christie, Holborn.

2 vols, 6s

I. A⁶ (–A1,2 + π⁴) B–2Q⁶, ($3 signed; 'VOL. I.' on $1), 236 leaves.

Pp. Engr. front. inserted + on ᴬπ1 *i* Gen. t., *ii* blk, *iii* t., *iv* blk, *v* Advertisement to Encyclopædia 'London, November, 1819.', *vi* blk, *vii* Contents vol. 1, *viii* blk, on A3 *5* Advertisement, *6* blk, *7* 8–468 text Cowley–Prior, 460 coloph: [wavy rule] | Stereotyped and Printed by James Fergusson, Newman Street, Oxford Street.', *Explicit*: END OF THE FIRST VOLUME.

II. π⁴ A–2N⁶ 2O⁴ (2O4 blk), ($3 signed; 'VOL. II.' on $1), 224 leaves.

Pp. *i* Gen. t., *ii* blk, *iii* t., *iv* blk, *v* Advertisement ('Nov. 1819.'), *vi* blk, *vii* Contents, *viii* blk, on A1 *1* 2–437 text Congreve–Lyttelton, 437 coloph. as vol.

1, *Explicit*: END OF JOHNSON'S LIVES OF THE POETS., *438* blk, *439–40* (2O4) blk.

Paper: White, wove; Demy (uncut: 7½ × 4⅞ in.); wmk.: '1818'.

Type: Bourgeois (2.9 mm), thinly leaded (0.6 mm).

Plate: Port. of SJ: 'Samuel Johnson, L.L.D. Engraved by J. Hawksworth, from the original picture by Sir Joshua Reynolds, for the Encyclopædia of British Literature. Published Decr. 1. 1819. by J. Fergusson Newman Street.'

References: Courtney 144 (to 1819 edn., 79.4LP/29, above; but NB '2 vols. 8°' which is a problem).

Notes: A reimpression of Fergusson's 1819 plates (79.4LP/29, above), which are reimpressed in Halifax in 1835, 1836 (79.4LP/52, 53, below), and again in Glasgow in 1839 (79.4LP/55, below).

Copies: *USA*: MH (10453.17); *Japan*: [Kyoto]; *UK*: O (Vet. A6 e.1435).

[**79.4LP/37**   Lives of the Poets,   1824
Dove's English Classics

The Lives of the English Poets, by Samuel Johnson, LL.D.
London: Printed by J. F. Dove
2 vols., 12°. Not seen.
Perhaps a ghost arising from a misreport of Dove's later edn. 1826, 79.4LP/43, below.
Copies: Unlocated.]

79.4LP/38   Lives of the Poets, Tegg   1824

THE | LIVES | OF THE MOST EMINENT | ENGLISH POETS: | WITH | CRITICAL OBSERVATIONS | ON THEIR | WORKS. | [medium rule] | BY SAMUEL JOHNSON, LL.D. | [medium rule] | A NEW EDITION, CORRECTED AND REVISED. | IN THREE VOLUMES. | VOL. I [–III]. | [short parallel rule] | LONDON: | PRINTED FOR THOMAS TEGG, 73, CHEAPSIDE; G. OFFOR; | G. AND J. ROBINSON; J. EVANS AND CO.; ALSO R. GRIFFIN | AND CO, GLASGOW; AND J. CUMMING, DUBLIN. | [short rule] | 1824.
   3 vols., 8°

I. π² a² B–2F⁸ 2G⁶, ($2 signed; 'VOL. I.' on $1), 234 leaves.
Pp. π1 ½t LIVES OF THE POETS. | [short rule] | VOL. I., π1ᵛ blk, π2 *i* t., *ii* coloph: 'LONDON: PRINTED BY T. DAVISON, WHITEFRIARS.', on a1 *iii* Contents, *iv* blk, *v–vi* Advertisement, on B1 *1* 2–459 text Cowley–Dryden, 459 END OF VOL. I., *460* blk.

II. *A*² B–2C⁸ 2D⁶, ($2 signed; 'VOL. II.' on $1), 208 leaves.

Pp. A1 t., A1ᵛ coloph., A2 Contents, A2ᵛ blk, on B1 *1* 2–410 text Smith–Savage, 410 END OF VOL. II., *411* blk, *412* coloph.

III. *A*² B–2B⁸ 2C⁴ (–2C4 ? blk), ($2 signed; 'VOL. III.' on $1), 198 leaves.

Pp. A1 t., A1ᵛ coloph., A2 Contents, A2ᵛ blk, on B1 *1* 2–389 text Swift–Lyttelton, 389 THE END., *390* coloph.

Notes: Paper is medium (9 × 5¾ in.), and wmk.: '1823'; but type (pica: 4.1 mm) is same as in 79.4LP/34 (1821), above, of which this is therefore probably a sterotyped reimpression.

Copies: L (1493. k.19, uncut); *USA*: [CtY, Liebert, NcU].

79.4LP/39   Lives of the Poets, Christie   1824

The Lives of the most eminent English Poets. With critical Observations on their Works. By Samuel Johnson, LL.D. In two volumes. Vol. I [– II]. **London**: Published by James Christie, Holborne; J. Richardson; I. Offor, I. Bumpus; T. Mason; J. Harrison; S. Wilkins; W. Sharpe; R. Baynes; J. Lester; W. Wright; T. Hughes; A.K. Newman & Co.; T. Fisher; C. Taylor; W. Darton; T. Wilson; I. Walker; R. Edwards; J. Clarke; M. Burton; J. Goodwyn; J. Murray; W. Moore; T. Gale; R. Anderson; J. Tindale; W. Martin; and Baynes & Son, Paternoster Row; also, R. Griffin & Co. Glasgow; M. Comerford, Portsmouth; I. Hinton, Oxford; and J. Hatt, Cambridge. 1824.

2 vols., 12°

I. *B*¹² C–U¹² X⁶, ($1,5 ($5 as $2 (–B, X5 as X3)) signed; 'VOL. I.' on $1), 234 leaves.

Pp. Engr. port. SJ front. ('Engraved by Freeman from an Original by Bartolozzi. London John Bumpus 1824') + on B1 *1* t., *2* blk, *3* Advertisement, *4* blk, *5* Contents of the First Volume, *6* blk, *7* 8–468 text Cowley–Prior, 468 END OF THE FIRST VOLUME.

II. *A*² B–T¹² U⁴ (U4 ? blk), ($1,5 (as vol. 1) signed; 'VOL. II.' on $1), 222 leaves.

Pp. A1 t., A1ᵛ blk, A2 Contents, A2ᵛ blk, on B1 *1* 2–437 text Congreve–Lyttelton, 437 THE END., *438* blk.

Paper: White, wove; Small post (uncut: 7⅝ × 4¾ in.); no vis. wmk.
Type: Brevier (2.7 mm).
Copies: O (Vet. A6 e.1435 (1–2)); *UK*: BMp (495373–4).

79.4LP/40   Lives of the Poets, ed. Lynam   1825

THE | LIVES | OF THE | ENGLISH POETS. | BY | SAMUEL JOHNSON, LL. D. | [short rule] | EDITED | BY THE REV. ROBERT

LYNAM, A.M. | ASSISTANT CHAPLAIN TO THE MAGDALEN HOSPITAL. | [short rule] | IN TWO VOLUMES. | VOL. I [–II]. | [medium rule] | LONDON: | PRINTED FOR GEORGE COWIE AND CO. | IN THE POULTRY. | 1825.

2 vols., 8°

I. π² *B⁴ *C–*2G⁸ *2H², ($2 (all starred; *T2 as *2T2) signed; 'VOL. I.' on $1), 232 leaves.

Pp. *i* t., *ii* coloph: 'Printed by J.F. DOVE, St. John's Square.', *iii* Contents, *iv* blk, on *B1 ²*i*–ii Original Advertisement to 1779–80 edn., on *B2 pp. *3* 4–460 text Cowley–Sheffield, 460 coloph. as p. ii.

II. *A*⁴ (A2 + *B²) *C–*2G⁸ *2H⁶, ($2 (as vol. 1) signed; 'VOL. II.' on $1 ('VOL. IV.' on K1)), 236 leaves.

Pp. *i* t., *ii* coloph. (as vol. 1), *iii* Contents, *iv* blk, on *B1 pp. *3* 4–470 (264 as 204) text Prior–Lyttelton, 470 coloph. as vol. 1.

Paper: White, wove; Medium (uncut: 9 × 6 in.); wmk.: '1824'.
Type: Pica (4.1 mm).
Notes: This edn. is not a separate issue of the sheets carrying the 'Lives': L–2U (III) and B–2E (IV) from vols. 3–4 of Lynam's edn. of SJ's *Works*, 8°, 6 vols., 1824 (87.3W/19a) or 1825 (87.3W19b, below). The faulty direction line in II. K1 and the mispagination of II. 264 (in *Pope*) are oversights.
Copies: O (Vet. A6 e.1438 (1–2));
USA: Hyde ('William Adams' — 'The gift of Serjeant Adams Bonchurch 184' — 'Edmund Peel' — 'E.L.J.H.' — 'A.F. Owen Jones'), [Liebert = CtY], [PV]; *UK*: BMp (393789–90).

79.4LP/41   Lives of the Poets,   1825
Jones's University Edition

THE | LIVES | OF THE | ENGLISH POETS; | BY | SAMUEL JOHNSON, LL.D. | [medium rule] | LONDON: | PUBLISHED BY JONES & COMPANY, | 3, ACTON PLACE, KINGSLAND ROAD. | [short rule] | 1825.

8°, π² A² B–2Z⁴, ($1 signed), 184 leaves.

Pp. *i* t., *ii* blk, *iii* Contents, *iv* blk, on A1 pp. *1* 2–363 text Cowley–Lyttelton, 363 *Explicit*: THE END., *364* blk.
Pagination: unnumbered 1, 59, 67, 83, 91, 202, 320, 323, 351.
Paper: White, wove; Demy (uncut: 8¾ × 5⅝ in.); no vis. wmk.
Type: Minion (2.3 mm), leaded (0.5 mm); 2 cols./p.
Notes: Annotation signed by 'H'[awkins], 'C'[halmers], Malone, and James Boswell jun. In MH copy wraps. incl. advts. for *Lives* in Jones's University Edition of British Classic Authors, as 'The Four Volumes complete in One. Price 6s. 6d.'

Copies: E (AB. 3. 75.49);
USA: DLC, ICU, [Liebert = CtY], MH (10453.18); *Japan*: [Kyoto]; *UK*: AWn.

79.4LP/42   Lives of the Poets, Philadelphia   1825

Lives . . . Philadelphia: H.C. Carey and J. Lea. 1825.
  Pp. 520. Not examined.
  Notes: Apparently a separate impression of vol. v of Carey & Lea's edn. of SJ's *Works*, 6 vols., Philadelphia, 1825 (87.3W/24, below).
  Copies: DcU ('1 vol of Works').

79.4LP/43   Lives of the Poets, Dove's English Classics   1826

[DOVE's ENGLISH CLASSICS.] | [medium rule] | THE | LIVES | OF | THE ENGLISH POETS: | BY | SAMUEL JOHNSON, LL.D. | [short rule] | IN TWO VOLUMES. | VOL. I [–II]. | [short rule] | LONDON: | PRINTED BY J.F. DOVE; | *And Sold by all the* | BOOKSELLERS in ENGLAND, SCOTLAND, and IRELAND. | 1826.
  2 vols., 12°

  I. A^2 B–S^{12}, ($1,5, $5 as $2, signed; 'VOL. I.' on $1), 206 leaves.
  Pp. Engr. front. and t. 2 leaves + *1* t., *2* blk, *3* Contents, *4* blk, on B1 *5* 6–412 (141 as 41) text Cowley–Sheffield.

  II. A^2 B–S^{12} T^8, ($1,5 (as vol. 1), signed; 'VOL. II.' on $1), 214 leaves.
  Pp. Engr. front. and t. 2 leaves + *1* t., *2* blk, *3* Contents, *4* blk, on B1 *5* 6–424 text Prior–Lyttelton, *425–8* (T7–8) Dove's advts.

  References: Courtney 144.
  Notes: The advts. at the end of vol. 2 show that this edn. retailed at 9s. in boards. There was evidently an export sale in USA too.[1]
  Copies: Hyde ('John Colston' — 'Georgina S. Colston');
  USA: [Liebert = CtY], NN, TxU, [KU]; *UK*: BMp (875045–6).

[1] In their Trade *Catalogue*, 1835, Oliver & Boyd, of Edinburgh, offered this edn. (p. 30), at 4s. 6d. to the trade, 9s. retail (E: MS Acc. 5000, no. 1414); and witness *30th New York Trade Sale by Bangs, Richards, & Platt*, 26 Aug. 1839, p. 57, offering '*Scott & Webster, and Dove's English Classical Library*: 15 Johnson's Lives of the Poets [$] 1.50.'

79.4LP/44   Lives of the Poets, Bumpus   1827

Lives of the most eminent Poets, with the Correspondence, Prayers and Meditations. . . . London: Bumpus. 1827

4 vols., 12°. Not examined.
References: Cf. Sandars (Oxford), *Cat*. 99 (1981), 349. @ £24.00.
Notes: The 'Lives' (inc. 'Eminent Persons'), occupy vols. 1–3 and Prayers &
Meditations are in vol. 4. Cf. SJ's *Works*, 1824 (87.3W/20, below), of which this
appears to be a separate issue.
Copies: *USA*: IU; *UK*: [WLAp].

79.4LP/45   Lives of the Poets, Jones's edition   1827

THE | LIVES | OF THE | ENGLISH POETS; | BY | SAMUEL
JOHNSON, LL.D. | [medium rule] | LONDON: | PUBLISHED BY
JONES & COMPANY, | 3, ACTON PLACE, KINGSLAND ROAD. |
[short rule] | 1827.
  8°, π² A² B–2Z⁴, ($1 signed), 184 leaves.
  Pp. *i* t., *ii* blk, *iii* Contents, *iv* blk, on A1 *1* 2–363 text, *364* blk.
  Not examined.
  Notes: Probably another impression of Jones's edn. 1825 (79.4LP/41), above.
  Copies: Unlocated (Clifton Books, *Cat*. '18th Century' (Feb. 1990), 18, £85).

79.4LP/46   Lives of the Poets, Jones's edition   1828

THE | LIVES | OF THE | ENGLISH POETS; | BY | SAMUEL
JOHNSON, LL.D. | [medium rule] | LONDON: | PUBLISHED BY
JONES & COMPANY, | 3, ACTON PLACE, KINGSLAND ROAD. |
[short rule] | 1828.
  8°, π² A² B–2Z⁴, ($1 signed), 184 leaves.
  Pp. *i* t., *ii* blk, *iii* Contents, *iv* blk, on A1 *1* 2–363 text, *364* blk.
  Notes: Another impression of Jones's edn. 1825 (79.4LP/41), above.
  Copies: BMp (829599).

79.4LP/47   Lives of the Poets, Jones's edition   1829

THE | LIVES | OF THE | ENGLISH POETS; | BY | SAMUEL
JOHNSON, LL.D. | [medium rule] | LONDON: | PUBLISHED BY
JONES & COMPANY, | 3, ACTON PLACE, KINGSLAND ROAD. |
[short rule] | 1829.
  8°, π² A² B–2Z⁴, ($1 signed), 184 leaves.
  Pp. *i* t., *ii* blk, *iii* Contents, *iv* blk, on A1 *1* 2–363 text, *364* blk.
  Notes: Another impression of Jones's edn. 1825 (79.4LP/41), above.
  Copies: BMp (921398).

79.4LP/48   Lives of the Poets, Tilt's Edition   1831

THE | LIVES OF THE ENGLISH POETS. | WITH | [BL] **Critical Observations on their Works.** | AND | LIVES OF SUNDRY EMINENT PERSONS. | [short rule] | BY | SAMUEL JOHNSON, LL. D. | [Vignette engr. profile port. of SJ] | LONDON: | CHARLES TILT, 86, FLEET STREET. | [5 dots] | M DCCC XXXI.

8°, *A*² B–2I⁸ 2K⁴ (2K4 ? blk), ($1 signed), 254 leaves.

Pp. *i* t., *ii* coloph: CHISWICK: | PRINTED BY C. WHITTINGHAM., *iii* Contents (ordered alphabetically), *iv* blk, on B1 pp. *1* 2–394 text Cowley–Lyttelton, *395* 396–502 Lives of Sundry Eminent Persons: Sarpi, Boerhaave, Blake, Drake, Barretier, Morin, Burman, Sydenham, Cheynel, Cave, King of Prussia, Browne, and Ascham), 502 *Explicit*: THE END., coloph. as p. ii, *503–4* (2K4) blk.

Notes: Paper is white, wove, but no vis. wmk.; type is ruby (2.0 mm), leaded, 2 cols./p. Some drop-heads have an engr. portrait, viz. *Cowley* (p. 1), *Denham* (23), *Milton* (27), *Butler* (63), *Otway* (69), *Waller* (71), *J. Phillips* (91), *Dryden* (98), *Parnell* (157), *Garth* (159), *Rowe* (161), *Addison* (166), *Prior* (192), *Congreve* (201), *Gay* (216), *Tickell* (226), *Somervile* (230), *Swift* (270), *Pope* (287), *Thomson* (339), *Watts* (345), *A. Philips* (349), *Dyer* (356), *Shenstone* (358), *Young* (362), *Akenside* (383), *Gray* (386), and *Lyttelton* (391), and of *Sarpi* (395), *Boerhaave* (398), *Blake* (408), *Drake* (415), *Morin* (446), *Burman* (449), *Sydenham* (453), *Cave* (463), *King of Prussia* (467), and *Ascham* (495).

Copies: Op ('Bessy Morland October 15th 1833' — 'Edward J. Sage 1891'— Stoke Newington PL); *UK*: BMp (820800); SPAg (–t.).

79.4LP/49   Lives of the Poets, Sharpe   1831

Lives of the English Poets. By Samuel Johnson, LL.D. . . . . Chiswick: J. Sharpe . . . 1831. Not seen.

References: Courtney 144.
Copies: *USA*: MB, NN, NRU, [AU, WShe].

79.4LP/50   Lives of the Poets, Jones's edition   1832

The Lives of the English Poets; by Samuel Johnson, LL.D. London: Published by Jones & Company, 3, Acton Place, Kingsland Road. 1832

Notes: Another impression of Jones's edn. 1825 (79.4LP/41, above).
Copies: AWn.

[79.4LP/51   Lives of the Poets, Cadell's edition   [1834 ?]

Alexander Chalmers noted in his diary for 1833, '*November* 28. — Cadell called and informed me of the intention of the booksellers to publish a new edition of Johnson's Poets, in two volumes, and invited me to read the proofs, &c., which I declined, as I thought I could not undertake anything of the kind with the pressure of my Biog. Dict. *November* 29. — Looked over Johnson's Poets, but am determined to have nothing to do with Cadell's plan, and wrote him to that effect. *December*, 6. — Richardson called, and informed me I might expect a visit from R. Baldwin, to talk about the scheme of the Poets, &c.' (James Chalmers, *In Memoriam* [1884], 29 ff.).

No edn. in 2 vols. with the names of any of these booksellers at this date has been traced, and it seems that the project was abortive.]

79.4LP/52   Lives of the Poets, Halifax   1835

THE LIVES | OF THE | MOST EMINENT | ENGLISH POETS, | WITH | CRITICAL OBSERVATIONS | ON | THEIR WORKS. | BY SAMUEL JOHNSON, LL.D. | IN TWO VOLUMES. | VOL. I [–II]. | HALIFAX: | PUBLISHED BY WILLIAM MILNER. | [HARTLEY AND WALKER, PRINTERS.] | MDCCCXXXV.

2 vols., 12s

I. *B*¹² C–U¹² X⁶, ($1,4, $4 as $2, signed; 'VOL. I.' on $1), 234 leaves.

Pp. *1* t., *2* blk, *3* Advertisement, *4* blk, *5* Contents, *6* blk, *7* 8–468 text Cowley–Prior, 468 coloph: 'Printed at Hartley & Walker's Office, Halifax.', *Explicit*: 468 END OF THE FIRST VOLUME.

II. *A*² B–T¹² U⁴ (U4 blk), ($1,4 (as vol. 1) signed; 'VOL. II.' on $1), 222 leaves.

Pp. A1 t., A1ᵛ blk, A2 Contents, A2ᵛ blk, *1* 2–437 Congreve–Lyttelton, 437 *Explicit*: THE END., coloph: 'Hartley and Walker, Printers, Halifax.', *438* blk, *439–50* (U4) blk.

References: Courtney 144.

Notes: The plates are badly worn and are evidently derived from those of Ferguson's edn. 1819 (79.4LP/29, above). The wove paper gives no assistance in the detection of the imposition.

Copies: O (279 e. 142–3; 'D. James Clk 1835'; vol. 2 undated);

USA: CtY (Ib.55. F779Geh); *UK*: HAF³ (in 1st copy vol. 1 is undated).

79.4LP/53   Lives of the Poets, Halifax   1836

The Lives of the most eminent English Poets, with critical Observations on their Works. By Samuel Johnson, LL.D. In two volumes. Vol. I [– II]. Halifax: Published by William Milner. 1836.

2 vols., 12s. Collation as 79.4LP/52, above.

References: Courtney 144.

Notes: A reimpression of prec. (79.4LP/52, and of 79.4LP/29, above), but var. imprint, and coloph. on I. 2: 'Printed from Stereotype Plates, by Hartley & Walker.' On I. 468: 'HALIFAX: | PRINTED BY HARTLEY AND WALKER, CHEAPSIDE.', and II. 437: 'HARTLEY AND WALKER, PRINTERS, HALIFAX.'

Copies: BMp (470943–4, lacks II. U4 blk);

USA: NIC; *UK*: BRu, JDF (in publisher's mauve stippled cloth, within dec. compartment on spine, gilt: 'JOHNSON's | LIVES | OF THE MOST | EMINENT | ENGLISH | POETS. | VOL. I [– II] | 2 VOLS | *10s.*)', HAF.

79.4LP/54   Lives of the Poets, Jones's Edition   1838

THE | LIVES | OF | THE ENGLISH POETS. | BY | SAMUEL JOHNSON, L.L.D. | [dash] | LONDON: | PUBLISHED BY JONES AND CO. | [dash] | MDCCCXXXVIII.

8s, *A*⁴ (? –A1) B–2A⁸ 2B⁴, ($1 signed), 191 leaves.

Pp. [? A1 ½t, *or* blk] + Engr. front. + A2 t., A2ᵛ blk, A3 *v* vi–vii Contents, *viii* blk, on B1 *9* 10–384 text, 384 *Explicit*: THE END., coloph: [rule] | W.F. PRATT, Printer, Howden.

Notes: Small (trimmed: 5 × 3 in., wove paper), brevier (2.6 mm). Front. port. 'Dr. Johnson'.

Copies: E (BCL B.5703, 'St Mary's College Library, Blairs';[1] spine t., gilt: 'Johnson's Lives of the Poets 3/6.').

---

[1] A. Cherry, 'The Library of St Mary's College, Blairs, Aberdeen', *Bibliotheck*, xii (1985), 61.

79.4LP/55   Lives of the Poets, Glasgow   1839

THE LIVES | OF THE MOST | EMINENT ENGLISH POETS. | WITH | CRITICAL OBSERVATIONS | ON | THEIR WORKS. | [medium rule] | BY SAMUEL JOHNSON, LL.D. | [medium rule] | IN TWO VOLUMES. | VOL. I [–II]. | GLASGOW: | W. R. M'PHUN, PUBLISHER, 86, TRONGATE; | N. H. COTES, LONDON; W. WHYTE & CO., EDINBURGH. | [short rule] | MDCCCXXXIX.

2 vols., 12°

I. *B*¹² C–U¹² X⁶, ($1,5, $5 as $2 (–H5, L5, + X3) signed; 'VOL. I.' on $1), 234 leaves.

II. *A*² B–T¹² U⁴ (–U4 ? blk), ($1,5 (as vol. 1) (–C5, L5) signed; 'VOL. II.' on $1 (–G)), 222 leaves.

Notes: This is another battered reimpression of the plates of Fergusson's stereotype of 1819 (79.4LP/29), above, but without the special titles and the 1819 advts. Colophons have been eliminated and the plates imposed in 12s. with adjustments to the signatures, but Contents and pagination are the same. The tt. here are **not** cancels and are integral to the structure. There is no vis. wmk. in the paper.
Copies: Gp (B.69727); *UK*: ABu, BMp, E (Jac. V 4/2).

79.4LP/56 Lives of the Poets, Tilt's Cabinet Library 1840

THE | LIVES OF THE ENGLISH POETS. | WITH | [BL] **Critical observations on their Works.** | AND | LIVES OF SUNDRY EMINENT PERSONS. | BY | SAMUEL JOHNSON, LL. D. | . . . LONDON: | CHARLES TILT, 86, FLEET STREET. | . . . MDCCCXL.
8°, *A*² B–2I⁸ 2K⁴, 254 leaves. . . . Not examined.
References: Courtney 144.
Notes: Probably a reissue of Tilt's 1831 edn. (79.4LP/48), above.
Copies: C (1840. 7. 84); *USA*: MH.

[79.4LP/57 Lives of the Poets, Kent's edition [? 1844]

References: In Sampson Low's *English Catalogue, 1835–63*, i (1864), under Johnson, is: 'Lives 12°. 6s. Kent. 1844', and '2s. H. Bohn. 1848', reporting an edn. or edns. of which no copies have yet been traced. W. Kent & Co. of Paternoster-row, are recorded in Hodson's *Directory* (1855), 71]

79.4LP/58 Lives of the Poets, Aberdeen 1847

THE LIVES | OF THE MOST EMINENT | ENGLISH POETS: | WITH | CRITICAL OBSERVATIONS | ON | THEIR WORKS. | [short rule] | BY SAMUEL JOHNSON, LL.D. | [short rule] | A NEW AND COMPLETE EDITION. | FOUR VOLUMES IN ONE. | [short rule] | ABERDEEN: | PUBLISHED BY GEORGE CLARK AND SON. | IPSWICH:— J. M. BURTON. | [short rule] | MDCCCXLVII.
12s, A–2D¹², ($1,5 (M as 2M, Q5 as 2Q) signed), 324 leaves.
Pp. *1* ½t: LIVES OF THE ENGLISH POETS., *2* blk, *3* t., *4* blk, *5–6* Advertisement, on A4 pp. 7 8–642 (199 as 399, 218, 306, 371 unnumbered, 315 as 314) text Cowley–Lyttelton, 642 *Explicit: FINIS.*, coloph: '[rule] | James Clark, Printer, Aberdeen.', *643–644* Index (not alphabetical), *645–7* Catalogue of New & Cheap publications, *648* blk.
Paper: Newsprint, white, wove; uncut: 7⅜ × 4¼ in. No vis. wmk.

Type: Brevier (2.6 mm), leaded (0.5 mm); apparently stereotyped, though I
have found no predecessor.

References: Courtney 144–5.

Notes: The advts. (645–7) at the end name: 'W. Milner, Halifax, G. Clarke &
Son, Aberdeen, and J.M. Burton, of Ipswich', as concerned with the publica-
tions which include: 'Johnson's Complete English Dictionary, 8vo. 3s. 6d.,
Johnson's Lives of the Poets, 2s. 6d., Boswell's Life of Johnson . . ., Dodd's
Beauties of Shakespeare, 1s.'

Copies: Eu (.82463, with advts.);

USA: DLC, [MdBG, MH, NNUT], OCi; *Can*: [CaBViP]; *UK*: ABu,
BMp², E (NG.1570 a.13), Eu, Gp (B.766751), JDF ('J. Grant Robinson'),
[WLAp].

79.4LP/59   Lives of the Poets, Jones's edition   1848

THE | LIVES | OF THE | ENGLISH POETS; | BY SAMUEL
JOHNSON, LL.D. | [medium rule] | *COMPLETE IN ONE VOLUME.* |
[medium rule] | LONDON: | JONES AND CO., THE TEMPLE OF THE
MUSES. | 1848.

8° , π1 2π² A–2Z⁴, ($1 signed), 187 leaves.

Pp. Engr. port. SJ ('Engraved by Mr R. Page from the admired Painting by
Sir Joshua Reynolds') front. + π1 *i* t., *ii* blk, on 2π1 *iii* ½t: THE | LIVES |
OF THE | ENGLISH POETS. | BY | SAMUEL JOHNSON, LL.D., *iv*
blk, *v* Contents, *vi* blk, on A1 *1* 2–363 text Cowley–Lyttelton, *364* blk.

Paper: White, wove; Demy (uncut: 8¾ × 5⅝ in.).

Type: Brevier (2.5 mm), 2 cols./p.

Notes: From markedly worn stereos, presumably a reimpression from Jones's
1825 edn. (79.4LP/41), above.

Copies: Gp (B.709180); *USA*: CtY, MH (10453. 21); *UK*: BMp (481014).

79.4LP/60   Lives of the Poets, ed. Hazlitt   1854

JOHNSON'S LIVES | OF THE | BRITISH POETS | [BL] **Completed by** |
WILLIAM HAZLITT. | [Engr. vignette: putto with lyre, riding a lioness] |
IN FOUR VOLUMES. — VOL. I [–IV]. | LONDON: | NATHANIEL
COOKE, MILFORD HOUSE, STRAND. | MDCCCLIV.

Var. vol. 4: LONDON: | NATHANIEL COOKE, | THE NATIONAL
ILLUSTRATED LIBRARY, | MILFORD HOUSE, MILFORD LANE,
STRAND: | W.S. ORR & CO., AMEN CORNER, PATERNOSTER
ROW. | [short rule] | 1854.

4 vols., 8°

I. *A*⁴ B–X⁸ Y⁴, ($1 signed; 'VOL. I.' on $1 (–C, F)), 168 leaves.

Pp. Engr. front. and t. 2 leaves, + *i–vii* Dedication (To Richard Monckton Milnes, M.P.), *viii* blk, *ix–*x Preface ('Chelsea, Feb. 1854'), *xi* xii–xiii Contents, *xiv* blk, on B4 pp. *1* 2–322 (151 as 15) text Amergin–Waller, 322 coloph: 'Robson, Levey, and Franklyn, Great New Street and Fetter Lane.'

Plates: inserted facing pp. 10, 72, 144, 240, & 288.

II. *A*² B–U⁸ X⁶, ($1 signed, 'VOL. II.' on $1), 160 leaves.

Pp. *i* ½t: JOHNSON's | LIVES OF THE POETS. | [rule] | VOL. II., *ii* coloph. as I. 322, Engr. front. and t. 2 leaves + *iii* Contents, *iv* blk, on B1 *1* 2–316 (128 as 182) text Nabbes–Pomfret, 316 coloph. as vol. 1.

Plates: inserted facing pp. 89, 129, 135, 139, 181 & 244.

III. *A*1 B–U⁸ X⁸ (–X8 = A1), ($1 signed; 'VOL. III.' on $1), 160 leaves.

Pp. Engr. front. & t. 2 leaves + *i* Contents, *ii* blk, on B1 *1* 2–318 text Swift–Mason, 318 coloph. as vol. 1.

Plates: inserted facing pp. 13, 62, 86, 146, 158, 211.

IV. *A*² B–U⁸ X², ($1 signed; 'VOL. IV.' on $1), 156 leaves.

Pp. *i* ½t: as vol. 2 . . . VOL. IV., *ii* coloph. as vol. 2, Engr. front. and t. 2 leaves + *v–*vi Contents, on B1 *1* 2–297 text Lillo–Landor, 297–304 Characteristics, 304 coloph. as vol. 2, *305* 306–8 Index.

Plates: inserted facing pp. 120, 122, 128, 139, 147.

References: Courtney 145, 147; Low's *English Catalogue, 1835–63,* i (1864), 'ed. Hazlitt, 4 vols. post 8vo. 10s. Ingram, 1854'.

Notes: There are line engravings throughout the work. No ½tt in vols. 1 and 3. The additional Lives were the work of W.C. Hazlitt, and include a 'Life of Johnson', IV. 70–93.

Copies: O (210 c. 162–5);

USA: Hyde ('Williams'; blind stamped covers with devices incorporating words 'National Illustrated Library'), ICN, ICU, [Liebert = CtY], MH, NN², TxU, ViU, [KU, NRU, PJB, PLT, WaSpG]; *UK*: ABu, AWu, BMp, C, Csj, E (x. x. 5), SAN, [WLAp]; *Fr*: BN.

79.4LP/61a   Lives of the Poets, ed. Cunningham   1854
Murray's British Classics

LIVES | OF THE | MOST EMINENT | ENGLISH POETS, | WITH | CRITICAL OBSERVATIONS ON THEIR WORKS. | BY SAMUEL JOHNSON. | [medium wavy rule] | WITH NOTES CORRECTIVE AND EXPLANATORY, | BY PETER CUNNINGHAM, F.S.A. | [medium wavy rule] | IN THREE VOLUMES. — VOL. I [–III]. | LONDON: | JOHN MURRAY, ALBEMARLE STREET. | 1854. | *The Proprietor of the Copyright of this Work reserves to himself the right | of Translation in Foreign Countries.*

3 vols., 8°

I. a^8 b^8 B–2B^8 2C^4 2D^2, + [^{2}B–C^8], ($2 signed), 214 + [16] leaves.

Pp. *i* ½t, *ii* blk, *iii* t., *iv* coloph: 'LONDON: PRINTED BY WILLIAM CLOWES AND SONS, STAMFORD-STREET, | AND CHARING CROSS.', *v* vi–xxvii Editor's Preface ('Sept. 21, 1854'), *xxviii* blk, *xxix–xxx* Advertisement, *xxxi–xxxii* Contents, on B1 *1–2* 3–395 text Cowley–Dryden, [+ ^{2}B–C^8 = 32 pp. Murray's advts. (ptd. by Bradbury & Evans)].

II. A^4 B–2E^8 2F^6, + [χ^8 (χ4 + $^2\chi^2$)], ($2 signed), 226 + [10] leaves.

Pp. *i* ½t, *ii* blk, *iii* t., *iv* coloph. as vol. 1, *v* vi–viii Contents, on B1 *1–2* 3–444 text Pomfret–Savage, [+ χ^{10} = 20 pp. Murray's advts. (ptd. by Bradbury & Evans, 'October 1854')].

III. a^4 b^2 B–2F^8 2G^4, + [^{2}B–C^8], ($2 signed), 234 + [16] leaves.

Pp. *i* ½t, *ii* blk, *iii* t., *iv* coloph. as vol. 1, *v–vii* Editor's Postscript ('Nov. 29, 1854'), *viii* blk, *ix* x–xii Contents, on B1 *1–2* 3–420 text Pope–Gray, 423–31 Additional Notes, 432 (432 as 43) Errata, 433–56 Index, + [^{2}B–C^8 = 32 pp. Murray's advts. (ptd. by Bradbury & Evans, 'April 1854')].

References: Courtney 145–6; Low's *English Catalogue, 1835–63*, i (1864), '3 vol. 8vo. 22s. 6d. Murray, 1854'.

Notes: This appears to have been Murray's first essay with the *Lives* in his series 'Murray's British Classics', to which it belongs.

The Lives are printed in the order of the original *Prefaces* (79.4LP/1.2, above), of which the text is also followed. At Christie's, 3 May 1967, lot 36 was a letter from Sir Egerton Brydges to Murray, suggesting an edn. of the *Lives*, for which he had collected in his mind 'matter for notes and comments, moral, biographical and critical.' It is not known whether Brydges conveyed these matters to Cunningham for use.[1] Cunningham's papers included interesting Johnsoniana, and were dispersed at Sotheby's &c., 26 Feb. 1855. He made use of much MS and primary material (noticed in Preface, I. v–vii), which is valuable, and not all was noticed by G.B. Hill for his edn. of 1905 (79.4LP/71a, below). Cunningham consulted SJ's copy of Collins and Hammond's *Elegies*, now NNC (*Booklist* 76).

Copies: O (210 a. 209–11);

USA: CSmH, CtY, Hyde^2 (1. 'A.D. Toogood' — R.B. Adam; 2. 'Robert F. Metzdorf'), IU, [Liebert], MB, MH (10453.23), NjP^2, NN, PPL, TxU, [DLC, PBm, PP, PPT, PU]; *UK*: ABu, AWn, AWu (lacks vol. 3), BMp, BRu, C, Ck (Keynes), E, Eu, Gu, LICj, MRc, MRu, SAN, [WLAp]; *Fr*: BN.

---

[1] In C.R. Johnson's *Catalogue* 32 (1991), 37(7) was an 'Autobiographical Fragment' in MS by Brydges (from Phillipps MSS), adverting to the strong influence which the *Lives* had exerted upon him as a young man.

79.4LP/61b   Lives of the Poets, ed. Cunningham,   1854
first Boston issue

Lives of the most eminent English Poets, with critical Observations on their Works. By Samuel Johnson. With notes corrective and explanatory, by Peter Cunningham, F.S.A. In three volumes. Vol. I [– III]. Boston: Little, Brown &c.

2 vols. Not examined.
Copies: IU.

79.4LP/61c   Lives of the Poets, ed. Cunningham,   [1854]
second Boston issue

Lives . . . Boston: S.E. Cassimo & Co., n.d.
2 vols. Not examined.
Copies: MeB, NN, UCLA.

79.4LP/61d   Lives of the Poets, ed. Cunningham,   1857
first New York issue

Lives . . . New York: Derby and Jackson.
2 vols. Not examined.
Copies: CtY[2] (2 vols.), DLC, ICU (2 vols.), NN (2 vols.), OClJC, PHi (2 vols.), PMA.

79.4LP/61e   Lives of the Poets, ed. Cunningham,   1859
second New York issue

Lives . . . New York: Derby & Jackson.
2 vols. Not examined.
Copies: NN (2 vols. in 1).

79.4LP/61f   Lives of the Poets, ed. Cunningham,   1861
third New York issue

Lives . . . New York: Derby & Jackson.
2 vols. Not examined.
Copies: CtY, [Liebert].

79.4LP/61g   Lives of the Poets, ed. Cunningham,   1864
                      first Philadelphia issue

Lives . . .
   2 vols. Not examined.
   Copies: ViU.

79.4LP/61h   Lives of the Poets, ed. Cunningham,   1868
                      second Philadelphia issue

Lives . . . Philadelphia: Claxton . . . &c.
   2 vols. Not examined.
   Copies: [Liebert = CtY].

79.4LP/61i   Lives of the Poets, ed. Cunningham   1870
                      third Philadelphia issue

Lives . . . Philadelphia: Claxton, Remsem, & Haffelfinger.
   2 vols. Not examined.
   Copies: ICU, NjP, [OrP].

79.4LP/61j   Lives of the Poets, ed. Cunningham   1878

Lives . . . Not seen.
   Copies: Unlocated.

79.4LP/61k   Lives of the Poets, ed. Cunningham   1886

Lives . . . Not seen.
   Copies: Unlocated.

79.4LP/62   Lives of the Poets, Tauchnitz   1858

[½t] Collection of British Authors. Vol. CCCCXVIII [– CCCCXIX].
Johnson's Lives. In Two Volumes. Vol. I [– II].
   [Title] The Lives of the English Poets, by Samuel Johnson, LL.D. In Two
Volumes. Vol. I [– II]. Leipzig Bernhard Tauchnitz. 1858
   2 vols., 8°

   I. π1–3 1–25^8 26$_1$, 204 leaves.

Pp. π1 ½t, π2 t., π3 *v*–vi Contents, on 1₁ *1* 2–402 text Cowley–Sheffield, 402 *Explicit*: END OF VOL. I., coloph: Printed by Bernhard Tauchnitz.

II. π 1–3 1–25⁸ 26⁸ (–26₈ ? blk), 211 leaves.

Pp. π1 ½t, π2 t., π3 *v*–vi Contents, on 1₁ *1* 2–414 text Prior–Lyttelton, 414 *explicit*: THE END., coloph. as vol. 1.

References: Courtney 146; Todd and Bowden, *Tauchniz International Editions* (1988), 106.

Notes: Published 18 Feb. 1858, and reissued November 1886, July 1888; vol. 2 apparently reissued in August 1896 (T&B).

Copies: O;

USA: [Liebert = CtY], MB, MH (vol. 1 only), NN (2 vol. > 1), OCi, PU, ViU, [NBuG, OClW]; *Can*: CaBVU; *UK*: C, E (AB.1.80.58, 'Signet Library').

79.4LP/63   Lives of the Poets, Oxford English Classics   1864–65

[Within double rules] THE LIVES | OF THE MOST EMINENT | ENGLISH POETS; | WITH CRITICAL OBSERVATIONS ON THEIR WORKS. | BY SAMUEL JOHNSON. | VOL. I [–III]. | [2 cols. list of names] | [BL] **Oxford and London:** | JOHN HENRY AND JAMES PARKER. | 1864

3 vols., 12s

I. *A*⁴ B–S¹² T⁶ ($1,5, $5 as $2 signed), 214 leaves.

Pp. *i* t. (1864), *ii* coloph: 'Printed by Messrs. Parker, Cornmarket, Oxford.', *iii*–iv Advertisement (to 79.4LP/1b), *v* Advertisement to present edn. ('Oxford, July 1, 1864'), *vi* blk, *vii* Contents, *viii* blk, on B1 pp. *1* 2–413 Cowley–Dryden, 413 coloph., *414* blk, + 3 leaves advts.

II. *A*² B–S¹² T¹⁰, ($1,5 signed), 216 leaves.

Pp. i t. (1864), *ii* coloph., *iii* Contents, *iv* blk, on B1 pp. *1* 2–421 Pomfret–Savage, 421 coloph., *422* blk, + 3 leaves advts.

III. *A*² B–Q¹² R¹⁰, ($1,5 signed), 192 leaves.

Pp. *i* t. (1865), *ii* coloph., *iii* Contents, *iv* blk, on B1 pp *1* 2–380 Pope–Gray, 380 coloph.

References: Courtney 146.

Notes: A reprint from 1783 edn. (79.4LP/7, above), with very few notes. Low's *English Catalogue, 1863–72*, ii (1873), '3 vols. 18mo. ea. 3s. 6d. 1865, reduced 2s. 6d. each, Parker 1870'.

Copies: O (210 g. 7,8,8*); *USA*: NjP; *UK*: C, Csj, E (s. s.8), [WLAp '1869'].

79.4LP/64a   Lives of the Poets, Crocker, first issue   1868

LIVES | OF THE | MOST EMINENT ENGLISH | POETS: | WITH | CRITICAL OBSERVATIONS ON THEIR WORKS. | BY | SAMUEL JOHNSON, LL. D. | *CAREFULLY COLLATED WITH THE BEST EDITIONS.* | LONDON: ALFRED THOMAS CROCKER, 303 & 304 STRAND. | 1868.

16°, A^4 (–A1 ?= 2L1) B–2I^8 2K^4 2L1, ($2 signed), 256 leaves.

Pp. *i* t., *ii* blk, *iii* Author's Notice (1779 & 1783 Advertisement), *iv–v* Preliminary Notice (signed: 'F.C.'), *vi* Contents, on B1 pp. *1* 2–505 Cowley–Lyttelton, 505 *Explicit*: THE END., *506* coloph: 'London: Savill, Edwards and Co., Printers, Chandos Street, | Covent Garden.'

References: Courtney 146; Low's *English Catalogue, 1863–72*, ii (1873), 'new ed. post 8vo. 3s. 6d. Crocker. 1870'.

Notes: 'F.C.' is unidentified, unless one of the Crocker brothers. This edn. appears to have been taken over by Frederick Warne, see below, 79.4LP/65.

Copies: O (210 g. 211; maroon cloth);
USA: MB, NN; *UK*: AWu, BMp, C, E, Gp (B.563599); *Aust*: CNL.

79.4LP/64b   Lives of the Poets, Crocker, second issue   1871

The Lives of the most eminent English Poets: with critical Observations on their Works. To which are added The "Preface to Shakespeare," and the Review of the "Origin of Evil." By Samuel Johnson, LLD. With a Sketch of the Author's Life, by Sir Walter Scott. London: Albert J. Crocker and Brothers, The Mermaid, Temple Bar, 227, Strand. 1871.

8s, a^4 b^8 B–2M^8 2N^4, ($2 signed), 288 leaves.

Pp. a1 *i* ½t, *ii* blk, *iii* t., *iv* blk, *v–vi* Preliminary note, *vii* Author's (= SJ's) Advertisement, *viii* blk, on b1 *ix* x–xviii Synoptic Conts., *xix* xx–xxiv Scott's 'Sketch', on B1 *1* 2–505 text, 506 note, 507–34 Pref. to Sh., 534–49 Review of Jenyns, 549 *Explicit*: THE END., 550 coloph: (as prec. 79.4LP/67a), *551–2* advts. for Mermaid series of 'Our old English Dramatists'.

Notes: The MS of Scott's brief biography of SJ is Es. It was written for Ballantyne's *Novelist's Library*, 1823; see *Rasselas*, 59.4R/110, above.

Copies: AWn, BMp (470945).

79.4LP/65a   Lives of the Poets, Chandos Classics,   [? 1871–80]
No. 9

THE "*CHANDOS CLASSICS.*" | LIVES | OF THE | MOST EMINENT ENGLISH | POETS: | *WITH CRITICAL OBSERVATIONS ON THEIR WORKS.* | TO WHICH ARE ADDED | THE "PREFACE TO

SHAKESPEARE," AND THE REVIEW OF | "THE ORIGIN OF EVIL." | BY | SAMUEL JOHNSON, LL.D. | WITH A SKETCH OF THE AUTHOR'S LIFE BY | SIR WALTER SCOTT. | [BL] New Edition, with a Complete Index. | [Device: inverted horseshoe flanked by wings] | LONDON AND NEW YORK: | FREDERICK WARNE AND CO.

Var: omits first line, and then as: . . . SCOTT. | [device, as above] | LONDON: | FREDERICK WARNE AND CO. | AND NEW YORK. (Hyde)

8°, *a*² b⁸ B–2O⁸ 2P⁶, ($2 signed), 304 leaves.

Pp. *i* t., *ii* coloph: 'Richard Clay & Sons, Limited, | London & Bungay.', *iii*–iv Preliminary Notice (signed 'F.C.'), *v* vi–xiv Contents, *xv* xvi–xx Samuel Johnson (by Scott), on B1 pp. *1* 2–505 text Cowley–Lyttelton, 506 note on Polonius, 507–33 Preface to Shakespeare (dated '1768'), 534–49 Review of Jenyns &c., 550–51 Post-Praefatio, *552* 553–88 Index, 588 coloph. as p. ii (some copies have publisher's code number below coloph., as JDF: 'O52915988525')

Notes: This derives from Crocker's edn. (79.4LP/64, above) with additional items from p. 506 onwards. Also issued as 'The Lansdowne Poets', [n.d.]: (Liebert = CtY), and in 'The Chandos Library' series (AWn ?).

Copies: O (279 e. 200);

USA: CSmH, DFo, DLC, Hyde ('C.F. Tucker Brooke'), [Liebert = CtY], MB, [MdBJ], MH, [MWelC, NcRS], NjP, NN, [NRU, OCl, OCIRC, OClW, ODW, OO, PBm, PHC], TxU, ViU; *UK*: AWu, BMp (553553), DUNu, JDF² (1. In mustard cloth, black, green & gilt titling & decorations 'The Chandos Clasics Lives of the Poets Samuel Johnson L.L.D.', spine: Johnson's Lives of the Poets Chandos Classics F Warne & Co.' back (blind): 'The Chandos Classics Lives of the Poets Frederick Warne & Co. London.'; 2. Plain blue cloth, ptd. spine label, publisher's code no. on p. 588), Gu, NCu², SAN; [C ('? 1871'), En ('? 1872')].

79.4LP/65b   Lives of the Poets, Chandos Classics,   [? 1880]
                                            another issue

[Title] THE "CHANDOS CLASSICS." | [medium rule] | LIVES | OF THE | MOST EMINENT ENGLISH | POETS: | WITH CRITICAL OBSERVATIONS ON THEIR WORKS. | TO WHICH ARE ADDED | THE "PREFACE TO SHAKESPEARE," AND THE REVIEW OF | "THE ORIGIN OF EVIL." | BY | SAMUEL JOHNSON, LL.D. | WITH A SKETCH OF THE AUTHOR'S LIFE BY | SIR WALTER SCOTT. | [BL]: New Edition, with a Complete Index. | [Circular device: F. Warne, Oxford St. Covent Garden] | LONDON: | FREDERICK WARNE & CO. | BEDFORD STREET, STRAND. | NEW YORK: SCRIBNER, WELFORD, & ARMSTRONG.

Var: . . . FREDERICK WARNE & CO., | BEDFORD STREET, COVENT GARDEN, | NEW YORK: SCRIBNER, WELFORD & ARMSTRONG.

Collation &c., as prec., but Port. of Shakespeare ('Chandos Portrait') as front.

References: Low's *English Catalogue, 1872–80*, iii (1882), 'new ed. post 8vo. 3s. 6d. Warne, 1872–7'.

Notes: There may be a colophon on p. *ii* as: [BL] 'Bungay: | Clay and Taylor, Printers.', or none, and where none (BmP **1**.) the coloph. on p. 588 is: '*Printed by* Morrison & Gibb Limited, *Edinburgh*.', but BmP **2**., and JDF have no colophons at all.

Copies: BMp² (**1**. 473244, no coloph on ii, but M & G on 588; **2**. 518893 no colophs.); *UK*: JDF (var., no coloph on ii, or 588).

79.4LP/66   Lives of the Poets,   1886–1891
               Cassell's National Library

Vols. 17 (1886), 37 (1886), 131 (1888), 159 (1889), 166 (1889).

Vol. 17 (1886): CASSELL'S NATIONAL LIBRARY. | [medium rule] | LIVES | OF THE | English Poets | [BL] **Waller Milton Cowley** | BY | SAMUEL JOHNSON, LL.D. | [Cassell's circular device: La Belle Sauvage] | CASSELL & COMPANY, Limited: | *LONDON, PARIS, NEW YORK & MELBOURNE*. | 1886.

16s, *A*¹⁶ B–F¹⁶, ($1 as '$–17' signed), 96 leaves.

Pp. *1* ½t: LIVES OF THE ENGLISH POETS | [BL] **Waller Milton Cowley**, *2* advts., *3* t., *4* blk, *5* 6–8 Introduction (signed 'H[enry]. M[orley].'), *9* 10–54 text Waller, 55–134 text Milton, 135–92 text Cowley, 192 *Explicit*: THE END., coloph: [medium rule] | Printed by Cassell & Company, Limited, La Belle Sauvage, London, E.C.

References: Courtney 146.

Copies: O (2794 f. 1; ptd. paper wraps); *UK*: JDF² (brown cloth, black & gilt titling).

Vol. 37 (1886): CASSELL'S NATIONAL LIBRARY. | [medium rule] | LIVES | OF THE | English Poets. | [BL] **Butler, Denham, Dryden, Roscommon,** | **Spratt, Dorset, Rochester, Otway.** | BY | SAMUEL JOHNSON, LL.D. | [circular device: La Belle Sauvage] | CASSELL & COMPANY, Limited: | *LONDON, PARIS, NEW YORK & MELBOURNE*. | 1886.

16s, *A*¹⁶ B–F¹⁶, ($1 as '$–37'), 96 leaves.

Pp. *1* ½t: LIVES OF THE ENGLISH POETS. [**No names**], *2* advts., *3* t., *4* blk, *5* 6–11 Introduction ('H.M.'), *12* blk, *13* 14–26 Butler, *27* 28–36 Denham, *37* 38–159 Dryden, 160–69 Roscommon, 170–5 Sprat, 176–9 Dorset, 180–7 Rochester, 188–92 Otway, 192 *Explicit* & coloph. as vol. 17.

References: Courtney 146.

Notes: Reissued '1892' in blind-stamped blue cloth, with addendum to coloph. as '78–692'.

Copies: JDF (brown cloth, black & gilt titling).

Vol. 131 (1888): CASSELL'S NATIONAL LIBRARY. | [medium rule] | LIVES | OF THE | Enɢʟɪsʜ Poets. | [BL] **Addison Savage Swift.** | BY | SAMUEL JOHNSON, LL.D. | [circular device: La Belle Sauvage] | CASSELL & COMPANY, Lɪᴍɪᴛᴇᴅ: | *LONDON, PARIS, NEW YORK &* *MELBOURNE.* | 1888.

16s, A^{16} B–F^{16}, ($1 as '$–131'), 96 leaves.

Pp. *1* ½t: LIVES OF THE ENGLISH POETS, *2* advts, *3* t., *4* blk, *5*–6 Introd. ('H.M.'), *7* 8–59 Addison, *60* 61–154 Savage, *155* 156–92 Swift, 192 *Explicit* & coloph. as vol. 17.

References: Courtney 146.

Copies: O (2794 f. 1ᶜ; paper wraps); *USA*: IaU, ICU; *UK*: BRu.

Vol. 159 (1889): CASSELL'S NATIONAL LIBRARY. | [medium rule] | LIVES | OF THE | Enɢʟɪsʜ Poets | [BL] **Prior Congreve Blackmore Pope** | BY | SAMUEL JOHNSON, LL.D. | [circular device: La Belle Sauvage] | CASSELL & COMPANY Lɪᴍɪᴛᴇᴅ: | *LONDON, PARIS, NEW YORK &* *MELBOURNE.* | 1889.

16s, A^{16} B–F^{16}, ($1 as '$–159'), 96 leaves.

Pp. *1* ½t: LIVES OF THE ENGLISH POETS | [BL] **Prior Congreve Blackmore Pope**, *2* advts., *3* t., *4* blk, 7 8–28 text Prior, *29* 30–42 text Congreve, *43* 44–61 text Blackmore, *62* 63–192 text Pope, 192 coloph: as vol. 17.

References: Courtney 146.

Copies: O (2794 f.1ᵈ; paper wraps); *UK*: BRu, Op (Vernon 72178, boards).

Vol. 166 (1889): THE | Enɢʟɪsʜ Poets | [BL] **Gay Thomson Young Gray etc.** | BY | SAMUEL JOHNSON, LL.D. | [circular device: La Belle Sauvage] | CASSELL & COMPANY Lɪᴍɪᴛᴇᴅ: | *LONDON, PARIS, NEW YORK &* *MELBOURNE.* | 1889.

16s, A^{16} B–F^{16}, ($1 as: '$–166'), 96 leaves.

Pp. *1* ½t: LIVES OF THE ENGLISH POETS | [BL] **Gay Thomson Young Gray etc.**, *2* advts., *3* t., *4* blk, *5* 6–7 Introduction ('H.M.'), *8* blk, *9* 10–192 text Lives of King, Halifax, Parnell, Garth, Rowe, Gay, Tickell, Somerville, Thomson, Watts, A. Philips, West, Collins, Shenstone, Young, Akenside, Gray, and Lyttelton, 192 coloph: as vol. 17, above, + 1 leaf advts.

References: Courtney 146.

Notes: Published in weekly volumes, grey paper covers printed in red at 3d. each, or in brown cloth-covered boards, with black and gold decorated titling, viz. Front cover: JOHNSON'S | LIVES OF THE POETS | [short rule] | Wᴀʟʟᴇʀ, Mɪʟᴛᴏɴ, Cᴏᴡʟᴇʏ; CASSELL'S | NATIONAL | LIBRARY;

EDITED BY PROFESSOR HENRY MORLEY. On spine: JOHNSON'S LIVES: WALLER, MILTON, COWLEY. at 6d., &c.

There were frequent reimpressions from the plates of these vols. Low's *English Catalogue*, notices 1886, 1891, 1892, &c.

Copies: O (2794 f. 1ᵃ⁻ᵉ).

79.4LP/67 Lives of the Poets, New York 1889

Lives of the Poets
Second Edition New York: Holt & Co. Not examined.
Copies: ICU.

79.4LP/68 Lives of the Poets, ed. Napier, 1890
Bohn's Standard Library

JOHNSON'S | LIVES OF THE POETS. | EDITED, WITH NOTES, BY | MRS ALEXANDER NAPIER. | AND AN INTRODUCTION BY J. W. HALES, M.A., | PROFESSOR OF ENGLISH LITERATURE IN KING'S COLLEGE, LONDON, AND | CLARK LECTURER AT TRINITY COLLEGE, CAMBRIDGE. | VOL. I [–III]. | LONDON: GEORGE BELL & SONS, YORK STREET, | COVENT GARDEN. | 1890.
3 vols., 8°

I. A⁸ (A1 blk) b⁸ B–2K⁸ 2L², ($1 signed (+ A); 'I.' on $1), 274 leaves.
Pp. A1 blk, on A2 *i* ½t, *ii* blk, *iii* t., *iv* coloph: 'Chiswick Press:— C. Whittingham and Co., Tooks Court, | Chancery Lane.', *v* Dedication, *vi* blk, *vii* viii–ix Preface ('Robina Napier, Bromley College, Dec. 22, 1889.'), *x* blk, *xi* Contents, *xii* blk, *xiii* xiv–xxvi Introduction ('John W. Hales, King's College, London. August 3, 1889.'), *xxvii* facsimile of (79.4LP/7) 1783 t., *xxviii* blk, xxix–xxx Advertisement to 1783, on B1 *1* ½t 'COWLEY.' *2* Pref. note, *3* 4–496 text Cowley–Dryden, 496–515 Appendix & notes, 515 *Explicit*: END OF VOL. I., coloph. (on single line), *516* blk.

II. A⁴ B–2D⁸ 2E⁴ 2F², ($1 (+ A) signed; 'II.' on $1), 218 leaves.
Pp. A1 *i–ii* blk, on A2 *iii* ½t, *iv* blk, *v* t., *vi* coloph., *vii* Contents, *viii* blk, on B1 *1* ½t 'SMITH.', *2* blk, *3* 4–420 text Smith–Savage, *421* ½t Appendix, *422* blk, *423* 424–7 text Appx., 427 *Explicit*: END OF VOL. II., coloph. as vol. 1.

III. A⁴ B–2D⁸ 2E⁶, ($1 (+ A) signed; 'III.' on $1), 218 leaves.
Pp. A1 blk, *iii* ½t, *iv* blk, *v* t., *vi* coloph., *vii* Contents, *viii* blk, on B1 *1* ½t 'SWIFT.', *2* Prelim. note, *3* 4–395 text Swift–Lyttelton, *396* blk, *397* ½t Index, *398* blk, *399* 400–28 Index (2 cols./p.), 428 *errata* & coloph.

References: Courtney 146; Low's *English Catalogue 1890–97*, v (1898), 'Lives 3 vols. 3s. 6d. each. Bell. Oct. 90.'; Cordasco, *Bohn Libraries* (1951) 143.

Notes: Follows the text of 1783 (79.4LP/7) above. Published in grey-green cloth, blind-stamped on covers in circle: 'Bohn's Standard Library.', gilt spine title 'Johnson's | Lives of | the Poets.'

Copies: O (279 e. 23–5); *USA*: DLC, ICU, IU, [Liebert= CtY], MB, MH (vol. 2 only), NjP, PPD; *UK*: BMp, C, DUNu, E (S. 153 g), Eu (.82463).

79.4LP/69a   Lives of the Poets, ed. Henley,   1896
                              English Classics

THE LIVES OF | THE MOST EMINENT | [red] ENGLISH POETS | BY | SAMUEL JOHNSON | LL.D. | IN THREE VOLUMES | VOL. I [–III]. | METHUEN AND CO. | 36 ESSEX STREET: STRAND | LONDON | 1896

3 vols., 8°

I. *a*⁸ b⁸ A–X⁸ Y⁶, ($1 signed), 190 leaves.

Pp. *i* ½t: English Classics | Edited by W.E. Henley | Johnson's Lives of | The English Poets | With an Introduction | by John Hepburn Millar | I [–III], *ii* blk, + Litho. port. front. 1 leaf + *iii* t., *iv* blk, *v* Contents, *vi* blk, *vii* viii–xxxi Introduction (by Millar), *xxxii* blk, on A1 *1* 2–348 text Cowley–Dryden, 348 coloph: 'Edinburgh: T. and A. CONSTABLE, Printers to Her Majesty.'

II. π⁴ (π1 blk) A–T⁸ U² (U2 blk), ($1 signed), 158 leaves.

Pp. *i–ii* blk, *iii* ½t, *iv* blk, *v* t., *vi* blk, *vii* Contents, *viii* blk, on A1 *1* 2–305 text Smith–Savage, *306* coloph. as vol. 1, *307–8* (U2) blk.

III. π⁴ (π1 blk) A–S⁸ ($1 signed), 148 leaves.

Pp. *i–ii* blk, *iii* ½t, *iv* blk, *v* t., *vi* blk, *vii* Contents, *viii* blk, on A1 *1* 2–287 text Swift–Lyttelton, *288* coloph. as vol. 1.

References: Courtney 146–7.

Notes: Third line of t. in red; no notes. Low's *English Catalogue, 1890–97*, v (1898), 'Lives 3 vols. 8vo. 10s. 6d. Eng. Class. Methuen. Mar. 96'.

Copies: O (279 e. 35–7);

USA: Hyde (glazed green cloth, uncut: 7⅝ × 5⅛ in.), IU, [Liebert = CtY], MB, MH; *UK*: BMp, BRp, BRu, Cp, DUNu, E (NF. 1317 c.4), NCu, SAN.

79.4LP/69b   Lives of the Poets, ed. Henley   1896
                         English Classics, Chicago issue

THE LIVES OF | THE MOST EMINENT | [red] ENGLISH POETS | BY | SAMUEL JOHNSON | LL.D. | IN THREE VOLUMES | VOL. I

[–III]. | CHICAGO: STONE & KIMBALL | LONDON: METHUEN & Co. | 1896

3 vols., 8°. Not examined.

Notes: This is the American issue of 79.4LP/69a.

Copies: ICN.

79.4LP/70a   Lives of the Poets, ed. Waugh   1896

[Within broad decorated border; **Red**] JOHNSON'S | LIVES OF THE POETS | *A NEW EDITION* | WITH NOTES AND INTRODUCTION | BY | ARTHUR WAUGH, | AUTHOR OF 'ALFRED, LORD TENNYSON: A STUDY | OF HIS LIFE AND WORK.' | IN SIX VOLUMES. | VOL. I [–VI]. | [**Red**] **LONDON**: | KEGAN PAUL, TRENCH, TRÜBNER & CO. LD. | PATERNOSTER HOUSE, CHARING CROSS ROAD. | [**Red**] MDCCCXCVI.

6 vols., 8°

I. π^8 a^8 B–R^8, ($2 signed), 144 leaves.

Pp. *i* ½t: Johnson's | Lives of the Poets | Vol. I [–VI]., *ii* blk, Front. port. of SJ inserted 1 leaf + *iii* t., *iv* blk, *v* vi–viii Preface, *ix* Contents, *x* Portraits, *xi* xii–xxx Introduction (by Waugh), *xxxi*–xxxii Chronological Table, on B1 *1* Facsimile of 1783 t. (79.4LP/7, above), *2* blk, *3*–4 Advertisement to 1783 edn. (79.4LP/7), *5–7* 8–253 text Cowley–Roscommon, 253 coloph: 'Printed by | Spottiswoode and Co., New-Street Square | London.', *254* blk, *255–6* (R8) advts.

Plates: facing pp. t., 6, 90, 206, 228.

II. A^4 B–S^8 T^4, ($2 signed), 144 leaves.

Pp. *i* ½t, *ii* blk, *iii* t., *iv* blk, *v* Contents, *vi* blk, *vii* Portraits, *viii* blk, on B1 *1–3* 4–280 text Otway–Dryden, 280 coloph. as vol. 1.

Plates: facing pp. 2, 12, 94, 122.

III. *^{4} B–P^8 Q^4 R^2, ($2 (–*, + *4) signed), 122 leaves.

Pp. *i* ½t, *ii* blk, *iii* t., *iv* blk, *v* Contents, *vi* blk, *vii* Portraits, *viii* blk, on B1 *1–3* 4–235 text Smith–Prior, 235 coloph. as vol. 1, *236* blk.

Plates: facing pp. 56, 66, 74, 102, 204.

IV. A^4 B–S^8, ($2 signed), 140 leaves.

Pp. *i* ½t, *ii* blk, *iii* t., *iv* blk, *v* Contents, *vi* blk, *vii* Portraits, *viii* blk, on B1 *1–3* 4–265 text Congreve–Savage, *266* blk, *267* ½t: Appendix, *268* blk, *269* 270–71 text Appendix, 271 coloph. as vol. 1, *272* blk.

Plates: facing pp. 2, 66, 132.

V. A^4 B–R^8, ($2 signed), 132 leaves.

Pp. *i* ½t, *ii* blk, *iii* t., *iv* blk, *v* Contents, *vi* blk, *vii* Portraits, *viii* blk, on B1 *1–3* 4–256 text Swift–Pitt, 256 coloph. as vol. 1.

Plates: facing pp. 2, 68.

VI. *A*⁴ B–R⁸, ($2 signed), 132 leaves.

Pp. *i* ½t, *ii* blk, *iii* t., *iv* blk, *v* Contents, *vi* blk, *vii* Portraits, *viii* blk, on B1 *1–3* 4–207 text Thomson–Lyttelton, *208* blk, *209* ½t Notes on the Portraits, *210* blk, *211* 212–13 text Notes on Portraits, *214* blk, *215* ½t Index, *216* blk, *217* 218–54 Index, 254 coloph. as vol. 1, *255–56* (R8) advts.

Plates: facing pp. 2, 60, 86, 174.

References: Courtney 147.
Notes: Low's *English Catalogue, 1890–97*, v (1898), 'Lives ed. Waugh. 6 vols. 12mo. 6s. each. Paul. Ap.–Sept. 96'.
Copies: O (279 e. 38);
USA: [CoU], Hyde² (1. 'Edmund Gosse' pres. 'Henry James'; uncut: 6⅞ × 4½ in.; 2. R.B. Adam, uncut), IU; *UK*: BMp, C, E (282 f.), Ep (PR.503.J69), Eu, LICj, SHp, [WLAp].

79.4LP/70b   Lives of the Poets, ed. Waugh,   [1896]
American issue

Johnson's Lives of the Poets A New Edition With Notes and Introduction by Arthur Waugh, . . . In Six Volumes. Vol. I [– VI]. . . . NEW YORK: | SCRIBNER'S SONS. [n.d.]
6 vols., 8°. Not examined.
Notes: A variant impression of prec. 79.4LP/70a.
Copies: MH; *USA*: [Liebert (vols. 2–3, 5–6 only) = CtY], PU.

79.4LP/71a   Lives of the Poet's, Hill's edition   1905

LIVES OF THE | ENGLISH POETS | BY SAMUEL JOHNSON, LL.D. | EDITED BY | GEORGE BIRKBECK HILL, D.C.L. | SOMETIME HONORARY FELLOW OF PEMBROKE COLLEGE, OXFORD | WITH BRIEF MEMOIR OF DR. BIRKBECK HILL, BY HIS NEPHEW | HAROLD SPENCER SCOTT, M.A., NEW COLLEGE, OXFORD | IN THREE VOLUMES | VOL. I [–III]. | COWLEY–DRYDEN [II. SMITH–SAVAGE, III. SWIFT–LYTTELTON] | OXFORD | AT THE CLARENDON PRESS | M DCCCC V
3 vols., 8°

I. *a*⁸ b⁶ B–2H⁸ 2I⁴, ($2 signed), 258 leaves.
Pp. *i* t., *ii* coloph: 'HENRY FROWDE, M.A. | PUBLISHER TO THE UNIVERSITY OF OXFORD | LONDON, EDINBURGH | NEW YORK AND TORONTO', iii–v Contents, vi Alphabetical list of Poets, vii Prefatory

Note, viii Addenda &c., ix–xxii Memoir of GBH by Scott, *xxiii–xxiv* Bibliography, *xxv* xxvi–xxvii Advertisement to third edn. 1783 (79.4LP/7), *xxviii* blk, on B1 *1* 2–487 text and Appendixes and Additional Notes Cowley–Dryden, *488* coloph: 'OXFORD | PRINTED AT THE CLARENDON PRESS | BY HORACE HART, M.A. | PRINTER TO THE UNIVERSITY'.

II. A^2 B–2E^8 2F^4, ($2 signed), 222 leaves.
Pp. *i* t., *ii* coloph. as I. ii, *iii* Contents, *iv* Alphabetical list, on B1 *1* 2–440 text &c. Smith–Savage, 440 coloph: 'Oxford: Printed at the Clarendon Press by HORACE HART, M.A.'

III. A^2 B–2N^8 2O^4, ($2 signed), 286 leaves.
Pp. *i* t., *ii* coloph. as I. ii, *iii* Contents, *iv* Alphabetical list, on B1 *1* 2–461 text &c. Swift–Lyttelton, *462* blk, *463* 464–558 Index, *559* 560–68 List of Works quoted, 568 coloph. as II. 440.

References: Courtney 147.
Notes: Published in ¼ roan at £2. 2s., and maroon cloth at £1. 1s., but cf. Low's *English Catalogue, 1901–5*, vii (1906), 'Lives ed. Hill. 3 vols. 36s. Frowde. Dec. 05'. Until the advent of the Yale edn., this text, despite many shortcomings, must be considered as indispensable and its historical notes and index are always of interest.
Copies are common in large libraries.
Copies: O^2 (**1**. 279 d. 10–12; **2**. 279 d. 65–7);
USA: CtY, Hyde (R.B. Adam), ICU, IU, NIC, NjP, MH;   *UK*: BMp, BRu, C, E, Eu, JDF ('R.W. Chapman'), L, MRu, Oef, Op.

79.4LP/71b   Lives of the Poets, Hill's edition   1968

This edn. was reprinted by Georg Olms Verlag, Hildesheim, 1968

79.4LP/72   Lives of the Poets, World's Classics,   [1906]
                                  Vols. 83–4

LIVES OF THE | ENGLISH POETS | BY | SAMUEL JOHNSON | WITH AN INTRODUCTION | BY ARTHUR WAUGH | VOL. I [–II]. | [Rectangular interlaced device inc. words: 'THE WORLD'S CLASSICS'] | HENRY FROWDE | OXFORD UNIVERSITY PRESS | LONDON, NEW YORK AND TORONTO.
Note: The styling of tt. varies with later impressions, e.g.:
[Within decorated frame: single rule and flowers] LIVES OF THE ENGLISH | [hollow] POETS | BY SAMUEL JOHNSON | *With an*

Introduction by | *Arthur Waugh* | VOLUME I [– II]. | LONDON | OXFORD UNIVERSITY PRESS

   2 vols., 16°

   I. *a²* b⁸ A–2G⁸ (2G8 blk), ($1 signed; 'VOL. I.' on $1), 250 leaves.

   Pp. Litho. port. (within green dec. border: 'SAMUEL JOHNSON') front. & t. (within green dec. border: LIVES OF THE | ENGLISH POETS | BY | SAMUEL JOHNSON, LL.D., inc. in lower border: HENRY FROWDE | OXFORD UNIVERSITY PRESS | LONDON, NEW YORK AND TORONTO.) + *i* t., *ii* SJ's dates and publisher's statement, coloph: 'Edinburgh: T. and A. CONSTABLE, Printers to His Majesty.', *iii* ½t: [BL] **The World's Classics** | LXXXIII [–LXXXIV] | JOHNSON'S LIVES OF | THE ENGLISH POETS — I [–II], *iv* blk, on b1 *v* vi–xvii Introduction (signed: 'ARTHUR WAUGH.'). *xviii* blk, *xix*–xx Contents, on A1 *1* 2–478 text Cowley–Sheffield, 478 *Explicit*: END OF VOL. I., coloph: [medium rule] | Printed by T. and A. CONSTABLE, Printers to His Majesty | at the Edinburgh University Press.

   II. π⁴ (π1 blk) A–2H⁸ (2H8 blk), ($1 signed; 'VOL. II.' on $1), 252 leaves.

   Pp. π1 blk, + *i* ½t: LXXXIV . . . II, *ii* blk, Litho. port. of SJ front. and t. (as vol. 1) 2 leaves inserted + *iii* t., *iv* SJ's dates, publisher's statement and coloph. as I. ii, *v*–vi Contents, on A1 *1* 2–493 text Prior–Lyttelton, 493 *Explicit*: END OF VOL. II., coloph: as I. 478, *494* blk.

   References: Courtney 147; Low's *English Catalogue, 1906–10*, viii (1911), 'Lives 2 vols. W. Classics 1s. ea. leather 1s. 6d. Frowde Nov. 06'.

   Notes: Waugh's Introd. derives from 1896 (79.4LP/70) above. The text is not accurate and includes many misreadings.

   The earlier issues were advertised as published in the following binding styles:
(a) Ordinary edition
      [Green] cloth boards, gilt spines   1s.
      Sultan-red Leather, limp, gilt top   1s. 6d.
      Buckram, paper label, gilt top   1s. 6d.
      Quarter parchment, gilt top   1s. 8d.
      Lambskin, limp, gilt top   2s.
      Quarter Vellum, hand-tooled, panelled lettering-piece, gilt top.
      Superior library style   4s.
      Half Calf, marbled edges   4s.
      Whole Calf, marbled edges   5s. 6d.
      Tree Calf, marbled edges   5s. 6d.
   (b) Pocket edition (on thin paper)
      Limp cloth, gilt back, gilt top   1s.
      Sultan-red Leather, limp, gilt top   1s. 6d.
      Quarter Vellum, hand-tooled, panelled
      lettering-piece, gilt top   4s.

This edn. of the *Lives* was published in both series, but specimens of all these binding styles are difficult to find, and it may be that many were discontinued. It was stereotyped and frequently reissued. Reissues have not been treated separately, but the following is a list of such as have been noticed:

1906	2 vols.	IU
1912	2 vols.	NN; ENc
1920	2 vols.	NN
1926	2 vols.	
1929	2 vols.	
1932	Vol. 2	ViU
1933	Vol. 1	ViU
1936	Vol. 2	
1938	Vol. 1	
1942	Vol. 2	
1946	Vol. 1	
1948		
1949	Vol. 2	

New and reset impression was prepared and published in:

1952	2 vols.	
1955	Vol. 1	
1956	Vol. 2	
1959	Vol. 1	
1961	2 vols.	
1964	2 vols.	Oef
1967	Vol. 2	
1968	Vol. 1	
1977	2 vols	Oef

Copies: No record has been attempted of copies of these issues and impressions.

79.4LP/73   Lives of the Poets, Everyman's Library   1925
                 Vols. 413 and 400, ed. L. Archer-Hind

SAMUEL JOHNSON | LIVES OF | THE ENGLISH POETS | IN TWO VOLUMES · VOLUME ONE [– TWO] | COWLEY to PRIOR [CONGREVE TO LYTTELTON] | INTRODUCTION BY | L. ARCHER HIND | [device: E/L + fish and anchor] | LONDON J.M. DENT & SONS LTD | NEW YORK E.P. DUTTON & CO INC.

16s, 2 vols.

I. a^{16} B–N^{16} ($1,5, $5 as *$ signed; 'I^{770}' on $1), 208 leaves.

Pp. 1 blk, a2 gen. t., a2^v note on SJ, a3 t., a3^v coloph, a4 viii–xiv Introduction (signed 'L. A.-H.'), xiv–xv bibliography, xvi Advertisement to 1781 edn., xvii–xviii Contents vols. I–II, on a10 1–395 text: Cowley–Prior, *396* blk + *397–8* (N16) blk leaf.

II. A–M¹⁶ N⁸ ($1,5 signed, $5 as *$; 'II⁷⁷¹' on $1), 200 leaves.

Pp. A1 blk, A2 gen. t., A2ᵛ note on SJ, A3 t., a3ᵛ coloph., a4 vii Contents, *viii* blk, on A5 1–392 text: Congreve–Gray.

References: Clifford & Greene, p. 257.

Notes: The text derives from the 'Prefaces' (1779–81), 79.4LP/1b, above. Initially this set formed vols. 413 and 400 of the 'Everyman Library' series, though this was later changed to vols. 770–771. They were first published in October 1925, at 2s. each. The publisher's code on the verso of each t., is I: Y 138/5 m, and II: Y 150/12½ m. The editor was L. Archer-Hind. This edn. was frequently reissued. No record has been attempted of copies of later impressions and issues.

Copies: BMp, E, O; *USA*: IU.

79.4LP/A/1   Abridged Lives of the Poets,   1784
                       Philadelphia

The Lives of the British Poets. Philadelphia. 1784
  8°, pp. 145. Not examined.
  References: Evans 18543; ESTC: w009288.
  Notes: Parts I–III only, comprising Cowley, Denham, and Milton.
  Copies: MH, NN.

79.4LP/A/2   Lives of the Poets,   1797
                       Newbery's Abridgement

JOHNSON's LIVES | OF THE | ENGLISH POETS, | *ABRIDGED:* | WITH | NOTES AND ILLUSTRATIONS | BY THE EDITOR. | DESIGNED FOR | *THE IMPROVEMENT OF YOUTH* | IN THE KNOWLEDGE OF | POLITE LITERATURE, | AND AS | A USEFUL AND PLEASING COMPENDIUM FOR | PERSONS OF RIPER YEARS. | [medium swelled rule] | To which is prefixed, | SOME ACCOUNT | OF THE | LIFE OF Dʀ. JOHNSON. | [bevelled parallel rule] | *LONDON:* | PRINTED FOR E. NEWBERY, AT THE CORNER OF | ST. PAUL's CHURCH-YARD. | 1797.

12°, A–L¹², ($6 (B6 as B5) signed), 132 leaves.

Pp. Engr. front. + *i* t., *ii* blk, *iii*–iv Preface, *v* vi–xxi Life of Johnson, *xxii* blk, *xxiii–xxiv* Contents, on B1 pp. *1* 2–239 text (abridged) of Lives, *240* blk.

Pagination: no errors; *Press-figures*: none; *Catchwords*: not recorded.
Explicit: 239 THE END.

Paper: White, laid; La. post (uncut: 7 × 4½ in.); no vis. wmk.

Type: Long primer (3.4 mm).

Plate: Engr. five medallion heads, SJ (after Trotter) in centre, of Milton, Pope, Dryden, & Thomson. 'H. Richter del. et sc. Published Jan.ʸ. 12. 1797, by E. Newbery, corner of Sᵗ Paul's.'

References: Courtney 143; Welsh 242; Roscoe, *Newbery* (1973), J191A; ESTC: n007296.

Copies: O (Vet. A5. f. 2742);

USA: CLU, CtY ('1795'), Hyde ('Robertson'), [Liebert], MH (10453.6.3), NIC, NjP, NN (misdated '1795'), NRU, PPL, [IEN, MiU]; *Can*: CaOHM; *UK*: ABu, BMp (484967), Gu, SAN (ˢPR553.J6D97); *Eir*: Dt.

79.4LP/A/3   Abridged Lives of the Poets, Paris   1805

[Engr. t.] THE LIVES | [*Copperplate italic*] *of the most celebrated English Poets,* | *with Criticisms* | *Extracted from Dʳ Johnson.* | [Oval port. of SJ after Trotter: *'Johnson'*] | *Paris.* | *Published* | *by Parsons and Galignani.* | 1805.

6s, A–2C⁶ ($1 (U as V) signed), 156 leaves.

Pp. Engr. t. + on A1 pp. *1–2* Preface dh: 'To THE READER.' ht: 'PREFACE.', *3* 4-22 dh: SOME ACCOUNT | OF THE LIFE | OF | DR. JOHNSON. | [wavy rule], rt: SOME ACCOUNT OF | THE LIFE OF DR. JOHNSON. (pp. 4, 6, 10: 'ACCOUNT ON'), *23* 24–312 dh: LIVES | OF THE | ENGLISH POETS. | [wavy rule] | COWLEY. [&c.] text Cowley–Gray (abridged) [incl: 252–70 Benjamin Jonson, 270–81 Spenser, 282–305 William Shakespeare (from Rowe's 2nd edn. 1709, n. by Steevens, p. 305), 306–7 SJ's horse-holding anecdote and Steevens's note, 308–12 Verse eulogies of Shakespeare (incl. ll. 1–8 of SJ's *Drury Lane Prologue*, 1747, (47.10DLP/1, above)]; 312 *Explicit*: THE END.

Paper: White, laid; cut: 6⅛ × 3⅝ in.; wmk.: P & J PELLERIN | A MAUZE + Grapes.¹

Type: Petit romain [= long primer] (3.4 mm), leaded (1.5 mm). Metal ornn. pp. 2, 22 (angel).

Notes: Some annotation from Seward's *Anecdotes* (5 vols., 1795–7), apparently new to this edn. In 'Shakespeare' some notes from 'Reed'. In 'Life' of SJ an approving mention of *Olla Podrida*. Text is significantly abridged.

Copies: O (279 f. 23; marbled paper boards, red leather spine label 'Lives of English poets' (in *copperplate* as t.) 'R.E. Gathorne-Hardy');

USA: NRU; *UK*: Unlocated (John Hart, *Cat.* 20 (1992), 76, £85); *Fr*: BN.

---

¹ This is an uncertain reading. The letters may also form 'MAITZE'.

79.4LP/A/4   Lives of the Poets, Jones's abridgement   1838

THE | LIVES | OF | THE ENGLISH POETS, | BY SAMUEL JOHNSON, L.L.D. | [short rule] | LONDON: | PUBLISHED BY JONES AND CO. | [short rule] | MDCCCXXXVIII.

8s, A^4 (−A1 = ? ½t) B–2A^8 2B^4, ($1 signed), 192 leaves.

Pp. ? A1 ½t, A2 t., A2^v blk, A3 pp. v vi–vii Contents (Gray misdirected to p. 376 [= 374]), *viii* blk, on B1 pp. *9* 10–384 texts Cowley–Lyttelton, 384 coloph: '[rule] | W. F. PRATT, Printer, Howden.', *Explicit*: THE END.

Paper: White, wove; pot (uncut: 5 × 3⅛ in.); no vis. wmk.

Type: (2.5 mm), leaded (0.2 mm).

Notes: The only copy seen has no ½t, but the structure and pagination require one.

Copies: E (BCL. B5703, 'St Mary's College Library, Blairs',[1] in publisher's binding: light brown cloth, gilt spine: 'Johnson's Lives of the Poets 3/6.').

---

[1] Cherry, 'The Library of St Mary's College, Blairs, Aberdeen', *Bibliothek*, xii (1985), 61.

79.4LP/S/1a   Lives of the Poets, Selections,   1878
Arnold's Six Chief Lives

THE | SIX CHIEF LIVES | FROM | JOHNSON'S "LIVES OF THE POETS," | WITH | MACAULAY'S "LIFE OF JOHNSON." | *EDITED, WITH A PREFACE,* | BY | MATTHEW ARNOLD. | [BL] **London:** | MACMILLAN AND CO. | 1878. [*The Right of Translation and Reproduction is Reserved.*]

8°, a^8 b^6 B–2G^8 2H^2, (? + ^{2}a–c^8), ($4 signed), 248 (+ ? 24) leaves.

Pp. *i* ½t, *ii* blk, *iii* t., *iv* coloph: 'R. Clay, Sons, and Taylor. Bread Street Hill.', *v* Contents, *vi* blk, *vii* viii–xxv Preface, *xxvi* blk, *xxvii* ½t, *xxviii* blk, on B1 pp. *1* 2–42 Macaulay's Life of SJ, *43* ½t, *44* blk, *45* 46–120 Milton, *121* 122–234 Dryden, *235* 236–71 Swift, *272* blk, *273* 274–326 Addison, *327* 328–454 Pope, *455* 456–66 Gray, *467* coloph. as p. ii, *468* blk, (+ *1* 2–46 *47–8* Macmillan's advts.).

References: Courtney 148; *Tinker* 175.

Notes: For further frequent issues and impressions, see below. In his Preface Arnold confesses to having struck out 'a few things in them which might be thought objectionable reading for girls and young people'.

Copies: O (210 o. 187);

USA: Hyde ('H.S. Wyatt'–'R.B. Adam'), PPL, PPM; *UK*: C, E, En, Eu, LICj, [WLAp].

79.4LP/S/1b   Lives of the Poets, Selections,   1879
  Arnold's Six Chief Lives, first New York issue

————New York, Henry Holt, 1879.
Not examined.
USA: CtY, PHC.

79.4LP/S/1c   Lives of the Poets, Selections,   1880
  Arnold's Six Chief Lives, second New York issue

————New York, Henry Holt, 1880
Unlocated.

79.4LP/S/1d   Lives of the Poets, Selections,   1881
  Arnold's Six Chief Lives, Macmillan

————London: Macmillan, 1881.
Not examined.
UK: DdU.

79.4LP/S/1e   Lives of the Poets, Selections,   1882
  Arnold's Six Chief Lives, New York

————New York, Henry Holt, 1882.
Not examined.
USA: OC.

79.4LP/S/2a   Lives of the Poets, Selections,   1886
  Arnold's Six Chief Lives

————London: Macmillan, 1886
References: Courtney 148, 'A few passages were excised or condensed in this edition. Some notes are contained on pp. 457–63, in the compilation of which Arnold received much assistance.' Low's *English Catalogue, 1881–89*, iv (1891), 'Six Poets, Arnold, post 8vo. 4s. 6d. Macmillan 1886'; Courtney 145.
UK: C, E, O (279 e.13), Oef.

79.4LP/S/2b   Lives of the Poets, Selections,   1889
                         Arnold's Six Chief Lives

———London: Macmillan, 1889
   Not examined.
   UK: NCu.

79.4LP/S/2c   Lives of the Poets, Selections,   1889
                 Arnold's Six Chief Lives, New York

———New York: Henry Holt, 1889
   Not examined.
   USA: PSC, PTC.

79.4LP/S/2d   Lives of the Poets, Selections,   1908
                         Arnold's Six Chief Lives

Further reprints in London, in 1908, and 1927.
   Not examined.

79.45LP/S/3   Lives of the Poets, Selections,   1917
                         Aphorisms on Authors

Aphorisms on Authors and their Ways; with some general observations on the
humours, habits, and methods of composition of poets — good, bad, and indif-
ferent Diligently collected from Johnson's "Lives" By A. B. (The source of each
quotation is indicated by the name of the Poet from whose "Life" it is extracted)
One Hundred Copies Privately Printed. 1917.
   Pp. 1 blk leaf, *3* ½t, *4* blk, *5* t., *6* coloph: London Eyre and Spottiswoode
Ltd. His Majesty's Printers East Harding Street, E.C. 4., *7* Dedication (signed
from: 'The Pightle, Sheringham, Norfolk. *October*, 1917.'), *8* blk, *9* 10–12
Contents, *13* 14–60 text, + 2 blk leaves.
   Copies: O (2699 e. 272).

79.4LP/S/4   Lives of the Poets, Selections,   1955
                         Gateway edition

Samuel Johnson. Lives of the English Poets. Introduction by Warren L.
Fleischauer. Gateway Editions, Inc. Distributed by Henry Regnery Company
New York Chicago Los Angeles

Pp. xiv + 402. Paperback. Printed by Thomas Moran's Sons, Inc. Baton Rouge, Louisiana.

References: Clifford & Greene 22.2.

Copies: Hyde, [DLC, MB, MiU, OClJC, OrP, OU]; *Can*: [CaBViP].

79.4LP/S/5   Lives of the Poets, Selections,   1963
                     Fontana Library

Samuel Johnson. The Lives of the English Poets. Selected and Introduced by S. C. Roberts. Collins: The Fontana Library.

Pp. 384 (Cowley, Milton, Pomfret, Dryden, Smith, Congreve, Gay, Thomson, Watts, Shenstone, Akenside, Gray, Lyttelton). Paperback, 8s. 6d.

References: Clifford & Greene 22.2.

79.4LP/S/6   Lives of the Poets, Selections,   [? 1964]
                     Avon Library, NS 5

Avon Library NS 5. Samuel Johnson's Lives of the Poets Edited by Edmund Fuller. A classic work of biography and criticism. Milton, Butler, Dryden, Addison, Congreve, Gay, Pope, Swift, Thomson and others. Also included is Johnson's famous Preface to Shakespeare.

[Subt.] Selections from The Lives of the English Poets & Preface to Shakespeare by Samuel Johnson Edited, with an Introduction, by Edmund Fuller. An Avon Library Book.

Pp. [8] + 9–14 Introduction, 15–409 Lives, 410–32 Preface to Shakespeare and notes.

Copies: T.M. Bonnell, Esq;.

79.4LP/S/7   Lives of the Poets, Selections,   1965
                     ed. Montagu

Samuel Johnson Lives of the English Poets Selected and Edited by Robert Montagu   Milton Cowley Shenstone Congreve Rochester Thomson Gay Pope Gray Otway Dryden The Folio Society London MCMLXV

Pp. Front. SJ, *1* t., *2* coloph., *3* Contents, *4* List of illustrations, *5* 6–10 Introduction, *11* ½t, *12* blk, *13* Advert. to 1779 ed., *14* blk, *15* 16–420 text.

Copies: O; *USA*: NN; *UK*: BMp (821734), DUNu.

79.4LP/S/8   Lives of the Poets, Selections,   1971
                          Oxford Paperback

Oxford Paperback English Texts. General Editor John Buxton Johnson's Lives of the Poets A Selection. ed. J.P. Hardy Oxford Clarendon Press.
  Includes: Cowley, Milton, Dryden, Pope, Thomson, and Gray, annotated.
  ISBN: 0-19-871052-6.

79.4LP/S/9   Lives of the Poets, Selections,   1975
                          Everyman

Lives of the English Poets. A Selection Introduction by John Wain.
  Dent Everyman's Library Hardback No. 770; Paperback Bo. 1770.
  Includes: Cowley, Milton, Rochester, Dryden, Addison, Savage, Pope, Swift, Thomson, Collins, and Gray; without notes.
  ISBN (Hbk): 0-460-00770-x; (pbk): 0-460-01770-5.
  Reprinted in 1977.

79.4LP/TD/1   Lives of the Poets, Dutch translation,   1824
                          Amsterdam

Not seen, despite its ghostly appearance this is an unlikely fiction.
  Copies: Unlocated.

79.4LP/TF/1   Lives of the Poets, French translation,   1823
                          Paris

Vies des Poètes Anglais les plus célèbres, avec des Observations critiques sur leurs ouvrages, Par le Docteur Samuel Johnson; traduites de l' anglais par E. Didot et E. Mahon. Paris, J. Didot. 1823
  2 vols. Not examined.
  References: Brunet (1860–5), iii. 552; Quérard, *La France Littéraire*, iv (1830), 230, notes as above, and '(Tome 1ᵉʳ et unique). Paris, J. Didot. 1823. in-8. 7fr. 50. «ce n'est point une traduction pure et simple; les traducteurs y ont ajoutés des notes; il est à regretter que le second et dernier volume n' ait pas vu le jour».'
  Copies: *Fr*: BN (vol. 1 only).

**79.4LP/TF/2   Lives of the Poets, French translation,   1842
Paris**

[½t] VIES | DES POÈTES ANGLAIS | LES PLUS CÉLÈBRES.

[Title] VIES | DES POÈTES ANGLAIS | LES PLUS CÉLÈBRES, | AVEC | DES OBSERVATIONS CRITIQUES SUR LEURS OUVRAGES, | PAR LE DOCTEUR SAMUEL JOHNSON; | TRADUITES DE L' ANGLAIS | PAR E. DIDOT ET E. MAHON. | [medium ornamental rule] | PARIS. | *LIBRAIRIE DE LEBAILLY* | rue Dauphine, n. 24. | [short dash] | 1842

2 vols., 8°

I. π^2 1–28⁸, ($2 ($2 as $) signed; 'I.' on $1 (1–7 only)), 226 leaves.

Pp. *i* ½t, *ii* coloph: [rule] | PARIS.– Imprimerie d' Amédée Saintin, 38, rue Saint-Jacques., *iii* t., *iv* blk, on 1₁ pp. ²*1* 2–24 Vie de Johnson dh: [double rule] | VIE | DE SAMUEL JOHNSON, | DOCTEUR EN DROIT. | [short rule], *25*–26 Avertissement (to 'Prefaces'), *27* 28–448 text Cowley–Walsh dh: VIE [*sic*] | DES POÈTES ANGLAIS. | [wavy rule], 448 *Explicit*: FIN DU PREMIER VOLUME.

II. 1–10⁸, ($2 signed; 'II.' on $1), 80 leaves.

Pp. *1* 2–159 text Dryden–Gray dh: VIES | DES POÈTES ANGLAIS. | [wavy rule], 159 *Explicit*: FIN., coloph: [rule] | Imprimé d' Amédée Saintin, rue Saint Jacques, 38., *160* blk.

Paper: White, laid; cut: 8 × 4½ in.; wmk.: P | F

Type: Philosophie (= sm. pica, 3.8 mm), notes: gaillard (= bourgeois, 3.0 mm).

Notes: Various notes signed: 'N.D.T.' [Note du Traducteur], and 'N.D.L' ED. ANGL.' [Note de l'Editeur Anglais]. Quotations are in English but supplemented with Fr. translations. O copy is dated '1843' but has no ½tt so that whether the t. is a cancel or not is uncertain; there is no coloph. on II. 159. It is probably a reissue.

Copies: CtY (J637. Eh.823. v.b.); *UK*: O (279 e. 167, '1843', 'R.W. Chapman').

**79.4LP/TG/1   Lives of the Poets,   1781–83
German translation, Altenburg**

[Fraktur] Samuel Johnson's | biographifche und critifche | Nachrichten | von | einigen englifchen Dichtern. | Aus dem Englifchen überfetzt | und | mit Anmerkungen vermehrt. | Erfter [–Zweiter] Theil. | [Engr. vignette: I. Telescope and globe; II. Tree] | [heavy parallel rule] | Altenburg, | in der Richterifchen Buchhandlung. 1781 [1783].

2 vols., 8°

I. (1781):)(⁸ A–Z⁸, ($5 signed), 192 leaves.

Pp. *i* t., *ii* blk, *iii–xvi* **Vorbericht** (signed 'Blankenburg'), on A1 pp. *1* 2–164 Cowley, 165–223 Rochester, 224–54 Roscommon, 255–88 Denham, 289–91 Duke, 292–324 Dorset, 325–42 Yalden, 347–67 Sprat, *368* blk.

Pagination: 22 (1st '2' *inverted*), 23 as 32, 143 as 14, 164 as ↖, 241–72 as 231–62.

Catchwords: not recorded; *Explicit*: none.

II. (1783): A–Z⁸ 2A⁴, ($5 signed), 188 leaves.

Pp. *i* t., *ii* blk, *iii–xii* **Vorbericht**, *13* 14–201 Milton, 202–32 Butler, 233–339 Waller, 340–48 Halifax, 349–57 Garth, 358–60 Pomfret, 361–8 King, 369–72 Walsh, *373–6* **Druckfehler u. Verbeßerungen.**

Pagination: 303 as 203.

Catchwords: not recorded; *Explicit*: none.

Paper: White, laid; cut: 6⅜ × 3⅞; wmk.: crowned posthorn.

Type: Garmond (= long primer, 3.2 mm).

References: Price, *English Humaniora in Germany in the 18th Century* (1955), 103.

Notes: This is a translation of the first instalment only of the *Prefaces* (1779), 79.4LP/1b, above. There seems to have been no complementary translation of the second instalment.

Copies: O (Vet. D5 f.70–1, 'Lionel R.M. Strachan . . . 1905');

USA: Hyde (MS spine labels); *Ger*: [Bayerische Staatsbibliothek, 2 pts.].

79.4LP/TJ/1   Live of the Poets, Japanese translation   1943

Johnson's Lives of the English Poets. Translated by Rintarô Fukuhara. Kenkyusha British and American Classics. 1943. 3 vols.

Not seen, but apparently comprising only the Lives of Milton, Dryden, and Pope as texts with annotations.[1]

[1] Reported to me by Prof. Daisuke Nagashima, to whom I am indebted for much friendly assistance.

79.4LP/SS   LIVES, SHORTER SELECTIONS

Under this heading are listed collections of select lives comprising two or three biographies, together with single lives either published separately or prefixed to collections of the works of the authors. These are arranged strictly in alphabetical order of the names of the Poets, and in the case of small groups are described under the first alphabetical name, with a cross-reference from the others as appropriate.

This record is the result of very desultory inquiry, and the compiler is conscious of many more omissions than usual. Few of the following pieces have been examined, but a full description shows which have been so. Adumbrations of and selections from Johnson's *Lives* form the staple of many biographical or critical accounts, and the following list is only a beginning of what should eventually form a part of the account of the basis of Johnson's reputation and influence as a literary critic.

79.4LP/SS/1   Lives, Shorter Selections, Addison   1807

The Poets of Great Britain . . . London: Cadell and Davies. 1807
    Vols. 1–2: The Poetical Works of Joseph Addison, with a Life by Samuel Johnson
    SJ's Life.
    Copies: NCu.

79.4LP/SS/2   Lives, Shorter Selections, Addison   1810

The Works of the English Poets, from Chaucer to Cowper . . . by Alexander Chalmers, F.S.A. In twenty-one volumes . . . 1810
    SJ's Life, ix. 485–520.

79.4LP/SS/3   Lives, Shorter Selections, Addison   1822

The British Poets . . . Chiswick: Whittingham. 1822
    Vol. xxvi (Addison and J. Philips)
    SJ's Life of Addison, and Life of Philips.
    Copies: DLC, ICU.

79.4LP/SS/4   Lives, Shorter Selections, Addison   1877

The Lives of Dryden, Pope, and Addison . . . by Samuel Johnson. Edited by T.A. Oxford: James Parker & Co. 1877
    References: Courtney 149; Low's *Eng. Cat. 1872–80*, iii (1882), '18mo. 2s. & 1s. Parker. 1875–7'.
    Copies: C, E (W. 8/2), O (210 m. 597).

79.4LP/SS/5   Lives, Shorter Selections, Addison   1878

The Six Chief Lives from Johnson's Lives of the Poets, ed. Matthew Arnold. London: Macmillan and Co. 1878

SJ's Life of Addison, pp. 273–326 (79.4LP/S/1, above). Courtney 148.
Copies: Gp; *USA*: Hyde.

79.4LP/SS/6   Lives, Shorter Selections, Addison   [? 1888]

Cassell's National Library '1887'
  Cassell's National Library. London: Cassell & Co. 1888
  SJ's Life of Addison, see above 79.4LP/66.
  Copies: C (88.5.209, '30 Jul. 1888').

79.4LP/SS/7   Lives, Shorter Selections, Addison   1893

Bell's English Classics. Johnson's Life of Addison, edited with an Introduction
and Notes, by F. Ryland, M.A. London: George Bell and Sons;– Chiswick
Press: Charles Whittingham & Co . . . 1893
  8°, cloth, schoolbook, pr. 2s. 6d.
  References: Courtney 148.
  Copies: C, E (211.g), O (2695 e.44); MWElC, TxU.

79.4LP/SS/8   Lives, Shorter Selections, Addison   [1895]

Bell's English Classics. The Life of Addison, edited with an Introduction and
Notes by F. Ryland, M.A. London: George Bell and Sons. [1895]
  Copies: Unlocated.

79.4LP/SS/9   Lives, Shorter Selections, Addison   1900

Blackwood's English Classics.
  Johnson. The Lives of Milton and Addison. By J. Wight Duff. Edinburgh:
William Blackwood & Sons. 1900
  References: Courtney 149; Low's *Eng. Cat., 1898–1900*, vi (1901), 'ed. Duff.
12mo. 2s. 6d. Apr. 00'.
  Copies: E (S.143.i), O (2695 e.75).

79.4LP/SS/10   Lives, Shorter Selections, Addison   1913

Bell's English Classics.
  Life of Addison, edited with an Introduction and Notes by F. Ryland, M.A.
London: George Bell & Sons. 1913.
  References: Clifford & Greene 22.3.
  Copies: BMp.

79.4LP/SS/11   Lives, Shorter Selections, Addison   1915

Essays on Addison, by Johnson, Macaulay and Thackeray. With the Life by Johnson. ed. Grace E. Hadow. Oxford, 1915
References: Clifford & Greene 22.3; Low's *Eng. Cat., 1911–15*, ix (1916) '2s. 6d. . . . Oct. 15'.
Copies: O (2695 e.130); *USA*: ICU.

79.4LP/SS/12(TF)   Lives, Shorter Selections,   1797
                Addison, French translation

Vie d' Addison . . . Paris: Imprimerie-Librairie Chrétienne. An V [= 1797]
12°. Not seen.
Copies: Unlocated.

79.4LP/SS/13(TF)   Lives, Shorter Selections,   1804
                Addison, French translation

[Quérard, *La France Littéraire*, iv (Paris, 1830), 230:
   Vies de Milton et d' Addison, auxquelles on a joint un jugement sur les ouvrages de Pope; le tout traduit de l' Anglais (par A-M-H. Broulard), et suivi de divers morceaux de littérature (composés ou traduits par le même). Paris, Perlet. 1804
   2 vols. in-18. 2fr. Noting: «[Dès 1797 Broulard avait déjà publié la traduction de la *Vie de Milton* in-12»].

79.4LP/SS/14(TF)   Lives, Shorter Selections,   1805
                Addison, French translation

Vies d' Addison et de Milton. Strassburg. 1805
Notes: Presumably a reissue of Broulard's Paris edn. of 1804.
Copies: Unlocated.

79.4LP/SS/15   Lives, Shorter Selections, Akenside   1781

Bell's British Poets . . . Edinburg: The Apollo Press.
   Vol. 104, Akenside, 1781.
   SJ's Life (acknowledged and quoted), pp. v–xvi.

79.4LP/SS/16   Lives, Shorter Selections, Akenside   1810

The Works of the English Poets, from Chaucer to Cowper . . . by Alexander
Chalmers, F.S.A. In twenty-one volumes . . . 1810
  SJ's Life of Akenside, xiv. 53–6.

79.4LP/SS/17   Lives, Shorter Selections, Akenside   1823

The Poetical Works of Mark Akenside . . .
  SJ's Life, pp. iii–xii.
  References: Courtney 150.

79.4LP/SS/18   Lives, Shorter Selections, Akenside   1855

The Poetical Works of Mark Akenside . . . 1855
  SJ's Life, pp. iii–xii.
  References: Courtney 150.

79.4LP/SS/19   Lives, Shorter Selections, Broome   1781

Bell's British Poets . . . Edinburg: The Apollo Press.
  Vol. 83 Broome, 1781.
  SJ's Life (abbreviated paraphrase, with material from Fenton and Pope), pp.
v–x.

79.4LP/SS/20   Lives, Shorter Selections, Broome   [? 1796]

The Poetical Works of Broome . . . London: W. Cooke. [? 1796]
  SJ's Life (unacknowledged adaptation), pp. 5–10.
  References: Courtney 150; ESTC: t093238.

79.4LP/SS/21   Lives, Shorter Selections, Broome   1807

The Poetical Works of Broome
  SJ's Life, pp. 7–12.
  References: Courtney 150.

79.4LP/SS/22   Lives, Shorter Selections, Broome   1810

The Works of the English Poets, from Chaucer to Cowper . . . by Alexander
Chalmers, F.S.A. In twenty-one volumes . . . 1810
  SJ's Life, xii. 3–5.

79.4LP/SS/23   Lives, Shorter Selections, Butler   [? 1803]

The Poetical Works of Samuel Butler. London: Charles Cooke. [? 1803]
   2 vols. SJ's Life, i. 7–18.
   References: Courtney 150.

79.4LP/SS/24   Lives, Shorter Selections, Butler   [? 1804]

The Works of the English Poets, ed. John Aikin. [? n.d.]
   The Poetical Works of Samuel Butler. Vol. X.
   References: Courtney 150.

79.4LP/SS/25   Lives, Shorter Selections, Butler   1806

The Poetical Works of Samuel Butler, ed. John Aikin. 1806
   2 vols. SJ's Life, i. i–xxvi.
   References: Courtney 150.

79.4LP/SS/26   Lives, Shorter Selections, Butler   1810

The Works of the English Poets, from Chaucer to Cowper . . . by Alexander
Chalmers, F.S.A. In twenty-one volumes . . . 1810.
   SJ's Life, viii. 87–94.

79.4LP/SS/27   Lives, Shorter Selections, Butler   1822

The British Poets . . . Chiswick: Whittingham 1822
   Vols. XXI–XXII, The Poems of Samuel Butler.
   Copies: DLC.

79.4LP/SS/28   Lives, Shorter Selections, Butler   1886

Cassell's National Library 1886
   Vol. 37.
   SJ's Life of Butler, see above 79.4LP/66
   Copies: C² (86.5.260 '2 Nov. 1886'; 86.5.283 '24 Nov. 1886').

79.4LP/SS/29(TF)   Lives, Shorter Selections,   1816
                         Butler, French translation

La Vie de Butler, traduit A-M-H. B[roulard]. Paris: Warée oncle & Jannet.
1816
8°.

References: Quérard, *La France Littéraire*, iv (Paris, 1830), 230: 'Vie de
Samuel Butler, traduite de l' Anglais, par A-M-H. Broulard, (extrait du
Mercure Ètranger), Paris, de l' imprimerie d' Egron. 1816, i-8. de 20 pag. 75c.'
Copies: *Fr*. BN² (var: with and without name of translator on tt.).

79.4LP/SS/30   Lives, Shorter Selections, Collins   1781

Bell's British Poets . . . Edinburg: The Apollo Press.
   Vol. 97, pt. ii, Poetical Works of William Collins. 1781
   SJ's Life (some extracts and fnn., amalgamated with Langhorne's *Memoirs*
from *The Poetical Works of Mr William Collins*, 1765), pp. v–xii.

79.4LP/SS/31   Lives, Shorter Selections, Collins   1798

THE | POETICAL WORKS | OF | *WILLIAM COLLINS*, | ENRICHED
WITH | ELEGANT ENGRAVINGS. | TO WHICH IS PREFIXED | A
LIFE OF THE AUTHOR, | *BY DR. JOHNSON*. | [medium total rule] |
LONDON: | *PRINTED BY T. BENSLEY*, | FOR E. HARDING, Nº 98,
PALL-MALL. | [short swelled rule] | 1798
   8°, *A*⁸ B–C⁸ D⁸ (±D8) E–L⁸ M⁴ (-M1 ? = 'D8'), 91 leaves.
   Pp. *i* t., *ii* blk, *iii* iv–xiv SJ's Life, *xv–xvi* Contents, on B1 *1* ½t, *2* blk, *3*
4–165 text, *166* blk.
   References: Courtney 150; ESTC t125340.
   Notes: The cancelled leaf bears the text of the 'Ode written . . . the year 1746'
(p. 47). The Engravings (20) by S. Harding & Gardiner, are printed with the
letterpress, and are variously dated 1797–98.
   Copies: Hyde ('Mrs Duff of Muirtown Paisley Decʳ 1798').
   USA: [Liebert = CtY], TxU; *Can*: CaOHM; *UK*: AWn, Ct ('1799'), Oef.

79.4LP/SS/32   Lives, Shorter Selections, Collins   1800

THE | POETICAL WORKS | OF | *WILLIAM COLLINS*, | ENRICHED
WITH | ELEGANT ENGRAVINGS. | TO WHICH IS PREFIXED | A
LIFE OF THE AUTHOR, | *BY DR. JOHNSON*. | [medium parallel rule] |
SECOND EDITION. | [medium total rule] | LONDON: | PRINTED BY

T. BENSLEY, | *Bolt Court, Fleet Street,* | FOR VERNOR AND HOOD, POULTRY; HARDING, PALL-MALL; WRIGHT, | PICCADILLY; SAEL, STRAND; AND LACKINGTON, | ALLEN, AND CO. FINSBURY SQUARE. | [short swelled rule] | 1800.

8°, A–K⁸ L⁴ M², 86 leaves.

Pp. *i* t., *ii* blk, *iii* iv–xiii SJ's Life, *xiv* blk, *xv–xvi* Contents, on B1 *1* ½t, *2* blk, *3* 4–155 text, *156* coloph: Engr. plates as in 1798 (above) but on separate leaves facing pp. 3, 7, 14, 16, 17, 25, 27, 29, 33, 37, 40, 45, 63, 66, 71, 72, and 83.

References: Courtney 150; ESTC: t125259.

Copies: DLC, Hyde (imperfect 'Webb'–'Geo. Digby'), [Liebert], TxU; *Can*: CaOHM; *UK*: AWn, Ct.

79.4LP/SS/33   Lives, Shorter Selections, Collins   1804

The Poetical Works of William Collins . . . 1804
SJ's Life, pp. 3–11.
References: Courtney 150.
Copies: SHu; *USA*: CtY, NN, TxU.

79.4LP/SS/34   Lives, Shorter Selections, Collins   1808

The Poetical Works of William Collins . . . 1808
SJ's Life, pp. 5–10 (also includes Lives of Pomfret and Hammond).
References: Courtney 150.

79.4LP/SS/35   Lives, Shorter Selections, Collins   1810

The Works of the English Poets, from Chaucer to Cowper . . . by Alexander Chalmers, F.S.A. In twenty-one volumes . . . 1810
SJ's Life, xiii. 191–93.

79.4LP/SS/36   Lives, Shorter Selections, Collins   1811

'The Life of William Collins' in *The European Magazine*, lx (1811), 208–10.
References: Courtney 150.

79.4LP/SS/37   Lives, Shorter Selections, Collins   1821

The Poetical Works of William Collins, ed. Revd. William Crowe . . . 1821
SJ's Life (enlarged), pp. i–xvi.
References: Courtney 150.

79.4LP/SS/38   Lives, Shorter Selections, Collins   1827

The Poetical Works of William Collins, ed. Alexander Dyce. London: William Pickering . . . Talboys. 1827
    8°, SJ's Life, pp. 1–8 (with notes by Dyce pp. 9–38, and additional notes by Revd. J. Mitford 39*–40*).
    References: Courtney 150.
    Copies: LCu; *USA*: CLU-C, [Liebert], MB; *UK*: AWn.

79.4LP/SS/39   Lives, Shorter Selections, Collins   1828

The Poetical Works of William Collins, edited by the Rev. William Crowe . . . Bath: E. Collings. 1828
    8°, SJ's Life (enlarged).
    Copies: [Liebert = CtY]; *UK*: BAT.

79.4LP/SS/40   Lives, Shorter Selections, Collins   1834

The Poetical Works of William Collins . . . New York: Gladding. 1834
    Copies: DFo.

79.4LP/SS/41   Lives, Shorter Selections, Collins   1848

The Poetical Works of William Collins, ed. Revd. William Crowe . . . 1848
    SJ's Life (as in 1821, above), pp. iii–vii.
    References: Courtney 150.

79.4LP/SS/42   Lives, Shorter Selections, Congreve   1810

The Works of the English Poets, from Chaucer to Cowper . . . by Alexander Chalmers, F.S.A. In twenty-one volumes . . . 1810
    SJ's Life, x. 257–65.

79.4LP/SS/43   Lives, Shorter Selections, Congreve   1897

Bell's English Classics. Johnson's Lives of Prior and Congreve. Edited with Introduction and Notes by F. Ryland, M.A. London: George Bell & Sons:– Chiswick Press: Charles Whittingham & Co. . . . 1897
    8°, cloth, schoolbook, pr. 2s. 6d.
    References: Courtney 149.
    Copies: E (258.h), O (2795 e.20).

79.4LP/SS/44   Lives, Shorter Selections, Cowley   1805

The English Poets, ed. J. Aikin, vol. VII. 1805
  References: Courtney 150.

79.4LP/SS/45   Lives, Shorter Selections, Cowley   1808

The Poetical Works of Abraham Cowley . . . London. 1808
  Copies: CtY.

79.4LP/SS/46   Lives, Shorter Selections, Cowley   1809

The Works in Prose and Verse of Abraham Cowley, ed. J. Aikin. London. C.
Whittingham for John Sharpe. 1809
  3 vols. Engr. tt. Vol. I. SJ's Life, pp. i–xcix.
  References: Courtney 150.
  Copies: *USA*: PU; *UK*: AWn, LEu, NCu.

79.4LP/SS/47   Lives, Shorter Selections, Cowley   1810

The Works of the English Poets, from Chaucer to Cowper . . . by Alexander
Chalmers, F.S.A. In twenty-one volumes . . . 1810
  SJ's Life, vii. 3–40.

79.4LP/SS/48   Lives, Shorter Selections, Cowley   1879

The Lives of the English Poets, ed. Carl Böddeker, pt. 1. Berlin. 1879
  References: Courtney 150.

79.4LP/SS/49   Lives, Shorter Selections, Cowley   1884

The Lives of Cowley, Milton and Waller. Leipzig. 1884
  References: Courtney 150.

79.4LP/SS/50 No entry.

79.4LP/SS/51   Lives, Shorter Selections, Cowley   1945

Critical Remarks on the Metaphysical Poets. An Interlude. [ed. Horace Gregory] With 12 line-drawings by Kurt-Roesch. Mount Vernon, N.Y.: Golden Eagle Press. 1945

   Pp. 54, with 12 full-page illus.; Janson type; 1,000 copies on Winterbourne's mould-made paper, in slip-case. Clifford & Greene 12.4.
   Copies: NIC.

79.4LP/SS/52   Lives, Shorter Selections, Denham   1779

Bell's British Poets . . . Edinburg: The Apollo Press.
   Vol. 35, 1779
   SJ's Life (very slightly rearranged, and paraphrased[1]), pp. v–xviii.

---

  [1] This version of Johnson's Life of Denham led to the investigation of a possible lawsuit against Bell. In the Hyde Collection there is a document canvassing this infringement of the London proprietors' copyright in SJ's work.

79.4LP/SS/53   Lives, Shorter Selections, Denham   1810

The Works of the English Poets, from Chaucer to Cowper . . . by Alexander Chalmers, F.S.A. In twenty-one volumes . . . 1810
   SJ's Life, vii. 223–9.

79.4LP/SS/54   Lives, Shorter Selections, Dorset   [? 1796]

The Poetical Works of . . . Dorset. London: Charles Cooke. [? 1796]
   References: Courtney 150.

79.4LP/SS/55   Lives, Shorter Selections, Dorset   1810

The Works of the English Poets, from Chaucer to Cowper . . . by Alexander Chalmers, F.S.A. In twenty-one volumes . . . 1810
   SJ's Life, viii. 339–40.

79.4LP/SS/56   Lives, Shorter Selections, Dryden   1779

Extracts from the Life of Dryden were printed in the *Caledonian Mercury*, no. 9044 (1779), of which a single copy is preserved in NIC; a run of the newspaper is E.

79.4LP/SS/57   Lives, Shorter Selections, Dryden   1800

The Prose Works of John Dryden, ed. Edmond Malone . . . 1800
  SJ's Criticism of Dryden extracted from the Life, I. i, pp. viii–xix.
  References: Courtney 150.

79.4LP/SS/58   Lives, Shorter Selections, Dryden   1807

The Poetical Works of John Dryden . . . 10 vols. 1807
  References: Courtney 150.

79.4LP/SS/59   Lives, Shorter Selections, Dryden   1810

The Works of the English Poets, from Chaucer to Cowper . . . by Alexander
Chalmers, F.S.A. In twenty-one volumes . . . 1810
  SJ's Life, viii. 423–91.

79.4LP/SS/60   Lives, Shorter Selections, Dryden   1811

The Poetical Works of John Dryden. ed. T. Warton. London: Rivington . . . 4
vols. 1811
  References: Courtney 150.
  Copies: CtY, ICU; *UK*: E (Ak.4.7).

79.4LP/SS/61   Lives, Shorter Selections, Dryden   [? 1817]

The British Drama, ed. Richard Cumberland. London: Printed for C. Cooke.
[? 1817]
  Vol. IX: Dryden's Tragedy of *All for Love* . . . &c., with a Life by Dr Johnson,
and a Critique by R. Cumberland.
  Copies: *USA*: MB (E.229.7.9 '1817'), NRU.

79.4LP/SS/62   Lives, Shorter Selections, Dryden   [? 1822]

The British Poets, vols. 23–25.
  The Poems of John Dryden . . . Chiswick: Whittingham. 3 vols. [1822]
  Copies: ICU.

79.4LP/SS/63   Lives, Shorter Selections, Dryden   1856

Dryden's Poetical Works . . . 1856
Copies: NCu.

79.4LP/SS/64   Lives, Shorter Selections, Dryden   1867

Dryden's Poetical Works. London: Routledge. 1867
Pp. xii + lx + 445.
Copies: Oef.

79.4LP/SS/65   Lives, Shorter Selections, Dryden   1876

The Lives of Dryden and Pope, . . . by Samuel Johnson. Edited by T.A.
Oxford: James Parker & Co. 1876
References: Courtney 148.

79.4LP/SS/66   Lives, Shorter Selections, Dryden   1877

The Lives of Dryden, Pope, and Addison . . . by Samuel Johnson. Edited by
T. A. Oxford: James Parker & Co. 1877
References: Courtney 149.
Copies: E (WW. 8/2), O (210 m. 597).

79.4LP/SS/67   Lives, Shorter Selections, Dryden   1878

The Six Chief Lives from Johnson's Lives of the Poets, ed. Matthew Arnold.
London: Macmillan and Co. 1878
SJ's Life, pp. 121–234 (79.4LP/S/1, above). Courtney 148.
Copies: Hyde.

79.4LP/SS/68   Lives, Shorter Selections, Dryden   1878

[BL] **Clarendon Press Series.** Johnson Select Works Edited *with Introduction
and Notes* by Alfred Milnes, B.A. (Lond.) Late Scholar of Lincoln College,
Oxford. *Lives of Dryden and Pope, and Rasselas* **Oxford** At the Clarendon Press
MDCCCLXXVIII.

SJ's Life of Dryden, pp. *1–3* 4–121, with Notes pp. *383* 384–423. See
59.4R/290, above.

Notes: In his Notes (383), dated 'January 1879', Milnes refers to the proofs of
Dryden in L (C.28.e.10), and notes (p. xxxii) that he had adopted the text of

1783 (79.4LP/7, above). This is the first recorded consultation of the proofs,[1] though because he follows 1783, Milnes missed the revision of the cancellandum of f8 preserved in those proofs. Published in 'Extra fcp. 8vo., 4*s*. 6*d*.'

[1] They were noticed by John P. Anderson in the 'Bibliographical Appendix' to F.R.C. Grant's *Life of Johnson* (1887), pp. v–vi.

79.4LP/SS/69   Lives, Shorter Selections, Dryden   1879

Clarendon Press Series Johnson Select Works Edited with Introduction and Notes by Alfred Milnes, B.A. . . . Lives of Dryden and Pope Oxford At the Clarendon Press MDCCCLXXIX
  A reimpression of 1878.
  References: Courtney 149. Published in 'stiff covers, 2*s*. 6*d*.'
  Copies: C (G.49.106).

79.4LP/SS/70   Lives, Shorter Selections, Dryden   1880

Clarendon Press Series. Johnson Select Works Edited with Introduction and Notes by Alfred Milnes, B.A. . . . Lives of Dryden and Pope Oxford At the Clarendon Press MDCCCLXXX [*All rights reserved*]
  SJ's Life, pp. 3–121, notes 259–300.

79.4LP/SS/71   Lives, Shorter Selections, Dryden   1885

Clarendon Press Series. Johnson Select Works Edited . . . by Alfred Milnes . . . Lives of Dryden and Pope Oxford At the Clarendon Press MDCCCLXXXV
  SJ's Life, pp. 3–121, notes 259–300.
  References: Courtney 149.
  Notes: A reimpression of 1879, without the *Rasselas*. Low's *Eng. Cat., 1881–89*, iv (1891), '12mo. 2s. 6d. Oxford Warehouse 1885'.
  Copies: C, DUNu, E ([Ao] 8/3), En ('1886'), O (2795 f.2); *USA*: MH, NN, OOxM.

79.4LP/SS/72   Lives, Shorter Selections, Dryden   1886

Clarendon Press Series. Johnson Select Works Edited . . . by Alfred Milnes . . . Lives of Dryden and Pope Oxford At the Clarendon Press MDCCCLXXXVI
  SJ's Life, pp. 3–121, notes 259–300.
  Notes: Another impression of 1879.
  Copies: En (B15/b 5).

79.4LP/SS/73 Lives, Shorter Selections, Dryden   [? 189–]

Select Poetical Works of John Dryden. The Penny Poets No. 34. Masterpiece Library. [? 189–]
  Not examined.
  Copies: [Eu (P. 82148)].

79.4LP/SS/74 Lives, Shorter Selections, Dryden   1891

Johnson Select Works Edited by Alfred Milnes. Dryden and Pope. Oxford. 1891
  SJ's Life, pp. 3–121, notes 259–300.
  Copies: *USA*: NcD.

79.4LP/SS/75 Lives, Shorter Selections, Dryden   1894

Johnson Select Works Lives of Dryden and Pope Edited by Alfred Milnes. Oxford. 1894
  SJ's Life, pp. 3–121, notes 259–300.
  Copies: *USA*: WaSpG.

79.4LP/SS/76 Lives, Shorter Selections, Dryden   1895

Bell's English Classics. The Life of Dryden, by Samuel Johnson. With Introduction and Notes by F. Ryland, M.A . . . London: George Bell & Sons:–Chiswick Press: Charles Whittingham & Co. . . . 1895
  Johnson's Life of Dryden with Introduction and Notes by F. Ryland, M.A. Author of "A Student's Handbook of Psychology and Ethics," "Chronological Outlines of English Literature," Etc. London George Bell & Sons 1895
  8°, *xxxiv* + 192 pp., cloth; schoolbook, at 2s. 6d.
  References: Courtney 148; Clifford & Greene 22.5; Low's *Eng. Cat., 1890–97*, v (1898), 'ed. Ryland, 8vo. E. Class. 2s. 6d. Bell. Mar. 95'.
  Copies: *USA*: Hyde, OCl; *UK*: C, E.

79.4LP/SS/77 Lives, Shorter Selections, Dryden   1896

The Life of Dryden, ed. F. Ryland . . . 1896
  Another impression of prec. 1895.
  Copies: CaBVaU, WaU.

79.4LP/SS/78   Lives, Shorter Selections, Dryden   1899

Johnson Selected Works Lives of Dryden and Pope Edited by Alfred Milnes. Oxford. 1899.
  Copies: [WLAp].

79.4LP/SS/79   Lives, Shorter Selections, Dryden   1899

English Classics.
  Johnson's Life of Dryden, edited by Peter Peterson [and C.D. Punchard] London: Macmillan and Co. 1899
  SJ's Life is summarized, and annotated.
  References: Courtney 148; Clifford & Greene 22.5; Low's *Eng. Cat., 1898–1900*, vi (1901), 'Cr. 8vo. pp. 202. 2s. 6d. . . . Oct. 99'.
  Copies: ABu, DUNu², E (S.143.h), O (2795 e.24), SAN; *USA*: MH.

79.4LP/SS/80   Lives, Shorter Selections, Dryden   1913

Clarendon Press Series The Life of Dryden, edited with Introduction and Notes, by Alfred Milnes . . . Oxford At the Clarendon Press. 1913
  A reimpression from 1879 edn. but without the Pope and *Rasselas*. Clifford & Greene 22.5; Low's *Eng. Cat., 1911–15*, ix (1916), '12mo. p. 196. 1s. 6d. Clar. Milford. Nov. 13'.
  Copies: AWn, E (T.164.b), LEu, O (2795 f.24); *USA*: MiU.

79.4LP/SS/81   Lives, Shorter Selections, Dryden   1914

The Life of Dryden, edited by A.J. Collins. University Tutorial Press. 1914
  References: Clifford & Greene 22.5; (? from Life by S.E. Goggin?); Low's *Eng. Cat., 1911–15*, ix (1916), 'Collins 8vo. 2s. Clive. Feb. 14'.
  Copies: AWn, E (1914.10), O (2795 f.26); *USA*: CLU-C.

79.4LP/SS/82   Lives, Shorter Selections, Dryden   1915

Clarendon Press Series The Lives of Dryden and Pope, edited by Alfred Milnes . . . New Edition. Oxford At the Clarendon Press. 1915
  A reimpression from 1879.
  Copies: Eu (.82463).

79.4LP/SS/83   Lives, Shorter Selections, Dryden   1917

The Life of Dryden, ed. A.J. Collins. University Tutorial Press. London: W.B. Clive. 1917
  8°. Published at 2s. 6d. A reimpression from 1914, above.

79.4LP/SS/84   Lives, Shorter Selections, Dryden   1925

Dryden: Poetry and Prose. Edited by D. Nichol Smith. Oxford. Clarendon Press. 1925

79.4LP/SS/85   Lives, Shorter Selections, Dryden   1937

Masterpieces of English. Vol. 15. Johnson's Life of Dryden, ed. [? G.S. Dickson /? A.J. Collins]. London: Nelson. 1937
  References: Clifford & Greene 22.5. Published at 10s. in Sept. 1937.
  Copies: AWn, E (T.187.f).

79.4LP/SS/86   Lives, Shorter Selections, Dryden   [1943]

Kenkyusha English Classics. Vol. 51. Lives of the English Poets. Vol. II. Dryden By Samuel Johnson With Introduction and Notes by Rintaro Fukuhara. Tokyo Kenkyusha [1943]

79.4LP/SS/87   Lives, Shorter Selections, Dryden   1951

Kenkyusha English Classics. Vol. 51. Johnson's English Poets, Vol. II. Dryden New Series. With Introduction and Notes by Rintaro Fukuhara. Tokyo Kenkyusha 1951
  Copies: Hyde.

79.4LP/SS/88   Lives, Shorter Selections, Dyer   1810

The Works of the English Poets, from Chaucer to Cowper . . . by Alexander Chalmers, F.S.A. In twenty-one volumes . . . 1810
  SJ's Life, xiii. 221–2.

79.4LP/SS/89   Lives, Shorter Selections, Dyer   1819

The Works of the British Poets, ed. Sanford [and Walsh], 1819
  The Poetical Works of John Dyer, vol. XIX, SJ's Life, pp. 251–61.
  References: Courtney 150.

79.4LP/SS/90   Lives, Shorter Selections, Gay   1795

The Poetical, Dramatic, and Miscellaneous Works of John Gay. Simpkin &
Marshall. 6 vols. 1795
  SJ's Life, i., pp. v–xxiv.
  References: Courtney 150; ESTC: t013742.
  Copies: [OCi].

79.4LP/SS/91   Lives, Shorter Selections, Gay   1810

The Works of the English Poets, from Chaucer to Cowper . . . by Alexander
Chalmers, F.S.A. In twenty-one volumes . . . 1810
  SJ's Life, x. 427–33.

79.4LP/SS/92   Lives, Shorter Selections, Gay   1811

The Poems or Fables of John Gay. 1811
  SJ's Life, pp. iii–xvii.
  References: Courtney 150.

79.4LP/SS/93   Lives, Shorter Selections, Gay   1812

The Poems or Fables of John Gay. 1812
  SJ's Life, pp. v–xx.
  References: Courtney 150.

79.4LP/SS/94   Lives, Shorter Selections, Gay   1820

The Poems or Fables of John Gay. 1820
  SJ's Life, pp. v–xii.
  References: Courtney 150.

79.4LP/SS/95   Lives, Shorter Selections, Gay   1824

The Poems or Fables of John Gay. 1824
  SJ's Life, pp. xii–xxi.
  References: Courtney 150.

79.4LP/SS/96   Lives, Shorter Selections, Gay   1828

The Poems or Fables of John Gay. 1828
  SJ's Life, pp. v–xii.
  References: Courtney 150.

79.4LP/SS/97   Lives, Shorter Selections, Gay   1841

THE | [metal block sorts spaced with black blocks] LIVES | OF | JOHN GAY, ESQ. | DR NATHANIEL COTTON, | AND | EDWARD MOORE, ESQ. | [short rule] | BY DR JOHNSON. | [short rule] | [Armorial device 'Favente Deo'] | BERWICK: | PRINTED BY D. WEATHERLY, HIGH-STREET. | [short rule] | M,DCCC,XLI.
  Note: comma after 'M' in date is broken.
  8°, A⁸ ($3 signed), 8 leaves.
  Pp. *1* t., *2* blk, *3* 4–13 dh: THE | LIFE OF JOHN GAY, Esq. | [wavy rule], 13–14 DR NATHANIEL COTTON., 14–15 EDWARD MOORE, Esq. *Explixit*: 15 FINIS. coloph: [rule] | J. Weatherly, Printer, Berwick., *16* blk.
  Notes: A8 is folded back into first place as an unsigned prelim leaf. The Life of Gay is SJ's; the other Lives are not his but Isaac Reed's. A note signed 'R' [= Reed] suggests the origin, probably from *Lives*, Montrose 1800 (79.4LP/13, above).
  Copies: E (RB. 5.1376(5), in vol. of chapbooks, some others by Weatherly).

79.4LP/SS/98   Lives, Shorter Selections, Gay   1854

The Poems or Fables of John Gay. Boston. Little, Brown & Co. 2 vols. 1854
  SJ's Life, I. ix–xxiii.
  References: Courtney 150.
  Copies: *USA*: MB⁴, NRU.

79.4LP/SS/99   Lives, Shorter Selections, Gay   1855

The Poems or Fables of John Gay. Boston. 2 vols. 1855
  SJ's Life, pp. vii–xxi.
  References: Courtney 150.

79.4LP/SS/100   Lives, Shorter Selections, Gay   1864

The Poetical Works of John Gay. Boston. Little, Brown & Co. 2 vols. 1864
  Copies: USA: ICU; *UK*: E (Zm.10.2$^{1-2}$), MRu (R58591).

79.4LP/SS/101   Lives, Shorter Selections, Gay   1870

'British Poets.' The Poetical Works of John Gay. Boston: Fields. 2 vols. 1870
  Copies: USA: NRU, PU ('1871').

79.4LP/SS/102   Lives, Shorter Selections, Gay   [? 1923]

'The Abbey Classics.' The Plays of John Gay . . . ornamented by Martin
Travers. Boston: Small. 2 vols. (illus.), n.d.
  References: Clifford & Greene 22.6 (London: Chapman & Dodd, ? [1923]).
  Copies: USA: NRU.

79.4LP/SS/103   Lives, Shorter Selections, Gray   1808

The Works of Thomas Gray, in Select British Poets. 1808
  References: Courtney 151.

79.4LP/SS/104   Lives, Shorter Selections, Gray   1810

The British Poets. The Works of Milton, Young, Thomson and Gray, with
Lives by Johnson; and Pope's Homer. London: G. Hazard. 7 parts. 1810
  SJ's Life in pt. IV, 3–8 with t.: The Poetical Works of Thomas Gray, with
the Life of the Author, by Samuel Johnson, LL.D. London: Printed for the
Proprietors, by G. Hazard, Beech-Street. 1810.
  Copies: Hyde ('MacGeagh').

79.4LP/SS/105   Lives, Shorter Selections, Gray   1810

The Works of the English Poets, from Chaucer to Cowper . . . by Alexander
Chalmers, F.S.A. In twenty-one volumes . . . 1810
  SJ's Life, xiv. 137–43.

79.4LP/SS/106 Lives, Shorter Selections, Gray 1855

The Poetical Works of Thomas Gray, Thomas Parnell, . . . &c. with Lives by
Johnson . . . 1855
  Copies: Eu (S.11.18).

79.4LP/SS/107 Lives, Shorter Selections, Gray 1878

Six Chief Lives from Johnson's Lives of the Poets, ed. Matthew Arnold . . .
London: Macmillan and Co. 1878
  SJ's Life, pp. 455–66 (794LP/S/1, above).
  References: Courtney 145.
  Copies: Hyde.

79.4LP/SS/108 Lives, Shorter Selections, Gray 1879

The Poems of Thomas Gray, edited by Francis Storr. 1879
  SJ's Life, pp. 1–15.
  References: Courtney 151.

79.4LP/SS/109 Lives, Shorter Selections, Gray 1882

The Poems of Thomas Gray, edited by Francis Storr. 1882
  SJ's Life, pp. 1–15.
  References: Courtney 151.

79.4LP/SS/110 Lives, Shorter Selections, Gray 1886

The Poems of Thomas Gray, edited by Francis Storr. 1886
  SJ's Life, pp. 1–15.
  References: Courtney 151.
  Copies: E (Hall.264.g).

79.4LP/SS/111 Lives, Shorter Selections, Gray 1915

Oxford Plain Texts Gray Oxford, 1915
  References: Clifford & Greene 22.7; Low's *English Cat., 1911–15*, ix (1916),
'4s. 3d. pp. 14. Clar. Milford. Jan. 15'.
  Copies: *USA*: MH.

79.4LP/SS/112   Lives, Shorter Selections, Gray   1926

Thomas Gray. Poetry and Prose. Edited with an Introduction and Notes by J. Crofts. Oxford Clarendon Press. 1926
  References: Clifford & Greene 22.7.
  Copies: E (T.7.g).

79.4LP/SS/113   Lives, Shorter Selections, Gray   1928

Thomas Gray. The Poetry and Prose, with Life by Johnson. Edited with Introduction and Notes by J. Crofts. Oxford Clarendon Press 1928
  Copies: Eu (.82161).

79.4LP/SS/114 Lives, Shorter Selections, Hammond   1808

The Poetical Works of William Collins . . . 1808
  With Lives of Collins and Pomfret.
  References: Courtney 150.

79.4LP/SS/115 Lives, Shorter Selections, Hammond   1810

The Works of the English Poets, from Chaucer to Cowper . . . by Alexander Chalmers, F.S.A. In twenty-one volumes . . . 1810
  SJ's Life, xi. 137–8.

79.4LP/SS/116   Lives, Shorter Selections, Hughes   1779

Bell's British Poets . . . Edinburg: The Apollo Press.
  Vol. 70. Poems of John Hughes. 1779
  SJ's Life (partly, with material from John Duncombe's *Account* prefixed to Hughes's *Poems on Several Occasions*, 1735), pp. v–xxvi.

79.4LP/SS/117   Lives, Shorter Selections, Hughes   1810

The Works of the English Poets, from Chaucer to Cowper . . . by Alexander Chalmers, F.S.A. In twenty-one volumes . . . 1810
  SJ's Life, x. 3–5.

79.4LP/SS/118   Lives, Shorter Selections, King   1807

The Poetical Works of King, London. 1807
  Copies: MB.

79.4LP/SS/119   Lives, Shorter Selections, King   1810

The Works of the English Poets, from Chaucer to Cowper . . . by Alexander
Chalmers, F.S.A. In twenty-one volumes . . . 1810
  SJ's Life, ix. 237–9.

79.4LP/SS/120   Lives, Shorter Selections, Lyttelton   1781

Bell's British Poets . . . Edinburg: The Apollo Press.
  Vol. 96. Poems of Lyttelton. 1781
  SJ's Life (brief critical notes, acknowledged), pp. v–xii.

79.4LP/SS/121   Lives, Shorter Selections, Lyttelton   1801

The Poetical Works of George, Lord Lyttelton. With Additions, to which is
prefixed an Account of his Life. London: C. Whittingham, for Cadell and
Davies, . . . &c. 1801
  SJ's Life (substantially), pp. iii–x.
  References: Courtney 151.

79.4LP/SS/122   Lives, Shorter Selections, Lyttelton   1810

The Works of the English Poets, from Chaucer to Cowper . . . by Alexander
Chalmers, F.S.A. In twenty-one volumes . . . 1810
  SJ's Life, xiv. 161–5.

79.4LP/SS/123   Lives, Shorter Selections, Mallet   18—

Select Poems of David Mallet, in The British Poets, ed. Sanford [& Walsh],
vol. XXVI. 18—
  References: Courtney 151.

79.4LP/SS/124   Lives, Shorter Selections, Mallet   1810

The Works of the English Poets, from Chaucer to Cowper . . . by Alexander Chalmers, F.S.A. In twenty-one volumes . . . 1810
SJ's Life, xiv. 3–6.

79.4LP/SS/125   Lives, Shorter Selections, Milton   1784

Milton's Works in: The Works of the English Poets [with Prefaces] . . . Göttingen: Printed for I. C. Dieterich. 8°, 2 vols. 1784
References: ESTC: t152379.
Not seen. ESTC reports a LP copy at Göttingen, and others at CLSU, MH, MnU, NcU, NIC.

79.4LP/SS/126   Lives, Shorter Selections, Milton   1796

Paradise Lost. London: J. Parsons. 2 vols. 1796
SJ's Life (abridged), i, pp. i–xxxviii, and Criticism of PL at xxxix–lxxv.
References: Courtney 151.
Copies: CaOHM (C.491).

79.4LP/SS/127   Lives, Shorter Selections, Milton   1795–6

The Poems of John Milton. 2 vols. 1795–96
SJ's Life (Criticism of PL only), i, pp. xvii–xli.
References: Courtney 151.
Copies: MRu (R35390).

79.4LP/SS/128   Lives, Shorter Selections, Milton   1799

[Engr. t.]: Milton's Paradise Lost, with the Life of the Author To which is pre-fixed the Celebrated Critique by Sam¹ Johnson LLD. [Vignette Adam and Eve] Outstretch'd he lay on the cold ground, and oft Curs'd his creation Book X, line 851. London Printed by C. Whittingham Dean Street Fetter Lane, for T. Heptinstall N°. 304 Holborn. And Sold by H.D. Symonds Paternoster Row; J.H. Hookham Bond Street; J.J. Black Leadenhall Street; R.H. Wesley Strand; and all the principal Booksellers in England, Scotland, Ireland, & America. 1799.
8°, [π²] + a–f⁴ B⁴ C–3B⁴, 214 leaves.
Pp. Engr. t. + engr. port. Milton + *iii* iv–xxxi Sketch of the Life and Writings of John Milton. By the Rev. John Evans, A.M. ('May 9, 1800. Pullins

Row, Islington.'), *xxxii* blk, *xxxiii* xxxiv–xlix Criticism on Paradise Lost by Samuel Johnson, LL.D., on B1 *1* 2–371 text, *372* advts., *373–6* list of subscribers.
   Notes: Edited by Revd. John Evans (1767–1827*), who added three footnotes to extracts from SJ 'I am now to examine . . . &c.' (Hill, paras. 207–64, 277).
   Copies: CSmH (146920); CaOHM; *UK*: [? BMp (535972)].

79.4LP/SS/129   Lives, Shorter Selections, Milton   1801

Milton's Poetical Works, ed. Revd. H. J. Todd, 6 vols. 1801.
   SJ's on M's Versification, i. 195–241.
   Copies: Eu (.82147/B1).

79.4LP/SS/130   Lives, Shorter Selections, Milton   1802

Paradise Lost, New Edition [? ed. Revd. John Evans]. 1802
   SJ's Life (= Critique of PL; Life by Fenton), pp. xix–xliii.
   Copies: NOu.

79.4LP/SS/131   Lives, Shorter Selections, Milton   1805

The Works of the English Poets, ed. J. Aikin. 'Milton' vol. XII. 1805
   SJ's Life, pp. i–cliii.
   References: Courtney 151.

79.4LP/SS/132   Lives, Shorter Selections, Milton   1805

Works of the English Poets, ed. Park. London: J. Sharpe. 1805
   Vol. III. Critique on Paradise Lost by Addison, with Remarks on Milton's Versification, by Johnson.
   SJ's Life (= critique of PL).
   Copies: DLC, ICU.

79.4LP/SS/133   Lives, Shorter Selections, Milton   1806

The Poetical Works of John Milton, ed. J. Aikin, 3 vols. 1806
   SJ's Life, pp. 3–102.
   References: Courtney 151.

79.4LP/SS/134   Lives, Shorter Selections, Milton   1807

Paradise Lost, A Poem, in Twelve Books. To which is prefixed The Life of the Author . . . and a Criticism by Dr. Johnson . . . London: Printed for Thomas Tegg, No. 111, Cheapside. 1807.

79.4LP/SS/135   Lives, Shorter Selections, Milton   1808

The Works of the British Poets. Vol. III. 'Milton'. 1808
  SJ's critique of Milton's Versification, pp. 135–66.

79.4LP/SS/136   Lives, Shorter Selections, Milton   1808

Paradise Lost. 1808
  SJ's Life, pp. xix–xlii.

79.4LP/SS/137   Lives, Shorter Selections, Milton   1809

Milton's Poetical Works. 3 vols. 1809
  SJ's Life, pp. 3–102.

79.4LP/SS/138   Lives, Shorter Selections, Milton   1810

Select British Poets. 1810

79.4LP/SS/139   Lives, Shorter Selections, Milton   1810

The Works of the English Poets, from Chaucer to Cowper . . . by Alexander Chalmers, F.S.A. In twenty-one volumes . . . 1810
  SJ's Life, vii. 271–42.

79.4LP/SS/140   Lives, Shorter Selections, Milton   1810

The Poetical Works of John Milton, with the Life of the Author, by Samuel Johnson, LL.D. London: Printed for the Proprietors, by G. Hazard. Beech-Street. 1810.
  8°, 7 pts. in 1 vol. Milton in pt.1, SJ's Life, pp. 3 4–28.
  Copies: Hyde ('MacGeagh').

79.4LP/SS/141   Lives, Shorter Selections, Milton   1817

Paradise Lost, by John Milton. To which are prefixed, The Life of the Author; and a Criticism on the Poem, by Samuel Johnson, LL.D. London: Printed for F.C. and J. Rivington; J. Nichols and Son; G. Wilkie; J. Nunn; W. Clarke and Sons; Cadell and Davies; Carpenter and Son; Longman, Hurst, Rees, Orme, and Brown; Scatcherd and Letterman; Lackington and Co.; W. Lowndes; E. Jeffery; J. Otridge; R. Scholey; J. Mawman; John Richardson; Baldwin, Cradock, and Joy; Gale and Fenner; Walker and Edwards; G. Cowie and Co.; and R. Hunter. 1817

2 vols., 8°. SJ's Life (Critique of PL), I. xix–xliii.
References: Courtney 151.
Copies: Hyde; *UK*: JDF (vol. 1 only).

79.4LP/SS/142   Lives, Shorter Selections, Milton   [? 1817]

The British Drama, ed. Richard Cumberland. London: C. Cooke. [? 1817]
Vol. IV. Milton: The Masque of Comus, with the Life of the author.
Copies: ICU, NRU.

79.4LP/SS/143   Lives, Shorter Selections, Milton   1817

Paradise Lost . . . To which are prefixed, the Life of the Author; and a Criticism on the Poem, by Samuel Johnson, LL.D. London: Printed for F. C. & J. Rivington &c., 1817

8°. The 'Life' is by Fenton, but the critique is SJ's.

79.4LP/SS/144   Lives, Shorter Selections, Milton   1821

Paradise Lost. London: J. Bumpus. 1821
SJ's Life, pp. xix–xlviii.
Copies: [Liebert]; *UK*: BMp (828134).

79.4LP/SS/145   Lives, Shorter Selections, Milton   1826

The Poetical Works of John Milton, ed. H.J. Todd, Third edition. 6 vols. 1826
See Todd's first edn. 1801, above.
Copies: Eu (.82147/B1).

79.4LP/SS/146   Lives, Shorter Selections, Milton   1833

John Milton, His Life and Times, by Joseph Ivimey. London. 1833
  SJ's Life adapted.

79.4LP/SS/147   Lives, Shorter Selections, Milton   1850

The Poetical Works of John Milton. London. 1850
  SJ's Life (complete).
  Copies: Eu (.82147/B1).

79.4LP/SS/148   Lives, Shorter Selections, Milton   1878

The Six Chief Lives from Johnson's Lives of the Poets, ed. Matthew Arnold.
London: Macmillan and Co. 1878
  SJ's Life of Milton, pp. 45–120 (79.4LP/S/1, above).
  References: Courtney 148.

79.4LP/SS/149   Lives, Shorter Selections, Milton   1884

The Life of Milton, edited by Carl Böddeker. Berlin. 1884
  References: Courtney 151.

79.4LP/SS/150   Lives, Shorter Selections, Milton   1884

Lives of Cowley, Milton, and Waller. Leipzig. 1884
  References: Courtney 150.

79.4LP/SS/151   Lives, Shorter Selections, Milton   1888

Johnson's Lives of the Poets. Milton. Edited by C.H. Firth. Oxford University
Press. 1888
  Pp. xii + 144.
  References: Courtney 149. (Reimpressed 1891, 1892, 1894, 1904, 1907, 1908,
1920, 1927, 1934, 1939); Clifford & Greene 22.8.
  Copies: C ('2 Jul 1888'), E ([An] 6/3), O (2795 f.5).

79.4LP/SS/152   Lives, Shorter Selections, Milton   1891

Johnson's Life of Milton, edited by C. H. Firth. Oxford. 1891
References: Courtney 149.
Reimpression of 1888.

79.4LP/SS/153   Lives, Shorter Selections, Milton   1892

Johnson's Lives of the Poets. Milton. Edited with an Introduction and Notes by K. Deighton. London. Macmillan and Co. 1892 Glasgow: Printed at the University Press by Robert Maclehose and Co.
Pp. xxxviii + 139.
Reimpressed 1893, 1899 (twice), 1900, 1906, 1934, 1949, 1953, 1956, 1960, 1963, 1965.
References: Courtney 149; Clifford & Greene 22.8; Low's *Eng. Cat., 1890–97*, v (1989), '8vo. 1s. 9d. Macmillan. July 92'.
Copies: DUNu, E (245.h), O (2794 e.4), SAN.

79.4LP/SS/154   Lives, Shorter Selections, Milton   1894

Bell's English Classics. Johnson's Life of Milton, edited with an Introduction and Notes by F. Ryland. London: George Bell & Sons. 1894
8°, cloth, schoolbook, at 2s. 6d.
References: Clifford & Greene 22.8; Low's *Eng. Cat., 1890–97*, v (1898), 'ed. Ryland. 8vo. 2s. 6d. Bell. Oct. 94'.
Copies: C ('1894'), E (211.g. '1894'), O (2795 e.14): *USA*: OCl.

79.4LP/SS/155   Lives, Shorter Selections, Milton   [? 1895]

The Penny Poets, nos. 10, 15. Masterpiece Library. Paradise Lost [Abridged]. [? 1895]
Copies: Eu (P.82147).

79.4LP/SS/156   Lives, Shorter Selections, Milton   1900

Blackwood's English Classics.
Johnson. The Lives of Milton and Addison, edited by John Wight Duff. Edinburgh: William Blackwood & Sons. 1900
References: Clifford & Greene 22.8; Low's *Eng. Cat., 1898–1900*, vi (1901), '12mo. 2s. 6d. Aug. 00'.
Copies: DUNu, C, E (S.143.i), O (2695 e.75); *USA*: NIC.

79.4LP/SS/157   Lives, Shorter Selections, Milton   [1900]

Berry's PT and SS Series of English Classics. Johnson's Life of Milton, ed. T.W. Berry and T.P. Marshall. Newport, Salop. [? & Simpkin & Marshall 1900]
References: Clifford & Greene 22.8; Low's *Eng. Cat., 1898–1900*, vi (1901), '8vo. 2s. Simpkin. July 00'.
Copies: C, E (1900.24(11)).

79.4LP/SS/158   Lives, Shorter Selections, Milton   1900

English Classics.
Johnson's Lives of the Poets. Milton. With an Introduction and Notes by K. Deighton. London: Macmillan and Co. Ltd. 1900
Mentions 1st edn. 1892, and reprints 1893, 1899 (twice), and 1900.
References: Low's *Eng. Cat., 1898–1900*, vi (1901), '2s. 6d. Macmillan 00'.
Copies: JDF.

79.4LP/SS/159   Lives, Shorter Selections, Milton   1906

Macmillan's English Classics. Johnson's Life of Milton, edited by K. Deighton. London: Macmillan and Co. 1906
Copies: [Liebert].

79.4LP/SS/160   Lives, Shorter Selections, Milton   1907

Johnson's Life of Milton, edited by C.H. Firth. Oxford University Press. 1907
Reimpression of 1888, q.v.
References: Courtney 149; Clifford & Greene 22.8.
Copies: E (T.163.h).

79.4LP/SS/161   Lives, Shorter Selections, Milton   1907

University Tutorial Series. Johnson's Life of Milton, edited by S.E. Goggin, B.A. London. 1907
References: Clifford & Greene 22.8; Low's *Eng. Cat., 1906–10*, viii (1911), '8vo. p. 118. 1s. 6d. Clive. Jan. 08'.
Copies: E (1907.30), O(2795 e.39 (ii.1), '1908').

79.4LP/SS/162   Lives, Shorter Selections, Milton   1915

Bell's English Classics. Johnson's Life of Milton, edited F. Ryland. London:
George Bell & Sons. 1915
Copies: *USA*: MH.

79.4LP/SS/163   Lives, Shorter Selections, Milton   1920

Milton Poetry and Prose Selected by Beatrice G. Madan. Oxford Clarendon
Press. 1920
References: Clifford & Greene 22.8

79.4LP/SS/164   Lives, Shorter Selections, Milton   1922

Milton's Poetry and Prose, edited by A.M.D. Hughes. Oxford. 1922
Reissued 1930.
Copies: Eu (.82147/A).

79.4LP/SS/165   Lives, Shorter Selections, Milton   [1949]

British and American Classics. Vol. 50 'Milton'. Kenkyusha English Classics.
Lives of the English Poets. Vol. I: Milton By Samuel Johnson With
Introduction and Notes by Rintaro Fukuhara. Tokyo Kenkyusha. [1949]
Copies: Hyde.

79.4LP/SS/166   Lives, Shorter Selections, Milton   1951

Kenkyusha English Classics. New Series. 'Milton' Edited by Rintaro Fukuhara.
Tokyo. 1951

79.4LP/SS/167   Lives, Shorter Selections, Milton   1956

Macmillan's English Classics. Johnson's Life of Milton, with Introduction and
Notes by K. Deighton. London: Macmillan and Co. 1956
Pp. xxxviii + 139.
Copies: Eu (.82463).

79.4LP/SS/168(TF)   Lives, Shorter Selections,   1797
Milton, French translation

Vie de Milton, et Jugement sur ses Écrits. Ouvrage traduit de l' Anglais de feu Samuel Johnson, et pouvant faire suite au poëme du Paradis Perdu. A Paris, A l' Imprimerie-Librairie Chrétienne, rue St.-Jacques, n°. 278 et 279, vis-à-vis celle du Plâtre. An V de la Republique. [= 1797]

12°, π² A–Z⁶ 2A⁴, ($3 (–E1, M2 as L2; U as V) signed), 144 leaves.

Pp. *i* ½t Vie de Milton, *ii* Advertissement ('On publiera incessament les vies d' *Adisson* [!] et de *Pope*, par le même auteur.') and imprint, *iii* t., *iv* blk, on A1 pp. *1* 2–273 text, 274–84 Table Sommaire ('Tiré des vies des poëtes anglais par Samuel Johnson, morte en 1784, dont plusieurs ont été traduites dans le Censeur universel anglais.' p. 274 n). Quérard, *La France Littéraire*, iv (1830), 230 identifies the translator as A-M-H Broulard (cf. 'Addison', above).

Copies: Hyde; *UK*: C (X.16.54).

79.4LP/SS/169(TF)   Lives, Shorter Selections,   1805
Milton, French translation

Vies de Milton et Addison. Strassburg. 1805
Cf. Addison, 79.4LP/SS/14(TF), above.

79.4LP/SS/170(TG)   Lives, Shorter Selections,   1784
Milton, German translation

The Works of the English Poets. With Prefaces, biographical and critical, by Samuel Johnson. Miltons Werke . . . Göttingen. Printed for I.C. Dieterich, MDCCLXXXIV.

8°, 2 vols. SJ's Life, in i. 3–104, followed by Par. Lost.; vol. 2 contains other poems. (Apparently part of an edition of Die Werke der englischen Dichteren.) Port. of SJ, after Reynolds, engr. 'J.G. Sturm' as front. vol. 1, and port of Milton as front. to vol. 2.

Copies: NIC; *Ger*: [Bayerische Staatsbibliothek], GöttU.

79.4LP/SS/171(TG)   Lives, Shorter Selections,   1813
Milton, German translation

Miltons Verlorenes Paradies. Übersetzt von J.F. Pries. Rostock und Leipzig. 1813

Miltons Leben, nach Johnson, pp. ix–xxxii.
Copies: MRu (R19687).

79.4LP/SS/172(TJ)   Lives, Shorter Selections,   1974
Milton, Japanese translation

[Johnson's Life of Milton] Translated by Natsuo Shumuta, Tokyo: Chikuma-shobo, 1974, in: Sekai-hihyo-taikei, vol. I.

79.4LP/SS/173   Lives, Shorter Selections, Otway   1812

The Works of Otway, consisting of his Plays, Poems and Letters. With a Sketch of his Life enlarged from that of Dr. Johnson. London: Rivington . . . &c., 2 vols. 1812
    SJ's Life, i. 3–13 (expanded).
    References: Courtney 151.
    Copies: Eu (OS. .82245).

79.4LP/SS/174   Lives, Shorter Selections, Otway   1817

Venice Preserved 1817
    SJ's Life included.
    Copies: E (NE. 1017 i.16(2)).

79.4LP/SS/175   Lives, Shorter Selections, Parnell   1810

The Works of the English Poets, from Chaucer to Cowper . . . by Alexander Chalmers, F.S.A. In twenty-one volumes . . . 1810
    SJ's Life, ix. 345–7.

79.4LP/SS/176   Lives, Shorter Selections, Parnell   1855

The Poetical Works of Thomas Gray, Parnell . . . &c. with Lives by Samuel Johnson . . . 1855
    Copies: E (S.11.18).

79.4LP/SS/177   Lives, Shorter Selections, Parnell   [? 188–]

The Poetical Works of Churchill, Parnell, and Tickell, with Lives. Boston and New York: H. Mifflin. [188–?], 4 vols. in 2.
    Copies: ICU.

79.4LP/SS/178　　　　Lives, Shorter Selections,　　　　1781
　　　　　　　　　　　　　Ambrose Philips

Bell's British Poets . . . Edinburg: The Apollo Press.
　Vol. 93, 1781
　SJ's Life, pp. v–xxii (partly from SJ, with some of his criticism, but mainly
from Cibber's *Lives of the Poets* (1753), v. 122–42)

79.4LP/SS/179　　　　Lives, Shorter Selections,　　　　1810
　　　　　　　　　　　　　Ambrose Philips

The Works of the English Poets, from Chaucer to Cowper . . . by Alexander
Chalmers, F.S.A. In twenty-one volumes . . . 1810
　SJ's Life, xiii. 99–103.

79.4LP/SS/180　　　　Lives, Shorter Selections,　　　　1781
　　　　　　　　　　　　　John Philips

Bell's British Poets . . . Edinburg: The Apollo Press.
　Vol. 66, 1781
　SJ's Life, pp. v–xxxix (partially derived from SJ and acknowledged, but mainly
from George Sewell, *The Life and Character of Mr John Philips*, 1712, acknowledged).

79.4LP/SS/181　　　　Lives, Shorter Selections,　　　　1810
　　　　　　　　　　　　　John Philips

The Works of the English Poets, from Chaucer to Cowper . . . by Alexander
Chalmers, F.S.A. In twenty-one volumes . . . 1810
　SJ's Life, viii. 367–75.

79.4LP/SS/182　　　　Lives, Shorter Selections,　　　　1822
　　　　　　　　　　　　　John Philips

The British Poets . . . Chiswick: Whittingham. 1822
　Vol. xxvi (Poems of Addison and J. Philips).
　Cf. Addison, 79.4LP/SS/3, above.
　Copies: DLC.

79.4LP/SS/183   Lives, Shorter Selections, Pitt   1782

Bell's British Poets . . . Edinburg: The Apollo Press.
  Vol. 90, 1782
  SJ's Life, pp. v–xiv (a few critical observations only, remainder from Cibber's
Lives of the Poets (1753), v. 298–307).

79.4LP/SS/184   Lives, Shorter Selections, Pitt   1810

The Works of the English Poets, from Chaucer to Cowper . . . by Alexander
Chalmers, F.S.A. In twenty-one volumes . . . 1810
  SJ's Life, xii. 365–6.

79.4LP/SS/185   Lives, Shorter Selections, Pitt   1819

The British Poets, ed. Sanford [& Walsh], vol. XXI.
  SJ's Life, pp. 337–9.
  References: Courtney 151.

79.4LP/SS/186   Lives, Shorter Selections, Pomfret   1808

The Poetical Works of William Collins . . . 1808
  With Lives of Collins and Hammond.
  References: Courtney 150.

79.4LP/SS/187   Lives, Shorter Selections, Pomfret   1810

The Works of the English Poets, from Chaucer to Cowper . . . by Alexander
Chalmers, F.S.A. In twenty-one volumes . . . 1810
  SJ's Life, viii. 303.

79.4LP/SS/188   Lives, Shorter Selections, Pope   1794

The Poetical Works of Alexander Pope, to which is prefixed a Life of the
Author. Edinburgh. 1794
  Copies: O (2804 d.35).

79.4LP/SS/189   Lives, Shorter Selections, Pope   1806

The Works of Alexander Pope in Verse and Prose, edited by W.L. Bowles. London: J. Johnson. 10 vols. 1806
   Copies: Eu (V*14.1–10), O (270 e. 126–35), Oef.

79.4LP/SS/190   Lives, Shorter Selections, Pope   1807

Bell's Poets of Great Britain.
   The Poetical Works of Alexander Pope, with a Life by Samuel Johnson. 1807
   Copies: O (2804 f. 320–5).

79.4LP/SS/191   Lives, Shorter Selections, Pope   1810

The Works of the English Poets, from Chaucer to Cowper . . . by Alexander Chalmers, F.S.A. In twenty-one volumes . . . 1810
   SJ's Life, xii. 51–119 (+ Epitaphs 119–28).

79.4LP/SS/192   Lives, Shorter Selections, Pope   1812

The Works of Alexander Pope, with a selection of explanatory notes, and the account of his Life by Dr Johnson. 8 vols. London. 1812.
   16°
   Copies: O (2799 f. 539–46).

79.4LP/SS/193   Lives, Shorter Selections, Pope   1819

The Works of the British Poets, ed. Sanford [& Walsh]. The Works of Alexander Pope, vols. XX——. 1819
   SJ's Life, xx. 1–69.
   References: Courtney 151.

79.4LP/SS/194   Lives, Shorter Selections, Pope   1824

The Poetical Works of Alexander Pope. 1824
   References: Courtney 151.
   Copies: O (2795 e. 149).

79.4LP/SS/195   Lives, Shorter Selections, Pope   1824–5

The Poetical Works of Alexander Pope. Ed. W. Roscoe. 10 vols. 1824–5.
Copies: O (2799 d. 215–25).

79.4LP/SS/196   Lives, Shorter Selections, Pope   1827

The Poetical Works of Alexander Pope. 1827
References: Courtney 151.

79.4LP/SS/197   Lives, Shorter Selections, Pope   1830

The Poetical Works of Alexander Pope, including his Translation of Homer.
With a Life of the Author, by Dr. Johnson. London: Published by Jones and
Co., Temple of the Muses (Late Lackington's), Finsbury Square. 1830.
    The engr. t. is dated 'July 3, 1824'; 2 cols./p.
    SJ's Life and Epitaphs pp. *iii* iv–xxxi.
    Copies: LICj.

79.4LP/SS/198   Lives, Shorter Selections, Pope   1830

The Poetical Works of Alexander Pope. Philadelphia: J.J. Woodward. 1830
References: Courtney 151.
Copies: [Liebert], PU.

79.4LP/SS/199   Lives, Shorter Selections, Pope   1849

The Poetical Works of Alexander Pope. Boston. 1849
Copies: O (2799 e. 779).

79.4LP/SS/200   Lives, Shorter Selections, Pope   1874

The Life of Pope . . . 2 vols. 1874
SJ's Life of Pope (from Oxford edn. 1825).
Copies: MH.

79.4LP/SS/201   Lives, Shorter Selections, Pope   1876

The Lives of Dryden and Pope, . . . by Samuel Johnson. Edited by T.A.
Oxford: James Parker & Co. 12°, 1876

The Lives are analysed by 'T.A.'
References: Courtney 148.

79.4LP/SS/202   Lives, Shorter Selections, Pope   1877

The Lives of Dryden, Pope, and Addison . . . by Samuel Johnson. Edited by
T.A. Oxford: James Parker & Co. 12°, 1877
References: Courtney 149.
Copies: E, O (210 m.597).

79.4LP/SS/203   Lives, Shorter Selections, Pope   1878

The Six Chief Lives from Johnson's Lives of the Poets, ed. Matthew Arnold.
London: Macmillan and Co. 1878
SJ's Life of Pope, pp. 327–454 (79.4LP/S/1, above).
References: Courtney 148.

79.4LP/SS/204   Lives, Shorter Selections, Pope   1879

Clarendon Press Series. Johnson Select Works Lives of Dryden, Pope, and
Rasselas. Edited with Introduction and Notes by Alfred Milnes, M.A.. Oxford.
MDCCCLXXIX
SJ's Life, pp. 125–257. Published at 4s. 6d.
References: Courtney 149.

79.4LP/SS/205   Lives, Shorter Selections, Pope   1885

Clarendon Press Series. Johnson Select Works Lives of Dryden and Pope
Edited with an Introduction and Notes by Alfred Milnes, M.A. Oxford.
MDCCCLXXXV.
References: Courtney 149; Clifford & Greene 22.9.
Copies: *USA*: MH, NN, OOxM; *UK*: DUNu, En ('1886'), O (2795 f.2).

79.4LP/SS/206   Lives, Shorter Selections, Pope   1891

Clarendon Press Series. Johnson Select Works Lives of Dryden and Pope
Edited with an Introduction and Notes by Alfred Milnes, M.A. Oxford.
MDCCCXCI.
Copies: *USA*: NcD.

79.4LP/SS/207   Lives, Shorter Selections, Pope   1894

Clarendon Press Series. Johnson Select Works Lives of Dryden and Pope Edited with an Introduction and Notes by Alfred Milnes, M.A. Oxford. MDCCCXCIV.
   Copies: *USA*: [WaSpG].

79.4LP/SS/208   Lives, Shorter Selections, Pope   1894

Bell's English Classics. Johnson's Life of Pope, edited with an Introduction by F. Ryland, M.A. London: George Bell & Sons. 1894
   Cloth, schoolbook, 2s. 6d.
   Copies: *USA*: MBtS, TxU.

79.4LP/SS/209   Lives, Shorter Selections, Pope   1896

Bell's English Classics. Johnson's Life of Pope, edited with an Introduction by F. Ryland, M.A. London: George Bell & Sons. 1896
   Cloth, schoolbook, 2s. 6d.
   Copies: Eu (.82463); *Can*: CaBVaU.

79.4LP/SS/210   Lives, Shorter Selections, Pope   1897

Johnson's Life of Pope, edited by Kate Stephens. New York: Harper & Brothers. 2 pts. 12°, 1897.
   References: Clifford & Greene 22.9.
   Copies: *USA*: [Liebert], MB, MH (15451.240), NN.

79.4LP/SS/211   Lives, Shorter Selections, Pope   1899

Johnson's Life of Pope, edited by Peter Peterson [& C.D. Punchard]. London: Macmillan and Co. 8°, 1899
   References: Courtney 149; Low's *Eng. Cat., 1898–1900*, vi (1901), 'Cr. 8vo. 2s. 6d. Macmillan. Oct. 99'.
   Copies: ABu, DUNu³, E (S.143.h), NOu, O (2795 e.23), SAN; *USA*: MH, PU.

79.4LP/SS/212   Lives, Shorter Selections, Pope   1900

Bell's English Classics. Johnson's Life of Pope, edited with an Introduction and Notes by F. Ryland, M.A. London: George Bell & Sons. 1900
   References: Courtney 149.

79.4LP/SS/213   Lives, Shorter Selections, Pope   1906

Bell's English Classics. Johnson's Life of Pope, edited with an Introduction and
Notes by F. Ryland, M.A. London: George Bell & Sons. 1906
    References: Clifford & Greene 22.9.
    Copies: *USA*: CtY, NcD.

79.4LP/SS/214   Lives, Shorter Selections, Pope   1910

Johnson's Life of Pope, edited with an Introduction and Notes By Peter
Peterson [& C.D. Punchard]. London: Macmillan and Co. 1910
    Copies: *USA*: NjP.

79.4LP/SS/215   Lives, Shorter Selections, Pope   1915

Clarendon Press Series Lives of Dryden and Pope, edited by Alfred Milnes.
Oxford. 1915
    Copies: *UK*: Eu (.82463).

79.4LP/SS/216   Lives, Shorter Selections, Pope   1917

University Tutorial Series. Johnson Life of Pope, edited by A. R. Weekes, M.A.
Editor of Shakespeare: "As You Like It," "The Tempest" Shelley: "Adonais,"
Keats: "Odes," etc. London: W.B. Clive. University Tutorial Press, Ltd. High
St., New Oxford St., W.C. 1917
    8°, cloth, schoolbook at 2s. 6d.
    References: Clifford & Greene 22.9.
    Copies: *UK*: E (T.127.i), O (2795 e.65); *USA*: Hyde ('Huxley').

79.4LP/SS/217   Lives, Shorter Selections, Pope   1920

Bell's English Classics. Johnson's Life of Pope, edited with an Introduction and
Notes, by F. Ryland, M.A. London: George Bell and Sons. 1920
    References: Clifford & Greene 22.9.
    Copies: *USA*: MH; *UK*: BMp.

79.4LP/SS/218   Lives, Shorter Selections, Pope   1928

Barnet H. Clark, Great Short Biographies. New York: Robert M. McBride. 1928
    SJ's Life, pp. 731–86.
    References: Clifford & Greene 22.9.

79.4LP/SS/219   Lives, Shorter Selections, Pope   1935

Oxford Anthology of English Prose, ed. A. Whitridge and J.W. Dodds. New York: Oxford University Press. 1935.
SJ's Life, pp. 278–300.
References: Clifford & Greene 22.9.

79.4LP/SS/220   Lives, Shorter Selections, Pope   [1950]

Kenkyusha English Classics. Vol. 52. Johnson's English Poets.
  Lives of the English Poets Vol. III: Pope By Samuel Johnson With Introduction and Notes by Rintaro Fukuhara. Tokyo Kenkyusha. [1950]
Copies: *USA*: Hyde.

79.4LP/SS/221   Lives, Shorter Selections, Pope   1951

Kenkyusha English Classics. Ed. Rintaro Fukuhara. New Series. 'Pope'. Tokyo. 1951

79.4LP/SS/222(TG)   Lives, Shorter Selections,   1782
                    Pope, German translation

In *Göttingiſches Magazin*, iii (1782).
  Cf. Price, *English Humaniora in Germany in the 18th Century* (1955), 103.

79.4LP/SS/223(TG)   Lives, Shorter Selections,   1844–67
                    Pope, German translation

G.C. Lichtenbergs Vermiſchte Schriften, vermehrte von deſſen Söhnen ver-anſtaltete. Göttingen. 8 vols. 12°, 1844–67
  SJ's Life of Pope: 'Nachricht von Popes Leben und Schriften, aus Johnſon's Prefaces . . . 1781', v. 33–70.
Copies: MRu (R.26567).

79.4LP/SS/224   Lives, Shorter Selections, Prior   1810

The Works of the English Poets, from Chaucer to Cowper . . . by Alexander Chalmers, F.S.A. In twenty-one volumes . . . 1810
SJ's Life, x. 105–18.

79.4LP/SS/225   Lives, Shorter Selections, Prior   1897

Bell's English Classics. Johnson's Lives of Prior and Congreve. Edited with Introduction and Notes by F. Ryland, M.A. London: George Bell & Sons:- Chiswick Press: Charles Whittingham & Co . . . 1897
    8°, cloth, schoolbook, at 2s. 6d.
    References: Courtney 149; Clifford & Greene 22.10; Low's *Eng. Cat., 1890–97*, v (1898), 'ed. Ryland, 12mo. 2s. Bell Nov. 97', and *Eng. Cat., 1898–1900*, vi (1901), '12mo. 2s. Bell. Feb. 98'. Possible var. dates.
    Copies: C (98.7.900), E (258.h), O (2795 e.20).

79.4LP/SS/226   Lives, Shorter Selections, Prior   [? 19—]

The Abbey Classics. The Shorter Poems of Matthew Prior. With an Introduction by Francis Bickley. Ornamented by Martin Travers. Boston: Small, Maynard and Co.
    [? London: Simpkin & Marshall 19—; *sometimes* Chapman & Dodd]
    Copies: NRU.

79.4LP/SS/227   Lives, Shorter Selections, Rochester   1782

SOME | PASSAGES | IN THE | LIFE AND DEATH | OF | JOHN Earl of Rochefter, | Written by his own Direction on his Death-bed. | By GILBERT BURNET, D.D. | Bishop of SALISBURY. | WITH A | SERMON, | Preached, at the FUNERAL of the faid EARL, | By the Rev. ROBERT PARSONS, A.M. | To this Edition is prefixed | Some ACCOUNT of the LIFE and WRITINGS | of the EARL of ROCHESTER, | By Dr. SAMUEL JOHNSON. | [rule] | The Account of Burnet's falutary Conferences (with Rochester) are given | by him in a Book, entitled — Some Paffages in the Life and Death of John | Earl of Rochester; which the Critic ought to read for its Elegance, the | Philofopher for its Arguments, and the Saint for its Piety. | Johnfon's Poets, Vol. I. | [heavy parallel rule] | LONDON: | Printed for T. DAVIES, RUSSEL-STREET, | COVENT-GARDEN. | M.DCC.LXXXII.
    8°, A–I⁸ K⁴, ($4 signed), 76 leaves.
    Pp. Engr. port. front. ('John Wilmot, Earl of Rochester') + *i* t., *ii* Advertisement, iii–x SJ's Life, xi–xvi Preface, on B1 1–95 text: Some Passages . . . &c., *96* blk, *97* ½t: Sermon, *98* Advertisement, 99–136 text of Sermon.
    References: Courtney 151–2; *Tinker* 446; ESTC: t130071.
    Notes: This Life enjoyed considerable popularity among the evangelicals into the early part of the 19th century.
    Copies: Hyde ('H. Matson'–'D.H. Parry');
    USA: [Liebert], NRU; *Can*: CaOHM (B.15755); *UK*: Ljh ('Henry Edm. Peach'–'A.J. Finney, 1917'–'P.R. Finney').

79.4LP/SS/228   Lives, Shorter Selections, Rochester   1787

SOME PASSAGES IN THE | LIFE and DEATH | OF | JOHN Earl of
Rocheſter, | WRITTEN BY | GILBERT BURNET, D.D. | BISHOP of
SALISBURY. | WITH A | SERMON, | Preached at the FUNERAL of the ſaid
EARL, | By the Rev. ROBERT PARSONS, A.M. | TO THIS EDITION IS
PREFIXED | An ACCOUNT of the LIFE and WRITINGS | OF THE |
EARL OF ROCHESTER, | By Dr. SAMUEL JOHNSON. | [parallel rule] |
LONDON: | Printed for W. LOWNDES, No. 77, Fleet-ſtreet. |
M,DCC,LXXXVII.

12°, A–F¹², ($6 signed), 72 leaves.

Pp. *i* t., *ii* blk, *iii–iv* Advertisement, '3–9' [=5–11] 12 SJ's Life, 13–18
Preface, *19* 20–106 Some Passages, *107* ½t Sermon, *108* Advertisement,
109–44 text.

References: Courtney 152; ESTC: t110321.

Copies: *USA*: Hyde ('Jas. C. Hozier'), [Liebert], NjP; *UK*: En², MRu, [SPu].

79.4LP/SS/229   Lives, Shorter Selections, Rochester   1791

Some Passages in the Life and Death of John Earl of Rochester. Written by his
own Direction on his Death-bed. By Gilbert Burnet, D.D. Bishop of Salisbury.
With a Sermon, preached at the Funeral of the said Earl, by the Rev. Robert
Parsons, A.M. To this Edition is prefixed Some Account of the Life and
Writings of the Earl of Rochester, By Dr. Samuel Johnson. The Account of
Burnet's salutary Conferences (with Rochester) are given by him in a Book,
entitled — Some Passages in the Life and Death of John Earl of Rochester;
which the Critic ought to read for its Elegance, the Philosopher for its
Arguments, and the Saint for its Piety. Johnson's Poets, Vol. I. Dublin: Printed
by B. Dugdale, No. 150, Capel Street. M,DCC,XCI.

12°, A–I⁶ K⁴, ($3 signed), 58 leaves.

Pp. *i* t., *ii* Advertisement, *iii* iv–viii SJ's Life, ix–xii Preface, *13* 14–84 Some
Passages, *85* ½t: Sermon, *86* Advertisement, 87–116 text.

References: ESTC: t160264.

Copies: *UK*: C (Hib.7.791.28¹).

79.4LP/SS/230   Lives, Shorter Selections, Rochester   1805

Some Passages in the Life and Death of John Earl of Rochester, written by
Gilbert Burnet, D.D. Bishop of Salisbury. With a Sermon, preached at the
Funeral of the said Earl, by the Rev. Robert Parsons, A.M. A New edition. To
which is now prefixed an Account of the Life and Writings of the Earl of
Rochester, By Dr. Samuel Johnson. London: Printed by W. Nicholson,
Warner-street, for W. Baynes, 54, Paternoster-Row. 1805.

12°, π1 A–F¹², ($6 (–A2,3) signed), 73 leaves.

Pp. Engr. port. front. (by Freeman: John Wilmot, Earl of Rochester. Born 1648. Died 1680. 'Pubᵈ. by W. Baynes, Janʸ. 1. 1805') + *1* t., *2* blk, *3–4* Advertisement, 5–12 SJ's Life, 13–18 Preface, *19* 20–106 Some Passages, *107* ½t Sermon, *108* Advertisement, 109–44 text.

References: Courtney 152.

Notes: published at 2s.

Copies: *USA*: CLU-C, Hyde (blue bds. uncut; 'Richᵈ. Wade'), NRU; *UK*: ABu, En, LEu.

79.4LP/SS/231   Lives, Shorter Selections, Rochester   1810

Some Passages in the Life and Death of John, Earl of Rochester, written by Gilbert Burnet, D.D. Bishop of Salisbury. With a Sermon, preached at the Funeral of the said Earl, by the Rev. Robert Parsons, A.M. A New Edition: to which is now prefixed an Account of the Life and Writings of the Earl of Rochester, By Dr. Samuel Johnson. London: Printed by W. Nicholson, Warner-street, for W. Baynes, 54, Paternoster-Row. 1810.

SJ's Life, pp. 5–12.

References: Courtney 152. This is apparently a reissue of prec. 1805.

Copies: [Liebert]; *UK*: En (B13/a6, 'William Lomax: "Denique Coelum"').

79.4LP/SS/232   Lives, Shorter Selections, Rochester   1810

The Works of the English Poets, from Chaucer to Cowper . . . by Alexander Chalmers, F.S.A. In twenty-one volumes . . . 1810

SJ's Life, viii. 231–4.

79.4LP/SS/233   Lives, Shorter Selections, Rochester   1816

Evidences of the Christian Religion. Vol. IV. Some Passages . . . London . . . 1816

Not seen.

79.4LP/SS/234   Lives, Shorter Selections, Rochester   1819

Some Passages . . . London: Ogle, Duncan & Co., 37 Paternoster Row, & 295 Holborn. 1819

References: Courtney 152.

79.4LP/SS/235   Lives, Shorter Selections, Rochester   1820

Some Passages . . . London: W. Baynes & Son, 23 & 54 Paternoster Row. 1820
  References: Courtney 152.
  Copies: E.

79.4LP/SS/236   Lives, Shorter Selections,   1780
                             Roscommon

Bell's British Poets . . . Edinburg: The Apollo Press.
  Vol. 43, 1780
  SJ's Life, pp. v–xvi, taken directly from Cibber's *Lives of the Poets*, 1753, ii.
344–53, which is itself from SJ's account in *Gents. Mag.* xviii (May, 1748),
214–17 (48GM18, above), with additional paras. 27–39 from *Prefaces*, 1779
(79.4LP/1.2, above).

79.4LP/SS/237   Lives, Shorter Selections,   1807
                             Roscommon

Poetical Works of Earl of Roscommon . . . London. 1807
  Copies: MB.

79.4LP/SS/238   Lives, Shorter Selections,   1810
                             Roscommon

The Works of the English Poets, from Chaucer to Cowper . . . by Alexander
Chalmers, F.S.A. In twenty-one volumes . . . 1810
  SJ's Life, viii. 255–60.

79.4LP/SS/239   Lives, Shorter Selections,   1820
                             Roscommon

Poetical Works of Wentworth Dillon, Earl of Roscommon . . . London. 1820
  SJ's Life, pp. 5–7.
  Copies: MB.

79.4LP/SS/240   Lives, Shorter Selections, Rowe   1781

Bell's British Poets . . . Edinburg: The Apollo Press.
  Vol. 58, 1781

SJ's Life, pp. v–xxv, mainly from Cibber's *Lives*, 1753, and some details from *Biographia Britannica*, but some material from SJ incorporated.

79.4LP/SS/241   Lives, Shorter Selections, Rowe   1792

The Works of Nicholas Rowe, Esq; A New Edition. 2 vols. 12°, London: W. Lowndes . . . 1792
   SJ's Life, i. 1–11.
   References: Courtney 152.
   Copies: *USA*: ICU, MB; *UK*: BMp, E.

79.4LP/SS/242   Lives, Shorter Selections, Rowe   1810

The Works of the English Poets, from Chaucer to Cowper . . . by Alexander Chalmers, F.S.A. In twenty-one volumes . . . 1810
   SJ's Life, ix. 457–62.

79.4LP/SS/243   Lives, Shorter Selections, Savage   1810

The Works of the English Poets, from Chaucer to Cowper . . . by Alexander Chalmers, F.S.A. In twenty-one volumes . . . 1810
   SJ's Life, xi. 243–98. See 44.2LS/1 &c., above.

79.4LP/SS/244   Lives, Shorter Selections, Shenstone   [? 1799]

Essays on Men and Manners, by W. Shenstone. London: C. Cooke. [? 1799]
   References: Courtney 152.
   Copies: [Liebert = CtY].

79.4LP/SS/245   Lives, Shorter Selections, Shenstone   1807

Essays on Men and Manners, by W. Shenstone . . . London. 12°, 1807
   Copies: E (Newb. 1930).

79.4LP/SS/246   Lives, Shorter Selections, Shenstone   1810

The Works of the English Poets, from Chaucer to Cowper . . . by Alexander Chalmers, F.S.A. In twenty-one volumes . . . 1810
   SJ's Life, xiii. 257–61.

79.4LP/SS/247   Lives, Shorter Selections, Smith   1781

Bell's British Poets . . . Edinburg: The Apollo Press.
   Vol. 102, pt. 2, 1781
   SJ's Life, pp. v–xii, mainly from Cibber's *Lives*, 1753, iv. 303–12, with additional material from SJ.

79.4LP/SS/248   Lives, Shorter Selections, Smith   1810

The Works of the English Poets, from Chaucer to Cowper . . . by Alexander Chalmers, F.S.A. In twenty-one volumes . . . 1810
   SJ's Life, ix. 165–76.

79.4LP/SS/249   Lives, Shorter Selections, Swift   1810

The Works of the English Poets, from Chaucer to Cowper . . . by Alexander Chalmers, F.S.A. In twenty-one volumes . . . 1810
   SJ's Life, xi. 345–66.

79.4LP/SS/250   Lives, Shorter Selections, Swift   1819

The Works of the British Poets, ed. Sanford [& Walsh]. XVIII (Swift). 1819
   SJ's Life is a derivative version, afforced with material from Scott, pp. 36–
   References: Courtney 152.

79.4LP/SS/251   Lives, Shorter Selections, Swift   1878

The Six Chief Lives from Johnson's Lives of the Poets ed. Matthew Arnold. London: Macmillan and Co. 1878.
   SJ's Life, pp. 235–71 (79.4LP/S/1, above).
   References: Courtney 148.

79.4LP/SS/252   Lives, Shorter Selections, Swift   1894

Bell's English Classics. Johnson's Life of Swift, edited with an Introduction and Notes by F. Ryland, M.A. London: George Bell & Sons:– Chiswick Press: Charles Whittingham & Co . . . 1894
   8°, cloth, schoolbook, at 2s.
   References: Courtney 149; Clifford & Greene 22.11.
   Copies: *UK*: C (94.7.819), E (213.g), O (2695 e.47); *USA*: MWelC.

79.4LP/SS/253   Lives, Shorter Selections, Swift   1896

Bell's English Classics. Johnson's Life of Swift, edited with an Introduction and Notes by F. Ryland, M.A. London: George Bell and Sons. 1896
8°, cloth, schoolbook, at 2s.
Copies: *USA*: MB.

79.4LP/SS/254 Lives, Shorter Selections, Thomson   1788

The Seasons . . . Philadelphia: Printed and sold by Prichard and Hall, in Market Street near Front Street. M.DCC.LXXXVIII.
18°, pp. xviii + 196. Includes SJ's Life. ESTC: w003005. Not examined.

79.4LP/SS/255 Lives, Shorter Selections, Thomson   1790

The Seasons . . . Philadelphia: Printed by H. Taylor for R. Campbell, North-East Corner of Second and Chesnut-Streets. M.DCC.XC.
12°, pp. xii + 190. Includes SJ's Life. ESTC: w003006. Not examined.

79.4LP/SS/256 Lives, Shorter Selections, Thomson   1792

The Seasons . . . London: J. Strahan . . . 1792
    SJ's Life is condensed with that of Patrick Murdoch from *Seasons*, 1762. Cf. ESTC: t051947.
Copies: *UK*: L. (11631. g.24).

79.4LP/SS/257 Lives, Shorter Selections, Thomson   1793

The Seasons . . . ed. Percival Stockdale. 1793.
    SJ's Life (an edited version: 8 paras. *om* (31–2, 40–2, 49, 51–2) and some verbal changes by Stockdale).
References: Courtney 152; cf. ESTC: t018661.

79.4LP/SS/258 Lives, Shorter Selections, Thomson   1793

The Seasons . . . edited McKenzie. Dublin: W. McKenzie. 8°, 1793
SJ's Life, pp. iii–xxi.
References: Courtney 152; ESTC: t051944.
Copies: BMp (425080), O (Vet. A5 e.2762).

79.4LP/SS/259   Lives, Shorter Selections, Thomson   1794

The Seasons: by James Thomson. With the Life of the Author. London: Printed for J. Creswick, and Co. M DCC XCIV.
    12°. Pp. xix + 196; with plates.
    References: *Tinker* 2131; ESTC: t088947.
    Copies: CtY.

79.4LP/SS/260   Lives, Shorter Selections, Thomson   1795

The Seasons. Containing, Spring. Summer. Autumn. Winter. By James Thomson. With the Life of the Author, by Dr. Samuel Johnson. Philadelphia: Printed by Jacob Johnson & Co. No. 147, High-street. M DCC XCV.
    12°. Pp. xix + 194. Includes SJ's Life.
    References: Evans 29628; *Tinker* 2132; ESTC: w022101.
    Copies: CtY, [Liebert].

79.4LP/SS/261   Lives, Shorter Selections, Thomson   1800

The Seasons . . . By James Thomson. Printed at Wrentham, Massachusetts: by and for Nathaniel Heaton, jun, Also for David Heaton, Providence; Oliver Farnsworth, Newport; Henry Cushing, Providence; Thomas C. Cushing, Salem; Ephraim Goodale, Mendon, &c. &c. 1800
    12°. Pp. xv + 168. Includes SJ's Life. ESTC: w029097.
    Copies: *USA*: [Liebert = CtY], MWA, NRU; *UK*: [L].

79.4LP/SS/262   Lives, Shorter Selections, Thomson   1800

The Seasons . . . By James Thomson. 1800
    Copies: L (1507/502).

79.4LP/SS/263   Lives, Shorter Selections, Thomson   1801

The Seasons. Containing, Spring. Summer. Autumn. Winter. By James Thomson. With the Life of the Author, By Dr. Samuel Johnson. Philadelphia: Printed by John Bioren, No. 88, Chesnut Street, for Benjamin and Jacob Johnson, No. 174, High-Street. 1801
    12°.
    Copies: Hyde, [Liebert = CtY].

79.4LP/SS/264 Lives, Shorter Selections, Thomson   1805

The Seasons . . . By James Thomson. London: J. Wallis. 1805
8°, 286 pp., (some engr. illus. after Bewick).
Copies: L² (11632 bb. 40; *LP* L.c.70 f.s).

79.4LP/SS/265 Lives, Shorter Selections, Thomson   1806

The Seasons . . . 1806
Copies: [? A.T. Hazen].

79.4LP/SS/266 Lives, Shorter Selections, Thomson   1807

The Seasons . . . By James Thomson. Brookfield [Mass.]: E. Merram. 1807
16°.
Copies: [Liebert = CtY].

79.4LP/SS/267 Lives, Shorter Selections, Thomson   1808

Select British Poets . . . 1808 'Thomson'.
References: Courtney 152. Not seen.
Copies: [? O (Vet. A6 e. 340)].

79.4LP/SS/268 Lives, Shorter Selections, Thomson   1809

Thomson's Poetical Works, Gloucester. 1809
References: Courtney 152.

79.4LP/SS/269 Lives, Shorter Selections, Thomson   1809

The Seasons . . . Edinburgh: Printed by J. Ballantyne & Co. for R. Scholey, J.
Walker, . . . 1809
8°, 262 pp.
References: Courtney 152
Copies: L (11631. b.44).

79.4LP/SS/270 Lives, Shorter Selections, Thomson   1810

The British Poets. The Works of Milton, Young, Thomson and Gray. London:
G. Hazard. 1810.

8°, 7 parts.
Copies: Hyde ('MacGeagh').

79.4LP/SS/271 Lives, Shorter Selections, Thomson 1810

The Works of the English Poets, from Chaucer to Cowper . . . by Alexander
Chalmers, F.S.A. In twenty-one volumes . . . 1810
SJ's Life, xii. 405–12.

79.4LP/SS/272 Lives, Shorter Selections, Thomson 1811

Thomson's Seasons, and Castle of Indolence, and Other Poems. Edinburgh:
James Ballantyne & Co. 1811
8°. Pp. xxii [2] 215 [6], 216–88; SJ's Life, pp. v–xxii.
Copies: E (ABS.1.81.56).

79.4LP/SS/273 Lives, Shorter Selections, Thomson 1811

The Seasons . . . By James Thomson. London: Walker . . . 1811
16°.
Copies: [Liebert = CtY]; *UK*: L (11658. de.5).

79.4LP/SS/274 Lives, Shorter Selections, Thomson 1812

The Seasons . . . By James Thomson. New York: Van Winkle . . . 1812
16°.
Copies: [Liebert = CtY].

79.4LP/SS/275 Lives, Shorter Selections, Thomson [? 1815]

The Works of James Thomson . . . London: Offor. 10 vols. [? 1815]
Copies: E (ABS.2.86.39).

79.4LP/SS/276 Lives, Shorter Selections, Thomson 1815

The Seasons . . . By James Thomson. Alnwick: W. Davison. 1815
12°, pp. 163. Coloph (163): 'Printed by H. Mozley, Printer, Gainsborough.'
Burman, p. 25 (s.d. '1815').

79.4LP/SS/277   Lives, Shorter Selections, Thomson   1815

The Seasons, By James Thomson. To which is prefixed a Life of the Author, by
Samuel Johnson. Middlebury, Vt. Printed and Published by William Slade, Jun.
1815.
    Pp. 262, SJ's Life, pp. 3–23.
References: McCorison, *Vermont Imprints* (1963), 1785.

79.4LP/SS/278   Lives, Shorter Selections, Thomson   1816

The Seasons . . . By James Thomson. Oxford: Nathaniel Bliss. 1816
    Copies: *UK*: AWn, O (2799 f.124).

79.4LP/SS/279   Lives, Shorter Selections, Thomson   1817

The Seasons . . . By James Thomson. . . . 1817
    Copies: *USA*: PU.

79.4LP/SS/280   Lives, Shorter Selections, Thomson   1822

The Seasons, and a Poem to the memory of Sir Isaac Newton, by James
Thomson. To which is prefixed an Account of his Life and Writings by Samuel
Johnson. Kilmarnock: Printed by and for R. Mathie. 1822
    Pp. 203.
    Copies: *UK*: E (ABS.1.90.167), Eu (S.B. 82156); *USA*: NUC (807).

79.4LP/SS/281   Lives, Shorter Selections, Thomson   1822

The Seasons . . . By James Thomson. Boston. 1822
    Copies: CtY.

79.4LP/SS/282   Lives, Shorter Selections, Thomson   1823

Jones's British Poets. Vol. 7. The Seasons by James Thomson, with a biographical Sketch of the Author. London. 1823

79.4LP/SS/283   Lives, Shorter Selections, Thomson   1824

The Works of James Thomson, New Edition. 12 vols. 1824
    Copies: E (PCL. 407–18).

79.4LP/SS/284   Lives, Shorter Selections, Thomson   1824

The Seasons . . . By James Thomson. London: G.& W.B. Whitaker. 1824
8°, 276 pp. SJ's Life (with notes).
Copies: *UK*: L (11633 bb.47 + MS notes by the editor), O (2799 e.487).

79.4LP/SS/285   Lives, Shorter Selections, Thomson   1824

The Seasons . . . By James Thomson. Edinburgh: Oliver & Boyd. 1824
8°, 168 pp.
Copies: *UK*: Ep, L (1568/5037).

79.4LP/SS/286   Lives, Shorter Selections, Thomson   1825

University Edition: Diamond British Poets in Miniature. The Works of James
Thomson. Jones & Co. 2 vols. 1825
SJ's Life (criticism of Thomson).
Copies: *UK*: E (AB.3.79.53), O (2799 g.27; ? 2799 g.40).

79.4LP/SS/287   Lives, Shorter Selections, Thomson   1829

The Seasons . . . Edinburgh: Oliver & Boyd. 1829
Copies: *UK*: E² (NG.1169.c.28; ABS.1.80.70).

79.4LP/SS/288   Lives, Shorter Selections, Thomson   [? 1829]

The Seasons . . . Edinburgh. [Oliver & Boyd] n.d.
Copies: *UK*: Eu (D.S.g.13.26); *Can*: CaOHM (A.21).

79.4LP/SS/289   Lives, Shorter Selections, Thomson   [? 1830]

The Seasons . . . By James Thomson. London: T. Allman. [? 1830]
32°, 180 pp.
Copies: *UK*: L (1481. a.4).

79.4LP/SS/290   Lives, Shorter Selections, Thomson   1834

The Seasons . . . By James Thomson. London. 1834
Copies: E.

79.4LP/SS/291   Lives, Shorter Selections, Thomson   1835

The Seasons . . . By James Thomson. Belfast. 1835
Copies: Ep.

79.4LP/SS/292   Lives, Shorter Selections, Thomson   1836

The Seasons . . . By James Thomson. With Illustrations by Corbould. London:
Scott, Webster & Geary. 1836
Copies: O (2799 f.495).

79.4LP/SS/293   Lives, Shorter Selections, Thomson   1837

The Seasons and The Castle of Indolence . . . 1837
SJ's Life (slightly adapted).
References: Courtney 152.
Copies: E.

79.4LP/SS/294   Lives, Shorter Selections, Thomson   1838

The Seasons and The Castle of Indolence . . . By James Thomson. London.
1838
SJ's Life, pp. iii–xii.
Copies: MB.

79.4LP/SS/295   Lives, Shorter Selections, Thomson   1839

The Seasons . . . By James Thomson. London: Printed for the Booksellers by
William Walker of Otley. 1839
32°, 174 pp., SJ's Life (abridged).
Copies: L (11645. de.55).

79.4LP/SS/296   Lives, Shorter Selections, Thomson   1841

The Seasons . . . By James Thomson. Halifax: William Milner. 1841
16°, 174 pp.
Copies: L (11647. dg. 78).

79.4LP/SS/297   Lives, Shorter Selections, Thomson   1845

The Seasons . . . 1845
  Copies: [? Gp].

79.4LP/SS/298   Lives, Shorter Selections, Thomson   [? 1849]

The Seasons and The Castle of Indolence . . . London: Charles Daly. [? 1849]
  References: Courtney 152.

79.4LP/SS/299   Lives, Shorter Selections, Thomson   1852

The Seasons and The Castle of Indolence . . . By James Thomson. London.
1852
  SJ's Life, pp. v–xvi.
  References: Courtney 152.

79.4LP/SS/300   Lives, Shorter Selections, Thomson   1853

The Seasons and The Castle of Indolence . . . 1853

79.4LP/SS/301   Lives, Shorter Selections, Thomson   1862

The Poetical Works of James Thomson . . . 1862
  Copies: AWn.

79.4LP/SS/302   Lives, Shorter Selections, Thomson   [? 1880]

The Works of James Thomson . . . Edinburgh [? 1880]
  Copies: E (BCL. D6399).

79.4LP/SS/303   Lives, Shorter Selections, Tickell   1781

Bell's British Poets . . . Edinburg: The Apollo Press.
  Vol. 80, 1781
  SJ's Life (some admixture), pp. v–xii.

79.4LP/SS/304   Lives, Shorter Selections, Tickell   1810

The Works of the English Poets, from Chaucer to Cowper . . . by Alexander
Chalmers, F.S.A. In twenty-one volumes . . . 1810
SJ's Life, xi. 97–99.

79.4LP/SS/305   Lives, Shorter Selections, Tickell   1854

The British Poets. Edited by F.J. Child. The Poetical Works of Thomas
Tickell, with a Life by Dr Johnson. [With Poetical Works of Thomas Parnell]
Boston: Little, Brown and Co. 1854
References: Courtney 152.
Copies: NRU.

79.4LP/SS/306   Lives, Shorter Selections, Tickell   [? 188–]

The Poetical Works of Churchill, Parnell, and Tickell, with Lives. Boston and
New York: H. Mifflin. [188-?], 4 vols in 2.
Copies: ICU.

79.4LP/SS/307   Lives, Shorter Selections, Waller   1810

The Works of the English Poets, from Chaucer to Cowper . . . by Alexander
Chalmers, F.S.A. In twenty-one volumes . . . 1810
SJ's Life, viii. 3–27.

79.4LP/SS/308   Lives, Shorter Selections, Waller   1884

The Lives of Cowley, Milton, and Waller . . . Leipzig. 1884
References: Courtney 150.

79.4LP/SS/309   No entry.

79.4LP/SS/310   Lives, Shorter Selections, Watts   1785

THE | LIFE | OF THE | Rev. ISAAC WATTS, D.D. | By SAMUEL
JOHNSON, L.L.D. | With NOTES | CONTAINING | ANIMADVER
SIONS and ADDITIONS. | [medium swelled rule] | TO WHICH ARE

SUBJOINED, | A diftinguifhing Feature of the DOCTOR's CHARACTER, | omitted by his BIOGRAPHERS; | An authentic ACCOUNT of his laft SENTIMENTS on | the TRINITY; and | A COPY of a MANUSCRIPT of his never before publifhed. | [medium swelled rule] | *Veritatis amator fincerus et pacificus cultor.* | [medium swelled rule] | LONDON: | PRINTED FOR J.F. AND C. RIVINGTON, IN ST. PAUL's | CHURCH-YARD; AND J. BUCKLAND, IN PATER-NOSTER- | ROW. MDCCLXXXV.

8°, A–I⁸, ($4 (–A1,2) signed), 72 leaves.

Pp. *i* ½t, *ii* blk, *iii* t., *iv* blk, *v–x* Preface, *xi–xv* Contents, *xvi* advts, on B1 pp. *1* 2–32 SJ's Life, *33* 34–41 Supplement to Gibbons's Account, 42–100 Watts on the Trinity, 101–12 Address to the Deity, *113* 114–28 Appendices.

References: Courtney 149–50; *Tinker* 1368, Clifford & Greene 22.12; ESTC: t083968.

Notes: The editor was Samuel Palmer (1741–1813*).

Copies: *USA*: CtY, Hyde ('Madan'), IEN, IU, [Liebert² (pres. copy)], MH, NN, NPM, NRU ('R.B. Adam'); *UK*: C (7100 c.237), MRc, O (Vet. A5. e.4058).

79.4LP/SS/311   Lives, Shorter Selections, Watts   1786

Biographia Evangelica, by Erasmus Middleton. London. 1786
SJ's Life, IV. 265–72.
References: Courtney 152; ESTC: t016667.

79.4LP/SS/312   Lives, Shorter Selections, Watts   1791

The Life of Isaac Watts, D.D. By Samuel Johnson, L.L.D. Second Edition. 1791
SJ's Life, pp. 1–32; This is only a reissue of 1785 edn. above.
References: Courtney 149–50; Clifford & Greene 22.12; ESTC: t083969.
Copies: O (Vet. A5 e.2043/1), En; *USA*: CoU, ICN, [Liebert], TxU.

79.4LP/SS/313   Lives, Shorter Selections, Watts   1792

The Life of Isaac Watts, D.D. By Samuel Johnson, L.L.D. London: J. Johnson and T. Knott, &c. 1792
SJ's Life, pp. *33* 34–41. This is another issue of Palmer's 1785 edn., above. Not seen.
References: *Göttingen Catalogue*, ed. B. Fabian, 1987–8. ('Second Edition').
Copies: [? Göttingen U].

79.4LP/SS/314   Lives, Shorter Selections, Watts   1810

The Works of the English Poets, from Chaucer to Cowper . . . by Alexander Chalmers, F.S.A. In twenty-one volumes . . . 1810
  SJ's Life, xiii. 3–7.

79.4LP/SS/315   Lives, Shorter Selections, Watts   1810

The Improvement of the Mind . . . by Isaac Watts. London. 1810
  12°. Not examined.
  Copies: *UK*: AWn, NOu, SHu.

79.4LP/SS/316   Lives, Shorter Selections, Watts   1819

The Works of the British Poets, ed. Sanford [& Walsh], XXIII. 1819
  SJ's Life of Watts, pp. 3–11.

79.4LP/SS/317   Lives, Shorter Selections, Watts   1821

The Improvement of the Mind . . . by Isaac Watts. Edinburgh: Printed for Fairbairn & Anderson (Successors to Mr Creech), 55 North Bridge Street; Bell & Bradfute; William Whyte & Co; William Oliphant; James Robertson; Waugh & Innes; John Robertson; and Macredie & Co. 1821
  12°.
  Copies: JDF.

79.4LP/SS/318   Lives, Shorter Selections, Watts   1824

The Improvement of the Mind, by Isaac Watts. 1824
  Copies: E (NG.1177 b.7).

79.4LP/SS/319   Lives, Shorter Selections, Watts   1825

The Improvement of the Mind, by Isaac Watts. 23rd edition. London. 1825
  Copies: Ep.

79.4LP/SS/320   Lives, Shorter Selections, West   1781

Bell's British Poets . . . Edinburg: The Apollo Press.
  Vol. 95, 1781
  SJ's Life (criticisms, acknowledged), pp. v–vi.

79.4LP/SS/321   Lives, Shorter Selections, West   1810

The Works of the English Poets, from Chaucer to Cowper . . . by Alexander
Chalmers, F.S.A. In twenty-one volumes . . . 1810
  SJ's Life, xiii. 135–7.

79.4LP/SS/322   Lives, Shorter Selections, Young   [? 1784]

The Complaint: or Night-Thoughts . . . [Dublin] No. 63 Dame Street
McKenzie Printer Bookseller & Stationer to the University of Dublin. [?
1784–]
  SJ's Life 'From the Prefaces, Biographical and Critical'. ESTC: t204411. Not
examined.
  Copies: T. Bonnell, Esq;

79.4LP/SS/323   Lives, Shorter Selections, Young   [? 1809]

Select British Poets . . . London.
  References: Courtney 152.

79.4LP/SS/324   Lives, Shorter Selections, Young   1810

The Works of the English Poets, from Chaucer to Cowper . . . by Alexander
Chalmers, F.S.A. In twenty-one volumes . . . 1810
  SJ's Life, xiii. 339–66.

79.4LP/SS/325   Lives, Shorter Selections, Young   1810

The British Poets. The Works of Milton, Young, Thomson and Gray. London:
G. Hazard. 1810
  8°, 7 parts.
  Copies: Hyde ('MacGeagh').

79.4LP/SS/326   Lives, Shorter Selections, Young   1819

Works of The British Poets, ed. Sanford [& Walsh], XXV. 1819
  SJ's Life (with modifications 'After Johnson and others').
  References: Courtney 152.

79.6M/1   Maurice's Poems and Translation   1779
                                of Sophocles

POEMS | AND | MISCELLANEOUS PIECES, | WITH A | FREE
TRANSLATION | OF THE | OEDIPUS TYRANNUS OF
SOPHOCLES. | BY | THE REV. THOMAS MAURICE, A.B. | OF |
UNIVERSITY COLLEGE, OXFORD. | *LONDON,* | Printed for the
AUTHOR, | And fold by J. Dodsley, Pall-mall; G. Kearsly, in Fleet-ftreet; |
Meffrs. Fletcher, Prince, Parker and Bliss, Oxford; and | Meffrs.
Woodyer and Merryl, in Cambridge. | M.DCC.LXXIX.

4°, A⁴ χ² B–2H⁴, ($2 signed), 126 leaves.

Pp. A1 *i* t., *ii* blk, iii–iv Dedication dh: TO HIS GRACE | THE DUKE
OF MARLBOROUGH.' (dated '15 June 1779'), v–vi Preface, vii–x List of
Subscribers, *xi* Contents, *xii* blk, on B1 *1* 2–238 *239* text, *240* blk.

Pagination: [↑]; 230–31 duplicated at 2G4; blks. 68, 74; ½tt. 69–70, 101–2,
135–6, 147–8; 118 *sometimes* as 105, 119 *sometimes* as 112.

Press-figures: A4(vii)–3, χ1ᵛ(x)–3, B1ᵛ(2)–1, C3ᵛ(14)–2, D4(23)–1,
F3ᵛ(38)–2, F4ᵛ(40)–1, G4(47)–3, H2ᵛ(52)–3, H4(55)–3, I4ᵛ(64)–1, K4(71)–3,
L3(77)–1, M4(87)–3, N4ᵛ(96)–3, O1ᵛ(98)–3, P3(109)–1, Q4(119)–3,
Q4ᵛ(120)–3, R4ᵛ(128)–3, S1ᵛ(130)–3, T1ᵛ(138)–3, U4(151)–1, X4(159)–1,
Y4(167)–1, Z3ᵛ(174)–1, 2A2ᵛ(180)–2, 2B4(191)–1, 2C3ᵛ(198)–1,
2D2ᵛ(204)–2, 2E3ᵛ(214)–2, 2F1ᵛ(218)–3, 2G1ᵛ(226)–3, 2G3(229)–1,
2H2ᵛ(236)–3.

Catchwords: 107 From (Hence), 146 A BRIEF (A FREE).

Explicit: 237 THE END.

Paper: White, laid; Demy (11⅛ × 8⅞ in.), wmk.: fleur-de-lys.

Type: Dedication and text: english (4.5 mm), Preface: pica (4.2 mm),
Subscribers and notes: small pica (3.6 mm).

References: Courtney 129; CH 154; Hazen 136–42; Keast, in *Eighteenth
Century Studies* (1970), 63–80 is not wholly reliable. See also Maurice, *Memoirs
of the Author of Indian Antiquities*, 1819; Subscriptions no. 42. ESTC: t042583.

Notes: SJ wrote the 'Preface' to the *Oedipus Tyrannus* (pp. 149–52), and may
have helped with the 'Dedication' to the D. of Marlborough,¹ though I doubt it.
Maurice published 'Proposals', of which a copy is in O, though there is no evidence to connect SJ with it. SJ was also a subscriber (p. ix: 'Samuel Johnson
L.L.D.'), and his own copy (untraced), was sold to 'W[right]' for 16s. 6d. in his
sale Christie, 16 Feb. 1785. Though there were just over 300 copies subscribed
for, it is unlikely that the edn. was remarkably small: probably 500 were printed.
Maurice published verses on SJ 'To Samuel Johnson, LL.D.' (written in 1778)
in his *Poems, Epistolary, Lyrical and Elegiacal. In Three Parts . . . London: Printed
by W. Bulmer & Co. for J. Wright*, 8°, 1800, pp. 61–3.

Copies: O (Vet. A5 d.260, 'Thomas Williams');
USA: CSmH², CtY, [FU], [Goldberg], Hyde⁴ (**1.** unopened; **2.** uncut; **3.**

Adam; **4**. R.W. Rogers), [Liebert (blue wraps. uncut, 'R. Farmer. From the Author'²) = CtY], ICN, NIC, NN, PPL; *UK*: C, Ct, E, L (11630 e.8(1)).

¹ George Spencer (1739–1817), 4th D.
² Now CtY: *YULG* lii (1978), 93.

79.6M/2   Maurice's Westminster Abbey and   1813
Translation of Oedipus

WESTMINSTER | ABBEY; | WITH | OTHER OCCASIONAL POEMS, | AND A | FREEE TRANSLATION | OF THE | OEDIPUS TYRANNUS | OF SOPHOCLES. | ILLUSTRATED WITH ENGRAVINGS. | [medium parallel rule] | BY THE AUTHOR OF INDIAN ANTIQUITIES. | [medium total rule] | LONDON: | [medium total rule] | PRINTED FOR THE AUTHOR. | BY W. BULMER AND CO. CLEVELAND-ROW, ST. JAMES'S. | AND SOLD BY WHITE, COCHRANE, AND CO. FLEET-STREET, | AND THE AUTHOR AT THE BRITISH MUSEUM. | 1813.

4°, *A*⁶ B–P⁸ Q², ($1 signed), 120 leaves.

Pp. A1 *i* ½t: [short rule] | WESTMINSTER ABBEY. | &c. &c. &c. | [short rule], *ii* blk, *iii* t., *iv* blk, *v* Dedication to the Earl of Carysfort, *vi* blk, *vii* Contents, *viii* blk, on A4 ²*i* ii–iv Subscribers, on B1 *1* 2–217 text, *218* blk.

Pagination: no errors; *Press-figures*: none; *Catchwords*: none.

Explicit: 217 THE END.

Paper: White, wove: an uncut copy measures just over 9½ × 6½ in. which is hardly an octavo size, but the wove paper makes it difficult to ascertain a quarto arrangement. As a quarto it answers to a small post (uncut: 9½ × 7⅝ in.), but if an octavo then the uncut sheet should have been a royal (10 × 6¼ in.). Wmk.: 'W BALSTON 1809' and '1806' and '1808'.

Type: Text: english (4.7 mm), notes: small pica (3.5 mm).

Plates: (3) 1. Front. 'Moonlight View of Westminster Abbey from the Surrey side of the Thames', 2. North portico of Westminster Abbey, 3. Sophocles.

References: Courtney 129, [Subscriptions no. 42A].

Notes: There is some duplication of text at pp. 104–5 arising from proof revision. The Dedication to Carysfort is evidently Maurice's.¹ SJ's 'Preface' to the Sophocles is pp. 123–9. SJ was one of the 199 subscribers (taking 263 copies) to the first edn. of 1784 (ESTC: t052343), but that edn. did not include the 'Sophocles', nor did the reprint of Maurice's *Poems*, London: Bulmer, 1800. 8° (ESTC: t085995).

Copies: O (GA Westm. 4° 64); *USA*: CtY, DFo, [Goldberg], [Liebert (uncut) = CtY], MH, NN; *Can*: CaOHM; *UK*: BMp, En, L.

¹ John Joshua Proby (1751–1828*), 1st. E., was himself a poet.

79.6M/3   Maurice's Translation of Oedipus   1822

A free Translation of the Oedipus Tyrannus of Sophocles; the noblest Production of the Greek dramatic Muse. London: Printed for the Author, by W. Bulmer and W. Nicol, Cleveland-Row; and sold by Messrs. Rivington, Waterloo-Place. 1822.

8°, *A*⁸ B–E⁸ F⁴ G², ($1 signed), 46 leaves.

Pp. A1 ½t Oedipus Tyrannus, A1ᵛ blk, A2 t., A2ᵛ blk, A3 Maurice's Dedication to Samuel Parr ('Janry 1, 1822.'), A3ᵛ blk, A4–4ᵛ Advertisement (misspelt A4ᵛ ht: 'ADVETISEMENT.') by TM, A5 *i* ii–v Preface, *vi* blk, A8 *vii* The Argument, *viii* Dram. Pers., on B1 *1* 2–74 text of Oedipus, 74 *Explicit*: THE END., coloph: 'London: Printed by W. Bulmer and W. Nicol, Cleveland-row, St. James's.', *75* advts., *76* blk.

Notes: There is nothing of SJ in this edn.

Copies: L (11705. d. 23).

79.12LP   Henry Lucas's Poems   1779

[½t] [rule] | POEMS | TO | HER MAJESTY. | &c. &c. | [rule]

[Title] POEMS | TO | HER MAJESTY: | TO WHICH IS ADDED | A NEW TRAGEDY, | ENTITLED THE | EARL of SOMERSET; | LITERALLY FOUNDED ON HISTORY: | WITH A | PREFATORY ADDRESS, &c. | [rule] | By HENRY LUCAS, A.M. | STUDENT of the MIDDLE TEMPLE, | AUTHOR of the TEARS of ALNWICK, VISIT from the SHADES, *&c.* | [rule] | ——*Tentanda via eſt, quâ me quoque poſſim* | *Tollere humo*—— VIRGIL. | 'Tis Nature's precept, to attempt to riſe, | On virtuous pinions, ſoaring to the ſkies. | [heavy parallel rule] | LONDON: | PRINTED *FOR THE* AUTHOR, | By WILLIAM DAVIS, N°. 25, LUDGATE-HILL. | Sold alſo by J. DODSLEY, *Pall-Mall*; J. RIDLEY, *St. James's*-Street; J. MURRAY, *Fleet-* | *Street*; and by the AUTHOR, N°. 1, *Spur-Street, Leiceſter-Fields*; near *Panton-Street.* | [short heavy parallel rule] | M,DCC,LXXIX.

4°, *A*⁴ B–2E⁴ χ⁴, ($2 (–$1 BE; –$2 CKLNY 2B2C2E) signed), 116 leaves.

Pp. A1 ½t, + Engr. front. + A2 t., on A3 *i* ii–iv Dedication to the Queen¹ (signed 'Henry Lucas, June 4, 1779'), on B1 *1* ½t, *2* blk, *3* 4–24 text Poems, on E1 *²i* ½t Poems, &c., *ii* blk, *iii* iv–xl Prefatory Address ('Henry Lucas, July 1, 1779.'), *xli* xlii–xliv Prologue, *xlv* Persons, *xlvi* blk, on K4 *1* 2–146 text 'Earl of Somerset', on χ⁴ (8 pp.) Subscribers, (incl. 'Samuel Johnson, L.L.D.').²

Pagination: 10, 12 blk; 9, 11, 13 unnumbered; *Press-figures*: none.

Catchwords: xxv ˏwhence, ("~,), xxvi ˏAnd ("~), 41 Haſt (Has), 72 Thenceˏ (~,), 82–3, 114 *om.* before ACT, 127 *The* (SCENCE, *The*), 131 Suit [t *ſlipt*], 132 Ha! (*ᵗ*~!).

Explicit: 146 THE END.

Paper: White, laid; La. post (uncut: 10½ × 8¼ in.); no vis. wmk.

Type: Dedication: double pica (7.0 mm), text: great primer (5.7 mm), notes: english (4.7 mm).

Plates: (2) Front. facing t. in red, and p. xlvi (K3ᵛ) The Earl of Somerset 'H. L. Eſq. invᵗ. W. Sharp ſculpᵗ.' 'H.L.' is presumably Lucas himself.

References: Liebert, *PBSA* xli (1947), 231–8; *Boswell Papers*, xiii. 219 (s.d. '11 April 1779', *JB: Laird of Auchinleck*, 75); *Life* iii. 552; Subscriptions no. 36; ESTC: t042678.

Notes: Published at 10s. 6d., or 1 gn. bound, on 9 December 1779 (*Public Advertiser*). Lucas acknowledged SJ's assistance in his Prefatory Address (p. xxxv), 'Dr Samuel Johnson — to whom permit me thus publicly to express my gratitude, for the peculiar kindness of his perusal, emendations, and good opinion of this work.' On 28 August 1777 the *Morning Chronicle* noted that Lucas ('Author of the *Tears of Alnwick*') had written a tragedy which Johnson had revised and which will be played in the coming season. SJ had been 'compelled' to read it in May 1777 (*Letters* 516, Hyde, iii. 20–21).

Lucas had tried to get his play staged in 1773 (*Priv. Corr. of Garrick*, ed. Boaden, i (1831), 579–80, Geo. Faulkner to DG, 9 Oct. 1773). It was noticed with slight approval, by Edmund Cartwright in *Monthly Review*, lxiii (Sept. 1780), 230–1. In his 'Ejaculation; occasioned by seeing the Royal Children on His Majesty's Birth-Day', Lucas involves SJ in the butter which is so lavishly spread throughout this collection:

> Language, by Johnson tho' ſublimely dreſt,
> Speaks now the rapture, that my ſoul poſſeſt,
> The rich idea lives but in my breaſt. (p. 6)

SJ's copy of the book was lot 335 in the sale of his library at Christie's, 16 Feb. 1785.[3] The copy presented by Lucas to Qu. Charlotte, in full red morocco, was sold as lot 669 at Sotheby (James Bohn), 19 April 1854.

Copies: O (Harding C. 3721, 'Sir John Dashwood King'[4]); *USA*: CSmH² (2. lacks ½t), CtY (= [Liebert]), DLC (imperfect *Earl of Somerset* only, detached from this book), CtY (no ½t), ICN (no ½t), MH (17454.69*), NIC, [NL]; *Can*: CaOHM (D 1658); *UK*: C, L² (1. 11630. e.8 (2); 2. 97. k.14), LEu; *Eir*: Dt.

---

[1] Charlotte Sophia, of Mecklenburg-Strelitz (1744–1818*).

[2] 100 names took 146 copies, among them Lord LeDespencer (10 books), James Dodsley, Mrs [Eliza] Griffith, Sir Joshua Reynolds (2), John Walcot Esq. (2), and Benjamin West.

[3] Together with John Nichols's 'A collection of royal wills, 1780' it went to 'Money' for 9s. 6d. (cf. Greene, *Samuel Johnson's Library* (1975), 118.

[4] For the connections between Dashwood-King, DeSpencer, and Walcot among the subscribers, see SJ's *Journey* (1985), 247 n. 1.

80.5DMG/1   Davies's Memoirs of Garrick,   1780
                          first edition

MEMOIRS | OF THE | LIFE | OF | DAVID GARRICK, Efq. | INTERSPERSED WITH | CHARACTERS and ANECDOTES | OF | HIS THEATRICAL CONTEMPORARIES. | THE WHOLE FORMING | A HISTORY OF THE STAGE, | WHICH INCLUDES | A Period of Thirty-Six Years. | [rule] | By THOMAS DAVIES. | ————Quem populus Romanus meliorem virum quam | hiftrionem effe arbitratur, qui ita digniffimus eft fcena propter | artificium, ut digniffimus fit curia propter abftinentiam. | Cicero pro Q. Rofcio Comœdo. | [rule] | VOL. I. [– II.] | [double rule] | LONDON: | Printed for the Author, and fold at his Shop in Great | Ruffell-Street, Covent-Garden. | [short rule] | M.DCC.LXXX.

2 vols., 8°

I. A⁸ b² B–U⁸ *X⁴ X–Y⁸, ($4 (–B4, I4; F4 as F3) signed; 'Vol. I' on $1 (–A, b)), 182 leaves.

Pp. Front. engr. port. Garrick + A1 *i* t., *ii* blk, *iii–v* Dedication dh: TO | Richard Brinfley Sheridan, Efq. ('April 22. 1780'), *vi* blk, *vii–ix* ADVERTISEMENT., *x Errata* Vols. I & II., on A6 *xi–xx* Contents dh: [double rule] | CONTENTS | OF THE | FIRST VOLUME., on B1 *1* 2–304 *305–*312 305–36 text Life of Garrick dh: THE | LIFE | OF | DAVID GARRICK, Esq. | [medium swellled rule], rt: THE LIFE OF | DAVID GARRICK, Efq.

Pagination: The interpolated *X⁴ carries the duplicated starred pp. *305–12 containing chapter XXVII* (an account of Margaret Woffington).

Press-figures: none throughout.

Catchwords: 55 place‸ (~*,), 163 [*con-*]*fidered*‸ (~,), 202 [fen-] fibility‸ (~,).

Explicit: 336 End of the First Volume.

II. A–N⁸ O⁸ (O5 + χ²) P–2D⁸, ($4 (2C3 as C3) signed; 'Vol. II.' on $1(+ ᵒχ1, [= p. *203])), 218 leaves.

Pp. A1 blk, on A2 *i* t., *ii* blk, *iii–xv* Contents, *xvi* blk, on B1 *1* 2–202 *203–*206 (χ²), 203–389 text, *390* blk, *391* 392–416 Appendix dh: APPENDIX. | [medium swelled rule] | TESTIMONIES | OF | Mr. Garrick's GENIUS and MERITS., ht: APPENDIX.

Pagination: The inserted bifolium following O5 carries the duplicated starred pp. *203–6 (containing an account of Giffard's and others' *The Golden Calf*), 297 as 279.

Catchwords: 57 [no-] bleman‸ (~,), 72 [af-] fured (fnred), 79 ‸One (*~).

Explicit: 416 FINIS.

Paper: White, laid; La. post (uncut: 8¼ × 5⅛ in.); wmk.: fleur-de-lys + LVG.

Type: English: I. Advertisement (4.5 mm), text (4.3 mm).

Plate: Port. of Garrick 'Engraved from Mr Pingo's Seal for the Theatrical Fund. | Published by T. Davies, April the 25ᵗʰ. 1780.' (*Fettercairn* 226, 1094).

References: *Life* iii. 434 (Courtney 152); CH 160; *Tinker* 1367; Arnott and Robinson (1970), 2930; ESTC: t072058.

Notes: The interpolation in vol. 1 is an account of Margaret Woffington. Davies acknowledged SJ's aid 'with the early part of Mr. Garrick's life' in his *Advertisement* (I. A4 p. *vii*), but as CH observed his help 'was probably substantial'. The work includes the letter from Gilbert Walmesley to Colson, 1737 (i. 9–10), and of March 2 (i. 11–12), SJ's Drury-Lane Prologue (i. 108–11), an account of *Irene* (i. 119–23), and the reference to DG from SJ's *Life of Smith* (ii. 392). It was undertaken by Davies largely to recoup his fortunes after his bankruptcy of 1778, and SJ was among those who promoted and gave assistance.[1]

The opening paragraph is certainly SJ's. The book was published on 6 May 1780 (*Gazetteer*), and reviewed at length by Ralph Griffiths in *Monthly Review*, lxiii (Aug. 1780), 116–20, (Sept. 1780), 207–14, and (Nov. 1780), 363–8. Other notices include the *Critical Review*, xxiv (May 1780), 329–36, *Westminster Mag.* viii (May, 1780), 277–8, *Political Mag.* i (May 1780), 349, 352 and 389, and *Gents. Mag.* l (July 1780), 330–33.

Copies: O (12 θ. 1112–3);

USA: CSmH, CtY, DFo (extra-illus. to 4 vols), Hyde, ICU, [Liebert (orig. boards. uncut 'Plymouth'²)], MB, MH (extra-illus.), NjP, NN, NPM (extra-illus. to 4 vols.); *Can*: CaOHM (B. 8089–90); *UK*: BRp², Cf ('Fitzwilliam 1780'), Cq, En ('Adam Smith'), Ep, [Es], HLu, JDF (annot. by Alexander Chalmers, with newspaper clippings, — 'J.J. Vernon' (Radley Coll. Prize) — Mary Lascelles), L, LICj (inscr. TD: 'To His honour'd Freind & Patron Dr Samuel Johnson from the Authour.' *Booklist* 55), Ljh (MS notes), MRp, MRc, MRu², NCp, Om.

[1] Davies had earlier produced the *Works of William Browne*, 3 vols., 1772, the *Miscellaneous and Fugitive Pieces*, 3 vols. 1773–4 (above 73.12DM), the *Lives of Elias Ashmole and William Lilly*, 1774, and the *Works of John Eachard*, 1774, but his major literary works came after the collapse of 1778 with the *Works of Massinger*, 1779, the Garrick, followed by *Dramatic Miscellanies*, 3 vols. 1783–4 (*Lit. Anec.* vii (1813), 421–43).
[2] The last (7th) E. Plymouth, Henry Other-Arthur (1768–1843), *o.s.p.*

80.5DMG/2   Davies's Memoirs of Garrick,   1780
second edition

MEMOIRS | OF THE | LIFE | OF | DAVID GARRICK, Efq. | INTERSPERSED WITH | CHARACTERS ᴀɴᴅ ANECDOTES | OF | HIS THEATRICAL CONTEMPORARIES. | THE WHOLE FORMING | A HISTORY OF THE STAGE, | WHICH INCLUDES | A Period of Tʜɪʀᴛʏ-Sɪx Yᴇᴀʀs. | rule] | By THOMAS DAVIES. | ——Quem populus Romanus meliorem virum quam | hiftrionem effe arbitratur, qui ita digniffimus

eſt ſcena propter | artificium, ut digniſſimus ſit curia propter abſtinentiam. | Cicero pro Q Roſcio Comoedo. | [rule] | A NEW EDITION. | [rule] | VOL. I [– II]. | [total rule]. | LONDON: | Printed for the Author, and ſold at his Shop in Great | Ruſſell-Street, Covent-Garden. | [short rule] | M.DCC.LXXX.
2 vols., 8°

I. A–Y⁸ Z⁴, ($4 (–A4, T4, A4ᵛ as A4) signed; 'Vol. I.' on $1), 180 leaves.

Pp. Engr. port. front. + A1 *i* t., *ii* blk, *iii–v* Dedication dh: TO | Richard Brinſley Sheridan, Eſq., *vi* blk, *vii–viii* Advertisement, on A5 ²*i* ii–viii Contents, on B1 *1* 2–344 text Life of Garrick.

Pagination: no errors; *Press-figures*: none.

Catchwords: 55 place,ᴧ (~,*), 69 months,ᴧ (~,).

Explicit: 344 END OF THE FIRST VOLUME.

II. A–2E⁸, ($4 (–A1) signed; 'Vol. II.' on $1), 224 leaves.

Pp. A1 *i* ½t THE | LIFE | OF | DAVID GARRICK, Eſq. | VOL. II., *ii* blk, *iii* t., *iv* blk, *v–xv* Contents, *xvi* blk. on B1 *1* 2–396 text, 397–429 Appendix, *430* blk, *431* Proposals for Dramatic Miscellanies ('Feb. 1. 1781'), *432* blk.

Pagination: [↑] 397.

Press-figures: B1ᵛ(2)–1, B7(13)–4, C1ᵛ(18)–4, D6(43)–2, E2ᵛ(52)–1, F3ᵛ(70)–1, G1ᵛ(82)–3, G2ᵛ(84)–2, H3ᵛ(102)–1, I5ᵛ(122)–4, I6ᵛ(124)–1, K7ᵛ(142)–2, K8ᵛ(144)–4, L1ᵛ(146)–4, L6ᵛ(156)–1, M4ᵛ(168)–2, N4ᵛ(184)–3, N5ᵛ(186)–5, O1ᵛ(194)–2, P6ᵛ(220)–1, Q6(235)–4, R8ᵛ(256)–2, S1ᵛ(258)–4, S5(265)–2, T6(283)–1, U1ᵛ(290)–1, U2ᵛ(292)–4, X2ᵛ(308)–1, X8(319)–4, Y2ᵛ(324)–4, Y5ᵛ(330)–1, Z5ᵛ(346)–1, Z7(349)–5, 2A4ᵛ(360)–1, 2A5ᵛ(362)–4, 2B1ᵛ(370)–4, 2C5ᵛ(394)–1.

Catchwords: 352 Amongſt (To eſtablish); but 'amongst' catches with the opening of the second para. on p. 353, reflecting adjustment of type in proof.

Explicit: 429 FINIS.

Paper: White, laid; crown (uncut: 7½ × 5 in.); wmk.: fleur-de-lys.

Type: Dedication: great primer (5.9 mm), text: english (4.7 mm), notes, quotes and appendix: small pica (3.5 mm).

Plate: NOT in O.

References: Arnott & Robinson (1970), 2932; ESTC: t072057.

Notes: The distribution of press-figures points to shared printing of the two volumes.

Copies: O (M. Adds. 1237 e. 25–6);

USA: CtY, DFo² (extra-illus.), Hyde ('Jonathan Pytts'), MH², NN; *UK*: ABu, BRu, Eu, IPS, L², Ljh, LVu, SHu.

80.5DMG/3   Davies's Memoirs of Garrick, Dublin   1780

MEMOIRS | OF THE | LIFE | OF | DAVID GARRICK, Efq. | INTERSPERSED WITH | CHARACTERS AND ANECDOTES OF HIS | THEATRICAL CONTEMPORARIES. | THE WHOLE FORMING | A HISTORY OF THE STAGE, WHICH INCLUDES A | PERIOD OF THIRTY-SIX YEARS. | By THOMAS DAVIES. | ——Quem populus Romanus meliorem virum quam hift-| rionem effe arbitratur, qui ita digniffimus eft fcena propter | artificium, ut digniffimus fit curia propter abftinentiam. | Cicero pro Q. Rofcio Comoedo. | VOL. I [– II]. | DUBLIN: | Printed by *JOSEPH HILL,* | FOR | J. Williams, W. Halhead, E. Cross, C. Jenkin, L. | Flin, W. Gilbert, T. Walker, W. Wilson, L. | White, J. Beatty, and R. Burton, Bookfellers. | M DCC LXXX.

2 vols., 12°

I. A⁸ B–M¹² N⁶ (N6 blk), ($5 (–A5, N4,5) signed; 'Vol. I.' on $1 (–A)), 146 leaves.

Pp. Engr. port. ('D. GARRICK ... W. Efdall fculpᵗ') + on A1 *i* t., *ii* blk, *iii–iv* Dedication ('April 22, 1780'), *v–vii* Advertisement, *viii* blk, *ix–xvi* Contents, on B1 *1* 2–274 text, *275–6* (N6) blk.

Pagination: no errors; *Press-figures*: none.

Catchwords: 8 ∧and ("~), 9 ∧hopes ("~), 89 Perhaps∧ (~,), 94]*Lady* ([~), 147 [him-] felf (himfelf), 306 light∧, (~*,).

Explicit: 274 End of the First Volume.

II. A⁶ B–O¹², ($5 (–A1,4,5) signed; 'Vol. II.' on $1 (–A)), 162 leaves.

Pp. A1 *i* t., *ii* blk, *iii–xi* Contents, *xii* blk, on B1 *1* 2–292 text, *293* 294–311 Appendix, *312* Errata in vol. 2.

Catchwords: 89 A SOLILOQUY (A Soliloquy), 126 [fuperiori-] rity (ty), 195 tende∧ (tender).

Explicit: 311 FINIS.

Paper: White, laid; Crown [or Grand cornet] (uncut: 6⅔ × 3¾ in.); no vis. wmk.

Type: Dedication: paragon (6.5 mm), advertisement: english (4.4 mm), leaded (1.6 mm), text: pica (4.0 mm), notes: bourgeois (3.2 mm).

References: Arnott & Robinson (1970), 2931; ESTC: t066307.

Copies: O (Vet A5 f. 2463–4, 'Charles Andrew Caldwell');

USA: ICU, TxU; *UK*: C, L, SAN; *Eir*: Dt.

80.5DMG/4   Davies's Memoirs of Garrick,   1781
third London edition

MEMOIRS | OF THE | LIFE | OF | DAVID GARRICK, Efq. | INTERSPERSED WITH | CHARACTERS and ANECDOTES | OF |

HIS THEATRICAL CONTEMPORARIES. | THE WHOLE FORMING | A HISTORY OF THE STAGE, | WHICH INCLUDES | A Period of Thirty-Six Years. | [rule] | By THOMAS DAVIES. | [rule] | ——Quem populus Romanus meliorem virum quam | hiftrionem effe arbitratur, qui ita digniffimus eft fcena propter | artificium, et digniffimus fit curia propter abftinentiam. | Cicero pro Q Rofcio Comoedo. | [rule] | THIRD EDITION. | [rule] | VOL. I [– II]. | [total rule] | LONDON: | Printed for the Author, and fold at his Shop in Great | Ruffell-Street, Covent-Garden. | [short rule] | M.DCC.LXXXI.

2 vols., 8°

I. A–Z⁸, ($4 (–A1, E6 as E3) signed; 'Vol. I.' on $1 (–A)), 184 leaves.

Pp. Engr. port. front. ('J.K. Sherwin') + A1 *i* t., *ii* blk, *iii–v* Dedication, *vi–vii* Advertisement, *viii–xv* Contents, *xvi* blk, on B1 *1* 2–352 text.

Pagination: no errors; *Press-figures*: none; *Catchwords*: not recorded.

Explicit: 352 End of the First Volume.

II. A–2E⁸ 2F², ($4 (–2F2) signed; 'Vol. II.' on $1 (–A)), 226 leaves.

Pp. A1 *i* ½t, *ii* blk, *iii* t., *iv* blk, *v–xv* Contents, *xvi* blk, on B1 *1* 2–400 text of Life, 401–34 Appendix, *435* Proposals for *Dramatic Miscellanies* ('February 1. 1781'), *436* Conditions.

Pagination: [↑] 401.

Press-figures: B5(9)–3, B7ᵛ(14)–1, C5ᵛ(26)–1, C8ᵛ(32)–3, D1ᵛ(34)–3, D2ᵛ(36)–4, E8(63)–1, E8ᵛ(64)–4, F5(73)–5, F8(79)–4, G5(89)–1, H1ᵛ(98)–5, H8ᵛ(112)–1, I3ᵛ(118)–1, K7ᵛ(142)–5, L5ᵛ(154)–4, M2ᵛ(164)–5, M5ᵛ(170)–2, N7ᵛ(190)–5; cetera desunt.

Catchwords: not recorded.

Explicit: 434 THE END.

Paper: White, laid; sm. post (uncut: 7⅝ × 4¾ in.); wmk.: fleur-de-lys.

Type: english (4.4 mm).

Plate: Port. of DG, engr. J.K. Sherwin.

References: Arnott & Robinson (1970), 2934; ESTC: t065970.

Notes: The missigning of I. E6 follows that in the second edn. 80.5DMG/2, above. The compositor set not only the text of p. 53 in 2nd edn. as p. 59 here, but also reproduced the faulty signature. There is no cancel.

Copies: O (Mal. I. 168–9; with set-off of ¹352 on blk recto of engr. front.);

USA: CtY, DFo (extra-illus.), DLC, Hyde (extra-illus. 'Edmond Malone' with some annotation, — 'George Daniel'), ICN, MH (extra-illus.), NN; *UK*: BAT, BMp, C, E, Felbrigg, L, LEu, MRu, NCp, NOu.

80.5DMG/5   Davies's Memoirs of Garrick,   1784
fourth London edition

MEMOIRS | OF THE | LIFE | OF | DAVID GARRICK, Efq. | INTERSPERSED WITH | CHARACTERS and ANECDOTES | OF | HIS THEATRICAL CONTEMPORARIES. | THE WHOLE FORMING | A HISTORY OF THE STAGE, | WHICH INCLUDES | A Period of Thirty-Six Years. | [rule] | By THOMAS DAVIES. | [rule] | ——Quem populus Romanus meliorem virum quam hif- | trionem effe arbitratur, qui ita digniffimus eft fcena propter | artificium, et digniffimus fit curia propter abftinentiam. | Cicero pro Q. Rofcio Comœdo. | FOURTH EDITION. | To which is added an accurate INDEX. | [rule] | VOL. I [– II]. | [total rule] | LONDON: | Printed for the Author, and sold at his Shop in Great Russell-Street, Covent-Garden. | M.DCC.LXXXIV.

2 vols., 8°

I. A–2A⁸, ($4 signed; 'Vol. I.' on $1 (–A)), 192 leaves.

Pp. Engr. port. DG front. ('J K Sherwin') + A1 t., A1ᵛ blk, A2–4 Dedication to Sheridan, A4ᵛ advert. for 4th edn., A5–8ᵛ Contents, on B1 *1* 2–354 text, 355–68 Index.

Pagination: (↑) 355–68.

Press-figures: none throughout; *Catchwords*: not recorded.

Explicit: 354 End of the First Volume. 368 THE END.

II. A–2G⁸ 2H⁴, ($4 (–2H3,4) signed; 'Vol. II.' on $1 (–A, 2B)), 244 leaves.

Pp. A1 ½t THE | LIFE | OF | DAVID GARRICK, Efq. | VOL. II., A1ᵛ blk, A2 t., A2ᵛ blk, A3–8 Contents, A8ᵛ blk, on B1 *1* 2–419 text, *420* blk, *421* 422–56 Appendix, 457–71 Index, 471 Errata, *472* blk.

Pagination: (↑) 457; *Catchwords*: not recorded.

Explicit: 471 THE END.

Paper: White, laid; small post (uncut: 7⅝ × 4¾ in.); no vis. wmk.

Type: Dedication: great primer (6.0 mm), Advertisement: english (4.9 mm), text: english (4.6 mm), notes: sm. pica (3.6 mm).

References: Arnott and Robinson (1970), 2934; ESTC: t072056.

Notes: There is no ½t for vol. 1. An invoice dated 30 Dec. 1785, from George Robinson to John Bell, of Bell & Bradfute (Edinburgh), includes '2 [Copies] Garrick's Life 2vs. 8° q[ires] 13s. 8d.' (E: MS Dep. 317, Box 1).

Copies: O (Vet. A5 e. 5102/1–2, 'Richard Smith' — William Pratten 1836' — 'H.L.F. Guermonprez Pratten legacy 1889');

USA: DFo, MH² (extra-illus.), PPL; *UK*: Gp, L³, Ljh, LVu.

80.5DMG/6   Davies's Memoirs of Garrick   1808

MEMOIRS | OF THE | LIFE | OF | DAVID GARRICK, ESQ. | INTERSPERSED WITH | [BL] Characters and Anecdotes | OF | HIS THEATRICAL CONTEMPORARIES. | THE WHOLE FORMING | *A HISTORY OF THE STAGE,* | WHICH INCLUDES A PERIOD OF THIRTY-SIX YEARS. | [medium swelled rule] | BY THOMAS DAVIES. | [medium swelled rule] | ——Quem populus Romanus meliorem virum quam histrionem | esse arbitratur, qui ita disgnissimus est scena propter artificium, ut | dignissimus sit curia propter abstinentiam. | CICERO pro Q. Roscio Comœdo. | [short parallel rule] | A NEW EDITION, | *WITH AMPLE ADDITIONS AND ILLUSTRATIONS,* | IN THE FORM OF NOTES. | [short total rule] | IN TWO VOLUMES. | VOL. I [– II]. | [medium parallel rule] | *LONDON:* | PRINTED FOR LONGMAN, HURST, REES, AND ORME, | PATERNOSTER ROW, | 1808.

2 vols., 8°

I. π⁴ A⁸ (–A8 ? blk) B–2A⁸ 2B⁸ (–2B8 ? blk), ($4 (–B1) signed; 'VOL. I.' on $1), 204 leaves.

Pp. π1 *i* ½t, *ii* blk, Engr. port. front. + π2 *iii* t., *iv* blk, *v* vi–vii Dedication to Sheridan ('April 22. 1780'), *viii* blk, *ix*–x 'Author's Advertisement (1781)', *xi*–xii Editor's Advertisement (signed 'S[tephen] J[ones]' ?), *xiii* xiv–xxi Contents, *xxii* Errata, (? *xxiii–xxiv* A8 blk), on B1 *1* 2–381 text of Life, *382* coloph: [medium rule] | S. GOSNELL, Printer, Little Queen Street., *383–4* (2B8) ?blk.

Pagination: ↑.

Press-figures: A6ᵛ(xx)–4, B8(15)–4, C8(31)–3, D8(47)–3, E2ᵛ(52)–3, F7ᵛ(78)–4, G2ᵛ(84)–5, H8ᵛ(112)–4, I6(123)–5, I7(125)–4, K1ᵛ(130)–5, K8ᵛ(144)–4, L7(157)–3, L8(159)–4, M8(175)–3, N2ᵛ(180)–3, O2ᵛ(196)–5, P8(223)–4, Q8(239)–3, R5ᵛ(250)–5, S1ᵛ(258)–4, S8ᵛ(272)–5, T3ᵛ(278)–5, U8ᵛ(304)–4, X7ᵛ(318)–5, Y5(329)–3 [*inverted*], Y7ᵛ(334)–5, Z3ᵛ(342)–3, 2B3ᵛ(374)–4.

Catchwords: none throughout.

Explicit: 381 END OF THE FIRST VOLUME.

II. π² A⁴ B–2I⁸ 2K⁴, ($4 (2G4 as GG) signed; 'VOL. II.' on $1), 258 leaves.

Pp. π1 *i* ½t, *ii* blk, *iii* t., *iv* blk, on A1 *v* vi–xii Contents, on B1 *1* 2–430 text of Life, on 2E8 *431* 432–502 Appendix, 502 coloph: as vol. 1, *503–4* advt. for Mrs Inchbald's *British Theatre*.

Pagination: ↑ as vol. 1.

Press-figures: B7(13)–3, C6(27)–4, D8(47)–4, E4ᵛ(56)–5, F8ᵛ(80)–3, G7(93)–5, H6ᵛ(108)–3, I1ᵛ(114)–5, K5ᵛ(138)–3, L1ᵛ(146)–5, M5ᵛ(170)–5, N7(189)–4, O2ᵛ(196)–3, P2ᵛ(212)–3, Q5ᵛ(234)–5, Q8ᵛ(240)–3, R5ᵛ(250)–5, R7ᵛ(254)–3, S1ᵛ(258)–3, S4ᵛ(264)–4, T8ᵛ(288)–4, U7(301)–5, X6(315)–3,

Y3^v(326)–5, Z6^v(348)–3, 2A6(363)–4, 2B5(377)–5, 2C8^v(400)–4, 2D1^v(402)–3, 2E1^v(418)–4, 2F5(441)–3, 2H8(479)–5, 2I7(493)–4, 2K1^v(498)–5.

Explicit: 502 FINIS.

Paper: White, wove; small post (uncut: 7⅝ × 4¾ in.), wmk.: '1807'.

Type: Pica (4.0 mm).

Plate: Engr. port. front. of DG after Reynolds, 'Engraved by Evans from a Picture by Sir J. Reynolds. Published by Longman and Co. 1806.'

References: J. Allen, *Bibliotheca Herefordiensis* (1821), 64.[1]

Notes: Edited by 'S. J.' [= ? Stephen Jones].

On 19 Sept. 1808, Robert Douglas, bookseller in Galashiels ordered 'Davies's Life of Garrick' for the Selkirk Library from Messrs Bell & Bradfute of Edinburgh (E: MS Dep. 317, Box 5).

Copies: O (M. Adds. 123 c. 71);

USA: CSmH, CtY, DFo, Hyde (Adam), ICU, MB, MH[2], NjP, NN, TxU, ViU; *UK*: BAT, BMp, L[3], LCu, LICj ('W. Bladon, Junr.'), MRu.

---

[1] Allen records an edition of '1801', though no such edn. is known. Garrick was b. in Hereford and properly a subject, but Allen merely mentions Davies's first edn. of 1780, and reports only the two publications of '1801', and 1808. His uneven record (cf. 74.10TH/1–2, above) makes him unreliable, and I dismiss the '1801' edn. as a fiction.

80.5DMG/7 Memoirs of Garrick, Boston 1808

Memoirs of the Life of David Garrick . . . Boston . . . 2 vols.

Not seen.

Copies: [PPL].

80.5DMG/8 Davies's Memoirs of Garrick 1818

Memoirs of the Life | OF | David Garrick, Esq. | INTERSPERSED WITH | [BL] **Characters and Anecdotes** | OF | HIS THEATRICAL CONTEMPORARIES. | THE WHOLE | Forming a History of the Stage, | WHICH INCLUDES | A PERIOD OF THIRTY-SIX YEARS. | [short rule] | By THOMAS DAVIES. | [short rule] | [Quote] | FROM THE LAST LONDON EDITION. | VOL. I [– II]. | BOSTON: | PUBLISHED BY WELLS AND LILLY. | . . . | 1818.

2 vols., 12°

I. π² 1/1*–20/20*²/⁴ 21⁴ (–21₄ ? blk), 125 leaves.

Pp. π1 *i* t., *ii* blk, *iii* iv–vii Dedication, *viii* blk, *ix–x* Advertisement, *xi*–xvii Contents, *xviii* blk, on 2₂ *13* 14–246 text.

II. π⁴ 2/2*–25/25*²/⁴ 26², 150 leaves.

Pp. π1 *i* t., *ii* blk, *iii–viii* Contents, on 2₁ *13* 14–304 text.
Notes: The CSmH copy has the dates on the tt. amended in pencil to '1823' suggesting the existence of a possible reissue with that date.[1]
Copies: CSmH (121655); *USA*: CtY, MH[2], NN.

[1] I am indebted to Prof. O M Brack for notes on this copy.

80.5DMG/TG/1   Davies's Memoirs of Garrick,   1782
                 German translation

[Fraktur] Leben | von | David Garrik | Aus dem Englifchen des Herrn Davies. | [rule] | Nach der neuften Englifchen Ausgabe. | [medium rule] | Erfter [–Zweiter] Theil. | [rule] | Leipzig, | im Schwickertfchen Verlage 1782.
2 vols., 8°

I. π1 a–b⁸ c⁴ *d⁶* A–Y⁸ (–Y8 ? blk), ($1 signed), 202 leaves.
Pp. π1 t., π1ᵛ blk, on a1 *I* II–VI Vorbericht des Ueberfetzers, *VII* VIII–XL Kurtzgefaßte Gefchichte der Englifchen Bühne, on d1 *III* IV–VI Vorbericht des Verfaffers, *VII* VIII–XIV Inhalt, on A1 ½t Nachrichten von David Garriks Leben und Character, A1ᵛ *2* blk, *3* 4–350 text, 350 Ende des erften Theils.

II. π⁴ 2π² A–2F⁸ 2G² 2H⁴, ($1 signed), 244 leaves.
Pp. π1 *I* t., *II* blk, *III* IV–XII Inhalt, on A1 *1* 2–398 text, *399* ½t Anhang, *400* blk, *401* 402–74 Anhang., 474 Ende des zweiten Theils.

Paper: White, laid; Beinenkorb (7 × 4 in.); wmk. visible but unidentified.
Type: Brevier (3.5 mm).
Notes: The last sections of vol. II might be described as: 2G⁴ (–2G3,4 + 2H⁴).
Copies: L (10825 aaa.20).

80.9TE   Election Address for Henry Thrale   1780

4 September   Election Address for Henry Thrale
  Published in *Public Advertiser*, 5 Sept.
  References: Courtney 152; *Thraliana* i. 449, 453–4; Fleeman in *Johnson, Boswell and their Circle* (1965), 185–6; *DNB* 'Missing Persons' (1993), s.n. Sir Richard Hotham (1722–99).

4 September   Election Address for Henry Thrale
  Published in *Public Advertiser*, 6 Sept.
  References: Fleeman, in *Johnson, Boswell and their Circle* (1965), 186–7.

5 September   Election Address for Henry Thrale
  MS draft dated '5 Sept.' but published in *Public Advertiser*, 7 Sept.

References: Fleeman, in *Johnson, Boswell and their Circle* (1965), 185.
MS in PPRF (*MS Handlist* 166, *MS Index* JoS 195).

80LEE   Latin Translation of Epitaph on Lady Elibank   1780

Latin translation of Epitaph on Lady Elibank.

Translated at a meeting of the Club, reported by Langton to JB, *Life* iv. 10,
477, Waingrow, 362, but without precise dating.

The epitaph was composed in English by Patrick Murray, Lord Elibank, on
Mary Margaret his wife, who died 8 June 1762. SJ produced Murray's version at
the meeting, and rendered it into Latin. The final text in Latin is on the monument in Aberlady Parish Church, E. Lothian, though the church was rebuilt in
1887 (*Life* iv. 477). Murray's seat, Ballencrieff, is in the parish, and was visited
by SJ and JB, 13–15 Nov. 1773 (*Journey* (1985), 317).

81.4BG   Baretti's Guide to the Royal Academy   [1781]

A | GUIDE | THROUGH THE | ROYAL ACADEMY, | BY | JOSEPH
BARETTI | SECRETARY FOR FOREIGN CORRESPONDENCE | TO
THE ROYAL ACADEMY. | [medium swelled rule] | LONDON: |
PRINTED BY T. CADELL, | PRINTER TO THE ROYAL ACADEMY.
| [PRICE ONE SHILLING.]

4°, A–D⁴, ($2 (–A1) signed), 16 leaves.

Pp. A1 *1* t., *2* blk, *3* 4–32 text dh: A | GUIDE | THROUGH THE |
ROYAL ACADEMY.

Pagination: [↑].

Press-figures: A4(7)–1 *or* 3, A4ᵛ(8)–3, B2ᵛ(12)–2, B4(15)–1, C1ᵛ(18)–5,
C3(21)–5, D3(29)–1, D4(31)–6.

Catchwords: *no errors*, 8 it, 16 [eſta-] bliſhed, 24 was

Explicit: 32 FINIS.

Paper: White, laid; Double post with vertical chain lines (uncut: 10¼ × 8¼
in.); no vis. wmk., but cmk.: ? small 5-pt. star.

Type: Text: small pica (3.8 mm), notes in long primer (3.25 mm).

References: Hazen 11–12; ESTC: t083915.

Notes: The variant press-fig. on A4 (p. 7), is not associated with any resetting
of the type or with any variation in the text.

The *Guide* was produced for the opening of the exhibition on 30 Apr. 1781,
and noticed in *London Mag.* xlix (Apr–Jun, 1781), *Critical Rev.* xxvi (June
1781). Hazen cites Walpole's notice of it in his letter to Mason of 6 May 1781.

SJ's contribution was at least the opening sentence.

Copies: O⁴ (John Johnson, **1.** uncut, sewn, A4–3; **2.** uncut, disbound A4–1; **3.**
cut. disbound, A4–1; **4.** Douce B 816, A4–1);

USA: CtY[2] (**1**. Im. J637. 780Gb, A4–1; **2**. ~780g, A4–3), Hyde (disbound 'William A. Jackson, 3 Dec. 1949', A4–3), ICN, [Liebert[2] (**1**. uncut, unbound, sewed, A4–3; **2**. disbound 'Jos. Spilsbury', A4–1)], MH (Lowell), NcU, NN; *UK*: Cf, Csj, L[3] (**1**. 101. i.58; **2**. 131. c.22; **3**. 679. e.10(1)), Lg, NCl.

81.4BPA   Petition for the Member for Ayrshire   1781

Petition to the House of Commons by the Member of Parliament for Ayrshire
   References: Life iv. 73–4; *Boswell Papers*, xiv. 184; *JB: Laird of Auchinleck*, 307–8, and *passim*.
   Notes: Boswell presented this petition respecting the 1780 election of Hugh Montgomerie, after consultation with and advice from SJ on Sunday, 1 April 1781. He published SJ's observation in *Life* (1791), ii. 372–3.
   Copies: Unlocated.

81.4ET   Epitaph on Henry Thrale   d. 4 April 1781

Marble monument by John Flaxman on the interior South wall of St Leonard's parish church, Streatham, erected 20 Sept. 1782. The memorial was damaged in a fire in the church in the 1980s. It is in small capitals throughout and read (1965):

HIC CONDITUR QUOD RELIQUUUM EST | HENRICI THRALE. | QUI RES SEU CIVILES SIVE DOMESTICAS ITA EGIT. | UT VITAM ILLI LONGIOREM MULTI OPTARENT. | ITA SACRAS, | UT QUAM BREVEM ESSENT HABITURAS PRÆSCIRE VIDERETUR, | SIMPLEX, APERTUS SIBIQUE SEMPER SIMILIS, | NIHIL OSTENTAVIT AUT ARTE FICTUM AUT CURA LABORATUM, | IN SENATU REGI PATRIÆQUE FIDELITER STUDIT, | VULGI OBSTREPENTIS CONTEMPTOR ANIMOSUS, | DOMI INTER MILLE MERCATURÆ NEGOTIA, LITERARUM | ELEGANTIAS MINIME NEGLEXIT. | AMICIS QUOCUNQUE MODO LABORANTIBUS, | CONSILIIS, AUCTORITATE, MUNERIBUS, ADFUIT. | INTER FAMILIARES, COMITES, CONVIVAS, HOSPITES, | TAM FACILE FUIT MORUM SUAVITATE, | UT OMNIUM ANIMOS AD SE ALLICERET; | TAM FELICIT SERMONIS LIBERTATE, | UT NULLI ADULATUS OMNIBUS PLACERET. | NATUS 1728. | OBIIT 1781. | CONSORTES TUMULI HABET RADULPHUM PATREM, | STRENUUM, PRUDENTUMQUE, VIRUM, ET HENRICUM | FULIUM UNICUM, QUEM SPEI PARENTIUM | MORS INOPINA DECENNEM PRÆRIPUIT. | ITA DOMUS FELIX ET OPULENTA, QUAM | EREXIT AVUS, AUXITQUE PATER, CUM NEPOTE | DECIDIT. | ABI LECTOR ET VICIBUS RERUM | HUMANARUM PERSPECTIS, | ÆTERNITATEM COGITA.[1]

A SJ's draft MS.[2] Though undated it was probably composed in June 1781 (*Diaries &c.*, (1958), i. 307–9). Since it has never been published a transcription follows:

Hic conditur quod reliquum eſt
Henrici Thrale
Qui res ſeu civiles ſive domeſticas ita egit
Ut illi vitam longiſsimam multi optarent,
ita ſacras
Ut quam brevis efset futura præſenſio videretur.
Simplex, apertus, ſibique ſemper ſimilis
Nihil oſtentavit aut arte fictum, aut cura laboratum.
In Senatu, Regi Patriæque fideliter ſtuduit
Vulgi obſtrepentis contemptor animoſus.
Domi inter multa mercaturæ negotia literarum
elegantias minime neglexit.
Amicis quocunque modo laborantibus
conſiliis, auctoritate, muneribus adfuit.

[f. 1ᵛ]inter Familiares, Comites, Convivas, Hoſpites
tam ſuavis fuit illi morum facilitas
ut omnium animos ad ſe alliceret;
tam grata ſermonis libertas
ut nullius adulator, omnibus placeret.
Natus
Obijt
Conſortes [tu] tumuli ha<be>t Radulphum patrem, pru-
dentem ſtrenuumque virum, et Henricum filium uni-
cum quem ſpei Parentium mors inopina decennem
præripuit. Sic domus felix et opulenta quam erexit
Avus, a[x]uxitque Pater, cum Nepote decidit. Abi,
Lector, et [hu] rerum humanarum vicibus perſpectis
Æternitatem cogita.

B Revised version (Lost: see **C**, below).

C HLT transcript in MS *Thraliana* (MS: CSmH (vol. IV); *Thraliana* i. 543), but in a revised version of **A**, and with a few transcriptional errors. It seems probable that this version is not directly copied from **A** but from an intermediate version (**B**), possibly in SJ's hand, though perhaps as likely in a transcript by HLT which SJ then corrected.[3]

D The fair copy, taken from the lost revised transcript **B**, above, and used by the sculptor, Flaxman, when cutting the memorial stone.

E The memorial stone on the wall of St Leonard's, Streatham. This exhibits a text which is centred on the slab, as was SJ's draft **A** on the page, a procedure which called for some management of the text by the sculptor, but this is, nevertheless, the only reliable version.

Printed versions soon followed:

F Henry Maty, *A New Review: with Literary Curiosities, and Literary Intelligence* . . . &c., v (Apr. 1784), 269–71, prints a version which derives from either **B** or **D** above since it shows misreadings of SJ's hand, and unaccountably produces two unwarranted readings, in l. 20, 'Natus 1724' for *Natus 1728*, and in l. 29, 'Abi Viator' for *Abi Lector*. It may be that Maty was given access to (D) which, if it had already been used by the mason, would have suffered from much dust and handling, and was no doubt less than readily legible.

G When HLT prepared her 'Anecdotes' for publication, she did not recur to the version she had transcribed in her *Thraliana* **C**, but followed Maty's *New Review*, to which she refers (pp. 133–4), and so she reports the wrong date of her husband's birth, and gives the 'Abi Viator' reading too. It is tempting to suggest that she used Maty's reading because she knew he had made use of an authoritative MS version, and that she need not therefore return to the monument itself. Her MS is a transcription from Maty (NPM: MS MA 322 p. 80), and despite the cancellation by Samuel Lysons, of sig. K in the first edition of *Anecdotes*, the text of the epitaph remains unchanged in the printed version.[4]

H George Kearsley published another version from Maty's text in his edition of *The Poetical Works of Samuel Johnson*, 1785, 192–3 (85.2PW/1, below), with a few transcriptional errors, as 'neglexerit' (line 12), for *neglexit*.

I Hawkins in *Life87*, followed HLP's *Anecdotes*, 1785, and Isaac Reed, in *Works*, xiv (1788), 544–5 (**K**), followed Hawkins, but both suffer from the corruptions in Maty's *New Review*.

K Reed's version (**I**, above) is derivative

L Daniel Lysons's *Environs of London*, (1792), i. 484 either derives from HLT's transcript **B**, which he might have acquired by the agency of his brother,[5] or from Maty's *Review*, **F**.

M Manning and Bray published a version in their *Surrey* (1814), iii. 391–2, which is evidently taken from Lysons's *Environs*, **L**, above.[6]

The stemma of this text appears to be:

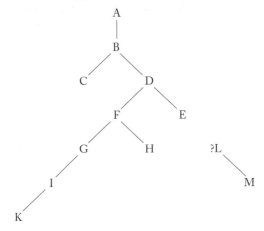

¹ *Thraliana* i. 542. Flaxman was paid £31. 13s. 4d. for the work ('Thrale Estate Book' quoted by Mary C. Hyde, *The Thrales of Streatham Park* (1977), 226 n.) It may be noted that the close of the incised epitaph does not use the words 'Abi viator' as sometimes charged, but 'Abi lector' (*Life* iv. 85 n.).

² Owned by the Hon. Diana Holland-Hibbert. I am indebted to her for permission to publish a transcription, to her late father the 4th Visc. Knutsford for the privilege of examining this MS, and to Mr Alan Bell, who first drew it to my attention. *MS Index* JoS 199. Though it comprises two leaves 4°, the epitaph occupies only the first two pp., the third p. is blank, and the 4th is docketed, 'Dr Johnson's Epitaph on *Mr Thrale* The original Copy in Dr. Johnson writing.' It has been folded and some text is lost at the folds. It is bound in a 19th-century autograph album.

³ As was the case with the epitaph on Hester Maria Salusbury, 1775 (75.6ES, above).

⁴ Clifford, *BJRL* xx (1936), 157–72, and Brownley, *BJRL* lxvii (1985), 623–40 both mention this matter, which is examined in more detail by Riely, *PQ* li (1972), 961–5.

⁵ They collaborated on the *Magna Britannia*.

⁶ F. Arnold, *The History of Streatham* (1886), 74–5, follows HLP's *Anecdotes* (G). H.W. Bromhead, *The Heritage of St Leonard's Parich Church, Streatham* (1932), gives only an English translation of the epitaph (pp. 24–5), and gives the date of birth as '1724'; he also calls HLT's mother 'Hester Lynch Salusbury' (p. 35), though correctly 'Hester Maria' on p. 37. His consultation of the inscriptions was not careful.

81.6BAR   Boswell's Answers for the Robertsons   1781

[Drop-h]: JUNE 21. 1781. | ANSWERS | FOR | THOMAS ROBERTSON Printer in Edinburgh, and | JOHN ROBERTSON alſo Printer in Edinburgh, his | Father and Adminiſtrator-in-law; | TO THE | PETITION of ROBERT GROOM Preſident, JOHN WATSON Trea- | ſurer, and the other Members of the Society of Solicitors before | the Commiſſary, Sheriff, and City Courts of Edinburgh.

4°, A–C², ($1 signed), 6 leaves.

Pp. *1* 2–12 text (signed 12: 'JAMES BOSWELL.').

Pagination: [↑], no errors; *Press-figures*: none.

Catchwords: no errors; *Explicit*: none.

Paper: White, laid; crown (uncut: 10 × 7½ in.); no vis. wmk.

Type: Scotch face: english (4.5 mm), leaded (0.3 mm).

References: *Life* iv. 129–31, 497; *Boswell Papers* ix. 226, 246, xv. 43; *JB: Laird of Auchinleck*, 407 n. 5, 409; Ballantyne, *Session Papers*, 810621.

Notes: The Robertsons were printers and proprietors of the *Caledonian Mercury* and the *Edinburgh Gazette*, which was alleged to have libelled the Society of Solicitors in its number of 28 April 1780. The Court of Session awarded damages of £20 instead of the £2,250 sued for, and this petition is for a review of the award. Other printed papers relative to the case are in Es.

SJ's contribution to the composition of this statement which is dated 21 June 1781, is on pp. 11–12 (last four paragraphs), and was again published in *Life* (1791), ii. 407–8. JB's annotated copy was discovered at Malahide Castle in 1961 and is now Hyde.¹ It was dictated to JB on 4 June 1781.² On p. 11 the Horatian phrase '*genus irritabile*' is misprinted as '*genius irritabile*', but is corrected in *Life*.

Copies: *USA*: Hyde ('Boswell'); *UK*: Es (598:7).

[1] D. Buchanan, *The Treasure of Auchinleck* (1975), 309.

[2] JB did not send his MS of what SJ dictated to him to the printer (CtY: MS Boswell, C 1604), but sent instead the printed version in which he had made one verbal change which he remarks: 'I printed it Verbatim in the Answers for Robertson against the Solicitors with the single change of *jocandi* for *irritandi*, Robertson having suggested that Blackstone holds irritating to be actionable' (*Life* iv. 130 n.).

81.7SE/1   William Shaw, Enquiry into Ossian   1781

[½t] AN | ENQUIRY | INTO THE | AUTHENTICITY | OF THE | Poems afcribed to OSSIAN. | [medium swelled rule] | [Price 1*s*. 6*d*.]

[Title] AN | ENQUIRY | INTO THE | AUTHENTICITY | OF THE | Poems afcribed to OSSIAN. | [medium swelled rule] | BY | W. SHAW, A.M. F.S.A. | Author of the GALIC DICTIONARY and GRAMMAR. | [parallel rule] | LONDON: | PRINTED FOR J. MURRAY, N° 32, FLEET-STREET. | [short rule] | M.DCC.LXXXI.

8°, *A*² B–F⁸ G⁴, ($4 (–G3,4) signed), 46 leaves.

Pp. A1 ½t, A1ᵛ blk, A2 t., A2ᵛ blk, on B1 1–87 text dh: [medium swelled rule], *88* blk.

Pagination: [↑].

Press-figures: B2ᵛ(4)–1, C7(29)–9, D1ᵛ(34)–3, E7ᵛ(62)–3, F6(75)–3.

Catchwords: no errors *Explicit*: 87 FINIS.

Paper: White, laid; Medium (uncut: 9 × 5¾ in.); no vis. wmk.

Type: English (4.7 mm), leaded.

References: Courtney 153–4; ESTC: t143497; Curley, in *Aberdeen and the Enlightenment*, edd. Carter and Pittock (1987), No. 42, 375–431, proposing SJ's involvement.

Notes: Published 7 July 1781 at 1s. 6d. (*London Chronicle*); extracts appeared in the *St James's Chronicle*, 19 June, and in the *Gents. Mag.* for June, pp. 251–2. For an episode involving Thomas Percy relative to this work, see *Lit. Illus.* vi (1831), 567–9, B.H. Davis, *Thomas Percy* (1989), 256–9, and Sher, in *Ossian Revisited*, ed. Gaskill (1991), 207–46. Shaw identified Macpherson as the intruder into McNicol's *Remarks*, 1779 (pp. 82–4).[1] This work provoked John Clark's *An Answer to Mr Shaw's Inquiry into the Authenticity of the Poems of Ossian*, late in 1781, rebutting Shaw's arguments, and provoking a pamphlet war between the two.

Copies: O (G. Pamph. 347);

USA: CtY, Hyde, ICN, ICU, MH, NN, [CLU, OCl]; *Can*: CaOHM; *UK*: ABu, E³ (1. H.M. uncut, 'Lauriston Castle' — 'Hew Morrison', no ½tt), Eu, Gu, L² (1. 1461. f.10; 2. 116. i.7), MRp; *Aust*: CNL (DNS 6990).

[1] R.F. Metzdorf, 'McNicol, Macpherson, and Johnson', in *Eighteenth-century Studies* (New York, 1970), 45–61, esp. 55–6.

81.7SE/2 Shaw's Enquiry, Dublin 1782

AN | ENQUIRY | INTO THE | AUTHENTICITY | OF THE | Poems aſcribed to Ossian. | By W. SHAW, A.M. F.S.A. | Author of the Galic Dictionary and Grammar. | PRINTED BY [**in red**: Engr. oval with 3 cherubs supporting a wreathed cartouche: 'Pat Byrne [**BL**] **Bookſeller** Stationer &c. Nº 36 College Green **Dublin**'] | M.DCC.LXXXII.

12°, *A*1 B–H¹² I⁴, ($5 signed), 89 leaves.

Pp. A1 t., A1ᵛ blk, on B1 1–172 text, on I3–4 *173–6* advts.

Pagination: [↑]; *Press-figures*: none; *Catchwords*: no errors.

Explicit: 172 FINIS.

Paper: White, laid; Lombard (uncut: 7½ × 4⅞ in.); no vis. wmk.

Type: English (4.8 mm), leaded.

References: ESTC: t115886.

Copies: O (270 g.380, + final leaves advts.);

USA: DLC (PR 3544.S5), [NcU, NN, PWW]; *UK*: C, E (OSS 208, 'Anne Palmer' — 'Richard Williams'), L (270. g.380).

81.7SE/3 Shaw's Enquiry, second London edition 1782

AN | ENQUIRY | INTO THE | AUTHENTICITY | OF THE | POEMS ascribed to OSSIAN. | WITH A | Reply to Mr. CLARK's Answer. | [medium swelled rule] | BY | W. SHAW, A.M. F.S.A. | Author of the Galic Dictionary and Grammar. | [double rule] | LONDON. | Printed for J. Murray, Nº 32 Fleet-Street. | [short rule] | M.DCC.LXXXII.

8°, π1 A–L⁴, ($2 signed), 45 leaves.

Pp. π1 t., π1ᵛ blk, on A1 *1* 2–48 text dh: AN | ENQUIRY, *&c.*, *49* ½t APPENDIX, | CONTAINING | A REPLY to Mr. CLARK., *50* blk, *51* 52–80 text dh: APPENDIX. | [medium swelled rule], *81* 82–88 text dh: APPENDIX. | [medium swelled rule].

Pagination: [↑]; *Press-figures*: none.

Catchwords: 28 *om.* (Mr.), 34 *om.* (deſtroy), 48–50 *om.*, 74 [High-] landers₍ (–,); *Explicit*: 88 FINIS.

Paper: White, laid; Demy (uncut: 8¾ × 5½ in.); no vis. wmk.

Type: Pica (4.0 mm).

References: *Life* iv. 252, 526 (Courtney 153); ESTC: t118399; *Diaries* 317.

Notes: Published 3 April 1782 (*Morning Chronicle*). Samuel Parr thought SJ helped to revise this second edition, 'The Doctor [Shaw] published two books against the authenticity of Ossian. His style, in the first, is clumsy and obscure, but in the second it was much improved, by the assistance of Dr. Johnson'.[1] The attribution is plausible, and Curley, in Carter and Pittock (1987), argues for SJ's part in the 'Appendix', i.e. the 'Reply to Clark'. Sher, in Gaskill (1991), adduces evidence from the archives of John Murray, the publisher, showing that

Murray had sent Shaw's 'Reply to Clark' in MS to Johnson, and that SJ made some alterations, though, as Sher points out, these were probably not substantial but stylistic, quoting SJ's note to Murray, 'I have done for this what can be done easily; but it cannot be made of much use' (Sher, p. 210 & refs). SJ also read, and presumably corrected the proofs (*Diaries*, 18 and 23 March 1782). The controversy continued with Clark's *An Answer to Mr Shaw's Reply*, Edinburgh, 1783, and Shaw's *A Rejoinder to an Answer from Mr Clark on the Subject of Ossian's Poems*, Rochester, 1784 (ESTC: t152127).[2] There is no evidence of SJ's further involvement.

Copies: O (G. Pamph. 333);
USA: CSmH, CtY, [PPAmP], PPL; *UK*: ABu, E[3], Eu, Gu, L (687. g.32(1)).

---

[1] *Bibliotheca Parriana* (Bohn, 1827), item 700. The catalogue was compiled by Henry S. Bohn (Cordasco, *Bohn Libraries* (1951), 103), and is at times discursively anecdotal. Parr was not a wholly reliable judge of SJ's style, cf. *Works* (Yale), ii, 'Adventurer', 330–1.
[2] Announced as a 'New publication' in *Gents. Mag.* lv (June 1785), 472, at 1s. 6d. and published by 'Crowder'.

81.11B(Part 1)/1	Beauties of Johnson,	1781
	Part 1, first edition	

THE | BEAUTIES of JOHNSON: | CONSISTING OF | MAXIMS and OBSERVATIONS, | MORAL, CRITICAL, and MISCELLANEOUS, | BY | Dr. SAMUEL JOHNSON. | (Accurately extracted from his works, and arranged in | Alphabetical Order, after the manner of the Duke de | la ROCHE-FOUCAULT's Maxims.) | [rule] | "We frequently fall into error and folly, not becaufe the true principles | "of action are not known, but becaufe for a time they are not re- | "membered: he may therefore be juftly numbered among the bene- | "factors of mankind, who CONTRACTS THE GREAT RULES OF | "LIFE INTO SHORT SENTENCES, that may be eafily impreffed | "on the memory, and taught by frequent recollection to recur habi- | "tually to the mind." | RAMBLER. | [bevelled parallel rule] | LONDON: | Printed for G. KEARSLY, at No. 46, in Fleet-ftreet. | M.DCC.LXXXI.

8°, A⁴ χ² B–2D⁴, ($2 signed), 110 leaves.

Pp. Engr. front. + A1 *i* t., *ii* blk, *iii* iv–vii Preface ('Nov. 1781'), *viii* blk, on χ1 *ix–xii* A TABLE of the SUBJECTS, ht: INDEX., on B1 *1* 2–206 text dh: [parallel rule] | MAXIMS, &c. | [medium swelled rule], *207* advt. for *The Peerage*, *208* blk.
Pagination: (↑).
Press-figures: B4ᵛ(8)–4, E3(29)–4, F1ᵛ(34)–4, G4(47)–4, H2ᵛ(52)–4, I3ᵛ(62)–4, L4(79)–4, P3(109)–4, Q4(119)–4, R3(125)–4, S4ᵛ(136)–4, T3ᵛ(142)–4, X4ᵛ(160)–4, Y2ᵛ(164)–4, Z4ᵛ(176)–4, 2A3ᵛ(182)–3, 2B3(189)–4, 2C2ᵛ(196)–4.
Catchwords: 21 BEAUTY. (B. | BEAUTY.), 63 *om*. (F. | FAME.), 91 IN- (I. | INDUSTRY.), 127 negligence‿ (~,), 189 the (pride).

Explicit: 206 THE END.

Paper: white, laid; small post (7⅝ × 4¾ in.); no vis. wmk.

Type: Pica (4.0 mm).

Plate: Engr. port. SJ (Left profile): 'Drawn from the Life by J. Harding. Etched by T. Trotter.'

References: Courtney 154–5; CH 160–1; *Rothschild* 1268; *Tinker* 1369; Hazen, *MP* xxxv (1938), 289–95; ESTC: t116315.

Notes: In the Table of Contents the sequence of cwdd. is broken at vii with 'MAXIMS' catching with B1. The complete work was eventually published in two parts (81.11B(Parts 1+2)/1, below). Part I was published 22 Nov. 1781 (*Morning Chron.*). It was probably compiled by William Cooke (Hazen, art. cit.), but SJ did not know (*Letters* 781, 15 May 82, to Lancelot St Albyn; Hyde, iv. 39-41).[1] The epigraph is from *Rambler* 175 (par. 3).

William Dodd's *Beauties of Shakespeare*, 1771, seems to have led the way to such anthologies; Kearsley had published *The Beauties of Biography*, 2 vols., 12° in 1777. No references are given for the extracts.

Copies: O (2699 e. 176, *cropt*);

USA: Hyde[2] (1. 'Wm. Nash, Royston'; 2. 'R.W. Chapman'), ICU, IU, [Liebert ('John Ireland Blackburne 1874' — 'R.W. Chapman') = CtY], NcU, NIC, NjP ('R.W. Rogers'), NN; *Can*: CaOHM ('R.W. Chapman'); *UK*: BMp (489051), Ljh.

---

[1] The apparent recommendation of suicide in an extract in the *Beauties* to which St Albyn had referred, had been raised in the *Morning Chron.*, 12 Dec. 1781, and repeated in the *Morning Herald*, 13 Dec. (McGuffie, *SJ in the British Press* (1976), 269).

81.11B(Part 1)/2   Beauties of Johnson,   1782
Part 1, second edition, first issue

THE | BEAUTIES OF JOHNSON: | CONSISTING OF | MAXIMS AND OBSERVATIONS, | MORAL, CRITICAL, AND MISCELLANEOUS, | Accurately extracted from the Works of | DR. SAMUEL JOHNSON, | and arranged in Alphabetical Order, after the manner of | the Duke de la ROCHE-FOUCAULT's Maxims. | [rule] | 'We frequently fall into error and folly, not becaufe the true principles | 'of action are not known, but becaufe for a time they are not re- | 'membered: he may therefore be juftly numbered among the bene- | 'factors of mankind, who CONTRACTS THE GREAT RULES OF | 'LIFE INTO SHORT SENTENCES, that may be eafily impreffed | 'on the memory, and taught by frequent recollection to recur habi- | 'tually to the mind.' | RAMBLER. | [rule] | SECOND EDITION, | Enlarged and corrected, and the References added. | LONDON: | Printed for G. KEARSLY, at No. 46, in Fleet-ftreet. | M.DCC.LXXXII.

12°, A–S⁶ T⁴, ($3 (–M3, Q3) signed), 112 leaves.

Pp. A1 *i* t., *ii* blk, *iii* iv–vii Preface to First Edition ('Nov. 24, 1781.'), *viii* Postscript ('December 20, 1781'), *ix–xii* Table of Subjects, on B1 *1* 2–209 text, 209 *210–11* Advts., *212* blk.

Pagination: (↑), 208 as 172; *Press-figures*: M4(127)–4.

Catchwords: 16 *om.* (Tedioufneff,), 17 *om.* (He), 21 *om.* (B.), 34 *om.* (CHANCE.), 46 *om.* (The), 63 FAME. (F. | ~.), 71 may (think), 77 courts (s *slipt*), 91 IN- (I. | INDUSTRY.), 105 *om.* (Acquifitions), 137 [de-] ftroyed; (deftroyed;), 190 fhall, (~₌).

Explicit: 209 FINIS.

Paper: White, laid; La. post (7¼ × 4 in.); no vis. wmk.

Type: Pica (4.0 mm).

Plate: Engr. port. SJ (as 81.11B(Part 1)/1): 'Drawn from the Life by J. Harding. Etched by T. Trotter'.

References: ESTC: t119481.

Notes: Published 31 December 1781 (*Morning Chron.*, noting that references had been added), following a preliminary announcement of it as 'A Christmas-Box or New-Year's Gift' in *St James's Chron.*, 22–25 Dec. 1781.

Copies: O (2699 e. 279);

USA: CtY, [Liebert ('Harriet Wynne Fletcher')]; *Can*: CaOHM ('Rippey').

81.11B(Part 1)/3   Beauties of Johnson,   1782
                              Part 1, Dublin

[½t] [row of flowers] | THE | BEAUTIES of JOHNSON, | &c. &c. | [row of flowers]

[Title] THE | BEAUTIES of JOHNSON: | CONSISTING OF | MAXIMS and OBSERVATIONS, | MORAL, CRITICAL, and MISCELLANEOUS, | BY | Dr. SAMUEL JOHNSON. | (Accurately extracted from his Works, and arranged | in Alphabetical Order, after the manner of the Duke de | la Roche-Foucault's Maxims.) | [rule] | "We frequently fall into error and folly, not becaufe the | "true principles of action are not known, but becaufe for | "a time they are not remembered: he may therefore be | "juftly numbered among the benefactors of mankind, | "who 'contracts the great rules of life into fhort fen- | 'tences,' that may be eafily impreffed on the memory, | "and taught by frequent recollection to recur habitually | "to the mind." | RAMBLER. | [double rule] | DUBLIN: | PRINTED FOR MESSRS. PRICE, WHITE- | STONE, WALKER, MONCREIFFE, GIL- | BERT, WHITE, MILLS, BEATTY, | BURTON, PARKER, | AND BYRNE. | [short rule] | M DCC LXXXII.

12°, A⁸ (A1 blk) χ⁴ B–M¹² (M12 blk), ($5 signed), 144 leaves.

Pp. A1 blk, A2 *iii* ½t, *iv* blk, *v* t., *vi* blk, *vii* viii–xv Preface, xvi blk, on χ1–4 Index, χ4ᵛ blk, on B1 *1* 2–262 text dh: [double rule] | MAXIMS, &c. | [short swelled rule], *263–4* (M12) blk.

Pagination: [↑]; *Press-figures*: none; *Catchwords*: no errors.
Explicit: 262 THE END.
Paper: White, laid; La. post (7 × 4½ in.); wmk.: fleur-de-lys.
Type: Pica (4.0 mm).
References: ESTC: t186151.
Notes: The paper appears to be English. The extracts are still without refer-
ences.
Copies: O (Vet. A5 e. 5001);
USA: CtY, NcU ('Isabella Moutray'); *UK*: BMp (563230); *Eir*: Dt (190
u.106).

81.11B(Part 1)/4   Beauties of Johnson, Part 1,   1782
                      second ['third'] London edition, second issue

THE | BEAUTIES of JOHNSON: | CONSISTING OF | MAXIMS and
OBSERVATIONS, | MORAL, CRITICAL, and MISCELLANEOUS, |
Accurately extracted from the Works of | Dr. SAMUEL JOHNSON, | and
arranged in Alphabetical Order, after the manner of | the Duke de la ROCHE-
FOUCAULT's Maxims. | [rule] | "We frequently fall into error and folly, not
becaufe the true principles | "of action are not known, but becaufe for a time
they are not re- | "membered: he may therefore be juftly numbered among the
bene- | "factors of mankind, who CONTRACTS THE GREAT RULES OF | "LIFE INTO
SHORT SENTENCES, that may be eafily impreffed | "on the memory, and taught
by frequent recollection to recur habi- | "tually to the mind." | RAMBLER. |
[rule] | THIRD EDITION, | Enlarged and corrected, and the References
added. | [rule] | LONDON: | Printed for G. KEARSLY, at No. 46, in Fleet-
ftreet. | M.DCC.LXXXII.

12°, A⁶ (± A4) B–S⁶ T⁴ (–T4 ? = 'A4'), ($3 (–M3, Q3) signed), 112 leaves.

Pp. A1 *i* t., *ii* blk, *iii* iv–vii Preface to First Edition ('Nov. 24, 1781.'), *viii*
Advertisement to the Third Edition, *ix–xii* Table of Subjects, on B1 *1* 2–209
text, 209–*210* advts.

Pagination: (↑), 208 as 172; *Press-figures*: M4(127)–4.

Catchwords: 16 *om.* (Tedioufneff,), 17 *om.* (He), 21 *om.* (B.), 34 *om.*
(CHANCE.), 46 *om.* (The), 63 FAME. (F. | ~.), 71 may (think), 77 courts (s
slipt), 91 IN- (I. | INDUSTRY.), 105 *om.* (Acquifitions), 137 [de-] ftroyed;
(deftroyed;), 190 fhall, (~ₐ).

Explicit: 209 FINIS.

Paper: White, laid; La. post (7¼ × 4 in.); no vis. wmk.

Type: Pica (4.0 mm).

Plate: Engr. port. SJ (as 81.11B(Part 1)/1): 'Drawn from the Life by J.
Harding. Etched by T. Trotter.

References: Courtney 154; ESTC: t116316.

Notes: A reissue of the 2nd. edn. (81.11B(Part 1)/2, above) with a reworded t., and a new 'Advertisement to the Third Edition' on p. viii (A4). Published 21 January 1782, at 2s. (*Morning Chron.*). On the wrappers of NIC copy is an engr. t: 'Beauties | of | Johnson. | Price Two Shillings.'

Copies: O (Vet. A5 f. 1236);

USA: [Liebert ('George Chetwynde' — R.W. Chapman) = CtY], NIC (uncut, blue wrappers); *Can*: CaOHM ('Rippey'); *UK*: BMp (876743), C ('John Dorrington' 'Lypiatt Park 349'), L, NCu; *Aust*: CNL (DNS 4758).

81.11B(Part 1)/5   Beauties of Johnson,   1782
Part 1, second ['fourth'] London edition, third issue

THE | BEAUTIES of JOHNSON: | CONSISTING OF | MAXIMS and OBSERVATIONS, | MORAL, CRITICAL, and MISCELLANEOUS, | Accurately extracted from the Works of | Dr. SAMUEL JOHNSON, | And arranged in Alphabetical Order, after the manner of | the Duke de la ROCHE-FOUCAULT's Maxims. | [rule] | "We frequently fall into error and folly, not becaufe the true principles | "of action are not known, but becaufe for a time they are not re- | "membered: he may therefore be juftly numbered among the bene- | "factors of mankind, who CONTRACTS THE GREAT RULES OF | "LIFE INTO SHORT SENTENCES, that may be eafily impreffed | "on the memory, and taught by frequent recollection to recur habi- | "tually to the mind." | RAMBLER. | [rule] | FOURTH EDITION, | Enlarged and corrected, and the References added. | [rule] | LONDON: | Printed for G. KEARSLY, at No. 46, in Fleet-ftreet. | M.DCC.LXXXII.

12°, A⁶ (± A1, A4) B–S⁶ T⁴, ($3 (–M3, Q3, R3) signed), 112 leaves.

Pp. Engr. front. (as 81.11B(Part 1)/2) + A1 *i* t., *ii* blk, *iii* iv–vii Preface to First Edition ('*November* 24, 1781.'), *viii* Advertisement to the Fourth Edition ('February 9, 1782'), *ix–xii* A Table of the Subjects, on B1 *1* 2–209 text, 209–*210* advts, 211–*12* blk.

References: Courtney 154; CH 160–1; *Tinker* 1372; ESTC: t064463.

Notes: A reissue of the sheets and frontispiece of 81.11B(Part 1)/2, above, with new t., and advert. leaf on p. viii. Published 19 February 1782, at 2s. (*Morning Chron.*). Advt. on 209 for Part II, as 'In the Press, and speedily will be published'.

Copies: O (2699 f. 249(1));

USA: CtY, Hyde³ (1. Adam; 2. 'J.B. Lowe', no front.; 3. Adam, no front.), NIC; *UK*: JDF ('Ino. Grant', uncut); *Aust*: CNL (DNS 4758).

81.11B(Part 1)/6   Beauties of Johnson,   1782
Part 1, third ['fifth'] London edition, first issue

[Engr. t.] ——*The*—— | Beauties of Johnson: | *consisting* of | [BL] **Maxims** and **Observations** | *Moral, Critical, & Miscellaneous,* | accurately extracted from the works of | *D': Samuel Johnson,* | And arranged in Alphabetical order, | *after the manner of the Duke de la Roche Foucault's Maxims.* | *THE FIFTH EDITION*, | *Enlarged and Corrected.* | [circle containing head of SJ, after Trotter] | [BL] **LONDON** | *Printed for G. Kearsley Fleet Street* —— *1782* | *Harman Scrip:* | Price Half a Crown Sewed.

12°, a⁶ A–U⁶, ($3 signed), 126 leaves.

Pp. Engr. t. + a1 *i–v* A Table of the Subjects, *vi* blk, on a4 ² *iii* iv–vii Preface to the First Edition ('November 24th 1781.'), *viii* Advertisement to the Fifth Edition ('April 16th, 1782'), on A1 ³*vii* viii–xv Memoirs of the Life and Writings of Dr. Samuel Johnson, *xvi–xvii* Kearsly's advts., *xviii* blk, on B1 *1* 2–228 text *Beauties &c.*, 228 advts. for *Beauties of Sterne,* and *Beauties of Goldsmith, Fielding, and Watts.*

Pagination: (↑) a, B–U (sloped parens as **a** (↑) 13, 19, 56, 59; **b** (↑) 18, 28, 54, 58, 68; **c** (↑) 3, 4, 44, 60, 61); [↑] A; (↑) 8.

Press-figures: none.

Catchwords: 23 [prin-] ting (*slipt*) (ing), 142 negli- (negligence,), 164 PRE- (PERFECTION.), 176 *om.* (Though), 177 Whoever (*slack*) (Whoſoever), 182 expences (s *slipt*), 194 SOLI- (SEDUCTION.), 195 many (y *slipt*).

Explicit: 228 FINIS.

Paper: White, laid; La. post (7 × 4½ in.); no vis. wmk.

Type: Pica (4.0 mm).

References: Brack and Kelley, *Early Biographies of SJ* (1974), 122; ESTC: n015747.

Notes: Some additional material taken from the Notes to SJ's *Shakespeare.* Published 23 April, 1782 with Part II as 2 vols. @ 5s., or 2s. 6d. each.

Copies: O (2699 e. 187 (1));

USA: Hyde (Adam), NIC, NjP; *UK*: JDF ('Mary Whitley' — 'Mary Parry, Mold, Flintshire, N. Wales'), Op ('Vernon').

81.11B(Part 1)/7   Beauties of Johnson,   1782
Part 1, third ['sixth'] London edition, second issue

[Engr. t.] ——*The*—— | Beauties of Johnson: | *consisting* of | [BL] **Maxims** and **Observations** | *Moral, Critical, & Miscellaneous,* | accurately extracted from the works of | *D': Samuel Johnson,* | And arranged in Alphabetical order, | *after the manner of the Duke de la Roche Foucault's Maxims.* | *THE SIXTH EDITION*, | *Enlarged and Corrected.* | [circle containing head of SJ, after Trotter] | [BL]

LONDON | *Printed for G. Kearsley Fleet Street —— 1782* | *Harman Scrip:* | Price Half a Crown Sewed.

12°, a⁶ A–U⁶, ($3 signed), 126 leaves.

Pp. Engr. t. + a1 *i–v* Table of Subjects, *vi* blk, on a4 ²*iii* iv–vii Preface, on a6ᵛ *viii* Advertisement to the Fifth Edition, on A1 ³*vii* viii–xv Memoirs of Johnson, *xvi–xvii* Kearsly's advts, *xviii* blk, on B1 *1* 2–228 text of Beauties, 228 advt. for *Beauties of Sterne*.

References: ESTC: t075745.

Notes: A reissue of the 'fifth' edn. 1782 (81.11B(Part 1)/6, above), with new engr. t. Published 1 Aug. 1782.

Copies: O (2699 e. 217);

USA: CtY, Hyde ('John Knott M.D.' — Adam), MB, NIC; *UK*: BMp (561717), Csj, L (1490 pp.17), Ljh.

81.11B(Part 2)/1   Beauties of Johnson,   1782
                        Part 2, first edition

[½t] [med. swelled rule] | THE BEAUTIES OF JOHNSON. | PART II: | With the Head of the Author, drawn from Life, and etched. | [med. swelled rule] | [Price Two Shillings and Six pence, sewed.]

[Title] THE | BEAUTIES OF JOHNSON: | CONSISTING OF | MAXIMS AND OBSERVATIONS, | MORAL, CRITICAL, AND MISCELLANEOUS, | Accurately extracted from the Works of | Dʀ. SAMUEL JOHNSON, | And arranged in Alphabetical Order, after the Manner | of the Duke de la Roche-Foucault's Maxims. | [rule] | "We frequently fall into error and folly, not becaufe the true | "principles of action are not known, but becaufe for a time | "they are not remembered: he may therefore be juftly num- | "bered among the benefactors of mankind, who contracts | "ᴛʜᴇ ɢʀᴇᴀᴛ ʀᴜʟᴇs ᴏꜰ ʟɪꜰᴇ ɪɴᴛᴏ sʜᴏʀᴛ sᴇɴᴛᴇɴᴄᴇs, | "that may be eafily impreffed on the memory, and taught by | "frequent recollection to recur habitually to the mind." | Rᴀᴍʙʟᴇʀ. | [rule] | PART II. | [parallel rule] | LONDON, | Printed for G. Kᴇᴀʀsʟʏ, at No. 46, in Fleet ftreet. | M.DCC.LXXXII.

12°, A–S⁶, ($3 (–A1, D3, N3, S3; H3 as H5) signed; 'Part II.' on $1), 108 leaves.

Pp. Engr. front. + on A1 *i* ½t, *ii* blk, *iii* t., *iv* blk, *v–vi* Advertisement ('February 9, 1782'), *vii* viii–x Table of the Subjects, *xi* blk, *xii* advt. for *The Beauties of Sterne*, on B1 *1* 2–204 text, 204 advt. for Chesterfield's *Letters upon Ancient History*.

Pagination: (↑) except in A; *Press-figures*: none.

Catchwords: 30 *om.* (COMPLAINT.), 31 *om.* (He), 45 *om.* (EUROPEAN), 79 *om.* (HEALTH.), 83 *om.* (INNOCENCE.), 84 *om.* (There), 87 *om.* (The),

94 *om.* (K.), 101 LEARN- (LIBERTY.), 131 *om.* (PLAYER.), 136 *om.* (*Boſſu*), 154 *om.* (The), 184 *om.* (The), 195 *om.* (The).

Explicit: 204 FINIS.

Paper: White, laid; La. post (7¼ × 4 in.); no vis. wmk.

Type: Pica (4.0 mm).

Plate: Engr. port. SJ (in sepia), 'Drawn from the Life by J. Harding Etch'd by T. Trotter. Publish'd as the Act directs by G. Kearsly N°. 46 Fleet Street Feby. 10th. 1782.'

References: Courtney 154; ESTC: t064462.

Notes: Published 19 February 1782, together with the 'Fourth' edition of Part I (81.11B(Part 1)/5 above)

Copies: O² (1. Vet. A5. f. 1237; 2. 2699 e. 215(2));

USA: CtY, Hyde³ (1. 'R.W. Chapman'; 2. 'J. B. Lowe'; 3. Adam), [Liebert], NIC; *Can*: CaOHM; *UK*: C, JDF ('Mary Whitley' — 'Mary Parry, Mold, Flintshire'), Op ('Vernon').

81.11B(Part 2)/2   Beauties of Johnson,   1782
Part 2, first edition, second issue

THE | BEAUTIES of JOHNSON: | CONSISTING OF | MAXIMS and OBSERVATIONS, | MORAL, CRITICAL, and MISCELLANEOUS, | Accurately extracted from the Works of | Dr. SAMUEL JOHNSON, | And arranged in Alphabetical Order, after the Manner | of the Duke de la Roche-Foucault's Maxims. | [rule] | "We frequently fall into error and folly, not becauſe the true | "principles of action are not known, but becauſe for a time | "they are not remembered: he may therefore be juſtly num- | "bered among the benefactors of mankind, who contracts | "the great rules of life into short sentences, | "that may be eaſily impreſſed on the memory, and taught by | "frequent recollection to recur habitually to the mind." | Rambler. | [rule] | PART II. | [rule] | THE SECOND EDITION. | [parallel rule] | LONDON, | Printed for G. Kearsly, at No. 46, in Fleet-ſtreet. | M.DCC.LXXXII.

12°, A⁶ (± A2) B–S⁶, ($3 (–A1, D3, N3, S3; H3 as H5) signed; 'Part. II.' on $1), 108 leaves.

References: ESTC: n032418.

Notes: A reissue of 81.11B(Part 2)/1, above with a cancelled t., but no other changes. Published 23 April 1782, together with the 'Fifth' edition of Part I (81.11B(Part 1)/6, above)

Copies: O (2699 f. 279); *USA*: Hyde (Adam, −A1.6), NIC.

81.11B(Part 2)/3　　　　Beauties of Johnson,　　　　1782
Part 2, first edition, third issue

[Engr. t.] *THE* | Beauties of Johnson, | ——*Confifting of*—— | [BL]
Maxims, Obfervations | &c. &c. | *THE FIFTH EDITION.* | Part II. |
[medium swelled rule] | LONDON: | Printed for G. Kearsly, in Fleet Street.
| 1782. | *Price 2ˢ 6ᵈ Sewed.* | [short orn. flourish]

　　12°, A⁶ (± A2) B–S⁶, ($3 (–A1, D3, N3, S3; H3 as H5) signed; 'Part II.' on
$1), 108 leaves.

　　References: ESTC: t141519.

　　Notes: Another issue with new engraved t. of the first edn. of Part II
(81.11B(Part 2)/1, above).

　　Copies: O (2699 e.187 (2));

　　USA: CtY, Hyde ('John Knott', imperfect lacks front. and A1), MB; *UK*: Csj,
L (1490. pp. 17), LICj.

81.11B(Parts 1+2)/1　　　Beauties of Johnson,　　　　1787
Two Parts in One, 'seventh' edition

A NEW EDITION, being the SEVENTH, | WHEREIN THE TWO
VOLUMES ARE COMPRISED IN | ONE, AND ARRANGED UNDER
ONE ALPHABET, | WITH CONSIDERABLE ADDITIONS. | [medium
swelled rule] | the | BEAUTIES | of | *Samuel Johnfon*, ll.d. | CONSISTING
OF | MAXIMS and OBSERVATIONS, | Moral, Critical, and
Miscellaneous, | TO WHICH ARE NOW ADDED, | BIOGRAPHICAL
ANECDOTES | OF THE | DOCTOR, | SELECTED FROM | THE
LATE PRODUCTIONS OF | Mrs. Piozzi, Mr. Boswell, | AND OTHER
AUTHENTIC TESTIMONIES. | ALSO, | HIS WILL, AND THE SER
MON HE WROTE FOR THE | LATE DOCTOR DODD. | [medium
parallel rule] | LONDON. | PRINTED FOR G. KEARSLEY, NO. 46, FLEET
STREET. | *Price Three Shillings and Sixpence fewed.* | MDCCLXXXVII.

　　12°, a–f⁶ g⁴ B–2C⁶, ($3 signed), 190 leaves.

　　Pp. Engr. front. port. + a1 *iii* t., *iv* blk, on a2 *v* Advertisement ('November
6, 1786.'), *vi* vii–viii Preface, *ix* x–xiv Contents, *xv* xvi–lxvii Biographical
Anecdotes, lxviii–lxix Dodd's Speech to the Court, lxx–lxxx text: Convict's
Address, *lxxxi–lxxxii* advts., on B1 *1* 2–294 text: Beauties &c., + engr. leaf:
facsimile of SJ's handwriting + *295* 296–97 Catalogue of SJ's Works, 297
298–300 Kearsley's advts.

　　Pagination: 1 as 'L'.

　　Press-figures; *Catchwords*; *Explicit*: not recorded.

　　Paper: White, laid; La. Post (7 × 4½ in.).

　　Type: Not recorded.

Plates: 1. Engr. port. SJ, after Trotter: 'Samuel Johnson, *L.L.D.* From the original Drawing, in the poffeffion of Mr. John Simco. taken from the life, a Short time before his decease, and Etched by T. Trotter. Price 1ˢ. Publish'd as the Act directs Novʳ. 16. 1786, by G. Kearsley, Nᵒ. 46 Fleet Street, London.';

2. Facsimiles of SJ's handwriting (i.e. *Letters* 782, SJ — Kearsley, 20 May 1782).

References: Courtney 155; Hazen, *MP* xxxv (1938), 289–95; Pottle, *Literary Career of JB* (1929), § 106, p. 201; ESTC: t116308.

Notes: George Kearsley I died in 1790, so this is the last edn. for which he could have any direct responsibility, though his widow Catherine (who seems to have d. about 1796), and son George, continued in business until 1813 (Maxted 127). The additional material, pp. xxvii–xlvi, allegedly from Boswell's *Tour* is really from *Johnson's Table Talk* (Pottle § 69)[1], and is not entirely authentic.

Copies: *USA*: CLU, Hyde, [Liebert = CtY], NIC, NRU[2], WiM (lacks pp. 215–16); *Can*: CaOHM; *Japan*: [Kyoto]; *UK*: BMp, C, Ljh, Oef.

---

[1] Compiled by D.E. McDonnell (Lustig, *PBSA* lxxi (1977), 83–8). His receipt for the work, dated 24 Dec. 1785, is MS Hyde.

81.11B(Parts 1+2)/2   Beauties of Johnson,   1787
Philadelphia

The Beauties of Johnson: consisting of maxims and observations, moral, critical, and miscellaneous. By Dr. Samuel Johnson. (Accurately extracted from his Works, and arranged in alphabetical order, after the manner of the Duke de la Roche-foucault's Maxims.) To which is prefixed, The Life of Dr. Johnson; with some Papers written by him, in behalf of a late unfortunate Character. Philadelphia: Printed by W. Spotswood. MDCCLXXXVII.

12°, Pp. Engr. port. & t., + *1 ½*t, *3* t., *5* 6–103 Life of SJ (inc. Catalogue of his Works, 100–3), *104* blk, [2] *1* 2–138 text of Beauties, *139–43* Index, *144* advt. Not examined.

References: Hazen (1938), 295; Evans 20433; ESTC: w023115.
Copies: *USA*: [CtY, MWA, PPL, PSC, RPJCB].

81.11B(Parts 1+2)/3   Beauties of Johnson,   1792
'eighth' edition

A NEW EDITION, being the EIGHTH, | WHEREIN THE TWO VOLUMES ARE COMPRISED IN | ONE, AND ARRANGED UNDER ONE ALPHABET, | WITH VERY CONSIDERABLE ADDITIONS. | THE | BEAUTIES | of | *Samuel Johnſon*, LL.D. | CONSISTING OF | MAXIMS AND OBSERVATIONS, | *MORAL, CRITICAL, and MISCELLANEOUS:* |

TO WHICH ARE NOW ADDED, | BIOGRAPHICAL ANECDOTES | OF THE | DOCTOR, | SELECTED FROM | The Works of Mrs. PIOZZI; —His LIFE, | recently published by Mr. BOSWELL, | and other authentic Testimonies, | ALSO, | HIS WILL, AND THE SER MON HE WROTE FOR THE | LATE DOCTOR DODD. | [medium parallel rule] | LONDON: | PRINTED FOR C. AND G. KEARSLEY, NO. 46, | FLEET-STREET. | [dash] | M DCC,XCII.   *Stet*: M͵DCC,XCII.

12°, a¹² (± a4) b–d¹² e⁶ f⁴ (–f4 = 'a4') B–N¹² O⁶, ($6 (–e, f, N6) signed), 207 leaves.

Pp. Engr. front. port. + a1 *iii* t., *iv* blk, on a2 *v* Advertisement and note on this edn., *vi* vii–viii Preface, *ix* x–xiv Contents, *xv* xvi–cii Biographical Anecdotes, ciii–civ Dodd's Speech to the Court, cv–cxv Convict's Address, *cxvi* advt., + facs. of SJ's handrwiting + on B1 *1* 2–294 text: Beauties &c., *295* Catalogue of SJ's Works, 296–300 Kearsley's advts.

Pagination: (↑); *Press-figures*: none; *Catchwords*: not recorded.

Explicit: 294 *The End of the Beauties*.

Paper: White, laid; La. post (7 × 4½ in.); no vis. wmk.

Type: Preface: pica (4.0 mm), text: long primer (3.3), references: brevier (2.6).

Plates: Engr. port. SJ. front., and facs. of SJ's handwriting, as 7th edn. 1787 (81.11B(Parts 1+2)/1, above)

References: Courtney 155; Hazen (1938), 295; Pottle, *Literary Career of JB* (1929) §106, pp. 200–1; ESTC: t116309.

Notes: A reprint of '7th' edition of 1787, with additional material (pp. li–lxxx, and xcv–xcvii), derived from Boswell's *Life*, 1791. The origin of the *cancellans* 'a4' (first leaf of 'Contents'), is demonstrated by the Hyde (Fergusson — Adam) copy which contains the *cancellandum* as a4, and the *cancellans* bound as f4.

Copies: O (Vet A5. f. 1783);

USA: Hyde² (1. 'W.J.C.' — 'James R. Fergusson' — Adam; 2. 'Neville Fellows Beard' — 'Kingsford'), [Liebert ('E. Dinsdale') = CtY], NIC, NjP, NRU, PU, TxU; *Can*: CaOHM²; *UK*: BAT, BMp (472061); *Aust*: CNL (DNS 4806).

81.11B(Parts 1+2)/4   Beauties of Johnson,   1797
'ninth' edition

A NEW EDITION, being the NINTH, | WHEREIN THE TWO VOLUMES ARE COMPRISED IN | ONE, AND ARRANGED UNDER ONE ALPHABET, | WITH VERY CONSIDERABLE ADDITIONS. | THE | BEAUTIES | OF | *Samuel Johnſon*, LL.D. | CONSISTING OF | MAXIMS and OBSERVATIONS, | *MORAL, CRITICAL, and MISCELLANEOUS:* | TO WHICH ARE NOW ADDED, | BIOGRAPHICAL ANECDOTES | OF THE | DOCTOR, | SELECTED FROM | The Works of Mrs. PIOZZI; His LIFE, | recently published by Mr. BOSWELL, | and

OTHER AUTHENTIC TESTIMONIES, | ALSO, | HIS WILL, AND THE SER
MON HE WROTE FOR THE | LATE DOCTOR DODD. | [medium
parallel rule] | LONDON: | PRINTED FOR G. KEARSLEY; J. WALKER;
| J. SCATCHARD; VERNOR & HOOD; LEE | & HURST; LACKING-
TON, ALLEN, | & CO. and HAMILTON & CO. | [short swelled rule] |
M,DCC,XCVII.

12°, a–d¹² e⁸ (e4 + 'e5') B–N¹² O⁶, ($6 (–e6) signed), 207 leaves.

Pp. Engr. port. front. + on a1 *i* t., *ii* blk, on a2 *v* Advertisement, *vi* vii–viii
Preface, *ix* x–xiv Contents, *xv* xvi–cii Biographical Anecdotes, ciii–civ Dodd's
Speech to the Court, cv–cxv Convict's Address, *cxvi* blk + facs. of SJ's handwriting + on B1 *1* 2–294 text: Beauties &c., *295* Catalogue of SJ's Works,
296–300 Kearsley's advts.

Pagination: (↑).

Press-figures: a11ᵛ(xxii)–3, a12ᵛ(xxiv)–1, b11(xlv)–1, c1ᵛ(l)–4, c12ᵛ(lxxii)–3,
d12ᵛ(xcvi)–2, e1ᵛ(xcviii)–3, e8(cxi)–5, B5(9)–5, B8ᵛ(16)–4, C12(47)–5,
C12ᵛ(48)–3, D2ᵛ(52)–3, D12(71)–1, E7ᵛ(86)–1, E8ᵛ(88)–5, F11ᵛ(118)–3,
G12(143)–4, G12ᵛ(144)–3, H6ᵛ(156)–4, H10(163)–3, I12(191)–3,
I12ᵛ(192)–5, K12ᵛ(216)–1, L11(237)–1, L12(239)–4, M2ᵛ(244)–3, M8(255)–4,
N4ᵛ(272)–2, N11ᵛ(286)–3.

Catchwords: not recorded; *Explicit*: 294 THE END.

Paper: White, laid; La. post (7 × 4½ in.); no vis. wmk.

Type: Preface: pica (4.0mm), text: long primer (3.6 mm), references: brevier
(2.5 mm).

Plates: Engr. port. front., and facs. of SJ's hand, as 81.11B(Parts 1+2)/1, above.

References: Courtney 155; Hazen (1938), 295; ESTC: t116664.

Copies: O (Vet. A5 e.2161);

USA: DFo, DLC, Hyde² (1. 'Barry' — 'L.F. Powell';[1] 2. 'Kemp' — Adam,
imperfect), IU, [Liebert = CtY], MH, PPL; *UK*: BMp (497734); *Aust*: CNL
(DNS 4807).

---

[1] Powell noted in my copy of *Catalogus Bibliothcae Hydeianae* (1965), iii. 457, 'Barry was I believe
the artist. I noticed there was a mark in the margin against his name L.F.P.'

81.11B(Parts 1+2)/5   Beauties of Johnson,   1804
new edition

THE | BEAUTIES | OF | [hollow] SAMUEL JOHNSON, LL. D. |
CONSISTING OF | MAXIMS and OBSERVATIONS, | *Moral, Critical.*
and Miscellaneous, | TO WHICH ARE NOW ADDED, | Biographical
Anecdotes of the Doctor, | SELECTED FROM | *THE WORKS OF MRS.*
PIOZZI, | His LIFE recently published by Mr. BOSWELL, | And other
authentic Testimonies, | ALSO | HIS WILL, | AND THE | SERMON HE
WROTE FOR THE LATE DR. DODD. | [short swelled rule] | A NEW

EDITION. | [short swelled rule] | *LONDON;* | Printed for G. KEARSLEY; J. WALKER; SCATCHARD and | LETTERMAN; LACKINGTON, ALLEN, and Co.; LONGMAN, | HURST, and Co.; and B. CROSBY. | 1804. | [short swelled rule] | W. Thorne, Printer, Red Lion Court, Fleet Street.

12°, A⁶ B–R¹² S⁶, ($6 signed), 204 leaves.

Pp. Engr. port. front. + A1 *i* t., *ii* blk, *iii* Advertisement, *iv* v–vi Preface, *vii* viii–xii Contents, on B1 *1* 2–88 Biographical Anecdotes, 89–90 Dodd's Speech to the Court, 91–101 Convict's Address, *102* blk, 103–394 text: Beauties &c.

Pagination: [↑];

Press-figures: B8(15)–2, E7(85)–2, F11ᵛ(118)–2, I12ᵛ(192)–2, L6ᵛ(228)–2, M7(253)–2, N11ᵛ(286)–2, P7ᵛ(326)–2.

Catchwords: 10 reply;) (reply):), 41 *om.* (and), 101 *om.* (BEAUTIES,), 243 which (those), 319 accurate (observer,), 357 SHAKSPEA‸E. (SHAKSPEARE.).

Explicit: 394 THE END.

Paper: White, wove; medium (7⅝ × 4½ in.).

Type: Long primer (3.2 mm), 'Beauties' small pica (3.6 mm).

Plate: As in 7th edn. 1787 (81.11B(Parts 1+2)/1, above).

References: Courtney 155; Hazen (1938), 295.

Copies: O (2699 e. 114);

USA: Hyde² (1. 'Godfrey Massy' — Adam, uncut; 2. 'Johnson's Hill Mission School, South Shields'), [Liebert = CtY], NIC, NjP, NN, NRU, TxU; *Japan*: [Kyoto]; *UK*: AWn, BMp² (1. 60642; 2. 467489), BRp, Ep, JDF², STA.

81.11B(Parts 1+2)/6   Beauties of Johnson,   1817
                       Beauties of Literature, Vol. 23

The Beauties of Literature, vol. 23.

The Beauties of Johnson, consisting of selections from his works. By Alfred Howard, Esq. London: Printed by T. Davison, for Thomas Tegg, no. 73, Cheapside; R. Griffin and Co. Glasgow; and J. Cumming, Dublin. [n.d.]

12°, *A*² B–H¹² I¹⁰, ($1,5 ($5 as $2), signed), 96 leaves.

Pp. Engr. front. port. SJ 'Engraved by W.T. Fry Published by Thoˢ. Tegg, Cheapside.' + A1 t., A1ᵛ blk, A2 *iii*–iv Contents, on B1 *1* 2–188 text. *Explicit*: 188 THE END. coloph: LONDON: | PRINTED BY THOMAS DAVISON, WHITEFRIARS.

References: [? Courtney 155].

Notes: See below 81.11B(Parts 1+2)/12 and 15. Issued in ptd. brown boards at 7s. per volume.

Copies: L (1506/649; 'J.L. Scott' — 'Blanche Hartnell 1923').

UK: BMp (518887, undated), JDF (undated, 'Mrs Sharp Fern Hall').

81.11B(Parts 1+2)/7   Beauties of Johnson,   1819
                                 Glasgow

The Beauties of Samuel Johnson, LL.D. consisting of Maxims and
Observations, Moral, Critical, and Miscellaneous. A New Edition. Glasgow:
Printed by W. Falconer, for James Scott, Bookseller, Cross. 1819

  Var: The Beauties . . . L.L.D. . . . . Moral ∧ Critical, . . . Edinburgh: Printed
for J. Robertson, Parliament Square, and T. & J. Allman, London. 1819.

  12°, π1 A⁴ B–N¹² O², ($5 (–E3,4, FG4, H3, IKLM4, N3,4) signed), 151 leaves.

  Pp. π1 t., π1ᵛ blk, on A1 *v*–vi Preface to the First Edition ('The Editor,
November 24th, 1781.'), *vii* viii–xii Contents, on B1 *13* 14–304 text, 304
  Explicit: THE END.
  References: Courtney 155; Hazen (1938), 295.
  Notes: On 4 May 1922 R.W.Chapman told D. Nichol Smith, 'I have *A New
Edition Edinburgh* 1819. It has no biographical section. RWC.' (*Aust*: CNL —
DNS copy of *Courtney*). Both tt. are singletons, but the 'Edinburgh' t. is on
paper distinct from the sheets of the volume, and is presumed a substitute and
therefore the variant, from the 'Glasgow' norm; but priority is not established.
  Copies: *UK*: BMp² (**1**. 469803, Glasgow; **2**. 561718, Edinburgh).

81.11B(Parts 1+2)/8   Beauties of Johnson,   1828
                                 new edition

THE | BEAUTIES | OF | *SAMUEL JOHNSON, LL.D.* | CONSISTING
OF | MAXIMS AND OBSERVATIONS, | *Moral, Critical, and Miscellaneous;*
| TO WHICH ARE NOW ADDED, | BIOGRAPHICAL ANECDOTES
OF THE DOCTOR, | SELECTED FROM | THE WORKS OF Mʀs.
PIOZZI, | HIS LIFE BY MR. BOSWELL, | [BL] **And other authentic
Testimonies;** | ALSO, | THE SPEECH AND SERMON | HE WROTE
FOR THE LATE DR. DODD. | [short rule] | A NEW EDITION. | [short
rule] | LONDON: | PRINTED AND PUBLISHED BY J. KAY, | 95,
WOOD STREET, CHEAPSIDE. | 1828.

  18°, *A*⁶ B–R⁹ S², ($5 &c.), 152 leaves.

  Pp. A1 *i* ½t, *ii* blk + Engr. front. port. (SJ after Reynolds: 'Sʳ. J. Reynolds
pinxᵗ. L. How. Sculpᵗʳ'), + A2 *iii* t., *iv* blk, *v*–vi Preface, *vii* viii–xii Index, on
B1 *1* 2–102 Biographical anecdotes, *103* 104–292 text: Beauties &c., 292
coloph: Printed by J. Kᴀʏ, 95, Wood Street, Cheapside.
  Pagination: no errors; *Press-figures*: none; *Catchwords*: none.
  Explicit: 292 THE END.
  Paper: White, wove; royal (6⅝ × 4¼ in.); wmk.: '1826'.
  Type: Long primer (3.2 mm).
  References: Courtney 155; Hazen (1938), 295.

Notes: The signing is irregular, though predominantly as $5, but –BCS2, and –BC4,5; BC3 as $2, O5 as O6, B6 as B3, C7 as C3, DLMNOPQR8 as $6, BC9 as BC4, EFGHIK9 as $6.
   Copies: O (2699 f. 155, green dimpled cloth, 'F. Benwell');
   USA: Hyde (uncut, Adam), NjP, NRU; *Japan*: [Kyoto]; *UK*: BMp (487613).

81.11B(Parts 1+2)/9   Beauties of Johnson,   1828
                          Edinburgh

A New collection arranged by Sources. Not seen.
   References: Hazen (1938), 295.
   Copies: [? NjP].

81.11B(Parts 1+2)/10   Beauties of Johnson,   1828
                            Boston

THE | [hollow] BEAUTIES | OF | JOHNSON, | CONSISTING OF | SELECTIONS FROM HIS WORKS. | [short parallel rule] | BOSTON: | N. H. WHITAKER. | [short rule] | 1828.
   16°, *1*⁸ 2–10⁸, ($1 signed), 80 leaves.
   Pp. 1₁ *1* t., *2* blk, *3* 4–160 text 'Johnson'.
   References: Hazen (1938), 295; S&S 33723 [MBAt, MeBaT, MiD, OHi, PSC-Hi, RJa].
   Notes: This selection derives from the 7th, London edn. 1787, (81.11(Parts 1 + 2)/1, above)
   Copies: Hyde² (**1**. 'A. Wardner'; **2**. 'Ketchum' — 'New Hampshire Antiquarian Society'); *USA*: CtY, DLC, [Liebert = CtY], MB, MH.

81.11B(Parts 1+2)/11   Beauties of Johnson,   1830
                            Edinburgh

BEAUTIES | OF | SAMUEL JOHNSON, LL.D. | EXHIBITING | THE BEST THOUGHTS AND MOST INTERESTING | PASSAGES | OF THAT EMINENT AUTHOR. | [short parallel rule] | EDINBURGH: | PETER BROWN AND THOMAS NELSON. | [short rule] | MDCCCXXX.
   12°, *A*² B–2D⁶ 2D⁴, ($3 (–2D3) signed), 162 leaves.
   Pp. Engr. port. SJ front. + A1 *i* t., *ii* blk, *iii* Advertisement, *iv* blk, on B1 *1* 2–314 text as 'Extracts from . . .' &c., *315* 316–20 Index, 320 coloph: [medium rule] | Printed by James Clarke & Co.
   Pagination: no errors; *Press-figures*: none; *Catchwords*: none.

Explicit: 320 THE END.
Paper: White, wove; no vis. wmk.
Type: Advertisement: sm. pica (3.5 mm), text: brevier (2.7).
Notes: See also Boston, 1834 (81.11B(Parts 1+2)/14) below.
Copies: ABu (*82463/B); *UK*: BMp (813434), JDF ('F.G.L. Nill').

81.11B(Parts 1+2)/12   Beauties of Johnson,   1833
Beauties of Literature, Vol. VII

[Gen. t.] The Beauties of Literature. Consisting of classic selections from the [BL] **most eminent British and Foreign Authors.** By Alfred Howard, Esq. In fifteen volumes. Vol. viii. London: Printed by Thomas Davison, for T.T. and J. Tegg, 73, Cheapside; R. Griffin and Co., Glasgow; J. Cumming and Co., Dublin; and M. Baudry, Paris. 1833.

[Title] The Beauties of Johnson, consisting of Selections from his Works. By Alfred Howard, Esq. London: Printed by T. Davison, for Thomas Tegg, No. 73, Cheapside; R. Griffin and Co., Glasgow; and J. Cumming, Dublin.

12°, π1 A^2 B–H^{12} I^{12} (−I6.7), ($1,5 ($5 as $2) signed), 97 leaves.

Pp. π1 Gen. t., + [Engr. port. SJ after Opie, front. 'Engraved by W.T. Fry. Published by Thos. Tegg. Cheapside.'] + A1 *i* t., *ii* blk, *iii*–iv Contents, on B1 *1* 2–188 text, 188 coloph: 'London: Printed by Thomas Davison, Whitefriars.'

Notes: See 81.11B(Parts 1+2)/6 (1817), above, and 81.11B(Parts 1+2)/15 (1834), below.

Copies: O (3963 f.63 (8); contemp. dark green cloth, leather spine label, gilt; 'C. Fulljames').

81.11B(Parts 1+2)/13   Beauties of Johnson,   1833
Boston

THE | LIFE OF JOHNSON: | WITH | [BL] **Maxims and Observations,** | MORAL, CRITICAL, AND MISCELLANEOUS, | ACCURATELY SELECTED FROM THE WORKS OF | DR. SAMUEL JOHNSON, | And arranged in Alphabetical Order. | FROM THE FIFTH LONDON EDITION. | Enlarged and Corrected. | [short orn. rule] | BOSTON: | MARSH, CAPEN & LYON, AND B.H. GREENE. | [short wavy rule] | 1833.

12°, *1*^{6} 2–24^6 (24$_6$ blk), ($3 ($3 as $*) signed), 144 leaves.

Pp. 1$_1$ *i* t., *ii* Licence, *iii* iv–vi Table of Subjects, *vii* viii–x Preface, *xi* Advertisement, *xii* blk, on 2$_1$ *xiii*–xiv Preface to American edition, *15* 16–61 Murphy's Memoir of SJ, *62* blk, *63* 64–285 The Maxims of SJ, *286* blk, *287–88* (24$_6$) blk.

Pagination: no errors.

References: Hazen (1938), 295.

Notes: The arrangement of the material follows that of *Beauties*, 81.11B(Part 1)/6 and 81.11B(Part 2)/3 (1782), above.

Copies: Hyde ('White' — 'Rogers'; *viii*–ix misimposed); *USA*: DLC.

81.11B(Parts 1+2)/14   Beauties of Johnson,   1834
       Boston

THE | LIFE OF JOHNSON: | WITH | [BL] **Maxims and Observations,** | MORAL, CRITICAL, AND MISCELLANEOUS, | ACCURATELY SELECTED FROM THE WORKS OF | DR. SAMUEL JOHNSON, | And arranged in Alphabetical Order. | FROM THE FIFTH LONDON EDITION. | Enlarged and Corrected. | [short orn. rule] | BOSTON: | MARSH, CAPEN & LYON, AND B.H. GREENE. | [short wavy rule] | 1834.

12°, a stereotype reimpression of the preceding 1833 Boston edn. with redated t., and 'Licence', an undated Preface, and with the last sentence removed from the 'Advertisement' (p. xi).

References: Hazen (1938), 295.

Copies: Hyde ('George Howland'); *USA*: MB.

81.11B(Parts 1+2)/15   Beauties of Johnson,   1834
Howard's Beauties of Literature, Vol. VIII

Howard's Beauties of Literature. Consisting of Classic Selections from the most eminent British and Foreign Authors. By Alfred Howard, Esq. In Fifteen Volumes: Vol. VIII. With the Beauties of Goldsmith. [1834]

The Beauties of Johnson, consisting of Selections from his Works, by Alfred Howard, Esq. London: Printed by T. Davison, for Thomas Tegg, No. 73, Cheapside; R. Griffin and Co. Glasgow; and J. Cumming, Dublin.

12°, A^2 B–H^{12} I^{10}, ($1,5 ($5 as $2) signed), 96 leaves.

Pp. Engr. port. front. + A1 *i* t., *ii* blk, *iii*–iv Contents, on B1 *1* 2–188 text, 188 coloph: London: Printed by Thomas Davison, Whitefriars.

Explicit: 188 THE END.

References: Courtney 155 (undated); Hazen (1938), 295.

Notes: See 1830 (81.11B(Parts 1+2)/12, above), of which this appears to be a stereotype reimpression. The date at AWn is presumably a cataloguer's guess.

Copies: ABu (*82463); *USA*: [Liebert = CtY]; *Can*: CaOHM; *UK*: AWn ('1828').

81.11B(Parts 1+2)/16   Beauties of Johnson,   1837
                              Boston

The Beauties of Johnson. Selected Thoughts of Samuel Johnson . . . [with] a Sketch of his Life. Sixth American Edition from the Fifth London Edition. Boston: J. Dawe.

   8°, 285 pp. Not examined.

   References: Hazen (1938), 295; S&S 44998 [MBelm], 45000 [MB, PPL, RBa, TxU].

   Notes: A stereotype reimpression of Boston, 1833 (81.11B(Parts 1+2)/13, above).

   Copies: NRU.

81.11B(Parts 1+2)/17   Beauties of Johnson,   1843
                              Cooperstown

The Beauties of Johnson. Not seen.

   References: Hazen (1938), 295 notes this edn.

   Notes: A copy at PPA is reported as dated '1841'.

   Copies: Unlocated [? PPA].

81.11B(Parts 1+2)/18   Beauties of Johnson,   1851
                              New York

The Beauties of Johnson. New York. Not seen.

   References: Hazen (1938), 295 notes this edn.

   Copies: [MH], [? PPFr].

81.11B(Parts 1+2)/19   Beauties of Johnson,   1853
                              New York

The Beauties of Johnson, choice selections from his Works. New York: Leavitt & Allen, 27 Dey-Street. 1853.

   16°, *1*⁸ 2–10⁸, 80 leaves; Pp. *1* t., *2* blk, *3* 4–160 text.

   A stereotype reimpression from the Boston edn., 1828 (81.11B(Parts 1+2)/10, above), with adjusted t. Trimmed: 3¼ × 2½ in.

   Copies: Hyde; *USA*: NRU.

81.11B(Parts 1+2)/20　　Beauties of Johnson　　　　1885

The Beauties of Samuel Johnson, with Biographical Anecdotes. . . 1885.
　Not seen.
　Copies: [BMp (60642)].

82.2DL　　Announcement of Death of Robert Levet　　1782

February　　Newspaper announcement of death of Robert Levet.

　In SJ's letter of 14 Feb. 1782 to Charles Patrick inquiring after Levet's family, 'I therefore gave notice of his decease in the papers, that an heir, if he has any, may appear.' (*Letters* 760; Hyde iv. 11). A brief notice in *Lond. Chron.*, 26 Jan. 1782, reads simply: 'Last week died at the house of his friend, Dr. Samuel Johnson, Dr. Levet, a Practitioner in Physic.' No fuller notice has been traced.

82.11NH/1a　　Nichols's History of Hinckley　　　　1782

THE | HISTORY and ANTIQUITIES | OF | HINCKLEY, | IN THE COUNTY OF | LEICESTER; | INCLUDING THE HAMLETS OF | STOKE, DADLINGTON, WYKIN, and THE HYDE. | WITH A LARGE APPENDIX, | CONTAINING | Some Particulars of the ancient Abbey of Lira in Normandy; | Aftronomical Remarks, adapted to the Meridian of Hinckley; | and Biographical Memoirs of feveral Perfons of Eminence. | By JOHN NICHOLS, F.S.A. Edinb. *Correfp.* | and Printer to the Society of Antiquaries of London. | MDCCLXXXII.

[Sub-t.] BIBLIOTHECA | TOPOGRAPHICA | BRITANNICA. | N° VII. | CONTAINING | The Hiftory and Antiquities of Hinckley, | in the County of Leicester; including the | Hamlets of Stoke, Dadlington, Wykin, | and The Hyde. | With a large Appendix. | [medium swelled rule] | LONDON, | PRINTED BY AND FOR J. NICHOLS, | PRINTER TO THE SOCIETY OF ANTIQUARIES; | AND SOLD BY ALL THE BOOKSELLERS IN GREAT-BRITAIN AND IRELAND. | MDCCLXXXII. | [Price Seven Shillings and Six Pence.]

4°, *a*1 b² B–D⁴ E⁴ (±E4) F⁴ (±F4) G⁴ H⁴ (H3 + *I3) I⁴ K⁴ (±K4) L–2B⁴ 2C² 2D–2H⁴ 2I² ($2 (+ cancels, −$2 of $²) signed), 124 leaves.

Pp. a1 *i* t., *ii* blk, *iii* sub-t, *iv* blk, v–vi Dedication dh: 'To Mr. John Robinson of Hinckley.' ('J. NICHOLS. *Nov.* 1, 1782.'), on B1 1–54, *55–*56 (=ᴴ*I3), 55–240 text.

Pagination: [↑] v–vi; 156 as 1ˏ6.

Press-figures: B2ᵛ(4)–3, C1ᵛ(10)–6, C2ᵛ(12)–7, D2ᵛ(20)–3, D3ᵛ(22)–6, E2ᵛ(28)–5, 'E4'ᵛ(32)–4, F3(37)–1, G3ᵛ(46)–3, H4(55)–3, I3(61)–2, K2ᵛ(68)–4, L4ᵛ(80)–4, M4ᵛ(88)–3, N1ᵛ(90)–3, O2ᵛ(100)–2, P4(111)–7, Q4(119)–1,

R1^v(122)–4, T1^v(138)–5, T2^v(140)–4, U2^v(148)–3, X2^v(156)–7, Y3(165)–1, Z3(173)–7, 2B4^v(192)–1, 2C2(195)–3, 2D3^v(202)–1, 2G3(225)–4, 2H4^v(236)–4.

Catchwords: 27 The ('e' *slipt*), 45 21 "Here (last 'e' *slipt*), 54 BENE-(BENEFACTIONS), 70 ICH (IHC), 72 RECORDS, (RECORDS,), 120 N° XVII (APPENDIX, N° XVII.), 132 *om.* (and), 135 *om.* (JOHN), 142 *om.* (Genealogy), 143 *om.* (3. EMME), 144 *om.* (NOTES), 150 PEDIGREE (PEGI-GREE), 150 *om.* ([E]), 167 8.Captain (9.~), 196 *om.* (The), 204 The (VENUS.), 223 a (and).

Explicit: none.

Paper: White, laid; Demy (uncut: 11¼ × 8¾ in.); no vis. wmk.

Type: Dedication: pica (4.1 mm), leaded (1.2 mm); text: english (4.5 mm), leaded (1.4 mm); notes: pica (4.1 mm), leaded (0.2 mm); Appendix: small pica (3.9 mm), leaded (0.4 mm); notes: bourgeois (3.0 mm), unleaded.

Plates: 13, listed at p. 240.

References: ESTC: t079945; *Lit. Anec.* vi. 632, ix. 73; *Letters* 822; Hyde iv. 184 (SJ to JN, 10 Jan. 1783); *Lit. Anec.* ii. 551 n., ix. 190–1; *Gleanings* v. 76.

Notes: There is an account of Sir Cordell Firebrace at p. 167. Despite Nichols's assertion that SJ contributed towards the life of Anthony Blackwall (pp. 177–79), this cannot mean that SJ wrote it. The composition of the account is entirely in Nichols's manner and lacks every characteristic of SJ's style. In the account of Revd. John Dyer (pp. 183–4) there are further references to SJ, whose own Life of Dyer is cited briefly.

Copies: O (Gough Leic. 3(1), annotated by Richard Gough); *UK*: BMp, E, L⁴.

82.11NH/1b   Nichols's History of Hinckley,   1790
          Collections towards History of Leicestershire

COLLECTIONS | TOWARDS | THE HISTORY AND ANTIQUITIES | OF THE | Town and County of LEICESTER. | Publiſhed by JOHN NICHOLS, F.S.A. EDINB. & PERTH. | [Engr. vign.: 'LABOR IPSE VOLUPTAS'] | LONDON: | PRINTED BY AND FOR THE EDITOR. | MDCCXC.

References: *Lit. Anec.* ix. 71–3; ESTC: t084191.

Notes: A reissue of 82.11NH/1a, above. The t. of 82.11NH/1a is a2 on a bifolium bearing on a1 the t. of 82.11NH/1b.

Copy: O (4° BS 511).

82.11NH/1c   Nichols's History of Hinckley,   1790
Additional Collections towards History of Leicestershire

Further materials were added to the previous volume, as *Additional Collections towards the History of Leicestershire*, 1790, these *Additional Collections* included SJ's epitaph on Elizabeth Johnson (84.7/EEJ, below), at p. 519.
  Copy: O: (4° BS. 512).

82.11NH/2   Nichols's History of Hinckley,   1795–1815
The History and Antiquities of the County of Leicestershire

4 vols. This is a further enlargement of the preceding compilations.
  Copies: O² (**1**. Vet. A5 b.49; **2**. Gough Leic. 14–20).

82.12RD   Reynolds's 11th Presidential Discourse   1782

[½t] A | DISCOURSE, *&c.* | [Price Three Shillings.]
  [Title] A | DISCOURSE, | DELIVERED TO THE | STUDENTS | OF THE | ROYAL ACADEMY | ON THE | Diftribution of the Prizes, *December* 10, 1782, | BY THE | PRESIDENT. | [medium swelled rule] | LONDON: | Printed by THOMAS CADELL, PRINTER to the | ROYAL ACADEMY. | M.DCC.LXXXIII.
  4°, *A*² B–G², ($1 signed), 14 leaves.
  Pp. A1 *1* ½t, *2* blk, *3* t., *4* blk, on B1 *5* 6–28 text, dh: [orn. hp.] | A | DISCOURSE, *&c.* | GENTLEMEN,.
  Pagination: [↑], no errors; *Press-figures*: none; *Catchwords*: none.
  Explicit: 28 THE END.
  Paper: White, laid; crown (uncut: 10 × 7½ in.); wmk.: fleur-de-lys + Strasburg bend.
  Type: Text: great primer (5.7 mm), leaded (2.0 mm), notes: long primer (3.4 mm).
  References: Hilles, *Literary Career of Reynolds* (1936), 134–137 and *illus.* facing p. 135; *Discourses . . . by Reynolds*, ed. Robert R. Wark (1959); Brownell, *Johnson's Attitude to the Arts* (1989), 83–6; ESTC: t031957.
  Notes: The 11th Discourse of which (**a**) the MS draft is preserved at the Royal Academy of Arts, bearing MS corrections and alterations by SJ (*MS Index* JoS 337), and (**b**) a single leaf, similarly corrected by SJ, in the possession of Paul Mellon, Esq. (*MS Index* JoS. 338). This is the only Discourse in which SJ's involvement with the text is demonstrable, though it may reasonably be suspected of some of the others.[1]
  Copies:[2] O (Vet. A5 d. 667, 'Dr George Fordyce from the Author');

USA: CSmH, CtY², InU, MH², NjP, NIC, PPL; *UK*: C, E (Pres.), L² (1. Pres. Sir Joseph Banks; 2. Pres. F.M. Newton³), Lu, MRu.

¹ JR certainly invited Malone to revise some later Discourses, specifically the 13th of 11 Dec. 1786 (Hilles, ed., *Letters of . . . Reynolds* (1929), cxii, pp. 170–1, and *Literary Career of Reynolds* (1936), 142–3, and was commonly supposed to have enlisted SJ's assistance in the same way.
² A copy inscribed by JR: 'Dr Burney from the Author' was Maggs Bros. *Cat.* 1038 (1984), 414 (5).
³ Secretary to the Royal Academy.

83.1DL   Erasmus Darwin's Translation of Linnaeus   1782–3

[½t] [rule] | A | SYSTEM | OF | VEGETABLES, | IN TWO VOLUMES. | VOL. I [– II]. | [rule]

[Title] A | SYSTEM | OF | VEGETABLES, | ACCORDING TO THEIR | [2 cols., col. a:] *CLASSES* | *GENERA* | [col. b:] *ORDERS* | *SPECIES* | WITH THEIR | CHARACTERS AND DIFFERENCES. | [rule] | TRANS LATED FROM THE THIRTEENTH EDITION | (AS PUBLISHED BY DR. MURRAY) | OF THE | SYSTEMA VEGETABILIUM | OF THE LATE PROFESSOR | LINNEUS; | AND FROM THE | SUPPLEMENTUM PLANTARUM | OF THE PRESENT PROFESSOR | LINNEUS. | [rule] | BY A BOTANICAL SOCIETY, AT LICHFIELD. | [rule] | LICHFIELD: | PRINTED BY JOHN JACKSON, FOR LEIGH AND | SOTHEBY, YORK STREET, COVENT GARDEN, | LONDON. MDCCLXXXII.

Var: DIFFERENCES. | IN TWO VOLUMES | [rule] | TRANSLATED . . . LINNEUS. | [rule] | VOL. I. | [double rule] | BY A BOTANICAL . . . LONDON. | MDCCLXXXIII. (SAN)

II. . . . DIFFERENCES. | IN TWO VOLUMES. | [rule] . . . LINNEUS. | [rule] | VOL. I [– II]. | [double rule] | BY A BOTANICAL . . . &c. [as vol. 1] (Hyde).

2 vols., 8°

I. π² *a*² (a2 + χ1) *b*⁴ *C–*F⁴ *G² *H⁴ + [22], ²A–3G⁴, ($2 (b1 as '2', –*C1, U2) signed), 243 leaves.

Pp. π1 ½t, π2 t., on a1 *i*–ii Dedication to Sir Joseph Banks, on a2 ²*i* ii–xii Preface of the Translators, *xiii* ½t Botanical Terms, *xiv* blk, xv–xl terms, xli–xlvii Index, *xlviii* Errata, *xlix* l–lvi Alphabetical Index, 11 leaves unsigned of printed descriptions with 11 engr. plates inserted + on A1 ½t on A2 *3* 4–424 text.

Pagination: 44 *sometimes* at inner margin ↖.
Press-figures: b1(v)–2; *Catchwords*: not recorded; *Explicit*: none.

II. A–Z⁴ 2A⁴ (–2A4) 2B–3O⁴ *3P–3S*⁴, ($2 (–A1,2, + A3 as A2, –K2) signed), 255 leaves.

Pp. A1 ½t, A2 t., on A3 *425* 426–897 text, *898* blk, on 3P1 ½t Alphabetical Catalogue of English and Scottish Names of Plants (1784), 3P1ᵛ blk, on 3P2–3S3ᵛ text (unpaged), 354 blk.

Pagination: 890 at inner margin ↖.
Press-figures: 3P2–3, 3Q1–1, 3Q2–3, 3R1–1, 3R2–3, 3S1–1, 3S2–3.
Catchwords: not recorded.
Explicit: 897 FINIS. 3S2ᵛ FINIS.

Paper: White, laid; La. post (uncut: 8¼ × 5½ in.); wmk.: fleur-de-lys.
Type: Preface: english (4.4 mm), leaded (0.5 mm), text: sm. pica (3.5 mm), notes: brevier (2.6 mm).
Plates: The inserted 11 plates in vol. 1 are furnished with facing letterpress pp. of printed descriptions.[1]
References: Courtney 156; A.H. Stevenson (1961), 665; Simms, *Bibliotheca Staffordiensis* (1894), 281; Soulsby, *A Catalogue of the Works of Linnaeus*, 2nd. edn. (1933); T. Williams, *A Checklist of Linneana, 1735–1834* (1964); King-Hele, *Letters of Erasmus Darwin* (1981), 109–22; ESTC: t081060.
Notes: The *Catalogue* at the end of vol. 2 comprises 4 unsigned and unpaged gatherings. This section is the only one to carry press-figures.

SJ's contribution is acknowledged, I. xi: 'to that great Master of the english tongue Dr. SAMUEL JOHNSON, for his advice in the formation of the botanic language'; also named is 'John Sneyd, Esq; *Belmount, Staffordshire.*' SJ's involvement is mentioned in ED's letters to Joseph Banks of 29 Sept. 1781 (114), and to J.C. Lettsome, 8 Oct. 1787 (171–2).[2]

The Lichfield Botanical Society was Erasmus Darwin himself, who also published Linnaeus's *The Families of Plants, with their Natural Character . . . By a Botanical Society at Lichfield*, 2 vols., 8°, Lichfield, 1787 (O: 8° D. 184–5. BS), with Brooke Boothby (1744–1824*), and Revd. William Jackson (1735–98), of Lichfield. The course of publication is traced by King-Hele in *Letters of Erasmus Darwin* (1981), showing that the translation was made from J.A. Murray's edition of *Systema Vegetabilium*, 13th. edn. (Göttingen, 1774). Specimens were distributed by Darwin in 1781 (*Letters*) on which King-Hele reports: 'Two 7-page specimens bound in the back of a copy of Linnaeus's *Fundamenta Botanica* in the Linnean Society Library' (112 n. 2).[3]

The work was issued in four parts between 1783 and 1785, and in two volumes dated '1783'. The titles, which do not mention the volumes, were evidently intended to precede the collected numbers. No date of publication has yet been discovered but it may be presumed to have been early in 1783.[4]

Copies: O (Vet. A5 e.908–9);
USA: [CLSU], CtY ('1787'), DLC, Hyde ('Constable'), [KyBgW], [Liebert], MB, MH, PPAmP (580.L641sy, vol. 1 only, var), [PPPH, PWcT]; *Can*: CaOHM (C 2766–67); *UK*: Eu, L² (2. imperfect), LCu, [LEu], Llis, LVp (var. tt.), MRu, NOu, SAN (ˢQK91.S8V4, + extra and variant t.), SHu.

---

[1] See T. Martyn, *38 Plates* [by Frederick Polydore Nodder] *to illustrate Linnaeus's System* (1794), 8° (L: 7028. bb. 58; O: 19113 e.4), and ?reissued by William White, London, 1799 (NCu: 582).
[2] Darwin was anxious to retain the descriptive force of Linnaeus' Latin terminologies in his

English versions mentioned in his letter to Banks of 29 Sept. 1781: 'awl-pointed, for acuminatum, edge-hollow'd for sinuatum; scollop'd for retusum; wire-creeping for sarmentosum . . .' (*Letters of Erasmus Darwin*, ed. King-Hele (1981), 113), and worried about the adjectival use of past-participial forms, 'Some of our friends think the word eggshape should be written egg**shaped** — we thought sword-form and eggshape and halbert-shape etc might be used adjectivally better . . .' (113), adding 'Of these niceties of language I will endeavour to get the opinion of Dr. Johnson, and with it egg**shaped**, and thread-form**ed**, if it be esteemed better' (114). He later wrote to Banks, 23 Feb. 1782, 'They [*sc*. the Botanical Society] have at length after much advice and consideration determined the botanical language; which is much more similar to the original than that they first proposed' (121–22). Some of these details are mentioned in the 'Preface' p. iii. It is not easy to determine just how much of a contribution all this required from SJ. The 'Botanical language' and pronunciation were noticed by 'P.B.C.' in *Gents. Mag.* lv (Oct. 1785), 757–58).

   ³ *Catalogue of the Linnaean Society of London* (1825), 456 'probably proof'.
   ⁴ The work was announced in *Gents. Mag.* lv (Sept. 1785), 716 'New Publications', as 'Lichfield Botany, 2 vols. 8vo. sewed, 18s. *Leigh*.' but this is presumably a late advt.

83.2EH   Obituary of Coleborne Hancock   1783

Published in an unidentified newspaper, reporting the death of Hancock, a glass-manufacturer, on 13 February 1783.

References: Waingrow, *Corr.* 539–40, and a transcript from a newspaper preserved in Boswell papers, with a letter to JB from James Sedgewick, 3 June 1793 (CtY: MS Boswell C 2452), reporting that SJ had composed a new 'Shop card' for Hancock's widow, and sending the transcription of the obituary. JB did not adopt this into the *Life* (1791 or later), presumably because he was unable to identify the source of the obituary, or perhaps to verify SJ's association with Hancock.

Copies: CtY (MS Boswell C 1610).

83.5CV/1   Crabbe's The Village   1783

[½t] [medium swelled rule] | THE | VILLAGE: | A | POEM. | [medium swelled rule] | [Price 2s. 6d.]

   [Title] THE | VILLAGE: | A | POEM. | IN TWO BOOKS. | [short swelled rule] | BY | THE REVᴰ GEORGE CRABBE, | CHAPLAIN TO HIS GRACE THE DUKE OF RUTLAND, &c. | [parallel rule] | LONDON: | PRINTED FOR J. DODSLEY, PALL-MALL. | [short rule] | M.DCC.LXXXIII.

   4°, *A*² B–F⁴ (F4 blk), ($2 signed), 22 leaves.

   Pp. A1 ½t, A1ᵛ blk, A2 t., A2ᵛ blk, on B1 *1* 2–23 text of Bk. 1 dh: [triple rule] | THE | VILLAGE. | [short swelled rule] | BOOK I., *24* blk, *25* 26–38 text of Bk. 2 dh: [as Bk. 1, but 'BOOK II.'), *39–40* (F4) blk.

   Pagination: [↑].

   Press-figures: B4(7)–1, C1ᵛ(10)–1, D2ᵛ(20)–3, D3ᵛ(22)–2, E4(31)–6, E4ᵛ(32)–1, F1ᵛ(34)–3, F3(37)–1.

Catchwords: no errors.
Explicit: 38 FINIS.
Paper: White, laid; Demy (uncut: 11 × 8¾ in.); no vis. wmk.
Type: Great primer (6.1 mm), leaded (4.1 mm).
References: *Life* iv. 175, 509–10 (Courtney 155–6); Bareham and Gatrell, *A Bibliography of George Crabbe* (1978), no. 11; *George Crabbe Complete Poetical Works*, ed. Lady N. Dalrymple-Champneys and A. Pollard, 3 vols. (Oxford, 1988), no. 49, i. 155–75, 662–71; ESTC: t000481.
Notes: GC's MS (last recorded in 1834 as showing variants in i. 99–100, 143 ff., 219, ii. 161–2), was revised by SJ (*Letters* 830, to Reynolds, 4 Mar. 1783; Hyde iv. 116-17); later revisions by GC for his *Poetical Works*, 1807, are not Johnsonian. Published at 2s. 6d. on 23 May 1783.
Copies: O (GP 1491 (2));
USA: CSmH, CtY³, DLC, Hyde², ICN, ICU, IU, [Liebert (uncut. 'Loveday')], MB, MH³, NjP², NN, NPM, PPL, TxU²; *Can*: CaOHM (C.296); *UK*: C², Ct, L², LVu, MRp, MRu.

83.5CV/2   Crabbe's The Village, New York   1791

The Village: a Poem. In two books. By the Revd. George Crabbe, Chaplain to His Grace the late Duke of Rutland, &c. The Fifth Edition. London: printed. New-York: re-printed for Berry and Rogers, no 35, Hanover-Square; and sold by Thomas and Andrews, Boston. — 1791 —
12°, Pp. 36. Not examined.
References: Evans 23297, ESTC: w035268.
Copies: [MWA].

83.11EHC   Rules of the Essex Head Club   1783

The Club was established in December 1783 (SJ to Reynolds, 4 Dec. 1783, *Letters* 916, Hyde iv. 256-7, and *Life* iv. 253–254 and n. 5), and SJ drew up the Rules.[1] These were published in *Gents. Mag.* lv (Feb. 1785), 99, and thence by William Cooke, *Life of Johnson*, 1785 (2nd. edn., 26 Feb. 1785, *Morning Chron.*), 66–9, together with a list of members (69–70); the Rules were also printed in the 'Life' of SJ prefixed to Jarvis & Fielding's edn. of *Dictionary*, 1785–6 (55.4D/10, above); see below 85GM55.

---

[1] He promised to let HLT have the 'names and the regulations' on 27 Dec. 1783 (*Letters* 921, iii. 118; Hyde iv. 264-5), but on 31 Jan. 1784, he wrote to HMT with a further promise to transmit to her 'our numbers, our names, and our laws' (*Letters* 929.1; Hyde iv. 278-80), showing that the composition of the rules was a slow process.

84.6AC   Account of Archibald Campbell   1784

15 June   Account of Archibald Campbell
   Written in JB's notebook whilst at Pembroke College, Oxford, and published in *Journal of a Tour* (1785), 448–9 (3rd. edn. (1786), 371); in *Life* (1791), dated to '9 June 1784'.
   References: *Journal of a Tour*, ed. Pottle and Bennett (1963), 354, with facs. of MS; *Life* iv. 286, v. 357, 562.
   Notes: The MS is CtY (MS Boswell C. 1605; *MS Handlist* 217; *MS Index* JoS 230).

84.7EEJ   Epitaph on Elizabeth Johnson   1784

Memorial stone, now on the ambulatory wall of the rebuilt parish church of St Peter and St Paul, Bromley, Kent.[1]
   Elizabeth Johnson (b. 1689), died 17 March 1752 OS, and was buried at Bromley as the burial register shows, on 26 March with an affidavit given by 'Mr Denenen' and the note that she was 'of yᵉ Parish of Sᵗ. Brides London'.[2]
   SJ composed this epitaph in summer 1784 (*Life* iv. 352). On 12 July 1784 he wrote to Revd. Thomas Bagshaw, the incumbent,

> Perhaps You may remember that in the year 1753, You committed to the ground my dear Wife; I now entreat your permission to lay a stone upon her, and have sent the inscription that if You find it proper, You may signify your allowance.
>
> You will do me a great favour by showing the place where she lies, that the stone may protect her remains.
>
> Mr. Ryland will wait on You for the inscription, and procure it to be engraved. You will easily believe that I shrink from this mournful office. When it is done, if I have strength remaining, I will visit Bromley once again, and pay you part of the respect to which You have a right from,
>
> Reverend Sir, Your most humble Servant,
>
> July 12, 1784   Sam. Johnson
> Bolt court, Fleetstreet.[3]

On the same day he also wrote to Ryland:

> Mʳ Payne will pay you fifteen pounds towards the stone of which You have kindly undertaken the care. The Inscription is in the hands of Mʳ Bagshaw, who has a right to inspect it, before he admits it into his Church.
>
> Be pleased to let the whole be done with privacy, that I may elude the vigilance of the papers (*Letters* 977; Hyde iv. 350–1; MS Hyde).

By October 1784 it seems that the memorial stone had been put in place, for SJ wrote again to Ryland on 30th from Lichfield:

Accept my sincere thanks for your care in laying down the stone; what You and young Mr Ryland have done, I doubt not of finding well done, if ever I can make my mind firm enough to visit it (*Letters* 1029.2; Hyde iv. 429-30; MS Hyde).

Ryland acknowledged this letter in a lost reply which appears to have included a copy of the inscription, for SJ replied on 4 November, still from Lichfield:

I saw the draught of the stone. I am afraid the date is wrong. I think it should be 52. We will have it rectified. You say nothing of the cost but that You have paid it. My intention was the [= that] Mr Payne should have put into your hands fifteen pounds which he received for [? = from] me at Midsummer. If he has not done it, I will order You the money, which is in his hands.

Shall I ever be able to bear the sight of this stone? In your company, I hope, I shall. You will not wonder that I write no more. God bless you for Christs sake (*Letters* 1032; Hyde iv. 434-5; MS Hyde).[4]

On 2 December he wrote to Lucy Porter:

I laid this summer a stone over Tetty in the Chapel of Bromley in Kent. The Inscription is in Latin of which this is the English.

Here lie the remains of Elizabeth, descended from the ancient house of Jarvis at Peatling in Leicestershire; a Woman of beauty, elegance, ingenuity, and piety. Her first Husband was Henry Porter; her second, Samuel Johnson, who having loved her much, and lamented her long, laid this stone upon her. She died in March. 1752 (*Letters* 1041; Hyde iv. 444; MS Hyde).[5]

(**A**) The stone is evidently the authoritative version, despite the erroneous date of Tetty's death.

(**B**) It was first published in *Gents. Mag.* liv (Dec. 1784), 884, in a version directly descended from the stone or possibly, if from a Johnsonian source, from a copy of SJ's own draft. It differs from the extant inscription in minor details of punctuation and capitalization, and gives the date 'MDCCLIII.'

(**C**) William Cooke in his hasty *Life of Johnson*, 2nd edn. ([26 Feb.] 1785), 37, followed (**B**), with no variants.[6]

(**D**) Revd. William Shaw published a version in his *Memoirs of Johnson* (1785), 114, with several minor misprints: 'Pentlingae' for *Peatlingae*, 'culta' for *cultae*, 'amatum' for *amatam*, 'dinque' for *diuque* and 'Londin.' for *Londini*, though this last reading is actually what stands on the stone but in no other printed version, and a few slight variations of punctuation. These errors are attributable to Shaw's transcription of his source.

(**E**) William Mavor included the epitaph in his account of SJ, prefixed to Harrison's edn. of the *Dictionary*, 1786 (55.4D/7, above).

(**F**) Hawkins, *Life87*, 315, next printed the text in a version which in the details of punctuation owes more to the *Gents. Mag.* (**B**) above, than to any other source.

(G) The unknown author of the brief biography of SJ prefixed to Jarvis & Fielding's edn. of the *Dictionary* (1786; 55.4D/10 above), adopted Cooke's version (**C** above).

(H) That Great Peatling in Leicestershire was Tetty's birthplace, induced John Nichols to notice her in his *Collections towards the History . . . of Leicester,* 1790 (82.11NH/1b, above), and to record SJ's epitaph on p. 519 from the *Gents. Mag.* version (**B**), above.

(I) Boswell (*Life* (1791), ii. 536), mentioned the epitaph as in *Works*, 1787, apparently meaning (F) above. Malone added the text to *Life* (1804), i. 212 n. JB's papers and a transcript are CtY: MS Boswell M 164. The transcript is marked 'Dr. J. has written v. for u. throughout' which may mean that it was taken directly from SJ's lost MS, perhaps (B) above.

¹ The inscription as it appears on the stone was defaced by the German bombing of the church on 16 April 1941 (when seven churches were destroyed in Bromley), and when it was also cracked across, but it is printed by Richard Holworthy, *The British Archivist,* 'Supplement' (1922), p. 2, no. 10. It is also printed in Horsburgh, *Bromley, Kent* (1929), 126, and Peter Cochrane printed a transcription from the stone in *The Saturday Review of Literature,* 12 Sept. 1953, 51. There is a photograph in Halliday, *Dr Johnson and His World* (1968), 40.
  The stone survived the bombing raid of 1941, but was thereafter taken from the floor of the church and affixed to the wall of the ambulatory when the church was rebuilt. H. M. The Queen, then The Princess Elizabeth, laid the foundation stone for the present church in 1949. The church had undergone various reconstructions during the 19th Century. *JNL* xix, no. iv (1959), 7. I am indebted to Mr. John Dempster, of Bickley, for his considerable assistance in preparing this note, and to Miss Helen D. Moore for more recent information.
² The entry in the burial register appears to be in the hand of Revd. Thomas Bagshaw 'Curate' (p. 3, *s.a.* 1752); it is printed in the *Parish Registers and Records in the Diocese of Rochester,* ed. W.E. Buckland (1912), under 'Bromley, St Peter and St Paul', p. 55, with the apparently mistaken addition of 'Minister' after Denenen's name. There is a small mystery about 'Denenen', whose name is otherwise unrecorded: it seems to be an error for John Denne, prebendary of Rochester until his death on 5 Aug. 1767 (*Gents. Mag.* xxxvii (Aug. 1767), 430), who is not to be confused with John Denne, Archdeacon of Rochester, who died 28 June 1747 (*Gents. Mag.* xvii (June 1747), 297), as happens in Hennessy's *Novum Repertorium Ecclesiasticum Parochiale Londinense* (1898), p. CLVII, note h126. It is to this John Denne that the biographical notices in L: Add. MS 5852 p.252, and 5886 p. 23, refer.
³ *Letters* 975, Hyde iv. 348-9; MS in the possession of Mrs Sarah Markham, of Wootton-under-Edge, Glos., to whom I am deeply indebted for much kindness and assistance.
⁴ The erroneous date 'MDCCLIII.' was never rectified, and still stands on the stone, as it appears also in all the early printed versions. It surely arose from SJ's recollection of the change of the calendar which took place in September 1752.
⁵ Malone made a copy of the epitaph which passed into the Boswell papers and is now CtY (MS Boswell M 164; *MS Index* JoS 198), see (I), above.
⁶ The December number of the *Gents. Mag.* 1784, would ordinarily be published about mid-January 1785; Cooke's first edition, with an 'Advertisement' dated 28 Dec. 1784, had been published about a fortnight after SJ's death on 13 Dec. 1784, and his second, slightly enlarged edition, was advertised on 26 Feb. 1785 (*Morning Chron.*). SJ's reference to a 'draught of the stone' on 4 Nov. 1784 to Ryland, is presumably to a drawing or a sketch recording its appearence, and perhaps the inscription, though the latter would be superfluous to the composer. If this 'draught' escaped from SJ's effects at his death, it is plausible that Cooke or Kearsley may have obtained it.

84.9LS   Projected Life of Scott of Amwell   1784

John Scott (†12 Dec. 1783), was one of a group of Quaker friends of SJ centred mainly on John Hoole. Towards the end of his life Scott prepared a collection of 'Critical Essays' for which SJ promised to write a biographical sketch. SJ began the task in Sept. 1784, as his letter of 16th to David Barclay attests (*Letters* 1012.1; Hyde iv. 404–5), but SJ was then at Ashbourne and did not return to London until 16 November (*Letters* 1036, 1037; Hyde iv. 437–9), when he was soon busied with other affairs including the placing and preparation of the epitaphs for his wife and parents. Such materials as Barclay may have accumulated in September therefore had little hope of completion. In the event it was John Hoole who furnished Scott's *Essays* with a brief biography, and it is reasonable to suppose that SJ communicated whatever he had to Hoole, who attended him during his own last days.[1] Johnson's contribution to the memoir is not recoverable, unless some MS material remains to be found or until the parts composed by John and Samuel Hoole can be identified.

Reference: Liebert, *Johnson's Last Literary Project* (1948).

[1] Hoole's brother Samuel (1719–88) also contributed to the memoir, having published an undated 'Memoir of the Last Illness of John Scott' (probably early in 1784). Hoole's attendance on the dying Johnson is recorded in his account in *European Mag.* xxxv (Sept. 1799), 153–8, partly reprinted in *Johns. Misc.* ii. 145–60, and in a MS (now CtY) published by Brack, *Journal Narrative Relative to Dr Johnson's Last Illness* (1972), and in four letters to William Bowles, of Heale (MS: O). The implications of Hoole's accounts are discussed by Brack in *YULG* xlvii (1973), 107–8, and Korshin, in *Johnson after Two Hundred Years* (1986), 55–76.

84.11EP   Epitaph on Michael and Sarah Johnson   1784

SJ composed this epitaph about a month before his own death on 13 December 1784, and certainly before 2 December. The inscription is on a stone in the floor of the centre aisle of St Michael's Church in Lichfield, of which the original has been lost so that the present stone (prepared in 1884), represents a renewed version.

References: *Life* iv. 393, noting that SJ's MS text was sent to Richard Greene, of Lichfield, with a letter dated 2 Dec. 1784 (*Letters* 1040; Hyde iv. 443-4); and n. 3, recounting the obscure history of the stone, suggesting that the stone was not then set up, but that the present inscription, cut in 1884,[1] probably derives from Croker's edn. of Boswell (1848), 798 n., where it is taken from SJ's *Works*, 1787.[2] Nevertheless William Thompson the mason's, bill for 7 gns. was paid by Greene on 1 July 1785:[3]

The Ex^rs of the late D^r. Johnson
    To W^m. Thompson D^rs.

1785

| To a Gravestone laid down in S^t. Margaret's | £ S D |
| Church Lichfield, to the Memory of the said | 7 – 7 – 0 |

To a Gravestone laid down in S^t. Margaret's £ S D
Church Lichfield, to the Memory of the said 7 – 7 – 0
D^r. Johnson's Father, Mother, and Brother.
July 1st: 1785, Rec^d. by the hands of M^r. Rich^d. Greene
the above contents.   W^m. Thompson.

A translation of the epitaph, which may be in the hand of Richard Greene, is also preserved in the Birthplace (MS 22/4).[4]

The text was first printed in *Gents. Mag.* lv (Jan. 1785), i. 9, taken into Cooke's *Life of Johnson* (2nd edn. 1785), 48–9, and into the *European Mag.* vii (Feb. 1785), 83–4, whence perhaps Hawkins took it for his *Life87*, 577–8, (2nd. edn.), 578–9, and then by Isaac Reed for supp. vol. xiv (1788), 539–40. Cooke's and the *European. Mag.* debts are clear, but Hawkins and Reed vary in punctuation and their relationship is not demonstrable.

---

[1] The statement in the *City and County of Lichfield: Programme of Commemorative Celebrations of the 250th Anniversary of the Birth of Dr. Samuel Johnson* (Lichfield, 15–20 September 1959), p. 7, item 6, that: 'The original lettering on the tombstone became worn, and indecipherable, and was removed, but in 1854 a new "deep, massy and hard stone" with the epitaph engraved "on a large size" replaced the old one', misprints the date.

[2] Not in Croker's *Boswell* (1831), v. 303, but in 1848 &c., p. 798 n. The text of the epitaph seems to have been published first by John Nichols in *Gents. Mag.* lv (Jan. 1785), 9, as having 'been transmitted to me by a friend at Lichfield', an almost certain reference to Greene.

[3] With the copy of SJ's letter to Greene which was made for JB was also the note: 'To Mrs. Porter. Madam, be pleased to pay to Mr Greene ten pounds Sam. Johnson. £10 = 0 = 0. Decem. 2^d 1784.' (LICj: MS. 22/3; *Letters* iii. 251, n. on 1040). SJ's stress on the urgency of the matter and the disregard of cost is clear from the letter.

[4] I am indebted to Dr Graham Nicholls, curator of the Birthplace Museum at Lichfield, for generous assistance with these notes.

84.12W/1   Johnson's Will   1784

The Will was drafted by Sir John Hawkins, but SJ's responsibility for the wording and the contents, which he dictated to George Strahan, is clear.[1] As his legal advisor and executor, Hawkins reported fully on the composition, which he urged on SJ on 27 November, and noted a series of abortive dictations (*Life87*, 580 ff.). On 8 December Hawkins recorded another Will dictated to Revd. George Strahan, and on 9 Dec. a Codicil was composed in the same way disposing of his property in more detail (*Life87*, 588).

SJ's signature was witnessed by Revd. George Strahan and John Desmoulins. The Codicil was witnessed by John Copley, William Gibson, and Henry Cole, presumably SJ's neighbours.

The probate copy of the document is Ljh, and another MS copy is in L: (MS Egerton 24476, fo. 56).

[1] John Hoole also reports on the composition, showing that various of SJ's friends made suggestions on the first draft of 27 November 1784 (*Johns. Misc.* ii. 148–9). Hoole's account of SJ's last days was published in *European Mag.* xxxv (Sept., 1799), 153–8, from his MS which was lot 370 at Sotheby's (Mitchell-Ellis), 20 May 1968, to Traylen, and CtY (Osborn), and again published by Brack in *YULG* xlvii (1973), 103–8, and separately in a limited edn. from the Windhover Press, Iowa City, (1972). Hoole gave further reports in his letters to William Bowles, 30 Nov. 1784 and 5 Dec. (O: MS Don. c.52, fos. 94–97ᵛ), and 13 and 14 Dec. (MSS: Hyde), and in a letter to Beattie (pmk: 12 MR [?1785]; E: Fettercairn/Forbes-Beattie papers). The relation between the letters and the published account is canvassed by Korshin, in *Johnson after Two Hundred Years* (1986), 55–76. Other minor anecdotes of SJ by Hoole formed lot 369 in the above sale, and are now CtY, but are not relevant here.

84.12W/2   Johnson's Will and Codicil,   1784
London Chronicle etc.

The Will and Codicil were first published in the newspapers (e.g. *London Chron.*, 25 Dec. 1784, *St James's Chron.*, 25 Dec., and *Public Advertiser*, 26 Dec.), where JB first noticed it (*JB: Applause*, 274, s.d. 28 Dec. 1784), probably in the *London Chron.*[1] It was also printed in *Gents. Mag.* liv (Dec. 1784), 2. 946–7 as 'extracted from the Prerogative Court of Canterbury'.

[1] Further details are considered in *Gleanings* ii. 38–9, iii. 168–9, and iv. 20. Public comment began almost immediately after SJ's death, and that Frank Barber was favoured as the residuary legatee excited much contemporary comment (*Public Advertiser, Gen. Evening Post, St James's Chron.*, 14 Dec. 1784; *Gazetteer, London Packet, Morning Chron., Public Advertiser* (again), 15 Dec.; *Morning Herald, Gen. Evening Post* (again), 16 Dec.; *Morning Chronicle*, 17 Dec. and in minor observations elsewhere); see McGuffie, *SJ in the British Press* (1976), 330 ff. Hawkins disapproved strongly of this bequest and expressed his views at some length in *Life87*, 1st. edn., 586 n., and 596–7, 2nd. edn., 589 n. and 599–600.

84.12W/3a   Johnson's Will and Codicil,   1784
Cooke's Life of Samuel Johnson

Within a few days both Will and Codicil were also printed by William Cooke in his *The Life of Samuel Johnson, LL.D. With Occasional Remarks on his Writings, an Authentic Copy of his Will, and a Catalogue of his Works. . .*, &c., London: Printed for G. Kearsley, No. 46, Fleet-Street, M DCC LXXXV. [Entered at Stationers Hall]., 8°, on pp. 121–7, published on 28 December 1784,

84.12W/3b   Johnson's Will and Codicil,   1785
Cooke's Life of Samuel Johnson, second edition

The Will and Codicil were also printed in Cooke's second edn., also dated 1785, 12°, pp. 106–14, published 26 Feb. 1785 (*Morning Chron.*).

84.12W/4   Johnson's Will and Codicil,
Jarvis & Fieldings's edition of the Dictionary

The Will and Codicil were again reprinted in the anonymous biography of SJ which was prefixed to Jarvis & Fielding's edn. of the *Dictionary* (1786, above 55.4D/10).

84.12W/5   Johnson's Will and Codicil,   1787
Hawkins Life87, first and second editions

The Will and Codicil were published authoritatively by Hawkins (SJ's executor), in *Life87*, 1st edn., 591–5, 2nd edn., 595–98.

84.12W/6   Johnson's Will and Codicil, Boswell's Life   1791

Will and Codicil were published by JB in *Life* (1791), ii. 572–3, with JB's observations on 574–5 n. (*Life* iv. 402–5 n., 440–45).

84GM54   Gentleman's Magazine, Vol. LIV   1784

Life of Styan Thirlby (1686–1753)

April 260–2, Dec. 893 n.   Letter to 'Mr. Urban, *April* 8', signed 'J.N.'
Reprinted in facsimile in Fleeman, *Early Biographical Writings* (1973), 520–22. SJ's account is absorbed in an enlarged version by Nichols in *Lit. Anec.* iv (1812), 264–71.
References: *Life* iv. 161 n; *Johnsonian Miscellanies*, ii. 430–1; a note by 'Leicestrensis'[1] in *Gents. Mag.* lv (1785), i. 36, reflects upon SJ's account.
Notes: The MS is Hyde (*MS Handlist* 214; *MS Index* JoS 214).

December, ii. 892   Letter to Nichols, dated '*Dec.* 6, 1784', identifying contributors to vols. i–vii of the *Ancient Universal History*.
References: *Life* iv. 382–3 (Courtney 156); Murphy *Essay* (1792), 129–31; *Letters* 1042; Hyde iv. 445.
Notes: The MS of the letter itself is L (Add. MS 5159).

[1] Revd. Aulay Macaulay (Kuist 90b).

85.2BH/1a   Burney's Commemoration of Handel   1785

AN | ACCOUNT | OF THE | MUSICAL PERFORMANCE | IN | WESTMINSTER-ABBEY, | AND THE | PANTHEON, | May 26th, 27th,

29th; and June the 3d, and 5th, 1784. | IN | COMMEMORATION | OF | HANDEL. | By CHARLES BURNEY, Muſ.D. F.R.S. | ——All | The multitude of Angels, with a ſhout | Loud as from numbers without number, ſweet | As from bleſs'd voices, uttering joy, heav'n rung | With jubilee, and loud Hoſannas fill'd | Th' eternal regions. Milt. Parad. Lost, Book III. | [double rule] | LONDON, | Printed for the Benefit of the Musical Fund; and Sold by T. Payne and | Son, at the Meuſe-Gate; and G. Robinson, Pater-noſter-Row. | MDCCLXXXV.

Var. Tinker 1377 notes 'Menſe-Gate'.

4°, A⁴ a–b⁴ B⁴ *B⁴ C⁴ D⁴ (–D2,3 + ˣD⁴, ˣD4 + *D'1), E⁴ F⁴ (–F4), G–H⁴ I1, ²B–C⁴ ²D⁴ (²D4 + χ1) ²E⁴ (–²E4 + *E1.*F1'), ²F⁴ (–²F1) ²G⁴ (²G2 + ²χ1) ²H–I⁴ K–M⁴ N⁴ (N1 + ³χ1) O–S⁴ T² ⁴χ1, ($2 signed; ²B–T in *italic* caps.), 113 leaves.

Pp. Engr. front. + A1 *i* t., *ii* blk, *iii–vi* Dedication dh: TO THE | KING., ht: DEDICATION., vii Contents dh: [double rule] | [double rule] | CONTENTS., *viii* 'Directions for the Plates', on a1 ²*i* ii–xvi Preface dh: [double rule] | [double rule] | PREFACE., ht: PREFACE., on B1 *1* 2–8 *1–*8 9–20 *19–*24 21–41 Sketch of the Life of Handel, on G2ᵛ *42* 43–6 List of Handel's Works, on H1 *47* Proposals for Handel's Music ('*June* 22, 1783.'), *48* 49–56 Addenda to the 'Preface' and the 'Life', on ²B1 ½t 'Commemoration', ²B1ᵛ blk, on ²B2 *1* 2–15 Introduction, *16–17* 18–21 'The Orchestra' &c., *22* blk, *23* ½t 'First Performance', *24* blk, on χ1 'List of Compositions', *25* 26–41 Account, *42* blk, *43* ½t 'Second Performance', *44* blk, on ²χ1 recto blk, verso 'List of Pieces', on ²G³ *45* 46–70 Account, *71* ½t 'Third Performance', *72* blk, 73–90 Account, on ³χ1 recto blk, verso 'Selection of Sacred Music', on N2 *91* ½t 'Fourth Performance', *92* blk, *93* 94–107 Account, *108* blk, *109* ½t 'Fifth Performance', *110* blk, 111–25 Account, *126* blk, *127* ½t 'Appendix', *128* blk, 129–39 text of Appendix, *140* advt. for Burney's *History of Music*, vols. I–II (76.1BH/1, above), on ⁴χ1 *Errata* and Binder's Directions.

Pagination: 48, 97 unnumbered; starred page numbers in above are found on the starred signatures, and are within brackets.

Press-figures: none.

Catchwords: xiii kind‸ (~;), *8 *om.* (when), 18 ‸have ("~), 25 ‸Strong ("~), 38 *om.* (CHARACTER), 48 ‸That ("~), 56 *om.* (COMMEMORATION), ²19 Mr. (Baron), 25 examined‸ (~,), 40 Indeed, (Nothing,), 93 BY ("By), 130 5."That (V."~).

Explicit: none.

Paper: White, laid; (**a**) Large paper: Royal (uncut: 11⅝ × 9⅛ in.), wmk.: fleur-de-lys + Strasburg bend; this is also appreciably heavier paper; (**b**) ordinary paper — medium (uncut: 11⅝ × 9 in.), wmk.: fleur-de-lys.

Type: Dedication: double pica (7.0 mm), leaded (2.0 mm), Preface: great primer (6.0 mm), leaded (2.0 mm), Life and text: english (4.5 mm), leaded (1.5 mm), notes: bourgeois (3.1 mm), leaded (0.6 mm).

Plates: (8), though the list on A4ᵛ (*viii*) 'Directions for the Plates', calls for seven only:[1] **1**. inserted facing t. Front. Allegory, 'Publish'd January 8ᵗʰ. 1785-', **2**. facing p. 1 (B1) View of Handel's Monument in Westminster Abbey 'E.F. Burney delin. I.M. Delattre sculp.', **3**. 23 (²D4) Design of monument 'B. Rebecca delt. I.K. Sherwin Engraver to His Majesty &c His Royal Highness the Prince of Wales sculpsit.', **4**. 25 (²E1) 'From Harmony, From heavenly Harmony This Universal Frame began' 'I.B. Cipriani R.A. Inventᵗ. F. Bartolozzi R.A. Engraver to His Majesty Sculpᵗ.', **5**. 43 (²G2) The Dead Shall Live, the Living Die. Allegory of Messiah 'May 29. Messiah', 'R. Smirke pinxᵗ. F. Haward sculp. R.A. Publish'd 29ᵗʰ May 1784', **6**. 71 (K4) View of the Gallery . . . &c. 'E.F. Burney del. J. Spilsbury sculp.', **7**. 91 (N2) View of the Orchestra and Performers 'Published January 14ᵗʰ. 1785', and **8**. 109 (P3).

Plates were evidently available separately as two of them are found in L copies of *Newcastle Musical Festival, in St. Nicholas's Church, August 25th. 1791. A Selection of Sacred Music*. Newcastle-on-Tyne, 1791 (L²: 1. 1560/2240; 2. 1560/2238).

References: CH 161–2; Hazen 30–33; Lonsdale, *Burney* (1965), 29, 285, 314, 400, ch. 7, esp. 307; *Rothschild* 544; *Tinker* 1377; *Letters* 1000.1, 1004, Hyde iv. 384-86, 392-3; ESTC: n014660.

Notes: A stub in the Hyde (Leeds) copy shows that F⁴ (−F4) was bound in the sequence: F1.4 (−F4), F2.3. The Binder's Directions clarify the disposition of the various insertions. Some of these changes have been attributed to George III (Hazen), though Lonsdale is doubtful (*Burney* (1965), 305). CB stated that he had 'cancelled the 1st sheet . . .' (Lonsdale, 307 n. 3).[2] SJ supplied the Dedication, part of the composition of which is revealed in SJ's letters to Burney of Aug.–Sept. 1784. 2,000 copies, with some on Large Paper (*USA*: CtY; *UK*: L), were printed and published. Early copies were issued, perhaps privately, dated '1784' (ESTC: t149607; L (785. 1.209)). The plates occasioned a good deal of delay (n. 1, below), but the work eventually appeared on 1 Feb. 1785 (*St. James's Chron.*), and was reviewed in *Gents. Mag.* lv (Feb. 1785), 129–30 and (Mar. 1785) 200–2, *Critical Rev.* lix (Feb. 1785), 130–8 (by Thomas Twining, Lonsdale, 311–12), the *Monthly Rev.* lxxii (Feb. 1785), 279–86 (by George Colman, Lonsdale, 312–13), in the *European Mag.* vii (Mar. 1785), 193–7, and in Maty's *New Review* vii (1785), 56–62. It is also noticed in Burney's own *History of Music*, iv (1789), 518–9. Some extracts are found in G.F. Graham, *Account of the First Edinburgh Musical Festival held between the 30th October and 5th November 1815*, Edinburgh 1815 (Lonsdale, 500). An *obiter dictum* of SJ on age, is cited pp. 30–31.

'Miscellaneous materials relating to the Handel Commemorations of 1784 and 1834' were lot 417 at Puttick & Simpson (Fillinham), 6 Aug. 1862. An extra-illustrated copy of this book (2 vols. with scores and over 90 portraits) was lot 219 at Christie's, 5 Dec. 1906. The performances were described in *St James's Chron.*, 5 June 1784, and in other newspapers.

Copies:[3] O² (a: Douce B. subt. 272; b: GG 49.Art);
USA: [CLSW], CLU-C, CSmH² (a 'Britwell', and b), [CSt, CTM], CtY²
(1. Tinker, notes 'Menſe' in imprint; 2. Music school), [CU], DFo ('Wᵐ.
Frere'), DLC², Hyde³ (1. a uncut, full red morocco, gilt 'Presentation to Her
Majesty' [= Qu. Charlotte-Sophia];[4] 2. b 'John Meade Falkner' — 'Chauncey
Brewster Tinker'; 3. b 'Duke of Leeds'), ICN², ICU, [Liebert (uncut) = CtY],
MB, [MdBP], MH², [MHi, MiW, MRNEcM, NBC], NIC, NjP, NPM, NN,
NNC, [NRU], PPL, [OOxM, OU, PPCI, PPiU, PU-W], PPL, [PPL-R],
TxU², ViU; *Can*: CaOHM² (1. D. 438; 2. D. 1688); *UK*: BAT, [W.R. Batty],
BMp, C, Cf² (1. 'Fitzwilliam 1785. From the Author'), Ct (Rothschild),
DUNu, E (Mus. pr. 4/1), Ep, [Es], Gp, L⁶, LEu, LICj ('Arthur F. Hill, FSA'),
MRc, MRu, NCl, NOu, [L.F. Powell], SHp, SHu; *Aust*: CNL (DNS 2455).

¹ Hazen 31–2 notes only seven, and the reviewer in the *European Mag.* vii (March 1785), commented, 'The work is embellished with seven copper-plates', but his list shows that the frontispiece was disregarded (196). The same explanation accords with the notice in *Gents. Mag.* lv (Mar. 1785), 22, 'embellished with seven plates'. Such a work is, however, likely to attract insertions, and Hazen 31 n. and Lonsdale, *Burney* (1965), 306–7, 310, comment on the delay occasioned by the plates.

² In Blackwell's *Catalogue* B 107 (1993), 62, @ £350, was a copy retaining the original *cancellantia* of D2–3 (pp. 19–22), and their replacements.

³ A copy presented to Edmund Ayrton, Master of the Chapel Royal, was item 42 in E.M. Lawson, *Catalogue* 175 (1969), but is not located; it is likely that CB made several presentations. Lonsdale notes that the LP copies were intended for the Directors of the Commemoration (*Burney* (1965), 311).

⁴ Lonsdale, *Burney* (1965), 310–11.

85.2BH1b   Burney's Commemoration of Handel,   1964
facsimile

A facsimile reprint of the first edition was published at Amsterdam, in 1964
Copies: O; *UK*: NCp, SAN.

85.2BH/2   Burney's Commemoration of Handel,   1785
Dublin

AN | ACCOUNT | OF THE | MUSICAL PERFORMANCES | IN |
WESTMINSTER-ABBEY, | AND THE | PANTHEON, | May 26th, 27th,
29th; and June the 3d, and 5th, 1784. | IN | COMMEMORATION | OF |
HANDEL. | By CHARLES BURNEY, Muſ.D. F.R.S. | —-All | The multitude
of Angels, with a ſhout | Loud as from numbers without number, ſweet | As
from bleſſ'd voices, uttering joy, heav'n rung | With jubilee, and loud Hoſannas
fill'd | Th' eternal regions. | MILT. PARAD. LOST, Book III. | [short swelled
rule] | DUBLIN: | Printed for Meſſrs. MONCREIFFE, JENKIN, WHITE, | H.
WHITESTONE, BURTON, and BYRNE. | [short ornam. rule] | MDCCLXXXV.

8°, A⁴ a⁸ B–P⁸ (P8 blk), ($2 signed), 124 leaves.

Pp. A1 *i* t., *ii* blk, *iii–vi* Dedication dh: TO THE | KING., vii Contents, *viii* blk, on a1 *i* ii–xvi Preface, on B1 *1* 2–74 Life of Handel, on F6 p. ²*1* ½t, *2* blk, *3* 4–25 Introduction and performers, on H2 *25* ½t Commemoration, *26* blk, 27–131 text, *132* blk, *133* ½t Appendix, *134* blk 135–45 Appendix ('St Martin's-street, July 1784.'), *146* blk, *147–8* (P8) blk.

Pagination: [↑] vii, 67, ²61, 77, 89, 100, 102–4, 117, 135; (↑) 56; unnumbered 'Dedication', ²i, 1, 59, 63–4, 75–7, ²17–18, 25–9, 44–9, 75–6, 78, 95–9, 115–6, 132–4; H3 not included in numeration, 79 as 97.

Press-figures: none.

Catchwords: 30 ₐany ("~), 63 *om.* (ADDENDA), 74 *om.* (COMMEMORATION), ²17 *om.* (ASSISTANT), 57 *om.* (but), 94 *om.* (Selection), 95–8 *om.*, 99 BY ("By), 100 *om.* ("By), 115–16 *om.*, 129 *om.* (STATE), 132–4 *om.*

Explicit: none.

Paper: White, laid; Carré (8¼ × 5¼ in.); wmk.: F DANGO[UMOIS] + fleur-de-lys.

Type: Preface: english (4.6 mm), leaded (0.6 mm); text: pica (4.0 mm), leaded (0.3 mm), notes: bourgeois (3.0 mm). Dhh have heavy parallel rules.

Plates: none.

References: CH 161–2; Hazen 31; ESTC: t150538.

Copies: E (Hall 149. i, 'Lauriston Castle');

USA: [CSt], [Liebert ('N.W. Bruel') = CtY], MBAt, NN, PPL; *UK*: L (7895. aaa.35), Lv (Dyce, 1659); *Eir*: D, Dt².

85.2BH/3   Burney's Commemoration of Handel   1834

AN ACCOUNT | OF THE | MUSICAL PERFORMANCES | IN | WESTMINSTER ABBEY, | AND | *THE PANTHEON*, | May 26th, 27th, 29th, and June the 3rd and 5th, 1784, | IN | COMMEMORATION | OF | HANDEL; | By CHARLES BURNEY, Mus.D. F.R.S.| To which is added, | A NOTICE OF THE FORTHCOMING | ROYAL MUSICAL FESTIVAL | OF 1834. | [short rule] | "—All | The multitude of Angels, with a shout | Loud as from numbers without number, sweet | As from bless'd voices, uttering joy, heav'n rung | With jubilee, and loud Hosannas fill'd | Th' eternal regions." | MILT. PARAD. LOST, Book III. | [short rule] | [**Black letter**] **London:** | PUBLISHED BY DUFF AND HODGSON, 65, OXFORD STREET, | AND TO BE HAD OF ALL MUSIC AND BOOKSELLERS. | [short rule] | 1834. | *Price One Shilling*.

8°, A–B⁸ C⁴, ($2 (–C2) signed), 20 leaves.

Pp. Engr. front. + A1 *i* t., *ii* coloph: 'Entered at Stationers' Hall | [medium rule] | ALFRED ROBINS, Printer, 29 Tavistock Street, Covent Garden.', *iii–iv*

Dedication 'To the King', *v* vi–xiv Preface, *xv* xvi–xxvii Commemoration, xxviii–xxxv Performers and Performances, *xxxvi* Statement of Funds, *xxxvii* ½t 'Royal Musical Festival', xxxviii text, xxxix Patrons &c., *xl* Order of Performances.

Pagination: ↑, but iv ↖.

Press-figures: none; *Catchwords*: none; *Explicit*: none.

Paper: White, wove; royal (10 × 6¼ in.); no vis. wmk.

Type: Small pica (3.5 mm).

Plate: 'The Orchestra, Westminster Abbey. G.E. Maddey, lith. 3, Wellington St. Strand.'

References: Lonsdale, *Burney* (1965), 500.

Notes: SJ's 'Dedication' is reprinted pp. iii–iv.

Copies: O (34. 696); *USA*: DLC, ViU; *UK*: C, E (552), Gu, L².

| 85.2BH/TG/1a | Burney's Commemoration of Handel, German translation | 1785 |

[Fraktur] Dr. Karl Burney's | Nachricht | von Georg Friedrich Händel's | Lebensumſtänden | und | der ihm zu London im Mai und Jun. 1784 angeſtellten | Gedächtnißfeyer. | [rule] | Aus dem Engliſchen überſetzt | von | Johann Joachim Eſchenburg, | Profeßor in Braunſchweig. | [Woodcut vign.] | Mit Kupfern. | [ornamental double rule] | Berlin und Stettin, | bei Friedrich Nicolai, 1785.

4°, *–***⁴ ****² a–f⁴ g² A–N⁴ (*1 ? ½t or blk), ($3 signed; BD: **Burney** on $1), 92 leaves.

Pp. (*1 ?), Engr. front. + *2 ½t Dedicatory, *2ᵛ blk, on *3–4ᵛ Dedication ('**Allergnädigste Königin**'), on **2–***3ᵛ **Vorbericht des Verfaßers**, ***4–****2ᵛ **Vorbericht des Ueberſetzers**, on a1 *I* ½t **Abriss von Händels Leben**, *II* blk, *III* IV–LII text, on A1 *1* ½t **Händels Gedächnißfeyer**, *2* blk, *3* 4–102 text, *103* **Inhalt**, *104* blk.

Pagination: I–III, XLIX, 1–3, 19–21, 35–7, 57–8, 73–5, 85 unnumbered.

Press-figures: none.

Catchwords: XXVII ˄er („~), XLVI **Händel**˄ (Händel's), 89 ˄**ein** („~).

Explicit: none; 102 [Engr. of commemorative medal].

Paper: White, laid; ? Register (*c.* 10 × 8in.); no vis. wmk.

Type: **Vorbericht**: cicero (4.5 mm), text: brevier (4.0 mm), notes: garmond (3.5 mm).

Plates: (2) 1. Front. 'Haendels Denkmal in der Westmünster Abley' (*stet*: Abley), and 2. plate (fold.) 'Plan des Orchesters und dessen Vertheilung', facing p. 13.

References: Lonsdale, *Burney* (1965), 500.

Notes: It is not clear why the modified version of SJ's Dedication to the King

should now be rendered as addressed to the Queen. It is signed by 'allerun-
terthänigst treugehorsamster Johan Joachim Eschenburg'. Eschenburg's translation is mentioned by Burney in his *History* (76.1BH, above), iv (1789), 603–4.[1]

Copies: L² (**1**. 785. k.9, 'Herrn Planta . . . von den Uebersetzer'; **2**. Hirsch I.
645); *USA*: DLC, CtY ('Lowell' — 'Mason', lacks *1).

---

[1] 'Professor Eschenburg, of Brunswick, the celebrated translator of Shakespeare into German,
Brown's Dissertation on the Rise, &c. of Music and Poetry, Webb on the same subject, and the ora-
torio of Judas Maccabæus, has done me the honour to translate the Dissertation on the Music of the
Ancients, prefixed to the first volume of this work, and my Account of the Commemoration of
Handel.' The Dissertation appeared as *Dr. Karl Burney's Abhandlung über die Musik der Alten . . .
übersetzt und mit einigen Anmerkungen begleitet von J. J. Eschenburg*, Leipzig, in Schwickerischen
Verlage. 1781, 4° (Lonsdale, *Burney* (1965), 499). It contains nothing Johnsonian.

85.2BH/TG/1b   Burney's Commemoration of   [1965]
Handel, German translation, facsimile

A facsimile of the above edition was published in Leipzig [1965]. Nachricht
von Georg Friedrich Händels Lebensumständen Faksimiliedruck im Veb
Deutscher Verlag für Musik Leipzig.

Notes: The Nachwort is signed, Walther Siegmund-Schultze. The facsimile
was taken from a copy in the Staatsbibliothek zu Leipzig.

Copy: L (X.431/194).

85.2PW/1   Poetical Works, ed. Kearsley   1785

THE | POETICAL WORKS | OF | *SAMUEL JOHNSON*, ll.d. | NOW
FIRST COLLECTED | IN ONE VOLUME. | [orn. device: interlaced 'G K']
| LONDON. | PRINTED FOR THE EDITOR, | AND SOLD BY G.
KEARSLEY, NO. 46, FLEET | STREET, 1785. | [Price Two Shillings
and Six Pence.]

8°, A⁴ B–N⁸ O⁴, ($4 signed), 104 leaves.

Pp. A1 *i* t., *ii* blk, iii–vi Advertisement dh: ADVERTISEMENT. |
[medium swelled rule], vii–viii Contents dh: TABLE of CONTENTS. |
[medium swelled rule], on B1 *1* ½t: [medium parallel rule] | LONDON: | A
SATIRE. | CORRECTED FROM A COPY PRINTED AT THE |
CLARENDON PRESS, | At Oxford. | [medium total rule], 4–196 text, 196
Errata (5), *197–200* (O3–4) Kearsley's advts.

Pagination: [↑] iii–viii; (↑) 4–196; i–ii, 1–3, 22, 37–8, 42, 152–4, 197–200
unpaged, 152, 154 blk.

Press-figures: none.

Catchwords: *om.* pp. 1–2, 4, 6, 8, 10, 12, 14, 16, 18, 20, 36–8, 42, 114, 150–4,
171, 178; 41 The (PERSONS), 103 ACT. (~ₐ), 122 Cali· (~.).

Explicit: 196 FINIS.

Paper: White, laid; Foolscap (uncut: 6¾ × 4¼ in.); wmk.: Britannia.

Type: Small pica (3.5 mm), leaded (0.6 mm); notes minion (2.3 mm).

References: Courtney 157; CH 162; *Tinker* 1874, *Poems*² xv–xvi; ESTC: t082914.

Notes: This first issue contains no cancelled leaves. The solecism stands on p. iii, l. 6: 'little remains for me, than to state', and the text of 'Messia' (pp. 180–4), is faulty. The 5 *errata* usually occupy six lines of type, but there are said to be copies with only 4 lines of *errata*, though none has been seen.

This edition was published on 15 February 1785 (*Morning Chron.* and *St James's Chron.*). Kearsley's responsibility for the collection is clarified in the 'Advertisement' prefixed to the 1789 edn. (85.2PW/5, below). The dh to *London* associates this version with the text of *Two Satires*, 1759 (38.5L/9, above).

Copies:[1] O (Vet. A5 f.205);

USA: CtY², Hyde (Adam), [Liebert ('H. Harvey Frost', uncut, marbled wraps) = CtY], MH (16477.31*), NIC, NjP, ViU ('Clement Shorter' — McGeorge, uncut, marbled wraps), [? WiM]; *Can*: CaOHM; *Japan*: [Kyoto²]; *UK*: [W.R. Batty ('Mrs Annie Jeaffreson' — 'R.E. Gathorne-Hardy')²], BMp² (60170, no advts., 60185), Ck, L² (11633. aa.29 + MS notes; 11630. aaa.41); *Aust*: CNL (DNS 4808).

[1] Robert Burns's copy was sold by Phillips Son & Neale (Edinburgh), 19 August 1981, 72, £120; a copy of this first state was lot 113 at Sotheby's, 19 May 1980, and went to Quaritch for £170. An undifferentiated copy with the bookplate of Sir Robert Salusbury Cotton was in Maggs Bros, *Catalogue* 299 (1934), 349, £4. 10s.

[2] This appears to be the same copy sold by Maggs Bros, *Catalogue* 1038 (1984), 176.

85.2PW/2   Poetical Works, ed. Kearsley, Dublin   1785

THE | POETICAL WORKS | OF | *SAMUEL JOHNSON*, LL.D. | NOW FIRST COLLECTED | IN ONE VOLUME. | [medium swelled rule] | DUBLIN: | PRINTED FOR L. WHITE, P. BYRNE, AND | R. MARCHBANK. | M,DCC,LXXXV.

12°, A⁴ B–I¹² K², ($2,5 signed), 102 leaves.

Pp. A1 *i* t., *ii* blk, iii–vi Advertisement, vii–viii Contents, on B1 *1–3* 4–196 text.

Pagination: (↑); [↑] iii–viii; *Press-figures*: none.

Catchwords: 28 The (~*), 36 *om.* (IRENE), 41–2 *om.*, 114 *om.* (SCENE), 150 *om.* (SCENE), 151–4 *om.*, 171. *om.* (To).

Explicit: 196 FINIS.

Paper: White, laid; Grand cornet [or Crown ?] (6⅔ × 3¾ in.); no vis. wmk.

Type: Advertisement: small pica (3.6 mm), text: long primer (3.2 mm), notes: bourgeois (2.6 mm).

References: Courtney 157; Cole, *PBSA* lxxv (1981), 235–55; ESTC: t082915.

Notes: The paper may be English: the absence of a wmk. makes it difficult to identify. This is a direct reprint of 85.2PW/1 above, retaining the uncorrected texts of the 'Advertisement' and in the 'Messia'. It was announced in the *Dublin Evening Post*, 10 May 1785 (Cole).

Copies: O² (1. 2799 f.469, 'Nathaniel Taylor'; 2. Vet. A5 f.1023(1));

USA: CSmH ('Beverley Chew'), CtY (TCD prize), Hyde ('Bindon Blood Aug^st. 17th. 1792' — 'W. Burton June 12th 1800' — 'T.C. Burton Septr. 1831'), IU, [Liebert = CtY], NIC, NRU; *Can*: CaOHM; *Japan*: [Kyoto]; *UK*: C, Gu (P.19——k.33), L (11607. aaa.3); *Eir*: Dt (54 t.91).

85.2PW/3   Poetical Works, ed. Kearsley,   1785
                           second London issue

THE | POETICAL WORKS | OF | *SAMUEL JOHNSON*, LL.D. | NOW FIRST COLLECTED | IN ONE VOLUME. | [orn. device: interlaced 'G K'] | LONDON. | PRINTED FOR THE EDITOR, | AND SOLD BY G. KEARSLEY, NO. 46, FLEET | STREET, 1785. | [Price Two Shillings and Six Pence.]

8°, A⁴ (± A2) B–M⁸ N⁸ (−N2,3,4 + N2, N3.4) O⁴, ($4 (−A1,3,4, D3, L4, O2–4) signed), 104 leaves.

Pp. A1 *i* t., *ii* blk, iii–vi Advertisement, vii–viii Contents, *1–3* 4–196 text, 196 *Errata* (5), *197–200* (O3–4) Kearsley's advts. (For details see 85.2PW/1, above, from which this issue differs only in the cancelled leaves.)

References: Courtney 157; CH 162; *Tinker* 1374; ESTC: t082914 (undifferentiated from the first issue, 85.2PW/1, above).

Notes: The cancelled leaves correct a solecism in A2 (p. iii), and several errors in the text of 'Messia'. This issue appears to have been announced separately on 24 March 1785 (*St James's Chron.*), at '2s. 6d. sewed' (*Gents. Mag.* lv (Apr. 1785), 302. The 5 *errata* (affecting the text of *Irene*) still stand on p. 196, and the text is unchanged.

Copies: O (12 θ. 667);

USA: CSmH ('Thomas Eyre, 25 March 1785'), CtY, DLC, Hyde² (1. 'Mrs Vesey'; 2. 'Norman'), ICN, ICU, [Liebert ('Miss Eleanor Poole, July 22. 1812' — A.E. Newton) = CtY], NN [NRo], TxU, WiM ('Le Cte Le Pelletier' — 'Brackenbury' [= Hugh Walpole]); *Can*: CaOHM; *UK*: AWn, BAT, [W.R. Batty ('J. Maundy Gregory')], BRu, C, Ep (no advts.), [?En], JDF ('C.F. Parker,[1] Pemb. Coll. Oxon.'— 'Gordon Tidy, 1914'), STA (uncut), Yc (XII.B, lacks N3.4).

---

[1] 1787–1870, *Al. Ox.* 1065/37, Fellow until 1819 then Rector of Ringshall, Suffolk. Macleane, *History of Pembroke College, Oxford* (1897), 463–4.

85.2PW/4   Poetical Works, new edition   1785

[½t] [medium swelled rule] | POEMS. | [medium swelled rule]

[Title] THE | POETICAL WORKS | OF | *SAMUEL JOHNSON*, L.L.D. | COMPLETE | IN ONE VOLUME. | [medium swelled rule] | A NEW EDITION. | [medium swelled rule] | *LONDON:* | Printed for W. Osborne and T. Griffin, | in St. Paul's Church-yard; and | J. Mozley, Gainsborough. | M.DCC.LXXXV.

8°, *A*⁴ B–U⁴, ($2 (L2 as K2) signed), 80 leaves.

Pp. π1 *i* ½t, *ii* blk, *iii* ½t: *Dr. JOHNSON's* | *POETICAL* | *WORKS.*, *iv* blk, *v* t., *vi* blk, vii–viii CONTENTS., on B1 *1–3* 4–152 text.

Pagination: [↑] vii–viii, (↑) 4–152; i–vi, 1–3, 20, 71–2, 76 unnumbered.

Press-figures: H4ᵛ(56)–2, I1ᵛ(58)–2, K1ᵛ(66)–2, L4ᵛ(80)–3, M4ᵛ(88)–2, N4ᵛ(96)–2, S1ᵛ(130)–2, U1ᵛ(146)–2; (56, 66, 88 sometimes unfigured).

Catchwords: *om.* i–vi, 2, 4, 6, 8, 10, 12, 14, 16, 18, 71–2, 76; 17 Scarce (S *inverted*), 35 Here (*slipt*), 39 *om.* (In), 106 Abdalla, (~.), 131 Two (With . . .| Two), 132 Conſtrain'd (Conſtrains), 133 Caraza. (Carara.), 141 Abdalla. (Aspasia.), 146 Cou'd (Caraza. | Could).

Explicit: 152 THE END.

Paper: White, laid; Foolscap (uncut: 6¾ × 4¼ in.); wmk.: Britannia.

Type: Long primer (3.2 mm), leaded (1.0 mm), but text of *Irene* (pp. 77–152) unleaded; notes: bourgeois (2.8 mm).

References: Courtney 157; *Tinker* 1375, *Poems*¹ xv, *Poems*² xv–xvi; ESTC: t042748.

Notes: This edition is reprinted from the second issue of 1785 (85.2PW/3, above), adopting the corrected readings in 'Messia'. *Irene* is here placed at the end of the collection.

Copies: O (12 θ.930);

USA: CSmH, CtY² (2. uncut), Hyde² (1. 'Richardson of Pitfour';¹ 2. 'Lomeshaye' — Adam), IU, [Liebert ('Brindley Hone, 46 York Street Dublin Ireland', blue boards uncut) = CtY], MH (16477.31.3), NIC, NjP, NN ('To Willᵐ. Cowper Esqʳ. from his affectionate friend Samuel Rose' + autograph and bookplate of WC, and ALS John Johnson to Thomas Hill), NRo ('R.W. Chapman'), TxU; *Japan*: [Kyoto]; *UK*: BMp (561716), C, E, En, JDF, Gp (uncut), Gu, L (11644. ee.78 (1)), MRu, Oef, Om; *Aust*: CNL (DNS 4809).

¹ John Richardson (1780–1864*), of Pitfour Cas., by Perth.

85.2PW/5   Poetical Works, ed. Kearsley   1789

[½t] [medium swelled rule] | POEMS. | [medium swelled rule]

[Title] THE | POETICAL WORKS | OF | *SAMUEL JOHNSON*, LL.D. | A NEW EDITION CONSIDERABLY ENLARGED. | [orn. device of interlaced 'G K'] | [BL] London: | PRINTED FOR GEORGE KEARSLEY, | JOHNSON'S HEAD, | FLEET-STREET, | 1789.

8°, A–P⁸, ($4 (–A1,2, D3, L4) signed), 120 leaves.

Pp. A1 *i* ½t, *ii* blk, *iii* t., *iv* blk, v–x Advertisement dh: ADVERTISE-MENT. | short swelled rule], (signed: 'G. K. Fleet-Street, *March* 1789.'), xi–xv TABLE OF CONTENTS. | [short swelled rule], *xvi* blk, on B1 *1* ½t London, *2–3* 4–212 text, on P3 *213–24* Kearsley's advts.

Pagination: [↑], but i–iv, xvi, 1–3, 22, 37–8, 42, 152–4 unnumbered; xvi, 38, 152, 154 blk.

Press-figures: A6(xi)–3, B8(15)–2, C4ᵛ(24)–2, C6(27)–3, D7ᵛ(46)–2, D8ᵛ(48)–3, E1ᵛ(50)–2, F5(73)–2, G7ᵛ(94)–3, H5(105)–2, I5(121)–3, K8ᵛ(144)–2, L2ᵛ(148)–3, M7(173)–2, N3ᵛ(182)–2, O7ᵛ(206)–3, P5–3, P5ᵛ–2.

Catchwords: om. i–iv, x, xvi, 1, 2, 4, 6, 8, 10, 12, 14, 16, 18, 20, 36–8, 42, 114, 151–4; v twenty; (~*;), xii *Anacreon*, (*~,), xiii *Impromptu* (*~), 241 [Iᴙᴇɴᴇ. (ᴧ~.), 176 ANACREON. (~,).

Explicit: 212 FINIS.

Paper: White, laid; Foolscap (uncut: 6¾ × 4¼ in.); wmk.: Britannia + GR.

Type: Long primer (3.3 mm), leaded (1.0 mm); notes brevier (2.7 mm).

References: Courtney 157; CH 162; ESTC: t082913.

Notes: Kearsley's Advertisement clarifies his responsibility for this and for the first collection (85.2PW/1, above). This edition was published at 3s. in boards.

Among the advts. in 8th edn. of *Beauties*, 1792 (81.11B(Parts 1+2)/3, above), p. 297 is: 'Poems of Dr. Johnson, just published in One Volume, by C. and G. Kearsley; & Posthumous Pieces. Translation of the *Bellum Catilinarium*, from Sallust. One Volume of Latin Pieces. One ditto of Memoirs of his own Life* And some Greek Epigrams. * *Consisting of loose memorandums. Another volume was burned by Dr. Johnson in a mistake, a few days before his death, along with other manuscripts.*' The 'Sallust' survives as a fragment (MS Hyde, *MS Handlist* 204; *MS Index* JoS 327) but it was never printed in any edn. of SJ's *Poems*, and remained unpublished until Sept. 1993 when a facsimile was privately printed for 'The Johnsonians' of New York, edited by G.T. Tanselle and D.L. Vander Meulen.[1] The 'Latin pieces' and the 'Greek Epigrams' appear to be the material published by Langton in *Works* (1787), i. 383–9, 407–26, and the 'Memoirs' may be identified with what was eventually published by Richard Wright as *An Account of the Life of Dr. Samuel Johnson, from his birth to his eleventh year, written by himself* (1805), commonly called 'Annals'. There is more than an air of opportunism about this.

Copies: JDF (lacks ½t; 'Carleton-Greene');

USA: CtY (no ½t), Hyde (Adam), ICU, [Liebert (uncut) = CtY], MH (16477.32), NIC ('H.G. Pollard'), NjP², NRo; *Can*: CaOHM; *Japan*: [Kyoto]; *UK*: [W.R. Batty ('James P. Murray')], BMp (472060), C, L² (11631. aa.16; 11630. aaa.43), O (Vet. A5 f.3396), Oef; *Aust*: CNL (DNS 4810).[2]

¹ SJ recommended Sallust among other authors, to his cousin, Samuel Ford in 1735 (*Letters* 3.3; Hyde i. 11–12), perhaps together with the 'Scheme for the Classes of a Grammar School', since both were published by 'S.P.' in *Gents. Mag.* lv (Apr. 1785), 266. 'S.P.' may have been either Samuel Pegge, or John Nichols (*Life* i. 99–100), but the document is lost. Sallust is cited in the drafts for *Irene* (*Poems*² 374 and n.), and the detail from *Bellum Catilinarium*, xv. 5, is repeated in the published text of the tragedy at *Irene*, IV. viii. 3–7. The same detail is repeated in *Rambler* 60, and a further well-known line from *Catiline*, xx. 4 is the motto for *Rambler* 64. Another mention of Catiline's immoderate ambition occurs in *Adventurer* 99 (*Catiline*, v. 5). SJ's continuing interest is reflected in his having taken a copy with him on his Scottish travels in 1773 (*Life* v. 122), and in inquiry of Richard Owen Cambridge in 1783 after a Spanish translation (*Life* iv. 195). On 15 July 1783 he commented further to Langton on Sallust's debts to Plato and Xenophon (*Diaries* 360–1). The concentration of his interest emerges in 1783, and the translation is reported in his diary for 15 September 1783: 'I finished Sallust' (*Diaries* 367). It was mentioned by Malone in his letter to Percy on 2 March 1785, commenting on possible losses of Johnsoniana after the fire at Sir John Hawkins's house: 'The translation of Sallust was merely done . . . as a passtime, I believe, at Brighthelmstone, for he was then observed to have that book often in his hand' (*Percy Letters* (Percy–Malone) (1944), 20–1). That locates some of the work in the autumn of 1782. Malone went on to say that the executors intended to publish it, though 'It has I am told, no remarkable merit'. Hawkins presumably decided against publication for this reason: 'so flatly and insipidly rendered that the suffering it to appear would have been an indelible disgrace to his memory' (*Life87* 541), and Boswell also commented 'it seems to have no very superiour merit to mark it as his' *Life* iv. 383 n.). Both observations are true. The extant MS is incomplete but what remains exhibits marks of haste and inattention, and of syntactic clumsiness characteristic of a very preliminary literal version needing considerable revision.

² Inscribed: 'E Libris Jacobi Boswell 1793 | Dono dedit | J W D' (probably Revd. James William Dodd, †1820, JB jun's tutor at Westminster), and, in another hand, 'This Volume was purchased at the sale of Mr. Boswell's Books in 1825 & contains Notes & various readings which he had transcribed from Dr. Johnson's own handwriting'. On the ½t of *London*, JB jun. wrote: 'These notes & various readings I have transcribed from Johnsons own hand writing on a copy of the 5th edition', and on p. 22 ('Vanity') he wrote: 'compared with the 1st Edition'. The volume figured in Sotheby, *Biblotheca Boswelliana*, 24 May 1825, lot 1489, where it was purchased by Edward Jesse for 15s.

85.2PW/6   Poetical Works, English Poets, Vol. 72   1790

[½t] THE | SEVENTY-SECOND VOLUME | OF THE | ENGLISH POETS; | CONTAINING | JOHNSON, | AND | PART of W. WHITEHEAD.

[Title] The Works of the English Poets. With Prefaces, Biographical and Critical. By Samuel Johnson. Volume the Seventy-Second. London: Printed by M. Brown; For J. Buckland, J. Rivington and Sons, T. Payne and Sons, L. Davis, B. White and Son, T. Longman, B. Law, J. Dodsley, H. Baldwin, J. Robson, C. Dilly, T. Cadell, J. Nichols, J. Johnson, G. G. J. and J. Robinson, R. Baldwin, H.L. Gardner, P. Elmsly, T. Evans, G. Nicol, Leigh and Sotheby, J. Bew, N. Conant, J. Murray, J. Sewell, W. Goldsmith, W. Richardson, T. Vernor, W. Lowndes, W. Bent, W. Otridge, T. and J. Egerton, S. Hayes, R. Faulder, J. Edwards, G. and T. Wilkie, W. Nicoll, Ogilvie and Speare, Scatcherd and Whitaker, W. Fox, C. Stalker, E. Newbery. 1790.

8°, *A*² B–Z⁸ 2A² (2A2 blk), ($4 signed; 'Vol. LXXII.' on $1), 180 leaves.

Pp. A1 ½t, A1ᵛ blk, A2 t., A2ᵛ blk, on B1 *1* ½t: THE | POEMS | OF | SAMUEL JOHNSON, L.L.D., *2* blk, 3–133 text dh: Dr. JOHNSON's |

POEMS. | [medium swelled rule], 134–7 Contents dh: THE | CONTENTS.,
138 blk, *139* ½t Whitehead, *140* blk, 141–352 Whitehead's Poems, 355–6
Contents, *357–8* (2A2) blk.

Pagination: [↑] 3, 17, 31, 75, 129, 134; 86 as 6; 74, 140, 357–8 blk.

Press-figures: none.

Catchwords: 8 The (ᵐThe), 9 Well (ᵘWell), 14 In (ᴵIn), 15 Much (ᵒMuch), 17
But (Impeachment . . .| . . .| But), 73 *om.* (POEMATA.), 87 His︿ (~,), 89 *om.*
(VERSUS,), 90 *om.* (Eis), 102–4 *om.*, 108 *om.* (ME,), 110–24 *om.*, 126 Ruffia,
(ᵏ~,), 133 *om.* (THE | CONTENTS.), 134–7 *om.*

Explicit: 352 END OF VOLUME SEVENTY-TWO.

References: Courtney 157; ESTC: t152606.

Notes: see above, 79.4LP/8a.

Copies: O (2804 f.76).

85.2PW/7   Poetical Works, Works of the British Poets,   1792–5
Vol. 11, ed. Anderson

[Engr. t.] A Complete Edition of the Poets of Great Britain. Volume the
Eleventh. Containing Wilkie, Dodsley, Shaw, Smart, Langhorne, Bruce,
Chatterton, Graeme, Glover, Lovibond, Penrose, Mickle, Jago, Scott, Johnson,
W. Whitehead, Jenyns, Logan, Warton, Cotton & Blacklock. [Vignette
Caesar's Dream. Langhorne's Poems. 'Burney del. Chesham sculp.'] London:
Printed for John & Arthur Arch, 23 Gracechurch Street: and for Bell &
Bradfute and J. Mundell & Co. Edinburgh.

[Title] The Works of the *British Poets*, with Prefaces, biographical and critical, *by Robert Anderson. M.D. Volume Eleventh.* Containing [3 cols., col. a:]
Wilkie, Dodsley, Smart, Shaw, Smart, Langhorne, Bruce, Chatterton, Graeme,
[col. b:] Glover, Lovibond, Penrose, Mickle, Jago, Scott, [col. c:] Johnson, W.
Whitehead, Jenyns, Logan, Warton, Cotton, Blacklock. London: Printed for
John & Arthur Arch; and for Bell & Bradfute, and J. Mundell, Edinburgh.
1794.

Vol. xi ('1794'), 8°; Pp. *777* t., *779* 780–836 Life of SJ (by Anderson) 2
cols./p., *837* 838–68 Poems.

References: Courtney 158; ESTC: t002891.

Notes: The *Works*, in 13 vols. were published 1792–95, and vol. 11, despite
the date, appeared in 1795. The 'Life' by Anderson was also published separately in 1795 with minor typographical adjustments and a change to the final
paragraph, forming a 'second edition' (strictly a second impression), upon which
Anderson based his 'Third' edition of 1815, which was enlarged with notes
from Thomas Percy. In the 1815 'Introduction', Anderson explains the evolution of his biography of SJ, p. *v*.[1]

Copies: O (2804 d. 38);

USA: NN³, WiM ('1795'); *Can*: CaOHM²; *UK*: Eu, L (11607. ff.1/11); *Fr*: BN.

---

¹ Anderson to Percy, 29 Oct. 1804; *Percy Letters* (Percy–Anderson) (1988), LV. 169–76, esp. 172, and Robert Anderson, *The Life of Samuel Johnson (1815)*, ed. P.J. Korshin (1973), vi–vii (see also Korshin, *HLQ* xxxvi (1973), 239–53).

85.2PW/8   Poetical Works, Cooke's edition   [1797]

[Engr. t.] JOHNSON's WORKS. | forming part of | [BL] **Cooke's Pocket Edition of** | *the Original & Complete Works of* | SELECT BRITISH POETS, | *or Entertaining Poetical Library* | containing the moſt Eſteemed | [BL] **Poetic Productions** | *Superbly Embelliſhed.* | [Vignette of 2 shepherds with goat beneath tree] | *R. Corbould del Cole sculpᵗ.* | Embellished under the Direction of C. Cooke, July 7. 1797 | Vide Pastoral I. page 74. line 20

[½t] THE | POETICAL WORKS | OF | SAMUEL JOHNSON, LL.D. | CONTAINING HIS | [2 cols., col. a:] LONDON: A SATIRE. | VANITY OF HUMAN WISHES. | ODES. | [vertical rule, col. b:] PROLOGUES. | MISCELLANIES. | EPITAPHS. | [across the full measure] *&c. &c. &c.* | [medium parallel rule] | [8 lines verse] *Mr. Courtney's Poetical Review.* | [medium total rule] | [BL] **London:** | PRINTED AND EMBELLISHED | Under the Direction of | C. COOK. [*Stet*: COOK.]

[Title] THE | POETICAL WORKS | OF | [hollow] S. JOHNSON, LL.D. | WITH | THE LIFE OF THE AUTHOR. | [medium parallel rule] | [BL] **Cooke's Edition.** | [medium total rule] | [14 lines verse] | *Mr. Murphy's Poetical Epiſtle to Johnſon.* | [parallel rule] | EMBELLISHED WITH SUPERB ENGRAVINGS. | [total rule] | [BL] **London:** | Printed for C. COOKE, No. 17, Paternoſter-Row | and ſold by all the Bookſellers in | Great-Britain and | Ireland.

18°, π² A–C⁶ D⁴ E–G⁶ H², ($3 (−D3) signed), 44 leaves.

Pp. Engr. t. + π1 *i* t., *ii* blk, *iii* ½t, *iv* blk, on A1 *1* 2–36 dh: LIFE OF | DR. JOHNSON, L.L.D. | [short total rule], on D1 *37* 38–83 text of Poems, *84* CONTENTS.

Pagination: 51 as 5; *Press-figures*: E4ᵛ(52)–2.

Catchwords: 17 Chronicle,' (nicle,'), 36 *om.* (LONDON:); no cwds in text of Poems (37–83).

Explicit: 83 FINIS.

Paper: White, laid; wmk.: '1795' and '1796'.

Type: Bourgeois (2.8 mm), leaded (0.3 mm), notes: ? pearl (1.0 mm).

Plates: (3): 1. Engr. t., as above; 2. Oval port. of SJ ('Blinking Sam'), 'Engraved by Granger from a Drawing by W.H. Brown. JOHNSON. | Engraved for C. Cook. March 4. 1797.' 3. Circle enclosing polymastoid female suckling putto, with cornucopia watched by rabbit, the whole supported by putti and cornucopia. At head: 'painted by T. Kirk Printed for C. Cook. July 11. 1797. Engraved by J. Chapman. | And nature on her naked breafts | Delights to catch the gales of Life. | Vide Spring. Page 57. line 2.[1]

References: Courtney 157; ESTC: t082918.

Notes: The date of publication must postdate that of the paper, and in view of the dates on the plates, 1797 seems most likely. Copies are bound variously with other of Cooke's poets, reflecting the decision of owners rather than Cooke's publishing policy.

Copies: O[3] (**1**. Vet. A5 f.2182; **2**. Vet. A5 f.959(2); **3**. 2804 f. 116);

USA: Hyde ('William Bland'), [Liebert = CtY], MB, MH (KC. 13094), NcD, NN, NRo; *UK*: BMp (641791), E (ABS.1.81.101(2)), JDF[3] (**1**. Contemp. sheep 'Arthur Viscount Dillon'; **2**. bound with *Congreve*; **3**. bound with *Moore*), Gu, L[3] (**1**. 1066. a.12; **2**. 11613. h.1/30;[2] **3**. Cup. 501 a.7/19(1), uncut, bound with *Garth*), LVu, MRc, SHu.

---

[1] The text reads 'naked breast' (*Poems*[2] 102): Kirk got carried away.
[2] L: (Cup. 501 a.7/19(1)), appears to be a reissue of about 1816.

85.2PW/9   Poetical Works, ed. Park   1805

THE | POETICAL WORKS | OF | *SAMUEL JOHNSON.* | COLLATED WITH THE BEST EDITIONS: | BY | *THOMAS PARK, ESQ. F.S.A.* | [parallel rule] | LONDON; | [BL] **Printed at the Stanhope Press,** | BY CHARLES WHITTINGHAM, | *Union Buildings, Leather Lane*; | FOR JOHN SHARPE, OPPOSITE YORK-HOUSE, | PICCADILLY. | [diamond rule] | 1805.

16°, *A*[2] B–F[8] G[4] (G4 ? blk), ($1 signed), 46 leaves.

Pp. A1 *1* t., *2* blk, *3–4* Contents, on B1 *5* 6–8 Encomium (by 'T.H. 1785',[1] and Arthur Murphy's *Poetical Epistle*), *9* 10–89 text, *90* blk, (? *91–2* blk).

Pagination: 1–5, 9, 30, 45, 57, 66, 75, 87, 90 unpaged.

Press-figures, *Catchwords*, and *Explicit*: none.

Paper: White, wove; probably royal (16° gives uncut leaf of 5 × 3⅛ in.); no vis. wmk.

Type: Brevier (2.5 mm), leaded (0.5 mm); notes: nonpareil (2.0 mm).

Plate: A fearful traveller. JOHNSON. | New fears in dire viciffitude invade, | The ruftling brake alarms, and quivering fhade. | *Vanity of Human Wishes.* | Painted by Rob[t]. Smirke, R.A. Engraved by Anth[y]. Cardon | Published 1st. Jan[y]. 1805, by John Sharpe, | Piccadilly.

References: Courtney 158.

Copies: JDF ('Hon[ble]. Arthur Dillon',[2] bound with *Poetical Works* of Joseph Warton);

USA: DLC, [Liebert = CtY], MH (10487.38); *Japan*: [Kyoto]; *UK*: ABu, BMp[2] (166851, 866012), BRp, L (1066. d.5, 16), MRu, STA (uncut).

¹ 'T.H.' is not identified and I doubt Thomas Harwood whose brief sketch of SJ was proposed in his letter to JB of 12 Mar. 1787, and adumbrated in his *History & Antiquities of the Church & City of Lichfield* (Gloucester, 1806); see Waingrow, *Corr.* 208-10 and refs.
    ² Not Hon. Col. Arthur Richard Dillon (1750–94*), 2nd s. of Henry, 11th Visc., guillotined in the French Terror, but probably Arthur Richard, 2nd s. of John (1740?–1805), 1st Bt. (1801) of Lismullen, Co. Meath, later general, who d. *b.s.p.* 1845.

85.2PW/10   Poetical Works, Philadelphia   1805

THE | POETICAL WORKS | OF | *SAMUEL JOHNSON, L.L.D.* | WITH THE | LIFE OF THE AUTHOR. | [medium parallel rule] | *PHILADELPHIA:* | PRINTED FOR BENJAMIN JOHNSON, | JACOB JOHNSON, AND | ROBERT JOHNSON. | [12 points] | 1805.

12°, A–L⁶, ($1,3 ($3 as $2, but 'D5'; −A1, H1) signed), 66 leaves.

Pp. Engr. front. port. of SJ + A1 *1* t., *2* blk, *3* 4–52 dh: THE | LIFE OF DR. JOHNSON. | [parallel rule], rt: LIFE OF | DR. JOHNSON., on E3 *53* 54–129 text of Poems, *130* 131–2 Contents.

Pagination: ↑ at 81, 83, 109; 54 as 45, 79 as 97, 1–3, 130 unnumbered.

Paper: Dull white (foxed), wove; foolscap (uncut: 5⅔ × 3¼ in.); no vis. wmk.

Type: Text: bourgeois (2.9 mm), leaded; Life: brevier (2.7 mm).

References: Courtney 157; S&S 8706 [NcGW].

Notes: The poems are arranged with *London* and *Vanity* together, followed by 'Prologues', 'Odes', and 'Miscellanies'.

Copies: BMp (541768, 'W.S. Chase 1883. Anyone may borrow but a Gentleman returns');

USA: CSmH, CtY, [Liebert = CtY], MB, MH (116477.32.10*), MWA, NjP, NN, PPL.

85.2PW/11   Poetical Works, ed. Blagdon   1806

THE | POEMS | OF | Dʀ. SAMUEL JOHNSON. | To which is prefixed, | A | *LIFE OF THE AUTHOR.* | [medium parallel rule] | Bʏ F.W. BLAGDON, Esǫ. | [medium total rule] | LONDON: | Published by W. SUTTABY, and B. CROSBY | and Co. *Stationers'-Court.* | 1806.

16°, *A*⁸ B–D⁸, ($1 signed), 32 leaves.

Pp. Engr. front. + A1 *1* t., *2* coloph: 'R. Edwards, Printer, | Crane Court, Fleet-Street.', *3* 4–16 Life of SJ, 16 Contents, on B1 *17* 18–64 text, 64 coloph: 'R. Edwards, Printer.'

Pagination: no errors; *Explicit*: 64 FINIS.

Paper: White, wove; Demy (4¾ × 2¾ in.).

Type: Ruby (1.9 mm).

Plate: Allegorical figure of Justice 'R. Corbould Reg. del. F. Englehart Sculp. JOHNSON, [4 lines from *London*] page 20. Pub^d by W. Suttaby, Stationer's Court, Feby. 1, 1805'.

Notes: Printed covers give price as 8d. and list Charles Corrall as a publisher; back cover lists 26 uniform vols. 'Published by W. Suttaby, Crosby and Co., and C. Corrall', including 'The Laurel' @ 2s., and *Rasselas* @ 1s. 6d. (cf. 85.2PW/13b, below, and 59.4R/47, above, where James Cundee is named as printer of 'Sharpe's Superb Edition of the British Classics').[1]

Copies: O (2803 g.1 (1), ptd. back wrapper only; bound with Rusher's *Galloping Guide to the ABC*, @ 1d. (see 59.4R/42a–b, above);

USA: Hyde ('Joseph Balestier', orig. wraps), NjP; *Can*: CaOLUI; *UK*: L (11568. de. 35), SHu.

---

[1] I have a fragmentary note of a copy dated '1805' but suppose that it lacked the t., and the date was derived from the engr. front. *DNB* (Supp. xxii, s.n. Francis William Blagdon, 1830–97), ascribes his Life of SJ to '"The Laurel" (London, 1808, 24mo).' cf. 85.2PW/13b, below.

85.2PW/12   Poetical Works, Poets of Great Britain,   1807 Vol. LX

[Gen. t.] THE | POETS | OF | [hollow] *GREAT BRITAIN*, | IN SIXTY-ONE DOUBLE-VOLUMES. | [short parallel rule] | VOL. LX. | [short total rule] | *ARMSTRONG, GOLDSMITH and JOHNSON*. | [short swelled rule].

[**Var. Gen. t.**] THE | POETS | OF | [hollow] *GREAT BRITAIN*, | IN ONE HUNDRED AND TWENTY-FOUR VOLUMES. | [medium parallel rule] | VOL. CXXII. | [medium total rule] | *JOHNSON*. | [short swelled rule].

[Title] *THE* | [Hollow] POETICAL WORKS | OF | SAMUEL JOHNSON, LL.D. | WITH | *THE LIFE OF THE AUTHOR*. | [double rule] | Happy the bard . . . [6 lines] . . . inform the mind. COWPER. | [double rule] | *IN ONE VOLUME*. | [short swelled rule] | [**BL**] **London:** | Printed for Cadell and Davies; Longman, Hurst, Rees and Orme; | Nichols and Son; J. Walker; Wilkie and Robinson; W.J. and | J. Richardson; F.C. and J. Rivington; Lackington, Allen, and | Co.; R.H. Evans; Cuthell and Martin; Scatcherd and Letter- | man; Otridge and Son; Vernor, Hood, and Sharpe; R. Faul- | der; T. Payne; J. Nunn; R. Lea; J. Deighton; J. Johnson; | W. Clarke and Sons; W. Lowndes; J. Hatchard; Black and | Parry; J. Harding; E. Jeffery; J. Carpenter; W. Miller; | Leigh and Sotheby; Payne and Mackinlay; Mathews and | Leigh; P. Wynne; J.Booker; and Samuel Bagster. | 1807.

18°, *A*² B–M⁶ N⁴, ($3 (−N3) signed), 72 leaves.

Pp. A1 gen. t., A1ᵛ coloph: '[rule] | Printed by Mercier and Co. Northumberland-Court, Strand.' + engr. front. + A2 t., A2ᵛ blk, on B1 *5* 6–8 Life of SJ., *9* 10–141 text of J's Poems, *142* 143–44 Contents, 144 coloph. as A1ᵛ.

Pagination: ↑ 17–23, 73–75, 81, 84, 91, 120, 127; 39 as 99.
Press-figures: D6(39)–2, D6ᵛ(40)–1, H6ᵛ(88)–2.
Explicit: 141 END OF JOHNSON'S POEMS.
Copies: O (2804 f.341, 'Waterstock'¹).

¹ By Wheatley, Oxon. seat of Ashhurst family.

85.2PW/13a   Poetical Works, ed. Blagdon   1808

THE | [hollow] POEMS | OF | DR. SAMUEL JOHNSON. | TO WHICH IS PREFIXED, | A | *LIFE OF THE AUTHOR*, | BY | F.W. BLAGDON, ESQ. | [double rule] | LONDON: | Published by W. SUTTABY, B. CROSBY, and SCATCHARD | and LETTERMAN, Stationers Court; | and | C. CORRALL, 38 Charing Cross. | 1808. | [short rule] | Corrall, Printer.

Stet: SCATCHARD

12°, A–C¹² D⁶, ($1,5 (+ D3, −D6) signed), 42 leaves.

Pp. On A1 *1* t., *2* blk, *3* 4–22 Life of Johnson, *xxiii*–xxiv Contents, on B1 *25* 26–84 text, 84 FINIS., coloph: [medium rule] | Corrall, Printer, Charing Cross.

Plate: Front. 'Painted by H. Singleton. Engraved by I. Romney. *JOHNSON* 'He turns . . . till he dies' Vanity of Human Wishes. pa. 38. London: Published by W. Suttaby, Septʳ. 24, 1808.'

References: [? Courtney 158].

Notes: The paper is foolscap. Published as 'The Laurel', perhaps with an appropriate engr. t. In Constable's sale of the 'Stock in Quires' of John Fairbairn (Edinburgh), 1809, is 'Johnson's Poetical Works. fcp. 8vo. £0. 1. 0. [Trade] £0. 2. 0. [retail in boards]'.¹

Copies: O (Vet. A6 f.142, uncut: 5¾ × 3 in.);

USA: PPL; *UK*: IPS, L (1346. a. 37), Ljh (+ 'Collins' with Life by Langhorne), LvU (P.683.2.179).

¹ E: (MS Acc. 5000, no. 1389).

85.2PW/13b   Poetical Works, The Laurel   [1808]

[Engr. t.] The | **LAUREL** | CONTAINING THE POETICAL | **Works of** | Collins | Dr. Johnson, | Pomfret | & Hammond. | [vignette: Muses with laurel-crowned plinth bearing above four names. 'R. Cook del. C. Heath fculp.'] | Publish'd by W. Suttaby, & B. Crosby & Cº. Stationer's Court, London.

Collation &c., as preceding 85.2PW/13a, but Engr. front. [The Miser] 'Painted by H. Singleton Engraved by I. Romney. JOHNSON. [4 lines,

287–90] Vanity of Human Wishes, p.a. 36. London. Published by W. Suttaby, Septr. 24. 1808.' With F.W. Blagdon's Life of SJ.
  Copies: L (11602. aa. 12) Ljh ('E.C. McLaughlin, January 29th. 1921').

**85.2PW/14   Poetical Works, The Cabinet of Poetry,   1808
Vol 6**

Poetical Works: The Cabinet of Poetry, vol. 6. 1808, pp. 103–31.
  Not examined.
  Copies: [BMp (992523)], [L (1346. a. 37(2))].

**85.2PW/15   Poetical Works, Works of the English   1810
Poets, ed. Chalmers, Vol. XVI**

[½t] The Works of the English Poets, from Chaucer to Cowper. Vol. XVI.
  [Title] The Works of the English Poets, from Chaucer to Cowper; including the Series Edited with Prefaces, Biographical and Critical, by Dr. Samuel Johnson: and the most approved translations. The Additional Lives by Alexander Chalmers, F.S.A. In Twenty-one volumes. Vol. XVI. Smart, Wilkie, P. Whitehead, Fawkes, Lovibond, Harte, Langhorne, Goldsmith, Armstrong, Johnson. London: Printed for J. Johnson; J. Nichols and Son; R. Baldwin; F. and C. Rivington; W. Otridge and Son; Leigh and Sotheby; R. Faulder and Son; G. Nicol and Son; T. Payne; G. Robinson; Wilkie and Robinson; C. Davies; T. Egerton; Scatcherd and Letterman; J. Walker; Vernor, Hood, and Sharpe; R. Lea; J. Nunn; Lackington, Allen, and Co.; J. Stockdale; Cuthell and Martin; Clarke and Sons; J. White and Co.; Longman, Hurst, Rees, and Orme; Cadell and Davies; J. Barker; John Richardson; J.M. Richardson; J. Carpenter; B. Crosby; E. Jeffery; J. Murray; W. Miller; J. and A. Arch; Black, Parry, and Kingsbury; J. Booker; S. Bagster; J. Harding; J. Mackinlay; J. Hatchard; R.H. Evans; Matthews and Leigh; J. Mawman; J. Booth; J. Asperne; P. and W. Wynne; and W. Grace. Deighton and Son at Cambridge; and Wilson and Son at York. 1810.
  8°, *A*⁸ (−A1 ? blk) B–2R⁸, ($1 signed), 319 leaves
  Pp. A1 ? blk, A2 series t., A2^v blk, A3 t., A3^v coloph: '[short rule] | C. WHITTINGHAM, Printer, | Goswell Street, London.', A4 *v* vi–xiii Contents (xiii coloph.), *xiv* blk, on B1 *1* ½t Smart, *3* 4–15 Life, *16* blk, *17* 18–106 Smart's poems, *107* ½t Wilkie, *108* blk, *109* 110–21 Life, *122* blk, *123* 124–95 Wilkie's poems, *196* blk, *197* ½t Paul Whitehead, *198* blk, *199* 200–5 Life, *206* blk, *207* 208–30 Whitehead's poems, *231* ½t Fawkes, *232* blk, 233–4 Life, *235* 236–79 Fawkes's poems, *280* blk, *281* ½t Lovibond, *282* blk, *283*–284 Life, *285* 286–307 Lovibond's poems, *308* blk, *309* ½t Harte, *310* blk, *311* 312–18 Life, *319* 320–403 Harte's poems, *404* blk, *405* ½t Langhorne, *406* blk, *407* 408–13

Life, *414* blk, *415* 416–75 Langhorne's poems, *476* blk, *477* ½t Goldsmith, *478* blk, *479* 480–7 Life, *488* blk, *489* 490–512 Goldsmith's poems, *513* ½t Armstrong, *514* blk, *515* 516–19 Life, *520* blk, *521* 522–45 Armstrong's poems, *546 blk*, 547 ½t: The Poems of Samuel Johnson, LL.D., *548* blk, *549* 550–70 The Life of Johnson, By Mr. Chalmers., *571* 572–624 Poems of Dr. Johnson., 624 *Explicit*: END OF VOL. XVI., coloph: '[short rule] | Printed by W. Flint, | Old-Bailey.'

References: Courtney 158.

Notes: 2 cols./p. throughout. See 79.4LP/22.

Copies: O (280 i. 400); *USA*: ICU, MH² (1. 10481.1(16)), NN; *UK*: Ep, Eu, Gp (E 19036), HLu, L (11613. c.1), MRu.

85.2PW/16   Poetical Works, Charlestown   1810

Poetical Works of Samuel Johnson: with an Account of the Author.

Charlestown (Mass.): Printed for Asahel Brown, by Samuel T. Armstrong. 1810.

24°. Not examined.

References: S&S 20459 [MBAt, MC, OT].

Notes: The Life of SJ is pp. 5–57.

Copies: MH (*EC75 G5745.B810p); *USA*: MB, MWA.

85.2PW/17   Poetical Works, ed. Park   1811

The Poetical Works of Samuel Johnson. Collated with the Best Editions, by Thomas Park, F.S.A. London: Suttaby, Evance, and Fox . . . &c. 1811

Var: London: Stanhope Press. Printed by Whittingham and Rowland: Published by Suttaby, Evance, and Fox. 1811

? 24°, vol. xix; pp. Engr. front. port. + 133 + 1 pl. Not examined.

References: Courtney 158.

Notes: Also issued as vol. xxv in the series 'Park's British Poets', 1811.

Copies: [Liebert = CtY];

USA: ICU, MH (10487.40(19)), NN²; *UK*: Gu (Bf.70——m.6); *Fr*: BN.

85.2PW/18   Poetical Works, ed. Blagdon   1815

The Poetical Works of Samuel Johnson, edited with a Life by F.W. Blagdon. London: Suttaby, Evance, & Co. 1815

24°; Pp. Front. port. + 84 pp. Not examined.

Notes: Cf. *The Laurel*, London, 1808 (85.2PW/13b, above), incl. Poems of Collins, Johnson, Pomfret, and Hammond. J. Burmester, *Catalogue*, 19 (1992),

212, describes a copy with the engr. t. for 'The Laurel. Containing the Poetical Works of Collins, Dr. Johnson, Pomfret & Hammond. London: Published by Suttaby, Evance and Fox; and Baldwin, Cradock and Joy', dated 1815, but prefixed to later impressions of the various poets from 1818 to 1823.

Copies: NN; *USA*: [IU 'The Laurel']; *UK*: Ljh.

85.2PW/19   Poetical Works, Edinburgh   1815

Appended to: The Lives of the most eminent English Poets: with . . . a Life of the Author, and his Poetical Works. Edinburgh: Printed for Peter Hill, Printer to the Church of Scotland. 1815.

   4 vols. 12°, iv. 227–307. Not seen.
   References: See 79.4LP/25, above.
   Copies: Unlocated.

85.2PW/20   Poetical Works, Burlington, NJ   1816

THE | POETICAL WORKS | OF | *SAMUEL JOHNSON, L.L.D.* | WITH | AN ACCOUNT | OF | THE AUTHOR'S LIFE. | [medium swelled rule] | *BURLINGTON, N.J.* | Printed and sold, by | David Allinson, | [short dotted (10) rule] | 1816.

   12°, π² 1–11⁶ 12⁴, ($1,3 signed; $3 as $*), 72 leaves.
   Pp. π1 t., π1ᵛ blk, on π2 *1* Quotation, *2* Contents, *3* 4–61 Life of Johnson, *62* blk, *63* 64–140 text of Poems, *141–2* (12₄) Allinson's advts.
   References: *Tinker* 1376; S&S 37958 [NjR, ViSwC].
   Copies: Hyde² (1. 'Ingraham' — Goodspeed; 2. 'Shanks' — 'Leslie');
   USA: [Liebert = CtY], MH (KC 12488), MWA, NjP, OCi, PHi, PU.

85.2PW/21   Poetical Works, ed. Blagdon   1820

[Printed grey wraps. Within wavy rule frame]: THE | POEMS | OF | DR. SAMUEL JOHNSON. | [diamond rule] | To which is prefixed, | A LIFE OF THE AUTHOR. | [short parallel rule] | LONDON: | PUBLISHED BY SUTTABY, EVANCE, AND | FOX, STATIONERS' COURT; | AND BALDWIN, CRADOCK, AND JOY, | PATERNOSTER ROW. | 1820. | Price 1s.
   [Title] THE | [hollow] POEMS | OF | DR. SAMUEL JOHNSON. | To which is prefixed, | *A LIFE OF THE AUTHOR.* | [double rule] | LONDON: | PUBLISHED BY SUTTABY, EVANCE, AND | FOX, STATIONERS' COURT; | AND BALDWIN, CRADOCK, AND JOY, | PATERNOSTER-ROW. | [short rule] | 1820.

12s, A^{12} B–C^{12} D^6, ($1,5 (−D5, + D3) signed), 42 leaves.

Pp. Engr. port. front (as 1806, 85.2PW/11, above) + A1 *1* t., *2* coloph: '[rule] | Printed by J. Seeley, Buckingham. | [rule]', *3* 4–22 dh: LIFE OF DR. JOHNSON. | [short total rule] (2 Quot. 1. Horace, 2. Roscommon] | short parallel rule], rt: LIFE OF DR. JOHNSON., *23*–24 Contents, on B1 *25* 26–84 text of Poems, 84 coloph. (as above).

Pagination: 1–3, 23, 25, 32, 52, 68, 83, unpaged; *Explicit*: 84 FINIS.

References: Courtney 157.

Notes: See 1806 above (85.2PW/11). It is difficult to settle the format of this edn. The size (5⅝ × 3 in.) suggests a 24° (*c*.23 × 18 sheet = medium).

The printed back-wrapper carries advts. for uniform titles, including 'The J——el, containing Collins, Johnson, Pomfret, and Hammond. 4s.', evidently a variant form of 'The Laurel' (85.2PW/13b, 85.2PW/18, above), and 'Rasselas, A Tale, by Dr. Johnson 2s.' (presumably 59.4R/95 (1820)).

Copies: O (2805 f.620(2)); *USA*: NIC; *Japan*: [Kyoto]; *UK*: JDF (uncut, wraps), L (11612. a. 32, 'Suttaby & Co.').

85.2PW/22   Poetical Works, British Poets,   1822
Vol. LXVII

The British Poets. Including Translations. In one hundred volumes. LXVII. Armstrong and Johnson. Chiswick: Printed by C. Whittingham, College House; for J. Carpenter, J. Booker, Rodwell and Martin, G. and W.B. Whittaker, R. Triphook, J. Ebers, Taylor and Hessey, R. Jennings, G. Cowie and Co, N. Hailes, J. Porter, B.E. Lloyd and Son, C. Smith, and C. Whittingham. 1822.

LXVII. Pp. *128* 129–50 Life of SJ, 151–4 Encomiums on SJ, 155–228 Poems, 229–72 Poemata.

References: Courtney 158.

Notes: Life of SJ by S.W. Singer. Cp. 79.4LP/35, above.

Copies: O (2804 f.180/67);

USA: DLC, NN; *UK*: Cp, E, Gp (E 15737), L (11603. aa.8), LVu.

85.2PW/23   Poetical Works, The British Anthology,   1825
Vol. VII

The British Anthology; or, Poetical Library. Vol. VII. Armstrong, Warton, Johnson, Cowper. London: Published by John Sharpe, Duke Street, Piccadilly. 1825.

6s, B–K^6 L1, ^{2}B–D^6, ^{3}B–D^6, ^{4}B–D^6, ($1,3 signed), 109 leaves.

Pp. B1 ½t: The British Anthology. Vol. VII., B1^v coloph: 'Printed by

Thomas Davison, Whitefriars.', B2 Gen. t., B2ᵛ blk, B3 *v–vi* Contents, *vii* ½t Armstrong and Wartons, *viii* blk, *9* 10–74 text Armstrong, *75* 76–103 text T. Warton, *104* 105–8 J. Warton, on ²B1 ½t: 'Johnson. The Vanity of Human Wishes, and Other Poems.', ²B1ᵛ blk, ²B2 *3* 4–36 text (English poems only, without 'Irene'), ³B1 ½t Cowper, *2* blk, *3* 4–36 text, ⁴B1 *1* ½t 'John Gilpin', *2* blk, *3* 4–36 text.
  Copies: BMp (516251).

85.2PW/24   Poetical Works, Philadelphia   1835

The Poems of Samuel Johnson . . . Philadelphia: Gibbons. 1835.
  Not examined.
  Copies: [PPL].

85.2PW/25   Poetical Works,   1853
Routledge's British Poets

[½t] Routledge's British Poets.
  The Poems of Oliver Goldsmith, Tobias Smollett, Samuel Johnson, and William Shenstone. With Biographical Notices, and Notes. Illustrated by John Gilbert. London: George Routledge & Co. Farringdon Street. 1853
  8°, π² M–R⁸ S⁴, 54 leaves; Pp. π1 ½t: The Poetical Works of Samuel Johnson, π1ᵛ–2ᵛ Contents, on M1 *i* ii–xvi Life, on N1 *1* 2–88 text of Poems.
  References: Courtney 158; Low, *English Catalogue, 1835–63*, i (1864), '12°. 5s. Routledge 1853'. For reimpressions, see 85.2PW/26 and 30, below.
  Copies: Gp, L (11603. e. 6).

85.2PW/26   Poetical Works, Routledge   1855

The Poetical Works of Goldsmith, Smollett, Johnson, and Shenstone. London: George Routledge & Co. 1855
  Notes: Another impression of preceding 1853 85.2PW/25.
  Copies: *UK*: L (1568/898), NCu.

85.2PW/27   Poetical Works, ed. Gilfillan   1855

[The Works of the British Poets, vol. 22]
  [½t] THE | POETICAL WORKS | OF | JOHNSON, PARNELL, GRAY, | AND | SMOLLETT.
  [Title] THE | POETICAL WORKS | OF | JOHNSON, PARNELL, GRAY, | AND | SMOLLETT. | [short rule] | [BL] **With Memoirs, Critical**

Dissertations, and | Explanatory Notes, | BY THE | REV. GEORGE GILFILLAN. | [short rule] | EDINBURGH: | JAMES NICHOL, 9 NORTH BANK STREET. | LONDON: JAMES NISBET AND CO. | DUBLIN: W. ROBERTSON. | M.DCCC.LV.

8°, π⁴ A–I⁸ *L⁸ L–Q⁸ (Q8 blk), ($1 signed), 132 leaves.

Pp. π1 *i* ½t, *ii* blk, *iii* t., *iv* blk, *v* vi–vii Contents, *viii* blk, on A1 *1* ½t 'Johnson', *2* blk, *3* 4–16 Life of SJ, *17* 18–81 text of J's Poems, *82* blk, on F2 *83* ½t 'Parnell', *84* blk, *85* 86–145 text of Parnell, *146* blk, on *L2 *147* ½t 'Gray', *148* blk, *149* 150–208 text of Gray, on O1 *209* ½t 'Smollett', *210* blk, *211* 212–54 text of Smollett, 254 coloph: [medium rule] | BALLANTYNE AND COMPANY, PRINTERS, EDINBURGH.', *255–6* (Q8) blk.

Pagination: no errors; *Explicit*: 82 END OF JOHNSON'S POEMS.
Paper: White, wove; Demy (uncut: 8¾ × 5½ in.); no vis. wmk.
Type: Pica (4.0 mm).
References: Courtney 158 (8); Low, *English Catalogue 1835–63*, i (1864), 'Gilfillan 8vo. 4s. 6d. Nisbet. 1856', but no copy so dated has been found.
Notes: The interpolated sheet signed '*L' carries the Memoir of Gray; it may have been a cancel, for there is no sheet signed 'K'. Issued in ribbed blue-green cloth with blind foliage decorations, gilt t. on spine.
Copies: O (280 p. 107);
USA: Hyde, ICU, [Liebert = CtY], NRo, ViU; *UK*: ABu, AWn, BMp (829428), BRu, C, Ck, Cp, DUNu, E, Ep, Eu, Gp, Gu, GTc, HLu, IPS, JDF², LCu, LVu, MRp, Oef.

85.2PW/28   Poetical Works,   1862
Nichol's Library Edition of the British Poets, No. 26

Nichol's Library Edition of the British Poets, No. 26.
    The Poetical Works of Johnson, Parnell, Gray, and Smollett, with Memoirs, Critical Dissertations, and Explanatory Notes by the Rev George Gilfillan. Edinburgh: James Nichol, 9 North Bank Street. London: James Nisbet and Co. Dublin: W. Robertson. 1862
    8°, π⁴ A–I⁸ *L⁸ L–Q⁸ (Q8 blk), ($1 signed), 132 leaves.
Notes: Another impression of 85.2PW/27. The text was edited by Charles Cowden Clarke. Coloph: Ballantyne and Company, Printers, Edinburgh.
Copies: NOu.

85.2PW/29   Poetical Works, ed. Gilfillan   1863

The Poetical Works of Johnson, Parnell, Gray, and Smollett, with Memoirs &c., by Rev. George Gilfillan. Edinburgh: James Nichol . . . 1863
    8°, π⁴ A–I⁸ *L⁸ L–Q⁸ (Q8 blk), ($1 signed), 132 leaves.

Notes: Another impression of preceding 85.2PW/27.
Copies: *UK*: ABu, NOu.

85.2PW/30   Poetical Works,   1865
Routledge's British Poets

[½t] Routledge's British Poets. The Poems of Goldsmith, Smollett, Johnson, and Shenstone.
[Title] The Poetical Works of Oliver Goldsmith, Tobias Smollett, Samuel Johnson, and William Shenstone. With Biographical Notices and Notes. Illustrated by John Gilbert. New Edition. London: Routledge, Warne, and Routledge, Broadway, Ludgate Hill. New York: 129, Grand Street. 1865
8s, *A*⁸ B–2H⁸ 2I² [+ 6 leaves R, W & R's advts.], ($1 signed), 250 [+ 6] leaves.
Pp. A1 ½t, A2 t., A3 Contents, A4 *i* ii–xvi Account of OG, *1* 2–84 Poems of OG, on G7 ½t, G8 *i–ii* Contents, *iii* iv–xv Account of TS, *xvi* blk, on H8 *1* 2–33 Poems of TS, *34* blk, on L1 ½t The Poetical Works of Samuel Johnson., L1ᵛ–L2ᵛ Contents, on L3 *i* ii–xvi Account of SJ, on M3 *1* 2–88 Poems of SJ, on R7 ½t WS, R7ᵛ–R8ᵛ Contents, on S1 *i* ii–xxxi Account of WS (**not** by SJ) + Description of Leasowes by R. Dodsley, *xxxii* blk, on U1 *1* 2–192 Poems of WS, *193* 194–6 Index (of titles) + 6 leaves advts.
Illustrations: front., (Goldsmith) facing pp. 4, 26, (Smollett) 10, (Johnson) 10 'Fall of Wolsey', (Shenstone) 84, 161.
Notes: Advertised as 'Fcp 8vo. cloth, gilt edges price 3s. 6d. each; or morocco, elegant or antique 7s.' as 'Presents and School Prizes', also as 'Best Edition. Edited by the Rev. R.A. Willmott, . . . Fcp. 8vo. cloth, bevelled boards, gilt and gilt edges, price 5s. each; or morocco, elegant or antique, gilt edges 10s.' This is a stereo reimpression of 85.2PW/25, above.
Copies: E (ABS.1.89.78, 'Elm Bank House, Kilburn July 21ˢᵗ. 1868. The 1st Class prize presented by Miss Richardson to Miss Spooner' bound in 'morocco, elegant, gilt edges').

85.2PW/31   Poetical Works, ed. Gilfillan,   1867
Edinburgh

The Poetical Works of Johnson, Parnell, Gray, and Smollett, with Memoirs &c., by Rev. George Gilfillan. Edinburgh: James Nichol . . . 1867
8°, π⁴ A–I⁸ *L⁸ L–Q⁸ (Q8 blk), ($1 signed), 132 leaves.
Notes: Another impression of 85.2PW/27, above.
Copies: *USA*: ICU.

85.2PW/32   Poetical Works, ed. Clarke, Edinburgh   1868

The Poetical Works of Johnson, Parnell, Gray, and Smollett. With Memoirs, Critical Dissertations, and Explanatory Notes. The Text edited by Charles Cowden Clarke. Edinburgh: William P. Nimmo. 1868

8°, π⁴ A–I⁸ *L⁸ L–Q⁸ (Q8 blk), ($1 signed), 132 leaves.

Notes: A reissue, with new ½t and title of 85.2PW/27, above.

Copies: BMp (519059); *USA*: MH (16477.32.25).

85.2PW/33   Poetical Works,   1878
Cassell's Library of British Poets, Part 95

Cassell's Library Edition of British Poets, part 95
  Poetical Works of Johnson and Parnell. 1878
  References: Courtney 158 (9).
  Notes: The editing and annotation is that of George Gilfillan, 85.2PW/27, above.
  Copies: E; *UK*: O (280 j. 802(2)).

85.2PW/34   Poetical Works, ed. Clarke   [? 1878]

The Poetical Works of Johnson, Parnell, Gray, and Smollett. With Memoirs, Critical Dissertations, and Explanatory Notes. The Text edited by Charles Cowden Clarke. Cassell Petter & Galpin: London, Paris & New York. [? 1878]

16s, π⁴ A² B⁸ C–I¹⁶ J⁸, ($1,5 ($5 as $2) signed), 134 leaves.

Pp. π1 ½t, π1ᵛ blk, π2 t., π2ᵛ blk, π3–4 Contents, π4ᵛ blk, on A1 *3* 4–16 Account of SJ, *17* 18–81 text of Poems, *82* blk, *83* ½t Parnell, *84* Pope's verses, *85* 86–91 Account of Parnell, *92* blk, *93* 94–145 Parnell's poems, *146* blk, *147* ½t Gray, *148* blk, *149* 150–60 Account of Gray, *161* 162–208 Gray's poems, *209* ½t Smollett, *210* blk, *211* 212–17 Account of Smollett, *218* blk, *219* 220–54 Smollett's poems; 254 coloph: 'Cassell Petter & Galpin, Belle Sauvage Works, London, E.C.'

Notes: Cassell, Petter & Galpin were the founders of the first half-penny newspaper, *The Echo*, in 1868, which collapsed under John Passmore Edwards (1823–1911*) in 1905. The firm became Cassell's.

Copies: L (11607. e. 14(2)).

85.2PW/35   Poetical Works, Routledge, Excelsior   1880

Routledge's 'Excelsior' Series.
  The Poetical Works of Samuel Johnson. Not seen.

References: Courtney 158.
Copies: Unlocated.

85.2PW/36a   Poetical Works, The Muses Library   1905

[½t] [BL] **The Muses Library** THE POEMS OF | JOHNSON, GOLDSMITH, GRAY, | AND COLLINS.

The Poems of Johnson, Goldsmith, Gray, and Collins Edited with an Introduction and Notes by Colonel T. Methuen Ward [Device 'R'] London: George Routledge & Sons, Limited New York: E.P. Dutton & Co.

8s, *A*1–5 B–Z⁸ 2A1–3 (A ≡ 2A), ($1 signed), 184 leaves.

Pp. A1 *i* ½t, *ii* advts., *iii* t., *iv blk,* v Prefatory Note (signed 'T.M.W. *March,* 1905.'), *vi* blk, *vii* viii–x Contents, on B1 *²i* ii–xlix Introduction, *l* blk, on E2 *51* ½t 'Johnson', *52* blk, 53–108 Johnson's Poems, *109–10* 111–210 Goldsmith, *211–12* 213–70 Gray, *271–2* 273–338 Collins, *339–40* 341–54 Notes (Johnson 341–3), 355–8 Index of First Lines, 358 coloph: 'Plymouth William Brendon and Son, Ltd. Printers.'

References: Courtney 158; Low's *English Catalogue, 1901–5*, vii (1906), 'Johnson's Poems, 1s. 2s. net. July 05' implying two issues, perhaps in var. bindings. The usual binding is in dark blue cloth with gilt decorated spine, from top 'JOHNSON | GOLDSMITH | GRAY, &C.', middle: 'THE | MUSES' | LIBRARY', and at foot: 'ROUTLEDGE'. The paper quality also varies, some copies bulk 180 mm, others on rougher paper: 240 mm.

Notes: Derived from Gilfillan's edition of 1855 (above 85.2PW/27).

85.2PW/36b   Poetical Works, The Muses Library   1912

Reprint of 85.2PW/36a.

85.2PW/36c   Poetical Works, The Muses Library   1922

Reprint of 85.2PW/36b, with a colophon on p. *iv*: '*Printed in Great Britain by Wm. Brendon & Son, Ltd., Printers, Plymouth.*'

Copies: O (2804 f.38, dated '1906');

USA: [Liebert = CtY]; *UK*: E ('1906'), JDF², L, ('1905'), LEu (B.4862K.MAN; pres. by editor), MRu, SAN.

85.2PW/37 Poetical Works,   1941
ed. Nichol Smith and McAdam

The Poems of Samuel Johnson Edited by David Nichol Smith and Edward L. McAdam. Oxford At the Clarendon Press. [1941]
Pp. xxvi + 420.
References: Press-code — 917.23.
Notes: The first scholarly edition of the 20th century. There was a lithographic reprint in 1952, and another impression in 1962.

85.2PW/38 Poetical Works,   1964
ed. McAdam and Milne, Yale Edition, Vol. VI

The Yale Edition of the Works of Samuel Johnson. Vol. VI. Poems.
Samuel Johnson Poems Edited by E.L. McAdam, Jr. with George Milne. New Haven and London, Yale University Press, 1964.
References: Published in UK April 1965, ISBN: 0-300-00734-5
Notes: This edition abandoned the traditional arrangement and offered the poems in strict chronological sequence. The editors exploited many MSS which had emerged since 1941.

85.2PW/39a Poetical Works, English Poems,   1971
ed. Fleeman

(Penguin Education) Penguin English Poets. General Editor: Christopher Ricks.
Samuel Johnson The Complete English Poems. Edited by J.D. Fleeman. Penguin Books.
12s, 1^{12} 2–11^{12} (11_{11-12} blk), ($1 signed), 132 leaves.
Pp. 260 + 4 blk.
References: ISBN: 0-14-080.165.0
Notes: First issued in perfect binding, paperback, May 1971.

85.2PW/39b Poetical Works, English Poems,   1974
ed. Fleeman

Penguin English Poets. &c. as above. Allen Lane. 1974
16s, 1–8^{16}, 128 leaves.
References: ISBN 0-7139-0573-5.
Notes: This reprint is in hardback.

85.2PW/39c   Poetical Works, English Poems,   1982
                          ed. Fleeman

Penguin English Poets. Penguin Books. 1982
   References: ISBN 0-14-042-296X
   Notes: Paperback reprint, coloph: 'Made and printed in Great Britain by
Hazell Watson & Viney Ltd, Aylesbury Bucks Set in Monotype Ehrhardt'.

85.2PW/39d   Poetical Works, Yale English Poets,   1982
                          No. 11

'Yale English Poets' no. 11. New Haven and London Yale University Press
   References: ISBN: 0-300-02826-1.
   Notes: Paperback issue from the plates of 85.2PW/39a, above.

85.2PW/39e   Poetical Works, The English Poets,   1982
                          Yale

'The English Poets' New Haven and London Yale University Press
   References: ISBN: 0-300-02824-5
   Notes: Hardback issue of preceding 85.2PW/39d.

85.2PW/40   Poetical Works, Oxford English Texts,   1974
                   ed. Nichol Smith and McAdam, rev. Fleeman

Oxford English Texts
   The Poems of Samuel Johnson Edited by David Nichol Smith and Edward
L. McAdam Second Edition Oxford At the Clarendon Press 1974
   References: ISBN 0-19-812702-2
   Notes: Revised by JDF from 85.2PW/37, above, with the pieces in strict
chronological sequence, and published May 1974.

85.7RE/1a   Frances Reynolds's Enquiry   1785

AN | ENQUIRY | CONCERNING THE | PRINCIPLES of TASTE, |
AND | OF THE ORIGIN | OF OUR | IDEAS of BEAUTY, &c. | [medium
swelled rule] | Sunt certi denique fines, | Quos ultra citraque nequit confiftere
rectum. | HOR. | [triple rule] | LONDON: | Printed by BAKER and
GALABIN, | INGRAM-COURT, FENCHURCH STREET. | M.DCC.LXXXV.
   8°, A⁴ (–A4 = H1) B–G⁴ *H*1, ($2 signed), 28 leaves.

Pp. A1 *i* t., *ii* blk, iii–v Dedication dh: [parallel rule] | To Mrs. MONTAGU. | Madam, ('The AUTHOR.'), *vi* blk, on B1 1–49 text dh: [parallel rule] | CHAPTER I. &c., *50* blk.

Pagination: (↑); *Press-figures*: none.
Catchwords: 46 ₐs (is); *Explicit*: 49 THE END.
Paper: White, laid; Demy (8¾ × 5⅝ in.); wmk.: W.
Type: Small pica (3.5 mm), leaded.
References: 85.7RE/1b, below. ESTC: t100606.
Notes: The fourth leaf of A⁴ stands in the final place.

An early draft was seen by SJ in 1781 (*Letters* 738, 777; Hyde iii. 355–6, iv. 30–1), and the work was overseen and criticized by him before eventual publication in July 1785.[1] 250 copies only of this edn. were printed. On p. 49 is a quotation of the last two lines of SJ's translation of Boethius (III. ix), which had formed the motto of *Rambler* 7 (*Poems*² 140–1).

Copies: L (11825. d.11); *USA*: NNC.

---

[1] FR wrote to Elizabeth Montagu, 12 July 1785, 'I had conceived of Johnson being strongly prejudiced against women's literary productions, But I deceived myself. He was sincere, he judged fully of the work, & his opinions greatly corresponded with yours' (CSmH: MS. MO 4650; cf. also FR to EM, 5 Feb. 1789, MO 4651).

85.7RE/1b   Frances Reynolds's Enquiry, facsimile   1951

A facsimile edition of 85.7RE/1, with Introduction (which marshals the known facts) by J.L. Clifford, was no. 27 in the Augustan Reprint Society series.

85.7RE/2   Frances Reynolds's Enquiry   1789

AN | ENQUIRY | CONCERNING THE | PRINCIPLES OF TASTE, | AND | OF THE ORIGIN | OF OUR | IDEAS OF BEAUTY, &c. | [short swelled rule] | ——Sunt certi denique fines, | Quos ultra citraque nequit confiftare rectum. | HOR. | [medium orn. swelled rule] | LONDON: | PRINTED BY J. SMEETON, IN ST. MARTIN'S LANE, | CHARING CROSS. | [short swelled rule] | M: DCC: LXXXIX.

8°, *A*² B–H⁴ (H4 blk), ($2 signed), 30 leaves.

Pp. A1 *i* t., *ii* blk, *iii*–iv Dedication: TO | Mrs. MONTAGUE. | MADAM, (Signed: 'THE AUTHOR.'), + Engr. plate (diagram) + on B1 1–47 text dh: [parallel rule] | CHAPTER I., 48 Letter to Banks, 49–50 Letter to Jenkinson, 51–2 Letter to Dodd, *53* ERRATA., *54* blk.

Pagination: (↑); *Press-figures*: none.
Catchwords: 16 [influence] of (pain,), 21 [for-] titude₍ₐ₎ (~.), 47 *om.*
Explicit: 47 THE END.

Paper: White, laid; La. post (uncut: 8¼ x 5¼ in.); no vis. wmk.; Plate wmk.: [WHA]TMAN.

Type: Dedication: pica (4.2 mm), leaded (1.2 mm), text: pica (3.9 mm), leaded (1.5 mm), footnotes: long primer (3.2 mm).

References: ESTC: n001744.

Notes: Three letters by SJ are added: **1**. To Joseph Banks, 27 Feb. 1772 (*Letters* 272; Hyde i. 386) with text of motto, **2**. to Charles Jenkinson, 20 June 1777 (*Letters* 520; Hyde iii. 29), **3**. to William Dodd, 26 June 1777 (*Letters* 523; Hyde iii. 32–3). FR's text is here revised from the first edn. (85.7RE/1, above). This edn. was noticed in *European Mag.* xi (July 1789), 5.

Copies: O (G. Pamph. 1317 (3)); *USA*: DLC, MH.

85.8PM/1   Prayers and Meditations   1785

PRAYERS | AND | MEDITATIONS, | COMPOSED BY | SAMUEL JOHNSON, LL.D. | AND |PUBLISHED FROM HIS MANUSCRIPTS, | By GEORGE STRAHAN, A.M. | VICAR OF ISLINGTON, MIDDLESEX; AND RECTOR OF | LITTLE THURROCK, IN ESSEX. | [swelled rule] | LONDON: | PRINTED FOR T. CADELL, IN THE STRAND. | MDCCLXXXV.

8°, A–P⁸ Q², ($4 (–Q2) signed), 122 leaves.

Pp. A1 *i* t., *ii* blk, *iii* iv–xvi Preface dh: [parallel rule] | PREFACE., ht: PREFACE. (signed: 'GEORGE STRAHAN. Iſlington, | Auguſt 6, 1785'), on B1 *1* 2–227 text dh: [parallel rule] | PRAYERS | AND | MEDITATIONS. | [rule] | 1738. | short swelled rule], rt: PRAYERS AND | MEDITATIONS. (on 123: MEDITATIO$_\wedge$), *228* advt. for SJ's *Works* ed. Hawkins.

Pagination: 46 and 123 may be unnumbered.

Press-figures: A3ᵛ(vi)–7, B8(15)–2, C8(31)–4, D7(45)–6, D8(47)–3, E6(59)–5, F5(73)–4, G5ᵛ(90)–3, H7ᵛ(110)–7, I6(123)–8, K6(139)–6, L1ᵛ(146)–7, L7(157)–1, M1ᵛ(162)–6, N1ᵛ(178)–8, O5ᵛ(202)–1, P8(223)–2.

Catchwords: om. xvi, 3–6, 8–9, 12, 14, 16–21, 23–4, 26, 30, 32, 35, 37, 39–40, 42, 44, 49–50, 53–4, 56, 59–63, 65, 69, 70–4, 76, 78, 80, 83, 89, 93, 96, 101–2, 107, 109, 113–14, 118–19, 122, 126–7, 130–3, 136–8, 141–5, 148, 150, 155–6, 160–1, 165–6, 170–2, 175, 177–83, 185, 187–91, 193–4, 196, 205–10, 212, 215, 217, 220–2, 224–5; 36 O Al$_\wedge$ (O Almighty), 91 then (*broken* n).

Explicit: 227 FINIS.

Paper: White, laid; Demy (uncut: 8¾ × 5½ in.), no vis. wmk.

Type: Text: english (4.4 mm), notes: pica (4.0 mm).

References: Courtney 158–9; CH 163; *Tinker* 1378; *Life* iv. 376; *Diaries* xvi–xviii; ESTC: t004079.

Notes: Andrew Strahan printed 750 copies of this edn. in August 1785 on the account of Thomas Cadell (L: Add. MS 48809, fo. 82ᵛ), and it was published

13 August 1785 (*Lond. Chron.*). Not all copies suffer from the misprinting on p. 123 which led to the loss of the last letter of the running title and the page number.

A transcription of this collection, docketed 'The Prayers are in the writing of my late Wife Arabella Mellor Hetherington 10th July 1814', is MS Hyde.

The copy described in ESTC: n041989 at ViRCU, ending at I6v with p. 124, appears to be an imperfect copy of the 2nd edn. (ending with the note for Easter Saturday, 1773), or of the 3rd or 4th (ending with the Prayer for April 10 [1773])

Copies: O (8° F. 118. BS);

USA: CSmH (uncut), CtY ('Jerome Kern', uncut), Hyde[3] (1. Pres. Geo. Strahan to W. Herringham; 2. 'Charles Lamb', bds. uncut; 3. 'W. B. Bemis', bds.), ICU, [Liebert (boards, uncut)], ICN, ICU, IU, MB, MH (16477.23*), NIC, NjP (Pres. Geo. Strahan to Boswell — Robert H. Taylor[1]), NN, NPM, NRU, PPL, TxU, ViU; *Can*: CaOHM; *UK*: ABu, BMp (87283), C, Csj, Eu[2], Gu, JDF ('Jane Palmer, August 7th 1827'), L[3], LEu, LICj, MRu, SAN, STA (uncut, sewn in sheets); *Aust*: CNL (DNS 4813).

An interesting annotated copy was lot 324 at Sotheby's, 17 May 1973, but is untraced, and another from the library of Alan G. Thomas, Sotheby, 21 June 1993, 198 (with notes by Sarah Adams).

---

[1] *Princeton University Library Chronicle*, xxxviii (1977), 168.

85.8PM/2   Prayers and Meditations, Dublin   1785

PRAYERS | AND | MEDITATIONS, | COMPOSED BY | SAMUEL JOHNSON, LL.D. | AND | PUBLISHED FROM HIS MANUSCRIPTS, | By GEORGE STRAHAN, A.M. | VICAR OF ISLINGTON, MIDDLESEX; AND RECTOR OF | LITTLE THURROCK, IN ESSEX. | [medium swelled rule] | DUBLIN: | PRINTED FOR MESS. WHITE, BYRNE AND CASH. | [short swelled rule] | M.DCC.LXXXV.

12°, A1–9 B–M¹² N1–3, ($5 (A2 as A, A2v as A2; –A2,3,4,5, C3,4, D4, I4, K4, L4, M4; K9 as K3) signed), 144 leaves.

Pp. A1 *i* t., *ii* blk, *iii* iv–xviii Preface ('Islington, August 6, 1785'), on B1 *1* 2–269 text, *270* blk.

Pagination: No errors; *Press-figures*: none.

Catchwords: *om.* pp. xviii, 3, 5, 7, 9–10, 12, 14, 16, 18–19, 21–2, 24, 26–7, 30, 33, 35, 38–9, 41–2, 44–6, 48, 50, 52–3, 56, 59, 63–4, 67, 71–3, 78, 81, 84–9, 91, 95, 96–7, 100–107, 115, 119, 122, 129–31, 133, 142–3, 147, 150, 152–3, 156–8, 165, 172–3, 177, 179, 181, 187, 190, 194, 196, 204, 207, 210, 215–19, 222, 225–30, 232–3, 235, 246–7, 250, 255, 258–60, 262–4, 266–8; 118 informed∧ (∼,), 243 Tu. (Th.).

Explicit: 269 FINIS.

Paper: White, laid; crown (uncut: 6⅔ × 3¾ in.); wmk.: DANGOUMOIS | FIN | V C

Type: Preface: english (4.5 mm), text: pica (3.8 mm), notes: small pica (3.5 mm).

References: Courtney 159; Cole, *PBSA* lxxv (1981), 244; ESTC: t115788.

Notes: Sigg. A ≡ N of which A1 (t.) seems to have belonged to N1–3 as the separated strip of the 12° by cutting.

Copies: O (Vet. A5 f.2638, 'Mary McKeown [?] August 10th 1786 [?] Mary Miss Bennet', and much other scribbling on endpapers);

USA: Hyde ('Bolton' — 'Duff'), [IEN], [Liebert], NIC; *Can*: CaOHM ('Rippey'); *Japan*: [Kyoto]; *UK*: C, L (3458. e.21), Lv (Dyce: 'John Mitford'); *Eir*: D.

85.8PM/3   Prayers and Meditations,   1785
                    second London edition

PRAYERS | AND | MEDITATIONS, | COMPOSED BY | SAMUEL JOHNSON, LL.D. | AND | PUBLISHED FROM HIS MANUSCRIPTS, | By GEORGE STRAHAN, A.M. | VICAR OF ISLINGTON, MIDDLESEX; AND RECTOR OF | LITTLE THURROCK, IN ESSEX. | [short swelled rule] | THE SECOND EDITION. | [swelled rule]| LONDON: | PRINTED FOR T. CADELL, IN THE STRAND. | MDCCLXXXV.

8°, A–P⁸ Q⁴ R² (R2 blk), ($4 (–A1, R3,4) signed), 126 leaves.

Pp. A1 *i* t., *ii* blk, *iii* iv–xvi Preface dh: [parallel rule] | PREFACE., ht: PREFACE. (sgd: 'GEORGE STRAHAN. Iflington, | Auguft 6, 1785.'), on B1 *1* 2–233 text dh: [double rule] | PRAYERS | AND | MEDITATIONS. | rule] | 1738. | [short swelled rule], rt: PRAYERS AND | MEDITATIONS., *234* advt. for SJ's *Works*, *235–6* (R2) blk.

Pagination: 156 ('1' *slipt*).

Press-figures: A3ᵛ(vi)–9, B7ᵛ(14)–4, C8(31)–8, D8(47)–8, E5ᵛ(58)–7, F8(79)–4, G8ᵛ(96)–9, H5ᵛ(106)–1, I3ᵛ(118)–8, K3ᵛ(134)–1, L1ᵛ(146)–8, M5(169)–‡, N3ᵛ(182)–6, N5(185)–8, O6(203)–‡, P3ᵛ(214)–4, Q3(229)–3.

Catchwords: *om.* pp. xvi, 3, 5–6, 8–9, 11, 13, 15, 18, 20, 22–7, 29–30, 32, 36, 38, 41, 43, 45–6, 48, 50, 55–6, 59–60, 62, 65–9, 72, 75–80, 82, 84, 86, 89, 95, 99, 102, 107–8, 113, 115, 119–20, 124–5, 128, 132–3, 136–9, 142–4, 147–51, 154, 156, 161–2, 166–7, 171–2, 176, 178, 181, 183–9, 191, 193–7, 199–200, 202, 211–16, 218, 221, 223, 226–8, 230–2.

Explicit: 233 FINIS.

Paper: White, laid; Demy (uncut), no vis. wmk.

Type: Text: (4.3 mm), Preface: (4.5 mm) notes: (3.9 mm)

References: Courtney 159; CH 163; *Tinker* 1379; ESTC: t115787.

Notes: Andrew Strahan printed 1,000 copies in Nov. 1785, again for Thomas Cadell (L: Add. MS 48809, fo. 83ᵛ), and it was published on Sat. 12 November 1785 (*Public Advertiser*). Three prayers (24, 25 April, and 6 May, 1752)[1] were added to this edn. at pp. 10–15. On 31 Jan. 1787 George Strahan signed a receipt of Thomas Cadell for £47. 7s. 2d. 'On account of Dr Johnson's Prayers' (MS: H.W. Liebert = ?CtY).[2]

Copies: O (12 θ. 1918);

USA: CSmH (352311), Hyde (Adam), [Liebert ('Fanny Reynolds from her affectionate children. March 18' — 'William Whitehead' — 'G. Madan')], NcU, NIC, NjP, NN, PU, TxU, H.D. Weinbrot, Esq; WiM; *Can*: CaOHM; *Japan*: [Kyoto]; *UK*: BMp (463099), En, JDF ('E. Taswell, August 31st. 1796' — Esme Nicoll), L (3456 h.2), MRu, NOu, Oef, STA; *Aust*: CNL (DNS 4813).

---

[1] *Diaries* 44–7. Transcripts of these prayers are L: Egerton MS 2182, fo. 9, apparently made by or for George Strahan.
[2] Sotheby, 22 April 1958, 532, to Liebert, and subsequently to ? CtY.

85.8PM/4   Prayers and Meditations,   1796
                                 third London edition

PRAYERS | AND | MEDITATIONS, | COMPOSED BY | SAMUEL JOHNSON, LL.D. | AND | PUBLISHED FROM HIS MANUSCRIPTS, | By GEORGE STRAHAN, A.M. | VICAR OF ISLINGTON, MIDDLESEX; AND RECTOR OF | CRANHAM, IN ESSEX. | [short swelled rule] | THE THIRD EDITION. | [short swelled rule]| LONDON: | Printed for T. CADELL Jun. and W. DAVIES, | (Succeſſors to Mr. CADELL,) in the Strand. | MDCCXCVI.

8°, A⁸ a⁸ B–P⁸ Q⁴, ($4 (a1 as '†a') signed), 132 leaves.

Pp. A1 *i* t., *ii* blk, *iii* iv–xvi Preface to First edition dh: PREFACE | TO THE | FIRST EDITION in 1785., rt: PREFACE TO | THE FIRST EDITION. (signed: 'GEORGE STRAHAN. Islington, | Auguſt 6, 1785.'), on a1 *xvii* xviii–xxxii Advertisement to this Edition dh: ADVERTISEMENT | TO THIS | THIRD EDITION., rt: ADVERTISEMENT | TO THIS EDITION. (signed: 'GEORGE STRAHAN. Islington, | May 2, 1796.'), on B1 *1* 2–230 text dh: [parallel rule] | PRAYERS | AND | MEDITATIONS. | [rule] | 1738. | [short swelled rule], rt: PRAYERS AND | MEDITATIONS., *231* Cadell & Davies's advts, *232* blk.

Pagination: 94 as 64, 98 as 60.

Press-figures: A6ᵛ(xii)–14, a7(xxix)–11, B1ᵛ(2)–10, C8(32)–9, D6(43)–*3, E2ᵛ(52)–8, F5(73)–4, G3ᵛ(86)–8, H7ᵛ(110)–7, I5ᵛ(122)–10, K7ᵛ(142)–1, L3ᵛ(150)–9, M6(171)–10, N7(189)–3, O6(203)–1, P7ᵛ(222)–10, Q1ᵛ(226)–8.

Catchwords: *om.* pp. xvi, xxxii, 3, 5–6, 8, 10, 12, 14–15, 18, 20, 22–6, 28–9,

31, 35, 37, 40, 42, 44–5, 47, 54, 58–9, 61, 64–8, 70, 74–9, 81, 83, 85, 88, 94, 98–9, 101, 106–7, 112, 114, 118–19, 123–4, 127, 131–2, 135–8, 141–3, 146, 148–9, 152, 154, 159–60, 164–5, 168–9, 173, 175, 178, 180–6, 188, 190–4, 196–7, 199, 208–13, 215, 218, 220, 223–5, 227–9.

Explicit: 230 FINIS.

Paper: White, laid; Demy (uncut: 8¾ × 5⅝ in.); wmk. (in sig. a): Fleur-de-lys + IV 1794.

Type: Preface: english (4.6 mm), text: pica (4.5 mm), notes: small pica (3.5 mm).

References: Courtney 159; CH 163; ESTC: t115199.

Notes: Andrew Strahan printed 1,000 copies in Apr. 1796 (L: Add. MS 48811, fo. 69ᵛ), noting that two sheets were cancelled. In view of Strahan's letters to Revd. Mr Swire attached to the O copy (below),[1] of which the first particularly deals with the question of apparitions and is a reply to observations by Swire on the topic, it is likely that the 'Advertisement to this Edition', occupying †a⁸, was one of the cancelled sheets since it discusses SJ's belief in such things arising from the new prayer for 26 April 1752 (of which Strahan noted 'now in my possession', Preface),[2] which was added to this edn. at p. 15 (sig. B8). The cancellations, whatever their reasons, delayed publication, as Strahan's letter of 20 June 1796 shows (n. 6, below). George Strahan sent a note to Davies, 22 May 1804, asking for a copy of the acount for this edn., and signed a receipt for £51. 19s. 3d. on 15 June 1805 (MSS Hyde).[3] A presentation copy by Strahan to William Windham is noticed in *Windham Papers* (1913), ii. 12–13.

Copies: O (1409 e.3; 'The Gift of the Editor G: S:'[4]);

USA: Hyde ('James Palmer' — 'T.F. Peacock 1872' — Adam), [Liebert ('J.G. Weddell')], NIC, NjP, NRU; *Can*: CaOHM; *UK*: BMp (87284), JDF, L (1478. b.2), MRu; *Aust*: CNL (DNS 4814).

---

[1] Swire was Revd. Samuel (1740–1816), a Fellow of University College from 1763 and perhaps George Strahan's tutor. *Al. Ox.* iv. 1378/34.

[2] *Diaries* 46-7. Boswell also saw it (*Life* i. 235). This prayer is also found in the transcript in L: Egerton MS 2182, fo. 9, cf. n. 3, above. In the final sentence JB read 'influences' whereas Strahan printed 'influencies'. If that reading reflects haste, it may be that sig. B was cancelled to accept the new text, but it is difficult to detect any physical grounds for supposing that to have happened. Neither the paper nor the running heads shows any differences from the remainder of the book, but both could still have been available from the original setting. The press-figure *3 in D(i) is the only other feature which might signal a cancellation.

[3] A letter from George Strahan, 21 May 1796, relative to this edn. was sold at Puttick & Simpson, 8 Mar. 1858, lot 129, and again P & S (Johnston), 12 Aug. 1863. It is not yet traced, but it may be that it relates to some problems which led to the cancellation.

[4] Two letters from Strahan to 'Revd. Mr. Swire', of 6 and 20 June 1796, are tipped in with a specimen of Strahan's wax seal bearing the head of SJ to which reference is made in the first letter; the second mentions that he had 'delayed this acknowledgement till I could procure a copy of the new Edition of Dr Johnson's Prayers &c. to accompany it. But now we are ready for publication I know of no conveyance . . . by which this little Volume may be transmitted to you.' MS transcripts (? by Swire) of a note on SJ by George Horne from *Olla Podrida*, xiii (1787), 132–41, and of prayers from Hawkins's *Works* (1787), xi (viz. 1 Jan. 1750/1, 1 Jan. 1784 PM 11, Ashbourne 1 Aug. 1784, Ashbourne 5 Sept. 1784, and Ashbourne 18 Sept. 1784) are also inserted, as is a copy of Trotter's engraving of SJ from Kearsley's *Beauties*, '7th ed.', dated 'Nov. 16, 1786' facing the t.

85.8PM/5   Prayers and Meditations, Dublin   1796

[½t] [short parallel rule] | PRAYERS | AND | MEDITATIONS. | [short parallel rule]

[Title] PRAYERS | AND | MEDITATIONS, | COMPOSED BY | SAMUEL JOHNSON, LL.D. | AND PUBLISHED FROM HIS MANUSCRIPTS. | [short swelled rule] | BY GEORGE STRAHAN, A.M. | VICAR OF ISLINGTON, MIDDLESEX; AND RECTOR | OF CRANHAM, IN ESSEX. | [short swelled rule] | FOURTH EDITION. | [medium parallel rule]| DUBLIN: | PRINTED FOR H. COLBERT, NO. 136, CAPEL-STREET. | [short parallel rule] | 1796.

12°, A–I¹² (A1 blk), ($1,2,5 (–A1,2, H5; C5 as C3) signed), 108 leaves.

Pp. A1 blk, on A1 ½t, on A3 *i* t., *ii* blk, *iii* iv–xx Preface, on B1 *1* 2–192 text (rt: PRAYERS AND | MEDITATIONS.)

Pagination: no errors; *Press-figures*: none.

Catchwords: *om.* pp. xx, 10, 43, 147; xi reftriction︿ (~*,), 11 And︿ (~,), 16 Boothby, (whom), 95 Almighty (Aʟmighty), 145 thoughts︿ (~,).

Explicit: 192 FINIS.

Paper: Preface: white wove, no vis wmk.; text: white, laid; La. post (uncut: 7 × 4½ in.); wmk.: E B

Type: Pica (4.4 mm), notes: long primer (3.3 mm).

References: Cole, *PBSA* lxxv (1981), 244; ESTC: n020972.

Notes: The text is a reprint of the first London edn. 1785 (85.8PM/1, above), and takes no account of the additional material in 85.8PM/2 or 85.8PM/4.

Copies: O (Vet. A5 f.3087, 'James Smyth November 5th 1805');

USA: Hyde, [Liebert = CtY]; *Japan*: [Kyoto]; *Eir*. Dt.

85.8PM/6a   Prayers and Meditations,   1806
             Vernor, Hood, and Sharpe

PRAYERS | AND | MEDITATIONS, | COMPOSED BY | SAMUEL JOHNSON, LL.D. | AND | *PUBLISHED FROM HIS MANUSCRIPTS,* | BY | GEORGE STRAHAN, A.M. | Vicar of Islington, Middlesex, and Rector of Cranham, in Essex. | [short swelled rule] | *A NEW EDITION.* | [short swelled rule] | LONDON: | PRINTED FOR | VERNOR, HOOD, AND SHARPE, IN THE POULTRY. | [diamond] | 1806.

8°, A⁴ B–N⁸ O² (A1 blk), ($4 signed), 102 leaves.

Pp. A1 blk, A2 t., A2ᵛ coloph: PRINTED BY A. TOPPING, | PLAYHOUSE-YARD, BLACKFRIARS., A3 ADVERTISEMENT. (no date), A3ᵛ blk, A4 Quotation from Murphy's *Essay*, A4ᵛ blk, on B1 *1* 2–192 text dh: PRAYERS | AND | [Hollow] MEDITATIONS., rt: PRAYERS AND | MEDITATIONS., *193–6* dh: INDEX ᴛᴏ ᴛʜᴇ PRAYERS.

Pagination: no errors; *Press-figures*: none; *Catchwords*: none.
Explicit: 192 THE END.
Paper: White, laid; crown (uncut: 7¾ × 5 in.); no vis. wmk.
Type: Pica (4.0 mm), leaded (1.5 mm).
References: Courtney 160.
Copies: O (Vet. A6 e.71);
USA: NjP (with MS notes); *Japan*: [Kyoto]; *UK*: BMp (499575), Ct, L (4410. ccc.17).

85.8PM/6b   Prayers and Meditations,   1807
Vernor, Hood, and Sharpe

PRAYERS | AND | [hollow] MEDITATIONS, | COMPOSED BY | SAMUEL JOHNSON, LL.D. | AND | *PUBLISHED FROM HIS MANUSCRIPTS*, | BY | GEORGE STRAHAN, A.M. | Vicar of Islington, Middlesex, and Rector of Cranham, in Essex. | [medium parallel rule] | *A NEW EDITION*. | [medium total rule] | LONDON: | PRINTED FOR | TAYLOR AND HESSEY, 93, FLEET-STREET, | AND | VERNOR, HOOD, AND SHARPE, IN THE POULTRY. | [short swelled rule] | 1807.

8°, A⁶ B–N⁸ (A1 blk), ($4 signed), 102 leaves.

Pp. A1 blk, A2 t., A2ᵛ coloph: PRINTED BY A. TOPPING, | PLAYHOUSE-YARD, BLACKFRIARS., A3 ADVERTISEMENT. (no date), A3ᵛ blk, A4 Quotation from Murphy's *Essay*, A4ᵛ blk, on B1 *1* 2–192 text dh: PRAYERS | AND | [hollow] MEDITATIONS., rt: PRAYERS AND | MEDITATIONS., 192 coloph: 'TOPPING, PRINTER, PLAYHOUSE.YARD, BLACKFRIARS.', *193–6* dh: INDEX ᴛᴏ ᴛʜᴇ PRAYERS.

Pagination: no errors; *Press-figures*: none; *Catchwords*: none.
Explicit: 192 THE END.
Paper: White, laid; crown (uncut: 7¾ × 5 in.); no vis. wmk.
Type: Pica (4.0 mm), leaded (1.5 mm).
Notes: Another issue of 85.8PM/6a (1806), above.
Copies: NIC; H.D. Weinbrot, Esq; ('Robᵗ Thorp.' [p. 148]: '28 July 1841').

85.8PM/7   Prayers and Meditations, 'fourth' edition   1807

PRAYERS | AND | MEDITATIONS, | COMPOSED BY | SAMUEL JOHNSON, LL.D. | AND | PUBLISHED FROM HIS MANUSCRIPTS, | By GEORGE STRAHAN, D.D. | PREBENDARY OF ROCHESTER, AND VICAR OF ISLINGTON | IN MIDDLESEX. | [short swelled rule] | THE FOURTH EDITION. | [short swelled rule] | LONDON: | PRINTED FOR T. CADELL AND W. DAVIES, IN THE STRAND. | MDCCCVII.

8°, A⁸ a⁸ B–P⁸ Q⁴, ($4 (–Q3,4) signed), 132 leaves.

Pp. A1 *i* t., *ii* coloph: 'Strahan and Preston, | Printers-Street, London.', *iii* iv–xvi Preface to first edition dh: PREFACE | TO THE | FIRST EDITION in 1785., rt: PREFACE TO | THE FIRST EDITION., on a1 *xvii* xviii–xxxii Advertisement to this edition dh: ADVERTISEMENT | TO | THIS EDITION., rt: ADVERTISEMENT | TO THIS EDITION., on B1 *1* 2–230 text dh: [parallel rule] | PRAYERS | AND | MEDITATIONS. | [rule] | 1738. | [short swelled rule], rt: PRAYERS AND | MEDITATIONS. (230 PRAYERS, &c.), 230 coloph: as p. ii, *231* advts., *232* blk.

Pagination: no errors.

Press-figures: A7ᵛ(xiv)–6, a5ᵛ(xxvi)–1, a7(xxix)–9, B2ᵛ(4)–1, C8ᵛ(32)–2, D3ᵛ(38)–9, D5(41)–7, E4ᵛ(56)–8, F3ᵛ(70)–2, F5(73)–2, G7(93)–9, G8(95)–8, H2ᵛ(100)–1, I5ᵛ(122)–2, K6ᵛ(140)–1, L7(157)–9, L7ᵛ(158)–1, M7ᵛ(174)–†, M8ᵛ(176)–8†, N6(187)–8, O4ᵛ(200)–3, P3ᵛ(214)–8, Q1ᵛ(226)–1; P and Q *sometimes* unfigured.

Catchwords: *om.* pp. xvi, xxxii, 3, 5–6, 8, 10, 12, 14–15, 18, 20, 22–6, 28–9, 31, 35, 37, 40, 42, 44–5, 47, 54, 58–9, 61, 64–8, 70, 74–9, 81, 82, 85, 88, 94, 98–9, 101, 106–7, 112, 114, 118–19, 123–4, 127, 131–2, 135–8, 141–3, 146, 148–9, 152, 154, 159–60, 164–5, 168–9, 173, 175, 178, 180–6, 188, 190–4, 196–7, 199, 208–13, 215, 218, 220, 223–5, 227–9.

Explicit: 230 FINIS.

Paper: White, wove; La. post (uncut: 8¼ × 5¼ in.); wmk.: '1806₉'[1]

Type: Preface and text: pica (4.4 mm), notes: small pica (3.5 mm).

References: Courtney 160.

Notes: 1,000 copies printed by Strahan in August 1807 (L: Add. MS 48815, fo. 18ᵛ). The 'Advertisement' is extensively revised from that of the 3rd edn. (85.8PM/4, above), but no new material is added to the collection.

In Vernor, Hood, & Sharpe's Trade Catalogue (Jan.–July, 1810), was 'Johnson's Prayers, 8vo. [Trade] 0. 2s. 6d.' 'Sells in boards' [= Retail] 0. 4s. 0d.', showing a discount of 37½% (E: MS Acc. 5000, no. 1389).

Copies: O (1409 e.32);

USA: CLU, Hyde ('Sarah Harriet Burney 1809' — 'Marquess of Crewe'), ICU ('Philip Twells M.A.'), [Liebert], NIC, NjP, NRU, TxU; *Japan*: [Kyoto]; *UK*: BMp² (1. 382158; 2. 835859 '1807'), BRu, DUu (Routh), E (L.116.a), Ep, En, JDF ('H.W. Ryland'), L (20039. b.10).

---

[1] It is tempting to suppose that the subscript '9' in this watermark date represents the month (September), but I know of no evidence to corroborate the conjecture.

85.8PM/8   Prayers and Meditations   1809
(with Knox's Considerations)

CONSIDERATIONS | ON THE | NATURE AND EFFICACY | OF THE | LORD'S SUPPER. | [short orn. swelled rule] | *BY VICESIMUS KNOX, D.D.* | MASTER OF TUNBRIDGE SCHOOL, AND LATE | FELLOW OF ST. JOHN'S COLLEGE, OXFORD. | [short orn. swelled rule] | *TO WHICH ARE ADDED,* | PRAYERS | COMPOSED AND USED | BY SAMUEL JOHNSON, L.L.D. | ALSO, | A SERMON, | BY THE LATE | REV. WILLIAM ROMAINE, A.M. | OF LONDON. | [medium parallel rule] | *NEW-YORK:* | PRINTED FOR JOHN SHEDDEN, BOOKSELLER, | NO. 94, WATER-STREET. | [short swelled rule] | *FROM THE PRESS OF T. KIRK, BROOKLYN.* | [short dotted (14) rule] | 1809.

12°, A⁶ ²A⁶ B–P⁶ R–U⁶ W⁶ X–Y⁶, ($3 (P5 as Q) signed), 138 leaves.

Pp. A1 *i* t., *ii* blk, *iii*–iv Recommendation, *v*–vi Preface, *vii* viii–xii Contents, on ²A1 *13* 14–163 Considerations, *164* blk, *165* 166–88 Appendix, on P5 *189* ½t SJ's Prayers, *190* blk, *191* 192–232 text, on U3 *233* ½t Romaine's Sermon, *234* blk, *235* 236–71 text of Sermon, 272–4 Hymns, *275–6* (Y6) Shedden's advts.

Notes: The text of SJ's Prayers (189–232) is taken from the third London edn. (1796), 85.8PM/4, above: Strahan is described as 'Rector of Cranham' on the ½t.

Copies: *USA*: Hyde, [Liebert = CtY], MH.

85.8PM/9   Prayers and Meditations   1813

[½t] PRAYERS | AND | MEDITATIONS.
[Title] PRAYERS | AND | MEDITATIONS, | COMPOSED BY | SAMUEL JOHNSON, LL.D. | AND | *PUBLISHED FROM HIS MANUSCRIPTS,* | BY | GEORGE STRAHAN, A.M. | VICAR OF ISLINGTON, MIDDLESEX; AND RECTOR OF CRANHAM, IN | ESSEX. | [short swelled rule] | [**BL**] **A New Edition.** | [medium parallel rule] | *LONDON:* | PRINTED FOR TAYLOR AND HESSEY, FLEET-STREET; | SHARPE AND HAILES, PICCADILLY; CRADOCK AND | JOY, AND J. CARR, PATERNOSTER ROW; AND J. MAR- | TIN, HOLLES STREET, CAVENDISH SQUARE. | [short swelled rule] | 1813.

18°, a⁶ B–P⁶, ($1,3 ($3 as $2) signed), 90 leaves.

Pp. a1 *i* ½t, *ii* blk, *iii* t., *iv* coloph: [rule] | PRINTED BY WHITTINGHAM AND ROWLAND, | GOSWELL STREET., *v* Extract from Murphy's 'Essay' on SJ, *vi* blk, *vii*–xi Contents dh: CONTENTS. | [short total rule], *xii* blk, on B1 *1* 2–168 text dh: PRAYERS | AND |

MEDITATIONS. | [short parallel rule], rt: PRAYERS AND | MEDITATIONS., 168 coloph: [short rule] | Whittingham and Rowland, Printers, | Goswell Street, London.

Explicit: 168 THE END.

Paper: White, wove; Royal (uncut: 6⅔ × 4⅓ in.); no vis. wmk.

Type: Small pica (3.5 mm), notes: brevier (2.7 mm).

References: Courtney 160.

Notes: This follows the second edn. 1785 (85.8PM/3), but does not include the prayer for 26 April 1752, added in the third 1796 (85.8PM/4), above. It appears not to be an authorized edn., but the initial copyright (1785) was presumably supposed lapsed after 28 years, even though the editor, Strahan, was still alive.

Copies: JDF ('Mary Lascelles 1937', blue boards, uncut);

UK: BMp (354688, 'Henry Brooke'), Gp (A 95951), L (3457. cc.13(1)).

85.8PM/10   Prayers and Meditations, 'fifth' edition   1817

PRAYERS | AND | MEDITATIONS, | COMPOSED BY | SAMUEL JOHNSON, LL.D. | AND | PUBLISHED FROM HIS MANUSCRIPTS, | By GEORGE STRAHAN, D.D. | PREBENDARY OF ROCHESTER, AND VICAR OF ISLINGTON | IN MIDDLESEX. | [short swelled rule] | THE FIFTH EDITION. | [short swelled rule]| LONDON: | PRINTED FOR T. CADELL AND W. DAVIES, | IN THE STRAND. | 1817.

8°, A⁸ a⁸ B–P⁸ Q⁴, ($4 (–Q3,4) signed), 132 leaves.

Pp. A1 *i* t., *ii* (and 230) coloph: 'Printed by A. Strahan, | Printers-Street, London.', *iii* iv–xvi Preface to First edition, *xvii* xviii–xxxii Advertisement to the Fourth edition (misdated p. xxxii as '1769'), on B1 *1* 2–230 text, *231–2* advts.

Pagination: 152 as 15.

Press-figures: A4ᵛ(viii)–15, a7ᵛ(xxx)–12, B1ᵛ(2)–15, C7ᵛ(30)–12, D1ᵛ(34)–14, E1ᵛ(50)–14, F7ᵛ(78)–10, G3ᵛ(86)–8, H7ᵛ(110)–11, I7ᵛ(126)–2, K1ᵛ(130)–11, L7ᵛ(158)–4*, M7ᵛ(174)–11, N3ᵛ(182)–11, O7ᵛ(206)–13, P4ᵛ(216)–11, P7ᵛ(222)–7.

Catchwords: *om.* pp. xvi, xxxii, 3, 5, 6, 8, 10, 12, 14–15, 18, 20, 22–6, 28–9, 31, 35, 37, 40, 42, 44–5, 47, 54, 58–9, 61, 64–8, 70, 74–9, 81, 83, 85, 88, 94, 98, 101, 106–7, 112, 114, 118–19, 123–4, 127, 131–2, 135–8, 141–3, 146, 148–9, 152–4, 159–60, 164–5, 168–9, 173, 175, 178, 180–6, 188, 190–4, 196–7, 199, 208–13, 218, 220, 223–5, 227–9 (no errors).

Explicit: 230 FINIS.

Paper: White, wove; medium (9 × 5¾ in.); wmk.: 1806.

Type: Pica (4.3 mm), notes: small pica (3.5 mm).

References: Courtney 160.

Notes: A reprint of the 4th edn. 1807 (85.8PM/7), above.

Copies: O (1409 d.6; blue boards, uncut);

USA: Hyde[2] (1. 'Attwood' — 'Tivetts' — 'Stanton' + MS notes; 2. 'Squibb' — Adam + MS notes[1]), [Liebert (uncut)], NRU, TxU; *Japan*: [Kyoto]; *UK*: BMp (53662), Es (176 e.1), L (3456. h.3), LVu.

---

[1] Puttick & Simpson (G. J. Squibb), 9 July 1859, 223, 'In this copy is contained a MS copy of an unpublished Prayer communicated by Sir Harris Nicolas, also some MS memoranda relative to the Originals of the above Prayers, & of the Dr's Pew in St Clement's Church, by G.J. Squibb, Esq.' cf. *Johns. Misc.* ii. 114 n. and *Diaries* 362–3.

85.8PM/11   Prayers and Meditations, Dorchester   1821

[Hollow] PRAYERS, | ON SEVERAL OCCASIONS. | [short wavy rule] | BY | SAMUEL JOHNSON, LL.D. | [short wavy rule] | *A NEW EDITION.* | DORCHESTER: | PRINTED BY G. CLARK, HIGH-STREET. | 1821.

18°, A–D[9] E[12], ($1,3,4,9 as $1,2,3 signed; '$' in lower case (–A4) A–D; + E4), 48 leaves.

Pp. A1 *1* ½t, *2* blk, *3* t., *4* blk, *5* 6–95 text of Prayers, *96* coloph: 'Printed by G. Clark, Dorchester.'

Pagination: no errors; *Press-figures*: none; *Catchwords*: none.

Explicit: 95 THE END.

Paper: White, wove; La. post (uncut: 5½ × 3½ in.); no vis. wmk.

Type: Text: small pica (3.6 mm), leaded (1.0 mm).

References: Courtney 160.

Notes: The ½t is formed by folding back E12 to stand in first place.

Copies: O (138. i. 508, with facsimile t. from Hyde); *USA*: Hyde ('Hart'), NIC.

85.8PM/12   Prayers and Meditations, Glasgow   1823

PRAYERS | AND | MEDITATIONS, | COMPOSED BY | SAMUEL JOHNSON, LL.D. | AND | PUBLISHED FROM HIS MANUSCRIPTS | BY | GEORGE STRAHAN, A.M. | Vicar of Islington, Middlesex, and rector of Cranham, in Essex. | [BL] GLASGOW, | PRINTED FOR RICHARD GRIFFIN AND CO. GLASGOW; | AND THOMAS TEGG, LONDON. | [short rule] | 1823.

12°, *A*[4] B–M[6] N[2], ($1 signed), 72 leaves.

Pp. Engr. port. front. + A1 t., A1[v] coloph: 'James Starke, Printer.', A2 Quotation from Murphy's *Essay*, A2[v] blk, on A3 *i* ii–iv Contents, on B1 *1* 2–134 text, on N2 *1*–2 'New and Interesting Works published by Richard Griffin & Co. Hutcheson-street, Glasgow; and Thomas Tegg, Cheapside, London.'

Pagination: no errors; *Explicit*: 134 THE END.

Paper: White, wove; foolscap (uncut: 5⅔ × 3¼ in.); no vis. wmk.

Type: Text: long primer (3.1 mm), notes: minion (2.4 mm).

References: Courtney 160–1.

Notes: Probably a reprint of 1813 (85.8PM/9, above), since the t. ignores GS's ecclesiastical promotions of 1817.

BMp copy is in printed brown boards: [within ornam. frame] PRAYERS | AND | MEDITATIONS, | COMPOSED BY | SAMUEL JOHNSON, LL.D. | AND | PUBLISHED FROM HIS MANUSCRIPTS, | BY GEORGE STRAHAN, A.M. | Vicar of Islington, Middlesex, and Rector of Cranham, in Essex. | PRINTED FOR RICHARD GRIFFIN AND CO. GLASGOW; | AND THOMAS TEGG, LONDON. | [short rule] | 1823.

Copies: BMp (381611, 'Mary Hudson's 1824');

USA: CtY; *Japan*: [Kyoto]; *UK*: L (3456. aaa.44).

85.8PM/13   Prayers and Meditations, Dorchester   1826

PRAYERS, | ON SEVERAL OCCASIONS. | [short wavy rule] | BY SAMUEL JOHNSON, LL.D. | [short wavy rule] | *A NEW EDITION.* | DORCHESTER: | PRINTED BY G. CLARK, CORNHILL. | 1826.

16°, A–F⁸ G⁴ (G4 ? blk), ($2 signed), 52 leaves.

Pp. A1 *1* t., *2* blk, *3* 4–102 text of Prayers, 102 coloph: 'PRINTED BY G. CLARK, | *Cornhill, Dorchester.*', *103–4* (G4) ? blk.

Pagination: no errors; *Explicit*: 102 THE END.

Paper: White, wove; ? foolscap (uncut: 3¾ x 4¼ in.); no vis. wmk.

Type: Brevier (2.6 mm), unleaded.

Notes: A reprint of the text of Dorchester 1821 (85.8PM/11, above).

Copies: O (1409 g.44); *USA*: Hyde; *UK*: C (8100 e.81), LICj².

85.8PM/14   Prayers and Meditations, Glasgow   1826

PRAYERS | AND | MEDITATIONS, | COMPOSED BY | SAMUEL JOHNSON, LL.D. | AND | PUBLISHED FROM HIS MANUSCRIPTS. | By GEORGE STRAHAN, A.M. | *Vicar of Islington, Middlesex, and Rector* | *of Cranham, in Essex.* | [medium rule] | [BL] **Glasgow:** | PRINTED FOR RICHARD GRIFFIN & CO. | AND THOMAS TEGG, LONDON. | [dash] | MDCCCXXVI.

Stet: **Glasgow:** (roman colon).

12°, π⁴ A–L⁶ M² ($1,3 signed; $3 as 2), 84 leaves.

Pp. Engr. port. SJ. front. ('Kerr, sc. 30. Trongate. JOHNSON. GLAS-GOW, Published by Richard Griffin & Co. 1825.') + π1 t, π1ᵛ coloph: 'R. MALCOLM, PRINTER.', π2 Advertisement (Extract from Murphy's *Essay*

1792), π2ᵛ blk, on π3 *i* ii–iv Contents, on A1 *1* 2–134 text dh: PRAYERS AND MEDITATIONS. | [short rule], rt: PRAYERS AND | MEDITATIONS., *135–6* Griffin's advts. (incl. tt. by Washington Irving).

Pagination: no errors; *Explicit*: 134 THE END.

Paper: White, wove; Sm. post (uncut: 6 × 3¾ in.); no vis. wmk.

Type: Long primer (3.2 mm), leaded (1.0 mm).

References: Courtney 161.

Notes: Cf. 1813 (85.8PM/9, above). En copy in printed boards, front cover: [within double orn. rules] PRAYERS | AND | MEDITATIONS, | COMPOSED BY | SAMUEL JOHNSON, LL.D. | AND | PUBLISHED FROM HIS MANUSCRIPTS. | BY GEORGE STRAHAN, A.M. | *Vicar of Islington, and Rector | of Cranham, in Essex.* | [short swelled rule] | [**BL**] **Glasgow:** | PRINTED FOR RICHARD GRIFFIN & CO. | AND THOMAS TEGG, LONDON. | [short rule] | MDCCCXXVI., on back cover: advts. as pp. 135–7 above.

Copies: En ('Boyd Rennach Wilson'); *Japan*: [Kyoto]; *UK*: L (3456. e. 16), STA.

85.8PM/15   Prayers and Meditations,   [? 1826]
                       Renshaw and Kirkman

Prayers and Meditations, composed by Samuel Johnson, L.L.D. and published from his Manuscripts. A new Edition. London: Published by Renshaw and Kirkman, and sold by all Booksellers. [n.d.]

8s, *A*⁴ B–H⁸ (H8 blk), ($1 signed), 60 leaves.

Pp. Engr. port. front. + A1 t., A1ᵛ coloph: 'Lymington: Printed by R. Galpin.', A2 Advertisement, A2ᵛ blk, A3 *i* ii–iv Contents: 'Index to the Prayers', on B1 *1* 2–109 text, 109 THE END., *110* coloph., *111–12* (H8) blk.

Notes: Probably a 32° from a Large post sheet (21 x 16½ in.) which would produce the dimensions of the extant copy.

Copies: LICj (1498; purple cloth, gilt edges; cut: 4 × 2⅝ in.).

85.8PM/16   Prayers and Meditations,   [? 1826]
                       Philadelphia, Jacobs

Prayers and Meditations. Philadelphia: Jacobs. No date.

Not examined.

Copies: Pennsylvania: Weston Theological School.

85.8PM/17   Prayers and Meditations, Washbourne   1836

The Prayers of Samuel Johnson, LL.D. London: Henry Washbourne, Salisbury Square, Fleet Street, Bowdery & Kerby, Oxford Street. 1836.

8°, *A²* B–F⁸ G⁶ (G6 blk), ($1 signed), 48 leaves.

Pp. A1 t., A1ᵛ coloph: 'Bradbury and Evans, Printers, Whitefriars.', A2–2ᵛ Contents, on B1 *1* 2–90 text, *Explicit*: 90 THE END., *91–92* blk.

References: Courtney 161.

Notes: L copy measures 4 × 2⅝ in. (cut), in black ribbed cloth, gilt titled spine, blind arabesques on front and back covers.

Copies: L (3456. a. 17).

[85.8PM/18   Prayers and Meditations,   1840
introd. Gresley

Prayers and Meditations, composed by Samuel Johnson, LL.D. With a Preface by the Rev. William Gresley, M.A., Prebendary of Lichfield. Lichfield: Printed and published by T.G. Lomax, at the Johnson's Head. 1840

References: Courtney 161.

Notes: Cp. 1860 (85.8PM/21), below. This is probably a ghost conjured by a confusion of the date. No copies have been found; Courtney based most of his record on L copies.

Copies: Unlocated.]

85.8PM/19   Prayers and Meditations, Allman   1845

[Within a single rule] The Prayers of Samuel Johnson, LL.D. London: T. Allman, Holborn Hill; 1845.

8s, *A²* B–F⁸ G⁸ (–G6,7,8 ? = A / advts. ?), ($1 signed), 47 leaves.

Pp. A1 t., A1ᵛ blk, A2–2ᵛ Contents, on B1 *1* 2–90 text, *Explicit*: THE END.

Notes: Miniature book: 4 1/16 × 4⅝ in.

Copies: BMp (497733; blue ribbed blind stamped cloth, gilt titling, all edges gilt).

85.8PM/20   Prayers and Meditations, Glasgow   1846

Prayers and Meditations, composed by Samuel Johnson, LL.D., and published from his manuscripts by George Strahan . . . Glasgow: R. Griffin . . . 1846

Not examined.

References: Courtney 161.

Notes: This is most likely to be a reimpression of Griffin's edn. 85.8PM/14 (1826), above.

Copies: [CtY].

85.8PM/21   Prayers and Meditations, introd. Gresley   1860

[Within rules, circles at corners]: PRAYERS & MEDITATIONS, | COMPOSED BY | SAMUEL JOHNSON, LL.D. | WITH A PREFACE BY THE REV. WILLIAM GRESLEY, M.A., | PREBENDARY OF LICHFIELD. | [device: cross] | LICHFIELD: | PRINTED AND PUBLISHED BY T.G. LOMAX, | AT THE JOHNSON'S HEAD. | LONDON: SOLD BY JOSEPH MASTERS. | MDCCCLX.

8s, a² b–c⁸ B–I⁸ K⁴, 86 leaves.

Pp. a1 *i* t., *ii* coloph: 'LICHFIELD: | PRINTED BY THOMAS GEORGE LOMAX, | THE JOHNSON'S HEAD.', *iii* Dedication to the citizens of Lichfield ('Lichfield, January 1860.'), *iv* blk, on b1 *v* vi–xvi Preface to first edition (85.8PM/1) dh: PREFACE TO THE FIRST EDITION | IN 1785. | [medium rule], *xvii* xviii–xxiv Preface to this Edition dh: PREFACE TO THIS EDITION. | [medium rule], (p. xxiv 'W. GRESLEY.'), on B1 *1* 2–148 text, 149 coloph: [**BL**] 'Lichfield: | PRINTED BY T. G. LOMAX, AT 'THE JOHNSON'S HEAD'.

Paper: White, wove; slightly foxed. Dark pink end-papers.

Type: All pp. within rules, as t.

References: Courtney 161; Low, *English Catalogue 1835–63*, i (1864), 'Preface by Gresley. 18°. 2s. 6d. *Masters* 1860'.

Notes: Gresley consulted the MSS at Op, and inserted a deleted line on p. xx from the meditation for 6 Apr. 1777 (*Diaries* 266). Published in devotional style binding: dark blue cloth, blind tooled, gilt t. (in L) on front: 'Prayers & Meditations' and 'Samuel Johnson, L.L.D.' with 'JOHNSON'S | PRAYERS' (roman caps) on spine; red edges.

Copies: O (138 d. 288);

UK: BMp (89041), C (8100 e. 200), E (L 9.a), JDF ('A Haywood | Stafford'), L (3455. b. 43), LICj, [WLAp].

85.8PM/22   Prayers and Meditations,   1903
ed. Bradley, New York

[Decorated t. of upright leaves in blue with compartments, and ornamental lettering in black]: The Prayers of Doctor SAMUEL JOHNSON Edited by W.A. Bradley New York McClure, Phillips and Company MCMII

8s, 1⁶ 2⁴ 3–6⁸ 7⁶ 8⁸, (unsigned), 56 leaves.

Pp. 1₁ ½t The Prayers of Dr Samuel Johnson. + Portrait (after Reynolds) inserted + 1₂ t., 1₂ᵛ coloph: 'Copyright MCMII', 1₃ ½t I. Introductory, 1₄ text, 1₅ ½t: II. New Year Prayers, 1₆ 7–17 text (nos. *I*, II–XVIII), *18* blk, on 3₁ *19* ½t Easter Day Prayers, 21–34 text (nos. *I*, II–XXI), on 4₁ *35* ½t IV. In Memory of his Wife, *36* blk, 37–42 text (nos. *I*, II–IX), *43–44* blk, on 4₆ *45 ½t: V.* On his Birthday, 46 blk, 47–56 text (nos. *I*, II–XVI), on 5₄ *57* ½t: VI. On Several Occasions, *58* blk, 59–78 text (nos. *I*, II–XXXV), *79* Explicit:, *80* blk, on 6₈ *81* ½t: Notes, *82* blk, 83–108 text of Notes, *109* coloph. (Note on issues and limitations), *110* blk.

Paper: 3 issues: (a) 50 copies on Imperial Japanese vellum, numbered 1–50; (b) 200 on Kelmscott hand-made, nos. 51–250 (in blue-grey boards, gilt spine titling), and (c) 500 on machine paper, nos. 251–750.

Notes: Publication was intended for November 1902, and coloph. on verso of t. reads 'MCMII' but a further 'I' may be hand-stamped in to correct the date of publication which was, in fact, February 1903. This may also be done to the date on the t. A printed apology should be laid in, explaining the delay. The designs were the work of William Jordan.

Copies: Hyde² (**1**. 'MCMII' no. 582; **2**. 'MCMIII' no. 403 (DLC duplicate, with access. date: 'Feb 27 1903'); *USA*: DLC, MH, NN.

85.8PM/23   Prayers and Meditations, ed. Higgins   [1904]

[½t] PRAYERS AND MEDITATIONS

[title] PRAYERS | AND MEDITATIONS | BY SAMUEL JOHNSON, LL.D. | A NEW EDITION WITH NOTES | BY | THE REV HINCHCLIFFE HIGGINS | AND A PREFACE BY | AUGUSTINE BIRRELL, K.C. | Also some Opinions of Dr. Johnson on | THE CHRISTIAN RELIGION. | [orn. flower] | LONDON: ELLIOT STOCK | 62 PATERNOSTER ROW

16s, a⁶ A–I⁸ K⁶ (a1, K6 blk), ($1 signed), 84 leaves.

Pp. a1 blk, on a2 *i* ½t, *ii* blk, *iii* t., *iv* blk, v–viii Preface ('AUGUSTINE BIRRELL.'), *ix* Contents, *x* blk, on A1 *1* 2–9 Introduction. The Religious Side of Dr. Johnson's Character (signed 'H.H.'), *10* blk, *11* ½t Prayers & Meditations, *12* blk, on B1 13–19 Preface to the first edition (85.8PM/1, above), *20* blk, 21–130 text of Prayers &c., *131* ½t Opinions, *132* blk, 133–43 text (from *Life*), *144* blk, *145* ½t: BIOGRAPHICAL NOTES, *146* blk, *147–51* text, *152* Johnson's London Residences, *153–154* Table of Dates, 154 coloph: *Elliot Stock, 62 Paternoster Row, London, E.C.*

Paper: Hand-made; wmk.: Abbey Mills | Greenford. Deckle edges preserved.

Type: Bold, long primer (3.2 mm), and ? minion (2.5 mm).

References: Courtney 161; Low, *English Catalogue, 1901–5*, vii (1906), 'ed. Higgins and Birrell. 5/-. E. Stock. Dec. 04.'

Notes: Published in light blue cloth, gilt titling and black decoration; black end-papers.
Copies: O (1409 e. 24, '1905');
UK: AWn, BMp (433378), C, E (L.123.b), En, JDF ('F.R. Bracey'[1]), Gp (A 231877), L (3455. f. 38).

[1] Bracey noted in pencil p. 89 on the Prayer for 18 Sept. 1775, composed at Calais and used at Notre Dame, 'I read aloud this prayer in the same church, 1911, F.R.B.' and added, 'This Church since blown up — 1940'. This copy is imperfect (Contents, Introd. and ½t = A6, torn out).

| 85.8PM/24 | Prayers and Meditations, Little Masterpieces Library | 1905 |

Little Masterpieces Library. Johnson's Conversation, Prayers and Meditations, and Essays. 1905. Not examined.
Copies: [Gu (G 583042)].

| 85.8PM/25 | Prayers and Meditations, new and revised edition | 1906 |

[½t] PRAYERS | AND | MEDITATIONS.
[Title] PRAYERS | AND | MEDITATIONS | COMPOSED BY | SAMUEL JOHNSON, LL.D. | NEW AND REVISED EDITION | WITH | ADDITIONAL MATTER | LONDON: H.R. ALLENSON, LIMITED | RACQUET COURT, FLEET STREET | 1906
16s, *A*⁸ B–L⁸, ($1 signed), 88 leaves.
Pp. A1 *i* ½t, *ii* blk, *iii* t., *iv* blk, v–xiv Introduction (signed: 'H.C.'), xv–xvi Index of Prayers, on B1 1–157 text of Prayers, *158* coloph: 'Printed by Turnbull and Spears, Edinburgh.', *159–60* (L8) advts.
Explicit: none.
Paper: White with horizontal dandy-roll chain lines.
Type: Sm. pica (3.5 mm), with some parts of text in long primer (3.2 mm), notes in bourgeois (2.9 mm); initial words, htt. and rtt. are in **Black letter**, great primer (6.0 mm) and english (4.9 mm).
References: Courtney 161; Low, *English Catalogue 1906–10*, viii (1911), '16°. p. 174. 2/6. Allenson. Nov. 06.'
Notes: The advts. specify the format as 'Demy 16mo' and show the sale price as 2s. 6d. The brown paper wraps comprise:

1. front cover: [within rules] Rich Purple Cloth, Demy 16mo, 2/6 net. Prayers === and Meditations by DR. JOHNSON. These devotional compositions of the old Doctor of Fleet Street will be found full of human nature delightfully expressed, in conjunction with deepest reverence for divine and

holy things and aspirations after the highest aims in life. Many very interesting side lights of the customs of his time are incidentally conveyed. London: H.R. ALLENSON, Limited.

2. [Spine]: Prayers and Meditations SAMUEL JOHNSON LL.D. 2/6 NET ALLENSON.,

3. [back]: Framed advt. for 'A Daily Message from Many Minds: Thoughts for the Quiet Hour from Fenelon, Jeremy Taylor, Hawthorne, Wordsworth, Phillips Brooks, Robertson, &c. &c. &c. . . . 2/6 nett.',

4. [inside front flap]: advt. for Sixth edn. of 'Great Souls at Prayer. Fourteen Centuries of Prayer, Praise and Aspiration, from St. Augustine to Christina Rosetti [*sic*] and Robert Louis Stevenson, selected by M.W. Tileson.',

5. [Inside back flap]: advt. for 'The Practice of the Presence of God'.

The binding is in a devotional style: full royal blue cloth, gilt titling, black and blind rules, bevelled boards, red edges.

The colophon has sometimes led to this edn. being described as an 'Edinburgh' edn., of 1906, but no such edn. has been found.

Copies: O (1409 f.66);

USA: Hyde; *UK*: C, E (L. 126.f), JDF (with dust wrapper), GTc, L (3455. h. 36), LICj, MRu, [WLAp].

85.8PM/26	Prayers and Meditations, third new and revised edition	[1927]

[½t] PRAYERS | AND | MEDITATIONS.

[Title] PRAYERS | AND | MEDITATIONS | COMPOSED BY | SAMUEL JOHNSON, LL.D. | THIRD | NEW AND REVISED EDITION | WITH | ADDITIONAL MATTER | LONDON: | H.R. ALLENSON, LIMITED | RACQUET COURT, FLEET STREET

16s, A^8 B–L^8, ($1 signed), 88 leaves.

Pp. A1 *i* ½t, *ii* blk, *iii* t., *iv* coloph: '*Printed in Great Britain | by Turnbull & Spears, Edinburgh.*', v–xiv Introduction (signed 'H.C.'), xv–xvi Index of Prayers, on B1 1–157 text of Prayers, *158* blk, *159–60* (L8) advts.

References: *English Catalogue, 1926–30* (1931), 'pp. 173, 3/6d. Oct. 27'.

Notes: A reimpression from stereo plates of the 1906 edn. (85.8PM/25, above) with the word 'THIRD' added to the t., and the coloph. standing on p. iv. The advts. are also new. It is not clear how the *English Catalogue* reckons the pagination.

Copies: En (ˢUU.8/JOH);

USA: Hyde, [PHC]; *UK*: AWn ('1928'), E ('1928'), L (03456. df. 75), MRp.

85.8PM/27   Prayers and Meditations, introd. Savage   1927

PRAYERS AND MEDITATIONS | COMPOSED BY | SAMUEL JOHNSON, LL.D.; | WITH AN INTRODUCTION | BY | THE VERY REV. | HENRY EDWIN SAVAGE, D.D., | DEAN OF LICHFIELD. | [small decorated cross] | LICHFIELD: | LOMAX'S SUCCESSORS (F.H. BULL & E. WISEMAN), | THE "JOHNSON'S HEAD." | MCMXXVII.

16s, A^8 B–K^8 L^4 (A1, L3,4 blk), ($1 signed), 84 leaves.

Pp. A1 *i* blk, *ii* blk, on A2 *iii* t., *iv* coloph: 'LICHFIELD: | PRINTED BY LOMAX'S SUCCESSORS, | THE 'JOHNSON'S HEAD.", *v* vi–xix Introduction (signed 'H.E.S. The Deanery, Lichfield, | June, 1927.'), xx List of editions, *xxi* xxii–xxix Preface to the first edition 1785, *xxx* blk, on B8 *1* 2–133 text of Prayers, *134* coloph: (as iv), *135–8* (L3–4) blk. *Explicit*: none.

Paper: White, wove; uncut: 6⅝ × 4¼ in.; no vis. wmk.

Type: Long primer (3.2 mm) and brevier (2.5 mm).

References: *English Catalogue, 1926–30* (1931), 'pp. 163, 3s. 6d. Nov. 1927'.

Notes: The list of editions (xx) is acknowledged from Courtney, noting a copy of 85.8PM/13 (1826), in LICj. The binding is full royal blue cloth with gilt titling.

Copies: BMp (341352);

USA: Hyde, MH, [PU]; *Japan*: [Kyoto]; *UK*: C, E, JDF, L (03456. de. 83), LEu.

85.8PM/28   Prayers and Meditations,   1937
Archetype Deluxe

[Decorative lettering] ARCHETYPE DELUXE EDITION | [in a rectangle in yellow] Prayers | COMPOSED | BY | DOCTOR | SAMUEL | JOHNSON | [device of inverted triangle of 3 asterisks] | [below the yellow rectangle] AT THE GOLDEN EAGLE PRESS | 1937

1^6 2^4 (–2_1) *3*–4^4, (no signatures), 17 leaves.

Pp. $1_{1–4}$ blk, Front. port. inserted + 1_5 t., 1_5^v blk, 1_6 Contents, on 2_1 *1* ½t, *2* blk, *3*–15 text, *16* blk, *17* coloph. 'S. A. Jacobs, The Golden Eagle Press, Mount Vernon, New York.', *18* blk, $4_{2–4}$ blk.

Paper: 'Charles I, hand-made.'

Type: 'Dutch old style Jansen & Goudy'.

Notes: The colophon gives details of the edn. which was limited to 418 copies, published in a slipcase. This edn. contains 13 prayers only.

Copies: Hyde (uncut, no. 21);

USA: ICN (Wing), NIC, NN, NRU; *Can*: CaOLUI; *UK*: L (Cup. 510 sat. 3).

85.8PM/29   Prayers and Meditations, ed. Trueblood   1945

[**Red** and Black]: DOCTOR | JOHNSON'S | PRAYERS | *INTRODUCTION* | *BY ELTON TRUEBLOOD* | [Vignette: head of SJ after Trotter] | James Ladd Delkin | Stanford University, California

8s, *1–6*⁸ *7*⁴ (1₁, 7₄ blk), (unsigned), 52 leaves

Pp. 1₁ *i–ii* blk, *iii* t., *iv* blk, *v* Quotation, *vi* blk, vii Contents, *viii* blk, ix–xxxii Introduction, on 3₁ *1* ½t, *2* blk, 3–68 text, *69* blk, *70* coloph [**Red** and Black]: 'Printed by Taylor & Taylor, San Francisco.', *71–2* (7₄) blk.

Paper: 'Worthy Hand and Arrows'.

Type: 'Centaur by Bruce Rogers, and Arrighi italic by Frederique Warde'.

References: *Tinker* 1380.

Notes: Privately printed and limited to 300 [?/ 350] copies.

Copies: Hyde (red paper boards, white canvas backstrip, gilt, in cellophane wraps); *USA*: MH, NN.

85.8PM/30   Prayers and Meditations, ed. Trueblood   [1947]

Doctor Johnson's | PRAYERS | [rule] | *Edited by* Elton Trueblood | [Quotation] | [rule] | Published by Harper & Brothers |NEW YORK *and* LONDON

8s, *1–6*⁸ *7*⁴ *8*⁸ (1₁₋₄, 8₅₋₈ blk), (unsigned), 60 leaves.

Pp. 1₁₋₄ blk, on 1₅ *i* ½t, *ii* blk, 1₆ *iii* t., *iv* Copyright statement and coloph., on 1₇ v–viii Order of Prayers, ix–xxxv Introduction, *xxxvi* blk, on 3₈ 1–66 text of Prayers, 8₅₋₈ blk.

References: *Tinker* 1381.

Notes: Coloph: 'Hand set in Weiss type by Arthur and Edna Rushmore at The Golden Hind Press, Madison, New Jersey'.

Copies: *USA*: T.M. Curley, Esq; ('Maurice J. Quinlan'), CtY, MH, NN, NRU.

85.8PM/31   Prayers and Meditations, ed. Trueblood   1947

[½t] DOCTOR | JOHNSON'S | PRAYERS

[Title] [within parallel rules] DOCTOR | JOHNSON'S | PRAYERS | EDITED BY ELTON TRUEBLOOD | [woodcut: head of SJ by John R. Biggs, after Reynolds] | SCM PRESS LIMITED

8s, *A*⁸ B–E⁸ F¹⁰, ($1 (F2 as '*F') signed), 50 leaves.

Pp. A1 *i* ½t, *2* Quotation, *3* t., *4* coloph: 'First published October 1947 from 56 Bloomsbury Street, London, W.C. 1 Distributed in Canada by our exclusive agents The Macmillan Company of Canada Limited 70 Bond Street, Toronto Printed in Great Britain by the Shenval Press, London and Hertford', *5*

Contents, *6* blk, 7–29 Introduction, *30* Flaxman medallion,[1] *31* ½t (as A1), *32* blk, 33–100 texts of Prayers.

Notes: Published (October 1947), at 6s., with printed paper wrappers.
Copies: BMp (589816); AWn, En, JDF[2], L, [STIu].

---

[1] Tinker, *The Wedgwood Medallion of Samuel Johnson* (1926). See also *Life* iv. 462, and Liebert, *Lifetime Likenesses of Samuel Johnson* (1974).

85.8PM/32   Prayers and Meditations, ed. McAdam   1958

Samuel Johnson Diaries, Prayers, and Annals Edited by E.L. McAdam, Jr. with Donald and Mary Hyde New Haven: Yale University Press, 1958 London: Oxford University Press [1958]

Forming vol. 1 of The Yale Edition of the Works of Samuel Johnson.

Notes: This is still the most complete collection of Johnson's private diaries, prayers, and 'meditations'. A few further readings from the Pembroke MSS (85.8PM/33, below), are proposed by JDF, *RES* n.s. xix (1968), 172–9.

85.8PM/33   Prayers and Meditations, MSS facsimile   [1974]

[Facsimile edition of the MSS at Pembroke College, Oxford][1]

Published to commemorate the 350th anniversary of the Royal Charter of June 1624, converting the College from Broadgates Hall, to Pembroke College.

1,000 copies of 14 sewed notebooks in decorated paper wraps enclosed in dustproof polythene envelopes, photogravure facsimiles of all inscribed pages (original blanks omitted), by Cotswold Collotype, of Wootton-under-Edge, Glos. Issued in Oxford blue slip-case box with gilt spine t.: JOHNSON'S | PRAYERS | AND | MEDITATIONS | [Arms of Pembroke College at tail]; with inserted bifolium printed note: A NOTE ON THE | FACSIMILES (by JDF, but unsigned).

Note: This edn. does not include material from any source other than the Pembroke MSS (*MS Handlist* 85–6, 89, 94, 102, 108, 114, 126, 145, 151–2, 156, 181, 221; *MS Index* pp. 125–6).

---

[1] The originals were presented to G.W. Hall (Master 1809–34), by Maria-Isabella Rose, daughter of Revd. George Strahan, and received by him on 30 May 1826. Maria-Isabella married William Rose (b. 1781), of Wolston Grange, Warwicks. Revd. Charles Rose (1788-1845), of Lincoln Coll., Oxford (*Al. Ox.* 1225/3), who owned SJ's copy of Landesius (*Booklist* 196), was a younger brother. Croker cited other prayers in his edn. of Boswell (e.g. 'Scruples', *Diaries* 70, and a Latin memo. of 6 Oct. 1782), as from 'Rose MSS' which suggests that not all the documents acquired by or known to Strahan were presented to the college. The lineage of the Rose family is fully reported in Burke, *Landed Gentry* (1921), 'Rose of Wolston Grange', but surviving descendants have eluded me. The family held the advowson of Whilton by Daventry, Northants, but the last presentation by Mrs D.M. Rose in 1960 led nowhere in 1967. For an investigation of Strahan's acquisition of these MSS, see Clingham, in *The Age of Johnson*, iv (1991), 83–95.

85.8PM/TJ/1   Prayers and Meditations,   1933
                         Japanese translation

PRAYERS | AND | MEDITATIONS | COMPOSED BY SAMUEL
JOHNSON, LL.D. | JAPAN: | THE ICHIRYUSHA | 18
NAGAREKAWA-CHO, NAKAKU, NAGOYA.

Pp. *i* Japanese title, *iii* English t., 1–3 Preface, 5–182 text, *183* coloph:
[Japanese, stating printed '20th June 1933']

Notes: The translator was Suzuki Jirô.[1]

Copies: A. Nakahara, Esq; (Kyoto).

[1] I am indebted to Prof. Akio Nakahara, of Kyoto, and to Prof. Hitoshi Suwabe, of Tokyo, for information on this translation.

85.8PM/Setting/1   Prayers and Meditations,   1909
                              Setting, Last Prayer

Price 3d. net. The Prayer. (Dr. Johnson's Last Prayer) Arthur B. Plant, Mus.
Doc. Oxon. A. Weekes & Co. Ltd. 14 Hanover St. London. W.1. Clayton F.
Summy Co. 429 S. Wabash Ave. Chicago USA.

4 leaves. Pp. *1* 2–3 text and score, *4* blk.

Notes: Code no. 'W. 5690.' Sheet-music. Prayer of 5 Dec. 1784, set to music
by Arthur B. Plant.

Plant (b. Lichfield, 1855),[1] also composed *The 'Johnson' Anthem*, intended for
the 'bicentenary Service, Sunday 19th. September, 1909, in Lichfield
Cathedral', for the same publishers, at 1s. The 'Prayer' formed part of the
'Anthem'.

Copies: Hyde; *UK*: LICj.

[1] Simms, *Bibliotheca Staffordiensis* (1894), 362, and *Al. Ox.* iii. 1121.

85.8PM/Setting/2   Prayers and Meditations,   1984
                              Setting, Engaging in Politicks

Prayer: 'Almighty God, Who Art the Giver of All Wisdom' ('Engaging in
Politicks. Nov. 1765 with H—n'[1]), set to music by Bernard Rose, for performance in Lichfield Cathedral, 15 July 1984.

[1] This is the form of the title in the MS (Pembroke book 4, fo. 2), modified by the editors of
Diaries 98.

85PT   [Joseph Simpson] The Patriot, a Tragedy   1785

[½t] [rule] | THE | PATRIOT, | A | TRAGEDY. | [rule] | [Price One Shilling and Six-pence.]

[Title] THE | PATRIOT, | A | TRAGEDY. | From a Manuscript of the Late | Dr. SAMUEL JOHNSON, | Corrected by Himself. | LONDON: | Printed for G. Goulding, No. 25, James-Street, | Covent-Garden; W. Brown, Corner of Effex-Street, | Strand; and J. Scatcherd and J. Whitaker, Ave- | Mary-Lane. | M.DCC.LXXXV.

8°, *A*⁴ (–A1) B–H⁴ I1 (= A1), ($2 (–D2) signed), 32 leaves.

Pp. A2 *i* ½t, A2ᵛ *ii* blk, A3 *iii* t., A3ᵛ *iv* '[Entered at Stationers-Hall.].', A4 *v* Prologue, A4ᵛ *vi* Dramatis Personae, on B1 *9* 10–66 text.

Pagination: pp. 7–8 omitted from numeration.

Press-figures: A4(vii)–3, B2ᵛ(12)–1, C4ᵛ(24)–5, D2ᵛ(28)–1, E1ᵛ(34)–3, F3(45)–1, G4ᵛ(56)–3, H4(63)–5.

Catchwords: 9 Xerxes. (XERXES.), 27 *om.* (ACT III.), 29 Ariana (ARIANA), 30 Teribazus. (TERIBAZUS.), 31 Euriclea. (EURICLEA.), 45 Hype- (HYPERANTHES.), 46 Hyper- (HYPERANTHES.), 51 Agis. (AGIS.), 52 *om.* (ACT V.).

Explicit: 66 FINIS.

Paper: White, laid; La. post (uncut: 8¼ × 5¼ in.); no vis. wmk.

Type: Pica (4.0 mm), leaded (0.8 mm).

References: Courtney 156; *Gleanings* viii. 69; *Life* iii. 28, 475;[1] Clifford & Greene 9:34; ESTC: t043776.

Notes: The implied attribution to SJ appears to be no more than a booksellers' ploy: JB explicitly denied it, giving it to Joseph Simpson (1721–68), from whom, rightly, no one has attempted to take it.[2] The Harvard MS is entitled 'Leonidas, a Tragedy. 1750', and is a fair copy. Reade reports an attempted publication as *Leonidas* in 1764.

Copies: O (Malone B.34); *USA*: CSmH, DLC, Hyde², NjP; *UK*: C, E (1966.5/3), Gu, L.

---

[1] At the Roxburghe sale, Evans, 18 May 1812, James Boswell, jun. bought a copy as lot 5205 for 3s. 6d. It next appeared in the Boswell sale, Sotheby, 24 May 1825, 2594, as 'Simpson's (Jos.) Patriot, a Tragedy 1785 *See note by Mr. Boswell relative to the Author*', and was bought by Webster for 6d. It is untraced.

[2] Simpson was the author of *Rambler* 107, signed 'Amicus'; *BQR* vii (1934), 508–9; *Thraliana* ii. 696. The work was, however, earlier associated with SJ by James Scott, *Fugitive Political Essays, which have appeared in the Public Advertiser under the several Names of Old Slyboots, Faction, Hortensius, &c.* (1770).

85GM55   Gentleman's Magazine, Vol. LV   1785

February 99   Rules of the Essex Head Club

References: *Life* iv. 253 ff., esp. 254 n. 5; Courtney 163.

Notes: This version did not include the 'Nightly Rules' which were first printed in Cooke's *Life of Johnson*, 2nd. edn. Kearsley (1785), 66–69. The two pieces were combined by Isaac Reed in Supp. *Works*, xiv (1788), 550–51. It is unusual to find JB differing from Reed in that he omitted the 'Nightly Rules' from his note in *Life* (1791), ii. 476, and they have not yet been included in any edn. of *Life*, not even by Croker.[1] The Essex Head Club was established in December 1783 (SJ to Reynolds, 4 Dec. 1783, *Letters* 916, Hyde iv. 256-7), see above 83.11EHC.

April 266   Scheme for the Classes of a Grammar School.
Communicated from 'Ross, Herefordsh. Apr. 6' by 'S.P.' from a MS composed by SJ in early summer 1735, see 35.6SC, above.

October 764–5   Speech on the Rochefort Expedition
'A Speech *dictated* by Dr Johnson, without premeditation or hesitation, on the subect of an Address to the Throne, after the Expedition to Rochfort, in September, 1757, at the desire of a friend, who delivered it, the next day, at a certain repectable *talking* Society.'
Notes: See above, s.d. 1757 (57.9SR).

[1] The authenticity of these, as well as their origin, remains uncertain. It may be presumed that JB deliberately rejected them.

87.3W/1   The Works of Samuel Johnson, ed. Hawkins   1787

[½t] THE | WORKS | OF | SAMUEL JOHNSON, LL.D. | IN ELEVEN VOLUMES.
[Title] THE | WORKS | OF | Samuel Johnſon, LL.D. | TOGETHER WITH | HIS LIFE, | AND | NOTES ON HIS LIVES OF THE POETS, | By Sir JOHN HAWKINS, Knt. | IN ELEVEN VOLUMES. | VOL. I [– XI]. | [bevelled parallel rule] | LONDON: | Printed for J. Buckland, J. Rivington and Sons, T. Payne and Sons, L. Davis, | B. White and Son, T. Longman, B. Law, J. Dodſley, H. Baldwin, J. Robſon, | J. Johnſon, C. Dilly, T. Vernor, W. Nicoll, G. G. J. and J. Robinſon, | T. Cadell, T. Carnan, J. Nichols, J. Bew, R. Baldwin, N. Conant, P. Elmſly, | W. Goldſmith, J. Knox, R. Faulder, Leigh and Sotheby, G. Nicol, J. Murray, | A. Strahan, W. Lowndes, T. Evans, W. Bent, S. Hayes, G. and T. Wilkie, | T. and J. Egerton, W. Fox, P. M'Queen, D. Ogilvie, B. Collins, E. Newbery, | and R. Jameſon. | M DCC LXXXVII.
    11 vols., 8°

I. A⁶ B⁸ (± B4) C⁸ (± C2,3) D⁸ (± D1) E–L⁸ M⁸ (± M5) N–R⁸ S⁸ (± S7) T⁸ (± T2) U⁸ X⁸ (± X4) Y⁸ (± Y1,4,6) Z–2B⁸ 2C⁸ (± 2C4) 2D–2F⁸ 2G⁸ (± 2G7) 2H–2I⁸ 2K⁸ (± 2K8) 2L⁸ (–2L1,8 + 2L1.8) 2M⁸ 2N⁸ (± 2N3) 2O⁸ 2P⁸

(± 2P1) 2Q⁴ 2R1 2S⁸, ($4 (+ M5, S7, Y6, 2G7, 2K8, 2L8) signed; 'Vᴏʟ. I.' on $1), 315 leaves.

Pp. A1 ½t Works, A1ᵛ blk, + Engr. port. of SJ front. + A2 t., A2ᵛ blk, A3 *v* Dedication to King George III., *vi* blk, *vii* viii–x ADVERTISEMENT. (signed 'J.H.'), *xi* ½t Life, *xii* blk, on B1 *1* 2–595 text: Life of Johnson, 596–602 POSTSCRIPT., on 2S1 Index (8 leaves, unpaged), 2S8ᵛ Errata.

Pagination: [↑] viii–x, 596.

Press-figures: A5(ix)–5, B4ᵛ(8)–7, B6ᵛ(12)–1, B8(15)–2, C3ᵛ(22)–11, C6(27)–3, C7(29)–9, D3ᵛ(38)–2, D6ᵛ(44)–5, E8(63)–11, E8ᵛ(64)–2, F1ᵛ(66)–2, F5(73)–11, G6ᵛ(92)–12, G7ᵛ(94)–7, H3ᵛ(102)–7, H8ᵛ(112)–8, I5ᵛ(122)–2, I8ᵛ(128)–5, K2ᵛ(132)–1, K3ᵛ(134)–11, L2ᵛ(148)–7, L5ᵛ(154)–8, M6(171)–4, M8ᵛ(176)–8, N5ᵛ(186)–11, N8ᵛ(192)–7, O3ᵛ(198)–2, O7(205)–5, P2ᵛ(212)–3, P8(223)–6, Q3ᵛ(230)–9, Q8ᵛ(240)–7, R7(253)–7, R7ᵛ(254)–4, S5(265)–6, T7ᵛ(286)–7, T8ᵛ(288)–8, U2ᵛ(292)–5, U5ᵛ(298)–11, X4ᵛ(312)–11, X7(317)–2, X7ᵛ(318)–3, Y1ᵛ(322)–10, Y5ᵛ(330)–5, Y7(333)–2, Z7ᵛ(350)–7, Z8ᵛ(352)–8, 2A3ᵛ(358)–3, 2A8ᵛ(368)–5, 2B8(383)–12, 2B8ᵛ(384)–10, 2C3ᵛ(390)–9, 2D5(409)–8, 2D8(415)–10, 2E5(425)–6, 2E5ᵛ(426)–10, 2F5ᵛ(442)–1, 2F8ᵛ(448)–8, 2G3ᵛ(454)–6, 2H2ᵛ(468)–8, 2H7ᵛ(478)–11, 2I2ᵛ(484)–3, 2I5ᵛ(490)–7, 2K5(505)–7, 2L5(521)–1, 2L6(523)–2, 2M2ᵛ(532)–6, 2M3ᵛ(534)–10, 2N2ᵛ(548)–5, 2O1ᵛ(562)–9, 2P2ᵛ(580)–9, 2P3ᵛ(582)–4, 2S5ᵛ–3, 2S6ᵛ–1; 2Q and 2R unfigured; B, C, X, Y figured 3 times.

Catchwords: 8 but, (but͙,), 28 ͙paper, ('~,), 51 view͙ (~,), 53 particular͙ (~,), 81 n. ͙provements ('~), 172 n. 'for [*slipt*], 213 Richardfon͙, (~*,), 250 [learn-] ing͙ (~,), 254 philofophers, (~,), 279 ͙Milton. ('~.), 304 'time, ('~͙,) 320 afked, (~͙,), 322 languages͙ (~,), 352 n. ͙of ('~), 387 [involu-] tions͙ (~,), 396 and͙ (~,), 439 n. fcore͙ (~,), 475 chieftains͙ (~,), 512 truft, (~.), 531 was͙ (~,), 578 literature͙. (~*.), 582 29th͙(~.).

Explicit: 602 END OF THE FIRST VOLUME.

II. *A*² B–F⁸ G⁸ (± G5) H–X⁸ Y⁸ (± Y2) Z–2H⁸, ($4 signed; 'Vᴏʟ. II.' (–X) on $1), 242 leaves.

Pp. A1 t., A1ᵛ blk, A2 Contents, A2ᵛ blk, on B1 *1* ½t 'Lives of the Poets' *2* blk, 3–4 Advertisement (dated '1783', from 79.4LP/7, above[1]), 5–477 text of Lives (5–70 Cowley, 71–81 Denham, 82–176 Milton, 177–95 Butler, 196–204 Rochester, 205–15 Roscommon, 216–21 Otway, 222–76 Waller, 277–9 Pomfret, 280–3 Dorset, 284–6 Stepney, 287–304 J. Philips, 305–7 Walsh, 308–448 Dryden, 449–75 Smith, 476–7 Duke), *478–80* blk.

Pagination: [↑] 3, 5, 71, 81, 177, 196, 205, 216, 222, 277, 280, 284, 287, 305, 308, 449, 476; 330 *sometimes* as 30.

Press-figures: B3ᵛ(6)–4, B7(13)–1, C6ᵛ(28)–1, C7ᵛ(30)–6, D6ᵛ(44)–5, D7ᵛ(46)–1, E6ᵛ(60)–3, E8(63)–4, F1ᵛ(66)–3, G6ᵛ(92)–2, G8(95)–7, H7ᵛ(110)–6, H8ᵛ(112)–1, I2ᵛ(116)–1, I6(123)–7, K5(137)–7, K5ᵛ(138)–5, L7(157)–7, L8(159)–5, M5(169)–1, M7ᵛ(174)–6, N4ᵛ(184)–7, N7ᵛ(190)–6,

O4ᵛ(200)–2, O6(203)–1, P6ᵛ(220)–4, P7ᵛ(222)–6, Q7(237)–4, Q7ᵛ(238)–2, R5ᵛ(250)–4, R8ᵛ(256)–7, S6(267)–1, S7(269)–5, T3ᵛ(278)–5, T7(285)–7, U8(303)–5, X4ᵛ(312)–5, X7ᵛ(318)–6, Y1ᵛ(322)–3, Y2ᵛ(324)–2, Y8ᵛ(336)–6, Z4ᵛ(344)–7, 2A7ᵛ(366)–7, 2B2ᵛ(372)–5, 2B6(379)–1, 2C1ᵛ(386)–7, 2C5(393)–5, 2D4ᵛ(408)–3, 2D6(411)–5, 2E5(425)–1, 2E8(431)–5, 2F6(443)–5, 2G2ᵛ(452)–6, 2G6(459)–7, 2H4ᵛ(472)–3, 2H5ᵛ(474)–1; Y figured 3 times.

Catchwords: 17 [merri-] ment. (~*.), 45 [ple-] nitude (tude).

Explicit: 477 END OF THE SECOND VOLUME.

III. *A*² B–2D⁸ 2E1, ($4 signed; 'Vᴏʟ. III.' ON $1), 211 leaves.

Pp. A1 t., A1ᵛ blk, A2 Contents, A2ᵛ blk, on B1 1–418 text of Lives (1–5 King, 6–11 Sprat, 12–16 Halifax, 17–21 Parnell, 22–7 Garth, 28–41 Rowe, 41–111 Addison, 112–18 Hughes, 119–28 Sheffield, Buckingham, 129–54 Prior, 155–71 Congreve, 172–93 Blackmore, 194–202 Fenton, 203–15 Gay, 216–25 Granville, 226–30 Yalden, 231–6 Tickell, 237–40 Hammond, 241–3 Somervile, 244–369 Savage, 370–413 Swift, 414–18 Broome).

Pagination: [↑] 1, 6, 12, 17, 22, 41, 112, 119, 129, 172, 194, 203, 216, 231, 237, 241, 244, 370, 414; (↑) 28, 155, 226; 27 as 2.

Press-figures: B7(13)–3, C8ᵛ(32)–6, D2ᵛ(36)–7, D5ᵛ(42)–3, E5ᵛ(58)–5, E7(61)–3, F7ᵛ(78)–7, G7ᵛ(94)–5, G8ᵛ(96)–6, H7(109)–3, I1ᵛ(114)–7, I5(121)–1, K5(137)–3, K8(143)–6, L4ᵛ(152)–1, L5ᵛ(154)–5, M1ᵛ(162)–7, M6ᵛ(172)–1, N3ᵛ(182)–5, O8(207)–7, O8ᵛ(208)–6, P3ᵛ(214)–6, P8ᵛ(224)–3, Q7(237)–2, Q7ᵛ(238)–6, R1ᵛ(242)–5, R8ᵛ(256)–3, S5ᵛ(266)–5, S7(269)–6, T8(287)–5, T8ᵛ(288)–6, U1ᵛ(290)–4, U8ᵛ(304)–6, X6ᵛ(316)–7, X7ᵛ(318)–1, Y6ᵛ(332)–1, Y7ᵛ(334)–2, Z8(351)–6, Z8ᵛ(352)–5, 2A7ᵛ(366)–2, 2A8ᵛ(368)–3, 2B3ᵛ(374)–1, 2B5(377)–5, 2C7(397)–4, 2C8(399)–1, 2D8(415)–1, 2D8ᵛ(416)–6.

Catchwords: 17 bee‸ (been), 98 Well‸ (Well !), 264 [Dedica-] tions; (~:), 317 in (inferted).

Explicit: 418 END OF THE THIRD VOLUME.

IV. A² B–2F⁸ 2G⁸ (± 2G5) 2H–2S⁸ (2S8 blk), ($4 (+ G5) signed; 'Vᴏʟ. IV.' on $1 (+ G5)), 322 leaves.

Pp. A1 *i* t., *ii* blk, *iii*–iv Contents, on B1 1–317 Lives of Poets (1–158 Pope, 159–62 Pitt, 163–78 Thomson, 179–88 Watts, 189–98 A. Philips, 199–203 West, 204–9 Collins, 210–13 Dyer, 214–22 Shenstone, 223–78 Young, 279–85 Mallet, 286–93 Akenside, 294–308 Gray, 309–17 Lyttelton), *318* blk, *319* ½t Lives of sundry Eminent Persons, *320* blk, 321–637 text (321–8 Sarpi, 329–57 Boerhaave, 358–78 Blake, 379–460 Drake, 461–71 Barretier, 472–9 Morin, 480–91 Burman, 492–500 Sydenham, 501–20 Cheynel, 521–30 Cave, 531–80 King of Prussia (Frederick the Great), 581–616 Browne, 617–37 Ascham, *638* blk, *639–40* (2S8) blk.

Pagination: [↑] iv, 1, 159, 163, 179, 189, 199, 204, 210, 214, 223, 279, 286, 294, 309, 321, 329, 358, 379, 461, 472, 480, 492, 501, 521, 531, 581, 617.

Press-figures: B2ᵛ(4)–4, B8(15)–3, C1ᵛ(18)–3, C5(25)–6, D1ᵛ(34)–1, D6ᵛ(44)–4, E5(57)–1, E5ᵛ(58)–4, F7(77)–4, G5ᵛ(90)–7, G7(93)–4, H8ᵛ(112)–3, I5ᵛ(122)–2, I7(125)–6, K6ᵛ(140)–6, K7ᵛ(142)–4, L8ᵛ(160)–4, M5ᵛ(170)–3, N5(185)–2, N6(187)–3, O1ᵛ(194)–4, O5(201)–3, P6(219)–3, P7(221)–1, Q1ᵛ(226)–1, Q8ᵛ(240)–3, R2ᵛ(244)–4, S6ᵛ(268)–2, S8(271)–1, T2ᵛ(276)–3, T7ᵛ(286)–4, U2ᵛ(292)–5, U6(299)–1, Y5ᵛ(330)–1, Y8ᵛ(336)–3, Z1ᵛ(338)–5, Z4ᵛ(344)–1, 2A8ᵛ(368)–5, 2B7(381)–5, 2C6(395)–5, 2C7(397)–1, 2D2ᵛ(404)–2, 2D8(415)–3, 2E2ᵛ(420)–2, 2F5(441)–7, 2G1ᵛ(450)–2, 2G5(457)–7, 2H2ᵛ(468)–7, 2I6ᵛ(492)–3, 2I7ᵛ(494)–1, 2K2ᵛ(500)–1, 2K8(511)–7, 2L2ᵛ(516)–3, 2L3ᵛ(518)–7, 2M2ᵛ(532)–1, 2M3ᵛ(534)–3, 2N1ᵛ(546)–4, 2N2ᵛ(548)–5, 2O5ᵛ(570)–7, 2O8ᵛ(576)–2, 2P4ᵛ(584)–7, 2P5ᵛ(586)–3, 2Q2ᵛ(596)–4, 2Q7ᵛ(606)–3, 2R7ᵛ(622)–7, 2R8ᵛ(624)–4; X unfigured.

Catchwords: 327 'tha‸ ('than).
Explicit: 637 END OF THE FOURTH VOLUME.

V. A⁴ B–2F⁸, ($4 signed; 'VOL. V.' on $1), 228 leaves.
Pp. A1 *i* t., A1ᵛ *ii* blk, *iii–v* Contents, A3ᵛ *vi* Errata, A4 *vii* ½t Rambler, *viii* blk, on B1 *1* 2–446 text Ramblers I–LXX dh: [parallel rule] | THE | RAMBLER. | [medium swelled rule] | NUMB. I. TUESDAY, *March* 20, 1750, *447–8* blk.
Pagination: no errors.
Press-figures: B1ᵛ(2)–5, B4ᵛ(8)–6, C6ᵛ(28)–5, C8(31)–6, D7(45)–5, D7ᵛ(46)–6, E8ᵛ(64)–5, F7(77)–5, F7ᵛ(78)–6, G5ᵛ(90)–5, H7ᵛ(110)–6, I6(123)–6, I7(125)–5, K5ᵛ(138)–5, K8ᵛ(144)–6, L2ᵛ(148)–6, L8(159)–5, M8(175)–6, N7ᵛ(190)–5, O7(205)–6, P7ᵛ(222)–5, Q5(233)–5, Q6(235)–6, R7(253)–6, R8(255)–5, S6ᵛ(268)–6, S8(271)–5, T6(283)–6, T7(285)–5, U2ᵛ(292)–5, U7ᵛ(302)–6, X2ᵛ(308)–5, X8(319)–6, Y1ᵛ(322)–5, Y8ᵛ(336)–6, Z8(351)–6, 2A1ᵛ(354)–5, 2B1ᵛ(370)–5, 2C6(395)–5, 2D8(415)–6, 2D8ᵛ(416)–5, 2E7ᵛ(430)–6, 2F3ᵛ(438)–5.
Catchwords: *om.* i–ii, v–viii, 13, 19, 26, 32, 39, 52, 65, 72, 87, 94, 109, 115, 143, 149, 155, 161, 167, 174, 180, 187, 193, 206, 224, 244, 250, 256, 269, 275, 281, 288, 294, 300, 312, 318, 324, 331, 337, 343, 350, 363, 369, 375, 386, 393, 399, 405, 411, 417, 434, 440.
Explicit: 446 END OF THE FIFTH VOLUME. (Small caps).

VI. a⁴ (a1 blk) B–2E⁸ 2F⁶, ($4 signed (a3 as a); 'VOL. VI.' on $1), 226 leaves.
Pp. a1 blk, a2 t., a2ᵛ blk, a3 *v–vii* Contents, a4ᵛ *viii* blk, on B1 *1* 2–443 text Ramblers LXXI–CXL (120 as '121' p. 319), *444* blk.
Pagination: no errors.
Press-figures: B8(15)–6, B8ᵛ(16)–5, C1ᵛ(18)–5, C2ᵛ(20)–6, D1ᵛ(34)–5, D8ᵛ(48)–6, E7ᵛ(62)–5, E8ᵛ(64)–6, F2ᵛ(68)–5, F7ᵛ(78)–6, G1ᵛ(82)–5, G4ᵛ(88)–6, H1ᵛ(98)–6, H7(109)–5, I5ᵛ(122)–6, I7(125)–5, K1ᵛ(130)–5, K6ᵛ(140)–6, L5ᵛ(154)–5, L7(157)–6, M7(173)–6, M7ᵛ(174)–5, N5(185)–6, N7ᵛ(190)–5, O8(207)–5, P6(219)–6, Q8(239)–6, Q8ᵛ(240)–5, R7ᵛ(254)–5, S5ᵛ(266)–6,

S7^v(270)–6, T8(287)–5, U8(303)–6, X1^v(306)–5, X2^v(308)–6, Y8^v(336)–5, Z7(349)–5, Z8(351)–6, 2A3^v(358)–6, 2A8^v(368)–5, 2B1^v(370)–5, 2C3^v(390)–6, 2D1^v(402)–6, 2D7(413)–5, 2E4^v(424)–6, 2E6(427)–5, 2F4(439)–5.

Catchwords: *om.* i–ii, 11, 23, 30, 35, 53, 59, 70, 76, 83, 89, 96, 102, 114, 121, 127, 137, 151, 163, 171, 177, 188, 201, 208, 214, 220, 226, 232, 238, 245, 252, 264, 277, 284, 291, 299, 305, 312, 319, 326, 332, 338, 343, 350, 357, 363, 369, 375, 382, 393, 399, 410, 416, 422, 428.

Explicit: 443 END OF THE SIXTH VOLUME. (Small caps).

VII. A^4 (A1 blk) B–2C^8, ($4 signed; 'VOL. VII.' on $1), 204 leaves.

Pp. A1 blk, A2 *i* t., *ii* blk, *iii–v* Contents, vi blk, on B1 *1* 2–397 text Ramblers CXLI–XXVIII, *398–400* blk.

Pagination: no errors.

Press-figures: A3^v–2, B2^v(4)–6, B7^v(14)–5, C5^v(26)–5, C6^v(28)–6, D8(47)–5, E8(63)–6, F1^v(66)–5, G8(95)–6, H7^v(110)–5, I1^v(114)–6, I8^v(128)–5, K2^v(132)–5, K7^v(142)–6, L5(153)–5, L8(159)–6, M6(171)–6, N8(191)–5, O7^v(206)–6, P8(223)–5, Q6(235)–6, Q8^v(240)–5, R2^v(244)–6, R3^v(246)–5, S3^v(262)–5, S6^v(268)–6, T7(285)–1, U1^v(290)–1, X7^v(318)–1, Y1^v(322)–1, Z7^v(350)–1, 2A3^v(358)–1, 2B3^v(374)–1, 2C6(395)–1.

Catchwords: *om.* i–ii, 6, 13, 21, 27, 38, 44, 50, 56, 62, 68, 74, 87, 94, 100, 106, 117, 122, 134, 141, 152, 157, 163, 168, 174, 180, 193, 198, 204, 214, 220, 225, 230, 236, 242, 248, 253, 258, 264, 270, 276, 281, 286, 292, 298, 304, 309, 315, 321, 326, 331, 338, 345, 351, 357, 362, 367, 373, 379, 385, 391; 111 (The), 126 [ceil-] ing$_\wedge$ (~,).

Explicit: 397 END OF THE SEVENTH VOLUME. (Small caps).

VIII. a^4 B–2C^8 2D^6 (2D6 blk), ($4 (a2 as a, a4 as b) signed; 'VOL. VIII.' on $1 (+ a, b)), 210 leaves.

Pp. a1 *i* t., *ii* blk, *iii–v* Contents, *vi* ADVERTISEMENT., *vii* ½t Idler, *viii* blk, on B1 *1* 2–410 text Idlers 1–103, *411–12* (2D6) blk.

Pagination: no errors.

Press-figures: B8(15)–1, C5^v(26)–1, D6(43)–6, E1^v(50)–6, E8^v(64)–5, F2^v(68)–5, F6(75)–6, G5^v(90)–6, G8^v(96)–5, H2^v(100)–5, H8(111)–6, I7(125)–5, I7^v(126)–6, K1^v(130)–5, K2^v(132)–6, L1^v(146)–5, L8^v(160)–6, M8(175)–6, M8^v(176)–5, N2^v(180)–5, N8(191)–6, O7^v(206)–5, O8^v(208)–6, P5^v(218)–5, P8(224)–6, Q1^v(226)–5, Q4^v(232)–6, R3^v(246)–6, R4^v(248)–5, S7(269)–6, S7^v(270)–5, T7^v(286)–5, U7^v(302)–6, X2^v(308)–6, X7^v(318)–5, Y8(335)–5, Z2^v(340)–5, 2A7(365)–6, 2A8(367)–5, 2B2^v(372)–6, 2B8(383)–5, 2C6(395)–5, 2D1^v(402)–6.

Catchwords: *om.* 4, 8, 16, 20, 24, 44, 48, 52, 59, 63, 70, 74, 79, 83, 87, 91, 95, 99, 104, 108, 110, 112, 116, 120, 124, 128, 137, 138, 144, 148, 154, 158, 162, 166, 174, 190, 193, 201, 205, 209, 214, 219, 227, 231, 234, 237, 243, 247, 251, 262, 265, 271, 278, 282, 291, 295, 299, 303, 311, 316, 320, 324, 328, 334, 338, 342, 353, 356, 360, 371, 374, 377, 381, 385, 389, 392, 400, 404, 407.

Explicit: 410 END OF THE EIGHTH VOLUME. (Small caps).

IX. *A*² B–2D⁸ 2E⁸ (–2E6) 2F⁸, ($4 signed; 'VOL. IX.' on $1), 225 leaves.

Pp. A1 t., A1ᵛ blk, A2 Contents, on B1 *1* 2–161 Adventurers (24 papers only²), *162* blk, *163* ½t Philological Tracts, *164* blk, *165* 166–446 texts.

Pagination: unnumbered 1, 162–5, 193, 230, 239, 303, 337, 350, 360, 364, 369, 374, 401, 422, 431, 436; 36 *sometimes* unnumbered, 191 as 189.

Press-figures: A2–2, B1ᵛ(2)–6, B2ᵛ(4)–5, C3ᵛ(22)–5, D8(47)–5, E8(63)–6, F1ᵛ(66)–5, F8ᵛ(80)–6, G1ᵛ(82)–6, G7(93)–5, H3ᵛ(102)–5, H6ᵛ(108)–6, I2ᵛ(116)–5, I3ᵛ(118)–6, K1ᵛ(130)–1, K4ᵛ(136)–6, L6ᵛ(156)–5, L8(159)–6, M5ᵛ(170)–6, M6ᵛ(172)–5, N6ᵛ(188)–5, N7ᵛ(190)–6, O6(203)–6, P2ᵛ(212)–6, Q1ᵛ(226)–6, Q8ᵛ(240)–5, R5ᵛ(250)–6, S7(269)–5, S7ᵛ(270)–6, T7(285)–5, T7ᵛ(286)–6, U1ᵛ(290)–5, X2ᵛ(308)–5, X5ᵛ(314)–6, Y7(333)–6, Y8(335)–5, Z8(351)–5, Z8ᵛ(352)–6, 2A1ᵛ(354)–5, 2A6ᵛ(364)–6, 2B8ᵛ(384)–3, 2C2ᵛ(388)–2, 2D7ᵛ(414)–5, 2F5ᵛ(440)–3, 2F7(443)–5; 2E unfigured.

Catchwords: *om.* 7, 13, 19, 25, 31, 46, 53, 67, 76, 89, 96, 115, 122, 128, 141, 148, 155, 161–4, 192, 229, 238, 302–3, 336, 349, 359, 363, 368, 373, 400, 421, 430, 435; 286 [*Up-*] *ton*, (∼*,).

Explicit: 446 END OF THE NINTH VOLUME. (small caps).

X. π² (π1 blk) a² B–2K⁸ 2L⁶, ($4 signed; 'VOL. X.' on $1), 266 leaves.

Pp. π1 blk, π2 t., a1–2 Contents, on B1 *1* ½t Political Tracts, *2* blk, *3* 4–143 text, *144* blk, *145* 146–82 Political Essays, *183* ½t Miscellaneous Essays, *184* blk, *185* 186–312 text, *313* ½t Journey, *314* blk, *315* 316–522 text, *523–4* blk.

Pagination: unnumbered 1, 34, 80, 93, 144–5, 158, 183–5, 194, 199, 220, 259, 275, 283, 286, 290, 299, 306, 313–5.

Press-figures: B4ᵛ(8)–5, B5ᵛ(10)–6, C6ᵛ(28)–5, C7ᵛ(30)–6, D8ᵛ(48)–2, E1ᵛ(50)–3, F1ᵛ(66)–2, G2ᵛ(84)–6, G7ᵛ(94)–5, H2ᵛ(100)–6, H3ᵛ(102)–5, I7ᵛ(126)–5, K6ᵛ(140)–5, K7ᵛ(142)–6, L6(155)–6, L8ᵛ(160)–5, M7(173)–5, M7ᵛ(174)–6, N1ᵛ(178)–6, O1ᵛ(194)–5, O7(205)–5, P7ᵛ(222)–6, Q5ᵛ(234)–6, R1ᵛ(242)–5, R2ᵛ(244)–6, S6(267)–6, T8(287)–2, U1ᵛ(290)–5, U8ᵛ(304)–6, X7ᵛ(318)–6, X8ᵛ(320)–5, Y1ᵛ(322)–6, Y2ᵛ(324)–5, Z7ᵛ(350)–6, 2A8(367)–6, 2A8ᵛ(368)–2, 2B8(383)–2, 2C8(399)–6, 2C8ᵛ(400)–5, 2D3ᵛ(406)–2, 2D6ᵛ(412)–6, 2E1ᵛ(418)–6, 2E2ᵛ(420)–4, 2F5ᵛ(442)–5, 2F7(445)–6, 2G2ᵛ(452)–2, 2H1ᵛ(466)–2, 2I5ᵛ(490)–6, 2I7(493)–5, 2K1ᵛ(498)–2, 2L3ᵛ(518)–2.

Catchwords: *om.* 33, 79, 92, 143–4, 157, 182–5, 193, 198, 219, 258, 274, 282, 285, 289, 295, 298, 305, 312–4.

Explicit: 522 END OF THE TENTH VOLUME. (Small caps).

XI. A⁴ B–2K⁸ 2L⁴, ($4 (–A1, 2L3,4) signed; 'VOL. XI.' on $1), 264 leaves.

Pp. A1 *i* t., *ii* blk, *iii–vi* Contents, *vii* ½t Rasselas, *viii* blk, on B1 *1* 2–188 text, *189* ½t Prayers, *190* blk, *191* 192–94 text, *195* ½t Apophthegms, *196* blk, *197* 198–216 text, *217* ½t Irene, *218* blk, *219–20* 221–314 *315* text, *316* blk,

317 ½t Poems *318* blk, *319* 320–430 text, on 2E8–2L4ᵛ (45 leaves, 90 pp. unpaged) Index.

Pagination: [↑] 221, 331, 344, 374, 383; unnumbered 1, 145, 163, 189–91, 195–7, 217–20, 315–19, and Index.

Press-figures: A3ᵛ–2,   B7ᵛ(14)–2,   C7(29)–2,   D1ᵛ(34)–2,   E8(63)–2, F2ᵛ(68)–2,   F5ᵛ(74)–4,   G7(93)–5,   G7ᵛ(94)–2,   H2ᵛ(100)–2,   I1ᵛ(114)–2, K1ᵛ(130)–2, L1ᵛ(146)–2, M6(171)–2, N1ᵛ(178)–2, O6(203)–2, P8(223)–4, Q7(237)–2, R8(255)–2, S5(265)–2, T1ᵛ(274)–2, U8ᵛ(304)–2, X2ᵛ(308)–4, Y8(335)–2,   Z8(351)–4,   2A1ᵛ(354)–2,   2B8(383)–2,   2C8(399)–2, 2E1ᵛ(418)–2, 2F4ᵛ–7, 2G1ᵛ–9, 2G6ᵛ–8, 2H4ᵛ–7, 2H5ᵛ–8, 2I1ᵛ–2, 2I6ᵛ–3, 2K3ᵛ–7, 2K5–4; 2D unfigured.

Catchwords: *om.* 7, 9, 47, 57, 59, 62, 65–6, 70, 76, 87, 92, 107, 117, 119, 127, 142, 144, 162, 188–90, 194–6, 216–20, 313–18, 330, 343, 348, 371, 375–9, 381–2, 393, 395–7, 401–4, 406–9, 411–25, 427, 430, 2G8, 2H2ᵛ, 2H4; 73 [foli-] litude: (tude:), 322 ˏBut (¹¹~), 325 ˏBy (²³~), 328 ˏPrepare (³²~), 332 ˏBut (*~), 357 How (Mark), 392 [Infula (INSULA).

Explicit: 2L4ᵛ FINIS.

Paper: White, laid; medium (uncut: 9 × 5¾ in.); wmk.: fleur-de-lys + IV.

Type: Pica (4.0 mm), leaded.

Plate: Front. vol. 1, Port. of SJ in oval frame with circular cartouche top left: 'Natus Sept. vii, 1709', and top right: 'Mortuus 13 Decem. 1784', centre foot: 'Samuel Johnson, L.L.D.'; 'Engraved by John Hall, Engraver to his Majesty. Publish'd as the Act directs, by the Proprietors, Janʸ. 1st. 1787.' (*Life* iv. 461, no. 13).

References: Courtney 161–2; CH 163–4; *Tinker* 1382; ESTC: t083967.

Notes: The sheets of vol. 1 (*Life87*) were issued separately with a new t. (see next entry, below) and without the portrait, Dedication, and Advertisement. The t. for this separate issue (with some minor variations) was printed with the cancels. For the cancels in vol. 1 (Hawkins's *Life87*), see next entry.

In vol. 8 the prelims were printed as stated, but in some copies (e.g. JDF) the two bifolia are bound in series, producing a1 t., a4 ½t Idler, a2–3 Contents.

Andrew Strahan printed vols. V–XI in January 1787, in 1,250 copies (L: Add. MS 48809, fo. 97ᵛ). It is certain that II–IV (*Lives of the Poets*) were printed by John Nichols. The Booksellers' agreement to publish this edn., to be 'conducted by Sir John Hawkins', dated 24 December 1784, was owned by the late Arthur A. Houghton, Jr., of New York.³ The complete edn. was advertised for sale on Tuesday, 20 March 1787 (*Lond. Chron.* and *Morning Chron.*). On 7 March 1787, Thomas Spence wrote to John Bell, of Bell & Bradfute (Edinburgh), 'Johnson's Works have been just divided. Seven Copies have this day been ship't for You aboard the Diligence, Cᵗ Butler who sails tomorrow or next day. — When the exchange was made I made a trifling mistake in saying 12 in place of Eleven \volumes/ of which the work consists — as a very short number has been printed, and as I am pretty confident you will have no difficulty in selling . . .' (E: MS Dep. 317, Box 1).

As the title makes plain, Hawkins not only superintended the edn., but was responsible for writing the Life (vol. 1), and supplying many notes to the *Lives of the Poets*. Other texts were not much attended to.[4] The edn. was severely reviewed by Arthur Murphy in *Monthly Rev.* lxxvi–lxxvii (Apr.–Aug. 1787), 273–92, 369–84 (Life), 56–70, 131–40 (Works), as a prelude to his own edn. of 1792, below.[5]

Copies: O (2699 e. 123–33);

USA:[6] CSmH, CtY, Hyde[3] (1. Red morocco, uncut, 'Laetetia Matilda Hawkins' (with notes) — 'Charles Sidney Hawkins'), ICN, IU, [Liebert (boards, uncut)], MH[2] (1. 16461.3; 2. A10.10.5* 'John Adams'), NN, NjP[2], PPL, PU; TxU; *Can*: CaOHM; *Japan*: [Kyoto]; *UK*: AWn, BMp (445201–11), C, Ck, Ct, E, JDF ('Sir Edward B. Baker, Bart.'), Gp, Gu, L (93 e.1–13), LICj[2], LVu (lacks vol. 11), MRu[2], OeF ('John Cam Hobhouse'), SAN; *Aust*: CNL (DNS 4831); *Fr*: BN.

[1] With the change in the final paragraph from 'Mr Steevens and other friends' to 'Mr Steevens and others'.

[2] Nos. 34, 41, 45, 50, 53, 58, 62, 69, 84, 85, 92, 95, 99, 102, 107, 108, 111, 115, 119, 120, 126, 131, 137, and 138. Hawkins adopted this selection and the texts from the edn. of 1778, 52.11Ad/12, above.

[3] To whom I am deeply indebted for the opportunity of examining it; *MS Handlist* 232.

[4] A brief account of the edn. is given by Alexander Chalmers in his *Biographical Dictionary* (1812–17), s.nn. 'Hawkins', xvii (1814), 244–54, and 'Johnson', xix (1815), 75–6; and a little tendentiously in Laetitia-Matilda Hawkins's *Memoirs* (1824), i. 155–9, 170–1, 173–5. John Sidney Hawkins defended his father's conduct of the work in *Gents. Mag.* lxxxiv (June 1814), i. 552. See further in my 'A Critical Study of the Transmission of the Texts of the Works of Dr. Samuel Johnson' (Oxford D.Phil. thesis, 1965).

[5] Murphy was employed regularly by the *Monthly* from July 1786 onwards (Emery, *Arthur Murphy* (1946), 152).

[6] Mrs Piozzi's copy (comprising 15 volumes) inscribed 'H: L: Piozzi, Streatham, 1790' was lot 170 at the Swann Galleries, New York, 24 May 1973. There were marginal notes in her hand in vol. XIV, 98–99.

[**87.3W/2** follows the sub-series tracing the publication of pieces first published or first collected in the Works.]

87.3W/1.1/1   Works, Hawkins's Life of Johnson   1787

THE | LIFE | OF | *SAMUEL JOHNSON*, ll.d. | [short swelled rule] | BY | Sir JOHN HAWKINS, Knt. | [medium swelled rule] | LONDON: | Printed for J. Buckland, J. Rivington and Sons, T. Payne and Sons, | L. Davis, B. White and Son, T. Longman, B. Law, J. Dodſley, | H. Baldwin, J. Robſon, J. Johnſon, C. Dilly, T. Vernor, W. Nicoll, | G. G. J. and J. Robinſon, T. Cadell,

T. Carnan, J. Nichols, | J. Bew, R. Baldwin, N. Conant, P. Elmſly, W. Goldſmith, | J. Knox, R. Faulder, Leigh & Sotheby, G. Nicol, | J. Murray, A. Strahan, W. Lowndes, T. Evans, | W. Bent, S. Hayes, G. and T. Wilkie, | T. & J. Egerton, W. Fox, P. Macqueen, | D. Ogilvie, B. Collins, | and E. Newbery. | [short rule] | M.DCC.LXXVII.

Notes: The imprint varies from the parent vol. 1 of *Works*, 1787 (above) not only in the tapering arrangement, but also in the omission of the name of 'R. Jameson', and in the spelling of 'P. Macqueen'. The separate issue was offered at 7s. in boards, in the *Lond. Chron.* and *General Evening Post*, 22 March 1787, but at 8s. in *Gents. Mag.* lvii (March 1787), 255. It was severely handled in various notes in the *Gents. Mag.* lvii, pp. 253, 345, 435, 522, 652, 751, 810, 847, 946, and 1146 (of which those in Aug., 652–3, Sept., 751–3, and Oct., 847–52, were by 'Sundry Whereof', *alias* Richard Porson); by Murphy in the *Monthly Rev.* (see 87.3W/1, above), by 'Philo-Johnson' in the *European Mag.* xi (Apr. 1787), 223–27, and further by William Julius Mickle in the same, xi (May 1787), 310–13, 319–23, xii (July 1787), 20–23, (Sept. 1787), 193–200.[1]

The *Collation* &c., are the same with vol. 1, above, save that the Portrait, the Dedication and the Advertisement are here omitted. Binder's Directions are removed from $1. The same leaves are cancelled here, as above, viz: B4, C2,3, D1, M5, S7, T2, X4, Y1,4,6, 2C4, 2G7, 2K8, 2L1, 2L8, 2N3, and 2P1.

The *cancellanda* (19) of the leaves in vol. 1 (i.e. Hawkins's *Life*) are preserved in the Hyde Collection (B4, C2,3, D1, M5, S7, T2, X4, Y1,4,6, 2C4[2], 2G7, 2K8, 2L1,8, 2N3, 2P1), and are annotated by Malone (noting the variants), who made transcriptions from them. These transcripts are in STA.[2] 2C4 was cancelled twice.[3] On the *cancellanda* are the following press-figures: S7^v(270)–9, 2C4^v (392, *first* version)–2, 2C4^v (392, *second* version)–4, 2G7(461)–9, 2K8(511)–1, 2N3^v(550)–6.

References: Courtney 162; CH 163–4; *Tinker* 1382; *Lit. Illus.* vii (1848), 475–6, 473; B.H. Davis, *Johnson before Boswell* (1960); ESTC: t082917.

Copies: O² (1. Douce HH. 77; 2. 2695 e.53);[4]

USA: CtY², Hyde⁴ (1. Original board and vellum spine, uncut; 2. 'Thomas Bond' — Adam; 4. grangerized with 182 engravings to 3 vols. Adam), [IU, InI, MA], MH, [MiU], NcU, [NjM], NPM, PHi, [PPT, OClW, OU, UC], ViU; *Can*: CaOHM (C.1424); *UK*: ABu, BMp, BRp, C, Csj, E, Ep, Eu, Felbrigg, Gu, L, LICj, LVp, LVu, NCl, SAN.

---

[1] Sherbo, *SB* xxxvii (1984), 210–27, esp. 224 n. 12.

[2] For a printed version of Malone's transcripts, see B.H. Davis, *Johnson Before Boswell* (1960), Appx. D, pp. 195–7.

[3] In O: (Percy 74, fo. 59), is preserved a *cancellans* of 2C4, bearing on p. 391 an inverted offset of X4 (p. 311, ll. 1–12) and of Y6^v (332, ll. 1–21, with l. 7 illegible at a fold), and on 392 an inverted offset of 2N3^v (550, ll. 1–11), and of 2L1 (513, ll. 1–20), apparently in the corrected versions.

[4] Horace Walpole's annotated copy was lot 735 in Part I of Jerome Kern's sale (Anderson Galleries, New York), 7 January 1929, and Thomas Park's copy, also annotated with reviews, notes and newspaper cuttings, was lot 1714 in William Pickering's sale at Sotheby &c., 20 March 1854.

87.3W/1.1/2   Works, Hawkins's Life of Johnson,   1787
                        Dublin

THE | LIFE | OF | SAMUEL JOHNSON, LL.D. | [medium swelled rule] |
BY | Sɪʀ *JOHN HAWKINS,* Kɴᴛ. | [medium swelled rule] | [metal block
device: cherub with scroll 'PRINTED BY CHAMBERS'] | FOR MESSRS. |
CHAMBERLAIN, COLLES, BURNET, | WOGAN, EXSHAW,
WHITE, BYRNE, WHITESTONE, | MOORE, AND JONES. | [short
swelled rule] | DUBLIN: MDCCLXXXVII.

8°, *A*1 B–2M⁸ 2N⁴, ($3 (+ C4, –S3, 2A3) signed), 277 leaves.

Pp. A1 *i* t., *ii* blk, on B1 *1* 2–533 text of Life, *534* blk, on 2M4–2N4ᵛ (9
leaves, unpaged) Index.

Pagination: 238–9 as 138–9, 324 *inverted* '3', 525 as 425.

Press-figures: none; *Catchwords*: not recorded.

Explicit: 533 FINIS.

Paper: White, laid; Carré (uncut: 8¼ × 5¼ in.); wmk.: indecipherable.

Type: Long primer (3.3 mm), notes: brevier (2.6 mm).

References: Courtney 162; ESTC: t110273.

Notes: The text follows Hawkins's first London edn., either as it appeared in
Works, or in the separate issue of his Life.

Copies: O (Vet. A5 e.2160, 'Maria Edgeworth from Dr. Brinkley');
USA: CtY, Hyde² (**1**. 'E. of Aldborough';¹ **2**. Adam), [InU, MdBP], MH,
NN, [OCl, PBm, PHi], PPU, [PV], WiM; *Can*: CaOHM²; *Japan*: [Kyoto];
UK: BMp, C, Cp, L, LCu, Owo; *Aust*: CNL (DNS 4326).

¹ Either Edward Stratford, 2nd E († 1801*), or his brother John, 3rd E (†1823).

87.3W/1.1/3   Hawkins's Life of Johnson,   1787
                    second London edition

THE | LIFE | OF | *SAMUEL JOHNSON,* ʟʟ.ᴅ. | BY | Sɪʀ JOHN
HAWKINS, Kɴᴛ. | [short swelled rule] | THE SECOND EDITION, |
REVISED AND CORRECTED. | [medium swelled rule] | LONDON: |
Printed for J. Buckland, J. Rivington and Sons, T. Payne and Sons, L. Davis, |
B. White and Son, T. Longman, B. Law, J. Dodſley, H. Baldwin, | J. Robſon,
C. Dilly, T. Vernor, W. Nicoll, G. G. J. and J. Robinſon, | T. Cadell, T.
Carnan, J. Nichols, T. Bowles, J. Bew, R. Baldwin, N. Conant, | P. Elmſly, W.
Goldſmith, J. Knox, R. Faulder, Leigh & Sotheby, G. Nicol, | W. Otridge, J.
Murray, A. Strahan, W. Lowndes, T. Evans, J. Phillips, | W. Stuart, J. Sewell,
H.L. Gardner, W. Bent, S. Hayes, G. and T. Wilkie, | T. & J. Egerton, W.
Fox, P. Macqueen, Scatcherd & Whitaker, D. Ogilvie, | R. Jameſon, J. Barker,
B. Collins, and E. Newbery. | [short rule] | M.DCC.LXXXVII.

8°, *A*1 B–E⁸ F⁸ (–F3,5 + F3.5) G–2O⁸ 2P⁸ (–2P3,6 + 2P3.6) 2Q⁸ 2R⁶, ($4 signed; 'VOL. I.' on $1 PQRSTU), 311 leaves

Pp. A1 *i* t., *ii* blk, on B1 *1* 2–598 Life dh: [bevelled parallel rule] | THE | LIFE | OF | Dr. SAMUEL JOHNSON. | [short swelled rule], ht: THE LIFE OF | Dr. SAMUEL JOHNSON, 599–605 Postscript dh. and ht: POSTSCRIPT., *606–20* (2Q7ᵛ–2R6ᵛ) Index (8 leaves, unpaged), dh: [bevelled double rule] | INDEX., ht: INDEX

Pagination: no errors.

Press-figures: B7ᵛ(14)–3, B8ᵛ(16)–1, C1ᵛ(18)–2, C5(25)–4, D2ᵛ(36)–4, D8(47)–2, E8(63)–4, F4ᵛ(72)–5, G8(95)–3, H1ᵛ(98)–4, H6ᵛ(108)–8, I2ᵛ(116)–8, K1ᵛ(130)–3, L1ᵛ(146)–4, X1ᵛ(307)–4, Y8(2350–4, Z4(343)–7, Z5ᵛ(346)–3, 2A8ᵛ(368)–3, 2B2ᵛ(372)–3, 2B5ᵛ(378)–4, 2C7ᵛ(398)–7, 2C8ᵛ(400)–4, 2D6(411)–5, 2E5ᵛ(426)–4, 2E7(429)–3, 2F1ᵛ(434)–3, 2F2ᵛ(436)–4, 2G6ᵛ(460)–3, 2G8(463)–2, 2H3ᵛ(470)–4, 2H5(473)–3, 2I6(491)–4, 2I8ᵛ(496)–9, 2K2ᵛ(500)–8, 2L5ᵛ(521)–4, 2L8ᵛ(528)–7, 2M1ᵛ(530)–8, 2M8ᵛ(544)–1, 2N4ᵛ(552)–2, 2N8(559)–3, 2O4ᵛ(568)–1, 2O6(571)–4, 2P1ᵛ(578)–7, 2P2ᵛ(580)–2, 2P3ᵛ(582)–7, 2Q4ᵛ(600)–3, 2Q5ᵛ(602)–8, 2R2ᵛ(612)–7, 2R3ᵛ(614)–4; there are no figg. in sigg. M–U, three in 2P.

Catchwords: 28 ˌpaper, ('~,), 57 ˌpleaſure ('~), 62 ˌnot ('~), 81n [im-] ˌprovements ('~), 172 ˌgraphia, ('~,), 182 ˌApropos: ('~:), 197 Ahˌ (~!), 213 Richardſonˌ (~*,), 254 philoſophers, (~ˌ), 279 ˌMilton. ('~.), 391 'manˌ (ˌ~,), 304 'time, ('~ˌ), 320 aſked, (~ˌ), 424 Dye (Dyer,), 448 [pe-] 'tition, (tion,), 512 truſt, (~.), 579 literature. (~*.).

Explicit: none.

Paper: White, laid; demy (8¾ × 5⅝ in.); wmk.: LVG.

Type: Pica (4.0 mm), leaded (1.0mm).

References: Courtney 162; P.A. Scholes, *Hawkins* (1953), 192, B. H. Davis, *Johnson Before Boswell* (1960); ESTC: t113903.

Notes: The imprint differs from that of the first separate edn. (87.3W/1.1/1, above), in the omission of the names 'J. Johnſon', and the addition of T. Bowles, W. Otridge, J. Phillips, W. Stuart, J. Sewell, H.L. Gardner, Scatcherd & Whitaker, R. Jameſon, J. Barker.

The headlines show that the book was printed in four sections to expedite production: B–L, M–U, X–2G and 2H–2Q.[1] The anomalous Binder's Directions in P–U show that section was set up from a copy of vol. I of *Works*, not from a copy of the first separate issue of the Life. This edn. was published 7 June 1787 (*Morning Chron.*). Hawkins made considerable revisions to his text and this second edn. represents the authoritative version of his biography. Some changes between this and the first edn. were noticed in *Gents. Mag.* lvii (June 1787), 522 (cf. also October 1787, 847, by 'Sundry Whereof').

Copies: O (2695 e. 152);

USA: CSmH, DLC, Hyde (Adam), MH, [MiU, NNC], NRU, PPL, TxU,

ViU; *Can*: CaOHM; *Japan*: [Kyoto]; *UK*: BAT, BMp, Cf, DUu, Gu, L, LVu, MRp, NCu, Op ('Vernon'), SHp, STA; *Aust*: CNL (DNS 4327).

¹ Scholes reproduced (facing p. 192) JH's letter (in the handwriting of his son, John Sidney Hawkins) of 8 April 1787, apparently to John Nichols, corroborating this division (*Lit. Anec.* v (1812), 54, 56).

87.3W/1.2/1a   Works, Vols. XII–XIII,   1787
                         Debates in Parliament

[½t] THE | WORKS | OF | Samuel Johnſon, LL.D. | [medium swelled rule, 64 mm] | IN THIRTEEN VOLUMES. | VOL. XII [– XIII]. | [parallel rule] | LONDON: | PRINTED FOR JOHN STOCKDALE, | OPPOSITE BURLINGTON HOUSE, PICCADILLY. | M,DCC,LXXXVII.

Vol. XIII: [medium swelled rule, 40 mm] . . . BURLINGTON-HOUSE, . . . M.DCC.LXXXVII.

[Debates t.] DEBATES | IN | PARLIAMENT. | By SAMUEL JOHNSON, LL.D. | [medium swelled rule] | IN TWO VOLUMES. | VOL. I [– II]. | [parallel rule] | LONDON: | PRINTED FOR JOHN STOCKDALE, | OPPOSITE BURLINGTON HOUSE, PICCADILLY. | M,DCC,LXXXVII.

Vol. II: . . .BURLINGTON-HOUSE, . . . M.DCC.LXXXVII.

2 vols., 8°

I. A⁶ (A5 + χ² (= 2C4.5), χ2 + 2χ1) B–2B⁸ 2C⁸ (–2C4.5, 2C8 blk), ($4 (–A1,2) signed; 'VOL. I.' on $1), 207 leaves.

Pp. A1 *i* Works t., *ii* blk, *iii* Debates t., *iv* blk, *v* vi–x Preface (dated 'March 1st. 1787'), on χ1 (=2C4) xi–xiv List of Fictitious Terms, *xv* Contents, *xvi* blk, *xvii* References to the Speakers, *xviii* blk, on B1 *1* 2–394 text of Debates, *395–6* (2C8) blk.

Pagination: no errors; *Press-figures*: none.

Catchwords: 75 appearance, (∼∧), 267 Sir, (∼∧), 348 opponents∧(∼,), 377 Publ∧ck (Publick).

Explicit: 394 END OF VOL. I. (small caps).

II. A⁴ (A3 + χ1) B–2K⁸ 2L², ($4 (–2L2) signed; 'VOL. II.' on $1), 263 leaves.

Pp. A1 Works t., A1ᵛ blk, A2 Debates t., A2ᵛ blk, A3 xv (for v) List of Fictitious Characters, *xvi* blk, *xvii* Contents, *xviii* References to Speakers, *xix–xx* Advertisement, on B1 *1* 2–516 text of Debates.

Pagination: no errors.

Press-figures: B3ᵛ(6)–2, C3ᵛ(22)–5, D1ᵛ(34)–4, E8(63)–8, F8ᵛ(80)–2, G1ᵛ(82)–8, G4ᵛ(88)–2, H3ᵛ(102)–4, H8ᵛ(112)–1, I4ᵛ(120)–2, I5ᵛ(122)–8, I6(123)–8, K4ᵛ(136)–5, K8(143)–8, L5ᵛ(154)–2, L6ᵛ(156)–5, M1ᵛ(162)–4,

M6ᵛ(172)–5, N6(187)–6, O1ᵛ(194)–4, O4ᵛ(200)–6, P2ᵛ(212)–7, P8(223)–2,
Q8(239)–5, R7(253)–2, T8(287)–8, U7(301)–5, X8ᵛ(320)–2, Y4(327)–2,
Y5ᵛ(330)–5, Z2ᵛ(340)–5, Z7ᵛ(350)–4, 2A8ᵛ(368)–6, 2B6(379)–5, 2B7(381)–2,
2C2ᵛ(388)–1,   2C8(399)–8,   2D5ᵛ(410)–6,   2E7(429)–2,   2E8(431)–3,
2F8ᵛ(448)–6,   2G7ᵛ(462)–4,   2H3ᵛ(470)–5,   2I6(491)–5,   2K5(505)–5,
2L2(515)–5.

Catchwords: 120 That (For), 160 is, (, *slipt*), 163 But͵ (~,), 451 *Friday*
(*February*).

Explicit: 516 THE END.

Paper: White, laid; demy (uncut: 8¾ × 5⅝ in.); wmk.: fleur-de-lys.

Type: Preface: pica (4.0 mm), leaded (2.2 mm); text: sm. pica (3.6 mm),
leaded (1.1 mm).

References: Courtney 5, 162; Hawkins *Life87* 101–2, 124–8 n.; *Life* i. 115–18,
150, 501–12; Hoover, *SJ's Parliamentary Reporting* (1953), 44–6, 50–3; *Tinker*
1382; ESTC: t144270.

Notes: The preliminary gatherings are awkward. Watermarks show that in
vol. 1, the Contents and References (I. xv–xvii) formed the innermost fold of an
original 2C⁸, with a single extra leaf tucked in, so adding three leaves to the initial A⁴. In vol. 2 The 'References to the Speakers' and the 'Advertisement' are
on conjugate leaves, so that the leaf bearing the 'Contents' is the intruder,
though its birthplace is not clear.

Stockdale's 'Introduction' (dated 'LONDON March 1st, 1787') asserts SJ's
responsibility for the Lilliputian Debates of the *Gents. Mag.* from 19 November
1740 to 23 February 1743 (vi), offers a survey of the history of Parliamentary
reporting, adding that Cave's Debates were first compiled by Guthrie, and then
by Johnson, who was succeeded by Hawkesworth (ix),[1] and claims that the volumes constitute either a supplement to Johnson's *Works*, or an independent
specimen of his writings. Boswell however, was 'well assured' that the editor was
George Chalmers (1742–1825*), though there is no corroborating evidence.[2]
The Lilliputian names are replaced by the real ones (x).

Published 24 April 1787, as vols. XII and XIII of Johnson's *Works*, ed.
Hawkins (*Lond. Chron.*), the 13 vols at £3. 18s. in boards, or £4. 17s. 6d. 'ele-
gantly calf gilt'.[3] The 2 vols of *Debates* were offered at 12s. The *Works* had
already been announced on 20 March 1787 in *Morning Chron.*, which had
stated on 22 March that the two volumes of Stockdale's *Debates* would appear
'On Saturday next. . .' [= 24 March]. In the last leaf of Reed's supplementary
vol. xiv to *Works* (87.3W/1.3, below), Stockdale advertised these volumes at
'12s. in Boards. ☞ The Publisher particularly requests those Gentlemen who
intend to complete Dr JOHNSON'S WORKS, will do it as soon as possible, otherwise they may not have an Opportunity, as there are but few remaining of the
12th and 13th Volumes.' This notice had already appeared in the *Lond. Chron.*,
22 Nov. 1787, p. 496, and in the *Morning Chron.*, 29 November 1787: it does

not sound like a rapid seller. The *Debates* were noticed briefly in the *Monthly Rev.* lxxvii (Sept. 1787), 250.

Copies: O (2699 e. 134–5);

USA: CSmH, CtY, Hyde[3] (**1**. 'Clement K. Shorter', uncut, unopened), ICN, IU ('R. Montgomery'), [Liebert], MH (16461.3), NjP, NPM, NN, PPL, TxU, ViU; *Can*: CaOHM; *Japan*: [Kyoto]; *UK*: AWn, C, Cf, Ck, E ([Ao] 3.1), L, LICj, MRu[2], Oef ('John Cam Hobhouse'), SHu, SPAg; *Aust*: CNL[2] (DNS **1**. 4764–5; **2**. 4832); *Fr*: BN.

---

[1] In this the writer was anticipated by William Shaw, *Memoirs of the Life and Writings of . . . Johnson* (1785), 42: 'His predecessor in this Herculean labour was Guthrie, . . . Hawkesworth, his friend and imitator, succeeded him likewise in these cursory productions'.

[2] The *DNB* also credits George Chalmers, with the 'Prefatory Introduction to Dr Johnson's 'Debates in Parliament', London 1794, 8vo.' citing a reissue of these vols. The authority for this attribution does not appear (but was probably JB, cf. also p. 5 of the Introduction), though in view of Chalmers's many publications of a political, constitutional and parliamentary nature, it is not an implausible one. His library, sold by R.H. Evans (1841), included many printed and MS pieces which could have contributed to the editing of these Debates, including a complete set of the *Gents. Mag.* and SJ's *Works* in 15 vols. See further his general correspondence: L: (Add MS 22900–22903, 27952, fo. 132, and 28653, fos. 80b, 84). Stockdale was a bookseller of 'much eccentricity of conduct and great coarseness of manners' (*Gents. Mag.* lxxxv (1815), i. 649), and not a very likely editor himself.

[3] Announced also as 'On Saturday next will be published . . .' in *Morning Chron.*, Thurs. 22 March 1787, but no advt. noted on Sat. 24th.

87.3W/1.2/1b   Works, Vols. XII–XIII,   1972
                    Debates in Parliament, facsimile

Facsimiles of these two volumes were published by Gregg International, Farnborough, Hants. in November 1972, at £74.00. ISBN: 0-576-02939-4

87.3W/1.2/1c   Works, Debates in Parliament,   1792
                              reissue

THE | WORKS | OF | Samuel Johnſon, L.L.D. | A NEW EDITION | [short swelled rule] | IN FOURTEEN VOLUMES. | VOL. XII [– XIII]. | [double rule] | LONDON: | PRINTED FOR T. VERNOR, AND THE REST OF | THE PROPRIETORS. | M,DCC,XCII.

2 vols., 8°. Collation as prec.

References: ESTC: n035965.

Notes: A reissue with cancelled tt. of 87.3W/1.2/1a, above, and appended to Murphy's edn. of SJ's Works, 12 vols. 1792 (87.3W/2, below), leading to the renumbering of the vols.

Copies: PPU (vol. 13 only), TxU; *Can*: [CaAEU].[1]

---

[1] B.J. McMullin, *News from the Rare Book Room*, xii (1970), 76–77.

87.3W/1.2/2   Works, Debates in Parliament   1811

The Works of Samuel Johnson, LL.D. A New edition. With an Essay on his Life and Genius, by Arthur Murphy, Esq. [medium parallel rule] Volume the Thirteenth [–Fourteenth] forming the First [–Second] Volume of Debates in Parliament. [medium parallel rule] LONDON; | Printed for T. Longman, B. White and Son, B. Law, J. Dodsley, H. Baldwin, | J. Robson, J. Johnson, C. Dilly, T. Vernor, G.G.J. and J. Robinson, | T. Cadell, J. Nichols, R. Baldwin, N. Conant, P. Elmsly, F. and C. | Rivington, T. Payne, W. Goldsmith, R. Faulder, Leigh and Sotheby, | G. Nicol, J. Murray, A. Strahan, W. Lowndes, T. Evans, W. Bent, | S. Hayes, G. and T. Wilkie, T. and J. Egerton, W. Fox, P. M'Queen, | Ogilvie and Speare, Darton and Harvey, G. and C. Kearsley, W. Millar, | B.C. Collins, and E. Newbery. | M DCC XCII.

     2 vols., 8°

XIII. A–2G⁸ 2H², ($2 (–A1, 2H2) signed; 'VOL. I.' on $1), 236 leaves.

Pp. A1 t., A1ᵛ coloph: 'Printed by S. Hamilton, Weybridge.', A2 *iii* iv–vii Preface ('London, March 1st, 1787.'), *viii* note on 'Lilliputian terms', ix–xiii Key to Names, xiv Key to terms, *xv* Contents, *xvi* blk, on B1 *1* 2–467 text of Debates, 467 *Explicit*: END OF VOL. I., coloph: as A1ᵛ, *468* blk.

XIV. *A²* B–2G⁸ 2H², ($2 (–2H2) signed; 'VOL. II.' on $1), 244 leaves.

Pp. A1 t., A1ᵛ coloph., A2 Contents, A2ᵛ blk, on B1 *1* 2–466, *Explicit*: THE END, 467–8 References to the Speakers, 468 coloph.

References: Courtney 165; Hoover, *SJ's Parliamentary Reporting* (1953), 50.
Notes: These volumes are directly reprinted from Stockdale, 1787, above.
Copies: O (8° H. 76–7 BS); *UK*: Eu, HLu.

87.3W/1.2/3   Works, Debates in Parliament,   1812
                      Cobbett's Parliamentary History

Cobbett's Parliamentary History of England From the Norman Conquest, in 1066, to the Year 1803. From which last-mentioned Epoch it is continued downwards in the Work entitled 'Cobbett's Parliamentary Debates'. London: 1806–12.

     12 vols., 8°

Vols. xi–xii. Not examined.

References: Hoover, *SJ's Parliamentary Reporting* (1953), 50–1
Notes: The editors were Cobbett and John Wright.
Copies: O; *UK*: E (GHC.5).

87.3W/1.2/4   Works, Debates in Parliament,   1825
Oxford English Classics

Vols. x–xi of Works, 1825. Not examined.
References: Hoover, *SJ's Parliamentary Reporting* (1953), 52–3.
Copies: USA: Hyde.

87.3W/1.3/1a   Works, Supplementary Vol., XIV   1788

THE | WORKS | OF | Samuel Johnſon, LL.D. | [medium swelled rule] | IN
FOURTEEN VOLUMES. | VOL. XIV. | [double rule] | LONDON: |
Printed for JOHN STOCKDALE, Piccadilly; and | G. G. J. and J.
ROBINSON, Pater-noster-Row. | M.DCC.LXXXVIII.

8°, A⁴ b² B–2N⁸, ($4 (–D3, Z4) signed), 286 leaves.

Pp. A1 *i* t., *ii* blk, *iii–vi* Preface, *vii–xii* Contents, on B1 *1–3* 4–556 text,
557–8 (2N8) advts.

Pagination: 511–12 duplicated at 2L, 523 as 52; unnumbered 36–8, 59–60,
115–16, 123, 125–7, 156, 164–9, 190–1, 199, 210, 216, 220, 232, 239, 241,
244, 249, 310, 330, 342–4, 355, 357–9, 377–8, 381–3, 398, 413, 421, 427, 456,
467, 490, 552; 164 blk.

Press-figures: A3–3, B5(9)–8, C6(27)–7, D8(47)–5, E3ᵛ(54)–2, F5ᵛ(74)–7,
G5ᵛ(90)–8, H1ᵛ(98)–1, I4ᵛ(120)–3, I8(127)–8, K1ᵛ(130)–1, L3ᵛ(150)–2,
M5ᵛ(170)–5, M6ᵛ(172)–7, N3ᵛ(182)–3, N5(185)–5, O1ᵛ(194)–3, P7(221)–8,
P8(223)–5, Q1ᵛ(226)–3, R1ᵛ(242)–8, R6ᵛ(252)–4, S1ᵛ(258)–8, S7(269)–3,
T5ᵛ(282)–1, U8ᵛ(304)–5, X8(319)–7, Y3ᵛ(326)–3, Y6ᵛ(332)–2, Z1ᵛ(338)–4,
2A7ᵛ(366)–8, 2B1ᵛ(370)–8, 2B2ᵛ(372)–1, 2C6(395)–5, 2D6ᵛ(412)–7 [*om.* in
CtY], 2D8(415)–1, 2E8(431)–1, 2F1ᵛ(434)–2, 2F2ᵛ(436)–6, 2G3ᵛ(454)–8,
2G4ᵛ(456)–2,   2H7ᵛ(478)–2,   2I6ᵛ(492)–2,   2K5ᵛ(506)–8,   2L7ᵛ(524)–3,
2M1ᵛ(528)–8, 2N3ᵛ(548)–8, 2N6ᵛ(554)–6.

Catchwords: 56 [for-] tune, (ture,), 64 ‸6. That ('~. ~), 87 1 — As ((1) ——
As), 116 n. ‸ſo ('~), 140 TES- (Testimonies), 160 [compu-] tation‸ (~,), 231
A RE- (OBSERVATIONS), 530 *om.* (LETTER).

Explicit: 556 FINIS.
Paper: White, laid; demy (8¾ × 5⅝ in.); no vis. wmk.
Type: Pica (4.0 mm), leaded (1.0 mm).
Plate: Inserted facing p. 165 'A Correct Table of the Magnetical Variations
. . . ' &c.
References: Courtney 162; CH 165; *Tinker* 1382; ESTC: n025884.
Notes: The editor was almost certainly Isaac Reed, though the evidence is cir-
cumstantial.[1] This volume represents an important supplement to the canon
established in Hawkins's collection of 1787, and apparently influenced JB in
several of his attributions in the *Life* (1791). It was announced as published at

7s. in boards, on 29 November 1787 (*Lond. Chron.* and *Morning Chron.*), and was noticed in the *Monthly Rev.* lxxix (Oct. 1788), 380.

Copies: O (2699 e. 174);

USA: CSmH, CtY, Hyde (with *Works*), ICN, IU ('B. Rollo'), [Liebert], MH (16461.3), NjP, NN, NPM, PPL, TxU, ViU; *Japan*: [Kyoto]; *UK*: AWn, C, Cf, E, LICj, MRu², Op, SHu; *Aust*: CNL (DNS 4833); *Fr*: BN.

---

¹ Quite apart from the association of Reed with two MS lists of SJ's minor works (referring to many of the obscure pieces in vol. xiv), one of which he marked for JB (CtY), the other preserved in Ljh, there is the foggy attribution in his obituary notice by James Bindley, in *European Mag.* li (Feb. 1807), 83–6, 'To these [Reed's publications] we may add two supplemental volumes, a thirteenth and fourteenth, to Dr Johnson's *Works*, 1788.' Letters from Reed to Stockdale on a new edn. of SJ's *Works* showing the help given by Reed to Stockdale, were included in lot 1050 in Robert Cole's sale at Puttick & Simpson, 29 July 1861. I do not know their present whereabouts. Two copies of this volume (xiv) were in Reed's sale, King: *Bibliotheca Reediana*, 2 Nov. 1807, 2359 — Nott, 7s., and 2360 — Sharpe, 6s. 6d., but again, their present whereabouts are unknown. See further, Sherbo, *Isaac Reed, Editorial Factotum* (1989).

87.3W/1.3/1b   Works, Supplementary Vol., XIV,   1792
                                    reissue

ADDITIONAL VOLUME | TO THE | WORKS | OF | Samuel Johnſon, LL.D. | [short parallel rule] | LONDON: PRINTED FOR S. HIGHLEY, FLEET-STREET. | MDCCXCII.

Var. **87.3W/1.3/1c**: . . . LONDON: PRINTED FOR T. VERNOR, AND THE REST OF THE PROPRIETORS. M,DCC,XCII.

8°, A⁴ (± A1) b² B–2N⁸, . . . &c., as prec.

A reissue with variant cancel tt. of 87.3W/1.3/1a, above. Cf. 87.3W/1.2/1c (1792), above, and refs. *Can*: Edmonton, U. Alberta.

References: CH 165; (b) ESTC: n042268.

Copies: (b) Op ('M: F: Fothergill Epsom July yᶜ 26 1796' — 'Edward Sage 1892'); *USA*: CtY (Im J637. B787. v.14b), MB (G 3947.38), PPU; *Can*: CaOHM.

87.3W/1.4   Works, Supplementary Vol., XV   1789

See Lobo's *Voyage to Abyssinia*, 35.2LV/2, above.

[½t] THE | WORKS | OF | Samuel Johnſon, ʟʟ.ᴅ. | [medium swelled rule] | IN FIFTEEN VOLUMES. | VOL. XV. | [double rule] | LONDON: | Pʀɪɴᴛᴇᴅ ꜰᴏʀ ELLIOT ᴀɴᴅ KAY, N° 332. Sᴛʀᴀɴᴅ, | Aɴᴅ C. ELLIOT, Eᴅɪɴʙᴜʀɢʜ. | M,DCC,LXXXIX.

[Title] A | VOYAGE TO ABYSSINIA, | BY FATHER JEROME LOBO, | *A PORTUGUESE MISSIONARY.* | CONTAINING THE | HISTORY, NATURAL, CIVIL, AND ECCLESIASTICAL, | OF THAT

REMOTE AND UNFREQUENTED COUNTRY, | Continued down to the beginning of the *Eighteenth Century:* | WITH | FIFTEEN DISSERTATIONS | On various Subjects, | RELATING TO THE ANTIQUITIES, GOVERNMENT, RELIGION, | MANNERS, AND NATURAL HISTORY, OF ABYSSINIA. | BY M. LE GRAND. | [rule] | TRANSLATED FROM THE FRENCH BY | Samuel Johnſon, ll.d. | [rule] | TO WHICH ARE ADDED, | VARIOUS OTHER TRACTS | BY THE SAME AUTHOR, | Not Publiſhed by Sir John Hawkins or Mr Stockdale. | [short swelled rule] | LONDON: | Printed for ELLIOT and KAY, N° 332. Strand, | And C. ELLIOT, Edinburgh. | M,DCC,LXXXIX.

8°, *a*⁸ b⁸ A–2G⁸ (a1 blk), ($4 (–a1,2,3) signed), 256 leaves.

Pp. a1 blk, on a2 ½t 'Works' (as above), a2ᵛ blk, a3 t., a3ᵛ blk, a4 Dedication ('To Arthur Murphy, Esq.'), a4ᵛ blk, on a5 *1* 2–10 General Preface (signed 'GEORGE GLEIG. Stirling, Dec. 1. 1788.'), *11* 12–15 SJ's Preface to Lobo's Abyssinia, *16* blk, *17* 18–23 Contents, *24* blk, *25* 26–500 Voyage to Abyssinia, &c., *501–2* (2G8) advts.

References: Courtney 3–4, 163; ESTC: t110318. See above, 35.1LV/2 (1789).

This volume was reviewed in *Gents. Mag.* lix (June 1789), 543–6, with long extracts, and, despite the 'Dedication', by Arthur Murphy, in *Monthly Rev.* 2 Ser. (1790), i. 281.

Gleig attributed the 'Preface' to Lindsay's *Evangelical History*, 1757 (57.4LEH, above) to SJ,[1] though JB was to reject it (wrongly) in *Life* (1791), ii. 559 n.; iv. 381 n. = 383). He also gave him (with some hesitation in 'Introduction', p. 7), the 'Picture of Human Life, from the Table of Cebes', first printed in Dodsley's *Museum* (1747), iii. 233–46 (46.3DM, above) and reprinted in the *Preceptor* (1748), ii. 541–6 (48.4DP, above) following the text of perhaps the third or fourth edn. of the latter (pp. 382–402).[2] The 'Memoirs of Bishop Berkeley' which had been given to SJ by Reed in *Works*, xiv (1788), 421–6 (87.3W/1.3/1a, above), he authoritatively rejected.[3] He printed two letters, one from SJ to Thomas Lawrence (*Letters* 650, 20 Jan. 1780, Hyde iii. 222–3),[4] the other to Charles Lawrence (*Letters* 704, 30 Aug. 1780, Hyde iii. 310–13).[5] The 'Dedication' to Kennedy's *Complete System of . . . Scripture Chronology*, 1762 (62.3KC, above), was correctly printed (pp. 486–7); six reviews were taken from the *Literary Mag.* 1756 (56.4LM, above) (pp. 403–80).[6] The 'Account of the Cock-Lane Ghost' was reprinted from *Gents. Mag.* xxxii (Jan. 1762), 43–44 (62GM32, above) and attributed to SJ (pp. 487–93). The verses 'Nugæ Anapæsticæ', also from a Lawrentian MS, were first printed here (pp. 499–500).[7] All Gleig's texts are but loosely taken from their copies with marked divergences in accidentals, and some substantive errors.

Copies: O² (1. 2699 e. 175; 2. 20742 e.13);

USA: CSmH (132151), CtY² (1. lacks a1–2), DLC, Hyde² (1. 'William Johnston', of Limekilns), InU, [Liebert (orig. blue boards, uncut)], MB, MH,

NcU, NIC, NjP, NN², OCl, [PPAN], PPU; *Can*: CaOHM² (C. 2526); *Japan*: [Kyoto]; *UK*: Abb, [W. R. Batty], BRp, C, Ct, DUNu, E, En, Eu, Gu, L (10097 d.2), LICj, Lsm, MRu, Op ('T. Holt White, 1818' — 'Henry W. Chandler'), SAN, SHu; *Aust*: CNL (DNS. 5215); *Fr*: BN.

¹ He took his text however from the version printed in the *Literary Mag.* II. xiii. 180–82 (56.4LM, above), and not from Lindsay's book itself.
² It was rejected as uncanonical by Alexander Chalmers in *Works*, 1806, I (Advertisement), iii–iv, 'The truth is it was translated by Mr Spence'.
³ Introduction (1789), 3–6, quoting a letter from his friend George Monck Berkeley, the son of the Bishop, expressly denying the 'Memoir' to SJ. This was overlooked by Sir G. Keynes in *BC* xxx (1981), 177–81. Gleig's intimacy with the Bishop and with G.M. Berkeley, is attested by correspondence in L: (Add. MS 39312, fos. 24, 33, 43, 45, 49, 65, 67, 84, and 144).
⁴ It was reprinted in *European Mag.* xv (Apr. 1789), 282, which appeared after Gleig's vol. xv, published on 6 April 1789 (*Morning Chron.*). Both versions diverge in minor details from the extant MS (Hyde).
⁵ Despite Gleig's claim to have followed the MS (CtY) of this letter (p. 498 n.), his text is demonstrably and carelessly taken from the *European Mag.* vii (May, 1785), 332–3 which is itself closer to the MS.
⁶ Reviews of the Natural History of Aleppo (*Lit. Mag.* ii. 80–86), of Memoirs of Sully (*Lit. Mag.* vi. 281–2), of Lucas's Essay on Waters (*Lit. Mag.* iv. 167–8, v. 225–9, vi. 288–93), of Evans's Geographical Essays (*Lit. Mag.* vi. 293–9), of Warton's Essay on Pope (*Lit. Mag.* i. 35–8), and the opening paragraphs of that of Harrison's Miscellanies (*Lit. Mag.* vi. 282–88).
⁷ *Poems²* 231–2. Gleig dated the verses 'March 21, 1782' but the extant MS (CSmH; *MS Handlist* 189, *MS Index* JoS 1) is undated, and the transcript which JB obtained from Elizabeth Lawrence (CtY: Boswell MS. M 145), is dated 'May 1782', but that may mean that she wrote it in reply to SJ's letter of 22 May 1782 (*Letters* 782.2, Hyde iv. 42). The date is canvassed by Chapman (*Letters* 770.1 n.).

87.3W/2   Works, ed. Murphy   1792

THE | WORKS | OF | Samuel Johnſon, ll.d. | A NEW EDITION, | IN TWELVE VOLUMES. | WITH | An ESSAY on his LIFE and GENIUS, | By ARTHUR MUPHY, Esq. | [short swelled rule] | VOLUME THE FIRST [– TWELFTH]. | [short swelled rule] | LONDON: | Printed for T. Longman, B. White and Son, B. Law, J. Dodsley, H. Baldwin, | J. Robson, J. Johnson, C. Dilly, T. Vernor, G. G. J. and J. Robinson, | T. Cadell, J. Nichols, R. Baldwin, N. Conant, P. Elmsly, F. and C. | Rivington, T. Payne, W. Goldsmith, R. Faulder, Leigh and Sotheby, | G. Nicol, J. Murray, A. Strahan, W. Lowndes, T. Evans, W. Bent, | S. Hayes, G. and T. Wilkie, T. and J. Egerton, W. Fox, P. M'Queen, | Ogilvie and Speare, Darton and Harvey, G. and C. Kearfley, W. Millar, | B.C. Collins, and E. Newbery. | M DCC XCII.
    12 vols., 8°

    I. π² a–l⁸ m⁶ B–O⁸ P⁴, ($4 (–m4, P3,4) signed; 'Vol. I.' on $1 (–F)), 204 leaves.
    Pp. Engr. port. of SJ front. + π1 *i* t., *ii* blk, iii–iv Contents, on a1 *1* 2–187 Murphy's Essay, *188* blk, on B1 *²1* ½t 'Poems', *2* blk, 3–215 text, *216* blk.

Pagination: [↑] ²iii, 3, ²15, 28, 33, 129, 168; unpaged 31–2, 34; blk. 32, 130, 216.

Press-figures: a4ᵛ(8)–5, a7ᵛ(14)–2, b6(27)–2, b6ᵛ(28)–3, c1ᵛ(34)–2, c4ᵛ(40)–1, d7ᵛ(62)–2, d8ᵛ(64)–3, e2ᵛ(68)–2, e8(79)–7, f3ᵛ(86)–5, f5(89)–4, g5ᵛ(106)–5, g7(109)–3, h3ᵛ(118)–4, h7(125)–3, i5ᵛ(138)–6, i8ᵛ(144)–4, k6(155)–2, k8ᵛ(160)–3, l4ᵛ(168)–3, l7ᵛ(174)–4, m1ᵛ(178)–4, m5(185)–1, B7ᵛ(14)–2, C1ᵛ(18)–4, C6ᵛ(28)–2, D2ᵛ(36)–7, D6(43)–1, E5(57)–4, E7ᵛ(62)–2, F8(79)–2, G5ᵛ(90)–7, G6ᵛ(92)–4, H8(111)–1, I3ᵛ(118)–2, I5(121)–1, K4ᵛ(136)–1, L3ᵛ(150)–4, L7(157)–3, M2ᵛ(164)–5, M5ᵛ(170)–7, N1ᵛ(178)–4, N2ᵛ(180)–5, O2ᵛ(196)–2, P3ᵛ(214)–5.

Catchwords: ²6 ˏBut ('~), ²9 By (²³ ~), 12 Prepare (³² ~), 15 But (* ~), 20 The (~*), 128 *om.* (EPILOGUE.), 129 *om.*, 186 O Qui (*~ ~), 188 Sen (*~), 190 E EAL~ (*E WALTONI), 212 His (*~).

Explicit: 215 END OF THE FIRST VOLUME.

II. *A²* B–2E⁸ 2F⁴ (2F4 blk), ($4 signed; 'VOL. II.' on $1), 222 leaves.

Pp. A1 t., 1ᵛ blk, A2 Contents, on B1 *1–3* 4–438 text Tracts and Essays, *439–40* (2F4) blk.

Pagination: [↑] 31; unnumbered 68, 77, 141, 171, 184, 194, 198, 203, 208, 235, 256, 265, 270, 281, 294, 319, 328, 334, 349, 360, 368, 371, 375, 384, 391, 398, 416.

Press-figures: A2(iii)–5, B6(11)–3, C3ᵛ(22)–3, D1ᵛ(34)–3, E7ᵛ(62)–3, F1ᵛ(66)–3, G1ᵛ(82)–3, H1ᵛ(98)–3, I5(121)–3, K2ᵛ(132)–3, L3ᵛ(150)–3, M8ᵛ(176)–3, N2ᵛ(180)–3, O3ᵛ(198)–3, P1ᵛ(210)–3, Q1ᵛ(226)–3, R6ᵛ(252)–3, S6ᵛ(268)–3, T1ᵛ(274)–3, U6(299)–3, X8ᵛ(320)–3, Y3ᵛ(326)–3, Z7(349)–3, 2A2ᵛ(356)–3, 2B5ᵛ(378)–3, 2C2ᵛ(388)–3, 2D8ᵛ(416)–3, 2E8ᵛ(432)–3, 2F2ᵛ(436)–3.

Catchwords: 30 *om.* (PREFACE), 67 *om.* (PROPOSALS), 76 *om.* (PREFACE), 125 [Mr. *Up-*] *ton*, (~*,), 140 *om.* (GENERAL), 170 *om.* (AN), 183 *om.* (AN), 193 *om.* (SOME), 197 *om.* (A), 202 *om.* (PRELIMINARY), 207 *om.* (INTRODUCTION), 234 *om.* (TIME), 255 *om.* (PREFACE), 264 *om.* (PREFACE), 269 *om.* (AN), 280 *om.* (POLITICAL), 293 *om.* (AN), 318 *om.* (MISCELLANEOUS), 327 *om.* (REVIEW), 332 *om.* (REVIEW), 348 *om.* (REVIEW), 359 *om.* (REPLY), 367 *om.* (INTRODUCTION), 370 *om.* (ON), 374 *om.* (CONSIDERATIONS), 380 *om.* (LETTER), 383 *om.* (SOME), 390 *om.* (FURTHER), 397 *om.* (THE), 415 *om.* (THE).

Explicit: 438 END OF THE SECOND VOLUME.

III. *A²* B–2E⁸ 2F⁴ 2G² (2G2 blk), ($4 (–2F3,4) signed; 'VOL. III.' on $1), 224 leaves.

Pp. A1 t., A1ᵛ blk, A2 Contents, on B1 *1* 2–442 text, *443–4* (2G2) blk.

Pagination: unnumbered 61, 81–2, 137, 298–9; blk 298.

Press-figures: B8ᵛ(16)–3, C1ᵛ(18)–3, D7ᵛ(46)–3, E3ᵛ(54)–3, F1ᵛ(66)–3, G2ᵛ(84)–3, H4ᵛ(104)–3, I7ᵛ(126)–3, K6ᵛ(140)–3, L2ᵛ(148)–3, M6(171)–3,

N2ᵛ(180)–3, O1ᵛ(194)–3, P3ᵛ(214)–3, Q7(237)–3, R1ᵛ(242)–3, S7(269)–3, T1ᵛ(274)–3, U3ᵛ(294)–3, X7ᵛ(318)–3, Y3ᵛ(326)–3, Z8(351)–3, 2A2ᵛ(356)–3, 2B7ᵛ(382)–3, 2C7ᵛ(398)–3, 2D7(413)–3, 2E1ᵛ(418)–3, 2F1ᵛ(434)–3.

Catchwords: 11 gods. (~*.), 17 ridicules ('~), 20 written ('~), 60 *om.* (GENERAL), 64 [go-] vernment, (~ₐ), 80 *om.* (MISCELLANEOUS), 136 *om.* (THE), 143 *om.* (Numb.) and 155, 161, 167, 182, 189, 203, 212, 225, 232, 252, 258, 264, 277, 284, 291; 297 *om.* (THE), 361 wouldₐ (~,).

Explicit: 442 END OF THE THIRD VOLUME.

IV. *A*⁴ (A1 blk) B–2F⁸ (2F8 blk), ($4 signed; 'VOL. IV.' on $1), 228 leaves.

Pp. A1 blk, A2 t., A2ᵛ blk, A3–4 Contents, A4ᵛ Errata, on B1 *1* 2–446 text Ramblers 1–70, *447–8* (2F8) blk.

Pagination: no errors.

Press-figures: B1ᵛ(2)–2, B2ᵛ(4)–2, C2ᵛ(20)–2, G8(95)–*, Q8(239)–5, Y8(335)–5, Z5ᵛ(346)–2, 2A8(367)–2, 2B6(379)–2, 2C6(395)–3, 2D8(415)–2, 2E8(431)–3, 2F5ᵛ(442)–2.

Catchwords: *om.* (Numb.) 13, 19, 26, 32, 39, 52, 65, 72, 87, 94, 109, 115, 143, 149, 155, 161, 167, 174, 180, 187, 193, 206, 225, 244, 250, 256, 269, 275, 281, 288, 294, 300, 312, 318, 324, 332, 337, 343, 350, 363, 369, 375, 386, 393, 399, 405, 411, 417, 434, 440.

Explicit: 446 END OF THE FOURTH VOLUME.

V. π1 *A*² B–2E⁸ 2F⁶, ($4 (–2F4) signed; 'VOL. V.' on $1), 225 leaves.

Pp. π1 t., A1–2 Contents, on B1 *1* 2–443 text Ramblers 71–140, *444* blk.

Pagination: no errors.

Press-figures: B7ᵛ(14)–2, C8(31)–2, D8(47)–2, E8(63)–2, F1ᵛ(66)–2, G1ᵛ(82)–2, H5ᵛ(106)–2, I3ᵛ(118)–3, K1ᵛ(130)–2, L1ᵛ(146)–2, M3ᵛ(166)–2, N7ᵛ(190)–3, O5ᵛ(202)–2, P5ᵛ(218)–2, Q8(239)–2, R7ᵛ(254)–2, S1ᵛ(258)–2, T1ᵛ(274)–2, U1ᵛ(290)–2, X1ᵛ(306)–2, Y1ᵛ(322)–2, 2A1ᵛ(354)–2, 2B6(379)–2, 2C5ᵛ(394)–2, 2D4ᵛ(408)–*, 2E6(427)–2, 2F1ᵛ (434)–2; Z unfigured.

Catchwords: *om.* (Numb.) 11, 23, 30, 35, 53, 58, 70, 76, 83, 89, 96, 102, 114, 121, 127, 137, 151, 163, 171, 177, 188, 201, 208, 214, 220, 226, 232, 238, 245, 252, 264, 277, 284, 291, 299, 305, 312, 319, 326, 332, 338, 343, 350, 357, 363, 369, 375, 382, 393, 399, 410, 416, 422, 428.

Explicit: 443 END OF THE FIFTH VOLUME.

VI. *A*⁴ (A1 blk) B–2C⁸ (2C8 blk), ($4 signed; 'VOL. VI.' on $1), 204 leaves.

Pp. A1 blk, A2 t., A2ᵛ t., A3–4 Contents, A4ᵛ blk, on B1 *1* 2–397 text Ramblers 141–208, *398–400* (2C8) blk.

Pagination: 138 as 118, 328 (with '3' *inverted*).

Press-figures: A3–2, B7ᵛ(14)–3, D8(47)–3, E8(63)–3, F3ᵛ(70)–3, G5ᵛ(90)–3, H8(111)–3, I3ᵛ(118)–3, K1ᵛ(130)–3, L8(159)–3, M8ᵛ(176)–2, N8(191)–3, O8(207)–3, P8(223)–3, Q6(235)–3, R3ᵛ(246)–3, S5ᵛ(266)–3, S7(269)–7,

T8(287)–7, U7ᵛ(302)–7, X3ᵛ(310)–7, Y8(335)–7, Z5ᵛ(346)–7, 2A7ᵛ(366)–7, 2B3ᵛ(374)–7, 2C1ᵛ(386)–7.

Catchwords: *om.* (NUMB.) 6, 13, 21, 27, 38, 44, 50, 56, 62, 68, 74, 87, 94, 100, 106, 112, 117, 122, 134, 141, 152, 157, 163, 168, 174, 180, 193, 198, 204, 214, 220, 225, 230, 236, 242, 248, 253, 258, 264, 270, 276, 281, 286, 292, 298, 304, 309, 315, 321, 326, 331, 338, 345, 351, 357, 362, 367, 373, 379, 385, 391; 176 [mo-] ther˄ (∼,).

Explicit: 397 END OF THE SIXTH VOLUME.

VII. π² a² B–2C⁸ 2D⁴ 2E² (2E2 blk), ($4 (–C3, 2D3) signed; 'VOL. VII.' on $1), 210 leaves.

Pp. π1 ½t [med. swelled rule] | THE | WORKS | OF | Samuel Johnſon, ll.d. | [med. swelled rule], π1ᵛ blk, π2 t., π2ᵛ blk, a1–2 Contents, a2ᵛ Advertisement [to the *Idler*], on B1 *1* 2–410 text Idlers 1–103, *411–12* (2E2) blk.

Pagination: 105 as 051.

Press-figures: B7(13)–4, B8(15)–2, C3(21)–1, C8(31)–5, D3ᵛ(38)–3, D7(45)–5, E3ᵛ(54)–1, E7(61)–4, F6(75)–4, F8ᵛ(80)–1, G3ᵛ(86)–5, G7(93)–4, H6(107)–4, H7(109)–1, I8(127)–1, K4ᵛ(136)–2, K8(143)–4, L6ᵛ(156)–1, L8(159)–2, M5(169)–5, M8(175)–2, N4ᵛ(184)–3, N5ᵛ(186)–2, O1ᵛ(194)–5, O4ᵛ(200)–4, P8ᵛ(224)–1, Q6(235)–1, Q8ᵛ(240)–3, R7(253)–5, R7ᵛ(254)–1, S2ᵛ(260)–5, S8(271)–3, T1ᵛ(274)–3, T8ᵛ(288)–2, U3ᵛ(294)–1, U6ᵛ(300)–4, X4ᵛ(312)–2, X6(315)–7, Y6(331)–4, Z6(347)–1, Z6ᵛ(348)–2, 2A6(363)–4, 2A8ᵛ(368)–1, 2B5ᵛ(378)–7, 2B8ᵛ(384)–4, 2C7(397)–5, 2C7ᵛ(398)–4, 2D3ᵛ(406)–7, 2D4ᵛ(408)–3.

Catchwords: NUMB. is consistently used as a cwd., but *om.* 371.

Explicit: 410 END OF THE SEVENTH VOLUME.

VIII. *A*² B–2D⁸, ($4 (–B4) signed; 'VOL. VIII.' on $1), 210 leaves.

Pp. A1 t., A1ᵛ blk, A2 Contents, on B1 *1* 2–416 text (Miscellaneous essays, Political Tracts, and Journey).

Pagination: unnumbered 7–9, 62–5, 96, 142, 206–9; blk. 62, 64, 206, 208.

Press-figures: B7ᵛ(14)–7, C1ᵛ(18)–7, D3ᵛ(38)7, E3ᵛ(54)–7, F3ᵛ(70)–7, G3ᵛ(86)–7, H3ᵛ(102)–7, I1ᵛ(114)–7, K8(143)–7, L8(159)–7, M6(171)–7, N8(191)–7, O6(203)–7, P8(223)–7, Q7ᵛ(238)–7, R6(251)–7, S1ᵛ(258)–7, T7ᵛ(286)–7, U5ᵛ(298)–7, X1ᵛ(306)–7, Y7ᵛ(334)–7, Z1ᵛ(338)–7, 2A7ᵛ(366)–7, 2B1ᵛ(370)–7, 2C1ᵛ(386)–7, 2D7ᵛ(414)–7.

Catchwords: 7–8, 61–4, 205–8 *om.*, 22 *om.* (REVIEW), 61 *om.* (POLITI-CAL), 95 *om.* (THOUGHTS), 141 *om.* (THE), 154 *om.* (Taxation), 205 *om.* (A).

Explicit: 416 END OF THE EIGHTH VOLUME.

IX. a² B–2F⁸ 2G⁴ 2H², ($4 (–2G3,4, 2H1) signed; 'VOL. IX.' on $1), 232 leaves.

Pp. a1 t., a1ᵛ blk, a2 Contents, a2ᵛ blk, on B1 1–460 text Lives: Cowley–Dryden.

Pagination: (↑) 1, 72, 183, 201, 211, 223, 229, 285, 287, 291, 294, 312, 315; [↑] 84; 131 as 1313.

Press-figures: B7ᵛ(14)–3, C7(29)–3, C7ᵛ(30)–5, D6ᵛ(44)–4, E1ᵛ(50)–5, E8ᵛ(64)–2, F7ᵛ(78)–1, F8ᵛ(80)–4, G4ᵛ(88)–2, G8(95)–3, H2ᵛ(100)–1, H5ᵛ(106)–7, I5ᵛ(122)–1, I6ᵛ(124)–2, K6(139)–2, K6ᵛ(140)–3, L7ᵛ(158)–1, L8ᵛ(160)–5, M8(175)–4, M8ᵛ(176)–1, N5(185)–4, N5ᵛ(186)–1, O7ᵛ(206)–2, O8ᵛ(208)–7, P3ᵛ(214)–2, Q5(233)–3, Q7ᵛ(238)–1, R4ᵛ(248)–1, R7ᵛ(254)–4, S7ᵛ(270)–6, T2ᵛ(276)–3, T8(287)–1, U7(301)–1, U7ᵛ(302)–6, X4ᵛ(312)–2, Y2ᵛ(324)–2, Y8(335)–1, Z7(349)–2, 2A5ᵛ(362)–1, 2A8ᵛ(368)–2, 2B3ᵛ(374)–1, 2C7ᵛ(398)–1, 2D7(413)–2, 2E5(425)–2, 2F7ᵛ(446)–3, 2F8ᵛ(448)–4, 2G3(453)–2.

Catchwords: 128 *that*ʌ (∼,), 313 *A col-* (*A Collection*), 320 ʌMonk] ('∼']), 367 'having'ʌ ('∼,), 368 'Jefferies, ('∼;), 455 'there ('If).

Explicit: 460 End of the Ninth Volume.

X. a² B–2C⁸ 2D², (\$4 (O4 as O, –T2) signed; 'Vol. X.' on \$1), 204 leaves.

Pp. a1 t., a1ᵛ blk, a2 Contents, a2ᵛ blk, on B1 1–404 text Lives: Smith–Savage.

Pagination: (↑) 1, 29, 31, 36, 43, 49, 54, 60, 73, 142, 148, 157, 185, 202, 226, 236, 250, 261, 267, 274, 278, 281.

Press-figures: B1ᵛ(2)–3, B8ᵛ(16)–1, C8ᵛ(32)–4, D7ᵛ(46)–2, E7ᵛ(62)–2, F7ᵛ(78)–3, G8(95)–4, G8ᵛ(96)–5, H6ᵛ(108)–7, H7ᵛ(110)–3, I7(125)–3, I8(127)–5, K5(137)–7, L7ᵛ(158)–3, L8ᵛ(160)–5, M2ᵛ(164)–5, M3ᵛ(166)–2, N8(191)–3, O2ᵛ(196)–1, O5ᵛ(202)–2, P5ᵛ(218)–7, P8ᵛ(224)–3, Q2ᵛ(228)–7, R7ᵛ(254)–7, S4ᵛ(264)–3, S8(271)–5, T8ᵛ(288)–3, U7ᵛ(302)–1, X1ᵛ(306)–5, X5(313)–7, Y6(331)–6, Z5(345)–7, Z7ᵛ(350)–6, 2A5(361)–6, 2A8(367)–1, 2B7ᵛ(382)–1, 2C4ᵛ(392)–4, 2C6(395)–3.

Catchwords: 2 'Ego ('—Ego), 27 Oden (oden), 70 works'ʌ (∼;), 231 Popeʌʌ (∼*;), 301 *Dealer*, (∼*,).

Explicit: 404 End of the Tenth Volume.

XI. a² B–2B⁸ 2C⁴, (\$4 (+ a2, –2C3,4) signed; 'Vol. XI.' on S1) 198 leaves.

Pp. a1 t., a1ᵛ blk, a2 Contents, a2ᵛ blk, on B1 1–389 text Lives: Swift–Lyttelton, *390* blk, on 2C4 *391* printed spine labels for vols. I–XII, 1792, *392* blk.

Pagination: (↑) 1, 49, 54, 217, 221, 238, 249, 259, 265, 272, 276, 286, 347, 355, 364, 380.

Press-figures: B8(15)–3, B8ᵛ(16)–4, C2ᵛ(20)–1, C7ᵛ(30)–4, D7(45)–3, D7ᵛ(46)–4, E5(57)–1, E7ᵛ(62)–4, F3ᵛ(70)–4, F8ᵛ(80)–7, G7ᵛ(94)–1, G8ᵛ(96)–2, H7(109)–4, H8(111)–2, I2ᵛ(116)–4, I6(123)–1, K5ᵛ(138)–1, K7(141)–7, L5(153)–1, L5ᵛ(154)–3, M2ᵛ(164)–4, M8(175)–1, N7ᵛ(190)–3, N8ᵛ(192)–2, O1ᵛ(194)–2, P8(223)–7, P8ᵛ(224)–4, Q8ᵛ(240)–2, R1ᵛ(242)–4,

R5(249)–2, S6(267)–7, S8ᵛ(272)–2, T4ᵛ(280)–1, T8(287)–7, U2ᵛ(292)–3, U7ᵛ(302)–3, X4ᵛ(312)–3, X6(315)–1, Y5(329)–1, Z3ᵛ(342)–1, 2A7ᵛ(366)–1, 2B3ᵛ(374)–7, 2C1ᵛ(386)–2.

Catchwords: 194 *om*. (of), 272 ‸1727 ('~').

Explicit: 389 END OF THE ELEVENTH VOLUME.

XII. *A*² B–2M⁸ (2M8 blk), ($4 signed; 'VOL. XII.' on $1), 274 leaves.

Pp. A1 t., A1ᵛ blk, A2 Contents, A2ᵛ blk, on B1 1 ½t, *2* blk, *3* 4–450 text (Lives of Sundry Eminent Persons, Letters, and Prayers), on 2G2–2M7ᵛ (46 leaves, 92 pp., unpaged) *Index*, 2M8 blk.

Pagination: [↑] 11, 41, 63, 149, 160, 168, 180, 190, 210, 220, 271, 308, unnumbered 1–3, 329–31, 439–41; blk 3, 330, 440, 2M8; Index unpaged.

Press-figures: B6(11)–2, C8(31)–2, D1ᵛ(34)–2, E1ᵛ(50)–2, F3ᵛ(70)–2, G1ᵛ(82)–2, H8(111)–2, I1ᵛ(114)–2, K7ᵛ(142)–2, L1ᵛ(146)–2, M7ᵛ(174)–2, N1ᵛ(178)–2, O8(207)–2, P1ᵛ(210)–2, Q8(239)–2, R6(251)–2, S1ᵛ(258)–2, T1ᵛ(274)–2, U1ᵛ(290)–2, X1ᵛ(306)–2, Y2ᵛ(324)–2, Z6(347)–2, 2A1ᵛ(354)–2, 2B1ᵛ(370)–2, 2C3ᵛ(390)–2, 2D3ᵛ(406)–2, 2E1ᵛ(418)–2, 2E8ᵛ(432)–2, 2F2ᵛ(436)–2, 2G3ᵛ–2, 2G7–7, 2H1ᵛ–2, 2I7ᵛ–6, 2I8ᵛ–11, 2K1ᵛ–6, 2L5ᵛ–5, 2M1ᵛ–2.

Catchwords: *om*. 2, 10, 40, 62, 148, 159, 167, 179, 189, 209, 219, 270, 307, 328–9, 438–50; LETTER *om*. 332, 337–40, 346, 377, 409, 414–17, 421, 426–8, 435; 442 *om*. (Compoſed), 443 *om*. (May), 448 *om*. (June), 449 *om*. ([The), 2G5 *om*. (B), 2I5 *om*. (I.), 2I6ᵛ *om*. (L.), 2K4 *om*. (N.), 2L3 *om*. (Q.); 153 theſe (thoſe), 183 of (f *broken*).

Explicit: 2M7ᵛ FINIS.

Paper: White, laid; Medium (uncut: 9⅛ × 6 in.); wmk.: 'W T'.

Type: Text: pica (3.9 mm), notes: bourgeois (3.1 mm).

Plate: As 1787 (above), SJ by John Hall, after Reynolds, 'Publiſh'd as the Act directs, by the Proprietors, Janʸ. 1ˢᵗ 1787.'

References: Courtney 163–4; ESTC: t083955.

Notes: Murphy reordered the *Poems* and *Poemata* from Hawkins's arrangement, and contributed the introductory Essay. JB reported to Malone '8' [=9] Mar. 1791, that Murphy got £200 for it.[1] Various editorial notes in the *Lives of the Poets* (vols. ix–xii), are signed 'R' [Reed], 'N' [Nichols], and 'H' [Hawkins]; they derive from *Lives*, 1790 (79.4LP/8, above). The 'Life of Young' is here revised by Croft. A letter from Murphy to Cadell (21 June 1790) relative to the preparation of this edn. is MS Hyde,[2] and one from James Robson to HLP (28 Jan. 1788) asking for assistance is CtY (Osborn).

1,250 copies of vols. IV–VI, VIII, and XII were printed by Andrew Strahan for Thomas Cadell in March 1792, incorporating an 'extra' charge for 6 sheets of the Index (L: Add. MS 48811, fo. 26). Some features of the typography and information on the subsequent distribution of parts of the work, show that Nichols was the printer of vols. IX–XI (*Lives*), together with vol. I, and perhaps that the Hughs-Hansard partnership was responsible for the rest (II–III, and VII). Strahan recorded a payment of £52. 10s. on July 9, 1792 'By Cash from the Proprietors of the Works for the Use of Johnson's Letters' (L: Add. MS 48804, fo. 9).

The sheets (I. a–1⁸ m⁶) bearing Murphy's *Essay* were issued separately in the same year, with new prelims and some resetting of the final leaf (see next entry). JB 'found Murphy at Elmsly's shop' on 14 Feb. 1791, and noted then that Murphy had already written his 'Essay'.³ Elmsly was not however, a printer. For Murphy's involvement in this edn., cf. *Lit. Anec.* ix (1815), 159.

Copies: O (2699 d. 18–29);

USA: CSmH, CtY, Hyde² (1. uncut, boards, paper spines, printed paper labels, 'John Walters Philipps'; 2. Adam), ICN, IU, MH (16461.4), NjP (lacks vol. 6), NN, [PPA, PPFr, PPT, PU], TxU, ViU, WiM; *Can*: CaOHM; *Japan*: [Kyoto]; *UK*: BMp (483954–65), BRu, C, Eu, Felbrigg, JDF, L (96. c.1–12), LICj, NCl, NOu (lacks vol. 9), [SPu, WLAp]; *Aust*: CNL (DNS 4835); *Ger*: [GöttU].

---

¹ *Correspondence of JB with Garrick, Burke, & Malone*, ed. Peter S. Baker, *et al.*, (1986), 413. Nichols, *Lit. Anec.* ix (1815), 159, said '£300', but he misdated the first edn. of the *Essay* to '1793'.

² 'I have considered what you mentioned to me relative to Doctʳ. Johnson's Life, and a new edition of his Works, and, having well weighed the matter, am writing to Undertake it. My intention is to write *An Essay on the Life and Genius of Doctʳ Johnson*: The Works must have a new arrangement, as near as may be in Chronological order, and the Pieces, which are most Certainly not his, must be discarded. Will you allow the best of his Letters to be inserted in this Edition? & what say you to the Parliamentary debates ? I think they should be added, in order to make a Complete Edition.

When you send the Volumes, I will in a few days after, give you the Arrangement Volume by Volume, that it may be shown to his friends for their Judgement; for I would rather hear, what Criticism has to say on the Subject, before Publication than after it. As [to] the Essay *on the Life & Genius*, I have calculated my own avocations and find that I can promise to deliver it to you, also for the Inspection of some select friends, *on or before the Last Day* of Octʳ. next.' (*Adam Catalogue*, iii. 179). An even earlier intention to write an account of SJ is intimated in a letter from Lord Chedworth, 19 May 1789, 'I have heard that a Life of Johnson may be expected from Murphy: I hope he will provide one' (*Letters from the late Lord Chedworth to the Rev. Thomas Crompton* (1828), 159, Letter LXXIII).

³ *JB: The Great Biographer* (1989), 124.

87.3W/2.1/1   Works, Murphy's Essay, separate issue   1792

[½t] [short swelled rule] | AN | ESSAY | ON THE | LIFE AND GENIUS | OF | SAMUEL JOHNSON, LL.D. | [short swelled rule] | *⁎* *Entered at* STATIONERS HALL.

[Title] AN | ESSAY | ON THE | LIFE AND GENIUS | OF | SAMUEL JOHNSON, LL.D. | By ARTHUR MURPHY, Esq. | [short swelled rule] | LONDON: | Printed for T. Longman, B. White and Son, B. Law, J. Dodfley, H. Baldwin, | J. Robfon, J. Johnfon, C. Dilly, T. Vernor, G. G. J. and J. Robinfon, | T. Cadell, J. Nichols, R. Baldwin, N. Conant, P. Elmfly, F. and C. | Rivington, T. Payne, W. Goldfmith, R. Faulder, Leigh and Sotheby, | G.

Nicol, J. Murray, A. Strahan, W. Lowndes, T. Evans, W. Bent, | S. Hayes, G. and T. Wilkie, T. and J. Egerton, W. Fox, P. M'Queen, | Ogilvie and Speare, Darton and Harvey, G. and C. Kearſley, W. Millar, | B.C. Collins, and E. Newbery. | M DCC XCII.

8°, π² a–l⁸ m⁶, ($4 (–m4) signed; 'VOL. I.' on $1 (m1ᵛ as '—N°1')), 96 leaves.

Pp. π1 *i* ½t, *ii* blk, *iii* t., *iv* blk, on a1 1–187 text of Essay, *188* blk.

Pagination: no errors.

Press-figures: a6(11)–2, b2ᵛ(20)–4, c2ᵛ(36)–2, d5(57)–1, e2ᵛ(68)–1, e8(79)–6, f7(93)–5, g8(111)–6, h1ᵛ(114)–4, h8ᵛ(128)–6, i1ᵛ(130)–1, k6ᵛ(156)–6, l8(175)–5, m5(185)–4.

Catchwords: no errors, (as 87.3W/2, vol. 1, above).

Explicit: 187 FINIS.

Paper: White, laid; medium (uncut: 9¼ × 6 in.); wmk.: 'W T'.

Type: Pica (3.9 mm), as 87.3W/2, above.

Plate: No plate in this issue.

References: Courtney 163; Roscoe, *Newbery* (1973), A373 (1); ESTC: t087884.

Notes: A separate issue of the sheets of Murphy's *Essay* from the 1792 Works, above, with new prelims. (½t + t.), different press-figures, and a re-set final page (187), adding 'FINIS.' and removing the former cwd: 'POEMS'. The Binder's Direction Lines ('VOL. I.') are however, retained. The misprint p. 72, l. 11, 'fuud' is not corrected.

This issue is noticed (adversely) in *St. James's Chron.*, 19–22, May 1792, at 4s. in boards, and was reviewed by Moody in *Monthly Rev.* xi (1792), 361. Nichols thought that it was first published in 1793, and reported that Murphy got £300 for it (*Lit. Anec.* ix (1815), 159).[1] Chalmers described it, rightly for an historian, as 'a very careless sketch' (*Biog. Dict.*, 'Murphy', xxii (1815), 526). Mrs Piozzi acquired a copy before publication (*Lit. Illus.* viii (1858), 293).

Copies: O² (1. Douce M. 12; 2. 8° D 44. BS);

USA: CtY, Hyde³, NcU, NRU, PP, TxU; *UK*: ABu, C, Ck (Keynes), Ct, E, L, LICj², LVu; *Aust*: CNL (Nichol Smith).

---

[1] But cf. p. 1647 n. 1, above.

87.3W/2.1/2   Murphy's Essay, second edition   1793

[½t] [short swelled rule] | AN | ESSAY | ON THE | LIFE AND GENIUS | OF | SAMUEL JOHNSON, LL.D. | [short swelled rule] | *⁎* *Entered at* STATIONERS HALL.

[Title] AN | ESSAY | ON THE | LIFE AND GENIUS | OF | SAMUEL JOHNSON, LL.D. | BY ARTHUR MURPHY, ESQ. | [short swelled rule] | LONDON: | Printed for T. Longman, B. White and Son, B. Law, J. Dodſley, H. Baldwin, | J. Robſon, J. Johnſon, C. Dilly, T. Vernor, G. G. J. and J.

Robinſon, | T. Cadell, J. Nichols, R. Baldwin, N. Conant, P. Elmſly, F. and C. | Rivington, T. Payne, W. Goldſmith, R. Faulder, Leigh and Sotheby, | G. Nicol, J. Murray, A. Strahan, W. Lowndes, T. Evans, W. Bent, | S. Hayes, G. and T. Wilkie, T. and J. Egerton, W. Fox, P. M'Queen, | Ogilvie and Speare, Darton and Harvey, G. and C. Kearſley, W. Millar, | B.C. Collins, and E. Newbery. | M DCC XCIII.

8°, π^2 a–l^8 m^6, ($4 (–m4) signed), 96 leaves.

Pp. π1 *i* ½t, *ii* blk, *iii* t., *iv* blk, on a1 *1* 2–187 text of Essay, *188* blk.

Pagination: no errors.

Press-figures: a6(11)–2, b2^v(20)–4, c2^v(36)–2, d5(57)–1, e2^v(68)–1, e8(79)–6, f7(93)–5, g8(111)–6, h1^v(114)–3, h8^v(128)–7, i1^v(130)–1, k7^v(158)–7, l8(175)–5, m5(185)–3.

Catchwords: no errors.

Explicit: 187 FINIS.

Paper: wmk.: 'T W' (Thomas Whatman).

Type: Pica (3.9 mm).

References: Courtney 163; *Tinker* 1407; Roscoe, *Newbery* (1973), A373 (2); ESTC: t004523.

Notes: There are few variants from the former edns., and it is doubtful if Murphy revised it. The misprint 'fuud' on p. 72, l. 11 (87.3W/2, 1792, above), is here corrected to 'fund'. Published at 4s.

Copies: O (GP 2906/3);

USA: Hyde^3 (**1.** uncut 'C. Dering'; **2.** uncut; **3.** 'Ridge'); *UK*: L (T. 1563 (1), 'Isaac Reed'), [Lu], Op (Vernon, uncut), MRu, STA (boards, uncut).

87.3W/2.1/3   Murphy's Essay, third edition   1820

AN | ESSAY | ON | THE LIFE AND GENIUS | OF | SAMUEL JOHNSON, LL.D. | [medium rule] | BY ARTHUR MURPHY, ESQ. | [short parallel rule] | LONDON: | PRINTED FOR W. SHARPE & SON, W. ALLASON, C. CHAPPPLE, W. ROBINSON | & SONS, J. MOLLISON, T. FISHER, J. BUMPUS, G. & J. OFFOR, J. CRANWELL, | J. EVANS & SONS, J. MAYNARD, E. WILSON, W. BAYNES & SON, T. MASON, | J. ROBINS & CO. AND W. HARWOOD, LONDON; ALSO W. STEWART & CO. | AND J. CARFRAE, EDINBURGH; AND W. TURNBULL, GLASGOW. | [short rule] | 1820.

8°, π1 A–H^8 I^4 (–I4 ? = π1), ($1 signed), 68 leaves.

Pp. π1 *i* t., *ii* blk, on A1 *1* 2–133 text of Essay, *134* blk.

Pagination: no errors.

Press-figures: A8^v(16)–26, B5^v(26)–17, C1^v(34)–17, D1^v(50)–28, E8^v(80)–56, F8^v(96)–17, G8(111)–28, H5^v(122)–28.

Catchwords: none.

Explicit: not recorded.
Paper: White, wove; Demy (uncut: 8¾ × 5⅝ in.); wmk.: '1817'.
Type: not recorded.
Notes: Separate impression of sigg. A–D, from *Works*, 1820 (87.3W/17, below), vol. 1 with variant press-figg., but reissue of sigg. E–I from same vol. To I3 (p. 133) is added a coloph: 'Printed by Walker and Greig, | Edinburgh.' The text is a reprint of the version in Works, 1801 (87.3W/5, below).
Copies: Hyde (boards, uncut; Adam); *USA*: DLC.

87.3W/3   Works, ed. Murphy, Dublin   1793

THE | WORKS | OF | SAMUEL JOHNSON, LL.D. | A NEW EDITION. | IN SIX VOLUMES. | WITH | AN ESSAY ON HIS LIFE AND GENIUS, | By ARTHUR MURPHY, Esq. | [short swelled rule] | VOLUME THE FIRST [– SIXTH]. | [short swelled rule] | DUBLIN: | PRINTED FOR LUKE WHITE. | [short rule] | 1793.

6 vols., 8°

I. π⁴ (–π1 ? blk) a–h⁸ i⁴, B–2E⁸ 2F⁴, ($4 signed; 'Vol. I.' on $1), 291 leaves.

Pp. Engr. port. SJ + π2 t., π2ᵛ blk, π3 *iii* iv–vi Contents, on a1 ᵀ*1* 2–136 Murphy's Essay, *1* ½t Poems, *2* blk. *3* 4–155 text Poems, *156* blk, *157* ½t, *158* blk, *159* 160–337 text Philological Tracts, *338* 339–61 Political essays, *362* 363–440 Miscellaneous essays, 440 *Explicit*: END OF THE FIRST VOLUME.

II. *A*⁴ B–2Q⁸, ($2 signed), 308 leaves.

Pp. A1 t., A1ᵛ blk, A2 *iii* iv–vii Contents, *viii* blk, on B1 *1* 2–98 Literary essays, 99–206 Adventurers (24), 207–306 Rasselas, 307–608 Ramblers 1–71, 608 *Explicit*: END OF THE SECOND VOLUME.

III. *A*⁴ B–2M⁸ 2N², ($2 signed), 278 leaves.

Pp. A1 t., A1ᵛ blk, A2 *iii* iv–viii Contents, on B1 *1* 2–547 text Ramblers 72–208, 547 *Explicit*: END OF THE THIRD VOLUME., *548* blk.

IV. A⁴ B–2M⁸ 2N⁴ (2N4 blk), ($2 signed), 280 leaves.

Pp. A1 t., A1ᵛ blk, A2 *iii* iv–vii Contents, *viii* blk, on B1 *1* 2–268 text Idlers (1–103), *269* 270–311 Miscellaneous essays, *312* blk, *313* ½t, *314* blk, *315* 316–409 Political Tracts, *411* ½t, *412* blk, *413* 414–550 text Journey, 550 *Explicit*: END OF THE FOURTH VOLUME., *551–2* blk.

V. *A*² B–2N⁸ 2O⁸ (O8 blk), ($2 signed), 290 leaves.

Pp. A1 t., A1ᵛ blk, A2 *iii*–iv Contents, on B1 *1* 2–574 Lives (Cowley–Savage), 574 *Explicit*: END OF THE FIFTH VOLUME., *575–6* blk.

VI. a⁴ (–a4 ? blk) B–2O⁸, ($2 signed), 291 leaves.

Pp. a1 t., a1ᵛ blk, a2 *iii* iv–v Contents, *vi* blk, on B1 *1* 2–268 Lives (Swift–Lyttelton), *269* 270–491 Eminent Persons, *492* blk, *493* 494–567 Letters, *568* blk, *569* 570–76 Prayers, 576 *Explicit:* FINIS.

Plate: A reversed version of that in Works, 1792 (87.3W/2, above), with SJ facing right, 'Painted by Sir Joshua Reynolds. Engraved by H. Broc<a ?>'.

References: ESTC: t126667.

Notes: White's responsibility for this edn. is likely to have been that of financial backer rather than as producer, though the identity of the printer remains unknown.[1]

Copies: O (Vet. A5 e. 2527–32);

USA: CtY, MB, [NcU, NIC], NjP, NRo, PPL; *Can*: CaOHM; *Japan*: [Kyoto]; *UK*: BMp (852740–5), L (1609/3909); *Eir*: [D], Dt.

---

[1] M. Pollard, *Dublin's Trade in Books* (1989), 194–5.

87.3W/4   Works, ed. Murphy   1796

[Medium swelled rule] | THE | WORKS | OF | Samuel Johnſon, LL.D. | TO WHICH IS PREFIXED | AN ESSAY ON HIS LIFE AND GENIUS, | BY ARTHUR MURPHY, ESQ. | A NEW EDITION, | IN TWELVE VOLUMES. | M DCC XCVI. | [medium swelled rule]

[Tt. vol. 2, &c.] THE | WORKS | OF | Samuel Johnſon, LL.D. | A NEW EDITION | IN TWELVE VOLUMES. | WITH | AN ESSAY ON HIS LIFE AND GENIUS, | BY ARTHUR MURPHY, ESQ. | [short swelled rule] | VOLUME THE SECOND [– TWELFTH]. | [short swelled rule] | LONDON: | Printed for T. Longman, B. Law, J. Dodſley, H. Baldwin, J. Johnſon, C. Dilly, | G. G. and J. Robinſon, P. Elmſley, J. Nichols, R. Baldwin, H.L. | Gardner, F. and C. Rivington, W. Otridge and Son, W. Richardſon, B. and | J. White, A. Strahan, Leigh and Sotheby, R. Faulder, G. Nicol, T. Payne, | W. Lowndes, T. Evans, S. Hayes, G. and T. Wilkie, C. Davis, J. Matthews, | T. Egerton, W. Fox, J. Edwards, P. M'Queen, Ogilvie and Speare, J. | Scatcherd, I. Taylor, Hookham and Co. C. and G. Kearſley, J. Walker, B.C. Collins, E. Newbery, Vernor and Hood, J. Deighton, Darton and | Harvey, J. Nunn, Lackington, Allen, and Co. J. Stockdale, J. Cuthell, D. | Walker, J. Anderſon, Clarke and Son, T. Cadell, jun. and W. Davis, J. | Barker, W. Miller, *and* Murray and Highley. | MDCCXCVI.

12 vols., 8°

I. π² a–l⁸ m⁸ (–m4.5 = vol. X 2D²) B–O⁸ P⁴, ($4 (l3 as I3) signed; 'VOL. I.' on $1 (–m1)), 204 leaves.[1]

Pp. Engr. port. front. + π1 t., π1ᵛ blk, on π2 ½t AN | ESSAY | ON THE | LIFE AND GENIUS | OF | SAMUEL JOHNSON, LL.D. | BY ARTHUR MURPHY, ESQ. | [swelled rule] | LONDON | [Imprint as vol. 2 &c.], π2ᵛ blk, on a1 *1* 2–187 text ('Essay'), *188* blk, on B1 ²*1* ½t 'Poems', *2* blk 3–215 text Poems, *216* blk.

Pagination: 'Essay' 111 as 11, 115 *broken* 5, 153 as 1, 188 blk; ²31–2, 34 and 130 unnumbered, 130 and 216 blk; [↑] ²3, 15, 28, 33, 35, 129, 168.

Press-figures: a7ᵛ(14)–1, a8ᵛ(16)–2, b1ᵛ(18)–6, b2ᵛ(20)–4, c1ᵛ(34)–1, c2ᵛ(36)–6, d5(57)–6, e5ᵛ(74)–3, f7ᵛ(94)–5, f8ᵛ(96)–6, g1ᵛ(98)–4, h3ᵛ(118)–1, i5ᵛ(138)–4, i6ᵛ(140)–5, l1ᵛ(162)–6, l4ᵛ(168)–4, B5ᵛ(10)–7, B6ᵛ(12)–3, C4ᵛ(24)–7, D5ᵛ(42)–5, D7(45)–7, E8(63)–7, E8ᵛ(64)–1, F3ᵛ(70)–7, F4ᵛ(72)–4, G3ᵛ(86)–7, G5(89)–3, H4ᵛ(104)–3, H8(111)–2, I3ᵛ(118)–4, I5(121)–3, K7(141)–2, L5(153)–3, L6(155)–2, M4ᵛ(168)–2, M7ᵛ(174)–1, N8(191)–6, O5(201)–2, O5ᵛ(202)–4.

Catchwords: 32 [Groſve-] nor⌃ (nor-ſquare); ²6 ⌃But (¹¹∼), 9 ⌃By (²¹∼), 12 ⌃Prepare (³²∼), 15 ⌃But, (*∼,), 20 ⌃The (*∼), *om.* 31–2, 34, 181 INSULA (A *broken*), 186 ⌃O Qui (*∼ ∼), 188 ⌃Sᴇᴜ (*∼), ⌃E WAL- (*∼ ∼), 212 ⌃Hɪs (*∼).

Explicit: 215 Eɴᴅ ᴏꜰ ᴛʜᴇ ꜰɪʀsᴛ Vᴏʟᴜᴍᴇ.

II. *A*² B–2E⁸ 2F⁴ (2F4 blk), ($4 signed; 'Vᴏʟ. II.' on $1), 222 leaves.

Pp. A1 t., A1ᵛ blk, A2 Contents, on B1 *1* ½t Philological Tracts, *2* blk, *3* 4–438 text (3–280 Philological Tracts, 281–318 Political essays, 319–438 Miscellaneous essays), *439–40* (2F4) blk.

Pagination: [↑] 31, unnumbered 68, 77, 141, 171, 184, 194, 198, 203, 208, 235, 256, 265, 270, 281, 294, 319, 328, 333, 349, 360, 368, 371, 375, 384, 391, 398, and 416.

Press-figures: B2ᵛ(4)–9, C6(27)–x, C8ᵛ(32)–*, D3ᵛ(38)–7, E1ᵛ(50)–x, F3ᵛ(70)–x, G5ᵛ(90)–x, H7ᵛ(110)–x, I1ᵛ(114)–x, K1ᵛ(130)–x, L8ᵛ(160)–x, M2ᵛ(164)–x, N1ᵛ(178)–4, O6(203)–x, P5ᵛ(218)–x, Q1ᵛ(226)–x, R5ᵛ(250)–x, S5ᵛ(266)–4, T7ᵛ(286)–4, U1ᵛ(290)–x, X5ᵛ(314)–*, Y6(331)–x, Z6(347)–5, 2A5ᵛ(362)–6, 2B5ᵛ(378)–§, 2C7ᵛ(398)–*, 2E1ᵛ(418)–1, 2F1ᵛ(434)–1.

Catchwords: *om.* 30, 67, 76, 140, 170, 183, 193, 197, 202, 207, 234, 255, 264, 269, 280, 293, 318, 327, 332, 348, 359, 367, 370, 374, 380, 383, 390, 397, 415; 124 [*Up-*] *ton*, (∼*,).

Explicit: 438 ᴇɴᴅ ᴏꜰ ᴛʜᴇ sᴇᴄᴏɴᴅ ᴠᴏʟᴜᴍᴇ.

III. *A*² B–2E⁸ 2F⁴ 2G² (2G2 blk), ($4 (–2F3,4) signed; 'Vᴏʟ. III.' on $1), 224 leaves.

Pp. A1 t., A1ᵛ blk, A2 Contents, on B1 *1* 2–442 text (1–80 Brumoy, 81–136 Macbeth, 137–297 Adventurers, 299–442 Rasselas), *443–44* (2G2) blk.

Pagination: unnumbered 61, 81, 137, and 299, 298 blk.

Press-figures: B1ᵛ(2)–x, C1ᵛ(18)–6, D6(43)–x, E1ᵛ(50)–†, F1ᵛ(66)–x, G3ᵛ(86)–x, H7ᵛ(110)–x, I5ᵛ(122)–6, K1ᵛ(130)–6, L1ᵛ(146)–9, M3ᵛ(166)–x, N5ᵛ(186)–§, O5(201)–3, P8(223)–3, Q6ᵛ(236)–3, R1ᵛ(242)–3, S5(265)–3, T8(287)–*, U1ᵛ(290)–8, X3ᵛ(310)–8, Y3ᵛ(326)–9, Z3ᵛ(342)–8, 2A3ᵛ(358)–x, 2B1ᵛ(370)–1, 2C5ᵛ(394)–x, 2D6(411)–§, 2D8ᵛ(416)–x, 2E6ᵛ(428)–2, 2F1ᵛ(434)–1.

Catchwords: 11 gods. (∼*.), 60 *om.* (GENERAL), 80 *om.* (MISCELLA-
NEOUS), 81 *om.* (NOTE), 136 *om.* (THE), *om.* pp. 143, 149, 155, 161,
167, 182, 189, 196, 203, 212, 225, 232, 251, 258, 264, 277, 284, 291, 297; no
errors.

Explicit: 442 END OF THE THIRD VOLUME.

IV. *b*1 c² B–2F⁸ (2F8 blk), ($4 signed; 'VOL. IV.' on $1), 227 leaves.

Pp. b1 t., b1ᵛ blk, c1–2ᵛ Contents, on B1 *1* 2–446 text Ramblers 1–70, *447–8*
(2F8) blk.

Pagination: no errors.

Press-figures: B7ᵛ(14)–5, C7ᵛ(30)–x, D1ᵛ(34)–1, E5ᵛ(58)–8, F6(75)–x,
G5ᵛ(90)–8, H7ᵛ(110)–6, K1ᵛ(130)–x, L8(159)–x, M1ᵛ(162)–7, N3ᵛ(182)–6,
O5(201)–6, P7(221)–6, Q2ᵛ(228)–§, R1ᵛ(242)–4, S5ᵛ(266)–§, T6ᵛ(284)–*,
U6(299)–§, Y7ᵛ(334)–2, Z8(351)–x, 2A3ᵛ(358)–6, 2A8ᵛ(368)–4, 2B4ᵛ(376)–x,
2B7ᵛ(382)–2, 2C7ᵛ(398)–2, 2C8(399)–9, 2D8ᵛ(416)–4, 2E7(429)–6,
2E7ᵛ(430)–5, 2F6(443)–4.

Catchwords: *om.* between essays: 13, 19, 26, 32, 39, 52, 65, 72, 87, 94, 102,
109, 115, 143, 149, 155, 161, 167, 174, 180, 187, 193, 206, 225, 244, 250, 256,
269, 275, 281, 288, 294, 300, 312, 318, 324, 331, 337, 343, 350, 363, 369, 375,
386, 393, 399, 405, 411, 417, 434, 440; 336 who∧ (∼,).

Explicit: 446 END OF THE FOURTH VOLUME.

Notes: Essays separated by parallel rules 7, 46, 58, 81, 123, 131, 137, 199,
213, 219, 232, 238, 263, 307, 357, 381, 423, (total rule) 429.

V. π1 a² B–2E⁸ 2F⁸ (–2F4.5 = a²; 2F8 blk), ($4 signed; 'VOL. V.' on $1),
225 leaves.

Pp. π1 t., π1ᵛ blk, a1–2 Contents, a2ᵛ blk, on B1 *1* 2–443 text Ramblers
71–140, *444–6* (2F8) blk.

Pagination: no errors.

Press-figures: B7ᵛ(14)–3, C3ᵛ(22)–2, D1ᵛ(34)–2, E5ᵛ(58)–2, F8(79)–2,
G1ᵛ(82)–2, H8ᵛ(112)–2, I8(127)–3, K6(139)–3, L7ᵛ(158)–1, M7ᵛ(174)–1,
N8(191)–1, O5ᵛ(202)–2, P8(223)–1, Q6(235)–2, R7(253)–1, S1ᵛ(258)–2,
T2ᵛ(276)–3, U8ᵛ(304)–2, X1ᵛ(306)–2, Y1ᵛ(322)–3, Z8ᵛ(352)–3, 2A7ᵛ(366)–3,
2B5(377)–3, 2C5ᵛ(394)–3, 2E5(425)–3, 2F2ᵛ(436)–3; unfigured 2D.

Catchwords: *om.* between essays: 11, 24, 30, 35, 53, 58, 70, 76, 83, 89, 96,
102, 114, 121, 127, 137, 151, 163, 171, 177, 188, 201, 208, 214, 220, 226, 232,
238, 245, 252, 264, 277, 284, 291, 299, 305, 312, 319, 326, 332, 338, 343, 350,
357, 363, 369, 375, 382, 393, 399, 410, 416, 422, 428; 146 *om.* (The), 261
[oppo-] ſition (poſition).

Explicit: 443 END OF THE FIFTH VOLUME.

Notes: Essays separated by parallel rules: 6, 18, 42, 48, 64, 109, 143, 158, 183,
195, 258, 271, 388, 405, 436.

VI. π1 *A*² B–2C⁸ (–2C8 ? = π1), ($4 signed; 'VOL. VI.' on $1), 202 leaves.

Pp. π1 t., π1ᵛ blk, A1–2 Contents, A2ᵛ blk, on B1 *1* 2–397 text Ramblers 141–208, *398* blk.

Pagination: 133 as 233, 314 as 144.

Press-figures: B7ᵛ(14)–2, C5(25)–3, D8(47)–2, E2ᵛ(52)–1, F5(73)–3, G1ᵛ(82)–1, H8(111)–2, I5(121)–3, K8(143)–2, L8ᵛ(160)–2, M7(173)–3, N8(191)–3, P1ᵛ(218)–3, R3ᵛ(246)–3, S3ᵛ(262)–3, T4ᵛ(280)–3, U1ᵛ(290)–3, X7(317)–1, Y8ᵛ(336)–1, Z3ᵛ(342)–8, 2A7(365)–2, 2B4ᵛ(376)–2, 2C5ᵛ(394)–2.

Catchwords: *om.* between essays: 6, 13, 21, 27, 38, 44, 50, 56, 62, 68, 74, 87, 94, 100, 106, 112, 117, 122, 134, 141, 152, 157, 163, 168, 174, 180, 193, 198, 204, 214, 220, 225, 230, 236, 242, 248, 253, 258, 264, 270, 276, 281, 286, 292, 298, 304, 309, 315, 321, 326, 331, 338, 345, 351, 357, 362, 367, 373, 379, 385, 391; 344 and (ₐnd).

Explicit: 397 END OF THE SIXTH VOLUME.

Notes: Essays separated by parallel rules: 33, 82, 129, 146, 188, 210.

VII. π1 a² B–2C⁸ 2D⁸ (–2D4.5 = a², 2D8 blk), ($4 signed; 'VOL. VII.' on $1), 209 leaves.

Pp. π1 t., π1ᵛ blk, a1–2 Contents, a2ᵛ Advertisement, on B1 *1* 2–410 text Idlers 1–103, *411–12* (2D8) blk.

Pagination: no errors;.

Press-figures: B8(15)–8, C6(27)–2, D7ᵛ(46)–2, E7ᵛ(62)–4, F6ᵛ(76)–3, G7(93)–3, H2ᵛ(100)–8, I7ᵛ(126)–2, K1ᵛ(130)–8, L3ᵛ(150)–8, M7(173)–2, N3ᵛ(182)–5, O2ᵛ(196)–5, P8(223)–8*, Q7ᵛ(238)–5, R2ᵛ(244)–*8, 2C3ᵛ(390)–3; S–2B unfigured.

Catchwords: *om.* between essays: 4, 8, 12, 16, 20, 24, 44, 48, 52, 59, 63, 70, 74, 79, 83, 87, 91, 95, 99, 104, 108, 112, 116, 120, 124, 128, 137, 141, 145, 149, 154, 158, 162, 166, 174, 190, 193, 201, 205, 209, 214, 219, 227, 231, 234, 237, 243, 247, 251, 262, 265, 271, 278, 282, 291, 295, 299, 303, 311, 316, 320, 324, 328, 334, 338, 342, 349, 353, 356, 360, 371, 374, 377, 381, 385, 389, 392, 400, 404, 407. No errors.

Explicit: 410 END OF THE SEVENTH VOLUME.

Notes: Essays separated by parallel rules: 33, 37, 41, 56, 67, 134, 178, 182, 186, 198, 224, 255, 259, 275, 288, 308, 346, 364, 368, 396; (double rule) 171.

VIII. *A*² B–2D⁸, ($4 (–B4) signed; 'VOL. VIII.' on $1), 210 leaves.

Pp. A1 t., A1ᵛ blk, A2–2ᵛ Contents, on B1 *1* 2–416 text (1–61 Misc. essays, 65–205 Political Tracts, 209–416 Journey).

Pagination: 7–9, 23, 62–5, 96, 142, 155, 206–9 unnumbered; 62, 64, and 206 blk.

Press-figures: B6(12)–5, C7(29)–6, D1ᵛ(34)–4, E6(59)–4, F6ᵛ(76)–x, G5ᵛ(90)–9, H5ᵛ(106)–x, I8(127)–9, K4ᵛ(136)–§, L1ᵛ(146)–§ M5(169)–x, N5ᵛ(186)–4, O5ᵛ(202)–§, P6(219)–1, Q8ᵛ(240)–1, R7ᵛ(254)–2, S6(267)–6, T3ᵛ(278)–*, U5(297)–6, X5ᵛ(314)–6, Y1ᵛ(322)–2, Z5ᵛ(346)–*, 2A3ᵛ(358)–5, 2A8ᵛ(368)–1, 2B3ᵛ(374)–9, 2C5ᵛ(394)–2, 2C6ᵛ(396)–5, 2D5ᵛ(410)–*.

Catchwords: *om.* 7–8, 22, 61–4, 95, 141, 154, 205–8; 261 *Highlanders*, (~ₐ), 387 [vir-] ing. (gin.), 400 decₐared (declared).
Explicit: 416 END OF THE EIGHTH VOLUME.

IX. a² B–2F⁸ 2G⁸ (–2G4.5 = a²), ($4 signed; 'VOL. IX.' on $1), 232 leaves.
Pp. a1 t., a1ᵛ blk, a2 Contents, a2ᵛ blk, on B1 1–460 text Lives: Cowley–Dryden.
Pagination: (↑) 1, 72, 183, 201, 211, 223, 229, 285, 287, 291, 294, 312, 315; [↑] 84; 396 unnumbered.
Press-figures: B1ᵛ(2)–5, B8ᵛ(16)–2, C3ᵛ(22)–6, C7(29)–2, D7(45)–3, D7ᵛ(46)–6, E6ᵛ(60)–3, F3ᵛ(70)–1, F5(73)–3, G6ᵛ(92)–3, G8(95)–6, H7(109)–2, H8(111)–6, I5ᵛ(122)–3, K7(141)–6, L6ᵛ(156)–3, M3ᵛ(166)–4, M5(169)–6, N6(187)–3, N7(189)–6, O2ᵛ(196)–1, O5ᵛ(202)–5, P2ᵛ(212)–5, P8(223)–3, Q4ᵛ(232)–4, Q8(239)–6, R7(253)–3, S1ᵛ(258)–5, S2ᵛ(260)–4, T2ᵛ(276)–6, T3ᵛ(278)–7, U8(303)–6, U8ᵛ(304)–1, X2ᵛ(308)–4, X6(315)–3, Y1ᵛ(322)–1, Y6ᵛ(332)–5, Z5(345)–2, Z8(351)–4, 2A1ᵛ(354)–4, 2A7(365)–5, 2B3ᵛ(374)–3, 2B4ᵛ(376)–1, 2C6ᵛ(396)–3, 2C8(399)–6, 2D5ᵛ(410)–5, 2D6ᵛ(412)–6, 2E5(425)–1, 2E8(431)–6.
Catchwords: 128 *that*ₐ (~,), 152 That [*bruised*], 187 „or [r *inverted*] ('of'), 231 fancy [y *damaged*] (~.), 256 made; (~:), 295 appear [r *damaged*] (appears), 298 tedioₐ (tedious), 320 „Monk] ('~]), 367 „defign ('~), 368 'Jefferies, ('~;), 423 [in-] deedₐ (~,), 445 *Pan*, [*damaged*].
Explicit: 460 END OF THE NINTH VOLUME.

X. a² B–2C⁸ 2D² ($4 (–2D2) signed; 'VOL. X.' on $1), 204 leaves.
Pp. a1 t., a1ᵛ blk, a2 Contents, a2ᵛ blk, on B1 1–404 text Lives: Smith–Savage.
Pagination: (↑) 1, 29, 31, 36, 43, 49, 54, 60, 73, 142, 148, 157, 185, 202, 226, 236, 250, 261, 267, 274, 278, 281; 40 occasionally unnumbered.
Press-figures: B6ᵛ(12)–3, B8(15)–5, C3ᵛ(22)–4, D2ᵛ(36)–1, D3ᵛ(38)–2, E2ᵛ(52)–6, E7ᵛ(62)–3, F5(73)–2, G5ᵛ(90)–4, G6ᵛ(92)–6, H5ᵛ(106)–2, H8ᵛ(112)–5, I3ᵛ(118)–2, I8ᵛ(128)–6, K5(137)–6, K5ᵛ(138)–1, L2ᵛ(148)–6, L7ᵛ(158)–2, M2ᵛ(164)–6, N5ᵛ(186)–4, N8ᵛ(192)–3, O3ᵛ(198)–3, O7ᵛ(206)–5, P3ᵛ(214)–5, Q8(239)–6, R5ᵛ(250)–2, S1ᵛ(258)–2, S8ᵛ(272)–6, T6(283)–2, U7(301)–6, X7ᵛ(318)–6, Y7(333)–5, Y8(335)–6, Z2ᵛ(340)–4, Z5ᵛ(346)–2, 2A1ᵛ(354)–2, 2B3ᵛ(374)–2, 2C2ᵛ(388)–4, 2C5ᵛ(394)–5, 2D1ᵛ(402)–4.
Catchwords: 2 '„Ego ('—Ego), 5 proₐ (proportion), 115 *well*ₐ (*well-fung*), 149 whichₐ (~,), 229 thouₐ (thoufand), 231 Popeₐₐ (~*;), 301 *Dealer*ₐₐ (~*,), 341 But, (~ₐ).
Explicit: 404 END OF THE TENTH VOLUME.

XI. a² B–2B⁸ 2C⁴ (–2C4 ? blk), ($4 signed; 'VOL. XI.' on $1), 190 leaves.
Pp. a1 t., a1ᵛ blk, a2 Contents, a2ᵛ blk, on B1 1–389 Lives: Swift–Lyttelton, *390* blk.

Pagination: no errors; (↑) 1, 49, 54, 238, 249, 259, 265, 272, 276, 286, 347, 355, 364, 380; [↑] 218, 221.

Press-figures: B2ᵛ(4)–4, B6(11)–5, C2ᵛ(20)–6, C3ᵛ(22)–1, D5(41)–3, D7ᵛ(46)–6, E1ᵛ(50)–4, E4ᵛ(56)–1, F1ᵛ(66)–1, F6ᵛ(76)–5, G2ᵛ(84)–4, G7ᵛ(94)–3, H8(111)–6, H8ᵛ(112)–5, I6ᵛ(124)–6, I7ᵛ(126)–3, K4ᵛ(136)–6, K6(139)–2, L1ᵛ(162)–1, L5(170)–6, M4ᵛ(168)–1, O8(207)–3, P8ᵛ(224)–2, Q4ᵛ(232)–2, Q8(239)–5, R3ᵛ(246)–4, R8ᵛ(256)–3, S2ᵛ(260)–5, S6(267)–3, T2ᵛ(276)–1, U6(299)–2, U7(301)–4, X6(315)–1, X8ᵛ(320)–6, Y4ᵛ(328)–5, Y8(335)–6, Z6(347)–5, Z8ᵛ(352)–2, 2A2ᵛ(356)–4, 2A3ᵛ(358)–1, 2B3ᵛ(374)–1, 2B7(381)–6; N unfigured.

Catchwords: 194 'Exple- (ₐExpletives), 272 1727 ('∼), 289 'thatₐ ('∼,), 320 Whoₐ (∼,).

Explicit: 389 ᴇɴᴅ ᴏꜰ ᴛʜᴇ ᴇʟᴇᴠᴇɴᴛʜ ᴠᴏʟᴜᴍᴇ.

XII. *A*² B–2M⁸ (–2M8 ? blk), ($4 signed; 'ᴠᴏʟ. XII.' on $1), 274 leaves.

Pp. A1 t., A1ᵛ blk, A2–2ᵛ Contents, on B1 *1* ½t Lives &c., *2* blk, *3* 4–450 text (3–328 Lives of sundry Eminent Persons, 331–438 selected Letters, 441–50 Prayers), on 2G3–2M7ᵛ *Index* (45 leaves, unpaged).

Pagination: [↑] 11, 41, 63, 149, 160, 168, 180, 190, 210, 220, 271, 308; 329–31, 439–41 unnumbered, Index unpaged.

Press-figures: K1ᵛ(130)–8, L3ᵛ(150)–8, P3ᵛ(214)–8, Q7(237)–*3, R8(255)–2*, X8(319)–8, 2C7ᵛ(398)–8; B–I, M–O, S–U, Y–2B, 2D–2M unfigured.

Catchwords: *om.* 10, 40, 62, 148, 159, 167, 179, 189, 209, 219, 270, 307, 328–30, 332, 337–40, 346, 377, 409–10, 414–17, 421, 426–8, 435, 438–40, 442–3, 448–9; 2G5, 2I5, 2I6, 2K4, 2L3; 137 oₐher (other), 2H8ᵛ *Fores,* (∼ₐ), 2K2ᵛ *Metrodorus*ₐ (∼,), 2L8 [Maſ-] ter's (ſter's).

Explicit: 2M7ᵛ FINIS.

Paper: White, wove; Demy (8¾ × 5⅝ in.); wmk.: 'W | 1794 P' and 'W T | 1795'.

Type: I. 'Essay': english (4.5 mm), leaded, text: pica (4.0 mm), notes: bourgeois (3.1 mm).

Plate: Engr. port. SJ, as 1787 'Publish'd as the Act directs, by the Proprietors, Janʸ. 1ˢᵗ 1787.'

References: Courtney 164; ESTC: t082916.

Notes: Andrew Strahan printed 1,250 copies of vols. V–VII and XII (with the Index), for Thomas Cadell in Sept. 1796 (L: Add. MS 48811, fo. 39). This is a direct reprint from Murphy's first edn. of 1792, without correction or rearrangement. The *Lives of the Poets* are annotated by 'H'[awkins], 'N'[ichols], and 'R'[eed].

Copies: O (8° S. 1–12. Linc.);

USA: Hyde ('Richard Marshall' — 'Michael Pepper', lacks VIII. O8), ICU, IU, MH (*57–1684), NIC, PPU, TxU, WiM; *Japan*: [Kyoto]; *UK*: BMp (396488), Csj, DUu, E (Jac.I.3/2), L (12269. d.1), LICj, MRp, NCu, Ol, Op.

¹ Somerville Rare Books (Dublin), *Catalogue* 1 (Nov. 1971), recorded a copy demonstrating this construction of sig. m. Most copies are too tightly bound to discover it.

87.3W/5   Works, ed. Murphy   1801

THE | WORKS | OF | Samuel Johnſon, LL.D. | A NEW EDITION, | IN TWELVE VOLUMES. | WITH | AN ESSAY ON HIS LIFE AND GENIUS, | BY ARTHUR MURPHY, ESQ. | [medium parallel rule] | VOLUME THE FIRST [– TWELFTH]. | [medium total rule] | *LONDON:* | *Printed by Nichols and Son, Red-Lion-Paſſage, Fleet-Street,* | For H. Baldwin, J. Johnſon, G. G. and J. Robinſon, P. Elmſly, | J. Nichols, R. Baldwin, H.L. Gardner, F. and C. Rivington, | W. Otridge and Son, W.J. and J. Richardſon, A. Strahan, J. Sewell, | Leigh and Sothebys, R. Faulder, G. and W. Nicol, T. Payne, W. | Lowndes, G. Wilkie, C. Davis, J. Matthews, T. Egerton, J. | Edwards, P. M'Queen, Ogilvie and Son, J. Scatcherd, J. Walker, | B.C. Collins, E. Newbery, Vernor and Hood, R. Lea, J. Deighton, | Darton and Harvey, J. Nunn, Lackington Allen and Co. J. Stockdale, | G. Cuthell, D. Walker, Clarke and Son, G. Kearſley, C. Law, | J. White, Longman and Rees, Cadell jun. and Davies, J. Barker, | Carpenter and Co. T. Hurſt, W. Miller, Murray and Highley, S. Bagſter, | J. Harding, J. Hatchard, J. Wallis, R.H. Evans, and J. Mawman. | 1801.

Stent: Sothebys, . . . G. Cuthell,

Var: II–IV, VIII. *Printed by Luke Hansard, Great Turnstile, near Lincoln's-Inn Fields . . .*

> V–VII, XII. *Printed by A. Strahan, Printers-Street.*

> IX–XI. *Printed by Nichols and Son; Red-Lion-Paſſage, Fleet Street.*

12 vols., 8°

I. A⁴ a–l⁸ m⁶ B–O⁸ P⁴, ($4 (–P3,4) signed; 'VOL. I.' on $1), 206 leaves.
Pp. 1–32 Murphy's Essay, 33–407 Poems and Poemata.

II. A² B–2E⁸ 2F⁴ (2F4 blk), ($4 signed), 222 leaves,
Pp. 3–438 Philological Tracts, Political essays, and Miscellaneous essays.

III. A² B–2E⁸ 2F⁴ 2G² (2G2 blk), ($4 signed), 224 leaves.
Pp. 1–136 Brumoy and Macbeth, 137–297 Adventurers (24), 299–442 Rasselas.

IV. π1 C² B–2E⁸ 2F⁶ (–2F6 ? blk), ($4 signed), 225 leaves.
Pp. 1–446 Ramblers (1–70).

V. π1 a² B–2E⁸ 2F⁶, ($4 signed), 230 leaves.
Pp. 1–443 Ramblers (71–140).

VI. a⁴ (–a3) B–2C⁸ (2C8 blk), ($4 signed), 203 leaves.
Pp. 1–397 Ramblers (141–208).

VII. π² a² B–2C⁸ 2D⁶ (2D6 blk), ($4 signed), 210 leaves.
Pp. 1–410 Idlers (1–103).

VIII. A² B–2D⁸, ($4 signed), 210 leaves.
Pp. 1–54 Miscellaneous essays, 65–204 Political Tracts, 205–416 Journey.

IX. a² B–2F⁸ 2G⁴ 2H², ($4 signed), 232 leaves.
Pp. 1–460 Lives: Cowley–Dryden.

X. a² B–2C⁸ 2D², ($4 signed), 204 leaves.
Pp. 1–404 Lives: Smith–Savage.

XI. a² B–2B⁸ 2C⁴ (2C4 blk), ($4 signed), 198 leaves.
Pp. 1–309 Lives: Swift–Lyttelton.

XII. A² B–2L⁸ 2M⁸ (2M8 blk), ($4 signed), 274 leaves.
Pp. 3–328 Eminent Persons, 331–438 Letters, 441–50 Prayers.

Plates: Front. vol. 1, engr. port. of SJ ('Blinking Sam') in oval frame, plain surround, entitled: 'Samuel Johnson, L.L.D.', and 'Painted by Sir Joshua Reynolds. Engraved by James Fittler, A.R.A.', n.d., but as 1787.

References: Courtney 164.

Notes: The printing was shared between the printers as recorded in the imprints, reflecting their particular proprietorial strengths in the various works included in the volumes. Strahan's share (vols. V–VII and XII) in 1,250 copies, is recorded in his ledgers (L: Add. MS 48811, fo. 39) under July 1801, where the round total of sheets (114), shows the validity of the several final blanks in his volumes, which were printed for Thomas Cadell. Strahan also printed the 6 sheets of Index. For a separate issue of IX–XI, see 79.4LP/15, above. The text is reprinted from 1792 (above), without corrections, though there are some differences in the texts of SJ's Latin Poems (*Poemata*, i. 168–235). Langton who had edited them for *Works*, 1787, died 18 Dec. 1801, so that the changes may have been his. It is reasonable to suppose that Murphy, who lived to 1805, continued to be responsible for the edition which bears his name.

Copies: O (2699 e. 279–90);

USA: DLC, Hyde ('Lambe' — 'Cowper'), MH (1461.6), NIC, NjP, NRU (lacks vol. 1), PPL, TxU, ViU; *Can*: CaOHM; *Japan*: [Kyoto]; *UK*: BMp (470020–31), Ep, [Es], L (633. i. 1–12), LICj, Oef, SAN; *Fr*: BN.

87.3W/6   Works   1801

The Works of Samuel Johnson, LL.D. . . . London.
    12 vols., 12°. Not examined.
    Copies: *USA*: [MH (16463.5)].

THE | WORKS | OF | SAMUEL JOHNSON, LL.D. | A NEW EDITION, | IN FIFTEEN VOLUMES. | WITH | A LIFE OF THE AUTHOR. | [short parallel rule] | VOL. I [– XV]. | [short total rule] | EDINBURGH: | PRINTED FOR BELL & BRADFUTE, JAMES M'CLEISH, AND | WILLIAM BLACKWOOD; | GILBERT & HODGES, DUBLIN; AND S. CAMPBELL, | NEW YORK. | 1806.

15 vols., 18°

I. A1–3 b–k⁶ B–S⁶ (–S6 ? blk), ($3 signed), 158 leaves.

Pp. A1 t., A1ᵛ coloph: 'G. CAW, Printer, | Edinburgh.', A2–3 Contents, A3ᵛ blk, on b1 *i* ii–cviii Life of Johnson, on B1 *1* ½t Poems, *2* blk, *3* 4–155 Poems, *156* 157–201 Poemata, 201 *Explicit*: END OF THE FIRST VOLUME. *202* blk.

II. A² B–2H⁶, ($3 signed), 182 leaves.

Pp. A1 t., A1ᵛ coloph., A2–2ᵛ Contents, 3–280 Philological tracts, *281* 282–318 Political essays, *319* 320–60 Miscellaneous essays, no *Explicit*.

III. A² B–2H⁶, ($3 signed), 182 leaves.

Pp. A1 t., A1ᵛ coloph., A2–2ᵛ Contents, on B1 *1* 2–216 Miscellaneous essays, *217* 218–360 Rasselas, 360 *Explicit* and coloph.

IV. πA1–3 A–2G⁶, ($3 signed), 183 leaves.

Pp. πA1 t., A1ᵛ coloph., A2–3ᵛ Contents, on A1 *1* 2–360 Ramblers 1–57, 360 *Explicit* and coloph.

V. πA1–3 A–2K⁶ (–2K6 ? blk), ($3 (2K3 as K) signed), 200 leaves.

Pp. πA1 t., A1ᵛ coloph., A2–3ᵛ Contents, on A1 *1* 2–394 Ramblers 58–120, no *Explicit*.

VI. π1–3 A–2G⁶, ($3 (–2G2) signed), 183 leaves.

Pp. π1 t., π1ᵛ coloph., π2–3 Contents, π3ᵛ blk, on A1 *1* 2–360 Ramblers 121–81, no *Explicit*.

VII. π1–3 A–2B⁶ 2C⁴ 2D⁴, ($3 signed), 161 leaves.

Pp. π1 t., π1ᵛ coloph., π2–3 Contents, π3ᵛ blk, on A1 *1* 2–152 Ramblers 182–208, *153* 154–315 Adventurers (24), 315 *Explicit*, *316* blk.

VIII. A1–3 B–2E⁶, ($3 signed), 165 leaves.

Pp. A1 t., A1ᵛ coloph., A2–3 Contents, A3ᵛ blk, on B1 *1* 2–323 Idlers 1–84, 324 blk, no *Explicit*.

IX. A1–3 B–2F⁶ 2G², ($3 signed), 173 leaves.

Pp. A1 t., a1ᵛ coloph., A2–3 Contents, A3ᵛ blk, on B1 *1* 2–69 Idlers 85–103; 65–9 no 22*, *70* blk, *71* 72–131 Misc. essays, *132* blk, *133* 134–339 Journey, 399 *Explicit* and coloph., *340* blk.

X. *A*² B–2E⁶ (–2E6 ? blk), ($3 signed), 163 leaves.

Pp. A1 t., A1ᵛ coloph., A2 Contents, A2ᵛ blk, on B1 *1* ½t, *2* blk, *3* 4–143 Political tracts, *144* blk, *145–146* advert., *147* 148–322 Lives of the Poets: Cowley–Milton, 322 *Explicit*.

XI. A² B–2G⁶, ($3 signed), 176 leaves.

Pp. A1 t., A1ᵛ blk, A2 Contents, A2ᵛ blk, on B1 *1* 2–348 Lives: Butler–Rowe, 348 *Explicit*.

XII. A² B–2E⁶ 2F², ($3 signed), 166 leaves.

Pp. A1 t., A1ᵛ blk, A2 Contents, A2ᵛ blk, on B1 *1* 2–328 Lives: Addison–Savage, 328 *Explicit*.

XIII. A² B–2H⁶, ($3 signed), 182 leaves.

Pp. A1 t., A1ᵛ coloph., A2 Contents, A2ᵛ blk, on B1 *1* 2 1–344 Lives: Swift–Young, 344 *Explicit*.

XIV. A² B–2G⁶ 2H², ($3 signed), 178 leaves.

Pp. A1 t., A1ᵛ coloph., A2 Contents, A2ᵛ blk, on B1 *1* 2–42 Lives: Mallet–Lyttelton, *43* ½t, *44* blk, *45* 46–352 Eminent Persons, 352 *Explicit*.

XV. A² B–Q⁶, a–k⁶ 11–3, ($3 (12ᵛ as 'h') signed), 155 leaves.

Pp. A1 t., A1ᵛ coloph., A2–2ᵛ Contents, on B1 *1* 2–22 Life of Ascham, *23* ½t Letters, *24* blk, *25* 26–132 Letters, *133* ½t Prayers, *134* 135–44 Prayers, *145* ½t, *146* blk, *147* 148–76 Supplementary Letters, on a1 Index (unpaged), 13.
Explicit: FINIS. and coloph., 13ᵛ blk.

Notes: The editor of this collection is unidentified but appears to have been a Scot, judging by the discussions of afforestation in the Highlands (I. li–lii), and of 'Ossian' (I. lv–lix). The 'Life' is not derived from Murphy, but is an adumbration of Boswell,[1] and the 'Supplementary Letters' in vol. 15, are from the same source, though *Idler* 41 is presented as a letter on the death of Elizabeth Johnson.[2]

Bell & Bradfute of Edinburgh were significantly involved in the distribution of this edition (E: MS Dep. 317, Box. 5); Samuel Campbell, of New York, had been apprenticed to Bell.[3] The various accounts show that there were two issues, one on demy (ordinary) paper, the other on royal, both 18°, and that the trade price in 1806 was £1. 6s. 3d. for the former, and £1. 16s. 3d. for the latter. Thomas Ostell, and his successors (1806), Cradock and Joy, were the main London agent. An undated Trade catalogue of 'Books in Quires', from Ogle & Aikman (Edinburgh), prices these volumes at £1. 8s. 9d. for the demy, and £2. for the royal paper copies.[4] These prices reflect a marked rise in prices at this time.

This edition was published in the summer of 1806, and preceded the London 8° (87.3W/8, below). Several letters relative to the publication of this edn. and to its advertising, distribution and sale, extending through 1810 to 1819, are among the papers of Bell & Bradfute.[5]

Copies: BMp (528101–15);

USA: Hyde ('Glyn'), NN, PPSwarth; *UK*: BRp, E (Newb. 1597–1611), LICj (B.10; 'George Todd Jun. Writer. Edinb. 1806' — 'Hay Hunter', boards, uncut: 6½ × 4 in.).

---

¹ It does include some independent material however.

² See *Life* i. 238 n., and *Gents. Mag.* lxiv (Feb. 1794), 100–1.

³ E: (MS Dep. 317, Box. 5) includes a letter from Campbell to Bradfute, condoling on the death of 'Mr Bell' and asserting that his 'kindness in aiding me when I left his service in 1785 will never be obliterated from my breast' (20 Dec. 1806). Cole, *Irish Booksellers* (1986), 57–9, shows him trading extensively in Irish books and issuing a catalogue in 1794.

⁴ E: (MS Acc. 5000, no. 1388). In the catalogue of William Creech's Stock, 7 July 1815, p. 24, a copy of this edn. is listed as '12 vols. royal 8vo' (E: MS Acc. 5000, no. 1413), and in J. Mawman's Trade *Catalogue* (July 1809), it is given as '[Trade] £2. 14s. 0. [Retail] £4. 4s. 0d.' Mawman is there styled as 'Agent to the University' [of Cambridge] (E: MS Acc. 5000, no. 1389).

⁵ E: (MS Dep. 317, Box 5). The priority of this edn. is clear from a letter of 19 Dec. 1806 from Bell & Bradfute to their London agent, Thomas Ostell: 'the London edit. is nearly ready in which I am a proprietor'.

87.3W/8   Works, ed. Chalmers   1806

THE | WORKS | OF | Samuel Johnſon, LL.D. | A NEW EDITION, | IN TWELVE VOLUMES. | WITH | AN ESSAY ON HIS LIFE AND GENIUS, | BY ARTHUR MURPHY, ESQ. | [medium parallel rule] | VOLUME THE FIRST [– TWELFTH]. | [medium total rule] | *LONDON:* | *Printed by Luke Hanſard, near Lincoln's-Inn Fields,* | For J. Johnſon, J. Nichols and Son, R. Baldwin, F. and C. Rivington, | Otridge and Son, W. J. and J. Richardson, A. Strahan, Leigh and Sotheby, | R. Faulder, G. Nicol and Son, T. Payne, W. Lowndes, Wilkie and Robinſon, | C. Davis, T. Egerton, P. M'Queen, Ogilvie and Son, Scatcherd and | Letterman, J. Walker, B.C. Collins, Vernor and Hood, R. Lea, J. Deighton, | Darton and Harvey, J. Nunn, Lackington Allen and Co. J. Stockdale, Cuthell | and Martin, Clarke and Son, Wynne and Son, G. Kearſley, C. Law, | J. White, Longman Hurſt Rees and Orme, Cadell and Davies, J. Barker, | T. Booker, Carpenter and Co. E. Jeffery, W. Miller, J. and A. Arch, | B. Croſby, Blacks and Parry, S. Bagſter, J. Harding, Payne and Mackinlay, | J. Hatchard, R. Phillips, R.H. Evans, J. Mawman, T. Oſtell, *and* Matthews | and Leigh. | 1806.

Var: IV–VII: Printed for J. Johnſon, . . .

IX–XII: *Printed by J. Nichols and Son, Red-Lion-Paſſage, Fleet-Street,* | For J. Johnſon, . . .

12 vols., 8°

I. A⁴ B–2C⁸ 2D⁴, ($4 (–2C3,4) signed; 'VOL. I.' on $1), 208 leaves.

Pp. Engr. port. front. + A1 *i* t., *ii* blk, iii–v Advertisement ('Alexʳ Chalmers. London, January 1806'), *vi* blk, *vii*–viii Contents, on B1 *1* 2–191 Murphy's Essay, *192* blk, 193 ½t Poems, *194* blk, *195* 196–407 text Poems &c., 407 coloph: Luke Hansard, printer, Great Turnstile, Lincoln's-Inn Fields., *408* blk.

Pagination: [↑] iii, 225, 227; (↑) 193, 207, 223, 321, 323, 360; blk. vi, 192, 194, 224, 322.

Press-figures: B4ᵛ(8)–9, C3ᵛ(22)–4, D7ᵛ(46)–§ (*sideways*), E5ᵛ(58)–3, F7ᵛ(78)–1, G6ᵛ(92)–3, H1ᵛ(98)–8, I3ᵛ(118)–4, K4ᵛ(136)–6, L4ᵛ(152)3, M4ᵛ(168)–11, N2ᵛ(180)–11, P4ᵛ(216)–8, Q2ᵛ(228)–5, R1ᵛ(242)–3, R6ᵛ(252)–7, S7ᵛ(270)–5, T8(287)–11, U4ᵛ(296)–6, Y2ᵛ(324)–4, Z1ᵛ(338)–8, 2A5(361)–7, 2A7ᵛ(366)–8, 2B3ᵛ(374)–2, 2C7ᵛ(398)–13, 2D2ᵛ(404)–12.

Catchwords: 33 ‸with- ('without), 191 *om.*, 199 ‸Illuſtrious (¹⁴~), 200 ‸Studious (¹⁸~), 203 ‸Should (²⁸~), 205 ‸Scarce (³⁶~), 206 *om.* (THE), 207 ‸But (*~), 212 ‸The (*~), 223–6 *om.*, 257 *om.* (MAHOMET.), 259–61 *om.*, 265–70 *om.*, 272–5 *om.*, 277–8 *om.*, 281–2 *om.*, 284–5 *om.*, 287–8 *om.*, 291–4 *om.*, 297–302 *om.*, 304–5 *om.*, 307–9 *om.*, 314–15 *om.*, 317–22 *om.*, 325 *om.* (PROLOGUE.), 338 *om.* (TO), 339 *om.* (VERSES), 340 *om.* (To), 343 *om.* (EPITAPH), 344 Hære (Hæres), 348 *om.* (PARAPHRASE), 350 *om.* (☞ *The*), 352 *om.* (PARODY), 353–6 *om.*, 358–9 *om.*, 363–5 *om.*, 368 *om.* (LUCE), 373–4 *om.*, 376–81 *om.*, 383–6 *om.*, 389–402 *om.*, 404 *om.* (*HIS).

Explicit: 407 END OF THE FIRST VOLUME.

II. *A*² B–2G⁸ 2H⁴, ($4 (–2H3,4) signed; 'VOL. II.' on $1), 238 leaves.

Pp. A1 *i* t., *ii* blk, *iii*–iv Contents, on B1 *1* ½t Philological Tracts, *2* blk, *3* 4–471 text, 471 coloph. as vol. 1, *472* blk.

Pagination: [↑] 31, 124, 133, 197, 227, 240, 250, 254, 259, 264, 291, 312, 321, 326, 337, 350, 375, 384, 389, 405, 413, 424, 427, 431, 440, 447, 454; unnumbered 68–9; blk 68, 472.

Press-figures: B3ᵛ(6)–7, C1ᵛ(18)–6, D3ᵛ(38)–8, E5ᵛ(58)–1, F1ᵛ(66)–6, G7ᵛ(94)–13, H8ᵛ(112)–8, I2ᵛ(116)–13, K3ᵛ(134)–1, L1ᵛ(146)–1, N1ᵛ(178)–1, O1ᵛ(194)–2, P5ᵛ(218)–11, Q7ᵛ(238)–11, R5ᵛ(250)–3, S7ᵛ(270)–12, T8ᵛ(288)–2, U5ᵛ(298)–10, X5ᵛ(314)–4, Y6ᵛ(332)–11, Z1ᵛ(338)–4, 2A1ᵛ(354)–10, 2B2ᵛ(372)–4, 2C1ᵛ(386)–2, 2C8ᵛ(400)–1, 2D3ᵛ(406)–1, 2D8ᵛ(416)–9, 2E8ᵛ(432)–12, 2F5ᵛ(442)–6, 2G8ᵛ(464)–6, 2H1ᵛ(466)–4.

Catchwords: 30 *om.* (PREFACE), 67 *om.* (MISCELLANEOUS), 73, 82, 84, 95, 106, 116, *om.* (NOTE), 102 A (As), 123 *om.* (PROPOSALS), 132 *om.* (PREFACE), 168 though‸ (~,), 180 *Upton*, (~*,), 196 *om.* (GENERAL), 197 *om.* (TWO), 201 *om.* (MERCHANT), 215 *om.* (TITUS), 224 *om.* (OTHELLO), 226 *om.* (AN), 239 *om.* (AN), 249 *om.* (SOME), 253 *om.* (A), 258 *om.* (PRELIMINARY), 263 *om.* (INTRODUCTION), 290 *om.* (THE), 311 *om.* (PREFACE), 320 *om.* (PREFACE), 325 *om.* (AN), 336 *om.* (POLITICAL), 349 *om.* (AN), 374 *om.* (MISCELLANEOUS), 383 *om.* (REVIEW*), 388 *om.* (REVIEW), 404 *om.* (REPLY), 412 *om.* (REVIEW*), 423 *om.* (INTRODUCTION), 426 *om.* (ON), 430 *om.* (CONSIDERATIONS), 436 *om.* (LETTER), 439 *om.* (SOME), 446 *om.* (FURTHER), 453 *om.* (THE).

Explicit: 471 END OF THE SECOND VOLUME.

III. *A*² B–2E⁸ 2F⁶, ($4 (–[? I3 as 3], 2F4) signed; 'VOL. III.' on $1), 224 leaves.

Pp. A1 *i* t., *ii* blk, *iii*–iv Contents, on B1 *1* 2–444 text (inc. 83–103 Dedications, 109–300 Adventurers, 303–444 Rasselas), 444 coloph. as vol. 1.

Pagination: [↑] 3, 61, 81, 104–7, 109, 301–3; blk 108.

Press-figures: B1ᵛ(2)–10, C4ᵛ(24)–13, D2ᵛ(36)–5, D5ᵛ(42)–6, E8ᵛ(64)–13, F6ᵛ(76)–6, G6ᵛ(92)–6, H1ᵛ(98)–7, [I3(117)–3], K1ᵛ(130)–4, L7ᵛ(158)–10, M7ᵛ(174)–1, O3ᵛ(198)–4, P1ᵛ(210)–13, Q4ᵛ(232)–13, R4ᵛ(248)–5, S1ᵛ(258)–13, T7ᵛ(286)–3, U2ᵛ(292)–10, X4ᵛ(312)–11, Y8ᵛ(336)–10, Z1ᵛ(338)–13, 2A8ᵛ(368)–9, 2B5ᵛ(378)–11, 2C8ᵛ(400)–13, 2E7ᵛ(430)–13, 2E8ᵛ(432)–8, 2F1ᵛ(434)–10, 2F2ᵛ(436)–5.

Catchwords: *om.* 2 (A), 11 gods_∧. (~*.), 60 *om.* (GENERAL), 80 *om.* (DEDICATIONS.), 83–4 *om.*, 88 *om.* (The), 93–4 *om.*, 99 *om.* (ANGELL's), 102–3 *om.*, 107–8 *om.*, NUMB. *om.*, pp. 115, 122, 128, 134, 140, 146, 154, 169, 176, 189, 196, 211, 217, 224, 231, 256, 262, 268, 274, 281, 294; 300–2 *om.* (THE); *om.* (CHAP.) 326, 348, 358, 360, 363, 366, 367, 371, 377, 408, 418, 420, 428.

Explicit: 444 END OF THE THIRD VOLUME.

IV. *A*⁴ (–A1) B–2F⁸ (2F8 blk), ($4 signed; 'VOL. IV.' on $1), 227 leaves.

Pp. A2 *i* t., *ii* blk, *iii*–*v* Contents, *vi* blk, on B1 *1* 2–446 text Ramblers 1–70, 446 coloph: Strahan and Preſton, New-Street Square, London, 447–8 blk.

Pagination: no errors.

Press-figures: A3(iii)–2, A3ᵛ(iv)–1, B8ᵛ(16)–1, C7(29)–1, D7ᵛ(46)–1, E7(61)–1, F7ᵛ(78)–1, G8(95)–1, H8ᵛ(112)–1, K1ᵛ(130)–1, L8ᵛ(160)–1, M5ᵛ(170)–1, M8ᵛ(176)–1, N7(189)–1, O6(203)–1, P6ᵛ(220)–1, Q4ᵛ(232)–1, R3ᵛ(246)–1, S5ᵛ(266)–1, T5ᵛ(282)–1, U6(299)–1, X5ᵛ(314)–1, Y4ᵛ(328)–1, Z8(351)–1, 2A7ᵛ(366)–1, 2B7ᵛ(382)–1, 2C7ᵛ(398)–1, 2D5ᵛ(410)–7, 2E2ᵛ(420)–1, 2E8(431)–1, 2F3ᵛ(438)–1, 2F5(441)–2.

Catchwords: *om.* (NUMB.) 13, 19, 26, 32, 39, 52, 65, 72, 87, 94, 102, 109, 115, 143, 149, 155, 161, 174, 180, 187, 193, 206, 225, 244, 250, 256, 269, 275, 281, 288, 294, 300, 312, 318, 324, 331, 337, 343, 350, 363, 369, 375, 386, 393, 399, 405, 411, 417, 434, 440; 16 [com-] plicate_∧ (~,), 192 formidable, (~_∧), 336 who_∧ (~,).

Explicit: 446 END OF THE FOURTH VOLUME.

V. π1 a² B–2E⁸ 2F⁶, ($4 (–2F4) signed; 'VOL. V.' on $1), 225 leaves.

Pp. π1 *i* t., *ii* blk, a1 *iii*–*v* Contents, *vi* blk, on B1 *1* 2–443 text Ramblers 71–140, 443 coloph. as vol. 4, *444* blk.

Pagination: no errors.

Press-figures: B3ᵛ(6)–1, C8ᵛ(32)–2, D7(45)–1, E5(57)–1, E8(63)–2, F7ᵛ(78)–2, G2ᵛ(84)–1, G6(91)–2, H8(111)–2, H8ᵛ(112)–1, I3ᵛ(118)–1, I8ᵛ(128)–2, K6ᵛ(140)–2, K8(143)–1, L7(157)–1, L8(159)–2, M5(169)–1, M7ᵛ(174)–2, N2ᵛ(180)–1, N7ᵛ(190)–2, O6(204)–2, O8(207)–1, P4ᵛ(216)–1, P6(219)–2, Q8(239)–2, Q8ᵛ(240)–1, R8ᵛ(256)–2, S6(267)–1, T1ᵛ(274)–2,

U4ᵛ(296)–8, X1ᵛ(306)–1, X6ᵛ(316)–2, Y7(333)–2, Z2ᵛ(340)–8, Z5ᵛ(346)–2, 2A7(365)–2, 2A7ᵛ(366)–8, 2B5(377)–2, 2C7ᵛ(398)–8, 2D5(409)–1, 2D8(415)–2, 2E5(425)–1, 2F2ᵛ(436)–1.

Catchwords: *om.* (Numb.) 11, 23, 30, 35, 53, 58, 70, 76, 83, 89, 96, 102, 114, 121, 127, 137, 151, 163, 171, 177, 188, 201, 208, 214, 220, 226, 232, 238, 245, 252, 264, 277, 284, 291, 299, 305, 312, 319, 326, 332, 338, 343, 350, 357, 363, 369, 375, 382, 393, 399, 410, 416, 422, 428; 216 'pleafure, ('~:), 431 *om.* (In).

Explicit: 443 END OF THE FIFTH VOLUME.

VI. π1 a² B–2B⁸ 2C⁶, ($4 (–2C4) signed; 'Vol. VI.' on $1), 201 leaves.

Pp. π1 *i* t., *ii* blk, a1 *iii*–v Contents, *vi* blk, on B1 *1* 2–396 text Ramblers 141–208, 396 coloph. as vol. 4.

Pagination: no errors.

Press-figures: B6(11)–1, B6ᵛ(12)–4, C3ᵛ(22)–1, C8ᵛ(32)–8, D7(45)–2, D8(47)–1, E3ᵛ(54)–2, E6ᵛ(60)–8, F8ᵛ(80)–8, G5ᵛ(90)–1, G8ᵛ(96)–8, H1ᵛ(98)–1, H5(105)–2, I6ᵛ(124)–2, K2ᵛ(132)–2, K6(139)–1, L3ᵛ(150)–1, L5(153)–2, M1ᵛ(162)–2, M7(173)–1, N8(191)–1, N8ᵛ(192)–6, O2ᵛ(196)–1, O8(207)–2, P7(221)–1, P8ᵛ(224)–2, Q5ᵛ(234)–2, Q8ᵛ(240)–1, R8(255)–1, R8ᵛ(256)–8, S5ᵛ(266)–2, S8ᵛ(272)–1, T5ᵛ(282)–1, T8ᵛ(288)–2, U6ᵛ(300)–1, X3ᵛ(310)–2, X7(317)–7, Y2ᵛ(324)–2, Z6(347)–2, Z6ᵛ(348)–1, 2A3ᵛ(358)–7, 2A8ᵛ(368)–1, 2B4ᵛ(376)–2, 2B7ᵛ(382)–8, 2C4ᵛ(392)–8, 2C6(395)–8.

Catchwords: *om.* (Numb.) 6, 13, 21, 27, 38, 44, 50, 56, 62, 68, 74, 87, 94, 100, 106, 112, 116, 122, 134, 140, 152, 157, 163, 168, 174, 180, 193, 198, 204, 214, 220, 225, 230, 236, 242, 248, 253, 258, 264, 270, 277, 281, 286, 292, 298, 304, 309, 315, 321, 326, 331, 338, 345, 351, 357, 362, 367, 378, 384, 390; 317 laughter (l *inverted*).

Explicit: 396 END OF THE SIXTH VOLUME.

VII. π1 *a²* B–2D⁸, ($4 signed; 'Vol. VII.' on $1), 211 leaves.

Pp. π1 t., π1ᵛ blk, a1–2 Contents, a2ᵛ Advertisement, on B1 *1* 2–410 text Idlers 1–103, *411* 412–15 Idler *22, 415 coloph. as vol. 4, *416* blk.

Pagination: 305 as 30.

Press-figures: a1ᵛ–1, B6(11)–2, B7(13)–1, C8(31)–8, D8(47)–2, E5(57)–2, F6(75)–8, F7(77)–1, G7(93)–8, H5(105)–2, I7(125)–2, K2ᵛ(132)–1, M8(175)–1, N5(185)–8, N5ᵛ(186)–1, O8(207)–2, P1ᵛ(210)–1, P7(221)–2, Q2ᵛ(228)–2, Q8(239)–1, R2ᵛ(244)–1, S7(269)–1, S7ᵛ(270)–2, T5(281)–1, T6(283)–2, U7(301)–1, U7ᵛ(302)–8, X1ᵛ(306)–1, X7(317)–2, Y6(331)–1, Y6ᵛ(332)–2, Z4ᵛ(344)–8, 2A5ᵛ(362)–7, 2A7(365)–2, 2B8(383)–2, 2C2ᵛ(388)–1, 2C8(399)–2, 2D6(411)–7, 2D6ᵛ(412)–1.

Catchwords: *om.* (Numb.) 4, 8, 12, 16, 20, 24, 44, 48, 52, 59, 63, 70, 74, 79, 83, 87, 91, 95, 99, 104, 108, 110, 112, 116, 120, 124, 128, 137, 141, 145, 149, 154, 158, 162, 166, 174, 190, 193, 201, 205, 209, 214, 219, 227, 231, 234, 237, 243, 247, 251, 262, 265, 271, 278, 282, 291, 295, 299, 303, 311, 316, 320, 325,

328, 334, 338, 342, 349, 353, 356, 360, 371, 375, 377, 381, 385, 389, 392, 400, 404, 407, 410.

Explicit: 415 END OF THE SEVENTH VOLUME.

VIII. *A²* B–2C⁸ 2D⁶, ($4 (–2D4) signed; 'VOL. VIII.' on $1), 208 leaves.

Pp. A1 *i* t., *ii* blk, *iii*–iv Contents, on B1 *1* 2–412 text (1–61 Essays, 64–204 Political Tracts, 205–412 Journey), 412 coloph: 'Luke Hanfard, printer, | near Lincoln's-Inn Fields.'

Pagination: [↑] 64; unnumbered 7–9, 23, 62–3, 65, 96, 142, 155, 205; blk: 62.

Press-figures: B1ᵛ(2)–6, C6ᵛ(28)–1, D7ᵛ(46)–10, E1ᵛ(50)–10, F5ᵛ(74)–12, G1ᵛ(82)–2, H1ᵛ(98)–13, I7ᵛ(126)–7, K5ᵛ(138)–12, L1ᵛ(146)–8, M4ᵛ(168)–5, N7ᵛ(190)–4, O7ᵛ(206)–5, P2ᵛ(212)–10, Q8ᵛ(240)–8, R8ᵛ(256)–5, S1ᵛ(258)–3, T4ᵛ(280)–5, U3ᵛ(294)–10, X4ᵛ(312)–8, Y1ᵛ(322)–9, Z1ᵛ(338)–2, 2A1ᵛ(354)–9, 2B5ᵛ(378)–13, 2C3ᵛ(390)–10, 2D4ᵛ(408)–1, 2D6(411)–3.

Catchwords: *om.* 6–8, 22, 61–4, 95, 141, 154, 204, 228 (ELGIN.); 234 lands (s *slipt*), 331 which (by).

Explicit: 412 END OF THE EIGHTH VOLUME.

IX. A⁴ B–2F⁸ 2G⁶, ($4 (–2G4) signed; 'VOL. IX.' on $1), 234 leaves.

Pp. A1 *i* t., *ii* blk, iii–v General Advertisement to Lives, *vi* blk, vii Contents, *viii* blk, on B1 1–460 text Lives: Cowley–Dryden, 460 coloph: [medium parallel rule] | *Printed by* NICHOLS *and* SON, *Red Lion-Passage, Fleet-Street, London.*

Pagination: (↑) iii, vii, 1, 72, 84, 183, 201, 211, 223, 229, 285, 287, 291, 294, 312, 315.

Press-figures: B5(9)–2, C2ᵛ(20)–3, D4ᵛ(40)–2, D7ᵛ(46)–5, H6ᵛ(108)–2, K6ᵛ(140)–5, T8(287)–5.

Catchwords: 81 'N‚ ('No), 128 *that*‚ (∼,), 256 made; (∼:), 333 ‚thief: ('∼:), 368 'Jefferies, ('∼;).

Explicit: 389 END OF THE NINTH VOLUME.

X. a² B–2C⁸ 2D², ($4 (–2D2) signed; 'VOL. X.' on $1), 204 leaves.

Pp. a1 *i* t., *ii* blk, iii Contents, *iv* blk, on B1 1–404 text Lives: Smith–Savage, 404 coloph. as vol. 9.

Pagination: (↑) iii, 1, 29, 31, 36, 43, 49, 54, 60, 73, 142, 148, 157, 185, 202, 226, 236, 250, 261, 267, 274.

Press-figures: Q3ᵛ(230)–2, X8(319)–2.

Catchwords: 127 ‚*Syph.* ('∼.), 153 [Shef-] field‚ (∼.), 235 *om.* (GAY.), 243 'Polly‚ ('∼,), 396 be (he).

Explicit: 404 END OF THE TENTH VOLUME.

XI. a² B–2B⁸ 2C⁴ (–2C4 ? blk), 198 leaves.

Pp. a1 *i* t., *ii* blk, iii Contents, *iv* blk, on B1 1–389 text Lives: Swift–Lyttelton, 389 coloph. as vol. 9, *390* blk, *391–2* (2C4) ? blk.

Pagination: (↑) iii, 1, 49, 54, 218, 221, 238, 249, 259, 265, 272, 276, 286, 347, 353, 364, 380.

Press-figures: none.

Catchwords: 128 [*Uſe of*] *Riches*, ('Riches,'), 137 'If ('March . . . | 'If), 173 [de-] light; (~:), 220 *om.* (THOMSON.), 230 [com-] mencemen‸ (mencement), 289 'that‸ ('~,), 290 *om.* (After), 320 Who‸ (~,), 369 ‸ſtudy; ('~;).

Explicit: 389 END OF THE ELEVENTH VOLUME.

XII. *a*² B–2M⁸ (–2M8 ? blk), 274 leaves.

Pp. a1 *i* t., *ii* blk, iii–iv Contents, on B1 *1* ½t Eminent Persons, *2* blk, 3–328 text, *329* ½t Letters, *330* blk, 331–438 text, *439* ½t Prayers, *440* blk, 441–50 text, on 2G2–2M7ᵛ *Index* (47 leaves, unpaged), 2M7ᵛ coloph: 'Nichols and Son, Printers, Red Lion Paſſage, Fleet-Street.'

Pagination: (↑) iii, 3, 11, 41, 63, 149, 160, 168, 180, 190, 210, 220, 271, 308, 331, 441; unnumbered 329–30, 439–40; blk: 330, 440; 247 as 24.

Press-figures: none.

Catchwords: 181 tim (time), 216 *om.* (He), 329–30 *om.*, 385 ſhoud (ſhould), 439–40 *om.*, 450 *om.* (INDEX.), 2G5 *om.* (B.), 2H8ᵛ *Fores*, (~‸), 2I3 Th (The), 2I5 *om.* (I. and J.), 2I6ᵛ *om.* (L.), 2L3 *om.* (Q.).

Explicit: 2M7ᵛ FINIS.

Paper: White, wove, often foxed; Demy (uncut: 8¾ × 5⅝ in.); wmk.: '1804', '1805'.

Type: Pica (4.0 mm). Very minor differences are discernible between the types of the different printers.

Plate: Engr. port. front. vol. 1: Oval frame, plain surround. Centre foot: 'Samuel Johnson, L.L.D.', 'Painted by Sir Joshua Reynolds. Engraved by James Fittler, A.R.A.', n.d. (as in 1801, above).

References: Courtney 164.

Notes: Andrew Strahan printed 1,500 copies of vols. IV–VII in December 1805 (L: Add. MS 48811, fo. 54ᵛ), overrunning 750 copies of the *Rambler* (IV–VI) as the '15th edition' (50.3R/43, above); and Nichols issued vols. IX–XI separately, see 79.4LP/19, above.

The editor was Alexander Chalmers who made several adjustments to the canon (I. iii–v) and improved the texts, notably of the periodical essays which he had already edited thoroughly for his *British Essayists*, (1802–3),[1] enlarging SJ's contribution to the *Adventurer* from Hawkins's 24, to a total of 29, by reprinting nos. 39, 67, 74, 81, and 128. Other canonical additions were: Dedications to Kennedy's *Scripture Chronology* (1751, iii. 83), to Gwynne's *London & Westminster Improved* (1766, iii. 84), to Adams's *Globes* (1766, iii. 85), to Pearce's *Works* (1777, iii. 86–7), to Hoole's *Tasso* (1763, iii. 87–8), to James's *Medicinal Dictionary* (1743, iii. 88), to Lennox's *Female Quixote* (1752, iii. 89–90) and her *Shakespeare Illustrated* (1753–4, iii. 90–3), to Payne's *Draughts* (1756, iii. 94), to Lindsay's *Evangelical History* (1757, iii. 95–9),[2] to Angell's *Stenography* (1758, iii. 100–1), to Baretti's *Dictionary* (1760, iii. 101–2), to Bennet's *Ascham* (1762, iii. 103), and the 'Preface' to Payne's *Tables of Interest*

(1758, iii. 104–7); he also included the original of *Idler* 22 ('Vultures', vii. 411–15), and the 'Life of Roscommon' (*Gents. Mag.* 1748, ix. 211–22). He rejected the *Table of Cebes* ('Preface', I. iii–iv, from Dodsley's *Museum*, 1747, as 'translated by Mr Spence'). Chalmers's reason for these adjustments was less that many (though not all) of these pieces had appeared in *Works*, xiv (1788), than that they had been attributed to SJ by Boswell, who had, however, been influenced by *Works*, xiv, in making some of his own attributions. This edition established Chalmers's canon and arrangement as the standard for future editions of the Collected Works.

Copies: O (2699 e. 291–302);[3]

USA: CLU, CtY, Hyde (uncut, grey bds., paper labels), ICU, MH (16462.6), NjP, [NRU, PPWag], ViU; [CaOLUI ('Nichols')]; *UK*: BAT, BMp, BRp, Cp, JDF ('Sir James Graham Domville, Bart.'[4]), GTc, HLu (lacks vol. 1), VuU[2], SAN ([s]PR3520.E06), WNs; *Aust*: CNL.

[1] This is most marked in the case of the *Rambler*, of which Chalmers's annotated copy of the folio edn. (50.3R/1, above) is still extant (NRU).
[2] Chalmers did not take his text from Gleig's reprint (*Works*, xv (1789); 87.3W/1.4, above) of the original 1757 text (57.4LEH, above), but from the slightly revised version in the *Lit. Mag.*, 1756 (56.4LM, above; cf. Hazen 116–25).
[3] Dickens's copy of this edn. was Sotheby (Yates), 21 Jan. 1895, 261.
[4] 3rd. Bt., of St. Albans, b. 1812.

87.3W/9   Works, ed. Chalmers   1806

THE | WORKS | OF | Samuel Johnson, LL.D. | A NEW EDITION. | IN TWELVE VOLUMES. | WITH | *AN ESSAY ON HIS LIFE AND GENIUS*, | By ARTHUR MURPHY, Esq, | [short parallel rule] | VOLUME THE FIRST [– TWELFTH] | [short total rule] | LONDON: | *Printed by E. Blackader, Took's Court, Chancery Lane.* | For J. Johnson, J. Nichols & Son, R. Baldwin, F. & C. Rivington, | Otridge & Son, W. J. & J. Richardson, A. Strahan, Leigh & | Sotheby, R. Faulder, G. Nicol & Son, T. Payne, W. Lowndes, | Wilkie and Robertson, C. Davis, T. Egerton, P. M'Queen, | Ogilvie & Son, Scatcherd & Letterman, J. Walker, B.C. Collins, | Vernor & Hood, R. Lea, J. Deighton, Darton & Harvey, J. Nunn, | Lackington, Allen, & Co; J. Stockdale, Cuthell & Martin, | Clarke & Son, Wynne & Son, G. Kearsley, C. Law, J. White, | Longman, Hurst, Rees & Orme, Cadell & Davies, J. Barker, | T. Booker, Carpenter & Co. E. Jeffery, W. Miller, G. & A. Arch, | B. Crosby, Blacks & Parry, S. Bagster, J. Harding, Payne & | Mackinley, J. Hatchard, R. Phillips, R.H. Evans, J. Mawman, | T. Ostell, *and* Matthews & Leigh. | [short rule] | 1806.

12 vols., 12°

Var. imprints: i–ii. Printed by E. Blackader, Took's Court, Chancery Lane, for J. Johnson, . . . &c.

iii, xii. Printed by J. & E. Hodson, Cross Street, Hatton Garden.
iv–v. Printed by Joyce Gold, Shoe-Lane.
vi–vii. Printed by R. Taylor & Co., Shoe-Lane.
viii–ix. Printed by Luke Hansard, near Lincoln's-Inn Fields.
x–xi. Printed by J. M'Creery, Black-Horse Court, Fleet-Street.

I. A^4 B–2E^6 2F^2, ($3 signed), 168 leaves.
Pp. A1 *i* t., *ii* blk, *iii* iv–vi advert. ('ALEX$_R$ CHALMERS. *London*, January 1806.'), *vii*–viii Contents, on B1 *1* 2–141 Murphy's Essay, *142* blk, *143* ½t, *144* blk, *145* 146–327 Poems & Poemata, 327 Explicit: END OF THE FIRST VOLUME. and coloph. (Blackader) as imprint, *328* blk.

II. A^2 B–2N^6 2O^2, ($3 signed), 214 leaves.
Pp. A1 *i* t., *ii* blk, *iii*–iv Contents, on B1 *1* ½t, *2* blk, *3* 4–299 Philological Tracts, *300* 301–22 Political Essays, *334* 335–423 Miscellaneous Essays, 423 Explicit and coloph. (Blackader) as imprint, *424* blk.

III. A^2 B–2N^6 2O^4 (2O4 blk), ($3 signed), 216 leaves.
Pp. A1 t., A1^v blk, A2–2^v Contents, on B1 *1* 2–103 Essays, *104* blk, *105* 106–286 Adventurer (29), *287* ½t, *288* note, *289* 290–426 Rasselas, 426 Explicit and coloph. (Hodson), *427–8* blk.

IV. A^4 B–2L^6 2M^4, ($3 signed), 206 leaves.
Pp. A1 *i* t., *ii* blk, *iii* iv–viii Contents, on B1 *1* 2–403 Ramblers 1–70, 403 explicit and coloph. (Gold), *404* blk.

V. A^4 B–2M^6 (2M6 ? blk), ($3 signed), 208 leaves.
Pp. A1 *i* t., *ii* blk, *iii* iv–vii Contents, *viii* blk, on B1 *1* 2–406 Ramblers 71–140, 406 explicit and coloph. (Gold), + ? blk leaf.

VI. A 1–3, B–2F^6, ($3 signed), 171 leaves.
Pp. A1 *i* t., *ii* blk, *iii* iv–vi Contents, on B1 *1* 2–336 Rambler 141–208, 336 Explicit and coloph. (Taylor).

VII. A 1–3 B–2F^6, ($3 signed), 171 leaves.
Pp. A1 *i* t., *ii* blk, *iii* iv–vi Contents, on B1 *1* 2–336 Idler (1–103 + *22 333–36), 336 Explicit and coloph. (Taylor).

VIII. A^2 B–2H^6 2I^4 (2I4 ? blk), ($3 signed), 186 leaves.
Pp. A1 *i* t., *ii* blk, iii–iv Contents, on B1 *1* 2–55 Miscellaneous Essays, *56* blk, *57* ½t, *58* note, *59* 60–183 Political Tracts, *184* 185–366 Journey, 366 Explicit and coloph. (Hansard), + ? blk leaf.

IX. A^4 B–2M^6, ($3 signed), 208 leaves.
Pp. A1 *i* t., *ii* blk, iii–v Original Advert., *vi* blk, vii Contents, *viii* blk, on B1 1–408 Lives: Cowley–Dryden, 408 Explicit and coloph. (Hansard).

X. A^2 B–2E^6 ²2D–2E^6 2F^4 (2F4 ? blk), ($3 signed), 180 leaves.

Pp. A1 *i* t., *ii* blk, iii Contents, *iv* blk, on B1 1–353 Lives: Smith–Savage, 353 Explicit and coloph. (M'Creery), *354* blk, + ? blk leaf.

XI. *A²* B–2F⁶ *2G²* (2G2 ? blk), ($3 signed), 172 leaves.
Pp. A1 *i* t., *ii* blk, iii Contents, *iv* blk, on B1 1–337 Lives: Swift–Lyttelton, 337 Explicit (no coloph.), *338* blk + ? blk leaf.

XII. *A²* B–2Z⁶, ($3 signed), 272 leaves.
Pp. A1 *i* t., *ii* blk, *iii*–iv Contents, on B1 *1* ½t, *2* blk, *3* 4–315 Eminent persons, *316* blk, *317* ½t, *318* blk, *319* 320–423 Letters, *424* 425–32 Prayers, on 2P1–2Z6ᵛ Index, 2Z6ᵛ FINIS. and coloph. (Hodson).

Plates: Engr. port. front. vol. 3. Oval in plain surround: Samuel Johnson, L.L.D., 'W. Evans sculpsit'.
References: Courtney 164.
Notes: In J. Mawman's Trade *Catalogue* (July 1809), this edn. is listed as '12 vols. 18mo. [Trade] £1. 10s. [Retail] £2. 8s. 0d.' and in William Creech's stock sale, 7 July 1815, a copy is listed as '12 vols. royal 18mo.' (E: MS Acc. 5000, no. 1389, and Ep: Creech papers).

The 12° format is proposed with some hesitation, but on the whole seems more likely than an 18°, given the dimensions of the extant copies. The wove paper is unhelpful in deciding the question.

This is a parallel edition of Chalmers's 8° edn. 1806 (87.3W/8, above), but is less carefully printed. Subsequent 12° edns. of SJ's *Works* derive from this, with minor textual corruptions but with no evidence of editorial intervention. There are some press-figures in various volumes, not recorded, and various paper stocks occur throughout.

Copies: O (2699 f.287–98, 'George Taylor 1806');
USA: CtY, NIC ('Hester Williams Wynne the Gift of my dear Papa June 1814'), NN (vols. 5–8 only); *UK*: BMp (lacks t. in vol. 10).

87.3W/10   Works, Boston and New York   1809–12

THE | WORKS | OF | SAMUEL JOHNSON, LL.D. | A NEW EDITION. | IN TWELVE VOLUMES. | WITH | AN ESSAY ON HIS LIFE AND GENIUS, | BY ARTHUR MURPHY, ESQ. | VOL. I [–XII]. | [short parallel rule] | [BL] **Boston**; | PUBLISHED BY HASTINGS, ETHERIDGE AND BLISS. | STATE STREET. | [short dotted rule] | 1809.

Var: III. . . . NEW YORK; | PUBLISHED BY WILLIAM DURRELL. | [short dotted rule] | 1811.

IV–V. . . . NEW YORK; | PUBLISHED BY WILLIAM DURRELL. | *Paul & Thomas, Printers.* | [short dotted rule] | 1811.

VI. NEW YORK; | PUBLISHED BY WILLIAM DURRELL. | *George Long, Printer.* | [short swelled rule] | 1811.[1]

VII. NEW YORK; | PUBLISHED BY WILLIAM DURRELL. | J. ORAM, Printer. | [short swelled rule] | 1811.

VIII–XI. NEW YORK; | PUBLISHED BY WILLIAM DURRELL. | [short swelled rule] | 1811.

XII. NEW YORK; | PUBLISHED BY WILLIAM DURRELL. | [short swelled rule] | 1812.

12 vols., 12°

I. Pp. *i* t., *ii* coloph: 'Charlestown, Mass. Printed by Hastings, Etheridge & Bliss.', *iii* iv–v Advertisement ('ALEX. CHALMERS, *London*, January, 1806.'), *1* 2–129 Murphy's *Essay*, *133* 134–247 Poems &c., 247 END OF THE FIRST VOLUME.

II. Pp. *i* t., *ii* coloph. as vol. 1, *1* 2–328 Philological Tracts, 329–66 Political Essays, 367–466 Miscellaneous essays, + 2 pp. advts., 466 END OF THE SECOND VOLUME.

III. Pp. 1–81 Brumoy, 83–108 Dedications, 109–280 Adventurer (29), 281–408 Rasselas, 408 END OF THE THIRD VOLUME., no coloph.

IV. Pp. 3–368 Ramblers 1–66, 368 END OF VOL. IV., no coloph.

V. Pp. *1* 2–356 Ramblers 67–131, 356 END OF VOL. V., no coloph.

VI. Pp. *5* 6–400 Ramblers 132–208, 400 END OF VOL. VI., no coloph.

VII. Pp. *1*–2 Advertisement, ²*1* 2–363 Idler 1–103, 363 END OF VOLUME VII., no coloph.

VIII. Pp. 5–59 Miscellaneous Essays, *61–3* 64–189 Political tracts, *190* 191–373 Journey, 373 coloph: 'JANE AITKEN, PRINTER, No 71, Third-street, Philadelphia.'² and explicit: END OF THE EIGHTH VOLUME.

IX. Pp. *7* 8–408 Lives: Cowley–Dryden, 408 coloph: '[rule] | A. FAGAN, PRINTER.'

X. Pp. *5* 6–363 Lives: Smith–Savage, 363 coloph: 'JANE AITKEN, PRINTER, No 71, Third-street, Philadelphia.' and explicit: END OF THE TENTH VOLUME.

XI. Pp. *5* 6–351 Lives: Swift–Lyttelton, 351 coloph: 'JANE AITKEN, PRINTER, No 71, Third-street, Philadelphia.' and explicit: END OF THE ELEVENTH VOLUME.

XII. Pp. *1* 2–279 Lives of Eminent Persons, 283–373 Letters, 374–82 Prayers and Meditations; no *Explicit*, no coloph.

Plates: Engr. port. of SJ as front., no titling: 'New York'.
References: S&S 17840–2 [DLC, IaK, ICP, KyLOP, NBuG, NdFM, NjR, POU, ViAl, WvW].

Notes: Vols. IX–XI containing the *Lives of the Poets* are variously gathered: vol. IX in 12s, and vols. X–XI in 6s (79.4LP/24, above), suggesting different printers. The variant imprints and changing colophons also imply that Durrell quickly became the senior proprietor and enlisted the aid of various printers to produce the collection as quickly as possible. Separate issues of the various volumes as edns. of *Rambler*, *Idler*, *Journey*, or *Lives of the Poets* vary in imprints but they either retain these colophons or eliminate them; no variations in the colophons have been found.

This edn. reprints Chalmers's 1806 text, probably from the 12° edn. (87.3W/9, above), since there are minor textual inaccuracies.

Copies: MH (16466.2);

USA: CtY[2] (**1**. NY: D. imperfect, lacks vol. 1; **2**. = vols. 1–2 only), DLC (lacks vol. 1), MB, MWA[3], NN, PPU, ViU (imperfect), WiM (imperfect); *UK*: LICj ('T.P. Chandler' — 'Wᵐ. Schlatter 1816').

[1] Vols. v and vi have this imprint in LICj copy.
[2] Not in LICj copy.

87.3W/11(Prop)   Proposals for an Edition of   1809–10
                               Johnson's Works

Dr. Abercrombie's Edition of Johnson's Works. Proposals by J. and A.Y. Humphreys, Philadelphia, for publishing by subscription The Works of Samuel Johnson, L.L.D. . . . By James Abercrombie, D.D.

Some part of Abercrombie's proposal is quoted in Waingrow, *Corr.* 462 n. Nathan Drake's *Essays on the Rambler. . .* &c., (1809),[1] are cited in support of the need for a new edition, remarking deficiencies in the existing edns. The Proposals estimate an edition in about 14 vols. 8°, but it never materialized.

[1] Drake expatiated on SJ's revisions of the text of the *Rambler* as revealed by Chalmers, in i. 273–80.

87.3W/12   Works, ed. Chalmers   1810

THE | WORKS | OF | | Samuel Johnſon, ʟʟ.ᴅ. | A NEW EDITION, | IN TWELVE VOLUMES. | WITH | Aɴ ESSAY ᴏɴ ʜɪs LIFE ᴀɴᴅ GENIUS, | Bʏ ARTHUR MURPHY, Esǫ. | [short parallel rule] | VOLUME THE FIRST [–TWELFTH]. | [short total rule] | *LONDON:* | *Printed by Luke Hansard & Sons, near Lincoln's-Inn Fields,* | For J. Nichols & Son; F. &. C. Rivington; Otridge & Son; A. Strahan; Leigh & | Sotheby; G. Nicol & Son; T. Payne; W. Lowndes; G. Robinson; Wilkie | & Robinson; C. Davis; T. Egerton; Scatcherd & Letterman; J. Walker; | Vernor, Hood, & Sharpe; R. Lea; Darton & Harvey; J. Nunn; Lackington, | Allen, & Co.; J. Stockdale; J.

Cuthell; Clarke & Sons; G. Kearsley; C. Law; | J. White & Co.; Longman, Hurst, Rees, & Orme; Cadell & Davies; J. Barker; | John Richardson; J.M. Richardson; J. Booker; J. Carpenter; B. Crosby; | E. Jeffery; J. Murray; W. Miller; J. & A. Arch; Black, Parry, & | Kingsbury; S. Bagster; J. Harding; J. Mackinlay; J. Hatchard; R. H. Evans; | Matthews & Leigh; J. Mawman; J. Booth; J. Asperne; R. Scholey; | R. Baldwin; J. Faulder; Sherwood, Neely, & Jones; J. Johnson & Co.; and | T. Underwood — Deighton & Son at Cambridge; and Wilson & Son at York. | [dash] | 1810.

12 vols., 8°

I. A⁴ B–2C⁸ 2D⁴, ($4 signed), 208 leaves.

Pp. Engr. port. SJ + A1 t., A2 iii–v Advertisement ('Alexʳ. Chalmers, London, January 1806.'), *vi* vii–viii Contents, on B1 *1* 2–191 Murphy's Essay, 193–359 Poems, 360–407 Poemata, 407 coloph: 'London: Printed by Luke Hansard & Sons, near Lincoln's-Inn Fields.', *408* blk.

II. A² B–2G⁸ 2H⁴, ($4 signed), 238 leaves.

Pp. A1 t., A1ᵛ blk, A2 iii–iv Contents, on B1 *1* ½t: Philological Tracts, *2* blk, *3* 4–336 Philological Tracts, 337–75 Political essays, 376–471 Miscellaneous Essays, 471 coloph., *472* blk.

III. *A*² B–2E⁸ 2F⁴ 2G², ($4 signed), 224 leaves.

Pp. A1 t., A2 *iii*–iv Contents, On B1 *1* 2–107 Dissertation, Dedications and Preface, *108* blk, 109–300 Adventurer (29), 301–444 Rasselas, 444 coloph.

IV. A⁴ B–2F⁸ (2F8 blk), ($4 signed), 228 leaves.

Pp. A1 ½t Works vol. iv., A1ᵛ blk, A2 t., A2ᵛ blk, A3 v–viii Contents, on B1 *1* 2–446 text Ramblers 1–70, *447–48* blk.

V. *a*² b² B–2E⁸ 2F⁶, ($4 signed), 226 leaves.

Pp. a1 ½t vol. v., a1ᵛ blk, a2 t., a2ᵛ blk, b1 v–viii Contents, on B1 *1* 2–443 text Ramblers 71–140, 443 coloph., *444* blk.

VI. A² b² B–2B⁸ 2C⁶, ($4 signed), 202 leaves.

Pp. A1 ½t vol. vi., A1ᵛ blk, A2 t., A2ᵛ blk, b1 v–vii Contents, *viii* blk, on B1 *1* 2–396 text Ramblers 141–208, 396 coloph.

VII. A⁴ B–2D⁸, ($4 signed), 212 leaves.

Pp. A1 ½t vol. vii., A1ᵛ blk, A2 t., A2ᵛ blk, A3 v–vii Contents, *viii* Advertisement, on B1 *1* 2–410 Idlers (1–103), *411* 412–15 Idler 22*, 415 coloph., *416* blk.

VIII. *a*² B–2C⁸ 2D⁶, ($4 signed), 208 leaves.

Pp. a1 t., a1ᵛ blk, a2 *iii*–iv Contents, on B1 *1* 2–61 Miscellaneous essays, *62* blk, *63* ½t Political Tracts, 64 Note, *65* 66–204 text, *205* 206–412 Journey, 412 coloph.

IX. A⁴ B–2F⁸ 2G⁴ 2H², ($4 signed), 234 leaves.

Pp. A1 t., A1ᵛ blk, A2 iii–v Original Advertisement (1779–80), *vi* blk, vii Contents, *viii* blk, on B1 1–460 Lives: Cowley–Dryden, 460 coloph: 'Printed by John Nichols and Son, Red Lion Passage, Fleet Street, London.'

X. a² B–2C⁸ 2D², ($4 signed), 204 leaves.

Pp. a1 t., a1ᵛ blk, a2 iii Contents, *iv* blk, on B1 1–404 Lives: Smith–Savage, 404 coloph. as vol. 9.

XI. a² B–2B⁸ 2C⁴ (–2C4 ? blk), ($2 signed), 198 leaves.

Pp. a1 t., a1ᵛ blk, a2 iii Contents, *iv* blk, on B1 1–389 Lives: Swift–Lyttelton, 389 coloph. as vol. 9, *390* blk + 1 blk leaf.

XII. *A²* B–2M⁸, ($2 signed), 274 leaves.

Pp. A1 t., A1ᵛ blk, A2 iii–iv Contents, on B1 *1* ½t Lives of Eminent Persons, *2* blk, 3–328 text Eminent persons, *329* ½t Letters, *330* blk, *331* 332–438 text Letters, *439* ½t Prayers, *440* blk, 441–50 Prayers, on 2G2–2M8 Index, 2M8 coloph. as vol. 9, 2M8ᵛ blk.

Plates: Engr. port. front. vol. 1: (as. 87.3W/8, 1806, above)
References: Courtney 164–5.
Notes: 'Advertisement' at I. iii–v, by Alexander Chalmers, 'London. January 1806.'

Two volumes of *Debates* were appended to this edn. dated 1811, with '. . . Thirteenth [–Fourteenth], Forming the First [–Second] Volume of Debates in Parliament.' (87.3W/1.2/2, above). The coloph. (t.ᵛ) reads: 'Printed by S. Hamilton, Weybridge.' This edn. is a reprint of Chalmers's 8° of 1806 (87.3W/8, above) without further editorial attention.

Vols. 4–6 were overrun to form a separate issue as the 'Sixteenth Edition' of *The Rambler*, 3 vols. 1810 (50.3R/48, above), and vols. 9–11 were similarly overrun in a separate issue of the *Lives of the Poets*, 3 vols. 1810 (79.4LP/21, above).

Copies: O (2699 d. 34–49 [Camera]); *Debates* (8° H. 76. BS);

USA: Hyde (Adam), ICN, ICU, IU, NjP, ViU (imperfect); *Can*: CaOHM; *Japan*: [Kyoto]; *UK*: AWn (imperfect), AWu, BMp (164876–87), Ck, DUc, E, Eu (Debates), L (1509/1349), MRu², Op ('G. Collier' — Stoke Newington PL), SHu.

87.3W/13   Works, ed. Chalmers   1816

THE | WORKS | OF | Samuel Johnſon, ʟʟ.ᴅ. | *A NEW EDITION* | IN TWELVE VOLUMES. | WITH | *AN ESSAY ON HIS LIFE AND GENIUS,* | Bʏ ARTHUR MURPHY, Esǫ. | [short parallel rule] | VOLUME THE FIRST [– TWELFTH]. | [short total rule] | LONDON: | PRINTED FOR

NICHOLS AND SON; F. C. AND J. RIVINGTON; A. STRAHAN; LEIGH | AND SOTHEBY; G. NICOL AND SON; G. WILKIE; C. DAVIS; T. EGERTON; J. | DEIGHTON AND SONS; J. NUNN; LACKINGTON AND CO.; J. CUTHELL; CLARKE | AND SONS; LAW AND WHITTAKER; LONGMAN, HURST, REES, ORME, AND | BROWN; CADELL AND DAVIES; J. OTRIDGE; J. BOOKER; CARPENTER AND SON; | E. JEFFERY; J. AND A. ARCH; BLACK AND CO; J. BLACK AND SON; J. BOOTH; | JOHN RICHARDSON; S. BAGSTER; J. HATCHARD; W. GINGER; R.H. EVANS; | J. MAWMAN; R. SCHOLEY; BALDWIN, CRADOCK, AND JOY; J. ASPERNE; SHER- | WOOD, NEELEY AND JONES; GALE AND FENNER; T. HAMILTON; J. PORTER; | JOHN ROBINSON; J. SHELDON; R. SAUNDERS; WALKER AND EDWARDS; AND | SIMPKIN AND MARSHALL. | 1816
  12 vols., 8°

  I. A^4 B–2C^8 2D^6, (\$2 signed; 'VOL. I.' on \$1), 210 leaves.
  Pp. A1 t., A1^v coloph: 'Printed by Nichols, Son, and Bentley, Red Lion Passage, Fleet Street, London.' A2 *iii* iv–v Advert. (Chalmers, 1806), v Note on Malone's notes to Lives, *vi* blk, *vii*–viii Contents, on B1 *1* 2–191 Murphy's Essay, 192 Parr's Epitaph on SJ, *193* ½t, *194* blk, 195–359 Poems, 360–411 Poemata, *Explicit*: 411 END OF THE FIRST VOLUME. *412* coloph: as A1^v (Nichols).

  II. A^2 B–2G^8 2H^4 (–2H4 ? blk), 237 leaves.
  Pp. A1 t., A1^v coloph. as vol. 1, a2–2^v Contents, on B1 *1* ½t, *2* blk. *3* 4–280 Philological Tracts, 281–318 Political essays, 319–415 Misc. essays, 416–70 Appendix: Misc. Obs. on Macbeth, 470 *Explicit*: END OF THE SECOND VOLUME. and coloph. as vol. 1.

  III. A^2 B–2G^8, 234 leaves.
  Pp. A1 t., A1^v blk, A2–2^v Contents, on B1 *1* 2–107 Dissertations &c., *108* blk, 109–300 Adventurers (29), *301* ½t, *302* note, 303–444 Rasselas, 445–63 Tales, *464* coloph.

  IV. A^4 (–A4 ? blk) B–2F^8 (–2F7 ? blk), 226 leaves.
  Pp. A1 t., A1^v coloph: 'Printed by A. Strahan, New-Street-Square, London.', A2 *iii* iv–vi Contents, on B1 *1* 2–464 Ramblers 1–70, 464 *Explicit* and coloph. (Nichols, as prec.).

  V. A^4 (–A4 ? blk) B–2E^8 2F^6, 225 leaves.
  Pp. A1 t., A1^v coloph. (Strahan), A2 *iii* iv–vi Contents, on B1 *1* 2–443 Ramblers 71–140, *444* coloph. (Nichols, as prec.).

  VI. A^4 (–A4 ? blk) B–2B^8 2C^8 (–2C8 ? blk), 202 leaves.

Pp. A1 t., A1ᵛ coloph. (Strahan), A2 *iii* iv–vi Contents, on B1 *1* 2–397 Ramblers 141–208, 397 *Explicit* and coloph. (Nichols), *398* blk.

VII. *A*⁴ (–A4 ? blk) B–2C⁸ 2D⁴ 2E1, 208 leaves.

Pp. A1 t., A1ᵛ coloph. (Strahan), A2 *iii* iv–v Contents, on B1 *1* 2–410 Idlers 1–103, 410 *Explicit* and coloph. (Strahan).

VIII. *A*² B–2C⁸ 2D⁶, 208 leaves.

Pp. A1 t., A1ᵛ coloph. (Strahan), A2 *iii*–iv Contents, on B1 *1* 2–61 Miscellaneous essays, *62* blk, *63* ½t, 64 note, *65* 66–204 Political Tracts, *205* 206–412 Journey, 412 *Explicit* and coloph. (Strahan).

IX. a⁴ B–2F⁸ 2G⁶, ($2 signed), 234 leaves.

Pp. a1 t., a1ᵛ coloph. (Strahan), a2 *iii* iv–v Original advert. to Prefaces, *vi* blk, *vii* Contents, *viii* blk, on B1 *1* 2–460 Lives: Cowley–Dryden, 460 *Explicit* and coloph. (Strahan).

X. A² B–2C⁸ 2D⁴, 206 leaves.

Pp. A1 t., A1ᵛ coloph. (Strahan), A2 Contents, A2ᵛ blk, on B1 *1* 2–408 Lives: Smith–Savage, 408 *Explicit* and coloph. (Strahan).

XI. *A*² B–2B⁸ 2C⁴, 198 leaves.

Pp. A1 t., A1ᵛ coloph. (Strahan), A2 Contents, A2ᵛ blk, on B1 *1* 2–391 Lives: Swift–Lyttelton, 391 *Explicit* and coloph. (Strahan), *392* blk.

XII. *A*² B–2M⁸, 274 leaves.

Pp. A1 t., A1ᵛ coloph. (Strahan), A2 *iii*–iv Contents, on B1 *1* ½t, *2* blk *3* 4–328 Lives of Eminent persons, *329* ½t, *330* blk, *331* 332–438 Letters, *439* ½t, *440* blk, 441–50 Prayers, on 2G2–2M8ᵛ Index (unpaged), 2M8ᵛ coloph. (Strahan).

Plate: Engr. port. front. vol. 1: in square frame: 'Engraved by W.T. Fry from an original Picture by Sir Joshua Reynolds. Samuel Johnson LLD. Published May 29 1816, by T. Cadell, & W. Davies, Strand.'

References: Courtney 165.

Notes: This edn. is mainly a reprint of Chalmers's 8° of 1806 (87.3W/8, above), save that he added 'The Fountains' (1766; iii. 445–63), and two poems: Translation of Medea ('The rites derived . . .' *Poems*² 221; i. 411), and 'Friendship, an Ode' (*Poems*² 36; i. 409), together with Malone's annotation on the *Lives of the Poets*, (Preface, I. v).

Andrew Strahan printed 1,500 copies of vols. VII–XII, with tt. for vols. IV–XII, in August 1816 (L: Add. MS 48816, fo. 147); the set was published at £4. 16s. in boards (*Morning Chron.* 6 Sept. 1816). Notes by Malone on the *Lives of the Poets* were included in this edn. and 500 copies of these vols. were separately issued as 79.4LP/26, above; similarly 500 copies of vol. 7, *Idler* (58.4Id/27, above), and vol. 8, *Journey* (75.1J/17) were also overprinted and separately issued.

Baldwin, Cradock, & Joy invoiced Bell & Bradfute (Edinburgh) for 2 copies of this edn. at £3. 2s. each, on 16 Jan. 1819, and a further invoice from Francis, Charles, & John Rivington, for 2 more copies on 10 March 1819 is docketed '[none left]'.[1]

Copies: O (8° H. 64–75 BS);

USA: CtY (– vol. 3), Hyde ('Ewart' — Adam), NN, [PBm, PPSwarth], ViU, WiM; *UK*: [BMp ? 8°/12° 835765–76)], Gu, HLu (+ *Debates*, 1811), LCu, NCu (lacks vols. 2, 5, 8), NOu, NOW, Oef.

---

[1] E: (MS Dep. 317, box 5). The docket may mean only that Bell & Bradfute had run out of stock, but it is more likely that the whole edition was exhausted.

87.3W/14 Works, ed. Chalmers 1816

THE | WORKS | OF | Samuel Johnson, LL.D. | A NEW EDITION. | IN TWELVE VOLUMES. | WITH | *AN ESSAY ON HIS LIFE AND GENIUS;* | By ARTHUR MURPHY, Esq. | [short double rule] | VOLUME THE FIRST [– TWELFTH]. | [short double rule] | LONDON: PRINTED BY | *G. Woodfall, Angel Court, Skinner Street,* | For Nichols and Son, F. C. and J. Rivington, A. Strahan, | G. Nicol and Son, G. Wilkie, C. Davis, T. Egerton, | J. Deighton and Sons, J. Nunn, Lackington, Allen and Co. | J. Cuthell, Clarke and Sons, Law and Whittaker, Longman, | Hurst, Rees, Orme and Brown, Cadell and Davies, J. Otridge, | J. Booker, Carpenter and Son, E. Jeffery, J. and A. Arch, | Black and Co. J. Black and Son, J. Booth, John Richardson, | S. Bagster, J. Hatchard, W. Ginger, R.H. Evans, | J. Mawman, R. Scholey, Baldwin, Cradock and Joy, | J. Asperne, Sherwood, Neely and Jones, Gale and Fenner, | T. Hamilton, J. Porter, John Robinson, R. Sheldon, | R. Saunders, Walker and Edwards, *and,* Simpkin and | Marshall. | [short rule] | 1816.

Var: VII–XII . . . *Luke Hansard & Sons, near Lincoln's-Inn Fields,* . . .

12 vols., 18°

I. a⁴ B–2E⁶ 2F², ($3 signed; 'VOL. I.' on $1), 168 leaves.

Pp. Engr. front. port. + a1 t., a1ᵛ blk, a2 *iii* iv–vi Advert. (Chalmers, 'July, 1816.'), *vii*–viii Contents, on B1 *1* 2–141 Murphy's Essay, *142* blk, *143* ½t Poems., *144* blk, *145* 146–285 Poems, *286* 287–326 Poemata, 327–8 Additional poems, 328 coloph: 'G. Woodfall, Printer, Angel Court, Skinner Street, London.'

II. *A*² B–2M⁶ 2N⁴ 2O⁴, 214 leaves.

Pp. A1 t., A1ᵛ blk, A2 Contents, on B1 *1* ½t, *2* blk, *3* 4–299 Philological Tracts, *300* 301–33 Political essays, *334* 335–423 Essays & Tales, 423 coloph. (Woodfall), *424* blk.

III. *A*² B–2N⁶ 2O 1–3, 215 leaves.

Pp. A1 t., A1ᵛ blk, A2 *iii*–iv Contents, on B1 *1* 2–103 Essays, *104* blk, *105* 106–286 Adventurers (29), *289* 290–426 Rasselas, 426 coloph. (Woodfall).

IV. a⁴ B–2L⁶ 2M² 2N², 206 leaves.
Pp. a1 t., a1ᵛ blk, a2 iii–vii Contents, *viii* blk, on B1 *1* 2–403 Ramblers 1–70, 430 coloph. (Woodfall), *404* blk.

V. a⁴ B–2M⁶ (–2M6 ? blk), 207 leaves.
Pp. a1 t., a1ᵛ blk, a2 iii–vii Contents, *viii* blk, on B1 *1* 2–406 Ramblers 71–140, 406 coloph. (Woodfall).

VI. a 1–3 B–2F⁶, 171 leaves.
Pp. a1 t., a1ᵛ blk, a2 *iii* iv–vi Contents, on B1 *1* 2–336 Ramblers 141–208, 336 coloph. (Woodfall).

VII. *A*⁴ B–2F⁶, 172 leaves.
Pp. A1 t., A1ᵛ blk, A2 iii–vii Contents, *viii* blk, on B1 *1* 2–333 Idlers (1–103), 333–6 Idler *22, 336 coloph: 'Printed by Luke Hansard & Sons, near Lincoln's-Inn Fields, London.'

VIII. *A*² B–2H⁶ 2I 1–3, ($3 (2H1 as H) signed), 185 leaves.
Pp. A1 t., A1ᵛ blk, A2 iii–iv Contents, on B1 *1* 2–55 Miscellaneous essays, *56* blk, 57 ½t, 58 note, *59* 60–183 Political Tracts, *184* 185–366 Journey, 366 coloph. (Hansard).

IX. *A*² B–2M⁶, 206 leaves.
Pp. A1 t., A1ᵛ blk, A2 iii Contents, *iv* blk, on B1 1–408 Lives: Cowley–Dryden, 408 coloph. (Hansard).

X. *A*² B–2G⁶ 2H1–3, 179 leaves.
Pp. A1 t., A1ᵛ blk, A2 iii Contents, *iv* blk, on B1 1–353 Lives: Smith–Savage, *354* coloph. (Hansard).

XI. *A*² B–2F⁶, 170 leaves.
Pp. A1 t., A1ᵛ blk, A2 iii Contents, *iv* blk, on B1 1–336 Lives: Swift–Lyttelton, 336 coloph. (Hansard).

XII. *A*² B–2Z⁶, 272 leaves.
Pp. A1 t., A1ᵛ blk, A2 iii–iv Contents, on B1 *1* ½t, *2* blk, *3* 4–315 Lives of Eminent persons, *316* blk, *317* ½t. *318* blk, 319–423 Letters, 424–32 Prayers, on 2P1–2Z6ᵛ Index (unpaged), 2Z6ᵛ coloph. (Hansard), *Explicit*: FINIS.

Notes: Published as 'a pocket edition, Royal 18mo. £2. 14s. in boards'. Preface is signed by Alex. Chalmers, 'July, 1816'. It is a reprint of Chalmers's 12° edn. of 1806 (87.3W/9, above), with all textual faults, and without the pieces added to the canon in 1816, 8° (87.3W/13, above), save that the Translation from Euripides is retained (i. 328).

Copies: O (Vet. A6 f.143);
USA: CtY (imperfect lacks vol. 3), MH; *UK*: [C], Gu, L (12269. b.23).

87.3W/15a   Works, Alnwick edition   1816

THE | [BL] **Works** | OF | SAMUEL JOHNSON, LL.D. | WITH | *HIS LIFE,* | BY | JAMES BOSWELL, ESQ. | [short wavy rule] | IN TWELVE VOLUMES. | [short wavy rule] | VOL. I [– XII]. | [parallel rule] | [*NAMED CONTENTS*] | [parallel rule] | [BL] **Alnwick:** | PRINTED BY AND FOR J. GRAHAM. | [short swelled rule] | 1816.
   10 vols., 12°

   I. A^2 B–2L⁶ 2M⁴ (–2M4 ? blk), 204 leaves.
   Pp. Port. front. + A1 *i* t., *ii* blk, *iii*–iv Contents, on B1 *1* 2–402 text (1–158 Poems, 161–402 Philological Tracts).

   II. A^4 (–A4 = ? 2I1) B² C–2H⁶ 2I1, ($3 (2F1 as F1) signed), 180 leaves.
   Pp. A1 *i* t., *ii* blk, *iii*–iv Contents, on B1 *1* 2–354 text Ramblers 1–77.

   III. A^4 (–A4 ? blk) B² C–2H⁶ 2I⁴, 184 leaves.
   Pp. A1 *i* t., *ii* blk, *iii* iv–v Contents, *vi* blk, on B1 *1* 2–360 text Ramblers 78–154; p. 331 as 319.

   IV. A^4 (–A4 ?) B–2G⁶ 2I², 180 leaves.
   Pp. A1 *i* t., *ii* blk, *iii* iv–v Contents, *vi* blk, on B1 *1* 2–368 text (1–226 Ramblers 155–208, 227–368 Adventurers (29)).

   V. A^4 (–A4 ?) B–2L⁶ 2M², 203 leaves.
   Pp. A1 *i* t., *ii* blk, *iii* iv–v Contents, *vi* Advertisement, on B1 *1* 2–399 text (1–287 Idlers 1–103, 287–90 Idler *22; 293–399 Rasselas), *400* blk.

   VI. [π1] A² B² C–2L⁶ 2M⁴ (–2M4 ?), 200 leaves.
   Pp. *i* t., *ii* blk, *iii*–iv Contents, on B1 *1* 2–394 text Lives: Cowley–Rowe.

   VII. π1 *A*1 B–2K⁶ 2L⁶ (± 2L6) 2M⁶, 206 leaves.
   Pp. *i* t., *ii* blk, *iii* Contents, *iv* blk, on B1 *1* 2–407 text Lives: Addison–Pope, *408* blk.

   VIII. A² B⁴ C–2I⁶ 2K², 188 leaves.
   Pp. *i* t., *ii* blk, *iii*–iv Contents, on B1 *1* 2–126 text Lives: Pitt–Lyttelton, *127–8* blk, 129–372 Eminent persons.

   IX. A^2 B² C–2K⁶ 2L⁴ (–2L4 ? blk), 193 leaves.
   Pp. *i* t., *ii* blk, *iii*–iv Contents, on B1 *1* 2–382 text (1–154 Journey, 157–290 Political Tracts, essays &c.).

   X. A^2 B² C–2D⁶ 2E², ²A–B² C–M⁴, (F2 as 'L2'), 200 leaves.

Pp. *i* t., *ii* blk, ²*i*–ii Contents, on B1 *1* 2–310 text (279 as 297) (1–222 Miscellanies and Dedications, 223–301 Letters, 303–10 Prayers), on ²A–M Index (44 leaves).

References: Burman 26.

Notes: Published with Boswell's *Life* as suppl. vols. XI–XII (though paged as 4 vols.). For a reissue in 1818, see below 87.3W/15b. Murphy's *Essay* is not included. Some additions were made to the canon on the basis of attributions by Boswell but mainly deriving from *Works*, xiv (1788), viz. Account of Tytler's *Enquiry* (*Gents. Mag.* 1760; x. 180–8), Advertisement to Lennox's *Brumoy* (1759, iii. 128; ix. 320–1), Papers concerning Dr Dodd (1777; x. 64–88), 'The Fountains' (1766; xi. 31–44), Letter on behalf of Milton's Granddaughter (*Gen. Adv.* 1750; x. 50), *Marmor Norfolciense* (1739; x. 89–112), 'Observations on the Treaties' (*Lit. Mag.* 1756; ix. 298–302), Preface to Payne's *Draughts* (1756; x. 201), 'Reflections upon Portugal' (*Univ. Vis.*, 1756; ix. 291–7). Though the text is mainly that of 1801 (87.3W/5, above), there is textual evidence of some independent editorial activity.

Copies: BMp (484427–38); *USA*: CtY (Im J637 B816), NIC; *UK*: [E].

87.3W/15b   Works, Alnwick edition, reissue   1818

THE | [hollow and shaded] WORKS | OF | SAMUEL JOHNSON, LL.D. | [short wavy rule] | *A NEW EDITION.* | [short diamond rule] | IN TEN VOLUMES. | [short diamond rule] | VOL. I [– X]. | [medium wavy rule] | POEMS | AND PHILOLOGICAL TRACTS. [– &c.] | [double rule] | *LONDON:* | PRINTED FOR G. OFFOR, TOWER-HILL; J. REID, BERWICK; | J. FINLAY, NEWCASTLE; W. BARNES, NORTH SHEILDS; | J. GRAHAM, SUNDERLAND; G. ANDREWS, DURHAM; AND | J. GRAHAM, ALNWICK. | [short rule] | 1818.

Stet: NORTH SHEILDS; Hyde *reads* SHIELDS;

10 vols., 12°. Collation and contents as 87.3W/15a, above.

Paper: (uncut: 7½ × 4½ in.).

References: Courtney 165–6.

Notes: A reissue of Graham's Alnwick, edn. 1816 (87.3W/15a, above), with cancelled tt. The companion reissue of Boswell's *Life* is in 4 vols. For Offor, see *DNB*, and Boase, *Modern English Biography* (1892-1921), ii. 1216–17.

Copies: O (2699 e. 104–13);

USA: Hyde (Adam; boards, uncut); *Can*: CaOHM (in 5 vols.); *Japan*: [Kyoto]; *UK*: BMp (515994–6003), E (ABS.2.86.39), JDF, L (12268. aaaa.17).

87.3W/16a   Works, Dublin   1816–17

THE | WORKS | OF | [BL] **Samuel Johnson, L.L.D.** | CONSISTING OF | [2 cols., col. a:] THE RAMBLER. | PAPERS of THE ADVENTURER. | THE IDLER. | A JOURNEY TO THE WEST- | ERN ISLAND OF SCOT- | LAND. | LIVES OF THE ENGLISH | POETS. | POEMS. | [vertical rule, col. b:] LIVES OF EMINENT PER- | SONS. | THE HISTORY OF RASSELAS, | PRINCE OF ABISSINIA. | PHILOLOGICAL TRACTS. | MISCELLANEOUS ESSAYS. | POLITICAL TRACTS. | POLITICAL ESSAYS. | LETTERS, ETC. | [across the measure:] *IN EIGHT VOLUMES.* | VOL. I [– VIII]. | DUBLIN: | PRINTED BY J. CHRISTIE, 17, ROSS-LANE. | 1816. [– 1817.]

8 vols., 8°

I. A^8 (–A8 ? = 4C1) B–4B^4 4C1, ($1 (4C1 as 4B) signed; 'VOL. I.' on $1), 288 leaves.

Pp. A1 gen. t., A1^v blk, A2 Rambler t., A2^v blk, A3 *iii* iv–vi Contents, on A4 *3* 4–570 text Ramblers 1–102.

II. A^4 B–4B^4 4C^2, 286 leaves.

Pp. A1 gen. t., A1^v blk, A2 Rambler t., A2^v blk, A3 *v* vi–viii Contents, on B1 *1* 2–563 text: Ramblers 103–208, *564* blk.

III. A^4 B–4B^4 4C^2, 286 leaves.

Pp. A1 gen. t., A1^v blk, A2 Idler t., A2^v advert., A3 *v* vi–viii Contents, on B1 *1* 2–352 text Idlers 1–103, 352–6 Idler *22, *357* ½t Adventurer, *358* blk, *359* 360–502 text Adventurers (24), *503* ½t Poems, *504* blk, *505* 506–64 Poems (English, and 'Messia' 561–4).

IV. A^4 (–A4 ? blk), B–4A^4 4B^4 (–4B4 ? blk), 284 leaves.

Pp. A1 gen. t., A1^v blk, A2 Contents, A3 Journey t., A3^v blk, on B1 *1* 2–195 text: Journey, *196* blk, *197* ½t, *198* blk, *199* 200–501 Eminent persons, *502* blk, *503* ½t Essays, *504* blk, *505* 506–54 Tales, *555* 556–66 Observations on State of Affairs.[1]

V. A^4 B–4B^4 4C^2, 286 leaves.

Pp. A1 gen. t. '1817', A1^v blk, A2 Lives t., A2^v blk, A3 Contents, A3^v blk, A4–4^v advert., on B1 *1* 2–564 Lives: Cowley–Fenton.

VI. A^4 (–A4 ? = 4D1) B–4C^4 4D1, 288 leaves.

Pp. A1 gen. t. '1817', A1^v blk, A2 Lives t., A2^v blk, A3 Contents, A3^v blk, on B1 *1* 2–569 Lives: Prior–Lyttelton, *570* blk.

VII. A^4 (–A4 ? = 4D1) B–4C^4 4D1, 288 leaves.

Pp. A1 gen. t. '1817', A1^v blk, A2 *iii*–iv Contents, *v* ½t Rasselas, *vi* blk, on B1 *1* 2–136 text Rasselas, *137* ½t 'Irene', *138* Note, *139–41* 142–221 text Irene,

222 blk, *223* ½t, *224* 225–532 Philological essays, *533* ½t, *534* blk, *535* 536–69 Political tracts, *570* blk.

VIII. *A*⁴ (–A4 ? = 4D1) B–4C⁴ 4D1, 288 leaves.

Pp. A1 gen. t. '1817', A1ᵛ blk, A2 *i*–ii Contents, A3–3ᵛ List of Subscribers, on B1 *1* 2–119 Political tracts, *120* blk, *121* ½t, *122* blk, *123* 124–270 Political essays, *271* ½t Letters, *272* blk, 273–416 Letters, *417* 418–71 Essays and reviews, *472* blk. *473* 474–510 Poemata, *511* 512–19 Prayers, *520* blk. *521* 522–48 Life of SJ, on 4A3–4D1ᵛ Index (unpaged), 4D1ᵛ *Explicit*: FINIS.

Notes: The latter four volumes are dated 1817. This is a reprint from the 1801 edn. (87.3W/5, above), with the addition in vol. 3 of the 'Ode on Friendship' (545–6; *Poems*² 36–9) and in vol. 8, of several letters (*Letters* 107, 140, 147, 352, 373, 378, 380, and 517, all of which were to be found in Boswell's *Life*). This edition does not however adopt Chalmers's canonical modifications of 1806 (87.3W/8, above).

   Copies: BMp (650042–9, '1816–17');

   USA: Hyde ('Reade', uncut); *Japan*: [Kyoto].

---

¹ A separate copy of vol. 4, formerly 'Arthur Conan Doyle', containing the *Journey* and *Lives of Eminent Persons*, pp. 566, is catalogued as an edn. of *Journey*, 1816, at TxU (DA.880.H4.J6.1816. HRC), but does not constitute a distinct issue.

87.3W/16b   Works, Dublin, reissue   1817

A reissue of Christie's Dublin edn., 1816–7, above, with all vols. dated '1817'. Not examined.

   Copies: *Eir*: Dt.

87.3W/17   Works, new edition   1820

THE | WORKS | OF | SAMUEL JOHNSON, LL.D. | A NEW EDITION. | IN TWELVE VOLUMES. | TO WHICH IS PREFIXED, | AN ESSAY ON HIS LIFE AND GENIUS, | BY ARTHUR MURPHY, ESQ. | [short diamond rule] | VOL. I [– XII]. | CONTAINING LIFE AND POEMS. [– &c.] | [medium total rule] | LONDON: | PRINTED FOR G. WALKER, J. AKERMAN, E. EDWARDS, J. HARWOOD, W. ROBINSON | AND SONS, LIVERPOOL; E. THOMSON, MANCHESTER; J. NOBLE, HULL; | J. WILSON, BERWICK; W. WHYTE AND CO. EDINBURGH; AND R. GRIFFIN | AND CO. GLASGOW. | J. Haddon, Printer, Tabernacle Walk. | [dash] | 1820.

   12 vols., 8°

I. *a*² A–X⁸ Y⁴, 174 leaves.

Pp. Engr. port. 1 leaf + a1 *i* t., *ii* blk, *iii* iv–v Contents, *vi* blk, on A1 *1* 2–133 Murphy's *Essay*, *135–7* 138–344 Poems and Poemata.

II. a² B–2E⁸ 2F⁴ (2F4 blk), 222 leaves.
Pp. a1 t., a1ᵛ blk, a2 *iii*–iv Contents, B1 *1* ½t, *2* blk, *3* 4–280 Philological Tracts, *281* 282–318 Political essays, *319* 320–438 Miscellaneous essays, + blk leaf.

III. *A²* B–2E⁸ 2F⁴ 2G² (2G2 blk), 224 leaves.
Pp. A1 t., A1ᵛ blk, A2 *iii*–iv Contents, on B1 *1* 2–136 Essays, *137* 138–297 Adventurers (24), *298* blk, *299* 300–442 Rasselas, + blk leaf.

IV. π² a² B–2F⁸ (2F8 blk), (a in *italic*), 228 leaves.
Pp. π1 blk, π2 t., π2ᵛ blk, a1 *iii* iv–vi Contents, B1 *1* 2–446 Ramblers 1–70 + blk leaf.

V. *A⁴* (–A1) B–2F⁸ (2F7–8 blk), 227 leaves.
Pp. A2 t., A2ᵛ blk, A3 *iii* iv–v Contents, *vi* blk, on B1 *1* 2–443 Ramblers 71–140, *444* blk, + 2 blk leaves.

VI. π1 *A²* B–2C⁸ (−2C8 blk ? = π1), 202 leaves.
Pp. π1 t., π1ᵛ blk, A1 *iii* iv–v Contents, *vi* blk, on B1 *1* 2–397 Ramblers 141–208, *398* blk.

VII. π² A² B–2C⁸ 2D⁴, 208 leaves.
Pp. π1 blk, π2 t., π2ᵛ blk, A1 *iii* iv–v Contents, *vi* blk, on B1 *1* 2–408 Idlers (1–103, only).

VIII. *A²* B–2C⁸ 2D⁶, 208 leaves.
Pp. A1 t., A1ᵛ blk, A2 *iii* iv Contents, on B1 *1* 2–61 Miscellaneous essays, *62* blk, *63* ½t, *64* 65–204 Political Tracts, *205* 206–412 Journey.

IX. *A²* B–2F⁸ 2G² (2G2 blk), 228 leaves.
Pp. A1 t., A1ᵛ blk, A2 *iii* Contents, *iv* blk, on B1 *1* 2–447 Lives: Cowley–Dryden (383–4 repeated), *448* blk, + 1 blk leaf.

X. *A²* B–2C⁸ 2D² (2D2 blk), 204 leaves.
Pp. A1 t., A1ᵛ blk, A2 Contents, A2ᵛ blk, on B1 *1* 2–402 Lives: Smith–Savage, + 1 blk leaf.

XI. *A²* B–2B⁸ 2C⁴ (2C4 blk), 198 leaves.
Pp. A1 t., A1ᵛ blk. A2 Contents, A2ᵛ blk, on B1 *1* 2–389 Lives: Swift–Lyttelton, *390* blk, + 1 blk leaf.

XII. *a*1 b² A–2E⁸ 2F⁴, 231 leaves.
Pp. a1 t., a1ᵛ blk, b1 *iii* iv–vi Contents, on A1 *1* 2–334 Lives of Eminent persons, *335* ½t, *336* blk, *337* 338–444 Selected Letters, *445* 446–55 Prayers, *456* blk.

Colophon: I (344), XII (455): 'Printed by Walker & Greig, Edinburgh.' II (438), III (442): 'Barnard and Farley, Skinner-Street, London.' XI (389): 'Printed by J. Haddon, Tabernacle Walk, Finchley.' No colophons in IV–X.

Plate: Engr. port. front., Square frame with orn. corners: 'Samuel Johnson, LLD. Engraved by Freeman from an original Drawing by Bartolozzi. London Published by Thomas Tegg, No. 111, Cheapside, May 20ᵗʰ 1819.'

References: *Adam Library* ii. 31.

Notes: The wove paper (wmk.: '1819') does not help towards the establishment of the inferred blank leaves. The absence of colophons may point to intended separate publication of the periodical essays (cf. Rambler, 1820, 50.3R/54, above), and of the Lives of the Poets. There is no index to this collection.

Published at £4. 4s., but by 1823 reduced to £2. 18s.[1] Murphy's *Essay* was issued separately, see above 87.3W/2.1/3. This edition did not adopt the canonical changes made by Chalmers in 1806 (87.3W/8, above) but derives from Murphy's last edn. of 1801 (87.3W/5, above).

Copies: O (2699 e. 390, 'James Cazalet, Halsted, Kent.');
USA: CtY, Hyde (Adam), MH² (**1**. 16464.4), NN, PPL, PPU; *Japan*: [Kyoto]; *UK*: BMp (477477–88), DUNu (lacks vol. 9), LICj (vol. 1 only, uncut); *Eir*: Dt ('Broadhead', boards, uncut).

[1] D. A. Talboys, *Catalogue* (1822–3), part III (O: 2593 e.86).

87.3W/18 Works, ed. Chalmers 1823

THE | WORKS | OF | SAMUEL JOHNSON, LL.D. | *A NEW EDITION* | IN TWELVE VOLUMES. | WITH | *AN ESSAY ON HIS LIFE AND GENIUS*, | By ARTHUR MURPHY, Esǫ. | [short rule] | VOLUME THE FIRST [– TWELFTH]. | [short rule] | LONDON: | PRINTED FOR F. C. AND J. RIVINGTON; G. AND W. NICOL; T. EGERTON; | LONGMAN, HURST, REES, ORME, AND BROWN; T. CADELL; J. NUNN; | J. CUTHELL; J. AND W.T. CLARKE; J. BOOKER; J. CARPENTER; JEF- | FERY AND SON; J. AND A. ARCH; J. BOOTH; J. RICHARDSON; HATCHARD | AND SON; W. GINGER; R.H. EVANS; J. MAWMAN; R. SCHOLEY; BALD- | WIN, CRADOCK, AND JOY; SHERWOOD AND JONES; T. HAMILTON; J. | ROBINSON; R. SAUNDERS; HARDING, MAVOR, AND LEPARD; G. AND W. | B. WHITTAKER; LLOYD AND SON; J. BOHN; T. TEGG; T. WILKIE; OGLE | AND CO.; SIMPKIN AND MARSHALL; KINGSBURY, PARBURY, AND ALLEN; | G. MACKIE; J. PORTER; G. GREENLAND; W. MASON; J. COLLINGWOOD; | W. WOOD; HURST AND ROBINSON; J. RACKHAM; AND DEIGHTON AND | SONS, CAMBRIDGE; BRODIE, DOWDING, AND CO. SALISBURY;

AND BELL | AND BRADFUTE; AND J. FAIRBAIRN, AT EDINBURGH. | 1823.

12 vols., 8°

I. *A*⁴ B–2D⁸, 210 leaves.

Pp. A1 t., A1ᵛ coloph., A2 *iii* iv–vii Contents, *viii* blk, on B1 *1* 2–191 Murphy's Essay, 192 Parr's epitaph on SJ; *193* ½t, *194* note, *195* 196–415 Poems and Poemata, *416* blk.

II. *A*1–3 B–2F⁸ (2F8 blk), 227 leaves.

Pp. A1 t., A1ᵛ coloph., A2 *iii* iv–vi Contents, on B1 *1* 2–446 Ramblers 1–70, + 1 blk leaf.

III. *A*1–3 B–2E⁸ 2F⁶, 225 leaves.

Pp. A1 t., A1ᵛ coloph., A2 *iii* iv–vi Contents, on B1 *1* 2–443 Ramblers 71–140, *444* coloph.

IV. *A*1–3 B–2C⁸ (2C8 ? blk), 203 leaves.

Pp. A1 t., A1ᵛ coloph., A2 *iii* iv–vi Contents, on B1 *1* 2–397 Ramblers 141–208, *398* blk, + 1 blk leaf.

V. *A*1–3 B–2C⁸ 2D⁸ (–D8) 2E–2N⁸ 2O² (2O2 blk), 284 leaves.

Pp. A1 t., A1ᵛ coloph., A2 *iii* iv–v Contents, *vi* advert., on B1 *1* 2–410 Idlers (1–103), 411–15 Idler *22, *416* blk, *417* ½t, *418* note, 419–560 Rasselas + 1 blk leaf.

VI. *A*⁴ B–2F⁸ 2G⁶, 234 leaves.

Pp. A1 blk, A2 t., A2ᵛ coloph., A3 Contents, A3ᵛ blk, A4–4ᵛ advert. to Prefaces, on B1 *1* 2–460 Lives: Cowley–Dryden.

VII. *A*² B–2C⁸ 2D⁴, 206 leaves.

Pp. A1 t., A1ᵛ coloph., A2 Contents A2ᵛ blk, on B1 *1* 2–408 Lives: Smith–Savage.

VIII. *A*² B–2B⁸ 2C⁴, 198 leaves.

Pp. A1 t., A1ᵛ coloph., A2 Contents, A2ᵛ blk, on B1 *1* 2–391 Lives: Swift–Lyttelton, *392* coloph.

IX. *A*² B–2O⁸, 290 leaves.

Pp. A1 t., A1ᵛ coloph., A2 *iii*–iv Contents, on B1 *1* ½t, *2* blk, *3* 4–338 Lives of Eminent Persons, *339* ½t, *340* blk, *341* 342–448 Selected Letters, *449* ½t, *450* blk, *451* 452–67 Prefaces, *468* 469–575 Prayers, *576* blk.

X. *A*² B–2D⁸, 210 leaves.

Pp. A1 t., A1ᵛ coloph., A2 *iii*–iv Contents, on B1 *1* ½t, *2* blk, *3* 4–416 Philological Tracts and miscellaneous essays.

XI. *A*² B–2N⁸ 2O² (2O2 + χ1), 285 leaves.

Pp. A1 t., A1ᵛ coloph., A2 *iii*–iv Contents, on B1 *1* ½t, *2* blk, 3–143 *144* Miscellaneous tracts, 145–185 Dedications, *186* 187–210 Legal opinions, *211* ½t, *212* blk, *213* 214–330 Reviews and criticisms, *331* ½t, *332* blk, *333* 334–68 Tales, *369* ½t, *370* blk, *371* 372–565 Adventurers (29), *566* blk.

XII. *A²* B–2M⁸ 2N⁴, 278 leaves.

Pp. A1 t., A1ᵛ coloph., A2 *iii*–iv Contents, on B1 *1* ½t, *2* blk, *3* 4–84 Essays, *85* ½t, *86* note, *87* 88–226 Political Tracts, *227* ½t, *228* blk, *229* 230–434 Journey, *435* ½t, *436* blk, *437* 438–60 Sermons (two: X and XXV), 2G7–2N4ᵛ Index.

Coloph: 'LONDON: PRINTED BY S. AND R. BENTLEY, DORSET-STREET.' at I. A1ᵛ, 416; II. A1ᵛ, 446; III. A1ᵛ, 444; IV. A1ᵛ, 397; V. A1ᵛ, 560; VI. A2ᵛ, 460; VII. A1ᵛ, 408; VIII. A1ᵛ, 392; IX. A1ᵛ, 575; X. A1ᵛ, 416; XI. A1ᵛ, 365; XII. A1ᵛ, 2N4ᵛ.

Plate: Engr. port. front. as 1816 87.3W/13, above.

References: Courtney 166.

Notes: The Advertisement is signed by Alexander Chalmers, 'London, Feb. 1823.' describing this as the 'seventh' edition. It is based on the 1816 edn. (87.3W/13, above), with some adjustments in the canon, all later adopted by Walesby in 1825 (87.3W/22, below) through the 1824 ed (87.3W/20, below).[1] Chalmers noted in his Diary, '1822. *February* 28. — Engaged with Mr Cadell to edit a new edition of Dr. Johnson's works, which I arranged anew, and made many improvements' (Chalmers, *In Memoriam* [1884], p. 27 ff., s.d.). These involved the addition of the *Lines on the Tender Infant (i. 360, *Poems²* 185, from *Works* (1787), xi. 377), on a *Portrait of Mrs Montagu (i. 362, *Poems²* 219–20 where it is erroneously given to 87.3W/13, from *Works* (1787), xi. 373), the verses 'To Sir John Lade' (i. 363, *Poems²* 225–7, from Piozzi, *Letters*, 1788), *Epitaphs on his parents (i. 364), *Elizabeth Johnson (i. 365), *Jane Bell (i. 365–6), *Mrs Salusbury (i. 366), *Goldsmith (i. 367), and *Henry Thrale (i. 377–8); *Dryden's Epigram on Milton (i. 414, *Poems²* 42–3), the *Epilogue to Baretti's *Carmen Seculare* (1779; i. 415, *Poems²* 218–19), and the translation of a *Welch Epitaph on Prince Madoc' (i. 415, *Poems²* 448). Further additions were the *Advertisement' to the 4th folio edn. of *Dictionary* (1773; x. 68–9), *Preface' to the octavo *Dictionary* (1756; x. 70–2), *Z. Williams, *Attempt to Ascertain the Longitude* (1755; x. 368–91), 'Considerations on the Corn Laws' ([1766] 1806; x. 402–10); *A Compleat Vindication* (1739; xi. 3–23), *Preface' to the *Gents. Mag.* 1738 (xi. 24–7), *Appeal to the Public' (*Gents. Mag.* 1739; xi. 28–33), *Considerations on Trapp's Sermons' (*Gents. Mag.* 1787; xi. 34–41), the 'Letter on Fireworks' (*Gents. Mag.* 1749; xi. 42–4), *Proposals for Anna Williams's *Essays* (1750; xi. 45), 'Project for the Employment of Authors' (*Univ. Vis.* 1756; xi. 46–56), *Preface' to *Lit. Mag.* (1756; xi. 57–60), 'Additional Account of Barretier' (*Gents. Mag.* 1742; ix. 159–69), *Gwynne's *Thoughts on the Coronation* (1761; xi. 171–82), *Preface' to the Artists' *Catalogue* (1762; xi. 183–5), the Legal Opinions for JB on †School Chastisement (xi.

186–9), †Vitious Intromission (xi. 190–97), †Lay Patronage (xi. 198–203) and †Pulpit Censure (xi. 204–10; all from *Life*), **Letter on Du Halde's *History of China*' (1738, *Gents Mag.* 1742; xi. 213–17), Reviews of the 'Account of the Duchess of Marlborough' (*Gents Mag.* 1742; xi. 218–24) and of Tytler's 'Enquiry' (*Gents. Mag.* 1760; xi. 319–30), and, from the *Literary Magazine* (56.4LM), of Birch's 'History of the Royal Society' (xi. 314–15), of Hampton's 'General History of Polybius' (xi. 316–17), of Harrison's 'Miscellanies' (xi. 317–18). **Marmor Norfolciense* (1739; xii. 3–33), was also added, though it had appeared in *Works* (Alnwick, 1816, 87.3W/15, above, &c.), as were additional 'Prayers and Meditations' (ix. 468 ff.), and two *Sermons* (X and XXV; xii. 437–60). Chalmers rejected the 'Review' of the Account of Benvenuto Cellini (1771, implicitly given to SJ by Davies in *Misc. & Fugitive Pieces*, iii (1774), 296–9, and adopted in *Works* (1787), ix. 360–3, and subsequent edns.) Unfortunately he did not spend much effort on the texts of most of these pieces, which were taken without editorial attention from the 1816 edn. (87.3W/13, above).

Copies: O² (**1**. 2699 e. 394, 'Miss Jones Stamford Hill'; **2**. 2699 d. 59–70, lacks vol. 10);

USA: Hyde (Adam), MH (16464.6), PPU; *Japan*: [Kyoto]; *UK*: ABu (*82463), BMp (495957–68), [C], E ([Ao].3.18), LCu, LEu, Oef, SAN (ˢPR3520.E23), SHu, WIS, Yc.

---

¹ In the following list, items marked with an asterisk * are taken from *Works*, xiv (1788), and those with a dagger † are from Boswell's *Life*.

87.3W/19a Works, ed. Lynam 1824

THE | WORKS | OF | SAMUEL JOHNSON, LL.D. | WITH | MURPHY'S ESSAY. | [short rule] | EDITED | BY THE REV. ROBERT LYNAM, A.M. | ASSISTANT CHAPLAIN TO THE MAGDALEN HOSPITAL. | [short rule] | IN SIX VOLUMES. | VOL. I [– VI]. | [medium rule] | LONDON: | PRINTED FOR GEORGE COWIE AND CO. | IN THE POULTRY. | 1824.

6 vols., 8°

I. *a*⁴ b–g⁸ h⁴, B–2N⁸ 2O⁴, ($2 signed), 340 leaves.

Pp. a1 t., a1ᵛ coloph: 'Printed by J.F. Dᴏᴠᴇ, St John's Square.', a2 *iii*–iv advert. to present edn., a3 *v* vi–viii Contents, on b1 ²*i* ii–cii Murphy's *Essay*, *ciii* Parr's epitaph, *civ* blk, on B1 *1* 2–568 text Ramblers 1–120, 568 *Explicit*: END OF VOL. I., and coloph.

II. *A*⁴ B–2X⁸ 2Y², ($2 signed), 350 leaves.

Pp. A1 t., A1ᵛ coloph., A2 *iii* iv–vii Contents, *viii* blk, on B1 *1* 2–386 Ramblers 121–208, *387* ½t, *388* advert., *389* 400–683 Idlers 1–103 (*22 pp. 680–83), 683 *Explicit*: END OF VOL. II., and coloph., *684* blk.

III. A^2 B–2U^8 (2U8 ? blk), ($2 signed), 338 leaves.

Pp. A1 t., A1^v coloph., A2 Contents, A2^v blk, on B1 *1* 2–144 Adventurers (29), *145* ½t, *146* advert. to original edn., *147* 148–662 Lives: Cowley–Fenton, 662 *Explicit*: END OF VOL. III., and coloph, *663–4* blk.

IV. A^2 B–2U^8 2X^6, ($2 signed), 344 leaves.

Pp. A1 t., A1^v coloph., A2 Contents, A2^v blk, on B1 *1* 2–410 Lives: Gay–Lyttelton, *411* 412–664 Lives of Eminent Persons, 664 *Explicit*: END OF VOL. IV., and coloph.

V. A^2 B–2Y^8 2Z^4, ($2 signed), 358 leaves.

Pp. A1 t., A1^v coloph., A2 *iii*–iv Contents, on B1 *1* ½t, *2* blk, *3* 4–306 Philological Tracts, *307* 308–474 Political Tracts, *475* 476–711 Miscellaneous Tracts, 711 *Explicit*: END OF VOL. V., and coloph., *712* blk.

VI. A^2 B–2Z^8, ($2 signed), 362 leaves.

Pp. A1 t., A1^v coloph., A2 *iii*–iv Contents, on B1 *1* 2–160 Journey, *161* ½t, *162* note, *163* 164–272 Rasselas, *273* 274–99 Tales, *300* blk, *301* ½t, *302* note, *303* 304–422 Poems, *423* 424–6 Epitaphs, *427* 428–60 Poemata, *461* ½t, *462* blk, *463* 464–544 Letters, *545* ½t, *546* blk, *547* 548–59 Prefaces, *560* 561–641 Prayers, *642* 643–668 Sermons (nos. X, XXII, and XXV), *669* 670–715 Index, 715 *Explicit*: THE END., and coloph., *716* blk.

Notes: Copies were exported to USA: M. & S. Thomas's *Trade Sale Catalogue* (Philadelphia, 5 Sept. 1825), shows William H. Woodward, of Philadelphia offering 50 copies, at $6.00 to the trade, $18.00 retail, and in the *Seventh Philadelphia Trade Sale* (17 Sept. 1827), Carey, Lea & Carey, offered 8 copies at $9.00 trade, for $18.00 retail (MWA).[1]

Copies: L (12275. de. 3); *USA*: Hyde[2] (1. 'Avery' — 'Morgan' — 'Houghton'; 2. 'Butler' — Adam), NjP; *UK*: LICj.

----

[1] I am indebted to Dr. Michael Winship for this and much other information of a like kind.

87.3W/19b   Works, ed. Lynam, reimpression   1825

THE | WORKS | OF | SAMUEL JOHNSON, LL.D. | WITH | MURPHY'S ESSAY. | [short rule] | EDITED | BY THE REV. ROBERT LYNAM, A.M. | ASSISTANT CHAPLAIN TO THE MAGDALEN HOSPITAL. | [short rule] | IN SIX VOLUMES. | VOL. I [– VI]. | [medium rule] | LONDON: | PRINTED FOR GEORGE COWIE AND CO. | IN THE POULTRY. | 1825.

6 vols., 8°

I. a^4 b–g^8 h^4, B–2N^8 2O^4, ($2 signed), 340 leaves.

Pp. a1 t., a1^v coloph: 'Printed by J.F. Dove, St John's Square.', a2 *iii*–iv advert. to present edn., a3 *v* vi–viii Contents, on b1 ²*i* ii–cii Murphy's *Essay, ciii* Parr's epitaph, *civ* blk, on B1 *1* 2–568 text: Ramblers 1–120, 568 *Explicit*: END OF VOL. I., and coloph.

II. *A*⁴ B–2X⁸ 2Y², ($2 signed), 350 leaves.

Pp. A1 t., A1ᵛ coloph., A2 *iii* iv–vii Contents, *viii* blk, on B1 *1* 2–386 Ramblers 121–208, *387* ½t, *388* advert., *389* 400–683 Idlers 1–103 (*22 pp. 680–83), 683 *Explicit*: END OF VOL. II., and coloph., *684* blk.

III. *A*² B–2U⁸ (2U8 ? blk), ($2 signed), 338 leaves.

Pp. A1 t., A1ᵛ coloph., A2 Contents, A2ᵛ blk, on B1 *1* 2–144 Adventurers (29), *145* ½t, *146* advert. to original edn., *147* 148–662 Lives: Cowley–Fenton, 662 *Explicit*: END OF VOL. III., and coloph, *663–4* blk.

IV. *A*² B–2U⁸ 2X⁶, ($2 signed), 344 leaves.

Pp. A1 t., A1ᵛ coloph., A2 Contents, A2ᵛ blk, on B1 *1* 2–410 Lives: Gay–Lyttelton, *411* 412–664 Lives of Eminent Persons, 664 *Explicit*: END OF VOL. IV., and coloph.

V. *A*² B–2Y⁸ 2Z⁴, ($2 signed), 356 leaves.

Pp. A1 t., A1ᵛ coloph., A2 *iii*–iv Contents, on B1 *1* ½t, *2* blk, *3* 4–306 Philological Tracts, *307* 308–474 Political Tracts, *475* 476–711 Miscellaneous Tracts, 711 *Explicit*: END OF VOL. V., and coloph., *712* blk.

VI. *A*² B–2Z⁸, ($2 signed), 362 leaves.

Pp. A1 t., A1ᵛ coloph., A2 *iii*–iv Contents, on B1 *1* 2–160 Journey, *161* ½t, *162* note, *163* 164–272 Rasselas, *273* 274–99 Tales, *300* blk, *301* ½t, *302* note, *303* 304–422 Poems, *423* 424–6 Epitaphs, *427* 428–60 Poemata, *461* ½t, *462* blk, *463* 464–544 Letters, *545* ½t, *546* blk, *547* 548–59 Prefaces, *560* 561–641 Prayers, *642* 643–668 Sermons (nos. X, XXII, and XXV), *669* 670–715 Index, 715 *Explicit*: THE END., and coloph., *716* blk.

References: Courtney 167; *CBEL* ii. 614
Notes: A reimpression of 1824, 87.3W/19a, q.v. above.
Copies: O (2699 e. 273–8, 'Charles Camnell');
USA: IU, MB, MH (Lamont), NIC (boards, cloth spine, ptd. labels, uncut), NjP, PPU; *UK*: BMp (2251–6), L (1609/1625), LVu, MRu, NOu, [WLAp]; *Eir*: Dt.

87.3W/20   Works, Baynes and Son   1824

THE | WORKS | OF | SAMUEL JOHNSON, LL.D. | *A NEW EDITION,* | IN TWELVE VOLUMES. | WITH | AN ESSAY ON HIS LIFE AND GENIUS, | By ARTHUR MURPHY, Esq. | [medium rule] | VOLUME THE FIRST [– TWELFTH]. | [medium rule] | LONDON: | PRINTED

FOR W. BAYNES AND SON, PATERNOSTER ROW; J. | CHRISTIE; J.
RICHARDSON; T. SETCHELL; W. SIOR; T. CRAW- | FORD; W.
CLARK; C. TAYLOR; J. GOODWIN; BLACK AND CO.; | J. HARRIS;
T. BIGG; J. BUMPUS; TOLBOYS, OXFORD; THORP, | CAMBBIDGE;
AND BARRETT, BATH. | [short rule] | 1824.

Stet (vol. 1, only; *correct* in some copies): TOLBOYS, . . . CAMBBIDGE;
12 vols., 12°

I. *A*⁴ B–2F⁶, ($3 signed), 172 leaves.

Pp. A1 t., A1ᵛ coloph: 'London: Printed by Cox and Baylis, Great Queen
Street.', A2 *iii* iv–v advert. ('*December*, 1824.'), *vi* blk, *vii* General Contents, *viii*
blk, on B1 *1* 2–133 Murphy's *Essay*, *134* blk, *135* ½t, *136* blk, *137* 138–336
Poems and Poemata, 336 *Explicit*: END OF THE FIRST VOLUME. and
coloph. as above.

II. *A*1–3 B–2O⁶ 2P1–3 (2P3 blk), ($3 signed), 222 leaves.

Pp. A1 t., A1ᵛ coloph. as vol. 1, A2 *iii* iv–vi Contents, on B1 *1* 2–435
Ramblers 1–70, *Explicit*: END OF THE SECOND VOLUME. and coloph.
as vol. 1, *436* blk, + 1 blk leaf.

III. *A*1–3 B–2O⁶ 2P1–3 (2P2,3 blk), ($3 signed), 222 leaves.

Pp. A1 t., A1ᵛ coloph. as vol. 1, A2 *iii* iv–vi Contents, on B1 *1* 2–433
Ramblers 71–140, 433 *Explicit*: END OF THE THIRD VOLUME. and
coloph. as vol. 1, *434* blk. + 2 blk leaves.

IV. *A*1–3 B–2K⁶, ($3 signed), 195 leaves.

Pp. A1 t., A1ᵛ coloph. as vol. 1, A2 *iii* iv–vi Contents, on B1 *1* 2–384
Ramblers 141–208, 384 *Explicit*: END OF THE FOURTH VOLUME. and
coloph. as vol. 1.

V. *A*⁴ B–2X⁶ 2Y², ($3 signed), 264 leaves.

Pp. A1 t., A1ᵛ coloph: 'D. Cartwright, Printer, 91 Batholomew Close.', A2 *v*
vi Contents [no iii–iv], *x* Advert., on B1 *1* 2–371 Idlers (1–103; pp. 372–76
Idler *22), *377* 378–520 Rasselas, 520 *Explicit*: THE END. and coloph. as A1ᵛ.

VI. π1 A² B–2N⁶ 2O⁴, ($3 signed), 217 leaves.

Pp. π1 t., π1ᵛ coloph: 'W. McDowall, Printer, Pemberton Row, Gough
Square.', A1 *iii* Contents, A1ᵛ *iv* blk, A2 *v*–vi Advert. to Original edn., on B1 *1*
2–428 Lives: Cowley–Dryden, 428 *Explicit*: END OF THE FIRST VOL-
UME., no coloph.

VII. *A*² B–2I⁶, ($3 signed), 188 leaves.

Pp. A1 t., A1ᵛ coloph. as vol. 6, A2 Contents. A2ᵛ blk, on B1 *1* 2–372 Lives:
Smith–Savage, 372 *Explicit*: END OF THE SECOND VOLUME., no
coloph.

VIII. *A*² B–2H⁶ 2I², ($3 signed), 184 leaves.

Pp. A1 t., A1ᵛ coloph. as vol. 6, A2 Contents. A2ᵛ blk, on B1 *1* 2–363 Lives: Swift–Lyttelton, 363 *Explicit*: END OF THE THIRD VOLUME., no coloph., *364* coloph. as vol. 6.

IX. *A²* B⁴ C–3A⁶, ($3 signed; 'VOL. IV.' on $1), 276 leaves.
Pp. A1 t., A1ᵛ coloph. as vol. 6, A2 *iii*–iv Contents, on B1 *1* 2–320 Lives of Eminent Persons, *321* ½t, *322* blk, 323–426 Letters, *427* ½t, *428* blk, *429* 430–44 Prefaces, *445* 446–546 Prayers, 546 explicit: END OF THE NINTH VOLUME. and coloph. as vol. 6, *547–8* advts. for 'Popular Books lately published.'

X. *A²* B–2L⁶, ($3 signed), 200 leaves.
Pp. A1 t., A1ᵛ coloph: 'D. Cartwright, Printer, Bartholomew Close.', A2 *iii*–iv Contents, on B1 *1* ½t, *2* blk, *3* 4–395 Philological Tracts, 395 *Explicit*: END OF THE TENTH VOLUME., *396* coloph. as A1ᵛ.

XI. *A²* B–2Y⁶ (2Y6 ? blk), ($3 signed), 266 leaves.
Pp. A1 t., A1ᵛ coloph. as vol. 10, A2 *iii*–iv, on B1 *1* ½t, *2* blk, *3* 4–137 Miscellaneous Tracts, 137–98 Dedications, 198–307 Reviews, 307–41 Tales, 342–525 Adventurers (29), 525 *Explicit*: END OF THE ELEVENTH VOLUME., *526* coloph. as vol. 10, + ? 1 blk leaf.

XII. *A²* B–2N⁶ 2O², ($3 signed), 214 leaves.
Pp. A1 t., A1ᵛ coloph. as vol. 10, A2 *iii*–iv Contents, on B1 *1* 2–216 Political Tracts, 217–424 Journey, 424 *Explicit*: THE END. and coloph. as vol. 10; no index.

Plates: I. Port. front. 'Engraved on Steel by R. Page. | Dr. JOHNSON. | London: Pubᵈ. by John Bumpus, 1822.'
References: Courtney 166.
Notes: Vols. 6–8 were clearly intended for separate issue (explicits), though no such issue of the *Lives of the Poets* has been located. There is no Index. The unsigned Advertisement (I. iii–v. '*December*, 1824'), describes this edn. as 'an essential benefit . . . conferred upon society.' It is based on Chalmers's edn. of 1823 (87.3W/18, above), omitting the verses on 'Sir John Lade' (*Poems²* 225–7), rejecting the epitaphs and Sermons which had appeared in 1823, and several Prayers,[1] and with one independent editorial addition to the canon in the inclusion of the 'Preface' to vol. III of the *Harleian Catalogue* (1743; x. 229–35). There is evidence therefore of editorial attention independent of Chalmers. This edition appears to have formed the working copy-text for Walesby's Oxford edn. 1825 (87.3W/22, below).
Copies: O (2699 f.354);
USA: Hyde; *UK*: BMp (438729–40), BRp, E (PCL. 407–18), Eu (Zz.9. 14–25; Conts. vol. 2 mistitled and bound in vol. 4), L (12275. de. 3), LICj (imperfect lacks vols. 5–11).

¹ Viz. On his Birthday, 1738 (*Diaries* 37–8), on the *Rambler*, 1750 (*Diaries* 43), death of his wife, 1752 (*Diaries* 44–5), 6 May 1752 (*Diaries* 47), Anniversary of d. of wife, 1754 (*Diaries* 54–7), death of mother, 1759 (*Diaries* 66–8), 1 Jan. 1770 (*Diaries* 125), 1 Jan. 1777 (*Diaries* 262–3), Birthday 1779 (*Diaries* 298), 22 June 1781 (*Diaries* 307–8), leaving Thrales 1782 (*Diaries* 338), and 5 Dec. 1784 (*Diaries* 417–18).

87.3W/21   *Works, Tegg's edition*   1824

THE | WORKS | OF | SAMUEL JOHNSON, LL.D. | WITH | AN ESSAY | ON | HIS LIFE AND GENIUS. | [medium rule] | BY ARTHUR MURPHY, ESQ. | [medium rule] | *A NEW EDITION*, | IN TWELVE VOLUMES. | VOL. I [– XII]. | [short total rule] | LONDON: | PRINTED FOR THOMAS TEGG; W. SHARPE AND SON; G. | OFFOR; G. AND J. ROBINSON; J. EVANS AND CO.: ALSO | R. GRIFFIN AND CO. GLASGOW; AND J. CUMMING, DUBLIN. | [dash] | 1824.

Var: III. . . . 1823.

12 vols., 8°

I. π² a–l⁸ m⁶, B–O⁸ P⁴, ($2 signed), 204 leaves.
Pp. π1 t., π1ᵛ coloph., π2 Contents, on a1 *1* 2–187 Murphy's *Essay*, *188* blk, on B1 ²*1* ½t, *2* blk, *3* 4–215 Poems and Poemata, 215 *Explicit*: END OF VOL. I., *216* coloph.

II. *A*² B–2E⁸ 2F⁴ (2F4 ? blk), ($2 signed), 222 leaves.
Pp. A1 t., A1ᵛ coloph., A2 *iii*–iv Contents, on B1 *1* ½t, *2* blk, *3* 4–280 Philological Tracts, *281* 282–318 Political Essays, *319* 320–438 Miscellaneous essays, 438 *Explicit*: END OF VOL. II. and coloph., + 1 ? blk leaf.

III. *A*² B–2E⁸ 2F⁶, ($2 signed), 224 leaves.
Pp. A1 t., A1ᵛ coloph., A2 *iii* Contents, *iv* blk, on B1 *1* 2–136 Essays, *137* 138–297 Adventurers (24), *298* blk, *299* 300–442 Rasselas, 442 *Explicit*: END OF VOL. III., *443* blk, *444* coloph.

IV. a⁴ B–2F⁸ (2F8 ? blk), ($2 signed), 228 leaves.
Pp. a1 t., a1ᵛ coloph., a2 ½t: THE | RAMBLER. | Nullius addictus jurare in verba magistri, | Quo me cunque rapit tempestas, deferor hospes. | Hor. | [short rule] | VOL. I., a2ᵛ blk, a3 *v* vi–vii Contents, *viii* blk, on B1 *1* 2–446 Ramblers 1–70, 446 *Explicit*: END OF VOL. I., and coloph., + 1 ? blk leaf.

V. a⁴ B–2E⁸ 2F⁶, ($2 signed), 226 leaves.
Pp. a1 t., a1ᵛ coloph., a2 ½t, a2ᵛ blk, a3 *v* vi–vii Contents, *viii* blk, on B1 *1* 2–443 Ramblers 71–140, 443 *Explicit*: END OF VOL. II., *444* coloph.

VI. a⁴ B–2B⁸ 2C⁴ 2D², ($2 signed), 202 leaves.
Pp. a1 t., a1ᵛ coloph., a2 ½t, a2ᵛ blk, a3 *v* vi–vii Contents, *viii* blk, on B1 *1* 2–396 Ramblers 141–208, 396 *Explicit*: END OF VOL. III., and coloph.

VII. *A*1–3 B–2C⁸ 2D1–5, ($2 signed), 208 leaves.

Pp. A1 t., A1ᵛ coloph., A2 *iii* iv–v Contents, *vi* advert., on B1 *1* 2–410 Idlers 1–103, 410 *Explicit*: END OF VOL. VII., and coloph.

VIII. *A*² B–2D⁸, ($2 signed), 210 leaves.

Pp. A1 t., A1ᵛ coloph., A2 *iii*–iv Contents, on B1 *1* 2–61 Miscellaneous Essays, *62* blk, *63* ½t, 64 blk, *65* 66–205 Political Tracts, *206* blk, *207* ½t, *208* blk, *209* 210–416 Journey, 416 *Explicit*: END OF THE EIGHTH VOLUME, and coloph.

IX. a² ²a² B–2F⁸ 2G⁶, ($2 signed), 234 leaves.

Pp. a1 t., a1ᵛ coloph., a2 ½t: LIVES OF THE POETS. | [dash] | VOL. I., a2ᵛ blk, ²a1 Contents, ²a1ᵛ blk, ²a2 *v*–vi advert. to original edn., on B1 *1* 2–459 Lives: Cowley–Dryden, *460* coloph.

X. *A*1–3 B–2C⁸ 2D⁶ (–2D6 = ? A1), ($2 signed), 208 leaves.

Pp. A1 t., A1ᵛ coloph., A2 ½t, A2ᵛ blk, A3 Contents, A3ᵛ blk, on B1 *1* 2–410 Lives: Smith–Savage, 410 *Explicit*: END OF VOL. X., and coloph.

XI. *A*1–3 B–2B⁸ 2C⁴, ($2 signed), 199 leaves.

Pp. A1 t., A1ᵛ coloph., A2 ½t, A2ᵛ blk, A3 Contents, A3ᵛ blk, on B1 *1* 2–389 Lives: Swift–Lyttelton, 389 explicit: END OF VOL. XI., *390* coloph., 2C4 blk, 2C4ᵛ ptd spine labels for 3 vols. of Lives, as: [rule] | DR. JOHN-SON's | LIVES | OF THE | POETS. | [short rule] | IN THREE VOLS. | [short rule] | VOL. I [– III]. | [rule].

XII. *A*² B–2M⁸ (? 2M8 blk), ($2 signed), 274 leaves.

Pp. A1 t., A1ᵛ coloph., A2 *iii*–iv Contents, on B1 *1* ½t, *2* blk, *3* 4–328 Lives of Eminent Persons, *329* ½t, *330* blk, *331* 332–438 Letters, *439* ½t, *440* blk, *441* 442–450 Prayers, on 2G2 *451* 452–542 Index, + 1 ? blk leaf.

Coloph: (versos of all tt.): 'London: Printed by Thomas Davison, Whitefriars.'
Plates: Engr. port. front. vol. 1: 'JOHNSON. | Engraved by E. Mitchell, from a Painting by Sir Joshua Reynolds, In the possession of James Boswell, Esq.'
Notes: The Review of the 'Account of Benvenuto Cellini', rejected by Chalmers in *Works*, 1823, above, is here retained (ii. 194–7). This appears to be a reprint of *Works*, 1820 (87.3W/17, above). The dating of the t. to vol. 3 cannot be an error, though an explanation is elusive. Some copies of vols. 4–6 have extra tt. as:
THE | RAMBLER. | BY S. JOHNSON, LL.D. | [short swelled rule] | IN THREE VOLUMES. | Nullius addictus jurare in verba magistri, | Quo me cunque rapit tempestas, deferor hospes. Hor. | [short rule] | THE SEVEN TEENTH EDITION. | [short swelled rule] | [BL] **London:** | PRINTED BY R. AND A. TAYLOR, SHOE-LANE, | FOR G. WALKER; J. AKERMAN; E. EDWARDS; G. & J. ROBINSON; | T. TEGG; E. THOMSON, MANCHESTER; J. NOBLE, HULL; | WILSON, BERWICK; AND R. GRIFFIN & SON, GLASGOW. | [short rule] | 1822.

For separate issuance, see above 50.3R/57; and some of vols. 9–11 have extra tt. as:

THE | LIVES | OF THE MOST EMINENT | ENGLISH POETS: | WITH | CRITICAL OBSERVATIONS | ON THEIR WORKS. | [short rule] | BY SAMUEL JOHNSON, LL.D. | [short rule] | A NEW EDITION, CORRECTED AND REVISED. | IN THREE VOLUMES. | VOL. I [– III]. | [short double rule] | LONDON: | PRINTED FOR THOMAS TEGG, 73, CHEAPSIDE; G. OFFOR; | G. AND J. ROBINSON; J. EVANS AND CO.: ALSO R. GRIFFIN | AND CO. GLASGOW; AND J. CUMMING, DUBLIN. | [short rule] | 1824. (See above 79.4LP/38).

It is likely that the prelims and final sig. 2D in vol. 7 were a whole sheet, but firm evidence has proved inconclusive. Other odd missing leaves (? blk) were also perhaps used to provide tt., but most copies are too tightly bound and wmks. too unclear to point to certain conjugacies.

Copies: O (2699 e.399, with spine labels in vol. xi);
USA: Hyde ('Skegg'), NjP, PPL, [PPT], ViU; *UK*: ABu (82463/2), BMp (971941–8, lacks vols. 9–12), LICj.

87.3W/22a   *Works, Oxford English Classics*   1825

THE | WORKS | OF | SAMUEL JOHNSON, LL.D. | IN NINE VOLUMES. | [short rule] | VOLUME THE FIRST [– NINTH]. | [circular device including arms of University] | [short swelled rule] | OXFORD. | PRINTED FOR WILLIAM PICKERING, LONDON; | AND TALBOYS AND WHEELER, OXFORD. | MDCCCXXV.

Var.[1] OXFORD, | PUBLISHED BY TALBOYS AND WHEELER; | AND W. PICKERING, LONDON.

OXFORD: | . . .

OXFORD. | PRINTED FOR WILLIAM PICKERING, LONDON; AND | . . .

LONDON, | PUBLISHED BY W. PICKERING, CHANCERY LANE; AND | TALBOYS AND WHEELER, OXFORD.

LONDON, | . . . LANE; | AND . . .

9 vols., 8°

I. a^4 (–a1 ?= 2D1) b–f^8 g^4, ^{2}a^2 B–2B^8 2C^4 2D1 (? =a1), ($2 signed), 246 leaves.

Pp. a1 *i* ½t: [BL] **Oxford English Classics.** | [short rule] | DR. JOHNSON'S WORKS. | [short rule] | LIFE, POEMS, AND TALES., *ii* blk. + Engr. port. front ('Painted by Sir Joshua Reynolds. [Facs. of signature: 'Sam: Johnſon'] Engraved by W.H. Worthington Published by W. Pickering London, & Talboys & Wheeler Oxford 1825'), on a2 *iii* t., *iv* blk, *v*–vi Contents, on b1 ^2i ii–lxxxvi Murphy's *Essay*, *lxxxvii* ½t POEMS., *lxxxviii* blk,

²a1 *i* ii–iv Prefatory Observations, on B1 *1* 2–149 text Poems, 150–4 Epitaphs, *155* 156–94 Poemata, *195–8* Prefatory Observations, *199* 200–310 text: Rasselas, *311* 312–94 text Letters, 394 *Explicit*: [short rule] | END OF VOL. I. | [short rule], coloph: TALBOYS AND WHEELER.

II. *a*² b⁸ (–b8) B–2I⁸ 2K², ($2 signed), 259 leaves.

Pp. a1 ½t: [BL] **Oxford English Classics.** | [short rule] | DR. JOHNSON'S WORKS. | [short rule] | THE RAMBLER. | VOL. I., *ii* coloph: [medium rule] | TALBOYS AND WHEELER, PRINTERS, OXFORD., *iii* t., *iv* blk, on b1 *v* vi–xii Prefatory Notice, *xiv* blk, *xv* xvi–xvii Contents, *xviii* blk, on B1 *1* 2–499 text Ramblers 1–105, *Explicit*: [short rule] | END OF VOL. II. | [short rule], coloph: TALBOYS AND WHEELER., *500* blk.

Notes: Pickering noted (below) cancels for a2 (t.), b2, I6, M7, Q1, R8, S3, T2, U4, 2A1, 2B8, 2G5, and supplied *cancellantia* for I6, Q1, R8, S3, 2A1, 2G5, **and** H8 and 2C⁸. No *cancellantia* for a2 (t.), b2, M7, T2, U4 or 2B8 are reported. The *cancellantia* for b2, M7, T2 and U4 were printed together as a ½-sheet; the remaining leaves formed a whole sheet, but there is no provision in this sum for *cancellantia* for a2 (t.) and 2B8.

III. *A*⁴ B–2G⁸ *2H*1, ($2 signed), 237 leaves.

Pp. a1 ½t . . . THE RAMBLER. | VOL. II., *ii* coloph., *iii* t., *iv* blk, *v* vi–viii Contents, on B1 *1* 2–465 text Ramblers 106–208, *Explicit*: . . . VOL. III., and coloph., *466* blk.

Note: The text of the final page 465 (2H1) does not catch properly with its antecedent (464) apparently because of a slip in casting off. The cancelled leaves in this vol. are B4 (7–8), B5 (9–10), C1 (17–18), C4 (23–4), F2 (67–8), H1 (97–8), H4 (103–4), H7 (109–10), L7 (157–8), Q2 (227–8), Q5 (233–4), Y1 (321–2), 2E4 (423–4), 2F5 (441–2), 2G5–6 (457–60), a total of two whole sheets. These are bound in at the end of vol. 3 in O (copy 2).

IV. *A*⁸ B–2F⁸ 2G⁴ (–2G4 ? blk), ($2 signed), 235 leaves.

Pp. A1 ½t . . . THE | ADVENTURER AND IDLER., *ii* blk, *iii* t., *iv* coloph., *v* vi–viii Prefatory Notice to the Adventurer, *ix* x–xii Prefatory Notice to the Idler, *xiii–xiv* xv–xvi Contents, on B1 *1* 2–148 text: Adventurers (29 papers), *149* ½t THE IDLER., *150* Advertisement, *151* 152–453 text Idlers (with *22 at end), *Explicit*: . . . VOL. IV., and coloph., *454* blk, *455–6* (2G4) ?blk.

V. *A*⁴ (–A4) B–2H⁸ 2I⁴ (–2I4), ($2 signed), 246 leaves.

Pp. A1 *i* ½t . . . MISCELLANEOUS PIECES., *ii* blk, *iii* t., *iv* blk, *v*–vi Contents, on B1 *1* 2–486 text: Miscellaneous Pieces, *Explicit*: . . . VOL. V., coloph.

VI. *A*⁴ (–A4) B–2K⁸ 2L⁴, ($2 signed), 263 leaves.

Pp. A1 ½t . . . REVIEWS, POLITICAL TRACTS, | AND | LIVES OF

EMINENT PERSONS., *ii* blk, *iii* t., *iv* blk, *v*–vi Contents, on B1 *1* 2–520 text Reviews, Political Tracts, Lives of Eminent Persons, *Explicit*: . . . VOL. VI., coloph.

VII. A^6 B–2H^8 2I^4 (–2I4), (\$2 signed), 249 leaves.

Pp. A1 *i* ½t . . . LIVES OF THE POETS. | VOL. I., *ii* blk, *iii* t., *iv* blk, *v* Advertisement (1783 Lives), viii ix–xii [sic] Prefatory Notice, *xiii* Contents, *xiv* blk, on B1 *1* 2–485 text Lives Cowley–Sheffield, *Explicit*: '. . . VOL. VII.', coloph., *486* blk.

Notes: The pagination of the prelims presumes an extra leaf at the beginning, but there is no function for any such.

VIII. π^2 a1 B–2I^8, (\$2 signed), 251 leaves.

Pp. π1 ½t . . . LIVES OF THE POETS. | VOL. II., *ii* coloph., *iii* t., *iv* blk, on a1 *v* Contents, *vi* blk, on B1 *1* 2–495 text: Lives Prior–Gray, *Explicit*: . . . VOL. VIII., coloph., *496* blk.

IX. π^2 2π1 B–2K^8 2L^8 (–2K8 ?= 2π1), 2M–2S^4 2T^2, (\$2 (–2M–T) signed), 296 leaves.

Pp. π1 *i* ½t . . . JOURNEY TO THE HEBRIDES. | TALES OF THE IMAGINATION. | PRAYERS AND SERMONS., *ii* coloph., *iii* t., *iv* blk, *v* Contents, *vi* blk, on B1 *1* 2–161 text Journey, 162–75 Vision of Theodore, *176* 177–90 Fountains, *191* 192–286 Prayers and Meditations, *287* ½t SERMONS | LEFT FOR PUBLICATION | BY | JOHN TAYLOR, LL.D., *288* blk, *289* 290–525 Sermons (25), *Explicit*: . . . VOL. IX., *526* blk, on 2M1 ^2i ii–lix Index, coloph., *lx* blk.

Notes: O5 (201–2) may be a cancel.

Paper: 2 issues (a) 75 copies on Large Paper (uncut), at £1. 1s. per vol.; (b) Ordinary paper; demy (uncut: 8¾ × 5½ in.), 9 vols. at 8s. per volume, or £3. 12s. the set.

Type: Pica (3.7 mm), leaded: (0.8 mm); footnotes: bourgeois (3.0 mm, leaded: 0.8 mm).

Plates: Engr. port. front. vol. 1: Square frame: 'Painted by Sir Joshua Reynolds. Sam: Johnſon Engraved by W.H. Worthington Published by William Pickering, London, & Talboys & Wheeler, Oxford, 1825.'

References: Courtney 166–7; Keynes, *William Pickering, Publisher* (1969); Warren, *Whittinghams* (New York, 1896); Sherbo, *PBSA* xlvii (1953), 376–8 (for cancels). Copies in sheets were sold in bulk at Lewis's sale of Pickering's stock, 12 May 1854, lot. 795.

Notes: The edn. was printed at Oxford by David Alphonso Talboys (?1790–1840*, Keynes),[2] and James Luff Wheeler (1798–1862, Boase, iii. 1299, s.n. 'James Talboys Wheeler', his son), published as a volume per month from 1 Nov. 1824,[3] and completed in summer (July) 1825.[4] All copies are dated 'MDCCCXXV'. A printed notice dated '*Oxford*, 1825' states that the edn. is

'Handsomely printed upon a fine laid paper, in demy 8vo. publishing in volumes at 8s. each, of which the sixth is just published. — The whole will be completed in nine volumes. by June, 1825.' Large paper volumes were priced at 21s. each. Copies were still advertised for sale in Talboys's catalogue of 1832 at the same prices as 1825. The claims of the prospectus that the typography and paper are new may be disputed since an identical face had been used in 1816 for the Oxford edn. of *Rasselas* (59.4R/80, above).

The ordinary paper issue was published in a glazed red cloth with printed paper spine labels, perhaps the first work so to appear.[5] Large paper copies are usually more sumptuously bound.

The edn. was 'superintended' by Francis Pearson Walesby.[6]

Cancels: A note on the cancels in vol. ix (O: copy 2, and *Aust.* CNL 'Pickering') states:

> The Binder is desired to insert the following Cancels given at the end of Vol. IX.
>
> Vol. II. — vii, 173, 275, 295. — Printed as a half sheet
> iii, 123, 225, 255, 261, 353, 383, 457. — A sheet.
> Vol. III. — 7, 9, 17, 23, 67, 97, 103, 109. — Ditto.
> 157, 227, 233, 321, 423, 441, 457, 459. — Ditto.
>
> *NB. The binder may find some of the above* inserted in some copies, which he need not displace.
>
> The Prefatory Notice to the Lives of the Poets must be taken from the beginning of Vol. VIII. and placed before Vol. VII. and the advertisement found in Vol. IX. must be placed immediately after the title in Vol. I.

The italicized 'NB.' shows that the insertion of the cancellantia was not regular, and accounts for variations within and between different copies.[7]

This edn. enjoyed a peculiar authority, presumably on account of the 'Oxford' association, which was unwarranted; it did, however, perpetuate the canon established by Chalmers in 1823, *via* the 1824 edn. (87.3W/20, above) from which the 'Preface' to vol. III of the *Harleian Catalogue* was taken, and to which were added the texts of all the sermons from Taylor's posthumous collection (88.5S/1, below), and the 'Epigram on Colley Cibber' (*Poems*[2] 92), and the Greek Tetrastich on Goldsmith (*Poems*[2] 198). Only the quality of printing, which may not appeal to everyone, marked it out: textually it is seriously corrupt and the punctuation is almost entirely faulty.

Two volumes of SJ's *Parliamentary Debates* from Stockdale's *Works*, 1787, xii–xiii (87.3W/1.2/1a), were appended.

Copies: O[2] (**1**. 2699 d. 116; **2**. 270 e. 426–34 with cancels);

USA: (**LP**) Hyde ('Jefferson' — Adam), MH (*58H-21), NjP; (**OP**) CLU, CtY[2], DLC, ICN, ICU[2] (**var.**), IU, MH, NIC[2], NjP, NN[2], [PBm, PP], PPU, [PV], TxU; *Can*: CaOHM; *Japan*: [Kyoto]; *UK*: (**LP**) BFq; (**OP**) AWn, BMp (266215–23, no Debates), BRu, C, Cp, Ct, E, Ep, JDF ('Thomas C. Humble'),

GTc, L (a. 12270 r.1), LCu, LEu, LICj, MRc, MRp, MRu, NCu, Oa, Oef, SPAg; *Aust*: CNL ('Pickering' DNS); *Fr*: BN.

[1] These variant imprints are so differently distributed that no clear pattern emerges. I have not seen a copy with a 'London' version in vols. I, III–V, VII–IX, but only 22 copies have been checked for these features; the other variations appear to be random. It is evident that titles were printed *ad hoc*, to meet the demand for individual volumes. In these circumstances it is perhaps fruitless to expect regularity in any given set, unless the LP copies are more consistent, but I have seen too few of those to reach a conclusion.

[2] *Gents. Mag.* (1840), ii. 220, and *Oxford Chron.*, 30 May 1840. Also *Al. Ox.* s.n., Saunders, *Salad for the Social* (1856), 27, and *Recollections of Oxford by an old Freeman* (1899).

[3] Sherbo, *PBSA* xlvii (1953), 376, and R.W. Chapman, *Cancels* (1930), 66–7.

[4] In *Aust*: CNL ('Pickering' — D. Nichol Smith), vol. IV was an advertisement: 'The Publishers of the *Oxford English Classics* present their grateful acknowledgements to the Public for the encouragement, already extended to their plan; and beg leave to assure their Subscribers, that no diligence shall be wanting on their part to merit a continuance of the same kind patronage.

Wherever a typographical error may occur, a reprinted leaf will be given: "and every exertion will be made to render their editions as complete and immaculate, as unwearied diligence can effect."

They also earnestly solicit any communication, that may tend to the improvement of their editions, and to the illustration of Johnson's life and writings.

Oxford, December, 1824.'

[5] Boase, *Modern English Biography*, ii. 1524–5, s.n. 'William PICKERING' gives this development from red boards to red cloth, to 1825. In a letter to David Hall, of Philadelphia, 19 March 1772, Strahan complained of the scarcity of sheepskin 'which makes it necessary to cover some of our small Books with Cloth' (I quote from Hoffman & Freeman, *Catal.* 33 (Apr. 1971), 217: I have not pursued the original). The precedence of the cloth binding of this edn. is an established tradition, but its reliability is not demonstrated.

[6] So stated in Pickering's advts. Walesby (1798–1858), of Lincoln College, Oxford (1823–37), became Professor of Anglo-Saxon (1829–34) and died as Recorder of Woodstock. See *NQ* 2nd ser., xi (1861), 269 (by Charles Sprengel Greaves (1801–81) and 335 (by James Heywood Markland (d. 1864), of Bath), *Al. Ox.*, *Gray's Inn Admissions Register*, ed. Foster (1889), 425, *Gents. Mag.* n.s., v (1858), 317, s.d. 'Aug. 5.', *The Times*, 7 Aug. 1858, 9 (col. 6), *Law Times*, 6 Nov. 1858, 79, *Registers of Wadham College*, ed. Gardiner (1889–95), ii. '1719–1871', 273–4, *Annual Register*, c (Rivington, 1858), 423. Walesby, a Lincolnshire man, contributed to agricultural literature, cf. *Baxter's Library of Practical Agriculture*, 4th. edn., 2 vols. (1846), p. vi, from which his *Memoir of . . . John Ellman, Esq. of Glynde*, was separately published in 1847. Greaves's note on Walesby asserted that he had before him Walesby's MS notebook in preparation of this edn., and showing his further responsibility for Talboys's edn. of Boswell's *Life*, 1826 (Pottle, *Literary Career of JB* (1929), 176–7). I have been unable to trace it. Letters by Walesby are in L: (Add. MSS 34570, fo. 207, 34572, fo. 446, and 34573, fo. 347 (to Philip Bliss)).

[7] Sherbo, *PBSA* xlvii (1953), 376–8.

87.3W/22b   Works, Oxford English Classics,   1968
                  facsimile, New York

A facsimile reprint of the Oxford English Classics edition was published in New York, 1968, by AMS Press.

87.3W/23a   Works, Jones's University Edition   1825

[Engr. t. within a Gothic decoration] Jones's University Edition of British Classic Authors The Works of Sam¹ Johnson, L.L.D. Vol. I [– II] [Vignette:

Obidah, Rambler. 65] 'Afraid to go forward lest he should go wrong' No. 65. London Published by Jones & Co. June 1. 1825.

THE | WORKS | OF | SAMUEL JOHNSON, LL.D. | A NEW EDITION, | WITH | AN ESSAY | ON HIS LIFE AND GENIUS, | BY | ARTHUR MURPHY, Esq. | [medium rule] | LONDON: | PUBLISHED BY JONES & COMPANY, | 3, ACTON PLACE, KINGSLAND ROAD. | [short rule] | 1825.

2 vols., 8°

I. *a*⁴ b–e⁴ *A*⁴ B–2Y⁴ ²*a*⁴ ²b² ²B–P⁴ π² ³A–2Z⁴, ($1 (c–e *italic*) signed; '*Idler*' on ²b1), 448 leaves.

Pp. Engr. port. front. ('Samuel Johnson, L.L.D. Engraved by Mʳ. Page from the admired Painting by Sir Joshua Reynolds. London. Published by Jones & Co. Janʸ. 1. 1826') and engr. t. + a1 t., *ii* coloph: 'Glasgow: Andrew & John M. Duncan, Printers to the University', *iii* iv–xl Murphy's Essay, on A1 *i* t. Rambler 1825, *ii* coloph., *iii*–iv Historical Preface, *v* vi–viii Contents, on B1 *1* 2–351 text Ramblers 1–208, *352* blk, on ²a1 *i* t. Idler 1825, *ii* coloph., *iii*–iv Contents, *v* vi–xii Biographical and Historical Preface, on ²B1 *1* 2–111 text Idlers (inc. *22), *112* blk, on π1 *i* t. Lives of Poets 1825, *ii* coloph., *iii* Contents, *iv* blk, on ³A1 *1* 2–363 text, *364* coloph.

II. *A*⁴ B–4R⁴, ($1 signed), 344 leaves.

Pp. Engr. t. (as vol. 1, 'Vol. 2.' and var. vignette: 'The Prince & Princess leaving the Valley. Rasselas. Stalker & Neale sc. 13 New Street, Strand.'), on A1 *1* t. Rasselas 1825, *2* coloph., *3* 4–44 text, *45* ½t 'Poems', *46* blk, *47* 48–104 *105* text, *106* Contents, *107* ½t Lives of Eminent Persons *108* blk, *109* 110–207 text, *208* blk, *209* ½t Letters, *210* blk, *211* 212–42 text, *243* ½t Prayers and Meditations, *244* blk, *245* 246–50 Preface and advertisement, *251* 252–84 text, *285* Contents, *286* blk, *287* ½t Tracts &c., *288* blk, *289* 290–687 text (511–64 Papers in the Adventurer, 512–627 Political Tracts, 628–87 Journey), *688* Contents.

References: Courtney 167–8.

Notes: The major sections of vol. 1 with separate tt. were evidently designed to be issued separately as well as jointly in this collection. See entries for Rambler (50.3R/69), Idler (58.4Id/35–6), Rasselas (59.4R/122), and Lives of the Poets (79.4LP/41). Texts are printed as 2 cols./p.

Advertised with MH copy (79.4LP/41, above) as:

> 54 numbers at 6d. or 27 parts 1s. each, beautifully printed in double columns 8vo on the finest vellum paper, hot pressed, and embellished with superior Engravings; the Complete Works of Dr. Samˡ. Johnson: Comprising the Rambler — Idler — Rasselas — Lives of the Poets — Letters — Poems — Miscellanies, &c. with an Essay on his Life and Genius, by Arthur Murphy, Esq. ⁎⁎ This Correct University Edition, will form 2 beautiful Library

Volumes, in Octavo, price 27s. and comprise with-out the smallest mutilation or abridgement, the whole of the 8vo edition in 12 vols. published at Four Guineas.

Jones's advts. for his 'Library Editions' are found in most copies offered in weekly 6d. numbers or monthly 1s. parts:

The British Classics, or Essayists; . . . Rambler, Idler, Adventurer . . . The Complete Dramatic Works of Shakspeare, Printed from the Texts of Johnson, Steevens, and Reed . . . a most Elegant, Single, Library Volume. . . . Rambler and Idler: uniformly printed in one beautiful volume, five plates, extra boards, 9s. . . . Johnson's (Dr.) Complete Works, by Murphy (comprising the same, verbatim, as the original edition in 12 volumes, published at £4. 4s.) in 2 beautiful volumes, boards, with fine engravings, £1. 8s.

Copies were exported to N. America, appearing in trade sale catalogues of 1838–39: J.J. Woodward (Philadelphia), *Tenth Philadelphia Trade Sale* (20 March 1838), by Lord & Carlisle, offered 10 copies, as did J.H. Wilkins & R.B. Carter (Boston), in '2 vols. royal 8vo. with plates, folded [= in quires] $3.50'; George Dempster & Co. (New York), offered 10 sets 'folded' at $3.00; In the *Thirtieth New York Trade Sale* (26 Aug. 1839) by Bangs, Richards & Platt, A.V. Blake (New York), offered 10 copies '2 vols. 8vo. fine edition, cloth $3.50'; and 10 copies '[ditto] sheep $4.00.'[1]

The plates of this edn. eventually passed to Henry G. Bohn, who reissued them in 1850 (87.3W/23b, below).

Copies: JDF; *USA*: CtY (Im J637 B792gk), MB, MH (KF 17175), [NRU], PPL, PPU; *UK*: [? BRp], E (AB.3.79.53), LICj.

---

[1] E: (MS Acc. 5000, no. 1401).

87.3W/23b   Works, Jones's edition, Bohn   1850

The Works of Samuel Johnson, LL.D. A new edition, with an Essay . . . London: Henry G. Bohn. 1850

2 vols., 8°. Not examined.

I. Pp. *i* t., *iii* iv–xl Murphy's Essay, *²i* t. Rambler 1825, *ii* coloph., *iii*–iv Historical Preface, *v* vi–viii Contents, on B1 *1* 2–351 text Ramblers 1–208, *352* blk, on *²a1* *i* t. Idler 1825, *ii* coloph., *iii*–iv Contents, *v* vi–xii Biographical and Historical Preface, on *²B1* *1* 2–111 text Idlers (inc. *22), *112* blk, on π1 *i* t. Lives of Poets 1825, *ii* coloph., *iii* Contents, *iv* blk, on *³A1* *1* 2–363 text, *364* coloph.

II. Pp. *1* t. Rasselas 1825, *2* coloph., *3* 4–44 text, *45* ½t Poems, *46* blk, *47* 48–104 *105* text, *106* Contents, *107* ½t Lives of Eminent Persons *108* blk, *109* 110–207 text, *208* blk, *209* ½t Letters, *210* blk, *211* 212–42 text, *243* ½t

Prayers and Meditations, *244* blk, *245* 246–50 Preface and advertisement, *251* 252–84 text, *285* Contents, *286* blk, *287* ½t Tracts &c., *288* blk, *289* 290–687 text (511–64 Papers in the Adventurer, 512–627 Political Tracts, 628–87 Journey), *688* Contents.

> *References*: Courtney 168.
> *Notes*: A reimpression from plates of Jones's edn., 1825 (87.3W/23a, above).
> *Copies*: Unlocated.

87.3W/23c Works, Jones's edition, Bohn 1854

Works of Samuel Johnson, LL.D. . . . A new edition, with an Essay . . . London: Henry G. Bohn. 1854
  2 vols., 8°

I. Pp. *i* t., *iii* iv–xl Murphy's Essay, *²i* t. Rambler 1825, *ii* coloph., *iii*–iv Historical Preface, *v* vi–viii Contents, on B1 *1* 2–351 text Ramblers 1–208, *352* blk, on *²*a1 *i* t. Idler 1825, *ii* coloph., *iii*–iv Contents, *v* vi–xii Biographical and Historical Preface, on *²*B1 *1* 2–111 text Idlers (inc. *22), *112* blk, on π1 *i* t. Lives of Poets 1825, *ii* coloph., *iii* Contents, *iv* blk, on *³*A1 *1* 2–363 text, *364* coloph.

II. Pp. *1* t. Rasselas 1825, *2* coloph., *3* 4–44 text, *45* ½t Poems, *46* blk, *47* 48–104 *105* text, *106* Contents, *107* ½t Lives of Eminent Persons *108* blk, *109* 110–207 text, *208* blk, *209* ½t Letters, *210* blk, *211* 212–42 text, *243* ½t Prayers and Meditations, *244* blk, *245* 246–50 Preface and advertisement, *251* 252–84 text, *285* Contents, *286* blk, *287* ½t Tracts &c., *288* blk, *289* 290–687 text (511–64 Papers in the Adventurer, 512–627 Political Tracts, 628–87 Journey), *688* Contents.

> *Notes*: A reimpression of Jones's edn., 1825 (87.3W/23a, above).
> *Copies*: *USA*: CtY, PP; *UK*: BMp.

87.3W/23d Works, Jones's edition, Bohn 1862

Works of Samuel Johnson, LL.D. . . . London: Bohn
  2 vols., 8°

I. Pp. *i* t., *iii* iv–xl Murphy's Essay, *²i* t. Rambler 1825, *ii* coloph., *iii*–iv Historical Preface, *v* vi–viii Contents, on B1 *1* 2–351 text Ramblers 1–208, *352* blk, on *²*a1 *i* t. Idler 1825, *ii* coloph., *iii*–iv Contents, *v* vi–xii Biographical and Historical Preface, on *²*B1 *1* 2–111 text Idlers (inc. *22), *112* blk, on π1 *i* t. Lives of Poets 1825, *ii* coloph., *iii* Contents, *iv* blk, on *³*A1 *1* 2–363 text, *364* coloph.

II. Pp. *1* t. Rasselas 1825, *2* coloph., *3* 4–44 text, *45* ½t Poems, *46* blk, *47* 48–104 *105* text, *106* Contents, *107* ½t Lives of Eminent Persons *108* blk, *109* 110–207 text, *208* blk, *209* ½t Letters, *210* blk, *211* 212–42 text, *243* ½t Prayers and Meditations, *244* blk, *245* 246–50 Preface and advertisement, *251* 252–84 text, *285* Contents, *286* blk, *287* ½t Tracts &c., *288* blk, *289* 290–687 text (511–64 Papers in the Adventurer, 512–627 Political Tracts, 628–87 Journey), *688* Contents.

Notes: A reimpression of Jones's edn., 1825 (87.3W/23a, above).
Copies: BMp (500664–5).

87.3W/23e   Works, Jones's edition, Bohn   [? 1863]

Works of Samuel Johnson, LL.D. . . . London: Bohn [n.d.]
2 vols., 8°. Not examined.

I. Pp. *i* t., *iii* iv–xl Murphy's Essay, ²*i* t. Rambler 1825, *ii* coloph., *iii*–iv Historical Preface, *v* vi–viii Contents, on B1 *1* 2–351 text Ramblers 1–208, *352* blk, on ²a1 *i* t. Idler 1825, *ii* coloph., *iii*–iv Contents, *v* vi–xii Biographical and Historical Preface, on ²B1 *1* 2–111 text Idlers (inc. *22), *112* blk, on π1 *i* t. Lives of Poets 1825, *ii* coloph., *iii* Contents, *iv* blk, on ³A1 *1* 2–363 text, *364* coloph.

II. Pp. *1* t. Rasselas 1825, *2* coloph., *3* 4–44 text, *45* ½t Poems, *46* blk, *47* 48–104 *105* text, *106* Contents, *107* ½t Lives of Eminent Persons *108* blk, *109* 110–207 text, *208* blk, *209* ½t Letters, *210* blk, *211* 212–42 text, *243* ½t Prayers and Meditations, *244* blk, *245* 246–50 Preface and advertisement, *251* 252–84 text, *285* Contents, *286* blk, *287* ½t Tracts &c., *288* blk, *289* 290–687 text (511–64 Papers in the Adventurer, 512–627 Political Tracts, 628–87 Journey), *688* Contents.

Notes: A reimpression of Jones's edn., 1825 (87.3W/23a, above).
Copies: BMp (456410–11).

87.3W/24   Works, second American edition   1825

THE | WORKS | OF | SAMUEL JOHNSON, L.L.D. | A NEW EDITION, | IN SIX VOLUMES. | WITH | AN ESSAY ON HIS LIFE AND GENIUS, | BY ARTHUR MURPHY, ESQ. | VOL. I [– VI]. | [short rule] | [**BL**] **Philadelphia**: | H.C. CAREY & I. LEA, TOWER & HOGAN, R.H. SMALL, ROBT. | DESILVER, AND MAROT & WALTER; | AND | COLLINS & HANNAY, COLLINS & CO., W.B. GILLEY, WILDER & CAMPBELL, | J.V. SEAMAN, AND D. MALLORY, NEW-YORK. | William Brown, Printer. | 1825.

6 vols., 8°. Not examined.

References: Courtney 168; S&S 21066 [CtHT-W, LN, LNH, MA, MdBS, MnMohC, NNF, NWM, TNJ, TxAuPT, Wv].

Copies: MH² (**1**. KE 24097); *USA*: DLC, Hyde ('Van Hoostraad'), ICU, MWA, NN, PHi ('New York'), PU ('New York'), ViU.

87.3W/25a   Works, 'First Complete American   [1832]
              Edition', New York, Blake

THE | WORKS | OF | SAMUEL JOHNSON, LL.D. | WITH AN | ESSAY ON HIS LIFE AND GENIUS, | BY | ARTHUR MURPHY, ESQ. | [short rule] | FIRST COMPLETE AMERICAN EDITION. | [short rule] | IN TWO VOLUMES. | I [– II]. | NEW-YORK: | A. V. BLAKE … [1832]
2 vols., 8°. Not examined.

I. Pp. *i* ½t, *iii* t., *i* ii–xxxiii Murphy's *Essay*, *xxxiv* blk, ²*i*–ii Advert. ('New-York, 1832', unsigned), *iii* iv–vi Contents, *vii* viii–xii Historical and Biographical Preface, 13–570 text.

II. Pp. *i* ½t, *iii* t., *1–2* Contents, *3* 4–699 text, *700* blk.

References: S&S 13174 [CtY, NN].
Notes: This edition was stereotyped and reimpressed and reissued several times, with many variant imprints reflecting the publishers, the different places of publication, and the different printers of the plates (whose imprints are generally found on the versos of the tt.), see 87.3W/25b–u, below. There are likely to be more variants than those recorded below, but perhaps not many more. The collection is distinctive in that vol. 1 is signed alphabetically, but the gatherings in vol. 2 are numbered. An uncut copy measures 10¼ × 6½ in., i.e. a Royal size, and because the sheets are gathered in 4s it is often (wrongly) described or catalogued as 4°.
Copies: *USA*: [CtY, NN].

87.3W/25b   Works, 'First Complete American   1832
              Edition', New York, Dearborn

THE | WORKS | OF | SAMUEL JOHNSON, LL.D. | WITH AN | ESSAY ON HIS LIFE AND GENIUS, | BY | ARTHUR MURPHY, ESQ. | [short rule] | FIRST COMPLETE AMERICAN EDITION. | [short rule] | IN TWO VOLUMES. | I [– II]. | NEW-YORK: | GEORGE DEARBORN, PUBLISHER. | SOLD BY COLLINS & HANNAY, NEW-YORK; CARTER, HENDEE & CO. BOSTON; | DESILVER, JR.

& THOMAS, PHILADELPHIA; AND EDWARD | J. COALE & CO.
BALTIMORE. | [dash] | 1832.

  2 vols., 8°. Not examined.
  References: S&S 13175 [IEN, NcU, OClW, TU].
  Notes: A reimpression of 87.3W/25a, above.
  Copies: *USA*: CtY, ViU.

| 87.3W/25c | Works, 'First Complete American Edition', New York, Harper | 1832 |

THE | WORKS | OF | SAMUEL JOHNSON, LL.D. | WITH AN |
ESSAY ON HIS LIFE AND GENIUS, | BY | ARTHUR MURPHY, ESQ.
| [short rule] | FIRST COMPLETE AMERICAN EDITION. | [short rule] |
IN TWO VOLUMES. | I [– II]. | NEW-YORK: | HARPER & BROS.
1832.

  2 vols., 8°. Not seen.
  References: S&S 13176 [MHab, MMal, NbU, OWoC].
  Notes: A reimpression of 87.3W/25a, above.
  Copies: [Unlocated].

| 87.3W/25d | Works, 'First Complete American Edition', New York, Dearborn | 1834 |

THE | WORKS | OF | SAMUEL JOHNSON, LL.D. | WITH AN |
ESSAY ON HIS LIFE AND GENIUS, | BY | ARTHUR MURPHY, ESQ.
| [short rule] | FIRST COMPLETE AMERICAN EDITION. | [short rule] |
IN TWO VOLUMES. | I [– II]. | NEW-YORK: | GEORGE
DEARBORN, PUBLISHER. | SOLD BY COLLINS & HANNAY, NEW-
YORK; CARTER, HENDEE & CO., BOSTON; | DESILVER, JR. &
THOMAS, PHILADELPHIA; AND EDWARD | J. COALE & CO.,
BALTIMORE. | [dash] | 1834.

  2 vols., 8°. Not examined.
  References: S&S 25143 [Co-SC, IJ, MChi, OClW, TxH].
  Notes: A reimpression of 87.3W/25a, above.
  Copies: *USA*: DFo, Hyde ('Van Schoonhoven', uncut: 10¼ × 6½ in.), NN.

| 87.3W/25e | Works, 'First Complete American Edition', New York, Dearborn | 1835 |

THE | WORKS | OF | SAMUEL JOHNSON, LL.D. | WITH AN |
ESSAY ON HIS LIFE AND GENIUS, | BY | ARTHUR MURPHY, ESQ.

| [short rule] | FIRST COMPLETE AMERICAN EDITION. | [short rule] | IN TWO VOLUMES. | I [– II]. | NEW-YORK: | GEORGE DEARBORN, PUBLISHER. | SOLD BY COLLINS & HANNAY, NEW-YORK; CARTER, HENDEE & CO. BOSTON; | DESILVER, JR. & THOMAS, PHILADELPHIA; AND EDWARD | J. COALE & CO. BALTIMORE. | [dash] | 1835.

2 vols., 8°. Not examined.

References: S&S 32411 [GOgU, IaPeC, KRCBt, MiD, TxShA].

Notes: Another impression of 87.3W/25a, above.

Copies: NN.

87.3W/25f   Works, 'First Complete American   1836
                     Edition', New York, Dearborn

THE | WORKS | OF | SAMUEL JOHNSON, LL.D. | WITH AN | ESSAY ON HIS LIFE AND GENIUS, | BY | ARTHUR MURPHY, ESQ. | [short rule] | FIRST COMPLETE AMERICAN EDITION. | [short rule] | IN TWO VOLUMES. | I [– II]. | NEW-YORK: | GEORGE DEARBORN, PUBLISHER. | SOLD BY COLLINS & HANNAY, NEW-YORK; CARTER, HENDEE & CO. BOSTON; | DESILVER, JR. & THOMAS, PHILADELPHIA; AND EDWARD | J. COALE & CO. BALTIMORE. | [dash] | 1836.

2 vols., 8°. Not examined.

References: S&S 38309 [MoGl, OAk, PV, TxU, ViL].

Notes: A reimpression of 87.3W/25a, above.

Copies: MH; *USA*: CtY, DLC, NIC, ViU.

87.3W/25g   Works, 'First Complete American   1837
                     Edition', New York, Dearborn

THE | WORKS | OF | SAMUEL JOHNSON, LL.D. | WITH AN | ESSAY ON HIS LIFE AND GENIUS, | BY | ARTHUR MURPHY, ESQ. | [short rule] | FIRST COMPLETE AMERICAN EDITION. | [short rule] | IN TWO VOLUMES. | I [– II]. | NEW-YORK: | GEORGE DEARBORN, PUBLISHER. | SOLD BY COLLINS & HANNAY, NEW-YORK; CARTER, HENDEE & CO., BOSTON; | DESILVER, JR. & THOMAS, PHILADELPHIA; AND EDWARD | J. COALE & CO., BALTIMORE. | [dash] | 1837.

2 vols., 8°. Not examined.

References: S&S 45007 [KyBgW, KyLoP, PSC].

Notes: Another impression of 87.3W/25a, above.

Copies: *USA*: MH, ViU.

87.3W/25h Works, 'First Complete American 1837
Edition', New York, Dearborn

THE | WORKS | OF | SAMUEL JOHNSON, LL.D. | WITH AN | ESSAY ON HIS LIFE AND GENIUS, | BY | ARTHUR MURPHY, ESQ. | [short rule] | FIRST COMPLETE AMERICAN EDITION. | [short rule] | IN TWO VOLUMES. | I [– II]. | NEW-YORK: | GEORGE DEARBORN, PUBLISHER. | SOLD BY COLLINS, KEESE, & Co. NEW-YORK; OTIS, BROADEN, & Co., BOSTON; | DESILVER, THOMAS, & Co., PHILADELPHIA. | [rule] | 1837.

2 vols., 8°. Not examined.

References: S&S 45001.

Notes: Another impression of 87.3W/25a, above; coloph: 'New-York: Printed by Scatcherd & Adams. No. 38 Gold Street.'

Copies: *USA*: NIC ('William Andrus' — Pres. NIC by 'Miss Andrus, 1929').[1]

---

[1] I am indebted to D.D. Eddy for information on this copy.

87.3W/25i Works, 'First Complete American 1838
Edition', New York, Blake

THE | WORKS | OF | SAMUEL JOHNSON, LL.D. | WITH AN | ESSAY ON HIS LIFE AND GENIUS, | BY | ARTHUR MURPHY, ESQ. | [short rule] | FIRST COMPLETE AMERICAN EDITION. | [short rule] | IN TWO VOLUMES. | I [– II]. | NEW-YORK: | A. V. BLAKE . . . 1838

[Engr. t.] . . . GEORGE DEARBORN, PUBLISHER. | SOLD BY COLLINS & HANNAY, NEW-YORK; CARTER, HENDEE & CO. BOSTON; | DESILVER, JR. & THOMAS, PHILADELPHIA; AND EDWARD | J. COALE & CO. BALTIMORE. | [dash] | 1838.

2 vols., 8°. Not examined.

Notes: Another impression of 87.3W/25a, above.

Copies: *USA*: NN, NRo, PPU.

87.3W/25j Works, 'First Complete American 1840
Edition', New York, Dearborn

THE | WORKS | OF | SAMUEL JOHNSON, LL.D. | WITH AN | ESSAY ON HIS LIFE AND GENIUS, | BY | ARTHUR MURPHY, ESQ. | [short rule] | FIRST COMPLETE AMERICAN EDITION. | [short rule] | IN TWO VOLUMES. | I [– II]. | NEW-YORK: | GEORGE DEARBORN, PUBLISHER. | SOLD | BY COLLINS & HANNAY, NEW-YORK; CARTER, HENDEE & CO., BOSTON; | DESILVER, JR.

| THOMAS, PHILADELPHIA; AND EDWARD | J. COALE & CO., BALTIMORE. | [dash] | 1840.

2 vols., 8°. Not examined.

Notes: Another impression of 87.3W/25a, above. [PPL & PGirard, give '1842' with this imprint.] S&S 40-3641, give a Philadelphian imprint: 'Alexander V. Blake, publisher; sold by Collins, Keese & Co; Otis, Boadens & Co.; Thomas, Cowperthwaite & Co.', and locate: KyU, Nh-Hi, OC, OO, and TJaU.

Copies: *USA*: NN, OCi ('Blake' in imprint).

87.3W/25k   Works, 'First Complete American   1843
                    Edition', New York, Dearborn

THE | WORKS | OF | SAMUEL JOHNSON, LL.D. | WITH AN | ESSAY ON HIS LIFE AND GENIUS, | BY | ARTHUR MURPHY, ESQ. | [short rule] | FIRST COMPLETE AMERICAN EDITION. | [short rule] | IN TWO VOLUMES. | I [– II]. | NEW-YORK: | GEORGE DEARBORN, PUBLISHER. | SOLD | BY COLLINS & HANNAY, NEW-YORK; CARTER, HENDEE & CO., BOSTON; | DESILVER, JR. | THOMAS, PHILADELPHIA; AND EDWARD | J. COALE & CO., BALTIMORE. | [dash] | 1843.

2 vols., 8°. Not examined.

Notes: Another impression of 87.3W/25a, above.

Copies: *USA*: NN, PPL.

87.3W/25l   Works, 'Third American Edition',   1846
                    New York, Blake

THE | WORKS | OF | SAMUEL JOHNSON, LL.D. | WITH AN | ESSAY ON HIS LIFE AND GENIUS, | BY | ARTHUR MURPHY, ESQ. | [short rule] | THIRD AMERICAN EDITION. | [short rule] | IN TWO VOLUMES. | I [– II]. | NEW-YORK: | A. V. BLAKE . . . 1846

2 vols., 8°. Not examined.

Notes: Another impression of 87.3W/25a, above.

Copies: *USA*: ViU; [PPHatU has 'New York: Harper' with this date].

87.3W/25m   Works, 'Third Complete American   1851
                    Edition', New York, Dearborn

THE | WORKS | OF | SAMUEL JOHNSON, LL.D. | WITH AN | ESSAY ON HIS LIFE AND GENIUS, | BY | ARTHUR MURPHY, ESQ.

| [short rule] | THIRD COMPLETE AMERICAN EDITION. | [short rule] | IN TWO VOLUMES. | I [– II]. | NEW-YORK: | GEORGE DEARBORN, PUBLISHER. | SOLD | BY COLLINS & HANNAY, NEW-YORK; CARTER, HENDEE & CO., BOSTON; | DESILVER, JR. | THOMAS, PHILADELPHIA; AND EDWARD | J. COALE & CO., BALTIMORE. | [dash] | 1851.

2 vols., 8°. Not examined.

Notes: Another impression of 87.3W/25a, above.

Copies: *USA*: NRo² (1. PR 3520.1851).

87.3W/25n   Works, 'First Complete American   1851
                  Edition', New York, Harper

THE | WORKS | OF | SAMUEL JOHNSON, LL.D. | WITH AN | ESSAY ON HIS LIFE AND GENIUS, | BY | ARTHUR MURPHY, ESQ. | [short rule] | FIRST COMPLETE AMERICAN EDITION. | [short rule] | IN TWO VOLUMES. | I [– II]. | NEW-YORK: | HARPER & BROS. 1851.

2 vols., 8°. Not examined.

Notes: Another impression of 87.3W/25a, above.

Copies: *USA*: ViU; [PCC, PPCCH].

87.3W/25o   Works, 'First Complete American   1854
                  Edition', New York, Dearborn

THE | WORKS | OF | SAMUEL JOHNSON, LL.D. | WITH AN | ESSAY ON HIS LIFE AND GENIUS, | BY | ARTHUR MURPHY, ESQ. | [short rule] | FIRST COMPLETE AMERICAN EDITION. | [short rule] | IN TWO VOLUMES. | I [– II]. | NEW-YORK: | GEORGE DEARBORN, PUBLISHER. | SOLD | BY COLLINS & HANNAY, NEW-YORK; CARTER, HENDEE & CO., BOSTON; | DESILVER, JR. | THOMAS, PHILADELPHIA; AND EDWARD | J. COALE & CO., BALTIMORE. | [dash] | 1854.

2 vols., 8°. Not examined.

Notes: Another impression of 87.3W/25a, above.

Copies: *USA*: CtY, DLC.

87.3W/25p   Works, 'First Complete American   1856
                  Edition', New York, Dearborn

THE | WORKS | OF | SAMUEL JOHNSON, LL.D. | WITH AN | ESSAY ON HIS LIFE AND GENIUS, | BY | ARTHUR MURPHY, ESQ.

| [short rule] | FIRST COMPLETE AMERICAN EDITION. | [short rule] | IN TWO VOLUMES. | I [– II]. | NEW-YORK: | GEORGE DEARBORN, PUBLISHER. | SOLD | BY COLLINS & HANNAY, NEW-YORK; CARTER, HENDEE & CO., BOSTON; | DESILVER, JR. | THOMAS, PHILADELPHIA; AND EDWARD | J. COALE & CO., BALTIMORE. | [dash] | 1856.

2 vols., 8°. Not examined.

Notes: Another impression of 87.3W/25a, above.

Copies: *USA*: PPL.

87.3W/25q   Works, 'Third Complete American   1857
                  Edition', New York, Harper

THE | WORKS | OF | SAMUEL JOHNSON, LL.D. | WITH AN | ESSAY ON HIS LIFE AND GENIUS, | BY | ARTHUR MURPHY, ESQ. | [short rule] | THIRD COMPLETE AMERICAN EDITION. | [short rule] | IN TWO VOLUMES. | I [– II]. | NEW-YORK: | HARPER & BROS. 1857.

Var: [?. . . GEORGE DEARBORN, PUBLISHER. | SOLD | BY COLLINS & HANNAY, NEW-YORK; CARTER, HENDEE & CO., BOSTON; | DESILVER, JR. | THOMAS, PHILADELPHIA; AND EDWARD | J. COALE & CO., BALTIMORE. | [dash] | 1857.]

2 vols., 8°. Not examined.

Notes: Another impression of 87.3W/25a, above.

Copies: *USA*: MH (KF 3045).

87.3W/25r   Works, 'First Complete American   1859
                  Edition', New York, Harper

THE | WORKS | OF | SAMUEL JOHNSON, LL.D. | WITH AN | ESSAY ON HIS LIFE AND GENIUS, | BY | ARTHUR MURPHY, ESQ. | [short rule] | FIRST COMPLETE AMERICAN EDITION. | [short rule] | IN TWO VOLUMES. | I [– II]. | NEW-YORK: | HARPER & BROS. 1859.

[?**Var**: . . . GEORGE DEARBORN, PUBLISHER. | SOLD | BY COLLINS & HANNAY, NEW-YORK; CARTER, HENDEE & CO., BOSTON; | DESILVER, JR. | THOMAS, PHILADELPHIA; AND EDWARD | J. COALE & CO., BALTIMORE. | [dash] | 1857.]

2 vols., 8°. Not examined.

Notes: Another impression of 87.3W/25a, above.

Copies: *USA*: CtY ('Harper').

1708

Works, Nimmo

87.3W/25s   Works, Harper   1861

Works of Samuel Johnson, LL.D. . . . New York: Harper.
  2 vols., 8°. Not seen.
  Notes: Probably another impression of 87.3W/25a, above.
  Copies: *USA*: PPAmSwd, HMus.

87.3W/25t   Works, Harper   1862

Works of Samuel Johnson, LL.D. . . . New York: Harper.
  2 vols., 8°. Not examined.
  Notes: Probably a reimpression of 87.3W/25a, above.
  Copies: *USA*: PHC.

87.3W/25u   Works, 'Third American edition',   1873
                    New York, Harper

THE | WORKS | OF | SAMUEL JOHNSON, LL.D. | WITH AN |
ESSAY ON HIS LIFE AND GENIUS, | BY | ARTHUR MURPHY, ESQ.
| [short rule] | THIRD AMERICAN EDITION. | [short rule] | IN TWO
VOLUMES. | I [– II]. | NEW-YORK: | HARPER & BROS. 1873.
  2 vols., 8°. Not examined.
  Notes: Another impression of 87.3W/25a, above.
  Copies: *USA*: CtY, DLC, MB.

87.3W/26a   Works, Nimmo   1876

[Within a single rule] THE WORKS | OF | SAMUEL JOHNSON, LL.D. |
COMPRISING THE | LIVES OF THE ENGLISH POETS; |
RASSELAS; | LIVES OF EMINENT PERSONS; | AND A | JOURNEY
TO THE WESTERN ISLANDS OF SCOTLAND. | WITH AN
INTRODUCTORY ESSAY BY | ARTHUR MURPHY. | *AND THIRTY-
TWO PORTRAITS ON STEEL.* | WILLIAM P. NIMMO, | LONDON: 14
KING WILLIAM STREET, STRAND; | AND EDINBURGH. | 1876.
  8°, A^8 B–2P^8, ($1 signed), 304 leaves.
  Pp. Engr. port. front. ('Samuel Johnson, L.L.D. Engraved by Mr R. Page
from the admired Painting By Sir Joshua Reynolds. Johnson's Works.
Frontispiece'), guarded with loose tissue + A1 *1* t., *2* coloph: Murray and Gibb,
Edinburgh, | Printers to Her Majesty's Stationery Office., *3*–4 Contents, 4
Erratum, 5–42 Murphy's Essay, 43–405 Lives of the Poets, *406* blk, 407–48
Rasselas, *449* 450–547 Lives of Eminent Persons, *548* blk, 549–608 Journey.

Plates: Cowley, facing p. 43, Milton (66), Butler (95), Roscommon (103), Otway (107), Waller (109), Dorset (125), Stepney (126), John Philips (127), Walsh (133), Dryden (134), Parnell (190), Garth (191), Rowe (193), Addison (197), Sheffield (219), Prior (221), Congreve (229), Fenton (241), Gay (244), Tickell (252), Somervile (255), Pope (308), Thomson (357), Watts (362), West (368), Shenstone (372), Young (375), Akenside (395), Gray (397), Lyttelton (402), which with the frontispiece makes a total of 32. The *Erratum* on p. 4 notes: 'It will be seen that the Portraits in the present Edition of Johnson's Works are incorrectly paged, but they are in every case properly placed beside the Life of the Poet to which they correspond.'

Notes: All letterpress pages are enclosed in a single rule frame, and exhibit some type batter as from stereotyping. The antecedent impression is not certain, but the inscription on the frontispiece implies some descent from Jones's edn. 1825 (87.3W/23a, above), and it seems that this volume is made up of selected plates from that initial impression though probably more directly from Bohn's plates of 1850 (87.3W/23b, above).

A 16 pp. section of Nimmo's adverts. may be bound in at the end, listing this as no. 21 of 'Nimmo's Library Edition of Standard Works' (p. 5), 'In large demy 8vo, with Steel Portrait and Vignette, handsomely bound, roxburgh style, gilt top, price 5s. each.' and the additional note: 'This series is also kept bound in cloth extra, full gilt side, back, and edges, price 6s. 6d. each; and in half-calf extra, marbled sides, edges, and end papers, price 8s. 6d. each. Also in full calf, gilt back and edges.' Boswell's *Life* was no. 16 in the same series.

Copies: JDF ('R.G.R. Hill') in dark olive cloth with black endpapers, gilt spine title: Dᴿ. JOHNSON'S | WORKS | Lɪᴠᴇs ᴏꜰ Tʜᴇ Pᴏᴇᴛs | [short rule]| Rᴀssᴇʟᴀs | [short rule] | Jᴏᴜʀɴᴇʏ ᴛᴏ Wᴇsᴛᴇʀɴ Isʟᴀɴᴅs | *&c &c* | Wɪᴛʜ 32 Pᴏʀᴛʀᴀɪᴛs | NIMMO'S | STANDARD LIBRARY. *Can*: CaOTM (Wood 185).

87.3W/26b   Works, Nimmo   1877

[Within a single rule] THE WORKS | OF | SAMUEL JOHNSON, LL.D. | COMPRISING THE LIVES OF THE ENGLISH POETS; | RASSELAS; | LIVES OF EMINENT PERSONS; | AND A | JOURNEY TO THE WESTERN ISLANDS OF SCOTLAND. | WITH AN INTRODUCTORY ESSAY BY | ARTHUR MURPHY. | *AND THIRTY-TWO PORTRAITS ON STEEL.* | WILLIAM P. NIMMO, | LONDON: 14 KING WILLIAM STREET, STRAND; | AND EDINBURGH. | 1877.

8°. A reimpression of prec. 87.3W/26a, differing only in the date on t.

Copies: *USA*: Hyde ('Oakley'); *UK*: DUu, Gu; *Aust*: CNL.

87.3W/26c   Works, Nimmo   1878

[Within a single rule] THE WORKS | OF | SAMUEL JOHNSON, LL.D. | CONTAINING THE LIVES OF THE ENGLISH POETS; | RASSELAS; | LIVES OF EMINENT PERSONS; | AND A | JOURNEY TO THE WESTERN ISLANDS OF SCOTLAND. | WITH AN INTRODUCTORY ESSAY BY | ARTHUR MURPHY. | [BL] **With Portraits.** | WILLIAM P. NIMMO, | LONDON AND EDINBURGH. | 1878.

8°. Another issue of Nimmo's edn., 1876 (87.3W/26a, above), but no coloph. on p. 2.

Copies: BMp, JDF (ex: J. Clark-Hall, Ltd., *Cat.* 48 (1993), 21).

87.3W/26d   Works, Nimmo, The Standard Library   [c. 1881]

The Standard Library.

[Within a single rule] THE WORKS | OF | SAMUEL JOHNSON, LL.D. | CONTAINING THE | LIVES OF THE ENGLISH POETS; | RASSELAS; | LIVES OF EMINENT PERSONS; | AND A | JOURNEY TO THE WESTERN ISLANDS OF SCOTLAND. | WITH AN INTRODUCTORY ESSAY BY | ARTHUR MURPHY. | [BL] **With Portraits.** | EDINBURGH: | W.P. NIMMO, HAY, & MITCHELL.

8°. Another impression or issue of 87.3W/26a, above, undated, but published about 1881.

Copies: *USA*: CtY ['1881'], Hyde ('Start' — 'Cross' — 'Flower'), PPL ['1881']; *UK*: E (BCL.D.6399, '? 1888').

87.3W/27a   Works, Literary Club edition   1903

The Literary Club Edition.

Gen. t: THE WORKS OF SAMUEL JOHNSON LITERARY CLUB EDITION FROM TYPE IN SIXTEEN VOLUMES. VOLUME I [–XVI].

16 vols. 8°. Not examined.

I–IV. The Rambler; IV. Rambler and Adventurer; V. Adventurer and Idler; VI. Idler and Poems; VII. Rasselas and Letters; VIII–XI. Lives of the Poets; XI. Lives of the Poets, and other Pieces; XII. Miscellaneous essays; XIII. Reviews and Political Tracts; XIV. Lives of Eminent Persons; XV. Journey to the Hebrides; Vision of Theodore, and The Fountains; XVI. 'Book of Devotions' [= Prayers & Meditations].

Paper: (uncut: 9⅛ × 6 in.).

References: Courtney 168; Clifford & Greene 2.1.

Notes: Each vol. begins with the Gen. t., followed by a distinct t. listing the contents, (e.g. I: THE RAMBLER | BY SAMUEL JOHNSON | [orn.] | THE LAMB PUBLISHING COMPANY | NEW YORK). On the verso of this t. is: 'Of this Extra Illustrated Edition of the Works of Samuel Johnson, Fifty-seven Sets have been printed from type on Special Water Marked Paper, of which this Copy is No.   Pafraets Press, Troy, New York, 1903'. It was also issued in 8 vols., see next entry.

Copies: CSmH (no. 7);

USA: Hyde (no. 433), MB, TxU, WiM; *UK*: [Gu (LJ20.1903)], SAN (ʳPR 3520.FO3), [WLAp]; *Aust*: CNL.

87.3W/27b   Works, New Cambridge edition   [?? 1903]

New Cambridge Edition

The Works of Samuel Johnson . . . Cambridge, Mass.: Harvard Cooperative Society; New York: Bigelow, Smith, and Co.

8 vols. Not examined.

References: Clifford & Greene 2.1.

Notes: This is a reissue of prec. (87.3W/27a), bound in 8 vols. rather than 16.

Copies: IU.

87.3W/S   WORKS SELECTIONS

Selections from Johnson abound, and the following list has no claim to completeness. Copies are not listed because this section was not originally planned for inclusion in the bibliography. Selections are more often derived from Boswell than from Johnson's writing, but they have a claim to inclusion on the grounds that they may be better known to the general reader than are complete collections.

Both Davies's *Miscellaneous and Fugitive Pieces*, 3 vols. 1773–4 (73.12DM), and William Cooke's *Beauties of Johnson*, 1781 (81.11B), have been noticed in the appropriate chronological place above. To them may be addded the following selections.[1]

[1] I am indebted to the lists in Clifford and Greene 49–52, and Greene and Vance, *A Bibliography of Johnsonian Studies, 1970–1985* (1987), 7. Further notices of selections in less specific anthologies will also be found in these works.

87.3W/S/1   Selected Works, Harper's Family   1840
                        Library, Nos. CIX–CX

'Harper's Family Library', Nos. CIX–CX. The Life and Writings of Samuel Johnson, LL.D., selected and arranged by the Rev. William P. Page. New York: Harper and Brothers, 1840. 2 vols.

Notes: This was also issued as No. 122 in 'Harper Brothers School District Library', 1840 (*Copy*: NIC); and reimpressed and republished in 1844, and 1855. The selections are chiefly from SJ's periodical essays.

87.3W/S/2   Selected Works, Library of   [1875]
Thoughtful Books

'The Library of Thoughtful Books' The Wisdom and Genius of Samuel Johnson, selected from his prose writings by W.A. Clouston. London: Blackwood and Co. [n.d. 1875].

87.3W/S/3   Selected Works, Life, Works   1884
and Table Talk

Dr. Johnson His Life, Works and Table Talk. Centenary Edition. With a prefatory Note by James Macaulay, Editor of the 'Leisure Hour'. T. Fisher Unwin. 1884.

87.3W/S/4   Selected Works, Life, Works   [c.1884]
and Table Talk, Diprose's Miniature Library

Diprose's Miniature library. Dr. Johnson His Life, Works and Table Talk. Centenary Edition. With a prefatory Note by James Macaulay, Editor of the 'Leisure Hour'. London. Diprose & Bateman. [n.d.]

The *Table Talk* was published separately, n.d., (pp. 128), in the same series. Its prefatory note, signed 'Macaulay' is from T.B. Macaulay's account of SJ. (JDF copy of TT is signed 'R.S. Hutton, July 28th 1880'). No copy of the 'Centenary Edition', above, is located, but some confusion may be suspected.

87.3W/S/5   Selected Works, Characteristics,   1884
and Aphorisms

Johnson: His Characteristics and Aphorisms. By James Hay. Paisley and London: Alexander Gardner. 1884.

Notes: The 'Aphorisms' include many extracts from SJ's writings (as well as his conversation), and are classified by topics (pp. 9–173).

87.3W/S/6   Selected Works, Wit and Wisdom   1888

Wit and Wisdom of Samuel Johnson. Selected and Arranged by George Birkbeck Hill, D.C.L. Pembroke College, Oxford At the Clarendon Press. 1888. [All rights reserved]
  Pp. xxiii, *xxiv* + 323, *324.*

87.3W/S/7   Selected Works, Little Masterpieces   1905

[With red double rules, red and black] Little Masterpieces Edited by William Stead, Jr. Samuel Johnson Born September 18, 1709 Died December 13, 1784 Conversations Prayers and meditations Essays from the Rambler and Idler The English Dictionary Lives of the Poets London The Masterpiece Press 14 Temple House, Temple Avenue 1905
  Pp. *i* ½t, *ii* blk, *iii* t., *iv* blk, v–vi Conts., vii–xxiii Introd. (Thomas Carlyle), *xxiv* blk, on A1 *1* ½t, *2* blk, 3–201 *202* text, *202* coloph: The Riverside Press limited, Edinburgh. Printed pink paper wraps. 'One Shilling'.

87.3W/S/8   Selected Works, Arnold Prose Books,   [? 1905]
                                     No. 7

Arnold Prose Books, no. 7. Selections from Samuel Johnson. London: Edward Arnold & Co. [n.d. 1905]

87.3W/S/9   Selected Works, Wit and Wisdom   1908

The Wit and Wisdom of Samuel Johnson and His Friends: A Calendar for 1909. Philadelphia: Stern. 1908
  Notes: Privately printed for A.E. Newton as a Christmas keepsake.

87.3W/S/10   Selected Works, Wit and Sagacity   1909

The Wit and Sagacity of Dr. Johnson, selected by Norman J. Davidson. London: Seeley. 1909.

87.3W/S/11   Selections from the Works, ed. Osgood   1910

Selections from the Works of Samuel Johnson, ed. Charles G. Osgood. New York: Henry Holt & Co, 1909; London: George Bell & Sons, 1910.

**87.3W/S/12   Selected Works, ed. Meynell and   1911
                  Chesterton, Regent Library**

'The Regent Library' Samuel Johnson: Extracts from his Writings. ed. Alice
Meynell, and G.K. Chesterton. London: Herbert and Daniel. 1911
   Notes: Chesterton wrote the Preface.

87.3W/S/13   Selected Works, Johnson Calendar   1916

The Johnson Calendar or Samuel Johnson for every Day of the Year Being a
Series of Sayings and Tales, Collected from his Life and Writings, ΟΣ ΚΑΙ
ΘΝΗΤΟΣ ΕΩΝ ΕΠΕΤ ΑΘΑΝΑΤΟΙΣΙ ΘΕΟΙΣΙ, By Alexander
Montgomerie Bell. Oxford At the Clarendon Press. M DCCCC XVI.
   Pp. *1* t., *2* coloph., *3* Dedication ('The Author South Newington, Banbury,
October 1, 1916.'), *4* blk, *5–6* Conts., *7* 8–11 Chronology, *12* blk, *13* 14–22
'Johnson's Political and Social Opinions', *23* 24–234 Calendar, *235* coloph., *236*
blk. Buff cloth.

**87.3W/S/14   Selected Works, ed. Chapman,   1922
                  Clarendon Series of English Literature**

'Clarendon Series of English Literature' Johnson, Prose and Poetry. edited by
R.W. Chapman. Oxford: The Clarendon Press. 1922.
   Notes: This has frequently been reissued.

87.3W/S/15   Selected Works, ed. Roberts   1926

Samuel Johnson. Writer. Edited by S.C. Roberts. New York: Dial Press;
London: Herbert Jenkins. 1926.

**87.3W/S/16   Selected Works, Selected English   [1936]
                  Classics, ed. Reynolds**

'Selected English Classics' Selections from Johnson, edited by W. Vaughan
Reynolds. London: Ginn and Co. [n.d. 1936]

87.3W/S/17   Selected Works, The Reader's   [1940]
                         Johnson, ed. Conley

The Reader's Johnson A Representative Selection from His Writings Edited by
C.H. Conley Wesleyan University New York Cincinnati Chicago American
Book Company Boston Atlanta Dallas San Francisco [1940]
     Copy: O (2699 e. 371: Imprint overstamped: 'D. Appleton-Century
Company Inc., 34, Bedford Street, Strand, London, W.C. 2.').

87.3W/S/18   Selected Works,   [1947]
          The Portable Johnson and Boswell, ed. Kronenberger

The Portable Johnson & Boswell, edited with an Introduction, by Louis
Kronenberger. New York The Viking Press. [1947]
     Pp. *vi* + 1–437, *438* Selections from JB, *439–41* 442–737 *738* Selections
from SJ, *739–40* 741–62 Appendix.

87.3W/S/19   Selected Works,   1948
          Some Observations and Judgements, ed. Hayward

Dr. Johnson Some Observations and Judgements upon Life and Letters
chosen by John Hayward. London: Zodiac Books. 1948.

87.3W/S/20   Selected Works, Wisdom of   [1948]
                         Dr. Johnson, ed. Maxwell

The Wisdom of Dr. Johnson Being Comments on Life and Moral Precepts
chosen from his Writings compiled with an Introduction by Constantia
Maxwell   Lecky Professor of Modern History Trinity College Dublin
Illustrated. George G. Harrap and Company Ltd London Sydney Toronto
Bombay [1948]
     Pp. *1–4* prelims, 5 compiler's note, *6* blk, 7 Conts., *8* blk, 9 Illus., *10* blk,
11–55 Introd., *56* blk, 57–8 Bibliog., *59* blk, 60 Epigraphs, 61–184 text, 185–6
Index to Introd., 187–9 *190* Index to Extracts. Brown cloth bds, grey-green
printed paper wraps, code: APT/L678.

87.3W/S/21   Selected Works, Falcon Prose   1949
                         Classics, ed. Symons

Falcon Prose Classics. Selected Writings of Samuel Johnson, Edited and introduced by Julian Symons. London Falcon Press. 1949

87.3W/S/22   Selected Works, The Reynard Library,   1950
ed. Crow

'The Reynard Library' Johnson Prose and Poetry Selected by Mona Wilson London Rupert Hart-Davis. 1950.

Notes: The texts were edited by John Crow, usually from first editions. Reissued in 1957, 1963, 1966, 1967, &c.; also in pbk. (1967) ISBN: 246–64495–8.

87.3W/S/23a   Selected Works, Rinehart Editions,   1952
ed. Bronson

'Rinehart Editions' Selected Prose and Poetry, edited with an Introduction and Notes by Bertrand H. Bronson. New York: Rinehart and Co. 1952.

87.3W/S/23b   Selected Works, Rasselas etc.,   [1958]
ed. Bronson

Rasselas, Poems, and Selected Prose, edited with an Introduction and notes by Bertrand H. Bronson. Holt, Rinehart and Winston, Inc. New York Chicago San Francisco Atlanta Dallas Montreal Toronto London Sydney [1958]

Pp. xiv (+ xv–xvi PS on Rasselas) xvii–xxxii, 1–612 + leaf of adverts.

Notes: This is an enlarged edn. of 87.3W/S/23a, and has been reimpressed several times since, and issued in stiff cloth and pbk.

87.3W/S/24a   Selections from Samuel Johnson,   1955
ed. Chapman

Selections from Samuel Johnson, 1709–1784. Edited by R.W. Chapman. London: Oxford University Press. 1955.

87.3W/S/24b   Selections from Johnson,   1962
ed. Chapman, World's Classics

'World's Classics' Selections from Samuel Johnson, 1709–1784. Edited by R.W. Chapman. London: Oxford University Press. 1962.

**87.3W/S/25   Selected Works, A Johnson Sampler,   1963
ed. Curwen**

A Johnson Sampler Edited by Henry Darcy Curwen Harvard University Press
Cambridge Massachusetts 1963.
  Pp. xi *xii–xvi*, *1* 2–320 (with Index).

**87.3W/S/26   Selected Works, A Johnson Reader,   [1964]
ed. MacAdam and Milne**

A Johnson Reader, edited by E.L. MacAdam, Jr. and George Milne. Pantheon
Books A Division of Random House New York [1964]
  Pp. xv *xvi 1–4* 5–464.

**87.3W/S/27   A Johnson Selection, ed. Miles,   1965
English Classics**

'English Classics — New Series' A Johnson Selection, edited with Introduction
and Notes by F.R. Miles Senior English Master King's School, Wimbledon
Macmillan London St. Martin's Press New York 1965
  Pp. *i–iv* prelims, v Conts., vi Ackn., vii–viii Chronlogy, ix–xxxv Introd.,
xxxvi blk, *1* 2–130 text, *131* 132–64 Notes &c., coloph. (164) Printed by
Robert Maclehose and Co. Ltd. The University Press, Glasgow. Printed red
cloth boards.

87.3W/S/28   Selected Writings, ed. Davies   1965

Samuel Johnson Selected Writings Edited with an introduction and notes by R.
T. Davies. Faber and Faber 24 Russell Square London 1965
  Issued in USA with var imprint: . . . Faber and Faber 24 Russell Square
London Evanston, Ill. Northwestern University Press 1965
  Pp. 398 (with Index).

**87.3W/S/29   Selected Works, ed. Peake,   [1967]
Routledge English Texts**

'Routledge English Texts' 'Rasselas' and Essays Samuel Johnson Edited by
Charles Peake London Routledge and Kegan Paul [1967]
  Pp. *i–vii* viii prelims, *ix* ½t, *x* blk, *xi* xii–xlii Introd., *1* 2–105 Rasselas, *106*
blk, *107* 108–165 misc. essays, *166* blk, *167* 168–210 Notes, *211*–212 Further
Reading. (Gen. editor of series: T.S. Dorsch.) Green stiff printed cloth.

87.3W/S/30   Selected Works, ed. Cruttwell,   [1968]
                      Penguin English Library

'Penguin English Library' EL 33 Samuel Johnson Selected Writings, edited
with an Introduction and Notes by Patrick Cruttwell. Penguin Books. [1968]
   Pp. *i–vi* prelims, 7–8 Pref., 9–36 Introd., 37–8 Sel. bibliog., *39–40* 41–514
text, 515–71 Notes *572* blk, *573–6* advts. Ptd. paper covers.

87.3W/S/31   Selected Works, Sayings of   [1968]
                      Dr. Johnson, ed. Reeves

The Sayings of Dr. Johnson compiled by James Reeves John Baker 5 Royal
Opera Arcade, Pall Mall London SW1 [1968]
   Pp. xi *xii*, 1–58 text, 59–60 sources.
   Notes: ISBN: 212-99827-2.

87.3W/S/32   Selected Works, ed. Keats,   [1969]
                      Little Paperback Classics, No. 77

'Little Paperback Classics' No. 77. Selected Sayings of Dr. Johnson Compiled
by A N Keats General Editor A Little Paperback Classic. Pyramid Books New
York [1969]
   Pp. 62 *63–4* advts. for other tt. in series, all at 35¢.
   Notes: The port. on front cover is not of SJ.

87.3W/S/33   Selected Works, Johnson on Johnson,   [1976]
                      ed. Wain

Johnson on Johnson A selection of personal and autobiographical writings of
Samuel Johnson (1709–1784) Selected, with an introduction and commentary
by John Wain. J.M. Dent & Sons Ltd. London [1976]
   Pp. xxiii *xxiv*, 1–247 *248*. ISBN: 0-460-00003-9.

87.3W/S/34   Selected Poetry and Prose,   1977
                      ed. Brady and Wimsatt

Samuel Johnson Selected Poetry and Prose Edited with an Introduction and
Notes by Frank Brady and W.K. Wimsatt University of California Press
Berkeley Los Angeles London 1977
   Pp. xii + 642. ISBN: (pbk) 0-520-03552-6.

87.3W/S/35   Selected Writings, ed. Rogers   1981

The Selected Writings of Samuel Johnson, edited by Katharine Rogers. New York: Signet. 1981

87.3W/S/36   Selected Works, ed. Greene,   1984
                    The Oxford Authors

'The Oxford Authors' Samuel Johnson, edited by Donald Greene. Oxford and New York: Oxford University Press. 1984.

Notes: This is a new selection, breaking with tradition, and offering a distinct view of SJ's literary work.

87.5TL   Taylor's Letter on a Future State   1787

[½t] [double rule] | A | LETTER | TO | SAMUEL JOHNSON, L.L.D. | [double rule]

[Title] A | LETTER | TO | SAMUEL JOHNSON, L.L.D. | ON THE SUBJECT | OF A | FUTURE STATE. | By JOHN TAYLOR, L.L.D. | PREBENDARY OF WESTMINSTER, RECTOR OF BOSWORTH, LEICESTERSHIRE, | AND MINISTER OF ST. MARGARET'S, WESTMINSTER. | [medium swelled rule] | *LONDON:* | PRINTED FOR T. CADELL, IN THE STRAND. | M.DCC.LXXXVII.

4°, π1 *A*⁴ B–C⁴ D² (–D1 = π1) E², ($2 (–D1, E2) signed), 16 leaves.

Pp. π1 ½t, π1ᵛ blk, on A1 t., A1ᵛ blk, A2 Dedication: TO HIS GRACE | WILLIAM DUKE OF DEVONSHIRE. (signed: *'JOHN TAYLOR.'*), A2ᵛ blk, A3 Advertisement, A3ᵛ blk, A4 Verses to Taylor, by Brooke Boothby, Junior., A4ᵛ blk, on B1 *1* 2–18 Letter to Johnson dh: [parallel rule] | A | LETTER | TO | SAMUEL JOHNSON, L.L.D., on E1 19–22 Letters from SJ to Taylor.

Pagination: [↑], no errors.

Press-figures: B4(7)–1, C3ᵛ(14)–1, E1ᵛ(20)–1.

Catchwords: 18 *om.* (*The*), 19 *om.* (DEAR), no errors.

Explicit: none.

Paper: White, laid; Medium (11½ × 9 in.), wmk.: fleur-de-lys in crowned shield + GR (Heawood 1846)

Type: Advertisement and verses: long primer (3.5 mm), leaded (3.2 mm, and 2.4 mm respectively); text: english (4.6 mm), leaded (2.0 mm).

References: Courtney 171; CH 163; *Rothschild* 2391; Waingrow, *Corr.* 98–9 n. 1; Chapman, *RES* ii (1926), 338–9; *Works* (Yale), xiv, p. xxii–xxiii; Waingrow, *MS of Life* i. 172 n.; ESTC: t134055.

Notes: D² and E² were not imposed as a whole sheet ([Liebert: 'Loveday']), but as two distinct pairs. The pamphlet was published 24 May 1787 (*Morning Chron.*). It is noticed in *Gents. Mag.* lvii (1787), 521, 873, and lviii (1788), 37. SJ's letters to Taylor were pp. 19: 18 Mar. 1752 (*Letters* 42, Hyde i. 61–2); pp. 20–1: 17 June 1783 (*Letters* 848, Hyde iv. 148–9); and pp. 21–2: 12 Apr. 1784 (*Letters* 951, Hyde iv. 312). All were printed by JB in *Life*, and this was probably his source (Waingrow).[1]

SJ's responsibility for the *Letter* is glanced at in a note by William Langley, schoolmaster at Ashbourne and no friend to Taylor, reporting a conversation with Archbishop John Moore on 26 July 1790 in which Langley confirmed SJ's authorship of the *Sermons* (88.5S, below), adding 'particulars relative to the pretended Letter to Johnson . . . Met the Bishop alone, further Talk of the Letter. Anecdote of the Bp's presenting it to the King in Manuscript . . . Taylor a mean deceitful Man . . .'.[2] If there was a MS presented to the King, it is no longer to be found.

The translation from Callimachus (pp. 11–2) is attributed to SJ in *Poems*[2], 458–9.

Copies: O (2804 d.46(5));

USA: CSmH, CtY[2] (**1.** Im J637. +787; **2.** Tracts 39), Hyde[2], ICN, IU, [Liebert ('John Loveday', orig. wraps, uncut) = CtY], MH (no ½t); *UK*: [W.R. Batty ('The gift of the Author')], BMp (72794), C (Yorke b.91[10]), Ct-R, E (6.858 (4), disb., Lauriston Castle), [Es], L[2] (**1.** Kings 13; **2.** C.53. d.20), LVu, MRu.

---

[1] This point was anticipated by D. Nichol Smith in a note in his own copy of Courtney (Aust: CNL). In *MS of Life*, Waingrow states that JB's text was 'evidently transcribed from p. 19' of Taylor's publication (p. 172 n.).

[2] O: MS Don. d. 76, fo. 23. Langley added a few more details in a letter to William Davenport, 1 Aug. 1790: 'He (Abp. Cant) asked whence I came & being told, if I knew Dr Taylor. Talked about the Sermons publish'd by Hayes. His Suspicion of their being Johnson's confirm'd by Me: & also particulars relative to the pretended Letter to Johnson . . . Further Talk of the Letter. Curious Anecdote of his Grace's presenting it to the King in MSS.' (MS Don. d. 76, fo. 21).

87GM57   Gentleman's Magazine, Vol. LVII   1787

July 555–57   'Considerations on the Case of Dr. T——s Sermons, abridg'd by Mr Cave'

Composed in 1739 when Trapp's *Sermons* were published (above 39GM9, June 288–92), but first printed here, apparently from the MS (Hyde; *MS Handlist* 27; *MS Index* JoS 176). This version in *Gents. Mag.* was followed by Isaac Reed in *Works*, xiv (1788), 467–73. JB's attribution (*Life* i. 17, 140–1 n. 5), is supported by Reed's and may derive from it. The text is printed by Brack, *Shorter Prose*.

December 1004   Query from 'Index Indicatorius'

'The Doctor wrote a Sermon which was preached at St. James's (or some other capital pulpit) on a 5th of November, and was afterwards published by command of the Archbishop. Qu. in what year, and by whom, was it published ?' The author of the query was probably John Nichols, but no reply was forthcoming.

References: Johnson's Sermons, *Works* (Yale), xiv, p. xxiii, n. 5.

Notes: Further dim light on this sermon is shed by JB in his letters of 11 June 1792 and 28 July 1793 to James Abercrombie which associate it with 'the Bishop of Salisbury', viz. Dr John Douglas, who was in possession of the answer, but JB was unsuccessful.[1]

The topic was perhaps congenial as relating to a feast-day at Pembroke College,[2] and was certain to atttract Tory preachers. The 1745 Jacobite rising may have marked a likely period for such a composition, but of the 32 listed for that date (2 before the King, one before the Lords, one before the Commons, and ten before the Lord Mayor of London) to 1752, I have seen only twelve, of which none can be attributed to SJ.[3]

---

[1] *Life* iii. 507; Waingrow, *Corr.* 484–6, 548–50; CtY. MSS: Boswell, L1, L2.

[2] *Life* i. 60; *Poems*[2] 471 'Somnium'. John Pointer, *Oxoniensis Academica* (1749), 109, and Erasmus Phillipps's 'Diary' in *NQ*, 10 Nov. 1860, reprinted in Macleane, *History of Pembroke College* (1897), ch. xxiv, esp. p. 327.

[3] Sampson Lettsome, *The Preacher's Assistant* (1753), lists published sermons by the names of preachers, dates of publication, format, biblical text, and the occasion.

88.3L/1　　　Letters of Johnson, Piozzi edition[1]　　　1788

LETTERS | TO AND FROM THE LATE | Samuel Johnſon, LL.D. | TO WHICH ARE ADDED | SOME POEMS | NEVER BEFORE PRINTED. | PUBLISHED | FROM THE ORIGINAL MSS. IN HER POSSESSION, | BY HESTER LYNCH PIOZZI. | IN TWO VOLUMES. | VOL. I [– II]. | [parallel rule] | LONDON: | Printed for A. STRAHAN; and T. CADELL, in the Strand. | MDCCLXXXVIII.

2 vols., 8°

I. π² (π1 blk) a⁸ B–2C⁸, ($4 signed; 'VOL. I.' on $1), 210 leaves.

Pp. π1 blk, π2 t., on a2 *i* ii–vi Preface, *vii* viii–xv Contents, *xvi* blk, on B1 *1* 2–391, 389–97 [=399] text of Letters dh: LETTERS | TO AND FROM | Samuel Johnſon, LL.D. | [medium swelled rule], rt: LETTERS TO AND FROM | DR. SAMUEL JOHNSON., *400* blk.

Pagination: 390–91 duplicated at 2C3ᵛ–2C4.

Press-figures: a2ᵛ(ii)–8, a3ᵛ(iv)–1, B6ᵛ(12)–8, B8(15)–3, C8(31)–9, D4ᵛ(40)–2, D8(47)–9, E1ᵛ(50)–7, E8ᵛ(64)–8, F4ᵛ(72)–3, F5ᵛ(74)–4, G6(91)–2, G8ᵛ(96)–8, H1ᵛ(98)–1, H2ᵛ(100)–7, I2ᵛ(116)–8, I7ᵛ(126)–11, K5ᵛ(138)–4, K7(141)–1, L8ᵛ(160)–6, M3ᵛ(166)–6, M7(173)–1, N3ᵛ(182)–4, N5(185)–5, O1ᵛ(194)–1, O7(205)–9, P5ᵛ(218)–5, P8ᵛ(224)–2, Q6ᵛ(236)–10, Q8(239)–1, R3ᵛ(246)–3, R6ᵛ(252)–9, S7(269)–1, S7ᵛ(270)–5, T3ᵛ(278)–5, U5ᵛ(298)–9,

U7(301)–1, X7(317)–3, Y1ᵛ(322)–3, Y7(333)–2, Z1ᵛ(338)–2, Z2ᵛ(340)–3, 2A6ᵛ(364)–3, 2A7ᵛ(366)–8, 2B6ᵛ(380)–2, 2B7ᵛ(382)–9, 2C4ᵛ(392)–12, 2C7ᵛ(398)–10.

Catchwords: om. vi, (*Generally between letters*) 2, 5, 6, 7, 11, 14, 16, 17, 22, 29, 34, 36–41, 44, 51, 53, 58, 61–3, 65, 70, 73, 75, 77, 80, 95, 105, 119, 127, 142, 147, 165, 169, 176, 180–1, 183, 188, 207–9, 211, 214, 217, 221–2, 228, 233, 235, 237, 240, 243, 245, 254, 256, 262, 272, 276, 278, 280, 282, 284, 286, 290, 294, 297, 305, 310, 315, 319, 324, 326, 332, 336, 341–2, 344, 346–8, 350, 353, 355, 358, 363, 365, 367, 369, 372, 378, 381, 383, 385, 387, 390, 395; 8 dying- (dying bed), 356 the (tænia,), 359 diſtreſſ- (diſtreſſful,).

Explicit: 397 END OF THE FIRST VOLUME.

II. A⁶ B–2D⁸ 2E⁴, ($4 (–A1,4, 2E3,4) signed; 'Vᴏʟ. II.' on $1), 218 leaves.

Pp. A1 *i* t., *ii* blk, *iii* iv–xi Contents, *xii* blk, on B1 *1* 2–412 text of Letters, *413* ½t POEMS., *414* blk, *415* 416–24 text of Poems.

Pagination: 53 as 35.

Press-figures: A5(ix)–6, B5ᵛ(10)–8, C5(25)–7, C8(31)–5, D5(41)–9, D6(43)–7, E3ᵛ(54)–7, E7(61)–1, F5ᵛ(74)–1, G6(91)–8, G8ᵛ(96)–9, H2ᵛ(100)–17, H7ᵛ(110)–16, I1ᵛ(114)–1, I8ᵛ(128)–8, K8(143)–4, K8ᵛ(144)–14, L1ᵛ(146)–6, L8ᵛ(160)–5, M5ᵛ(170)–17, M7ᵛ(174)–14, N3ᵛ(182)–7, N8ᵛ(192)–8, O4ᵛ(200)–8, O7ᵛ(206)–5, P3ᵛ(214)–18, P4ᵛ(216)–10, Q1ᵛ(226)–16, Q6ᵛ(236)–9, R2ᵛ(244)–7, R6(251)–12, S6ᵛ(268)–10, S7ᵛ(270)–16, T3ᵛ(278)–12, T4ᵛ(280)–16, U6ᵛ(300)–18, U7ᵛ(302)–17, X6ᵛ(316)–8, X8(319)–16, Y7ᵛ(334)–4, Y8ᵛ(336)–3, Z5(345)–12, Z7ᵛ(350)–18, 2A7ᵛ(366)–9, 2A8ᵛ(368)–1, 2B7(381)–18, 2B7ᵛ(382)–10, 2C1ᵛ(386)–18, 2C8ᵛ(400)–17, 2D1ᵛ(402)–1, 2D5(409)–7, 2E4(423)–3.

Catchwords: om. xi, 3, 5, 7, 9, 11, 13, 15, 19, 23, 29, 36, 39, 48, 50, 53, 56–7, 59, 62, 66, 69, 71, 80, 89, 93, 101, 103, 113, 123, 126, 128, 134, 138, 140, 142, 153, 157, 161, 165, 178–9, 184, 188, 194, 197–8, 201, 203, 207, 209, 218, 220, 229–31, 234, 239–40, 242–3, 248, 252, 254, 256, 258, 260, 267, 272, 274, 276, 279, 281, 283, 285, 287, 289, 291, 293, 304, 309, 312, 317, 322, 324, 328, 330, 333, 338, 349, 351, 353, 355, 357, 371, 377, 390, 392, 395, 398–99, 404, 408, 411; 418–21; 105 *** (*****), 412 (POEMS.).

Explicit: 412 END OF THE LETTERS. 424 FINIS.

Paper: White, laid; demy (uncut: 8¾ × 5⅝ in.); wmk.: fleur-de-lys + LVG.

Type: English (4.5 mm), leaded (0.9 mm); notes: sm. pica (3.5 mm). Letters on same page separated by single rules.

References: Courtney 168–9; CH 165; *Tinker* 1383; *Rothschild* 1270–1; ESTC: t082906.

Notes: The preliminaries of vols. I–II (π² + A⁶) formed a single sheet. An *Errata* slip was printed to be inserted in the volumes (it is variously placed), and it is found in two states affecting the text of l. 9 as: (**a**) '*rend*', or (**b**) '*read*'.

2,500 copies were printed by Andrew Strahan (who held, with Cadell, a ½ share in the title, L: Add. MS 48804, fo. 9), in Feb. 1788 (Add. MS 48809, fo. 102ᵛ), and published 8 Mar. 1788 (*London Chron.* and *Morning Chron.*).[2] According to HLP '500 Guineas and 50£ if it came to a 2ᵈ Edition was my Bargain with Cadell at the Royal Hotel when we first came over — Lysons Witness' (*Thraliana* 694, '26 Oct. 1787, Hanover Square').

In II. 391–400 are SJ's letters to Hill Boothby, also printed in *Annals*, 1805 (805A/1, below). The additional poems form a notable supplement to Kearsley's collection (85.2PW/1 &c., above).

This collection was noticed in contemporary newspapers, *St. James's Chron.*, 27–9 March, 3–5 Apr., 8–10 Apr., and 12–15 Apr., as 'Dr Johnson's Ghost to Mrs Piozzi' 22–24 April, and again as 'The Quintessence of Johnson's Letters to Mrs Piozzi' 29 July–2 Aug. 1788. The *Morning Post*, 12 March 1788, was unfavourable, but Baretti was worse in *European Mag.* xiii (Mar. 1788), 165, and thereafter in xiii (May–June), 313–17, 393–99, and xiv (Aug.), 89–99. *Gents. Mag.* lviii (Mar. 1788), 233 was non-committal, but Murphy was enthusiastic in *Monthly Rev.* lxxviii (Mar. 1788), 326. Sales were slow, Strahan recording sales receipts of £45. 12s. as late as 1811 (Add. MS 48804, fo. 9), but the inclusion of the letters in editions of SJ's *Works* was no doubt a factor.[3]

Copies: O² (1. Percy 42–3; 2. 8° C 150–1. BS);

USA: CLU-C (Boards, uncut: Errata b), CSmH ('Robert Hoe', 11168: Errata a), CtY, DFo (no Errata), DLC (Errata a), Hyde[5] (1. uncut, Errata a, 'A. E. Newton'; 2. 'Lee' Errata a; 3. uncut, Errata b, 'Mrs Littlewood' — Adam; 4. 'John Loveday' (+ annotations), boards, uncut, no Errata; 5. 'Littledale', Errata b), ICN ('L.H. Silver', E.S.J. 63596, + annotations[4]), IU² (1. Nickell, Errata b), [Liebert (annotations with identifications by H.L. Piozzi, 'W.S. Lewis') = CtY], MB (Errata b), NcU² (Errata b), NIC², NjP², NN², NN-B ('W. Cooke'), NPM², NRU, PPAt (Errata a), PPL, PPU ('Elizabeth Coulson', Errata b), TxU² (1. Errata a; 2. 'Hanley' boards uncut, Errata b), ViU² (no Errata), WiM; *Can*: CaOHM²; *Japan*: [Kyoto]; *UK*: ABu (no Errata), BMp (no Errata), BRp (no Errata), BRu, C (no Errata), Cf (no Errata), Ck, Ct-R ('H.L. Piozzi' + annotations), DUu, E (no Errata), Ep² (1. no Errata; 2. Errata b), Eu (no Errata), Gu (no Errata), L² (1. C.45. e.5–6 'G. Baretti' + annotations — 'George Daniel . . . Canonbury, April 1857';[5] 2. 93. e. 14–5), LEu ('H. Holland Edwards, Pennant Ereithlyn, North Wales', no Errata), Ljh ('Samuel Lysons'[6]), Lu (Sterling), LVu, MRp (Errata b), MRu² (1. Spencer, no Errata; 2. Errata b), Oef, Op ('Birkbeck Hill' + annotations[7]), SHu (vol. 2 only), SPp (no Errata), WIS; *Aust*: CNL (DNS 4793); *Eir*: Dt (S.n. 44–5); *Ger*: GöttU.

---

[1] All published collections of SJ's Letters are to some degree 'selections', but I have designated smaller collections as such in the following list. No attempt has been made to record individual letters, especially those which were published in magazines and newspapers, though others published individually are generally listed, probably inconsistently. Facsimiles of individual letters have generally been disregarded. Most of these categories can be pursued in the lists in Clifford & Greene § 23, and in the Supplement for 1970–85, by Greene and Vance (1987).

² HLP recorded the publication in *Thraliana* 711: 'The Letters are out — they were published on Sat: 8: Mar: Cadell printed 200 copies, & says 1100 are already sold. . . . the Book is well spoken of upon the whole — yet Cadell murmurs — I cannot make out why.' Charles Dilly gave JB a copy the day before publication (*JB: The English Experiment*, 194, s.d. 7 Mar. 1788). According to Clifford, *Piozzi* (1952), 282, 289 ff., publication was delayed until *Works*, 1787 (87.3W/1) should have appeared.

³ Strahan reported the sale of these rights on 9 July, 1792 'By Cash from the Proprietors of the Works for the Use of Johnson's Letters [£] 52 — 10s.' (L: Add. MS 48804, fo. 9).

⁴ These are signed as by 'H.L.P.' but are not in her hand and appear to be copies from another source. A description of HLP's own copy of this work is O: (MS Eng. lett. d. 119).

⁵ This copy was sold by Sotheby (George Smith), 10 July 1867, 4603, and subsequently by Hodgsons, 29 May 1911, 240 for £9. Baretti's annotations formed the basis of his strictures in *European Mag.*, above.

⁶ Chapman, *NQ* clxxxv (1943), 242, misleadingly describes the proofs which are included with this copy, as containing material that was 'cancelled': there are no cancels in the published copies, and his expression refers only to portions of text which were printed in proof, but eliminated before publication. See further Clifford, *Piozzi* (1952), 57 n.

⁷ Hill's notes anticipate his own edn. of SJ's *Letters* (1892).

88.3L/2   Letters, Piozzi edition, Dublin   1788

LETTERS | TO AND FROM THE LATE | Samuel Johnſon, LL.D. | TO WHICH ARE ADDED, | SOME POEMS | NEVER BEFORE PRINTED. | PUBLISHED | FROM THE ORIGINAL MSS. IN HER POSSESSION, | BY HESTER LYNCH PIOZZI. | IN TWO VOLUMES. | [dentellé swelled rule] | VOL. I [– II]. | [dentellé swelled rule] | DUBLIN: | PRINTED FOR MESSRS. R. MONCRIEFFE, L. WHITE, | P. BYRNE, P. WOGAN, W. PORTER, H. | COLBERT, J. MOORE, J. JONES. | [short rule] | M.DCC.LXXXVIII.

2 vols., 8°

I. A–S⁸ T⁴, ($2 (–A1, T2) signed), 148 leaves.

Pp. A1 *i* t., *ii* blk, *iii* iv–viii Preface, *ix* x–xvi Contents, on B1 *1* 2–279 text of Letters, *280* blk.

Press-figures: none.

II. π² (–π2 = X1) A⁴ B–U⁸ X1, ($2 (a1 as A2) signed), 158 leaves.

Pp. π1 *i* t., *ii* blk, *iii* iv–ix Contents, *x* blk, on B1 *1* 2–296 text of Letters, *297* 298–306 text of Poems.

Pagination: 277 as 27.

Press-figures: E6(59)–3, E8ᵛ(64)–1, F4(71)–1, F7(77)–3, G8ᵛ(96)–2, H7(109)–1, I3ᵛ(118)–1, I7ᵛ(126)–2, K6ᵛ(140)–2, L1ᵛ(146)–1, M5ᵛ(170)–2, N2ᵛ(180)–1, N4(183)–2, O4ᵛ(200)–1, O8(207)–3, P5ᵛ(216)–3, Q1ᵛ(226)–3, Q8ᵛ(240)–1, R1ᵛ(242)–1, S4ᵛ(264)–3, T3(277)–1, U3ᵛ(294)–2, U8ᵛ(304)–3.

Paper: White, laid; Demy [or ? Lombard] (uncut: 8¾ × 5¼ in.); no vis. wmk.
Type: Pica (4.1 mm), unleaded.
References: Courtney 168; CH 165; *Rothschild* 1270; ESTC: t075351.

Notes: The presence of press-figures in a Dublin printing is uncommon, but not unknown. It does not necessarily imply English printing, perhaps no more than some migrant compositors.

An annotated copy inscribed 'Edmond Malone' with identifications added, is at Georgetown University.[1]

Copies: O (2695 e.193);

USA: CtY, Hyde (Blue boards, uncut, 'Mary Anne Thomas' — 'Gardiner Feb^r. 1815' — 'Kennedy' — 'Galpin' — 'Fletcher'; with disjunct extra leaf D8 (vol. 2, pp. 47–8) laid in), MH (Lowell), NIC, NjP, NPM, PPL, PPU; *Can*: CaOHM; *Japan*: [Kyoto]; *UK*: C (Hib.5 788.13), BMp (340475), L (1490. i.32); *Aust*: CNL (DNS 4791–2); *Eir*: Dt.

[1] It appeared in Harding, Lepard & Co., *General Catalogue of Books* (1826), 1293 @ £4. 4s., and was then sold by R.H. Evans, 11 June 1838, lot 845, and was later sold to Maggs Bros. for £10. 5s. as lot 269 at Sotheby's 30 July 1923. I am indebted to Mrs Margaret Smith for the discovery of the present whereabouts of this copy.

88.3L/3   Letters (Selection), To Chesterfield   1790

THE CELEBRATED | LETTER | FROM | SAMUEL JOHNSON, LL.D. | TO | Philip Dormer Stanhope, Earl of Chesterfield; | NOW FIRST PUBLISHED, | WITH NOTES, | By JAMES BOSWELL, Esq. | [medium swelled rule] | LONDON: | PRINTED BY HENRY BALDWIN; | FOR CHARLES DILLY, IN THE POULTRY. | M DCC XC. | [Price Half a Guinea.]

4°, $2. Pp. *1* t., *2* Imprimatur: 'Entered in the Hall-Book of the Company of Stationers.' on $2 *3*–4 text.

Pagination: 4 [↑].

Press-figures: $2(3)–4.

Paper: White, laid; demy (uncut: 11¼ × 8¾ in.). Despite Pottle's unease, the paper stock is not significantly different from that of *Life* (1791), though it may be that superior sheets were selected for this small printing run.

References: Courtney 171–2; Pottle, *Literary Career of JB* (1929), 135–6, § 73; Chapman, *London Mercury*, xv (Nov. 1926), 50–8 (reprinted in *Johnson & Boswell Revised* (1928), 21–50); *Letters* i. xxxi–xxxv, and no. 61 (Hyde i. 94–7); *Tinker* 1387; Waingrow *MS of Life* i. 184–93.

Notes: To Pottle's account there is little to add. This piece is primarily an adjusted offprint from *Life* (1791), i. 141-2 with changes to the typographical arrangement primarily affecting the opening lines of each paragraph. JB followed the text as dictated to him by SJ on 4 June 1781 (CtY: MS Boswell: C 1596; *Life* iv. 128). SJ also dictated the letter to Baretti, which was given to Langton (L: Add. MS 5713), and JB had one of his children make a copy of it and used that as copy for his printer for *Life*, 1791 (CtY: MS Boswell, M 155:2). Inevitably there are many variations. Other MS versions are of uncertain authority but probably derive from the printed text (CSmH, Hyde).[1]

It was apparently worked off in spring of 1790 but despite the date it was not entered at Stationers' Hall until 29 April 1791 (Pottle, 137), and published 12 May 1791 (*NCBEL* ii. 1214).[2] Pottle's view (139–40; see also Nichols, *Lit. Illus.* vii. 344), that the piece was printed in order to secure JB's copyright against invasion by other biographers is very probable.[3] JB's account from Baldwin for the printing is CtY (MS Boswell, A 59:2). Copies are scarce. R.B. Adam published a facsimile in 1927 (88.3L/16, below), and there was an edn. in 1931 (88.3L/18), and a French translation in 1829 (88.3L/TF/1).

Copies: O;
USA: CtY (Tinker), Hyde; *UK*: L.

[1] An unidentified MS version by Robert Jephson was in the John Bullock sale, Sotheby &c., 10 July 1848, 267. JB had asked SJ for a copy as early as 20 Sept. 1779 (CtY: MS Boswell, L 671).
[2] It was advertised in *Public Advertiser*, 30 Apr. 1791, with the *Conversation with . . . George III* (91.5CG, below).
[3] JB preserved in his papers a newspaper clipping from the *St James's Chron.*, 21 May 1791, entitled 'Literary Property' in which his magnanimity over his property in this piece is acknowledged after an infringement by the *London Packet* (CtY: MS Boswell, P 100:7).

88.3L/4   Letters (Selection), To Wilson   1793

[½t] AN | Archæological Dictionary; | OR, | CLASSICAL ANTIQUITIES | OF THE | *JEWS, GREEKS*, and *ROMANS*, | ALPHABETICALLY ARRANGED.

[Title] AN | *Archæological Dictionary;* | OR, | CLASSICAL ANTIQUITIES | OF THE | *JEWS, GREEKS, and ROMANS*, | Alphabetically Arranged: | CONTAINING | An Account of their MANNERS, CUSTOMS, DIVERSIONS, RELIGIOUS RITES, | PHILOSOPHY, FESTIVALS, ORACLES, LAWS, ARTS, ENGINES of | WAR, WEIGHTS, MEASURES, MONEY, MEDALS, COMPUTATION | and DIVISION of TIME, CHRONOLOGICAL TERMS, HERESIES in the | PRIMITIVE CHURCH, &c. &c. | [rule] | By the Rev. T. WILSON, | Of CLITHEROE. | [rule] | THE SECOND EDITION, | With Confiderable Additions. | [total rule] | [BL] **London:** | Printed for D. OGILVY and J. SPEARE, J. JOHNSON, J. WALLIS, | J. DEIGHTON, H. GARDNER, B. WHITE and SON, | T. VERNOR and J. HOOD, S. HAYES, | and J. BINNS, at LEEDS. | [dash] | M.DCC.XCIII.

8°, *A*⁴ B–U⁴ W⁴ X–2L⁴ (2L4 blk), *A–*Z⁴ ²2A–²2D⁴ (²2D4 blk), ($2 (–2H2, 2L2) signed), 248 leaves.

Pp. A1 *i* ½t, *iii* t., *v–vi* Dedication to SJ ('Sept. 30th. 1782'), vii–viii SJ's Letter to Wilson (31 Dec. 1782, *Letters* 820; Hyde iv. 101–2), *ix–xi* Preface, *xii* blk, on B3–2L3ᵛ text of *Dictionary* (A–MYTTOTON), 2L4 blk, on *A1–²2D4 text N–ZYGITAE) unpaged, *Explicit*: THE END., ²2D4ᵛ blk.

References: *Life* iv. 162, 507–8; ESTC: t116234.

Notes: Wilson's first edn., also dedicated to SJ, was published in 1783.[1] This edn. includes SJ's letter of acknowledgement (*Letters* 820, 31 Dec. 1782), of which Wilson was sufficiently proud to have published it in *Gents. Mag.* lv (March 1785), 187–8, whence Reed extracted it for inclusion in *Works*. xiv (1788), 530–1 (no. xxxiv), 87.3W/1.3/1, above.

Copies: JDF ('Rich[d] Newcombe, Esq[r].');

USA: CLU-C, CSmH, CtY, Hyde (boards, uncut), NIC, PPL, PU; *UK*: C, E, Gu, L², O.

---

[1] Reviewed in *British Magazine and Review*, Jan. 1783, 47–8 (McGuffie, *SJ in the British Press*, (1976), 293).

88.3L/5   Letters (Selection), To Granger   1805

LETTERS | BETWEEN THE | Rev. JAMES GRANGER, M.A. | RECTOR OF SHIPLAKE, | AND | MANY OF THE MOST EMINENT | *LITERARY MEN OF HIS TIME:* | COMPOSING | A COPIOUS HISTORY AND ILLUSTRATION | OF HIS | [BL] **Biographical Hiſtory of England.** | WITH | MISCELLANIES, | AND | NOTES OF TOURS | IN | FRANCE, HOLLAND, AND SPAIN, | BY THE SAME GENTLEMAN. | [short diamond rule] | *EDITED BY J.P. MALCOLM,* | AUTHOR OF LONDINIUM REDIVIVUM, | FROM THE ORIGINALS IN THE POSSESSION OF | MR. W. RICHARDSON. | [double rule] | LONDON: | *Printed by Nichols and Son, Red Lion Passage, Fleet Street,* | FOR LONGMAN, HURST, REES, AND ORME, | PATERNOSTER-ROW. | 1805.

8°, *A*1 B–2D⁸ 2E², ($4 signed; 'Vol. I.' on $1 (–B, 2E), 'Vol. II.' on K1), ²B–2G⁸ ²H–²I⁴ ²K1, ($4 signed; 'Vol. II.' on $1 (–²D–K)), 263 leaves.

Pp. A1 t., A1ᵛ blk, on B1 1–4 Contents, 4–420 text (of 'Vol. 1'), on ²B1 1–103 text, *104* Postscript and coloph: *Printed by* Nichols *and* Son, | *Red Lion Paſſage, Fleet Street.*, on ²I1 105–14 Index, 114 advt. for *Londinium Redivivum*.

Pagination: (↑) 1, ²B1 1, 105; [↑] 417.

Press-figures: E5ᵛ(58)–2, 2D4ᵛ(408)–2, 2D5ᵛ(410)–1, ²B5(9)–2, ²B8(15)–1, C7(29)–1, D5(41)–2, E5(57)–2, E5ᵛ(58)–4, F7ᵛ(78)–4, F8ᵛ(80)–2.

Catchwords: 84 hands; (∼:), 95 ˄ 9 Ed- (N° ˄ Edward I.), 144 and˄ (N°,), 216 'Sir, (MR.).

Explicit: none.

Paper: White (browned), wove; Demy (8¾ × 5½ in.); wmk.: '1802' and '1803'.

Type: Pica (4.0 mm), leaded (1.2 mm); notes: long primer (3.2 mm).

Plates: 1. Front. 'Published 1 Aug[t] 1799 by Malcolm Somers Place 22 Boston House BRENTFORD', 2–3. facing p. 5 facsimile autographs 'Malcolm Sc.', 4. facing p. 12 (Duchess of Portland) 'Opus Marmor M. RYSBRAKE Londini.',

5. facing p. 320 'The Rev^d. W^m. Cole, A.M. of Cambridge, & F.A.S. 1768. Engraved from an original Drawing. London Published Aug^st. 20th. 1805, by W^m. Richardson N° 31, Strand.', 6. facing p. 358 'Mr Henry Welby G^t: Ætatis Suæ. 84. [with Epitaph &c.] Pub^d. Feby. 16th. 1794. by W. Richardfon Caftle S^t. Leicefter Square.'

Notes: SJ's Letter to Granger, 15 Dec. 1772 (*Letters* 292, Hyde, i. 416–7) is at pp. 114–15. Other minor allusions are of interest, perhaps notably on the portrait of Cave with SJ's Life in *Gents. Mag.*, at p. 187.

Copies: JDF (boards, uncut). Not a rare book.

88.3L/6   Letters (Selection), Original Letters   1817

[BL] **Original Letters,** | FROM | [2 cols., col. a:] RICHARD BAXTER, | MATTHEW PRIOR, | LORD BOLINGBROKE, | ALEXANDER POPE, | Dr. CHEYNE, | [vertical double rule, col. b:] Dr. HARTLEY, | Dr. SAMUEL JOHNSON, | Mrs. MONTAGUE, | Rev. WILLIAM GILPIN, | Rev. JOHN NEWTON, | [centred] GEORGE LORD LYTTELTON, | Rev. Dr. CLAUDIUS BUCHANAN, &c. &c. | WITH | *BIOGRAPHICAL ILLUSTRATIONS.* | EDITED BY | REBECCA WARNER, | *Of Beech-Cottage, near Bath.* | [short swelled rule] | Blest be the gracious Powers, who taught mankind | To stamp a lasting image of the mind ! | Beasts may convey, and tuneful birds may sing, | Their mutual feelings in the op'ning spring; | But Man alone has skill and pow'r to send | The heart's warm dictates to the distant friend: | 'Tis his alone to please, instruct, advise, | Ages remote, and nations yet to rise. *Crabbe's Library.* | [medium swelled rule] | PRINTED BY | RICHARD CRUTTWELL, ST. JAMES'S-STREET, BATH; | AND SOLD BY | LONGMAN, HURST, REES, ORME, AND BROWN, | PATER- | NOSTER-ROW, LONDON. | 1817.

8°, *A*⁴ B–U⁸, ($4 signed), 156 leaves.

Pp. A1 *i* t., *ii* blk, *iii*–iv To the Reader, *v* vi–viii Contents, on B1 *1* 2–303 text, 303 coloph: 'Printed by Richard Cruttwell | St. James's-Street, Bath.' *304* blk.

References: Courtney 169; CH 166.

Notes: pp. 202–5 notes on SJ and Joseph Fowke, 205–6 Letter 'xlviii' (SJ—Fowke, 11 July 1776, *Letters* 495; Hyde ii. 350–2), 207–9 Letter 'lii' (SJ—Fowke, 19 Apr. 1783, *Letters* 834; Hyde iv. 129–31), and 209–10 Letter 'l' (SJ—Richardson, 17 May [1753], *Letters* 48, dated '17 April'; Hyde i. 69–70).

Copies: Hyde.

88.3L/7   Letters (Selection), To George Colman   1820

POSTHUMOUS LETTERS, | FROM | *VARIOUS CELEBRATED MEN:* | ADDRESSSED TO | FRANCIS COLMAN, ᴀɴᴅ GEORGE COLMAN,

THE ELDER: | WITH | ANNOTATIONS, AND OCCASIONAL REMARKS, BY GEORGE COLMAN, THE YOUNGER. | [short swelled rule] | EXCLUSIVE OF THE LETTERS, ARE | AN EXPLANATION OF THE MOTIVES OF *WILLIAM PULTENEY* (AFTERWARDS | *EARL OF BATH*) FOR HIS ACCEPTANCE OF A PEERAGE; | AND | PAPERS TENDING TO ELUCIDATE THE QUESTION RELATIVE TO THE PROPORTIONAL SHARES | OF AUTHORSHIP TO BE ATTRIBUTED TO THE *ELDER COLMAN* AND *GARRICK*, | IN THE COMEDY OF *THE CLANDESTINE MARRIAGE*. | [short swelled rule] | LONDON: | PRINTED FOR T. CADELL AND W. DAVIES, | IN THE STRAND. | 1820.

4°, π^4 a^4 B–2X^4 2Y^2, ($2 (–Y2) signed), 182 leaves

Pp. π1 *i* ½t, *ii* blk, *iii* t., *iv* blk, *v* vi–ix Preface, *x* blk, *xi* xii–xvi Contents, xvi errata, on B1 *1* 2–347 text of Letters &c. (45, 84, 106, 132, 231, 327 unnumbered; 230, 326 blk), *348* blk. Coloph: 'Printed by A. and R. Spottiswoode, Printers-Street, London.'

Notes: SJ's letters to GC the Elder are 19 Aug. 1767, pp. 137–8, and 17 Jan. 1769, pp. 139–40.

Copies: Hyde ('Glegg').

88.3L/8   Letters (Selection)   1822

(A) [E copy] LETTERS | OF | DR SAMUEL JOHNSON, | CAREFULLY SELECTED AND ARRANGED FROM | VARIOUS PUBLICATIONS, | WITH EXPLANATORY NOTES. | To which are added, | [BL] **Miscellaneous Essays,** | ON | INTERESTING SUBJECTS. | WITH A FINE PORTRAIT OF THE AUTHOR. | EDINBURGH: | PRINTED FOR BELL AND BRADFUTE, | WM. WHYTE AND CO., JAMES ROBERTSON AND | CO., WAUGH AND INNES, JOHN ROBERTSON, | MACREDIE AND CO., JOHN FAIRBAIRN, | JOHN ANDERSON, JUN. AND THOMSONS, BROTHERS. | [short rule] | 1822. | Andrew Jack & Co. Printers.

Var: (B) [NIC] . . . BELL AND BRADFUTE, WILLIAM WHYTE AND CO., JAMES ROBERTSON AND CO., WAUGH AND INNES, JOHN ROBERTSON, MACREDIE AND CO., JOHN FAIRBAIRN, JOHN ANDERSON, JUN. PETER BROWN, AND THOMSONS, BROTHERS, EDINBURGH; AND C. AND H. BALDWYN, AND BEILBY AND KNOTTS, LONDON. 1822. . . .

12°, π^6 A–T^{12} U^8, ($1,5 ($5 as $2, –U5) signed), 242 leaves.

Pp. π1 blk, π2 *i* t., *ii* blk, *iii* iv–v Advertisement, *vi* blk, *vii* viii–x Index to the principal letters, and subjects treated in them, on A1 *1* 2–407 texts of 'Letters of Samuel Johnson', *408* blk, on S1 *409* 410–69 Essays by Dr Samuel

Johnson, 469 coloph: 'Andrew Jack & Co. Printers.' *470* blk, U8 xi Contents of
the Essays, *xii* blk.

References: Courtney 169.

Notes: The final leaf, U8, was evidently intended to form part of the
'Contents' though the occasional misnumbering of the first page as 'x' meant a
duplication: it then became a problem to the binder. This volume does not seem
to be a separate issue of a volume from any Collected Works.

The 'Essays' carry synoptic htt, and include SJ's Legal Opinions, taken from
Boswell's *Life* (I. Vicious Intromission 409–15, II. Lay Patronage 410–21, III.
Censure from the Pulpit 322–8, IV. School Discipline 428–31), V. Foreign
Policy (= 'Political State of Great Britain') 454–7, and VI. 'The Bravery of the
English Common Soldiers' 454–7 from the *Literary and British Mags.*, extracts
from *Falkland's Islands* 458–9, VII. 'Thoughts on Agriculture' from the
Universal Visiter 461–6, and VIII. the 'Preface' to Rolt's *Dictionary* 466–9.

Copies: NIC (a); *UK*: Gp (G.376242), E (var. b., BCL. C1631, ptd. boards,
uncut: 5⅞ × 3½ in, with advts. for the 'Edinburgh Classics'), En, O.

88.3L/9   Letters (Selection), ed. Simeon   1860–1

Original Letters of Dr. Johnson. Edited by Sir John Simeon.

Miscellanies of the Philobiblon Society. London Philobiblon Society VI
(1860–1), 43.

References: Courtney 169.

Notes: SJ's Letters to Taylor are here printed.

Copies: Not recorded.

88.3L/10   Letters (Selection), Love Letters   1888

Love Letters of Famous Men and Women of the Past and Present Century
Edited by J. T. Merydew Two Volumes with Portraits Vol. I [–II]. London
Remington & Co., Publishers Henrietta Street Covent Garden 1888 All rights
reserved

2 vols., 8°.

I. *a*⁸ b⁴ c² A–Z⁸ (Z8 blk), ($1 signed), 198 leaves.

Pp. π1 *i* ½t: Love Letters Vol. I., *iii* t., *v* Contents and list of portraits, *vii*
viii–xxvii Preface, on A1 *1* 2–366 text, *367–8* (Z8) blk., Plates inserted facing
pp. 8, 104, 129, 177, 185, 249, 253, 256, 264, and 305.

II. π1 2π² A–T⁸ U⁴ X² (X2 blk), ($1 signed), 161 leaves.

Pp. π1 ½t Love Letters Vol. II., 2π1 t., 2π2 *i*–ii Contents &c., on A1 *1*
2–314 text, *315–16* (X2) blk; Plates facing pp. 2π2, 25, 40, 48, 56, 64, 81, 88,
104, 113, 128, 145, 217, 225, 289, and 297.

References: Courtney 169.

Notes: Inaccurate versions of 559, 27 Oct. 1777 (pp. 257–8), 900, 13 Nov. 1783 (259–60), 778, 25 Apr. 1782 (261), and 972, 8 July 1784 (263–4) are quoted, with HLP to SJ 969a, 30 June 1784 (261–2) Comments on SJ pp. 254–7.

Copies: Hyde (uncut).

88.3L/11　　　　　Letters, ed. Hill　　　　　1892

Letters of Samuel Johnson, LL.D. Collected and edited by George Birkbeck Hill, D.C.L. Oxford: At the Clarendon Press. MDCCCXCII.

2 vols., 8°

References: Courtney 169.

Notes: This was the first serious advance on HLP's initial edition, for Hill sought a complete collection. Hill was able to reap the advantage of the 19th-century interest in autograph collection, to which he himself contributed (*Talks about Autographs*, 1896).[1] Copies are not scarce.

Copies: Op ('G.B. Hill', annotated);

USA: Not recorded; *UK*: O, Op, JDF ('William Thomas Rabbits').

[1] Munby, *The Cult of the Autograph Letter in England* (1962).

88.3L/12　　　Letters (Selection),　　　1897
Eighteenth Century Letters

Eighteenth Century Letters edited by R. Brimley Johnson, with an Introduction by G. B. Hill. London: Innes. 1897

Notes: The selection includes letters by Chesterfield.

88.3L/13　　　Letters (Selection),　　　[1906]
Letters of Literary Men

Letters of Literary Men Sir Thomas More to Robert Burns Arranged and Edited by Frank Arthur Mumby London George Routledge & Sons Limited New York: E.P. Dutton & Co

2 vols. 8°.

I. π1 A^4 B–2A^8 2B^4 (–2B4 = ?π1), ($1 signed), 192 leaves.

Pp. π1 *i* ½t + Front. + A1 *iii* t., *v* Contents, *vi* blk, vii–x Preface, on B1 *1–2* 3–366 Letters (Parts i–iv), 367–74 Index.

II. A^4 B–2R^8 2S^4, ($1 signed), 320 leaves.

Pp. A1 *i* ½t + Front. + A2 *iii* t., v–vii Preface, *viii* blk, on B1 *1–2* 3–620 text (parts i–iv), 621–32 Index.

References: Courtney 169.
Notes: SJ's letters quoted (*Letters* nos: 61, 655, 900, 970, 972, 163, 275 and 378), pp. 211–22; Letters of JB quoted (*Tinker* nos: 27, 173 and 203) pp. 222–27.
Copies: Hyde (uncut).

88.3L/14   Letters (Selection),   [1915]
Some Unpublished Letters

Dr. Samuel Johnson. Some Unpublished Letters.
$\$^6$ (unsigned), 6 leaves.
Pp. \$1 *1* t., *3* Foreword (signed: 'Clement Shorter. March 9. 1915'), *5–12* text of letters with some facsimiles.
Notes: *Letters* 278.1, 1016.1, 589.2, 992.1, 1039.1, 1042.1, and 1042.2 are here printed, with facsimiles of 1042.1, Pension receipt (10 Dec. 1784, *MS Handlist* 229), and receipt for *Rasselas*, 1759 (*MS Handlist* 80). Limited to 20 copies.
Copies: Hyde (wrappers); *USA*: CSmH (28788).

88.3L/15   Letters (Selection), ed. Chapman   [1925]

Selected Letters of Samuel Johnson Humphrey Milford Oxford University Press London Edinburgh Glasgow Copenhagen New York Toronto Melbourne Cape Town Bombay Calcutta Madras Shanghai
Pp. *vii* viii–xix Introd. ('R.W.C.'), xx references, 1–264 text, *265* 266–7 Index of Correspondents (Tr. of Gk. Epitaph on Goldsmith, 267). Edited By R.W. Chapman.

88.3L/16   Letters (Selection), To Chesterfield   1927

Samuel Johnson's Celebrated Letter to the Earl of Chesterfield and His Interview with King George III as Published in 1790 by James Boswell. Buffalo, New York: Privately Printed for R.B. Adam. 1927
12 leaves, unpaged with facsimiles.
References: Pottle, *Literary Career of JB* (1929), 141, § 76.
Notes: A facsimile of Boswell's original offprint from *Life* (1791), i. 141–2 (88.3L/3, above), published as a Christmas Greeting.

88.3L/17   Letters (Selection),   1929
                    Johnson, Boswell, and Mrs Piozzi

Johnson Boswell and Mrs. Piozzi A suppressed Passage restored 'This falls out better than I could desire.' Midsummer Night's Dream. Oxford University Press London: Humphrey Milford 1929

$8, Pp. *1* ½t, *3* t., *5* Prefatory note, *7* ½t + 2 leaves (facsimile of *Letter* 408 &c.) + *9–11* transcript, *13* 'The Pasted Scrap', 15 Johnsonian Facsimiles.

Notes: The texts of *Letters* 408 and 408.1 are examined and recovered.

Copies: Hyde² (**1.** 'Smith' with note — R.W. Chapman — Adam'; **2.** unopened).

88.3L/18   Letters (Selection), Forty Four Letters   1931

Forty Four Letters from Samuel Johnson Annotated by L. D'O. Walters Published at the Swan Press Chelsea 1931

4s, *1–13*⁴ (unsigned), 52 leaves.

Unpaged: 1₁ ½t, 1₂ t., 1₃ Contents, 1₄ ½t Samuel Johnson, 1₄ᵛ notes on Letter I, on 2₁ Letters nos. I–XLIV with annotations on facing versos, 45 leaves, 13₂ colophon, 13₃₋₄ 2 blk leaves.

References: Ridler, *British Modern Press Books* (1975), 275–76.

Notes: Limited to 100 copies.

Copies: Hyde ('Whittington' — 'Metzdorf'); NN.

88.3L/19   Letters (Selection),   1931
                    Letter to Chesterfield

Patronage: being a Letter to the Earl of Chesterfield. Warlingham. 1931.

Copies: E (Aln. 356).

88.3L/20   Letters (Selection), Johnson and Queeney   1932

Johnson and Queeney. Edited by the Marquis of Lansdowne. Cassell & Company 1932

88.3L/21   Letters (Selection), The Queeney Letters   1934

The Queeney Letters being Letters addressed to Hester Maria Thrale by Doctor Johnson Fanny Burney and Mrs. Thrale-Piozzi Edited by the Marquis of Lansdowne Cassell & Company Ltd London Toronto Melbourne and Sydney 1934

8°, *A*⁸ B–S⁸ T⁸ (T1 + 'T2'.T9), 154 leaves.

Pp. A1 *i* ½t, *iii* t., *v* Dedication, *vii* Contents, *ix* x–xxix Introduction, *xxx* blk, *xxxi* Principal references, *xxxii* blk, on C1 *1–3* 4–261 text, *262* blk, *263–5* 266–75 Index, *276* blk.

Notes: The intruded leaves 'T2'.T9 affect only the Index. Lord Lansdowne published 32 letters from SJ to Queeney Thrale (the descent of these papers from Lady Keith is documented by Mary Hyde, *The Thrales of Streatham Park* (1977), 333–4 n.). This is not a scarce book.

Copies: Hyde.

88.3L/22   Letters (Selection),   1946
English Letters of XVIII Century

Pelican Books English Letters of the XVIII Century, edited by James Aitken. London Penguin Books 1946

Notes: SJ's Letters pp. 69–87.

88.3L/23   Letters, ed. Chapman   1952

The Letters of Samuel Johnson with Mrs. Thrale's genuine Letters to him Collected & Edited by R.W. Chapman Sometime Fellow of Magdalen College Oxford Volume I: 1719–1774 [–II: 1775–1782; –III: 1783–1784] Letters 1–369 [Letters 370–821.1 –821.2–1174] Oxford At the Clarendon Press 1952.

3 vols.

Notes: This represented a major advance on Hill's work of 1892 (88.3L/11, above), including the texts of well over a thousand letters, still in pursuit of the goal of a complete collection. Those from Mrs Thrale-Piozzi were taken from the MSS in Rylands. A series of appendixes considers several important problems arising in the history of SJ's correspondence, and there are the usual idiosyncratic Chapman 'Indexes'. A Photolitho reprint was published by Oxford University Press in 1984 (ISBN: 0-19-818536-7, ~537-5, ~538-3).

A new redaction by Bruce Redford in 5 vols. (Princeton and Oxford) was published in two instalments, vols. i–iii (1992), and vols. iv–v (1994). This edition excludes letters not represented by verifiable documents.

Copies: Hyde ('R.W. Chapman').

88.3L/24   Letters (Selection), ed. Littlejohn   1965

A Spectrum Book. S-126.

Dr Johnson His Life in Letters Selected and edited by David Littlejohn. Prentice-Hall Englewood Cliffs New Jersey. 1965

Pp. *xiv* + 1–10 Introduction, 11–219 text, 221–5 Chronology, 227–39 Index of Names (with illus.); L Congress card: 65-23293; C 21838. Paperback.

88.3L/TF/1   Letter to Chesterfield,   1829
                     French translation

The 'Letter to Chesterfield' was translated into French by N.P. Chaulin, in *Précis de Pièces dramatiques de Shakespeare* (1829), pp. 422–4 and 433–5.

88.3SW   Sermon on the Death of His Wife   1788

A | SERMON, | WRITTEN BY THE LATE | SAMUEL JOHNSON, L.L.D. | FOR THE | FUNERAL of his WIFE. | PUBLISHED BY THE | Rev. SAMUEL HAYES, A.M. | Usher of Westminster-School. | [short swelled rule] | LONDON: | Printed for T. CADELL, in the Strand. | MDCCLXXXVIII.

8°, A⁴ (–A3 = C1) B⁸ C1, ($4 signed), 12 leaves.

Pp. A1 *i* t., *ii* blk, *iii* Editorial note ('Great Dean's Yard, Westminster, March 18th, 1788'), *iv* blk, *v* blk, *vi* advts.: 'Lately Published' for Piozzi's *Letters* and *Anecdotes* (4th edn.), on B1 *1* 2–18 text dh: [2 double rules] | A | SERMON, &c. | [medium swelled rule].

Pagination: (↑); *Press-figures*: B8(15)–3, B8ᵛ(16)–2.

Catchwords: *om.* in A; no errors; *Explicit*: 18 THE END.

Paper: White, laid; Demy (uncut: 8¾ × 5⅝ in.); wmk.: fleur-de-lys.

Type: Pica (4.3 mm), leaded, with blank lines between paras. 'Advertisement' in italics.

References: *Life* i. 241 (Courtney 170); CH 166; *Tinker* 1384; *Works* (Yale), xiv, p. xx, 261–71; ESTC: t047958.

Notes: The uncut copies show that the t. and leaf of advts. form a bifolium, and that A2 is a singleton, separated from C1. Published 19 Mar. 1788 (*Morning Chron.*). It was reprinted in James Abercrombie's *The Mourner Comforted*, Philadelphia, 1812.

Copies: O³ (**1**. 8° C. 151.BS; **2**. GP 1016 (3); **3**. GP 1777(7));

USA: CSmH ('Anderson' 146532), CtY, DLC, Hyde⁵ (**1**. 'Sir Thomas Phillipps' uncut, blue wraps; **2**. uncut; **3**. 'Appleby'; **4**., **5**. 'Lt. Col. F.R.C. Grant' — Adam, lacks A4), ICU, IU, [Liebert ('J. Loveday', uncut, blue wraps)], NcU, NIC, NjP, NPM, TxU; *Can*: CaOHM (C 2882); *UK*: ABu, BMp (574366), C, DUc, Eu, JDF, LICj (wraps, uncut), MRp, Owo, STA².

88.5OT   Boswell's Johnson's Ode to Mrs Thrale   1788

ODE | by | Dr. SAMUEL JOHNSON | to | Mrs. THRALE, | upon their supposed approaching nuptials. | [medium swelled rule] | ———*Tauri ruentis* | *In venerem tolerare pondus.* —— Hor. | [medium swelled rule] | *LONDON:* | Printed for R. FAULDER, New-Bond-Street | M DCC LXXXIV.

Stet: Street͵ |

4°, *B*⁴ C⁴, ($2 signed), 16 leaves.

Pp. B1 ½t ODE | BY | Dr. SAMUEL JOHNSON | TO | Mrs. THRALE. | [medium swelled rule] | [Price One Shilling.], B1ᵛ '[Entered at Stationers' Hall.]', B2 t., B2ᵛ blk, B3 *5* 6–8 Preface, *9* Argument, *10* blk, *11* 12–16 text.

References: Pottle, *Literary Career of JB* (1929), 131–4, §72; *Life* iv. 550–1; *Tinker* 337; *JB: Laird of Auchinleck* (1977), 316–21; *Boswell Catalogue*, J 75, J 105, M 302, L 937-8, C 1915–16; ESTC; t002407.

Notes: This is not by SJ but was composed by JB on 12 Apr. 1781, shortly after the death of Henry Thrale (4 Apr.). There is a MS among his papers (CtY: MS Boswell, M 302). It was later modified in collaboration with Wilkes, and printed by his agency in 1788 with a false date. Copies were perhaps made surreptitiously available at that time (notice in *Public Advertiser*, 12 May 1788), though publication was somewhat informal (*JB: English Experiment*, 223, s.d. 9 May 1788). It is suprising that Malone did nothing to discourage the publication.[1] It was reviewed in *Monthly Rev.* lxxviii (June 1788), 528.[2] Copies are relatively uncommon, and all are stitched, uncut, without wrappers; some are simply printed sheets.[3] It has no place in the Johnson canon.

Copies: Hyde, CtY; *UK*: Eu, L, Lv (Dyce, with attr. to JB by Samuel Lysons).

[1] In a letter to JB, 27 Nov. 1788, William Johnson Temple, JB's old friend, found it objectionable (CtY: MS Boswell, C 2862). Perhaps JB kept Malone in ignorance.
[2] Malone reported to JB on 17 June 1788 that it had 'gone off badly' (CtY: MS Boswell, C 1914).
[3] Some copies and loose sheets of this piece were burned at Auchinleck in 1917: extant copies represent escapes. Pottle, *Pride and Negligence* (1982), 77.

88.5S/1.1   Sermons, Vol. I   1788

[½t] [medium swelled rule] | SERMONS, | LEFT FOR PUBLICATION | BY | JOHN TAYLOR, LL.D. | Late Prebendary of Westminster, &c. | [medium swelled rule]

[Title] SERMONS, | ON DIFFERENT SUBJECTS, | LEFT FOR PUBLICATION | BY | JOHN TAYLOR, LL.D. | Late Prebendary of Westminster, | Rector of Bosworth, Leicestershire, | and Minister of St. Margaret's | Westminster. | [medium swelled rule] | PUBLISHED |

By the Rev. SAMUEL HAYES, A.M. | Usher of Westminster School. | [medium swelled rule] | LONDON: | Printed for T. CADELL, in the STRAND. | M,DCC,LXXXVIII.

8°, a⁸ B–T⁸ (T8 blk), ($4 signed), 152 leaves.

Pp. a1 *i* ½t, *ii* blk, *iii* t., *iv* blk, v–vii Dedication (William, D. of Devonshire), *viii* blk, ix–xv Contents, *xvi* blk, on B1 1–285 text of Sermons I–XIII, *286* blk, *287–8* (T8) blk.

Pagination: (↑); xiii as xiv, 26, 70, 96, 160, 184, 242, 286–8 blks.

Press-figures: a5ᵛ(x)–3, a7(xiii)–4, B5ᵛ(10)–2, B6ᵛ(12)–3, C2ᵛ(20)–2, C3ᵛ(22)–4, D6ᵛ(44)–4, D8(47)–2, E6ᵛ(60)–2, E7ᵛ(62)–3, F1ᵛ(66)–3, F8ᵛ(80)–2, G4ᵛ(88)–3, G5ᵛ(90)–2, H1ᵛ(98)–3, H6ᵛ(108)–5, I1ᵛ(114)–1, I5(121)–5, K1ᵛ(130)–5, K2ᵛ(132)–4, L5ᵛ(154)–4, L6ᵛ(156)–3, M6ᵛ(172)–7, M7ᵛ(174)–1, N2ᵛ(180)–2, N7ᵛ(190)–5, O1ᵛ(194)–2, O4ᵛ(200)–7, P5ᵛ(218)–2, P7(221)–3, Q3ᵛ(230)–3, Q8ᵛ(240)–4, R4ᵛ(248)–3, R5ᵛ(250)–5, S6(267)–2, T2ᵛ(276)–5, T6(283)–7.

Catchwords: 15 [edu-] cation‸ (~,), 123 fouth‸ (~,), 128 him‸ (~;).

Explicit: 285 FINIS.

Paper: White, laid; Demy (uncut: 8¾ × 5⅝ in); no vis. wmk.

Type: Pica (4.2 mm), leaded (1.3). Drop-heads: (a) parallel rule pp. 71, 161, 185, 203, 243, 263; (b) parallel + total rules ix, 1, 49, 97, 121, 223; (c) double rule 27, 139. Tpp. (a) small crown 48, 120, 262; (b) flowers 69, 183, 241. The 25-line page depth with pagination and direction line (5¾ in.), leaves a generous tail margin to the page which is easily but wrongly supposed Large Paper.

References: Courtney 170; CH 166, 170; *Works* (Yale), xiv; ESTC: t134009.

Notes: Published 29 May 1788 (*London Chron.*); broadly attributed to SJ in *Monthly Rev.* lxxx (Dec. 1788), 528, and (2nd ser.), i (March 1790), 351, but SJ's authorship was never seriously doubted, cf. *Works* (Yale), xiv, Introd.[1]

Copies: O (Vet. A5 e.2894);

USA: Hyde, [Liebert = CtY], NIC, NjP; *Can*: CaOHM² (B 14666, C 1221); *UK*: BMp, C, Ct, E (OO.2/2. 31), Eu, Gu, MRc, L (224. k.30); *Aust*: CNL (DNS 7502).

---

[1] To the testimony of William Langley, cited p. xxxii, n. 4, may be added further letters and papers by Langley on the subject in O (MS Don. d.76; some published by Jewitt), and others in Derby Public Library. On 29 June 1789 Hannah More wrote to Mrs Garrick, mentioning 'a book written under the name of Dr Taylor, but probably by their poor friend Johnson' (MS: DFo). A letter of Thomas Taylor, 14 May 1841, alludes to SJ and mentions a 'Vol. of Sermons supposedly written by Johnson, Dr Taylor's name prefixed' (MS: CSmH).

88.5S/1.2 *Sermons, Vol. II* 1789

[½t] [Short swelled rule] | SERMONS, | LEFT FOR PUBLICATION | BY | JOHN TAYLOR, LL. D. | [short swelled rule]

[Title] SERMONS | ON | DIFFERENT SUBJECTS, | LEFT FOR PUBLICATION | BY | JOHN TAYLOR, LL.D. | LATE PREBENDARY OF WESTMINSTER, | RECTOR OF BOSWORTH, LEICESTERSHIRE, | AND MINISTER OF ST. MARGARET'S, | WESTMINSTER. | [short swelled rule] | VOLUME THE SECOND. | [short swelled rule] | PUBLISHED | BY THE REV. SAMUEL HAYES, A.M. | LATE SENIOR USHER OF WESTMINSTER-SCHOOL. | TO WHICH IS ADDED, | A SERMON, | WRITTEN BY | SAMUEL JOHNSON, LL.D. | FOR THE FUNERAL OF HIS WIFE. | [short swelled rule] | LONDON, | Printed for T. CADELL, in the Strand. | M DCC LXXXIX.

8°, a⁴ B–Q⁸, ($4 signed; 'VOL. II.' on $1), 124 leaves.

Pp. a1 *i* ½t, *ii* blk, *iii* t., *iv* blk, v–viii Contents, on B1 *1* 2–239 text of Sermons I–XII, *240* blk.

Pagination: [↑] v–viii, 39–56, 65–86, 110–12, 114, 119, 134–41, 144, 146–7, 149–57, 162, 165–73, 175–8, 180, 184, 188, 190, 194, 196, 200, 204–6, 211, 221, 224, 239; (↑) 2–38, 57–64, 87–109, 113, 115–18, 120–33, 143, 145, 148, 159–61, 163–4, 174, 179, 181–3, 185–7, 189, 191–3, 195, 197, 199, 201–3, 207–10, 212–20, 222–3, 225–38. The distribution of the brackets and parentheses conforms to no evident pattern. Pp. 78, 158, 176, 198, 240 blk.

Press-figures: a3ᵛ(vi)–4, B2ᵛ(4)–2, C5(25)–6, C7ᵛ(30)–3, D7ᵛ(46)–3, D8ᵛ(48)–6, E1ᵛ(50)–2, E7(61)–5, F1ᵛ(66)–2, F4ᵛ(72)–7, G4ᵛ(88)–7, G8(95)–3, H1ᵛ(98)–6, I1ᵛ(114)–4, I7(125)–1, K5(137)–4, K8(143)–1, L1ᵛ(146)–6, M6(171)–4, M7(173)–1, N5(185)–6, N5ᵛ(186)–1, O8(207)–6, P1ᵛ(210)–4, P5(217)–6, Q3ᵛ(230)–4.

Catchwords: 84 man, (∼ₐ *in some copies*), 88 ₐ*Many* (*∼), 94 *Fraud* (*d* ascender broken).

Explicit: 239 THE END.

Paper: White, laid; La. post (8¼ × 5¼ in.); no vis. wmk.

Type: Pica (4.4 mm), leaded (1.3 mm). Dhh: (a) parallel rule pp. 19, 57, 159; (b) parallel + total rules 1; (c) double rule 79, 97, 119, 177, 199, 221; (d) total rule pp. 34, 141.

References: *Life*, iii. 181–2, 506–7 (Courtney 170); CH 166, 170; *Tinker* 1385; *Works* (Yale), xiv, pp. xx–xxi.

Notes: The variations in typography and in paper-stock suggest that these two volumes were not produced by the same printer. Neither was printed by Strahan. Published 14 Oct. 1788 (*St James's Chron.*)

Copies: O (Vet. A5 e.2895);

USA: Hyde (Adam), [Liebert], NIC, NjP; *Can*: CaOHM; *UK*: BMp, C, Ct, E (OO. 2/2. 32), Eu, Gu, MRc, L (102. f. 7–8).

88.5S/2   Sermons, second edition   1790–2

SERMONS, | ON DIFFERENT SUBJECTS, | LEFT FOR
PUBLICATION | BY | JOHN TAYLOR, LL.D. | LATE PREBENDARY
OF WESTMINSTER, | RECTOR OF BOSWORTH,
LEICESTERSHIRE, | AND MINISTER OF ST. MARGARET'S, |
WESTMINSTER. | [short swelled rule] | PUBLISHED | BY THE REV.
SAMUEL HAYES, A.M. | Usher of Westminster School. | [short
swelled rule] | VOL. I. | [short swelled rule] | THE SECOND EDITION. |
[short rule] | LONDON: | Printed for T. CADELL, in the STRAND. |
M,DCC,XC.

2 vols. 8°

I. a⁸ B–T⁸ (T8 blk), ($4 signed; 'Vol. I.' on $1 (–DEF)), 152 leaves.

Pp. a1 *i* ½t, *ii* blk, *iii* t., *iv* blk, v–vii Dedication (William, D. of Devonshire),
viii blk, ix–xv Contents, *xvi* blk, on B1 1–285 text of Sermons, *286* blk, *287–8*
(T8) blk.

Pagination: (↑); xvi, 26, 70, 96, 160, 184, 242, 286–8 blk.

Press-figures: B8ᵛ(16)–1, C1ᵛ(18)–7, C2ᵛ(20)–4, D5(41)–4, D8(47)–1,
E1ᵛ(50)–1, E6ᵛ(60)–4, F5ᵛ(74)–1, G3ᵛ(86)–1, H1ᵛ(98)–3, I8ᵛ(128)–2,
K7ᵛ(142)–3, K8ᵛ(144)–1, L1ᵛ(146)–2, L2ᵛ(148)–5, M5ᵛ(170)–5, M7(173)–2,
N1ᵛ(178)–1, O7(205)–3, O7ᵛ(206)–7, P3ᵛ(214)–1, P8ᵛ(224)–2, Q7ᵛ(238)–5,
Q8ᵛ(240)–1, R8(255)–7, S5ᵛ(266)–5, S8ᵛ(272)–3, T5(281)–1, T6(283)–3.

Catchwords: 128 him_∧ (∼;).

Explicit: 285 END OF THE FIRST VOLUME.

Paper: White, laid; La. post (8¼ × 5¼ in.); no vis. wmk.

Type: Dedication: english (4.3 mm), leaded, text: english, unleaded. A small
crown is tp. at end of sermons pp. 25, 48, 69, 120, 159, 183, 241, and 262.

References: ESTC: t133769.

Notes: Only 'Vol. I' was published in 1790.

Copies: L (4454 ff.18); *USA*: CtY (Im J637. 789T; with vol. 2 1789), ICU,
[Liebert ('Wᵐ. Strong')], NIC; *Can*: CaOHM (C.1220); *UK*: Oef.

Sermons, Vol. II   1792

[½t] [short swelled rule] | SERMONS | ON | DIFFERENT SUBJECTS, |
LEFT FOR PUBLICATION | BY | JOHN TAYLOR, LL.D. | [short
swelled rule]

[Title] SERMONS | ON | DIFFERENT SUBJECTS, | LEFT FOR
PUBLICATION | BY | JOHN TAYLOR, LL.D. | LATE PREBENDARY
OF WESTMINSTER, | RECTOR OF BOSWORTH,
LEICESTERSHIRE, | AND MINISTER OF ST. MARGARET'S, |
WESTMINSTER. | [medium swelled rule] | VOLUME THE SECOND. |

[medium swelled rule] | PUBLISHED | BY THE REV. SAMUEL HAYES, A.M. | LATE SENIOR USHER OF WESTMINSTER-SCHOOL. | TO WHICH IS ADDED, | A SERMON, | WRITTEN BY | SAMUEL JOHNSON, LL.D. | FOR THE FUNERAL OF HIS WIFE. | [short swelled rule] | LONDON, | Printed for T. CADELL, in the Strand. | M DCC XCII.

8°, a⁴ B–Q⁸, ($4 (–a1,2, N4) signed; 'VOL. II.' on $1), 124 leaves.

Pp. a1 *i* ½t, *ii* blk, *iii* t., *iv* blk, v–viii Contents, on B1 *1* 2–239 text, *240* blk.

Pagination: (↑); 78, 158, 176, 198, 240 blk.

Press-figures: B4ᵛ(8)–2, C5(25)–6, D2ᵛ(36)–3, D6(43)–2, E7ᵛ(62)–2, E8ᵛ(64)–3, F2ᵛ(68)–2, G8(95)–5, H1ᵛ(98)–5, I1ᵛ(114)–1, I5(121)–3, K8(143)–2, L6ᵛ(156)–3, L8(159)–6, M2ᵛ(164)–5, N3ᵛ(182)–6, O6ᵛ(204)–3, P5(217)–4, P6(219)–6, Q7ᵛ(238)–3.

Catchwords: 58 menₐ (~,), 88 ₐ*Many* (*~).

Explicit: 239 THE END.

Paper: White, laid; Medium (uncut: 9 x 5½ in.), wmk.: fleur-de-lys + K & S. Sig. O on appreciably thicker paper, with fleur-de-lys and no cmk.

Type: Pica (4.3 mm), leaded (1.2 mm). Dhh: (a) 2 × parallel rules: pp. 1; (b) 1 × parallel rule: 19, 39, 57, 79, 119, 141, 159, 199, 221; (c) 1 × total rule: 97, 177.

References: Courtney 170; ESTC: t133769.

Notes: If sig. O is a cancelled sheet there is no textual evidence for it.

Copies: E (Jolly 2709).

88.5S/3   Sermons, Dublin   1793

SERMONS | ON | DIFFERENT SUBJECTS, | LEFT FOR PUBLICATION | BY | JOHN TAYLOR, LL.D. | LATE PREBENDARY OF WESTMINSTER, | RECTOR OF BOSWORTH, LEICESTERSHIRE, | AND MINISTER OF ST. MARGARET'S, WESTMINSTER. | [short parallel rule] | PUBLISHED BY | THE REV. SAMUEL HAYES, A.M. | USHER OF WESTMINSTER-SCHOOL. | [short total rule] | TO WHICH IS ADDED, | A SERMON | WRITTEN BY | SAMUEL JOHNSON, LL.D. | FOR THE FUNERAL OF HIS WIFE. | [parallel rule] | DUBLIN: | PRINTED BY P. BYRNE, GRAFTON-STREET. | [short swelled rule] | M.DCC.XCIII.

8°, π1 A⁴ B–2G⁸ (–2G8 = ? π1), ($2 signed), 236 leaves.

Pp. π1 t., on A1 *i*–ii Dedication (William, D. of Devonshire), *iii* iv–viii Contents, on B1 *1* 2–462 text of Sermons.

Pagination: (↑), no errors.

Press-figures: B3ᵛ(6)–4, C1ᵛ(18)–2, D2ᵛ(36)–4, E2ᵛ(52)–4, F1ᵛ(66)–2, I2ᵛ(116)–4, K2ᵛ(132)–2, L3ᵛ(150)–2, M3(165)–3, N5ᵛ(186)–1, O1ᵛ(194)–2, P4ᵛ(216)–3, Q4ᵛ(232)–3, R1ᵛ(242)–4, S2ᵛ(260)–2, T7ᵛ(286)–1, U6(299)–4,

X7^v(318)–3, Y5(329)–4, Z8(351)–3, 2A5^v(362)–2, 2B7^v(382)–1, 2C8^v(400)–2, 2D5^v(410)–3, 2E7^v(430)–4, 2F8^v(448)–4, 2G4(455)–2.

Catchwords: not recorded.

Explicit: 462 THE END.

Paper: white, laid; La. post [or ? Carré] (uncut: 8¼ × 5¼ in.); no vis. wmk.

Type: Pica (4.3 mm).

References: Courtney 170–1; ESTC: t133771.

Notes: The presence of press-figures is unusual though not unknown in Dublin books of this period. The absence of a wmk. obscures the origin of the paper.

Copies: L (4461. dd.22); *USA*: CSmH (X65276), CtY (Mhc9. T216.Se72), PPL, PPU (257.3.T21); *Can*: CaOHM (B.15920).

88.5S/4   Sermons, third London edition   1795

[½t] [short swelled rule] | SERMONS, | LEFT FOR PUBLICATION | BY | JOHN TAYLOR, LL.D. | Late Prebendary of Westminster, &c. | [short swelled rule].

[Vol. I] SERMONS | ON | DIFFERENT SUBJECTS | LEFT FOR PUBLICATION | BY | JOHN TAYLOR, LL.D. | Late Prebendary of Westminster, | Rector of Bosworth, Leicestershire, | and Minister of St. Margaret's | Westminster. | [medium swelled rule] | PUBLISHED | By the Rev. SAMUEL HAYES, A.M. | Usher of Westminster School. | [short swelled rule] | THE THIRD EDITION. | [short swelled rule] | VOLUME I. | [short swelled rule] | LONDON: | Printed for T. CADELL, junior, and | W. DAVIES (Successors to Mr. CADELL), in | the strand. | 1795.

Var (b): . . . Usher of Westminster . . . VOLUME I. | [short swelled rule] | THE THIRD EDITION. | [short swelled rule] | LONDON: . . . the Strand$_\wedge$ | 1795.

8°, a^8 B–T^8 (T8 blk), ($4 (–a1,2) signed), 152 leaves

Pp. a1 *i* ½t, *ii* blk, *iii* t., *iv* blk, v–vii Dedication: [medium parallel rule] | TO |HIS GRACE | WILLIAM, | DUKE OF DEVONSHIRE., *viii* blk, ix–xv Contents dh: [2 × total rules] | CONTENTS. | [short swelled rule], *xvi* blk, on B1 1–285 text, *286–88* blk.

Pagination: [↑] v, (↑) vi–vii, ix–xv, 1; 26, 70, 96, 160, 184, 202, 222, 242, 286–88 blk.

Press-figures: a3^v(vi)–2, B3(5)–3, B6(11)–5, C8(31)–6, D4^v(40)–7, E3^v(54)–3, F5(73)–7, F8(79)–5, G7(93)–6, G7^v(94)–4, H5^v(106)–5, I5^v(122)–2, K7^v(142)–5, L6(155)–1, M4^v(168)–2, N8^v(192)–4, O4^v(200)–1, O6(203)–2, P8^v(224)–6, Q7(237)–2, R2^v(244)–3, S8^v(272)–5, T5^v(282)–6.

Catchwords: 15 [edu- *hyphen slipt*] cation$_\wedge$ (~,), 48 *om.* (SERMON III.), 128 him$_\wedge$ (~;), 247 *all* (*all* 'a' *is roman*).

Explicit: 285 FINIS.

Paper: White, laid; medium (9 × 5¾ in.); wmk.: fleur-de-lys + CW + 1794.

Type: text: pica (4.2 mm), leaded (1.2 mm), notes: bourgeois (3.0 mm). D-hdd: parallel rule p. 27; parallel and total rules pp. 49, 71, 97, 121, 139, 185, 203, 222, 243, 263; Tpp. flowers: 25, 48, 183, 221; orn. device: 69, 120, 159; small crown: 262.

[Vol. II] SERMONS | ON | DIFFERENT SUBJECTS | LEFT FOR PUBLICATION | BY JOHN TAYLOR, LL.D. | Late PREBENDARY of WESTMINSTER, | RECTOR OF BOSWORTH, LEICESTERSHIRE, | and MINISTER of ST. MARGARET'S | WESTMINSTER. | [short swelled rule] | VOLUME THE SECOND. | [short swelled rule] | PUBLISHED | By the REV. SAMUEL HAYES, A.M. | USHER OF WESTMINSTER SCHOOL, | TO WHICH IS ADDED, | A SERMON, | WRITTEN BY | SAMUEL JOHNSON, LL.D. | FOR THE FUNERAL OF HIS WIFE. | [short swelled rule] | THIRD EDITION. | [short swelled rule] | LONDON: | Printed for T. CADELL, junior, and W. DAVIES | (fucceffors to Mr. CADELL,) in the Strand. | 1795.

8°.

II. Pp. Sermons XII–XXV.

No copy has been seen, and since many sets of the Sermons in 2 vols. are of mixed edns. it is possible that the '3rd ed.' of vol. 2 is a ghost; it may however be a re-dated issue of vol. 2, 1792 (88.5S/2).

References: ESTC: n023895.

Copies: O (994 e. 369, vol. 1, only; var. b);

USA: CtY (Divinity), MH (C.1359.2), NIC; *UK*: BMp, Cp, DUu (vol. 1 only), E (Jolly 2708, vol. 1 only).

88.5S/5   Sermons, fourth London edition   1800

[Hollow] SERMONS, | ON DIFFERENT SUBJECTS, | LEFT FOR PUBLICATION | BY | *JOHN TAYLOR, LL.D.* | LATE PREBENDARY OF WESTMINSTER, | RECTOR OF BOSWORTH, LEICESTERSHIRE, AND | MINISTER OF ST. MARGARET'S, WESTMINSTER. | [short parallel rule] | PUBLISHED | BY THE REV. *SAMUEL HAYES*, A.M. | USHER OF WESTMINSTER SCHOOL. | [short swelled rule] | VOLUME I [–II]. | THE FOURTH EDITION. | [parallel rule] | *LONDON:* | PRINTED FOR T. CADELL, JUN. AND W. DAVIES, | IN THE STRAND. | [short orn. rule] | 1800.

2 vols. 8°.

I. a⁸ B–T⁸, ($4 signed; 'VOL. I.' on $1), 152 leaves.

Pp. [? a1 ½t], a2 t., a2ᵛ blk, a3 v–vii Dedication (William, D. of Devonshire), *viii* blk, ix–xv Contents, *xvi* blk, on B1 1–287 Sermons I–XIII, 287 coloph: 'Printed by JOHN NICHOLS, Red-Lion-Paffage, Fleet-ftreet, London.', *288* blk.

Pagination: (↑) v–vii, ix, 1, 27, 49, 71, 97, 121, 141, 163, 187, 205, 225, 245, 265; blk: 26, 70, 96, 140, 162, 186, 244.

Press-figures: B7(13)–4, C7(29)–3, D5^v(42)–4, E6(59)–4, E7(61)–2, H7(109)–2.

Catchwords: 50 affirms$_\wedge$ (~,), 54 enmity, (~$_\wedge$), 80 [con-] fidered$_\wedge$ (~,), 180 *om.* (It).

Explicit: 287 END OF THE FIRST VOLUME.

II. *A*⁴ B–Q⁸ R⁴, ($4 signed; 'VOL. II.' on $1), 128 leaves.

Pp. [? A1 ½t], A2 t., A2^v blk, A3 v–viii Contents, on B1 1–248 text, 248 coloph.

Pagination: (↑) v, 1, 21, 43, 63, 85, 103, 125, 147, 165, 183, 205, 229; blk: 42, 62, 182, 228.

Press-figures: G4^v(88)–2, H5(105)–2, H6(107)–4, I5(121)–2, O2^v(196)–2.

Catchwords: 61 *om.* (SERMON), 196 wll (will).

Explicit: 248 THE END.

Paper: white, laid; demy (8¾ × 5⅝ in.); no vis. wmk.

Type: English (4.5 mm).

References: Courtney 171; ESTC: 134039.

Copies: L (4461. dd.23); *USA*: [CU], MH (vol. 1: C.1359.2); *UK*: ABu (*82463/5), Cf, LEu (vol. 1 only: Stack Theol.), LVu; *Aust*: CNL (DNS 7503).

[88.5S/6   Sermons   1806

London, 1806. Not seen: probably a ghost.]

88.5S/7   Sermons, Walpole, NH   1806

SERMONS | ON | *DIFFERENT SUBJECTS,* | LEFT FOR PUBLICATION | BY | JOHN TAYLOR, LL.D. | LATE PREBENDARY OF WESTMINSTER, | RECTOR OF BOSWORTH, LEICESTERSHIRE, | AND MINISTER OF ST. MARGARET'S, WESTMINSTER. | [wavy rule] | PUBLISHED BY THE REV. SAMUEL HAYES, A.M. | USHER OF WESTMINSTER-SCHOOL, | [short wavy rule] | TO WHICH IS ADDED | A SERMON, | WRITTEN BY | SAMUEL JOHNSON, LL.D. | FOR THE FUNERAL OF HIS WIFE. | [double rule] | WALPOLE, N.H. | PRINTED FOR THOMAS AND THOMAS, BY G.W. NICHOLS. | [short wavy rule] | 1806.

8°, *A*⁴ B–U⁴ W⁴ X–2H⁴, ($1 signed), 126 leaves

Pp. *i* t., *ii* blk, *iii* Dedication (William, D. of Devonshire), *iv* blk, *v–viii*, Contents, *9* 10–256 text.

Pagination: [↑].

Explicit: 256 THE END.

Paper: White (foxing), wove; demy (8¾ × 5½ in.); no vis. wmk.

Type: Bourgeois (3.1 mm).

References: Courtney 171.

Notes: CSmH inscr. 'Ballston | Moral Library N° 93' and 'Price $1.50'.[1]

Copies: L (4454. g.15);

USA: [CLU], CSmH (191114), CtY², [DLC], ICU, [Liebert], MB ('1808'), [MdBP], MH, [MnU], MWA, [Nh, NjNbS], NjP, NN, NRU, [OO, ViLxVV].

[1] I am indebted to Prof. O M Brack for notes on this copy.

88.5S/8   Sermons, fifth London edition   1812

SERMONS | ATTRIBUTED TO | SAMUEL JOHNSON, LL.D. | AND | LEFT FOR PUBLICATION | BY | JOHN TAYLOR, LL.D. | LATE PREBENDARY OF WESTMINSTER, &c. | [short parallel rule] | THE FIFTH EDITION. | [parallel rule] | LONDON: | PRINTED FOR JOHN EBERS, NEW BOND STREET; SHARPE | AND HAILES, PICCADILLY; AND TAYLOR AND HESSEY, | FLEET STREET. | [short swelled rule] | 1812.

8°, *A*⁸ (± A2) B–2C⁸ 2D⁴ 2E², ($2 (–2D2, 2E2) signed), 214 leaves.

Pp. A1 *i* ½t, *ii* blk, *iii* t., *iv* blk, *v–*vi Advertisement to the Fifth Edition, *xi–xii* Dedication (William, D. of Devonshire), *xiii* xiv–xvi Contents, on B1 *1* 2–410 text of Sermons, 410 coloph: WHITTINGHAM AND ROWLAND, PRINTERS, | GOSWELL STREET, LONDON., *411–12* advts.

Pagination: 92 unnumbered; *Press-figures*: none; *Catchwords*: none.

Explicit: 410 FINIS.

Paper: White, laid; La. post (8¼ × 5½ in.); no vis. wmk.

Type: Pica (4.0mm).

References: Courtney 171.

Notes: May have been issued as a companion to *Works*, 1810 (87.3W/12, above).

Copies: L (4455 ee.15, 'Lord Edmund O'Bryen');

USA: Hyde ('Lockhart' — Adam; imperfect, lacks A4.5 in prelims), [Liebert ('Mʳ Chˢ Burton his Book 1817')], NjP, WiM; *UK*: AWu.

88.5S/9   Sermons, 'fifth' edition   1812

SERMONS, | ON | DIFFERENT SUBJECTS, | ATTRIBUTED TO | SAMUEL JOHNSON, LL.D. | AND |LEFT FOR PUBLICATION | BY |

JOHN TAYLOR, LL.D. | LATE PREBENDARY OF WESTMINSTER, RECTOR OF BOSWORTH, | LEICESTERSHIRE, AND MINISTER OF ST. MARGARET'S | WESTMINSTER. | [short parallel rule] | PUBLISHED | by the Rev. SAMUEL HAYES, A.M. | USHER OF WESTMINSTER SCHOOL. | [short swelled rule] | THE FIFTH EDITION. | [short swelled rule] | LONDON: | PRINTED FOR T. CADELL AND N. DAVIES, STRAND, | BY J. M'CREERY, BLACK-HORSE-COURT, FLEET-STREET. | [dash] | 1812.

8°, π1 *a*² b² B–2B⁸ 2C⁴ (–2C4 ?= π1), ($2 signed), 200 leaves.

Pp. π1 t., π1ᵛ *ii* blk, a1 *iii–iv* Dedication, a2 *v–x* Contents, on B1 *1* 2–389 text, Sermons I–XXV, 389 coloph: [short parallel rule] | J. M'Creery, Printer, Black-Horse-Court, | Fleet-Street, London., *390* blk.

Pagination: blk pp. 34, 84, 98, 114, 146, 172, 216, 232, 246, 262, 276, 294, 312, 326, 340, 374, 390; unnumbered 19, 34–5, 49, 67, 84–5, 98–9, 114–15, 131, 146–7, 159, 172–3, 187, 203, 216–17, 232–3, 246–7, 262–3, 276–7, 294–5, 312–13, 326–7, 340–1, 357, 374–5, 390.

Press-figures: none.

Catchwords: *om.* b2ᵛ; 259 [su-] periority ('ty' *slipt*), 237 motions, (*comma slipt*).

Explicit: 389 FINIS.

Paper: White, wove; ? demy (uncut: 8¾ × 5⅝ in.); wmk.: 1812

Type: Pica (4.0 mm), leaded (1.2 mm).

Copies: O (Vet. A6 e.1439; 'United Service Club'), SAN (ˢPR 3531.S3.E12).

88.5S/10   Sermons   1812

Sermons attributed to Samuel Johnson
    8°. Not seen.
    Copies: [? PPL.]

88.5S/11   *Sermons, Philadelphia*   1812

Not seen. This and 88.5S/10 (prec.), are highly uncertain, and in view of the unsubstantiated Philadelphian location, may both be ghosts.[1]

    Copies: Unlocated.

----

[1] The *Sermons* did not form a part of SJ's *Works* until 1823 when Chalmers printed two in vol. xii of his edn. (87.3W/18, above). A companion volume to the Boston-New York edn. of *Works*, 1809–12 (87.3W/10, above) is possible and might help to account for variant imprints, but copies are too elusive even for guesswork.

88.5S/12   Sermons, Walpole, N.H.   1812

Sermons on different Subjects . . . Walpole, N.H. Thomas and Thomas

    8°. Not examined. Perhaps a reprint of 88.5S/7, 1806, above, or another issue of 88.5S/11, above.

    Copies: NjP.

88.5S/13   Sermons, British Prose, Vol. XV   1819

British Prose Writers. Vol. XV. in 2 vols. Dr Johnson's Sermons. London: Published by John Sharpe, Piccadilly. 1819

    [Engr. t.] D^r. Johnson's Sermons | Vol. I. | [Dictionary port. of SJ in frame, 'Sir J. Reynolds pinx. G. Murray sc.'] | London, Published by John Sharpe, Piccadilly. | 1819.

    [Title] Sermons | by | Samuel Johnson, LL.D. | Left for publication | by | John Taylor, LL.D. | Late Prebendary of Westminster. | [short rule] | Vol. I [– II]. | MDCCCXIX.

    2 vols., 12°

    I. [Engr. t.] + B–G¹² H⁶ (H6 ? blk), ($1,5 (+ H3 –H5) signed; 'VOL. I.' on $1), 78 leaves.

    Pp. [B1 ?] B2 *3* t., on B3 *5* 6–155 text Sermons I–XII, *156* Index, coloph: T. Davison, Printer, Whitefriars.

    Explicit: 156 END OF VOL. I.

    II. [Engr. t., as vol. 1, but Vignette: East window and altar, 'R.W. del. J. Pye sc.', &c.] + B–G¹² H¹⁰, ($1,5 signed; 'VOL. II.' on $1), 82 leaves.

    Pp. [Engr. t.] + *1* t., *2* coloph., on B1 *3* 4–162 text Sermons XIII–XXV, *163* Index, and coloph. as vol. 1, *164* blk.

    Explicit: 163 THE END.

    Paper: White, wove; ? Foolscap (5⅔ × 3¼ in.), no vis. wmk.

    Type: Brevier (2.5 mm), leaded (0.4 mm).

    References: Courtney 171.

    Notes: Usually bound as 1 vol.

    Copies: O (994 f.61; 2 vols.>1);

    USA: MB, NN (2vols.>1), NRU; *UK*: BMp, JDF (2vols.>1, lacks tt., label: 'H. Hoodless, Wigton'), LICj (vol. 2 only, uncut, ptd. wraps), STA.

88.5S/14a   Sermons, Boston   1820

Sermons by J. Taylor. . . Boston: Printed by Wells . . . 1820

    Vol. I. Not seen.

    References: S&S 1804 (PPLT).

    Copies: Unlocated.

| 88.5S/14b | Sermons, British Prose Writers, Vol. 8, Boston | 1821 |

'British Prose Writers', vol. 8.[1]
  Select Editions of British Prose. Boston: Wells and Lilly
  2 vols., 16°, 426 pp. Not examined.
  References: S&S 5727 [CtW, ICT, IEG, KTW, MA, MBC, MLes, MdBD, MdBLC, MeBat, NbCrD, OO, RNR]
  Copies: MH (16477.24); *USA*: CtY, MB, MWA, NN, PPL.

  [1] In 1828 at Moses Thomas's *Philadelphia Trade Sale* (5 Sept. 1825), Wells & Lily of Boston offered 25 copies of 'Prose Writers' (10 vols.), including 'Johnson's Sermons' for $1.25 per volumes, and again at the *Philadelphia Trade Sale* (8 Sept. 1828), p. 3, they offered 10 copies of 'Johnson's Sermons' at the retail price of $1.25 (MWA).

| 88.5S/15 | Sermons, ed. Chalmers | 1823 |

See *Works*, ed. Chalmers, 1823 (87.3W/18, above), which added sermons X and XXV.

| 88.5S/16 | Sermons, Works | 1824 |

See ? *Works*, 1824 (87.3W/19a, above).

| 88.5S/17 | Sermons, Ripon | 1835 |

SERMONS | BY | SAMUEL JOHNSON, LL.D. | LEFT FOR PUBLICATION | BY | JOHN TAYLOR, LL.D. | PREBENDARY OF WESTMINSTER. | [medium rule] | RIPON: | PRINTED BY T. PROCTER, MARKET-PLACE. | [short rule] | MDCCCXXXV.
  8°, A^2 B–3C[4] 3D[2], ($1 signed), 196 leaves.
  Pp. Engr. port. of SJ front + A1 t., A1[v] blk, A2 Contents, on B1 *1* 2–388 text, 388 coloph: 'PRINTED BY T. PROCTER, RIPON.'
  Pagination: ↑; 99 as 90; *Explicit*: none.
  Paper: White, wove; Fine demy (uncut: 8¾ × 5⅝ in.); no vis. wmk.
  Type: Pica (4.1 mm), notes and epigraphs: long primer (3.2 mm).
  Plate: Port. of SJ 'Sir J. Reynolds, pinx[t] Heath sculp. Samuel Johnson, L.L.D. Published by Longman & C°. June 10th. 1805'. Perhaps a sophistication.
  References: Courtney 171; *Tinker* 1386.
  Notes: The O (Cassels) copy is inscribed: ' "A book that I have been instrumental in having printed at Ripon — they having been hitherto printed under the description of Sermons left for publication by Dr. Taylor for whom Dr. Johnson wrote them — but so long ago that few people are now living besides

myself, who remember the fact. I sent them to an old friend, whose husband as well as Dr. Taylor was a prebendary of Westminster, when she heard him preach, exclaimed that Sermon was Dr. Johnsons — a circumstance I mention as additional evidence of the fact—" extracted from a letter of Mrs Lawrence——.'

Most copies are bound in coloured morocco, a feature which corroborates a privately sponsored publication for presentation.

Copies: O (994 e.268, 'The Reverend Andrew Cassels from Mrs. Lawrence Studley Park March 1835'[1]);

USA: CLU, Hyde[2] (1. 'Lawrence' — 'Harrison ' — 'Redmond', fore-edge painting: view of Lichfield), ICU, [Liebert ('Lady Louisa Lygon') = CtY], NIC; *Can*: CaOLUI; *UK*: BMp, L (1509/1339), LICj, [WLAp].

---

[1] 'Miss Lawrence' lived at Studley Royal, noted for its gardens and park designed by John Aislabie (1670–1742*), 2 miles from Ripon, according to Carey's *Roads* (1817), 390. Edward Baines, *History, Directory & Gazetteer of the County of York* (1822), i ('West Riding'), 250, noted that 'The borough [sc. Ripon] is under the patronage of Mrs Lawrence of Studley Royal, and returns two members to Parliament', and further identifies Mrs Lawrence 255 and 612, 'Studley Royal . . . Lawrence, Elizabeth Sophia, Studley Park', and 650, 'Studley Royal, 2½ m. SW of Ripon, Mrs Lawrence; and 26, Lower Brooke street, London.'

91.5CG   Conversation with George III   1791

A | CONVERSATION | BETWEEN | HIS MOST SACRED MAJESTY | GEORGE III. | AND | SAMUEL JOHNSON, LL.D. | ILLUSTRATED WITH OBSERVATIONS, | By JAMES BOSWELL, Esq. | [medium swelled rule] | LONDON: | PRINTED BY HENRY BALDWIN; | FOR CHARLES DILLY, IN THE POULTRY. | MDCCXC. | [Price Half a Guinea.]

4°, $4; Pp. *1* t., *2* Imprimatur: 'Entered in the Hall-Book of the Company of Stationers.' *3* 4-8 text.

Pagination: [↑] 4–8.

Paper: White, laid; demy (uncut: 11¼ × 8¾ in.).

References: Courtney 172; Pottle, *Literary Career of JB* (1929), 137-41, § 75; F. Taylor, 'Johnsoniana from the Bagshawe Muniments', *BJRL* xxxv (1952), 211–47 (and 249–50); ESTC: t012462.

Notes: See notes on Letter to Chesterfield above (88.3L/3), which was, like this, published 12 May 1791 (*NCBEL* ii. 1214), but advertised in *Public Advertiser*, 30 Apr. 1791, with the *Letter to Chesterfield*. JB's note in his *Tour* (1785), 134, and his letter to Malone of 17 Nov. 1788 show his early determination of a separate publication.[1] This item was worked off as the corresponding pages of *Life* (1791), i. 291–6, were going through the press, but the opening lines of each paragraph were modified for the new piece. Again a slightly superior paper seems to have been used, but the stock is not different from that of *Life* (1791). Baldwin's account for the printing is CtY: (MS

Boswell, A 59). R.B. Adam, printed a facsimile from his own copy for Christmas 1927 (Pottle § 76). Copies are scarce.[2]

JB's record of the conversation itself (*Life* ii. 33-42), derived from oral reports and from the 'Caldwell Minute' made of an account of the meeting sent by SJ to Sir James Caldwell in 1767 (MS: MRu), with consultation of a similar note made by William Strahan in c. 1768 (MS: Lawrence G. Blackmon, Esq;).[3]

The Conversation was reprinted from *Life* (1791), in *The Witticisms, Anecdotes, Jests, and Sayings, of Dr. Samuel Johnson, during the whole course of his life. . . By J. Merry, Esq. of Pembroke College.* 1791 (Pottle, *Literary Career*, § 105, pp. 199–200); *Copies*: CSmH, CtY, Hyde; Mp, O; CNL. There was a second edition ('greatly improved'), published in 1793 (*Copies*: Hyde, NN; Gp, SWS, O), and a third in 1797 (*Copy*: CLU-C). 'J. Merry' and his college affiliation, are fictitious.

Copies: O;
USA: Hyde; *UK*: L.

---

[1] *Correspondence of JB with . . . Malone*, ed. P.S. Baker et al. (1986), 360.
[2] D. Buchanan, *The Treasure of Auchinleck* (1975), 343, reported a copy derived from JB himself as then in the possession of Heyward Isham, Esq; son of Col. R.H. Isham.
[3] O M Brack, 'Samuel Johnson's Private Interview with George III: The Strahan Minute' (1993). Joseph Cockfield reported that Hoole had told him of the conversation by 19 March 1768 (*Lit. Illus.* v (1828), 779).

93MH On the Character and Duty of an Academick, 1793 Moir's Hospitality

[½t] [rule] | HOSPITALITY. | *Price Half a Crown.* | [rule]

[Title] *HOSPITALITY.* | A | DISCOURSE | OCCASIONED BY | HIS MAJESTY'S LETTER | IN BEHALF OF | THE EMIGRANT FRENCH CLERGY, | IN ST. DIONIS BACK CHURCH, MAY 26, 1793. | TO WHICH IS APPENDED, | *A FRAGMENT of the late Dr. JOHNSON,* | ON THE | CHARACTER AND DUTY OF AN ACADEMICK, | NEVER BEFORE PUBLISHED. | BY JOHN MOIR, A.M. | [medium double rule] | USE HOSPITALITY ONE TO ANOTHER WITHOUT GRUDGING. PETER. | [medium double rule] | LONDON: | SOLD BY MESSRS. RIVINGTON, ST. PAUL S CHURCH YARD; MR. OWEN, PICCADILLY; | AND AT THE AUTHOR S HOUSE, NO. 4, NEWINGTON PLACE, KENNINGTON ROAD, | SURREY. | [short swelled rule] | 1793.

4°, *A*² B–F⁴ G², ($1 signed), 24 leaves.

Pp. A1 ½t, A1ᵛ blk, A2 t., A2ᵛ blk, on B1 *1* 2–41 text of Discourse dh: *HOSPITALITY.* | A | DISCOURSE, &c. | [short total rule] | [Text from Hebrews, xiii. 2], ht: HOSPITALITY., on G1 *42–3* text of Fragment dh: *A FRAGMENT of the late Dr. JOHNSON,* | ON THE | CHARACTER AND DUTY OF AN ACADEMICK., 43 ht: A FRAGMENT., *44* advt. for 'One Thing Needful . . . Price in Sheets Eight Shillings. By the same Author.'

Pagination: no errors; *Press-figures*: none; *Catchwords*: none.

Explicit: 41 THE END.

Paper: White, wove; Sm. post (9½ × 5⅝ in.); no vis. wmk.

Type: English (4.5 mm), leaded (2.5 mm), the 'Fragment' in pica (4.0), leaded (1.3).

Notes: First noticed by Richard Hatchwell, Esq.[1] The 'Fragment' attributed to SJ is mentioned in Moir's introductory paragraph (p. 40) as 'by one of the most illustrious moralists in modern times, presented to me, in the Author's own hand-writing, by a friend whose confidence is one of my best comforts, and whose communications are all valuable, and merit the highest gratitude.'

SJ's authorship of the 'Fragment' is wholly convincing, from the opening sentence: 'The great effect of society is, that by uniting multitudes in one general co-operation, it distributes to different orders of the community the several labours and occupations of life', to the close: 'Ignorance in other men may be censured as idleness, in an academick it must be abhorred as treachery.' One reading perhaps derives from SJ's MS: e.g. 'national knowledge' (*recte*: 'rational . . .').[2]

It is difficult to guess when this brief and uncompromising survey of the duties of academic teachers was composed, or under what circumstances, and it is therefore placed under the date of publication.

Revd. John Moir M.A. is noticed as the author of *The History of the political Life and public Service of the Rt. Hon. Charles James Fox*, London: Debrett, 1783, in a review in *European Mag.* iv (Aug. 1788), 126–7, where other publications are also attributed to him, and where he is decribed as 'of the Borough of Southwark' and holding a 'curacy in the city of London, besides a lectureship', adding that 'It was his fate to be born in Scotland, though his parents were both from England', and that his 'education was among the religious sect of the *Seceders*', but that 'at the age of sixteen' he 'sought for improvement in all kinds of literature and science, in the most celebrated schools and universities of Scotland', and that he studied divinity at Edinburgh, and subsequently entered the English Church. A copy of the Foulis folio of *Paradise Lost*, 1770, inscribed 'To the Reverend Mr John Mair Minister of the Gospel at Raine this Book is presented in Testimony of Regard by the University of Glasgow. Will: Leechman. Prin: & Vice Chancellour', then in the hands of a Boston bookseller, was described to me by Prof. Thomas Bonnell, in October 1993. Though it is plausible that Mair or Moir held a living at Raine in Essex (in the suburbs of Braintree), the Glasgow connection is a problem. A few personal details are added in a review of his *Gleanings* in *Gents. Mag.* lviii (June 1788), 537–8, noting that he had a 'sickly wife and a numerous increasing family' which he supported by a 'lectureship of Dionis Backchurch, Fenchurch-Street', and that he occupied 'the house inhabited by the late Dr. S. Johnson in Bolt-court, which Mr. M. took with the hope of letting it out in lodgings'. A notice of his *Parish Church* in *Gents. Mag.* lxxiii (June, 1803), i. 539-40, describes him as 'an unsuccessful candidate for a London pulpit'. These details allow the inference that Moir was perhaps born in the 1750s, but no notice of his death has yet been discovered.[3]

The appeal on behalf of the exiled French clergy was noticed by 'Clericus' in *Gents. Mag.* lxiii (June 1793), 498, and led to other sermons on the topic (*idem*, Aug. 1793, 730).

Moir's *Gleanings*, were published at ½ gn., with the imprint: 'London: Printed for the Author; and sold at his house, No. 8, Bolt Court, Fleet Street'. This was the house in which SJ died. There is no mention, however, of the MS 'Fragment' in *Gleanings*, although there is a somewhat whiggish essay on SJ at i. 60–68 which mentions 'Boswell, a Piozzi, and other gleaners of oddity and imbecility' (61), and relates an anecdote of SJ and 'a bookseller of eminence' (66, perhaps Osborne). In vol. 2, in the 'Verses on Various Subjects' is one entitled 'The Wits' (135–50), which includes disparaging allusions to SJ (145–6). Moir's political views are revealed in his essay on 'Majesty' (ii. 55–62). At this period, then, although he lived on hallowed ground, Moir was unsympathetic to SJ: his comments on the 'Fragment' ('by one of the most illustrious moralists in modern times'), published in *Hospitality*, reflect a marked change. The fragmentary details of his career and the various tenor of his writings imply a tenacious and opinionated man whose personal history and circumstances militated against his acceptance into a church and society which preferred conformity to individualism.

The means by which Moir might have obtained the 'Fragment' are easier to conceive if he was living in London, had lived in SJ's house and in Southwark, and held a curacy in the City. A multitude of friends is possible in such circumstances: his Scottish connections might have led him to Barclay of Thrale's brewery, or to Percival Stockdale, a later occupant of Bolt Court; his clerical associations could have involved many others. Speculation is at a stand.

Copies: O (Vet. A5. d.1531).

---

[1] To whom I am deeply indebted for his generosity in allowing me to examine the piece, announced in his *Malmesbury Miscellany*, 50 (1993), 61. This copy had been recently bound in half calf and marbled boards, and the edges trimmed.

[2] Dr David Fairer pointed out to me the un-Johnsonian implications of 'national' in such a context.

[3] Moir's publications are miscellaneous, including 1. *Obedience the best Charter*, London: Richardson & Urquhart (1776); 2. *Discourses on practical Subjects*, London: T. Cadell (1776); 3. *Strictures on Thomson's 'Seasons'* (1777; rptd. in *Gleanings* (1785), i. 75–102); 4. *The Beauties of Natural History* (European Mag.); 5. *Letters from an old patriotic Quaker to the King* (European Mag.) 6. *History of the political Life, &c., of Charles James Fox* [1783]; 7a. *Female Tuition*, London: J. Murray [1784], b. ———2nd edn. London: J. Murray (1786), c. ———Dublin: W. Sleater (1787), d. ———new edn. London: Printed for the author [1800], e. ———new edn. London: Murray & Highley [1800]; 8. *Sermons on some of the most useful and interesting subjects*, London: J.F. & C. Rivington (1784); 9. *Gleanings; or, Fugitive Pieces*, 2 vols. London: Printed for the author [1785]; 10. *One Thing needful*, London: Printed for the author [1791]; 11. *Preventive Policy*, London: Printed for the author [1796]; 12. *Irreligion the Stigma of our public Profession* [1799]; 13. *The Parish Church, a Discourse* (1802); 14. *Philosophical Remarks on the Christian Religion*, Philadelphia (1807); 15. *Debtors to God, not Givers*, [n.d.]

94.4PBS/1a   Piozzi's British Synonymy   1794

[½t] [medium double rule] | BRITISH SYNONYMY. | [medium double rule] | [Title] BRITISH SYNONYMY; | OR, | AN ATTEMPT | AT | REGULATING THE CHOICE OF WORDS | IN | FAMILIAR CONVERSATION. | INSCRIBED, | With Sentiments of Gratitude and Refpect, to fuch of her | Foreign Friends as have made Englifh Literature | their peculiar Study, | BY | HESTER LYNCH PIOZZI. | [short swelled rule] | IN TWO VOLUMES. | VOL. I [– II]. | [medium double rule] | *LONDON:* | PRINTED FOR G. G. AND J. ROBINSON, PATERNOSTER-ROW. | MDCCXCIV.

2 vols., 8°

I. a^2 b^4 B–2D^8 2E^4, ($4 signed; 'VOL. I.' on $1), 218 leaves

Pp. a1 ½t, a1^v blk, a2 t., a2^v epigraph, on b1 *i* ii–viii Preface, on B1 *1* 2–423 text dh and ht: BRITISH SYNONYMY. *424* blk.

Pagination: 2 unnumbered, 218 as 18.

Press-figures: b2^v(iv)–8, B8^v(16)–2, C5^v(26)–8, C7(29)–6, D6^v(44)–1, D7^v(46)–2, E1^v(50)–8, F6^v(76)–1, G5^v(90)–8, H7^v(110)–5, I2^v(116)–3, I8(127)–5, K5^v(138)–3, K6^v(140)–1, L4^v(152)–1, L5^v(154)–3, M3^v(166)–1, M7(173)–5, N6(187)–7, N6^v(188)–3, O4^v(200)–2, O5^v(202)–4, P3^v(214)–8, P7(221)–3, Q6^v(236)–7, Q7^v(238)–2, R1^v(242)–7, R6^v(252)–2, S2^v(260)–5, S5^v(266)–4, T8(287)–3, U7^v(302)–8, X6(315)–2, Y7(333)–5, Y8(335)–3, Z6(347)–7, 2A7^v(366)–7, 2B1^v(370)–2, 2B7(381)–1, 2C3^v(390)–3, 2C5(393)–8, 2D3^v(406)–7, 2D6^v(412)–2, 2E3^v(422)–3.

Catchwords: 289 Gothic (Gothick).

Explicit: 423 END OF THE FIRST VOLUME.

II. A^2 B–2D^8, ($4 (–O1), signed; 'VOL. II.' on $1), 210 leaves

Pp. A1 ½t as vol. 1, A2 t., A2^v epigraph (as vol. 1), on B1 *1* 2–416 text.

Pagination: 212 as 112.

Press-figures: B5^v(10)–2, B6^v(12)–7, C6(27)–6, C7(29)–3, D1^v(34)–7, D7(45)–8, E5(57)–1, E8(63)–2, F5^v(74)–3, F7(77)–8, G3^v(86)–2, G4^v(88)–7, H5(105)–2, H8(111)–4, I1^v(114)–5, I4^v(120)–3, K3^v(134)–3, K6^v(140)–2, L5(153)–5, L8(159)–3, M5^v(170)–3, M6^v(172)–1, N8(191)–3, N8^v(192)–5, O4^v(200)–8, O8(207)–7, P5^v(218)–4, P6^v(220)–2, Q8(239)–3, R4^v(248)–5, R7^v(254)–7, S5^v(266)–3, T7^v(286)–7, T8^v(288)–5, U6^v(300)–2, U8(303)–7, X6^v(316)–2, X8(319)–6, Y5(329)–8, Y8(335)–2, Z6(347)–8, Z6^v(348)–7, 2A2^v(356)–2, 2A8(367)–7, 2B1^v(370)–2, 2B4^v(376)–7, 2C1^v(388)–1, 2C8(399)–6, 2D7(413)–2, 2D7^v(414)–8.

Catchwords: 163 term$_\wedge$ (~,).

Explicit: 416 FINIS.

Paper: White, wove; medium (uncut: 9 × 5½ in.); wmk.: fleur-de-lys + W [C].

Type: English (4.7 mm), leaded (2.5 mm).

References: Courtney 173; *Rothschild* 1552; Alston, iii. 524; Clifford, *Piozzi* (1952), 366–70; *Poems*² 225–7; Weinbrot, *HLQ* xxxiv (1970–1), 79–80; ESTC: t098289.

Notes: HLP's MS of this whole work is in MRu. Her assignment of the copyright, dated 10 April 1794, for £300, is MS Hyde (from Upcott: Evans, 22 June 1846, 20; Clifford 368–9). The book was published early (probably on 3rd) in April 1794 (Clifford 369–70). There are many allusions to SJ throughout, viz. i. 18–19, 24, 27, 50, 82, 90, 145, 173, 206, 213, 218, [261], [279], 303, 312, 323, 351, 355, 359–60, 369, 381, 422; ii. 1, 37, 43, 79, 84, 106–7, 120, 122–3, 158, 165, 183, 193–4, 197, 202, 237–8, 251, 256–7, 276, 290, 299, 302, 331–2, 337–8, 343, 354, 358, 366, 371–2, 377, 405. SJ's verses on Sir John Lade were first published here in full (i. 359–60), though st. 4 already in HLP's *Anecdotes*, 1786, 196. SJ's earliest autograph version is CSmH (HM 2583),¹ and several versions by HLP are listed in *Poems*². HLP was vexed by allegations that the work derived from material supplied by SJ, which she denied (*Thraliana* 905).

Copies:² O (302 e. 35–6);

USA: CSmH (82845), CtY², DFo, DLC, Hyde, ICN, [IaU], ICU, IU, [Liebert, blue wraps, uncut], MB, [MeB], MH², [MiU], NIC, NjP, NN, [OCIW, OCU, OO, OU], [PBm], PPL, [PPM, PV], PPU, TxU, ViU (no ½t vol. 2), [WaU]; *Can*: CaOHM; *UK*: ABu², AWn, BAT, [W.R. Batty, uncut], BMp, BRu, C, Cq, E, Eu, Gp², Gu, L (626. h.11), MRc, MRp, MRu, SAN, SHu; *Aust*: CNL (DNS 6783).

¹ It is discussed, together with SJ's covering letter (*Letters* 691, Hyde, iii. 296-7; MS: CSmH: HM. 6001), by Weinbrot, *HLQ* xxxiv (1970–1), 79–80. Pedigrees of the Lade family are in L: (Add. MSS 5520, fo. 238, and 5538, p. 135).
² Maggs Bros, *Catalogue* 1038 (1984), 395 was Susanna Arabella Thrale's copy, and 396 was inscribed by HLP: 'From the Author'.

94.4BS/1b   Piozzi's British Synonymy, facsimile   1968

A facsimile from L copy was published by the Scolar Press, 1968.

94.4BS/2   British Synonymy, Dublin   1794

Dublin: Printed by William Porter, for P. Byrne, and W. Jones. 1794.
8°, Pp. xx + 516. Not examined.
References: ESTC: t126974.
Copies: *USA*: CSmH (X65697), DFo, MiU, NjP, [PPAt], PPL, OU, ViU; *Can*: CaOHM; *UK*: AWn (PE 1591.P66), L; *Eir*: Dp, Dt.

94.4BS/3   British Synonymy, Paris   1804

Five instalments in Parsons & Galignani's *British Library*, vols. xiv, xvi, xviii, xx, and xxii.

[Engr. t.] British Synonymy; or, An Attempt At regulating the choice of words in familiar Conversation. By HESTER LYNCH PIOZZI. With additional Note By the Editors. [Oval vignette of HLP] PARIS Published by Parsons and Galignani. 1804

12°, A–Z⁶ 2A–M⁶ 2N1–3, ($1 signed), 213 leaves.

Pp. Engr. t. + A1 *1* 2–4 Preface by the Editors, *5* 6–354 text, *355* 356–416 Table of British Synonymy, *417* 418–27 Index.

Notes: The typography is evidently French, and the paper is wove, and though it carries a wmk. the design is not identified.

Copies: BMp (408981); *USA*: CSmH (150479).

805A/1a   Account of the Life   1805
                        (Letters to Hill Boothby)

AN | ACCOUNT | OF THE | LIFE | OF | [hollow] DR. SAMUEL JOHNSON, | FROM HIS BIRTH TO HIS ELEVENTH YEAR, | *WRITTEN BY HIMSELF.* | TO WHICH ARE ADDED, | ORIGINAL LETTERS | TO | DR. SAMUEL JOHNSON, | *BY MISS HILL BOOTHBY:* | *From the MSS. preserved by the Doctor, and* | *now in the Possession of* RICHARD WRIGHT, | *Surgeon; Proprietor of the Museum of* | *Antiquities, Natural and Artificial Curiosi-* | *ties, &c. Lichfield.* | [short double rule] | [BL] **London:** | PRINTED FOR RICHARD PHILLIPS, | No. 6, BRIDGE-STREET, BLACKFRIARS; | By NICHOLS and SON, Red Lion Passage, Fleet Street. | 1805.

8°, A–I⁸, ($4 signed), 72 leaves.

Pp. A1 *i* t., *ii* blk, iii–viii Preface, *9* 10–32 Annals, 33–144 Letters &c.

Pagination: (↑) iii, 33, 141–44.

Press-figures: G7(109)–2; *Catchwords*: none.

Explicit: 144 [tp. FINIS.]

Paper: White, wove; foolscap (uncut: 6¾ × 4⅓ in.); wmk.: 'HCo 1804'.

Type: Pica (4.0 mm), leaded (1.2 mm).

References: Courtney 173–4; *Rothschild* 1272; *Tinker* 1388; *Works* (Yale), i, pp. xiii–xv. For an account of Richard Phillips see W.E. Axon, *The Bibliographer* (Oct. 1883), iv.

Notes: Richard Wright (1777–1821), the editor of this collection, inherited Greene's Museum, and enlarged it.[1] The book is briefly noticed in *Gents. Mag.* lxxv (July 1805), i. 651/214. Some of the Letters from SJ to Hill Boothby had already appeared in HLP's *Letters*, 1788 (88.3L/1, above). Copies are frequently uncut in boards. Simms, *Bibliotheca Staffordiensis*, 527, wrongly describes it as 'very rare'.

Copies: O (210 m. 495);
USA: CSmH, CtY, DFo, Hyde[3] (**1**. blue boards, uncut, 'F.B. Bemis'; **2**. blue boards, uncut; **3**. grey boards, paper spine label, uncut), ICN, ICU, IU, [Liebert], MH, NIC[2], NjP ('R.H. Isham'), NN, NPM, NRo, TxU, ViU, WiM; *Japan*: [Kyoto]; *UK*: BMp, BRu, C, Ct(R), DUu, E, LICj, MRu (imperf.), NOu, Op[2] (uncut, boards), STA, [WLAp]; *Aus*: J.P. Hardy ('Peter Cunningham' — 'Mary Lascelles').

---

[1] His ? son, Henry Wright wrote on 16 Sept. 1802, that he had been the compiler of the *Catalogue* of the contents of Greene's Museum, 1785, and that he was the writer of the Preface. He described the dispersal of the collection and noted that Richard Wright had paid 70 guineas for the contents of 'an interior closet' (*Lichfield Telegraph*, xxxv, Aug. 1854). Greene issued various *Catalogues* from about 1773 (Simms, *Bibliotheca Staffordiensis* (1894), 198), and the Museum was noticed in Stebbing Shaw, *History and Antiquities of the County of Stafford* (1798), i. 331–33.

805A/1b	Account of the Life, facsimile, ed. Stockham	1984

A facsimile edition was published by P. Stockham, London, in December 1984, at £25.00. ISBN: 0-907-148-01-8.

805A/1c	Account of the Life, facsimile, ed. Stockham	1984

A limited issue of the prec. 25 copies at £50.00. ISBN: 0-907-148-02-6.

805A/1d	Account of the Life, facsimile, ed. Stockham	1984

A paperback issue of the prec., at £1.95. ISBN: 0-907-148-00-X.

816.DW/1 [=74.7DW, above]	Diary of a Journey into North Wales	1816

[½t] JOURNEY | INTO | NORTH WALES.
[Title] A | [BL] **Diary of a Journey** | INTO | NORTH WALES, | IN THE YEAR 1774; | BY | SAMUEL JOHNSON, LL.D. | [short swelled rule] | EDITED, WITH ILLUSTRATIVE NOTES, | By R. DUPPA, LL.B. | BARRISTER AT LAW. | [medium parallel rule] | *LONDON:* | PRINTED FOR ROBERT JENNINGS, 2, POULTRY, | BY JAMES MOYES, GREVILLE STREET. | [short rule] | M.DCCC.XVI.
8°, *A*[8] B–P[8] Q[2], ($1 signed), 122 leaves.

Pp. A1 *i* ½t, *ii* blk, *iii* t., *iv* blk, *v*–vi Dedication dh: TO | EDWARD SWINBURNE, Esq. ('R. DUPPA, Lincoln's Inn, Sept. 18. 1816'), *vii* viii–xi Preface, xi *Erratum*, *xii* blk, *xiii* xiv–xvi Contents, on B1 *1* 2–149 text dh: A | JOURNEY | INTO | NORTH WALES, | IN | THE YEAR 1774. | [short swelled rule], rt: A JOURNEY INTO | NORTH WALES., Opinions and Observations by Dr. Johnson, *157* 158–88 Appendix, *189* 190–212 Itinerary, *213* 214–26 Index, [*227* advt. for Duppa's *Works*, *228* Errata]; *see Notes below*.

Pagination: 150 ↑; *Press-figures*: none; *Catchwords*: none.

Colophon: 226 PRINTED BY J. MOYES, | Greville Street, Hatton Garden, London.

Explicit: 226 THE END.

Paper: White, wove; La. post (uncut: 8¼ × 5¼ in.); wmk.: 'W BALSTON & Co. | 1814'

Type: text: pica (4.2 mm), leaded (2.0 mm); shoulder notes and footnotes: bourgeois (2.9 mm).

Plates: (2): Facsimiles of SJ's handwriting (variously placed, usually facing t.), both taken from this Diary.

References: *Life* v. 427–61, 579–95 (Courtney 174); CH 166; *Tinker* 1389, *Works* (Yale), i, pp. xix, 163–223; Clifford, *Piozzi* (1952), 445.

Notes: There are two states: (a) retains the final leaf Q2 with advt. for Duppa's *Works* on *227*, and *errata* on p. *228*; (b) has no leaf Q2, but an *Errata* slip is inserted in the volume (variously placed).

Duppa's own copy of this book was presented to CtY by H.W. Liebert in 1978.[1] Two letters from Duppa to Mrs Piozzi ('1815' and '6 Aug. 1816') and a letter from HLP to Duppa ('26 Sept. 1816'),[2] relative to the preparation of this book are MSS Hyde, others are MRu (Rylands Eng. MS 555/60–63); see further in *European Mag.* lxix (1816), 5.

The holograph MS of SJ's Welsh Diary is L (Add. MS 12070; *MS Handlist* 128, *MS Index* JoS 381). Duppa's transcription is inaccurate. The history of the MS is given by Powell in *Life* v. 427–8 n.

Copies: (a) O (8°.P 18.BS);

USA: (a) Hyde ('F.W. Branston'), [Liebert[2] (1. blue boards, uncut; 2. 'Hugh Walpole', uncut) = CtY], NcU, NIC; (b) CSmH ('A.M. Broadley'), CtY ('R. Duppa' + notes, pres. by H.W. Liebert), Hyde[4] (1. 'J. W. Croker' + annotations — Adam; 2. Boards, uncut; 3. Boards, uncut; 4. 'Marg[t]. Holford' extra-illus, no *errata* slip — Adam), ICU ('A.A. Arnold, Cobham, Kent' — 'W. Starkey'), IU (no *errata* slip), MiW (no ½t, 'John Morgan, Rubislaw House, Aberdeen'[3]), NIC, NRo, TxU; [*Indeterminate*: CLU, CtY, DLC, ICN, NjP, NN, PPL];

UK: (a) BMp, BRp, DUu, LEu, NCl, STA, SHu; *Eir*: Dt; (b) ABu (uncut), AWn[2] (1. uncut), AWu, [B.S. Barlow], [W.R. Batty, 'James Forster 1846'], BMp, BRu, C, DUu, E, Gu, L (287. b.14), MC, Op[2] (1. 'Edward Dowden' — 'Frederick Vernon', + errata slip; 2. 'G.B. Hill' no errata slip), Owo, SAN ([s]PR 3524. E16), SPp, STIu, STA; [*Indeterminate*: WLAp].

[1] *YULG* lii (1978), 92. It was lot 449 in Duppa's sale (R.H. Evans), 3 Sept. 1831, and was purchased by Stonehill for Mr Liebert at Sotheby's, 27 Nov. 1950, lot 129, for £38. At Duppa's sale (1831), were two other copies (untraced), lots 448–9, of which the latter was also annotated by him.

[2] Lot 244 at Sotheby's, 25 Feb. 1946.

[3] Morgan is a branch of the Forbes family, cf. Alexander Forbes, *Memorials of the Family of Forbes of Forbesfield* (Aberdeen, 1905).

816.DW/2   Diary of Journey into North Wales,   1817
Philadelphia

DIARY OF A TOUR | IN | NORTH WALES, | IN THE YEAR 1774. | TO WHICH IS ADDED | AN ESSAY ON THE CORN LAWS. | BY SAMUEL JOHNSON, LL.D. | I should like to read ALL that Ogden has written. | *Johnson.* | PHILADELPHIA: | PUBLISHED BY HARRISON HALL, | AT THE PORT FOLIO OFFICE. | J. Maxwell, Printer. | 1817.

12°, A–M⁶ N⁴ (N4 ? blk), ($1,3 ($3 as $2) signed), 76 leaves.

Pp. A1 *1* ½t, *2* blk, Engr. facs. of SJ's handwriting + *3* t., *4* blk, *5–6* Dedication, *7* 8–11 Preface, *12* blk, on B1 *13* 14–106 text, *107* 108–30 Appendix, *131* ½t Considerations on Corn, *132* blk, *133* Introductory note, *134* blk, *135* 136–48 text of Considerations, *149–50* advts., *151–2* (N4) ? blk.

Pagination and *Explicit* not recorded.

Paper: Small post (uncut: 6 × 3¾ in.).

Type: Not recorded.

References: *Tinker* 1390; S&S 41162 [MdW, MH-AH, RNHS].

Notes: The epigraph is from *Life*, iii. 248, though its relevance is unclear. For 'Considerations on Corn' see *Parliamentary Logick*, 1808 (66.11CC/1, above).

Copies: CtY (Im J637. 816b, grey boards, uncut and partly unopened);

USA: DLC, Hyde (grey boards, ptd. labels on spine and front, uncut, lacks ½t and N4), [Liebert = CtY], MWA, NcU, PPL, ViU; *UK*: none located.

List of Manuscript and Documentary Sources

This is not a comprehensive record of all documentary material relating to Johnson and the book trade consulted in the course of preparing this study; it is largely confined to documents cited in evidence or directly related to matters discussed. A good many of the Johnsonian documents were noticed in my *Preliminary Handlist of Documents & Manuscripts of Samuel Johnson* (1967). That list has been partly superseded by the work of Dr Margaret M. Smith in her section on Johnson in *Index of English Literary Manuscripts*, III. ii (John Gay–Ambrose Philips) (1989), and I cite her numeration with the prefix 'JoS'. In the following list parenthetical numbers refer to the enumeration of my list of 1967, followed by the JoS number from the *Index*. Detailed citations are usually given at the appropriate point in the text and so the following is more of a survey of collections and groups of papers than a detailed description of individual items. The lists mentioned above, however, should still be consulted for further information. Items are listed in the alphabetical order of their locations, and in deference to my North American friends I treat them first.

USA

Cambridge, Massachusetts

Harvard University Library
   Diary of Thomas Hollis, 1759–70 (MS Eng. 1191)
   'Piozziana' (MS Eng. 1280)
   'Upcottiana' (MS Eng. 1178, ii)

Denver, Colorado

Mr Arthur G. Rippey[1]
   Rec. s. Shakespeare subscription

Ithaca, New York

Cornell University Library
   MS of John Payne's *Draughts*, c. 1756 +
   MS French translation of *Rasselas*, c. 1809

New Haven, Connecticut

Yale University Library
   Receipt s. Johnson, 1783 (195)
   Receipt s. John Payne 1755 (*Tinker* 1416)

---

[1] The greater part of Mr Rippey's collection was acquired by McMaster University Library, Hamilton, Ontario, Canada, in 1985, but some few items, including this document, were subsequently dispersed through Messrs. Stonehill, Inc., of New Haven, Conn. I do not know its present location.

Receipt of Thomas Percy for copyright of *Miscellaneous Pieces*, 1762, 25 March 1763 (*Tinker* 1659)

New York

Grolier Club
Ledgers of William Bowyer

Pierpont Morgan Library
Rec. s. Johnson, 1749 (44)
Agreement s. Johnson, 1752 (55)
Johnson's 'Life of Pope' (171; JoS 224)

Public Library (Berg Collection)
Rec. s. Johnson, 1759 (80)
Annotated copy of *Lives*, 1781, i. (183; JoS 216)

[Arthur A. Houghton, Jr.] [2]
Agreement for *Lives of the Poets*, 1781 (176)
Agreement for Johnson's *Works*, 1784 (232)

Philadelphia

American Philosophical Society
Papers of William Strahan: Journals 1751–77, 4 vols (B/St.83)
Correspondence with David Hall and Benjamin Franklin

Public Library
Rec. s. Johnson, 1776 (143)

Rosenbach Foundation
Rec. s. Shakespeare subscription

San Marino, California

The Henry E. Huntington Library
Rec. s. Shakespeare subscription (LO 9626)
Transcript of Johnson's 'Prologue' to Hugh Kelly's *A Word to the Wise*, 1777 in Larpent Collection (LA 434; JoS 68)
Notes by Thomas Percy on Chinese topics (HM. 6173, 6511; PeT 397–8)
ALS William Seward to Richard Bull, n.d. (HM. 20892)

Somerville, New Jersey

The Hyde Collection
ALS William Chambers to John Nourse, 1758
ALS J.S. Hollis to R. Grave, 1798
Johnson on Trapp's *Sermons*, 1739 (27; JoS 176)
Rec. for *Life of Savage*, [1738] (34)
Rec. s. Johnson, 1748 (43)
Rec. s. Theophilus Cibber, 1752

---

[2] After Mr Houghton's death in 1990, his collection was dispersed at auction in New York. I have not pursued the subsequent whereabouts of every item.

Rec. s. Johnson, 1757 (78)
Distribution List for *Journey*, 1775
Corrected proofs of *Preface* to Pope, 1779 (174a; JoS 225)
John Nichols, notes on expenses relating to *Prefaces* and *Lives*
Frances Reynolds, 'Recollections'
ALS Richard Rolt to William Hunter, 1769

Washington, D.C.
Folger Shakespeare Library
Commonplace books and correspondence of Hamilton Boyle, 6th E. of Corke & Orrery (N. b. 42–3)
Prologue to Garrick's *Lethe* (W. b. 464, fo. 136)
Letters and papers of Isaac Reed (C. b. 11, M. a. 117–41, M. b. 6)
Rec. s. Isaac Reed for edition of Shakespeare, 1785 (W. b. 475)
Letters and notes of Jacob Tonson (C. c. 1)
Tonson's payments to Shakespearian editors (S. a. 163)

UNITED KINGDOM

Birmingham
Public Library
Robert Dodsley: Letter Book, 1756–64 (149158)
Thomas Warren: Papers relating to Edward Cave, Lewis Paul, &c. (MSS. 185602, 190122)

Bury St Edmunds
West Suffolk Record Office
Henry Hervey [Aston]: Miscellaneous pieces, 2 vols. (Acc. 941/70/31–32)

Cambridge
Fitzwilliam Museum
ALS G.A. Arnold to William Hayley, 1780 (Hayley MSS. xiv)
University Library
Sharebook of John Nichols, c. 1769–1815 (MS Add. 8226)
Munby MSS: 'Hutton' collection of receipts and documents, mainly of John Nourse

Edinburgh
Public Library
Inventories of Estate of William Creech (1799–1814), 1814 (qYZ.325.C91)
National Library of Scotland
Papers of Bell & Bradfute, 1771- (MS Dep. 317)
Papers of Archibald Constable, (MSS Dep. 307, 319–32, 789–803)
Papers of T. & A. Constable (MS Acc. 7908, Dep. 307)
Fettercairn papers (MS Acc. 4796)

Newhailes papers relative to Hailes's *Annals of Scotland* (MSS Acc. 7228/18–23, 54–64)

Inventory of library at Newhailes (Newhailes MSS Acc.7228/589; Acc. 8987/34)

Papers of Oliver & Boyd, 1812– (MS Acc. 5000; MS Dep. 312)

Papers of Smith Elder & Co. (MS Acc. 7212)

New College

Isaac Reed, 'Memoranda from Mr Dodsley's Papers' (MS CHA: W13B 1/3)

Register House

Journals of William Creech, 1744–67 (16078 BK (GD.38))

Film of Correspondence of W. Creech and David Dalrymple (M/film. RH4/26)

Signet Library

The Session Papers of James Boswell in the Signet Library, Edinburgh. By G. H. Ballantyne, 1969 (with additions, 1971)

University Library

Letter Lord Hailes to Boswell (MS La. II. 603)

John Hoole to 'Hood', n.d. (MS La. II. 422/118)

Papers of Thomas Nelson & Sons, 1849–

Glasgow

University Library (Archives)

Papers of Blackie & Co, 1794–1959

Lichfield

Johnson Birthplace Museum[3]

Accounts of William Baily, Bookseller, 1710 (MS 16/30)

Indenture of apprenticeship of Benjamin Johnson, 1675 (MS 33)

Accounts of Michael Johnson, Bookseller (MS 22/2)

Indictment and defence of Michael Johnson for trading as a Tanner, 1717–18 (MS 12/1–3)

Agreements, promissory notes and letters between Johnson and Jacob Tonson (MS 19/1–6; 40, 76–7)

Lincoln

Lincolnshire Archives (Lincolnshire County Council)

Deposit by J.C.P. Langton, Esq;

Account Books of Bennet Langton (with Langton family papers)

London

Barclay's Bank, 19 Fleet Street

Accounts of Robert Gosling's bank including accounts of the Company of Stationers, William Strahan, and other members of the Book Trade

---

[3] Kai Kin Yung, *Handlist of Manuscripts & Documents in the Johnson Birthplace Museum* (Lichfield: Lichfield City Council, 1972).

British Library
ALS J. Ash to Thomas Warton, 1762 (Add. MS 42560 fo. 89)
Correspondence: Thomas Birch to Philip Hardwicke (Add. MS 35397–393400), and
    Letter (Add. MS 4316 no. 634)
Papers of Edward Cave (Stowe 748 fos. 120, 143–89)
Character of Edmund Curll (Add. 5825 fo. 4b)
Agreements with Robert Dodsley, 1743–53 (Egerton 738)
Letters to George Faulkner (Egerton 201)
Goldsmith's 'Prospect of Society', proofs (C.58. g.7)
J. Haberkorn, printing bill (Add. MS 38730 fo. 126)
[Johnson]: Copy assignment of *Life of Savage*, 1743 (Add. MS 38728 fo. 123)
Johnson: Welsh diary, 1774 (Add. MS 12070; 128–9; JoS 381)
Johnson: French diary, 1775 (Add. MS 35299; 138b; JoS 383)
Johnson: Rough notes towards the 'Life of Pope' (Add MS 5994, fos. 159–77; 170a;
    JoS 222)
Assignment for Mrs Lennox's *Memoirs of Madame de Maintenon*, 1757 (Add. MS
    38373)
Longman file of Book Trade sale catalogues
Assignment of Thomas Lowndes, 1778 (Add. MS 38730 fo. 68)
Papers of John Nourse (Add. MS 38729)
Diary of Thomas Percy, 2 vols. 1753–1811 (Add. MS 32336–7)
Papers of Charles Rivington (Add. MS 38730)
Accounts, ledgers, and papers of William and Andrew Strahan (Add. MSS
    48800–48918, esp. 48800–17; Add. Ch. 75421–7)
The Society for the Encouragement of Learning, 1736–9 (Add. MS 6190)
Papers of the Whittingham Press (Add. MSS 41867–960; 43975–89)

Johnson House, Gough Square, Fleet Street
  List of Johnson's Works by Isaac Reed (MS Reed)

Lambeth Palace
Papers of Messrs. Cadell & Davies, 1799–1830

University College Library
Papers of Messrs. Routledge & Co. 1853-

Victoria and Albert Museum
Proofs of the *Prefaces to the Poets* (Forster 298; 175; JoS 215)
Rough notes towards the 'Life of Pope' (Dyce 5316; 170b; JoS 223)

Westminster City Library
Papers of John & Edward Bumpus, 1910-

Manchester

John Rylands Library, University of Manchester
Catalogue of Books at Brynbella (1806–13) & misc. letters to SJ, &c., (R. 71063)
Mottos for the *Idler* (MS Eng. 629/28)
Mrs Thrale's transcript of 'The Fountains' (MS Eng. 654)

Oxford

Bodleian Library
  William Bowyer's Paper Stock Ledger (MS Don. b. 4)
  Rec. s. Thomas Cadell, 1769 (John Johnson: 'Copyright' Box. 6)
  [John] Hervey: Epitaph on Queen Caroline, 1737–8 (MS Add. A. 190)
  ALS Michael Johnson to John Bagford, 1701 (MS Rawl. D. 398 ff. 115–16)
  [Johnson]: Part proof of Preface to Cowley (MS Don c. 62; 160)
  Longman file of Book Trade sale catalogues (John Johnson)
  Assignments of Thomas Lowndes (MS Eng. misc. c. 297)
  Thomas Percy's MS notes on Boswell's *Life of Johnson*, 1791 (MS Percy d. 11)
  Percy's notes on Johnson's writings (MS Percy 87)
  Isaac Reed's annotated copy of: *Petition of the Booksellers for Relief from the Expenses of Correction and Improvement*, n.d. (4 x. 136 Jur)
  Receipt for Shakespeare subscription (GA Staffs 4 8, p. 487)

Pembroke College
  Trading accounts of Michael, Sarah, and Nathaniel Johnson, 1726–.
  Italian & French translations of parts of *Rasselas* by 'J. Baretti', *c*.1809

Reading, Berks.

Public Library
  Agreement for the *Universal Visiter*, 1756

University Library
  Papers of George Bell & Sons, 1860–
  Papers of Messrs. Longman & Co.
  Papers of Messrs. Macmillan & Co

List of Printed Works Consulted

This list consists of items that have been consulted in the preparation of the bibliography but are not cited in the text, and significant items cited in the text in abbreviated form.

Abbattista, Guido, 'The Business of Paternoster Row: towards a Publishing History of the *Universal History* (1736–65)', *PH* xvii (1985), 5–50.

Abbott, Claude Colleer (comp.), *A Catalogue of Papers relating to Boswell, Johnson, & Sir William Forbes found at Fettercairn House* (Oxford: Clarendon Press, 1936).

Abbott, John L., 'Dr. Johnson and the Amazons', *PQ* xliv (1965), 484–95.

—— 'Samuel Johnson's "A Panegyric on Dr. Morin" ', *RN* viii (1966), 55–7.

—— 'Dr. Johnson and the Making of "The Life of Father Paul Sarpi" ', *BJRL* xlviii (1966), 255–67.

—— *John Hawkesworth: Eighteenth-Century Man of Letters* (Madison: University of Wisconsin, 1982).

—— 'The Making of the Johnsonian Canon', in Paul J. Korshin (ed.), *Johnson after Two Hundred Years*, 127–39.

Abrahams, Aleck, 'Payne at the Mews Gate', *NQ* 10th ser. vii (1907), 409, with further discussion 492–3; 10th ser. viii (1907), 55.

—— 'Pall Mall Nos. 50, 50a, and 51', *NQ* 11th ser. viii (1913), 223–5.

—— 'Payments to Eighteenth-Century Authors for Corrections and Improvements', *NQ* 12th ser. i (1916), 125.

Acres, W. Marston, *The Bank of England from Within, 1694–1900*, 2 vols. (London: Bank of England, 1931).

Adam, R.B., *A Catalogue of the Johnsonian Collection of R.B. Adam*, introd. Charles F. Osgood (Buffalo, NY: Privately printed, 1921).

—— *The R.B. Adam Library relating to Dr. Samuel Johnson and His Era*, 3 vols. (London: Oxford University Press, 1929), vol. iv (1930).

Adams, Thomas R., *The British Look at America during the Age of Samuel Johnson: An Exhibition* (Providence, RI: John Carter Brown Library, 1971).

—— *The American Controversy: A Bibliographical Study of the British Pamphlets about the American Disputes, 1764–1783*, 2 vols. (Providence, RI: Brown University Press; New York: Bibliographical Society of America, 1980).

Addison, W. Innes, *The Matriculation Albums of the University of Glasgow from 1728 to 1858* (Glasgow: J. Maclehose, 1913).

Alden, John, 'Scotch Type in Eighteenth-Century America' *SB* iii (1950–1), 270–4.

—— 'Deception in Dublin: Problems in Seventeenth-Century Irish Printing', *SB* vi (1954), 232–7.

Alkon, Paul K., 'Johnson's Condemned Sermon', in Burke and Kay (eds.), *The Unknown Samuel Johnson*, 113–30.

Alkon, Paul K.,'Illustrations of *Rasselas* and Reader-Response Criticism', in Paul K. Alkon and Robert Folkenflik, *Samuel Johnson: Pictures and Words* (Los Angeles: William Andrews and Clark Memorial Library, 1984), 3–62.

Allen, John, *Bibliotheca Herefordiensis or, A Descriptive Catalogue of Books, Pamphlets, Maps, Prints, &c. &c. relating to the County of Hereford* (Hereford: J. Allen, 1821).

Allen, Robert R., 'Variant Readings in Johnson's "London"', *PBSA* lx (1966), 214–15.

Alston, Robin C. (comp.), *A Bibliography of the English Language from the Invention of Printing to the Year 1800*, vol. 5: *The English Dictionary* (Leeds: Printed for the author, 1966; rev. and corr. edn. Ilkley: Janus Press, 1974).

—— 'Thomas Gardner: Printer and Publisher, 1735–1747', *Library*, 6th ser. iv (1982), 426–7.

—— F.J.G. Robinson, and C. Wadham (comps.), *A Check-List of Eighteenth-Century Books containing Lists of Subscribers* (Newcastle: Avero, 1983).

Altick, Richard D., 'English Publishing and the Mass Audience in 1852', *SB* vi (1954), 3–24.

—— *The English Common Reader* (Chicago: University of Chicago Press, 1957).

—— 'From Aldine to Everyman: Cheap Reprint Series of the English Classics 1830–1906', *SB* xi (1958), 3–24.

—— 'Nineteenth-Century English Best-Sellers: A Further List', *SB* xxii (1969), 197–206.

Alumni Cantabrigiensis: A Biographical List of All Known Students, Graduates and Holders of Office at the University of Cambridge, from the Earliest Times to 1900, comp. John and J.A. Venn, 10 vols. (Cambridge: Cambridge University Press, 1922–54).

Alumni Oxonienses: The Members of the University of Oxford, 1715–1886, comp. Joseph Foster, 4 vols. (London: Joseph Foster; Oxford: Parker, 1887–8).

Amory, Hugh, ' "*De facto* Copyright"? Fielding's *Works* in Partnership, 1769–1821', *ECS* xvii (1983–4), 449–76.

—— ' "Proprietary Illustration": The Case of Cooke's *Tom Jones*', in Harvey, Kirsop, and McMullin (eds.), *An Index of Civilisation*, 137–47.

Anderson, Robert, *The Life of Samuel Johnson, LL.D., with Critical Observations on His Work*, 3rd edn. (Edinburgh: Doig and Stirling, 1815).

—— *Robert Anderson: The Life of Samuel Johnson (1815)* (Hildesheim: Georg Olms Verlag, 1973).

Andrews, Alexander, *The History of British Journalism, from the Foundation of the Newspaper Press in England to the Repeal of the Stamp Act in 1855*, 2 vols. (London, 1859).

'Archibald Leighton, the First Binder in Cloth', *Bookbinder*, i (1888), 99–101.

Arkle, A.H., 'Early Liverpool Printers', *TLCHS* lxviii (1917), 73–84.

Armytage, W.H.G., 'The 1870 Education Act', *BJES* xviii (1970), 121–33.

Arnott, James Fullarton, and John William Robinson, *English Theatrical Literature, 1559–1900* (London: Society for Theatre Research, 1970).

Ashton, John, *Chap-Books of the Eighteenth Century* (London: Chatto & Windus, 1882).

Ashton, Thomas, *An Economic History of England: The 18th Century* (London: Methuen, 1955).

Astbury, Raymond, 'The Renewal of the Licensing Act in 1693 and its Lapse in 1695'. *Library*, 5th ser. xxxiii (1978), 296–322.

Attenborough, John, *A Living Memory: Hodder and Stoughton, Publishers, 1868–1975* (London: Hodder and Stoughton, 1975).

Atto, Clayton, 'The Society for the Encouragement of Learning', *Library*, 4th ser. xix (1938–9), 263–88.

Austen-Leigh, Richard A., *The Story of a Printing House: A Short Account of the Strahans and the Spottiswoodes*, 2nd edn. (London: Spottiswoode, 1912).

—— 'William Strahan and His Ledgers' *Library*, 4th ser. iii (1922–3), 283–4.

Austin, R., 'Robert Raikes the Elder & the "Gloucester Journal" ', *Library* 3rd ser. vi (1915), 1–24; repr. (London: Alexander Moring Ltd., 1915).

Avis, Frederick C., *The First English Copyright Act, 1709* (London: F.C. Avis, 1965).

Bailyn, Bernard and J.B. Hench, *The Press and the American Revolution* (Worcester, Mass.: American Antiquarian Society, 1980).

Bain, Iain, *John Sharpe, Publisher and Bookseller, Piccadilly: A Preliminary Survey of His Activities in the London Book Trade, 1800–1840* (Welwyn, Herts.: Laverock Press, 1960).

—— 'Thomas Ross & Son: Copper- and Steel-Plate Printers since 1833', *JPHS* ii (1966), 3–22.

—— 'James Moyes and His Temple Printing Office of 1825', *JPHS* iv (1968), 1–10.

Baine, Rodney M., 'Percy's Own Copies of the Reliques, *HLB* v (1951), 246–51.

Baker, David Erskine, Isaac Reed, and Stephen Jones (eds.), *Biographia Dramatica, or, A Companion to the Playhouse*, 3 vols. (London: Longman, Hurst, Rees, Brown, 1812).

Bald, R.C., 'Early Copyright Litigation and Its Bibliographical Interest', *PBSA* xxxvi (1942), 81–96.

Balderston, Katharine C., *The History & Sources of Percy's Memoir of Goldsmith* (Cambridge: Cambridge University Press, 1926).

Balston, Thomas, *William Balston, Paper Maker, 1759–1849* (London: Methuen, 1954).

—— *James Whatman, Father and Son* (London: Methuen, 1957).

Barber, Giles G., 'J.J. Tourneisen of Basle and the Publication of English Books on the Continent *c.* 1800', *Library*, 5th ser. xv (1960), 193–200.

—— 'Galignani's and the Publication of English Books in France from 1800 to 1852', *Library*, 5th ser. xvi (1961), 267–86.

—— 'Pendred abroad: A View of the Late Eighteenth-Century Book Trade in Europe', in R.W. Hunt *et al.* (eds.), *Studies in the Book Trade*, 231–77.

—— 'Books from the Old World and for the New: The British International Trade in Books in the Eighteenth Century', *SVEC* cli (1976), 185–224.

Barbier, Antoine Alexandre, *Dictionnaire des ouvrages anonymes et pseudonymes* (Paris, 1872–4).

Bareham, T. and S. Gatrell, *A Bibliography of George Crabbe* (Folkestone: Dawson; Hamden, Conn.: Archon, 1978).

Barker, A.D., 'Edward Cave, Samuel Johnson and *The Gentleman's Magazine*', D.Phil. thesis (University of Oxford, 1981).

—— 'The Printing and Publishing of Johnson's *Marmor Norfolciense* (1739) and *London* (1738 and 1739)', *Library*, 6th ser. iii (1981), 287–304.

—— 'Samuel Johnson and the Campaign to Save William Dodd', *HLB* xxxi (1983), 147–80.

Barker, J.R., 'Cadell and Davies and the Liverpool Booksellers', *Library*, 5th ser. xiv (1959), 274–80.

Barker, Nicolas, 'Typographic Studies', in Davison (ed.), *The Book Encompassed*, 83–98.

Barker, Ronald E., and G.R. Davies (eds.), *Books are Different: An Account of the Defence of the Net Book Agreement before the Restrictive Practices Court in 1962* (London: Macmillan, 1966).

Barnes, James J., *Free Trade in Books: A Study of the London Book Trade since 1800* (Oxford: Clarendon Press, 1964).

—— 'Galignani and the Publication of English Books in France: A Postscript', *Library*, 5th ser. xxv (1970), 294–313.

Barnouw, A.J., '*Rasselas* in Dutch', *TLS* (11 April 1935), 244.

Bartlett, M.E., 'A Checklist of Hartford, Connecticut, Imprints for the Years 1832–33', diss. (Catholic University of America, 1967).

Bataille, Robert R., 'Hugh Kelly, William Jackson, and the Editorship of the *Public Ledger*', *PBSA* lxxix (1985), 523–7.

Bate, Walter Jackson, *Samuel Johnson* (London: Chatto & Windus, 1978).

Bateson F.W. (ed.), *The Cambridge Bibliography of English Literature*, 4 vols. (Cambridge: Cambridge University Press, 1940); supplement, ed. George Watson (1957).

Battersby, James L., 'John Nichols on a Johnson Letter', *SB* xxiii (1970), 179–83.

Beal, Peter, 'Bishop Percy's Notes on *A Voyage to Abyssinia*', *PLPLS* xvi (1975), 39–49.

Belanger, Terry, 'Booksellers' Sales of Copyright: Aspects of the London Book Trade, 1718–1768', Ph.D. diss. (Columbia University, 1970).

—— 'Tonson, Wellington and the Shakespeare Copyrights', in Hunt *et al.* (eds.), *Studies in the Book Trade*, 195–209.

—— 'Booksellers' Trade Sales, 1718–1768', *Library*, 5th ser. xxx (1975), 281–302.

—— (ed.), *Regulations concerning the Issue of Trade Books: 1828*, School of Library Services, Columbia Univ. (Privately printed, New York, 1976).

—— 'A Directory of the London Book Trade, 1766', *PH* i (1977), 7–48.

—— 'From Bookseller to Publisher: Changes in the London Book Trade 1750–1850', in *Book Selling and Book Buying. Aspects of the Nineteenth Century British and North American Book Trade*, ed. Richard G. Landon (Chicago: American Library Association, 1978), 7–16.

—— 'Publishers and Writers in Eighteenth-Century England', in Rivers (ed.), *Books and Their Readers in Eighteenth-Century England*, 5–25.

Beljame, Alexandre, *Men of Letters and the English Public in the Eighteenth Century 1660–1744, Dryden, Addison, Pope*, ed. Bonamy Dobrée, trans. E.O. Lorimer (London: Kegan Paul, Trench, Trübner & Co., 1948).

Bell, Alan S., 'Some Recent Acquisitions of Publishing Archives by the National Library of Scotland', *PH* iii (1978), 37–45.

Bell, Edward, *George Bell, Publisher: A Brief Memoir* (Printed for private circulation at the Chiswick Press, 1924).

Belloc, Hilaire, 'Mrs. Piozzi's *Rasselas*', *Saturday Review of Literature*, ii (15 Aug. 1925), 37–8.

Bentley, G.E., 'Copyright Documents in the George Robinson Archive: William Godwin and Others 1713–1820', *SB* xxxv (1982), 67–110.

Bernard, Frederick V., 'A Note on Two Attributions to Johnson', *NQ* ccix (1964), 64, 190–1.

—— 'New Evidence on the Pamphilus Letters', *MP* lxii (1964), 42–4.

1768

—— 'Johnson's Address "To the Reader" ', *NQ* ccx (1965), 455.

—— 'Johnson and the Authorship of Four Debates', *PMLA* lxxxii (1967), 408–19.

—— 'Common and Superior Sense: A New Attribution to Johnson', *NQ* ccxii (1967), 176–80.

—— 'The History of Nadir Shah: A New Attribution to Johnson', *BMQ* xxxiv (1970), 92–104.

—— 'A New Preface by Samuel Johnson', *PQ* lv (1976), 445–9.

Berry, William T., A.F. Johnson, and W.P. Jaspert, *The Encyclopaedia of Type Faces*, rev. edn. (New York: Pitman, 1958).

—— and H. Edmund Poole, *Annals of Printing: A Chronological Encyclopaedia from the Earliest Times to 1950* (London: Blandford, 1966).

Besterman, Theodore, *The Publishing Firm of Cadell & Davies: Select Correspondence and Accounts, 1793–1836* (Oxford: Oxford University Press, 1938).

Bewick, Thomas, *1800 Woodcuts by Thomas Bewick and His School*, ed. Blanche Cirker, with an introduction by Robert Hutchinson (New York: Dover, 1962).

Bidwell, John, 'The Size of the Sheet in America: Paper-Moulds Manufactured by N. and D. Sellers of Philadelphia', *PAAS* lxxxvii (1977), 299–342.

—— 'The Study of Paper as Evidence, Artefact, and Commodity', in Davison (ed.), *The Book Encompassed*, 69–82.

Birmingham Public Library, *Shakespeare Bibliography: The Catalogue of the Birmingham Shakespeare Library, Birmingham Public Libraries*, 7 vols. (London: Mansell, 1971).

Birrell, Augustine, *Seven Lectures on the Law and History of Copyright in Books* (London: Cassell, 1899).

Black, Gerard, 'Booksellers of Glasgow and Edinburgh', *NQ* 12th ser. iii (1917), 445.

Blackburne, F., *Memoirs of Thomas Hollis*, 2 vols. (1780).

Blackie, Agnes A.C., *Blackie & Son, 1809–1959* (Glasgow: Blackie, 1959).

Blagden, Cyprian, 'Booksellers' Trade Sales 1718–1768', *Library*, 5th ser. v (1950–1), 243–57.

—— *The Stationers' Company: A History, 1403–1959* (London: Allen & Unwin, 1960).

—— 'Thomas Carnan and the Almanack Monopoly', *SB* xiv (1961), 23–43.

Blake, J.B., *A Short Title Catalogue of Eighteenth Century Printed Books in the National Library of Medicine* (Bethesda, Md.: National Library of Medicine, 1979).

Blakey, Dorothy, *The Minerva Press, 1790–1820* (Oxford: The Bibliographical Society, 1939).

Blanck, Jacob (comp.), *Bibliography of American Literature* (New Haven, Conn.: Yale University Press, 1955–91).

Blatchly, John, *The Town Library of Ipswich provided for the Use of the Town Preachers in 1599: A History and Catalogue* (Woodbridge: Boydell, 1989).

Blondel, Madeleine, 'Eighteenth-Century Novels Transformed: Pirates and Publishers', *PBSA* lxxii (1978), 527–41.

Bloom, Edward A., 'Samuel Johnson on Copyright', *JEGP* xlvii (1948), 165–72.

—— *Samuel Johnson in Grub Street* (Providence, RI: Brown University Press, 1957).

Boase, Frederic, *Modern English Biography*, 6 vols. (Truro: Netherton and Worth, 1892–1921).

Böker, Uwe, 'Sprache, literarischer Markt und kulturelle Orientierung', in *Language and Civilization: A Concerted Profusion of Essays and Studies in Honour of Otto Heitsch*, ed. T. Kirschner (Frankfurt-am-Main: P. Lang, 1992).

Böker, Uwe, 'The Marketing of Macpherson', in Gaskill (ed.), *Ossian Revisited*, 73–93.

Bolgar, R.R., *The Classical Heritage and Its Beneficiaries* (Cambridge: Cambridge University Press, 1954).

Bolitho, Hector, and Derek Peel, *The Drummonds of Charing Cross* (London: Allen & Unwin, 1967).

Bond, Donovan H., and W. Reynolds McLeod (eds.), *Newsletters to Newspapers: Eighteenth-Century Journalism* (Morgantown: West Virginia University Press, 1977).

Bond, Richmond P. and Marjorie N. Bond, 'The Minute Books of the *St. James's Chronicle*', *SB* xxviii (1975), 17–40.

Bond, W.H. (ed.), *Eighteenth-Century Studies in Honor of Donald F. Hyde* (New York: Grolier Club, 1970).

—— 'Thomas Hollis and Samuel Johnson', in *Johnson and His Age*, ed. J. Engel (Cambridge, Mass.: Harvard University Press, 1984).

—— and Daniel E. Whitten, 'Boswell's Court of Session Papers: a Preliminary Check-List', in Bond (ed.), *Eighteenth-Century Studies in Honor of Donald F. Hyde*, 231–55.

Bonham-Carter, Victor, *Authors by Profession*, vol. i (London: Society of Authors, 1978).

Bonnard, George A., 'A Note on the English Translations of Crousaz' Two Books on Pope's *Essay on Man*', *Recueil des Travaux* (1937), 175–84.

Bonnell, T.F., 'The Historical Context of Johnson's *Lives of the Poets*: Rival Collections of English Poetry, 1777–1810', Ph.D. diss. (University of Chicago, 1983).

—— 'John Bell's *Poets of Great Britain*: The "Little trifling Edition" Revisited', *MP* lxxxv (1987–8), 128–52.

Boog Watson, C.B., *Registers of Edinburgh Apprentices, 1701–1775*, Scottish Record Soc. lxi, (1929).

The Bookworm: An Illustrated Treasury of Old-Time Literature, 2 vols. (London, 1888–94).

Boothby, Hill, *An Account of the Life of Dr. Samuel Johnson from His Birth to His Eleventh Year, Written by Himself . . . From the MSS. Preserved by the Doctor; and Now in the Possession of Richard Wright* (London: Phillips, Nichols, 1805).

Boswell, James, *The Life of Samuel Johnson, LL.D.*, ed. John Wilson Croker, 5 vols. (London: John Murray, 1831).

—— *Boswell's Note-Book 1776–1777, recording Particulars of Johnson's Early Life*, ed. R.W. Chapman (London: Humphrey Milford, 1925).

—— *The Private Papers of James Boswell from Malahide Castle in the Collection of Lt-Col. R.H. Isham*, ed. Geoffrey Scott and Frederick A. Pottle, 18 vols. (Mt Vernon, NY: Privately printed by W.E. Rudge, 1928–34).

—— *Boswell's Life of Johnson: Together with Boswell's Journal of a Tour to the Hebrides and Johnson's Diary of a Journey into North Wales*, ed. George Birkbeck Hill, rev. L.F. Powell, 6 vols. (Oxford Clarendon Press, 1934–50).

—— *The Correspondence* (Yale Editions of the Private Papers of James Boswell):
1. *The Correspondence of James Boswell and John Johnston of Grange*, ed. Ralph S. Walker (London: Heinemann, 1966).
2. *The Correspondence and Other Papers of James Boswell relating to the Making of the Life of Johnson*, ed. Marshall Waingrow (London: Heinemann, 1969).
3. *The Correspondence of James Boswell with Certain Members of The Club*, ed. Charles N. Fifer (London: Heinemann, 1976).
4. *The Correspondence of James Boswell with David Garrick, Edmund Burke, and Edmond Malone*, ed. George M. Kahrl, *et al.* (London: Heinemann, 1986).

—— *The Private Papers* (Yale Editions of the Private Papers of James Boswell):
Boswell for the Defence, 1769–1774, ed. William K. Wimsatt, Jr., and Frederick A. Pottle (London: Heinemann, 1960).
Boswell: The Ominous Years, 1774–1776, ed. Charles Ryskamp and Frederick A. Pottle (London: Heinemann, 1963).
Journal of a Tour to the Hebrides with Samuel Johnson, ed. Frederick A. Pottle and Charles H. Bennett (New York: McGraw-Hill, 1961).
Boswell in Extremes, 1776–1778, ed. Charles McC. Weis and Frederick A. Pottle (London: Heinemann, 1971).
Boswell, Laird of Auchinleck, 1778–1782, ed. Frederick A. Pottle and Joseph W. Reed (New York: McGraw-Hill, 1977).
Boswell: The Applause of the Jury, 1782–1785, ed. Irma S. Lustig and Frederick A. Pottle (London: Heinemann, 1981).
Boswell: The English Experiment, 1785–1789, ed. Irma S. Lustig and Frederick A. Pottle (London: Heinemann, 1986).
The General Correspondence of James Boswell 1766–1769, ed. Richard C. Cole with Peter S. Baker and Rachel McClellan (New Haven, Conn.: Yale University Press; Edinburgh: Edinburgh University Press, 1993–).
—— *Boswell: The Great Biographer*, ed. Marlies K. Danziger and Frank Brady (London: Heinemann, 1989).
—— *Catalogue of the Papers of James Boswell at Yale University*, i, ed. Marion S. Pottle, Claude Colleer Abbott, and Frederick A. Pottle (Edinburgh: Edinburgh University Press; New Haven, Conn.: Yale University Press, 1993).
—— *James Boswell's Life of Johnson: An Edition of the Original Manuscript*, i, ed. Marshall Waingrow (Edinburgh: Edinburgh University Press; New Haven, Conn.: Yale University Press, 1994).
Botting, Roland B., 'Johnson, Smart, and the *Universal Visiter*', *MP* xxxvi (1939), 293–300.
Boulton, James T., *Johnson: the Critical Heritage* (London: Routledge & Kegan Paul, 1971).
Bowers, Fredson, *Principles of Bibliographical Description* (Princeton: Princeton University Press, 1949).
Bowker, R.R., *Copyright: Its Law and Its Literature* (New York: Publisher's Weekly, 1886).
Boynton, Henry Walcott, *Annals of American Bookselling, 1638–1850* (New York: J. Wiley & Sons, 1932).
—— *Copyright: Its History and Its Law* (Boston: Houghton Mifflin, 1912).
Brack, OM, *Journal Narrative Relative to Doctor Johnson's Last Illness, Three Weeks before His Death* (Iowa City: Windhover Press, 1972).
—— 'John Hoole's Journal Narrative Relating to Johnson's Last Illness', *YULG* xlvii (1973), 103–8.
—— 'The *Gentleman's Magazine*, Concealed Printing, and the Texts of Samuel Johnson's Lives of Admiral Robert Blake and Sir Francis Drake', *SB* xl (1987), 140–6.
—— 'Samuel Johnson Edits for the Booksellers: Sir Thomas Browne's "Christian Morals" (1756), and "The English Works of Roger Ascham" (1761)', in *Essays in Honor of William B. Todd*, ed. D. Oliphant (Austin: Henry Ransom Humanities Research Center, University of Texas, 1991), 13–39.

Brack, OM, 'Samuel Johnson's Private Interview with George III: The Strahan Minute' (Tempe, Ariz.: Privately printed for the Friends of the Arizona State University Library, 1993).

—— 'Samuel Johnson and the Preface to Abbé Prévost's *Memoirs of a Man of Quality*', *SB* xlvii (1994), 155–64.

—— 'Samuel Johnson and the Translations of Jean Pierre de Crousaz's *Examen* and *Commentaire*', *SB* xlviii (1995), 60–84.

—— (ed.), *Writers, Books, and Trade: An Eighteenth-Century English Miscellany for William B. Todd* (New York: AMS Press, 1994).

—— and Mary Early, 'Samuel Johnson's Proposals for the *Harleian Miscellany*', *SB* xlv (1992), 127–30.

—— and Thomas Kaminski, 'Johnson, James and the *Medicinal Dictionary*', *MP* lxxxi (1984), 378–400.

—— and Robert E. Kelley, *Samuel Johnson's Early Biographers* (Iowa City: University of Iowa Press, 1971).

—— *The Early Biographies of Samuel Johnson* (Iowa City: University of Iowa Press, 1974).

Bradford, Curtis B., 'The Edinburgh *Ramblers*', *MLR* xxxiv (1939), 241–4.

—— 'Johnson's Revisions of *The Rambler*', *RES* xv (1939), 302–14.

Brady, Frank, *James Boswell: The Later Years, 1769–1795* (London: Heinemann, 1894).

Brain, W. Russell, 'Doctor Johnson on Science', *London Hospital Gazette* (Feb. 1947), 14–20.

Brenni, Vito J. (comp.), *Book Printing in Britain and America: A Guide to the Literature and a Directory of Printers* (Westport, Conn.: Greenwood Press, 1983).

Brett-Smith, H.F.B., 'Johnson's *Journey to the Western Islands* and His Shakespeare', *TLS* (15 May 1919), 265.

Briggs, Asa (ed.), *Essays in the History of Publishing in Celebration of the 250th Anniversary of the House of Longman* (London: Longmans, 1974).

Briscoe, J.P., 'Derby Printers and Booksellers of the 18th Century', *Bookworm*, v (Feb. 1892), 89–92.

Bristol, R.P., *An Index of Printers, Publishers and Booksellers indicated by Charles Evans in His American Bibliography* (Charlottesville: Bibliographical Society of the University of Virginia, 1961).

—— *Index to Supplement to Evans's 'American Bibliography'* (Charlottesville: Bibliographical Society of the University of Virginia, 1971).

Broomhead, Frank, *The Zaehnsdorfs (1842–1947): Craft Bookbinders* (Pinner: Private Libraries Association, 1986).

Brown, A., 'James Lackington, Bookseller, 1746–1815', *NR* (June 1965), 28–41.

Brown, H.G. and O. Maude, *A Directory of the Book-Arts and Book Trade in Philadelphia to 1820, including Painters and Engravers* (New York: New York Public Library, 1950).

Brown, Philip A.H., *London Publishers and Printers: A Tentative List, c. 1800–1870* (London: British Museum, 1961).

—— *London Publishers and Printers, c. 1800–1870* (London: British Library, 1982).

Brown, R.W., 'Northamptonshire Printing, Printers and Booksellers', *Journal of the Northamptonshire Natural History Society* xix (1918), 183–91; xx (1919), 20–6, 45–56.

Brownell, Morris R., *Samuel Johnson's Attitude to the Arts* (Oxford: Clarendon Press, 1989).

Brownley, Martine Watson, 'Samuel Johnson and the Printing Career of Hester Lynch Piozzi', *BJRL*, lxvii (1985), 623–40.

Brunet, Jacques-Charles, *Manuel du libraire et de l'amateur de livres*, 5th edn., 8 vols. (Paris: Firmin Didot, 1860–5).

Bruun, C.V., *Bibliotheca Danica: Systematisk Fortegnelse over den danske Literatur fra 1482 til 1830*, 4 vols. (Kjobenharn: Gyldendal, 1877–1902).

Bryden, D.J., 'A Short Catalogue of the Types Used by John Reid, Printer in Edinburgh, 1761–74', *Bibliotheck*, vi (1971), 17–21.

Buchanan, David, *The Treasure of Auchinleck: The Story of the Boswell papers* (London: Heinemann, 1975).

Buckland, W.E. (ed.), *Parish Registers and Records in the Diocese of Rochester: A Summary of the Information Collected by the Ecclesiastical Records Committee of the Rochester Diocesan Conference* (London: Printed for the Kent Archaeological Society by Mitchell, Hughes and Clarke, 1912).

Bulloch, J.M., 'Andrew Millar, Publisher', *NQ* clxi (1931), 244.

Burdekin, R., *Memoirs of the Life and Character of Mr. Robert Spence, of York* (York, 1827).

Burke, John J., and Donald Kay (eds.), *The Unknown Samuel Johnson* (Madison: University of Wisconsin Press, 1983).

Burkett, Eva Mae, *American Dictionaries of the English Language before 1861* (Metuchen, NJ: Scarecrow Press, 1979).

Burlingham, Roger, *Of Making Many Books: a Hundred Years of Reading, Writing and Publishing* (New York: Scribner, 1946).

Burman, C.C., *An Account of the Art of Typography as practised in Alnwick from 1781 to 1815* (Alnwick: Alnwick and County Gazette, 1896).

Burman, P., *An Account of the Art of Typography as Practised in Alnwick from 1748 to 1900* (Edinburgh, 1918).

Burney, Frances, *Diary and Letters of Madame d'Arblay, Edited by Her Niece [Charlotte Barrett]*, 7 vols. (London: Henry Colburn, 1842–6).

Bushnell, G.H., *Scottish Engravers: A Biographical Dictionary of Scottish Engravers and of Engravers Who Worked in Scotland to the Beginning of the Nineteenth Century* (London: Oxford University Press, 1949).

Butterfield, L.H., 'The American Interests of the Firm of E. and C. Dilly, with Their Letters to Benjamin Rush, 1770–1795', *PBSA* xlv (1951), 283–332.

Cale, W.E., 'A Checklist of Hartford, Connecticut, Imprints from 1826–28', diss. (Catholic University of America, 1967).

Camden, Caroll (ed.), *Restoration and Eighteenth-Century Literature: Essays in Honor of Alan Dugald McKillop* (Chicago: University Press for William Marsh Rice University, 1963).

Campbell, Thomas, *Dr Campbell's Diary of a Visit to England in 1775* (Cambridge: Cambridge University Press, 1947).

Canney, Margaret, *et al.*, *Catalogue of the Goldsmith's Library of Economic Literature*, 5 vols. (London: Cambridge University Press and Athlone Press, for University of London Library, 1970–95).

Carlson, Carl Lennart, *The First Magazine: A History of the Gentleman's Magazine* (Providence, RI: Brown University, 1938).

Carnie, Robert Hay, 'Publishing in Perth before 1807', *AHS* no. 6 (1960).

—— 'Scottish Printers and Booksellers 1668–1775: A Second Supplement (I)', *SB* xiv (1961), 81–96.

Carnie, Robert Hay, 'Scottish Printers and Booksellers 1668–1775: A Second Supplement (II)', *SB* xv (1962), 105–20.

—— and Ronald Paterson Doig, 'Scottish Printers and Booksellers 1668–1775: A Supplement', *SB* xii (1959), 131–59.

Carter, A.C., *Robert Carter. His Life and Work, 1807–89* (New York, 1891).

Carter, Elizabeth, *A Series of Letters between Mrs. Elizabeth Carter and Miss Catherine Talbot, from the year 1741 to 1770, to which are added, Letters from Mrs. Elizabeth Carter to Mrs. Vesey, between the Years 1763 and 1787*, ed. Montagu Pennington, 4 vols. (London: F.C. and J. Risington, 1809).

Carter, Harry, *A History of the Oxford University Press*, vol. 1: *To the Year 1780* (Oxford: Clarendon Press, 1975).

Carter, Jennifer J., and Joan H. Pittock (eds.), *Aberdeen and the Enlightenment* (Aberdeen: Aberdeen University Press, 1987).

Carver, J.D., 'Thomas Percy and the Making of the *Reliques* . . . 1756–1765', B.Litt. thesis (University of Oxford, 1973).

Case, A.E., *A Bibliography of English Poetical Miscellanies, 1521–1750* (Oxford: The Bibliographical Society, 1935).

Cassirer, Ernst, *The Philosophy of the Enlightenment*, tr. Fritz C.A. Koelln and James P. Pettegrove (Princeton: Princeton University Press, 1951).

Catalogue général de la Librairie Française, ed. Otto Henri Lorenz, 13 vols. (Paris, 1867–96).

Chalmers, James, *In Memoriam Alexander Chalmers, F.S.A. Editor of the Biographical Dictionary. Born 1759. Died 1834.* (Aberdeen: Privately printed, 1884).

Chambers, Sir Robert, *A Course of Lectures on the English Law Delivered at the University of Oxford, 1767–1775, composed in association with Samuel Johnson*, ed. Thomas M. Curley (Oxford: Clarendon Press, 1986).

Chandra, Mrinal Kanti, *History of the English Press in Bengal, 1780 to 1857* (Calcutta: K.P. Bagchi, 1987).

Chapman, Robert William, 'Johnson and the Longitude', *RES* i (1925), 458–60.

—— 'Dr. Johnson and Dr. Taylor', *RES* ii (1926), 338–9.

—— 'Boswell's Proof Sheets', *London Mercury*, xv (Nov. 1926), 50–8.

—— 'The Numbering of Editions in the Eighteenth Century', *RES* iii (1927), 77–9.

—— *Johnson & Boswell Revised by Themselves and Others* (Oxford: Clarendon Press, 1928).

—— 'Dr. Johnson and Dr. Taylor', *TLS* (13 Dec. 1928), 991.

—— 'Bennet's *Ascham*', *RES* v (1929), 69–70.

—— *Cancels* (London: Constable; New York: Smith, 1930).

—— 'Johnson's Works: A Lost Piece and a Forgotten Piece', *The London Mercury*, xxi (1930), 438–44.

—— 'Eighteenth-Century Imprints', *Library*, 4th ser. xi (1931), 503–4.

—— 'Johnsonian Bibliography', *Colophon* ii (1932), xii. 13–20.

—— 'Authors and Booksellers', in *Johnson's England*, ed. Arthur S. Turberville (Oxford: Clarendon Press, 1933), ii. 310–30.

—— 'Dodsley's *Collection* . . .', *Proceedings of the Oxford Bibliographical Society*, iii (1932–3), 269–316.

—— 'Johnsonian Bibliography, 1750–65', *Colophone* iv (1934), xvi. 1–8.

—— Review of A.T. Hazen, *Samuel Johnson's Prefaces and Dedications*, *RES* xiv (1938), 359–65.

—— 'Piozzi on Thrale', *NQ* clxxxv (1943), 242–7.

—— 'Crousaz on Pope', *RES* n.s. i (1950), 57.

—— and Allen T. Hazen, 'Johnsonian Bibliography: A Supplement to Courtney', *Proceedings of the Oxford Bibliographical Society*, v (1939), 117–66.

Chapple, J.A.V., 'Samuel Johnson's *Proposals for Printing the History of the Council of Trent*', *BJRL* xlv (1963), 340–69.

Chard, Leslie F., 'Bookseller to Publisher: Joseph Johnson and the English Book Trade, 1760 to 1810', *Library*, 5th ser. xxxii (1977), 138–54.

Charlton, Kenneth, *Education in Renaissance England* (London: Routledge, 1965).

Charvat, W., *Literary Publishing in America, 1790–1850* (Philadelphia: University of Pennsylvania Press, 1959).

—— *The Profession of Authorship in America, 1800–1870: The Papers of William Charvat*, ed. Matthew J. Bruccoli (Columbus: Ohio State University Press, 1968).

Chaytor, H.J., *From Script to Print: An Introduction to Medieval Literature* (Cambridge: Cambridge University Press, 1945).

Cheney, C.R., John Cheney, and W.G. Cheney, *John Cheney and His Descendants, Printers in Banbury since 1767* (Banbury: Privately printed, 1936).

Church, E.D., *Catalogue of Books relating to the Discovery of North and South America forming a Part of the Library of E.D. Church*, comp. and annotated by George Watson Cole (New York: Peter Smith, 1907).

Churchill, W.A., *Watermarks in Paper in Holland, England, France, etc. in the XVII and XVIII Centuries and Their Interconnection* (Amsterdam: M. Hertzberger, 1935).

Cioranescu, Alexandre, *Bibliographie de la Littérature Française du Dix-Huitième Siècle*, 3 vols. (Paris: Éditions du CNRS, 1969).

Clapp, Sarah L.C., 'The Beginnings of Subscription Publication in the 17th Century', *MP* xx (1931), 199–224.

—— 'Subscription Publishers prior to Jacob Tonson', *Library*, 4th ser. xiii (1932–3), 158–83.

Clapperton, R.H., *The Paper-Making Machine: Its Invention, Evolution, and Development* (Oxford: Pergamon Press, 1967).

Clifford, James L., 'Further Letters of the Johnson Circle', *BJRL* xx (1936), 268–85.

—— *Hester Lynch Piozzi (Mrs Thrale)* (Oxford: Clarendon Press; 1st edn. 1941; 2nd edn. 1952; rpr. with corrections and additions 1968; reissued, introd. Margaret Anne Doody, 1987).

—— 'The Printing of Mrs Piozzi's *Anecdotes of Dr Johnson*', *BJRL* xx (1936), 157–72.

—— (comp.), *Johnsonian Studies, 1887–1950: A Survey and Bibliography* (Minneapolis: University of Minnesota Press, 1951).

—— *Young Samuel Johnson* (London: Heinemann, 1955).

—— 'Some Problems of Johnson's Obscure Middle Years', in Lascelles (ed.), *Johnson, Boswell and Their Circle*, 99–110.

—— 'Johnson's Trip to Devon in 1762', in Bond (ed.), *Eighteenth-Century Studies in Honor of Donald F. Hyde*, 3–28.

—— 'Johnson and the Society of Artists', *The Augustan Milieu*, ed. Henry Knight Miller *et al.* (Oxford: Clarendon Press, 1970), 333–48.

—— 'Johnson and Lauder', *PQ* liv (1975), 342–56.

—— 'Problems of Johnson's Middle Years—the 1762 Pension', in *Studies in the Eighteenth Century*, David Nichol Smith Memorial Seminar, ed. R.F. Brissenden and J.C. Eade (Canberra: Australian National University Press, 1976), 1–20.

Clifford, James L. *Dictionary Johnson: Samuel Johnson's Middle Years* (New York: McGraw-Hill, 1979).

—— and Donald J. Greene (comps.), *Samuel Johnson: A Survey and Bibliography of Critical Studies* (Minneapolis: University of Minnesota Press, 1970).

Clingham, G.J., 'Johnson's *Prayers and Meditations* and the "Stolen Diary Problem": Reflections on a Biographical Quiddity', *The Age of Johnson*, iv (1991), 83–95.

Cochrane, J.A., *Dr Johnson's Printer: The Life of William Strahan* (London: Routledge & Kegan Paul, 1964).

Cochrane, J.G. (comp.), *Catalogue of the Library at Abbotsford* (Edinburgh: Privately printed, 1838).

Cole, Richard Cargill, 'Samuel Johnson and the Eighteenth-Century Irish Book Trade', *PBSA* lxxv (1981), 235–55.

—— *Irish Booksellers and English Writers 1740–1800* (London: Mansell, 1986).

Coleman, D.C., *The British Paper Industry 1495–1860: A Study in Industrial Growth* (Oxford: Clarendon Press, 1958).

Collins, Arthur S., 'Some Aspects of Copyright from 1700 to 1780', *Library*, 4th ser. vii (1926–7), 67–81.

—— *Authorship in the Days of Johnson, being a Study of the Relation between Author, Patron, Publisher, and Public, 1726–1780* (London: R. Holden, 1927).

—— *The Profession of Letters: A Study of the Relation of Author to Patron, Publisher and Public, 1780–1832* (London: Routledge, 1928).

Collison-Morley, Lacy, *Giuseppe Baretti, with an Account of His Literary Friendships and Feuds in Italy and in England in the Days of Dr. Johnson* (London: John Murray, 1909).

Compton, F.E., 'Subscription Books', *BNYPL* xliii (1939), 879–94.

Congleton, J.E., and Elizabeth Congleton, *Johnson's Dictionary: Bibliographical Survey 1746–1984* (Terre Haute, Ind.: Dictionary Society of North America, 1984).

Cordasco, F., *The Bohn Libraries: A History and a Checklist* (New York: B. Franklin, 1951).

Cordell, Warren N. and Suzanne B. Cordell, *English-Language Dictionaries 1604–1900: The Catalog of the Warren N. and Suzanne B. Cordell Collection*, comp. Robert Keating O'Neill (New York: Greenwood, 1988).

Couper, W.J., *Dr Johnson in the Hebrides* (Glasgow: Privately printed, 1916).

Courtney, William Prideaux and David Nichol Smith (comps.), *A Bibliography of Samuel Johnson* (Oxford: Clarendon Press, 1915; reissued (300 copies) with facsimiles, 1925; repr. 1968; repr. New Castle, Delaware: Gerald M. Goldberg, Oak Knoll Books, 1984).

Cox, Harold, and John E. Chandler, *The House of Longman, with a Record of Their Bicentenary Celebrations 1724–1924* (London: Longman, Green and Co., 1925).

Craig, M.E., *The Scottish Periodical Press, 1750–1789* (Edinburgh: Oliver and Boyd, 1931).

Crane, Ronald S., 'An Early Eighteenth-Century Enthusiast for Primitive Poetry: John Husbands', *MLN* xxxvii (1922), 27–36.

Crellin, J.K., 'Dr James's Fever Powders', *Transactions of the British Society for the History of Pharmacy*, i (1974), 136–43.

Crone, J.S., 'The Parlour Library', *Irish Book Lover*, ii (1911), 133–5.

Cross, Wilbur L., *The History of Henry Fielding* (New Haven, Conn.: Yale University Press, 1918).

Crossley, James, 'Dr Johnson's Contributions to Baretti's Introduction', *NQ* 1st ser. v (1852), 101.

Curley, Thomas M., 'Johnson's Secret Collaboration', in Burke and Kay (eds.), *The Unknown Samuel Johnson*, 91–112.

—— 'Samuel Johnson and Sir Robert Chambers', *Indian Journal for 18th-Century Studies*, I. i (New Delhi, 1986), 1–16.

—— 'Johnson's Last Word on Ossian: Ghostwriting for William Shaw', in Carter and Pittock (eds.), *Aberdeen and the Enlightenment*, 375–431.

Curtius, Ernst Robert, *European Literature and the Latin Middle Ages*, tr. Willard R. Trask (London: Routledge & Kegan Paul, 1953).

Curwen, Henry, *A History of Booksellers: The Old and the New* (London: Chatto, 1873).

D., T.C., 'Joseph Richardson, an Eighteenth-Century Bookseller', *NQ* 11th ser. v (1912), 148.

Darnton, R., 'Reading, Writing and Publishing in 18th-Century France', *Daedalus*, c (1971), 214–57.

Darwin, Erasmus, *The Essential Writings of Erasmus Darwin*, ed. Desmond King-Hele (London: MacGibbon & Kee, 1968).

—— *The Letters of Erasmus Darwin*, ed. Desmond King-Hele (Cambridge: Cambridge University Press, 1981).

Davis, Bertram Hylton, *Johnson before Boswell: A Study of Sir John Hawkins' Life of Samuel Johnson* (New Haven, Conn.: Yale University Press, 1960).

—— *A Proof of Eminence: The Life of Sir John Hawkins* (Bloomington: Indiana University Press, 1973).

—— *Thomas Percy* (Twayne's English Authors, 313; Boston: Twayne, 1981).

—— *Thomas Percy: A Scholar-Cleric in the Age of Johnson* (Philadelphia: University of Pennsylvania Press, 1989).

Davis, Herbert, 'Bowyer's Paper Stock Ledger', *Library*, 5th ser. vi (1951), 73–87.

Davis, William, 'Samuel Johnson's Prefaces and Dedications', *NQ* 2nd ser. xi (1861), 207–8.

Davison, Peter (ed.), *The Book Encompassed: Studies in Twentieth-Century Bibliography* (Cambridge: Cambridge University Press, 1992).

Dawson, Giles E., 'The Copyright in Shakespeare's Dramatic Works', in Prouty (ed.), *Studies in Honour of A.H.R. Fairchild*, 11–35.

—— 'Three Shakespeare Piracies in the Eighteenth Century', *SB* i (1948–9), 47–58.

—— 'Warburton, Hanmer, and the 1745 Edition of Shakespeare', *SB* ii (1949–50), 35–48.

—— 'Robert Walker's Editions of Shakespeare', in *Studies in the English Renaissance Drama*, ed. J.W. Bennett *et al.* (New York: New York University Press, 1959).

Delalain, P.A., *Essai de Bibliographie de l'Histoire de l'Imprimerie Typographique et de la Librairie en France* (Paris, 1903; repr. Geneva: Slatkine, 1970).

DeMaria, Robert, Jr., *The Life of Samuel Johnson: A Critical Biography* (Oxford: Blackwell, 1993).

DeMolen, Richard L. (ed.), *The Meaning of the Renaissance and Reformation* (Boston: Houghton Miflin, 1974).

Dempster, John A.H., 'Thomas Nelson and Sons in the Late Nineteenth Century: A Study in Motivation. Part 1', *PH* xiii (1983), 41–87.

Dent, J.M., *Memoirs 1849–1926, with Some Additions by Hugh R. Dent* (London: J.M. Dent and Sons, 1928).

Dent, J.M., *The House of Dent, 1888–1938, being the Memoirs of J.M. Dent* (London: J.M. Dent & Sons, 1938).

Dewhirst, Kenneth (ed.), *Dr Thomas Sydenham (1624–89): His Life and Original Writings* (London: Wellcome Historical Medical Library, 1966).

Dibdin, T.F., *The Bibliographical Decameron*, 3 vols. (London: Printed for the author, 1817).

D'Israeli, Isaac, *Curiosities of Literature*, 5 vols. (London: John Murray, 1823).

Ditchfield, G.M., 'Dr. Johnson at Oxford, 1759', *NQ* ccxxxiv (1989), 66–8.

Dix, E.R.M., 'The Powell Family, Printers in Dublin in the 18th Century', *PBSI* ii (1923), 85–7.

—— 'Some 18th-Century Catalogues of Books printed in Ireland and for Sale in Dublin by Booksellers', *PBI* iii (1927), 81–2.

—— 'The Works of Oliver Goldsmith—Hand List of Dublin Editions before 1801', *PBSI* ii (1928), 93–101.

Dix, Robin, 'Akenside's *Odes on Several Subjects*', *Library*, 6th ser. xiv (1992), 51–9.

—— and Trude Laura Darby, 'The Bibliographical Significance of the Turned Letter', *SB* xlvi (1993), 263–70.

Dodsley, Robert, *The Correspondence of Robert Dodsley, 1733–1764*, ed. James E. Tierney (Cambridge: Cambridge University Press, 1988).

Doig, Ronald P., 'Reactions to the *Journey to the Western Islands*', *TJSL* (1973), 19–31.

Draper, John W., 'Queen Anne's Act: A Note on English Copyright', *MLN* xxxvi (1921), 146–54.

Duffy, B.J., '[Luke] White, Printer, Fleet-Street [Dublin]', *Irish Book Lover*, xxx (1947), 37.

Duncan, D., *Thomas Ruddiman: A Study in Scottish Scholarship in the Eighteenth Century* (Edinburgh: Oliver & Boyd, 1965).

Dunn, R.D., 'Samuel Johnson's Prologue to *A Word to the Wise* and the Epilogue by "a Friend" ', *ELN* xxv (1988), 28–35.

Dunton, John, *The Life and Errors* (London: S. Malthus, 1705).

—— *The Life and Errors of John Dunton, Citizen of London, with the Lives and Character of More than a Thousand Contemporary Divines and Other Persons of Literary Eminence*, 2 vols. (London: J. Nichols, 1818).

Eastman, Arthur M., 'Johnson's Shakespearean Labors in 1765', *MLN* lxiii (1948), 512–15.

—— 'The Texts from which Johnson Printed His Shakespeare', *JEGP* xlix (1950), 182–97.

Eaves, T.C. Dunan, 'Dr Johnson's Letters to Richardson', *PMLA* lxxv (1960), 377–81.

—— and Ben D. Kimpel, *Samuel Richardson: A Biography* (Oxford: Clarendon Press, 1971).

Eddy, Donald D., 'Samuel Johnson's Editions of Shakespeare (1765)', *PBSA* lvi (1962), 428–44.

—— 'The Publication Date of the First Edition of "Rasselas" ', *NQ* ccvii (1962), 21–2.

—— 'Dodsley's *Collection of Poems by Several Hands* (Six Volumes), 1758: Index of Authors', *PBSA* lx (1966), 9–30.

—— *A Bibliography of John Brown* (New York: Bibliographical Society of America, 1971).

—— *Samuel Johnson: Book Reviewer in the Literary Magazine, or, Universal Review* (New York: Garland, 1979).

—— and J.D. Fleeman, 'A Preliminary Handlist of Books to Which Dr. Samuel Johnson Subscribed', *SB* xlvi (1993), 187–220.

Eisenstein, Elizabeth L., *The Printing Press as an Agent of Change: Communications and Cultural Transformations in Early-Modern Europe*, 2 vols. (Cambridge: Cambridge University Press, 1979).

Emery, John Pike, *Arthur Murphy: An Eminent English Dramatist of the Eighteenth Century* (Philadelphia: University of Pennsylvania Press for Temple University, 1946).

The English Catalogue of Books (London: Sampson Low, 1861–1968).

Erwin, Timothy, 'The "Life of Savage", Voltaire, and a Neglected Letter', *NQ* ccxxviii (1983), 525–6.

—— 'Voltaire and Johnson again: the *Life of Savage* and the Sertorius Letter (1744)', *SVEC* xiv (1991), 211–23.

Evans, Joan, *The Endless Web: John Dickinson & Co. Ltd. 1804–1954* (London: Cape, 1955).

Ewing, J.C., 'Brash and Reid; Booksellers in Glasgow, and Their Collection of Poetry . . .', *Glasgow Bibliographical Society* (1934).

Exman, Eugene, *The Brothers Harper: A Unique Publishing Partnership and Its Impact upon the Cultural Life of America from 1817 to 1853* (New York: Harper, 1965).

Fabian, Bernhard (ed.), *A Catalogue of English Books printed before 1801 at Göttingen held by the University Library*, comp. by Graham Jefcoate and Karen Kloth, 4 vols. (Hildesheim: Georg Olms Verlag, 1987–8).

Fairer, David, 'Authorship Problems in *The Adventurer*', *RES* n.s. xxv (1974), 135–51.

Farthing, J.C., 'Production in the Row', *Manchester Review*, xi (1967), 134–48.

Faý, Bernard, *Notes on the American Press at the End of the Eighteenth Century* (New York: Grolier Club, 1927).

Feather, John P., *Book Prospectuses before 1801 in the John Johnson Collection: A Catalogue with Microfiche* (Oxford: Oxford Microform Publications for the Bodleian Library, 1976).

—— 'Country Book Trade Apprentices 1710–1760', *PH* vi (1979), 85–99.

—— 'The Book Trade in Politics: The Making of the Copyright Act of 1710', *PH* viii (1980), 19–44.

—— *The English Provincial Book Trade before 1850: A Checklist of Secondary Sources* (Oxford: Oxford Bibliographical Society, 1981).

—— 'John Nourse and His Authors', *SB* xxxiv (1981), 205–26.

—— 'The English Book Trade and the Law 1695–1799', *PH* xii (1982), 51–75.

—— 'The Commerce of Letters: The Study of the Eighteenth-Century Book Trade', *ECS* xvii (1983–4), 405–24.

—— *The Provincial Book Trade in Eighteenth-Century England* (Cambridge: Cambridge University Press, 1985).

—— 'British Publishing in the Eighteenth Century: A Preliminary Subject Analysis', *Library*, 6th ser. viii (1986), 32–46.

—— 'The Publishers and the Pirates: British Copyright Law in Theory and Practice, 1710–1775', *PH* xxii (1987), 5–32.

—— *A History of British Publishing* (London: Routledge, 1988).

—— 'Publishers and Politicians: The Remaking of the Law of Copyright in Britain 1775–1842. Part II: the Rights of Authors', *PH* xxv (1989), 45–72.

Ferdinand, Christine Y., 'Benjamin Collins, the *Salisbury Journal*, and the Provincial Book Trade', *Library*, 6th ser. xi (1989), 116–38.
—— 'Richard Baldwin Junior, Bookseller', *SB* xlii (1989), 254–64.
Fergus, Jan, 'Eighteenth-Century Readers in Provincial England: The Customers of Samuel Clay's Circulating Library and Bookshop in Warwick, 1770–72', *PBSA* lxxviii (1984), 155–213.
Ferrero, Bonnie M., 'Samuel Johnson, Richard Rolt, and the *Universal Visiter*', *RES* n.s. xliv (1993), 176–86.
Fisher, R.A., *A Digest of the Reported Cases . . . of Copyright . . . 1756–1870* (San Francisco: S. Whitney, 1871).
Fleeman, J.D., 'Some Proofs of Johnson's *Prefaces to the Poets*', *Library*, 5th ser. xvii (1962), 213–30.
—— '18th-Century Printing Ledgers', *TLS* (19 Dec. 1963), 1056.
—— 'The Reprint of *Rambler* No. 1', *Library*, 5th ser. xviii (1963), 288–94.
—— 'Johnson's "Journey" (1775), and Its Cancels', *PBSA* lviii (1964), 232–8.
—— 'Dr. Johnson and Henry Thrale, M.P.', in Lascelles (ed.), *Johnson, Boswell and Their Circle*, 170–88.
—— 'A Critical Study of the Transmission of the Texts of the Works of Dr. Samuel Johnson' D.Phil. thesis (University of Oxford, 1965).
—— 'The Making of Johnson's *Life of Savage*, 1744', *Library*, 5th ser. xxii (1967), 346–52.
—— *A Preliminary Handlist of Documents & Manuscripts of Samuel Johnson* (Oxford: Oxford Bibliographical Society, 1967).
—— 'Some Notes on Johnsons's Prayers and Meditations', *RES*, n.s. xix (1968), 172–9.
—— *Early Biographical Writings of Dr. Johnson* (Farnborough: Gregg, 1973).
—— 'The Revenue of a Writer: Samuel Johnson's Literary Earnings', in R.W. Hunt *et al.* (eds.), *Studies in the Book Trade*, 211–30.
—— (ed.), *The Sale Catalogue of Samuel Johnson's Library*, a facs. edn. of the Christie sale catalogue, 16 Feb. 1785, ed. J.D. Fleeman (Victoria, BC: University of Victoria, 1975).
—— 'Concealed Proofs and the Editor', *Studies in the Eighteenth Century*, David Nichol Smith Memorial Seminar, ed. R.F. Brissenden and J.C. Eade (Canberra: Australian National University Press, 1979), 207–21.
—— *A Preliminary Handlist of Copies of Books associated with Dr. Samuel Johnson* (Oxford: Oxford Bibliographical Society, 1984).
—— 'Johnsonian Prospectuses and Proposals', in Patey and Keegan (eds.), *Augustan Studies*, 215–38.
—— 'Dr Johnson and "Miss Fordice"', *NQ* cxxi (1986), 59–60.
—— 'Johnson in the Schoolroom: George Fulton's *Dictionary* (1821)', in Harvey, Kirsop, and McMullin (eds.), *An Index of Civilisation*, 163–71.
—— 'Dr Johnson and Revd William Dodd', *Edinburgh Bibliographical Society Transactions*, vi (1993), 55–6.
—— 'Johnson's *Shakespeare* (1765): The Progress of a Subscription', in OM Brack (ed.), *Writers, Books, and Trade*, 355–65.
Forster, Harold B., *Supplements to Dodsley's Collection of Poems* (Oxford: Oxford Bibliographical Society, 1980).
—— 'Rarities and Oddities in the Works of Edward Young', *BC* xxxii (1983), 425–38.
Forster, John, *The Life and Times of Oliver Goldsmith*, 2 vols. (London: Ward, Lock, 1871).

Foster, Joseph (ed.), *The Register of Admissions to Gray's Inn, 1521–1889*, 2 vols. (London: Privately printed, 1889).

Foxon, D.F., *English Verse 1701–1750: A Catalogue of Separately Printed Poems with Notes on Contemporary Collected Editions*, 2 vols. (Cambridge: Cambridge University Press, 1975).

—— *Pope and the Early Eighteenth-Century Book Trade*, rev. and ed. James McLaverty (Oxford: Clarendon Press, 1991).

Francis, F.C., 'Drawback on Paper', *Library*, 5th ser. iv (1949–50), 73.

Freind, Joseph H., *The Development of American Lexicography, 1798–1864* (Hague: Mouton, 1967).

Friedman, Albert B., 'The First Draft of Percy's *Reliques*', *PMLA* lxix (1954), 1233–49.

—— 'The Problem of Indifferent Readings in the Eighteenth Century, with a Solution from *The Deserted Village*', *SB* xiii (1960), 143–7.

—— 'Two Notes on Goldsmith', *SB* xiii (1960), 232–5.

Fumagali, Giuseppe (ed.), *Bibliografia Etiopica* (Milan: U. Hoepli, 1893).

Fussell, Paul, *Samuel Johnson and the Life of Writing* (New York: Harcourt, Brace, Jovanovich, 1971).

Gaine, Hugh, *The Journals of Hugh Gaine*, ed. P.L. Ford, 2 vols. (New York: Dodd, Mead & Co., 1902).

Gardiner, Robert Barlow (ed.), *The Registers of Wadham College, Oxford*, 2 vols. (London: G. Bell, 1889–95).

Garrick, David, *The Letters of David Garrick*, ed. David M. Little and George M. Kahrl, 3 vols. (Cambridge, Mass.: Harvard University Press, 1963).

—— *The Private Correspondence of David Garrick*, ed. James Boaden, 2 vols. (London: H. Colburn and R. Bentley, 1831–2).

Garrison, Fielding H., and Leslie T. Morton, *Garrison and Morton's Medical Bibliography: An Annotated Check-list of Texts illustrating the History of Medicine*, 2nd edn. (London: Grafton, 1954).

Gaskell, Philip, 'Notes on Eighteenth-Century British Paper', *Library*, 5th ser. xii (1957), 34–42.

—— *A New Introduction to Bibliography*, 2nd edn. (Oxford: Clarendon Press, 1974).

Gaskill, Howard (ed.), *Ossian Revisited* (Edinburgh: Edinburgh University Press, 1991).

Geduld, Harry M., *Prince of Publishers: A Study of the Work and Career of Jacob Tonson* (Bloomington: Indiana University Press, 1969).

Gilreath, J., 'American Book Distribution', *PAAS* xcv (1985), 501–83.

Ginsberg, H., 'The J.B. Lippincott Company', diss. (Drexel Institute of Technology, Philadelphia, 1952).

Glynn, J., *Prince of Publishers: A Biography of George Smith* (London: Allison & Busby, 1986).

Goff, F.R., 'The First Decade of the Federal Act of Copyright, 1790–1800', in *Essays Honoring Lawrence C. Wroth* (Portland, Me.: Anthoensen Press, 1951), 101–28.

Gold, Joel J., 'Johnson's Translation of Lobo', *PMLA* lxxx (1965), 51–61.

Goldsmith, Oliver, *A Prospect of Society by Oliver Goldsmith, being the Earliest Form of His Poem, now first reprinted from the unique original, with a reprint of the first edition of The Traveller*, ed. Bertram Dobell (London: Published by the editor, 1902).

—— *A Prospect of Society*, ed. William B. Todd (Cambridge: Walter Lane Press, 1954).

Goldsmith, Oliver, *The Collected Works of Oliver Goldsmith*, ed. Arthur Friedman, 5 vols. (Oxford: Clarendon Press, 1966).

Goudy, Frederic W., *Typologia: Studies in Type Design & Type Making* (Berkeley: University of California, 1940).

Goulden, Richard J., *The Ornament Stock of Henry Woodfall 1719–1747* (London: Bibliographical Society, 1988).

Gove, Philip B., 'Notes on Serialization and Competitive Publishing: Johnson's and Bailey's *Dictionaries*', *Proceedings of the Oxford Bibliographical Society*, v (1936–9), 305–22.

—— 'Bailey's Folio *Dictionary*: A Supplementary Note', *Proceedings of the Oxford Bibliographical Society*, n.s. i (1947), 45–6.

Graham, W.J., *English Literary Periodicals* (New York: T. Nelson, 1930).

Granger, James, *Letters between the Rev. J. G., M.A. . . . and . . . the Most Eminent Men of His Time*, ed. J.P. Malcolm (London, 1805).

Grant, Douglas, *The Cock Lane Ghost* (London: Macmillan, 1965).

Grant, Francis Richard Charles, *Life of Samuel Johnson* (London: W. Scott, 1887).

Grant, I.R., 'William Creech', *Books and the Man: Antiquarian Booksellers' Associated Annual* (London: Dawson & Sons, 1953), 70–6.

Grant, John, 'James Ballantyne's Kelso Press', *NQ* 11th ser. iii (1911), 347, with further discussion 396–7, 435–6, 457.

Grat, W.F., 'Alexander Donaldson and His Fight for Cheap Books', *Juridical Review*, xxxviii (1926), 180–202.

—— 'Dr Johnson's Publisher', *Fortnightly Review*, cxxix (1931), 245–50.

Green, Boylston, 'Possible Additions to the Johnson Canon', *YULG* xvi (1942), 7 0–9.

Green, Samuel A., *Remarks on the Early History of Printing in New England* (Boston, 1897).

Greene, Donald J., 'The Johnsonian Canon: A Neglected Attribution', *PMLA* lxv (1950), 427–34.

—— 'Was Johnson Theatrical Critic of the *Gentleman's Magazine*?', *RES* n.s. iii (1952), 158–61.

—— 'Johnson's Contributions to the *Literary Magazine*', *RES* n.s. vii (1956), 367–92.

—— 'Johnson and the "Harleian Miscellany" ', *NQ* cciii (1958), 304–6.

—— 'Some Notes on Johnson and the *Gentleman's Magazine*', *PMLA* lxxiv (1959), 75–84.

—— *The Politics of Samuel Johnson* (New Haven, Conn.: Yale University Press, 1960).

—— '*The False Alarm* and *Taxation No Tyranny*: Some Further Observations', *SB* xiii (1960), 223–31.

—— 'The Development of the Johnson Canon', in Camden (ed.), *Restoration and Eighteenth-Century Literature*, 407–27.

—— 'Johnsonian Attributions by Alexander Chalmers', *NQ* ccxii (1967), 180–1.

—— *Samuel Johnson* (New York: Twayne, 1970).

—— *Samuel Johnson's Library: An Annotated Guide* (Victoria: University of British Columbia, 1975).

—— 'Samuel Johnson, Journalist', in Bond and McLeod (eds.), *Newsletters to Newspapers*, 87–101.

—— (ed.), *Samuel Johnson*, The Oxford Authors (Oxford, 1984).

—— and John A. Vance (comps.), *A Bibliography of Johnsonian Studies, 1970–1985*, ELS Monograph Series 39 (Victoria, BC: English Literary Studies, University of Victoria, 1987).

Greenwood, David, 'Doctor Samuel Johnson and the Principal of St. Mary Hall', *BLR* viii (1971), 285–8.

Greg, W.W., 'A Formulary of Collation', *Library*, 4th ser. xiv (1933–4), 365–82; repr. in *Collected Papers*, ed. J.C. Maxwell (Oxford: Clarendon Press, 1966), 298–313.

Griffin, Charles and Co., *The Centenary Volume of Charles Griffin and Company Ltd., Publishers 1820–1920* (London: Charles Griffin and Co., 1920).

Griffith, Reginald Harvey, *Alexander Pope: A Bibliography*, 2 vols. (Austin: University of Texas, 1922–7).

Grove, George, *The New Grove Dictionary of Music and Musicians*, ed. Stanley Sadie, 20 vols. (London: Macmillan, 1980).

Gulley, J.L.M., 'More Chiswick Press Papers', *BMQ* xxvi (1962–3), 83–5.

Gunther, A.E., *Introduction to the Life of Rev. Thomas Birch D.D., F.R.S., 1705–1766, Leading Editor of the General Dictionary, Secretary of the Royal Society and Trustee of the British Museum* (Halesworth: Halesworth Press, 1984).

H., O.N., 'W. Innys, Eighteenth-Century Publisher', *NQ* cxlix (1925), 297–8, with further discussion 339, 358, 447; cl (1926), 33.

Hagberg, Knut, *Carl Linnaeus*, trans. by Alan Blair (London: Cape, 1952).

Haig, Robert L., *The Gazetteer, 1735–1797: A Study in the Eighteenth-Century Newspaper* (Carbondale: Southern Illinois University Press, 1960).

Hall, David D. and John B. Hench, *Needs and Opportunities in the History of the Book: America, 1639–1876* (Worcester, Mass.: American Antiquarian Society, 1987).

Halliday, F.E., *Doctor Johnson and His World* (London: Thames & Hudson, 1968).

Hammelman, Hanns, *Book Illustrators in Eighteenth-Century England*, ed. T.S.R. Boase (New Haven, Conn.: Yale University Press for the Paul Mellon Center for Studies in British Art, 1975).

Hampshire, G.I., 'Johnson, Elizabeth Carter, and Pope's Garden', *NQ* ccxvii (1972), 221–2.

Hansard, Luke Graves, *Luke Graves Hansard, His Diary, 1814–1841: A Case Study in the Reform of Patronage*, ed. P. and G. Ford (Oxford: Blackwell, 1962).

Hanson, Laurence W., 'Johnson, Percy, and Sir William Chambers', *BLR* iv (1953), 291–2.

—— *Government and the Press 1695–1763* (London: Oxford University Press, 1936).

Hanson, T.W., 'Edwards of Halifax: a Family of Booksellers, Collectors, and Bookbinders', *Papers of the Halifax Antiquarian Society* (1912), 141–200.

Harlan, Robert D., 'Some Additional Figures of Distribution of Eighteenth-Century English Books', *PBSA* lix (1965), 160–70.

Harris, Eileen, with Nicholas Savage, *British Architectural Books and Writers, 1556-1785* (Cambridge: Cambridge University Press, 1990).

Harris, Elizabeth M., 'Experimental Graphic Processes in England, 1800–1859', Parts I–II, *JPHS* iv (1968), 33–86; Part III, *JPHS* v (1969), 41–80.

Harris, John, *Sir William Chambers, Knight of the Polar Star* (London: A. Zwemmer, 1970).

Harrison, C.R., and Harry George, *The House of Harrison: Being an Account of the Family and Firm of Harrison and Sons, Printers to the King* (London: Harrison and Sons, 1914).

Harrison, James, *Printing Patents: Abridgements of Patent Specifications relating to Printing 1617–1857* (London: Printing Historical Society, 1969).

Hart, C.W., 'Dr Johnson's 1745 Shakespeare Proposals', *MLN* liii (1938), 367–8.

Hart, Edward L., 'Some New Sources of Johnson's *Lives*', *PMLA* lxv (1950), 1088–111.

Hart, Horace, *Notes on a Century of Typography at the University Press, Oxford 1693–1794* (Oxford: Oxford University Press, 1900).

Harvey, R., W. Kirsop, and B.J. McMullin (eds.), *An Index of Civilisation: Studies of Printing and Publishing History in Honour of Keith Maslen* (Clayton, Victoria: Centre for Bibliographical and Textual Studies, Monash University, 1993).

Hausmann, Friedrich, *Repertorium der diplomatischen Vertreter aller Länder* (Zürich: Fretz & Wasmuth, 1950).

Hawkins, John, *The Life of Samuel Johnson, LL.D.*, 2nd edn. (London, 1787).

Hawkins, Laetitia-Matilda, *Memoirs, Anecdotes, Facts, and Opinions*, 2 vols. (London: Longman, Hurst, Rees, Orme, Brown, and Green: 1824).

Hayward, Abraham (ed.), *Autobiography, Letters and Literary Remains of Mrs. Piozzi (Thrale)*, 2 vols. (London, 1861).

Hayward, J. (comp.), *English Poetry: An Illustrated Catalogue of First and Early Editions Exhibited in 1947 at 7 Albemarle Street, London* (London: Published for the National Book League by Cambridge University Press, 1950).

Hazen, Allen T., 'A Johnson Preface', *TLS* (28 June 1934), 460.

—— 'Crousaz on Pope', *TLS* (2 Nov. 1935), 704.

Hazen, Allen T., 'Eighteenth-Century Quartos with Vertical Chain-Lines', *Library*, 4th ser. xvi (1935–6), 337–42.

—— 'Samuel Johnson and Dr Robert James', *Bulletin of the Institute of the History of Medicine*, iv (1936), 455–65.

—— *Samuel Johnson's Prefaces and Dedications* (New Haven, Conn.: Yale University Press, 1937).

—— 'The Beauties of Johnson', *MP* xxxv (1938), 289–95.

—— 'Johnson's Shakespeare: a Study in Cancellation', *TLS* (24 Dec. 1938), 820.

—— 'Cancels in Johnson's Shakespeare', *BLR* i (1939), 42–3.

—— and Edward L. McAdam, 'Dr Johnson and the Hereford Infirmary', *HLQ* iii (1939–40), 359–67.

—— 'The Cancels in Johnson's *Journey*, 1775', *RES* xvii (1941), 201–3.

—— *A Catalogue of Horace Walpole's Library* (London: Oxford University Press, 1969).

—— and T.O. Mabbott, 'Dr Johnson and Francis Fawkes's *Theocritus*', *RES* xxi (1945), 142–6.

Heal, Ambrose, 'Adams, Instrument-Makers, XVIII Century', *NQ* clxx (1936), 423–4.

Hearne, Thomas, *Remarks and Collections of Thomas Hearne*, ed. Charles Edward Doble, David Watson Rannie, and Herbert Edward Salter, 11 vols. (Oxford: Oxford Historical Society at Clarendon Press, 1885–1921).

Heawood, Edward, *Watermarks Mainly of the 17th and 18th Centuries* (Hilversum: Paper Publications Society, 1950).

Hebb, John, 'Watts's Printing Office, Little Wild Court, Drury Lane', *NQ* 8th ser. x (1896), 394–5.

Hecht, Hans (ed.), *Thomas Percy and William Shenstone: Ein Briefwechsel aus der Entstehungszeit der Reliques of Ancient English Poetry* (Strassburg: K.J. Trübner, 1909).

Heel, Dalmatius van, *De Goudse Drukkers en hun Uitgaven*, 4 vols. (Gouda, 1950–1).

Hennessy, George (comp.), *Novum Repertorium Ecclesiasticum Parochiale Londinense; or, London Diocesan Clergy Succession from the Earliest Time to the Year 1898* (London: S. Sonnenschein, 1898).

Henrey, Blanche, *British Botanical and Horticultural Literature before 1800, comprising a History and Bibliography of Botanical and Horticultural Books printed in England, Scotland, and Ireland from the Earliest Times until 1800*, 3 vols. (Oxford: Oxford University Press, 1975).

Hernlund, Patricia, 'William Strahan's Ledgers: Standard Charges for Printing, 1738–1785', *SB* xx (1967), 89–111.

—— 'William Strahan's Ledgers, II: Charges for Papers 1738–1785', *SB* xxii (1969), 179–95.

Hervey, John, *The Diary and Letter Books of John Hervey, First Earl of Bristol, with Extracts from His Book of Expenses, 1688 to 1742*, ed. by S.H.A. Hervey, 3 vols. (Wells: E. Jackson, 1894).

Hervey, William, *The Journals of William Hervey in North America and Europe from 1755 to 1814*, ed. by S.H.A. Hervey (Bury: Paul & Mathew, 1906).

Higgs, Henry, *Bibliography of Economics, 1751–1775* (Cambridge: Cambridge University Press, 1935).

Hildeburn, Charles S.R., *A Century of Printing: The Issues of the Press in Pennsylvania, 1685–1784*, 2 vols. (Philadelphia: Matlack & Harvey, 1885–6).

—— *Sketches of Printers and Printing in Colonial New York* (New York: Dodd, Mead, 1895).

Hill, Joseph, *Book Makers of Old Birmingham* (Birmingham: Shakespeare Press, 1907).

Hilles, Frederick Whiley, *The Literary Career of Sir Joshua Reynolds* (Cambridge: Cambridge University Press, 1936).

—— 'The Making of *The Life of Pope*', in *New Light on Dr. Johnson: Essays on the Occasion of His 250th Birthday*, ed. F.W. Hilles (New Haven, Conn.: Yale University Press, 1959), 257–84.

—— 'Johnson's Correspondence with Nichols: Some Facts and a Query', *PQ* xlviii (1969), 226–33.

—— 'Sir Joshua and the Empress Catherine', in Bond (ed.), *Eighteenth-Century Studies in Honor of Donald F. Hyde*, 267–77.

Hillyard, Brian, 'Scottish Bibliography for the Period ending 1801', in Peter Davison (ed.), *The Book Encompassed*, 182–92.

Hindley, C., *The Life and Times of James Catnach (Late of Seven Dials), Ballad Monger* (Welwyn Garden City: Seven Dials Press, 1970).

Hobbs, J.L., 'The Parentage and Ancestry of John Gwyn, the Architect', *NQ* ccvii (1962), 22–4.

Hodges, John C. (ed.), *William Congreve: Letters & Documents* (London: Macmillan, 1964).

Hodgson, Norma and Cyprian Blagden, *The Notebook of Thomas Bennet and Henry Clements (1686–1719)* (Oxford: Oxford Bibliographical Society, 1956).

Hogarth, William, *The Genuine Works of William Hogarth*, with Biographical Anecdotes, a Chronological Catalogue, and Commentary by John Nichols and George Steevens, 3 vols. (London, 1808–17).

Holt, Henry, 'The Archives of Henry Holt & Co.', *Princeton University Library Chronicle*, xiii (1952), 208–9.

Holt, Henry, *Garrulities of an Octogenarian Editor* (Boston & New York: Houghton Mifflin, 1923).

Holworthy, R., 'The Monumental Inscriptions in the Church and Churchyard of Bromley, Co. Kent', 'Supplement' to *The British Archivist* (1922).

Honour, F.M., 'James Lackington, Proprietor, Temple of the Muses', *JLH* ii (1967), 211–24.

Hoole, Samuel, *Anecdotes respecting the Life of the late Mr. John Hoole* (London, 1803).

Hoover, Benjamin B., *Samuel Johnson's Parliamentary Reporting* (Berkeley: University of California Press, 1953).

Horsburgh, E.L.S., *Bromley, Kent: from the Earliest Times to the Present Century* (London: Hodder and Stoughton, 1929).

Howard, William J., 'Dr Johnson on Abridgment—A Re-Examination', *PBSA* lx (1966), 215–19.

Howe, Ellic, *The London Compositor: Documents relating to Wages, Working Conditions and Customs of the London Printing Trade, 1785–1900* (London: Bibliographical Society, 1947).

Hugo, Thomas, *Bewick's Woodcuts: Impressions of upwards of Two Thousand Woodcuts* (London, 1870).

Hulbert, J.R., *Dictionaries, British and American*, rev. edn. (London: Deutsch, 1968).

Hunt, C.J., *The Book Trade in Northumberland and Durham to 1860: A Biographical Dictionary* (Newcastle upon Tyne: Thorne's Bookshop, 1975).

Hunt, R.H., 'William Mavor', *BQR* vi (1931), 259–60.

Hunt, R.W. *et al.* (eds.), *Studies in the Book Trade in Honour of Graham Pollard* (Oxford: Oxford Bibliographical Society, 1975).

Hunter, David, 'Copyright Protection for Engravings and Maps in Eighteenth-Century Britain', *Library*, 6th ser. ix (1987), 128–47.

Hutchinson, Robert, *1800 Woodcuts by Thomas Bewick and his School* (New York: Dover, 1962).

Huxley, Leonard, *The House of Smith, Elder* (London: Printed for private circulation by William Clowes & Sons, 1923).

Hyde, Mary, *The Thrales of Streatham Park* (Cambridge, Mass.: Harvard University Press, 1977).

Ing, Janet, 'A London Shop of the 1850s: The Chiswick Press', *PBSA* lxxx (1986), 153–78.

Irving, Joseph, *The Book of Scotsmen Eminent for Achievements* (Paisley, 1881).

Isaac, Peter C.G., *William Davison of Alnwick, Pharmacist and Printer 1781–1858* (Oxford: Clarendon Press, 1968).

—— 'William Davison of Alnwick, Pharmacist and Printer', *Library*, 5th ser. xxiv (1969), 1–32.

—— *William Davison's New Specimens of Cast-Metal Ornaments and Wood Types, introduced with an Account of His Activities as Pharmacist and Printer in Alnwick, 1780–1858* (London: Printing Historical Society, 1990).

Isles, Duncan E., 'The Lennox Collection', *HLB* xviii (1970), 317–44; xix (1971) 36–60, 165–86, 416–35.

Jackson, William A., *The Carl H. Pforzheimer Library: English Literature, 1475–1700*, 3 vols. (New York: Privately printed, 1940).

Jacob, Margaret C., *The Newtonians and the English Revolution, 1689–1720* (Ithaca, NY: Cornell University Press, 1976).

Jaggard, William, *Shakespeare Bibliography: A Dictionary of Every Known Issue of the Writings of Our National Poet and of Recorded Opinion thereon in the English Language* (Stratford-on-Avon: Shakespeare Press, 1911).

James, L., *Fiction for the Working Man, 1830–1850: A Study of the Literature Produced for the Working Classes in Early Victorian Urban England* (London: Oxford University Press, 1963).

Jarvis, Rupert C., 'The Paper-Makers and the Excise in the Eighteenth Century', *Library*, 5th ser. xiv (1959), 100–16.

Jeremy, D.J., 'Damming the Flood: British Government Efforts to Check the Outflow of Technicians and Machinery, 1780–1843', *Business History Review*, li (1977), 2–19.

Johnson, Samuel, *Letters of Samuel Johnson, LL.D.*, ed. George Birkbeck Hill, 2 vols. (Oxford: Clarendon Press, 1892).

—— *Johnsonian Miscellanies*, ed. George Birkbeck Hill (Oxford: Clarendon Press, 1897).

—— *Lives of the English Poets*, ed. George Birkbeck Hill (Oxford: Clarendon Press, 1905).

—— *Papers written by Dr. Johnson and Dr. Dodd in 1777*, ed. R.W. Chapman (Oxford: Clarendon Press, 1926).

—— *The Poems of Samuel Johnson*, ed. David Nichol Smith and Edward L. McAdam (Oxford: Clarendon Press, 1941).

—— *The Letters of Samuel Johnson, with Mrs. Thrale's Genuine Letters to Him*, ed. R.W. Chapman, 3 vols. (Oxford: Clarendon Press, 1952).

—— *The Yale Edition of the Works of Samuel Johnson*, gen. editors Allen T. Hazen and John H. Middendorf, (New Haven, Conn.: Yale University Press, 1958–).

—— *Samuel Johnson, Diaries, Prayers, and Annals*, ed. Edward L. McAdam, Jr., with Donald and Mary Hyde (New Haven, Conn.: Yale University Press; London: Oxford University Press, 1958).

—— *Account of the Life of Mr. Richard Savage*, ed. Clarence Tracy (Oxford: Clarendon Press, 1971).

—— *The Poems of Samuel Johnson*, ed. David Nichol Smith and Edward L. McAdam, 2nd edn., rev. J.D. Fleeman (Oxford: Clarendon Press, 1974).

—— *A Journey to the Western Islands of Scotland*, ed. J.D. Fleeman (Oxford: Clarendon Press, 1985).

—— *The Letters of Samuel Johnson*, The Hyde Edition, ed. Bruce Redford, 5 vols. (Princeton: Princeton University Press; Oxford: Clarendon Press, 1992–4).

—— *The Shorter Prose Writings of Samuel Johnson*, ed. O M Brack (New York: AMS Press, forthcoming).

Johnston, Shirley White, 'Samuel Johnson's Text of *King Lear*: "Dull Duty" reassessed', *Yearbook of English Studies*, vi (1976), 80–91.

—— 'From Preface to Practice: Samuel Johnson's Editorship of Shakespeare', in Korshin and Allen (eds.), *Greene Centennial Essays*, 250–70.

Jonard, Norbert, *Giuseppe Baretti (1719–1789): L'Homme et l'oeuvre* (Clermont-Ferrand: G. de Bussac, 1963).

Jones, Claude, 'Christopher Smart, Richard Rolt, and *The Universal Visiter*', *Library*, 4th ser. xviii (1937–8), 212–14.

Jones, K.W., *Carl Van Vechten: A Bibliography* (New York: Knopf, 1955).

Kahn, Louis E., *A Catalog of Dictionaries: English Language, American Indian and Foreign Languages . . . The Louis E. Kahn Collection*, comp. Jean Hamer (Cincinnati: Public Library of Cincinnati and Hamilton County, 1972).

Kaminski, Thomas, 'Johnson and Oldys as Bibliographers: an Introduction to the Harleian Catalogue', *PQ* lx (1981), 439–53.

—— *The Early Career of Samuel Johnson* (New York: Oxford University Press, 1987).

Kaser, David, 'The Chronology of Carey Imprints', *PBSA* l (1956), 190–3.

—— 'The Origin of the Book Trade Sales', *PBSA* l (1956), 296–302.

—— *Messrs Carey and Lea of Philadelphia: A Study in the History of the Booktrade* (Philadelphia: University of Pennsylvania Press, 1957).

—— (ed.), *The Cost Book of Carey & Lea, 1825–1838* (Philadelphia: University of Pennsylvania Press, 1963).

Katterfeld, A., *Roger Ascham: Sein Leben und Seine Werke* (Strassburg: Trübner, 1879).

Kaufman, Paul, 'A Bookseller's Record of Eighteenth-Century Book Clubs', *Library*, 5th ser. xv (1960), 278–87.

—— 'The Eighteenth-Century Forerunner of the London Library', *PBSA* liv (1960), 89–100.

—— 'Reading Vogues at English Cathedral Libraries of the 18th Century', *BNYPL* lxvii (1963), 655–72; lxviii (1964), 48–64, 110–32, 191–202.

—— *Libraries and Their Users: Collected Papers in Library History* (London: Library Association, 1969).

Keast, W.R., 'The Preface to *A Dictionary of the English Language*: Johnson's Revision and Establishment of the Text', *SB* v (1952–3), 129–46.

—— 'Samuel Johnson and Thomas Maurice', in Bond (ed.), *Eighteenth-Century Studies in Honor of Donald F. Hyde*, 63–79.

Keir, David, *The House of Collins: The Story of a Scottish Family of Publishers from 1789 to the Present Day* (London: William Collins, 1952).

Kelly, Thoms, *A History of Adult Education in Great Britain*, 2nd edn. (Liverpool: Liverpool University Press, 1970).

Kendall, Lyle H., Jr., 'A Note on Johnson's "Journey" (1775)', *PBSA* lix (1965), 317–18.

Kennedy, Arthur Garfield, *A Bibliography of the Writings on the English Language from the Beginning of Printing to the End of 1922* (Cambridge, Mass.: Harvard University Press; New Haven, Conn.: Yale University Press, 1927).

Kernan, Alvin, *Printing Technology, Letters & Samuel Johnson* (Princeton: Princeton University Press, 1987).

Keynes, Geoffrey, *A Bibliography of Sir Thomas Browne*, 2nd edn. (Oxford: Clarendon Press, 1968).

—— *William Pickering, Publisher: A Memoir and a Check-List of His Publications*, rev. edn. (London: Galahad, 1969).

—— 'Samuel Johnson and Bishop Berkeley', *BC* xxx (1981), 177–81.

King, Arthur, and A.F. Stuart, *The House of Warne: One Hundred Years of Publishing* (London, New York: F. Warne, 1965).

Kirsop, Wallace, 'A Note on Johnson's *Dictionary* in Nineteenth-Century Australia and New Zealand', in Harvey, Kirsop, and McMullen (eds.), *An Index of Civilisation*, 172–4.

Knapp, Mary E., 'Prologue by Johnson', *TLS* (4 Jan. 1947), 9.

Knight, Charles, *Passages of a Working Life during Half a Century*, 3 vols. (London: Bradbury & Evans, 1864–5).

—— *Shadows of the Old Booksellers* (London: Bell & Daldy, 1865).

Knight, Charles A., 'Bibliography and the Shape of the Literary Periodical in the Early Eighteenth Century', *Library*, 6th ser. viii (1986), 232–48.

Koda, Paul S., 'A Descriptive Catalogue of the Warren N. Cordell Collection of Dictionaries', Ph.D. diss. (University of Indiana, 1974).

Kohler, C.C., *Catalogue: Johnson's Dictionary*, with preface by G.J. Kolb (Dorking, 1986).

Kolb, Gwin J., 'A Note on the Publication of Johnson's "Proposals for Printing the Harleian Miscellany" ', *PBSA* xlviii (1954), 196–8.

—— 'John Newbery, Projector of the *Universal Chronicle*: A Study of the Advertisements', *SB* xi (1958), 249–51.

—— 'Dr. Johnson and the *Public Ledger*: A Small Addition to the Canon', *SB* xi (1958), 252–5.

—— 'More Attributions to Dr. Johnson', *SEL* i (1961), 77–95.

—— '*Rasselas*: Purchase Price, Proprietors, and Printings', *SB* xv (1962), 256–9.

—— 'Johnson's "Little Pompadour": A Textual Crux and a Hypothesis', in Camden (ed.), *Restoration and Eighteenth-Century Literature*, 125–42.

—— 'The Reception of *Rasselas*, 1759–1800', in Korshin and Allen (eds.), *Greene Centennial Essays*, 217–49.

—— 'Sir Walter Scott, "Editor" of *Rasselas*', *MP* lxxxix (1991–2), 515–18.

—— and James H. Sledd, 'The History of the Sneyd–Gimbel and Pigott–British Museum Copies of Dr Johnson's *Dictionary*', *PBSA* liv (1960), 286–9.

Korshin, Paul J. (ed), *Robert Anderson: The Life of Samuel Johnson (1815)* (Hildesheim: Georg Olms Verlag, 1973).

—— 'Robert Anderson's *Life of Johnson* and Early Interpretive Biography', *HLQ* xxxvi (1973), 239–53.

—— 'Types of Eighteenth-Century Literary Patronage', *ECS* vii (1974), 453–73.

—— (ed.), *The Widening Circle: Essays on the Circulation of Literature in Eighteenth-Century Europe* (Philadelphia: University of Pennsylvania Press, 1976).

—— (ed.), *Johnson after Two Hundred Years* (Philadelphia: University of Pennsylvania Press, 1986).

—— 'Johnson's Last Days: Some Facts and Problems', in Korshin (ed.), *Johnson after Two Hundred Years*, 55–76.

—— and R.R. Allen (eds.), *Greene Centennial Studies: Essays presented to Donald Greene in the Centennial Year of the University of Southern California* (Charlottesville: University Press of Virginia, 1984).

Krapp, George Philip, *The English Language in America*, 2 vols. (Oxford: Oxford University Press, 1925).

Kuist, James M., *The Nichols File of 'The Gentleman's Magazine': Attributions of Authorship and Other Documentation in Editorial Papers at the Folger Library* (Madison: University of Wisconsin Press, 1982).

—— 'A Collaboration in Learning: *The Gentleman's Magazine* and Its Ingenious Contributors', *SB* xliv (1991), 302–17.

Labarre, E.J., *Dictionary and Encyclopaedia of Paper and Papermaking with Equivalent of the Technical Terms in French, German, Dutch, Italian, Spanish & Swedish*, 2nd edn. (Amsterdam: Swets & Zeitlinger, 1952).

Lackington, James, *Memoirs of the First Forty-Five Year of the Life of James Lackington* (London: Printed for the author, 1791).

Lackington, James, *The Confessions of J. Lackington, Late Bookseller* (London: Printed for the author, 1804).

Lams, Victor J., 'The "A" Papers in the *Adventurer*', *SP* lxiv (1967), 83–96.

Landon, Richard G., 'Samuel Johnson's *Journey* (1775), with Uncancelled U4 Leaf', *PBSA* lxiv (1970), 449–50.

Landsdowne, Henry Petty FitzMaurice, 6th Marquis of (ed.), *Johnson and Queeney* (London: Cassell, 1932).

Lascelles, Mary *et al.* (eds.), *Johnson, Boswell and Their Circle: Essays presented to Lawrence Fitzroy Powell* (Oxford: Clarendon Press, 1965).

Laver, James, *Hatchards of Piccadilly, 1797–1947* (London: Hatchard, 1947).

Lawler, Thomas Bonaventure, *Seventy Years of Textbook Publishing: A History of Ginn and Company, 1867–1937* (Boston: Ginn and Co., 1938).

Leed, Jacob, 'Two New Pieces by Johnson in the *Gentleman's Magazine*?', *MP* liv (1957), 221–9.

—— 'Samuel Johnson and the "Gentleman's Magazine": An Adjustment of the Canon', *NQ* ccii (1957), 210–13.

—— 'Samuel Johnson and the *Gentleman's Magazine*: Studies in the Canon of his Miscellaneous Prose Writings, 1738–1744', Ph.D. diss. (University of Chicago, 1958).

—— 'Two Notes on Johnson and *The Gentleman's Magazine*', *PBSA* liv (1960), 101–10.

—— 'Johnson, Du Halde, and the Life of Confucius', *BNYPL* lxx (1966), 189–99.

—— 'Patronage in the *Rambler*', *Studies in Burke and His Time*, xiv (1972), 5–21.

Lehmann-Haupt, Hellmut *et al.*, *The Book in America: A History of the Making and Selling of Books in the United States*, 2nd edn. (New York: Bowker, 1951).

Leslie, Charles R. and Tom Taylor, *Life and Times of Sir Joshua Reynolds, with Notices of Some of His Contemporaries*, 2 vols. (London: J. Murray, 1865).

Liebert, Herman W., 'An Addition to the Bibliography of Samuel Johnson', *PBSA* xli (1947), 231–8.

—— *Johnson's Last Literary Project* (New Haven, Conn.: printed for the author, 1948).

—— 'This Harmless Drudge', *New Colophon*, i (1948), 175–83.

—— *Johnson's Last Literary Project: An Account of the Work He Contemplated on His Death-Bed but Did Not Survive to Execute* (New Haven, Conn.: Privately printed, 1948).

—— *Dr. Johnson and the Misses Collier* (New Haven, Conn.: Yale University Press, 1949).

—— 'Dr. Johnson's First Book', *YULG* xxv (1950), 23–8.

—— 'Johnson and Gay', *NQ* cxcvi (1951), 216–17.

—— 'We Fell upon *Sir Eldred*', in *New Light on Dr. Johnson: Essays on the Occasion of His 250th Birthday*, ed. F.W. Hilles (New Haven, Conn.: Yale University Press, 1959), 233–45.

—— *Who Dropped the Copy for Rambler 109?* (New Haven, Conn.: Yale University Press, 1966).

—— *Lifetime Likenesses of Samuel Johnson, reissued with Additional Plates* (Los Angeles: William Andrews Clark Memorial Library, 1974).

—— 'A Neglected Johnsonianum', *YULG* lviii (1984), 140–2.

Lievre, Auguste-François, *Catalogue général des manuscrits des bibliothèques de France* (Paris: Plon, 1894).

Lindeboom, G.A., *Herman Boerhaave: The Man and His Work* (London: Methuen, 1968).

Little, Brown, & Co., *One Hundred and Twenty-Five Years of Publishing, 1837–1962* (Boston: Little, Brown, 1962).

Littlejohn, David, *Dr Johnson and Noah Webster: Two Men and Their Dictionaries* (San Francisco: Book Club of California, 1971).

Liveing, Edward G.D., *Adventure in Publishing: The House of Ward Lock, 1854–1954* (London: Ward, Lock, 1954).

Longman, Charles James, *The House of Longman 1724–1800: A Bibliographical History with a List of Signs Used by Booksellers of that Period* (London: Longmans, Green and Co., 1936).

Lonsdale, Roger H., *Dr Charles Burney: A Literary Biography* (Oxford: Clarendon Press, 1965).

—— (ed.), *Eighteenth Century Women Poets: An Oxford Anthology* (Oxford: Oxford University Press, 1989).

Lustig, Irma S., 'The Compiler of *Dr. Johnson's Table Talk*, 1785', *PBSA* lxxi (1977), 83–8.

Lynch, Kathleen M., *Jacob Tonson, Kit-Kat Publisher* (Knoxville, Tenn.: University of Tennessee Press, 1971).

McAdam, Edward L., 'A Johnson Pamphlet', *TLS* (14 Mar. 1936), 228.

—— 'Dr Johnson's Law Lectures for Chambers: An Addition to the Canon', *RES* xv (1939), 385–91; xvi (1940), 159–68.

—— 'New Essays by Dr Johnson', *RES* xviii (1942), 197–207.

—— 'Johnson's Lives of Sarpi, Blake, and Drake', *PMLA* lviii (1943), 466–76.

—— 'Pseudo-Johnsoniana', *MP* xli (1944), 183–7.

—— *Dr Johnson and the English Law* (Syracuse, NY: Syracuse University Press, 1951).

—— 'Dr Johnson and Saunders Welch's *Proposals*', *RES* n.s. iv (1953), 337–45.

McCann, E.J.W., 'Thomas Lowndes and the Publication of Edward Long's *The History of Jamaica*: A Note on Perpetual Copyright', *Library*, 6th ser. v (1983), 60–3.

McCarthy, William, 'The Composition of Johnson's *Lives*: A Calendar', *PQ* lx (1981), 53–67.

—— *Hester Thrale Piozzi: Portrait of a Literary Woman* (Chapel Hill: University of North Carolina Press, 1985).

McCorison, Marcus A., *Vermont Imprints, 1778–1820: A Check List of Books, Pamphlets, and Broadsides* (Worcester, Mass.: American Antiquarian Society, 1963).

McDermott, Anne, 'The Reynolds Copy of Johnson's *Dictionary*: A Re-examination', *BJRL* lxxiv (1992), 29–38.

MacDonald, K.D., 'The Rev. William Shaw: Pioneer Gaelic Lexicographer', *TGSI* l (1976–8), 1–19.

McDougall, W., 'Copyright Legislation in the Court of Session, 1738–49, and the Rise of the Scottish Book Trade', *Edinburgh Bibliographical Society Transactions*, v, 2–31.

McGill, W., 'Bookselling and Publishing in Edinburgh in the Late 18th Century', *Publishers' Circular*, clxiii (1949), 5.

McGuffie, Helen Louise, *Samuel Johnson in the British Press 1749–1784: A Chronological Checklist* (New York: Garland, 1976).

McKenzie, D.F., *Stationers' Company Apprentices 1641–1700* (Oxford: Oxford Bibliographical Society, 1974).

McKenzie, D.F., *Stationers' Company Apprentices 1701–1800* (Oxford: Oxford Bibliographical Society, 1978).

—— and J.C. Ross, *A Ledger of Charles Ackers, Printer of The London Magazine* (Oxford: Oxford Bibliographical Society, 1968).

McKerrow, Ronald B., 'The Treatment of Shakespeare's Text by His Earliest Editors', *PBA* xix (1933), 89–122.

McKillop, Alan D., 'Supplementary Notes on Samuel Richardson as a Printer', *SB* xii (1959), 214–18.

McKinlay, R., 'Some Notes on Dr Johnson's *Journey to the Western Islands*', *RGBS* viii (1930), 144–50.

McKitterick, David, 'Thomas Osborne, Samuel Johnson and the Learned of Foreign Nations: A Forgotten Catalogue', *BC* xli (1992), 55–68.

Macleane, Douglas, *History of Pembroke College, Oxford, anciently Broadgates Hall* (Oxford: Oxford Historical Society, 1897).

Maclehose, James, *The Glasgow University Press, 1638–1931, with Some Notes on Scottish Printing in the Last Three Hundred Years* (Glasgow: Glasgow University Press, 1931).

Macleod, A.L., 'Notes on John Gay', *NQ* cxcvi (1951), 32–4.

Macleod, Robert Duncan, *The Scottish Publishing Houses* (W. and R. Holmes, 1953).

—— 'Some Scottish Publishers', *LR* xviii (1962), 435–40, 514–20, 597–603.

McLeod, W.R., and V.B. McLeod, *Graphical Directory of English Newspapers and Periodicals 1702–1714* (Morgantown, W.Va.: School of Journalism, West Virginia University, 1982).

Maclure, J. Stuart, *Educational Documents: England and Wales, 1816–1963*, 2nd edn. (London: Chapman & Hall, 1968).

McMullin, B.J., 'Johnson's *Works* 1787–92', *News from the Rare Book Room*, xii (1970), 76–7.

—— 'Press Figures and Concurrent Perfecting: Walker & Greig, Edinburgh, 1817–22', *Library*, 6th ser. xii (1990), 236–41.

McMurtrie, Douglas C., *A History of Printing in the United States* (New York: Bowker, 1936).

—— *A Bibliography of Books and Pamphlets Printed at Ithaca, N.Y., 1820–1850* (Buffalo, NY: Grosvenor Library, 1937).

Madison, Charles A., *The Owl among the Colophons: Henry Holt as Publisher and Editor* (New York: Holt, Rinehart and Winston, 1966).

Malton, T., *An Essay concerning the Publication of Works, on Science and Literature, by Subscription* (London, 1777).

Mann, Peter H., *Book Publishing, Book Selling, and Book Reading: A Report to the Book Marketing Council of the Publishers Association* (London: Book Marketing Council, 1979).

Marcuse, Michael J., 'The *Gentleman's Magazine* and the Lauder/Milton Controversy', *BRH* lxxxi (1978), 179–209.

—— 'The Pre-Publication History of William Lauder's *Essay on Milton's Use and Imitation of the Moderns in His Paradise Lost*', *PBSA* lxxii (1978), 37–57.

—— ' "The Scourge of Impostors, the Terror of Quacks": John Douglas and the Exposé of William Lauder', *HLQ* xlii (1978–9), 231–61.

Marshall, Edward, 'Wire in Bookbinding', *NQ* 9th ser. ii (1898), 125.

Marshman, J.C., *The Life and Times of Carey, Marshman, and Ward, embracing the History of the Serampore Mission*, 2 vols. (London: Longman, Brown, Green, Longman & Roberts, 1859).

Marston, Edward, *Sketches of Some Booksellers of Other Days* (London: S. Low, Marston & Co., 1901).

—— *Sketches of Some Booksellers of the Time of Dr Samuel Johnson* (London: S. Low, Marston & Co., 1902).

Maslen, K.I.D., 'The Bowyer Press', *TLS* (30 March 1967), 274.

—— 'Printing Charges: Inference and Evidence', *SB* xxiv (1971), 91–8.

—— 'Printing for the Author: From the Bowyer Printing Ledgers, 1710–1775', *Library*, 5th ser. xxvii (1972), 302–9.

—— *The Bowyer Ornament Stock* (Oxford: Oxford Bibliographical Society, 1973).

—— 'The Bowyer Ledgers: Their Historical Importance', *PBSA* lxxxii (1988), 139–49.

—— 'The Bowyer Ledgers: Retrospect and Prospect', in Harvey, Kirsop, and McMullin (eds.), *An Index of Civilisation*, 1–14.

—— and John Lancaster (eds.), *The Bowyer Ledgers: The Printing Accounts of William Bowyer, Father and Son* (London: The Bibliographical Society of America, 1991).

Maxted, Ian, *The London Book Trades, 1775–1800: A Preliminary Checklist of Members* (Folkstone: Dawson, 1977).

—— *The British Book Trades, 1710–1771: An Index of Masters and Apprentices Recorded in the Inland Revenue Registers at the Public Record Office, Kew* (Exeter: Ian Maxted, 1983).

Mayer, Jean, *Diderot, Homme de Science* (Rennes: Bretonne, 1959).

Mayo, Robert D., *The English Novel in the Magazines, 1740–1815* (Evanston, Ill.: Northwestern University Press, 1962).

Metzdorf, Robert F., 'Notes on Johnson's *Plan of a Dictionary*', *Library*, 4th ser. xix (1938–9), 198–201.

—— 'Isaac Reed and the Unfortunate Dr Dodd', *HLB* vi (1952), 393–6.

—— 'Samuel Johnson in Brunswick', *MLN* lxviii (1953), 397–400.

—— 'The First American "Rasselas" and Its Imprint', *PBSA* xlvii (1953), 374–6.

—— 'Grand Cairo and Philadelphia: The Frontispiece to the 1768 Edition of Johnson's *Rasselas*', in Wahba (ed.), *Bicentenary Essays on Rasselas*, 75–80.

Michot, P., 'Dr Johnson on Copyright', *Revue des langues vivantes*, xxiii (1957), 137–47.

Middendorf, John H., 'Johnson as Editor: Some Proofs of the *Prefaces*', in Bond (ed.), *Eighteenth-Century Studies in Honor of Donald F. Hyde*, 89–106.

—— (ed.), *English Writers of the Eighteenth Century* (New York: Columbia University Press, 1971).

Mild, Warren, 'Johnson and Lauder: A Re-Examination', *MLQ* xiv (1953), 149–53.

Mitford, J., 'The Rise and Progress of the Magazine', in *The General Index to the Gentleman's Magazine*, iii (1821), iii–lxxx.

Monghan, E. Jennifer, *A Common Heritage: Noah Webster's Blue-Back Speller* (Hamden, Conn.: Archon, 1983).

Mongahan, T.J., 'Johnson's Additions to His *Shakespeare* for the Edition of 1773', *RES* n.s. iv (1953), 234–48.

Montluzin, Emily Lorraine de., 'Attributions of Authorship in the *Gentleman's Magazine*, 1731–77: A Supplement to Kuist', *SB* xliv (1991), 271–302.

—— 'Attributions of Authorship in the *Gentleman's Magazine*, 1778–92', *SB* xlv (1992), 158–87.

—— 'Attributions of Authorship in the *Gentleman's Magazine*, 1793–1808', *SB* xlvi (1993), 320–49.

Montluzin, Emily Lorraine de., 'Attributions of Authorship in the *Gentleman's Magazine*, 1809–26', *SB* xlvii (1994), 164–95.

Moran, James, *Clays of Bungay* (Bungay: Richard Clay & Co., 1978).

Morgan, C., *The House of Macmillan (1843–1943)* (London: Macmillan, 1943).

Morgan, Paul, 'Book-Sale Catalogues in Eighteenth-Century Warwickshire', in Harvey, Kirsop, and McMullin (eds.), *An Index of Civilisation*, 89–97.

Morison, Stanley, *John Bell, 1745–1831, Bookseller, Printer, Publisher, Typefounder, Journalist, &c.* (Cambridge: Printed for the author at the University Press, 1930).

Morris, J.C., 'The Publishing Activities of S.C. Griggs and Co., 1848–96; Jansen McClurg and Co., 1872–86; and A.C. McClurg and Co., 1886–1900; with Lists of Publications', MA thesis (University of Illinois, 1941).

Mosley, James, *British Type Specimens before 1831: A Hand-List* (Oxford: Oxford Bibliographical Society, 1984).

Mugglestone, L.C., 'Samuel Johnson and the Use of /h/', *NQ* ccxxxiv (1989), 431–3.

Mumby, Frank Arthur, *Publishing and Bookselling*, 5th edn. pt. 1: *From the Earliest Times to 1870*; pt. 2: *1870–1970*, by Ian Norrie (London: Cape, 1974).

—— *The House of Routledge, 1834–1934, with a History of Kegan Paul, Trench, Trübner and Other Associated Firms* (London: Routledge, 1934).

Munby, A.N.L., 'Cancels in Percy's *Reliques*', *TLS* (31 Oct. 1936), 892, 908.

—— *The Cult of the Autograph Letter in England* (London: University of London, Athlone, 1962).

Mundy, P.D., 'Dryden Leach, 1708', *NQ* clxiv (1933), 209; clxxiii (1937), 302, 339.

Munroe, P. (ed.), *A Cyclopaedia of Education*, 5 vols. (New York, 1911–13; rptd. Detroit, 1969).

Munter, Robert L., *The History of the Irish Newspaper, 1685–1760* (Cambridge: Cambridge University Press, 1967).

Muris, Oswald, and Gert Saarmann, *Der Globus im Wandel der Zeiten: eine Geschichte der Globen* (Berlin: Columbus, 1961).

Murray, K.M. Elisabeth, *Caught in the Web of Words: James A.H. Murray and the Oxford English Dictionary* (New Haven, Conn.: Yale University Press, 1977).

Myers, Robin, and Michael Harris (eds.), *Spreading the Word: The Distribution Networks of Print 1550–1850* (Winchester: St Paul's Bibliographies, 1990).

Nagashima, Daisuke, 'A Catalogue of the Samuel Johnson Collection in the Library of Kyoto University of Foreign Studies', in Daisuke Nagashima and Yoshitaka Mizutori (eds.), *Essays in Honour of Professor Haruo Kozu* (Hirakata: Intercultural Research Institute, Kansai University, 1990), 143–62.

Nangle, Benjamin Christie, *The Monthly Review, First Series 1749–1789: Indexes of Contributors and Articles* (Oxford: Clarendon Press, 1934).

—— *The Monthly Review, Second Series 1790–1815: Indexes of Contributors and Articles* (Oxford: Clarendon Press, 1955).

Natarajan, S., *A History of the Press in India* (London: Asia Publishing House, 1962).

Neill, D.G., 'Printed Books, 1640–1800', *Library Trends*, vii (1959), 537–53.

Neuberg, Victor E., *Chapbooks: A Bibliography of References to English and American Chapbook Literature of the Eighteenth and Nineteenth Centuries* (London: Vine Press, 1964).

—— 'The Diceys and the Chapbook Trade', *Library*, 5th ser. xxiv (1969), 219–31.

—— 'The Reading of the Victorian Freethinkers', *Library*, 5th ser. xxviii (1973), 191–214.

—— *Popular Literature: A History and Guide, from the Beginning of Printing to the Year 1897* (London: Woburn, 1977).

Newth, J.D., *Adam and Charles Black, 1807–1957* (London: Adam and Chales Black, 1957).

Nichol, Donald W., 'On the Use of "Copy" and "Copyright": A Scriblerian Coinage?' *Library*, 6th ser. xii (1990), 110–20.

—— *Pope's Literary Legacy: The Book-Trade Correspondence of William Warburton and John Knapton* (Oxford: Oxford Bibliographical Society, 1992).

Nichols, John, *Literary Anecdotes of the Eighteenth Century*, 9 vols. (London: Printed for the Author, 1812–15).

—— *Illustrations of the Literary History of the Eighteenth Century*, 8 vols. (London: Printed for the Author, 1817–58).

—— *A General Index to the Gentleman's Magazine*, 4 vols. (London: 1818–21).

Nicoll, Allardyce, *A History of English Drama, 1660–1900*, 4th edn., 6 vols. (Cambridge: Cambridge University Press, 1952–9).

Northcote, James, *The Life of Sir Joshua Reynolds*, 2nd edn., 2 vols. (London: Henry Colburn, 1819).

Nowell-Smith, S.H., *The House of Cassell, 1848–1958* (London: Cassell, 1958).

—— *International Copyright Law and the Publisher in the Reign of Queen Victoria*, Oxford (Oxford: Clarendon Press, 1968).

O'Casaide, S., 'Fictitious Imprints on Books Printed in Ireland', *PBSI* iii (1927), 31–5.

O'Kelley, F., 'Irish Book-Sale Catalogues before 1801', *PBSI* vi (1953), 35–55.

Orr, Leonard, 'Johnson and the Penultimate Chapter of Lennox's *The Female Quixote*', *Enlightenment Essays*, viii (1977), 64–74.

Osborn, James M., 'Dr Johnson's Intimate Friend', *TLS* (9 Oct. 1953), 652.

Osler, William, *Bibliotheca Osleriana: A Catalogue of Books Illustrating the History of Medicine and Science* (Oxford: Clarendon Press, 1929).

P., P.T., 'Pope and Henry Woodfall', *NQ* 1st ser. xii (1855), 197.

—— 'The Ledger of Henry Woodfall, jun., 1737–1748', *NQ* 1st ser. xii (1855), 217–19.

Palmer, D.J., *The Rise of English Studies: An Account of the Study of the English Language and Literature from Its Origins to the Making of the Oxford English School* (London: Oxford University Press for the University of Hull, 1965).

Papali, G.F., *Jacob Tonson, Publisher: His Life and Work (1656–1736)* (Auckland: Tonson Publishing, 1968).

Parker, William Riley, *Milton: A Biography*, 2 vols. (Oxford: Clarendon Press, 1968).

Parks, Stephen, 'Justice to William Creech', *PBSA* lx (1966), 453–64.

—— 'Booksellers' Trade Sales', *Library*, 5th ser. xxiv (1969), 241–3.

Patey, Douglas Lane, and Timothy Keegan (eds.), *Augustan Studies: Essays in Honor of Irvin Ehrenpreis* (Newark: University of Delaware Press, 1985).

Patterson, L.R., *Copyright in Historical Perspective* (Nashville, Tenn.: Vanderbilt University Press, 1968).

Paul, C. Kegan, *Memories*, (1889; rptd. with foreword by Colin Franklin, London: Routledge & Kegan Paul, 1971).

Paul, Sir James Balfour, *The Scots Peerage, Founded on Wood's Edition of Sir Robert Douglas's Peerage of Scotland*, 9 vols. (Edinburgh: David Douglas, 1904–14).

Pegge, Samuel (comp.), *Anonymiana, or, Ten Centuries of Observations on Various Authors and Subjects*, 2nd edn. (London: Nichols, Son, and Bentley, 1818).

Peltrier, Karen V., 'Additions and Corrections to Hazen's *A Catalogue of Horace Walpole's Library*', *PBSA* lxxviii (1984), 473–88.

Pendred, John, *The Earliest Directory of the Book Trade, by John Pendred (1785)*, ed. Graham Pollard (London: The Bibliographical Society, 1955).

Percy, Thomas, *Thomas Percy und William Shenstone: Ein Briefwechsel aus der Entstehungszeit der Reliques of Ancient English Poetry*, ed. Hans Hecht (Strassburg: K.J. Trübner, 1909).

—— *Letters*, gen. eds. David Nichol Smith, Cleanth Brooks, and A.F. Falconer:

1. *The Correspondence of Thomas Percy & Edmond Malone*, ed. Arthur Tillotson (New Haven, Conn.: Yale University Press, 1944).

2. *The Correspondence of Thomas Percy & Richard Farmer*, ed. Cleanth Brooks (Baton Rouge: Louisiana State University Press, 1946).

3. *The Correspondence of Thomas Percy and Thomas Warton*, ed. M.G. Robinson and Leah Dennis (Baton Rouge: Louisiana State University Press, 1951).

4. *The Correspondence of Thomas Percy & David Dalrymple, Lord Hailes*, ed. A.F. Falconer (Baton Rouge: Louisiana State University Press, 1954).

5. *The Correspondence of Thomas Percy and Evan Evans*, ed. Aneirin Lewis (Baton Rouge: Louisiana State University Press, 1957).

6. *The Correspondence of Thomas Percy and George Paton*, ed. A.F. Falconer (New Haven, Conn.: Yale University Press, 1961).

7. *The Correspondence of Thomas Percy and William Shenstone*, ed. Cleanth Brooks (New Haven, Conn.: Yale University Press, 1977).

8. *The Correspondence of Thomas Percy and John Pinkerton*, ed. Harriet Harvey Wood (New Haven, Conn.: Yale University Press, 1985).

9. *The Correspondence of Thomas Percy and Robert Anderson*, ed. W.E.K. Anderson (New Haven, Conn.: Yale University Press, 1988).

Petition of the Booksellers for Relief from the Expenses of Correction and Improvement (London, 1778).

Philip, I.G., 'Doctor Johnson and the Encaenia Oration', *BLR* viii (1969), 122–3.

Phillips, James W., 'A Trial List of Irish Papermakers, 1690–1800', *Library*, 5th ser. xiii (1958), 59–62.

Piccioni, Luigi, 'Per la fortuna del *Rasselas* di Samuele Johnson in Italia', *Giornale Storico della Letteratura Italiana*, lv (1910), 339–56.

—— *Bibliografia Analitica di Giuseppe Baretti* (Torino: Società subalpina Editrice, 1942).

Piggott, Stuart, 'New Light on Christopher Smart', *TLS* (13 June 1929), 474.

Piozzi, Hester Lynch, *Anecdotes of the Late Samuel Johnson, LL.D., During the Last Twenty Years of His Life* (London: Cadell, 1786).

—— *Thraliana: The Diary of Mrs. Hester Lynch Thrale (later Mrs. Piozzi), 1776–1809*, ed. Katharine C. Balderston, 2 vols. (Oxford: Clarendon Press, 1942; 2nd edn. 1951).

Pitcher, Edward L., 'On the Letter to the *Idler* (No. 41) from X.Y.Z.', *American Notes and Queries* xviii (1979), 37–8.

Pitman, Sir Isaac, *The House of Pitman* (London: Isaac Pitman and Sons, 1930).

Plant, Marjorie, *The English Book Trade: An Economic History of the Making and Sale of Books*, 3rd edn. (London: Allen & Unwin, 1974).

Plomer, Henry R., 'On the Value of Publishers' Lists [Thomas Tegg]', *Library*, 2nd ser. iii (1902), 427–33.

—— 'The Booksellers of London Bridge', *Library*, 2nd ser. iv (1903), 28–46.

—— *A Dictionary of the Printers and Booksellers Who Were at Work in England, Scotland, and Ireland from 1668 to 1725* (London: The Bibliographical Society, 1922).

—— *A Dictionary of the Printers and Booksellers Who Were at Work in England, Scotland, and Ireland from 1726 to 1775* (London: The Bibliographical Society, 1932).

Pollard, Alfred W., 'Some Notes on the History of Copyright in England, 1662–1774', *Library*, 4th ser. iii (1922–3), 97–114.

Pollard, Henry Graham, 'The English Market for Printed Books' (unpublished Sandars Lectures, Cambridge University, 1959).

—— and A. Ehrman, *The Distribution of Books by Catalogue from the Invention of Printing to A.D. 1800* (Cambridge: Roxburghe Club, 1965).

—— *Hodson's Booksellers, Publishers and Stationers Directory 1855: A Facsimile of the Copy in the Bodleian Library, Oxford* (Oxford: Oxford Bibliographical Society, 1972).

—— 'The English Market for Printed Books', *PH* iv (1978), 7–48.

Pollard, M., *Dublin's Trade in Books 1550–1800* (Oxford: Clarendon Press, 1989).

Pomfret, J.E., 'Some Further Letters of William Strahan, Printer', *PMHB* lx (1936), 455–89.

Porter, Roy, *English Society in the Eighteenth Century* (London: Allen Lane, 1982).

Pottle, Frederick A., *The Literary Career of James Boswell, being the Bibliographical Materials for a Life of Boswell* (Oxford: Clarendon Press, 1929).

—— *Pride and Negligence: The History of the Boswell Papers* (New York: McGraw-Hill, 1982).

Povey, K., 'Working to Rule, 1600–1800: A Study of Pressmen's Practice', *Library*, 5th ser. xx (1965), 13–54.

Powell, L.F., 'Percy's *Reliques*', *Library*, 4th ser. ix (1928–9), 113–37.

—— 'Johnson and a Friend', *The Times* (25 Nov. 1938), 15.

—— 'An Addition to the Canon of Johnson's Writings', *ES* xxviii (1943), 38–41.

—— 'Johnson Exhibited', in Wahba (ed.), *Johnsonian Studies*, 9–13.

—— 'For Johnsonian Collectors', *TLS* (20 Sept. 1963), 712.

Pressnell, L.S., and John Orbell, *A Guide to the Historical Records of British Banking* (New York: St Martin's Press, 1985).

Price, Mary Bell, and Lawrence M. Price, *The Publication of English Humaniora in Germany in the Eighteenth Century*, University of California Publications in Philology, 44 (Berkeley: University of California Press, 1955).

Priolkar, A.K., *The Printing Press in India, Its Beginnings and Early Development* (Bombay: Marathi Samshodhana Mandala, 1958).

Prior, James, *The Life of Oliver Goldsmith, M.B., from a Variety of Sources*, 2 vols. (London: John Murray, 1837).

—— *The Life of Edmond Malone, Editor of Shakespeare* (London: Smith, 1860).

Prouty, Charles T. (ed.), *Studies in Honour of A.H.R. Fairchild* (Columbia, University of Missouri, 1946).

Putnam, G.P., *Memories of a Publisher, 1865–1915* (New York, London: G.P. Putnam's Sons, 1915).

Quennell, Peter, *Samuel Johnson: His Friends and Enemies* (London: Weidenfeld and Nicholson, 1972).

Quérard, Joseph-Marie, *La France Littéraire, ou Dictionnaire bibliographique des savants, historiens et gens de lettres de la France*, 10 vols. (Paris: Firmin Didot, 1827–39).

—— *La littérature française contemporaine: xix siècle*, 6 vols. (Paris: Daguin Frères, 1842–57).

Quinlan, Maurice J., 'Samuel Whyte's Anecdotes about Dr Johnson', *DCLB* v (1963), 56–65.

Raby, J.T., *Bi-Centenary of the Birth of Dr Samuel Johnson* (Stafford: J. & C. Mort, 1909).

Ramos, G.C., *Annotações ligeiras a traduçao de Johnson da 'Viageo a Abissinia' do Padre Jeronimo Lobo* (Lisbon, 1945).

Ramsden, Charles, *Bookbinders of the United Kingdom (outside London), 1780–1840* (1954; repr. London: Batsford, 1987).

—— *London Bookbinders 1780–1840* (1956; repr. London: Batsford, 1987).

Randall, D.A., 'Percy's *Reliques* and Its Cancel Leaves', *New Colophon*, i (Oct. 1948); iv. 404–7.

Ransom, H., 'The Rewards of Authorship in the 18th Century', *SE* (1938), 47–66.

—— *The First Copyright Statute: An Essay on An Act for the Encouragement of Learning, 1710* (Austin: University of Texas, 1956).

Rappaport, Steve, *Worlds within Worlds: Structures of Life in Sixteenth-Century London* (Cambridge: Cambridge University Press, 1989).

Reade, Aleyn Lyell, *Johnsonian Gleanings*, 11 vols. (London: P. Lund Humphries, 1909–52).

Reading, J., 'Poems by Johnson', *TLS*, 11 Sept. 1937, 656.

Reddick, Allen, *The Making of Johnson's Dictionary, 1746–1773* (Cambridge: Cambridge University Press, 1990).

Rees, T., *Reminiscences of Literary London from 1779 to 1853* (New York: F.P. Harper, 1896).

Revello, José Torre, *Bibliografia de las Islas Malvinas: Obras, Mapas y Documentos* (Buenos Aires: Imprenta de la Universidad, 1953).

Reynolds, Sir Joshua, *Letters of Sir Joshua Reynolds*, ed. Frederick Whiley Hilles (Cambridge: Cambridge University Press, 1929).

—— *Discourses*, ed. Robert R. Wark (San Marino, Calif.: Huntington Library, 1959).

Rich, Eric E., *The Education Act 1870: A Study of Public Opinion* (Harlow: Longmans, 1970).

Richardson, John, Jr., 'Correlated Type Sizes and Names for the Fifteenth through Twentieth Century', *SB* xliii (1990), 251–72.

Richardson, Samuel, *The Case of Samuel Richardson, Printer; with Regard to the Invasion of his Property in the History of Sir Charles Grandison, Before Publication, by certain Booksellers in Dublin* (London, 1753).

—— *Selected Letters of Samuel Richardson*, ed. John Carroll (Oxford: Clarendon Press, 1964).

Ridler, William, *British Modern Press Books: A Descriptive Check List of Unrecorded Items*, 2nd edn. (Folkstone: Dawson, 1975).

Riely, J.C., 'Lady Knight's Role in the Boswell-Piozzi Rivalry', *PQ* li (1972), 961–5.

Rivers, Isabel (ed.), *Books and Their Readers in Eighteenth-Century England* (Leicester: Leicester University Press, 1982).

Rivington, Septimus (ed.), *The Publishing House of Rivington* (London: Rivington, Percival, 1894).

—— *The Publishing Family of Rivington* (London: Rivingtons, 1919).

Rizzo, Betty, 'Christopher Smart, the 'C.S.' Poems, and Molly Leapor's Epitaph', *Library*, 6th ser. v (1983), 22–31.

—— 'The Elopement of Francis Barber', *ELN* xxiii (1985–6), 35–8.

—— ' "Innocent Frauds": By Samuel Johnson', *Library* 6th ser. viii (1986), 249–64.

Roberts, W., 'Tricks of the 18th-century Publishers', *Bookworm*, vi (1893), 305–12.

Roberts, W., 'A Publisher's Stock Book', *TLS* (4 Jan. 1936), 20, 40.

Robinson, A.M. Lewin, 'Richardson, James Mallcott', *NQ* ccv (1960), 191.

Robinson, F.J.G., and P.J. Wallis, *Book Subscription Lists: A Revised Guide* (Newcastle: H. Hill, 1975, with *Supplements*, 1976–).

Rogers, J.W., *U.S. National Bibliography and the Copyright Law: An Historical Study* (New York: Bowker, 1960).

Rogers, Pat, 'Johnson's *Lives of the Poets* and the Biographic Dictionaries', *RES* n.s. xxxi (1980), 149–71.

Roscoe, S., *Thomas Bewick: a Bibliography Raisonné of Editions of the General History of Quadrupeds, The History of British Birds, and The Fables of Aesop, Issued during His Lifetime* (London: Oxford University Press, 1953).

—— *John Newbery and His Successors 1740–1814* (Wormley, Herts.: Five Owls Press, 1973).

Rostenberg, Leona, 'Richard and Anne Baldwin, Whig Patriot Publishers', *PBSA* xlvii (1953), 1–42.

Rothschild, Baron Nathaniel M.V., *The Rothschild Library: A Catalogue of the Collection of Eighteenth-Century Printed Books and Manuscripts formed by Lord Rothschild*, 2 vols. (Cambridge: Cambridge University Press, 1954).

Rowan, D.F., 'Johnson's *Lives*: An Unrecorded Variant and a New Portrait', *BC* i (1952), 174–5.

Rudolph, Frederick, *Essays on Education in the Early Republic* (Cambridge, Mass.: Harvard University Press, 1965).

Rugen, Paul R., 'A Printer in New York: John Townley West's Receipt Book, 1831–1837', *BNYPL* lxxv (1971), 174–5.

Ruhe, Edward, 'The Two Samuel Johnsons', *NQ* cxcix (1954), 432–5.

Ryley, Robert M., 'Warburton's Copy of Theobald's *Shakespeare*', *TCBS* vii (1980), 449–56.

Sabin, Joseph, *A Dictionary of Books relating to America*, 29 vols. (New York: Joseph Sabin, 1868–1936).

Sale, William M., *Samuel Richardson: A Bibliographical Record of His Literary Career with Historical Notes* (New Haven, Conn.: Yale University Press, 1936).

—— *Samuel Richardson: Master Printer* (Ithaca, NY: Cornell University Press, 1950).

Sallander, Hans (comp.), *Bibliotheca Walleriana: The Books Illustrating the History of Medicine and Science Collected by Eric Waller* (Stockholm: Almquist & Wicksell, 1955).

Sargent, G.H., 'James Rivington, Tory Printer . . .', *American Collector*, ii (1926), 336–8.

Saunders, J.W., *The Profession of English Letters* (London: Routledge and Kegan Paul; Toronto: Toronto University Press, 1964).

Savage, William, *A Dictionary of the Art of Printing* (London: Longman, Brown, Green, and Longman, 1841).

Schoenbaum, S., *Shakespeare's Lives* (Oxford: Clarendon Press, 1970).

Scholes, Percy A., *The Life and Activities of Sir John Hawkins, Musician, Magistrate, and Friend of Johnson* (London: Oxford University Press, 1953).

Scholes, R.E., 'Dr Johnson and the Bibliographical Criticism of Shakespeare, *SQ* xi (1960), 163–71.

Schonveld, C.W., 'Samuel Johnson's *Life of Dr. Boerhaave* and a Dutch Translation', in *The Age of Boerhaave* (Leiden: E.J. Brill, 1983), 17–21.

Scott, G.K., 'Wright: Bathoe: Early Circulating Libraries', *NQ* clxxii (1937), 190, 321.

Seary, Peter, 'The Early Editors of Shakespeare and the Judgements of Johnson', in Korshin (ed.), *Johnson after 200 Years*, 175–86.

—— *Lewis Theobald and the Editing of Shakespeare* (Oxford: Clarendon Press, 1990).

Segar, Mary, 'Dictionary Making in the Early Eighteenth Century', *RES* vii (1931), 210–13.

Shaw, Graham, *Printing in Calcutta to 1800: A Description and Checklist of Printing in Late 18th-Century Calcutta* (London: Oxford University Press for the Bibliographical Society, 1981).

Shaw, Ralph R., and Richard H. Shoemaker, *et al.* (comps.), *American Bibliography: A Preliminary Checklist for 1800[–1819]*, 23 vols. (New York: Scarecrow, 1958–83), continued as *A Checklist of American Imprints*, 20 vols. (New York: Scarecrow, 1964–84).

Shaw, William, *Memoirs of the Life and Writings of the Late Dr. Samuel Johnson* (London: Printed for J. Walker, 1785).

Sher, R.B., 'Percy, Shaw and the Ferguson "Cheat": National Prejudice in the Ossian Wars', in Gaskill (ed.), *Ossian Revisited*, 207–45.

Sherbo, Arthur, 'Dr Johnson's *Dictionary*: A Preliminary Puff', *PQ* xxxi (1952), 91–3.

—— 'Dr. Johnson's Revision of His *Dictionary*', *PQ* xxxi (1952), 372–82.

—— 'The Making of *Ramblers* 186 and 187', *PMLA* lxvii (1952), 575–80.

—— 'The Proof-Sheets of Dr. Johnson's Preface to Shakespeare', *BJRL* xxxv (1952–3), 206–10.

—— 'Two Additions to the Johnson Canon', *JEGP* lii (1953), 543–8.

—— 'The Cancels in Dr Johnson's *Works* (Oxford 1825)', *PBSA* xlvii (1953), 376–8.

—— Review of T.J. Monagham (1953), *PQ* xxxiii (1954), 283–4.

—— 'Christopher Smart and *The Universal Visiter*', *Library*, 5th ser. x (1955), 203–5.

—— 'A Possible Addition to the Johnson Canon', *RES* n.s. vi (1955), 70–1.

—— 'Two Notes on Johnson's Revisions in Mrs Masters' Poems', *MLR* l (1955), 311–15.

—— *Samuel Johnson, Editor of Shakespeare* (Urbana: University of Illinois Press, 1956).

—— 'Solomon Mendes, a Friend of the Poets', *PQ* xxxvi (1957), 508–11.

—— 'Sanguine Expectations: Dr Johnson's *Shakespeare*', *SQ* ix (1958), 426–8.

—— 'Samuel Johnson and the *Gentleman's Magazine*', in Wahba (ed.), *Johnsonian Studies*, 133–59.

—— 'Samuel Johnson and Certain Poems in the May 1747 *Gentleman's Magazine*', *RES* n.s. xvii (1966), 382–90.

—— 'Samuel Johnson's "Essay" on Du Halde's *Description of China*', *Papers on Language and Literature*, ii (1966), 372–80.

—— 'Samuel Johnson and Giuseppe Baretti: A Question of Translation', *RES* n.s. xix (1968), 405–11.

—— 'Some Observations on Johnson's Prefaces and Dedications', in Middendorf (ed.), *English Writers of the Eighteenth Century*, 122–42.

—— '1773: The Year of Revision', *ECS* vii (1973), 18–39.

—— 'George Steevens's 1785 Variorum Shakespeare', *SB* xxxii (1979), 241–6.

—— 'Isaac Reed and the *European Magazine*', *SB* xxxvii (1984), 210–27.

—— 'Additions to the Nichols File of the *Gentleman's Magazine*', *SB* xxxvii (1984), 228–33.

—— *The Birth of Shakespeare Studies: Commentators from Rowe (1709) to Boswell-Malone (1821)* (E. Lansing, Mich.: Colleagues Press, 1986).

—— '*The Bibliographer, Book-Lore,* and *The Bookworm*', *SB* xl (1987), 207–19.

—— ' "Hesiod" Cooke and the Subscription Game', *SB* xli (1988), 267–70.

—— 'From the *Westminster Magazine*: Swift, Goldsmith, Garrick, *et al.*', *SB* xli (1988), 270–83.

—— *Isaac Reed, Editorial Factotum* (Victoria, BC: English Literary Studies, University of Victoria, 1989).

—— 'Further Additions to the Nichols File of the *Gentleman's Magazine*', *SB* xlii (1989), 249–54.

—— 'From the *Monthly Magazine, and British Register*: Notes on Milton, Pope, Boyce, Johnson, Sterne, Hawkesworth, and Prior', *SB* xliii (1990), 190–7.

—— *The Achievement of George Steevens* (New York: Peter Lang, 1990).

Sherwood, Irma Z., 'Johnson and *The Preceptor*: An Addition to the Canon', *Transactions of the Johnson Society Northwest*, vii (1974), 1–18.

Shorter, A.H., *Paper Mills and Paper Makers in England, 1495–1800* (Hilversum: Paper Publications Society, 1957).

Shrove, R.H., 'Cheap Book Production in the United States, 1870 to 1891', MA thesis (University of Illinois, 1937).

Siebert, Frederick Seaton, *Freedom of the Press in England, 1476–1776: The Rise and Decline of Government Controls* (Urbana: University of Illinois Press, 1952).

Simmons, J.S.G., 'Samuel Johnson "on the Banks of the Wolga" ', *Oxford Slavonic Papers*, xi (1964), 28–37.

Simms, R., *Bibliotheca Staffordiensis; or, a Bibliographical Account of Books and Other Printed Matter Relating to, Printed or Published in, or Written by a Native, Resident, or Person Deriving a Title from the County of Stafford* (Lichfield: Privately printed, 1894).

—— 'Dr Johnson: Dr John Swan: Dr Watts', *NQ* 10th ser. vii (1907) 348–9, with further discussion 475; viii (1908), 178.

Skeel, E.E., *A Bibliography of the Writings of Noah Webster*, ed. Edwin H. Carpenter, Jr. (New York: New York Public Library, 1958).

Skinner, Robert T., *A Notable Family of Scots Printers* (Edinburgh: Privately printed by T. and A. Constable, 1927).

Sledd, James H., and Gwin J. Kolb, *Dr Johnson's Dictionary. Essays in the Biography of a Book* (Chicago: University of Chicago Press, 1955).

Small, Miriam Rossiter, *Charlotte Ramsay Lennox: An Eighteenth Century Lady of Letters* (New Haven, Conn.: Yale University Press, 1935).

Smiles, Samuel, *A Publisher and His Friends: Memoir and Correspondence of the Late John Murray*, 2 vols. (London: John Murray, 1891).

Smith, Albert H., 'John Nichols, Printer and Publisher', *Library*, 5th ser. xviii (1963), 169–90.

Smith, B.T. Knight, 'Dr Johnson and the Chief Accountant', *The Old Lady* (Dec. 1928), 410–13.

Smith, David Nichol, 'Johnson's Revisions of His Publications', *Johnson & Boswell Revised by Themselves and Others: Three Essays by David Nichol Smith, R.W. Chapman and L.F. Powell* (Oxford: Clarendon Press, 1928), 7–18.

—— *Samuel Johnson's 'Irene'* (Oxford: Clarendon Press, 1929).

—— 'The Contributors to *The Rambler* and *The Idler*', *BQR* vii (1934), 508–9.

—— 'Thomas Warton's Miscellany: *The Union*', *RES* xix (1943), 263–75.

Smith, George and Frank Benger, *The Oldest London Bookshop: A History of Two Hundred Years* (London: Ellis, 1928).

Smith, John Thomas, *Nollekens and his Times, comprehending a Life of That Celebrated Sculptor and Memoirs of Several Contemporary Artists*, 2 vols. (London: Colburn, 1828).

Smith, Margaret (ed.), *Index of English Literary Manuscripts*, III. ii (John Gay–Ambrose Philips) (London: Mansell, 1989).

Smollett, Tobias, *The Letters of Tobias Smollett*, ed. Lewis M. Knapp (Oxford: Clarendon Press, 1970).

Solberg, Thorvald, *Copyright in Congress, 1789–1904* (Washington, DC: Government Printing Office, 1905).

Soulsby, B.H., *A Catalogue of the Works of Linnaeus (and Publications More Immediately relating Thereto) Preserved in the Libraries of the British Museum*, 2nd edn. (London: British Museum, 1933).

Speck, W.A., 'Politicians, Peers, and Publication by Subscription', in Rivers (ed.), *Books and Their Readers in Eighteenth-Century England*, 47–68.

Stenton, Michael and Stephen Lees (comps.), *Who's Who of British Members of Parliament: A Biographical Dictionary of the House of Commons*, 4 vols. (Hassocks: Harvester, 1976–81).

Stern, Madeleine B., *Publishers for Mass Entertainment in Nineteenth-Century America* (Boston: G.K. Hall, 1980).

—— *Books and Book People in 19th-century America* (New York: Bowker, 1978).

Steven, Sir Leslie, and Sir Sidney Lee (eds.), *The Dictionary of National Biography: From the Earliest Times to 1900* (London: Oxford University Press, 1921–2).

Stevenson, A.H., *Observations on Paper as Evidence* (Lawrence: University of Kansas Libraries, 1961).

—— *Catalogue of Botanical Books in the Collection of Rachel McMasters Miller Hunt* [including 'A Bibliographical Method for the Description of Botanical Books'], vol. ii, comp. A.H. Stevenson (Pittsburgh, Pa.: Hunt Botanical Library, 1961).

Stevenson, Edward Luther, *Terrestrial and Celestial Globes: Their History and Construction* (New Haven, Conn.: Yale University Press for the Hispanic Society of America, 1921).

Stewart, David, *Sketches of the Character, Manners, and Present State of the Highlanders of Scotland, with Details of the Military Service of the Highland Regiments*, 2 vols. (Edinburgh, 1822).

Stewart, James D., Muriel E. Hammond, and Erwin Saenger (comps.), *British Union-Catalogue of Periodicals: A Record of the Periodicals of the World, from the Seventeenth Century to the Present Day, in British Libraries* (London: Butterworths, 1955).

Stewart, Mary Margaret, 'Smart, Kenrick, Carnan and Newbery: New Evidence on the Paper War, 1750–51', *Library*, 6th ser. v (1983), 32–43.

Stiles, Robert E., 'Dr Samuel Johnson's *Taxation No Tyranny* and Its Half Title', *American BC* i (1932), 155–6.

Stockwell, L., 'The Dublin Pirates and the English Laws of Copyright', *Dublin Magazine*, n.s. xii (1937), 30–40.

Stoddard, Roger E., *Marks in Books, Illustrated and Explained* (Cambridge, Mass.: Houghton Library, Harvard University, 1985).

Stratman, Carl J. (comp.), *A Bibliography of English Printed Tragedy, 1565–1900* (Carbondale: Southern Illinois University Press, 1966).

Straus, Ralph, *Robert Dodsley: Poet, Publisher & Playwright* (London: Bodley Head, 1910).

—— *The Unspeakable Curll, being Some Account of Edmund Curll, Bookseller* (London: Chapman and Hall, 1927).

Streeter, Harold Wade, *The Eighteenth-Century English Novel in French Translation: A Bibliographical Study* (New York: B. Blom, 1970).

Sullivan, Alvin (ed.), *British Literary Magazines*, vol. 1: *The Augustan Age and the Age of Johnson, 1698–1788*; vol. 2: *The Romantic Ages, 1789–1836* (Westport, Conn.: Greenwood Press, 1983).

Sutherland, James, *The Restoration Newspaper and its Development* (Cambridge: Cambridge University Press, 1986).

Sutherland, John, 'The British Book Trade and the Crash of 1826', *Library*, 6th ser. ix (1987), 148–61.

'Sylvanus Urban', 'The Autobiography of Sylvanus Urban', *Gentleman's Magazine*, cci (1856), 1–9, 131–40, 267–77, 531–41, 667–77; ccii (1857) 3–10, 149–57, 282–90, 379–87.

Tannenbaum, Samuel A. and Dorothy R. Tannenbaum, 'Roger Ascham', *Elizabethan Bibliographies*, 10 vols. (Port Washington, NY: Kennikat Press, 1967), i. 1–10.

Tanselle, G. Thomas, 'The Historiography of American Literary Publishing', *SB* xviii (1965), 3–39.

—— 'Copyright Records and the Bibliographer', *SB* xxii (1969), 77–124.

—— *A Guide to the Study of United States Imprints*, 2 vols. (Cambridge, Mass.: Belknap Press of Harvard University Press, 1971).

Taylor, Charles, 'Recollections of Circumstances Connected with the History of the Arts in Great Britain: And Especially with the Progress of Public Exhibitions of Works of Art', in *The Literary Panorama, or National Register*, iii (London: Cox, Son, & Baylis, 1808), 1010–18.

Taylor, F., 'Johnsoniana from the Bagshawe Muniments in the John Rylands Library: Sir James Caldwell, Dr. Hawkesworth, Dr. Johnson, and Boswell's Use of the "Caldwell Minute" ', *BJRL* xxxv (1952), 211–47, 249–50.

Taylor, James Stephen, *Jonas Hanway, Founder of the Marine Society: Charity and Policy in Eighteenth-Century Britain* (London: Scolar, 1985).

Taylor, Sr M. Eustace, *William Julius Mickle (1734–1788): A Critical Study* (Washington, DC: Catholic University of America, 1937).

Taylor, Richard Vickerman, *The Biographia Leodiensis; or, Biographical Sketches of the Worthies of Leeds and Neighbourhood* (London, 1865–7).

Tegg, T., *A Memoir of the Late Thomas Tegg, Abridged from his Autobiography by Permission of His Son, William Tegg* (Privately printed, 1870).

Thomas, Eugene J., 'A Bibliographical and Critical Analysis of Dr Johnson's *Dictionary* with Special Reference to Twentieth-Century Scholarship', Ph.D. thesis (University of Wales Institute of Science and Technology, 1974).

—— 'Dr Johnson and His Amanuenses', *TJSL* (1974), 26–30.

Tierney, James E., 'More on George Faulkner and the London Book Trade', *Factotum*, xix (1984), 8–11.

Timperley, C.H., *A Dictionary of Printers and Printing* (London: H. Johnson, 1839).

—— *An Encyclopædia of Literary and Typographical Anecdotes* (London: Henry G. Bohn, 1842).

Tinker, Chauncey Brewster, *Rasselas in the New World* (New Haven, Conn.: Yale University Press, 1925).

—— *The Wedgwood Medallion of Samuel Johnson: A Study in Iconography* (Cambridge, Mass.: Harvard University Press, 1926).

—— *The Tinker Library: A Bibliographical Catalogue of the Books collected by Chauncey Brewster Tinker*, comp. Robert F. Metzdorf (New Haven, Conn.: Yale University Press, 1959).

Todd, William B., '18th-Century Printing and Publishing', *TLS* (6 June 1952), 377.

—— 'Concurrent Printing: An Analysis of Dodsley's *Collection of Poems by Several Hands*', *PBSA* xlvi (1952), 45–57.

—— 'Concealed Editions of Samuel Johnson', *BC* ii (1953), 59–65.

—— 'Johnson's *Marmor Norfolciense*', *BC* ii (1953), 73.

—— 'The Printing of Johnson's *Journey* (1775)', *SB* vi (1954), 247–54.

—— 'The "Private Issues" of *The Deserted Village*', *SB* vi (1954), 25–44.

—— 'The "Private Issues' of *The Deserted Village* [Addendum]', *SB* vii (1955), 239.

—— 'Quadruple Imposition: An Account of Goldsmith's *Traveller*', *SB* vii (1955), 103–11.

—— 'The First Editions of *The Good Natur'd Man* and *She Stoops to Conquer*', *SB* xi (1958), 133–42.

—— 'Reynolds's Discourses. 1769–1791', *BC* vii (1958), 417–18.

—— 'Variants in Johnson's *Dictionary*, 1755', *BC* xiv (1965), 212-13.

—— 'A Bibliographical Account of *The Gentleman's Magazine*, 1731–1754', *SB* xviii (1965), 81–109.

—— 'London Printers' Imprints, 1800–1840', *Library*, 5th ser. xxi (1966), 46–59.

—— (comp.), *A Directory of Printers and Others in Allied Trades: London and Vicinity 1800–1840* (London: Printing Historical Society, 1972).

—— and Ann Bowden, *Tauchnitz International Editions in English, 1841–1955: A Bibliographical History* (New York: Bibliographical Society of America, 1988).

—— and Peter J. Wallis, 'Provincial Booksellers *c*.1744: The *Harleian Miscellany* Subscription List', *Library*, 5th ser. xxix (1974), 422–40.

Tommey, R., 'Fielding Lucas, jr. First Major Catholic Publisher and Bookseller in Baltimore, Maryland, 1804–1854', diss. (Catholic University of America, 1952).

Tracy, Clarence R., *The Artificial Bastard: A Biography of Richard Savage* (Toronto: University of Toronto Press, 1953).

—— 'Johnson and the Common Reader', *DR* lvii (1977), 405–23.

Treadwell, Michael, 'London Printers and Printing Houses in 1705', *PH* vii (1980), 5–44.

—— 'London Trade Publishers 1675–1750', *Library*, 6th ser. iv (1982), 99–134.

Tredrey, F.D., *The House of Blackwood, 1804–1954: The History of a Publishing Firm* (Edinburgh: W. Blackwood, 1954).

Trewin, J.C., and E.M. King, *Printer to the House: The Story of Hansard* (London: Methuen, 1952).

Tryon, W.S., 'Book Distribution in Mid-Nineteenth Century America illustrated by the Publishing Records of Ticknor and Fields, Boston', *PBSA* xli (1947), 210–30.

Tuer, A.W., *Bartolozzi and His Works*, 2 vols. (London: Field & Tuer, 1881).

Turner, John R., 'Title-Pages Produced by the Walter Scott Publishing Co Ltd', *SB* xliv (1991), 323–31.

Turner, Michael L., 'Andrew Wilson: Lord Stanhope's Stereotype Printer', *JPHS* ix (1973–4), 22–65.

—— 'The Minute Book of the Partners in the *Grub Street Journal*', *PH* iv (1978), 49–94.

Twiss, R., *Miscellanies*, 2 vols. (London: T. Egerton, 1805).

Tyson, Gerald P., 'Joseph Johnson, an Eighteenth-Century Bookseller', *SB* xxviii (1975), 1–16.

—— *Joseph Johnson: A Liberal Publisher* (Iowa City: University of Iowa Press, 1979).

Tyson, Moses and Henry Guppy (eds.), *The French Journals of Mrs Thrale and Doctor Johnson* (Manchester: Manchester University Press, 1932).

University of London, *The Sterling Library: A Catalogue of Printed Books and Literary Manuscripts Collected by Sir Louis Sterling and Presented by Him to the University of London*, comp. Margaret Cannery (Cambridge: Privately printed, 1954).

Updike, Daniel Berkeley, *Printing Types: Their History, Forms, and Use*, 2nd edn., 2 vols. (Cambridge, Mass.: Harvard University Press, 1937).

Viets, Henry R., 'Johnson and Cheyne', *TLS* (5 Feb. 1954), 89.

Vizetelly, F.H., *The Development of the Dictionary of the English Language, with Special Reference to the Funk & Wagnalls New Standard Dictionary* (New York: Funk & Wagnalls, 1923).

Wahba, Magdi (ed.), *Bicentenary Essays on Rasselas* (Cairo, 1959).

—— *Johnsonian Studies* (Cairo, 1962).

Walker, W., *The Life of George Gleig* (Edinburgh, 1878).

Wallis, P.J., 'Book Subscription Lists', *Library*, 5th ser. xxix (1974), 255–86.

—— *The Book Trade in Northumberland and Durham to 1860: A Supplement to C.J. Hunt's Biographical Dictionary* (Newcastle upon Tyne: Thorne's Bookshop, 1981).

Walmsley, R., 'Gleanings amongst Old Manchester Bookmen and Booksellers', *MR* viii (1959), 190–303.

Walpole Society, 'The Papers of the Society of Artists of Great Britain', vi (1917–18), 113–23.

Walters, Gwyn, 'The Booksellers in 1759 and 1774: The Battle for Literary Property', *Library*, 5th ser. xxix (1974), 287–311.

Wanley, Humfrey, *The Diary of Humfrey Wanley, 1715–26*, ed. C.E. Wright and R.C. Wright, 2 vols. (London: The Bibliographical Society, 1966).

Ward, C.C., and R.E. Ward, 'Literary Piracy in the 18th Century Book Trade: the Case of George Faulkner and Alexander Donaldson', *Factotum*, xvii (1983), 25–35.

Ward, Robert E., *Prince of Dublin Printers: The Letters of George Faulkner* (Lexington: University of Kentucky Press, 1972).

Warren, Arthur, *The Charles Whittinghams, Printers* (New York: Grolier Club, 1896).

Warrington, Bernard, 'William Pickering, Bookseller and Book Collector', *BJRL* lxxi (1989), 121–38.

Watson, George (ed.), *The New Cambridge Bibliography of English Literature*, 5 vols. (Cambridge: Cambridge University Press, 1969–77).

Watson, Melvin R., *Magazine Serials and the Essay Tradition, 1746–1820* (Baton Rouge: Louisiana State University Press, 1956).

Watson, S.F., *Some Materials for a History of Printing and Publishing in Ipswich* (Ipswich, 1949).

Watt, Ian, 'Publishers and Sinners: The Augustan View', *SB* xii (1959), 3–20.

Weber, Carl J., 'American Editions of English Authors', in Gordon N. Ray, Carl J. Weber, and John Carter, *Nineteenth-Century English Books: Some Problems in Bibliography* (Urbana: University of Southern Illinois Press, 1952), 25–50.

Webster, Noah, *The Letters of Noah Webster*, ed. Harry R. Warfel (New York: Library Publishers, 1953).

Weedon, M.J.P., 'Richard Johnson and the Successors to John Newbery', *Library*, 5th ser. iv (1949–50), 25–63.

Weekley, Montague, *Thomas Bewick* (London: Oxford University Press, 1953).

Weinbrot, Howard D., 'Samuel Johnson's "Short Song of Congratulation" and the Accompanying Letter to Mrs. Thrale: The Huntington Library Manuscripts', *HLQ* xxxiv (1970–1), 79–80.

Welford, R., 'Early Newcastle Typography', *Archaeologia Aeliana*, 3rd ser. iii (1907), 1–134; iv (1908), 147–53.

Wellcome Historical Medical Library, *A Catalogue of Printed Books in the Wellcome Historical Medical Library*, 3 vols. (London, 1962–).

Wells, Charles, 'Bristol Booksellers and Printers', *NQ* 11th ser. ii (1910), 23–4.

Welsh, Charles, *A Bookseller of the Last Century, being Some Account of the Life of John Newbery and of the Books He Published* (London: Griffith, Farran, Okeden & Welsh; New York: E.P. Dutton, 1885; rpt. Clifton: Augustus M. Kelley, 1972).

Wendorf, Richard, 'Robert Dodsley as Editor', *SB* xxxi (1978), 235–48.

—— 'The Making of Johnson's "Life of Collins" ', *PBSA* lxxiv (1980), 95–115.

Werdet, Edmond, *De la Librairie française: son Passé, son Présent, son Avenir, avec des Notices Biographiques sur les Libraires-Éditeurs les plus distingués depuis 1789–1860* (Paris, 1840).

Westby-Gibson, John, *The Bibliography of Shorthand* (London: Pitman, 1887).

Whale, R.F., *Copyright: Evolution, Theory, and Practice* (Totawa, NJ: Roman & Littlefield, 1972).

Wheeler, J.T., *The Maryland Press, 1777–1790* (Baltimore, Md.: The Maryland Historical Society, 1938).

Whiston, J.W., 'Some Letters and Accounts of Michael Johnson', *TJSL* (1974), 31–51.

Wilding, Michael, 'Michael Johnson: An Auction Sale', *NQ* ccxiv (1969), 181–2.

Wiles, Roy M., *Serial Publication in England before 1750* (Cambridge: Cambridge University Press, 1957).

—— 'Dates in English Imprints, 1700–52', *Library*, 5th ser. xii (1957), 190–3.

—— *Freshest Advices: Early Provincial Newspapers in England* (Columbus: Ohio State University Press, 1965).

—— 'The Contemporary Distribution of Johnson's *Rambler*', *ECS* ii (1968–9), 155–71.

Williams, Iolo Aneurin, 'The Teggs (Thomas and William)', *NQ* 12th ser. vii (1920), 48, with further discussion 92.

—— *Seven XVIIIth Century Bibliographies* (London: Dulau & Co., 1924).

—— 'John Wesley, Publisher', *NQ* cxlviii (1925), 279, with further discussion 428.

Williams, Terence (comp.), *A Checklist of Linneana, 1735–1834 in the University of Kansas Libraries* (Lawrence: University of Kansas, 1964).

Wilson, C.H. (ed.), *Brookiana*, 2 vols. (London: R. Phillips, 1804).

Wiltshire, John, *Samuel Johnson in the Medical World: The Doctor and the Patient* (Cambridge: Cambridge University Press, 1991).

Winans, Robert B., 'Works by and about Samuel Johnson in Eighteenth-Century America', *PBSA* lxii (1968), 537–46.

Windham, William, *The Windham Papers: The Life and Correspondence of the Rt. Hon. William Windham, 1750–1810*, ed. L.S. Benjamin, 2 vols. (London: Herbert Jenkins, 1913).

Winterich, John T., *Early American Books and Printing* (Boston, Mass.: Houghton Mifflin, 1935).

Wolpe, Richard J., *Marbled Paper: Its History, Techniques, and Patterns* (Philadelphia: University of Pennsylvania Press, 1990).

Woodmansee, Martha, 'The Genius and the Copyright: Economic and Legal Conditions of the Emergence of the "Author" ', *ECS* xvii (1983–4), 425–48.

Woodruff, James F., 'Dr Johnson's Advertisement for "The Spectator", 1776, and the Source of Our Information about Johnson's Receipts from "Irene": Two Notes on a Volume of Johnsoniana once belonging to Isaac Reed,' *NQ* ccxvi (1971), 61–2.

—— 'The Background and Significance of the *Rambler*'s Format', *PH* iv (1978), 113–33.

—— 'A Possible Johnson Letter in the "Daily Advertiser" ', *NQ* ccxxiv (1979), 35–7.

Woodson, William C., 'The 1785 Variorum Shakespeare', *SB* xxviii (1975), 318–20.

—— 'The Printer's Copy for the 1785 Variorum Shakespeare', *SB* xxxi (1978), 208–10.

—— 'Isaac Reed's 1785 Variorum Shakespeare', *SB* xxxix (1986), 220–9.

Wooll, J., *Biographical Memoirs of Joseph Warton* (1806).

'Works of Samuel Johnson in America, 1768–1820', *PAAS* xxxviii (1929), 215–16.

Wright, Alexander Tremaine, *The Two Angells of Stenography* (London: Truelove & Bray, 1919).

Wright, C.E., 'Edward Harley, 2nd Earl of Oxford, 1689–1741' (Portrait of a Bibliophile VIII), *BC* xi (1962), 158–74.

Wright, J.D. 'Some Unpublished Letters to and from Dr. Johnson', *BJRL* xvi (1932), 32–76.

Wright, W., 'Vernor, Hood & Sharp', *NQ* 8th ser. vi (1894), 47, with further discussion 111–12.

Wrigley, E.A., and R.S. Schofield, *The Population History of England 1541–1871: A Reconstruction* (Cambridge: Cambridge University Press, 1981).

Wroth, Lawrence C., *The History of Printing in Colonial Maryland, 1686–1776* (Baltimore, Md.: Typothetae of Baltimore, 1922).

—— *The Colonial Printer* (Portland, Me.: Southworth-Anthoensen Press, 1938).

Yeowell, James, *A Literary Antiquary: Memoir of William Oldys* (London: Spottiswoode, 1862).

Yung, Kai Kin, *Handlist of Manuscripts & Documents in the Johnson Birthplace Museum* (Lichfield: Lichfield City Council, 1972).

—— *Samuel Johnson, 1709–1784: A Bicentenary Exhibition* (London: Arts Council of London, 1984).

Chronological List of Publications

This list presents the items treated in the bibliography chronologically, year by year, providing a chronological index to the bibliography by Fleeman number. Publications within a year are listed in the order of their numbers. The numbers are followed by short titles (usually those to be found in the body of the bibliography), and they in turn are followed by dates of publication. When the precise date of publication is unknown and a date of printing is available, the latter is supplied (ptd.), but it does not determine the place of the item in the chronological sequence. To avoid repetition, editions of the Miniature Dictionary (56.1MD) are grouped together each year, and collections with no independent number are listed under the first Fleeman number to which they are attached.

1731

31.10HM/1 John Husbands's Miscellany (Messia), Oct.

1733

33BJ Birmingham Journal
33BS Brodhurst's Sermons

1734

34.7PP Proposals for the Latin Poems of Politian, 5 Aug.

1735

35.2LV/1a Lobo's Voyage to Abyssinia, first issue, 1 Feb.
35.2LV/1b Lobo's Voyage to Abyssinia, second issue, ?19 June
35.?6SC A Scheme of Classes of a Grammar School, ?June

1736

36GM6 Gentleman's Magazine, Vol. VI

1737

37.10HAP Hon. Henry Hervey-Aston's Proposals for an edition of his Miscellaneous Poems, before 17 Oct.

1738

38.4PM/1a Prévost's Memoirs (Vol. I), 25 Apr.
38.5L/1a London, first edition, 13 May
38.5L/2 London, first Dublin edition, ?May
38.5L/3 London, 'second' edition, c.20 May
38.5L/4 London, 'London' [Edinburgh] edition, ?Summer
38.5L/5 London, 'third' edition, 15 July
38.10SP Proposals for Printing the History of the Council of Trent, 21 Oct.
38.10DA The Daily Advertiser, 21 Oct.
38.11HAE/1 Hon. Henry Hervey-Aston, Epitaph on Queen Caroline, ?Nov.
38GM8 Gentleman's Magazine, Vol. VIII

1739

38.5L/6 London, 'fourth' edition
39.4DA Daily Advertiser, 13 Apr.
39.4MN/1 Marmor Norfolciense, first edition, Apr.
39.5CV A Compleat Vindication, May
39.10CP/1a Crousaz, Commentary on Pope, first edition, first issue, Oct.
39GM9 Gentleman's Magazine, Vol. IX

1740

40.4GP Prologue to Garrick's Lethe, 15 Apr.

40.5TKK History of Tahmas Kuli Khan, May

40.7LB/1 Life of Blake, first separate publication, July or Aug.

40GM10 Gentleman's Magazine, Vol. X

40GM10/EE/1 Essay on Epitaphs, The Gentleman's, or Universal Museum, Sept.

1741

38.4PM/1b Prévost's Memoirs, Vol. I, second issue, ?Nov.

39.10CP/1b Crousaz, Commentary on Pope, first edition, second issue, Nov.

41.6JP Proposals for James's Medicinal Dictionary, 24 June

41GM11 Gentleman's Magazine, Vol. XI

1742

42.2JMD James's Medicinal Dictionary, 4 Feb. 1742-Jan. 1745

42.5MA/1a Monarchy Asserted, folio, May

42.5MA/1b Monarchy Asserted, octavo, May

42.11HP/1a Proposals for the Harleian Catalogue, 1 Nov.

42.11SW/1 Life of Sydenham, 16 Nov.

42.12MC Miscellaneous Correspondence, 10 Dec. 1742-July 1748

42GM12 Gentleman's Magazine, Vol. XII

1743

43.1CBH Harleian Catalogue, Jan. 1743-Apr. 1745

43.8GEP General Evening Post, 25 Aug.

43.12HMP Proposals for the Harleian Miscellany, ?30 Dec.

43GM13 Gentleman's Magazine, Vol. XIII

1744

44.2LS/1 Life of Savage, first edition, 11 Feb.

44.4LBa Life of Barretier, separate issue, Apr.

44.4HM/1a Harleian Miscellany, first edition, Apr.

44.4HM/1b Harleian Miscellany, Catalogue of Pamphlets, Apr.

44.9PP/1a Proposals for The Publisher, 24 Sept.

44GM14 Gentleman's Magazine, Vol. XIV

1745

45.4MM Miscellaneous Observations on Macbeth, ?6 Apr.

45.4SP Proposals for a New Edition of Shakespeare, ?6 Apr.

45.5HAS/1a Henry Hervey-Aston, Sermon, May

45.10MBM/1a Samuel Madden, Boulter's Monument, first edition, first issue, 25 Oct.

45.10MBM/1b Samuel Madden, Boulter's Monument, first edition, second issue

45.10MBM/2 Samuel Madden, Boulter's Monument, Dublin

45.11P The Publisher ?25 Dec.

45GM15 Gentleman's Magazine, Vol. XV

1746

42.2JMD/TF James's Medicinal Dictionary, French translation, 1746-8

46.3DM/1a Dodsley's Museum, 29 Mar.

46GM16 Gentleman's Magazine, Vol. XVI

1747

47.8LP Proposals for Lauder's Adamus Exsul, Aug.

47.8PD/1a Plan of a Dictionary, first edition, first state, 1–8 Aug.

47.8PD/1b Plan of a Dictionary, first edition, second state, 1–8 Aug.

47.10DLP/1a Prologue Spoken at Drury Lane, 8 Oct.

47.10DLP/2 Prologue Spoken at Drury Lane, piracy, '1747'

47GM17 Gentleman's Magazine, Vol. XVII

1748

38.5L/8 London, Dodsley's Collection of Poems, 1748-

44.2LS/2a Life of Savage, second edition

48.4DP/1 The Preceptor, first edition, 7 Apr.

48.4DP/2 The Preceptor, Dublin, before 8 Dec.

48.4DP/VT/1 Vision of Theodore, Gentleman's Magazine, Apr.

48GM18 Gentleman's Magazine, Vol. XVIII

1749

42.11SW/2 Life of Sydenham, second edition, Nov.

49.1VW/1 Vanity of Human Wishes, first edition, 9 Jan.

49.2I/1a Irene, first edition, 6 Feb.

49.2I/2 Irene, first Dublin edition

49.2I/5 Irene, plan and specimen, Gentleman's Magazine, Feb.

49.3GD/1 Gwynnes's Essay on Design, Mar.

49.3GD/2 Gwynnes's Essay on Design, Dublin .

49.12LEM/1a Lauder's Essay on Milton, first edition, first issue, 14 Dec.

49GM19 Gentleman's Magazine, Vol. XIX

1750

38.5L/7 London, 'fifth' edition

42.5MA/2 Monarchy Asserted, Somers's Tracts

48.4DP/VT/2 Vision of Theodore, Grand Magazine of Magazines, Aug.-Sept.

50.1St/1a The Student, Jan. 1750–1

50.3RI Raleigh's Interest, 18 Mar.

50.3R/1a The Rambler, first edition, 20 Mar. 1750–17 Mar. 1752

50.3R/2 The Rambler, first Edinburgh edition, I-IV June 1750; VII-VIII July 1752

50.4PC/1a New Prologue to Comus, first edition 5 Apr.

50.4PC/2 New Prologue to Comus, second edition

50.4GA The General Advertiser, 4 Apr.

50GM20 Gentleman's Magazine, Vol. XX

1751

49.12LEM/1b Lauder's Essay on Milton, first edition, second issue ?Jan.

50.3R/3 The Rambler, second Edinburgh edition, Vols. I-IV, 1751–3

51.1LLD Lauder's Letter to Douglas 3 Jan.

51.11DA Daily Advertiser 16 Nov.

51GM21 Gentleman's Magazine, Vol. XXI

51LSG Letter from Staffordshire, ?Aug.

1752

49.1VW/2 Vanity of Human Wishes, Dodsley's Collection

50.3R/4a The Rambler, second London edition, first issue

50.3R/4b The Rambler, second London edition, second issue I-IV; V-VI, July

50.3R/5 The Rambler, first Dublin edition, 12 Dec.

52.3LFQ/1 Lennox's The Female Quixote, first edition, 13 Mar.

52.3LFQ/2 Lennox's The Female Quixote, second edition June

52.3LFQ/3 Lennox's The Female Quixote, first Dublin edition,

52.3LFQ/A/1 Lennox's The Female Quixote, abridgement [1752]

52.11Ad/1 The Adventurer, first folio edition 1753–4, 7 Nov. 1752–9 Mar. 1754

52GM22 Gentleman's Magazine, Vol. XXII

1753

42.11SW/3 Life of Sydenham, third edition, 23 June

44.4HM/2 Harleian Miscellany, second edition of Vol. I

46.3DM/U/1 Dodsley's Museum, The Union, ?3 May

50.3R/1b The Rambler, '1753' titles

50.3R/1c The Rambler, '1750' titles, ?1753

50.3R/S/1 Rambler Selections, Cibber's Lives of the Poets

50.3R/S/2 Rambler Selections, Warton's Virgil

53.2GMI/1 General Index to Gentleman's Magazine, 17 Feb.

53.4BGD Bathurst's Scheme for a Geographical Dictionary

53.5LSI/1 Lennox's Shakespear Illustrated, 18 May 1753 (Vols. I and II), Feb. 1754 (Vol. III)

53GM23 Gentleman's Magazine, Vol. XXIII

1754

48.4DP/3 The Preceptor, 'second' edition, June

49.2I/3 Irene, 'second' edition

50.3R/TF/S/1 Rambler, French translation, Selections

50.3R/TG/1 Rambler, German translation

52.3LFQ/TG/1 Lennox's The Female Quixote, German translation

52.11Ad/2 The Adventurer, second edition, 5 Apr.

52.11Ad/3 The Adventurer, first Dublin edition

52.11Ad/TF/1 Adventurer, Le Traducteur, 10 Aug.

54GM24 Gentleman's Magazine, Vol. XXIV

1755

47.8PD/2 Plan of a Dictionary, second edition '1747', ptd. Apr.

49.1VW/3 Vanity of Human Wishes, Dodsley's Collection

50.3R/S/3a Rambler Selections, Matrimonial Preceptor, 18 Mar.

55.1WL Zachariah Williams on the Longitude, 29 Jan.

55.4MM/1 Mary Masters's Poems, Apr.

55.4MM/S/1 Mary Masters, Selection

55.4D/1a Dictionary, first edition, 15 Apr.

55.4D/2 Dictionary, second edition, 14 June (first weekly no.)

55.7OW Obituary of Zachariah Williams, died 12 July

55.7BIL Baretti's Introduction, 19 July

55.11HS Speech for W.G. Hamilton, 1 Nov.

55GM25 Gentleman's Magazine, Vol. XXV

56.11LS/1 Sully's Memoirs 1756, 8 Nov. 1755

1756

50.3R/6a The Rambler, 'fourth' edition, first issue, ptd. 7 Jan.

50.3R/6b The Rambler, 'fourth' edition, second issue

52.11Ad/4 The Adventurer, 'third' edition, 9 Dec.

56.1DA/1 Abridged Dictionary, first edition, 5 Jan.

56.1PD/1 Payne's Draughts 30 Jan.

56.1UV/1a Universal Visiter, 2 Feb. 1756-

56.2RDT/1a Rolt's Dictionary of Trade, first issue, 12 Feb.

56.3BCM/1a Browne's Christian Morals, second edition, first issue, 18 Mar.

56.4LM The Literary Magazine 1756–8, 15 May

56.6SP/1 Proposals for Shakespeare, 1 June

56GM26 Gentleman's Magazine, Vol. XXVI

1757

55.4MM/S/2 Mary Masters, Selection, Beauties

56.11LS/2 Sully's Memoirs, second edition, ptd. Mar.

57.1LC The London Chronicle, 1 Jan.

57.2BIL Baretti's Italian Library, 14 Feb.

57.2DA Daily Advertiser, 14 Feb.

57.3LMM/1 Lennox's Memoirs of de Maintenon, first edition, 12 Mar.

57.4LEH Lindsay's Evangelical History, 16 Apr.

57.5CA/1 Chambers's Chinese Architecture, ?May

57.5CA/2 Chambers's Chinese Architecture, French translation, ?May

57.9SR Speech on the Rochefort Expedition, Sept.

57.12LP/1 Lennox's Philander, first edition, 3 Dec.

57.12PBA/1 Proposals for Bennet's Ascham, first edition, advertised 7 Jan. 1758

57GM27 Gentleman's Magazine, Vol. XXVII

1758

48.4DP/4 The Preceptor, 'third' edition

50.3R/S/3/Add1 Rambler Selections, Moral Miscellany

56.1DA/2 Abridged Dictionary, Dublin edition

57.3LMM/2 Lennox's Memoirs of de Maintenon, Dublin

57.12LP/2 Lennox's Philander, second edition, Dublin, ?Jan.

58.1BP Proposals for Baretti's Poems [?Jan.]

58.2PT/1 Payne's Tables of Interest, 25 Feb.

58.4Id/1 The Idler, The Universal Chronicle, 8 Apr. 1758–5 Apr. 1760

58.5WPP Saunders Welch, Proposals to Remove Prostitutes, 22 May

58.10HP/1 History of Pompadour, 7 Oct.

58.10AS/1 Angell's Stenography

58ET Elmer's Tables, ?7 Feb. 1760.

1759

38.5L/9 and **49.1VW/4** London and Vanity of Human Wishes, Two Satires

48.4DP/VT/11 Vision of Theodore, Dutch translation in De Hollandsche Wysgeer

50.3R/S/3b Rambler Selections, Matrimonial Preceptor

56.4LM/IPS An Introduction to the Political State of Great Britain

58.10HP/2 History of Pompadour, second edition, 11 Jan.

59.4R/1 Rasselas, first edition, 19 Apr.

59.4R/2 Rasselas, Dublin edition, 12 May

59.4R/3 Rasselas, 'second' edition, 26 June

59.10WDA Advertisement for the World Displayed, 23 Oct.

59.11LEP London Evening Post, Advertisement, 24–7 Nov.

59.12WD/1a World Displayed, first edition, first issue, 1 Dec.

59.12WD/1b World Displayed, first edition, second issue

59.12DG Letters to the Daily Gazetteer, 1, 8, 15 Dec.

59.12CR8 The Critical Review, Vol. VIII, Dec.

1760

46.3DM/U/2 Dodsley's Museum, The Union, 2 Jan.

50.3R/S/4 Rambler Selections, Narrative Companion

52.11Ad/5 The Adventurer, second Dublin edition

56.1DA/3 Abridged Dictionary, 'second' edition, 14 Aug.

57.12PBA/2 Proposals for Bennet's Ascham, second edition, ptd. Aug.

59.4R/4 Rasselas, 'third, edition, 7 Apr.

59.4R/TDu/1 Rasselas, Translations, Dutch

59.4R/TF/4 Rasselas, Translations, French

59.12WD/2a World Displayed, second edition, first issue, 1759–60, ptd. May 1760

60.1PL The Public Ledger, Jan.-Dec.

60.2BM The British Magazine, Vol. I., Feb.

60.2LSA Letters for Society of Artists, 19 Jan.–26 Feb.

60.2LB Brumoy's Greek Theatre, 21 Feb.

60.3H Something for Lord Charles Hay, ?1760

60.4MM The Monthly Melody, 1 Apr.

60.4BD/1 Baretti's Italian Dictionary, first edition, 24 Apr.

60.5FBB Flloyd's Bibliotheca Biographica

60.8FP/1 Hollis's Committee for French Prisoners, Aug.

60.10JCM Robert James on Canine Madness, Oct.

60.12LSA Letter for the Society of Artists, after 25 Nov.

60GM30 Gentleman's Magazine, Vol. XXX

61.3LH/TF/1 Lennox's Henrietta, French translation of first edition

1761

46.3DM/U/3 Dodsley's Museum, The Union

48.4DP/5 The Preceptor, 'fourth' edition, Dublin

50.3R/7 The Rambler, 'fifth' edition, Jan.

50.3R/S/5 Rambler Selections, Anningait and Ajutt

56.2RDT/1b Rolt's Dictionary of Trade, second issue, ptd. Jan. 1757

56.3BCM/1b Browne's Christian Morals, second edition, second issue

56.11LS/3 Sully's Memoirs, third edition

58.4Id/2a The Idler, second edition, 13 Oct.

58.4Id/2b The Idler, Reynolds's Three Letters, ?Oct.

58.4Id/3 The Idler, first Dublin edition, 12 Dec.

59.12WD/2b World Displayed, second edition, second issue

61.1LG The London Gazette, 6–10 Jan.

61.3LH/1 Lennox's Henrietta, second edition, 19 Mar.

61.3CR11 Critical Review, Vol. XI, Apr. 1761

61.4SL/1 Sophronia

61.8GC Gwynne on the Coronation, Sept.

61.8BA/1a Life of Ascham, Bennet's Ascham, first edition, first issue, ptd. July

1762

38.5L/10 London, Newbery's Art of Poetry

52.11Ad/6 The Adventurer, 'fourth' edition, ptd. Jan. (Vol. I)

57.5CA/3 Art of Laying out Gardens, from Chambers's Chinese Architecture

58.4Id/TD/1 The Idler, Dutch translation

59.4R/TG/1 Rasselas, Translations, German

62.3KC Kennedy's Chronology, 29 Mar.

62.5SA/1 Society of Artists' Catalogue, 16 Mar.

62.7WP Proposals for Anna Williams's Miscellanies [?July]

62.11FC DuFresnoy's Tables, 19 Nov.

62GDP Proposals for Anchitell Grey's Debates [1762]

62GM32 Gentleman's Magazine, Vol. XXXII

1763

42.11SW/4a Life of Sydenham, fourth edition, first issue

48.4DP/6 The Preceptor, 'fourth' edition

49.1VW/5 Vanity of Human Wishes, Dodsley's Collection

50.3R/8 The Rambler, 'sixth' edition, ptd. Apr.

50.3R/S/6 Rambler Selections, Miscellaneous Letters

52.3LFQ/4 Lennox's The Female Quixote, second Dublin edition

56.1DA/4a Abridged Dictionary, second Dublin edition, 9 Aug.

56.11LS/4 Sully's Memoirs, fourth edition, 21 July (announced as published in monthy parts)

61.4SL/2 Sophronia, Dublin

63.1PC/1a Poetical Calendar, Jan.-Dec.

63.1PC/1b Poetical Calendar, second 'edition'

63.2HT/1 Hoole's Tasso, first edition, ?Feb.

63.4CR Critical Review, Vol. XII, Apr.

63.7KS Dr King's Speech at the Oxford Encænia, ?8 July

1764

48.4DP/7 The Preceptor, fourth/fifth edition, Dublin

56.1DA/4b Abridged Dictionary, second Dublin edition, variant

59.4R/TF/1 Rasselas, Translations, French [1764], imprimatur 23 Mar.

59.4R/TI/1 Rasselas, Translations, Italian

59.4R/TR/1 Rasselas, Translations, Russian, Apr.

63.2HT/2 Hoole's Tasso, second edition, Feb.

64.7LC London Chronicle, 3–5 July

64.710–12CR Critical Review, Oct. and Dec. 1764

64.12GT/1a Goldsmith's Traveller, first state, 19 Dec.

64.12GT/1b Goldsmith's Traveller, second state

64GH Preface to Guthrie's History, 1764–7

1765

48.4DP/TG/1 Der Lehrmeister, Leipzig, 1765–67

49.1VW/6 Vanity of Human Wishes, Dodsley's Collection

50.3R/S/7 Rambler Selections, Matrimonial Preceptor

55.4D/3 Dictionary, third edition, Oct.

56.1DA/5 Abridged Dictionary, 'third' edition, ptd. Aug.

64.12GT/1c Goldsmith's Traveller, third state

64.12GT/1d Goldsmith's Traveller, fourth state

64.12GT/2 Goldsmith's Traveller, second edition

64.12GT/3 Goldsmith's Traveller, third edition

64.12GT/4 Goldsmith's Traveller, fourth edition, 6 Aug.

65.2PR/1 Percy's Reliques, first edition, 12 Feb.

65.9TE Henry Thrale's Election Addresses, 23 Sept.–24 Dec.

65.10SP/1 Shakespeare, first edition, 10 Oct.

65.10SP/2a Shakespeare, second edition, 12 Nov.

65.10SP/2b Preface to Shakespeare

1766

46.3DM/U/4 Dodsley's Museum, The Union

49.1VW/7 Vanity of Human Wishes, Dodsley's Collection

50.3R/9 The Rambler, 'seventh' edition, 4 Dec.

52.11Ad/7 The Adventurer, 'fifth' edition

56.1DA/4c Abridged Dictionary, second Dublin edition, reissue

58.10AS/2a Angell's Stenography, second edition, first issue [1766]

59.4R/5 Rasselas, 'fourth' edition, ptd. Dec. 1765

65.2PR/2 Percy's Reliques, second edition, Dublin

65.10SP/3 Shakespeare, Dublin, Nov.

66.4BD/1 Blackrie's Disquisition, Apr.

66.4WM/1 Anna Williams's Miscellanies, 1 Apr.

66.4WM/A/1 Newspaper advertisement for Anna William's Miscellanies, 1 Apr.

66.4WM/F/1 The Fountains, HLT transcript [?1766]

66.4WM/F/2 The Fountains, HLP transcript [?1766]

66.4WM/F/3 The Fountains, British Magazine, May-June

66.4WM/F/4 The Fountains, Universal Museum, Apr.–May

66.4WM/F/5 The Fountains, London Chronicle, No. 1476 [?1766]

66.4WM/F/6 The Fountains, Caledonian Mercury, 11 June

66.6AG/1 Adams on the Globes, first edition, 10 June

66.6FS Fordyce's Sermons, June

66.7GLW/1 Gwynne's London and Westminster Improved, 14 June

66.8CL/1 Law Lectures for Robert Chambers, ?Aug.

66.11CC Considerations on Corn, Parliamentary Logick, 1808 [Nov. 1766]

1767

38.5L/11 London, Goldsmith's Beauties

44.2LS/3a Life of Savage, third edition, first issue

58.4Id/4 The Idler, 'third' edition, with additional essays, ?27 Apr.

59.12WD/3 World Displayed, third edition [?1767]

61.8BA/1b Life of Ascham, Bennet's Ascham, first edition, second issue [1767]

63.2HT/3 Hoole's Tasso, third edition

64.12GT/8 Goldsmith's Traveller, Dublin, 1767 [numbered out of sequence]

65.2PR/3a Percy's Reliques, 'second' edition, 3 Dec.

65.2PR/3b Percy's Reliques, 'second' edition, Four Essays,

67.1FT/1 Fawkes's Theocritus, first edition, ?Jan.

67.4PG/1 Payne's Geometry, first edition, Apr.

67.6HM Hoole's Metastasio, 20 June

1768

38.5L/12 London and 49.1VW/8 Vanity of Human Wishes, A Select Collection of Poems, Edinburgh

50.3R/S/8 Rambler Selections, Rasselas

56.1DA/6 Abridged Dictionary, third Dublin edition

59.4R/6 Rasselas, first American edition, Philadelphia, July

59.4R/TF/5 Rasselas, Translations, French

64.12GT/5 Goldsmith's Traveller, fifth edition

65.10SP/4 Shakespeare, Woodfall, ptd. Aug.

67.4PG/2 Payne's Geometry, second edition

68.1GGM/1 Goldsmith's Good Natur'd Man, 29 Jan.

68.2TE Henry Thrale's Election Addresses, 29 Feb.–23 Mar.

68.5LB/1 Letter to F. A. Barnard, 28 May 1768, pub. 1823

68.12HC/1a Hoole's Cyrus, first issue, 20 Dec.

68.12HC/1b Hoole's Cyrus, second 'edition' issue

1769

42.11SW/4b Life of Sydenham, fourth ['fifth'] edition, second issue

44.2LS/3b Life of Savage, third edition, second issue

48.4DP/8 The Preceptor, 'fifth' edition, ptd. Apr.-Sept.

58.4Id/S/1 Idler Selections, Thomas Percy, Sermon

63.1PC/2 Poetical Calendar, Flowers of Parnassus

66.6AG/2 Adams on the Globes, second edition

68.12HC/2 Hoole's Cyrus, Dublin

68.12HC/3 Hoole's Cyrus, third edition

69.3GNDA Letter to the Gazetteer, 13 Mar.

69.5LC London Chronicle, 29 Apr.–2 May

1770

38.4PM/2 Prévost's Memoirs, new edition

49.1VW/9 Vanity of Human Wishes, Dodsley's Collection

52.11Ad/8 The Adventurer, a new edition, ptd. Oct. (Vols. I-II)

52.11Ad/9a The Adventurer, second Dublin edition, second issue, 1770–1

56.1DA/7 Abridged Dictionary, 'fourth' edition, ptd. Apr.

58.10AS/2b Angell's Stenography, second edition, second issue, approved 25 Jan.

64.12GT/6 Goldsmith's Traveller, sixth edition

64.12GT/7 Goldsmith's Traveller, 'fifth' edition

64.12GT/9 Goldsmith's Traveller, Dublin

70.1FA/1a False Alarm, first edition, first impression, 16 Jan.

70.1FA/1b False Alarm, first edition, second impression, 6 Feb.

70.1FA/1c False Alarm, first edition, third impression, 24 Feb.

70.1FA/1d False Alarm, first edition, fourth impression, 13 Mar.

70.1FA/2 False Alarm, Dublin

70.6GD/1a Goldsmith's The Deserted Village

70.6GD/2 Goldsmith's The Deserted Village

70.6GD/3 Goldsmith's The Deserted Village

70.6GD/4 Goldsmith's The Deserted Village

70.6GD/5 Goldsmith's The Deserted Village

70.6GD/6 Goldsmith's The Deserted Village

70.11PA Fictitious Newsletters and Reports, The Public Advertiser, Oct.-Nov.

1771

44.2LS/TF/1 Life of Savage, French translation

50.3R/10 The Rambler, 'eighth' edition, ptd. Aug.

50.3R/S/9 Rambler Selections, [Anne Penney's] Poems [1771]

52.11Ad/9b The Adventurer, second Dublin edition, third issue

60.4BD/2 Baretti's Italian Dictionary, second edition, ptd. May

65.10SP/5 Shakespeare, Dublin

70–71LP Proposals for William Langley [?1771]

71.3FI/1a Falkland's Islands, first edition, first state, 16 Mar.

71.3FI/1b Falkland's Islands, first edition, second state, 21 Mar.

71.3FI/2 Falkland's Islands, Dublin

71.3FI/3 Falkland's Islands, first edition, second impression, 11 Apr.

71.3FI/4 Falkland's Islands, New York

71.3FI/TF/1 Falkland's Islands, French translation

1772

38.5L/13 London and **49.1VW/10** Vanity of Human Wishes, A Select Collection of Poems, Edinburgh, second edition

50.3R/11 The Rambler, 'eighth' edition [third Edinburgh edition]

57.5CA/4a Chambers's Dissertation, expanded from his Chinese Architecture ?May

57.5CA/TF/2 Chambers's Chinese Architecture, French translation

59.4R/TF/2 Rasselas, Translations, French

59.4R/TI/2 Rasselas, Translations, Italian

59.4R/TS/1(1) Rasselas, Translations, Spanish

63.2HT/4 Hoole's Tasso, fourth edition, ptd. Oct. 1771

66.6AG/3 Adams on the Globes, third edition

68.12HC/4 Hoole's Cyrus, 'third' edition

70.6GD/7 Goldsmith's The Deserted Village

72.2PT Payne's Trigonometry, Feb.

72.2MBG Latin motto for Sir Joseph Banks's Goat, 27 Feb. 1772 [July, 1789]

72.4BPH Boswell's Petition for Hastie, ?11 Apr.

72.7BPW/1a Boswell's Petition for James Wilson, 1 July

72.12HEIC Present State of East-India Company's Affairs, 21 Dec.

1773

48.4DP/VT/7 Vision of Theodore, Allegories and Visions for the Entertainment and Instruction of Younger Minds

55.4D/4a Dictionary, fourth edition, 25 Jan.

56.1DA/8 Abridged Dictionary, 'fifth' edition, ptd. June

57.5CA/4b Chambers's Dissertation, expanded from his Chinese Architecture, 7 Apr.

57.5CA/4c Chambers's Dissertation, expanded from his Chinese Architecture, 7 Apr.

65.10SP/6 Shakespeare, Bathurst

73.4GEP Verses from Dr. Johnson to Dr. Goldsmith, General Evening Post, 1 Apr.

73.5BLP Legal argument for Boswell, 1 May

73.?6SOE Lines for William Scott for Oxford Encænia, ? summer

73.6MD Macbean's Dictionary, 19 June

73.8EM Epitaph on Colin Maclaurin, 17 Aug.

73.8LP/1a Opinion on Literary Property, 17 Aug.

73.10MP Meditation on a Pudding, 24 Oct.

73.10ES Epitaph on Tobias Smollett, 28 Oct.

73.11EP Epitaph on Thomas Parnell, 22 Nov.

73.12DM/1 Davies's Miscellaneous and Fugitive Pieces (includes 48.4DP/VT/8 Vision of Theodore and 49.1VW/11 Vanity of Human Wishes), 23 Dec.

73EB Epitaph on Jane Bell [?1773]

1774

48.4DP/VT/3 Vision of Theodore (extract), Lloyd's Evening Post, 18 May

52.11Ad/10 The Adventurer, a new edition [?Edinburgh]

52.11Ad/TF/2 Adventurer, Contes traduits de l'Anglois

55.4D/5a Dictionary, Dublin edition, first issue, 24 Dec.

59.12WD/4 World Displayed, fourth edition

73.12DM/2a Davies's Miscellaneous and Fugitive Pieces, second edition, first issue, 28 Apr.

73.12DM/2b Davies's Miscellaneous and Fugitive Pieces, second edition, second issue

73.12DM/3 (Vol. 3) Davies's Miscellaneous and Fugitive Pieces, Vol. III, 31 May

73.12DM/4 Davies's Miscellaneous and Fugitive Pieces, Dublin

74.7DW Diary of a Journey into North Wales, 5 Jul.–30 Sept.

74.10P/1 The Patriot, first edition, 12 Oct.

74.10P/2 The Patriot, second edition, 5 Nov.

74.10P/3 The Patriot, Dublin

74.10TE Henry Thrale's Election Addresses, 1–13 Oct.

74.10TH/1 Hereford Infirmary Appeal, 20 Oct.

74.10TH/2 Hereford Infirmary Appeal, ?Oct.

1775

39.4MN/2 Marmor Norfolciense, second edition, June

44.2LS/3c Life of Savage, third edition, third issue

44.2LS/5 Life of Savage, Works of Savage

48.4DP/9 The Preceptor, 'sixth' edition

49.1VW/13 Vanity of Human Wishes, Dodsley's Collection

57.5CA/TG/1 Chambers's Chinese Architecture, German translation

59.4R/7 Rasselas, 'fifth' edition, ptd. Mar.

61.4SL/3 Sophronia, second edition

65.2PR/4 Percy's Reliques, 'third' edition, Dec.

70.6GD/8 Goldsmith's The Deserted Village

74.10P/4 The Patriot, third edition, 8 May

74.10P/5 The Patriot, Dublin, second edition

75.1J/1a Journey, first edition, 18 Jan.

75.1J/2a Journey, second edition, first issue, late Jan.

75.1J/3a Journey, Dublin, Williams, first issue, 1 Feb.

75.1J/3b Journey, 'Pope' [=Dublin, Williams, second issue]

75.1J/4 Journey, Dublin, Leathley, 6 Feb.

75.1J/5a Journey, Dublin, Walker, first issue

75.1J/5b Journey, Dublin, Walker, second issue '1775'

75.1J/TG/1 Journey, German translation

75.1MQS Inscription for Picture of Mary, Queen of Scots, 21 Jan.

75.2LP Proposals for Lennox's Works, 14 Feb.

75.3TT/1 Taxation no Tyranny, first edition, 8 Mar.

75.3TT/2 Taxation no Tyranny, second edition [?15 Mar.]

75.3TT/3 Taxation no Tyranny, third edition, 21 Mar.

75.3TT/4 Taxation no Tyranny, fourth edition

75.3TT/6a Taxation no Tyranny, Wesley's Calm Address [1775]

75.3TT/6b Taxation no Tyranny, Wesley's Calm Address [1775]

75.3TT/6c Taxation no Tyranny, Wesley's Calm Address [1775]

75.3BG W. Bell's Greek Grammar, 1775 [?Mar. 1776]]

75.5BL/1 Legal Argument for Boswell, 6 May

75.5BL/2 Legal Argument for Boswell, 7 May

75.5NR Notice on Macleod of Raasay, 27 May

75.6ES Epitaph on Mrs Salusbury, 1 June

75.9–11FJ Journal of a visit to France, 15 Sept.–13 Nov.

75.10BP/1a Baretti's Easy Phraseology, 5 Oct.

75.10BP/1b Baretti's Easy Phraseology

75.11MC A Humble Address to the King, Morning Chronicle, 18 Nov.

1776

50.3R/12 The Rambler, 'ninth' edition [fourth Edinburgh edition]

57.5CA/TF/3 Chambers's Chinese Architecture, French translation, privilège 15 Nov.

75.1J/A/1 Abridged Journey, Modern Traveller

76.1HA/1 Hailes's Annals of Scotland, first edition: I, 15 Jan, 1776; II, Feb. 1779

76.1BH/1a Burney's History of Music, first edition, 31 Jan.

76.4PT/1 Political Tracts, Apr.

76.5BL Legal Argument for Boswell, 10 and 13 May

76.6GE/1 Epitaph on Goldsmith, May-Jun.

76.8ML/1 Mickle's Lusiad, Aug.

76.11SP Proposals for The Spectator, 30 Nov.

1777

44.2LS/4 Life of Savage, fourth edition,

44.2LS/6 Life of Savage, Works of Savage

44.2LS/7 Life of Savage, Works of Savage, Dublin

48.4DP/VT/4 Vision of Theodore, Lady's Magazine, Sept.–Oct.

52.11Ad/11 The Adventurer, Long's edition

55.4D/5b Dictionary, Dublin edition, second issue

56.1DA/TI/1 Abridged Dictionary, Italian, ed. Bottarelli, London

56.1DA/TI/2 Abridged Dictionary, Italian, ed. Bottarelli, second edition [??1777]

59.4R/8 Rasselas, second Dublin ['eighth'] edition

66.6AG/4 Adams on the Globes, fourth edition

75.3TT/TG/1 Taxation no Tyranny, German translation

76.4PT/2 Political Tracts, Dublin

76.6GE/2a Epitaph on Goldsmith, Poems and Plays, first issue, 4 Aug.

76.6GE/2b Epitaph on Goldsmith, Poems and Plays, second issue

77.1CB Charade on Thomas Barnard, 17 Jan.

77.2PC/1 Zachary Pearce on the Evangelists (Dedication and Life), 18 Jan.

77.2LC/1 Defence of James's Fever Powders, London Chronicle, 20 Feb.

77.2LC/2 Defence of James's Fever Powders, Dissertation on Fevers [1778]

77.3SP Shaw's Proposals, Mar.

77.5KW/1 [Prologue to] Kelly's Word to the Wise, 13 and 29 May

77.5KW/2 Prologue to Kelly's Word to the Wise [1778]

77.5DS/1 Dodd's Speech, Gazetteer, 16 May

77.5DS/2 Dodd's Speech, folio

77.6CA/1a Dodd, Convict's Address, first edition, first issue, 19 June

77.6CA/1b Dodd, Convict's Address, first edition, second issue, 26 June

77.6CA/2 Dodd, Convict's Address, Bath [1777]

77.6CA/3 Dodd, Convict's Address, Dublin

77.6CA/4 Dodd, Convict's Address, Edinburgh

77.6CA/5 Dodd, Convict's Address, Edinburgh

[**77.6CA/6** Dodd, Convict's Address, Gainsborough, 1777]

77.6CA/7 Dodd, Convict's Address, ?London [1777]

77.6CA/8 Dodd, Convict's Address, ?London [1777]

77.6CA/9 Dodd, Convict's Address, ?London [1777]

77.6CA/10 Dodd, Convict's Address, London

77.6CA/11 Dodd, Convict's Address, [?London]

77.6CA/12 Dodd, Convict's Address, [?London]

77.6CA/13 Dodd, Convict's Address, [London, 1777]

77.6CA/14 Dodd, Convict's Adress, Villette's edition

77.6CA/15 Dodd, Convict's Address, first Newcastle edition [1777]

77.6CA/16 Dodd, Convict's Address, Newcastle, second edition

77.6CA/17 Dodd, Convict's Address, Salisbury

77.6CA/18 Dodd, Convict's Address, Taunton

[**77.6CA/19** Dodd, Convict's Address, Whitehaven]

77.6CA/21/A Dodd, Convict's Address (Abridged)

77.6WD/S/1a Isaac Reed's Account of Dodd, first issue, 27 June

77.6WD/S/1b Isaac Reed's Account of Dodd, second issue, 1 Aug.

77.6WD/S/2 Citizen of London's Account of Dodd

77.6WD/S/3 Life and Writings of Dodd, 27 June

77.6WD/S/4 The Apparition [1777]

77.6WD/S/6 An Authentic Account of Dodd

77.6WD/S/7 Authentic Memoirs of Dodd [1777]

77.6WD/S/8 A Dialogue in the Shades, after 5 July

77.6WD/S/9 Evidences of Christianity Not Weakened

77.6WD/S/10 A Full and Circumstantial Account of Dodd, Mar.

77.6WD/S/11 A Full and Particular Account of Dodd [?1777]

77.6WD/S/12 John Villette's Genuine Account of Dodd, 5 July

77.6WD/S/13a A Relation of Dodd's Behaviour in Newgate

77.6WD/S/13b A Relation of Dodd's Behaviour in Newgate, second edition, 11 July

77.6WD/S/13c A Relation of Dodd's Behaviour in Newgate, third edition

77.6WD/S/13d A Relation of Dodd's Behaviour in Newgate, fourth edition

77.6WD/S/14 A Genuine and Authentic Account of Dodd

77.6WD/S/15 The Genuine Life and Trial Dodd

77.6WD/S/16 Genuine Memoirs of Dodd, early Mar.

77.6WD/S/17 John Duncombe's Historical Memoirs, 3 July

77.6WD/S/18 A Letter to Messrs. Fletcher and Peach

77.6WD/S/19 Life and Writings of Dodd

77.6WD/S/20 Memoirs of the Late William Dodd, July

77.6WD/S/21 A New Song [on Dodd] [?1777]

77.6WD/S/22 Observations on the Case of Dodd, 5 July

77.6WD/S/23 Dodd's Behaviour in Newgate

77.6WD/S/24 Remarks on Sanguinary Laws, 7 July

77.6WD/S/25 Serious Reflections upon Dodd's Trial, 27 June

77.6WD/S/26 A Sketch of the Life of Dodd, Mar.-Apr.

77.6WD/S/27 Particulars of the late Dr Dodd, July

77.6WD/S/28 A Tear of Gratitude, 8 July

77.6WD/S/29 Dodd's Thoughts in Prison, first edition, ?Sept.

77.6WD/S/30 Dodd's Thoughts in Prison [?1777]

77.6WD/S/31 Sololoques ou Lament-ations du docteur Dodd

77.6WD/S/57 Thoughts of a Citizen of London on Dodd '1767', 30 Aug.

77.6WD/S/58 The Trial and the Life of Dodd

77.6WD/S/59 The Trial of Dodd [?1777]

77.6WD/S/60 The Trial of Dodd, Edinburgh

77.6WD/S/61 The Proceedings in the King's Commission

77.6WD/S/62 Der unglückliche Prädicant zu London [?1777]

77.7DOP Dodd, Occasional Papers, 11 July

77.9BL Boswell's Petition for Joseph Knight, 23 Sept.

1778

52.11Ad/12 The Adventurer, a new edi-tion, 1778, ptd. Dec. (Vols. I–II)

52.11Ad/13 The Adventurer, a new edi-tion, Dublin

56.1DA/9 Abridged Dictionary, 'fifth' edition

56.1DA/10 Abridged Dictionary, 'sixth' edition, ptd. Apr.

56.11LS/5 Sully's Memoirs, fifth edition

56.11LS/6 Sully's Memoirs, new edition

58.4Id/S/2 Idler Selections, Fatal Effects of Luxury

65.10SP/7 Shakespeare, Bathurst

76.6GE/4 Epitaph on Goldsmith, Camp-bell's Philosophical Survey, Mar.

76.6GE/5 Epitaph on Goldsmith, Camp-bell's Phlosophical Survey, second edi-tion, Dublin

76.6GE/6 Epitaph on Goldsmith, Westminster Abbey

76.8ML/2 Mickle's Lusiad, Oxford, Sept.

77.6WD/S/32 Dodd's Thoughts in Prison

78.5RD/1a Reynolds's Seven Discourses, 19 May

[78.5RD/TI/1 Reynolds's Discourses, Italian translation]

78.7SA/1a Shaw's Analysis of the Galic Language, July

78.7SA/2a Shaw's Analysis of the Galic Language, second edition

78.10EC Epitaph on Dr Collier, ?Oct.

78ME/1 More's Sir Eldred, second edition

1779

50.3R/13 The Rambler, 'ninth' edition, 27 Nov.

59.12WD/6a World Displayed, sixth edition, Dublin, first issue

79.3BC/1 Baretti's Carmen Seculare, performed 26 Feb., reported 3 Mar.

79.3BC/2 Baretti's Carmen Seculare [1779]

79.4LP/1.1 [Lives of the Poets], Works of the English Poets, 2 Apr.

79.4LP/1.2 [Lives of the Poets], Prefaces, first instalment (Vols. I-IV), 2 Apr.

79.4LP/2a(i) Lives of the Poets, first instalment, first Dublin edition, first issue, first state, ?Oct.

79.4LP/2a(ii) Lives of the Poets, first instalment, first Dublin edition, first issue, second state

79.4LP/2a(iii) Lives of the Poets, first instalment, first Dublin edition, first issue, third state

79.4LP/SS/52 Life of Denham, Bell's British Poets, Vol. 35

79.4LP/SS/56 Life of Dryden, Caledonian Mercury, No. 9044

79.4LP/SS/116 Life of Hughes, Bell's British Poets, Vol. 70

79.6M/1 Maurice's Poems and Translation of Sophocles, June

79.12LP Henry Lucas's Poems, 9 Dec.

1780

44.2LS/8 Life of Savage, Bell's British Poets

49.2I/S/1 Irene selection Poetical Preceptor, second edition

61.4SL/4 Sophronia, 'second' edition

65.10SP/7/S1 Shakespeare, Malone's Supplement

76.6GE/3 Epitaph on Goldsmith, Poems and Plays

77.6WD/S/5a [Mary Bosanquet], An Aunt's Advice to a Neice

77.6WD/S/5b [Mary Bosanquet], An Aunt's Advice to a Neice, second edition

77.6WD/S/33 Dodd's Thoughts in Prison

77.6WD/S/56/TF/1 Dodd's Prison Thoughts, French translation

79.4LP/2b Lives of the Poets, first instalment, first Dublin edition, second issue

79.4LP/SS/236 Life of Roscommon, Bell's British Poets, Vol. 43

80.5DMG/1 Davies's Memoirs of Garrick, first edition, 6 May

80.5DMG/2 Davies's Memoirs of Garrick, second edition

80.5DMG/3 Davies's Memoirs of Garrick, Dublin

80.9TE Election Address for Henry Thrale, 5–7 Sept.

80LEE Latin Translation of Epitaph on Lady Elibank

1781

48.4DP/VT/5 Vision of Theodore, Weekly Miscellany

49.1VW/14 Vanity of Human Wishes, The Lady's Poetical Magazine

49.2I/4 Irene, new edition, 24 July

50.3R/14 The Rambler, 'ninth' edition [fifth Edinburgh edition]

77.6WD/S/34 Dodd's Thoughts in Prison, second edition

79.4LP/2c Lives of the Poets, first instalment, first Dublin edition, third issue

79.4LP/3 Lives of the Poets, first instalment, second Dublin edition

79.4LP/4 [Lives of the Poets], Prefaces, second instalment (Vols. V–X), 15 May

79.4LP/5 Lives of the Poets, second London edition, ?7 June

79.4LP/6a Lives of the Poets, second instalment, first Dublin edition, first issue, July

79.4LP/6b Lives of the Poets, second instalment, first Dublin edition, second issue

79.4LP/TG/1 Lives of the Poets, German translation, Altenburg, 1781–83

79.4LP/SS/15 Life of Akenside, Bell's British Poets, Vol. 104

79.4LP/SS/19 Life of Broome, Bell's British Poets, Vol. 83

79.4LP/SS/30 Life of Collins, Bell's British Poets, Vol. 97

79.4LP/SS/120 Life of Lyttelton, Bell's British Poets, Vol. 96

79.4LP/SS/178 Life of Ambrose Philips, Bell's British Poets, Vol. 93

79.4LP/SS/180 Life of John Philips, Bell's British Poets, Vol. 66

79.4LP/SS/240 Life of Rowe, Bell's British Poets, Vol. 58

79.4LP/SS/247 Life of Smith, Bell's British Poets, Vol. 102, pt. 2

79.4LP/SS/303 Life of Tickell, Bell's British Poets, Vol. 80

79.4LP/SS/320 Life of West, Bell's British Poets, Vol. 95

80.5DMG/4 Davies's Memoirs of Garrick, third London edition

81.4BG Baretti's Guide to the Royal Academy, 30 Apr.

81.4BPA Petition for the Member for Ayrshire

81.4ET Epitaph on Henry Thrale, after 4 Apr. [June 1781]

81.6BAR Boswell's Answers for the Robertsons, 21 June

81.7SE/1 William Shaw, Enquiry into Ossian, 7 July

81.11B(Part 1)/1 The Beauties of Johnson, Part 1, first edition, 22 Nov.

81.11B(Part 1)/2 Beauties of Johnson, Part 1, second edition, first issue [31 Dec. 1781]

79.4LP/SS/183 Life of Pitt, Bell's British Poets, Vol. 90

79.4LP/SS/222(TG) Life of Pope, Göttingisches Magazin, iii

79.4LP/SS/227 Life of Rochester, Some Passages in the Life and Death of Rochester

80.5DMG/TG/1 Davies's Memoirs of Garrick, German translation

81.7SE/2 Shaw's Enquiry, Dublin

81.7SE/3 Shaw's Enquiry, second London edition, 3 Apr.

81.11B(Part 1)/3 Beauties of Johnson, Part 1, Dublin

81.11B(Part 1)/4 Beauties of Johnson, Part 1, second ['third'] London edition, second issue, 21 Jan.

81.11B(Part 1)/5 Beauties of Johnson, Part 1, second ['fourth'] London edition, third issue, 19 Feb.

81.11B(Part 1)/6 Beauties of Johnson, Part 1, third ['fifth'] London edition, first issue, 23 Apr.

81.11B(Part 1)/7 Beauties of Johnson, Part 1, third ['sixth'] London edition, second issue, 1 Aug.

81.11B(Part 2)/1 Beauties of Johnson, Part 2, first edition, 19 Feb.

81.11B(Part 2)/2 Beauties of Johnson, Part 2, first edition, second issue, 23 Apr.

81.11B(Part 2)/3 Beauties of Johnson, Part 2, first edition, third issue

82.2DL Announcement of Death of Robert Levet, Feb.

82.11NH/1a Nichols's History of Hinckley

82.12RD Reynolds's 11th Presidential Discourse, 10 Dec.

1782

49.1VW/15 Vanity of Human Wishes, Dodsley's Collection

58.4Id/S/3 Idler Selections, School for Scandal

66.6AG/5 Adams on the Globes, fifth edition

1783

48.4DP/10 The Preceptor, 'seventh' edition

50.3R/15 The Rambler, 'twelfth' edition

52.3LFQ/5 Lennox's The Female Quixote, Harrison's edition

55.4D/A/TG/1 Dictionary Adaptation, German translation, Leipzig, 1783–96

56.1DA/11 Abridged Dictionary, 'seventh' edition, Apr.

56.1DA/TG/1 Abridged Dictionary, German, ?1783–6

58.4Id/5a The Idler, 'fourth' edition, first issue, 5 July

58.4Id/5b The Idler, 'fourth' edition, second issue, 5 July

59.4R/9 Rasselas, 'sixth' edition, 1783, ptd. Mar.

63.2HT/5 Hoole's Tasso, fifth edition

65.10SP/7/S2 Shakespeare, Second Appendix to Malone's Supplement

79.4LP/7a Lives of the Poets, third London edition, Feb.

79.4LP/7b Lives of the Poets, Additions and Corrections in third London edition, Mar.

83.1DL Erasmus Darwin's translation of Linnaeus, 1782–3

83.2EH Obituary of Coleborne Hancock, 13 Feb.

83.5CV/1 Crabbe's The Village, 23 May

83.11EHC Rules of the Essex Head Club, Nov.

1784

38.5L/14 London and **49.1VW/16** Vanity of Human Wishes, Juvenal and Persius, ed. Knox

50.3R/16 The Rambler, 'tenth' edition, ptd. Dec. 1783

55.4D/6 Dictionary, 'fifth' edition, 25 Dec.

75.1J/2b Journey, second edition, second issue '1775'

79.4LP/A/1 Abridged Lives of the Poets, Philadelphia

79.4LP/SS/125 Life of Milton, Works of the English Poets, Göttingen

79.4LP/SS/170(TG) Life of Milton, Works of the English Poets, Miltons Werke, Göttingen

79.4LP/SS/322 Life of Young, The Complaint: or Night-Thoughts, [Dublin] [?1784–]

80.5DMG/5 Davies's memoirs of Garrick, fourth London edition

84.6AC Account of Archibald Campbell, 15 June

84.7EEJ Epitaph on Elizabeth Johnson, July

84.9LS Projected Life of Scott of Amwell, Sept.

84.11EP Epitaph on Michael and Sarah Johnson, before 2 Dec.

84.12W/1 Johnson's Will, 8 Dec.

84.12W/2 Johnson's Will and Codicil, London Chronicle etc., 25 Dec.

84.12W/3a Jonson's Will and Codicil, Cooke's Life of Samuel Johnson, 28 Dec.

84GM54 Gentleman's Magazine, Vol. LIV

1785

50.3R/17 The Rambler, 'eleventh' edition, Dublin

50.3R/18 The Rambler, Harrison's British Classicks, 15 Jan.

50.3R/TF/S/2 Rambler, French translation, Selections

52.11Ad/14 The Adventurer, Harrison's British Classicks, 23 Apr.–18 June

55.4D/7 Dictionary, Harrison's edition, 22 Oct. 1785–15 Sept. 1787

55.4D/8 Dictionary, 'sixth' edition, quarto, 19 Nov. 1785–30 June 1787

55.4D/9 Dictionary, 'seventh' edition, folio, ptd. Nov.

55.4D/10 Dictionary, Jarvis & Fielding's edition, Oct. 1785-Sept. 1786 (includes 84.12W/4 Johnson's Will)

58.4Id/S/5a Idler Selections, No. 41, London Evening Post, 8 Jan.

59.4R/10 Rasselas, first German edition, first impression

59.4R/11 Rasselas, first German edition, second impression

59.4R/TG/2 Rasselas, Translations, German

65.10SP/8a Shakespeare, Bathurst

75.1J/6 Journey, new edition, 12 Nov.

75.1J/TF/1 Journey, French translation

79.4LP/SS/310 Life of Isaac Watts, ed. Palmer

84.12W/3b Jonson's Will and Codicil, Cooke's Life of Samuel Johnson, second edition, 26 Feb.

85.2BH/1a Burney's Commemoration of Handel, 1 Feb.

85.2BH/2 Burney's Commemoration of Handel, Dublin

85.2BH/TG/1a Burney's Commemoration of Handel, German translation

85.2PW/1 Poetical Works, ed. Kearsley (includes 38.5L/15 London and 49.1VW/17 Vanity of Human Wishes), 15 Feb.

85.2PW/2 Poetical Works, ed. Kearsley, Dublin, 10 May

85.2PW/3 Poetical Works, ed. Kearsley, second London issue, 24 Mar.

85.2PW/4 Poetical Works, new edition

85.7RE/1a Frances Reynolds's Enquiry, July

85.8PM/1 Prayers and Meditations, 13 Aug.

85.8PM/2 Prayers and Meditations, Dublin

85.8PM/3 Prayers and Meditations, second London edition, 12 Nov.

85PT [Joseph Simpson] The Patriot, a Tragedy, Apr.

85GM55 Gentleman's Magazine, Vol. LV, Feb., Apr., Oct.

1786

48.4DP/11 The Preceptor, 'seventh' edition, Dublin

48.4DP/VT/6 Vision of Theodore, New Novelist's Magazine

50.3R/S/10a Beauties of the Rambler, Adventurer, Connnoisseur, World, and Idler (includes 52.11Ad/S/1 Adventurer and 58.4Id/S/4 Idler)

50.3R/TF/1 Rambler, French translation

56.1DA/12 Abridged Dictionary, 'eighth' edition, ptd. Nov. 1785

56.1MD/1 Miniature Dictionary [?1786]

56.4LM/M/1 Memoirs of the King of Prussia, 14 Oct. (no. 1)

56.4LM/M/2 Memoirs of the King of Prussia, Oct.

59.4R/12 Rasselas, 'seventh' edition, 1786, ptd. Sept.

59.4R/TG/3 Rasselas, Translations, German

61.3LH/3 Lennox's Henrietta, Dublin

65.10SP/TF/1 Shakespeare, French translation

66.6AG/6 Adams on the Globes

79.4LP/SS/311 Life of Watts, Biographia Evangelica, by Middleton

1787

50.3R/S/10b Rambler Selections, Beauties

50.3R/S/11 Rambler Selections, New Novelist's Magazine, 1786–7

50.3R/TF/S/3 Rambler, French translation, Selections

58.4Id/6a The Idler, Harrison's British Classicks Mar.-Apr.

58.10AS/3 Angell's Stenography, Dublin

59.4R/13 Rasselas, Wenman's edition

59.4R/14 Rasselas, Harrison's Novelist's Magazine, Vol. XXIII, 1787–8

59.4R/15 Rasselas, Dublin

59.4R/S/1 Rasselas, Selection, English Miscellanies

59.4R/TF/6 Rasselas, Translations, French

59.4R/TG/4 Rasselas, Translations, German

63.2HT/6 Hoole's Tasso, sixth edition

66.4WM/F/7 The Fountains, European Magazine XII, July

66.4WM/F/8 The Fountains, Edinburgh Magazine, VI, Sept.

66.4WM/F/9 The Fountains, Northern Gazette, I, 30 Aug.–13 Sept.

66.4WM/F/10 The Fountains, Hibernian Magazine, Oct.

78.7SA/2b Shaw's Analysis of the Galic Language, 'third' edition

79.4LP/SS/228 Life of Rochester, Some Passages in the Life and Death of Rochester

81.11B(Parts 1+2)/1 Beauties of Johnson, Two Parts in One, 'seventh' edition

81.11B(Parts 1+2)/2 Beauties of Johnson, Philadelphia

87.3W/1 The Works of Samuel Johnson, ed. Hawkins (includes 38.5L/17 London, 48.4 DP/VT/8 Vision of Theodore, 49.1VW/20 Vanity of Human Wishes, and 84.12W/5 Johnson's Will), 20 Mar.

87.3W/1.1/1 Works, Hawkins's Life of Johnson, 22 Mar.

87.3W1/1.1/2 Works, Hawkins's Life of Johnson, Dublin

87.3W/1.1/3 Works, Hawkins's Life of Johnson, second London edition, 7 June

87.3W/1.2/1a Works, Vols. XII–XIII, Debates in Parliament, 24 Apr.

87.3W/1.3/1a Works, Supplementary Vol. XIV, 29 Nov., (includes 66.4WM/F/11 The Fountains)

87.5TL Taylor's Letter on a Future State, 24 May

87GM57 Gentleman's Magazine, Vol. LVII, July, Dec.

1788

42.11SW/5 Life of Sydenham, 'sixth' edition

52.11Ad/15 The Adventurer, a new edition, illustrated, 24 July

52.11Ad/16 The Adventurer, Moore's edition, Dublin

56.1PD/2 Payne's Draughts, second edition, 1788–9

59.4R/TF/7 Rasselas, Translations, French

59.12WD/6b World Displayed, sixth edition, Dublin, second issue

61.3LH/2 Lennox's Henrietta, Harrison's Novelist's Magazine, Vol. XXIII

63.2HT/7 Hoole's Tasso, seventh edition

65.10SP/8b Shakespeare, Prefatory matter

65.10SP/9 Shakespeare, Bell's edition

66.4WM/F/12 The Fountains, English Lyceum, Jan.

79.3BC/3 Baretti's Carmen Seculare [19 May]

79.4LP/SS/254 Life of Thomson, The Seasons, Philadelphia

88.3L/1 Letters of Johnson, Piozzi edition, 8 Mar.

88.3L/2 Letters, Piozzi edition, Dublin

88.3SW Sermon on the Death of His Wife, 19 Mar.

88.5OT Boswell's Johnson's Ode to Mrs Thrale, 12 May

88.5S/1.1 Sermons, Vol. I, 29 May

88.5S/1.2 Sermons, Vol. II, 14 Oct.

1789

50.3R/19 The Rambler, 'eleventh' edition, ptd. Mar.

50.3R/S/12 Rambler Selections, Beauties

50.3R/TF/S/4 Rambler, French translation, Selections

52.11Ad/S/2 Adventurer Selections, Beauties

58.2PT/2 Payne's Tables of Interest, second edition? [?Jan.]

59.4R/16 Rasselas, first Edinburgh edition

66.6AG/7 Adams on the Globes, Astronomical and Geographical Essays, [?1789]

76.1BH/2 Burney's History of Music, second edition

77.6WD/S/35 Dodd's Thoughts in Prison, third edition

77.6WD/S/35/Add1 Dodd's Thoughts in Prison, Russian translation

85.2PW/5 Poetical Works, ed. Kearsley

85.7RE/2 Frances Reynolds's Enquiry

87.3W/1.4 Works, Supplementary Vol. XV, 6 Apr. (includes 35.2LV/2 Lobo's Voyage)

1790

44.2LS/9 Life of Savage, Works of English Poets

56.1DA/13 Abridged Dictionary, 'ninth' edition, ptd. Dec. 1789

56.4LM/M/3 Memoirs of the King of Prussia, Liverpool [?1790]

58.4Id/7 The Idler, 'fifth' edition

58.4Id/8 The Idler, 'sixth' edition

58.4Id/TF/1 The Idler, French translation

59.4R/17 Rasselas, 'eighth' edition, ptd. Dec. 1789

59.4R/18 Rasselas, new edition

65.10SP/10 Shakespeare, Malone's edition

79.4LP/8a The Works of the English Poets, second edition, ptd. Dec. 1789

79.4LP/8b Prefaces to the Works of the English Poets (I-VI), companion to second edition of Works

79.4LP/9 Lives of the Poets, new edition, 1790–91, Vols. 3–4 ptd. Jan. 1791

79.4LP/SS/255 Life of Thomson, The Seasons, Philadelphia

82.11NH/1b Nichols's History of Hinckley, Collections towards History of Leicestershire

82.11NH/1c Nichols's History of Hinckley, Additional Collections towards History of Leicestershire

85.2PW/6 Poetical Works, English Poets, Vol. 72

88.5S/2 Sermons, second edition, 1790–2

1791

50.3R/20 The Rambler, 'twelfth' edition [?Edinburgh]

50.3R/21 The Rambler, Hodges's edition

50.3R/22 The Rambler, Locke's edition [?Edinburgh], 1791–2

58.4Id/9 The Idler, a new edition

59.4R/19 Rasselas, second American edition, Philadelphia

65.10SP/11 Shakespeare, Ayscough's edition

65.10SP/12a Shakespeare, Boydell's edition [1791]–1800

66.4WM/F/13 The Fountains, Weekly Miscellany, 26 Oct.–23 Nov.

66.6AG/8 Adams on the Globes

75.1J/7 Journey, new edition, ptd. Aug.

76.8ML/3a Mickle's Lusiad, Dublin, 'third edition'

79.4LP/SS/229 Life of Rochester, Some Passages in the Life and Death of Rochester

79.4LP/SS/312 Life of Isaac Watts, 'second edition'

83.5CV/2 Crabbe's The Village, New York

84.12W/6 Jonson's Will and Codicil, Boswell's Life

88.3L/3 Letters (Selection), To Chesterfield, 12 May

91.5CG Conversation with George III, 12 May

1792

50.3R/22/Add1 The Rambler, Harrison's British Classicks, second issue

55.4D/A/1 Dictionary Adaptation

56.1DA/14a Abridged Dictionary, 'eighth' edition [?first] issue

56.1DA/14b Abridged Dictionary, 'eighth' edition [?second] issue

56.1DA/15a Abridged Dictionary, 'tenth' edition, first issue

56.1DA/15b Abridged Dictionary, 'tenth' edition, second issue

58.4Id/6b The Idler, Harrison's British Classicks, second issue

59.4R/20 Rasselas, Symonds's edition [1792–3]

63.2HT/8 Hoole's Tasso, 'seventh' edition

75.1J/8a Journey, Edinburgh, first issue

79.4LP/SS/241 Life of Rowe, Works of Nicholas Rowe

79.4LP/SS/256 Life of Thomson, The Seasons

79.4LP/SS/313 Life of Isaac Watts

81.11B(Parts 1+2)/3 Beauties of Johnson, 'eighth' edition

87.3W/1.2/1c Works, Vols. XII-XIII, Debates in Parliament, reissue

87.3W/1.3/1b Works, Supplementary Vol. XIV, reissue (includes 48.4DP/VT/8 Vision of Theodore)

87.3W/2 The Works of Samuel Johnson, ed. Murphy, before 22 May
87.3W/2.1/1 Works, Murphy's Essay, separate issue, 22 May

87.3W/3 Works, ed. Murphy, Dublin
88.3L/4 Letters (Selection), To Wilson
88.5S/3 Sermons, Dublin
93MH On the Character and Duty of an Academick, Moir's Hospitality

1793

44.4HM/3 A Selection from the Harleian Miscellany
48.4DP/12 The Preceptor, 'eighth' edition
50.3R/23 The Rambler, Parsons's Select British Classics
50.3R/24 The Rambler, 'twelfth' edition
50.3R/25a The Rambler, Moore's edition, Dublin [1793]
50.3R/25b The Rambler, Moore's edition, second issue, Dublin, **50.3R/S/13** Rambler Selections, British Classics, Dublin
52.11Ad/17 The Adventurer, a new edition, Edinburgh
52.11Ad/18 The Adventurer, Moore's edition, Dublin
52.11Ad/S/3 Adventurer Selections, British Classics, Dublin
56.1DA/14c Abridged Dictionary, 'eighth' edition [?third issue]
58.4Id/10 The Idler, Parsons's edition
59.4R/21 Rasselas, 'ninth' edition, ptd. June
59.12WD/5 World Displayed, fifth edition
65.10SP/12b Shakespeare, Preface (with Pope's) [?1793–4]
65.10SP/13 Shakespeare, second variorum, fourth edition
76.8ML/3b Mickle's Lusiad, London, 'third edition'
77.6WD/S/36 Dodd's Thoughts in Prison, fourth edition
79.4LP/10 Lives of the Poets, ?Piracy
79.4LP/SS/257 Life of Thomson, The Seasons, ed. Stockdale
79.4LP/SS/258 Life of Thomson, The Seasons, ed. McKenzie, Dublin
87.3W/2.1/2 Murphy's Essay, second edition

1794

44.2LS/10 Life of Savage, British Poets, ed. Anderson
49.1VW/22 Vanity of Human Wishes, Roach's Beauties of the Poets
50.3R/26 The Rambler, [Hodges's] edition, second impression
50.3R/27 The Rambler, [Hodges's] edition, third impression [Edinburgh]
50.3R/28 The Rambler, 'thirteenth' edition, ptd. Aug.
52.11Ad/19 The Adventurer, Parsons's Select British Classics, 4 Jan.–8 Feb.
52.11Ad/20 The Adventurer, a new edition
52.11Ad/21 The Adventurer, Harrison's British Classicks
56.1DA/16 Abridged Dictionary, 'tenth' edition, ptd. Nov. 1793
56.1DA/17 Abridged Dictionary, 'eleventh' edition
56.1MD/2–3 Miniature Dictionary
58.4Id/S/5b Idler Selections [No. 41], Gentleman's Magazine, Feb.
59.4R/22 Rasselas, Wenman's second edition
59.4R/23 Rasselas, Cooke's first edition [1794]
65.10SP/14 Shakespeare, Dublin
77.6WD/S/37 Dodd's Thoughts in Prison, Exeter, New Hampshire
79.4LP/11 Lives of the Poets, ptd. Nov.
79.4LP/SS/188 Life of Pope, Poetical Works of Alexander Pope
79.4LP/SS/259 Life of Thomson, The Seasons
94.4PBS/1a Piozzi's British Synonymy, ?3 Apr. 1794
94.4PBS/2 Piozzi's British Synonymy, Dublin

1795

50.3R/29 The Rambler, Parsons's Select British Classics, second edition, 1795–6

50.3R/S/14 Rambler Selections, Literary Miscellany

56.1DA/TI/3 Abridged Dictionary, Italian, ed. Bottarelli, third edition

56.1MD/4–5 Miniature Dictionary

58.4Id/6c The Idler, Harrison's British Classicks, third issue

58.4Id/11 The Idler, Cuthell and Fairbairn

58.4Id/12 The Idler, Parsons's second edition, 1795–96

59.4R/24 Rasselas, Literary Association first edition

59.4R/25 Rasselas, third American edition, Greenfield, Mass.

59.4R/26 Rasselas, Henshall's first edition, Dublin [1795–6]

59.4R/TR/2 Rasselas, Translations, Russian

59.12WD/7 World Displayed, Philadelphia, 1795–6

65.10SP/15 Shakespeare, Bioren & Madan, Philadelphia, 1795–6

66.6AG/9 Adams on the Globes

67.1FT/2 Fawkes's Theocritus, Poets of Great Britain

68.12HC/5 Hoole's Cyrus, Bell's British Theatre, Vol. XXIV

75.1J/8b Journey, Edinburgh, second issue

[76.8ML/3/Add1 Mickle's Lusiad, Anderson's British Poets]

79.4LP/2d Lives of the Poets, first instalment, first Dublin edition, fourth issue

79.4LP/12a Lives of the Poets, Dublin, Moore's edition, first issue, 1795–1800

79.4LP/12b Lives of the Poets, Dublin, Moore's edition, second issue

79.4LP/SS/90 Life of Gay, Poetical, Dramatic, and Miscellaneous Works of John Gay

79.4LP/SS/260 Life of Thomson, The Seasons, Philadelphia

82.11NH/2 Nichols's History of Hinckley, The History and Antiquities of Leicestershire, 1795–1815

85.2PW/7 Poetical Works, Works of the British Poets, Vol. 11, ed. Anderson, 1792–5

88.5S/4 Sermons, third London edition

1796

46.3DM/U/5 Dodsley's Museum, The Union

49.2I/6 Irene, Bell's British Theatre, Vol. XXV

49.2I/7 Irene, Bell's British Theatre, Vol. XXV, variant impression

50.3R/30 The Rambler, Harrison's British Classicks, third issue

50.3R/S/15 Beauties of the Rambler, Adventurer, Connoisseur, World, and Idler (includes 52.11Ad/S/4 Adventurer and 58.4Id/S/6 Idler)

56.1MD/6–8 Miniature Dictionary

58.4Id/6d Harrison's British Classicks, fourth issue

59.4R/27 Rasselas, Literary Association, second edition

59.4R/28 Rasselas, Harding's edition, ptd. 1 Mar.

59.4R/29a Rasselas, Henshall's second edition, Dublin [1796]

59.4R/29b Raselas, Henshall's second edition, Glasgow issue

77.6WD/S/38 Dodd's Thoughts in Prison, Cooke's edition [1796]

77.6WD/S/39 Dodd's Thoughts in Prison, Bath

79.4LP/SS/20 Life of Broome, Poetical Works of Broome [?1796]

79.4LP/SS/54 Life of Dorset, Poetical Works of . . . Dorset [?1796]

79.4LP/SS/126 Life of Milton, Paradise Lost

79.4LP/SS/127 Life of Milton, Poems of John Milton, 1795–96

85.8PM/4 Prayers and Meditations, third London edition, June

85.8PM/5 Prayers and Meditations, Dublin

87.3W/4 Works, ed. Murphy, ptd. Sept.

1797

48.4DP/VT/9 Vision of Theodore, The Aberdeen Magazine

49.2I/8 Irene, Bell's British Theatre, Vol. XXIII

52.11Ad/22 The Adventurer, a new edition, illustrated

52.11Ad/23 The Adventurer, a new edition, illustrated

55.4D/11a Dictionary, 'eighth' edition, Dublin, ?1797

56.1DA/18 Abridged Dictionary, Edinburgh, 'eleventh' edition

56.1MD/9–11 Miniature Dictionary

58.4Id/S/5c Idler Selections, No. 41, New York Gazette, 10 Mar.

59.4R/30 Rasselas, Cooke's second edition [1797]

59.4R/TF/8 Rasselas, Translations, French

59.4R/TI/3 Rasselas, Translations, Italian

63.2HT/9 Hoole's Tasso, J. Johnson, octavo

63.2HT/10 Hoole's Tasso, J. Johnson, duodecimo

63.2HT/11 Hoole's Tasso, Associated Booksellers

76.1HA/2 Hailes's Annals of Scotland, second edition

78.5RD/2 Reynolds's Discourses, Works

79.4LP/A/2 Lives of the Poets, Newbery's Abridgement, 12 Jan.

79.4LP/SS/12(TF) Vie d'Addison, Paris

79.4LP/SS/168(TF) Vie de Milton, Paris [1797]

81.11B(Parts 1+2)/4 Beauties of Johnson, 'ninth' edition

85.2PW/8 Poetical Works, Cooke's edition [1797]

1798

50.3R/31a The Rambler, Chapman's edition, Edinburgh

50.3R/31b The Rambler, [Chapman's] edition, London issue

50.3R/32 The Rambler, Cooke's edition [1798–9]

56.1DA/19 Abridged Dictionary, 'eleventh' edition

56.1DA/20 Abridged Dictionary, 'eleventh' edition

56.1MD/12–13 Miniature Dictionary

58.4Id/13? The Idler, Suttaby's British Classics

59.4R/31 Rasselas, 'tenth' edition

59.4R/TF/9 Rasselas, Translations, French

59.4R/TF/10 Rasselas, Translations, French

59.4R/TS/1(2) Rasselas, Translations, Spanish

75.1J/9 Journey, second Edinburgh edition

75.1J/A/2 Abridged Journey, British Tourists

76.8ML/4 Mickle's Lusiad

78.5RD/3 Reynolds's Discources, Works

79.4LP/SS/31 Life of Collins, Poetical Works of William Collins

1799

50.3R/33 The Rambler, [?Parsons's reprint]

52.3LFQ/6 Lennox's The Female Quixote, Cooke's edition [1799]

55.4D/12 Dictionary, 'eighth' edition, ptd. Dec.

56.1DA/21 Abridged Dictionary, 'eleventh' London edition, first issue

56.1DA/22 Abridged Dictionary, 'eleventh' London edition, second issue

56.1MD/14–16 Miniature Dictionary

58.4Id/14 The Idler, Cooke's edition [1799]

59.4R/32 Rasselas, Lackington's edition

59.4R/33 Rasselas, Cooke's third edition [1799]

63.2HT/12 Hoole's Tasso, J. Johnson

65.10SP/16 Shakespeare, Tourneisen, Basil, 1799–1800

66.6AG/10 Adams on the Globes, London, 'fourth' edition

79.4LP/55/128 Life of Milton, Paradise Lost

79.4LP/SS/244 Life of Shenstone, Essays on Men and Manners, by W. Shenstone [?1799]

1800

50.3R/25c The Rambler, Moore's edition, third issue, London [?1800]

50.3R/36 The Rambler, first Montrose edition

50.3R/37 The Rambler, New York edition

50.3R/38 The Rambler, British Classics

52.11Ad/23/Add1 The Adventurer, Harrison's British Classicks

52.11Ad/24 The Adventurer, Cooke's edition ?20 Dec. 1800–6 Feb. 1802

56.1DA/A/1 Abridged Dictionary, Adaptations, Union Dictionary

56.1MD/17 Miniature Dictionary

[58.4Id/15 The Idler, 'fifth' edition]

58.4Id/16 The Idler, Alnwick

[59.4R/34 Rasselas, Bridgeport, Backus]

59.4R/TF/11 Rasselas, Translations, French *c.*1800

65.10SP/17 Shakespeare, Harding's edition

66.6AG/11 Adams on the Globes, Philadelphia, 'fourth' edition

66.6AG/12 Adams on the Globes, Whitehall, Pennsylvania

75.1J/10 Journey, Alnwick

75.1J/A/3 Abridged Journey, British Tourists

78ME/2 More's Sir Eldred [1800]

79.4LP/12c Lives of the Poets, Dublin, Moore's edition, third issue

79.4LP/13 Lives of the Poets, Montrose

79.4LP/14 Lives of the Poets, 1800–1801, ptd. Dec. 1800

79.4LP/SS/32 Life of Collins, Poetical Works of William Collins, second edition

79.4LP/SS/57 Life of Dryden, Prose Works of John Dryden, ed. Malone

79.4LP/SS/261 Life of Thomson, The Seasons, Wrentham, Massachusetts

79.4LP/SS/262 Life of Thomson, The Seasons

88.5S/5 Sermons, fourth London edition

1801

44.2LS/11a Life of Savage, Poetical Works of Savage, ed. Cooke, first issue [?1801]

50.3R/39 The Rambler, 'fourteenth' edition, ptd. May

50.3R/S/15/Add1 Rambler Selections, Elegant Selections

56.1MD/18 Miniature Dictionary

58.4Id/17 The Idler, Strahan

59.4R/35 Rasselas, Whittingham

77.6WD/S/40 Dodd's Thoughts in Prison, new edition

78.5RD/4 Reynolds's Discourses, Works

79.4LP/15 Lives of the Poets

79.4LP/SS/121 Life of Lyttelton, Poetical Works of George, Lord Lyttelton

79.4LP/SS/129 Life of Milton, Milton's Poetical Works, ed. Todd

79.4LP/SS/263 Life of Thomson, The Seasons, Philadelphia

87.3W/5 Works, ed. Murphy, ptd. July

87.3W/6 Works

1802

50.3R/40 British Essayists, ed. Chalmers (includes The Rambler, 52.11AD/25 The Adventurer, and 58.4Id/18 The Idler), ptd. Dec.

56.1DA/23 Abridged Dictionary, Montrose ['twelfth'] edition

56.1DA/A/2 Abridged Dictionary, Adaptations, Perry's

56.1MD/19 Miniature Dictionary

59.4R/36 Rasselas, Bristol, Mills
59.4R/TF/12 Rasselas, Translations, French
63.2HT/13 Hoole's Tasso, 'eighth' edition
79.4LP/SS/130 Life of Milton, Paradise Lost [?ed. Evans]

1803

50.3R/41 The Rambler, Select British Classics, Philadelphia
52.11Ad/26 The Adventurer, Select British Classics, Philadelphia, first American edition
56.1MD/20–2 Miniature Dictionary
58.4Id/19 The Idler, Select British Classics, first American edition
59.4R/37 Rasselas, Harrison
59.4R/38 Rasselas, Miller
59.4R/39 Rasselas, Daunt's-Bridge, Morgan
59.4R/40 Rasselas, Hartford, Cooke
59.4R/TF/13 Rasselas, Translations, French
59.4R/TP/1 Rasselas, Translations, Polish
63.2HT/14 Hoole's Tasso, 'eighth' edition, royal paper
79.4LP/16 Lives of the Poets, Philadelphia
79.4LP/SS/23 Life of Butler, Poetical Works of Samuel Butler [?1803]

1804

49.2I/9 Irene, British Drama
56.1DA/A/3 Abridged Dictionary, Adaptations, Kearsley's, Mar.
56.1MD/23 Miniature Dictionary
58.4Id/20 The Idler, British Essayists, ed. Chalmers
59.4R/41 Rasselas, Lane and Newman
59.4R/42a Rasselas, Banbury, Rusher
59.4R/42b Rasselas, Banbury, Rusher
59.4R/43 Rasselas, Cambridge, Hilliard
59.4R/44 Rasselas, Paris, Barrois
59.4R/TF/14 Rasselas, Translations, French
73.12DM/5 Davies's Miscellaneous and Fugitive Pieces

75.1J/TF/2 Journey, French translation
79.4LP/17 Lives of the Poets, Moore's second Dublin edition
79.4LP/SS/13(TF) Vies de Milton et d' Addison, Paris
79.4LP/SS/24 Life of Butler, Works of the English Poets, ed. Aikin [?1804]
79.4LP/SS/33 Life of Collins, Poetical Works of William Collins
81.11B(Parts 1+2)/5 Beauties of Johnson, new edition
94.4BS/3 Piozzi's British Synonymy, Paris

1805

40.7LB/2 Life of Blake, second separate publication, chapbook, ?Oct.
49.2I/10 Irene, Cawthorn's Minor British Theatre, No. 73
50.3R/42 The Rambler, 'fifteenth' edition, Berwick
55.4D/13 Dictionary, 'ninth' edition
56.1DA/24 Abridged Dictionary, Philadelphia
56.1DA/A/4 Abridged Dictionary, Adaptations, Perry's
56.1DA/TI/4 Abridged Dictionary, Italian, ed. Bottarelli, fourth edition
56.1MD/24–6 Miniature Dictionary
58.4Id/S/5d Idler Selections, No. 41, Poulson's Almanac
59.4R/45a Rasselas, Miller
59.4R/45b Rasselas, Miller, Illustrations
59.4R/46 Rasselas, Lane and Newman
61.3LH/4 Lennox's Henrietta [?1805]
79.4LP/18 Lives of the Poets, Works of the British Poets, ed. Park, 1805–6
79.4LP/A/3 Abridged Lives of the Poets, Paris
79.4LP/SS/14(TF) Vies d' Addison et de Milton, Strassburg
79.4LP/SS/44 Life of Cowley, Works of the English Poets, ed. Aikin, Vol. VII
79.4LP/SS/131 Life of Milton, Works of the English Poets, ed. Aikin, Vol. XII
79.4LP/SS/132 Life of Milton, Works of the English Poets, ed. Park, Vol. III

79.4LP/SS/169(TF) Vies de Milton et Addison, Strassburg
79.4LP/SS/230 Life of Rochester, Some Passages in the Life and Death of Rochester
79.4LP/SS/264 Life of Thomson, The Seasons
85.2PW/9 Poetical Works, ed. Park
85.2PW/10 Poetical Works, Philadelphia
88.3L/5 Letters (Selection), To Granger
805A/1a Account of the Life (Letters to Hill Boothby)

Bowles
79.4LP/SS/265 Life of Thomson, The Seasons
85.2PW/11 Poetical Works, ed. Blagdon
85.8PM/6a Prayers and Meditations, Vernor, Hood, and Sharpe
87.3W/7 Works, Edinburgh, summer
87.3W/8 Works, ed. Chalmers
87.3W/9 Works, ed. Chalmers
[88.5S/6 Sermons]
88.5S/7 Sermons, Walpole, N.H.

1806

40GM10/EE/2 Essay on Epitaphs, A Collection of Epitaphs
50.3R/43 The Rambler, 'fifteenth' edition, ptd. Dec. 1805
50.3R/44 The Rambler, 'sixteenth' edition
50.3R/45 The Rambler, Bell & Bradfute, Edinburgh
55.4D/14 Dictionary, 'ninth' edition
55.4D/A/2 Dictionary Adaptation [1806]
56.1DA/A/5 Abridged Dictionary, Adaptations, Union Dictionary
56.1DA/A/6 Abridged Dictionary, Adaptations, Perry's
56.1MD/27–32 Miniature Dictionary
59.4R/47 Rasselas, Suttaby and Crosby
59.4R/48 Rasselas, Whittingham
59.4R/49 Rasselas, Edinburgh, Bell & Bradfute
75.1J/11 Journey, Edinburgh
77.6WD/S/41 Dodd's Thoughts in Prison, London
77.6WD/S/42 Dodd's Thoughts in Prison, Philadelphia
79.4LP/19 Lives of the Poets (from Works)
79.4LP/20 Lives of the Poets, Edinburgh (from Works)
79.4LP/SS/25 Life of Butler, Poetical Works of Samuel Butler, ed. Aikin
79.4LP/SS/133 Life of Milton, Poetical Works of John Milton, ed. Aikin
79.4LP/SS/189 Life of Pope, Works of Alexander Pope in Verse and Prose, ed.

1807

38.5L/19 London, Gay's Trivia
50.3R/S/16 Rambler Selections, Classic Tales
52.11Ad/27 The Adventurer, Sharpe's British Classics
55.4D/A/3 Dictionary Adaptation
56.1DA/24/Add1 Abridged Dictionary, 'twelfth' edition
56.1MD/33–5 Miniature Dictionary
58.4Id/21 The Idler, Taylor
59.4R/50 Rasselas, Walker's English Classics
59.4R/51 Rasselas, Classic Tales, ed. Leigh Hunt
59.4R/52 Rasselas, Coxhead
59.4R/53 Rasselas, Lane, Newman
59.4R/54 Rasselas, Wright
63.2HT/15 Hoole's Tasso, J. Johnson
75.1J/A/4 Abridged Journey, British Tourists
79.4LP/SS/1 Life of Addison, The Poets of Great Britain
79.4LP/SS/21 Life of Broome, Poetical Works of Broome
79.4LP/SS/58 Life of Dryden, Poetical Works of John Dryden
79.4LP/SS/118 Life of King, Poetical Works of King
79.4LP/SS/134 Life of Milton, Paradise Lost
79.4LP/SS/190 Life of Pope, Bell's Poets of Great Britain

79.4LP/SS/237 Life of Roscommon, Poetical Works of Earl of Roscommon

79.4LP/SS/245 Life of Shenstone, Essays on Men and Manners, by W. Shenstone

79.4LP/SS/266 Life of Thomson, The Seasons, Brookfield [Mass.]

85.2PW/12 Poetical Works, Poets of Great Britain, Vol. LX

85.8PM/6b Prayers and Meditations, Vernor, Hood, and Sharpe

85.8PM/7 Prayers and Meditations, 'fourth' edition, ptd. Aug.

79.4LP/SS/136 Life of Milton, Paradise Lost

79.4LP/SS/186 Life of Pomfret, Poetical Works of William Collins

79.4LP/SS/267 Life of Thomson, Select British Poets

80.5DMG/6 Davies's Memoirs of Garrick

80.5DMG/7 Davies's Memoirs of Garrick, Boston

85.2PW/13a Poetical Works, ed. Blagdon

85.2PW/13b Poetical Works, The Laurel [1808]

85.2PW/14 Poetical Works, The Cabinet of Poetry, Vol. 6.

1808

38.5L/TF/1 London, French translation

44.4HM/4 Harleian Miscellany, ed. Malham, 1808–11

44.4HM/5 Harleian Miscellany, ed. Park, 1808–13

50.3R/46 British Essayists, ed. Chalmers (includes The Rambler, 52.11AD/28 The Adventurer, and 58.4Id/22a-b The Idler), 1807–8, ptd. Feb.

52.3LFQ/TS/1 Lennox's The Female Quixote, Spanish translation

56.1DA/25 Abridged Dictionary

56.1MD/36–7 Miniature Dictionary

59.4R/55 Rasselas, Lane, Newman

59.4R/56 Rasselas, Boston, Pelham

62.5SA/2 Society of Artists' Catalogue, The Literary Panorama

77.6WD/S/43 Dodd's Thoughts in Prison

77.6WD/S/44 Dodd's Thoughts in Prison

77.6WD/S/45 Dodd's Thoughts in Prison, Philadelphia

79.4LP/SS/34 Life of Collins, Poetical Works of William Collins

79.4LP/SS/45 Life of Cowley, Poetical Works of Abraham Cowley

79.4LP/SS/103 Life of Gray, Works of Thomas Gray, Select British Poets

79.4LP/SS/114 Life of Hammond, Poetical Works of William Collins

79.4LP/SS/135 Life of Milton, Works of the British Poets, Vol. III

1809

50.3R/47 The Rambler, Suttaby's British Classics

50.3R/S/17 Rambler Selections, Punishment of Death

52.11Ad/29 British Essayists, ed. Chalmers (includes The Adventurer, 58.4Id/23 The Idler [and The Rambler?]), New York and Boston 1809–

53.5LSI/2 Lennox's Shakespear Illustrated, Philadelphia

56.1DA/26a Abridged Dictionary, Montrose ['twelfth'] edition

56.1DA/26b Abridged Dictionary, Montrose ['twelfth'] edition

56.1DA/27 Abridged Dictionary, Maver, Glasgow

56.1MD/38–40 Miniature Dictionary

58.4Id/S/9 Idler Selections, American Prose Miscellany

59.4R/57 Rasselas, Suttaby, Crosby

59.4R/58 Rasselas, Edinburgh, Ramsay

59.4R/59 Rasselas, Bridgeport, Backus

59.4R/TDa/1 Rasselas, Translations, Danish

59.4R/TF/3 Rasselas, Translations, French, May

59.4R/TI/4 Rasselas, Translations, Italian

63.2HT/16 Hoole's Tasso, Suttaby's Miniature Library

75.1J/A/5 Abridged Journey, British Tourist's

76.1BH/1b Burney's History of Music, second issue of Vol. II '1782', 1809–10

76.8ML/5 Mickle's Lusiad

77.6WD/S/46 Dodd's Thoughts in Prison

78.5RD/5 Reynolds's Discourses, Works

79.4LP/SS/46 Life of Cowley, Works in Prose and Verse of Abraham Cowley, ed. Aikin

79.4LP/SS/137 Life of Milton, Milton's Poetical Works

79.4LP/SS/268 Life of Thomson, Thomson's Poetical Works, Gloucester

79.4LP/SS/269 Life of Thomson, The Seasons, Edinburgh

85.8PM/8 Prayers and Meditations (with Knox's Considerations)

87.3W/10 Works, Boston and New York, 1809–12

87.3W/11 Proposals for an Edition of Johnson's Works, 1809–10

1810

50.3R/48 The Rambler, 'sixteenth' edition

52.3LFQ/7 Lennox's The Female Quixote, British Novelists

55.4D/15 Dictionary, 'tenth' edition Nov.

55.4D/A/4 Dictionary Adaptation

56.1DA/A/7 Abridged Dictionary, Adaptations, Union Dictionary

56.1MD/41 Miniature Dictionary

56.11LS/7 Sully's Memoirs, new edition

58.4Id/24 The Idler, Suttaby's British Classics

[58.4Id/25 The Idler, Cooke's edition]

59.4R/60 Rasselas, The British Novelists

59.4R/61 Rasselas, Wilson

59.4R/62a Rasselas, Baltimore, Nicklin

59.4R/62b Rasselas, Boston, Mallory

59.4R/63 Rasselas, Frederick-town, Thomson

63.2HT/17 Hoole's Tasso, English Poets, ed. Chalmers

63.2HT/18 Hoole's Tasso, first American edition

66.6AG/13 Adams on the Globes, thirteenth edition

67.1FT/3 Fawkes's Theocritus, Chalmers's English Poets

75.1J/12 Journey, first American edition

76.8ML/6 Mickle's Lusiad, Chalmers's English Poets

77.6CA/20 Dodd, Convict's Address [1810]

79.4LP/21 Lives of the Poets (from Works)

79.4LP/22 Lives of the Poets, Works of the English Poets, ed. Chalmers, contains the lives of the following, with 79.4LP/SS item numbers: Addison (2); Akenside (16); Broome (22); Butler (26); Collins (35); Congreve (42); Cowley (47); Denham (53); Dorset (55); Dryden (59), Dyer (88); Gay (91); Gray (105); Hammond (115); Hughes (117); King (119); Lyttelton (122); Mallet (124); Milton (139); Parnell (175); Ambrose Philips (179); John Philips (181); Pitt (184); Pomfret (187); Pope (191); Prior (224); Rochester (232); Roscommon (238); Rowe (242); Savage (243); Shenstone (246); Smith (248); Swift (249); Thomson (271); Tickell (304); Waller (307); Watts (314); West (321); Young (324).

79.4LP/23 Lives of the Poets, Charlestown, Massachusetts

79.4LP/SS/104 Life of Gray, The British Poets, Works of Milton (SS/138), Young (SS/325), Thomson (SS/270), and Gray

79.4LP/SS/123 Life of Mallet, British Poets, ed. Sanford [and Walsh], Vol. XXVI, 18—[?]

79.4LP/SS/140 Life of Milton, Poetical Works of John Milton

79.4LP/SS/231 Life of Rochester, Some Passages in the Life and Death of Rochester

79.4LP/SS/315 Life of Watts, The Improvement of the Mind

79.4LP/SS/323 Life of Young, Select British Poets

85.2PW/15 Poetical Works, Works of the English Poets, ed. Chalmers, Vol. XVI

85.2PW/16 Poetical Works, Charlestown

87.3W/12 Works, ed. Chalmers

1811

42.5MA/3 Monarchy Asserted, Tracts

49.2I/11 Irene, Modern British Drama

50.3R/49 The Rambler, British Essayists, ed. Chalmers, New York and Boston

56.1MD/42–5 Miniature Dictionary

58.4Id/26 The Idler, Durell, New York

59.4R/64 Rasselas, Walker

59.4R/65 Rasselas, Belcher

59.4R/66 Rasselas, Philadelphia, Bennet & Walton

63.2HT/19 Hoole's Tasso, 'tenth' edition

75.1J/13 Journey, Edinburgh

79.4LP/24 Lives of the Poets, New York (from Works)

79.4LP/SS/36 The Life of Collins, The European Magazine, lx (1811), 208–10

79.4LP/SS/60 Life of Dryden, Poetical Works of John Dryden, ed. Warton

79.4LP/SS/92 Life of Gay, Poems or Fables of John Gay

79.4LP/SS/272 Life of Thomson, Seasons, and Castle of Indolence, and Other Poems, Edinburgh

79.4LP/SS/273 Life of Thomson, The Seasons

85.2PW/17 Poetical Works, ed. Park

87.3W/1.2/2 Works, Vols. XIII-XIV, Debates in Parliament

1812

50.3R/50a The Rambler, Earle's edition, Philadelphia and New York

50.3R/50b The Rambler, Earle's edition, second state, Philadelphia

50.3R/S/18 Spirit of British Essayists (includes selections from Rambler, 52.11Ad/S/5 Adventurer and 58.4Id/S/7 Idler)

56.1DA/28 Abridged Dictionary, Wilson's stereotype edition, first impression

56.1MD/46–8 Miniature Dictionary

59.4R/67 Rasselas, Whittingham

59.4R/68 Rasselas, Oliver & Boyd

59.4R/69 Rasselas, Walker and Greig

[75.1J/14 Journey (with McNicol's Remarks) ['1812']]

75.1J/15 Journey, New York

77.6WD/S/47 Dodd's Thoughts in Prison

79.4LP/SS/93 Life of Gay, Poems or Fables of John Gay

79.4LP/SS/173 Life of Otway, Works of Otway

79.4LP/SS/192 Life of Pope, Works of Alexander Pope

79.4LP/SS/274 Life of Thomson, The Seasons, New York

87.3W/1.2/3 Works, Vols. XI-XII, Debates in Parliament, Cobbett's Parliamentary History

88.5S/8 Sermons, fifth London edition

88.5S/9 Sermons, 'fifth' edition

88.5S/10 Sermons

88.5S/11 Sermons, Philadelphia

88.5S/12 Sermons, Walpole, N.H.

1813

55.4D/A/5 Dictionary Adaptation

56.1DA/29 Abridged Dictionary, Tegg's edition

56.1DA/30 Abridged Dictionary, Philadelphia

56.1MD/49–52 Miniature Dictionary

59.4R/70 Rasselas, Fessenden

59.4R/71 Rasselas, Mirror of Amusement [1813]

59.4R/TS/2 Rasselas, Translations, Spanish

62.5SA/3 Society of Artists' Catalogue, Memoirs of Sir Joshua Reynolds

[75.1J/16 Journey, 'sixth edition', Cadell and Davies]

77.6WD/S/48 Dodd's Thoughts in Prison

77.6WD/S/49 Dodd's Thoughts in Prison, Edinburgh

79.4LP/SS/171(TG) Life of Milton, Miltons Verlorenes Paradies, Rostock and Leipzig

79.6M/2 Maurice's Westminster Abbey and Translation of Oedipus
85.8PM/9 Prayers and Meditations

1814

35.2LV/3 Lobo's Voyage to Abyssinia, Pinkerton's Collection
50.3R/S/19 Rambler Selections, Vices of the Tavern
55.4D/11b Dictionary, 'eighth' edition, Dublin, reissue [1814]
56.1DA/31 Abridged Dictionary, Tegg's edition, second impression
56.1MD/53–6 Miniature Dictionary
59.4R/72 Rasselas, Leeds, Dewhirst
75.1J/A/6 Abridged Journey, British Tourist's
77.6WD/S/50 Dodd's Thoughts in Prison

1815

55.4D/11c Dictionary, 'eighth' edition, Dublin, reissue [1815]
56.1DA/32 Abridged Dictionary, 'fourteenth' edition
56.1MD/57–8 Miniature Dictionary
58.4Id/S/8a Idler Selections, Imprisonment for Debt
59.4R/73 Rasselas, Suttaby, Evance, and Fox
59.4R/74 Rasselas, York, Spencer and Burdekin
59.4R/75 Rasselas, Paris, Barrois
61.8BA/2 Life of Ascham, Ascham's Works
77.6WD/S/51 Dodd's Thoughts in Prison
79.4LP/25 Lives of the Poets, Edinburgh
79.4LP/SS/275 Life of Thomson, Works of James Thomson [?1815]
79.4LP/SS/276 Life of Thomson, The Seasons, Alnwick
79.4LP/SS/277 Life of Thomson, The Seasons, Middlebury, Vt.
85.2PW/18 Poetical Works, ed. Blagdon
85.2PW/19 Poetical Works, Edinburgh

1816

50.3R/51 The Rambler, 'seventeenth' edition, ?6 Sept.
55.4D/18 Dictionary, 'eleventh' edition
55.4D/A/6 Dictionary Adaptation
56.1MD/59–60 Miniature Dictionary
58.4Id/27 The Idler, Cadell and Davies, 6 Sept.
58.4Id/S/8b Idler Selections, Imprisonment for Debt, 'second' edition
59.4R/76 Rasselas, Whittingham
59.4R/77 Rasselas, Rivington
59.4R/78 Rasselas, Mirror of Amusement [1816]
59.4R/79 Rasselas, New York, Durell
59.4R/80 Rasselas, Baxter
63.2HT/20 Hoole's Tasso
65.10SP/TG/1 Shakespeare, German translation
75.1J/17 Journey, Cadell and Davies, 6 Sept.
75.1J/18 Journey, Cadell and Davies, 6 Sept.
77.2PC/2 Life of Zachary Pearce
79.4LP/26 Lives of the Poets (from Works), ptd. Aug.
79.4LP/27 Lives of the Poets (from Works)
79.4LP/SS/29(TF) La Vie de Butler, Paris
79.4LP/SS/233 Life of Rochester, Evidences of the Christian Religion, Vol. IV, Some Passages
79.4LP/SS/278 Life of Thomson, The Seasons, Oxford
85.2PW/20 Poetical Works, Burlington, NJ
87.3W/13 Works, ed. Chalmers, 6 Sept.
87.3W/14 Works, ed. Chalmers
87.3W/15a Works, Alnwick edition
87.3W/16a Works, Dublin, 1816–17
816DW/1 Diary of a Journey into North Wales

1817

44.2LS/11b Life of Savage, Poetical Works of Savage, ed. Cooke, second issue

50.3R/52 British Essayists, ed. Chalmers (includes The Rambler, 52.11Ad/30 The Adventurer, and 58.4Id/28 The Idler), ptd. ?Apr.

56.1DA/33 Abridged Dictionary, Tegg's edition, third impression

56.1MD/61–4 Miniature Dictionary

59.4R/81 Rasselas, Howlett

59.4R/82 Rasselas, Sharpe

59.4R/83 Rasselas, Walker's British Classics

59.4R/84 Rasselas, Sharpe

59.4R/TF/15 Rasselas, Translations, French

59.4R/TGr/1 Rasselas, Translations, Greek

[75.1J/18/Add1 Journey, Philadelphia]

75.1J/19a Journey, Glasgow (with McNicol's Remarks), first impression

79.4LP/SS/61 Life of Dryden, The British Drama, ed. Cumberland, Vol. IX [?1817]

79.4LP/SS/141 Life of Milton, Paradise Lost

79.4LP/SS/142 Life of Milton, The British Drama, ed. Cumberland, Vol. IV [?1817]

79.4LP/SS/143 Life of Milton, Paradise Lost

79.4LP/SS/174 Life of Otway, Venice Preserved

79.4LP/SS/279 Life of Thomson, The Seasons

81.11B(Parts 1+2)/6 Beauties of Johnson, Beauties of Literature, Vol. 23

85.8PM/10 Prayers and Meditations, 'fifth' edition

87.3W/16b Works, Dublin reissue

88.3L/6 Letters (Selection), Original Letters

816DW/2 Diary of Tour in North Wales, Philadelphia

1818

44.2LS/12 Life of Savage, British Poets, ed. Chalmers

55.4D/20a Dictionary, Todd's edition, first issue

55.4D/20b Dictionary, Todd's edition, second issue

55.4D/21a Dictionary, first American edition, first issue, Philadelphia

55.4D/A/7 Dictionary Adaptation 1818–

56.1MD/65–9 Miniature Dictionary

59.4R/85 Rasselas, Whittingham

59.4R/86 Rasselas, Paris, Louis

59.4R/87 Rasselas, Philadelphia, Buzby

59.4R/TF/16 Rasselas, Translations, French

59.4R/TF/17 Rasselas, Translations, French

62.5SA/4 Society of Artists' Catalogue, Life of Sir Joshua Reynolds

63.2HT/21 Hoole's Tasso

77.6WD/S/52 Dodd's Thoughts in Prison

79.4LP/28a Lives of the Poets, Edinburgh

80.5DMG/8 Davies's Memoirs of Garrick

87.3W/15b Works, Alnwick edition, reissue

1819

44.2LS/13 Life of Savage, British Poets, ed. Sanford and Walsh

50.3R/53 British Essayists, ed. Ferguson (includes The Rambler, 52.11Ad/31 The Adventurer, and 58.4Id/29 The Idler)

55.4D/21b Dictionary, first American edition, second issue, Philadelphia

55.4D/22 Dictionary, Philadelphia, 1818–19

55.4D/24 Dictionary, Offor's edition

56.1DA/34 Abridged Dictionary, Wilson's stereotype edition, second impression

56.1DA/35 Abridged Dictionary, Tegg's edition, fourth impression

56.1DA/TI/5 Abridged Dictionary, Italian, Milan

56.1MD/70–4 Miniature Dictionary

59.4R/88 Rasselas, Lanark, Borthwick

59.4R/89 Rasselas, Baltimore, Fielding Lucas

59.4R/90 Rasselas, M'Lean

59.4R/91 Rasselas, Paris, Louis

59.4R/TF/18 Rasselas, Translations, French

63.2HT/22 Hoole's Tasso, Suttaby, Evance & Fox, 31 May

65.10SP/TI/1 Shakespeare, Italian translation

75.1J/20 Journey, Alnwick

75.1J/21 Journey, Edinburgh

76.1HA/3 Hailes's Annals of Scotland, third edition

78.5RD/6 Reynolds's Discourses, Works

79.4LP/28b Lives of the Poets

79.4LP/29 Lives of the Poets, Encyclopædia of British Literature

79.4LP/30 Lives of the Poets, Philadelphia

79.4LP/SS/89 Life of Dyer, Works of the British Poets (includes also lives of Pitt (SS/185), Pope (SS/193), Swift (SS/250), Watts (SS/316), and Young (SS/326)), ed. Sanford [and Walsh]

79.4LP/SS/234 Life of Rochester, Some Passages in the Life and Death of Rochester

81.11B(Parts 1+2)/7 Beauties of Johnson, Glasgow

88.5S/13 Sermons, British Prose, Vol. XV

56.1DA/36 Abridged Dictionary, Chalmers's abridgement of Todd, first edition

56.1MD/75–6 Miniature Dictionary

59.4R/93 Rasselas, The British Novelist

59.4R/94 Rasselas, Bumpus, 1 July

59.4R/95a Rasselas, Suttaby, Evance & Fox

59.4R/95b Rasselas, Suttaby, Evance, and Fox

59.4R/96 Rasselas, Philadelphia, Parker

[59.4R/97 Rasselas, Appleton's Miniature Classical Library [1820]]

59.4R/TF/19 Rasselas, Translations, French

78.5RD/7 Reynolds's Discourses, Sharpe's British Prose Writers, 1820/5

79.4LP/31 Lives of the Poets (from Works)

79.4LP/32 Lives of the Poets, British Classics

79.4LP/SS/94 Life of Gay, Poems or Fables of John Gay

79.4LP/SS/235 Life of Rochester, Some Passages in the Life and Death of Rochester

79.4LP/SS/239 Life of Roscommon, Poetical Works of Wentworth Dillon, Earl of Roscommon

85.2PW/21 Poetical Works, ed. Blagdon

87.3W/2.1/3 Murphy's Essay, third edition

87.3W/17 Works, new edition

88.3L/7 Letters (Selection), To George Colman

88.5S/14a Sermons, Boston

1820

39.4MN/3 Marmor Norfolciense, third edition

50.3R/54 The Rambler, 'eighteenth' edition

50.3R/55 The Rambler, miniature edition

52.3LFQ/8 Lennox's The Female Quixote, British Novelists

55.4D/25 Dictionary, Offor's second impression

1821

50.3R/56 The Rambler, Small's edition, Philadelphia

56.1DA/37 Abridged Dictionary

56.1MD/77–80 Miniature Dictionary

59.4R/98 Rasselas, Belfast, Simms & M'Intyre

59.4R/99 Rasselas, Paris, Barrois

59.4R/TF/20 Rasselas, Translations, French

59.4R/TF/21 Rasselas, Translations, French

63.2HT/23 Hoole's Tasso

78.5RD/8 Reynolds's Discourses, Boston

79.4LP/33 Lives of the Poets, Rivington

79.4LP/34 Lives of the Poets, Walker

79.4LP/SS/37 Life of Collins, Poetical Works of William Collins, ed. Crowe

79.4LP/SS/144 Life of Milton, Paradise Lost

79.4LP/SS/317 Life of Watts, The Improvement of the Mind, Edinburgh

85.8PM/11 Prayers and Meditations, Dorchester

88.5S/14b Sermons, British Prose Writer, Vol. 8, Boston

1822

44.2LS/14 Life of Savage, British Poets, Whittingham edition

50.3R/57 The Rambler, 'seventeenth' edition

50.3R/58 The Rambler, Richardson's edition

55.4D/26 Dictionary, Offor's third impression

56.1DA/38 Abridged Dictionary, Tegg's edition, fifth impression

56.1DA/A/8 Abridged Dictionary, Adaptations, Union Dictionary

56.1DA/TB/1 Abridged Dictionary, Bengali, Serampore

56.1MD/81–3 Miniature Dictionary

59.4R/100 Rasselas, Sharpe

59.4R/101 Rasselas, Whittingham's Cabinet Library

59.4R/102 Rasselas, Smith [?1822]

59.4R/103 Rasselas, Boulogne, Le Roy-Berger

59.4R/104 Rasselas (with Vicar of Wakefield)

59.4R/105 Rasselas, Philadelphia, Yardley

59.4R/TF/22 Rasselas, Translations, French

59.4R/TF/23 Rasselas, Translations, French

63.2HT/24 Hoole's Tasso, Rivington

75.1J/19b Journey, Glasgow (with McNicol's Remarks), second impression

76.8ML/7 Mickle's Lusiad, English Translations

77.6WD/S/53 Dodd's Thoughts in Prison

79.4LP/35 Lives of the Poets, British Poets, Chiswick edition

79.4LP/36 Lives of the Poets, Christie

79.4LP/SS/3 Life of Addison, The British Poets (includes also lives of Butler (SS/27), Dryden (SS/62), and John Philips (SS/182))

79.4LP/SS/280 Life of Thomson, The Seasons, and a Poem to the memory of Sir Isaac Newton, Kilmarnock

79.4LP/SS/281 Life of Thomson, The Seasons, Boston

79.6M/3 Maurice's Translation of Oedipus

85.2PW/22 Poetical Works, British Poets, Vol. LXVII

88.3L/8 Letters (Selection)

1823

50.3R/59 British Essayists, ed. Ferguson (includes The Rambler, 52.11Ad/35 The Adventurer, and 58.4Id/32 The Idler)

50.3R/60 British Essayists, ed. Chalmers (includes The Rambler, 52.11Ad/33 The Adventurer, 58.4Id/30 The Idler), ptd. Aug.

50.3R/61 British Essayists, ed. Berguer (includes The Rambler, 52.11Ad/34 The Adventurer, and 58.4Id/31 The Idler)

50.3R/62 The Rambler, 'eighteenth' edition

50.3R/63 The Rambler, Jones's edition

52.11Ad/32 The Adventurer, a new edition

56.1DA/39 Abridged Dictionary, Wilson's stereotype edition, third impression

56.1MD/84–91 Miniature Dictionary

59.4R/106 Rasselas, Wilson

59.4R/107 Rasselas, Sharpe

59.4R/108 Rasselas and Dinarbas

59.4R/109 Rasselas, Suttaby, Evans, & Fox

59.4R/110 Rasselas, Ballantyne's Novelist's Library

59.4R/TF/24 Rasselas, Translations, French

59.4R/TI/5 Rasselas, Translations, Italian

77.6WD/S/54 Dodd's Thoughts in Prison, 1823–4

79.4LP/TF/1 Lives of the Poets, French translation, Paris

79.4LP/SS/17 Life of Akenside, Poetical Works of Mark Akenside

79.4LP/SS/282 Life of Thomson, Jones's British Poets, Vol. 7

85.8PM/12 Prayers and Meditations, Glasgow

87.3W/18 Works, ed. Chalmers

88.5S/15 Sermons, ed. Chalmers

1824

50.3R/64 The Rambler, Jones's edition

50.3R/65 The Rambler, Baynes & Son

50.3R/66 The Rambler, Glasgow

50.3R/67 The Rambler, ed. Chalmers, Philadelphia

50.3R/S/20 Spirit of British Essayists (includes Rambler Selections, 52.11Ad/S/6 Adventurer Selections, and 58.4Id/S/10 Idler Selections)

55.4D/27 Dictionary, Offor's fourth impression

55.4D/A/8 Dictionary Adaptation [?1824]

56.1DA/40 Abridged Dictionary, Wilson's stereotype edition, fourth impression

56.1DA/41 Abridged Dictionary, Chalmers's, second 'edition'

56.1DA/42 Abridged Dictionary, Tegg's edition, sixth impression

56.1MD/92–5 Miniature Dictionary

58.4Id/33 The Idler, Baynes & Son

58.4Id/34 The Idler, Bumpus

58.4Id/35 The Idler, Jones's University edition

59.4R/111 Rasselas, Hailes

59.4R/112 Rasselas, Edinburgh Classics

59.4R/113 Rasselas, Hodgson and Co.

59.4R/114 Rasselas, Suttaby, Evance & Fox

[59.4R/115 Rasselas]

59.4R/116a Rasselas, Limbird's British Novelist

59.4R/116b Rasselas, Limbird's British Novelist [1824–6]

59.4R/117 Rasselas, White

59.4R/118 Rasselas, Smith [1824]

59.4R/119 Rasselas, from Works

59.4R/120 Rasselas, Paisley

59.4R/121 Rasselas, Brattleboro', Holbrook & Fessenden

59.4R/TDu/2 Rasselas, Translations, Dutch

66.8CL/2 Law Lectures for Robert Chambers, Treatise on Estates and Tenures

75.1J/22 Journey (and Political Tracts)

77.6WD/S/5c [Mary Bosanquet], An Aunt's Advice to a Neice

78.5RD/9 Reynolds's Discourses, Works

[79.4LP/37 Lives of the Poets, Dove's English Classics]

79.4LP/38 Lives of the Poets, Tegg

79.4LP/39 Lives of the Poets, Christie

79.4LP/TD/1 Lives of the Poets, Dutch translation, Amsterdam

79.4LP/SS/95 Life of Gay, Poems or Fables of John Gay

79.4LP/SS/194 Life of Pope, Poetical Works of Alexander Pope

79.4LP/SS/195 Life of Pope, Poetical Works of Alexander Pope, ed. Roscoe, 1824–5

79.4LP/SS/283 Life of Thomson, Works of James Thomson

79.4LP/SS/284 Life of Thomson, The Seasons

79.4LP/SS/285 Life of Thomson, The Seasons, Edinburgh

79.4LP/SS/318 Life of Watts, The Improvement of the Mind
87.3W/19a Works, ed. Lynam
87.3W/20 Works, Baynes and Son
87.3W/21 Works, Tegg's edition
88.5S/16 Sermons, Works

1825

50.3R/68 The Rambler, 'eighteenth' edition
50.3R/69 The Rambler, Jones's University edition
50.3R/70a The Rambler, British Essayists, ed. Lynam
50.3R/70b The Rambler, British Essayists, ed. Lynam
52.11Ad/36 The Adventurer, Jones's University edition 1825-
55.4D/28 Dictionary, Offor's fifth impression
56.1DA/43 Abridged Dictionary, Wilson's stereotype edition, fifth impression
56.1MD/96–9 Miniature Dictionary
57.5CA/TF/4 Chambers's Chinese Architecture, French translation
58.4Id/36 The Idler, Jones's edition [?1825]
59.4R/122a Rasselas, Jones
59.4R/122b Rasselas, University Edition, Jones
59.4R/122c Rasselas, Jones's Cabinet Edition of Classic Tales
59.4R/123a Rasselas and Dinarbas
59.4R/123b Rasselas and Dinarbas [?1825]
59.4R/124 Rasselas, Suttaby, Evans, & Fox
59.4R/125 Rasselas, Edinburgh, Wilson
59.4R/126 Rasselas, Hartford, Andrus
59.4R/127 Rasselas, Paris, Baudry
59.4R/TF/25 Rasselas, Translations, French
59.4R/TI/6 Rasselas, Translations, Italian
75.1J/23 Journey, Glasgow
77.5KW/3 Prologue to Kelly's A Word to the Wise, Dramatic Table Talk

79.4LP/40 Lives of the Poets, ed. Lynam
79.4LP/41 Lives of the Poets, Jones's University Edition
79.4LP/42 Lives of the Poets, Philadelphia
79.4LP/SS/286 Life of Thomson, University Edition: Diamond British Poets in Miniature
79.4LP/SS/319 Life of Watts, The Improvement of the Mind, 23rd edition
85.2PW/23 Poetical Works, The British Anthology, Vol. VII
87.3W/1.2/4 Works, Works, X-XI, Debates in Parliament, Oxford English Classics
87.3W/19b Works, ed. Lynam, reimpression
87.3W/22a Works, Oxford English Classics, 1 Nov. 1824-July 1825
87.3W/23a Works, Jones's University Edition
87.3W/24 Works, second American edition

1826

38.5L/20 London and **49.1VW/23** Vanity of Human Wishes, The British Satirist
50.3R/71 The Rambler, Tegg's edition
50.3R/72 The Rambler, Jones's edition
50.3R/73a The Rambler, ed. Lynam
50.3R/TI/S/1 Rambler, Italian translation, Selections
55.4D/A/9 Dictionary Adaptation [1826]
56.1DA/44 Abridged Dictionary, Chalmers's, second 'edition', second impression
56.1MD/100–4 Miniature Dictionary
58.4Id/37 The Idler, Lynam's edition
59.4R/128 Rasselas, Virtue
59.4R/129 Rasselas, Tegg
59.4R/130 Rasselas, Bedlington's Cabinet Library, Carter's Stereotype Edition
59.4R/TAr/1 Rasselas, Translations, Armenian
59.4R/TG/5a–b Rasselas, Translations, German

79.4LP/43 Lives of the Poets, Dove's English Classics

79.4LP/SS/145 Life of Milton, Poetical Works of John Milton, ed. Todd

85.8PM/13 Prayers and Meditations, Dorchester

85.8PM/14 Prayers and Meditations, Glasgow

85.8PM/15 Prayers and Meditations, Renshaw and Kirkman n.d. [?1826]

85.8PM/16 Prayers and Meditations, Philadelphia, Jacobs n.d. [?1826]

1827

50.3R/73b British Essayists, ed. Lynam (includes The Rambler, 52.11Ad/37 The Adventurer, and 58.4Id/38 The Idler)

50.3R/74 The Rambler, ed. Chalmers, Philadelphia

50.3R/75 The Rambler, Tegg's edition

50.3R/TF/2 Rambler, French translation

55.4D/29 Dictionary, Todd's second edition

55.4D/30 Dictionary, Heidelberg

56.1DA/45 Abridged Dictionary, Jameson's, first edition

56.1DA/46 Abridged Dictionary, Tegg's edition, seventh impression

56.1MD/105–8 Miniature Dictionary

59.4R/131 Rasselas, Dove's English Classics

59.4R/132 Rasselas, Jones's Cabinet Edition of Classic Tales,

59.4R/133 Rasselas, Hartford, Andrus

59.4R/134 Rasselas, Smith [?1827–28]

59.4R/TF/26 Rasselas, Translations, French

59.4R/TG/6 Rasselas, Translations, German

77.6WD/S/55 Dodd's Thoughts in Prison, Dove's English Classics

79.4LP/44 Lives of the Poets, Bumpus

79.4LP/45 Lives of the Poets, Jones's edition

79.4LP/SS/38 Life of Collins, Poetical Works of William Collins, ed. Dyce

79.4LP/SS/196 Life of Pope, Poetical Works of Alexander Pope

1828

50.3R/76a The Rambler, introd. Murphy, Philadelphia

50.3R/76b The Rambler, introd. Murphy, Princeton, N.J.

55.4D/31 Dictionary, Heidelberg

55.4D/32 Dictionary, Robertson's stereotype from the folio

56.1DA/47 Abridged Dictionary, Wilson's stereotype edition, sixth impression

56.1DA/48 Abridged Dictionary, Jameson's, second impression

56.1DA/49 Abridged Dictionary, Moon, Boys, & Graves

56.1DA/50 Abridged Dictionary, Chalmers's, ed. Worcester, Boston stereotype edition, first edition

56.1MD/109–13 Miniature Dictionary

59.4R/135 Rasselas, Sharpe

59.4R/TI/7 Rasselas, Translations, Italian

79.4LP/46 Lives of the Poets, Jones's edition

79.4LP/SS/39 Life of Collins, Poetical Works of William Collins, ed. Crowe

79.4LP/SS/96 Life of Gay, Poems or Fables of John Gay

81.11B(Parts 1+2)/8 Beauties of Johnson, new edition

81.11B(Parts 1+2)/9 Beauties of Johnson, Edinburgh

81.11B(Parts 1+2)/10 Beauties of Johnson, Boston

1829

49.1VW/24 Vanity of Human Wishes, Sequel to the English Reader

52.11Ad/38 The Adventurer, Jones's edition

55.4D/33 Dictionary, Galignani's [Robertson's] stereotype

56.1DA/51 Abridged Dictionary, Wilson's stereotype edition, seventh impression

56.1DA/52 Abridged Dictionary, Chalmers's, Boston stereotype edition, second impression

56.1MD/114–19b Miniature Dictionary

59.4R/136 Rasselas, Whittingham

59.4R/137 Rasselas, Paris, Baudry

59.4R/138 Rasselas, Jones's Diamond Classics, University Edition

59.4R/139 Rasselas, Limbird's British Novelist

59.4R/TF/27 Rasselas, Translations, French

59.4R/TG/7 Rasselas, Translations, German

59.4R/TG/8 Rasselas, Translations, German

79.4LP/47 Lives of the Poets, Jones's edition

79.4LP/SS/287 Life of Thomson, The Seasons, Edinburgh

79.4LP/SS/288 Life of Thomson, The Seasons, Edinburgh n.d. [?1829]

88.3L/TF/1 Letter to Chesterfield, French translation

1830

55.4D/34 Dictionary, second impression of Robertson's stereotype

56.1DA/53 Abridged Dictionary, Chalmers's, Boston stereotype edition, third impression

56.1DA/54 Abridged Dictionary, Chalmers's, Boston stereotype edition, fourth impression

56.1MD/120–6 Miniature Dictionary

59.4R/140 Rasselas and Dinarbas

59.4R/141a Rasselas, Jones's Diamond Classics

59.4R/141b Rasselas, Jones's University Edition

59.4R/141c Rasselas, Jones's Classic Tales [?1830]

59.4R/142 Rasselas, Brussels, Frank

59.4R/143 Rasselas, Hartford, Andrus

59.4R/TF/28 Rasselas, Translations, French

59.4R/TF/29 Rasselas, Translations, French

79.4LP/SS/197 Life of Pope, Poetical Works of Alexander Pope

79.4LP/SS/198 Life of Pope, Poetical Works of Alexander Pope, Philadelphia

79.4LP/SS/289 Life of Thomson, The Seasons [?1830]

81.11B(Parts 1+2)/11 Beauties of Johnson, Edinburgh

1831

38.5L/21 London, Juvenal, trans. Badham

48.4DP/VT/12 Vision of Theodore, with interlinear Danish translation

49.1VW/25 Vanity of Human Wishes, Juvenal, trans. Badham

55.4D/35 Dictionary, Tegg's impression of Offor's edition

55.4D/A/TF/1 Dictionary Adaptation, French translation

56.1MD/127–33 Miniature Dictionary

59.4R/144 Rasselas, Jones's Cabinet Edition of Classic Tales

59.4R/145 Rasselas, Bedlington's Cabinet Library, Carter's Stereotype Edition

59.4R/146 Rasselas, Paris, Baudry

59.4R/TF/30 Rasselas, Translations, French

79.4LP/48 Lives of the Poets, Tilt's Edition

79.4LP/49 Lives of the Poets, Sharpe

1832

50.3R/77 The Rambler, SPCK edition

55.4D/36 Dictionary, Tegg's second impression of Offor's edition

56.1DA/55a Abridged Dictionary, Chalmers's, Boston stereotype edition, fifth impression

56.1DA/55b Abridged Dictionary, Chalmers's, Boston stereotype edition, fifth impression

56.1MD/134–8 Miniature Dictionary

59.4R/147 Rasselas, SPCK

59.4R/148 Rasselas, Jones's Diamond Classics

59.4R/149 Rasselas, Limbird's British Novelist

59.4R/150 Rasselas, Paris

59.4R/151 Rasselas, Leipzig, Müller

59.4R/152 Rasselas, Carter's Stereotype Edition, Hartford, Andrus, [1832]

59.4R/TF/31 Rasselas, Translations, French

59.4R/TG/9 Rasselas, Translations, German

79.4LP/50 Lives of the Poets, Jones's edition

87.3W/25a Works, 'First Complete American Edition', New York, Blake [1832]

87.3W/25b Works, 'First Complete American Edition', New York, Dearborn

87.3W/25c Works, 'First Complete American Edition', New York, Harper

1833

50.3R/78 British Essayists (includes The Rambler, 52.11Ad/39 The Adventurer, and 58.4Id/39 The Idler)

55.4D/37 Dictionary, Tegg's third impression of Offor's edition

56.1DA/56 Abridged Dictionary, Chalmers's, Boston stereotype edition, sixth impression

56.1DA/57a Abridged Dictionary, Chalmers's, Boston stereotype edition, seventh impression

56.1DA/57b Abridged Dictionary, Chalmers's, Boston stereotype edition, ?seventh impression

56.1MD/139–48 Miniature Dictionary

59.4R/153 Rasselas (with Vathek)

59.4R/154 Rasselas, Hartford, Andrus and Judd [1833]

59.4R/155 Rasselas, Carter's Stereotype Edition, Boston

59.4R/TB/1 Rasselas, Translations, Bengali [dedication, 11 Mar.]

59.4R/TF/32 Rasselas, Translations, French

79.4LP/SS/146 Life of Milton, John Milton, His Life and Times, by Ivimey

81.11B(Parts 1+2)/12 Beauties of Johnson, Beauties of Literature, Vol. VII

81.11B(Parts 1+2)/13 Beauties of Johnson, Boston

1834

31.10HM/TE/1 Messia, Meikle's translation

55.4D/39 Dictionary, Tegg's fourth impression of Offor's edition

56.1DA/58 Abridged Dictionary, Chalmers's, Boston stereotype editon, eighth impression

56.1DA/59 Abridged Dictionary, Chalmers's, ?Boston stereotype edition, ninth impression, Philadelphia

56.1DA/60 Abridged Dictionary, Tegg's edition, eighth impression

56.1DA/61 Abridged Dictionary, Wilson's stereotype edition, eighth impression

56.1DA/A/9 Abridged Dictionary, Adaptations, National Library

56.1DA/TB/2 Abridged Dictionary, Bengali, Serampore, another edition

56.1MD/149–50 Miniature Dictionary, 149 ptd. 8 Mar.

59.4R/156 Rasselas, Limbird's British Novelist

59.4R/157 Rasselas, Republic of Letters, No. 9

59.4R/158 Rasselas, Hartford, Andrus and Judd

59.4R/159 Rasselas, Paris & Lyon, Baudry, Cormon & Blanc

59.4R/TF/33 Rasselas, Translations, French

59.4R/TS/3 Rasselas, Translations, Spanish

79.4LP/51 Lives of the Poets, Cadell's editon [?1834]

79.4LP/SS/40 Life of Collins, Poetical Works of William Collins, New York

79.4LP/SS/290 Life of Thomson, The Seasons

81.11B(Parts 1+2)/14 Beauties of Johnson, Boston

81.11B(Parts 1+2)/15 Beauties of Johnson, Howards' Beauties of Literature Vol. VIII

85.2BH/3 Burney's Commemoration of Handel

87.3W/25d Works, 'First Complete American Edition', New York, Dearborn

1835

49.1VW/26 Vanity of Human Wishes, with 59.4R/164 Rasselas *c*.1835

56.1DA/62 Abridged Dictionary, Jameson's, ['fourth edition'], third impression

56.1DA/63 Abridged Dictionary, ?Boston stereotype edition, tenth impression, Philadelphia

56.1DA/64 Abridged Dictionary, Boston stereotype edition, eleventh impression, Philadelphia

56.1MD/151–6 Miniature Dictionary

58.4Id/S/8c Idler Selections, Imprisonment for Debt, New York

59.4R/160 Rasselas, Jones's Diamond Classics

59.4R/161 Rasselas, Tilt's Miniature Classical Library

59.4R/162 Rasselas, English Classic Library [1835]

59.4R/163a Rasselas, Fisher

59.4R/163b Rasselas, Mirror of Amusement, Fisher [1835]

59.4R/164 Rasselas, Daly [?1835]

59.4R/165 Rasselas, Derby, Richardson

59.4R/166 Rasselas, Paris, Baudry

59.4R/TF/34 Rasselas, Translations, French

79.4LP/52 Lives of the Poets, Halifax

79.4LP/SS/291 Life of Thomson, The Seasons, Belfast

85.2PW/24 Poetical Works, Philadelphia

87.3W/25e Works, 'First Complete American Edition', New York, Dearborn

88.5S/17 Sermons, Ripon

1836

56.1DA/65 Abridged Dictionary, Chalmers's, Boston stereotype edition, twelfth impression

56.1DA/66 Abridged Dictionary, Kay edition, Philadelphia

56.1DA/A/10 Abridged Dictionary, Adaptations, Tuckey's

56.1MD/157–62 Miniature Dictionary

56.3BCM/2 Browne's Christian Morals, third edition

59.4R/167 Rasselas, Scott, Webster, and Geary

59.4R/168 Rasselas, Diamond Classics [?1836]

59.4R/169 Rasselas, Tilt's Miniature Classical Library

59.4R/170 Rasselas, Nürnberg & New York, Campe [1836]

59.4R/TG/10 Rasselas, Translations, German [?1836]

79.4LP/53 Lives of the Poets, Halifax

79.4LP/SS/292 Life of Thomson, The Seasons

85.8PM/17 Prayers and Meditations, Washbourne

87.3W/25f Works, 'First Complete American Edition', New York, Dearborn

1837

55.4D/40 Dictionary, Tegg's fifth impression of Offor's edition

56.1DA/67 Abridged Dictionary, Chalmers's, second 'edition', third impression

56.1MD/163–7 Miniature Dictionary

59.4R/171 Rasselas, Select Classics

59.4R/172 Rasselas, Daly

59.4R/173 Rasselas, Boston, Harrington Carter

59.4R/174 Rasselas, Jones

78.5RD/10 Reynolds's Discourses

79.4LP/SS/293 Life of Thomson, The Seasons and The Castle of Indolence

81.11B(Parts 1+2)/16 Beauties of Johnson, Boston

87.3W/25g Works, 'First Complete American Edition', New York, Dearborn

87.3W/25h Works, 'First Complete American Edition', New York, Dearborn

1838

55.4D/41 Dictionary, third impression of Robertson's stereotype edition

56.1DA/68 Abridged Dictionary, Chalmers's, Boston stereotype edition, thirteenth impression, Philadelphia

56.1DA/69 Abridged Dictionary, Wilson's stereotype edition, ninth impression

56.1MD/168–73 Miniature Dictionary

59.4R/175 Rasselas, Daly

59.4R/176 Rasselas, Lacey

59.4R/177 Rasselas, Tilt's Miniature Classical Library

59.4R/178 Rasselas, Classical Tales, Hague, Fuhri

59.4R/TDu/3 Rasselas, Translations, Dutch, Classical Tales

59.4R/TP/2 Rasselas, Translations, Polish, 1838–40

79.4LP/54 Lives of the Poets, Jones's Edition

79.4LP/A/4 Lives of the Poets, Jones's abridgement

79.4LP/SS/294 Life of Thomson, The Seasons and The Castle of Indolence

87.3W/25i Works, 'First Complete American Edition', New York, Blake

1839

50.3R/TH/S/1 Rambler, Hungarian translation, Selections 1839–44

56.1DA/70 Abridged Dictionary, Chalmers's, Boston stereotype edition, fourteenth impression, Philadelphia

56.1MD/174–8 Miniature Dictionary

59.4R/179 Rasselas, Carter's Stereotype Edition, Boston

75.3TT/5 Taxation no Tyranny, American Archives

79.4LP/55 Lives of the Poets, Glasgow

79.4LP/SS/295 Life of Thomson, The Seasons

1840

55.4D/42 Dictionary, Tegg's sixth impression of Offor's edition

56.1MD/179–84 Miniature Dictionary

59.4R/180a Rasselas, Smith's Standard Library

59.4R/180b Rasselas, Smith's Standard Library [?1840]

59.4R/181a Rasselas, Derby, Richardson

59.4R/181b Rasselas, Derby, Richardson [?1840]

59.4R/182 Rasselas and Dinarbas, Scott, Webster, and Geary [?1840]

59.4R/183 Rasselas, Baudry's European Library, No. 9

59.4R/TF/35 Rasselas, Translations, French

59.4R/TG/11 Rasselas, Translations, German

59.4R/THu/1 Rasselas, Translations, Hungarian

79.4LP/56 Lives of the Poets, Tilt's Cabinet Library

[85.8PM/18 Prayers and Meditations, introd. Gresley]

87.3W/25j Works, 'First Complete American Edition', New York, Dearborn

87.3W/S/1 Selected Works, Harper's Family Library, Nos. CIX–CX

1841

56.1DA/71 Abridged Dictionary, Chalmers's, Boston stereotype edition, fifteenth impression, Philadelphia

56.1MD/185–9 Miniature Dictionary

59.4R/184 Rasselas, Daly

59.4R/185 Rasselas, New York, Mack, Andrus & Woodruff

59.4R/186 Rasselas, Appleton's Miniature Classical Library, New York

59.4R/TG/12 Rasselas, Translations, German

79.4LP/SS/97 Lives of Gay, Cotton, and Moore, Berwick

79.4LP/SS/296 Life of Thomson, The Seasons, Halifax

1842

56.1DA/72 Abridged Dictionary, Wilson's stereotype edition, tenth impression, Halifax

56.1DA/73 Abridged Dictionary, Chalmers's, Boston stereotype edition, ?sixteenth impression, Philadelphia

56.1MD/190 Miniature Dictionary

59.4R/187 Rasselas, Jones's Classic Tales

59.4R/188 Rasselas, Hughes [1842]

59.4R/189 Rasselas, Carter's Stereotype Edition, Boston, Mussey

59.4R/190 Rasselas, Paris, Thiérot

59.4R/TF/36 Rasselas, Translations, French

59.4R/TF/37 Rasselas, Translations, French

59.4R/TG/13 Rasselas, Translations, German

77.6WD/S/56 Dodd's Prison Thoughts (with The Grave etc.)

[78.5RD/11 Reynolds's Discourses]

79.4LP/TF/2 Lives of the Poets, French translation, Paris

1843

55.4D/43 Dictionary, fourth impression of Robertson's stereotype edition

56.1DA/74 Abridged Dictionary, Chalmers's, Boston stereotype edition, seventeenth impression, Philadelphia

56.1DA/75 Abridged Dictionary, Chalmers's, second 'edition', fourth impression

56.1MD/191–3 Miniature Dictionary

59.4R/191 Rasselas, Pocket English Classics, No. 1

59.4R/192 Rasselas, Gouda, van Goor

59.4R/TDu/4 Rasselas, Translations, Dutch

81.11B(Parts 1+2)/17 Beauties of Johnson, Cooperstown

87.3W/25k Works, 'First Complete American Edition', New York, Dearborn

1844

56.1DA/76 Abridged Dictionary, Chalmers's, Boston stereotype edition, eighteenth impression, Philadelphia

56.1MD/194–6 Miniature Dictionary

58.4Id/40 The Idler, British Essayists, ed. Chalmers, Boston

59.4R/193 Rasselas, Carter's Stereotype Edition, Moral Library

59.4R/TG/14 Rasselas, Translations, German

[79.4LP/57 Lives of the Poets, Kent's edition [?1844]]

79.4LP/SS/223(TG) Life of Pope, G.C. Lichtenbergs Vermischte Schriften, vermehrte von dessen Söhnen veranstaltete, Göttingen, 1844–67

1845

55.4D/A/10 Dictionary Adaptation

56.1MD/197–204 Miniature Dictionary

56.3BCM/3 Browne's Christian Morals, Bohn's Standard Library

59.4R/194 Rasselas, Pocket English Classics [1845]

59.4R/195 Rasselas and Dinarbas, Manchester, Johnson

59.4R/196 Rasselas, Gouda, van Goor

59.4R/TDu/5 Rasselas, Translations, Dutch

59.4R/TF/38 Rasselas, Translations, French

62.5SA/5 Society of Artists' Catalogue, Patronage of British Art

78.5RD/12a Reynolds's Discourses, Works

79.4LP/SS/297 Life of Thomson, The Seasons

85.8PM/19 Prayers and Meditations, Allman

1846

55.4D/44 Dictionary, fifth impression of Robertson's stereotype edition

56.1DA/77 Abridged Dictionary, Wilson's stereotype edition, eleventh impression, Halifax

56.1DA/78 Abridged Dictionary, Wilson's stereotype edition, twelfth impression [?1846]

56.1DA/TF/1 Abridged Dictionary, French, Noel [?1846]

56.1DA/TF/2 Abridged Dictionary, French, London

56.1MD/205–10 Miniature Dictionary

59.4R/197 Rasselas, SPCK

59.4R/198 Rasselas, Leipzig, Renger

59.4R/199 Rasselas, New York, Mack, Andrus

59.4R/TF/39 Rasselas, Translations, French

59.4R/TF/40 Rasselas, Translations, French

77.6WD/S/56 Dodd's Prison Thoughts

78.5RD/12b Reynolds's Discourses, Works

85.8PM/20 Prayers and Meditations, Glasgow

87.3W/251 Works, 'Third American Edition', New York, Blake

1847

56.1MD/211–15 Miniature Dictionary

59.4R/200 Rasselas, introd. Boswell, Tegg

59.4R/201 Rasselas, Jones's Classic Tales

59.4R/202 Rasselas, Hartford, Andrus

59.4R/TF/41 Rasselas, Translations, French

59.4R/TF/42 Rasselas, Translations, French

79.4LP/58 Lives of the Poets, Aberdeen

1848

50.3R/S/21 Rambler Selections, Wisdom

52.11Ad/S/7 Adventurer Selections, Wisdom

56.1DA/79a Abridged Dictionary, Jameson's, fourth impression ['seventh edition']

56.1DA/79b Abridged Dictionary, Jameson's, fourth impression ['seventh edition']

56.1DA/79c Abridged Dictionary, Jameson's, fourth impression ['seventh edition']

56.1MD/216–18 Miniature Dictionary

58.4Id/S/11 Idler Selections, Wisdom

59.4R/203 Rasselas, New York, Appleton [1848]

59.4R/204 Rasselas and Elizabeth [1848]

79.4LP/59 Lives of the Poets, Jones's edition

79.4LP/SS/41 Life of Collins, Poetical Works of William Collins, ed. Crowe

1849

49.1VW/27 Vanity of Human Wishes, Jonsunz Select Wurcs (Pitman's Phonetic Edition)

55.4D/45 Dictionary, sixth impression of Roberston's stereotype edition

55.4D/A/11 Dictionary Adaptation

56.1DA/80 Abridged Dictionary, Jameson's, fifth impression ['seventh edition']

56.1MD/219a–22 Miniature Dictionary

59.4R/205 Rasselas, Pitman's Phonetic edition

59.4R/206 Rasselas, Hartford, Andrus

79.4LP/SS/199 Life of Pope, Poetical Works of Alexander Pope, Boston

79.4LP/SS/298 Life of Thomson, The Seasons and The Castle of Indolence [?1849]

1850

48.4DP/VT/10 Vision of Theodore, with Rasselas

50.3R/79 The Rambler (with 52.11Ad/40 The Adventurer and 58.4Id/41 The Idler)

56.1DA/81a Abridged Dictionary, Jameson's, sixth impression, first state, ['seventh edition']

56.1DA/81b Abridged Dictionary, Jameson's, sixth impression, second state, ['seventh edition']

56.1MD/223–8 Miniature Dictionary

58.4Id/41 The Idler (with the Rambler and Adventurer)

59.4R/207 Rasselas, first coloured illustrated edition

59.4R/208 Rasselas, Hartford, Andrus

59.4R/209 Rasselas, New York, Carter

59.4R/D/1 Rasselas, Lacy's Dramatic Adaptation

59.4R/TF/43 Rasselas, Translations, French

59.4R/TG/15 Rasselas, Translations, German [?1850]

66.4WM/F/14 The Fountains (with Rasselas), Philadelphia

79.4LP/SS/147 Life of Milton, Poetical Works of John Milton

87.3W/23b Works, Jones's edition, Bohn

1851

49.1VW/28 Vanity of Human Wishes, ed. Hoskins, July-Aug.

56.1DA/82 Abridged Dictionary, Jameson's, seventh impression ['seventh edition'], Halifax

56.1DA/TB/3 Abridged Dictionary, Bengali, Calcutta

56.1MD/229–31 Miniature Dictionary

59.4R/210 Rasselas, Appleton's Miniature Classical Library

59.4R/211 Rasselas, New York, Carter

81.11B(Parts 1+2)/18 Beauties of Johnson, New York

87.3W/25m Works, 'Third Complete American Edition', New York, Dearborn

87.3W/25n Works, 'First Complete American Edition', New York, Harper

1852

55.4D/46 Dictionary, seventh impression of Robertson's stereotype edition

56.1DA/TG/2 Abridged Dictionary, German, Leipzig

56.1MD/232–3 Miniature Dictionary

56.3BCM/4 Browne's Christian Morals, Bohn's Antiquarian Library

59.4R/212 Rasselas, New York, Francis

59.4R/213 Rasselas, Hartford, Andrus

59.4R/214 Rasselas, Bohn's Cabinet Edition

59.4R/TI/8 Rasselas, Translations, Italian

78.5RD/12c Reynolds's Discourses, Works

79.4LP/SS/299 Life of Thomson, The Seasons and The Castle of Indolence

1853

56.1DA/83 Abridged Dictionary, Chalmers's, second 'edition', fifth impression

56.1DA/84 Abridged Dictionary, Jameson's, eighth impression ['seventh edition']

56.1DA/85 Abridged Dictionary, Chalmers's, Boston stereotype edition, nineteenth impression, Philadelphia

56.1MD/234–7 Miniature Dictionary

59.4R/215 Rasselas, Bohn's Cabinet Edition

59.4R/216 Rasselas, Cheerful Visitor [1852–3]

59.4R/217 Rasselas, New York, Appleton

59.4R/218 Rasselas, New York, Francis

59.4R/219 Rasselas, Philadelphia, Hazard

59.4R/220 Rasselas, Baudry's European Library

59.4R/TF/44 Rasselas, Translations, French

[**78.5RD/13** Reynolds's Life and Discourses, Ohio]

79.4LP/SS/300 Life of Thomson, The Seasons and The Castle of Indolence

81.11B(Parts 1+2)/19 Beauties of Johnson, New York

1850

85.2PW/25 Poetical Works, Routledge's British Poets

1854

55.4D/47 Dictionary, eighth impression of Robertson's stereotype edition
56.1MD/238–9 Miniature Dictionary
59.4R/221 Rasselas, New York, Appleton
59.4R/222 Rasselas, New York, Francis
59.4R/223 Rasselas, Hartford, Andrus
79.4LP/60 Lives of the Poets, ed. Hazlitt
79.4LP/61a Lives of the Poets, ed. Cunningham, Murray's British Classics
79.4LP/61b Lives of the Poets, ed. Cunningham, first Boston issue
79.4LP/61c Lives of the Poets, ed. Cunningham, second Boston issue [1854]
79.4LP/SS/98 Life of Gay, Poems or Fables of John Gay, Boston
79.4LP/SS/305 Life of Tickell, The British Poets, ed. Child
87.3W/23c Works, Jones's edition, Bohn
87.3W/25o Works, 'First Complete American Edition', New York, Dearborn

1855

52.11Ad/42 The Adventurer, British Essayists, ed. Chalmers, 1855–6 (includes 58.4Id/42 The Idler
56.1DA/86 Abridged Dictionary, Chalmers's, [Boston stereotype edition, twentieth impression]
56.1MD/240–4 Miniature Dictionary
59.4R/224 Rasselas, Jones's Diamond Classics
59.4R/225 Rasselas, New York, Appleton
59.4R/226 Rasselas, New York, Appleton [1855]
59.4R/227 Rasselas, New York, Carter [?1855]
79.4LP/SS/18 Life of Akenside, Poetical Works of Mark Akenside
79.4LP/SS/99 Life of Gay, Poems or Fables of John Gay, Boston
79.4LP/SS/106 Life of Gray, Poetical Works of Thomas Gray, Thomas Parnell, &c.
79.4LP/SS/176 Life of Parnell, Poetical Works of Thomas Gray, Parnell &c.
85.2PW/26 Poetical Works, Routledge
85.2PW/27 Poetical Works, ed. Gilfillan

1856

49.1VW/29 Vanity of Human Wishes, with Rasselas *c.*1856
50.3R/80 British Essayists, ed. Chalmers, Boston (includes The Rambler, 52.11Ad/41 The Adventurer, and 58.4Id/43 The Idler)
56.1DA/87 Abridged Dictionary, Chalmers's, Boston stereotype edition, twenty-first impression, Philadelphia
56.1MD/245–8 Miniature Dictionary
56.3BCM/5 Browne's Christian Morals, Bohn's Standard Library
59.4R/228 Rasselas, Tilt's Miniature Classical Library [1856]
59.4R/229 Rasselas, New York, Derby & Jackson
59.4R/230 Rasselas, New York, Derby & Jackson [1856]
59.4R/231 Rasselas, New York, Francis
59.4R/232 Rasselas, Philadelphia, Hazard
79.4LP/SS/63 Life of Dryden, Dryden's Poetical Works
87.3W/25p Works, 'First Complete American Edition', New York, Dearborn

1857

56.1DA/88 Abridged Dictionary, Chalmers's, Boston stereotype edition, twenty-second impression
56.1MD/249–54 Miniature Dictionary
59.4R/233 Rasselas, Bohn's Cabinet Edition
59.4R/234 Rasselas, New York, Derby & Jackson
59.4R/235 Rasselas, Gouda, van Goor

59.4R/TDu/6 Rasselas, Translations, Dutch

79.4LP/61d Lives of the Poets, ed. Cunningham, first New York issue

87.3W/25q Works, 'Third Complete American Edition', New York, Harper

1858

56.1DA/89 Abridged Dictionary, Chalmers's, Boston stereotype edition, twenty-third impression, Philadelphia

56.1MD/255–6 Miniature Dictionary

59.4R/236 Rasselas, Miniature Classical Library

59.4R/237 Rasselas, New York, Derby & Jackson

79.4LP/62 Lives of the Poets, Tauchnitz, 18 Feb.

1859

49.1VW/30 Vanity of Human Wishes and Parnell's Hermit, ed. Lal Behari De

56.1DA/90 Abridged Dictionary, Chalmers's, Boston stereotype edition, twenty-fourth impression, Philadelphia

56.1MD/257–60 Miniature Dictionary

59.4R/238 Rasselas, New York, Derby & Jackson

59.4R/239 Rasselas, New York, Francis

79.4LP/61e Lives of the Poets, ed. Cunningham, second New York issue

87.3W/25r Works, 'First Complete American Edition', New York, Harper

1860

55.4D/48 Dictionary, ninth impression of Robertson's stereotype edition

56.1DA/91 Abridged Dictionary, Jameson's, ninth impression ['seventh edition'], Halifax

56.1DA/92 Abridged Dictionary, Chalmers's, Boston stereotype edition, twenty-fifth impression, Philadelphia

56.1MD/261–5 Miniature Dictionary

59.4R/240 Rasselas, ed. Hunter

59.4R/241 Rasselas, Bohn's Cabinet Edition

59.4R/242 Rasselas, introd. Boswell, Tegg

59.4R/243 Rasselas, New York, Phinney, Blakeman, & Mason

59.4R/244 Rasselas, Allman [?1860]

59.4R/TF/45 Rasselas, Translations, French

59.4R/TS/4 Rasselas, Translations, Spanish

85.8PM/21 Prayers and Meditations, introd. Gresley

88.3L/9 Letters (Selection), ed. Simeon, 1860–1

1861

56.1MD/266–9 Miniature Dictionary

59.4R/TGr/2 Rasselas, Translations, Greek

79.4LP/61f Lives of the Poets, ed. Cunningham, third New York issue

87.3W/25s Works, Harper

1862

50.3R/81 The Rambler, Tegg's edition

56.1DA/A/11 Abridged Dictionary, Adaptations, Johnson and Walker's, New York

56.1DA/A/12 Abridged Dictionary, Adaptations, Johnson and Walker's, New York n.d. [?1862]

56.1DA/A/13 Abridged Dictionary, Adaptations, National Library, n.d. [?1862]

56.1MD/270–1 Miniature Dictionary

59.4R/245 Rasselas, New York, Appleton

59.4R/246 Rasselas, Leipzig, Renger

62.5SA/6 Society of Artists' Catalogue, History of the Royal Academy

79.4LP/SS/301 Life of Thomson, Poetical Works of James Thomson

85.2PW/28 Poetical Works, Nichol's Library Edition of the British Poets, No. 26

87.3W/23d Works, Jones's edition, Bohn

87.3W/25t Works, Harper

1863

50.3R/82 The Rambler and **58.4Id/44** The Adventurer, Bohn's edition
52.11Ad/43 The Adventurer and the Connoisseur
56.1MD/272–3 Miniature Dictionary
56.3BCM/6 Browne's Christian Morals, Rivingtons
59.4R/247 Rasselas, Philadelphia, Lippincott
59.4R/TF/46 Rasselas, Translations, French
85.2PW/29 Poetical Works, ed. Gilfillan
87.3W/23e Works, Jones's edition, Bohn n.d. [?1863]

1864

56.1MD/274–6 Miniature Dictionary
59.4R/248 Rasselas, New York, Blakeman & Mason
59.4R/249 Rasselas, Bohn's Cabinet of Classic Tales
79.4LP/61g Lives of the Poets, ed. Cunningham, first Philadelphia issue
79.4LP/63 Lives of the Poets, Oxford English Classics, 1864–65
79.4LP/SS/100 Life of Gay, Poetical Works of John Gay, Boston

1865

50.3R/83 British Essayists, ed. Chalmers, Boston (includes The Rambler, 52.11Ad/44 The Adventurer, and 58.4 Id/46 The Idler)
56.1MD/277–9 Miniature Dictionary
59.4R/250 Rasselas, ed. Hunter
59.4R/251 Rasselas, Griffin's Universal Library [1865]
59.4R/252 Rasselas, Philadelphia, Lippincott
59.4R/253 Rasselas, New York, Miller [?1865]
85.2PW/30 Poetical Works, Routledge's British Poets

1866

50.3R/84 British Essayists, ed. Chalmers (includes The Rambler, 52.11Ad/45 The Adventurer, and 58.4Id/45 The Idler)
50.3R/85 British Essayists, ed. Chalmers (includes The Rambler, The Adventurer, and 58.4Id/46 The Idler), Boston
55.4D/49 Dictionary, tenth impression of Robertson's stereotype edition
55.4D/50a Dictionary, Latham's edition, first issue, 1866–70
56.1MD/280–2 Miniature Dictionary
59.4R/254 Rasselas, Bohn's Cabinet Edition

1867

56.1MD/283a Miniature Dictionary
59.4R/255 Rasselas, ed. West
59.4R/256 Rasselas, ed. Hunter
59.4R/257 Rasselas, Pitman
59.4R/258 Rasselas, Masterpieces of Fiction [?1867]
59.4R/259 Rasselas, New York, Miller
59.4R/TF/47 Rasselas, Translations, French
78.5RD/12d Reynolds's Discourses, Works, Bohn's Library
79.4LP/SS/64 Life of Dryden, Dryden's Poetical Works
85.2PW/31 Poetical Works, ed. Gilfillan, Edinburgh

1868

56.1MD/283b–4 Miniature Dictionary
59.4R/260 Rasselas, Universal Library of Standard Authors [?1868]
59.4R/261 Rasselas, Fireside Library, No. 2
59.4R/262 Rasselas, ed. West
59.4R/263 Rasselas, Lotus Library, ed. West [?1868]
79.4LP/61h Lives of the Poets, ed. Cunningham, second Philadelphia issue
79.4LP/64a Lives of the Poets, Crocker, first issue

85.2PW/32 Poetical Works, ed. Clarke, Edinburgh

1869

56.1MD/285 Miniature Dictionary
59.4R/264a Rasselas, ed. West
59.4R/264b Rasselas, ed. West
59.4R/264c Rasselas, ed. West
59.4R/265 Rasselas, New York, Appleton
59.4R/266 Rasselas, New York, Allen

1870

59.4R/267 Rasselas, Groombridge
59.4R/268a Rasselas, New York, Allen
59.4R/268b Rasselas, Cabinet Series
59.4R/268c Rasselas, Cabinet Series [?1870]
59.4R/269 Rasselas, New York, Appleton
59.4R/270 Rasselas, Tegg [?1870]
79.4LP/61i Lives of the Poets, ed. Cunningham, third Philadelphia issue
79.4LP/SS/101 Life of Gay, British Poets, Poetical Works of John Gay, Boston

1871

55.4D/50b Dictionary, Latham's second issue
56.1DA/A/14 Abridged Dictionary, Adaptations, Library Dictionary
56.1MD/286 Miniature Dictionary
59.4R/271 Rasselas, Cabinet Series
79.4LP/64b Lives of the Poets, Crocker, second issue
79.4LP/65a Lives of the Poets, Chandos Classics, No. 9 [?1871–80]

1872

56.1DA/A/15 Abridged Dictionary, Adaptations, Library Dictionary
56.1DA/TB/4 Abridged Dictionary, Bengali, Calcutta, second edition
56.1MD/287–9 Miniature Dictionary
59.4R/272 Rasselas, ed. Hunter
59.4R/273 Rasselas, Classic Tales

59.4R/274 Rasselas, ed. West
59.4R/275 Rasselas, Philadelphia, Lippincott
59.4R/276 Rasselas, introd. Boswell, Tegg
59.4R/277 Rasselas, ed. West
59.4R/278 Rasselas, Philadelphia, Lippincott

1873

59.4R/TF/48 Rasselas, Translations, French
87.3W/25u Works, 'Third American edition', New York, Harper

1874

56.1MD/290–1 Miniature Dictionary
59.4R/281 Rasselas, Philadelphia, Lippincott
59.4R/279 Rasselas, New York, Carter
59.4R/280 Rasselas, New York, Carter [?1874/5]
59.4R/TG/16 Rasselas, Translations, German
79.4LP/SS/200 Life of Pope

1875

59.4R/282 Rasselas, ed. West
59.4R/283 Rasselas, Philadelphia, Lippincott
59.4R/TR/3 Rasselas, Translations, Russian [1875]
87.3W/S/2 Selected Works, Library of Thoughtful Books n.d. [1875]

1876

38.5L/22a Johnson's Satires, ed. Fleming (includes London and 49.1VW/31 Vanity of Human Wishes)
49.1VW/32 Vanity of Human Wishes, ed. Payne
50.3R/86 The Rambler, Tegg's edition
50.3R/87 The Rambler, The Idler (58.4Id/47a), The Adventurer (52.11Ad/46), and The Connoiseur, Nimmo's edition

55.4D/50c Dictionary, Latham's third issue

56.1DA/93a Abridged Dictionary, Latham's

56.1MD/292–4 Miniature Dictionary

59.4R/284 Rasselas, The World Story Books

75.1J/24 Journey, London and Glasgow

79.4LP/SS/65 The Lives of Dryden and Pope (79.4LP/SS/201), ed. T.A.

87.3W/26a Works, Nimmo

1877

50.3R/88 The Rambler, Tegg's edition

50.3R/89 The Rambler, The Idler (58.4Id/47b), The Adventurer (52.11Ad/47), and The Connoisseur, Nimmo's edition

55.4D/51 Dictionary, eleventh impression of Robertson's stereotype edition

55.4D/52 Dictionary, twelfth impression of Robertson's stereotype edition

58.4Id/48 The Idler (and Rasselas), ?Nimmo

59.4R/285 Rasselas, The World Story Books

59.4R/286 Rasselas (with Idler), ?Nimmo

59.4R/287 Rasselas, Philadelphia, Lippincott

76.8ML/8 Mickle's Lusiad, fifth edition

79.4LP/SS/66 Lives of Dryden, Pope (79.4LP/SS/202), and Addison (79.4LP/SS/4), ed. T.A.

87.3W/26b Works, Nimmo

1878

59.4R/288 Rasselas, ed. West

59.4R/289 Rasselas, ed. West

59.4R/290 Rasselas, Clarendon Press Series, ed. Milnes

59.4R/291 Rasselas, Philadelphia, Lippincott

59.4R/292a Rasselas, Chicago, Hill [?1878]

59.4R/292b Rasselas, New York, Lupton [?1878]

59.4R/293a Rasselas, Century Series [1878]

59.4R/293b Rasselas, ?Donohoe Brothers [?1878]

79.4LP/61j Lives of the Poets, ed. Cunningham

79.4LP/S/1a Lives of the Poets, Selections, Arnold's Six Chief Lives (79.4LP/SS/5, 67, 107, 148, 203, 251)

79.4LP/SS/68 Life of Dryden, Clarendon Press Series, ed. Milnes

85.2PW/33 Poetical Works, Cassell's Library of British Poets, Part 95

85.2PW/34 Poetical Works, ed. Clarke [?1878]

87.3W/26c Works, Nimmo

1879

59.4R/294 Rasselas, ed. Hunter

59.4R/295 Rasselas, ed. Hunter [?1879+]

59.4R/296 Rasselas, Clarendon Press Series, ed. Milnes

59.4R/297 Rasselas, New York, Miller [?1879]

59.4R/298 Rasselas, Philadelphia, Lippincott

79.4LP/S/1b Lives of the Poets, Selections, Arnold's Six Chief Lives, first New York issue

79.4LP/SS/48 Life of Cowley, Lives of the English Poets, ed. Böddeker

79.4LP/SS/69 Life of Dryden, Clarendon Press Series, ed. Milnes

79.4LP/SS/108 Life of Gray, Poems of Thomas Gray, ed. Storr

79.4LP/SS/204 Life of Pope, Clarendon Press Series, ed. Milnes

1880

59.4R/299a Rasselas, ed. West

59.4R/299b Rasselas, ed. West

59.4R/300 Rasselas, Familiar Quotations Series [?1880]

59.4R/301 Rasselas, introd. Boswell, Tegg [?1880]

59.4R/302 Rasselas, Select Works, ed. Milnes

59.4R/303 Rasselas, New York, Lovell

59.4R/304 Rasselas, New York, Lovell [?1880+]

59.4R/305a Rasselas, The Acme Library of Modern Classics

59.4R/305b Rasselas, New York, Allison

59.4R/305c Rasselas, New York, Allison [?1880+]

59.4R/306 Rasselas, New York, Cogswell

59.4R/307 Rasselas, Philadelphia, Lippincott

79.4LP/65b Lives of the Poets, Chandos Classics, another issue n.d. [?1880]

79.4LP/S/1c Lives of the Poets, Selections, Arnold's Six Chief Lives, second New York issue

79.4LP/SS/70 Life of Dryden, Clarendon Press Series, ed. Milnes

79.4LP/SS/177 Poetical Works of Churchill, Parnell, and Tickell (includes Life of Parnell and 79.4LP/SS/306 Life of Tickell), Boston and New York [188-?]

79.4LP/SS/302 Life of Thomson, Works of James Thomson, Edinburgh [?1880]

85.2PW/35 Poetical Works, Routledge Excelsior

1881

44.2LS/15 Life of Savage, English Library, 1881–2

56.1DA/93b Abridged Dictionary, Latham's

59.4R/308 Rasselas, Dicks' Celebrated Works, No. 26 [?1881]

59.4R/309 Rasselas, Works

59.4R/310 Rasselas, Acme Library of Modern Classics

59.4R/311 Rasselas, New York, Carter

59.4R/312 Rasselas, New York, Cogswell

59.4R/313 Rasselas, Philadelphia, Lippincott

79.4LP/S/1d Lives of the Poets, Selections, Arnold's Six Chief Lives, Macmillan

87.3W/26d Works, Nimmo, The Standard Library [c.1881]

1882

55.4D/50d Dictionary, Latham's fourth issue

56.1MD/295 Miniature Dictionary

59.4R/314a Rasselas, Classic Tales

59.4R/314b Rasselas, Classic Tales

59.4R/315 Rasselas, Chicago

59.4R/316 Rasselas, Lovell's Library, 19 Oct.

59.4R/317 Rasselas, Lovell's Library, 19 Oct.

59.4R/318 Rasselas, Seaside Library [1882]

59.4R/319 Rasselas, New York, Crowell [?1882]

59.4R/TF/49 Rasselas, Translations, French

79.4LP/S/1e Lives of the Poets, Selections, Arnold's Six Chief Lives, New York

79.4LP/SS/109 Life of Gray, Poems of Thomas Gray, ed. Storr

1883

40.GM10/EE/3a Essay on Epitaphs, Gleanings

56.1MD/296–8 Miniature Dictionary

59.4R/320 Rasselas, Fisher Unwin

59.4R/321a Rasselas, Nimmo and Bain

59.4R/321b Rasselas, New York, Scribner, Welford

59.4R/322 Rasselas, New York, Alden

59.4R/323 Rasselas, New York, Allison

59.4R/324 Rasselas, Philadelphia, Lippincott

59.4R/325a Rasselas, Routledge [1883]

59.4R/325b Rasselas, Routledge [1883]

59.4R/TI/9 Rasselas, Translations, Italian

59.4R/TS/5 Rasselas, Translations, Spanish

1884

49.1VW/33 Vanity of Human Wishes, ed. Payne

56.1MD/299 Miniature Dictionary

59.4R/326 Rasselas, facsimile edition

59.4R/327 Rasselas, Morley's Universal Library, Vol. XIX, Nov.

59.4R/328 Rasselas, ed. West

59.4R/329 Rasselas, Chicago and New York, Belford, Clarke,

59.4R/330 Rasselas, Chicago, Belford, Clarke [1884]

59.4R/331 Rasselas, Franklin Edition

59.4R/332 Rasselas, Philadelphia, Lippincott

59.4R/TG/17 Rasselas, Translations, German

78.5RD/14 Reynolds's Discourses, Parchment Library

79.4LP/SS/49 The Lives of Cowley, Milton (79.4LP/SS/150) and Waller (79.4LP/SS/308), Leipzig

79.4LP/SS/149 The Life of Milton, ed. Böddeker, Berlin

87.3W/S/3 Selected Works, Life, Works, and Table Talk

87.3W/S/4 Selected Works, Life, Works, and Table Talk, Diprose's Miniature Library [*c.*1884]

87.3W/S/5 Selected Works, Characteristics and Aphorisms

1885

56.1MD/300 Miniature Dictionary [?1885]

59.4R/333a Rasselas, Philadelphia, Classic Tales

59.4R/333b Rasselas, Classic Tales, New York, Little, Brown, & Co.

59.4R/334 Rasselas, Select Works, ed. Milnes, Oxford

59.4R/335 Rasselas, Caxton Edition, Chicago and New York, Belford, Clarke

59.4R/336 Rasselas, New York, Alden

59.4R/337 Rasselas, Routledge

59.4R/338 Rasselas, facsimile edition

59.4R/339 Rasselas, Tokio Publishing Company

59.4R/340 Rasselas, Philadelphia, Potter [1885]

79.4LP/SS/71 Life of Dryden, Clarendon Press Series, ed. Milnes

79.4LP/SS/205 Life of Pope, Clarendon Press Series, ed. Milnes

81.11B(Parts 1+2)/20 Beauties of Johnson

1886

59.4R/341 Rasselas, Morley's Universal Library, Vol. XIX

59.4R/342 Rasselas, ed. West

59.4R/343a Rasselas, Boston, Ginn

59.4R/343b Rasselas, Home and School Library

59.4R/344 Rasselas, New York, Knox [?1886]

59.4R/345 Rasselas, Tokio and Osaka, Rikugôkan

59.4R/TF/50 Rasselas, Translations, French

59.4R/TJ/1 Rasselas, Translations, Japanese

61.8BA/3 Life of Ascham, Memoir of Roger Ascham

75.1J/25a Journey, Cassell's edition

79.4LP/61k Lives of the Poets, ed. Cunningham

79.4LP/66 Lives of the Poets, Cassell's National Library (includes 79.4LP/SS/28 Life of Butler, 79.4LP/SS/50 Life of Cowley, 79.4LP/SS/309 Lives of Waller, Milton, and Cowley) 1886–1891

79.4LP/S/2a Lives of the Poets, Selections, Arnold's Six Chief Lives

79.4LP/SS/72 Life of Dryden, Clarendon Press Series, ed. Milnes

79.4LP/SS/110 Life of Gray, Poems of Thomas Gray, ed. Storr

1887

35.2LV/4a Lobo's Voyage to Abyssinia, Cassell's National Library, No. 91, 24 Sept.

48.4DP/VT/13 Vision of Theodore, with Rasselas, ?1887

56.1MD/301–2 Miniature Dictionary

[59.4R/346 Rasselas, Pitman's Shorthand Edition]

59.4R/347 Rasselas, Clarendon Press Series, ed. Hill

59.4R/348 Rasselas, Spiers [?1887]

59.4R/349 Rasselas, Tokyo, Routledge [?1887]

59.4R/350 Rasselas, Home and School Library, Boston, Ginn [1887]

59.4R/351 Rasselas, Caxton Edition

59.4R/352 Rasselas, Elzevir Library, 9 July

59.4R/353 Rasselas, Franklin Library

59.4R/354 Rasselas, Philadelphia, Lippincott

59.4R/THi/1 Rasselas, Translations, Hindustani [1887]

75.1J/25b Journey, Cassell's edition, New York

75.1J/25c Journey, Cassell's edition, London [?1887]

78.5RD/15 Reynolds's Discourses, Camelot Series

1888

50.3R/S/22a Camelot Series, Essays from The Rambler, The Advnturer (52.11Ad/S/8a), and The Idler (58.4Id/S/12a)

50.3R/S/22b Scott Library Series, Essays from The Rambler, The Adventurer (52.11Ad/S/8b), and The Idler (58.4Id/S/12b), ?1888

59.4R/355 Rasselas, Morley's Universal Library

59.4R/356 Rasselas, ed. West

59.4R/357 Rasselas, Caxton Edition

59.4R/358 Rasselas, New York, Butler

78.5RD/16a Reynolds's Discourses, Cassell's National Library

78.5RD/16b Reynolds's Discourses, Cassell's National Library, New York

79.4LP/SS/6 Life of Addison, Cassell's National Library

79.4LP/SS/151 Lives of the Poets. Milton, ed. Firth

87.3W/S/6 Selected Works, Wit and Wisdom

88.3L/10 Letters (Selection), Love Letters

1889

50.3R/S/23 Temple Library, Selections from The Rambler, The Adventurer (52.11Ad/S/9), and The Idler (58.4Id/S/13)

59.4R/359 Rasselas, Morley's Universal Library

59.4R/360 Rasselas, Cassell's National Library, No. 191

59.4R/361 Rasselas, New York and Melbourne, Cassell [?1889]

59.4R/362 Rasselas, Caxton Edition

59.4R/363 Rasselas, Laurel Crowned Tales

59.4R/364 Rasselas, Echo Series, 13 May

59.4R/365 Rasselas, Seaside Library [?1889]

59.4R/366 Rasselas, Bayard Series, ed. West

59.4R/367 Rasselas, Arundel Edition [?1889]

59.4R/368 Rasselas, Aldine Edition [?1889]

59.4R/369 Rasselas, Oxford Edition [?1889]

59.4R/TJ/2 Rasselas, Translations, Japanese

75.1J/25d Journey, Cassell's National Library

79.4LP/67 Lives of the Poets, New York

79.4LP/S/2b Lives of the Poets, Selections, Arnold's Six Chief Lives

79.4LP/S/2c Lives of the Poets, Selections, Arnold's Six Chief Lives, New York

1890

38.5L/22b London, Johnson's Satires, sixth edition

56.1DA/A/16 Abridged Dictionary, Adaptations, Household Dictionary [?1890]

56.1MD/303–4 Miniature Dictionary

59.4R/370 Rasselas, New York, Alden

59.4R/371 Rasselas, Laurel Crowned Tales

59.4R/372a Rasselas, Classic Tales [?1890]
59.4R/372b Rasselas, Classic Tales [?1890]
59.4R/373 Rasselas, The Gladstone Series [?1890]
59.4R/374 Rasselas, Chicago, Belford, Clarke [?1890]
59.4R/TJ/3 Rasselas, Translations, Japanese, trans. Tamura
59.4R/TJ/4 Rasselas, Translations, Japanese, trans. Watanabe
61.8BA/4 Life of Ascham, Two Great Teachers
79.4LP/68 Lives of the Poets, ed. Napier, Bohn's Standard Library
79.4LP/SS/73 Life of Dryden, Select Poetical Works of John Dryden, The Penny Poets No. 34 [?189-]

1891

56.1MD/305–6 Miniature Dictionary
59.4R/375 Rasselas, Cassell's National Library, introd. Morley
59.4R/376 Rasselas, ed. West
59.4R/377a Rasselas, Student's Series, ed. Scott [1891]
59.4R/377b Rasselas, ed. Scott, Boston and Chicago, Sibley and Ducker [1891]
59.4R/378a Rasselas, Knickerbocker Nuggets, No. 36 [1891]
59.4R/378b Rasselas, Elia Series [?1891]
59.4R/379 Rasselas, Cornell Series [?1891]
59.4R/380 Rasselas, New York, Lupton [?1891]
59.4R/381 Rasselas, New York, Lupton [?1891]
59.4R/382 Rasselas, New York, Lovell, Coryell [?189—]
59.4R/383 Rasselas, Chicago, Donohoe, Henneberry [?189—]
78.5RD/16c Reynolds's Discourses, Cassell's National Library
79.4LP/SS/74 Life of Dryden, Johnson Selected Works, ed. Milnes
79.4LP/SS/152 Life of Milton, ed. Firth

79.4LP/SS/206 Life of Pope, Clarendon Press Series, ed. Milnes

1892

56.1MD/307–8 Miniature Dictionary [??1892]
59.4R/384 Rasselas, Classic Tales, Bell
59.4R/385 Rasselas, Classics for Children, Boston, Ginn
59.4R/386 Rasselas, Laurel Crowned Tales, Chicago, McClurg
59.4R/387 Rasselas, Knickerbocker Nuggets, No. 36, May
59.4R/388 Rasselas, Universal Library, No. 73, 17 Dec.
59.4R/389 Rasselas, World's Classics, New York and London [?1892]
59.4R/TJ/5 Rasselas, Translations, Japanese
75.1J/25e Journey, Cassell's edition, London & New York
79.4LP/SS/153 Lives of the Poets. Milton, ed. Deighton
88.3L/11 Letters, ed. Hill

1893

35.2LV/4b Lobo's Voyage to Abyssinia, Cassell's National Library, No. 91
38.5L/23 Johnson's Satires, ed. Ryland, Blackie's English Classics (includes London and 49.1VW/34 Vanity of Human Wishes) [1893]
56.1MD/309 Miniature Dictionary [?1893]
58.4Id/S/14 Idler Selections, Eighteenth Century Essays
59.4R/390 Rasselas, Morley's Universal Library, Vol. XIX, fourth edition
59.4R/391 Rasselas, Clarendon Press Series, ed. Hill
59.4R/392 Rasselas, Perkins Institution, Boston
59.4R/TJ/6 Rasselas, Translations, Japanese
78.5RD/TG/1 Reynolds's Discourses, German translation

79.4LP/SS/7 Life of Addison, Bell's English Classics, ed. Ryland

1894

59.4R/393 Rasselas, Classic Tales [1894]

59.4R/394 Rasselas, English Readings, ed. Emerson

59.4R/TJ/7 Rasselas, Translations, Japanese

79.4LP/SS/75 Life of Dryden, Johnson Selected Works, ed. Milnes

79.4LP/SS/154 Life of Milton, Bell's English Classics, ed. Ryland

79.4LP/SS/207 Life of Pope, Clarendon Press Series, ed. Milnes

79.4LP/SS/208 Life of Pope, Bell's English Classics, ed. Ryland

79.4LP/SS/252 Life of Swift, Bell's English Classics, ed. Ryland

1895

59.4R/395 Raselas, Classics for Children, Boston, Ginn

59.4R/396 Rasselas, Chicago, Conkey [?1895]

59.4R/397a Rasselas, Hearthstone Edition [?1895]

59.4R/397b Rasselas, Cambridge Classics, No. 80 [?1895]

59.4R/397c Rasselas, Arlington Edition [?1895]

59.4R/398 Rasselas, Classic Tales [1895]

59.4R/399 Rasselas, English Readings, ed. Emerson

79.4LP/SS/8 Life of Addison, Bell's English Classics, ed. Ryland [1895]

79.4LP/SS/76 Life of Dryden, Bell's English Classics, ed. Ryland

79.4LP/SS/155 Life of Milton, The Penny Poets, Nos. 10, 15 [?1895]

1896

49.1VW/35 Vanity of Human Wishes, ed. Payne [1896]

59.4R/400 Rasselas, English Readings, ed. Emerson [?1896]

59.4R/401 Rasselas, ed. West

59.4R/402 Rasselas, Laurel Crowned Tales

59.4R/TF/51 Rasselas, Translations, French [1896]

79.4LP/69a Lives of the Poets, ed. Henley, English Classics

79.4LP/69b Lives of the Poets, ed. Henley, English Classics, Chicago issue

79.4LP/70a Lives of the Poets, ed. Waugh

79.4LP/70b Lives of the Poets, ed. Waugh, American issue [1896]

79.4LP/SS/77 Life of Dryden, Bell's English Classics, ed. Ryland

79.4LP/SS/209 Life of Pope, Bell's English Classics, ed. Ryland

79.4LP/SS/253 Life of Swift, Bell's English Classics, ed. Ryland

1897

44.4HM/6 Harleian Miscellany, Pamphlet Library

59.4R/403 Rasselas, Cassell's National Library, No. 10

59.4R/404 Rasselas, Premium Library, 9 Sept.

59.4R/405 Rasselas, New York, Alden

59.4R/406 Rasselas, Elia Series, No. 10 [?1897]

79.4LP/SS/43 Life of Congreve, Bell's English Classics, ed. Ryland

79.4LP/SS/210 Life of Pope, ed. Stephens, New York

79.4LP/SS/225 Lives of Prior and Congreve, Bell's English Classics, ed. Ryland

88.3L/12 Letters (Selection), Eighteenth Century Letters

1898

59.4R/407 Rasselas, Birmingham, Vincent Press, 8 Dec.

59.4R/408 Rasselas, Clarendon Press Series, ed. Hill

59.4R/409 Rasselas, Chicago, Sibley

1899

59.4R/410 Rasselas, Cassell's National Library, New Series, No. 347

59.4R/411 Rasselas, New York, Hurst [?1899]

59.4R/412 Rasselas, Laurel Crowned Tales [1899]

59.4R/413 Rasselas, Rahway, NJ, Mershon [1899]

59.4R/414 Rasselas, Benn Pitman Phonography, by Fuller [Vol. 3 '1900']

79.4LP/SS/78 Life of Dryden, Johnson Selected Works, ed. Milnes

79.4LP/SS/79 Life of Dryden, ed. Peterson [and Punchard]

79.4LP/SS/211 Life of Pope, ed. Peterson [and Punchard]

1900

59.4R/415 Rasselas, New York, Mershon [1900]

59.4R/416 Rasselas, Cassell's National Library

59.4R/417 Rasselas, Greening's Masterpiece Library, introd. Hannaford, advts. Oct.

59.4R/418 Rasselas, Gem Classics, ed. West

59.4R/419 Rasselas, Burt's Home Library [?1900]

59.4R/420 Rasselas, New York, Hurst [1900]

59.4R/421a Rasselas, Low's Choice Classics for Collectors, ed. West [?1900]

59.4R/421b Rasselas, ed. West, New York, Pott [?1900]

59.4R/422 Rasselas, New York, Fenno [?1900]

59.4R/424 Rasselas, Exmoor Edition [?1900]

59.4R/425 Rasselas, Pocket English Classics [?1900]

59.4R/TM/1 Rasselas, Translations, Marathi

79.4LP/SS/156 Lives of Milton and Addison (79.4LP/SS/9), ed. Wight Duff, Blackwood's English Classics

79.4LP/SS/157 Life of Milton, Berry's PT and SS Series of English Classics, ed. Berry and Marshall [1900]

79.4LP/SS/158 Life of Milton, English Classics, ed. Deighton

79.4LP/SS/212 Life of Pope, Bell's English Classics, ed. Ryland

79.4LP/SS/226 Life of Prior, The Abbey Classics, Shorter Poems of Matthew Prior, introd. Bickley [?1900]

1901

40GM10/EE/3b Essay on Epitaphs, Gleanings, second edition

49.1VW/36 Vanity of Human Wishes, Blackie's English Classics, ed. Ryland

58.4Id/S/15 Idler Selections, Little Masterpieces

59.4R/426 Rasselas, Classic Tales

59.4R/427 Rasselas, Laurel Crowned Tales

1902

47.10DLP/1b Prologue Spoken at Drury Lane, facsimile

59.4R/428 Rasselas, introd. Hannaford

59.4R/429 Rasselas, The Home Library

59.4R/430 Rasselas, Ariel Booklets, No. 36 [1902]

59.4R/431 Rasselas, Wausau, Wis., Philosopher Press, Sept.

1903

50.3R/90 The Rambler, Pafraets, New York

59.4R/432 Rasselas, Boston, Ginn

59.4R/433 Rasselas, New York, Pafraets

85.8PM/22 Prayers and Meditations, ed. Bradley, New York, Feb.

87.3W/27a Works, Literary Club edition

87.3W/27b Works, New Cambridge edition n.d. [?1903]

1904

56.3BCM/7 Browne's Christian Morals, Bohn's Standard Library

59.4R/434a Rasselas, Cassell's National Library New Series 10, introd. Morley, 10 Jan.

59.4R/434b Rasselas, Cassells' Handy Classics No. 10 [1904]

59.4R/435 Rasselas, Gibson's New Literary Reader, No. 5 [1904]

59.4R/436 Rasselas, Home and School Library

59.4R/437 Rasselas, New York, Mershon [?1904]

59.4R/438 Rasselas, Ariel Booklets, No. 36

59.4R/439 Rasselas, The Home Library [?1904]

59.4R/440 Rasselas, Carlton Classics, introd. Bennett

59.4R/TI/S/10 Rasselas, Translations, Italian, Selection, 29 Oct.

75.1J/26 Journey, University Tutorial Series, ed. Thomas [1904]

85.8PM/23 Prayers and Meditations, ed. Higgins [1904]

1905

50.3R/S/24 Rambler Selections, Little Masterpieces

59.4R/441 Rasselas, Cassell's National Library, No. 10, introd. Morley

59.4R/442 Rasselas, The Home and School Library

59.4R/443 Rasselas, Laurel Crowned Tales

59.4R/444 Rasselas, The New Universal Library, Sept.

59.4R/TF/52 Rasselas, Translations, French

59.4R/TJ/8 Rasselas, Translations, Japanese, trans. Shibano, 20 June

59.4R/TJ/9 Rasselas, Translations, Japanese, Routledge [?1905]

78.5RD/17 Reynolds's Discourses, ed. Fry

79.4LP/71a Lives of the Poets, Hill's edition

85.2PW/36a Poetical Works, The Muses Library

85.8PM/24 Prayers and Meditations, Little Masterpieces Library

87.3W/S/7 Selected Works, Little Masterpieces

87.3W/S/8 Selected Works, Arnold Prose Books, No. 7. [?1905]

1906

49.1VW/37 Vanity of Human Wishes, ed. Payne

59.4R/445 Rasselas, The York Library, introd. Fearenside

59.4R/446 Rasselas, ed. West

75.1J/27 Journey, Paisley, ed. Holmes [1906]

78.5RD/18 Reynolds's Discourses, New Univeral Library [1906]

79.4LP/72 Lives of the Poets, World's Classics, Vols. 83–4 [1906]

79.4LP/SS/159 Life of Milton, Macmillan's English Classics, ed. Deighton

79.4LP/SS/213 Life of Pope, Bell's English Classics, ed. Ryland

85.8PM/25 Prayers and Meditations, new and revised edition

88.3L/13 Letters (Selection), Letters of Literary Men [1906]

1907

50.3R/S/25 Rambler Selections, ed. Hale White (with appendix 48.4DP/VT14 Vision of Theodore)

58.4Id/S/16 Idler Selections

59.4R/447 Rasselas, Cassell's Handy Classics, ed. Morley

59.4R/448 Rasselas, Cassell's National Library No. 10, introd. Morley

59.4R/449 Rasselas, ed. Emerson

59.4R/450 Rasselas, Boston, Educational Publishing [1907]

59.4R/451 Rasselas, New York, Chicago, Siegel-Cooper [?1907]

59.4R/452 Rasselas, Chicago, Donohoe, Henneberry [?1907]

59.4R/453 Rassalas [sic], New York, Lupton [?1907]

59.4R/TB/2 Rasselas, Translations, Bengali

62.5SA/7 Society of Artists' Catalogue, Society of Artists

78.5RD/19 Reynolds's Discourses, ed. Dobson

79.4LP/SS/160 Life of Milton, ed. Firth

79.4LP/SS/161 Life of Milton, University Tutorial Series, ed. Goggin

1908

59.4R/454 Rasselas, The New Universal Library, Vol. I [1908]

59.4R/455 Rasselas, Laurel Crowned Tales

79.4LP/S/2d Lives of the Poets, Selections, Arnold's Six Chief Lives (also 1926 and 1927)

87.3W/S/9 Selected Works, Wit and Wisdom

1909

59.4R/456 Rasselas, Cassell's Little Classics, No. 9

59.4R/457 Rasselas, Cassell's National Library, No. 10, introd. Morley

59.4R/458 Rasselas, Ariel Booklets: Old Favourites Series [1909]

59.4R/459 Rasselas, English Readings, ed. Emerson

59.4R/TJ/10 Rasselas, Translations, Japanese

59.4R/TJ/S/1 Rasselas, Translations, Japanese, Selection, Oct.

78.5RD/TF/1 Reynolds's Discourses, French translation

85.8PM/Setting/1 Prayers and Meditations, Setting, Last Prayer, 19 Sept.

87.3W/S/10 Selected Works, Wit and Sagacity

1910

59.4R/460 Rasselas, University Tutorial Series, ed. Collins

59.4R/461 Rasselas, Home and School Library [1910]

59.4R/462 Rasselas, Chicago, Donohoe [?1910]

59.4R/463 Rasselas, ed. West

59.4R/464 Rasselas, New York and London, Putnam's [?1910 +]

59.4R/465 Rasselas, Cornell Series [?1910]

59.4R/TF/53 Rasselas, Translations, French [?1910]

79.4LP/SS/214 Life of Pope, ed. Peterson [and Punchard]

87.3W/S/11 Selections from the Works, ed. Osgood

1911

59.4R/466a Rasselas, Laurel Crowned Tales

59.4R/466b Rasselas, Laurel Crowned Tales

59.4R/467 Rasselas, Kobunsha, Tokyo

87.3W/S/12 Selected Works, ed. Meynell and Chesterton, Regent Library

1912

59.4R/468 Rasselas, The Brocade Series

59.4R/TB/3 Rasselas, Translations, Bengali

85.2PW/36b Poetical Works, The Muses Library

1913

59.4R/469 Rasselas, Laurel Crowned Tales

79.4LP/SS/10 Life of Addison, Bell's English Classics, ed. Ryland

79.4LP/SS/80 Life of Dryden, Clarendon Press Series, ed. Milnes

1863

1914

59.4R/470 Rasselas, Cassell's National Library, introd. Morley
59.4R/471 Rasselas, The Lotus Library, ed. West [1914]
79.4LP/SS/81 Life of Dryden, ed. Collins, University Tutorial Press

1915

59.4R/472 Rasselas, Chicago, Donohoe [?1915]
59.4R/473 Rasselas, The Home Library [1915]
59.4R/474 Rasselas, New York, Platt & Peck [?1916]
59.4R/475 Rasselas, The Stoddard Library
79.4LP/SS/11 Life of Addison (with other essays), ed. Hadow,
79.4LP/SS/82 Life of Dryden, Clarendon Press Series, ed. Milnes
79.4LP/SS/111 Life of Gray, Oxford Plain Texts
79.4LP/SS/162 Life of Milton, Bell's English Classics, ed. Ryland
79.4LP/SS/215 Life of Pope, Clarendon Press Series, ed. Milnes
88.3L/14 Letters (Selection), Some Unpublished Letters [1915]

1916

87.3W/S/13 Selected Works, Johnson Calendar

1917

59.4R/476 Rasselas, University Tutorial Press [1917]
59.4R/477 Rasselas, Home and School Library [1917]
79.4LP/S/3 Lives of the Poets, Selections, Aphorisms on Authors
79.4LP/SS/83 Life of Dryden, ed. Collins, University Tutorial Press
79.4LP/SS/216 Life of Pope, University Tutorial Series, ed. Weekes

1920

59.4R/478 Rasselas, Laurel Crowned Tales
79.4LP/SS/163 Life of Milton, Milton Poetry and Prose, sel. Madan
79.4LP/SS/217 Life of Pope, Bell's English Classics, ed. Ryland

1921

58.4Id/S/17 Idler Selections, ed. Roberts

1922

79.4LP/SS/164 Life of Milton, Milton's Poetry and Prose, ed. Hughes
85.2PW/36c Poetical Works, The Muses Library
87.3W/S/14 Selected Works, ed. Chapman, Clarendon Series of English Literature

1923

56.6SP/2 Proposals for Shakespeare, facsimile
59.4R/479 Rasselas, Carlton Classics, introd. Bennett [Jan. 1924]
59.4R/480 Rasselas, Classic Tales, introd. Fearenside
59.4R/481 Rasselas, Clarendon Edition, ed. Hill
59.4R/TA/1 Rasselas, Translations, Arabic
79.4LP/SS/102 Life of Gay, The Abbey Classics, Plays of John Gay, Boston n.d. [?1923]

1924

47.10DLP/2b Prologue Spoken at Drury Lane, piracy, facsimile
59.4R/482 Rasselas, University Tutorial Press, Selected English Classics, ed. Collins [1924]
59.4R/483 Rasselas, From Beowulf to Thomas Hardy, ed. Shafer
75.1J/28a Journey, Oxford English Texts, ed. Chapman, June

75.1J/A/7 Abridged Journey, Abbey Classics, Vol. XXIV [1924]

78.5RD/20 Reynolds's Discourses, Glasgow

1925

49.1VW/38 Vanity of Human Wishes, ed. Blakeney

50.4PC/1b New Prologue to Comus, first edition, facsimile

59.4R/484 Rasselas, Ariel Booklets [1925]

73.8LP/1b Opinion on Literary Property, facsimile

75.1J/29 Journey, Pilgrim's Books [May 1925]

79.4LP/73 Lives of the Poets, Everyman's Library, Vols. 413 and 400, ed. L. Archer-Hind

79.4LP/SS/84 Life of Dryden, Dryden: Poetry and Prose, ed. Nichol Smith

88.3L/15 Letters (Selection), ed. Chapman [1925]

1926

42.11HP/1b Proposals for the Harleian Catalogue, facsimile

59.4R/485 Rasselas, introd. Chesterton

59.4R/486 Rasselas, The New Universal Library [1926]

59.4R/487 Rasselas, ed. Hill

59.4R/488 Rasselas, ed. West [1926]

79.4LP/SS/112 Life of Gray, Poetry and Prose, ed. Crofts

87.3W/S/15 Selected Works, ed. Roberts

1927

49.1VW/39 Vanity of Human Wishes, facsimile, ed. Chapman

56.3BCM/8 Browne's Christian Morals, ed. Roberts

59.4R/489 Rasselas, ed. Chapman

59.4R/490 Rasselas, ed. Hill

59.4R/491 Rasselas, Readings in English Literature, ed. Pace [?1927]

66.4WM/F/15 The Fountains, Baskerville Series, Apr.

85.8PM/26 Prayers and Meditations, third new and revised edition [1927]

85.8PM/27 Prayers and Meditations, introd. Savage

88.3L/16 Letters (Selection), To Chesterfield

1928

79.4LP/SS/113 Life of Gray, Poetry and Prose, ed. Crofts

79.4LP/SS/218 Life of Pope, Barnet H. Clark, Great Short Biographies, New York

1929

59.4R/492 Rasselas, ed. Hill

88.3L/17 Letters (Selection), Johnson, Boswell, and Mrs Piozzi

1930

38.5L/24 London and Vanity of Human Wishes (49.1VW/40), introd. Eliot

44.9PP/1b Proposals for The Publisher, facsimile

59.4R/493 Rasselas, Everyman's Library, No. 856, ed. Henderson

59.4R/494 Rasselas, University Tutorial Series, ed. Collins [1930]

1931

59.4R/495 Rasselas, ed. Hill

75.1J/28b Journey, Oxford Standard Authors, ed. Chapman, Jan.

75.1J/30 Journey, Travellers' Library, no. 158, June

88.3L/18 Letters (Selection), Forty-Four Letters

88.3L/19 Letters (Selection), Letter to Chesterfield

1932

59.4R/496 Rasselas, Nelson's English Series

88.3L/20 Letters (Selection), Johnson and Queeney

1933

85.8PM/TJ/1 Prayers and Meditations, Japanese translation

1934

88.3L/21 Letters (Selection), The Queeney Letters

1935

76.1BH/3 Burney's History of Music
79.4LP/SS/219 Life of Pope, Oxford Anthology of English Prose, ed. Whitridge and Dodds

1936

71.3FI/TS/1 Falkland's Islands, Spanish translation
87.3W/S/16 Selected Works, Selected English Classics, ed. Reynolds [1936]

1937

79.4LP/SS/85 Life of Dryden, Masterpieces of English, Vol. 15
85.8PM/28 Prayers and Meditations, Archetype Deluxe

1940

50.3R/S/26 Rambler Selections, ed. Evans [1940]
59.4R/497 Rasselas, The Reader's Johnson [1940]
87.3W/S/17 Selected Works, The Reader's Johnson, ed. Conley [1940]

1941

85.2PW/37 Poetical Works, ed. Nichol Smith and McAdam

1942

59.4R/498 Rasselas, ed. Hill

1943

79.4LP/TJ/1 Lives of the Poets, Japanese translation

79.4LP/SS/86 Life of Dryden, Kenkyusha English Classics, Vol. 51, ed. Fukuhara [1943]

1945

38.5L/25 London, School of Arts and Crafts, Dec.
59.4R/499 Rasselas, University Tutorial Series, ed. Collins [1945]
59.4R/TS/6 Rasselas, Translations, Spanish [1945]
78.5RD/21 Reynolds's Discourses, ed. Olsen [1945]
79.4LP/SS/51 Life of Cowley, Critical Remarks on the Metaphysical Poets [ed. Horace Gregory] Mount Vernon, NY
85.8PM/29 Prayers and Meditations, ed. Trueblood

1946

59.4R/TAm/1 Rasselas, Translations, Amharic
59.4R/TF/54 Rasselas, Translations, French
88.3L/22 Letters (Selection), English Letters of XVIII Century

1947

59.4R/500 Rasselas, ed. Hill
85.8PM/30 Prayers and Meditations, ed. Trueblood [1947]
85.8PM/31 Prayers and Meditations, ed. Trueblood, SCM, Oct.
87.3W/S/18 Selected Works, The Portable Johnson and Boswell, ed. Kronenberger [1947]

1948

59.4R/TJ/11 Rasselas, Japanese translation
65.10SP/TJ/1 Shakespeare (Proposals etc.), Japanese translation, 1948–9
71.3FI/5 Falkland's Islands, Thames Bank

87.3W/S/19 Selected Works, Some Observations and Judgements, ed. Hayward

87.3W/S/20 Selected Works, Wisdom of Dr. Johnson, ed. Maxwell [1948]

1949

59.4R/501 Rasselas, ed. Hill

59.4R/TJ/12 Rasselas, Translations, Japanese, 20 Aug.

59.4R/TL/S/1 Rasselas, Translations, Latin, Selection

79.4LP/SS/165 Life of Milton, British and American Classics, Vol. 50, Kenkyusha English Classics, ed. Fukuhara [1949]

87.3W/S/21 Selected Works, Falcon Prose Classics, ed. Symonds

1950

49.1VW/42 Vanity of Human Wishes, facsimile, ed. Bronson

79.4LP/SS/220 Life of Pope, Kenkyusha English Classics, Vol. 52, ed. Fukuhara, Tokyo [1950]

87.3W/S/22 Selected Works, The Reynard Library, ed. Crow (includes 59.4R/502 Rasselas)

1951

59.4R/TS/7 Rasselas, Translations, Spanish [1951]

60.8FP/2 Hollis's Committee for French Prisoners, French translation, Dec.

79.4LP/SS/87 Life of Dryden, Kenkyusha English Classics, Vol. 51, ed. Fukuhara

79.4LP/SS/166 Life of Milton, Kenkyusha English Classics. New Series, ed. Fukuhara

79.4LP/SS/221 Life of Pope, Kenkyusha English Classics, ed. Fukuhara, Tokyo

85.7RE/1b Frances Reynolds's Enquiry, facsimile

1952

59.4R/503 Rasselas, Rinehart Editions

59.4R/TI/S/11 Rasselas, Translations, Italian, Selection

87.3W/S/23a Selected Works, Rinehart Editions, ed. Bronson

88.3L/23 Letters, ed. Chapman

1953

44.2LS/16 Life of Savage, Great English Short Novels [?1953]

50.3R/S/27a Rambler Selections, Everyman [1953]

1954

59.4R/504 Rasselas, ed. Hill

1955

45.5HAS/1b Henry Hervey-Aston, Sermon, facsimile

59.4R/505 Rasselas, Selections, ed. Chapman

68.5LB/2 Letter to F. A. Barnard, 28 May 1768, facsimile

79.4LP/S/4 Lives of the Poets, Selections, Gateway edition

87.3W/S/24a Selections from Samuel Johnson, ed. Chapman

1956

79.4LP/SS/167 Life of Milton, Macmillan's English Classics, ed. Deighton

1958

44.2LS/17 Life of Savage, ed. Lyon

59.4R/506 Rasselas, Everyman's Library, No. 856 [1958]

85.8PM/32 Prayers and Meditations, ed. McAdam

87.3W/S/23b Selected Works, Rasselas etc., ed. Bronson [1958]

1959

59.4R/507 Rasselas, Rinehart Editions [1959]

59.4R/TA/2 Rasselas, Translations, Arabic

78.5RD/22a Reynolds's Discourses, ed. Wark

1960

50.3R/S/27b Rambler Selections, Everyman [196-]

65.10SP/TI/2 Shakespeare, Italian translation

1962

59.4R/508 Rasselas, Barrons' Educational Series [1962]

59.4R/509 Rasselas, Crofts Classics, ed. Kolb

59.4R/510 Rasselas, University Tutorial Series, ed. Collins

59.4R/TJ/13 Rasselas, Translations, Japanese, 20 Sept.

87.3W/S/24b Selections from Samuel Johnson, ed. Chapman, World's Classics

1963

56.1DA/A/17a Abridged Dictionary, Adaptations, McAdam and Milne [?1963]

56.1DA/A/17b Abridged Dictionary, Adaptations, McAdam and Milne

56.1DA/A/17c Abridged Dictionary, Adaptations, McAdam and Milne

58.4Id/49 Johnson's Idler Essays

59.4R/511 Rasselas, University Tutorial Series, ed. Collins

79.4LP/S/5 Lives of the Poets, Selections, Fontana Library,

87.3W/S/25 Selected Works, A Johnson Sampler, ed. Curwen

1964

59.4R/512 Rasselas, University Tutorial Series, ed. Collins

59.4R/TAm/2 Rasselas, Translations, Amharic, 1964-5

59.4R/TG/18 Rasselas, Translations, German

79.4LP/S/6 Lives of the Poets, Selections, Avon Library, NS 5, n.d. [?1964]

85.2BH/1b Burney's Commemoration of Handel, facsimile

85.2PW/38 Poetical Works, ed. McAdam and Milne, Yale Edition of Works, Vol. VI

87.3W/S/26 Selected Works, A Johnson Reader, ed. MacAdam and Milne (includes 59.4R/513a Rasselas) [1964]

1965

38.5L/26 Selected Poems of Samuel Johnson and Oliver Goldsmith, ed. Rudrum and Dixon (includes London and 49.1VW/44 Vanity of Human Wishes) [1965]

49.2I/11 Irene, Eighteenth Century Tragedy, ed. Booth

75.1J/31 Journey, Riverside edition, ed. Wendt, Boston

79.4LP/S/7 Lives of the Poets, Selections, ed. Montagu

85.2BH/TG/1b Burney's Commemoration of Handel, German translation, facsimile [1965]

87.3W/S/27 A Johnson Selection, ed. Miles, English Classics

87.3W/S/28 Selected Writings, ed. Davies

88.3L/25 Letters (Selection), ed. Littlejohn

1966

59.4R/513b Rasselas, A Johnson Reader, ed. McAdam and Milne [1966]

1967

55.4D/1b Dictionary, first edition, facsimile

59.4R/514 Rasselas, Routledge's English Texts, ed. Peake

87.3W/S/29 Selected Works, ed. Peake, Routledge English Texts [1967]

1968

38.11HAE/2 Hon. Henry Hervey-Aston, Epitaph on Queen Caroline, reprint, summer
50.3R/S/28 Rambler Selections, Yale
52.11Ad/S/10 Adventurer Selections, Yale
58.4Id/S/18 Idler selections, ed. Bate
59.4R/515 Rasselas, ed. Hardy
75.1J/1b Journey, first edition, facsimile
76.4PT/3 Political Tracts
79.4LP/71b Lives of the Poets, Hill's edition
87.3W/22b Works, Oxford English Classics, facsimile, New York
87.3W/S/30 Selected Works, ed. Cruttwell, Penguin English Library [1968]
87.3W/S/31 Selected Works, Sayings of Dr. Johnson, ed. Reeves [1968]
94.4BS/1b Piozzi's British Synonymy, facsimile

1969

53.2GMI/1.1 Book Index to Gentleman's Magazine, facsimile
59.4R/516 Rasselas, Major English Writers [1969]
65.10SP/2c Preface to Shakespeare, facsimile
66.7GLW/2 Gwynne's London and Westminster Improved, facsimile
87.3W/S/32 Selected Works, ed. Keats, Little Paperback Classics, No. 77 [1969]

1970

38.5L/1b London and Vanity of Human Wishes (49.1VW/45), facsimiles, introd. Fleeman
46.3DM/1b Dodsley's Museum, facsimile
52.3LFQ/9 Lennox's The Female Quixote, ed. Dalziel
58.4Id/S/19 Idler Selections, The Vulture

59.4R/TF/55 Rasselas, Translations, French
64.12GT/1e Goldsmith's Traveller, facsimile
70.6GD/1b Goldsmith's The Deserted Village, facsimile

1971

44.2LS/2b Life of Savage, second edition, facsimile
44.2LS/18 Life of Savage, ed. Tracy
50.1St/1b The Student, facsimile
59.4R/517 Rasselas, Rinehart Edition
59.4R/518 Rasselas, Oxford English Novels, ed. Tillotson and Jenkins
72.7BPW/1b Boswell's Petition for James Wilson, facsimile
75.1J/31 Journey, Yale edition, ed. Lascelles
78.5RD/1b Reynolds's Seven Discourses, facsimile
79.4LP/S/8 Lives of the Poets, Selections, Oxford Paperback
85.2PW/39a Poetical Works, English Poems, ed. Fleeman, May

1972

78.7SA/1b Shaw's Analysis of the Galic Language, facsimile
87.3W/1.2/1b Works, Vols. XII-XIII, Debates in Parliament, facsimile

1973

38.5L/27 London, Septentrio Press
49.2I/1b Irene, first edition, facsimile

1974

39.10CP/1c Crousaz, Commentary on Pope, first edition, second issue, facsimile
59.4R/519 Rasselas, Garland facsimile
79.4LP/SS/172(TJ) Life of Milton, trans. Shumuta, Tokyo
85.2PW/39b Poetical Works, English Poems, ed. Fleeman

85.2PW/40 Poetical Works, Oxford English Texts, ed. Nichol Smith and McAdam, rev. Fleeman, May

85.8PM/33 Prayers and Meditations, MSS facsimile [1974]

1975

44.2LS/TJ/1 Life of Savage, Japanese translation, Suwabe

44.2LS/TJ/2 Life of Savage, Japanese translation, Nakagawa

59.4R/520 Rasselas, Folio Society

59.4R/521 Rasselas, ed. Hardy

61.8BA/TJ/1 Life of Ascham, Japanese translation

78.5RD/22b Reynolds's Discourses, ed. Wark

79.4LP/S/9 Lives of the Poets, Selections, Everyman

1976

59.4R/522a Rasselas, The Penguin English Library, ed. Enright

59.4R/522b Rasselas, Penguin Books, American issue

59.4R/TI/S/12 Rasselas, Translations, Italian, Selection

68.5LB/3 Letter to F. A. Barnard, 28 May 1768, Toucan Press

87.3W/S/33 Selected Works, Johnson on Johnson, ed. Wain [1976]

1977

56.3BCM/9 Browne's Christian Morals, Works, ed. Patrides

59.4R/523 Rasselas, Oxford Paperbacks

59.4R/524 Rasselas, Selected Poetry and Prose, ed. Brady and Wimsatt [1977]

59.4R/525 Rasselas, ed. Desai [1977]

61.8BA/5 Life of Ascham, facsimile

87.3W/S/34 Selected Poetry and Prose, ed. Brady and Wimsatt

1978

55.4D/4b Dictionary, fourth edition, facsimile

65.10SP/TJ/2 Shakespeare (Proposals etc.), Japanese translation

66.4WM/F/16 The Fountains, Harmsworth, 28 Feb.

1979

55.4D/1c Dictionary, first edition, facsimile

56.1UV/1b Universal Visiter, facsimile

59.4R/S/2 Rasselas, Selection, Toronto, Greyn Forest Press

1981

38.5L/28 London and The Vanity of Human Wishes (49.1VW/48), ed. and trans. Rudd

87.3W/S/35 Selected Writings, ed. Rogers

1982

49.1VW/49 Studies in English Literature: The Vanity of Human Wishes and Rasselas, ed. Cunningham

56.1DA/A/17d Abridged Dictionary, Adaptations, McAdam and Milne [1982]

66.4WM/F/17 The Fountains, Hillside Press, New York

85.2PW/39c Poetical Works, English Poems, ed. Fleeman

85.2PW/39d Poetical Works, Yale English Poets, No. 11

85.2PW/39e Poetical Works, The English Poets, Yale

1983

55.4D/1d Dictionary, first edition, facsimile

59.4R/TI/13 Rasselas, Translations, Italian [1983]

75.1J/A/8 Abridged Journey, Macdonald edition

1984

49.1VW/52 Vanity of Human Wishes, introd. Hodgart

59.4R/527 Rasselas, illust. Margaret Lock

59.4R/TF/56 Rasselas, Translations, French

66.4WM/F/18 The Fountains, St. Lucia, Queensland

75.1J/32 Journey, Penguin edition

85.8PM/Setting/2 Prayers and Meditations, Setting, Engaging in Politicks, 15 July

87.3W/S/36 Selected Works, ed. Greene, The Oxford Authors (includes 49.1VW/51 Vanity of Human Wishes and 59.4R/526 Rasselas)

805A/1b Account of the Life, facsimile, ed. Stockham

805A/1c Account of the Life, facsimile, ed. Stockham

805A/1d Account of the Life, facsimile, ed. Stockham

[1986 **75.1J/TG/2** Journey, German translation]

Index of Items

Individual poems by SJ appearing in periodicals are not listed here. Detailed accounts are given in *Poems*². The following special abbreviations are used: GM (*Gentleman's Magazine*); LM (*Literary Magazine*).

Abridged Dictionary (1756) 486–556

Abuse of Poetry, On the [notice], GM (1752) 396

Academick, Character and Duty of an, in Hospitality by Revd John Moir (1793) 1750–2

Account of Barbarossa, GM (1754) 406

Account of Archibald Campbell (1784) 1564

Account of the Conduct of the Duchess of Marlborough [review], GM (1742) 82

Account of the Detection of the Imposture in Cock-Lane, GM (1762) 1040

Account of the Harleian Library, GM (1742) 84

Account of Himself, by William Dodd (1777) 1295

Account of An historical . . . Enquiry into the Evidence against Mary Queen of Scots, GM (1760) 1021

Account of the late Application to Parliament by the Merchants of London, by Richard Glover [summary], GM (1742) 82

Account of Life of Edward Cave, GM (1754) 405

Account of the Life of Johnson [Letters to Hill Boothby] (1805) 1755–6

Account of the Plague by Procopius [introd.], GM (1743) 94

Adams, George, Treatise on the Globes (1766) 1146–53

Adamus Exsul, by Grotius, William Lauder's Proposals (1747) 140–1; proposals for printing, GM (1747) 147–8

Address of the Painters, Sculptors and Architects to George III, London Gazette (1761) 1021

[Address] to the Public, LM (1756) 686

Address to the Reader, GM (1738) 34

Address of Thanks for Henry Thrale (1774) 1204

Adventurer, The (1753–4) 334–96; selections 393–5; translations 396; brief account, GM (1752) 397

Advertisement for Francis Barber, Daily Advertiser (1757) 709

Advertisement for Debates in the Senate of Lilliput, GM (1739) 49

Advertisement for Edial School, GM (1736) 13

Advertisement for the World Displayed (1759) 990

Agriculture, Further Thoughts on, Universal Visiter (1756) 662

Alexander, James, Legal argument for, by James Boswell [Paterson vs. Alexander] (1775) 1249

Amazons, Dissertation on the, by Abbé De Guyon [translation] GM (1741) 59

Anagrammata Rediviva, proposals for printing, GM (1738) 37

Analysis of beauty, The, by William Hogarth [notice], GM (1753) 404; account, GM 404

Analysis of the Galic Language, by William Shaw (1778) 1344–6; proposals (1777) 1290–1

Ancient Geography, Dictionary of, by Alexander Macbean (1773) 1189–90

Ancient Universal History, Letter on contributors, GM (1784) 1570

Angell, John, Stenography (1758) 781–4

Annals of Scotland, by David Dalrymple, Lord Hailes (1776) 1255–9

Anson, George, Voyage round the World, abridged, GM (1749) 186; (1750) 319

Answers for the Robertsons, by James Boswell (1781) 1536–7

Apotheosis of Milton, GM (1738) 35

Appeal for the Hereford Infirmary, by Thomas Talbot, Hereford Journal (1774) 1204–5

Appeal to the Public, GM (1739) 48

Architecture among the Ancients, Rise of, Universal Visiter (1756) 662

Architecture, Designs among the Chinese, by Sir William Chambers (1757) 714–22; translations 715–16

Arguments against the Regency Bill, Sum of, GM (1751) 322

Armstrong, John, History of Minorca [review] LM (1756) 686

Art of Laying out Gardens among the Chinese, Sir William Chambers, GM (1757) 726; (1762) 716–19

Artists, Society of, Catalogue (1762) 1035–7; Letters for (1760) 1002–3, 1020–1

Ascham, Roger, Life of, in Bennet's edn. of Works (1761) 1028–32; proposals (1757) 724–5

Attack on the London Magazine, GM (1739) 47–8

Authours, On, Public Ledger (1760) 1001

Ayrshire, Petition for the Member for, by James Boswell (1781) 1533

Baker, Henry, Employment for the Microscope [notice], GM (1753) 403

Banks, Sir Joseph, Latin motto on goat of (1772) 1185

Barbadoes; a poem, by Nathaniel Weekes [notice], GM (1754) 406

Barbarossa, Account of, GM (1754) 406

Barber, Francis, advertisement for, Daily Advertiser (1757) 709

Baretti, Carmen Seculare, [1778] 1349–51; Dictionary of the Italian Language (1760) 1010–16; Easy Phraseology (1775) 1253–4; Guide to the Royal Academy, [1781], 1532–3; Introduction to the Italian Language (1755) 483–5; Italian Library (1757) 707–8; Proposals for Poems [Le Poesie] [1758] 726–7

Barnard, Frederick Augusta, Letter to (1768) 1167–8

Barnard, Thomas, Charade on [1777] 1284

Barretier, John Philip, Life of (1744) 110–11; GM (1740) 55; (1741) 58; (1742) 83

Bathurst, Richard, Scheme for a Geographical Dictionary (1753) 399

Beauties of Johnson (1781) 1539–57

Beaver, Samuel, The Cadet, A military treatise [review], LM (1756) 686

Bell, Jane, Epitaph on [?1773], 1199–200

Bell, William, Greek Grammar (1775) 1248

Bennet, James, Works of Roger Ascham (1761) 1028–32; proposals (1757) 724–5

Bibliotheca Biographica, by Thomas Flloyd (1760) 1016

Bibliotheca Harleiana, Vols. Three and Four, advertisement, GM (1743) 94–5

Birch, Thomas, History of the Royal Society [review], LM (1756) 686

Birmingham Journal (1733) 3–4

Black-friars Bridge, Considerations on Construction of, Daily Gazetteer (1759) 998–9

Blackrie, Alexander, Disquisition on Medicines (1766) 1138–9

Blackwell, Thomas, Memoirs of the Court of Augustus [review], LM (1756) 686–7

Blake, Admiral Robert, Life of (1740) 51–3; GM (1740) 53

Boadicea, by Richard Glover [account], GM (1753) 404

Boerhaave, Dr. Herman, Life of, GM (1739) 48; Universal Chronicle (1758) 735

[Boothby, Hill, Letters to], Account of the Life of Johnson (1805) 1755–6

Borlase, William, Observations on the Islands of Scilly [review], LM (1756) 686

Boswell, James, Answers for the Robertsons (1781) 1536–7; argument on title of Doctor of Medicine for Dr. Memis (1775) 1248–9; argument on Lay Patronage (1773) 1188; argument for Paterson vs. Alexander (1775) 1249; argument on Pulpit Censure (1776) 1270; petition for John Hastie (1772) 1186; petition for Joseph Knight (1777) 1333; petition for the Member for Ayrshire (1781) 1533; petition for James Wilson (1772) 1186–7; Ode to Mrs Thrale (1788) 1737

Boulter's Monument, by Samuel Madden (1745) 127–31

Bravery of the English Common Soldier, British Magazine (1760) 1001–2

Brief account of The Adventurer, GM (1752) 397

British Magazine, The (1760) 1001–2

British Synonymy, Hester Lynch Piozzi (1794) 1753–5

Brodhurst, Edward, Sermons (1733) 4

Brothers, The, by Edward Young [account], GM (1753) 403

Browne, Isaac Hawkins, Immortality of the Soul, translation of [notice], GM (1754) 405, another translation, by Dr Grey [notice], GM (1754) 405

Browne, Patrick, Civil and Natural History of Jamaica [review], LM (1756) 687

Browne, Sir Thomas, Christian Morals (1756) 673–8; review, LM (1756) 687

Brumoy, Fr Pierre de, Greek Theatre, translated by Charlotte Lennox (1759) 1003–7

Bunyan, John, Pilgrim's Progress, advertisement for reprinting, London Evening Post (1759) 990

Burman, Peter, Life of, GM (1742) 83; (1748) 170

Burney, Charles, Commemoration of Handel (1785) 1570–6; translations 1575–6; History of Music (1776–89) 1259–68

Byng, Admiral John, Some further particulars in relation to [review], LM (1756) 687

Fever Powders, Defence of James's (1777) 1288–90

Fictitious Newsletters and Reports, Public Advertiser (1770) 1178

Fifteen Sermons upon Social Duties, Patrick Delany [comment], GM (1744) 123–4

Fireworks, GM (1749) 186

Flloyd, Thomas, Bibliotheca Biographica (1760) 1016; Chronological Tables of Lenglet DuFresnoy (1762) 1038–9

Flying warlike machine, Plan for, by Morke [comment on], GM (1742) 83; editorial note, GM (1743) 94

Fontenelle, Bernard le Bovier de, Panegyric on Morin, GM (1741) 59

Fordyce, Revd James, Sermons to Young Women (1766) 1153–4

Foreign Books, GM (1741) 60; (1742) 81; (1743) 93; (1753) 404; (1754) 405–6; (1755) 486; (1756) 706; (1757) 726;

Foreign History, GM (1741) 59; (1742) 81, 84; (1743) 93–4; (1747) 148; (1748) 170; (1749) 186; (1750) 319

Fountains, The (?1766) 1142–5, *see also* Miscellanies, by Anna Williams (1766)

Four Letters from Isaac Newton [review], LM (1756) 686

Four Sermons, by Joseph Trapp [extract from], GM (1739) 49; considerations on, GM (1787) 1721

France, Journal of a visit to (1775) 1252

Frederick the Great, *see* King of Prussia, Memoirs (1786) 691–4; Life of, LM (1756) 687

Free Inquiry into the Nature and Origin of Evil, Soame Jenyns [review], LM (1757) 688

French Prisoners of War, Proceedings of the Committee for, by Thomas Hollis (1760) 1016–19; translation, 1018–19; British Magazine (1760) 1002

French Refugee, Observations on the foregoing Letter from a, LM (1756) 686

Further Thoughts on Agriculture, Universal Visiter (1756) 662

Future State, Letter to Johnson on a, by John Taylor (1787) 1720–1

Gamester, The, Edward Moore [account], GM (1753) 403

Gardiner, Richard, History of Pudica [notice], GM (1754) 405; Letter on Pudica, Thomas Shadwell [notice], GM (1754) 405

Garrick, David, Memoirs of, by Thomas Davies (1780) 1523–31; Lethe (1740) 49–50

Gazetteer, Letter to (1769) 1171

General Advertiser, The (1750) 318

General Evening Post (1743) 90; (1773) 1188

General History of Polybius, translated by James Hampton [review], LM (1756) 686

General Index, GM (1753) 397–9

Gentleman, Francis, Narcissa and Eliza [notice], GM (1754) 405

Gentleman's Magazine, vi. (1736) 13; viii. (1738) 34–7; ix. (1739) 47–9, x. (1740) 53–5; xi. (1741) 58–60; xii. (1742) 81–4; xiii. (1743) 93–5; xiv. (1744) 123–4; xv. (1745) 132–3; xvi. (1746) 140; xvii. (1747) 147–8; xviii. (1748) 170; xix. (1749) 186; xx. (1750) 318–20; xxi. (1751) 322–3; xxii. (1752) 396–7; xxiii. (1753) 403–4; xxiv. (1754) 404–6; xxv. (1755) 485–6; xxvi. (1756) 706; xxvii. (1757) 726; xxx. (1760) 1021; xxxii. (1762) 1040; liv. (1784) 1570; lv. (1785) 1622–3; lvii. (1787) 1721–2

Geographical Dictionary, Scheme for a, by Richard Bathurst (1753) 399

Geographical, historical, political . . . Essays, by Lewis Evans [review], LM (1756) 687

Geography, Dictionary of Ancient, by Alexander Macbean (1773) 1189–90

Geometry, Introduction to, William Payne (1767) 1162–3

George III, Conversation with (1791) 1749–50

Gifford, Richard, Contemplation [notice], GM (1753) 403

Gil Blas, by Edward Moore, remarks, GM (1751) 322

Globes, Treatise on the, by George Adams (1766) 1146–53

Glover, Richard, Account of the late Application to Parliament by the Merchants of London [summary], GM (1742) 82; Boadicea [account], GM (1753) 404; Letter to Mr. Richard Glover [notice], GM (1754) 404

Goldsmith, Oliver, The Deserted Village (1770) 1174–7; Epitaph on (1776) 1271–8; Good Natur'd Man (1768) 1165–7; The Traveller (1764) 1062–6; notice, Critical Review (1764) 1062; Verses from Dr. Johnson to Dr. Goldsmith, General Evening Post (1773) 1188

Good Natur'd Man, by Oliver Goldsmith (1768) 1165–7

Graham, George, Telemachus [review], Critical Review (1763) 1060

Grainger, James, Sugar Cane [review], Critical Review (1764) 1061; review, London Chronicle (1764) 1061

Grand Impostor Detected, The, by William Lauder [notice], GM (1754) 405

Grasier's Advocate, The, Remarks on, GM (1743) 93

Gray's-Inn Journal, Arthur Murphy [review], LM (1756) 686

Index of Persons and Places

This index follows outlines established by David Fleeman. It lists authors and editors with individual entries in the bibliography, members of the book trade, and individual owners of copies of books. It does not index scholars (except selectively in the case of early attributions), or institutions holding copies, or catalogues, or shelfmarks, or authors appearing in collections. Many of the individuals indexed remain unidentified and therefore undated, and some distinctions between booksellers remain tentative; the general assumption is that the older member of a book-trade family remains in control until his death.

The following special abbreviations are used: auct: auctioneer, bkc: bookcollector, bks: bookseller, engr: engraver, pprmkr: papermaker, ptr: printer. An asterisk (*) indicates an entry in *DNB*; a dagger (†) denotes a date of death, and a query (?) expresses uncertainty.

Entries that begin with the same word follow the order: personal names, company names, place names. A company name beginning with a personal name (first name + surname) is entered as a personal name, i.e. with the surname first. The ampersand is used regularly in the names of firms and is ignored in alphabetization; 'Co.' is included in the alphabetization. Members of partnerships not appearing independently are not entered independently.

A., T. (ed. *fl.* 1876) 1472, 1496, 1497
Abbey Classics (*fl.* ?1923) 1236, 1479, 1501
Abbott, John 829
Abercrombie, Revd James (of Phil., 1758–1841) 1671, 1722, 1736
Aberdarn, Edward 675
Aberdeen 507, 944, 1219, 1409, 1434, 1435
Aberdeen Infirmary 1248
Aberlady Parish Church, E. Lothian 1532
Abernethy & Walker (ptr. Edin., *fl.* 1812) 307, 394, 775
Abreu & Bertodano, Joseph Antonio [Don Felix], Marq. of (†1775) 1010, 1015
Academicus (?= Lord Hailes or John Loveday) 189–90
Acheson, Archibald Brabazon Sparrow, E. of Gosford 130
Acland, Sir Arthur Herbert Dyke (1847–1926*) 1336
Acland, Mary (*fl.* 1839) 967
Acon, R. (engr. *fl.* 1826) 848
Adam, Sir Frederick (1781–1853*) 978
Adam, Lena Stephens (w. of Robert Borthwick II) 97, 125
Adam, Robert Borthwick II (1863–1940, bkc.) 2, 7, 10, 18, 19, 20, 21, 23, 25, 27, 39, 42, 89, 92, 96, 97, 98, 125, 129, 143, 144, 171, 177, 179, 185, 190, 198, 208, 210, 213, 217, 230, 235, 237, 251, 255, 264, 270, 277, 291, 306, 310, 326, 338, 341, 402, 429, 452, 487, 658, 675, 740, 745, 753, 761, 782, 788, 790, 791,

792, 794, 795, 796, 799, 802, 803, 806, 813, 816, 818, 837, 847, 849, 861, 956, 1013, 1018, 1030, 1066n, 1071, 1090, 1111, 1117, 1142, 1156, 1162, 1180, 1183, 1190, 1191, 1194, 1196, 1207, 1208, 1210, 1215, 1217, 1219, 1220, 1286n, 1304, 1334, 1342, 1387, 1416, 1418, 1437, 1448, 1449, 1454, 1516, 1520, 1530, 1543, 1544, 1545, 1546, 1549, 1550, 1551, 1553, 1577, 1579, 1580, 1603, 1604, 1610, 1631, 1632, 1633, 1647, 1650, 1673, 1676, 1679, 1683, 1686, 1687, 1696, 1724, 1727, 1733, 1734, 1736, 1739, 1745, 1750, 1757
Adams, Serjeant (*fl.* ?1840–) 1428
Adams, Dudley (*fl.* 1810) 1153
Adams, George elder (†1773) 1146–53, 1666
Adams, George younger (1750–95*) 1147, 1151–2, 1153
Adams, Isaac (bks. Portland, *fl.* 1815) 578
Adams, John (*fl.* 1787) 1630
Adams, Sarah (m. Benjamin Hyett, 1746–1804) 787, 1142, 1601
Adams, William (1706–89*, Master of Pembroke, Oxon.) 1207n, 1209
Adams, William (1814–48*, F. of Merton]) 1428
Addis Ababa, Ethiopia 954
Addison, Joseph (1672–1719*) 143n, 1283
Adee, Olivia 1044
Adel, R. (engr. *fl.* 1833) 858
Adelmann 66

Dobelbower, Key, & Simpson (bks. Phil., *fl.* 1795–6) 998

Dobell, Bertram (1842–1914*) 1062–3, 1064

Dobell, Percy John (bks. *fl.* 1918–41) 146

Doble, C. E. 742

Dobroe Namerenie 986

Dobson, Austin *see* Dobson, Henry Austin

Dobson, C. M. 816

Dobson, Henry Austin (1840–1921*) 145, 777, 1342

Dobson, J. (bks. 1819) 465

Dobson, R. (bks. *fl.* 1822–3) 283, 284, 388, 767, 768

Dodd (art. *fl.* 1787) 800

Dodd, Anne (mercury, *fl.* 1726–?43) 44, 49n, 50, 660, 662

Dodd, Benjamin (bks. 1745–64) 1081, 1090, 1096, 1123

Dodd, Revd James William (†1820) 1581n

Dodd, Mary (née Perkins, wife of Revd W., forger, *fl.* 1777) 1292, 1294, 1306, 1310, 1323, 1325, 1326, 1327, 1328, 1329, 1330

Dodd, Maurice (bks. Carlisle) 408

Dodd, Revd William (forger, 1729–1777*) 779, 1292, 1294–333, 1540, 1547, 1549, 1550, 1552, 1600, 1679

Dodd, Mead & Co. (bks. New York, *fl.* 1902) 146

Doddesley, R. *see* Dodsley

Dodds, J. W. (ed. *fl.* 1935) 1500

Dodgson, Charles Lutwidge (1832–98*) 866

Dodgson, Edward Spencer (b. 1858–1912+) 1049

Dodsley, James (bks. 1724–97*) 155, 158, 160, 162, 164, 167, 179, 247, 303, 342, 344, 346, 348, 350, 357, 363, 371, 373, 373, 411, 421, 425, 429n, 432, 437, 441, 491, 494, 496, 498, 499, 500, 502, 505, 507, 510, 704, 706, 719, 720, 791, 792, 794, 796, 799, 803, 806, 1030, 1041, 1048, 1049, 1050, 1052, 1067, 1074, 1076, 1077, 1153, 1155, 1160, 1240, 1280, 1291, 1351, 1354, 1362, 1367, 1370, 1371, 1375, 1380, 1382, 1385, 1390, 1519, 1521, 1522, 1562, 1581, 1623, 1630, 1632, 1637, 1641, 1647, 1648, 1651

Dodsley, P. (*fl.* 1794) 248

Dodsley, Robert (bks. 1703–64*) 19, 20, 21, 22, 23, 32, 43, 92, 127, 133–40, 141, 142, 144, 145, 148–59, 170, 171, 172, 176, 177, 179, 184, 300, 319, 342, 344, 346, 407, 411, 509 [pseud.], 698, 712n, 717, 1003, 1070, 1245n, 1360 and 1394 [pseud.], 1640, 1667

Dodsley, R. & J., 411, 417, 486, 489, 695, 699, 700, 702, 707, 709, 714, 717, 724, 727, 785, 787, 789, 790, 1028, 1041, 1045, 1047, 1125

Dodsworth, Alexander (tr. *fl.* 1797) 797

Doig, Ronald Paterson 771

Doig, Sylvester (bks. Edin., *fl.* 1794) 250, 365, 367, 503

Doig & Sterling (bks. Edin., 1813) 576

Dolman , C. (bks. *fl.* 1840) 620, 625

Dolphin (bkc.?) 1424

Domville, Sir James Graham, 3rd Bt. St Albans (b. 1812) 1667

Donaldson, Alexander (bks. Edin. *fl.* 1750–94*) 27, 222, 226, 355, 700, 1191, 1210

Donaldson, James (1751–1830, ptr. Edin.) 1191

Donaldson, John (bks. London, *fl.* 1763–77) 1290, 1344

Doncaster, Yorks. 306

Donkin, Henry 1218

Donington, Northants. (Sir Robert Clyfton) 487

Donnant, Denis François (tr. b. 1769) 963

Donohoe, Henneberry & Co. (bks. Chicago, *fl.* ?1878–85) 655, 895, 898, 899, 900, 901, 902, 906, 908, 909, 912, 913, 914, 916, 917, 920, 936, 938, 941

Donoughmore, Richard Hely-Hutchinson, 1st E. (1756–1825*) 1159

Dorchester, Dorset 1610, 1611

Dormer, Philip *see* Chesterfield, 4th E. of

Dorrington, John (of Lypiatt Park) 1543

Dorsch, T.S. (ed. *fl.* 1967) 950, 1718

Dorset *see* Sackville, Charles, 2nd D. of (1711–69*)

Doubleday Doran (bks. New York, *fl.* 1924) 943

Doubleday, Page (bks. New York, *fl.* 1901) 777

Douce, Francis (1757–1834*, bkc.) 1156

Douglas, James, 4th E. Morton (†1581) 1021

Douglas, Revd John DD , Bp. of Salisbury (1721–1807*) 185, 186, 320–1, 1060, 1722

Douglas, Noel, Replicas (*fl.* 1927) 1175

Douglas, Robert (bks. Galashiels, *fl.* 1808) 1530

Dovaston, H. M. 190

Dove, J. F. (ptr. & bks. *fl.* 1820–27) 281, 286, 290, 292, 387, 389, 769, 770, 834n, 851, 859, 861, 862, 865, 868, 873, 1330, 1422, 1426, 1428, 1429, 1686, 1687

Dowden, Edward (1843–1913*) 210, 1096, 1207, 1757

Dowdeswell, Revd G. Berens (? †1933) 402n

Dowdeswell, John 7, 122

Dowdeswell, William (of Pull Court, 1761–1828*) 402

Dowding, J. (bks. *fl.* 1827–40) 467, 536, 603, 613, 620, 625, 630

Dowson, B. U. (*fl.* 1807) 270

Dowson, Mary S. (*fl.* 1884) 270

Doyle, Sir Arthur Conan (1859–1930*) 1681n

Doyle, M. (bks. 1819) 465

Dradzowa, Martinus (art. *fl.* 1754) 333

Drake, Sir Francis (1540?–96*) 53–4, 58, 99, 100, 101, 102

Draper, Somerset (*fl.* 1743–53) 1118n
Drawback 558, 559, 1390
Dreghorn, L. *see* Maclaurin, John
Dreser (engr. 1850) 872
Drewerie, Robert (Robert Drury) 118
Droeshout, Martin (engr. *fl.* 1620–51*) 1088, 1095, 1119
Drogheda 197n
Drumminor Ho., Aberdeens. 712; *see also* Forbes family
Drummond (of Pitkellonie) 425
Drummond, James (*fl.* 1769) 493
Drummond, R. 425
Drury, Alexander 326
Drury, Robert (1567–1607*) 118
Drury, T. R. (ptr. *fl.* 1832–3) 606, 608
Drury Lane Theatre 145–7, 148, 176–80
Du Barry, Marie Jeanne Gomard de Vaubernier, comtesse (1741–93) 97
Du Fresne, Mme. (tr. *fl.* 1832) 967, 969
Du Resnel, Abbé Jean-François Resnel du Bellay (1692–1761) 43, 45
Dublin 18, 105, 130, 139, 152, 157, 159, 165, 172, 173, 178, 183, 197n, 208, 230, 246, 247, 271, 286, 289, 290, 291, 293, 301, 305, 318, 327, 328, 342, 345, 352, 353, 357, 359, 365, 368, 387, 394, 430, 431, 446, 448, 449, 465, 466, 471, 472, 473, 480, 487–8, 490, 491, 493, 494, 517, , 518, 519, 520, 522, 525, 527, 528, 529, 561, 576, 583, 587, 590, 593, 594, 598, 601, 604, 605, 607, 611, 612, 613, 615, 616, 618, 619, 623, 624, 625, 627, 631, 634, 711, 714n, 720, 723, 742, 743, 767, 769, 783–4, 788, 795, 801, 810, 813, 820, 823, 850, 859, 861, 863, 993, 996, 997, 1024, 1026, 1052, 1066, 1072, 1097–8, 1106, 1110, 1135, 1136, 1154, 1157, 1170, 1174, 1182, 1197, 1202, 1203, 1209, 1210, 1211, 1212, 1213, 1218, 1220, 1236, 1240, 1269, 1273, 1274, 1276, 1277, 1279, 1281, 1299, 1321, 1332, 1348, 1357, 1358, 1359, 1360, 1361, 1372, 1374, 1392, 1393, 1394, 1403, 1405, 1407, 1426, 1502, 1507, 1518, 1526, 1538, 1541, 1551, 1554, 1555, 1573, 1577, 1593, 1601, 1604, 1650, 1659, 1680, 1681, 1691, 1693, 1725, 1726, 1741, 1754
Ducarel, Andrew Coltee (1713–85*) 1077
Duchesne (bks. Paris, *fl.* 1760) 1024
Duchesne, La Veuve (bks. Paris, 1774) 396
Duchiron, M. (tr. *fl.* 1798) 962
Duck, Stephen (1705–56*) 136
Duff 1602
Duff, Mrs (of Muirtown, Paisley, *fl.* 1798) 1466
Duff, John Wight (ed. *fl.* 1900) 1462, 1488
Duff, William (? 1732–1815*; *fl.* 1791) 705
Duff & Hodgson (bks. *fl.* 1835) 1574

Duffy, James (bks. & ptr. Dublin, *fl.* 1847) 631, 634
Dufour, J. E. (bks. Maastricht, *fl.* 1786) 312
DuFresnoy, Nicolas Lenglet (1674–1755) 1038–9
Dugdale, B. (bks. Dublin *fl.* 1791) 1502
DuHalde, Jean Baptiste (1641–1743) 83, 1686
Dulau, A. B. (bks. *fl.* 1823) 285, 387, 767
Dulau, A. B., & Co. (bks. *fl.* 1826) 594
Dullingham, Cambs., (Christopher Jeaffreson) 503
Dumfries 465
Dumolard (bks. Milan, *fl.* 1883) 981
Duncan, Andrew & John M. (ptr. Glas. Univ., *fl.* 1817–25) 287, 291, 389, 585, 587, 789, 847, 848, 1223, 1698
Duncan, J. & A. (bks. Glas., 1802) 513, 515, 536
Duncan, James (bks. *fl.* 1823–36) 308, 394, 467, 590, 593, 601, 603, 604, 613, 614, 616
Duncan, James & A. (bks. Glas. 1798–1809) 256, 261, 571
Duncan, James, & Son (bks. Glas., 1792) 506
Duncan, William (1717–60*) 151
Duncan & Malcolm (bks. 1840) 620, 625
Duncombe, John (1729–86*) 405, 1044, 1317–18
Dunfermline, Thomson, Revd James
Dunk, George Montagu, 1st E. of Halifax (1716–71*) 1158
Dunlop & Wilson (bks. Glas., *fl.* 1777–92) 506, 1290
Dunn, Robert D. 1293
Dunn & Wright (ptr. Glas., *fl.*?1867) 885
Dunnichen, Forfars (George Dempster) 502, 1207
Dunvegan *see* Macleod of Dunvegan
Duppa, Richard (1770–1831*) 1756–8
DuPré, Isaac (of Wilton Park) 350
Durand (bks. Paris, *fl.* 1746–8) 67
Durell, William *see* Durrell
Durham 1679
Durrell, William (bks. New York, *fl.* 1808–12) 764, 1221, 1413, 1420, 1669, 1670, 1671
Dutton, E. P., & Co. [Inc.] (bks. New York, *fl.* 1905–53) 311, 312, 934, 936, 943, 944, 945, 948, 1335, 1341, 1451, 1596, 1732
Dutton, Robert (bks. *fl.* 1808–10) 122
Drake, Nathan (1766–1836*) 1671
Dwight, W. (*fl.* 1851) 226
Dyce, Alexander (1798–1869*, ed.) 25, 39, 177, 723, 1468
Dyer, Revd John (1700?-58*) 1070, 1558
Dyer, Richard (auth. of Carnation) 403
Dysart, Lionel Murray, 3rd E. of (1707–70*) 115

Fulton George (lexicog. *fl.* 1822) 585n, 587,
590, 592, 593, 595, 597, 599, 601, 607, 609,
610, 613, 615, 616, 617, 621, 625, 626, 629,
633, 636, 637, 639, 640n, 641, 644, 646, 649,
650, 655
Fulton, John Farquhar (1899–1960) 74
Furbo, A.M. 170n
Furness, Horace Howard (1833–1912) 125, 402
Fussell (art. *fl.* 1835) 860

G. 54
G., C. 714
G., J. H. (*fl.* 1806) 47
G., M. L. C. (*fl.* 1926) 943
G., W., (art. *fl.* ?1800) 53
Gage, W. J. & Co. (bks. Toronto, *fl.* 1888) 309
Gaine, Hugh (ptr. New York, *fl.* 1771) 1183
Gainsborough, Lincs. 28, 503, 513, 581, 1301,
1325, 1327, 1510, 1579
Galashiels, Borders 1530
Gale, T. (bks. *fl.* 1824) 1427
Gale, William 382
Gale, William (of Southwark) 762
Gale, Curtin, & Co. (bks. 1813) 575, 576
Gale, Curtis, & Fenner, (bks. *fl.* 1813–15) 519,
1329
Gale & Fenner (bks. *fl.* 1816–18) 278, 383,
459, 578, 581, 583, 765, 834, 1415, 1486,
1674, 1676
Galignani, A. & W. (bks. Paris, *fl.* 1804–29)
470, 843; *see also* Parsons & Galignani
Gallaudet, E. (art. *fl.* ?1829) 530
Gallie, George (bks. Glas. *fl.* 1834) 3
Gallo-Anglus (*fl.* 1755) 686
Galpin, R. (ptr. Lymington, *fl.* ?1826) 1612,
?1726
Garden, F. (engr. *fl.* 1761) 1028
Garden City Press (Letchworth) 1231
Gardener *see* Gardner
Gardiner (art. *fl.* 1797–8) 1466
Gardiner (*fl.* 1815) 1726
Gardiner, Mrs Ann (*fl.* 1756) 487, 662, 663n,
1029
Gardiner, Richard (*fl.* 1754) 405
Gardner 440
Gardner, Alexander (bks. & ptr. Paisley, *fl.*
1837–1906) 1229, 1713
Gardner, H. (bks. *fl.* 1793) 1727
Gardner, H. L. (bks. *fl.* 1778–1801) 1118,
1123, 1125, 1380, 1382, 1385, 1390, 1398,
1400, 1581, 1632, 1633, 1651, 1657
Gardner, Samuel 338
Gardner, Thomas (ptr. *fl.* 1735–56) 17–18, 38,
660, 661, 663n, 664–9
Garland Publishing (New York, *fl.* 1974) 47,
951
Garlick, John 81

Garlick, Thomas (schoolmaster, ?†1728/9) 84n
Garrick, Mrs. (?1725–1822) 1738n
Garrick, David (actor 1717–79*) 49–50, 136,
145–6, 148, 177, 196, 316, 317, 675, 680,
1044, 1090, 1142, 1165n, 1169, 1196, 1200n,
1208, 1241, 1265, 1279, 1309n, 1347,
1523–31, 1730
Garrick, Peter (1710–95) 50
Gaskell, Philip 111n
Gastrell, [Elizabeth] Jane (née Aston, 1710–91)
208
Gateway Editions (*fl.* 1955) 1456
Gathorne-Hardy, Robert E. (?1840–1906*)
144, 190, 1453, 1577
Gätschenberger, S. (tr. *fl.* 1874) 977
Gawler, Mr. [? William, 1750–1809*] 1334
Gay, John (1685–1732*) 29, 36, 1117
Geel, Jacob (1789–1862, tr.) 48
Geeves, T. (bks. *fl.* 1836–7) 536, 613, 620
Geneste, Lord 217
Geneva, Switz. 45, 1237
Gentleman, Francis (1728–84*) 405
George II, King (1683–1760*) 33–4, 111, 120
George III, King (1738–1820*; Prince of Wales
—1760) 149, 153, 154, 156, 158, 166, 714,
1003, 1021, 1026, 1033, 1146, 1148, 1149,
1150, 1151, 1152, 1153, 1155, 1206, 1254,
1284–5, 1294, 1307, 1333, 1334, 1335, 1336,
1337, 1338, 1339, 1340, 1341, 1342, 1343,
1571, 1572, 1575–6, 1624, 1733, 1749–50
George IV (1762–1830*; Prince of Wales—
1820) 1153
German, George 499
Gessner & Schramm (bks. Leipzig, *fl.* 1775)
1239
Giardini, D. (mus.) 1009
Gibbon, Edward (1737–94*) 787, 1071, 1344
Gibbons (bks. Phil., *fl.* 1835) 1592
Gibbons, James (*fl.* 1763) 75
Gibbons, Thomas (1720–85*) 1516
Gibbs, James (1682–1754*) 7
Gibbs, P. (*fl.* 1736) 782
Gibson, J. (engr. *fl.* 1756) 672–3
Gibson, Robert, & Sons (bks. Glas. *fl.* ?1904)
932–3
Gibson, William (*fl.* 1784) 1568
Giffard, Henry (1699–1772) 49–50, 1523
Gifford, Richard (1725–1807*) 403
Gilbert, Claudius (1670–1743*) 130, 478, 528,
606, 1159, 1394
Gilbert, Frederick (art. *fl.* ?1881) 899
Gilbert, Sir John (art. 1817–97*) 1592, 1594
Gilbert, R. (ptr. *fl.* 1823) 980
Gilbert, R. & R. (ptr. *fl.* 1816) 1287, 1288
Gilbert, William (1540–1603*) 408
Gilbert, W. (bks. Dublin *fl.* 1778–82) 1276,
1526, 1541

Gilbert & Hodges (bks. Dublin *fl.* 1806) 271,
823, 1218, 1407, 1659
Gilbert & Rivington (ptr. *fl.* 1832) 856
Giles, John Allen (ed. 1808–84*) 1031
Gilfillan, Revd George (1813–78*) 1592–3,
1594, 1595, 1596
Gillet, James (bk. *fl.* 1814–20) 1235
Gillet, T. (ptr. *fl.* 1805) 547
Gillies, J. (bks. Glas., 1802) 513
Gilley, W. B. (bks. New York, *fl.* 1825) 1701
Gilmer, George (*fl.* 1761) 66
Gilpin, George (?G.G. Brown, 1816–) 1366
Ginger, W. (bks. *fl.* 1816–23) 332, 548, 838,
1674, 1676, 1683
Ginn & Co. (pub. Boston, *fl.* 1886–1936) 909,
910, 912, 921, 923, 932, 933, 934, 938,
941–2, 1715
Gisborne, A. F. 837
Gladding (bks. New York, *fl.* 1834) 1468
Glanville (?Hon Frances, Mrs Boscawen,
†1805) 27
Glanville, S. 2n
Glasgow, 3, 29, 173, 174, 256, 261, 280, 282,
283, 284, 287, 288, 289, 290, 291, 293, 308,
388, 389, 390, 394, 465, 466, 471, 472, 473,
480, 503, 513, 515, 525, 527, 528, 551, 552,
564, 567, 569, 571, 579, 585, 587, 590, 593,
594, 598, 601, 603, 604, 607, 611, 612, 613,
614, 615, 616, 617, 618, 619, 620, 621, 624,
625, 627, 629, 631, 641, 651, 654, 656, 657,
767, 768, 769, 813, 836, 840, 847, 850, 853,
856, 867, 870, 883, 932–3, 1136, 1216, 1220,
1222, 1224, 1225, 1226, 1227, 1290, 1342,
1409, 1414, 1417, 1421, 1424, 1426, 1427,
1433, 1488, 1551, 1552, 1554, 1555, 1610,
1611, 1612, 1613, 1649, 1681, 1691, 1692,
1693, 1698, 1718, 1751
Glasgow University Library 1018
Glass, P. (bks. *fl.* 1758) 781
Glegg 1730
Gleig, George (ed. 1753–1840*) 9–10, 137n,
1034, 1640, 1641n, 1667n
Glendinning, W. (ptr. *fl.* 1803) 1152
Gloucester 1509
Glover, Richard (1712–85*) 82, 404, ?1273
Glyn 1661
Glynn, St John (1603–66*) 68
Goadby, Robert (1723–78*) 1331
Godine, David R. (bks. Boston, *fl.* 1970) 778
Godolphin, Francis, 2nd E. (1678–1766*)
1023n
Godolphin, Mary, D. of Leeds (*fl.* 1761) 1023
Goethe, Johann Wolfgang von (1749–1832)
841n, 1239
Goggin, S. E. (ed. *fl.* 1907–16) 1475, 1489
Gold, Charles (ptr. *fl.* ?1815) 449
Gold, Joyce (ptr. *fl.* 1806) 270, 1668

Goldberg, Gerald E. 120, 152, 325, 410, ?698,
782, 802, 1020, 1047, 1097, 1161, 1172,
1181, 1190, 1216, 1218, 1265, 1269, 1279,
1519, 1520
Golden Eagle Press, Mt Vernon, NY (*fl.*
1937–45) 1470, 1618
Golden Hind Press, Madison, NJ (*fl.* ?1947)
1619
Golding, Ellen (*fl.* 1839) 605
Goldney, H. (ptr. *fl.* 1779–90) 363, 1277, 1352,
1380
Goldney, Sarah (*fl.* 1776) 2
Goldsmith, Revd Henry (†1768) 1062, 1063,
1064, 1065, 1066
Goldsmith, Oliver (1730–74*) 27, 31, 175, 740,
1002, 1062–6, 1165–7, 1174–7, 1188,
1271–8, 1278, 1288, 1685, 1696
Goldsmith, W. (bks. *fl.* 1787–93) 219, 223,
228, 234, 244, 252, 357, 363, 371, 432, 435,
437–8, 441, 496, 498, 499, 500, 502, 505,
507, 509, 1380, 1382, 1385, 1390, 1581,
1623, 1631, 1632, 1637, 1641, 1647, 1649
Golightly, Frances M. 429
Gollancz, Victor (bks. *fl.* 1963) 552
Good, John Mason (1764–1827*) 480
Goodale, Ephraim (bks. Mendon, *fl.* 1800)
1508
Goodall, Charles MD (1642–1712*) 71, 72, 73,
74
Goodden, John Culliford (*fl.* 1773–80) 1097
Goodhugh, T. (bks. *fl.* 1823–4) 523, 524
Goodman & Piggot (engr. Phil., *fl.* 1821) 282
Goodnight (engr. *fl.* 1769) 1148
Goodsman, ?David (bks. *fl.* 1776) 1278
Goodspeed, George (bks. Boston) ?1590
Goodwin, J[ames] (bks. *fl.* 1813–27) 287, 517,
518, 519, 520, 522, 523, 524, 525, 527, 573,
1689
Goodwin, John (British Consulate, Palermo) 525
Goodwyn, J. (bks. *fl.* 1824) 1427
Goor, G. B. van (bks. Gouda, *fl.* 1843–57) 868,
869, 879, 958
Gordon, Gen. Charles George ('Chinese',
1833–85*) 642
Gordon, R. (bks. Edin., *fl.* 1795) 1216
Gordon, W. (bks. Edin., *fl.* 1792) 199–200,
203, 1135
Gordon-Lennox, Charles, 3rd D. of Richmond
& Lennox (1735–1806) 781, 782, 784
Gore, Charles 788
Gosford, Archibald Brabazon Sparrow
Acheson, E. (1841–1922) 130
Gosnell, S. (ptr. *fl.* 1803) 1529
Gosse, Sir Edmund William (1849–1928*)
1340, 1448
Gosse, P., & J. Neaulme (bks. Paris & La Haye
fl. 1728) 6

Harmondsworth, Middx. 952

Harmsworth, Alfred Charles William, Visc. Northcliffe (1865–1922*) 1321

Harmsworth, Esmond Cecil, 2nd Visc. Rothermere (1898–1978*) 279, 1395

Harmsworth, Thomas, Publishing (*fl*. 1978) 1145

Harper, J.(bks. *fl*. 1817) 278, 383, 765

Harper & Brothers (bks. New York, *fl*. 1832–1947) 1498, 1619, 1703, 1706, 1707, 1708, 1709, 1712–13

Harrap, George G. (pub. *fl*. 1948) 1715

Harrild, Thomas (ptr. *fl*. 1855) 876

Harrington, Joseph 1314

Harrington, Timothy Charles (1851–1910*) ?100

Harrington, Col. William (binder, *fl*. 1826) 851n

Harris, B. (bks. *fl*. 1831–41) 605, 624

Harris, H. (bks. *fl*. 1831–41) 605, 616, 624

Harris, J. (bks. *fl*. 1802–27) 277, 287, 381, 383, 517, 518, 519, 520, 522, 523, 524, 525, 527, 529, 762, 765, 824, 828, 1689

Harris, James (1709–80*) 1347

Harris, John (ed. *fl*. 1972) 719

Harris, Thomas (†1820*) 102, 103, 104, 1292

Harris, Isle of (Finlay J. Macdonald) 1236

Harrison (*fl*. 1835) 1749

Harrison, Elizabeth (1724–56) 687, 1641n, 1686

Harrison, James elder (†1769) 233

Harrison, James younger (*fl*. 1785–1824) 142, 232–4, 241, 255, 263, 361, 373, 376, 436–7, 523, 524, 529, 691, 694, 747–50, 1427, 1565

Harrison, Richard (*fl*. 1882–88) 341, 803

Harrison, Thomas (†1791) 233, 437

Harrison, W. sen. (engr. *fl*. 1795–6) 998

Harrison, W. jun. (engr. *fl*. 1803) 379

Harrison & Co. (bks. *fl*. 1783–94) 168, 232–4, 241, 304, 329, 361, 368, 373, 376, 436, 445, 691, 747–50, 800, 801, 819, 1023, 1240

Harrop, Revd Samuel (†1781) 7n

Hart 1610

Hart, Harris (ptr. *fl*. ?1765–87†) 1162, 1163, 1184

Hart, Horace (ptr. OUP, 1840–1916) 1449

Hart, John (ptr. *fl*. 1737–64) 1162

Hart, Marie L. (US) 842

Hart-Davis, Rupert (pub. *fl*. 1950) 947, 1717

Hartford, Conn. 849, 852, 855, 857–8, 870, 871, 872, 873, 876

Hartley, Cecil (ed., *fl*. 1824) 591, 593, 596, 597, 599

Hartley & Walker (ptr. Halifax, *fl*. 1835–6) 1432, 1433

Hartnell, Blanche (*fl*. 1923) 1551

Hartopp, E. S E. (*fl*. 1853) 415

Harvard Co-operative Society (pub. Camb. Mass., *fl*. 1903) 1712

Harvard University Press (*fl*. 1963) 1718

Harvey & Darton (bks. *fl*. 1826–9) 173, 524, 526, 586, 587, 589, 591, 595, 603, 620, 624; *see also* Darton & Harvey

Hartwig & Müller (bks. Hamburg, *fl*. 1826) 974

Harwood, J. (bks. *fl*. 1813–22) 517, 518, 519, 520, 522, 1681

Harwood, J. & F. (bks. *fl*. ?1829) 600

Harwood, Thomas (1767–1842*) 1200n, 1585n

Harwood, W. (bks. 1819–20) 465, 466, 1649

Haslewood, Joseph (1769–1833*) 125

Haslewood Books (pub. *fl*. 1930) 30

Hastie, John (of Campbelltown, *fl*. 1772) 1186

Hastings, Elizabeth (Ct. of Moira, †1808) 488

Hastings, J. D. 1034

Hastings, Sir John Rawdon, 1st E. of Moira (†1793) 488

Hastings, Selina, Ct. of Huntingdon (1707–91*) 1298, 1301, 1313, 1314

Hastings, Etheridge & Bliss (bks. Boston & Charlestown, *fl*. 1809) 1669, 1670

Hatchard, J. (bks. *fl*. 1800–16) 277, 383, 449, 454, 457, 459, 460, 765, 1058, 1398, 1400, 1406, 1409, 1411, 1415, 1586, 1588, 1657, 1661, 1667, 1672, 1674, 1676

Hatchard, T. (bks. *fl*. 1855) 639

Hatchard & Co. (bks. *fl*. 1866–76) 475, 476, 545, 653

Hatchard & Son (bks. *fl*. 1821–3) 284, 386, 467, 536, 603, 613, 619–20, 625, 630, 766, 1423, 1683

Hatchards (bks. *fl*. 1876–82) 477

Hatchwell, Richard (bks. Malmesbury) 556, 1751

Hatt, J. (bks. Camb., *fl*. 1824) 1427

Haward, F. (engr. *fl*. 1785) 1572

Hawes, Lacey (bks. *fl*. 1750–76) *see* Hitch, C. & L. Hawes; and Hawes, Clarke, & Collins

Hawes, [Lacey], [W.] Clarke, & [R.] Collins (bks. *fl*. 1765–73) 219, 348, 350, 421, 425, 491, 494, 496, 510, 1013, 1081, 1090, 1096, 1101, 1102, 1111

Hawes, L[acey], & Co. (bks. *fl*. 1767) 1160

Hawes & Co. (bks. *fl*. -1776) 359, 1122

Hawes, R. (bks. *fl*. ?1775) 1245, 1246

Hawes, William (1736–1808*) 1288n

Hawkes & Lea (bks. 1813–22) 517, 518, 519, 520, 522

Hawkesworth, John (1715?-73*) 298, 299, 337, 338, 339n, 341, 345, 358–9, 361, 364, 370, 372, 375, 376, 378, 380, 382, 384, 385, 388, 389, 390, 391, 392, 404, 736, 772, 838, 999, 1044, 1046, 1240, 1635

Hyde collection (*cont.*):
  960, 961, 964, 965, 973, 975, 979, 980, 984,
  988, 989, 995, 996, 999, 1007, 1013, 1017,
  1018, 1023, 1030, 1034, 1039, 1046, 1047,
  1061, 1062, 1066, 1071, 1080, 1090, 1096,
  1097, 1111, 1117, 1124, 1134, 1135, 1136,
  1138, 1142, 1147, 1148, 1150, 1152, 1156,
  1159, 1161, 1162, 1165, 1167, 1168, 1171,
  1172, 1173, 1180, 1181, 1182, 1183, 1184,
  1190, 1196, 1197, 1199, 1201, 1206, 1207,
  1208, 1210, 1211, 1212, 1214, 1215, 1216,
  1217, 1218, 1219, 1220, 1222, 1224, 1227,
  1231, 1238, 1241, 1242, 1243, 1245, 1251,
  1254, 1256, 1265, 1269, 1270, 1276, 1279,
  1286, 1291, 1294, 1296, 1297, 1299, 1304,
  1306, 1307, 1308, 1309, 1313, 1314, 1318,
  1320, 1322, 1324, 1325, 1329, 1331, 1332,
  1334, 1340, 1342, 1343, 1346, 1350, 1351,
  1358, 1360, 1363, 1366, 1371, 1374, 1379,
  1381, 1382, 1385, 1387, 1389, 1392, 1394,
  1400, 1402, 1407, 1410, 1412, 1415, 1416,
  1418, 1420, 1422, 1424, 1428, 1429, 1436,
  1437, 1442, 1446, 1448, 1449, 1453, 1454,
  1457, 1460, 1462, 1466, 1467, 1472, 1474,
  1476, 1479, 1480, 1485, 1486, 1490, 1491,
  1499, 1500, 1501, 1502, 1503, 1508, 1510,
  1516, 1518, 1519, 1524, 1525, 1527, 1530,
  1533, 1536, 1537, 1540, 1543, 1544, 1545,
  1546, 1547, 1548, 1549, 1550, 1551, 1553,
  1555, 1556, 1560, 1561, 1563, 1564, 1565,
  1570, 1572, 1573, 1577, 1578, 1579, 1580,
  1584, 1586, 1590, 1593, 1600, 1601, 1602,
  1603, 1604, 1605, 1607, 1608, 1610, 1611,
  1615, 1617, 1618, 1619, 1621, 1622, 1630,
  1631, 1632, 1633, 1636, 1638, 1639, 1640,
  1646, 1647, 1648, 1649, 1650, 1656, 1658,
  1661, 1667, 1673, 1676, 1679, 1681, 1683,
  1686, 1687, 1690, 1693, 1696, 1702, 1703,
  1710, 1711, 1712, 1721, 1724, 1726, 1727,
  1728, 1729, 1730, 1732, 1733, 1734, 1735,
  1736, 1737, 1738, 1739, 1745, 1749, 1750,
  1754, 1756, 1757, 1758

I. 54
Ichiryusha (bks. Nagoya, Japan, *fl.* 1933) 1621
Ilchester, Henry-Thomas Fox-Strangways, 2nd
  E. of (1747–1802) 1378, 1379
Ilkley, Yorks 178
Imhoff, Charlotte 503
Immerzeel. J. jun. (bks. Rotterdam, *fl.* 1824) 957
India 1278, 1280, 1281, 1282
Inge, Eliza 497
Ingelby (?mus. 1779) 1350
Ingraham (*fl.* 1816) 1590
Ingram (?bks. *fl.* 1854) 1436
Ingram, John Kells (1823–1907) 1358, 1360,
  1374

Innerpeffray 120, 1256, 1269
Insel (bks. Frankfurt, *fl.* 1964) 977
Inskeep (bks. New York, *fl.* 1809) 403
Ipswich, Suffolk 1434, 1435
Irby, Charles Frank (*fl.* 1836) 603
Irby, James Warwick (*fl.* 1841) 603
Ireland, T. jun. (bks. Edin., *fl.* 1829) 529
Isaac, Tuckey, & Co. (bks. *fl.* 1836) 549
Isaacs, A. J. (bks. *fl.* ?1857) 643
Isham, Heyward (son of next) 1750n
Isham, Col. Ralph Heyward (1890–1955) 25,
  39, 97, 146, 153, 659, 695, 728, 1194, 1196,
  1274, 1358, 1750n, 1756
Isles, Duncan E. 333
Ivimey, Joseph (ed. *fl.* 1833) 1487
Izumitani, Yutaka 790, 982n, 983, 984

——J* 118
J., S. 6, 34, 123
J——* 118
J——O. 118
Jack, Prof. & Mrs A. A. (of Aberdeen) 101
Jack, Andrew, & Co. (ptr. Edin. *fl.* 1822) 1730
Jackson, Christopher (bks. Dublin, *fl.* 1777)
  1332
Jackson, J. (bks. *fl.* 1756) 658, 659
Jackson, John (1686–1763*, theol.) 1034
Jackson, John (ptr. Lichfield, *fl.* 1783) 1560
Jackson, R. (bks. Dublin, *fl.* 1778) 1276
Jackson, W. (ptr. *fl.* 1819) 279, 384, 766
Jackson, Revd William (of Lichfield, 1735–98)
  1561
Jackson, William (ptr. & bks. Oxford, *fl.*
  1753–95) 138, 139
Jackson, William Alexander (1905–64) 89, 1533
Jackson & Lister (William Jackson & J. Lister,
  ptr. Oxford, *fl.* 1776) 1278, 1280
Jacobs (bks. Phil. *fl.* ?1826) 1612
Jacobs, S. A. (ptr. Golden Eagle, Mt Vernon,
  NY, *fl.* 1937) 1618
James, Charles (†1821) 461
James, D. (*fl.* 1835) 1432
James, George Payne Raynsford (1799–1860*)
  67n
James, Henry (1843–1916*) 1448
James, Revd John (?†1772) 281
James, R. (bks. Dublin *fl.* 1752) 172, 178
James, Robert MD (1705–76*) 48, 49n, 56–8,
  60–7, 90, 91, 132, 731, 1019–20, 1288–90,
  1666
Jameson, Noel 1358, ?1360
Jameson, R. (bks. *fl.* 1787–94) 234, 244, 252,
  1346, 1623, 1632, 1633
Jameson, R. S. (lexicog. *fl.* 1827) 526, 527–8,
  534, 540–2, 544–5
Jamieson, R. (bks. Edin., *fl.* 1778) 1345
Jannet (bks. Paris, *fl.* 1816) 1466

Keith, Peter 189
Keith, Robert (1681–1757*) 687
Kellett, W. 1359
Kelso 820
Kelly, Elizabeth (*fl*. 1773, thief) 429n
Kelly, E. M. 728n
Kelly, Hugh (1739–77*, dram.) 1001, 1291–4
Kemble, John Philip (1757–1823*, actor) 1165
Kamel el Mohandes (tr. *fl*. 1959) 955
Kemp 1550
Kempthorne, J. A. (Bp.) 452
Kenkyusha (pub. Tokyo, *fl*. ?1909–) 985, 1460, 1476, 1490, 1500
Kennedy 1726
Kennedy, Revd John (of Bradley, 1698–1782*) 1032–4, 1147n, 1640, 1666
Kennedy, Máire 43n
Kenney, Courtney S. (ed. *fl*. 1927) 1159
Kenrick, William (1725?-79*) 1089, 1297
Kent, W. (bks. *fl*. 1844–55?) 1434
Kent & Co. (bks. *fl*. 1876–82) 477, 653; *see also* Simpkin, Marshall, Hamilton, Kent & Co.
Keogh, George Rowse 213
Kern, Jerome (bkc. 1885–1945) 18, 39, 89, 97, 198, 317, 793, 994, 1097, 1379n, 1601, 1631n
Kerr (engr.?Glas., *fl*. 1825–6) 1226, 1611
Kershaw, John (1730?-97*) 402
Kersseboom, Willem 93
Ketchum (*fl*. 1828) 1553
Ketelby (?Albert William, 1875–1959*) 7
Kettilby, Samuel DD (of Gresham Coll., 1736–1808) 1034
Keynes, Sir Geoffrey Langdon (1887–1982) 1371, 1437, 1648
Keys, T. (bks. *fl*. 1819) 465
Keysler, John George 687
Kiernan, J. (ptr. Dublin, *fl*. 1777) 795
Kilkenny, Ire. 197n
Kilmarnock, E. Ays. 1191, 1220n, 1511
Kilvert, N. (*fl*. 1777) 1089
Kimball, Leonard 756
Kimber, Edward (1719–69*) 330, 399
Kimber & Sharpless (bks. Phil., *fl*. ?1838) 536, 537
King, Sir John Dashwood 1522
King, R. M. 803
King, Revd William DD (1685–1763*) 37n, 1060–1
King & Baird (ptr. Phil., *fl*. 1840) 622
King's Lynne, Norfolk 38, 40, 41
Kingsbury *see also* Black &c.
Kingsbury & Co. (bks. *fl*. 1823) 589, 591
Kingsbury, Parbury & Allen (bks. *fl*. 1822–3) 284, 386, 524, 526, 549, 593, 595, 766, 842, 1683
Kingsford, Thomas (*fl*. 1801) 244

Kingsford (poss. Thomas, prec.) 1549
Kingston, Evelyn Pierrepont, 2nd D. of (1711–73*) 1019
Kinishihôryû-dô (?pub. Tokyo, *fl*. 1893) 983
Kippis, Andrew (1725–95*) 1029
Kirby, R. S. (bks. *fl*. 1817–23) 277, 284, 383, 386, 765, 766
Kirk, T. (ptr. New York, *fl*. 1809) 1608; *see also* Eastburn, Kirk & Co.
Kirk, Thomas (1765–97*, art.) 331, 808, 814, 815, 819, 1054, 1057, 1584
Kirkleatham, Yorks. 61, 66
Kirkwood [E.] & Sons (engr. Edin. *fl*. 1800) 262, 1397
Kitchen, Thomas (engr.) *see* Kitchin
Kitchin, Thomas (engr. *fl*. 1750–8) 187, 781, 783, 784
Kite, B. & T. (bks. Philadelhia, *fl*. 1808) 1326
Knapp, Humphrey 208
Knapton. J[ohn] (bks. *fl*. 1756–60) 486, 489, 694
Knapton, J[ohn] & P[aul] (bks. *fl*. 1735–70) 141, 144, 411, 417
Kneass, W. (engr. USA, *fl*. 1803) 379
Kneller, Sir Godfrey (1646–1723*) 308, 1384, 1399, 1405
Knevett, Arliss, & Baker (bks. *fl*. 1811) 573
Knevett, Arliss, & Co. (bks. *fl*. 1809) 571
Knickerbocker Press (G. P. Putnam's Sons, New York, ?1891–?7) 919, 921, 922, 926
Knight, Ellis Cornelia (1757–1837*) 796
Knight, Joseph (*fl*. 1777) 1333
Knight, Phillipina, Lady (1727–99) 1140
Knott, John MD 1545
Knott, T. (bks. *fl*. 1792) 1516
Knox, John (bks. *fl*. 1787) 223, 228, 234, 244, 424, 425, 496, 498, 1623, 1631, 1632
Knox, Mary 802
Knox, Thomas R., & Co. (bks. New York, succ. James Miller, *fl*. ?1886) 910
Knox, Revd Vicesimus (1753–1821*) 28, 172, 1608
Knutsford, 4th Visc. 1536n
Kobe, Japan 110
Koda, Paul S. 449n, 556
Kolb, Gwyn Jackson (1919–) 773, 808, 819, 820, 821, 822, 823, 824, 825, 826, 827, 829, 831, 832, 833, 834, 835, 836, 837, 838, 839, 840, 842, 843, 845, 847, 848, 849, 850, 851, 852, 853, 854, 856, 859, 862, 863, 866, 867, 869, 872, 873, 874, 875, 876, 880, 882, 883, 884, 887, 890, 892, 893, 897, 900, 902, 903, 905, 906, 907, 909, 910, 912, 915, 916, 919, 920, 921, 922, 924, 925, 926, 927, 929, 931, 934, 935, 936, 940, 941, 942, 943, 944, 945, 946, 947, 948, 949, 950, 951, 952, 953, 955, 956, 960, 961, 962, 966, 977, 978, 979, 980, 988

Merrill, J. (bks. Cambridge, *fl.* 1750) 187, 189

Merrill, John & Joseph (bks. Cambridge, *fl.* 1773–95) 1519; *see also* Merryl

Merrill, T. & J. (bks. Cambridge, *fl.* 1758–75) 1160

Merrill & Sons (bks. Lowell, Mass., *fl.* ?1845) 628

Merry, J. (of Pembroke Coll., Oxon., pseud., *fl.* 1791) 1750

Mershon Company (Rahway, NJ, ?1899–?1904) 927, 933

Mershon Company Press (Rahway, NJ, 1895) 924

Mershon Company Publishers (Rahway, NJ, 1897) 925, 928

Merydew, J. T. (ed. *fl.* 1888) 1731

Merryl (bks. Cambridge, *fl.* 1779 = ?J. & J. Merrill) 1519

Mesnard, A. (bks. *fl.* 1829) 529

Messurier *see* Mesurier

Mesurier, T. Le (bks. Dublin, *fl.* 1844) 625, 627

Metastasio, Pietro Trapassi (1698–1782) 1009, 1163–5

Methuen & Co. (bks. *fl.* 1896) 1446, 1447

Metzdorf, Robert Frederic (*fl.* 1953) 787, 788, 794, 795, 798, 801, 806, 808, 809, 811, 812, 814, 816, 817, 818, 824, 825, 829, 834, 841, 846, 848, 849, 850, 853, 855, 857, 858, 860, 863, 867, 874, 877, 878, 884, 887, 888, 954, 956, 1325, 1422, 1437, 1734

Meurose, James (bks. Kilmarnock, *fl.* 1773) 1191

Mexico City 988

Meyer, H. (engr. *fl.* 1807) 573, 824

Meynell, Alice Christiana Gertrude (née Thompson, 1847–1922*) 1715

Meysey-Thompson, Sir Henry (1809–74*) 7n, 1269

Michie, John (*fl.* 1814) 308

Mickle, William Julius (1735–88*) 1058, 1078–83, 1631

Middlebury, Vt. 828, 1511

Middlemist (engr. *fl.* 1819) 583

Middlesex, Charles Sackville, ?3rd E. of (1711–69*, 2nd D. of Dorset 1765) 323, 325, 327, 328, 329, 331, 332

Middleton, Conyers (1683–1750*) 34

Middleton, Erasmus (1739–1805*) 1516

Mifflin (bks. & pub. Boston & New York) *see* Houghton Mifflin

Mifflin, J. (?bks. *fl.* 1777–8) 431, 497

Miglietta, Goffredo (ed. *fl.* 1983) 982

Milan, It. 555–6, 980, 981, 982

Miles, F. R. (ed. *fl.* 1965) 1718

Milford, Sir Humphrey Sumner (1877–1952*, ptr. OUP) 1230, 1733, 1734

Millan, John (*fl.* 1727–84) 52n

Millar, Andrew (bks. *fl.* 1707–68) 66n, 127, 141, 144, 211, 213, 214, 215, 217, 220, 325, 326, 346, 348, 400, 401, 411, 417, 421, 424, 483, 486, 489, 491, 492, 503, ?504, 510, 695, 698, 699, 700, 702, 707, 709, 710, 714, 716, 722, 781, 1003, 1021, 1038, 1039, 1153, 1394 [pseud.]

Millar, John Hepburn (ed. *fl.* 1896) 1446

Millar, W. (bks. *fl.* 1790–8) 235, 257, 752, 1637, 1641, 1648, 1649

Millekin [or Milliken], John (bks. Dublin) 353–4

Miller, Andrew (engr. †1763) 1405

Miller, J. (bks. *fl.* 1810–20) 331, 332, 827, 838

Miller, James (bks., succ. to F. C. Francis & Co., New York, *fl.* ?1865–79) 884, 886, 888, 892, 896, 910, 912, 913

Miller, Samuel Christie (of Britwell Court, †1889) ?25, 1573

Miller, T. (ptr. *fl.* 1815) 1329

Miller, William (bks. *fl.* 1794–1824) 181, 237, 247, 265, 373, 374, 377, 381, 523, 524, 706, 759, 762, 819, 821, 822, 1058, 1406, 1409, 1411, 1586, 1588, 1651, 1657, 1661, 1667, 1672

Miller, William Henry ('Foot-rule', of Britwell Court, 1789–1848) ?25, 1573

Milliken [or Millekin], J (bks. Dublin *fl.* 1771) 353–4

Mills (bks. Dublin, *fl.* 1782) 1541

Mills, J. (ptr. Bristol, *fl.* 1802) 819

Mills, M. (ptr. Dublin, *fl.* 1777–86) 1024, 1273

Mills, T. (? Miles, bks. Bristol, *fl.* 1777–85) 1298, 1299

Milne, George (*fl.* 1964) 20, 127, 175, 399, 552, 949, 950, 1018, 1597, 1718

Milner, William (ptr. & bks. Halifax, *fl.* 1835–46) 538, 539, 540, 541, 629, 1432, 1435, 1513

Milner & Carping (bks. *fl.* ?1860) 645

Milner & Co. (ptr. Halifax, *fl.* ?1860) 645

Milner & Sowerby (ptr. Halifax, *fl.* 1848–65) 540, 542, 545, 645, 647, 648, 649

Milnes, Alfred (ed. 1849–1921) 893–4, 896, 897, 907, 984, 1472, 1473, 1474, 1475, 1497, 1498, 1499

Milnes, Richard Monckton, 1st B. Houghton (1809–85*) 1436, ?1687

Milson, I. or J. (engr. *fl.* 1787) 1023

Milton, John (1608–74*) 35, 37n, 140, 141, 147, 173, 183–6, 316–18, 319, 320–1

Milton, William, Visc., & 4th E. Fitzwilliam (1748–1833) 519

Miner, E. N. (pub. New York, *fl.* 1899–1900) 928

Minerva Press (ptr. *fl.* 1804) 820, 822, 825; *see also* Lane & Newman

Moutadon, Alain (tr. *fl.* 1984) 973
Moutard (bks. Paris, *fl.* 1785) 1237
Moutray, Isabella 1542
Mower, A. (ptr. *fl.* 1809) 827
Moxon, Edward (1801–58*) 864
Moyes, James (ptr. *fl.* 1816–23) 1756, 1757
Moysey, F. 1030
Mozley, Henry (bks. Derby, *fl.* 1818–33) 285, 291, 387, 582, 585, 587, 589, 590, 593, 596, 600, 606, 608, 616, 767, 769
Mozley, Henry (ptr. & bks. Gainsborough, *fl.* 1801–15) 513, 1325, 1327, 1510
Mozley, J. (bks. Gainsborough, *fl.* 1785–7) 28, 513, 581, 1579
Mozley, John & Charles (bks. & ptr. Derby, *fl.* ?1841–59) 622, 643
Mozley & Co. (bks. Gainsborough, *fl.* 1792) 503
Muckrill, Thomas J. 611
Mudge, Revd Zacharaiah (1694–1769*) 1171–2
Mudie, W. (bks. Edin., *fl.* 1800) 1395
Mudie, W., & G. Gray (ptr. & bks., Edin, *fl.* 1800) 1395
Mukherjee, Purna Chandra (bks. Calcutta, *fl.* 1912) 956
Müller, Immanuel (bks. Leipzig, *fl.* 1832) 857, 975, 976
Mullett, Charles F. 429
Mulso, Hester (Mrs Chapone, 1727–1801*) 196, 337
Mumby, Frank Arthur (ed. *fl.* 1906) 1732
Mumford's Coffee House (1770) 1176
Munby, Alan Noel Latimer (1913–74*) 120, 1334n, 1360n, 1381
Mundell, Doig, & Stevenson (bks. Edin., *fl.* 1809–22) 515, 517, 518, 519, 520, 522, 570
Mundell, J. (bks. Glas. *fl.* 1798) 1216
Mundell, J. & Co. (bks. Edin., *fl.* 1792–5) 106, 547, 1582
Mundell & Co. (ptr. Edin., *fl.* 1813) 576
Mundell & Son (bks. Edin., *fl.* 1798) 1216
Munford, Revd George (1795–1871) 9
Munn, Daniel Rolfe 1096
Munro, George (pub. New York, ?1882–?89) 902, 915
Munroe & Francis (bks. New York) 275; *see also* Monroe, Francis & Parker
Münster, Ger. 976, 977
Muonier, A. (ptr. & bks. Paris, *fl.* 1905) 972
Murata, Yuji (ed., *fl.* 1892) 983
Murdoch, Patrick (†1774) 999n, 1507
Murdock, Harold (1862–1934) 18, 97, 98, 111, 144, 325, 675, 1217, 1366
Murphy, Arthur (1727–1805*) 9, 10n, 294, 295, 313, 446, 448, 685, 686, 688, 695, 817, 899, 1252n, 1402, 1554, 1584, 1611–12, 1630, 1631, 1636, 1637, 1640, 1641–58,

1660, 1661, 1668, 1669, 1673, 1674, 1682, 1683, 1688, 1689, 1691, 1693, 1698, 1699, 1700, 1701, 1701, 1703, 1704, 1705, 1706, 1707, 1707, 1708, 1709, 1710, 1711, 1724
Murray, Alexander, L. Henderland (1736–95*) 1008n
Murray, David (bks. Edin.) 138; *see also* Jackson, William, of Oxford
Murray, David Leslie (1888–1962) 1231
Murray, G. (engr. *fl.* 1819–35) 860, 864, 1337, 1747
Murray, H. (bks. *fl.* 1794) 252, 371, 507, 1390
Murray, J. A. (*fl.* 1774–82) 1560, 1561
Murray, James [Augustus] Henry (1837–1915*) 478, 653, 655
Murray, James P. 1580
Murray, John I (*né* McMurray, bks. *fl.* 1745–93) 228, 234, 244, 363, 432, 437–8, 441, 498, 499, 501, 502, 505, 1248, 1255, 1290, 1351, 1353, 1354, 1362, 1367, 1375, 1380, 1382, 1385, 1521, 1537, 1538–9, 1581, 1623, 1630, 1632, 1641, 1648, 1649
Murray, John II (1778–1843, bks.) 122, 272, 331, 332, 381, 457, 459, 460, 467, 509, 523, 524, 529, 762, 826, 827, 838, 1056, 1058, 1118, 1125, 1409, 1411, 1415, 1423, 1427, 1588, 1637, 1672
Murray, John III (1808–92*) 47, 475, 476, 545, 1436, 1437
Murray, Lindley (1745–1826*) 173, 306, 622, 632, 633, 648
Murray, Mary Margaret, Lady Elibank (†1762) 1532
Murray, Patrick, 5th B. Elibank(1703–78*) 1532
Murray, William, 1st E. Mansfield (1705–93*, LCJ) 1294, 1306, 1310, 1319, 1325, 1327, 1328, 1329
Murray & Gibb (ptr. Edin., *fl.* 1876–7) 298, 299, 393, 772, 1709
Murray & Highley 263, 265, 377, 450, 510–11, 512, 561, 562, 563, 565, 758, 759, 1400, 1651, 1657
Muses Library (Routledge, 1905–22) 1596
Mussey, R. B. (bks. Boston, *fl.* 1842) 867
Muston (engr. *fl.* 1794) 243
Myers, J. W. (ptr. *fl.* 1794–1800) 546, 557
Mylne, Robert (arch. 1734–1811*) 999
Mynde, J. (engr. *fl.* ?1753) 197

N., J. (*fl.* 1784) 1570
N., J. (*fl.* 1810) 1025
N., O. (*fl.* 1749) 186
Nadir Shah, Tahmas Kuli Khan (1688–1747) 50–1
Nagashima, Daisuke 110n, 982n, 1138n, 1460n
Nagoya, Japan 1621

Rivington & Marshall (ptr. *fl.* 1790) 1381
Rivingtons (bks. *fl.* 1863) 677
Roach, J. (bks. *fl.* 1794) 173
Roake & Varty (bks. *fl.* 1831–2) 605, 606, 616, 624
Robbins & Wheeler (bks. Winchester, *fl.* 1828) 528, 598
Roberts *see also* Robinson & Roberts
Roberts (engr. *fl.* 1794) 370
Roberts, Elizabeth (*fl.* 1810) 1025
Roberts, H. (art. *fl.* 1748) 151
Roberts, James (1766–1809*, art.) 240
Roberts, James (bks. *fl.* 1706–54) 60, 95, 110, 124
Roberts, Mrs James (w. of prec. bks.) 65
Roberts, Sir Sydney Castle (1889–1966) 311, 312, 677, 777, 1400n, 1457, 1715
Robertson 1453
Robertson, Alexander (ptr. Edin., *fl.* 1750–84) 1300
Robertson, D. (bks. Glas., *fl.* 1837) 616
Robertson, J. 198
Robertson, J. & M. (bks. Glas. *fl.* 1792–1802) 256, 506, 513, 1409
Robertson, James (bks. Edin. *fl.* 1809–21) 515, 836, 1517, 1552
Robertson, James, & Co. (bks. Edin., *fl.* 1822) 1730
Robertson, John (bks. & ptr. Edin., *fl.* 1821–2) 841, 1517, 1536–7, 1730
Robertson, John (bks. London, 1844) 625
Robertson, Joseph Ogle (bks. *fl.* 1828) 469, 470, 471, 472, 473, 474, 475, 477, 478, 481
Robertson, Thomas (ptr. Edin., *fl.* 1781) 1536–7
Robertson, W. (bks. Lanark, *fl.* 1819) 836
Robertson, W. (bks. Dublin, *fl.* 1855–62) 1593
Robertson, Revd William (hist. 1721–93*) 1021
Robertson, William John 1227
Robertson & Atkinson (?Thomas Atkinson, 1801?-33*; bks. Glas. *fl.* 1823–4) 308, 394, 590, 593
Robins, Alfred (ptr. *fl.* 1834) 1574
Robins, J. & Co. (bks. *fl.* 1820) 1649
Robins, J., & Sons (bks. *fl.* 1819) 465, 466
Robins, T. (bks. *fl.* 1823–9) 523, 524, 529
Robinson *see also* Hurst &c.; Wilkie & Robinson
Robinson, George (1737–1801*, bks.) 223, 228, 272, ?319, 331, 381, 425, 432, 435, 496, 498, 499, 704, 706, 1058, 1111, 1118, 1123, 1189, 1253–4, 1259, 1260, 1265, 1266, 1286n, 1351, 1353, 1354, 1362, 1367, 1370, 1371, 1375, 1528, 1571
Robinson, G. (bks. *fl.* 1808–13) 575, 762, 827, 1409, 1410, 1588; *see also* Robinson, G. & S.

Robinson, G. G. & J. (bks. *fl.* 1794–1801) 252, 263, 371, 374, 450, 505, 507, 510, 512, 560, 561, 562, 565, 1390, 1398, 1400, 1657, 1753
Robinson, G. G. J. & J (bks. *fl.* 1787–?96) 77, 78, 234, 244, 363, 437–8, 441, 500, 502, 1125, 1261, 1263, 1266, 1380, 1382, 1385, 1581, 1623, 1630, 1632, 1637, 1638, 1641, 1647, 1648–9, 1651
Robinson, G. & J. (bks. Liverpool, *fl.* 1802–55) 265, 282, 289, 377, 536, 603, 613, 620, 625, 630, 639, 1424
Robinson, G. & J. (bks. *fl.* 1824) 563, 565, 759, 1426, 1691, 1692, 1693
Robinson, G. & S. (bks. *fl.* 1814–17) 519, 576
Robinson, J. (bks. *fl.* 1783? ?1817 ?1820) 764, 765, 834, 1422; *see also* Robinson, James; Robinson, John
Robinson, J. (engr. 1813) 831n, 833n
Robinson, J. (ptr. Baltimore, *fl.* 1819) 836
Robinson, J. Grant 1435
Robinson, J. H. (engr. 1817) 834, 835
Robinson, James (bks. *fl.* 1821) ? 586, 844
Robinson, John (1774–1840, grammarian) 529
Robinson, John (bks. *fl.* 1816–23) 276, 278, 281, 383, 519, ?521, ?524, , 1674, 1676, 1683
Robinson, John (bkc. *fl.* 1783) 747
Robinson, John (of Hinckley) 1557
Robinson, Joseph (ptr. Baltimore, *fl.* 1810) 828, ?836
Robinson, Richard, 1st B. Rokeby (1689–1761*) ?402
Robinson, Sir Thomas, 1st Bt. Rokeby ('Long', 1700?-77?) ?402, 1018, 1090, 1290
Robinson, Thomas Philip, 1st E. de Grey, & B. Grantham (1781–1859*) 1156
Robinson, W .& Sons (bks. *fl.* 1820) 1649
Robinson, W. & Sons (bks. Liverpool, *fl.* 1819–23) 280, 285, 465, 466, 1421, 1681
Robinson & Co. (bks. *fl.* 1822–3) 283, 284, 388, 767, 768
Robinson & Roberts (bks. *fl.* 1767–70) 219, 220, 225, 494, 1013, 1102, 1160
Robinson, Son, & Holdsworth (bks. Leeds, *fl.* 1816) 459, 460
Robson, J. & Co. 363
Robson, J[ames] (1759–1806†, bks.) 228, 244, 371, 425, 432, 437–8, 441, 498, 499, 500, 502, 505, 507, 1102, 1111, 1118, 1123, 1125, 1259, 1260, 1265, 1280, 1351, 1354, 1362, 1367, 1375, 1380, 1382, 1385, 1390, 1581, 1623, 1630, 1632, 1637, 1641, 1646, 1647, 1648
Robson, Joseph (acc. of Hudson's Bay) 397
Robson, T., & Co. (bks. Newcastle upon Tyne, *fl.* ?1777) 1303, 1304
Robson & Clark (bks. *fl.* 1789) 234, 1261, 1262, 1266

Robson, Levey, & Franklyn (ptr. *fl.* 1854) 1436

Rochester, Kent 1314, 1539

Rochford, William Henry Nassau Zuylestein, 4th E. (1717–81*) 658, 659, 1184

Rochefort expedition (1757) 689n, 722, 1623

Rodd, Thomas jun. (bks. *fl.* 1796–1849*) 69

Rodwell, J. (bks. *fl.* 1813–15) 480, 519

Rodwell, W. (bks. *fl.* 1823–29) 523, 524, 529

Rodwell & Martin (bks. *fl.* 1817–26) 108, 278, 284, 332, 383, ?386, 460, 521, 524, 526, 765, 766, 838, 1415, 1423, 1425, 1591

Roe (bks. Mountmelick, *fl.* 1750) 197n

Roe, J. (bks. *fl.* ?1805) 52, 53

Roesch, Kurt– (art. *fl.* 1945) 1470

Roffe[e], R. (engr. *fl.* 1824) 845

Rogers (engr. *fl.* 1835) 860

Rogers, Bruce (typog. *fl.* 1945) 1619

Rogers, Katherine Muntzer (ed. *fl.* 1981) 1720

Rogers, J. (engr. *fl.* 1834) 533, 537

Rogers, J. I. 250

Rogers, Robert Wentworth 25, 40, 111, 125, 146, 321, 429, 675, 728, 1013, 1180, 1190, 1194, 1286, 1334, 1520, 1540, ?1555

Rogers, Samuel (1763–1855*) 1252, 1352n

Rogers, W. S. (art. *fl.* 1900) 928, 931

Rojas, R. Riera (bks. Barcelona, *fl.* ?1945) 989

Rokeby Hall, Yorks. (Richard Robinson, 1st B., & Sir Thomas Robinson) 402

Rolleston, Christopher (?f. of Lancelot) 1165

Rolleston, Sir Humphrey Davy (1862–1944*) 72

Rolleston, Lancelot (1786–1862) 1165

Rollo, B. 1639

Rolt, Richard (1725?–70*) 663, 664–9, 670–3

Romaine, Revd William (1714–95*) 1608

Rome 983

Romney, John (1758–1832*) 484

Romney, John (1786–1863, engr.) 1587

Romsey, Suffolk 961

Rooker, Edward (engr. 1749–57) 182, 715

Root, Robert K. (*fl.* 1932) 946

Roper, Charles Trevor, 18th B. Dacre (1745–94) 1276

Roscoe, William (ed. 1753–1831*) 1496

Roscommon, Wentworth Dillon, 4th E. (1633–86*) 170

Rose, Bernard (mus. *fl.* 1984) 1621

Rose, Revd Charles (of Wolston Grange, Warwicks, 1788–45) 1620

Rose, Mrs D. M. (?of Wolston Grange, Warwicks, *fl.* 1960) 1620n

Rose, George (?1817–82*) 1030

Rose, Maria-Isabella (of Wolston Grange, Warwicks, *fl.* 1826) 1620n

Rose, Samuel (1767–1804*) 1277, 1579

Rose, William (of Wolston Grange, Warwicks, b. 1781) 1620n

Rosebery, Archibald Philip Primrose, 5th E. (1847–1929) 177

Rosenbach, Abraham Simon Wolf (1876–1952) 145–6, 177

Rosez, J. (bks. Brussels, *fl.* 1863) 971

Rosoman, Thomas (? bks. *fl.* 1756) 663n, 669

Ross, Caroline (née Davy) 1219

Ross, Laurentia Dorothea 341

Ross, Lucy Catherine Davy 1219

Ross, R. (bks. Edin., *fl.* 1797) 508

Ross, W. 341

Ross & Blackwood (bks. Edin., *fl.* 1802) 512–13

Rossell's Prisoner's Directory 1303

Rosset (bks. Lyon, *fl.* 1787) 314

Rosslyn, Alexander Wedderburn, 1st E. (1733–1805*) 1007

Rosslyn, James St Clair-Erskine, 2nd E. (1762–1837*) 1007

Roster, J. (lexicog. *fl.* 1816) 1015

Rostock, Ger. 1491

Rota, Peter Ricco (It. lexicog. *fl.* 1790) 1015

Rotherham, Yorks. 308

Rothermere, Esmond Cecil Harmsworth, 2nd Visc. (1898–1978*) 279, 1395

Rothschild, L. R., 18n, 39, 52, 97, 103, 143, 171, 177, 415, 788, 1018, 1030, 1064, 1096, 1209, 1219, 1303

Rothschild, Nathaniel Mayer Victor, B. (1910–) 43, 123, 125, 126, 143, 171, 177, 198, 415, 1071, 1097, 1366, 1573

Rothwell, Richard, RA (engr. 1800–68*) 819

Rotterdam, Neth. 957

Routh, Martin Joseph (1755–1854*) 7, 185, 321, 675, 1071, 1174, 1209, 1241, 1607

Routledge, George & Co. (bks. *fl.* 1853–65) 634, 638, 640, 642, 913, ?1472, 1592

Routledge, George, & Son (bks. *fl.* ?1905) 934

Routledge, George, & Sons (1872–1906) 642, 647, 653, 655, 904, 905, 908, 909, 911, 913, 921, 922, 936, 944, 984, 1341, ?1595, 1596, 1732

Routledge & Kegan Paul (pub., *fl.* 1967–8) 950, 1270, 1718

Routledge, Warne, & Routledge (bks. *fl.* 1861–5) 635, 643, 644, 646, 647, 1594

Roux, Philippe (bks. Maastricht, *fl.* 1786) 312

Rowe, Nicholas (1674–1718*) 1081, 1091, 1098, 1106, 1107, 1112, 1117, 1118, 1126, 1453

Rowley, Revd Thomas (1797–1877) 1214

Rowson, Susannah (née Haswell, 1762–1824) 569, 578

Roxburghe, D. of (sale 1812) 1622n

Royal Academy 1037, 1532–3, 1559

Rudd, Niall (ed. *fl.* 1981) 32, 175

Index of Persons and Places

Spottiswoode & Co. (ptr. *fl.* 1860–96) 29, 475–6, 545, 881, 883, 885, 890, 1447

Spottiswoode & Shaw (ptr. *fl.* 1847) 630

Sprange (bks. Tonbridge, *fl.* 1775) 1240

Springvale (George Matthew) 448

Squibb, George John (*fl.* 1859) 97, 1610

Stables, D. Wintringham 809

Stace, Machell (bkc. *fl.* 1812–43) 185n

Stafford, George (ptr. *fl.* 1794–5) 557, 558, 559

Staffordshire 322–3

Stagg, J (bks. *fl.* 1745) 127

Stahel'schen Buch-und Kunsthandlung (Würzburg, *fl.* 1874) 977

Stalker, C. (bks. *fl.* 1790–2) 502, 505, 1380, 1382, 1385, 1581

Stalker & Neele [or Neale] (engr. *fl.* 1825) 847

Stanhope, Philip Dormer *see* Chesterfield, 4th E. of

Stanhope Press (Chiswick, Whittingham, *fl.* 1805–11) 1403, 1589

Stanhope Press (Glas., R. Chapman, *fl.* 1817) 1223

Stanley, Arthur Penrhyn (1815–81*) 1032

Stansbury, Abraham D. (bks. New York, *fl.* 1803) 379

Stansbury, Arthur & Abraham (bks. New York, *fl.* 1803) 266, 760

Stanton 1610

Stapylton, Martin, 7th Bt., of Myton, Yorks (1723–1801) 7

Staquet, J. (tr. *fl.* 1946) 972

Stark 2

Starke, James (ptr. Glas., *fl.* 1823–5) 1226, 1610

Starkey, W. 1757

Start (*fl.* 1881?) 1711

Stassin & Xavier (bks. Paris, *fl.* 1846) 969

Statham, M. P. 14

Stawell, J. 1216

Stead, William, jun. (ed. *fl.* 1905) 311, 1714

Stearns, Thomas (*fl.* 1826) 851n

Stechell & Son (bks. *fl.* 1820) 838

Steevens, George (1736–1800*) 37n, 1111, 1112, 1117, 1118, 1121, 1122, 1123, 1125, 1134, 1136, 1311, 1453, 1630n

Steinberg, Theodore 215

Stella & Figli (bks. Milan, *fl.* 1828) 980, 981

Stephen, Leslie (1832–1904*) 919, 929, 931, 933, 939, 941

Stephens, Kate (ed. New York, *fl.* 1897) 1498

Stephens [= Stephanus/Etienne], Robert (*fl.* 1643–97) 87

Stephens, Thomas 2

Stephens, Austin, & Sons (ptr. Hertford, *fl.* 1866–) 885n

Stereotype Office, Camden Town and Duke Street *see* Wilson, Andrew

Sterling, Sir Gilbert 28

Sterling, Sir Louis Saul (†1958) 18, 27, 39, 171, 787, 1196, 1209, 1371

Sterling & Co. (bks. Edin., *fl.* 1837) 536

Sterling & Kenney (bks. Edin., *fl.* 1826–7) 467, 526

Sterling & Slade (bks. Edin., *fl.* 1820–4) 332, 521, 524, 838

Stern (bks. Phil., *fl.* 1908) 1714

Sterne, Laurence (1713–68*) 1017, 1018

Stettin, Ger. 1575

Steuart, David Erskine, 11th E. Buchan (1742–1829*) 674

Steuart, James 1171

Steven, J. (bks. Glas., *fl.* 1817) 1223

Stevens, George Alexander (1710–84*) 397

Stevens, Richard or Robert (bks 1758–60) 729, 731, 732, 733–4

Stevens & Haynes (bks. *fl.* 1870–82) 475, 476, 477, 545

Stevens & Norton (bks. *fl.* 1843) 625, 630, 639

Stevens & Sons (bks. *fl.* 1866–76) 475, 476, 545, 653

Stevenson, Duncan (ptr. to Edin. Univ., *fl.* 1830) 601, 604, 609

Stevenson, Duncan, & Co. (bks. Edin., *fl.* 1819) 584

Stevenson, Margery (of Balladoole) 329

Stevenson & Co. (ptr. Edin., *fl.* 1831–41) 605, 616, 624

Stewardson, Thomas (of Phil.) 464

Stewart (of Isle of Man) 440

Stewart [or Stuart], Gilbert (1742–86*, historian) 1255, 1256

Stewart, Miss (?Grace or Clementina, daus. of Sir John S., †1797, of Grandtully, Perths.) 1348

Stewart, T. (bks. Dublin, *fl.* 1778) 1276

Stewart, W. (bks. *fl.* 1794) 357, 454, 457, 459, 460, 467, 557

Stewart, W., & Co. (bks. Edin., *fl.* 1820) 1649

Stirling, Sir Gilbert 28

Stirling & Kenney (bks. Edin., *fl.* 1830) 601, 604

Stirling, Kenney, & Co. (bks. Edin., *fl.* 1831) 604, 609, 616, 623

Stirling & Slade (bks. Edin., *fl.* 1819–23) 285, 386, 583, 766, 1225, 1423

Stirling 503, 515, 571, 577

Stirling Town Councillors 1249

Stirling-Maxwell, Sir William (9th Bt, 1818–78*) 1207

Stock, Elliot (bks. *fl.* 1884–1904) 905, 1615

Stockdale, John (bks. *fl.* 1749?–1814?) 452, 454, 457, 480, 510, 512, 514, 548, 557, 560, 561, 562, 563, 565, 566, 568, 569, 570, 573, 574, 1058, 1398, 1400, 1405, 1409, 1410,

765, 766, 767, 768, 821, 835, 840, 841, 844, 850, 853, 1226, 1329, 1426, 1485, 1551, 1554, 1555, 1610, 1611, 1612, 1683, 1691, 1692, 1693

Tegg, T[homas], & Son (bks. *fl*. 1834–4) 472, 611, 613, 615

Tegg, William (bks. *fl*. 1852–77) 296, 297, 298, 636, 644, 870, 881, 889, 890, 897

Tegg, W[illiam], & Co. (bks. *fl*. 1848–55) 540, 541, 638, 653

Tegg & Co. (bks. Dublin, *fl*. 1837–40) 472, 473, 618, 624

Tegg & Co. (bks. London, *fl*. 1855–76) 639, 653

Tegg, Wise, & Tegg (bks. Dublin, *fl*. 1835) 611

Telfer-Smollett, Maj. Patrick 1192

Temple, G. (ptr. Newcastle upon Tyne, *fl*. 1785) 1303

Temple, William Johnstone [or Johnson] (1739–96*) 1737

Temple Press (Letchworth, 1930) 945

Templeman, J. (bks. *fl*. 1823–4) 523, 524

Tencé, Louis, & Co. (ptr. Brussels, *fl*. 1830) 855

Tennant, A. (bks. Bath, *fl*. 1777) 1298

Terry (? Daniel, 1780?-1829*) 1208

Tesson & Lea (Pierre Tesson, ptr. Phil., *fl*. 1803) 266, 379, 760

Testu (ptr. Paris, *fl*. 1818–19) 835, 964

Thackeray, Francis (1793–1842*) 264

Thames Bank Publishing Co., Leigh on Sea, Essex (1948) 1183

Theobald, Lewis (1688–1744*) 126, 1081, 1091, 1098, 1106, 1107, 1112, 1117, 1118, 1126

Theocritus (*c*.310–250 BC) 1160–1

Thicknesse, Philip (1719–92*) 1307

Thiérot (bks. Paris, *fl*. 1842) 867, 969

Thirlby, Styan (1686–1753*) 1570

Thomas, Alan G. (†1992) 1372n, 1601

Thomas, Edward Joseph (ed. *fl*. 1878–1904) 1228

Thomas, Isaiah (ptr. *fl*. 1749–1831)

Thomas, J. (bks. Calcutta, *fl*. 1851) 553

Thomas, J. (bks. London, *fl*. 1843–55) 625, 630, 639

Thomas, Mary (*fl*. 1912) 600

Thomas, Mary Anne 1726

Thomas, Moses (bks. Phil., *fl*. 1827–9) 294, 462–3, 464, 529n, 590n, 842n, 1326n, 1421n, 1748n

Thomas, M[oses] & S. (bks. Phil., *fl*. 1825) 289, 463n, 571n, 1337n, 1687

Thomas & Andrews (bks. Boston, *fl*. 1791) 1563

Thomas, Cowperthwaite & Co. (bks. Phil., *fl*. 1838–53) 543, 618, 622, 1706

Thomas & Whipple (bks. Newburyport, *fl*. 1806) 568

Thomas & Thomas (bks. Walpole, NH, *fl*. 1806) 1744, 1747

Thompson (engr./art., *fl*. 1807) 1057

Thompson (?engr. 1812–40) 829, 840, 861, 865

Thompson, G. (bks. *fl*. 1783) 227

Thompson, Henry Yates (bkc., 1838–1928*) 25

Thompson, Isaac (ptr. Newcastle upon Tyne, *fl*. 1737–76) 1303

Thompson, James *see* Thomson

Thompson, John (ptr. Phil., *fl*. 1795–6) 998

Thompson, Robert D. (of Dingwall) 1346

Thompson, William (1712?-66*) 54

Thompson, William (mason, of Lichfield, *fl*. 1784) 1567–8

Thomson, E. (bks. Manchester, *fl*. 1819–22) 280, 282, 465, 1421, 1424, 1681, 1692

Thomson, E. W. (engr., *fl*. 1797) 1054

Thomson, J. jun [& Co.] (bks. Edin., *fl*. 1808–9) 570

Thomson, James (1700–48*) 109, 173, 1371

Thomson, Revd James (1699–1790) 1270

Thomson, John P. (ptr. & bks. Frederick Town) 828

Thomsons, Bros. (bks. Edin., *fl*. 1822) 1730

Thoreau, Henry David (1817–62) 535

Thorndike 1201

Thorne, William (ptr. *fl*. 1799–1818) 1551

Thornton, Bonnell (1724–68*) 189, 298, 299, 337, 392, 736–7

Thornton, Henry Mills 1402

Thornton, Marianne (?1797–1887) 825

Thorp (bks. Camb., *fl*. 1824) 287, 1689

Thorp, Robert (*fl*. 1841) 1606

Thorpe (bks. Camb., *fl*. 1824) 287

Thorpe, Thomas (bks. *fl*. 1823) 1252

Thorpe & Burch (bks. *fl*. 1823) 589

Thoyts, Samuel 1047

Thrale, Henry, MP (1728/9–81) 416, 962n, 1080–1, 1167, 1171, 1203–4, 1250, 1252, 1254, 1531–2, 1533–6, 1685, 1737, 1752

Thrale, Hester Lynch (née Salusbury; 1741–1821*) *see* Piozzi, Hester Lynch

Thrale, Hester Maria 'Queeney' (1764–1837) 1253, 1254, 1334, 1346, 1563n, 1734–5

Thrale, Sophia (1771–1824) 1346

Thrale, Susanna Arabella (1770–1858) 824, 1754n

Thurlbourn [or Thurlborne], W. (bks. Cambridge, *fl*. 1735–63) 1045

Thurloe, John (1616–68*) 68

Thurlow, Edward, 1st B. (1731–1806) 78

Thurm, Susanne (trs. *fl*. ?1775) 1238, 1239

Thursby, Revd George Augustus (1771–1836) 1196